THE NAVARRE

NEW TESTA

COMPACT ED

THE NAVARRE BIBLE

New Testament

in the Revised Standard Version
with a commentary by members of the
Faculty of Theology of the University of Navarre

COMPACT EDITION

FOUR COURTS PRESS • DUBLIN
SCEPTER PUBLISHERS • PRINCETON, NJ

Nihil obstat: Martin Hogan, LSS, PhD, *censor deputatus.*
Imprimi potest: Desmond, Archbishop of Dublin, 12 July 2001

Typeset by Carrigboy Typsetting Services for
FOUR COURTS PRESS
Fumbally Lane, Dublin 8, Ireland.
e-mail: info@four-courts-press.ie
http://www.four-courts-press.ie

and in North America for

SCEPTER PUBLISHERS, INC,
P.O. Box 1270, Princeton, NJ 08542
e-mail: general@scepterpublisher.org
http://www.scepterpublisher.org

A catalogue record for this title is available from the British Library,

ISBN 1–85182–680–7 (Four Courts Press)
ISBN 1–889334–59–6 (Scepter Publishers)

Library of Congress Cataloging-in-Publication Data

Bible. N.T. English. Revised Standard. 2001.
The Navarre Bible. New Testament in the Revised Standard Version / with a commentary by members of the Faculty of Theology of the University of Navarre.
p. cm.
Translation of: Sagrada Biblia. Nuevo Testamento.
Includes bibliographical references and index.
ISBN 1–889334–59–6 (alk. paper)
1. Bible. N.T. – Commentaries. I. Universidad de Navarra. Facultad de Teología. II. Title.
BS2091.A1 2001.P7
225.7'7–dc21 2001042676

ACKNOWLEDGMENTS

Original title: *Sagrada Biblia: Nuevo Testamento.*
Quotations from Vatican II documents are based on the translation in Vatican Council II:
The Conciliar and Post Conciliar Documents,
ed. A. Flannery, OP (Dublin 1981).

Printed and bound in England by MPG Books, Bodmin, Cornwall.

Contents

Preface

In the early 1970s the theology faculty of the University of Navarre embarked on the project of making a new Spanish translation of the Bible together with a commentary designed for the general reader—a project dear to the heart of the university's founder and first chancellor, Blessed Josemaría Escrivá de Balaguer. The first volume—St Matthew's Gospel—appeared in 1976; the New Testament was covered in a series of twelve volumes; the Old Testament in Spanish is almost completed.

THE NAVARRE BIBLE, the English-language version of this work, is issued in three editions, each of which uses for its translation of Holy Scripture the Revised Standard Version Catholic Edition (RSVCE). The translator and publishers of the Navarre Bible wish to thank the National Council of the Churches of Christ in the United States of America for its permission to use the RSV.

The three editions of the Navarre Bible are described below.

NAVARRE BIBLE, STANDARD EDITION

The Standard Edition consists of the Revised Standard Version; various general introductory essays together with special introductions to the individual book(s) of the Bible, and extensive commentary/notes; the Catholic Church's official Latin version of Scripture, the New Vulgate, in its *editio typica altera*, issued in 1986; the RSV's own footnotes (indicated by superior letters); and cross references to scriptural passages, given as marginal notes (these references are provided by the University of Navarre editors and not by the RSV).

The Standard Edition is at present available in twelve separate volumes for the New Testament (*c*.2,700 pages in all) and (so far) one volume for the Old Testament, the Pentateuch (comprising Genesis, Exodus, Leviticus, Numbers and Deuteronomy). The rest of the Old Testament will (it is planned) be covered in volumes on: the Historical Books (2); the Prophets; and the Psalms and Wisdom Books.

NAVARRE BIBLE, READER'S EDITION

The Reader's Edition differs from the Standard Edition in only two respects: it does not include the New Vulgate (Latin) text or the *general* introductory essays. To date, the only volume available in a Reader's Edition is one comprising the four Gospels and the Acts of the Apostles.

NAVARRE BIBLE: NEW TESTAMENT: COMPACT EDITION

This Compact Edition contains the entire New Testament (RSVCE); quite short introductions to each of the four Gospels, to the Acts, to the letters and to the book of Revelation; and new commentaries/notes—much less extensive than those in the Standard and Reader's Editions, and often drawn from different sources.

The introductions and commentaries are designed to help the reader become more and more familiar with the books of the New Testament. The commentaries try to explain the content and structure of each book, and to focus attention on the line of thought and on key passages. They seek to identify what each of the sacred writers was intent on getting across—conscious of our need to understand properly what God sought to convey by means of the writers he inspired. Additionally, the notes try to provide doctrinal and ascetical explanations that flow from the biblical text itself and that are in line with the Church's understanding of it. In support of this "reading of the Bible in the Church" the notes include many quotations which should help the reader see how the Magisterium, the Fathers, Doctors and Saints have intrepreted things that our Lord said and did, as also the words of the apostles and other sacred writers.

To be more specific, the notes on the Gospels aim to help the reader grasp the teachings of each evangelist about the person of Jesus and thereby learn more about the mystery of Christ. The Gospel story invites the reader to become involved in it, as Blessed Josemaría Escrivá put it, "as one more member of the cast". For those who approach the Gospels in a spirit of faith and see it not just as a book about the past, the text becomes a call to conform their lives to that of the Son of God became man. The notes on the Acts of the Apostles, following the thread of St Luke's account, try to show how the Church took shape under the guidance of the Holy Spirit and the apostles. They also draw attention to the example set by certain figures in the early Church as regards imitation of Christ and perseverance in the work of evangelization. The commentaries on the Letters explore the doctrinal, moral and ascetical message passed on by the apostles, who are forever encouraging us to rediscover the new life in Christ. Finally, the notes on the book of Revelation try to highlight the consolation and spirit of constancy and love that Christ's victory can provide to believers.

The divisions of the biblical text into parts and sections has been made by the Navarre Bible editors. Their notes are of three kinds:

- general notes to the so-called "parts" of the various biblical books; these are identified by the (double) symbol □ □ alongside the bold chapter/verse numbers of notes.
- notes to the sections which go to make up each part: these are identifed by a (single) symbol □ alongside the bold numbers.

- notes to shorter passages which form a sort of unit. The majority of notes are of this kind, and within them verses of particular importance are commented on. These notes are *not* preceded by a symbol.

Sometimes the New Testament author includes quotations from the Old Testament. Cross-references to these are provided by the Navarre Bible editors at the very bottom of the page.

References to parallel passages (in other Gospels, mainly) are provided by the Navarre editors, and appear aligned with section headings.

Asterisks printed in the biblical text refer to the "Explanatory Notes" in the RSVCE to be found on pages 691ff.

A short index is provided at the end of the volume; this is meant to cover the themes indicated in the part and section headings and in the body of the notes.

In their introduction to the Spanish edition of this volume, the editors acknowledge the help given by many members of the theology faculty of the University of Navarre.

Abbreviations

1. BOOKS OF HOLY SCRIPTURE

Acts	Acts of the Apostles
Amos	Amos
Bar	Baruch
1 Chron	1 Chronicles
2 Chron	2 Chronicles
Col	Colossians
1 Cor	1 Corinthians
2 Cor	2 Corinthians
Dan	Daniel
Deut	Deuteronomy
Eccles	Ecclesiastes (Qohelet)
Esther	Esther
Eph	Ephesians
Ex	Exodus
Ezek	Ezekiel
Ezra	Ezra
Gal	Galatians
Gen	Genesis
Hab	Habakkuk
Hag	Haggai
Heb	Hebrews
Hos	Hosea
Is	Isaiah
Jas	James
Jer	Jeremiah
Jn	John
1 Jn	1 John
2 Jn	2 John
3 Jn	3 John
Job	Job
Joel	Joel
Jon	Jonah
Josh	Joshua
Jud	Judith
Jude	Jude
Judg	Judges
1 Kings	1 Kings
2 Kings	2 Kings
Lam	Lamentations
Lev	Leviticus
Lk	Luke
1 Mac	1 Maccabees
2 Mac	2 Maccabees
Mal	Malachi
Mic	Micah
Mk	Mark
Mt	Matthew
Nah	Nahum
Neh	Nehemiah
Num	Numbers
Obad	Obadiah
1 Pet	1 Peter
2 Pet	2 Peter
Phil	Philippians
Philem	Philemon
Ps	Psalms
Prov	Proverbs
Rev	Revelation (Apocalypse)
Rom	Romans
Ruth	Ruth
1 Sam	1 Samuel
2 Sam	2 Samuel
Sir	Sirach (Ecclesiasticus)
Song	Song of Solomon
1 Thess	1 Thessalonians
2 Thess	2 Thessalonians
1 Tim	1 Timothy
2 Tim	2 Timothy
Tit	Titus
Tob	Tobit
Wis	Wisdom
Zech	Zechariah
Zeph	Zephaniah

2. OTHER ABBREVIATIONS

ad loc.	*ad locum*, commentary on this passage
Apost.	Apostolic
can.	canon
chap.	chapter
cf.	*confer*, compare
Decl.	Declaration
Dz-Sch	Denzinger-Schönmetzer, *Enchiridion Biblicum* (4th edition, Naples-Rome, 1961)
Enc.	Encyclical
Exhort.	Exhortation
f	and following (*pl.* ff)
ibid.	*ibidem*, in the same place
in loc.	*in locum,* commentary on this particular passage
loc.	*locum*, place or passage
pl.	plural
par.	parallel passages
Past.	Pastoral
RSVCE	Revised Standard Version, Catholic Edition
SCDF	Sacred Congregation for the Doctrine of the Faith
sess.	session
v.	verse (*pl.* vv.)

See also abbreviations in “Sources quoted” on pp. 709–12.

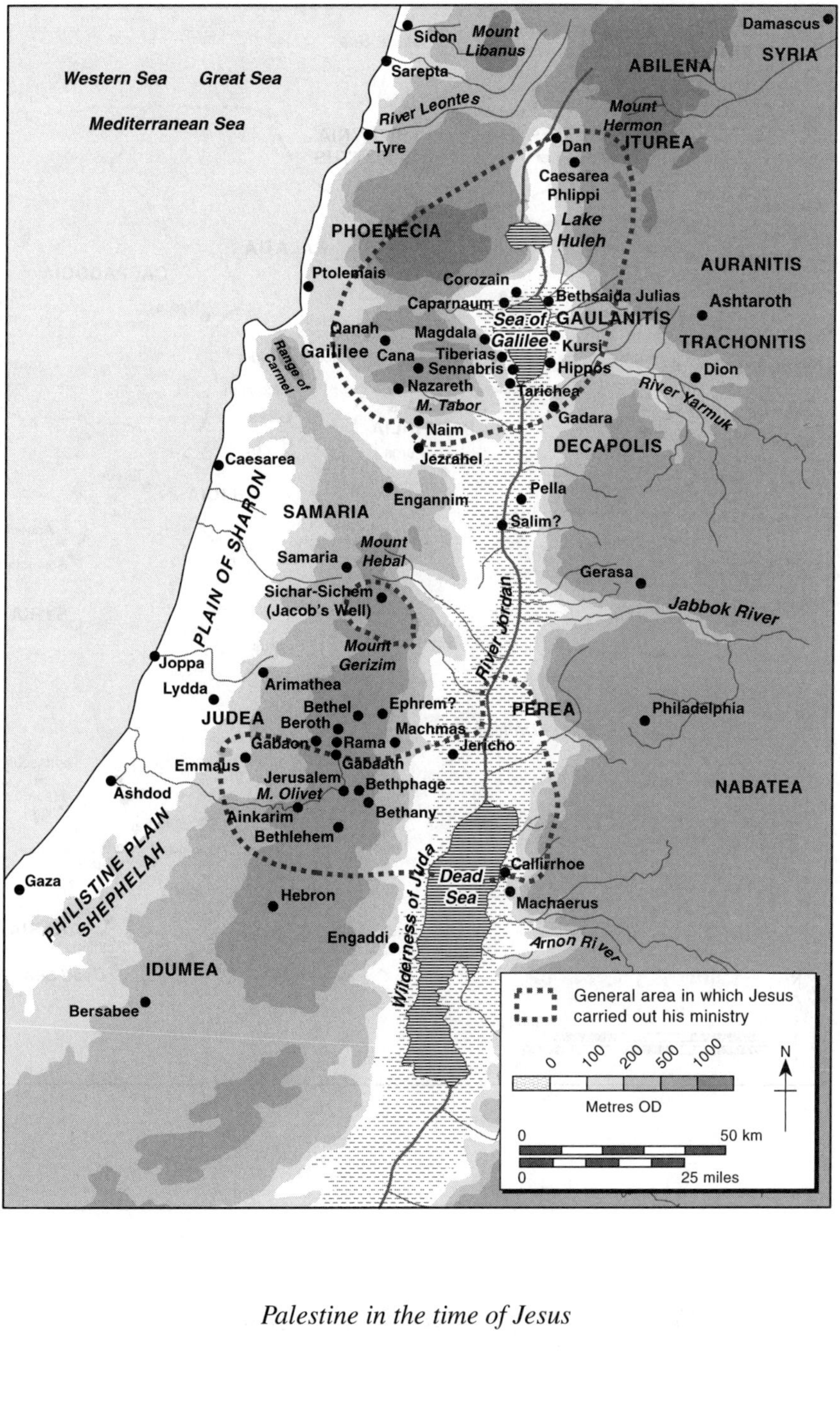

Palestine in the time of Jesus

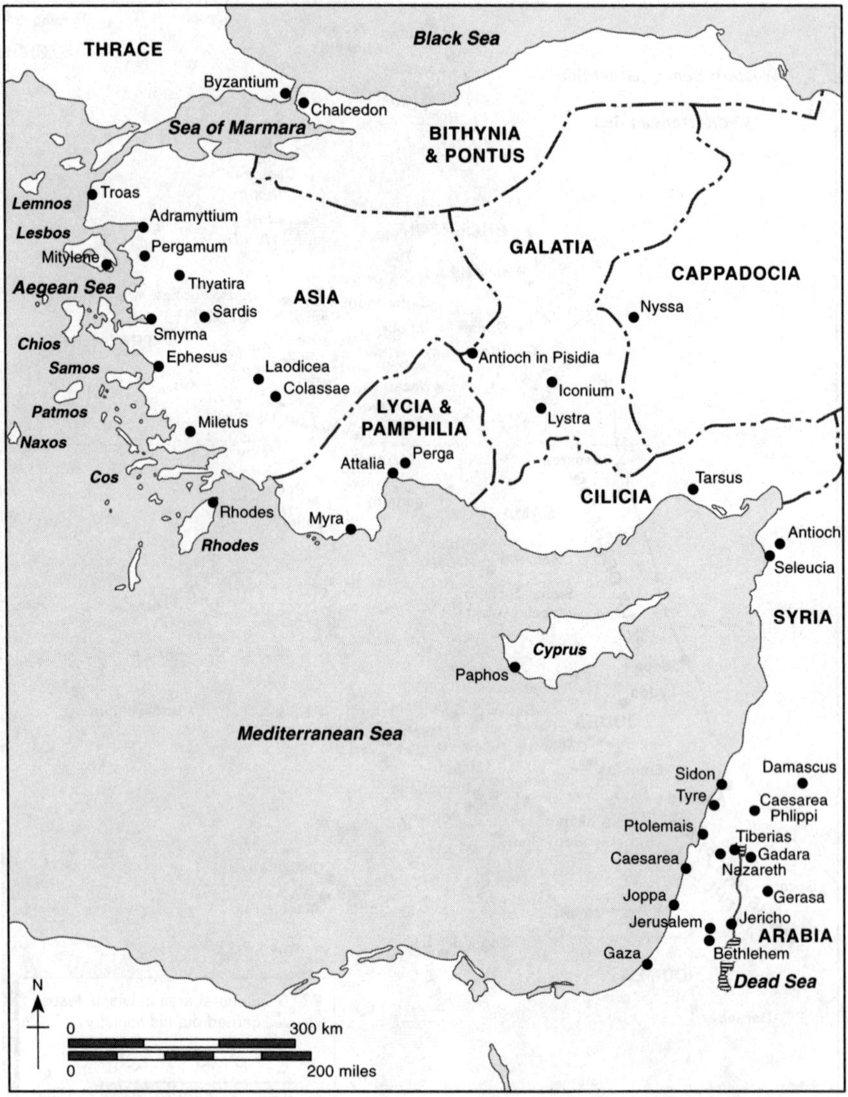

The Eastern Mediterranean Sea in the first century AD

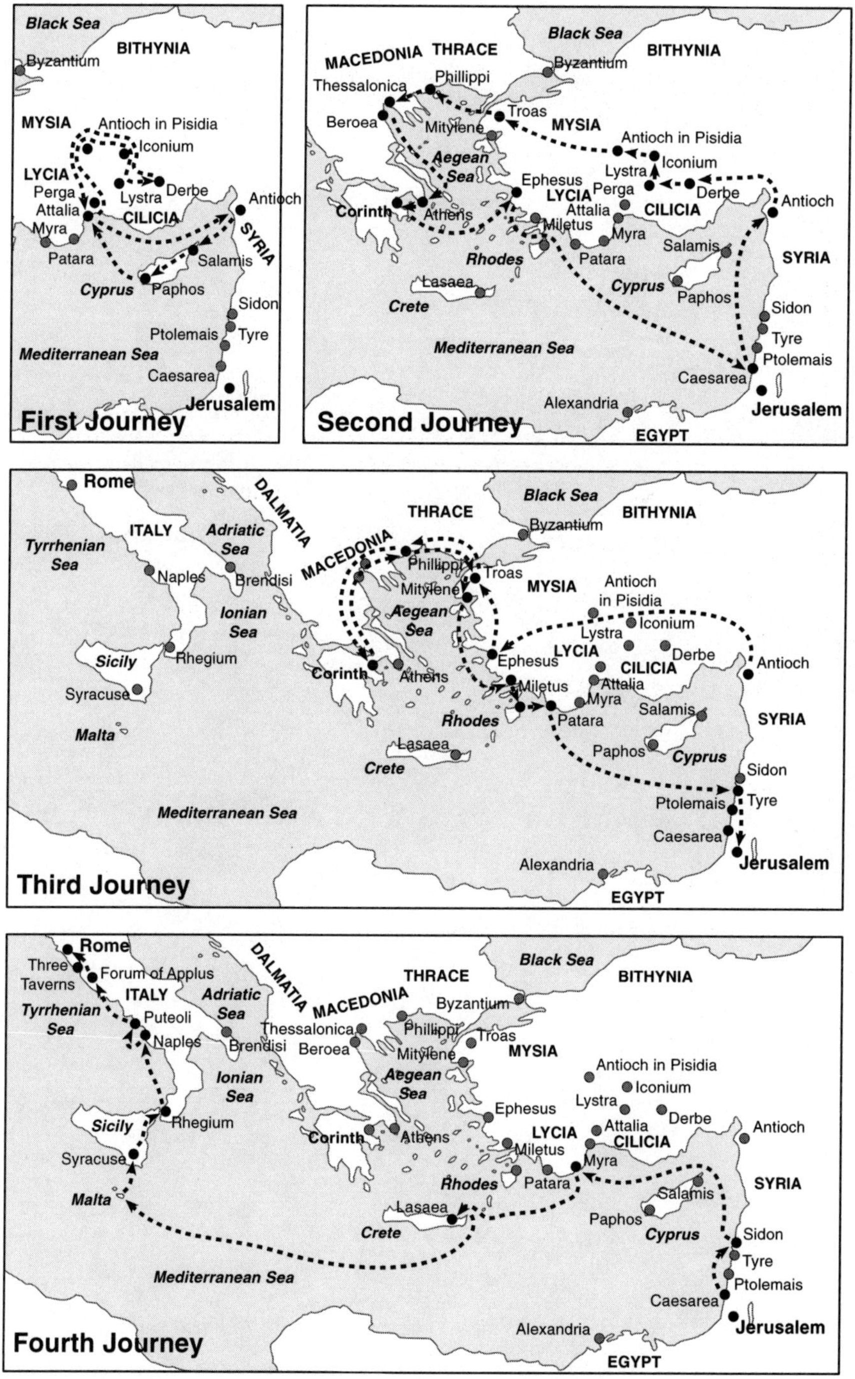

Missionary journeys of St Paul

The New Testament

The term "New Testament" means, first and foremost, the new and definitive Covenant established by God with mankind through Jesus Christ, in whom the Covenant offered to Israel found its fulfilment; that Covenant thereby became the "Old Testament". From the first century AD onwards, Christian writers used the terms "Old Testament" and "New Testament", that is, the Old and New Covenants, in that sense. From the second century onwards, the term "New Testament" acquired an additional meaning—the collection of books inspired by the Holy Spirit that bear divine and enduring testimony to the coming of Christ and to his work of salvation.

The canon of the New Testament consists of twenty-seven books, all of them written more or less in the second half of the first century. These books are often divided into three groups—*historical* books or narratives (the four Gospels and the Acts of the Apostles), *didactical* books or epistles (the thirteen letters of St Paul, the Letter to the Hebrews and the seven "catholic" letters); and the *prophetical* book or book of consolation (the Apocalypse or Revelation).

The entire New Testament tells us about Jesus Christ, revealing him to be "the Son of God made man, the Father's one, perfect and unsurpassable Word" (*CCC*, 65). That is why reading the New Testament is a very good way to get to know Jesus. The Gospels tell us what "Jesus, the Son of God, while he lived among men, really did and taught" (Vatican II, *DV*, 19). The other books, "in accordance with the wise design of God, firmly establish those matters which concern Christ the Lord, formulate more and more precisely his authentic teaching, preach the saving power of Christ's divine work, recount the beginnings and wonderful spread of the Church, and foretell its glorious consummation" (ibid., 20). This means that, by reading and reflecting on the books of the New Testament, Christians find a compass for their life's journey: the Gospels bear true witness to Jesus' life on earth and provide Christians with their Model; the letters help them to see what Christ's person and work mean for them today and for their Christian life; and the book of Revelation and other eschatological passages in the New Testament give them strength and encouragement to cope with difficulties and to keep alive their hope in ultimate victory.

The Gospels

The New Testament opens with the four Gospels; these are "the heart of all the Scriptures 'because they are our principal source for the life and teaching of the Incarnate Word, our Saviour' " (*CCC*, 125; Vatican II, *DV*, 18).

The word "gospel", of Greek origin, originally meant "good news" and was already in use to some degree in the time of Jesus. In Greek antiquity it was also used to mean the reward given to the bearer of that good news, or the offering made to the gods in thanksgiving for the benefits it brought. The Romans used the word to designate the contribution made by the emperor Augustus to mankind. In the Greek translation of the Old Testament (cf. Is 52:7) it is used to designate the messianic times, when God will save his people.

On beginning his public ministry (cf. Mk 1:13–14), Jesus preached the Gospel, the good news that it was he who would inaugurate the Kingdom of God. At the end of his life on earth (cf. Mk 16:15), he sent his apostles out to preach the Gospel to all creation. So, apostolic preaching about the life and message of Jesus is "the Gospel", good news. It is not surprising that as early as the middle of the second century AD the books reporting the actions and words of Jesus should be called the "memoirs of the apostles" or the "Gospels".

The origins of the Gospels lie in apostolic preaching. Jesus did not send his disciples out to write but to preach. They used every means available to them to spread the good news of Jesus and to make Jesus himself known, but the writing down of this apostolic teaching in the form of Gospels was not something that the disciples did during Jesus' lifetime; it was the result of a long process. The *Catechism of the Catholic Church* describes this process as follows: "We can distinguish three stages in the formation of the Gospels: 1. *The life and teaching of Jesus*. The Church holds firmly that the four Gospels, 'whose historicity she unhesitatingly affirms, faithfully hand on what Jesus, the Son of God, while he lived among men, really did and taught for their eternal salvation, until the day when he was taken up.' 2. *The oral tradition*. 'For, after the ascension of the Lord, the apostles handed on to their hearers what he had said and done, but with that fuller understanding which they, instructed by the glorious events of Christ and enlightened by the Spirit of truth, now enjoyed.' 3. *The written Gospels*. 'The sacred authors, in writing the four Gospels, selected certain of the many elements which had been handed on, either orally or already in written form; others they synthesized or explained with an eye to the situation of the churches, the while sustaining the form of preaching, but always in such a fashion that they have told us the honest truth about Jesus' " (*CCC*, 126; Vatican II, *DV*, 19).

The first three Gospels are also known as the "Synoptic Gospels". They show many similarities and also significant differences, from one to another. If the content of these Gospels is laid out in three parallel columns, one is able to see at a glance (*synopsis*) where they agree and where they differ. This "discordant concordance" applies both to the structure and the actual wording of these Gospels.

In their *structure* the three Gospels seem to follow the same pattern. After introducing Jesus, they recount his baptism by John, his activity in Galilee proclaiming the Kingdom of God, his going up to Jerusalem, and events of his time there, culminating in his passion, death and resurrection. Inside this pattern which they all share, we find that each evangelist has his own special characteristics: for example, St Matthew gives more space to Jesus' great discourses in Galilee; St Mark makes Peter's confession of faith the centre-piece of his account; while St Luke gives an extensive account of Jesus' preaching in his journey from Galilee to the Holy City, painting it as an unhurried journey up to Jerusalem.

As regards the content and wording of these three Gospels, they share about 350 verses. In addition to these, Matthew and Luke have another 230 verses or so in common; Matthew and Mark, some 180; and Mark and Luke, some 100. The fact that the Gospels all derive from the same apostolic tradition and that each evangelist is writing to meet the needs of his particular readers helps explain these similarities and differences. The degree to which one Gospel may owe something to another, or to which all of them owe something to earlier documents which have not survived, is something which scholars have not yet managed to work out.

The Gospel according to St John, although it has a different structure from that of the Synoptics and develops in a different way, also contains apostolic preaching, which is why it often concurs with the Synoptics, both as regards the public life of our Lord and in its account of his passion, death and resurrection.

The Gospel according to St Matthew

As is true of most of the sacred books, the author of the first Gospel does not identify himself in the text. From very early times, Tradition has attributed this Gospel to St Matthew, one of the twelve apostles. According to Papias, a second-century writer, Matthew wrote his Gospel "in the language of the Hebrews" (cf. Eusebius of Caesarea, *Eccl. Hist.*, 3, 39, 1). However, we have no written evidence of that version. The canonical Gospel of Matthew is a Greek version. Many features of the first Gospel lead us to think that it was written for a community which included Christians of both Jewish and pagan backgrounds; and for this reason scholars tend to think that it was written in Syria.

The evangelist begins his account with episodes from Jesus' infancy and from there on he follows the same structure as found in the other two Synoptics (cf. "The Gospels", above). However, the outstanding feature of the first Gospel is its inclusion of several long discourses by Jesus. Five of these—the sermon on the mount (5:1–7:27), the discourse to the twelve apostles (10:1–42), that of the parables (13:1–52), the so-called "discourse on the Church" (18:1–35) and the "eschatological discourse" (24:1–25:46)—conclude with words along the lines of "and when Jesus finished these sayings…" (cf. 7:28; 11:1; 13:53; 19:1; 26:1). Some scholars see this form of presentation of the Gospel as being evocative of the five books of the Pentateuch, the Jewish Law; certainly, they do show the evangelist's desire to make the point that Jesus is the Messiah who has come to bring the Law to fulfilment.

All the Gospels could claim to share the programme of the fourth evangelist when he tells his readers that he wrote his book "that you may believe that Jesus is the Christ, the Son of God, and that believing you may have life in you" (Jn 20:31). Within this general programme, each evangelist has laid stress on some particular aspect. St Matthew depicts Jesus as the *promised and rejected* Messiah. He shows, firstly, that Jesus is the promised Messiah, and to do this he presents Christ's words and actions in the light of various Old Testament passages. Very often he expressly makes the point that some particular event "took place to fulfil what the Lord had spoken by the prophet" (cf. 1:22–23; 2:5–6, 15, 17–18, 23; 3:3–4; 4:14–16; 8:17; 12:17–21; 13:35; 21:4–5; 27:9–10). For this and other reasons Matthew's book has been called the "Gospel of fulfilment". However, Israel rejects Jesus as the Messiah. Many passages in the first Gospel show the representatives of the Jewish establishment as being opposed to Jesus, and it also records Christ's sadness at the fact that Israel has failed to respond to God's plan. This is the reason why Jesus announces that God will form a new nation, a people "which produces its fruits" (21:43). This new people is the Church. And, so, the Gospel of St

Matthew has also been called the "Gospel of the Church" or the "ecclesiastical Gospel", because it is the one which is most at pains to explain how this new Israel is constituted: its foundation is enunciated in what Jesus says after Peter's profession of faith (16:16–18); its administration is evident from the "discourse on the Church" (18:1–34) and, above all, the fact of the Church (although it is not explicitly called "church") can be divined in many other passages—the parables about the Kingdom of heaven, the mission given to the apostles, etc. The members of the Church are asked to bear fruit in the form of deeds or works, so they will not go the way of the previous people of God (25:1–46); this means that Christians must observe all that Jesus has commanded (28:20), all that God has revealed to his people, because Christ did not come to abolish the Law and the Prophets but "to fulfil them" (5:17). Jesus, then, is the Master, the Teacher; but above all he is *Emmanuel*, God with us (1:23), who is in the midst of his Church (18:20), where he will abide until the end of the world (28:20).

Matthew

1. BIRTH AND INFANCY OF JESUS

The ancestry of Jesus Christ Lk 3:23–38

1 1The book of the genealogy of Jesus Christ, the son of David, the son of
Abraham.*
2Abraham was the father of Isaac, and Isaac the father of Jacob, and Jacob
the father of Judah and his brothers, 3and Judah the father of Perez and Zerah
by Tamar, and Perez the father of Hezron, and Hezron the father of Ram,[a] 4and
Ram[a] the father of Amminadab, and Amminadab the father of Nahson, and
Nahson the father of Salmon, 5and Salmon the father of Boaz by Rahab, and
Boaz the father of Obed by Ruth, and Obed the father of Jesse, 6and Jesse the
father of David the king.
And David was the father of Solomon by the wife of Uriah, 7and Solomon
the father of Rehoboam, and Rehoboam the father of Abijah, and Abijah the
father of Asa,[b] 8and Asa[b] the father of Jehoshaphat, and Jehoshaphat the father
of Joram, and Joram the father of Uzziah, 9and Uzziah the father of Jotham, and
Jotham the father of Ahaz, and Ahaz the father of Hezekiah, 10and Hezekiah the

---

1:1–2:23 ☐ St Matthew and St Luke begin their Gospels with episodes about Jesus' birth and infancy, thereby showing that the Good News about Jesus Christ includes (along with his death and resurrection, his teaching and public ministry) the proclamation of his human ancestry and the entirely unique way that the eternal Son of God (cf. Jn 1:14) became man. St Matthew shows Jesus to be the Messiah descended from David, the Saviour in whom God's promises to the people of Israel are fulfilled.

Matthew and Luke focus on essentially the same facts, though from different angles: Jesus was born in Bethlehem in Judea. His mother was the Virgin Mary, who was betrothed to St Joseph; but no man was involved in the conception of her child. The family eventually settled in Nazareth. In his account, St Matthew focuses particularly on St Joseph's role; St Luke, on the Blessed Virgin. St Matthew tells us that it was Joseph who received the news of Jesus' virginal conception; he then took Mary as his wife and it was he who gave the Child his name (1:18–25). After the Magi leave, Joseph is told to take the Child and his Mother and flee to Egypt. After Herod's death, Joseph is given another message by the angel—to return to the land of Israel (2:1–23).

1:1–17 Matthew provides this genealogy of Jesus going back to Abraham, to show that Jesus belongs to the chosen people of Israel, the recipient of God's

a. Greek *Aram* **b.** Greek *Asaph*

father of Manasseh, and Manasseh the father of Amos,[c] and Amos[c] the father
of Josiah, 11and Josiah the father of Jechoniah and his brothers, at the time of
the deportation to Babylon.
12And after the deportation to Babylon: Jechoniah was the father of
Shealtiel,[d] and Shealtiel[d] the father of Zerubbabel, 13and Zerubbabel the father
of Abiud, and Abiud the father of Eliakim, and Eliakim the father of Azor,
14and Azor the father of Zadok, and Zadok the father of Achim, and Achim the
father of Eliud,15 and Eliud the father of Eleazar, and Eleazar the father of
Matthan, and Matthan the father of Jacob, 16and Jacob the father of Joseph the
husband of Mary, of whom Jesus was born, who is called Christ.*
17So all the generations from Abraham to David were fourteen generations,
and from David to the deportation to Babylon fourteen generations, and from
the deportation to Babylon to the Christ fourteen generations.

The virginal conception of Jesus, and his birth Lk 1:26–38; 2:1–7

18Now the birth of Jesus Christ[f] took place in this way. When his mother Mary
had been betrothed to Joseph, before they came together she was found to be
with child of the Holy Spirit; 19and her husband Joseph, being a just man and
unwilling to put her to shame, resolved to send her away quietly. 20But as he
considered this, behold, an angel of the Lord appeared to him in a dream,

---

promises (cf. Gen 12:2–3). Luke, for his part, will take the genealogy back to Adam, to stress that Jesus belongs to all mankind (cf. Lk 3:23–38).

The genealogy presented here marks out three stages of salvation history (cf. v. 17), each consisting of fourteen generations not all of them the same length. Thus, he is making a play on the numbers fourteen and three. In Hebrew, the numerical value of the consonants of the word David totals fourteen; so, Matthew is showing that Jesus is the true Son of David (cf. 2 Sam 7:14).

For each link in the genealogy the evangelist uses the same verb—"was the father of" = "begot"; but for the last link he uses different wording (v. 16)—"Mary, of whom Jesus *was born*", indicating thereby the action of God in the virginal conception of Jesus.

1:18–25 Although Jesus was not the son of Joseph according to the flesh, he is however the Messiah descended from David. This is God's doing, because it is God who takes the initiative by calling Joseph to be the husband of Mary and the father of the Child. Joseph obediently accepted this calling and, in keeping with God's plan, truly acted as the father of Jesus, giving him the name of Jesus and taking care of the Child and the Blessed Virgin: "St Joseph really is a father and lord. He protects those who revere him and accompanies them on their journey through this life—just as he protected and accompanied Jesus when he was growing up. As you get to know him, you discover that the holy patriarch is also a

c. Other authorities read *Amon* **d.** Greek *Salathiel* **f.** Other ancient authorities *read of the Christ*

saying, "Joseph, son of David, do not fear to take Mary your wife, for that
which is conceived in her is of the Holy Spirit; 21 she will bear a son, and you
shall call his name Jesus, for he will save his people from their sins." 22 All this
took place to fulfil what the Lord had spoken by the prophet:

23 "Behold, a virgin shall conceive and bear a son,
and his name shall be called Emmanuel"

(which means God with us). 24 When Joseph woke from sleep, he did as the
angel of the Lord commanded him; he took his wife, 25 but knew her not until
she had borne a son; *and he called his name Jesus.

The adoration of the Magi

2 1 Now when Jesus was born in Bethlehem of Judea in the days of Herod
the king, behold, wise men from the East came to Jerusalem, saying,
2 "Where is he who has been born king of the Jews? For we have seen his star
in the East, and have come to worship him." 3 When Herod the king heard this,
he was troubled, and all Jerusalem with him; 4 and assembling all the chief
priests and scribes of the people, he inquired of them where the Christ was to
be born. 5 They told him, "In Bethlehem of Judea; for so it is written by the
prophet:

6 'And you, O Bethlehem, in the land of Judah,
are by no means least among the rulers of Judah;
for from you shall come a ruler
who will govern my people Israel.' "

---

master of the interior life—for he teaches us to know Jesus and share our life with him, and to realize that we are part of God's family" (Bl. J. Escrivá, *Hom.*, 1, 39).

2:1–12 St Matthew uses the story of the wise men, the Magi, to establish the historical context of events: "when Jesus was born in Bethlehem of Judea in the days of Herod the king" (v. 1). The wise men who seek Jesus out, not being Jews, are the first–fruits of the Gentiles who will receive the call of salvation in Christ: "May all the nations come to form part of the family of the patriarchs. And may the children of the promise receive the blessing of the people of Abraham, which was rejected by the children of his flesh. May all peoples, represented by the Magi, adore the creator of the universe, and may God be known not only in Judea but throughout the whole world, as it is written, his name shall be great in Israel" (St Leo the Great, *Serm. 3 in Epiph.*, 3).

As he did in the genealogy, Matthew teaches that Jesus is the Messiah, a king in the style of a new and greater David, in whom the prophecies are fulfilled which spoke of a star announcing his birth (cf. Num 24:17), the city of Bethlehem in which he is born (cf. Mic 5:1), and the kings of the earth doing obeisance to God, offering him gifts and worshipping him (Is 49:23; 60:5; Ps 72:10–15).

1:23 Is 7:14. **2:6** Mic 5:22.

7Then Herod summoned the wise men secretly and ascertained from them
what time the star appeared; 8and he sent them to Bethlehem, saying, "Go and
search diligently for the child, and when you have found him bring me word,
that I too may come and worship him." 9When they had heard the king they
went their way; and lo, the star which they had seen in the East went before
them, till it came to rest over the place where the child was. 10When they saw
the star, they rejoiced exceedingly with great joy; 11and going into the house
they saw the child with Mary his mother, and they fell down and worshipped
him. Then, opening their treasures, they offered him gifts, gold and frank-
incense and myrrh. 12And being warned in a dream not to return to Herod, they
departed to their own country by another way.

The flight into Egypt. The massacre of the Innocents

13Now when they had departed, behold, an angel of the Lord appeared to
Joseph in a dream and said, "Rise, take the child and his mother, and flee to
Egypt, and remain there till I tell you; for Herod is about to search for the
child, to destroy him." 14And he rose and took the child and his mother by
night, and departed to Egypt, 15and remained there until the death of Herod.
This was to fulfil what the Lord had spoken by the prophet, "Out of Egypt
have I called my son."

16Then Herod, when he saw that he had been tricked by the wise men, was
in a furious rage, and he sent and killed all the male children in Bethlehem and
in all that region who were two years old or under, according to the time which
he had ascertained from the wise men. 17Then was fulfilled what was spoken
by the prophet Jeremiah:

18"A voice was heard in Ramah,
wailing and loud lamentation,
Rachel weeping for her children;
she refused to be consoled,
because they were no more."

2:13–18 In recounting the mysteries of Christ's life, the evangelist shows their profound meaning. Jesus' flight into Egypt, and return to Palestine show him to be like Jacob (Gen 46:17) who went down into Egypt, and like the people of Israel who came up from there. Jesus is the new Israel/Jacob, and the new people of God, the Church, begins with him.

The episode of the holy innocents reveals the brutality of Herod, an upstart king, and it also shows Jesus' similarity to Moses, who was also providentially saved from death when still a child (Ex 2:1–10). The Church venerates these children because they "suffered as martyrs and confessed Christ *non loquendo, sed moriendo*, not by speaking, but by dying" (St Thomas Aquinas, *Com. on Mt*, in loc.).

2:15 Hos 11:1. **2:18** Jer 31:15.

The return to Nazareth Lk 2:51–52

19But when Herod died, behold, an angel of the Lord appeared in a dream to
Joseph in Egypt, saying, 20"Rise, take the child and his mother, and go to the
land of Israel, for those who sought the child's life are dead." 21And he rose
and took the child and his mother, and went to the land of Israel. 22But when
he heard that Archelaus reigned over Judea in place of his father Herod, he was
afraid to go there, and being warned in a dream he withdrew to the district of
Galilee. 23And he went and dwelt in a city called Nazareth, that what was
spoken by the prophets might be fulfilled, "He shall be called a Nazarene."

2. PRELUDE TO THE PUBLIC MINISTRY OF JESUS

The preaching of John the Baptist Mk 1:1–8; Lk 3:1–18; Jn 1:19–34

3 1In those days came John the Baptist, preaching in the wilderness of Judea,
2"Repent, *for the kingdom of heaven is at hand." 3For this is he who was
spoken of by the prophet Isaiah when he said,

"The voice of one crying in the wilderness:
Prepare the way of the Lord,
make his paths straight."

2:19–23 Everyone knew Jesus as being a native of Nazareth, the "Nazarene". The Jewish authorities used the word as a term of abuse (cf. Jn 1:46; 19:19). Even in St Paul's time, unbelieving Jews tried to humiliate Christians by calling them Nazarenes (cf. Acts 24:5). However, St Matthew sees the name "Nazarene" as fulfilling the prophecies and showing the messianic character of Jesus.

3:1–4:11 □ St Matthew describes Jesus' preparations immediately prior to his public ministry. The events related here happen in places which have enormous salvific meaning in the history of the people of Israel—the river Jordan, the gateway to the promised land (cf. Josh 3:8) and the wilderness, a place of trial and purification for the Jews (cf. Deut 8:2). This is the background against which the Kingdom of God is inaugurated by the coming of the Messiah; that coming is announced and confirmed by John the Baptist, the last of the prophets.

3:1–12 John the Baptist's style of life is in line with that of certain Old Testament prophets, particularly Elijah (cf. 2 Kings 1:8; 2:8–13ff). The quotation from Isaiah 40:3 shows that John's prophetic mission consists, firstly, in preparing the Jewish people to receive the Kingdom of God, and, secondly, in bearing witness to the fact that Jesus is the Messiah who is bringing that Kingdom into being. The Baptist teaches that the fact that someone is descended physically from Abraham does not mean he is saved: a personal conversion is needed which produces the good works of a holy life lived in God's presence.

3:3 Is 40:3.

[4]Now John wore a garment of camel's hair, and a leather girdle around his
waist; and his food was locusts and wild honey. [5]Then went out to him
Jerusalem and all Judea and all the region about the Jordan, [6]and they were
baptized by him in the river Jordan, confessing their sins.*
[7]But when he saw many of the Pharisees and Sadducees coming for
baptism, he said to them, "You brood of vipers! Who warned you to flee from
the wrath to come? [8]Bear fruit that befits repentance, [9]and do not presume to
say to yourselves, 'We have Abraham as our father'; for I tell you, God is able
from these stones to raise up children to Abraham. [10]Even now the axe is laid
to the root of the trees; every tree therefore that does not bear good fruit is cut
down and thrown into the fire.
[11]"I baptize you with water for repentance, but he who is coming after me
is mightier than I, whose sandals I am not worthy to carry; he will baptize you
with the Holy Spirit and with fire. [12]His winnowing fork is in his hand, and he
will clear his threshing floor and gather his wheat into the granary, but the
chaff he will burn with unquenchable fire."

Jesus is baptized Mk 1:9–11; Lk 3:21–22

[13]Then Jesus came from Galilee to the Jordan to John, to be baptized by him.
[14]John would have prevented him, saying, "I need to be baptized by you, and
do you come to me?" [15]But Jesus answered him, "Let it be so now; for thus it
is fitting for us to fulfil all righteousness." Then he consented.* [16]And when
Jesus was baptized, he went up immediately from the water, and behold, the
heavens were opened[g] and he saw the Spirit of God descending like a dove,
and alighting on him; [17]and lo, a voice from heaven, saying, "This is my
beloved son,[h] with whom I am well pleased."

Jesus fasts and is tempted Mk 1:12–13; Lk 4:1–13

4 [1]Then Jesus was led up by the Spirit into the wilderness to be tempted by
the devil. [2]And he fasted forty days and forty nights, and afterward he was

---

3:13–17 By seeking John's baptism, Jesus shows that he too supports the plan devised by God to prepare his people by means of the prophets. In this way our Lord "fulfils all righteousness" (v.15), that is, everything laid down by God.

The Gospel text makes it plain that Jesus is incomparably greater than the Baptist, and it also shows that the true Baptism given Jesus is the Holy Spirit descending on him: this anoints him for the mission on which he is about to embark. Jesus is the Anointed *par excellence*, that is, the Christ, the Messiah. And he is also declared Son of God by the one who has sent him—the Father. Cf. also the notes on Mk 1:9–13 and Lk 3:21–22.

4:1–11 Before beginning his work as Messiah and promulgating the New Law, in the sermon on the mount, Jesus prepares himself by prayer and fasting in the

g. Other ancient authorities add *to him* **h.** Or *my son, my* (or *the*) *Beloved*

hungry. [3]And the tempter came and said to him, “If you are the Son of God,
command these stones to become loaves of bread.” [4]But he answered, “It is
written,

> ‘Man shall not live by bread alone,
> but by every word that proceeds from the mouth of God.’ ”

[5]Then the devil took him to the holy city, and set him on the pinnacle of the
temple, [6]and said to him, “If you are the Son of God, throw yourself down; for
it is written,

> ‘He will give his angels charge of you,’

and

> ‘On their hands they will bear you up,
> lest you strike your foot against a stone.’ ”

[7]Jesus said to him, “Again it is written, ‘You shall not tempt the Lord your
God.’ ” [8]Again, the devil took him to a very high mountain, and showed him
all the kingdoms of the world and the glory of them; [9]and he said to him, “All
these I will give you, if you will fall down and worship me.” [10]Then Jesus said
to him, “Begone, Satan! for it is written,

> ‘You shall worship the Lord your God
> and him only shall you serve.’ ”

[11]Then the devil left him, and behold, the angels came and ministered to him.

---

desert. Moses acted in a similar way before proclaiming, in God’s name, the Old Law on Mount Sinai (Ex 34:28), and Elijah journeyed for forty days in the desert to equip himself for his mission to promote observance of the Law (cf. 1 Kings 19:5–8). The Church, too, invites us to interior renewal by means of penitential practices during the season of Lent: “Brothers, there are three means of ensuring that faith remains strong, and devotion and virtue constant—prayer, fasting and works of mercy. Prayer calls, fasting intercedes and works of mercy receive” (St Peter Chrysologus, *Serm.*, 43).

Matthew uses this episode of the temptations in the wilderness to depict Jesus as the new Israel, in contrast to the old. Jesus is tempted, as Moses and the chosen people were in their forty-year pilgrimage in the wilderness. The Israelites yielded to temptation: they complained against God on account of their hunger (Ex 16:1ff), demanded a miracle when they had no water (Ex 17:1–7), and adored the golden calf (Ex 32). But Jesus does not yield and, by overcoming the temptation, “reveals the way in which the Son of Man is Messiah, contrary to the way Satan proposes to him and the way men wish to attribute to him (cf. Mt 16:21–23)” (*CCC*, 540).

4.4 Deut 8:3. **4:6** Ps 91:11–12. **4:7** Deut 6:16. **4:10** Deut 6:13.

PART ONE: JESUS' MINISTRY IN GALILEE

Jesus begins to preach Mk 1:14–15; Lk 4:14–15

[12]Now when he heard that John had been arrested, he withdrew into Galilee;
[13]and leaving Nazareth he went and dwelt in Capernaum by the sea, in the
territory of Zebulun and Naphtali, [14]that what was spoken by the prophet
Isaiah might be fulfilled:

> [15]"The land of Zebulun and the land of Naphtali,
> toward the sea, across the Jordan, Galilee of the Gentiles—
> [16]the people who sat in darkness have seen a great light
> and for those who sat in the region and shadow of death
> light has dawned."

[17]From that time Jesus began to preach, saying, "Repent, for the kingdom of
heaven is at hand."

The first disciples are called Mk 1:16–20; Lk 5:1–11; Jn 1:35–51

[18]As he walked by the Sea of Galilee, he saw two brothers, Simon who is
called Peter and Andrew his brother, casting a net into the sea; for they were
fishermen. [19]And he said to them, "Follow me, and I will make you fishers of
men." [20]Immediately they left their nets and followed him. [21]And going on
from there he saw two other brothers, James the son of Zebedee and John his

---

4:12–16:20 □□ Jesus' ministry in Galilee now begins. By actions and words he proclaims that the Kingdom of God has come. First, he calls his disciples and assembles the new people of God (4:12–25). Then, as supreme Teacher, Lawgiver and Prophet, he proclaims the New Law of the Kingdom in the sermon on the mount (5:1–7:29). His teaching is vouched for by the "works of the Messiah", the miracles that confirm his authority (8:1–9:38).

The sending out of the apostles (10:1–42), and Jesus' actions (11:1–12:50) and words (13:1–52) show that he is more than a Teacher: he is the Messiah of Israel. The religious leaders of the chosen people (11:16–12:45) are bent on rejecting him, but the signs he works are so clear (14:13–15:39) that St Peter professes that Jesus is truly the Messiah, the Son of God (16:13–20).

4:12–25 The land which, in the time of Isaiah was ravaged by invaders and planted by sizeable numbers of foreigners, is now the first to receive the light of salvation and to hear the Messiah's preaching (cf. Is 8:23–9:1). Thus the prophecies are fulfilled.

Unlike John, who simply proclaims that the Kingdom is close at hand, our Lord begins to establish that Kingdom in human history by means of his actions and words. He calls his first disciples to leave all things—these men who will later

4:15–16 Is 9:1–2.

brother, in the boat with Zebedee their father, mending their nets, and he called
to them. 22Immediately they left the boat and their father, and followed him.
23And he went about all Galilee, teaching in their synagogues and preaching
the gospel of the kingdom and healing every disease and every infirmity
among the people. 24So his fame spread throughout all Syria and they brought
him all the sick, those afflicted with various diseases and pains, demoniacs,
epileptics, and paralytics, and he healed them. 25And great crowds followed
him from Galilee and the Decapolis and Jerusalem and Judea and from beyond
the Jordan.

3. THE SERMON ON THE MOUNT

The Beatitudes

Lk 6:20–26

5 1Seeing the crowds, he went up on the mountain, and when he sat down
his disciples came to him. 2And he opened his mouth and taught them,
saying:
3"Blessed are the poor in spirit, for theirs is the kingdom of heaven.
4"Blessed are those who mourn, for they shall be comforted.
5"Blessed are the meek, for they shall inherit the earth.
6"Blessed are those who hunger and thirst for righteousness, for they shall
be satisfied.
7"Blessed are the merciful, for they shall obtain mercy.
8"Blessed are the pure in heart, for they shall see God.
9"Blessed are the peacemakers, for they shall be called sons of God.

---

make up the group of the Twelve on which he will found his Church. The miracles he works are signs that Jesus is establishing the Kingdom of God, signs of the mercy and grace that God, through Jesus, is offering all men, as represented by the crowds that flock to him. "The Lord Jesus inaugurated his Church by preaching the Good News, that is, the coming of the Kingdom of God, promised over the ages in the scripture [. . .]. This kingdom shone out before men in the words, in the works and in the presence of Chirst" (Vatican II, *LG*, 5).

5:1–7:29 □ The sermon on the mount is the first of the five great discourses in which St Matthew brings together Jesus' teachings on the Kingdom of God. In this discourse we find a summary of the kinds of people who belong to the Kingdom (5:1–12) and what their attitudes should be to the Law (5:17–48; 6:16–18), to God (6:25–24), to their neighbour (6:1–4; 7:1–5), and what their approach to prayer should be (6:7–14; 7:7–11).

5:1–12 The beatitudes form the gateway to the sermon on the mount. In them Jesus includes the promises made to the chosen people from Abraham onwards;

[10]"Blessed are those who are persecuted for righteousness' sake, for theirs is the kingdom of heaven.

[11]"Blessed are you when men revile you and persecute you and utter all kinds of evil against you falsely on my account.

[12]"Rejoice and be glad, for your reward is great in heaven, for so men persecuted the prophets who were before you.

Salt of the earth and light of the world Mk 4:21; Lk 11:33; 14:34–35

[13]"You are the salt of the earth; but if salt has lost its taste, how shall its saltness be restored? It is no longer good for anything except to be thrown out and trodden under foot by men.

[14]"You are the light of the world. A city set on a hill cannot be hid. [15]Nor do men light a lamp and put it under a bushel, but on a stand, and it gives light to all the house. [16]Let your light so shine before men, that they may see your good works and give glory to your Father who is in heaven.

Jesus and his teaching, the fullness of the Law Lk 6:27–36; 12:58–59; 16:17–18

[17]"Think not that I have come to abolish the law and the prophets; I have come not to abolish them but to fulfil them.* [18]For truly I say to you, till heaven and

---

but he gives these promises a new orientation, focusing not just on possession of a land but on the Kingdom of heaven: "The Beatitudes depict the countenance of Jesus Christ and portray his charity. They express the vocation of the faithful associated with the glory of his passion and resurrection; they shed light on the actions and attitudes characteristic of the Christian life; they are the paradoxical promises that substain hope in the midst of tribulations; they proclaim the blessings and rewards already secured, however dimly, for Christ's disciples; they have begun in the lives of the Virgin Mary and all the saints" (*CCC*, 1717).

5:13–16 The similes of salt and light apply to those who practise the beatitudes, that is, Jesus' disciples, and they show the importance of good works (v. 16). Salt preserves food from corruption; in the offerings of the Old Law it symbolized the inviolability and enduring nature of the Covenant (cf. Lev 2:13). Our Lord makes it plain that his disciples are the salt of the earth, that is, they give a divine flavour to all human things, and preserve the world from corruption, by keeping alive the Covenant with God. "As the soul is in the body, so are Christians in the world" (Anon., *Letter to Diognetus,* 6, 1).

Moreover, like Jesus himself, his disciples should be light for those in darkness (cf. 4:16; Is 8:23–9:1). "It seems to me that this lamp stands for charity; it must shine out to cheer not only those I love best but all that are in the house" (St Thérèse of Lisieux, *Autobiography*, chap. 9).

5:17–48 In Jesus' time, in a climate of messianic expectancy, the role of being the definitive interpreter of the Law was attributed to the Messiah. Although he does

earth pass away, not an iota, not a dot, will pass from the law until all is
accomplished. 19Whoever then relaxes one of the least of these command-
ments and teaches men so, shall be called least in the kingdom of heaven; but
he who does them and teaches them shall be called great in the kingdom of
heaven. 20For I tell you, unless your righteousness exceeds that of the scribes
and Pharisees, you will never enter the kingdom of heaven.
21"You have heard that it was said to the men of old, 'You shall not kill; and
whoever kills shall be liable to judgment.' 22But I say to you that every one
who is angry with his brother[i] shall be liable to judgment; whoever insults[j] his
brother shall be liable to the council, and whoever says, 'You fool!' shall be
liable to the hell[k] of fire. 23So if you are offering your gift at the altar, and there
remember that your brother has something against you, 24leave your gift there
before the altar and go; first be reconciled to your brother, and then come and
offer your gift. 25Make friends quickly with your accuser, while you are going
with him to court, lest your accuser hand you over to the judge, and the judge
to the guard, and you be put in prison; 26truly, I say to you, you will never get
out till you have paid the last penny.
27"You have heard that it was said, 'You shall not commit adultery.' 28But I
say to you that every one who looks at a woman lustfully has already
committed adultery with her in his heart. 29If your right eye causes you to sin,

---

evoke this parallel with Moses, St Matthew shows that Jesus is much more than the interpreter: he is on the same level as God, he is above the Law. Jesus teaches the true meaning of the Law that God gave the Jewish people through Moses, and he perfects the Law by giving it a definitive interpretation, speaking with divine authority. To what "was said" (by God) to the men of old Jesus adds things which he himself now establishes. He does not abolish the precepts of the Old Law but he interiorizes them and perfects the Law's content, propounding teaching that was implicit in the Law's precepts but which men failed to appreciate.

In vv. 31–32 our Lord tackles the question of divorce. The Mosaic Law (Deut 24:1–4) tolerated divorce on account of the hardness of heart of the early Hebrews. Jesus re-establishes the original indissolubility of marriage as instituted by God (Gen 1:27; 2:24; cf. Mt 19:4–6; 1 Cor 7:10; Eph 5:31). The phrase "except on the ground of unchastity" should not be interpreted as an exception to the principle of indissolubility which Jesus has just re-established. It can almost definitely be said that the phrase refers to unions which some pagan peoples allowed as marriages but which, because they were incestuous, were banned by the Mosaic Law (cf. Lev 18)—unions, in other words, which were radically invalid on account of some impediment.

Verse 48 sums up the teaching contained in the entire chapter. Our Lord brings out the Law in all its fullness by teaching that we are to imitate the perfection of our Father who is in heaven. The goal behind keeping the Law is to attain the

i. Other ancient authorities insert *without cause* **j.** Greek *says Raca to* (an obscure term of abuse) **k.** Greek *Gehenna* **5:21** Ex 20:13; Deut 5:17. **5:27** Ex 20:11; Deut 5:18.

pluck it out and throw it away; it is better that you lose one of your members
than that your whole body be thrown into hell.[k]* 30And if your right hand
causes you to sin, cut it off and throw it away; it is better that you lose one of
your members than that your whole body go into hell.[k]
31"It was also said, 'Whoever divorces his wife, let him give her a cer-
tificate of divorce.' 32But I say to you that every one who divorces his wife,
except on the ground of unchastity,* makes her an adulteress; and whoever
marries a divorced woman commits adultery.
33"Again you have heard that it was said to the men of old, 'You shall not
swear falsely, but shall perform to the Lord what you have sworn.' 34But I say
to you, Do not swear at all, either by heaven, for it is the throne of God, 35or
by the earth, for it is his footstool, or by Jerusalem, for it is the city of the great
King. 36And do not swear by your head, for you cannot make one hair white
or black. 37Let what you say be simply 'Yes' or 'No'; anything more than this
comes from evil.[l]
38"You have heard that it was said, 'An eye for an eye and a tooth for a
tooth.' 39But I say to you, Do not resist one who is evil. But if any one strikes
you on the right cheek, turn to him the other also; 40and if any one would sue
you and take your coat, let him have your cloak as well; 41and if any one forces
you to go one mile, go with him two miles. 42Give to him who begs from you,
and do not refuse him who would borrow from you.
43"You have heard that it was said, 'You shall love your neighbour and hate
your enemy.' 44But I say to you, Love your enemies and pray for those who
persecute you, 45so that you may be sons of your Father who is in heaven; for
he makes his sun rise on the evil and on the good, and sends rain on the just
and on the unjust. 46For if you love those who love you, what reward have
you? Do not even the tax collectors do the same? 47And if you salute only your
brethren, what more are you doing than others? Do not even the Gentiles do
the same? 48You, therefore, must be perfect, as your heavenly father is perfect.

An upright intention in almsgiving, prayer and fasting Lk 11:1–4

6 1"Beware of practising your piety before men in order to be seen by them;
for then you will have no reward from your Father who is in heaven.

---

perfection or holiness of God. Strictly speaking this is not possible for a created being, but the holiness of God is the model towards which we should tend. "It is quite clear that all Christians in any state or walk of life are called to the fullness of Christian life and to the perfection of love, and by this holiness a more human manner of life is fostered also in earthly society" (Vatican II, *LG*, 40).

6:1–18 Jesus has more to say here about true "righteousness", the path that leads to salvation; he spells out the attitude that should motivate Christian behaviour.

l. Or *the evil one* **5:31** Deut 24:1. **5:33** Lev 19:12; Num 30:2. **5:35** Is 66:1; Ps 48:2. **5:38** Ex 21:24. **5:43** Lev 19:18.

2"Thus, when you give alms, sound no trumpet before you, as the hypocrites
do in the synagogues and in the streets, that they may be praised by men.
Truly, I say to you, they have their reward. 3But when you give alms, do not let
your left hand know what your right hand is doing, 4so that your alms may be
in secret; and your Father who sees in secret will reward you.

5"And when you pray, you must not be like the hypocrites; for they love to
stand and pray in the synagogues and at the street corners, that they may be
seen by men. Truly, I say to you, they have their reward. 6But when you pray,
go into your room and shut the door and pray to your Father who is in secret;
and your Father who sees in secret will reward you.*

7"And in praying do not heap up empty phrases as the Gentiles do; for they
think that they will be heard for their many words. 8Do not be like them, for
your Father knows what you need before you ask him. 9Pray then like this:

Our Father who art in heaven,
Hallowed by thy name.
10Thy kingdom come,
Thy will be done,
On earth as it is in heaven.
11Give us this day our daily bread;[m]
12And forgive us our debts,
As we also have forgiven our debtors;
13And lead us not into temptation,
But deliver us from evil.[n]

14For if you forgive men their trespasses, your heavenly Father also will
forgive you; 15but if you do not forgive men their trespasses, neither will your
Father forgive your trespasses.

16"And when you fast, do not look dismal, like the hypocrites, for they
disfigure their faces that their fasting may be seen by men. Truly, I say to you,

---

Almsgiving, prayer and fasting were the basic forms of personal piety among the chosen people, but Jesus teaches that true piety should go beyond the mere external; it should be practised with sincerity, in privacy with God and without any ostentation.

In his teaching on prayer our Lord stresses the simplicity and sincerity with which we should turn to God: "What we think should conform with what we say" (St Benedict, *Rule*, 19). Our Lord goes on to teach the Our Father as the distinctive prayer of the Christian. The tradition of the Church never ceases to sing the praises of this prayer: "The Lord's Prayer truly is a summary of the whole Gospel" (Tertullian, *De oratione*, 1). As St Thomas Aquinas puts it, "The Lord's Prayer is the most perfect of prayers [...]. In it we ask, not only for all the things we can rightly desire, but also in the sequence that they should be desired. This prayer teaches us not only to ask for things, but also in what order we should desire them" (*Summa theol.*, 2–2, 83, 9).

m. Or *our bread for the morrow.* **n.** Or *the evil one.* Other authorities, some ancient, add, in some form, *For thine is the kingdom and the power and the glory, for ever. Amen*

they have their reward. [17]But when you fast, anoint your head and wash your
face, [18]that your fasting may not be seen by men but by your Father who is in
secret; and your Father who sees in secret will reward you.

Trust in God's fatherly providence Lk 12:22–34

[19]"Do not lay up for yourselves treasures on earth, where moth and rust[o]
consume and where thieves break in and steal, [20]but lay up for yourselves
treasures in heaven, where neither moth nor rust[o] consumes and where thieves
do not break in and steal. [21]For where your treasure is, there will your heart be
also.

[22]"The eye is the lamp of the body. So, if your eye is sound, your whole
body will be full of light; [23]but if your eye is not sound, your whole body will
be full of darkness. If then the light in you is darkness, how great is the
darkness!

[24]"No one can serve two masters; for either he will hate the one and love
the other, or he will be devoted to the one and despise the other. You cannot
serve God and mammon.*

[25]"Therefore I tell you, do not be anxious about your life, what you shall eat
or what you shall drink, nor about your body, what you shall put on. Is not life
more than food, and the body more than clothing? [26]Look at the birds of the air;
they neither sow nor reap nor gather into barns, and yet your heavenly Father
feeds them. Are you not of more value than they? [27]And which of you by being
anxious can add one cubit to his span of life?[p] [28]And why are you anxious

---

6:19–34 This group of teachings again stresses the interior and spiritual nature of the Law which our Lord is bringing to perfection. Man's heart yearns for a treasure which will guarantee him security and happiness. Jesus teaches that the true treasure is good works, done with an upright intention; these will be eternally rewarded by God in heaven. That is where Christ's disciple should put his heart. Once again we can see that the righteousness of the Kingdom of God is the only thing that matters for man: a person who tries to do the will of the Father in line with Jesus' teaching will be given everything else as well (cf. v. 33).

Within this passage, vv. 22–23 are a little gem of Jesus' wisdom teaching. The Master uses the simile of the eye as a lamp which provides the body with light. Christian exegesis has interpreted this "eye" and this "lamp" as meaning the motivation behind our behaviour. "The eye refers to motive. When a person want to do something, he first forms an intention: thus, if your intention is sound—simple and clear—that is to say, if it is directed towards God, your whole body will be sound, sincerely directed towards good" (St Thomas, *Com. on Mt*, in loc.).

Verses 25–34 expand Jesus' teaching on the attitude we should have when saying the Lord's Prayer: we should trust in God our Father in the midst of our ordinary daily activities.

o. Or *worm* **p.** Or *to his stature*

about clothing? Consider the lilies of the field, how they grow; they neither toil
nor spin; [29]yet I tell you, even Solomon in all his glory was not arrayed like one
of these. [30]But if God so clothes the grass of the field, which today is alive and
tomorrow is thrown into the oven, will he not much more clothe you, O men of
little faith? [31]Therefore do not be anxious, saying, 'What shall we eat?' or
'What shall we drink?' or 'What shall we wear?' [32]For the Gentiles seek all
these things; and your heavenly Father knows that you need them all. [33]But
seek first his kingdom and his righteousness, and all these things shall be yours
as well.

[34]"Therefore do not be anxious about tomorrow, for tomorrow will be
anxious for itself. Let the day's own trouble be sufficient for the day.

Various precepts. Do not judge

Mk 4:24; Lk 6:37–42

7 [1]"Judge not, that you be not judged. [2]For with the judgment you pronounce
you will be judged, and the measure you give will be the measure you get.
[3]Why do you see the speck that is in your brother's eye, but do not notice the
log that is in your own eye? [4]Or how can you say to your brother, 'Let me take
the speck out of your eye,' when there is the log in your own eye? [5]You
hypocrite, first take the log out of your own eye, and then you will see clearly
to take the speck out of your brother's eye.

Respect for holy things

[6]"Do not give dogs what is holy; and do not throw your pearls before swine, lest
they trample them under foot and turn to attack you.

The effectiveness of prayer

Lk 11:5–13

[7]"Ask, and it will be given you; seek, and you will find; knock, and it will be
opened to you. [8]For every one who asks receives, and he who seeks finds, and
to him who knocks it will be opened. [9]Or what man of you, if his son asks him
for bread, will give him a stone? [10]Or if he asks for a fish, will give him a
serpent? [11]If you then, who are evil, know how to give good gifts to your
children, how much more will your Father who is in heaven give good things
to those who ask him!

7:1–12 St Matthew gathers together here various teachings of our Lord about the way his disciples should conduct themselves. We should practise brotherly love (vv. 1–5), treat Christ's teaching with respect and veneration (v. 6), and pray in the confidence that God will give us all we ask (vv. 7–11); basically, we should do good to others unconditionally, just as, quite reasonably, no one places conditions on the love he has for himself (v. 12).

The golden rule Lk 6–31
12So whatever you wish that men would do to you, do so to them; for this is the law and the prophets.

The narrow gate Lk 13:22–30
13"Enter by the narrow gate; for the gate is wide and the way is easy,[q] that leads to destruction, and those who enter by it are many. 14For the gate is narrow and the way is hard, that leads to life, and those who find it are few.

False prophets Lk 6:43–44
15"Beware of false prophets, who come to you in sheep's clothing but inwardly
are ravenous wolves. 16You will know them by their fruits. Are grapes gathered
from thorns, or figs from thistles? 17So, every sound tree bears good fruit, but
the bad tree bears evil fruit. 18A sound tree cannot bear evil fruit, nor can a bad
tree bear good fruit. 19Every tree that does not bear good fruit is cut down and
thrown into the fire. 20Thus you will know them by their fruits.

Doing the will of God Lk 13:25–30
21"Not every one who says to me, 'Lord, Lord,' shall enter the kingdom of
heaven, but he who does the will of my Father who is in heaven. 22On that day
many will say to me, 'Lord, Lord, did we not prophesy in your name, and cast
out demons in your name, and do many mighty works in your name?' 23And
then will I declare to them, 'I never knew you; depart from me, you evildoers.'

7:13–27 The last part of the sermon on the mount gives the conditions required for entering the Kingdom of God as seen from the angle of the final judgement. It takes a real effort to follow the route to the Kingdom, but the goal is Life, or eternal salvation (vv. 13–14). "The way of Christ 'leads to life'; a contrary way 'leads to destruction'. The Gospel parable of the *two ways* remains ever present in the catechesis of the Church; it shows the importance of moral decisions for our salvation" (*CCC*, 1696). It is not surprising that Christ's disciples should meet difficulties or be led astray by false prophets (who will not be judged worthy to enter the Kingdom: vv. 15–20). Our Lord stresses that a disciple of his will be judged in line with whether he did the Father's will during his life on earth (vv. 21–23). The parable about building on rock (vv. 24–27) sums up the way a person should act in order to enter the Kingdom of God, which is continually made present in the Church. A person who strives to put Jesus' teachings into practice, no matter what personal difficulties arise and even if he or she finds himself or herself surrounded by false doctrines, will remain steadfast in faith, like the wise man who builds his house on rock.

q. Other ancient authorities read *for the way is wide and easy*

Building on rock Lk 6:46–49

24 “Every one then who hears these words of mine and does them will be like
a wise man who built his house upon the rock; 25 and the rain fell, and the
floods came, and the winds blew and beat upon that house, but it did not fall,
because it had been founded on the rock. 26 And every one who hears these
words of mine and does not do them will be like a foolish man who built his
house upon the sand; 27 and the rain fell, and the floods came, and the winds
blew and beat against that house, and it fell; and great was the fall of it.”

The authority of Jesus’ teaching

28 And when Jesus finished these sayings, the crowds were astonished at his
teaching, 29 for he taught them as one who had authority, and not as their scribes.

4. THE MIRACLES OF THE MESSIAH

Curing of a leper Mk 1:40–45; Lk 5:12–16

8 1 When he came down from the mountain, great crowds followed him; 2 and
behold, a leper came to him and knelt before him, saying, “Lord, if you
will, you can make me clean.” 3 And he stretched out his hand and touched
him, saying, “I will; be clean.” And immediately his leprosy was cleansed.*
4 And Jesus said to him, “See that you say nothing to any one; but go, show
yourself to the priest, and offer the gift that Moses commanded, for a proof to
the people.”[r]

7:28–29 These verses marking the close of the sermon indicate (through Christ’s manner of teaching) that he is the Messiah, and they show the effect his discourse had on his listeners. They also act as a link with the next section that follows, reporting miracles of Jesus which ratify his authority.

8:1–9:38 □ In the previous section (5:1–7:29) we saw Jesus as the supreme lawgiver and teacher. Now he is depicted as being endowed with divine authority over disease, death, the elements of nature and evil spirits. The miracles worked by Jesus confirm the divine authority of his teaching, and his divinity.

8:1–4 For the third time (cf. 4:23; 5:1) the Gospel shows the following Jesus has acquired; there is no doubt about his popularity.

In this particular cure we can see the leper’s faith in Jesus’ power, and the way Jesus does not promote himself. It is plain to see that our Lord respects what the Law lays down: if a leper was cured, he had to present himself to a priest, who verified the cure and gave authorization for the person to resume his place in the civil and religious life of Israel (cf. Lev 14).

r. Greek *to them*

The centurion's faith
Lk 7:1–10; Jn 4:46–54

5 As he entered Capernaum, a centurion came forward to him, beseeching him 6 and saying, "Lord, my servant is lying paralyzed at home, in terrible distress." 7 And he said to him, "I will come and heal him." 8 But the centurion answered him, "Lord, I am not worthy to have you come under my roof; but only say the word, and my servant will be healed. 9 For I am a man under authority, with soldiers under me; and I say to one, 'Go,' and he goes, and to another, 'Come,' and he comes, and to my slave, 'Do this,' and he does it." 10 When Jesus heard him, he marvelled, and said to those who followed him, "Truly, I say to you, not even[s] in Israel have I found such faith. 11 I tell you, many will come from east and west and sit at table with Abraham, Isaac, and Jacob in the kingdom of heaven, 12 while the sons of the kingdom will be thrown into the outer darkness; there men will weep and gnash their teeth." 13 And to the centurion Jesus said, "Go; be it done for you as you have believed." And the servant was healed at that very moment.

Curing of Peter's mother-in-law
Mk 1:29–31; Lk 4:38–39

14 And when Jesus entered Peter's house, he saw his mother-in-law lying sick with a fever; 15 he touched her hand, and the fever left her, and she rose and served him.

Other cures
Mk 1:32–34; Lk 4:40–41

16 That evening they brought to him many who were possessed with demons; and he cast out the spirits with a word, and healed all who were sick. 17 This was to fulfil what was spoken by the prophet Isaiah, "He took our infirmities and bore our diseases."

8:5–13 If a Jew entered the house of a Gentile, he contracted legal impunity (cf. Jn 18:28; Acts 11:2–3). The centurion's refinement and faith can be seen from the way he makes his request to our Lord (vv. 8–10). Jesus uses this encounter with a Gentile believer to pronounce a solemn prophecy to the effect that the Gospel will be preached to all, and not just to Jews. "The closer an apostle is to God, the more universal his desires. His heart expands and takes in everybody and everything in its longing to lay the universe at the feet of Jesus" (Blessed J. Escrivá, *The Way*, 764).

8:14–17 St Matthew here offers the true interpretation of Jesus' miracles in the light of the prophecy of Isaiah: "Moved by so much suffering Christ not only allows himself to be touched by the sick, but he makes their miseries his own: 'He took our infirmities and bore our diseased' (Mt 8:17; cf. Is 53:4). But he did not heal all the sick. His healings were signs of the coming of the Kingdom of God. They announced a more radical healing: the victory over sin and death through his Passover" (*CCC*, 1505).

s. Other ancient authorities read *with no one* **8:17** Is 53:4

Following Christ is not easy Lk 9:57–62

[18]Now when Jesus saw great crowds around him, he gave orders to go over to
the other side. [19]And a scribe came up and said to him, "Teacher, I will follow
you wherever you go." [20]And Jesus said to him, "Foxes have holes, and birds
of the air have nests; but the Son of man has nowhere to lay his head."
[21]Another of the disciples said to him, "Lord let me first go and bury my
father." [22]But Jesus said to him, "Follow me, and leave the dead to bury their
own dead."

The calming of the storm Mk 4:35–41; Lk 8:22–25

[23]And when he got into the boat, his disciples followed him. [24]And behold,
there arose a great storm on the sea, so that the boat was being swamped by the
waves; but he was asleep. [25]And they went and woke him, saying, "Save, Lord;
we are perishing." [26]And he said to them, "Why are you afraid, O men of little
faith?" Then he rose and rebuked the winds and the sea; and there was a great
calm. [27]And the men marvelled, saying, "What sort of man is this, that even
winds and sea obey him?"

The demoniacs of Gadara Mk 5:1–20; Lk 8:26–39

[28]And when he came to the other side, to the country of the Gadarenes,[t] two
demoniacs met him, coming out of the tombs, so fierce that no one could pass
that way. [29]And behold, they cried out, "What have you to do with us, O Son

---

8:18–22 Jesus, who uses his authority to cure diseases, is at the same time the humble Messiah, rejected by his own people. Anyone who wants to be with him has to "follow him". Following Jesus means being his disciple (cf. 19:21). Occasionally we are told that the crowds "follow him" (4:25; 8:1; 20:29; etc.). But his true disciples are "those who follow him" all the time. This following calls for the same sort of detachment and self-surrender as our Lord himself practised.

8:23–27 Jesus has power not only over disease but also over the elements of nature. He is the Son of God. In the "ecclesiastical Gospel", as the Gospel of Matthew is sometimes called, the boat is a symbol for the Church. The faith which the disciples got from seeing the miracle continues to be found in the Church. The Church, in which Christ is present, is the universal vehicle of salvation. "The waves beat against her [the Church] but she holds firm, and though the elements of this world often rise up against her, she offers the sure port of salvation to all who are hard-pressed" (St Ambrose, *Letters*, 2,1).

8:28–34 Jesus has authority over demons and diabolical powers. These are able to act in man and also, if God so permits, in other creatures which lead man to set himself against God. The Jews regarded pigs as unclean (the same attitude obtains

t. Other ancient authorities read *Gergesenes*; some, *Gerasenes*

of God? Have you come here to torment us before the time?"* [30]Now a herd
of many swine was feeding at some distance from them. [31]And the demons
begged him, "If you cast us out, send us away into the herd of swine." [32]And
he said to them, "Go." So they came out and went into the swine; and behold,
the whole herd rushed down the steep bank into the sea, and perished in the
waters. [33]The herdsmen fled, and going into the city they told everything, and
what had happened to the demoniacs. [34]And behold, all the city came out to
meet Jesus; and when they saw him, they begged him to leave their neigh-
bourhood.

Curing of a paralyzed man

Mk 2:1–12; Lk 5:17–26

9 [1]And getting into a boat he crossed over and came to his own city. [2]And
behold, they brought to him a paralytic, lying on his bed; and when Jesus
saw their faith he said to the paralytic, "Take heart, my son; your sins are
forgiven." [3]And behold, some of the scribes said to themselves, "This man is
blaspheming." [4]But Jesus, knowing[u] their thoughts, said, "Why do you think
evil in your hearts? [5]For which is easier, to say, 'Your sins are forgiven,' or to say,
'Rise and walk'? [6]But that you may know that the Son of man has authority on
earth to forgive sins"—he then said to the paralytic—"Rise, take up your bed
and go home." [7]And he rose and went home. [8]When the crowds saw it, they
were afraid, and they glorified God, who had given such authority to men.

The call of Matthew

Mk 2:13–17, Lk 5:27–32

[9]As Jesus passed on from there, he saw a man called Matthew sitting at the tax
office; and he said to him, "Follow me." And he rose and followed him.

[10]And as he sat at table[v] in the house, behold, many tax collectors and
sinners came and sat down with Jesus and his disciples. [11]And when the
Pharisees saw this, they said to his disciples, "Why does your teacher eat with

---

in some Gentile countries); their meat could not be eaten (cf. Deut 14:8); so, in this passage the cure of the possessed man and the destruction of the swine indicate Jesus' complete victory over the demon.

9:1–8 By curing the paralytic by his word and nothing more, Jesus shows his critics that, just as he has power to cure the effects of sin (disease), so too does he have power to cure the cause of disease, that is, sin: he has divine power. Our Lord gives a share in this power to his apostles and their successors, that is, bishops and their co-workers, priests (cf. Jn 20–22).

9:9–13 Jesus calls whomever he wishes, without reference to the sort of distinctions the Pharisees used to make. Now he calls a tax collector, whom Mark

u. Other ancient authorities read *seeing*. **v.** Greek *reclined*

tax collectors and sinners?" [12]But when he heard it, he said, "Those who are
well have no need of a physician, but those who are sick. [13]Go and learn what
this means, 'I desire mercy, and not sacrifice.' For I came not to call the
righteous, but sinners."

A discussion on fasting Mk 2:18–22; Lk 5:33–39

[14]Then the disciples of John came to him, saying, "Why do we and the
Pharisees fast,[w] but your disciples do not fast?" [15]And Jesus said to them, "Can
the wedding guests mourn as long as the bridegroom is with them? The days
will come, when the bridegroom is taken away from them, and then they will
fast. [16]And no one puts a piece of unshrunk cloth on an old garment, for the
patch tears away from the garment, and a worse tear is made. [17]Neither is new
wine put into old wineskins; if it is, the skins burst, and the wine is spilled, and
the skins are destroyed; but new wine is put into fresh wineskins, and so both
are preserved."

The raising of Jairus' daughter and the curing of the woman with a hemorrhage Mk 5:21–43; Lk 8:40–56

[18]While he was thus speaking to them, behold, a ruler came in and knelt before
him, saying, "My daughter has just died; but come and lay your hand on her,
and she will live." [19]And Jesus rose and followed him, with his disciples.
[20]And behold, a woman who had suffered from a hemorrhage for twelve
years came up behind him and touched the fringe of his garment; [21]for she said
to herself, "If I only touch his garment, I shall be made well." [22]Jesus turned,
and seeing her he said, "Take heart, daughter; your faith has made you well."
And instantly the woman was made well. [23]And when Jesus came to the ruler's

---

and Luke name as Levi (cf. Mk 2:14; Lk 5:27) and whom tradition identifies as the author of the first Gospel. Many people were shocked to see Jesus do such a thing (Lk 11:19). But, using words of the prophet Hosea, Jesus identified his merciful approach to sinners with God's own attitude to them.

9:14–17 The teaching contained in these verses shows the significance of Jesus' action in calling sinners. He sets up a new relationship between man and God which involves complete regeneration. His spirit is too fresh, too powerful, to fit into old formulae, which are ceasing to be valid.

9:18–26 These two miracles show, once more, that faith is needed if one is to be able to receive the saving influence of Jesus—in the case of the woman, a faith which overcomes obstacles even though it is a faith timidly expressed; for his part, Jairus, a man of substance, humbles himself before Jesus in the sight of all and openly begs his help.

w. Other ancient authorities add *much* or *often* **9:13** Hos 6:6.

house, and saw the flute players, and the crowd making a tumult, [24]he said,
"Depart; for the girl is not dead but sleeping." And they laughed at him. [25]But
when the crowd had been put outside, he went in and took her by the hand, and
the girl arose. [26]And the report of this went through all that district.

Curing of two blind men. The dumb devil Lk 11:14–15

[27]And as Jesus passed on from there, two blind men followed him, crying
aloud, "Have mercy on us, Son of David." [28]When he entered the house, the
blind men came to him; and Jesus said to them, "Do you believe that I am able
to do this?" They said to him, "Yes, Lord." [29]Then he touched their eyes,
saying, "According to your faith be it done to you." [30]And their eyes were
opened. And Jesus sternly charged them, "See that no one knows it." [31]But
they went away and spread his fame through all that district.

[32]As they were going away, behold, a dumb demoniac was brought to him.
[33]And when the demon had been cast out, the dumb man spoke; and the crowds
marvelled, saying, "Never was anything like this seen in Israel." [34]But the
Pharisees said, "He casts out demons by the prince of demons."

The need for good pastors Mk 6:34; Lk 10:2

[35]And Jesus went about all the cities and villages, teaching in their synagogues
and preaching the gospel of the kingdom, and healing every disease and every
infirmity. [36]When he saw the crowds, he had compassion for them, because
they were harassed and helpless, like sheep without a shepherd. [37]Then he said
to his disciples, "The harvest is plentiful, but the labourers are few; [38]pray
therefore the Lord of the harvest to send out labourers in to his harvest."

9:27–34 The faith of these two blind men leads them to follow Jesus despite their disability. The evangelist makes it clear how opinions about Jesus were divided: those with simplicity of heart acknowledge his unique power; others, with more complicated minds, completely misinterpret the signs he works.

9:35–38 By his account of the sermon on the mount and the miracles Jesus works, the evangelist has shown how Jesus put into effect the programme of action summarized in v. 35 and announced earlier in 4:23. It is a programme which will have a world-wide scope and will extend across history through the mission of the apostles sent out to work in the fields of the Lord.

Jesus is moved when he sees the crowds. He sees as now being fulfilled the prophecy of Ezekiel 34 in which God, through the prophet, upbraids the false shepherds of Israel and promises to send the Messiah to be the people's new leader. The evangelist's words allow us to see into Jesus' heart: "This Divine Heart is a great abyss which holds all good, and he commands that all his poor people

9:36 Num 27:17.

5. FROM THE OLD TO THE NEW PEOPLE OF GOD

The calling of the twelve apostles Mk 3:12–19; Lk 6:12–16

10 [1]And he called to him his twelve disciples and gave them authority over
unclean spirits, to cast them out, and to heal every disease and every
infirmity. [2]The names of the twelve apostles are these: first, Simon, who is
called Peter, and Andrew his brother; James the son of Zebedee, and John his
brother; [3]Philip and Bartholomew; Thomas and Matthew the tax collector;
James the son of Alphaeus, and Thaddaeus;[x] [4]Simon the Cananaean, and Judas
Iscariot, who betrayed him.

The apostles' first mission Mk 6:6–13; Lk 9:1–6

[5]These twelve Jesus sent out, charging them, "Go nowhere among the
Gentiles, and enter no town of the Samaritans,* [6]but go rather to the lost sheep
of the house of Israel. [7]And preach as you go, saying, 'The kingdom of heaven

---

should pour their needs into it. It is an abyss of joy in which we cast away all our burdens; an abyss of humility in which we discard our pride. It is a fount of mercy for the wretched, an abyss of love in which to drown our weakness" (St Margaret Mary Alacoque, *Divine Office*, 16 October).

10:1–12:50 □ In this section the evangelist describes the confrontation between Jesus and his disciples, on the one hand, and unbelieving Jews, on the other. The change-over from the old to the new people of God is taking place. The section begins with the second of our Lord's five great discourses in this Gospel; it is usually called "the apostolic discourse" (10:1–42). Jesus prepares his twelve apostles for their mission, an apostolate which will be continued by the Church to the end of time. But, in reaction to the proclamation of Jesus as Messiah, the religious leaders of the chosen people become increasingly obstinate in their rejection of him (11:16–12:50).

10:1–4 In order to advance the Kingdom of God which he is inaugurating, Jesus founds a new people of God, the Church; this he does by empowering and instructing the twelve apostles, who succeed and take over from the twelve patriarchs of the twelve tribes of Israel and who form the seed of the Church: "He sent them first of all to the children of Israel and then to all peoples so that, sharing in his power, they might make all peoples his disciples and sanctify and govern them and thus spread the Church and, administering it under the guidance of the Lord, shepherd it all days until the end of the world" (Vatican II, *LG*, 19).

10:5–15 In his plan of salvation God made certain promises to the Hebrew people, along with a covenant and the Law, and sent prophets to them. The

x. Other ancient authorities read *Lebbaeus* or *Lebbaeus called Thaddaeus*.

is at hand.' 8Heal the sick, raise the dead, cleanse lepers, cast out demons. You
received without pay, give without pay. 9Take no gold, nor silver, nor copper
in your belts, 10no bag for your journey, nor two tunics, nor sandals, nor a staff;
for the labourer deserves his food. 11And whatever town or village you enter,
find out who is worthy in it, and stay with him until you depart. 12As you enter
the house, salute it. 13And if the house is worthy, let your peace come upon it;
but if it is not worthy, let your peace return to you. 14And if any one will not
receive you or listen to your words, shake off the dust from your feet as you
leave that house or town. 15Truly, I say to you, it shall be more tolerable on the
day of judgment for the land of Sodom and Gomorrah than for that town.

Jesus' instructions to the apostles Mk 13:9–13; Lk 12:1–12,49–53; 21:12–17

16"Behold, I send you out as sheep in the midst of wolves; so be wise as
serpents and innocent as doves. 17Beware of men; for they will deliver you up
to councils, and flog you in their synagogues, 18and you will be dragged before
governors and kings for my sake, to bear testimony before them and the
Gentiles. 19When they deliver you up, do not be anxious how you are to speak
or what you are to say; for what you are to say will be given to you in that
hour; 20for it is not you who speak, but the Spirit of your Father speaking
through you. 21Brother will deliver up brother to death, and the father his child,
and children will rise against parents and have them put to death; 22and you
will be hated by all for my name's sake. But he who endures to the end will be
saved. 23When they persecute you in one town, flee to the next; for truly, I say

---

Messiah, according to his human generation, would be born of this chosen people, which explains why the Messiah and the Kingdom of God should be preached first to the house of Israel and only later to Gentiles: the people of Israel were the medium through which all others could be reconciled to God.

The powers mentioned in v. 8 were the very sign the prophets predicted for the Kingdom of God or the reign of the Messiah. To begin with (8:1–9:38) it is Jesus Christ who exercises these powers; now the time has come for him to confer them on his disciples, to show that theirs is a divine mission (cf. Is 35:5–6; 40:9; 52:7; 61:1).

The peace that the apostles should bring with them (vv. 11–15) is the sign of God's blessings which Jesus' disciples, his envoys, are to pour out on those who give them a good reception.

10:16–42 Here we have a gathering together of instructions and markers about how the Gospel is to be spread. These words apply not only to the apostles but to all Christ's disciples; in the performance of their mission they will experience difficulties and persecution as our Lord himself did, for "a disciple is not above his teacher, nor a servant above his master" (v. 24).

to you, you will not have gone through all the towns of Israel, before the Son
of man comes.
[24]"A disciple is not above his teacher, nor a servant[y] above his master; [25]it is
enough for the disciple to be like his teacher, and the servant[y] like his master. If
they have called the master of the house Beelzebul, how much more will they
malign those of his household.
[26]"So have no fear of them; for nothing is covered that will not be revealed,
or hidden that will not be known. [27]What I tell you in the dark, utter in the light;
and what you hear whispered, proclaim upon the housetops. [28] And do not fear
those who kill the body but cannot kill the soul; rather fear him who can destroy
both soul and body in hell.[z] [29]Are not two sparrows sold for a penny? And not
one of them will fall to the ground without your Father's will. [30]But even the
hairs of your head are all numbered. [31]Fear not, therefore; you are of more value
than many sparrows. [32]So every one who acknowledges me before men, I also
will acknowledge before my Father who is in heaven; [33]but whoever denies me
before men, I also will deny before my Father who is in heaven.
[34]"Do not think that I have come to bring peace on earth; I have not come to
bring peace, but a sword. [35]For I have come to set a man against his father, and
a daughter against her mother, and a daughter-in-law against her mother-in-law;
[36]and a man's foes will be those of his own household. [37]He who loves father or
mother more than me is not worthy of me; and he who loves son or daughter
more than me is not worthy of me; [38]and he who does not take his cross and
follow me is not worthy of me. [39]He who finds his life will lose it, and he who
loses his life for my sake will find it.

Jesus describes himself as "the Son of man" (v. 23), indicating that he is the judge who, at the end of the world, will judge all mankind (cf. 25:31). The "coming" mentioned here in the Gospel is probably a reference to the destruction of Jerusalem and the temple in the year 70—events which are a sort of anticipated sign of the punishment which will be meted out at the end of time to those who reject Christ and his Gospel. Anyway, the passage does state that the task of preaching the Gospel will go on until the end of time.

In vv. 28–31, our Lord once again teaches the paternal providence of God, about which he had much to say in the sermon on the mount (cf. 6:19–34). Here he is speaking in the context of the persecution that awaits his disciples, but it is not something we should be afraid of. "If the birds, which are of such little worth, are not abandoned by God's providence and concern, how can you, who in the nature of your souls are eternal, fear that he whom you know as Father will not look after you with special care?" (St Jerome, in *Cat. aurea*, in loc.).

At the end of this passage he gives two key guidelines for Christian living—the radicalism involved in following Jesus (vv. 37–39), and the identification of the disciple with his or her teacher (vv. 40–42).

y. Or *slave* **z.** Greek *Gehenna* **10:35** Mic 7:6.

40“He who receives you receives me, and he who receives me receives him who sent me. 41He who receives a prophet because he is a prophet shall receive a prophet’s reward, and he who receives a righteous man because he is a righteous man shall receive a righteous man’s reward. 42And whoever gives to one of these little ones even a cup of cold water because he is a disciple, truly, I say to you, he shall not lose his reward.”

Messengers from John the Baptist

Lk 7:18–30

11 1And when Jesus had finished instructing his twelve disciples, he went on from there to teach and preach in their cities.

2Now when John heard in prison about the deeds of the Christ, he sent word by his disciples 3and said to him, “Are you he who is to come, or shall we look for another?”* 4And Jesus answered them, “Go and tell John what you hear and see: 5the blind receive their sight and the lame walk, lepers are cleansed and the deaf hear, and the dead are raised up, and the poor have good news preached to them. 6And blessed is he who takes no offence at me.”

7As they went away, Jesus began to speak to the crowds concerning John: “What did you go out into the wilderness to behold? A reed shaken by the wind? 8Why then did you go out? To see a man[a] clothed in soft raiment? Behold, those who wear soft raiment are in kings’ houses. 9Why then did you go out? To see a prophet?[b] Yes, I tell you, and more than a prophet. 10This is he of whom it is written,

> ‘Behold, I send my messenger before thy face,
> who shall prepare thy way before thee.’

11Truly, I say to you, among those born of women there has risen no one greater than John the Baptist; yet he who is least in the kingdom of heaven is greater than he. 12From the days of John the Baptist until now the kingdom of heaven has suffered violence,[c] and men of violence take it by force. 13For all the prophets and the law prophesied until John; 14and if you are willing to accept it, he is Elijah who is to come. 15He who has ears to hear,[d] let him hear.

11:1–15 In contrast to those who reject Jesus we have the figure of John the Baptist. Our Lord tells the Baptist’s disciples that they have seen performed before their very eyes the signs which the ancient prophecies foretold about the Messiah and his Kingdom (cf. Is 26:19; 29:18–19; 35:35; 66:1; etc.). He is telling them, in effect, that he is the prophet “who was to come” (cf. v. 3).

As regards the Baptist (vv. 7–14), Jesus shows them that John truly was his precursor, the one who had the same mission as Elijah, in line with the belief at the time that the prophet Elijah would have to come again in advance of the Messiah (cf. 17:10–13; Mk 9:10–13).

a. Or *what then did you go out to see? A man . . .* **b.** Other ancient authorities read *What then did you go out to see? A prophet?* **c.** Or *has been coming violently* **d.** Other ancient authorities omit *to hear*
11:5 Is 35:5–6; 61:1. **11:10** Mal 3:1.

Jesus reproaches his contemporaries Lk 7:31–35

16"But to what shall I compare this generation? It is like children sitting in the market places and calling to their playmates,

17'We piped to you, and you did not dance;
we wailed, and you did not mourn.'

18For John came neither eating nor drinking, and they say, 'He has a demon';
19the Son of man came eating and drinking, and they say, 'Behold, a glutton and a drunkard, a friend of tax collectors and sinners!' Yet wisdom is justified by her deeds."[e]

Jesus reproaches cities for their unbelief Lk 10:13–16

20Then he began to upbraid the cities where most of his mighty works had been done, because they did not repent. 21"Woe to you, Chorazin! woe to you, Bethsaida! for if the mighty works done in you had been done in Tyre and Sidon, they would have repented long ago in sackcloth and ashes. 22But I tell you, it shall be more tolerable on the day of judgment for Tyre and Sidon than for you. 23And you, Capernaum, will you be exalted to heaven? You shall be brought down to Hades. For if the mighty works done in you had been done in Sodom, it would have remained until this day. 24But I tell you that it shall be more tolerable on the day of judgment for the land of Sodom than for you."

Jesus thanks his Father Lk 10:21–24

25At that time Jesus declared, "I thank thee, Father, Lord of heaven and earth, that thou hast hidden these things from the wise and understanding and revealed them to babes; 26yea, Father, for such was thy gracious will.[f] 27All

---

11:16–19 Quoting some popular song or children's game of the time, Jesus reproaches for their empty excuses those who are slow to acknowledge him. The actions of Jesus and John the Baptist, each in their own way, provide clear evidence that God's plan for man's salvation is being accomplished: the fact that some people fail to acknowledge this is not going to prevent God's plan being put into effect.

11:20–24 Chorazin and Bethsaida were thriving cities on the north shore of the lake of Gennesaret, not far from Capernaum. During his public ministry Jesus often preached in these cities and worked many miracles there. Tyre and Sidon, two cities of Phoenicia, along with Sodom and Gomorrah (all notorious for loose living), were classical examples that the Jews used to cite in connexion with divine punishment for sin (cf. Ezek 26–28; Is 23).

11:25–30 In contrast to what he says about those who do not believe in him, Jesus rejoices over those who accept him—simple, humble people who don't trust in

e. Other ancient authorities read *children* (Luke 7.35). **f.** Or *so it was well-pleasing before thee*
11:23 Is 14:13–15.

things have been delivered to me by my Father; and no one knows the Son
except the Father, and no one knows the Father except the Son and any one to
whom the Son chooses to reveal him.* 28Come to me, all who labour and are
heavy laden, and I will give you rest. 29Take my yoke upon you, and learn
from me; for I am gentle and lowly in heart, and you will find rest for your
souls. 30For my yoke is easy, and my burden is light."

The law of the sabbath Mk 2:23–28; Lk 6:1–5

12 1At that time Jesus went through the grainfields on the sabbath; his
disciples were hungry, and they began to pluck ears of grain and to eat.
2But when the Pharisees saw it, they said to him, "Look, your disciples are
doing what is not lawful to do on the sabbath." 3He said to them, "Have you
not read what David did, when he was hungry, and those who were with him:
4how he entered the house of God and ate the bread of the Presence, which it
was not lawful for him to eat nor for those who were with him, but only for the
priests? 5Or have you not read in the law how on the sabbath the priests in the
temple profane the sabbath, and are guiltless? 6I tell you, something greater
than the temple is here. 7And if you had known what this means, 'I desire
mercy, and not sacrifice,' you would not have condemned the guiltless. 8For the
Son of man is lord of the sabbath."

---

their own wisdom like those who consider themselves prudent and worldly wise. "His exclamation, 'Yes, Father!', expresses the depth of his heart, his adherence to the Father's 'good pleasure', echoing his mother's *Fiat* at the time of his conception and prefiguring what he will say to the Father in his agony. The whole prayer of Jesus is contained in this loving adherence of his human heart to the mystery of the will of the Father (cf. Eph 1:9)" (*CCC*, 2603).

"Yoke" (v. 29) was a word used to describe the Law of Moses which, with the passage of time, had become encrusted and weighed down by all kinds of little rules and regulations which were impossible to bear (cf. Acts 15:10) and which gave people no peace of soul. Jesus, instead, tells them about his yoke and his burden: "Any other burden weighs upon you and crushes you, but Christ's yoke reduces the weight. Any other yoke is heavy, but Christ's yoke has wings. If you were to deprive a bird of its wings, you might seem to have reduced its weight, but the more you take that weight from it, the more you are tying it to the earth. You see there on the ground someone you wanted to relieve of a burden; restore to him the burden of his wings and you will see how he flies" (St Augustine, *Serm.*, 126, 12).

12:1–14 When Jesus, with divine authority, gives a definitive interpretation of the Law, he is opposed by some Pharisees who fail to accept his teaching even though it is underwritten by the miracles that accompany it. This happens, for instance, apropos of the sabbath. God instituted the sabbath and commanded the Jewish people to abstain from certain kinds of work on that day in order to make it easier

Curing of the man with a withered hand Mk 3:1–6; Lk 6:6–11
9And he went on from there, and entered their synagogue. 10And behold, there
was a man with a withered hand. And they asked him, "Is it lawful to heal on
the sabbath?" so that they might accuse him. 11He said to them, "What man of
you, if he has one sheep and it falls into a pit on the sabbath, will not lay hold
of it and lift it out? 12Of how much more value is a man than a sheep! So it is
lawful to do good on the sabbath." 13Then he said to the man, "Stretch out your
hand." And the man stretched it out, and it was restored, whole like the other.
14But the Pharisees went out and took counsel against him, how to destroy him.*

Jesus, the servant of God
15Jesus, aware of this, withdrew from there. And many followed him, and he
healed them all, 16and ordered them not to make him known. 17This was to
fulfil what was spoken by the prophet Isaiah:

18"Behold my servant whom I have chosen,
my beloved with whom my soul is well pleased.
I will put my Spirit upon him,
and he shall proclaim justice to the Gentiles.
19He will not wrangle or cry aloud,
nor will any one hear his voice in the streets;
20he will not break a bruised reed
or quench a smouldering wick,
till he brings justice to victory;
21and in his name will the Gentiles hope."

---

for them to spend time honouring God. In due course, this divine precept was made so complicated that, in Jesus' time, thirty-nine types of work were forbidden. Jesus often teaches that sabbath rest is not infringed by service of God or of one's neighbour and he rejects the Pharisees' criticism on four grounds—the example of David; the fact that priests work; divine mercy; and the fact that Jesus himself is lord of the sabbath. Then he goes on to corroborate his teaching by working the miracle.

12:15–21 By his quotation from the prophet Isaiah (vv. 18–21) the evangelist provides the key to the teaching contained in chapters 11 and 12 which shows the hardness of heart that brings the Jewish leaders to reject Christ: in Jesus is fulfilled the prophecy of the suffering Servant whose loving and gentle teaching would bring the light of truth to the world. Jesus' mission as suffering Servant, which began at his Baptism on the Jordan (3:17), can be seen again in Matthew's account of the way the Pharisees oppose Jesus; and he shows it very particularly in his account of Christ's passion and death (cf. 27:30).

12:7 Hos 6:6. **12:18–21** Is 42:1–14.

Allegations by the Pharisees.
The sin against the Holy Spirit Mk 3:22–30; Lk 6:43–45; 11:14–26

[22]Then a blind and dumb demoniac was brought to him, and he healed him, so
that the dumb man spoke and saw. [23]And all the people were amazed, and said,
"Can this be the Son of David?" [24]But when the Pharisees heard it they said,
"It is only by Beelzebul, *the prince of demons, that this man casts out
demons." [25]Knowing their thoughts, he said to them, "Every kingdom divided
against itself is laid waste, and no city or house divided against itself will
stand; [26]and if Satan casts out Satan, he is divided against himself; how then
will his kingdom stand? [27]And if I cast out demons by Beelzebul, by whom do
your sons cast them out? Therefore they shall be your judges. [28]But if it is by
the Spirit of God that I cast out demons, then the kingdom of God has come
upon you. [29]Or how can one enter a strong man's house and plunder his goods,
unless he first binds the strong man? Then indeed he may plunder his house.
[30]He who is not with me is against me, and he who does not gather with me
scatters. [31]Therefore I tell you, every sin and blasphemy will be forgiven men,
but the blasphemy against the Spirit will not be forgiven.* [32]And whoever says
a word against the Son of man will be forgiven; but whoever speaks against the
Holy Spirit will not be forgiven, either in this age or in the age to come.

[33]"Either make the tree good, and its fruit good; or make the tree bad, and
its fruit bad; for the tree is known by its fruit. [34]You brood of vipers! how can
you speak good, when you are evil? For out of the abundance of the heart the
mouth speaks. [35]The good man out of his good treasure brings forth good, and
the evil man out of his evil treasure brings forth evil. [36]I tell you, on the day of
judgment men will render account for every careless word they utter; [37]for by
your words you will be justified, and by your words you will be condemned."

12:22–37 Jesus rejects the Pharisees' malicious accusation (v. 24) by pointing out that his casting out of demons proves that the Kingdom of God has begun and that Satan is being ousted from his domains. Verse 30 sums up his whole line of argument: either one is with Him or with the devil. Such an absolute requirement made by Christ only goes to show his divinity.

The sin against the Holy Spirit (v. 32) "does not properly consist in offending against the Holy Spirit in words; it consists rather in the refusal to accept the salvation which God offers to man through the Holy Spirit, working through the power of the Cross. [...] Blasphemy against the Holy Spirit is the sin committed by the person who claims to have a '*right*' *to persist in evil*—in any sin at all—and who thus rejects Redemption" (John Paul II, *Dom. et Viv.*, 46). It is in this sense that it is described as unforgivable.

The sign of Jonah Lk 11:24–26, 29–32

38Then some of the scribes and Pharisees said to him, "Teacher, we wish to see
a sign from you." 39But he answered them, "An evil and adulterous generation
seeks for a sign; but no sign shall be given to it except the sign of the prophet
Jonah. 40For as Jonah was three days and three nights in the belly of the whale, so
will the Son of man be three days and three nights in the heart of the earth. 41The
men of Nineveh will arise at the judgment with this generation and condemn it;
for they repented at the preaching of Jonah, and behold, something greater than
Jonah is here. 42The queen of the South will arise at the judgment with this
generation and condemn it; for she came from the ends of the earth to hear the
wisdom of Solomon, and behold, something greater than Solomon is here.
43"When the unclean spirit has gone out of a man, he passes through
waterless places seeking rest, but he finds none. 44Then he says, 'I will return
to my house from which I came.' And when he comes he finds it empty, swept,
and put in order. 45Then he goes and brings with him seven other spirits more
evil than himself, and they enter and dwell there; and the last state of that man
becomes worse than the first. So shall it be also with this evil generation."

The true kinsmen of Jesus Mk 3:31–35; Lk 5:19–21

46While he was still speaking to the people, behold, his mother and his
brethren *stood outside, asking to speak to him.[g] 48But he replied to the man
who told him, "Who is my mother, and who are my brethren?"* 49And
stretching out his hand toward his disciples, he said, "Here are my mother and

---

12:38–45 Apropos of the sign they ask of him, perhaps a miracle or some other work of wonder, Jesus replies by announcing his death and resurrection, comparing himself with the prophet Jonah. By drawing this parallel he shows that he himself is the "sign" *par excellence*, the clinching proof of the divinity of his person, his mission and his teaching. The Ninevites did penance because they recognized the prophet Jonah and accepted his message. Jesus is greater than Jonah. And he is also greater than Solomon, whom Jewish tradition saw as the epitome of the wise man. The queen of the South was the queen of Sheba, a kingdom in the south of Arabia, who visited Solomon (1 Kings 10:1–13) and was amazed by the wisdom God had given him. The Ninevites and the queen will confront those Jews who fail to come over to Jesus or to seek the truth.

The rejection of Jesus by those Jews leads to a grave warning: if they continue to reject the light, their last state will be worst than the first.

12:46–50 Jesus regards as belonging to his own family those who accept him and do the will of God the Father. "Becoming a disciple of Jesus means accepting the invitation to belong to God's family, to live in comformity with his way of life" (*CCC*, 2233).

g. Other ancient authorities insert verse 47, *Some one told him, "Your mother and your brothers are standing outside, asking to speak to you"* **12:40** Jon 1:17.

my brethren! [50]For whoever does the will of my Father in heaven is my brother,
and sister, and mother."

6. THE PARABLES OF THE KINGDOM

Parable of the sower. The meaning of parables

Mk 4:1–20; Lk 8:4–15

13 [1]That same day Jesus went out of the house and sat beside the sea.
[2]And great crowds gathered about him, so that he got into a boat and sat
there; and the whole crowd stood on the beach. [3]And he told them many things
in parables, saying: "A sower went out to sow. [4]And as he sowed, some seeds
fell along the path, and the birds came and devoured them. [5]Other seeds fell on
rocky ground, where they had not much soil, and immediately they sprang up,
since they had no depth of soil, [6]but when the sun rose they were scorched;
and since they had no root they withered away. [7]Other seeds fell upon thorns,
and the thorns grew up and choked them. [8]Other seeds fell on good soil and
brought forth grain, some a hundredfold, some sixty, some thirty. [9]He who has
ears,[h] let him hear."

[10]Then the disciples came and said to him, "Why do you speak to them in
parables?" [11]And he answered them, "To you it has been given to know the

---

The "brethren" of Jesus mentioned here are relatives. Ancient languages—Hebrew, Aramaic, Arabic etc.—normally used this term to mean people belonging to the same family, clan or even tribe. The Church has always maintained as absolutely certain that Jesus had no brothers or sisters in the full sense of the term: it is a dogma that Mary was ever-Virgin (cf. ibid., 500).

13:1–52 □ The discourse of the parables, the third of those recounted in St Matthew, marks the start of a new section of the Gospel. It includes seven parables about the Kingdom of heaven. All three Synoptic Gospels (cf. Mk 4:1–34; Lk 8:4–18) record this discourse, and all refer to the same fact: after the first parable, that of the sower, the disciples ask our Lord what it means, and Jesus then explains the "secrets of the kingdom of heaven" (v. 11; cf. Mk 4:11; Lk 8:10). The parable of the sower tells us what our attitude should be to the Word of God; this may be why it is placed at the start of the discourse.

Matthew includes here two parables which Mark and Luke position elsewhere in their narratives—that of the weeds and that of the mustard seed. These are often called the "parables about growth" because they describe the conditions that allow the seed to grow and also the fact that the Kingdom is small to begin with but its internal vigour gives it a multiplying effect (cf. the note on Mk 4:1–34). Finally, this Gospel includes here additional parables—those of the treasure, the pearl and the net.

h. Other ancient authorities add here and in verse 43 *to hear*

secrets of the kingdom of heaven, but to them it has not been given. [12]For to him
who has will more be given, and he will have abundance; but from him who has
not, even what he has will be taken away.* [13]This is why I speak to them in para-
bles, because seeing they do not see, and hearing they do not hear, nor do they
understand. [14]With them indeed is fulfilled the prophecy of Isaiah which says:

'You shall indeed hear but never understand,
and you shall indeed see but never perceive.
[15]For this people's heart has grown dull,
and their ears are heavy of hearing,
and their eyes they have closed,
lest they should perceive with their eyes,
and hear with their ears,
and understand with their heart,
and turn for me to heal them.'

[16]But blessed are your eyes, for they see, and your ears, for they hear. [17]Truly,
I say to you, many prophets and righteous men longed to see what you see,
and did not see it, and to hear what you hear, and did not hear it.

[18]"Hear then the parable of the sower. [19]When any one hears the word of
the kingdom and does not understand it, the evil one comes and snatches away

---

13:1–23 Jesus used parables a great deal in his preaching. The rabbis of the time also used them to explain phrases in Scripture, but Jesus makes much more use of them and he does so with a purpose of his own—to reveal the mysteries of God. "Jesus' invitation to enter his kingdom comes in the form of parables, a characteristic feature of his teaching (cf. Mk 4: 33–34). Through his parables he invites people to the feast of the kingdom (cf. Mt 22:1–14), but he also asks for a radical choice: to gain the kingdom, one must give everything (cf. Mt 13:44–45). Words are not enough, deeds are required (cf. Mt 21: 28–31). The parables are like mirrors for man: will he be hard soil or good earth for the word (cf Mt 13:3–9) What use has he made of the talents he has received (cf. Mt 25: 14–30)? Jesus and the presence of the kingdom in this world are secretly at the heart of the parables. One must enter the kingdom, that is, become a disciple of Christ, in order to 'know the secrets of the kingdom of heaven' (Mt 13:11.). For those who stay 'outside' (Mk 4:11), everything remains enigmatic (cf. Mt 13:10–15)" (*CCC*, 546).

From the point of view of its form, a parable can be a simple comparison or a detailed story. Sometimes Jesus' parables have a paradoxical tone to them, in order to capture people's attention and awaken their curiosity. Because parables are based on things people are familiar with, they are something everyone can understand. However, in order to grasp their full message, one needs to go beyond the image or story. That is why, if someone has a closed mind, he never gets past

13:14–15 Is 6:9–10.

what is sown in his heart; this is what was sown along the path. [20]As for what was sown on rocky ground, this is he who hears the word and immediately receives it with joy; [21]yet he has no root in himself, but endures for a while, and when tribulation or persecution arises on account of the word, immediately he falls away.[i] [22]As for what was sown among thorns, this is he who hears the word, but the cares of the world and the delight in riches choke the word, and it proves unfruitful. [23]As for what was sown on good soil, this is he who hears the word and understands it; he indeed bears fruit, and yields, in one case a hundredfold, in another sixty, and in another thirty."

Parable of the weeds

[24]Another parable he put before them, saying, "The kingdom of heaven may be compared to a man who sowed good seed in his field; [25]but while men were sleeping, his enemy came and sowed weeds among the wheat, and went away. [26]So when the plants came up and bore grain, then the weeds appeared also. [27]And the servants [j] of the householder came and said to him, 'Sir, did you not sow good seed in your field? How then has it weeds?' [28]He said to them, 'An enemy has done this.' The servants [j] said to him, 'Then do you want us to go and gather them?' [29]But he said, 'No; lest in gathering the weeds you root up the wheat along with them. [30]Let both grow together until the harvest; and at harvest time I will tell the reapers, Gather the weeds first and bind them in bundles to be burned, but gather the wheat into my barn.' "

The mustard seed; the leaven Mk 4:30–34; Lk 13:18–21

[31]Another parable he put before them saying, "The kingdom of heaven is like a grain of mustard seed which a man took and sowed in his field; [32]it is the smallest of all seeds, but when it has grown it is the greatest of shrubs and becomes a tree, so that the birds of the air come and make nests in its branches."

[33]He told them another parable. "The kingdom of heaven is like leaven which a woman took and hid in three measures of meal, till it was all leavened."

[34]All this Jesus said to the crowds in parables; indeed he said nothing to them without a parable. [35]This was to fulfil what was spoken by the prophet:[k]

"I will open my mouth in parables,
I will utter what has been hidden
since the foundation of the world."

---

the surface of the parable. Jesus accuses people like that of not using their ears. On the meaning of vv. 14–15, see the note on Mk 4:10–12.

13:24–52 The parable of the weeds complements that of the sower. The devil also sows (v. 39); he sows his snares, and in some people they prove productive:

i. Or *stumbles* **j.** Or *slaves* **k.** Other ancient authorities read *the prophet Isaiah* **13:35** Ps 78:2.

The parable of the weeds explained

36Then he left the crowds and went into the house. And his disciples came to
him, saying, "Explain to us the parable of the weeds of the field." 37He answered,
"He who sows the good seed is the Son of man; 38the field is the world, and the
good seed means the sons of the kingdom; the weeds are the sons of the evil
one, 39and the enemy who sowed them is the devil; the harvest is the close of
the age, and the reapers are angels. 40Just as the weeds are gathered and burned
with fire, so will it be at the close of the age. 41The Son of man will send his
angels, and they will gather out of his kingdom all causes of sin and all
evildoers, 42and throw them into the furnace of fire; there men will weep and
gnash their teeth. 43Then the righteous will shine like the sun in the kingdom
of their Father. He who has ears, let him hear.

The hidden treasure; the pearl; the net

44"The kingdom of heaven is like treasure hidden in a field, which a man found
and covered up; then in his joy he goes and sells all that he has and buys that
field.

45"Again, the kingdom of heaven is like a merchant in search of fine pearls,
46who, on finding one pearl of great value, went and sold all that he had and
bought it.

47"Again, the kingdom of heaven is like a net which was thrown into the
sea and gathered fish of every kind; 48when it was full, men drew it ashore and
sat down and sorted the good into vessels but threw away the bad. 49So it will
be at the close of the age. The angels will come out and separate the evil from
the righteous, 50and throw them into the furnace of fire; there men will weep
and gnash their teeth.

51"Have you understood all this?" They said to him, "Yes." 52And he said
to them, "Therefore every scribe who has been trained for the kingdom of
heaven is like a householder who brings out of his treasure what is new and
what is old."*

---

inevitably, the children of God live alongside the children of the evil one; inevitably, good and evil happen all the time. But at the end of time, Christ, the victorious Son of God, will judge all and give each person what he or she deserves. We find a similar idea in the parable of the dragnet (cf. vv. 47–50).

Jesus uses the parables of the hidden treasure and the pearl (vv. 44–46) to show that what matters most of all is the Kingdom of heaven and a person's desire to attain it. There are slight differences in these two parables: the treasure means abundance of gifts; the pearl, the beauty of the Kingdom. The treasure is something stumbled on, the pearl, the result of a lengthy search. However, man always needs to make a generous effort because God "never fails to help someone who decides to leave all things for his sake" (St Teresa of Avila, *Way of Perfection*, 1, 2).

7. JESUS WITHDRAWS TO THE BORDER COUNTRY

No one is a prophet in his own country Mk 6:1–6; Lk 4:16–30
53And when Jesus had finished these parables he went away from there, 54and
coming to his own country he taught them in their synagogue, so that they
were astonished, and said, "Where did this man get this wisdom and these
mighty works? 55Is not this the carpenter's son? Is not his mother called Mary?
And are not his brethren James and Joseph and Simon and Judas?* 56And are
not all his sisters with us? Where then did this man get all this?" 57And they
took offence at him. But Jesus said to them, "A prophet is not without honour
except in his own country and in his own house." 58And he did not do many
mighty works there, because of their unbelief.

The martyrdom of John the Baptist Mk 6:14–29; Lk 3:19–20
14 1At that time Herod the tetrarch heard about the fame of Jesus; 2and he
said to his servants, "This is John the Baptist, he has been raised from
the dead; that is why these powers are at work in him." 3For Herod had seized
John and bound him and put him in prison, for the sake of Herodias, his
brother Philip's wife;[1] 4because John said to him, "It is not lawful for you to
have her." 5And though he wanted to put him to death, he feared the people,
because they held him to be a prophet. 6But when Herod's birthday came, the

---

13:53–16:20 □ After the discourse of the parables the evangelist reports various miracles and teachings of Jesus in Galilee and the surrounding area. These verses help to show that, with regard to Jesus, a person has to take sides—to be for him or against him. From the discourse of the parables onwards, Matthew identifies three groups of people more clearly—the disciples (especially Peter), who follow Jesus closely; the crowds, who follow him but fail to understand him; and the religious authorities, who set traps for him. The section ends with Peter's solemn profession of faith in which he proclaims Jesus to be the Messiah and the Son of God (16:6).

13:53–58 The Nazarenes' initial admiration (v. 54) seems in contrast to their eventual shock (v. 57): their familiarity with Jesus seems to prevent them from acknowledging the supernatural character of his mission.

14:1–12 Herod the tetrarch, Herod Antipas, is the same Herod as appears later in the account of the Passion (Lk 23:7ff). A son of Herod the Great (Mt 2:1ff), he governed Galilee and Perea. He was married to a daughter of an Arabian king, but in spite of this he lived in concubinage with Herodias. The historian Flavius Josephus (cf. *Ant.*, 18, 116–119) provides a little more information about this episode—that it took place in the palace fortress of Makeronte, that Herodias'

1. Other ancient authorities read *his brother's wife*

daughter of Herodias danced before the company, and pleased Herod, 7so that
he promised with an oath to give her whatever she might ask. 8Prompted by
her mother, she said, "Give me the head of John the Baptist here on a platter."
9And the king was sorry; but because of his oaths and his guests he com-
manded it to be given; 10he sent and had John beheaded in the prison, 11and his
head was brought on a platter and given to the girl, and she brought it to her
mother. 12And his disciples came and took the body and buried it; and they
went and told Jesus.

First miracle of the loaves and fish Mk 6:30–44; Lk 9:10–17; Jn 6:1–15
13Now when Jesus heard this, he withdrew from there in a boat to a lonely
place apart. But when the crowds heard it, they followed him on foot from the
towns. 14As he went ashore he saw a great throng; and he had compassion on
them, and healed their sick. 15When it was evening, the disciples came to him
and said, "This is a lonely place, and the day is now over; send the crowds
away to go into the villages and buy food for themselves." 16Jesus said, "They
need not go away; you give them something to eat." 17They said to him, "We
have only five loaves here and two fish." 18And he said, "Bring them here to
me." 19Then he ordered the crowds to sit down on the grass; and taking the five
loaves and the two fish he looked up to heaven, and blessed, and broke and
gave the loaves to the disciples, and the disciples gave them to the crowds.
20And they all ate and were satisfied. And they took up twelve baskets full of
the broken pieces left over. 21And those who ate were about five thousand men,
besides women and children.

Jesus walks on the water Mk 6:45–52; Jn 6:16–21
22Then he made the disciples get into the boat and go before him to the other
side, while he dismissed the crowds. 23And after he had dismissed the crowds
he went up into the hills by himself to pray. When evening came, he was there

---

daughter was called Salome, etc. In his account, the evangelist shows how close Jesus and John were (vv. 1–2, 12).

14:13–21 By the multiplication of the loaves and the fish, our Lord symbolically points to the establishment of the new people of God (cf. the note on Mk 6:30–44). St Matthew focuses particularly on Jesus' sensitivity to the needs of people. Thus, he includes, along with this miracle, mention of Jesus healing the sick (v. 14).

14:22–33 St Matthew is the only evangelist to report the episode of St Peter walking on the water (vv. 28–31). He is also the only one to record the solemn promise Jesus makes to Peter (16:17–19) and the episode of the temple tax (17:24–27). The Gospel of Matthew, which has been called the "ecclesiastical

alone, [24]but the boat by this time was many furlongs distant from the land,[m]
beaten by the waves; for the wind was against them. [25]And in the fourth watch
of the night he came to them, walking on the sea. [26]But when the disciples saw
him walking on the sea, they were terrified, saying, "It is a ghost!" And they
cried out for fear. [27]But immediately he spoke to them, saying, "Take heart, it
is I; have no fear."

[28]And Peter answered him, "Lord, if it is you, bid me come to you on the
water." [29]He said, "Come." So Peter got out of the boat and walked on the
water and came to Jesus; [30]but when he saw the wind,[n] he was afraid, and
beginning to sink he cried out, "Lord, save me." [31]Jesus immediately reached
out his hand and caught him, saying to him, "O man of little faith, why did you
doubt?" [32]And when they got into the boat, the wind ceased. [33]And those in
the boat worshipped him, saying, "Truly you are the Son of God."*

Cures in Gennesaret Mk 6:53–56

[34]And when they had crossed over, they came to land at Gennesaret. [35]And
when the men of that place recognized him, they sent round to all that region
and brought to him all that were sick, [36]and besought him that they might only
touch the fringe of his garment; and as many as touched it were made well.

The tradition of the elders. True cleanness Mk 7:1–23

15 [1]Then Pharisees and scribes came to Jesus from Jerusalem and said,
[2]"Why do your disciples transgress the tradition of the elders? For they
do not wash their hands when they eat." [3]He answered them, "And why do you
transgress the commandment of God for the sake of your tradition? [4]For God
commanded, 'Honour your father and your mother,' and, 'He who speaks evil
of father or mother, let him surely die.' [5]But you say, 'If any one tells his father

---

Gospel", thereby shows the importance Jesus wanted Peter to have in the Church. In this particular episode we can see the greatness and weakness of Peter, his faith and the difficulty he had in believing (cf. also the notes on 8:23–27; Mk 4:35–41; 6:45–52).

14:34–36 By contrast, we can see the faith of these men who drew near to Jesus and had their requests granted. They set an example for us: in our Saviour's adorable Humanity we can find relief from all our afflictions (cf. 11:28).

15:1–20 The first two Gospels (cf. the note on Mk 7:1–23) report this episode which greatly affected the early Christian's policy in regard to the laws of the Pharisees. Christ very clearly explains that in many instances the traditions of the Pharisees "made void" (v. 6) God's commandment; therefore, in those cases they should not be followed (v. 14). The passage is reminiscent of the sixth beatitude

m. Other ancient authorities read *was out on the sea* **n.** Other ancient authorities read *strong wind*
15:4 Ex 20:12; Deut 5:16; Ex 21:17.

or his mother, What you would have gained from me is given to God,[o] he need
not honour his father.'* 6So, for the sake of your tradition, you have made void
the word[p] of God. 7You hypocrites! Well did Isaiah prophesy of you, when he
said:

> 8'This people honours me with their lips,
> but their heart is far from me;
> 9in vain do they worship me,
> teaching as doctrines the precepts of men.'"

10And he called the people to him and said to them, "Hear and understand:
11not what goes into the mouth defiles a man, but what comes out of the
mouth, this defiles a man." 12Then the disciples came and said to him, "Do you
know that the Pharisees were offended when they heard this saying?" 13He
answered, "Every plant which my heavenly Father has not planted will be
rooted up. 14Let them alone; they are blind guides. And if a blind man leads a
blind man, both will fall into a pit." 15But Peter said to him, "Explain the
parable to us." 16And he said, "Are you also still without understanding? 17Do
you not see that whatever goes into the mouth passes into the stomach, and so
passes on?[q] 18But what comes out of the mouth proceeds from the heart, and
this defiles a man. 19For out of the heart come evil thoughts, murder, adultery,
fornication, theft, false witness, slander. 20These are what defile a man; but to
eat with unwashed hands does not defile a man."

The Canaanite woman Mk 7:24–30

21And Jesus went away from there and withdrew to the district of Tyre and
Sidon. 22And behold, a Canaanite woman from that region came out and cried,
"Have mercy on me, O Lord, Son of David; my daughter is severely possessed
by a demon." 23But he did not answer her a word. And his disciples came and
begged him, saying, "Send her away, for she is crying after us." 24He answered,

---

(cf. 5:8) which invites the pure of heart to see God. "'Pure in heart' refers to those who have attuned their intellects and wills to the demands of God's holiness, chiefly in three areas: charity; chastity or sexual rectitude, love of truth and orthodoxy of faith" (*CCC*, 2518).

15:21–28 The faith of this Canaanite woman is very well described: she makes her request even though she has to be persistent to do so (v. 23). She presses her case though she feels unworthy (vv. 24–26); she perseveres despite difficulties (v. 27); and she gets what she wants (v. 28). "We often find that our Lord does not grant us what we ask for immediately; he delays [meeting our request] so that our desire might increase in ardour, so that we might better appreciate the value of what we ask for. It is not a refusal but a test that prepares us to receive more abundantly what we desire" (St John B. M. Vianney, *Serm. on prayer*).

o. Or *an offering* **p.** Other ancient authorities read *law* **q.** Or *is evacuated* **15:8–9** Is 29:13.

"I was sent only to the lost sheep of the house of Israel."* 25But she came and knelt before him, saying, "Lord, help me." 26And he answered, "It is not fair to take the children's bread and throw it to the dogs." 27She said, "Yes, Lord, yet even the dogs eat the crumbs that fall from their master's table." 28Then Jesus answered her, "O woman, great is your faith! Be it done for you as you desire." And her daughter was healed instantly.

Curing of many sick people Mk 8:1–10

29And Jesus went on from there and passed along the Sea of Galilee. And he went up into the hills, and sat down there. 30And great crowds came to him, bringing with them the lame, the maimed, the blind, the dumb, and many others, and they put them at his feet, and he healed them, 31so that the throng wondered, when they saw the dumb speaking, the maimed whole, the lame walking, and the blind seeing; and they glorified the God of Israel.

Second miracle of the loaves Mk 8:11–21; Lk 12:54–56

32Then Jesus called his disciples to him and said, "I have compassion on the crowd, because they have been with me now three days, and have nothing to eat; and I am unwilling to send them away hungry, lest they faint on the way." 33And the disciples said to him, "Where are we to get bread enough in the desert to feed so great a crowd?" 34And Jesus said to them, "How many loaves have you?" They said, "Seven, and a few small fish." 35And commanding the crowd to sit down on the ground, 36he took the seven loaves and the fish, and having given thanks he broke them and gave them to the disciples, and the disciples gave them to the crowds. 37And they all ate and were satisfied; and they took up seven baskets full of the broken pieces left over. 38Those who ate were four thousand men, besides women and children. 39And sending away the crowds, he got into the boat and went to the region of Magadan.

15:29–31 At times (cf. 11:4–6; Lk 7:21–23) the evangelists gather up and summarize these cures worked by Jesus, cures which fulfilled what the prophet Isaiah said would happen in the time of the Messiah: "Then the eyes of the blind shall be opened, and the ears of the deaf unstopped; then shall the lame man leap like a hart, and the tongue of the dumb sing for joy" (Is 35:5–6).

15:32–39 As well as being concrete, real events, Jesus' miracles were also signs denoting things supernatural. In this instance (v. 37), the superabundance of ordinary food is a sign of the greatness of God's gifts, especially the Eucharist; and the assistance given by the disciples is a sign of the mediatory role of Church ministers. For the specific meaning of this second miracle of the loaves, see the note on Mk 8:1–10.

The Pharisees and Sadducees try to test Jesus

16 1And the Pharisees and Sadducees came, and to test him they asked
him to show them a sign from heaven. 2He answered them,[r] "When it is
evening, you say, 'It will be fair weather; for the sky is red.' 3And in the
morning, 'It will be stormy today, for the sky is red and threatening.' You know
how to interpret the appearance of the sky, but you cannot interpret the signs of
the times. 4An evil and adulterous generation seeks for a sign, but no sign shall
be given to it except the sign of Jonah." So he left them and departed.
5When the disciples reached the other side, they had forgotten to bring any
bread. 6Jesus said to them, "Take heed and beware of the leaven of the
Pharisees and Sadducees." 7And they discussed it among themselves, saying,
"We brought no bread." 8But Jesus, aware of this, said, "O men of little faith,
why do you discuss among yourselves the fact that you have no bread? 9Do you
not yet perceive? Do you not remember the five loaves of the five thousand, and
how many baskets you gathered? 10Or the seven loaves of the four thousand,
and how many baskets you gathered? 11How is it that you fail to perceive that
I did not speak about bread? Beware of the leaven of the Pharisees and
Sadducees." 12Then they understood that he did not tell them to beware of the
leaven of bread, but of the teaching of the Pharisees and Sadducees.

Peter's profession of faith and his primacy

Mk 8:27–30; Lk 9:18–21

13Now when Jesus came into the district of Caesarea Philippi, he asked his
disciples, "Who do men say that the Son of man is?" 14And they said, "Some
say John the Baptist, others say Elijah, and others Jeremiah or one of the
prophets."* 15He said to them, "But who do you say that I am?" 16Simon Peter
replied, "You are the Christ, the Son of the living God."* 17And Jesus answered

---

16:1–12 The Pharisees twice (cf. 12:38) turn to Jesus asking him for a sign. For our Lord (and also the reader of the Gospel) the two miracles of loaves (14:13–21; 15:32–39) are truly signs—as are the miracles he performed in the intervening period (cf. 15:29–31 and note). That is why Jesus reproaches them for failing to appreciate the meaning of these prodigies: "The miracles of Jesus demonstrate that the kingdom has already come on earth [...]. But principally the kingdom is revealed in the person of Christ himself, Son of God and Son of Man" (Vatican II, *LG*, 5).

16:13–20 Matthew's account of this episode has two distinct but interrelated features—Peter's profession of faith and the promise that our Lord makes him. Unlike all those who have failed to work out who Jesus is (v. 14; cf. 14:2; 16:2–4; etc.), Peter plainly acknowledges Jesus to be the promised Messiah and the Son of man. Peter's words should be taken literally because he speaks with the help of revelation from God (cf. *CCC*, 441–442).

r. Other ancient authorities omit the following words to the end of verse 3 him, "Blessed are you, Simon Bar-Jona! For flesh and blood has not revealed this to you, but my Father who is in heaven. 18And I tell you, you are Peter,[s] and on this rock[t] I will build my church, and the powers of death[u] shall not prevail against it.* 19I will give you the keys of the kingdom of heaven, and whatever you bind on earth shall be bound in heaven, and whatever you loose on earth shall be loosed in heaven." 20Then he strictly charged the disciples to tell no one that he was the Christ.

PART TWO: JESUS' MINISTRY ON THE WAY TO JERUSALEM

8. TOWARDS JUDEA AND JERUSALEM

Jesus foretells his passion and resurrection.
The law of Christian renunciation Mk 8:31–9:1; Lk 9:22–27

21From that time Jesus began to show his disciples that he must go to Jerusalem and suffer many things from the elders and chief priests and scribes, and be killed, and on the third day be raised. 22And Peter took him and began

---

In a play on words which is easier to see in Hebrew or Aramaic than in other languages (the word "John"—in "Bar-Jona", v. 17—means in fact "God is merciful"), Jesus reminds Peter that the act of faith he has just made is indeed a gift from God. In the same context, Jesus promises him something which he will later confer on him (cf. Jn 21: 15–23 and note)—the power to bind and loose in his Church (vv. 18–19). From the beginning, the Church has held that this gift is also passed on to the successors of St Peter as bishop of Rome: "The bishop of Rome, in whom rests the function given in a unique way to Peter, the first of the Apostles, and which he passed on to his successors, is head of the college of bishops, the Vicar of Christ and Pastor of the universal Church on earth; he has, therefore, by virtue of his function, ordinary power which is supreme, full, immediate and universal in the Church, and which he can exercise freely" (*Code of Canon Law*, 331; cf. Vatican II, *LG*, 18).

The saints have regarded love for the Church and the Pope as a true sign of love for Christ: "He who disobeys the Christ on earth [the Pope], who acts for Christ in heaven, will not partake of the fruit of the blood of the Son of God" (St Catherine of Siena, *Letters*, 207).

16:21–20:34 □□ After Peter's profession of faith at Caesarea Philippi (16:13–20), we can notice a new tone in the Gospel. Jesus now teaches his disciples about his

s. Greek *Petros* **t.** Greek *petra* **u.** Greek *the gates of Hades*

to rebuke him, saying, "God forbid, Lord! This shall never happen to you."
23 But he turned and said to Peter, "Get behind me, Satan! You are a hindrance[v]
to me; for you are not on the side of God, but of men."
24 Then Jesus told his disciples, "If any man would come after me, let him
deny himself and take up his cross and follow me. 25 For whoever would save
his life will lose it, and whoever loses his life* for my sake will find it. 26 For
what will it profit a man, if he gains the whole world and forfeits his life? Or
what shall a man give in return for his life? 27 For the Son of man is to come
with his angels in the glory of his Father, and then he will repay every man for
what he has done. 28 Truly, I say to you, there are some standing here who will
not taste death before they see the Son of man coming in his kingdom."

The Transfiguration Mk 9:2–13; Lk 9:28–36

17 1 And after six days Jesus took with him Peter and James and John his
brother, and led them up a high mountain apart. 2 And he was trans-
figured before them, and his face shone like the sun, and his garments became
white as light. 3 And behold, there appeared to them Moses and Elijah, talking

---

mission as the suffering Servant and about the future life of the Church. On the latter subject, chapter 18 has so much to say that it has been called the "discourse on the Church". Later, on the way to Jerusalem (19:1–20:34), other episodes are included which further illustrate aspects of the life of the Church—poverty, service of others, etc.

16:21–17:27 □ The Gospel account of Jesus' teaching about his passion, death and resurrection (16:21) and then his rebuking of Peter (16:23) point out clearly the "way of the cross". The two announcements of the Passion (16:21; 17:22–23) and the implications of the Transfiguration prepare the reader for what is going to happen. Our Lord knows that he must be handed over, and he is ready for his mission. But he also knows that the final outcome for him is not death but resurrection and glorification, and he tells the disciples this.

16:21–28 Jesus vigorously rejects Peter's attempt to dissuade him from accepting the death that is part of Jesus' mission as Messiah (cf. the note on Mk 8:31–9:1). He goes on to explain, in paradoxes, how radically his disciples must commit themselves to Him: "The way of perfection passes by way of the Cross. There is no holiness without renunciation and spiritual battle. Spiritual progress entails the ascesis and mortification that gradually lead to living in the peace and joy of the Beatitudes" (*CCC*, 2015).

17:1–13 In the Transfiguration, Jesus gives his disciples a glimpse of the glory he will merit through his passion (cf. the note on Lk 9:28–36). But the disciples are

v. Greek *stumbling block*

with him. [4]And Peter said to Jesus, "Lord, it is well that we are here; if you wish,
I will make three booths here, one for you and one for Moses and one for
Elijah."* [5]He was still speaking, when lo, a bright cloud overshadowed them, and
a voice from the cloud said, "This is my beloved Son,[w] with whom I am well
pleased; listen to him." [6]When the disciples heard this, they fell on their faces, and
were filled with awe. [7]But Jesus came and touched them, saying, "Rise, and have
no fear." [8]And when they lifted up their eyes, they saw no one but Jesus only.

[9]And as they were coming down the mountain, Jesus commanded them,
"Tell no one the vision, until the Son of man is raised from the dead." [10]And the
disciples asked him, "Then why do the scribes say that first Elijah must come?"
[11]He replied, "Elijah does come, and he is to restore all things; [12]but I tell you
that Elijah has already come, and they did not know him, but did to him
whatever they pleased. So also the Son of man will suffer at their hands." [13]Then
the disciples understood that he was speaking to them of John the Baptist.

Curing of an epileptic boy Mk 9:14–29; Lk 9:37–43

[14]And when they came to the crowd, a man came up to him and kneeling before
him said, [15]"Lord, have mercy on my son, for he is an epileptic and he suffers
terribly; for often he falls into the fire, and often into the water. [16]And I brought
him to your disciples, and they could not heal him." [17]And Jesus answered, "O

---

overawed (vv. 6–7) and fail to grasp what all this means (cf. the note on Mk 9:2–13). This episode also tells us something about Jesus' personality: he is the Lord (v. 4), the Son of God, in whom God is well pleased (v. 5; cf. Is 42:1); we must listen to him, for he reveals God to man: "he that would now question God, or seek any vision or revelation, would not only be acting foolishly, he would be committing an offence against God by not setting his eyes solely upon Christ, and seeking no new thing or aught beside. And God might answer him after this manner, saying: If I have spoken all things to you in my Word, which is My Son, and I have no other word, what answer can I now make to you, or what can I reveal to you which is greater than this? Set your eyes on him alone, for in him I have spoken and revealed all things to you, and in him you will find even more than what you ask and desire for […]. Listen to him, for I have no more faith to reveal, neither have I any more things to declare" (St John of the Cross, *Ascent of Mount Carmel,* 2, 22, 5).

17:14–20 Through the cure of this boy, Jesus teaches us the important place faith has in prayer. The force of the comparison our Lord makes (v. 20) stems from the fact that the mustard seed is very small and yet it produces a large shrub which can grow to three metres (ten feet) or more in height. So, a very small act of genuine faith can produce surprising results.

See the RSV note on v. 21, the text of which occurs in Mark 9:29.

w. Or *my Son, my* (or *the*) *Beloved*

faithless and perverse generation, how long am I to be with you? How long am I to bear with you? Bring him here to me.” [18]And Jesus rebuked him, and the demon came out of him, and the boy was cured instantly. [19]Then the disciples came to Jesus privately and said, “Why could we not cast it out?” [20]He said to them, “Because of your little faith. For truly, I say to you, if you have faith as a grain of mustard seed, you will say to this mountain, ‘Move hence to yonder place,’ and it will move; and nothing will be impossible to you.”[x]

Second announcement of the Passion. The temple tax Mk 9:30–32; Lk 9:43–45

[22]As they were gathering[y] in Galilee, Jesus said to them. “The Son of man is to be delivered into the hands of men, [23]and they will kill him, and he will be raised on the third day.” And they were greatly distressed.

[24]When they came to Capernaum, the collectors of the half-shekel tax went up to Peter and said, “Does not your teacher pay the tax?” [25]He said, “Yes.” And when he came home, Jesus spoke to him first, saying, “What do you think, Simon? From whom do kings of the earth take toll or tribute? From their sons or from others?” [26]And when he said, “From others,” Jesus said to him, “Then the sons are free. [27]However, not to give offence to them, go to the sea and cast a hook, and take the first fish that comes up, and when you open its mouth you will find a shekel; take that and give it to them for me and for yourself.”

9. THE DISCOURSE ON THE CHURCH

The “little ones” and the Kingdom. On leading others astray. The lost sheep Mk 9:33–50; Lk 9:46–50; 15:4–7

18 [1]At that time, the disciples came to Jesus, saying, “Who is the greatest in the kingdom of heaven?” [2]And calling to him a child, he put him in the midst of them, [3]and said, “Truly, I say to you, unless you turn and become like children, you will never enter the kingdom of heaven. [4]Whoever humbles himself like this child, he is the greatest in the kingdom of heaven.

[5]“Whoever receives one such child in my name receives me; [6]but whoever causes one of these little ones who believe in me to sin,[z] it would be better for

---

17:22–27 From the time of Peter’s confession of faith, Jesus begins to teach his disciples about the salvific events of his passion and resurrection, and about the future life of the Church. In the episode of the temple tax Jesus wants to make two things clear—the fact that he is the Son of God and Lord of the temple, and Peter’s involvement with him in the care of the Church.

18:1–20:34 □ This section begins with the fourth of our Lord’s discourses in Matthew’s Gospel, the discourse on the Church (18:1–35)—a series of instructions

x. Other ancient authorities insert verse 21, *But this kind never comes out except by prayer and fasting*
y. Other ancient authorities read *abode* **z.** Greek *causes . . . to stumble*

him to have a great millstone fastened round his neck and to be drowned in the
depth of the sea.
7"Woe to the world for temptations to sin![a] For it is necessary that tempta-
tions come, but woe to the man by whom the temptation comes! 8And if your
hand or your foot causes you to sin,[z] cut it off and throw it from you; it is
better for you to enter life maimed or lame than with two hands or two feet to
be thrown into the eternal fire. 9And if your eye causes you to sin,[z] pluck it out
and throw it from you; it is better for you to enter life with one eye than with
two eyes to be thrown into the hell[b]* of fire.
10"See that you do not despise one of these little ones; for I tell you that in
heaven their angels always behold the face of my Father who is in heaven.[c]
12What do you think? If a man has a hundred sheep, and one of them has gone
astray, does he not leave the ninety-nine on the hills and go in search of the one
that went astray? 13And if he finds it, truly, I say to you, he rejoices over it
more than over the ninety-nine that never went astray. 14So it is not the will of
my[d] Father who is in heaven that one of these little ones should perish.

Fraternal correction. The apostles' authority Lk 17:3–4

15"If your brother sins against you, go and tell him his fault, between you and
him alone. If he listens to you, you have gained your brother. 16But if he does

---

about the way the Church should work in the future: Jesus' teaching focuses mainly on Christians' relations with one another, and on the responsibilities and duties of those who hold positions of authority in the Church.

The section then moves to the journey into Judea in the direction of Jerusalem (19:1–20:34). The episodes which Matthew includes in this stage of Jesus' ministry contain teaching similar to that of the previous chapter—on the Christian calling, on precedence in the Church, etc.

18:1–14 To the disciples' questions about who is the greatest, Jesus seems to give a paradoxical answer: "If you ask me," St Augustine writes, "what is the most essential thing in the religion and morality of Jesus Christ, I will reply: first, humility, second, humility; and third, humility" (*Letters*, 118, 22).

Our Lord goes on to warn about the danger of scandal in the Church. "Scandal is an attitude or behaviour which leads another to do evil" (*CCC*, 2284). To show the gravity of scandal, Jesus exaggerates in order to make his point. Scandal is particularly serious when it affects those for whom our Lord has most regard—the weak, children, for example (v. 14).

See the RSV note on v. 11; these words seem to come from Lk 19:10.

18:15–20 This passage focuses on three aspects of the life of the Church—fraternal correction, the authority of pastors, and prayer in common. Christians,

a. Greek *stumbling blocks* **b.** Greek *Gehenna* **c.** Other ancient authorities add verse 11, *For the Son of man came to save the lost* **d.** Other ancient authorities read *your* **18:16** Deut 19:15.

not listen, take one or two others along with you, that every word may be
confirmed by the evidence of two or three witnesses. 17If he refuses to listen to
them, tell it to the church; and if he refuses to listen even to the church, let him
be to you as a Gentile and a tax collector. 18Truly, I say to you, whatever you
bind on earth shall be bound in heaven, and whatever you loose on earth shall
be loosed in heaven.* 19Again I say to you, if two of you agree on earth about
anything they ask, it shall be done for them by my Father in heaven. 20For
where two or three are gathered in my name, there am I in the midst of them."

Forgiveness of injuries. Parable of the unforgiving servant Lk 17:3–4

21Then Peter came up and said to him, "Lord, how often shall my brother sin
against me, and I forgive him? As many as seven times?" 22Jesus said to him,
"I do not say to you seven times, but seventy times seven.[e]
23"Therefore the kingdom of heaven may be compared to a king who
wished to settle accounts with his servants. 24When he began the reckoning,
one was brought to him who owed him ten thousand talents;[f] 25and as he could
not pay, his lord ordered him to be sold, with his wife and children and all that
he had, and payment to be made. 26So the servant fell on his knees, imploring
him, 'Lord, have patience with me, and I will pay you everything.' 27And out

---

particularly pastors, should watch over their brethren as Christ did, to avoid anyone being lost (cf. Jn 17:12). The practice of fraternal correction is one way of helping to save a brother who has gone astray (vv. 15–17). The last stage—treating him as a Gentile or a tax collector (v. 17)—is the equivalent of excommunication, a final recourse for saving his soul (cf. 1 Cor 5:4–5).

"The office of binding and loosing which was given to Peter was also assigned to the college of the apostles united to its head" (Vatican II, *LG*, 22). The Tradition of the Church has interpreted these words of our Lord (v. 18) as follows: "The words *bind and loose* mean: whomever you exclude from your communion, will be excluded from communion with God; whomever you receive anew into your communion, God will welcome back into his. *Reconciliation with the Church is inseparable from reconciliation with God*" (*CCC*, 1445).

At the end of this passage (vv. 19–20) Jesus emphasizes the effectiveness of prayer in common. For his disciples, these words would have shown his divine character; they were familiar with a contemporary saying that when two men meet together to study the words of the Law, God himself is there with them.

18:21–35 To Peter's question about the number of times one should forgive someone, Jesus replies with a circumlocution which means the same as the adverb "always" (cf. Gen 4:24). "The Lord did not confine forgiveness to a specific number [of instances]; he implied that one needs to forgive continuously and whenever the need arises" (St John Chryostom, *Hom. on Mt*, 61,1).

e. Or *seventy-seven times* **f**. A talent was more than fifteen years' wages of a labourer

of pity for him the lord of that servant released him and forgave him the debt.
28But that same servant, as he went out, came upon one of his fellow servants
who owed him a hundred denarii;[g] and seizing him by the throat he said, 'Pay
what you owe.' 29So his fellow servant fell down and besought him, 'Have
patience with me, and I will pay you.' 30He refused and went and put him in
prison till he should pay his debt. 31When his fellow servants saw what had
taken place, they were greatly distressed, and they went and reported to their
lord all that had taken place. 32Then his lord summoned him and said to him,
'You wicked servant! I forgave you all that debt because you besought me;
33and should not you have had mercy on your fellow servant, as I had mercy
on you?' 34And in anger his lord delivered him to the jailers,[h] till he should pay
all his debt. 35So also my heavenly Father will do to every one of you, if you
do not forgive your brother from your heart."

Marriage and virginity

Mk 10:1–12

19 1Now when Jesus had finished these sayings, he went away from
Galilee and entered the region of Judea beyond the Jordan; 2and large
crowds followed him, and he healed them there.
3And Pharisees came up to him and tested him by asking, "Is it lawful to
divorce one's wife for any cause?" 4He answered, "Have you not read that he
who made them from the beginning made them male and female, 5and said, 'For
this reason a man shall leave his father and mother and be joined to his wife, and
the two shall become one'?[i] 6So they are no longer two but one.[i] What therefore

---

The parable of the unforgiving servant, also, teaches the deepest reason for being forgiving: we are debtors of God. The parable is particularly eloquent if we bear in mind the amounts involved: a denarius was the equivalent of a working man's daily wage; and a talent was worth six thousand denarii. So, the king writes off seventy million denarii for the servant—an enormous sum, far beyond the man's ability to repay.

19:1–12 The Pharisees ask our Lord a trick question and he explains that marriage is indissoluble (cf. the note on Mk 10:1–12). The aside in v. 9 should not be seen as an exception (cf. the note on 5:17–48).

In the same context our Lord explains that celibacy is a gift from God: "Both the sacrament of Matrimony and virginity for the Kingdom of God come from the Lord himself. It is he who gives them meaning and grants them the grace which is indispensable for living them out in conformity with his will. Esteem of virginity for the sake of the kingdom and the Christian understanding of marriage are inseparable, and they reinforce each other: 'Whoever denigrates marriage also diminishes the glory of virginity. Whoever praises it makes virginity more admirable and resplendent' (St John Chrysostom, *De virg.*, 10,1)" (*CCC*, 1620).

g. The denarius was a day's wage for a labourer **h.** Greek *torturers* **i.** Greek *one flesh*
19:4–5 Gen 1:27; 2:24.

God has joined together, let no man put asunder." [7]They said to him, "Why then did Moses command one to give a certificate of divorce, and to put her away?" [8]He said to them, "For your hardness of heart Moses allowed you to divorce your wives, but from the beginning it was not so. [9]And I say to you: whoever divorces his wife, except for unchastity,[j] and marries another, commits adultery; and he who marries a divorced woman commits adultery."[k]*

[10]The disciples said to him, "If such is the case of a man with his wife, it is not expedient to marry." [11]But he said to them, "Not all men can receive this precept, but only those to whom it is given. [12]For there are eunuchs who have been so from birth, and there are eunuchs who have been made eunuchs by men, and there are eunuchs who have made themselves eunuchs for the sake of the kingdom of heaven. He who is able to receive this, let him receive it."*

Jesus blesses the children Mk 10:13–16; Lk 18:15–17

[13]Then children were brought to him that he might lay his hands on them and pray. The disciples rebuked the people; [14]but Jesus said, "Let the children come to me, and do not hinder them; for to such belongs the kingdom of heaven." [15]And he laid his hands on them and went away.

The rich young man. Christian poverty and renunciation Mk 10:17–31; Lk 18:18–30

[16]And behold, one came up to him, saying, "Teacher, what good deed must I do, to have eternal life?" [17]And he said to him, "Why do you ask me about what is good? One there is who is good. If you would enter life, keep the

---

19:13–15 Cf. the note on Mk 10:13–16.

19:16–30 The first three Gospels report this episode, but Matthew's description of the conversation between Jesus and the young man is the most detailed. The latter keeps all the commandments (vv. 18–20), and he asks Jesus what further "good works" (vv. 16, 20) he should do. In his first reply Jesus prepares him for his subsequent demand (v. 21): "This is not a matter only of disposing oneself to hear a teaching and obediently accepting a commandment. More radically, it involves *holding fast to the very person of Jesus*, partaking of his life and his destiny, sharing in his free and loving obedience to the will of the Father" (John Paul II, *Veritatis splendor*, 19).

In this sense, the present episode and the previous one dealing with marriage (cf. 19:1–12) very clearly spell out the fullness and perfection of the Law to be found in the lives of those who follow Christ's teaching and example. Our Lord teaches marriage to be indissoluble and says that the commandments must be kept; but he also asks celibacy and detachment from everything for the sake of the Kingdom of heaven, of those who have been given those gifts.

j. Other ancient authorities, after *unchastity*, read *makes her commit adultery* **k**. Other ancient authorities omit *and he who marries a divorced woman commits adultery* **19:7** Deut 24:1.

commandments." [18]He said to him, "Which?" And Jesus said, "You shall not kill, You shall not commit adultery, You shall not steal, You shall not bear false witness, [19]Honour your father and mother, and, You shall love your neighbour as yourself." [20]The young man said to him, "All these I have observed; what do I still lack?" [21]Jesus said to him, "If you would be perfect, go, sell what you possess and give to the poor, and you will have treasure in heaven; and come, follow me." [22]When the young man heard this he went away sorrowful; for he had great possessions.

[23]And Jesus said to his disciples, "Truly, I say to you, it will be hard for a rich man to enter the kingdom of heaven. [24]Again I tell you, it is easier for a camel to go through the eye of a needle than for a rich man to enter the kingdom of God." [25]When the disciples heard this they were greatly astonished, saying, "Who then can be saved?" [26]But Jesus looked at them and said to them, "With men this is impossible, but with God all things are possible." [27]Then Peter said in reply, "Lo, we have left everything and followed you. What then shall we have?" [28]Jesus said to them, "Truly, I say to you, in the new world, when the Son of man shall sit on his glorious throne, you who have followed me will also sit on twelve thrones, judging the twelve tribes of Israel. [29]And every one who has left houses or brothers or sisters or father or mother or children or lands, for my name's sake, will receive a hundredfold,[l] and inherit eternal life. [30]But many that are first will be last, and the last first.

Parable of the labourers in the vineyard

20 [1]"For the kingdom of heaven is like a householder who went out early in the morning to hire labourers for his vineyard. [2]After agreeing with the labourers for a denarius[m] a day, he sent them into his vineyard. [3]And going

---

After the rich young man leaves, Jesus expounds his teaching on the subject of riches (cf. the note on Mk 10:23–31). Then, in reply to Peter, he explains what lies in store for someone who sincerely follows Christ: following him means that the person believes in a regeneration (v. 28), a new birth, in which there will be an inversion of values. Those who now seem to be of no importance will become the judges; those who seem to be rejected will become the first; everything one gives up now will be multiplied by a hundred.

20:1–16 This parable explains the previous verse (19:30) and it seems to refer to the Jewish people: God called them at the first hour but at the end of the day he also called the Gentiles. The parable shows the goodness and mercy of God, which exceed anything that human standards of justice would indicate. We can also see from this parable how important it is to respond positively to God's call, irrespective of when he actually makes it. People should not judge God's way of

l. Other ancient authorities read *manifold* **m.** The denarius was a day's wage for a labourer
19:18–19 Ex 20:12–16; Deut 5:16–20

out about the third hour he saw others standing idle in the market place; [4]and to them he said, ‘You go into the vineyard too, and whatever is right I will give you.’ So they went. [5]Going out again about the sixth hour and the ninth hour, he did the same. [6]And about the eleventh hour he went out and found others standing; and he said to them, ‘Why do you stand here idle all day?’ [7]They said to him, ‘Because no one has hired us.’ He said to them, ‘You go into the vineyard too.’ [8]And when evening came, the owner of the vineyard said to his steward, ‘Call the labourers and pay them their wages, beginning with the last, up to the first.’ [9]And when those hired about the eleventh hour came, each of them received a denarius. [10]Now when the first came, they thought they would receive more; but each of them also received a denarius. [11]And on receiving it they grumbled at the householder, [12]saying, ‘These last worked only one hour, and you have made them equal to us who have borne the burden of the day and the scorching heat.’ [13]But he replied to one of them, ‘Friend, I am doing you no wrong; did you not agree with me for a denarius? [14]Take what belongs to you, and go; I choose to give to this last as I give to you. [15]Am I not allowed to do what I choose with what belongs to me? Or do you begrudge my generosity?’[n] [16]So the last will be first, and the first last.”

Third announcement of the Passion Mk 10:32–34; Lk 18:31–34

[17]And as Jesus was going up to Jerusalem, he took the twelve disciples aside, and on the way he said to them, [18]“Behold, we are going up to Jerusalem; and the Son of man will be delivered to the chief priests and scribes, and they will condemn him to death, [19]and deliver him to the Gentiles to be mocked and scourged and crucified, and he will be raised on the third day.”

The mother of the sons of Zebedee makes her request Mk 10:35–45

[20]Then the mother of the sons of Zebedee came up to him, with her sons, and kneeling before him she asked him for something. [21]And he said to her, “What do you want?” She said to him, “Command that these two sons of mine may

---

working, but should rather be grateful to him for choosing to involve them in his plan of salvation.

20:17–19 As he makes his way up to Jerusalem, Jesus for a third time confronts and foretells the death that awaits him. The evangelist wants to put on record Jesus’ determination to carry out the Father’s plan for him.

20:20–28 Jesus moderates the excessively human ambition and eagerness of the apostles and of the mother of the sons of Zebedee by reminding them that God’s will and a spirit of service must have priority.

n. Or *is your eye evil because I am good?*

sit, one at your right hand and one at your left, in your kingdom." 22But Jesus
answered, "You do not know what you are asking. Are you able to drink the
cup that I am to drink?" They said to him, "We are able." 23He said to them,
"You will drink my cup, but to sit at my right hand and at my left is not mine
to grant, but it is for those for whom it has been prepared by my Father." 24And
when the ten heard it they were indignant at the two brothers. 25But Jesus
called them to him and said, "You know that the rulers of the Gentiles lord it
over them, and their great men exercise authority over them. 26It shall not be
so among you; but whoever would be great among you must be your servant,
27and whoever would be first among you must be your slave; 28even as the Son
of man came not to be served but to serve, and to give his life as a ransom for
many."

Curing of the blind men of Jericho Mk 10:46–52; Lk 18:35–43

29And as they went out of Jericho, a great crowd followed him. 30And behold,
two blind men sitting by the roadside, when they heard that Jesus was passing
by, cried out,[o] "Have mercy on us, Son of David!" 31The crowd rebuked them,
telling them to be silent; but they cried out the more, "Lord, have mercy on us,
Son of David!" 32And Jesus stopped and called them, saying, "What do you
want me to do for you?" 33They said to him, "Lord, let our eyes be opened."
34And Jesus in pity touched their eyes, and immediately they received their
sight and followed him.

Speaking in the language of liturgical sacrifice, evocative of the suffering Servant of the prophet Isaiah (Is 52:13–53:12), Jesus makes it clear (v. 28) that in his case that service extends even to giving up his life. His disciples need to have the same attitude: "The Church, and each of her members, is thus called to share in the *munus regale* of the Crucified Christ […]. Jesus, then, is the living, personal summation of perfect freedom in total obedience to the will of God" (John Paul II, *Veritatis splendor*, 87).

20:29–34 All three Synoptic Gospels report both this miracle worked by Jesus in Jericho and the messianic title ("Son of David") that the blind men apply to him on the very threshold of his entry into Jerusalem. Each evangelist applies his own particular emphasis. Matthew, as on other occasions (cf. 8:28–34; 9:27–31), mentions that there are *two* blind men. And he is the only one to attribute the cure to Jesus' compassion (v. 34). "Jesus, above all through his way of life and his actions, has shown how operative *love is present in the world*, the love which is directed towards man and embraces the whole of humanity" (John Paul II, *Div. in mis.*, 3).

o. Other ancient authorities insert *Lord*

PART THREE: JESUS' MINISTRY IN JERUSALEM

10. CLEANSING OF THE TEMPLE. CONTROVERSIES

The Messiah enters the Holy City

Mk 11:1–11; Lk 19:28–40; Jn 12:12–19

21 1And when they drew near to Jerusalem and came to Bethphage, to the
Mount of Olives, then Jesus sent two disciples, 2saying to them, "Go into
the village opposite you, and immediately you will find an ass tied, and a colt with
her; untie them and bring them to me. 3If any one says anything to you, you shall
say, 'The Lord has need of them,' and he will send them immediately." 4This took
place to fulfil what was spoken by the prophet, saying,
5"Tell the daughter of Zion,
Behold, your king is coming to you,
humble, and mounted on an ass,
and on a colt, the foal of an ass."
6The disciples went and did as Jesus had directed them; 7they brought the ass
and the colt, and put their garments on them, and he sat thereon. 8Most of the
crowd spread their garments on the road, and others cut branches from the
trees and spread them on the road. 9And the crowds that went before him and
that followed him shouted, "Hosanna to the Son of David! Blessed is he who
comes in the name of the Lord! Hosanna in the highest!"* 10And when he

---

21:1–28:20 □ □ In their account of Jesus' last days on earth, the Synoptic Gospels all follow the same pattern and purpose. The account begins with a manifestation of Jesus as Messiah, and the cleansing of the temple (21:1–22). Controversies with Jewish leaders explain why Jesus will later be condemned (21:23–23:29), and the "eschatological discourse" rounds off our Lord's teachings (24:1–25:46). The narrative grows in intensity as it focuses on Jesus' last hours—his submission to the Father's will (26:26–46), his arrest, trial and sentencing (26:47–27:31), his death 27:32–66) and his resurrection (28:1–20).

Within this framework, Matthew's account highlights certain features—our Lord's serene submission to his role as the suffering Servant, Israel's rejection of God's plans, etc.

21:1–23:39 □ Jesus' controversies with the religious leaders tell us of the reasons which bring about his death. But there is an underlying cause which links up all the episodes: Israel has failed to respond to the gift of God and therefore God will found a new people which will produce fruits (21:43). Yet our Lord's words are also a warning to those who make up this new people, the Church: as he will explain later in chapter 25, faithfulness to the gift of God must always be expressed in deeds.

21:5 Is 62:1; Zech 9:9. **21:9** Ps 118:26.

entered Jerusalem, all the city was stirred, saying, "Who is this?"
11
And the crowds said, "This is the prophet Jesus from Nazareth of Galilee."

Jesus in the temple Mk 11:15–19; Lk 19:45–48; 2:13–25

12
And Jesus entered the temple of God[p] and drove out all who sold and bought
in the temple, and he overturned the tables of the money-changers and the
seats of those who sold pigeons.
13
He said to them, "It is written, 'My house
shall be called a house of prayer'; but you make it a den of robbers."

14
And the blind and the lame came to him in the temple, and he healed
them.
15
But when the chief priests and the scribes saw the wonderful things
that he did, and the children crying out in the temple, "Hosanna to the Son of
David!" they were indignant;
16
and they said to him, "Do you hear what these
are saying?" And Jesus said to them, "Yes; have you never read,

'Out of the mouth of babes and sucklings
thou hast brought perfect praise'?"

17
And leaving them, he went out of the city to Bethany and lodged there.

The cursing of the fig tree Mk 11:12–14, 20–25

18
In the morning, as he was returning to the city, he was hungry.
19
And seeing
a fig tree by the wayside he went to it, and found nothing on it but leaves only.
And he said to it, "May no fruit ever come from you again!" And the fig tree
withered at once.
20
When the disciples saw it they marvelled, saying, "How
did the fig tree wither at once?"
21
And Jesus answered them, "Truly, I say to
you, if you have faith and never doubt, you will not only do what has been

---

21:1–11 In his triumphant entry into Jerusalem, Jesus reveals himself as the Messiah. Matthew reads the fact that the ass was tied with her colt as the fulfilment of the prophecy of Zechariah (v. 5; cf. Zec 9:9). That prophecy describes the future Messiah as being just and humble, the Saviour. The Fathers see this episode as a symbolic one: the she-ass, the mother, representing the Jews under the yoke of the Law, and the colt represents the Gentiles. Jesus brings both Jews and Gentiles into the Church, the new Jerusalem.

21:12–17 In this day in Jerusalem Matthew includes three messianic signs which Jesus performed in the temple—the cleansing of the temple (vv. 12–13; cf. the note on Mk 11:12–25); the cures (v. 14); and the fact that the humble praise God (cf. v. 16) as is implied in Psalm 8, which Jesus sees as being fulfilled in the applause of the children. In his account of this episode, the evangelist gives us a glimpse of Jesus' divinity.

21:18–22 Cf. the note on Mk 11:12–25.

p. Other ancient authorities omit *of God* **21:13** Is 56:7; Jer 7:11. **21:16** Ps 8:2.

done to the fig tree, but even if you say to this mountain, 'Be taken up and cast into the sea,' it will be done. 22and whatever you ask in prayer, you will receive, if you have faith."

The authority of Jesus is questioned Mk 11:27–33; Lk 20:1–8

23And when he entered the temple, the chief priests and the elders of the people came up to him as he was teaching, and said, "By what authority are you doing these things, and who gave you this authority?"* 24Jesus answered them, "I also will ask you a question; and if you tell me the answer, then I also will tell you by what authority I do these things. 25The baptism of John, whence was it? From heaven or from men?" And they argued with one another, "If we say, 'From heaven,' he will say to us, 'Why then did you not believe him?' 26But if we say, 'From men,' we are afraid of the multitude; for all hold that John was a prophet." 27So they answered Jesus, "We do not know." And he said to them, "Neither will I tell you by what authority I do these things.

Parable of the two sons

28"What do you think? A man had two sons; and he went to the first and said, 'Son, go and work in the vineyard today.' 29And he answered, 'I will not'; but afterward he repented and went. 30And he went to the second and said the same; and he answered, 'I go, sir,' but did not go. 31Which of the two did the will of his father?" They said, "The first." Jesus said to them, "Truly, I say to you, the tax collectors and the harlots go into the kingdom of God before you. 32For John came to you in the way of righteousness, and you did not believe him, but the tax collectors and the harlots believed him; and even when you saw it, you did not afterward repent and believe him.

21:23–27 Cf. the note on Mk 11:27–33.

21:28–46 In these two parables our Lord is referring to Israel's rejection of its God and to God's decision to create a new people (v. 43). Matthew is the only evangelist to report the parable of the two sons; it underlines the need for conversion (v. 32): Israel is like the son who said yes to God but then failed to believe and produced no fruit (cf. v. 30), whereas sinners who are converted when they see the signs of God (v. 32) do the Father's will and enter the Kingdom of God (v. 31). The parable of the wicked tenants is a sort of compendium of salvation history (cf. the note on Mk 12:1–12). Matthew is the only evangelist whose account of the parable speaks of "a nation producing fruits" (cf. v. 43), a reference to the Church, the new people of God: "As Israel according to the flesh which wandered in the desert was already called the Church of God, so too, the new Israel, which advances in this present era in search of a future and permanent

Parable of the wicked tenants Mk 12:1–12; Lk 20:9–19

33"Hear another parable.* There was a householder who planted a vineyard,
and set a hedge around it, and dug a wine press in it, and built a tower, and let
it out to tenants, and went into another country. 34When the season of fruit
drew near, he sent his servants to the tenants, to get his fruit; 35and the tenants
took his servants and beat one, killed another, and stoned another. 36Again he
sent other servants, more than the first; and they did the same to them.
37Afterward he sent his son to them, saying, 'They will respect my son.' 38But
when the tenants saw the son, they said to themselves, 'This is the heir; come,
let us kill him and have his inheritance.' 39And they took him and cast him out
of the vineyard, and killed him. 40When therefore the owner of the vineyard
comes, what will he do to those tenants?" 41They said to him, "He will put
those wretches to a miserable death, and let out the vineyard to other tenants
who will give him the fruits in their seasons."

42Jesus said to them, "Have you never read in the scriptures:

'The very stone which the builders rejected
has become the head of the corner;
this was the Lord's doing,
and it is marvellous in our eyes'?

43Therefore I tell you, the kingdom of God will be taken away from you and
given to a nation producing the fruits of it. 44And he who falls on this stone
will be broken to pieces; but when it falls on any one, it will crush him."[q]

45When the chief priests and the Pharisees heard his parables, they
perceived that he was speaking about them. 46But when they tried to arrest
him, they feared the multitudes, because they held him to be a prophet.

Parable of the marriage feast Lk 14:15–24

22 1And again Jesus spoke to them in parables, saying, 2"The kingdom
of heaven may be compared to a king who gave a marriage feast for
his son, 3and sent his servants to call those who were invited to the marriage
feast; but they would not come. 4Again he sent other servants, saying, 'Tell

---

city, is called also the Church of Christ. It is Christ indeed who had purchased it with his own blood; he has filled it with his Spirit; he has provided means adapted to its visible and social union" (Vatican II, *LG*, 9).

22:1–14 This parable, which is very like another reported by St Luke (cf. Lk 14:15–24 and note) develops the teaching in the two preceding ones. Israel has rejected the invitation to salvation, and God, by convoking the Church, extends his call to everyone his messengers meet. The part about the man who comes without a wedding garment, is also a call to vigilance addressed to those who form part of the Church: Israel's downfall (v. 7) is a sign of what will happen to us if we prove

q. Other ancient authorities omit verse 44 **21:33** Is 5:1–7. **21:42** Ps 118:22–23.

those who are invited, Behold, I have made ready my dinner, my oxen and
my fat calves are killed, and everything is ready; come to the marriage feast.'
[5]But they made light of it and went off, one to his farm, another to his
business, [6]while the rest seized his servants, treated them shamefully, and
killed them. [7]The king was angry, and he sent his troops and destroyed those
murderers and burned their city. [8]Then he said to his servants, 'The wedding
is ready, but those invited were not worthy. [9]Go therefore to the thorough-
fares, and invite to the marriage feast as many as you find.' [10]And those
servants went out into the streets and gathered all whom they found, both bad
and good; so the wedding hall was filled with guests.
[11]"But when the king came in to look at the guests, he saw there a man who
had no wedding garment;* [12]and he said to him, 'Friend, how did you get in
here without a wedding garment?' And he was speechless. [13]Then the king said
to the attendants, 'Bind him hand and foot, and cast him into the outer
darkness; there men will weep and gnash their teeth.' [14]For many are called,
but few are chosen."

Tribute to Caesar Mk 12:13–17; Lk 20:20–26

[15]Then the Pharisees went and took counsel how to entangle him in his talk.
[16]And they sent their disciples to him, along with the Herodians, saying, "Teacher,
we know that you are true, and teach the way of God truthfully, and care for no
man; for you do not regard the position of men. [17]Tell us, then, what you think. Is
it lawful to pay taxes to Caesar, or not?" [18]But Jesus, aware of their malice, said,
"Why put me to the test, you hypocrites? [19]Show me the money for the tax." And
they brought him a coin.[r] [20]And Jesus said to them, "Whose likeness and
inscription is this?" [21]They said, "Caesar's." Then he said to them, "Render
therefore to Caesar the things that are Caesar's, and to God the things that are
God's." [22]When they heard it, they marvelled; and they left him and went away.

The resurrection of the dead Mk 12:18–27; Lk 20:27–40

[23]The same day Sadducees came to him, who say that there is no resurrection;
and they asked him a question, [24]saying, "Teacher, Moses said, 'If a man dies,

---

unworthy of God's grace (v. 13). "What are we to understand by the image of the wedding garment, if not charity? He who enters the wedding feast without the wedding garment is like one who belongs to the Church, having faith but no love" (St Gregory the Great, *Hom. on Gospel*, 2, 18, 9).

22:15–22 Cf. the note on Mk 12:13–17.

22:23–33 The Sadducees use the levirate law (described in the passage) to argue against belief in the resurrection of the dead. By outlining an extreme case they

r. Greek *a denarius* **22:24** Deut 25:5; Gen 38:8.

having no children, his brother must marry the widow, and raise up children for
his brother.' 25Now there were seven brothers among us; the first married, and
died, and having no children left his wife to his brother. 26So too the second and
third, down to the seventh. 27After them all, the woman died. 28In the resurrection,
therefore, to which of the seven will she be wife? For they all had her."
29But Jesus answered them, "You are wrong, because you know neither the
scriptures nor the power of God. 30For in the resurrection they neither marry
nor are given in marriage, but are like angels[s] in heaven. 31And as for the
resurrection of the dead, have you not read what was said to you by God, 32'I
am the God of Abraham, and the God of Isaac, and the God of Jacob'? He is
not God of the dead, but of the living." 33And when the crowd heard it, they
were astonished at his teaching.

The greatest commandment of all Mk 12:28–34; Lk 10:25–28

34But when the Pharisees heard that he had silenced the Sadducees, they came
together. 35And one of them, a lawyer, asked him a question, to test him.
36"Teacher, which is the great commandment in the law?" 37And he said to
him, "You shall love the Lord your God with all your heart, and with all your
soul, and with all your mind. 38This is the great and first commandment. 39And
a second is like it, You shall love your neighbour as yourself. 40On these two
commandments depend all the law and the prophets."

The divinity of the Messiah Mk 12:35–37; Lk 20:41–44

41Now while the Pharisees were gathered together, Jesus asked them a
question, 42saying, "What do you think of the Christ? Whose son is he?" They

---

make the law and belief in resurrection look ridiculous. In his reply Jesus shows up the frivolity of their objections and asserts the truth of the resurrection of the dead. At the end of the passage the evangelist is happy to note how impressed the people were by Jesus' teaching (cf. the note on Lk 20:27–40).

22:34–40 Here Jesus replies to a question posed by Pharisees whose main interest was in compliance with all the commandments in the Mosaic laws—of which there were as many as 613. Jesus teaches that the entire Law can be summed up in the two commandments of love (Deut 6:5; Lev 19:18). The first is the most important because love of one's neighbour is a consequence of love of God (cf. St Thomas, *Com. on Mt*, in loc.). As regards the intensity with which God should be loved, St Bernard wrote: "You ask me for what reason and by what method or means God ought to be loved. My answer is that the reason to love God is God; the method and means are to love him without method or means" (*De dilig. Dei*, 1, 1).

22:41–46 Jesus puts a question to the Pharisees but doesn't give them the answer. The answer, in fact, would imply the pre-existence and divinity of the Messiah

s. Other ancient authorities add *of God* **22:32** Ex 3:6. **22:37** Deut 6:5. **22:39** Lev 19:18.

said to him, "The son of David." 43He said to them, "How is it then that David, inspired by the Spirit,[t] calls him Lord, saying,

44'The Lord said to my Lord,
Sit at my right hand,
till I put thy enemies under thy feet'?

45If David thus calls him Lord, how is he his son?" 46And no one was able to answer him a word, nor from that day did any one dare to ask him any more questions.

Jesus indicts the scribes and Pharisees Mk 12:38–40; Lk 11:37–54; 20:45–47

23 1 Then said Jesus to the crowds and to his disciples, 2"The scribes and
the Pharisees sit on Moses' seat; 3so practise and observe whatever they
tell you, but not what they do; for they preach, but do not practise. 4They bind
heavy burdens, hard to bear,[u] and lay them on men's shoulders; but they
themselves will not move them with their finger. 5They do all their deeds to be
seen by men; for they make their phylacteries* broad and their fringes long, 6and
they love the place of honour at feasts and the best seats in the synagogues, 7and
salutations in the market places, and being called rabbi by men. 8But you are
not to be called rabbi, for you have one teacher, and you are all brethren. 9And
call no man your father on earth, for you have one Father, who is in heaven.*
10Neither be called masters, for you have one master, the Christ. 11He who is
greatest among you shall be your servant; 12whoever exalts himself will be
humbled, and whoever humbles himself will be exalted.

(who is prior to and greater than David) and also his truly being a man (the son of David, the Messiah)—something the Pharisees could not grasp. But the Christian reader, who knows the full truth about who Jesus is, can indeed answer the question.

23:1–36 Jesus severely criticizes the scribes and Pharisees for their behaviour, which was motivated more by a desire to project a good impression than to live in accordance with the truth. There are two parts to this discourse: the first (vv. 1–12) is addressed to the people and to his disciples, the second (the famous "woes": vv. 13–36) to the scribes and Pharisees. Throughout, Christ is making the same point; it is not his intention to abolish the teaching of the Law as enunciated by scribes and Pharisees (cf. vv. 3 and 23) but to purify and elevate it (cf. 5:17–20).

In the first part we can see the contrast between the way the scribes and Pharisees act and the way that Christians should act. The former "preach, but do not practise" (v. 3) and they want to be the first before all (v. 6); Christians should desire, rather, to serve and to be humble (vv. 11–12). Jesus gives some examples of this: rabbi, father and master were titles of honour that teachers of the Law of Moses gave themselves. When Jesus tells his disciples not to accept such titles, he is saying that a Christian should seek to serve others, not to be given honorary titles.

t. Or *David in the Spirit* **u.** Other ancient authorities omit *hard to hear* **22:44** Ps 110:1.

13"But woe to you, scribes and Pharisees, hypocrites! because you shut the kingdom of heaven against men; for you neither enter yourselves, nor allow those who would enter to go in.[v] 15Woe to you, scribes and Pharisees, hypocrites! for you traverse sea and land to make a single proselyte, and when he becomes a proselyte, you make him twice as much a child of hell[w] as yourselves.

16"Woe to you, blind guides, who say, 'If any one swears by the temple, it is nothing; but if any one swears by the gold of the temple, he is bound by his oath.' 17You blind fools! For which is greater, the gold or the temple that has made the gold sacred? 18And you say, 'If any one swears by the altar, it is nothing; but if any one swears by the gift that is on the altar, he is bound by his oath.' 19You blind men! For which is greater, the gift or the altar that makes the gift sacred? 20So he who swears by the altar, swears by it and by everything on it; 21and he who swears by the temple, swears by it and by him who dwells in it; 22and he who swears by heaven, swears by the throne of God and by him who sits upon it.

23"Woe to you, scribes and Pharisees, hypocrites! for you tithe mint and dill and cummin, and have neglected the weightier matters of the law, justice and mercy and faith; these you ought to have done, without neglecting the others. 24You blind guides, straining out a gnat and swallowing a camel!

25"Woe to you, scribes and Pharisees, hypocrites! for you cleanse the outside of the cup and of the plate, but inside they are full of extortion and rapacity. 26You blind Pharisee! first cleanse the inside of the cup and of the plate, that the outside also may be clean.

27"Woe to you, scribes and Pharisees, hypocrites! for you are like whitewashed tombs, which outwardly appear beautiful, but within they are full of dead men's bones and all uncleanness. 28So you also outwardly appear righteous to men, but within you are full of hypocrisy and iniquity.

29"Woe to you, scribes and Pharisees, hypocrites! for you build the tombs of the prophets and adorn the monuments of the righteous, 30saying, 'If we had

---

The "woes" (vv. 13–22) spell out the disastrous consequences and the inconsistency involved in a merely external fulfilment of the Law. At a particular juncture (v. 23) our Lord points out the route we should take: we should imitate the qualities God manifests towards his people—justice, mercy and fidelity.

The discourse ends with a prophetic lament (vv. 33–36): just as the prophets suffered (and died) as a result of the unbelief of their contemporaries, so too the first Christians will suffer due to the hardheartedness of the scribes and Pharisees.

See the RSV note on v. 14. This addition is attributable to the influence of Mark 12:20 and Luke 20:47.

v. Other authorities add here (or after verse 12) verse 14, *Woe to you, scribes and Pharisees, hypocrites! for you devour widows' houses and for a pretence you make long prayers; therefore you will receive the greater condemnation* **w.** Greek *Gehenna* lived in the days of our fathers, we would not have taken part with them in shedding the blood of the prophets.' [31]Thus you witness against yourselves, that you are sons of those who murdered the prophets. [32]Fill up, then, the measure of your fathers. [33]You serpents, you brood of vipers, how are you to escape being sentenced to hell?[w] [34]Therefore I send you prophets and wise men and scribes, some of whom you will kill and crucify, and some you will scourge in your synagogues and persecute from town to town, [35]that upon you may come all the righteous blood shed on earth, from the blood of innocent Abel to the blood of Zechariah the son of Barachiah, whom you murdered between the sanctuary and the altar. [36]Truly, I say to you, all this will come upon this generation.

Jerusalem admonished Lk 13:34–35

[37]"O Jerusalem, Jerusalem, killing the prophets and stoning those who are sent to you! How often would I have gathered your children together as a hen gathers her brood under her wings, and you would not! [38]Behold, your house is forsaken and desolate.[x] [39]For I tell you, you will not see me again, until you say, 'Blessed is he who comes in the name of the Lord.' "

11. THE ESCHATOLOGICAL DISCOURSE

Announcement of the destruction of the temple Mk 13:1–2; Lk 21:5–6

24 [1]Jesus left the temple and was going away, when his disciples came to point out to him the buildings of the temple.* [2]But he answered them, "You see all these, do you not? Truly, I say to you, there will not be left here one stone upon another, that will not be thrown down."

The beginning of tribulations.
Persecution on account of the Gospel Mk 13:3–13; Lk 21:7–19

[3]As he sat on the Mount of Olives, the disciples came to him privately, saying, "Tell us, when will this be, and what will be the sign of your coming and of the

---

23:37–39 Using the simile of the hen and her chicks, Jesus applies to himself the merciful action of God towards his people (cf. Deut 32:11; Ps 17:8; 36:8; 61:5); his mention of the prophets' fate reminds us what his own destiny will be. The evangelist's citation of these words of Jesus is a useful reminder to Christians not to harden their hearts against God's invitations.

24:1–25:46 □ Jesus' eschatological discourse (the fifth discourse in St Matthew's Gospel) occurs in all three Synoptic Gospels. Matthew's is the longest of the three and is, moreover, rounded off by the parables in chapter 25. The theme running

x. Other ancient authorities omit *and desolate* **23:38** Jer 22:5. **23:39** Ps 118:26.

close of the age?” [4]And Jesus answered them, “Take heed that no one leads you astray. [5]For many will come in my name, saying, ‘I am the Christ,’ and they will lead many astray. [6] And you will hear of wars and rumours of wars; see that you are not alarmed; for this must take place, but the end is not yet. [7]For nation will rise against nation, and kingdom against kingdom, and there will be famines and earthquakes in various places: [8]all this is but the beginning of the sufferings.

[9]“Then they will deliver you up to tribulation, and put you to death; and you will be hated by all nations for my name’s sake. [10]And then many will fall away,[y] and betray one another, and hate one another. [11]And many false prophets will arise and lead many astray. [12]And because wickedness is multiplied, most men’s love will grow cold. [13]But he who endures to the end will be saved. [14]And this gospel of the kingdom will be preached throughout the whole world, as a testimony to all nations; and then the end will come.

The great tribulation Mk 13:14–23; Lk 21:20–24

[15]“So when you see the desolating sacrilege spoken of by the prophet Daniel, standing in the holy place (let the reader understand), [16]then let those who are in Judea flee to the mountains; [17]let him who is on the housetop not go down to take what is in his house; [18]and let him who is in the field not turn back to take his mantle. [19]And alas for those who are with child and for those who give suck in those days! [20]Pray that your flight may not be in winter or on a sabbath. [21]For then there will be great tribulation, such as has not been from the beginning of the world until now, no, and never will be. [22]And if those days had not been shortened, no human being would be saved; but for the sake of the elect those days will be shortened. [23]Then if any one says to you, ‘Lo, here is the Christ!’or ‘There he is!’ do not believe it. [24]For false Christs and false prophets will arise and show great signs and wonders, so as to lead astray, if possible, even the elect. [25]Lo, I have told you beforehand. [26]So, if they say to you, ‘Lo, he is in the wilderness,’ do not go out; if they say, ‘Lo, he is in the inner rooms,’ do not believe it. [27]For as the lightning comes from the east and shines as far as the west, so will be the coming of the Son of man. [28]Wherever the body is, there the eagles[z] will be gathered together.

---

through the whole discourse is our Lord’s exhortation to vigilance and hope, as well as the need to make one’s talents bear fruit.

24:1–51 The language in this chapter is of an apocalyptic type: it uses symbolism and imagery to describe events at the end of time. There are two intermingling levels of reference—to the destruction of Jerusalem and to the end of this present world, indicating that the first is a figure or type of the second.

y. Or *stumble* **z.** Or *vultures* **24:15** Dan 9:27; 11:31; 12:11. **24:21** Dan 12:1; Joel 2:2.

The coming of the Son of man Mk 13:24–27; Lk 21:25–28

29"Immediately after the tribulation of those days the sun will be darkened, and
the moon will not give its light, and the stars will fall from heaven, and the powers
of the heavens will be shaken; 30then will appear the sign of the Son of man in
heaven, and then all the tribes of the earth will mourn, and they will see the Son
of man coming on the clouds of heaven with power and great glory; 31and he will
send out his angels with a loud trumpet call, and they will gather his elect from
the four winds, from one end of heaven to the other.

The end will surely come—the lesson of the fig tree Mk 13:28–31; Lk 21:29–33

32"From the fig tree learn its lesson: as soon as its branch becomes tender and
puts forth its leaves, you know that summer is near. 33So also, when you see
all these things, you know that he is near, at the very gates. 34Truly, I say to
you, this generation will not pass away till all these things take place. 35Heaven
and earth will pass away, but my words will not pass away.

The time of the second coming of Christ Mk 13:32–37; Lk 17:22–27

36"But of that day and hour no one knows, not even the angels of heaven, nor
the Son,[a] but the Father only. 37As were the days of Noah, so will be the
coming of the Son of man. 38For as in those days before the flood they were
eating and drinking, marrying and giving in marriage, until the day when Noah
entered the ark, 39and they did not know until the flood came and swept them
all away, so will be the coming of the Son of man. 40Then two men will be in
the field; one is taken and one is left. 41Two women will be grinding at the
mill; one is taken and one is left.

Vigilance. Parable of the faithful servant Lk 12:35–48; 21:34–36

42Watch therefore, for you do not know on what day your Lord is coming.
43But know this, that if the householder had known in what part of the night
the thief was coming, he would have watched and would not have let his house
be broken into. 44Therefore you also must be ready; for the Son of man is
coming at an hour you do not expect.

45"Who then is the faithful and wise servant, whom his master has set over
his household, to give them their food at the proper time? 46Blessed is that
servant whom his master when he comes will find so doing. 47Truly, I say to

---

Matthew's account of this discourse (cf. the notes on Mk 13:1–37) contains nuances not found in the other Synoptic Gospels: people, especially those who have a particular responsibility for their brethren (vv. 45–51), need to be watchful and to remember that severe tribulation can cause disciples to fall away (vv. 10–12). Also, Christians need to be alert and vigilant, for the Lord will come suddenly, like lightning (v. 27), when least expected (v. 50), without our realizing it (vv. 36–41).

a. Other ancient authorities omit *nor the Son* **24:29** Is 13:10; Joel 2:10–11.

you, he will set him over all his possessions. 48But if that wicked servant says to himself, 'My master is delayed,' 49and begins to beat his fellow servants, and eats and drinks with the drunken, 50the master of that servant will come on a day when he does not expect him and at an hour he does not know, 51and will punish[b] him, and put him with the hypocrites; there men will weep and gnash their teeth.

Parable of the wise and foolish maidens

25 1"Then the kingdom of heaven shall be compared to ten maidens who took their lamps and went to meet the bridegroom.[c] 2Five of them were foolish, and five were wise. 3For when the foolish took their lamps, they took no oil with them; 4but the wise took flasks of oil with their lamps. 5As the bridegroom was delayed, they all slumbered and slept. 6But at midnight there was a cry, 'Behold, the bridegroom! Come out to meet him.' 7Then all those maidens rose and trimmed their lamps. 8And the foolish said to the wise, 'Give us some of your oil, for our lamps are going out.' 9But the wise replied, 'Perhaps there will not be enough for us and for you; go rather to the dealers and buy for yourselves.' 10And while they went to buy, the bridegroom came, and those who were ready went in with him to the marriage feast; and the door was shut. 11Afterward the other maidens came also, saying, 'Lord, lord, open to us.' 12But he replied, 'Truly, I say to you, I do not know you.' 13Watch therefore, for you know neither the day nor the hour.

Parable of the talents Lk 19:11–27

14"For it will be as when a man going on a journey called his servants and entrusted to them his property; 15to one he gave five talents,[d] to another two,

---

25:1–13 This parable is a clear message about the call to vigilance which was the theme of the previous discourse. The bridegroom stands for Christ, the virgins for the people invited to the wedding, that is, to the spousal covenant between God and his Church. It is not enough for us to be in the Church; we need to have a lively faith and to do good works. "Watch with your heart, with faith, with hope, with charity, with good deeds […]; trim your lamps, make sure they do not go out, fuel them with the spiritual oil of a good conscience; stay united to your spouse by means of Love; then he will lead you into the banquet hall, where your lamp will never be put out" (St Augustine, *Serm.*, 93, 17).

25:14–30 A talent was not any kind of coin but a measure of value worth about thirty-four kilos (seventy-five pounds) of silver. In this parable our Lord teaches the need to respond to grace by making a genuine effort right through one's life. All the gifts of nature and grace which God has given us should yield a profit. It

b. Or *cut him in pieces* **c.** Other ancient authorities add *and the bride* **d.** A talent was more than fifteen years' wages of a labourer to another one, to each according to his ability. Then he went away. [16]He who had received the five talents went at once and traded with them; and he made five talents more. [17]So also, he who had the two talents made two talents more. [18]But he who had received the one talent went and dug in the ground and hid his master's money. [19]Now after a long time the master of those servants came and settled accounts with them. [20]And he who received the five talents came forward, bringing five talents more, saying, 'Master, you delivered to me five talents; here I have made five talents more.' [21]His master said to him, 'Well done, good and faithful servant; you have been faithful over a little, I will set you over much; enter into the joy of your master.' [22]And he also who had the two talents came forward, saying, 'Master, you delivered to me two talents; here I have made two talents more.' [23]His master said to him, 'Well done, good and faithful servant; you have been faithful over a little, I will set you over much; enter into the joy of your master.' [24]He also who had received the one talent came forward, saying, 'Master, I knew you to be a hard man, reaping where you did not sow, and gathering where you did not winnow; [25]so I was afraid, and I went and hid your talent in the ground. Here you have what is yours.' [26]But his master answered him, 'You wicked and slothful servant! You knew that I reap where I have not sowed, and gather where I have not winnowed? [27]Then you ought to have invested my money with the bankers, and at my coming I should have received what was my own with interest. [28]So take the talent from him, and give it to him who has the ten talents. [29]For to every one who has will more be given, and he will have abundance; but from him who has not, even what he has will be taken away.* [30]And cast the worthless servant into the outer darkness; there men will weep and gnash their teeth.'

The Last Judgment

[31]"When the Son of man comes in his glory, and all the angels with him, then he will sit on his glorious throne. [32]Before him will be gathered all the nations, and he will separate them one from another as a shepherd separates the sheep from the goats, [33]and he will place the sheep at his right hand, but the goats at

---

does not matter how many gifts we have received; what matters is our generosity in putting them to good use: "You think your life is for yourself? Your life is for God, for the good of all men, through your love for our Lord. Your buried talent, dig it up again!" (Bl. J. Escrivá, *Hom.,* 2, 47).

25:31–46 The three preceding parables (24:42–51; 25:1–13; 25:14–30) are rounded off by this other parable which announces the Lord's Judgment. Jesus depicts this Last Judgment in all its ceremony: "Then will the conduct of each one and the secrets of hearts be brought to light. Then will the culpable unbelief that counted the offer of God's grace as nothing be condemned. Our attitude to our neighbour will disclose acceptance or refusal of grace and divine love" (*CCC*, 678).

the left. 34Then the King will say to those at his right hand, 'Come, O blessed
of my Father, inherit the kingdom prepared for you from the foundation of the
world; 35for I was hungry and you gave me food, I was thirsty and you gave
me drink, I was a stranger and you welcomed me, 36I was naked and you
clothed me, I was sick and you visited me, I was in prison and you came to
me.' 37Then the righteous will answer him, 'Lord, when did we see thee
hungry and feed thee, or thirsty and give thee drink? 38And when did we see
thee a stranger and welcome thee, or naked and clothe thee? 39And when did we
see thee sick or in prison and visit thee?' 40And the King will answer them, 'Truly
I say to you, as you did it to one of the least of my brethren, you did it to me.'
41Then he will say to those at his left hand, 'Depart from me, you cursed, into the
eternal fire prepared for the devil and his angels; 42for I was hungry and you gave
me no food; I was thirsty and you gave me no drink, 43I was a stranger and you
did not welcome me, naked and you did not clothe me, sick and in prison and you
did not visit me.' 44Then they also will answer, 'Lord, when did we see thee
hungry or thirsty or a stranger or naked or sick or in prison, and did not minister
to thee?' 45Then he will answer them, 'Truly, I say to you, as you did it not to one
of the least of these, you did it not to me.' 46And they will go away into eternal
punishment, but the righteous into eternal life."

12. THE PASSION, DEATH AND RESURRECTION OF JESUS

The last announcement of the Passion. The conspiracy against Jesus

Mk 14:1–2; Lk 22:1–2; Jn 11:45–57

26 1When Jesus had finished all these sayings, he said to his disciples,
2"You know that after two days the Passover is coming, and the Son of
man will be delivered up to be crucified."

The parable also reveals the dimensions of love for God in earthly life: "the Lord asks only two things of us: love for His Majesty and love for our neighbour. It is for these two virtues that we must strive, and if we attain them perfectly we are doing his will [...]. The surest sign that we are keeping these two commandments is, I think, that we should really love our neighbour; for we cannot be sure that we love God, although we may have good reasons for believing that we do, but we can know quite well if we love our neighbour. And be certain that, the further advanced you find you are in this, the greater the love you will have for God; for so dearly does His Majesty love us that he will reward our love for our neighbour by increasing the love we bear to himself, and that in a thousand ways: I have no doubt of this" (St Teresa of Avila, *Interior Castle,* 5, 53, 7–8).

26:1–28:20 □ The events of our Lord's passion were deeply etched on the disciples' memory; we can see this from the apostles' discourses in the book of the

[3]Then the chief priests and the elders of the people gathered in the palace
of the high priest, who was called Caiaphas, [4]and took counsel together in
order to arrest Jesus by stealth and kill him. [5]But they said, "Not during the
feast, lest there be a tumult among the people."

The anointing at Bethany. Judas betrays Jesus Mk 14:3–11; Lk 22:3–6; Jn 12:1–11

[6]Now when Jesus was at Bethany in the house of Simon the leper, [7]a woman
came up to him with an alabaster jar of very expensive ointment, and she
poured it on his head, as he sat at table. [8]But when the disciples saw it, they
were indignant saying, "Why this waste? [9]For this ointment might have been
sold for a large sum, and given to the poor." [10]But Jesus, aware of this, said to
them, "Why do you trouble the woman? For she has done a beautiful thing to
me. [11]For you always have the poor with you, but you will not always have
me. [12]In pouring this ointment on my body she has done it to prepare me for
burial. [13]Truly, I say to you, wherever this gospel is preached in the whole
world, what she has done will be told in memory of her."

[14]Then one of the twelve, who was called Judas Iscariot, went to the chief
priests [15]and said, "What will you give me if I deliver him to you?" And they
paid him thirty pieces of silver. [16]And from that moment he sought an
opportunity to betray him.

Acts, and from the intensity of this narrative in all four Gospels. St Matthew puts special emphasis on two things—Jesus' serenity in the face of his perfidious accusers, and the reason why he tolerated all these affronts: he bore them because he was the suffering Servant, foretold by the prophets, who took our sins upon himself.

God's plans are fulfilled in the death of Jesus, and also in his resurrection. A new stage begins with the resurrection and the commission given to the apostles: the risen Jesus stays with the Church forever, the gates of heaven have been opened, and Christians must bring this message of salvation to all men.

26:1–16 The first three Gospels recount the start of this unfolding drama in very much the same way: the Jewish authorities were looking for a way to arrest Jesus without causing an uproar and they find an unexpected ally in Judas, "one of the twelve" (v. 14). However, each evangelist emphasizes some particular aspect. Matthew shows very clearly the way Jesus is in control of what is going to happen. These events are part of God's plan of salvation: even the thirty pieces of silver that Judas will receive for his betrayal (v. 15) fit the plan outlined by God in Scripture (cf. 27:9–10). On the anointing at Bethany, see the note on Mk 14:1–11.

26:15 Zech 11:12.

Preparations for the Last Supper
and announcement of Judas' treachery Mk 14:12–21; Lk 22:7–13; Jn 13:21–22

17Now on the first day of Unleavened Bread the disciples came to Jesus,
saying, "Where will you have us prepare for you to eat the passover?"* 18He
said, "Go into the city to such a one, and say to him, 'The Teacher says, My
time is at hand; I will keep the passover at your house with my disciples.'"
19And the disciples did as Jesus had directed them, and they prepared the
passover.

20When it was evening, he sat at table with the twelve disciples;[e] 21and as
they were eating, he said, "Truly, I say to you, one of you will betray me."
22And they were very sorrowful, and began to say to him one after another, "Is
it I, Lord?" 23He answered, "He who has dipped his hand in the dish with me,
will betray me. 24The Son of man goes as it is written of him, but woe to that
man by whom the Son of man is betrayed! It would have been better for that
man if he had not been born." 25Judas, who betrayed him, said, "Is it I,
Master?"[f] He said to him, "You have said so."

The institution of the Eucharist Mk 14:22–25; Lk 22:14–20; 1 Cor 11:23–26

26Now as they were eating,* Jesus took bread, and blessed, and broke it, and
gave it to the disciples and said, "Take, eat; this is my body." 27And he took a
cup, and when he had given thanks he gave it to them, saying, "Drink of it, all
of you; 28for this is my blood of the[g] covenant, which is poured out for many
for the forgiveness of sins. 29I tell you I shall not drink again of this fruit of the
vine until that day when I drink it new with you in my Father's kingdom."

26:17–25 Mark and Luke go into detail about the preparations for the Passover meal. Matthew, for his part, remembers that Jesus knew (v. 25) that Judas had betrayed him, but this does not deflect Him from his mission: "My time is at hand," he tells the owner of the house (v. 18): "The desire to embrace his Father's plan of redeeming love inspired Jesus' whole life, for his redemptive passion was the very reason for his Incarnation" (*CCC*, 607).

26:26–29 Jesus' actions and words during the Last Supper are especially full of meaning. In their accounts of the institution of the Eucharist (as elsewhere), the various evangelists chose different aspects to emphasize (cf. the notes on Mk 14:22–25 and Lk 22:7–20). St Matthew is the only one to report what Jesus says about what meaning his death will have for expiation of sins (v. 28). Jesus' words show the full extent of God's plan of salvation. "The Scriptures had foretold this divine plan of salvation through the putting to death of 'the righteous one, my Servant' as a mystery of universal redemption, that is, as the ransom that would free men from the slavery of sin [...]. In particular Jesus' redemptive death fulfils Isaiah's prophecy of the suffering Servant" (*CCC*, 601).

e. Other authorities omit *disciples* **f.** Or *Rabbi* **g.** Other ancient authorities insert *new*

The disciples' desertion foretold Mk 14:26–31; Lk 22:31–34; Jn 13:36–38
30And when they had sung a hymn, they went out to the Mount of Olives. 31Then
Jesus said to them, "You will all fall away because of me this night; for it is
written, 'I will strike the shepherd, and the sheep of the flock will be scattered.'
32But after I am raised up, I will go before you to Galilee." 33Peter declared to
him, "Though they all fall away because of you, I will never fall away." 34Jesus
said to him, "Truly, I say to you, this very night, before the cock crows, you will
deny me three times." 35Peter said to him, "Even if I must die with you, I will not
deny you." And so did all the disciples.

Gethsemane—the agony in the garden Mk 14:32–42; Lk 22:39–46
36Then Jesus went with them to a place called Gethsemane, and he said to his
disciples, "Sit here, while I go yonder and pray." 37And taking with him Peter
and the two sons of Zebedee, he began to be sorrowful and troubled. 38Then he
said to them, "My soul is very sorrowful, even to death; remain here, and
watch[h] with me." 39And going a little farther he fell on his face and prayed,
"My Father, if it be possible, let this cup pass from me; nevertheless, not as I
will, but as thou wilt." 40And he came to the disciples and found them sleeping;
and he said to Peter, "So, could you not watch[h] with me one hour? 41Watch[h]
and pray that you may not enter into temptation; the spirit indeed is willing, but
the flesh is weak." 42Again, for the second time, he went away and prayed, "My
Father, if this cannot pass unless I drink it, thy will be done." 43And again he

---

26:30–35 In advance of the great test, Jesus forewarns his disciples, Peter especially: they will all be scandalized (v. 31). They have acknowledged him as the Messiah (16:13–20), but they have not managed to accept the fact that his messianship is that of the suffering Servant (16:21–23). Now events are going to force them to do so. Even so, they are very slow to accept the fact: "This teaches us a great truth—that man's resolution is not enough: we need to be helped from on high" (St John Chrysostom, *Hom. on Mt*, 82, 4).

26:36–46 The three Synoptics (Mark's account particularly, cf. Mk 14:32–42 and note) contrast Jesus' dramatic prayer with the disciples' sheer inability to keep him company. Matthew focuses on the fact that in his prayer Jesus shows himself to be fully aware of God's will and embraces it. Thus, the start of the prayer (v. 39) shows how difficult it is for him to face what lies ahead; but, as his prayer advances, he entirely abandons himself to the Father's will (vv. 42 and 44) "All that the beginner in prayer has to do—and you must not forget this, for it is very important—is to labour, to be resolute and prepare himself with all possible diligence to bring his will into conformity with the will of God" (St Teresa, *Interior Castle*, 2, 8).

h. Or *keep awake* **26:31** Zech 13:7.

came and found them sleeping, for their eyes were heavy. 44So, leaving them again, he went away and prayed for the third time, saying the same words. 45Then he came to the disciples and said to them, "Are you still sleeping and taking your rest? Behold, the hour is at hand, and the Son of man is betrayed into the hands of sinners. 46Rise, let us be going; see, my betrayer is at hand."

The arrest of Jesus Mk 14:43–52; Lk 22:47–53; Jn 18:1–12

47While he was still speaking, Judas came, one of the twelve, and with him a great crowd with swords and clubs, from the chief priests and the elders of the people. 48Now the betrayer had given them a sign, saying, "The one I shall kiss is the man; seize him." 49And he came up to Jesus at once and said, "Hail, Master!"[i] And he kissed him. 50Jesus said to him, "Friend, why are you here?"[j] Then they came up and laid hands on Jesus and seized him. 51And behold, one of those who were with Jesus stretched out his hand and drew his sword, and struck the slave of the high priest, and cut off his ear.* 52Then Jesus said to him, "Put your sword back into its place; for all who take the sword will perish by the sword. 53Do you think that I cannot appeal to my Father, and he will at once send me more than twelve legions of angels? 54But how then should the scriptures be fulfilled, that it must be so?" 55At that hour Jesus said to the crowds, "Have you come out as against a robber, with swords and clubs to capture me? Day after day I sat in the temple teaching, and you did not seize me. 56But all this has taken place, that the scriptures of the prophets might be fulfilled." Then all the disciples forsook him and fled.

Jesus before the chief priests Mk 14:53–65; Lk 22:26–71; Jn 18:13–24

57Then those who had seized Jesus led him to Caiaphas the high priest, where the scribes and the elders had gathered. 58But Peter followed him at a distance,

---

26:47–56 This scene, so rich in contrasts, shows the majesty of our Lord. Judas betrays him with a kiss, the sign of friendship and respect (v. 49); whereas, for Jesus, Judas is the friend who does not even realize his true role in the drama of events (v. 50). Jesus is arrested under cover of darkness (v. 55), by an armed troop (v. 47), yet if he were to make a simple request to the Father all these people's plans would be undone (v. 53). The fact is that Jesus surrenders because he chooses to do so, because his decision to fulfil the Scriptures (vv. 54 and 56) is irrevocable even though it means his death (cf. 26:42).

26:57–75 In this episode, which is found in all four Gospels, we can see the contrasting attitudes of Jesus and Peter. St Matthew gives an orderly account of the affronts that Jesus suffers. First, he is falsely accused (v. 59) and then he is incriminated by being quoted out of context (v. 61). Jesus remains silent in the face

i. Or *Rabbi* **j.** Or *do that for which you have come*

as far as the courtyard of the high priest, and going inside he sat with the guards
to see the end. 59Now the chief priests and the whole council sought false
testimony against Jesus that they might put him to death,* 60but they found none,
though many false witnesses came forward. At last two came forward 61and said,
"This fellow said, 'I am able to destroy the temple of God, and to build it in three
days.'" 62And the high priest stood up and said, "Have you no answer to make?
What is it that these men testify against you?" 63But Jesus was silent. And the
high priest said to him, "I adjure you by the living God, tell us if you are the
Christ, the Son of God." 64Jesus said to him, "You have said so. But I tell you,
hereafter you will see the Son of man seated at the right hand of Power, and
coming on the clouds of heaven." 65Then the high priest tore his robes, and said,
"He has uttered blasphemy. Why do we still need witnesses? You have now heard
his blasphemy.* 66What is your judgment?" They answered, "He deserves death."
67Then they spat in his face, and struck him; and some slapped him, 68saying,
"Prophesy to us, you Christ! Who is it that struck you?"

Peter's denials Mk 14:66–72; Lk 22:54–62; Jn 18:15–18, 25–27

69Now Peter was sitting outside in the courtyard. And a maid came up to him,
and said, "You also were with Jesus the Galilean." 70But he denied it before
them all, saying, "I do not know what you mean." 71And when he went out to
the porch, another maid saw him, and she said to the bystanders, "This man
was with Jesus of Nazareth." 72And again he denied it with an oath, "I do not
know the man." 73After a little while the bystanders came up and said to Peter,
"Certainly you are also one of them, for your accent betrays you." 74Then he
began to invoke a curse on himself and to swear, "I do not know the man." And
immediately the cock crowed. 75And Peter remembered the saying of Jesus,
"Before the cock crows, you will deny me three times." And he went out and
wept bitterly.

Jesus is brought before Pilate Mk 15:1

27 1When morning came, all the chief priests and the elders of the people
took counsel against Jesus to put him to death; 2and they bound him
and led him away and delivered him to Pilate the governor.

---

of these accusations (v. 63). When he admits that he is the Messiah, he is accused of blasphemy (v. 65), judged worthy of death (v. 66), and insulted by the servants (vv. 67–68). The reader sees Peter's denial as the crowning insult.

But, as so often, the Gospel is paradoxical. Jesus uses an image which evokes the Last Judgment (cf. 24:30; 25:31); he who is now being judged will later be the one who judges.

27:3–10 We do not know what led Judas to betray Jesus; but we do know that, on seeing him condemned, he feels remorse and recognizes his sin. But he despairs

26:64 Dan 7:13; Ps 110:1.

Judas' despair and death
3When Judas, his betrayer, saw that he was condemned, he repented and
brought back the thirty pieces of silver to the chief priests and the elders,
4saying, "I have sinned in betraying innocent blood." They said, "What is that
to us? See to it yourself." 5And throwing down the pieces of silver in the
temple, he departed; and he went and hanged himself. 6But the chief priests,
taking the pieces of silver, said, "It is not lawful to put them into the treasury,
since they are blood money." 7So they took counsel, and bought with them the
potter's field, to bury strangers in. 8Therefore that field has been called the
Field of Blood to this day. 9Then was fulfilled what had been spoken by the
prophet Jeremiah, saying, "And they took the thirty pieces of silver, the price
of him on whom a price had been set by some of the sons of Israel, 10and they
gave them for the potter's field, as the Lord directed me."

Jesus' trial before Pilate Mk 15:1–15; Lk 23; 1–25; Jn 18:28–19:16
11Now Jesus stood before the governor; and the governor asked him, "Are you
the King of the Jews?" Jesus said to him, "You have said so." 12But when he
was accused by the chief priests and elders, he made no answer. 13Then Pilate
said to him, "Do you not hear how many things they testify against you?"
14But he gave him no answer, not even to a single charge; so that the governor
wondered greatly.
15Now at the feast the governor was accustomed to release for the crowd any
one prisoner whom they wanted. 16And they had then a notorious prisoner, called
Barabbas.[k] 17So when they had gathered, Pilate said to them, "Whom do you

---

of forgiveness and kills himself. "By *despair,* man ceases to hope for his personal salvation from God, for help in attaining it or for the forgiveness of his sins. Despair is contrary to God's goodness, to his justice—for the Lord is faithful to his promises—and to his mercy" (*CCC*, 2091).

The reaction of the chief priests is no less pathetic: when commenting on this passage, St Jerome (*Com. on Mt*, in loc.) remarks that they deserved our Lord's accusation about straining out a gnat and swallowing a camel (cf. 23:24). The evangelist sees the purchase of the potter's field as further proof that Jesus is the suffering Servant of God in whom Scripture's prophecies are fulfilled.

27:11–26 Matthew emphasizes Israel's rejection of the Messiah. This passage includes a number of scenes which show Jesus' dignity and the injustice of his sentence.

It begins with accusations by the chief priests, and Pilate's invitation to Christ to defend himself. But Jesus says nothing (vv. 12, 14). As Isaiah foretold of the suffering Servant (Is 53:7), "he was afflicted, yet he opened not his mouth; like a lamb that is led to the slaughter".

k. Other ancient authorities read *Jesus Barabbas* **27:9** Zech 11:12–13; Jer 32:6–15.

want me to release for you, Barabbas[k] or Jesus who is called Christ?" [18]For he knew that it was out of envy that they had delivered him up. [19]Besides, while he was sitting on the judgment seat, his wife sent word to him, "Have nothing to do with that righteous man, for I have suffered much over him today in a dream." [20]Now the chief priests and the elders persuaded the people to ask for Barabbas and destroy Jesus. [21]The governor again said to them, "Which of the two do you want me to release for you?" And they said, "Barabbas." [22]Pilate said to them, "Then what shall I do with Jesus who is called Christ?" They all said, "Let him be crucified." [23]And he said, "Why, what evil has he done?" But they shouted all the more, "Let him be crucified."

[24]So when Pilate saw that he was gaining nothing, but rather that a riot was beginning, he took water and washed his hands before the crowd, saying, "I am innocent of this righteous man's blood;[l] see to it yourselves." [25]And all the people answered, "His blood be on us and on our children!" [26]Then he released for them Barabbas, and having scourged Jesus, delivered him to be crucified.

The crowning with thorns Mk 15:10–20; Jn 19:1–3

[27]Then the soldiers of the governor took Jesus into the praetorium, and they gathered the whole battalion before him. [28]And they stripped him and put a scarlet robe upon him, [29]and plaiting a crown of thorns they put it on his head, and put a reed in his right hand. And kneeling before him they mocked him, saying, "Hail, King of the Jews!" [30]And they spat upon him, and took the reed and struck him on the head. [31]And when they had mocked him, they stripped him of the robe, and put his own clothes on him, and led him away to crucify him.

Then come two references to Jesus' innocence—Pilate's attempt to set him free (v. 18) and Pilate's wife interceding for "that righteous man" (v. 19). But the chief priests incite the crowd to call for Jesus' death, and the crowd does exactly that.

This brings us to the central scene. With a gesture whose significance his hearers could not miss (v. 24; cf. Deut 21:6–8) he puts all the responsibility for Jesus' death onto the people. Their reply (v. 25) should be read in a theological sense, that is, as rejection of the Messiah, on account of which God gives his vineyard to another nation which does produce the fruits of it (cf. 21:43): "neither all Jews indiscriminately at that time, nor Jews today, can be charged with the crimes committed during his passion. [...] The Jews should not be spoken of as rejected or accursed as if this followed from Holy Scripture" (Vatican II, *NA*, 4).

27:27–31 All Christ's sufferings have redemptive value: "Look at the spittle on my face that I have endured so as to return the first breath of life to you; contemplate the blows on my cheeks which I have borne in order to remake your deformed image in my image" (Ancient homily, *Divine Office,* Holy Saturday).

l. Other ancient authorities omit *righteous* or *man's*

The crucifixion and death of Jesus Jn 15:21–41; Lk 23:26–29; Jn 19:17–30

[32]As they were marching out, they came upon a man of Cyrene, Simon by name; this man they compelled to carry his cross. [33]And when they came to a place called Golgotha (which means the place of a skull), [34]they offered him wine to drink, mingled with gall; but when he tasted it, he would not drink it. [35]And when they had crucified him, they divided his garments among them by casting lots; [36]then they sat down and kept watch over him there. [37]And over his head they put the charge against him, which read, "This is Jesus the King of the Jews." [38]Then two robbers were crucified with him, one on the right and one on the left. [39]And those who passed by derided him, wagging their heads [40]and saying, "You who would destroy the temple and build it in three days, save yourself! If you are the Son of God, come down from the cross." [41]So also the chief priests, with the scribes and elders, mocked him, saying, [42]"He saved others; he cannot save himself. He is the King of Israel; let him come down now from the cross, and we will believe in him. [43]He trusts in God, let God deliver him now, if he desires him; for he said, 'I am the Son of God.'" [44]And the robbers who were crucified with him also reviled him in the same way.

[45]Now from the sixth hour there was darkness over all the land[m] until the ninth hour. [46]And about the ninth hour Jesus cried with a loud voice, "Eli, Eli, lama sabachthani?" that is, "My God, my God, why hast thou forsaken me?"* [47]And some of the bystanders hearing it said, "This man is calling Elijah." [48]And one of them at once ran and took a sponge, filled it with vinegar, and put it on a reed, and gave it to him to drink. [49]But the others said, "Wait, let us see

---

27:32–56 Our Lord's words on the cross probably caused his disciples to realize later on that in Jesus' crucifixion and death the Scriptures were perfectly fulfilled (cf. the note on Mk 15:12–41). Hence all the references here to passages from the Old Testament (Ps 22; 69; etc.) announcing that a righteous man must suffer in order that the name of God might be praised by all the nations: "The death of the Saviour was a perfect holocaust which he himself offered to the Father for our redemption; although the pains and sufferings of the passion were so great and strong that any other mortal would have been destroyed by them, Christ's death could not have been brought about without his consenting to it, if the fire of infinite love had not consumed his whole life. He was his own sanctifier; he offered himself to the Father and was consumed by love" (St Francis de Sales, *Treatise on the Love of God,* 10, 17).

In this connexion, St Matthew reports subsequent events (vv. 52–53), showing that by his death Jesus conquers death itself—which the Church professes in its belief in Christ's descent into hell: "Scripture calls the abode of the dead, to which the dead Christ went down, 'hell'—*Sheol* in Hebrew or *Hades* in Greek—because those who are there are deprived of the vision of God. [. . .] Jesus did not descend

m. Or *earth* **27:34** Ps 69:21. **27:35** Ps 22:18. **27:39** Ps 22:7–8. **27:43** Ps 22:8. **27:46** Ps 22:1. **27:48** Ps 69:21.

whether Elijah will come to save him."[n] 50And Jesus cried again with a loud
voice and yielded up his spirit.
51And behold, the curtain of the temple was torn in two, from top to
bottom; and the earth shook, and the rocks were split; 52the tombs also were
opened, and many bodies of the saints who had fallen asleep were raised, 53and
coming out of the tombs after his resurrection they went into the holy city and
appeared to many. 54When the centurion and those who were with him,
keeping watch over Jesus, saw the earthquake and what took place, they were
filled with awe, and said, "Truly this was the Son[x] of God!"
55There were also many women there, looking on from afar, who had
followed Jesus from Galilee, ministering to him; 56among whom were Mary
Magdalene, and Mary the mother of James and Joseph, and the mother of the
sons of Zebedee.

The burial of Jesus Mk 15:42–47; Lk 23:50–56; Jn 19:31–42

57When it was evening, there came a rich man from Arimathea, named Joseph,
who also was a disciple of Jesus. 58He went to Pilate and asked for the body of
Jesus. Then Pilate ordered it to be given to him. 59And Joseph took the body,
and wrapped it in a clean linen shroud, 60and laid it in his own new tomb,
which he had hewn in the rock; and he rolled a great stone to the door of the
tomb, and departed. 61Mary Magdalene and the other Mary were there, sitting
opposite the sepulchre.
62Next day, that is, after the day of Preparation, the chief priests and the
Pharisees gathered before Pilate 63and said, "Sir, we remember how that
imposter said, while he was still alive, 'After three days I will rise again.'
64Therefore order the sepulchre to be made secure until the third day, lest his
disciples go and steal him away, and tell the people, 'He has risen from the
dead,' and the last fraud will be worse than the first." 65Pilate said to them,

---

into hell to deliver the damned, nor to destroy the hell of damnation, but to free the just who had gone before him" (*CCC*, 633).

27:57–66 "In his plan of salvation, God ordained that his Son should not only 'die for our sins (1 Cor 15:3) but should also 'taste death', experience the condition of death, the separation of his soul from his body, between the time he expired on the cross and the time he was raised from the dead. The state of the dead Christ is the mystery of the tomb and the descent into hell" (*CCC*, 624). St Matthew reports details—the new tomb and the great stone (v. 60), the sealing and the guard (v. 66)—which show that Christ truly died and that there was no basis to the story subsequently put about (cf. 28:15).

n. Other ancient authorities insert *And another took a spear and pierced his side, and out came water and blood* **x.** Or *a son*

'You have a guard[o] of soldiers; go, make it as secure as you can."[p] 66So they went and made the sepulchre secure by sealing the stone and setting a guard.*

Jesus rises from the dead and appears to the women

Mk 16:1–8; Lk 24:1–12; Jn 20:1–10

28 *1Now after the sabbath, toward the dawn of the first day of the week, Mary Magdalene and the other Mary went to see the sepulchre. 2And behold, there was a great earthquake; for an angel of the Lord descended from heaven and came and rolled back the stone, and sat upon it. 3His appearance was like lightning, and his raiment white as snow. 4And for fear of him the guards trembled and became like dead men. 5But the angel said to the women. "Do not be afraid; for I know that you seek Jesus who was crucified. 6He is not here; for he has risen, as he said. Come, see the place where he[q] lay. 7Then go quickly and tell his disciples that he has risen from the dead, and behold, he is going before you to Galilee; there you will see him. Lo, I have told you." 8So they departed quickly from the tomb with fear and great joy, and ran to tell his disciples. 9And behold, Jesus met them and said, "Hail!" And they came up and took hold of his feet and worshipped him. 10Then Jesus said to them, "Do not be afraid; go and tell my brethren to go to Galilee; and there they will see me."

The soldiers are bribed

11While they were going, behold, some of the guard went into the city and told the chief priests all that had taken place. 12And when they had assembled with the elders and taken counsel, they gave a sum of money to the soldiers 13and said, "Tell people, 'His disciples came by night and stole him away while we

---

28:1–15 The signs which the evangelist reports as announcing the resurrection (vv. 2–4) show the magnitude of the event: "Faith in the Resurrection has as its object an event which is historically attested to by the disciples, who really encountered the Risen One. At the same time, this event is mysteriously transcendent insofar as it is the entry of Christ's humanity into the glory of God" (*CCC*, 656). And this fact has key importance for our lives, for "Christ, 'the first-born from the dead' (Col 1:18), is the principle of our own resurrection, even now by the justification of our souls (cf. Rom 6:4), and one day by the new life he will impart to our bodies (cf. Rom 8:11)" (ibid., 658).

The evangelist also gives a negative proof of the fact that Christ truly rose—the fact that people spread the story that his body was stolen (vv. 11–15): "Wretched craftiness," says St Augustine, "do you give us witnesses who were asleep? It is you who are really asleep if this is the only kind of explanation you have to offer" (St Augustine, *Enarr. in Ps*, 63, 15).

o. Or *take a guard* **p.** Greek *know* **q.** Other ancient authorities read *the Lord* were asleep.' [14]And if this comes to the governor's ears, we will satisfy him and keep you out of trouble." [15]So they took the money and did as they were directed; and this story has been spread among the Jews to this day.

Appearance in Galilee.
The mission to the world Mk 16:14–18; Lk 24:36–49; Jn 20:19–31

[16]Now the eleven disciples went to Galilee, to the mountain to which Jesus had directed them. [17]And when they saw him they worshipped him; but some doubted. [18]And Jesus came and said to them, "All authority in heaven and on earth has been given to me. [19]Go therefore and make disciples of all nations, baptizing them in the name of the Father and of the Son and of the Holy Spirit, [20]teaching them to observe all that I have commanded you; and lo, I am with you always, to the close of the age."

28:16–20 All four evangelists report how difficult it was for the apostles to accept the resurrection of Jesus. Mark (cf. Mk 16:9–20 and note) is more explicit on this than Matthew, who makes only a very short reference to their doubts (v. 17): "It is no great thing to believe that Christ died. Pagans, Jews [...] believe it too. Everyone believes that Christ died. Christians' faith consists in believing in the resurrection of Christ" (St Augustine, *Enarr. in Ps*, 120, 6).

Once they accept the resurrection, Christ charges his disciples with the mission of the Church—to sanctify men and show them what a Christian life means (vv. 19–20). But they are not going to be left on their own: he is the Emmanuel, "God with us" (1:23) and, being God (v. 18), he is with us until the end of time (v. 20).

The Gospel according to St Mark

Tradition attributes the second Gospel to St Mark, "the disciple and interpreter of Peter" (cf. St Irenaeus, *Adv. haer.*, 3, 1, 1), and tells us that St Mark wrote his Gospel in Rome, at the request of Christians who wanted to have a written account of St Peter's preaching. Close examination of this Gospel would tend to confirm some of this. For example, the evangelist seems to be addressing people who do not have a Jewish background, for he explains Jewish customs to them (7:3–4; 14:2; 15:42), and translates Aramaic words for them when they appear (3:17; 5:41; 7:11; 14:36; 15:22; 15:34). Moreover, the liveliness of the narrative and the author's penchant for picturesque details—the "cushion" on which Jesus slept on the boat (4:38), the "green" grass at the time of the miracle of the loaves (6:39), etc.—suggest that many passages in this Gospel must have come from an eyewitness to the events.

Unlike the other Synoptic Gospels, this one does not cover episodes from Jesus' infancy. Its structure seems to be a detailed development of Peter's address in the house of Cornelius the centurion (Acts 10:34–43): Jesus began to preach the Gospel in Galilee, he went about doing good, the Jews of Jerusalem put him to death by crucifying him, but God raised him from the dead and after he was risen he sent his disciples out to preach. In keeping with this outline, Mark gives an account of Jesus' activity in Galilee and the neighbouring regions, his journey up to Jerusalem, his controversy with Jewish leaders in the Holy City, and his death and resurrection. One could say that there is a "geographical" structure to this Gospel. But there is also what could be called a "theological" structure. What the evangelist is doing is showing how Jesus manifested himself by words and actions which led the people to ask: "Who is this?" St Peter, who is at the centre of this Gospel, is the only one to speak up: "You are the Christ" (8:29). From this point onwards, Jesus begins to reveal what his mission as Messiah means: he is the rejected Messiah who must die on the cross in order to rise again. This second part of the Gospel concludes with the profession of faith made by the centurion at the foot of the cross: "Truly this man was the Son of God" (15:39). These titles—Christ/ Messiah and Son of God—are the ones Mark gave Jesus at the start of his Gospel (1:1).

The first verse of the Gospel—"The beginning of the gospel of Jesus Christ, the Son of God"—seems to summarize the main content of Mark's account. Jesus is the Son of God: this is what the Father proclaims him to be at his Baptism and at the Transfiguration (1:11; 9:7) and this, too, is the confession made by the centurion (15:39); but it is a confession the reader of the Gospel will also make when he sees the miracles Jesus does (Mark is the evangelist who gives most space to our Lord's miracles) and when he sees his resurrection and glorification (16:19). Equally, Jesus is the *Christ*. Unlike Matthew, Mark does not use Old Testament texts to prove that Jesus is the Messiah, but by recounting Jesus' works he shows them to be the works of the promised Messiah. However, when performing these messianic actions, Jesus asked those who benefited from them to say nothing about them (1:44; 5:43; 7:36; 8:26) because he did not want his messianic mission to be interpreted in an earthly and political way, but rather to be seen in the light of the cross (8:27–33).

Mark is the only evangelist who uses the word "gospel" (it appears at the heading of his account). The Gospel is the Good News preached by Jesus (1:14–15), by his words and actions; thus, everything Christ does can truly be called the Gospel of Jesus Christ (1:1). Jesus sends his disciples out to preach it (16:15), telling them that to give one's life for the Gospel is as noble an action as to give it for Christ himself (10:29). Finally, Mark makes the point that he is relating only the *beginning* (1:1), because the Gospel must be preached "to the whole creation" (16:15). The evangelist tells us that Jesus carried out most of his public ministry in Galilee, a region which, in Christ's time, was a veritable crossroads of cultures where Jews and Gentiles intermingled. And therefore it is in Galilee that the Lord assembles his disciples after his resurrection (14:28; 16:7), to send them out from there to all parts of the world.

Mark

1. PRELUDE TO THE PUBLIC MINISTRY OF JESUS

The ministry of John the Baptist Mt 3:1–12; Lk 3:1–8; Jn 1:19–34

1 1 The beginning of the gospel of Jesus Christ, the Son of God.[a] 2 As it is
written in Isaiah the prophet,[b]

> "Behold, I send my messenger before thy face,
> who shall prepare the way;
> 3 the voice of one crying in the wilderness:
> Prepare the way of the Lord,
> make his paths straight—"

4 John the baptizer appeared[c] in the wilderness, preaching a baptism of
repentance for the forgiveness of sins. 5 And there went out to him all the
country of Judea, and all the people of Jerusalem; and they were baptized by
him in the river Jordan, confessing their sins. 6 Now John was clothed in
camel's hair, and had a leather girdle around his waist, and ate locusts and wild
honey. 7 And he preached, saying, "After me comes he who is mightier than I,
the thong of whose sandals I am not worthy to stoop down and untie. 8 I have
baptized you with water, but he will baptize you with the Holy Spirit."

1:1–13 □ These verses are a kind of prologue. They introduce Jesus to us in his two natures—as God, whose coming to his people must be heralded by his messenger (vv. 2–3; cf. Mal 3:1), and as man, who is subject to temptation and who is like all men except that he does not sin (vv. 12–13; cf. Heb 4:15). The Baptism of Jesus, which forms the centre of the narrative, reveals Jesus to be the Son of God.

The opening verse is like a gateway to the entire Gospel according to Mark: Jesus of Nazareth is the Messiah ("Jesus Christ") and also the Son of God; with him the moment of salvation arrives ("the beginning), for he himself is the Good News of salvation ("the gospel").

1:1–8 The evangelist uses a quotation from the prophets and references to John's prophet-like actions to show that the Baptist is the link between the Old and New Testaments: he is the last of the prophets, and the first witness to Christ.

The Baptist's austere lifestyle is very much in line with his message: people need to repent, to be cleansed, so as to be able to receive the Messiah. John shows

a. Other ancient authorities omit *the Son of God* **b.** Other ancient authorities read *in the prophets* **c.** Other ancient authorities read *John was baptizing* **1:3** Is 40:3

Jesus is baptized Mt 3:13–17; Lk 3:21–22

9In those days Jesus came from Nazareth of Galilee and was baptized by John
in the Jordan. 10And when he came up out of the water, immediately he saw
the heavens opened and the Spirit descending upon him like a dove; 11and a
voice came from heaven, "Thou art my beloved Son;[d] with thee I am well
pleased."

The tempting of Jesus Mt 4:1–11; Lk 4:1–13

12The Spirit immediately drove him out into the wilderness. 13And he was in
the wilderness forty days, tempted by Satan; and he was with the wild beasts;
and the angels ministered to him.

---

the greatness of Jesus, the Messiah; he regards himself as unworthy to untie his sandal strap (v. 7); the humility of this expression is made clear if one remembers that this was such a humiliating action that it was forbidden to make a Jewish slave do such a thing.

1:9–13 The account of the Baptism of Jesus reminds us that he went to John for baptism even though he had no need of a baptism of repentance. The evangelist focuses mainly on the fact that the Blessed Trinity manifests Jesus as Son and as Messiah, as can be seen from both the voice from heaven and the descent of the Spirit upon Jesus. The Fathers of the Church interpreted the Holy Spirit's appearing in the form of a dove as a sign of peace and reconciliation (cf. Gen 8:10–11) offered by God to men in Christ. As regards Jesus, his Baptism means "the acceptance and inauguration of his mission as God's suffering Servant. He allows himself to be numbered among sinners; he is already 'the Lamb of God, who takes away the sin of the world' (Jn 1:29). Already he is anticipating the 'baptism' of his bloody death (Mt 3:15). Already he is coming to 'fulfil all righteousness', that is, he is submitting himself entirely to his Father's will: out of love he consents to this baptism of death for the remission of our sins. The Father's voice responds to the Son's acceptance, proclaiming his entire delight in his Son" (*CCC*, 536).

1:12–13 Mark simply states that Jesus was tempted; unlike Matthew and Luke he does not describe each temptation. This allows him to move on directly to his account of Jesus' public activity, a ministry for which his time in the wilderness was a preparation.

d. Or *my Son, my* (or *the*) *Beloved*

PART ONE: JESUS' MINISTRY IN GALILEE

2. JESUS BEGINS HIS MINISTRY

Jesus begins to preach and calls his first disciples Mt 4:12–25; Lk 4:14–15; 5:1–11; Jn 1:31–51

14Now after John was arrested, Jesus came into Galilee, preaching the gospel of God, 15and saying, "The time is fulfilled, and the kingdom of God is at hand; repent, and believe in the Gospel."

1:14–8:30 □□ The Gospel of Mark is similar in structure to the early preaching of the apostles: "You know [...] the word which was proclaimed throughout all Judea, beginning from Galilee after the baptism which John preached: how God anointed Jesus of Nazareth with the Holy Spirit and with power; how he went about doing good and healing all that were oppressed by the devil, for God was with him" (Acts 10:37–38). In this first part (1:14–8:30) the evangelist describes the teaching and healing work of Jesus in Galilee and the neighbouring regions. His miracles and teachings lead people to ask, "Who is this?" (cf. 1:27; 2:7, 12; 3:32; 4:41; 6:2, 14–16; etc.) and they cannot work it out. St Peter is the only one who manages to acknowledge that Jesus is the Messiah (cf. 8:29). But, even then, Jesus asks his disciples not to say anything, because he must first undergo the suffering of the cross.

1:14–3:35 □The account of Jesus' public ministry begins with a summary of his preaching (1:14–15)—an urgent call to repentance, in order to enter the Kingdom of God. Then we are told about some episodes to do with Jesus' initial activity in Capernaum and thereabouts. His actions amaze and delight the people (1:27–28, 37, 45; 2:2, 12; etc.) but they provoke opposition from the scribes and Pharisees (2:6, 16, 23–24; 3:6; etc.). Also included here is our Lord's call to his disciples, leading to the formation of the group of twelve apostles (3:13–19). Thus we are introduced to the cast of characters who will later play a part in the drama that leads to Jesus' death.

Readers of the Gospel are shown what Jesus did and taught during the first stage of his public ministry: for example, we are given an account of a day in the Master's life (1:21–38), we see his exhausting schedule, his compassion (1:41), his indignation (3:5), etc.

1:14–15 The fact that Jesus' preaching begins when that of the Baptist ends is an indication that the stage of the promises is over; with Jesus and his words the Kingdom of God (and, therefore, salvation) commences. "Jesus himself, the Good News of God, was the first and greatest evangelist" (Paul VI, *Evang. nunt,* 7).

[16]And passing along by the Sea of Galilee, he saw Simon and Andrew the brother of Simon casting a net in the sea; for they were fishermen. [17]And Jesus said to them, "Follow me and I will make you become fishers of men." [18]And immediately they left their nets and followed him. [19]And going on a little farther, he saw James the son of Zebedee and John his brother, who were in their boat mending the nets. [20]And immediately he called them; and they left their father Zebedee in the boat with the hired servants, and followed him.

Jesus in the synagogue of Capernaum Lk 4:31–37

[21]And they went into Capernaum; and immediately on the sabbath he entered the synagogue and taught. [22]And they were astonished at his teaching, for he taught them as one who had authority, and not as the scribes. [23]And immediately there was in their synagogue a man with an unclean spirit; [24]and he cried out, "What have you to do with us, Jesus of Nazareth? Have you come to destroy us? I know who you are, the Holy One of God." [25]But Jesus rebuked him saying, "Be silent, and come out of him!" [26]And the unclean spirit, convulsing him and crying out with a loud voice, came out of him. [27]And they were all amazed, so that they questioned among themselves, saying, "What is this? A new teaching! With authority he commands even the unclean spirits, and they obey him." [28]And at once his fame spread everywhere throughout all the surrounding region of Galilee.

Curing of Peter's mother-in-law Mt 8:14–15; Lk 4:38–39

[29]And immediately he[e] left the synagogue, and entered the house of Simon and Andrew, with James and John. [30]Now Simon's mother-in-law lay sick with a fever, and immediately they told him of her. [31]And he came and took her by the hand and lifted her up, and the fever left her; and she served them.

1:16–20 In Jesus' time, devout young men seeking a better understanding and practice of the Law of Moses attached themselves to a teacher or rabbi: it was the disciple who chose the master. Jesus, on the contrary, takes the initiative, calling those he chooses to be his disciples, and his call is imperative.

The Son of God passes by and issues his call. If it is not responded to "immediately" (v. 18), he may continue on his way and we may lose sight of him.

1:21–28 Both the evangelist (v. 22) and the crowd (v. 27) are amazed to see that Jesus teaches "with authority". Over the course of these early chapters of the Gospel, Jesus will show that he has authority over many more things—diseases and demons (1:29–34), ritual laws (2:18–28), etc.

1:29–34 Jesus now shows that he also has authority over disease and over the devil. The end of the passage records that he forbids the demons to make known

e. Other ancient authorities read *they*

Jesus cures many sick people Mt 8:10–17; Lk 4:40–41

32That evening, at sundown, they brought to him all who were sick or possessed with demons. 33And the whole city was gathered together about the door. 34And he healed many who were sick with various diseases, and cast out many demons; and he would not permit the demons to speak, because they knew him.*

Jesus goes to a lonely place to pray Lk 4:42–44

35And in the morning, a great while before day, he rose and went out to a lonely place, and there he prayed. 36And Simon and those who were with him followed him, 37and they found him and said to him, "Every one is searching for you." 38And he said to them, "Let us go on to the next towns, that I may preach there also; for that is why I came out." 39And he went throughout all Galilee, preaching in their synagogues and casting out demons.

Curing of a leper Mt 8:1–4; Lk 5:12–16

40And a leper came to him, beseeching him, and kneeling said to him, "If you will, you can make me clean." 41Moved with pity, he stretched out his hand and touched him, and said to him, "I will; be clean." 42And immediately the leprosy left him, and he was made clean. 43And he sternly charged him, and sent him away at once, 44and said to him, "See that you say nothing to any one; but go, show yourself to the priest, and offer for your cleansing what Moses commanded, for a proof to the people."[f] 45But he went out and began to talk

---

who he is. This is a feature of the early stage of Christ's activity: he demands silence from his disciples (8:30; 9:9), the sick people whom he cures (1:44; 5:43; 7:36; 8:26) and the demons who recognize who he is (1:25, 34; 3:12) but whose testimony he does not accept. In this way he tries to refine the notion most of his contemporaries had about the Messiah: Jesus wants them to understand his mission in the light of the cross.

1:35–39 The New Testament often makes mention of Jesus' prayer, to set it as an example for the Christian. St Mark explicitly refers to Jesus praying "alone", at three important moments—here, at the start of his public ministry (1:35), midway through that ministry (6:46) and, finally, at Gethsemane (14:32). "When you start out each day to work by Christ's side and to look after all those souls who seek him, remember that there is only one way of doing it—by turning to the Lord. Only in prayer, and through prayer, do we learn to serve others" (Bl. J. Escrivá, *The Forge*, 72).

1:40–45 Leprosy, a disgusting disease, was regarded as a punishment from God (cf. Num 12:10–15; Lev 13ff). The Law declared lepers to be unclean and made

f. Greek *to them*

freely about it, and spread the news, so that Jesus[g] could no longer openly enter a
town, but was out in the country; and people came to him from every quarter.

Curing of a paralyzed man Mt 9:1–8; Lk 5:17–26

2 [1]And when he returned to Capernaum after some days, it was reported that
he was at home. [2]And many were gathered together, so that there was no
longer room for them, not even about the door; and he was preaching the word
to them. [3]And they came, bringing to him a paralytic carried by four men.
[4]And when they could not get near him because of the crowd, they removed
the roof above him; and when they had made an opening, they let down the
pallet on which the paralytic lay. [5]And when Jesus saw their faith, he said to
the paralytic, "My son, your sins are forgiven." [6]Now some of the scribes were
sitting there, questioning in their hearts, [7]"Why does this man speak thus? It is
blasphemy! Who can forgive sins but God alone?" [8]And immediately Jesus,
perceiving in his spirit that they thus questioned within themselves, said to
them, "Why do you question thus in your hearts? [9]Which is easier, to say to
the paralytic, 'Your sins are forgiven,' or to say, 'Rise, take up your pallet and

---

them live apart from everyone else in order not to pass their uncleanness on to other people and things they came into contact with (Num 5:12; 12:14ff). The curing of leprosy was seen as one of the blessings that would mark the arrival of the Messiah (cf. Is 35:8; Mt 11:5; Lk 7:22).

In the words and actions of the leper we can see his faithful prayer and his great desire to be cured; and Jesus' words and actions show his mercy, greatness and authority: "That man knelt prostrate on the ground (a sign of humility and of shame) so that all might be ashamed of their sins. Shame, however, must not come in the way of confession: the leper shows his wound and asks for the cure. His confession is full of piety and faith. 'If you will,' he says, 'you can': that is, he acknowledges that Christ has the power to cure him" (St Bede, *In Marci Evang. exp.*, in loc.).

2:1–12 The evangelist's account brings the whole scene to life—the reports of Jesus' arrival, the crush of people, the opening of the roof, etc. The Gospel helps us to get a new sense of the salvific effect of Jesus' actions: he cures the body of disease, and the spirit of sin. Here we see Jesus' divine power to forgive sins, the fact that he can read the scribes' thoughts and is able to cure the paralytic (vv. 5, 8, 11), and the resourceful faith of the man's friends who overcome obstacles to bring him to Jesus (vv. 3–5). "The Lord Jesus Christ, physician of our souls and bodies, who forgave the sins of the paralytic and restored him to bodily health, has willed that his Church continue, in the power of the Holy Spirit, his work of healing and salvation, even among her own members. This is the purpose of the two sacraments of healing: the sacrament of Penance and the sacrament of Anointing of the Sick" (*CCC*, 1421).

g. Greek *he*

walk'? [10]But that you may know that the Son of man has authority on earth to forgive sins"—he said to the paralytic—[11]"I say to you, rise, take up your pallet and go home." [12]And he rose, and immediately took up the pallet and went out before them all; so that they were all amazed and glorified God, saying, "We never saw anything like this!"

The calling of Matthew Mt 9:9–13; Lk 5:27–32

[13]He went out again beside the sea; and all the crowd gathered about him, and he taught them. [14]And as he passed on, he saw Levi* the son of Alphaeus sitting at the tax office, and he said to him, "Follow me." And he rose and followed him.

[15]And as he sat at table in his house, many tax collectors and sinners were sitting with Jesus and his disciples; for there were many who followed him. [16]And the scribes of[h] the Pharisees, when they saw that he was eating with sinners and tax collectors, said to his disciples, "Why does he eat[i] with tax collectors and sinners?" [17]And when Jesus heard it, he said to them, "Those who are well have no need of a physician, but those who are sick; I came not to call the righteous, but sinners."

A discussion on fasting Mt 9:14–17; Lk 33–39

[18]Now John's disciples and the Pharisees were fasting; and people came and said to him, "Why do John's disciples and the disciples of the Pharisees fast, but your disciples do not fast?" [19]And Jesus said to them, "Can the wedding guests fast while the bridegroom is with them? As long as they have the bridegroom with them, they cannot fast. [20]The days will come, when the

---

2:13–17 Here we are given a very brief account of the calling of "Levi, the son of Alphaeus". In the parallel passage in the first Gospel (Mt 9:9–13) the man is called "Matthew", one of the twelve apostles (Mk 3:18).

Eating a meal together was a clear sign of friendship and communion. The Gospels show us Jesus dining with Pharisees (Lk 7:36–50), with friends such as Lazarus of Bethany (Jn 12:2), with his disciples (3:20), and, here, with tax collectors and sinners. Moreover, Jesus often used the simile of the banquet when talking about the Kingdom (Mt 22:1–14; Lk 14:16–24). The meaning of this passage is crystal clear: Jesus excludes no one from his call to salvation: "I am not come for them to continue to be sinners, but to have them change and become better"' (St John Chrysostom, *Hom. on Mt*, 30, 3).

2:18–22 What is at issue here is the behaviour of Jesus' disciples. By accusing them of relaxing the demands of self-denial, they are also criticizing Jesus, their Master. His reply, drawing the comparison with the bridegroom, implies that he is more than a teacher—he is the Messiah (cf. Jn 3:29)—and it highlights an aspect

h. Other ancient authorities read *and* **i.** Other ancient authorities add *and drink*

bridegroom is taken away from them, and then they will fast in that day. [21]No
one sews a piece of unshrunk cloth on an old garment; if he does, the patch
tears away from it, the new from the old, and a worse tear is made. [22]And no
one puts new wine into old wineskins; if he does, the wine will burst the skins,
and the wine is lost, and so are the skins; but new wine is for fresh skins."[j]

The law of the sabbath Mt 12:1–8; Lk 6:1–5

[23]One sabbath he was going through the grainfields; and as they made their
way his disciples began to pluck ears of grain. [24]And the Pharisees said to him,
"Look, why are they doing what is not lawful on the sabbath?" [25]And he said
to them, "Have you never read what David did, when he was in need and
hungry, he and those who were with him: [26]how he entered the house of God,
when Abiathar was high priest, and ate the bread of the Presence, which it is
not lawful for any but the priests to eat, and also gave it to those who were
with him?" [27]And he said to them, "The sabbath was made for man, not man
for the sabbath; [28]so the Son of man is lord even of the sabbath."

Curing of the man with a withered hand Mt 12:9–14; Lk 6:6–11

3 [1]Again he entered the synagogue, and a man was there who had a withered
hand. [2]And they watched him, to see whether he would heal him on the

---

of his being accepted as the Messiah Saviour—the joy his coming brings. Penitential practices must take second place to this. The most important thing is to accept Jesus: to do this, we need to renew ourselves interiorly and to detach ourselves from the routine of a sterile life.

2:23–28 In Jesus' time, the Pharisees had laid down all kinds of detailed rules about how to keep the Law. These prescriptions, when separated from the spirit that informed them, became really burdensome (cf. 7:1–13; Acts 5:10; etc.). By quoting a particular example and a proverb (v. 27), Jesus explains that precepts of this sort must yield to the natural law: the precept of sabbath observance must not get in the way of sheer survival. The Second Vatican Council uses this passage to highlight the dignity of the human person: "The social order and its development must constantly yield to the good of the person, since the order of things must be subordinate to the order of persons and not the other way around" (*GS*, 26). But what this passage does, primarily, is show Jesus to be the "lord of the sabbath" (v. 28). If we bear in mind that the sabbath precept was instituted by God himself, we can see that Jesus is implying that he is God.

3:1–6 This episode confirms that Jesus is "lord of the sabbath". He is the Messiah with divine authority and he shows this in the cures he works. Those who criticize

j. Other ancient authorities omit *but new wine is for fresh skins*

sabbath, so that they might accuse him. 3And he said to the man who had the
withered hand, "Come here." 4And he said to them, "Is it lawful on the sabbath
to do good or to do harm, to save life or to kill?" But they were silent. 5And he
looked around at them with anger, grieved at their hardness of heart, and said
to the man, "Stretch out your hand." He stretched it out, and his hand was
restored. 6The Pharisees went out, and immediately held counsel with the
Herodians against him, how to destroy him.

Cures beside the Sea of Galilee

7Jesus withdrew with his disciples to the sea, and a great multitude from Galilee
followed; also from Judea 8and Jerusalem and Idumea and from beyond the
Jordan and from about Tyre and Sidon a great multitude, hearing all that he did,
came to him. 9And he told his disciples to have a boat ready for him because of
the crowd, lest they should crush him; 10for he had healed many, so that all who
had diseases pressed upon him to touch him. 11And whenever the unclean spirits
beheld him, they fell down before him and cried out, "You are the Son of God."
12And he strictly ordered them not to make him known.

Jesus chooses twelve apostles Mt 10:1–4; Lk 6:12–16

13And he went up into the hills, and called to him those whom he desired; and
they came to him. 14And he appointed twelve,[k] to be with him, and to be sent out
to preach 15and have authority to cast out demons: 16Simon whom he surnamed
Peter; 17James the son of Zebedee and John the brother of James, whom he
surnamed Boanerges, that is, sons of thunder; 18Andrew, and Philip, and
Bartholomew, and Matthew, and Thomas, and James the son of Alphaeus, and
Thaddaeus, and Simon the Cananaean, 19and Judas Iscariot, who betrayed him.

---

him fail to read the evidence. The hypocritical attitude of the Pharisees and Herodians justifies our Lord's indignation and sorrow.

3:7–12 The proclamation of the Gospel, by words and actions, now goes beyond the narrow confines of Galilee, and people from all Palestine flock to see him: it is a prelude to the universal spread of the Gospel (vv. 7–8). The thronging of the people (vv. 7, 9–10) reflects what Christians did in every age, because the holy Humanity of our Lord is our only way to salvation, the irreplaceable means of union with God.

3:13–19 In addition to the groups mentioned earlier (crowds, disciples, and even unclean spirits) the Gospel will now bring in others—scribes and Pharisees, relatives of Jesus, his Mother, etc. Each has his or her own reaction to Jesus. The evangelist stresses particularly the group of the Twelve (v. 14). The fact that Jesus chose exactly twelve apostles is very significant. Their number agrees with that of

k. Other ancient authorities add *whom also he named apostles*

Jesus' relatives are concerned about him
Then he went home; 20and the crowd came together again, so that they could
not even eat. 21And when his friends heard it, they went out to seize him, for
they said, "He is beside himself."

Allegations of the scribes. Sin against the Holy Spirit Mt 12:22–32; Lk 11:14–26
22And the scribes who came down from Jerusalem said, "He is possessed by
Beelzebul, and by the prince of demons he casts out the demons." 23And he
called them to him, and said to them in parables, "How can Satan cast out
Satan? 24If a kingdom is divided against itself, that kingdom cannot stand. 25And
if a house is divided against itself, that house will not be able to stand. 26And if
Satan has risen up against himself and is divided, he cannot stand, but is coming
to an end. 27But no one can enter a strong man's house and plunder his goods,
unless he first binds the strong man; then indeed he may plunder his house.
28"Truly, I say to you, all sins will be forgiven the sons of men, and
whatever blasphemies they utter; 29but whoever blasphemes against the Holy
Spirit never has forgiveness, but is guilty of an eternal sin"—30for they had
said, "He has an unclean spirit."

---

the twelve patriarchs of Israel: the apostles stand for the new people of God, the Church Christ founds (cf. the note on Mt 10:1–4).

In its description of what being apostles involves, the Gospel mentions four features—the fact that our Lord calls them, freely, without any merit on their part; the apostles' response; their link with Christ; and their being sent into the world to preach (cf. 1:16–18; 16:20). This shows the importance that contact and friendship with Jesus have for effective apostolate: "Christ, sent by the Father, is the source of the Church's whole apostolate; thus the fruitfulness of apostolate for ordained ministers as well as for lay people clearly depends on their vital union with Christ" (*CCC*, 864).

3:20–30 People think our Lord's activity makes no sense (v. 21). This is reported in various places in the New Testament (cf. 6:3); the prophets' doings often provoked a similar reaction (cf., for example, Jer 26). The criticism made by the scribes who came down from Jerusalem is much worse than the thoughts in the minds of Jesus' relatives. The scribes see that Jesus has authority over the demons but they actually credit to the devil things that are works of God. Making a number of comparisons (vv. 23–27), Jesus explains the inherent contradiction in the scribes' accusation. Later, on account of their hardness of heart, Jesus, who showed his compassion by forgiving sinners their sins and by eating with them, warns that it will be very difficult for people to gain forgiveness if they voluntarily close their minds to the truth (cf. the note on Mt 12:22–37).

The true kinsmen of Jesus Mt 12:46–50; Lk 8:19–21

31 And his mother and his brethren* came; and standing outside they went to
him and called him. 32 And a crowd was sitting about him: and they said to
him, "Your mother and your brethren[l] are outside, asking for you." 33 And he
replied, "Who are my mother and my brethren?" 34 And looking around on
those who sat about him, he said, "Here are my mother and my brethren!
35 Whoever does the will of God is my brother, and sister, and mother."

3. PARABLES OF THE KINGDOM OF GOD

Parable of the sower. The meaning of parables Mt 13:1–23; Lk 8:4–18

4 1 Again he began to teach beside the sea. And a very large crowd gathered
about him, so that he got into a boat and sat in it on the sea; and the whole
crowd was beside the sea on the land. 2 And he taught them many things in
parables, and in his teachings he said to them: 3 "Listen! A sower went out to
sow. 4 And as he sowed, some seed fell along the path, and the birds came and
devoured it. 5 Other seed fell on rocky ground, where it had not much soil, and
immediately it sprang up, since it had no depth of soil; 6 and when the sun rose
it was scorched, and since it had no root it withered away. 7 Other seed fell
among thorns and the thorns grew up and choked it, and it yielded no grain.
8 And other seeds fell into good soil and brought forth grain, growing up and
increasing and yielding thirtyfold and sixtyfold and a hundredfold." 9 And he
said, "He who has ears to hear, let him hear."

3:31–35 This passage explicitly distinguishes Jesus' Mother and "brethren" (v. 31) from the other relatives/friends (v. 21) who thought he was out of his mind. On the meaning of the expression "brethren of Jesus", see the note on Mt 12:46–50.

The episode reported here indicates a key feature of the Christian: doing the will of God implies a closer relationship to Christ than merely being a member of his family. Therefore, the inclusion of Jesus' Mother here is very significant, for she, more than anyone else, "received the words whereby, in extolling a kingdom beyond the concerns and ties of flesh and blood, he declared blessed those who heard and kept the word of God as she was faithfully doing" (Vatican II, *LG*, 58).

4:1–34 □ In this discourse recounted by St Mark we find three types of parable—that of the sower (vv. 3–20), those of the lamp and the measure (vv. 21–25) and those of the seed and the mustard seed (vv. 26–32). All have to do with the Kingdom of God, though from different angles (cf. the note on Mt 13:1–52).

At the start of his preaching, Christ proclaims the coming of the Kingdom of God (1:15). However, as the parable of the sower shows, this Kingdom is not depicted as something dramatic and overpowering, which is what many of Jesus'

l. Other early authorities add *and your sisters*

[10]And when he was alone, those who were about him with the twelve asked
him concerning the parables. [11]And he said to them, "To you has been given
the secret of the kingdom of God, but for those outside everything is in
parables; [12]so that *they may indeed see but not perceive, and may indeed hear
but not understand; lest they should turn again, and be forgiven." [13]And he said
to them, "Do you not understand this parable? How then will you understand
all the parables? [14]The sower sows the word. [15]And these are the ones along
the path, where the word is sown; when they hear, Satan immediately comes
and takes away the word which is sown in them. [16]And these in like manner
are the ones sown upon rocky ground, who, when they hear the word,
immediately receive it with joy; [17]and they have no root in themselves, but
endure for a while; then, when tribulation or persecution arises on account of
the word, immediately they fall away.[m] [18]And others are the ones sown among
thorns; they are those who hear the word, [19]but the cares of the world, and the
delight in riches, and the desire for other things, enter in and choke the word,
and it proves unfruitful. [20]But those that were sown upon the good soil are the
ones who hear the word and accept it and bear fruit, thirtyfold and sixtyfold
and a hundredfold."

Parables of the lamp and the measure Mt 7:1–2; Lk 8:16–18

[21]And he said to them, "Is a lamp brought in to be put under a bushel, or under
a bed, and not on a stand? [22]For there is nothing hid, except to be made

---

contemporaries expected it to be. It comes to birth with the person and preaching of Jesus, but its fruits depend on people's dispositions and on the reception they give it (vv. 14–20). We need to be alert (vv. 23–25), to be witnesses of the word of God (vv. 21–22), and not judge the Kingdom by its small beginnings; without our knowing how, it will bear fruit (vv. 26–29) far richer than we could possibly expect (vv. 30–32).

4:10–12 The Kingdom of God is a mystery. If the Twelve and the other disciples know about it and understand it (cf. Mt 13:51), they do so by God's gift (v. 11; cf. Mt 13:11). The disciples are distinguished from "those outside"—a reference which normally applied to the Gentiles but which here applies to Jews who chose not to appreciate the signs worked by Jesus (cf. Lk 12:41). Those signs fulfil the words of the prophet Isaiah (Is 6:9–10). When, in v. 12, Jesus says "so that …", we might at first sight find it disconcerting; our Lord is in fact using a wording often found in the Bible (cf. Ex 4:21; 7:3, 13, 22; etc.) which attributes to God the actions of men. It is a way of referring to the mystery of how God's grace and man's cooperation combine in salvific actions. We also find that when people sincerely seek God, he "opens hearts to understand" his words (cf. Acts 16:14).

m. Or *stumble* **4:12** Is 6:9–10.

manifest; nor is anything secret, except to come to light. [23]If any man has ears
to hear, let him hear." [24]And he said to them, "Take heed what you hear; the
measure you give will be the measure you get, and still more will be given
you. [25]For to him who has will more be given; and from him who has not, even
what he has will be taken away."

Parables of the seed and of the mustard seed Mt 13:31–33; Lk 13:18–19

[26]And he said, "The kingdom of God is as if a man should scatter seed upon
the ground, [27]and should sleep and rise night and day, and the seed should
sprout and grow, he knows not how. [28]The earth produces of itself, first the
blade, then the ear, then the full grain in the ear. [29]But when the grain is ripe,
at once he puts in the sickle, because the harvest has come."

[30]And he said, "With what can we compare the kingdom of God, or what
parable shall we use for it? [31]It is like a grain of mustard seed, which, when
sown upon the ground, is the smallest of all the seeds on earth; [32]yet when it is
sown it grows up and becomes the greatest of all shrubs, and puts forth large
branches, so that the birds of the air can make nests in its shade."

The end of the parables discourse Mt 13:34

[33]With many such parables he spoke the word to them, as they were able to
hear it; [34]he did not speak to them without a parable, but privately to his own
disciples he explained everything.

4. MIRACLES AND ACTIVITY IN GALILEE

The calming of the storm Mt 8:23–27; Lk 8:22–25

[35]On that day, when evening had come, he said to them, "Let us go across to
the other side." [36]And leaving the crowd, they took him with them just as he

---

4:35–6:6 □ After giving Jesus' teaching by way of parables, Mark reports a series of miracles. The section opens and closes with two passages which ask the Gospel's central question: "Who is this?" (cf. 4:41; 6:2–3). The disciples gradually begin to frame an answer, which St Peter will provide in due course (cf. 8:29). The wonderment of the disciples and the people steadily grows (cf. 4:41; 5:20, 42; 6:2); Jesus does not accept what the unclean spirits say about him (cf. 5:7); and his fellow-countrymen regard him as an upstart (cf. 6:3); meanwhile, readers are invited to continually assert their faith in him.

4:35–41 In many places in the Bible, the sea stands for antagonistic forces which only God can control (cf. Ps 65:8; 93:4; 107:23–30). Jesus controls the waves by the power of his voice (v. 39), which shows that he has the power of God: hence was, in the boat. And other boats were with him. [37]And a great storm of wind arose, and the waves beat into the boat, so that the boat was already filling. [38]But he was in the stern, asleep on the cushion; and they woke him and said to him, "Teacher, do you not care if we perish?" [39]And he awoke and rebuked the wind, and said to the sea, "Peace! Be still!" And the wind ceased, and there was a great calm. [40]He said to them, "Why are you afraid? Have you no faith?" [41]And they were filled with awe, and said to one another, "Who then is this, that even wind and sea obey him?"

The Gerasene demoniac Mt 8:28–34; Lk 8:26–39

5 [1]They came to the other side of the sea, to the country of the Gerasenes.[n] [2]And when he had come out of the boat, there met him out of the tombs a man with an unclean spirit, [3]who lived among the tombs; and no one could bind him any more, even with a chain; [4]for he had often been bound with fetters and chains, but the chains he wrenched apart, and the fetters he broke in pieces; and no one had the strength to subdue him. [5]Night and day among the tombs and on the mountains he was always crying out, and bruising himself with stones. [6]And when he saw Jesus from afar, he ran and worshipped him; [7]and crying out with a loud voice, he said, "What have you to do with me, Jesus, Son of the Most High God? I adjure you by God, do not torment me." [8]For he had said to him, "Come out of the man, you unclean spirit!" [9]And Jesus[o] asked him, "What is your name?" He replied, "My name is Legion; for we are many." [10]And he begged him eagerly not to send them out of the country. [11]Now a great herd of swine was feeding there on the hillside; [12]and

---

the disciples' question (v. 41). This scene has been interpreted as symbolic of the way Jesus acts in his Church. Sometimes we too think that Jesus is asleep, but our prayer "awakens" him, he comes to our rescue, and calm is restored.

5:1–20 Gerasa was in the Decapolis, whose inhabitants were mostly pagans of Greek or Syrian origin, as one can gather from the fact that there was this huge herd of swine; Jews were forbidden to raise pigs or eat pork (Lk 11:7). But Jesus' mission is not confined to Jews; it covers the whole world. Therefore, what Christ says at the end of this episode shows its whole meaning: this man, now that he is cured, is to proclaim throughout the region that the "mercy" of God extends to all who live there (vv. 19–20): "Those who have met Christ must not shut themselves in their own little world: what a sad a limitation that would be! They must open out like a fan in order to reach all souls. Each has to create (and widen) a circle of friends, whom he can influence through his professional prestige, his behaviour and his friendship, so that Christ may exercise his influence by means of that prestige, that behaviour and that friendship" (Bl. J. Escrivá, *Furrow*, 193).

n. Other ancient authorities read *Gergesenes*; some, *Gadarenes* they begged him, "Send us to the swine, let us enter them." [13]So he gave them leave. And the unclean spirits came out, and entered the swine; and the herd, numbering about two thousand, rushed down the steep bank into the sea, and were drowned in the sea.

[14]The herdsmen fled, and told it in the city and the country. And people came to see what it was that had happened. [15]And they came to Jesus, and saw the demoniac sitting there, clothed and in his right mind, the man who had had the legion; and they were afraid. [16]And those who had seen it told what had happened to the demoniac and to the swine. [17]And they began to beg Jesus[p] to depart from their neighbourhood. [18]And as he was getting into the boat, the man who had been possessed with demons begged him that he might be with him. [19]But he refused, and said to him, "Go home to your friends, and tell them how much the Lord has done for you, and how he has had mercy on you." [20]And he went away and began to proclaim in the Decapolis how much Jesus had done for him; and all men marvelled.

Jairus' daughter is restored to life.
Curing of the woman with a hemorrhage Mt 9:18–26; Lk 8:40–56

[21]And when Jesus had crossed again in the boat to the other side, a great crowd gathered about him; and he was beside the sea. [22]Then came one of the rulers of

---

5:21–43 In his description of these two miracles we can see how Mark likes to supply details which his readers can or will be able to readily recall. But, at the same time, everything he recounts is designed to teach the reader—about what faith in Jesus can do and about the advantage of getting to know him.

The woman with the hemorrhage suffered from an illness which meant that she was legally unclean (cf. Lev 15:25ff). The evangelist vividly shows how desperate she is; she actually dares to touch Jesus' garment. Jesus starts the conversation with her to show everyone that the cause of her cure is not some sort of magic but rather her faith and the power which comes out of him: "she touches, the crowd presses. What does 'touched' mean except 'believed'?" (St Augustine, *In Ioann. Ev.*, 26, 3).

The story of Jairus, too, shows the ruler's faith which, with Jesus' encouragement, overcomes the obstacles he meets. His daughter is about to die and, on that account, he does not let his social position hold him back but begs Jesus to come and cure her (vv. 22–23). After this, at two points (vv. 36, 40), despite the news of the girl's death and the people's taunts, Jesus encourages the man's faith with words and gestures. Eventually, Jairus' faith is rewarded by the raising of his daughter. "He who awakes good desires in his children obliges us to ask, seek and call [...]. This might seem strange, if we failed to realize that God our Lord [...] is trying to foster our desires in our prayers and to prepare us to receive what he is about to give us" (St Augustine, *Letters*, 130, 16–17).

o. Greek *he* **p.** Greek *him*

the synagogue, Jairus by name, and seeing him, he fell at his feet, [23]and besought him, saying, "My little daughter is at the point of death. Come and lay your hands on her, so that she may be made well, and live." [24]And he went with him.

And a great crowd followed him and thronged about him. [25]And there was a woman who had a flow of blood for twelve years, [26]and who had suffered much under many physicians, and had spent all that she had, and was no better but rather grew worse. [27]She had heard the reports about Jesus, and came up behind him in the crowd and touched his garment. [28]For she said, "If I touch even his garments, I shall be made well." [29]And immediately the hemorrhage ceased; and she felt in her body that she was healed of her disease. [30]And Jesus, perceiving in himself that power had gone forth from him, immediately turned about in the crowd, and said, "Who touched my garments?" [31]And his disciples said to him, "You see the crowd pressing around you, and yet you say, 'Who touched me?' " [32]And he looked around to see who had done it. [33]But the woman, knowing what had been done to her, came in fear and trembling and fell down before him, and told him the whole truth. [34]And he said to her, "Daughter, your faith has made you well; go in peace, and be healed of your disease."

[35]While he was still speaking, there came from the ruler's house some who said, "Your daughter is dead. Why trouble the Teacher any further?" [36]But ignoring[q] what they said, Jesus said to the ruler of the synagogue, "Do not fear, only believe." [37]And he allowed no one to follow him except Peter and James and John the brother of James. [38]When they came to the house of the ruler of the synagogue, he saw a tumult, and people weeping and wailing loudly. [39]And when he had entered, he said to them, "Why do you make a tumult and weep? The child is not dead but sleeping." [40]And they laughed at him. But he put them all outside, and took the child's father and mother and those who were with him, and went in where the child was. [41]Taking her by the hand he said to her, "Talitha cumi"; which means, "Little girl, I say to you, arise." [42]And immediately the girl got up and walked; for she was twelve years old. And immediately they were overcome with amazement. [43]And he strictly charged them that no one should know this,* and told them to give her something to eat.

The raising of the girl, although it is a public act, is done in the presence only of her parents and Jesus' three closest disciples. Even so, he "strictly charged them" (v. 43) not to spread news of the miracle. We have seen him do the same thing on other occasions, as if he wants to avoid people misunderstanding his mission as Messiah-Saviour: the complete work of Christ is comprised not just of miracles but also his death on the cross and his resurrection (cf. the note on 7:31–37).

q. Or *overhearing*. Other ancient authorities read *hearing*.

No prophet is honoured in his own country Mt 13:53–58; Lk 4:16–30

6 [1]He went away from there and came to his own country; and his disciples
followed him. [2]And on the sabbath he began to teach in the synagogue; and
many who heard him were astonished, saying, "Where did this man get all this?
What is the wisdom given to him? What mighty works are wrought by his
hands! [3]Is not this the carpenter, the son of Mary and brother of James and Joses
and Judas and Simon, and are not his sisters here with us?" And they took
offence[r] at him. [4]And Jesus said to them, "A prophet is not without honour,
except in his own country, and among his own kin, and in his own house." [5]And
he could do no mighty work there, except that he laid his hands upon a few sick
people and healed them. [6]And he marvelled because of their unbelief.

6:1–6 This passage about Jesus' visit to Nazareth concludes a section which contrasts the faith of Jairus and the woman with the hemorrhage (5:21–42) with the lack of faith of his disciples (4:35–41) and his fellow-countrymen (vv. 1–6). But these verses do tell us things about the sort of life Jesus led for most of the time he spent on earth—the ordinary life of an artisan, with his family, living in ordinary circumstances: "Your human vocation is a part—and an important part—of your divine vocation. That is why you must strive for holiness, giving a particular character to your human personality, a style to your life; contributing at the same time to the sanctification of others, your fellow men; sanctifying your work and your environment—the profession or job that fills your day" (Bl. J. Escrivá, *Hom.*, 1, 46).

6:6–8:30 □ Jesus' activity in Galilee extends further, thanks to that of his disciples (6:6–13). In Jesus' time, Galilee was a region which a special ethnic mix, and it was geographically different from the rest of Palestine. Its cities were populated by both Jews and pagans, and its trade and the sort of work people did meant that it had close ties with neighbouring regions inhabited by non-Jews. By going into these neighbouring regions (7:24–8:9)—as he also did earlier (cf. 5:1–20)—Jesus showed that, although his mission was directed first to the children of Israel (cf. 7:27), its scope was universal.

The people continue to ask who Jesus is (cf. 6:14–16; 8:27–28). In earlier passages, the evangelist showed that the unclean spirits knew the answer (cf. 1:24, 34; 3:11–12; 5:7), but Christ does not acknowledge what they have to say; what he wants is for people to acknowledge him as the Messiah. When this happens with Peter's profession of faith (8:29), a new stage of the Gospel begins in which the Master tells his disciples about the redemptive nature of his messianic mission.

r. Or *stumbled*

5. JESUS JOURNEYS WITH HIS APOSTLES

The mission of the Twelve Mt 10:5–15; Lk 9:1–6

And he went about among the villages teaching.
7And he called to him the twelve, and began to send them out two by two,
and gave them authority over the unclean spirits. 8He charged them to take
nothing for their journey except a staff; no bread, no bag, no money in their
belts; 9but to wear sandals and not put on two tunics. 10And he said to them,
"Where you enter a house, stay there until you leave the place. 11And if any
place will not receive you and they refuse to hear you, when you leave, shake
off the dust that is on your feet for a testimony against them." 12So they went
out and preached that men should repent. 13And they cast out many demons,
and anointed with oil many that were sick and healed them.

Opinions about Jesus Mt 14:1–2; Lk 9:7–9

14King Herod heard of it; for Jesus's[s] name had become known. Some[t] said,
"John the baptizer has been raised from the dead; that is why these powers are
at work with him." 15But others said, "It is Elijah." And others said, "It is a
prophet, like one of the prophets of old." 16But when Herod heard of it, he
said, "John, whom I beheaded, has been raised."

The martyrdom of John the Baptist Mt 14:3–12; Lk 3:19–20

17For Herod had sent and seized John, and bound him in prison for the sake of
Herodias, his brother Philip's wife; because he had married her. 18For John

---

6:6–13 After spending some time with Jesus, the Twelve are sent out to preach. This mission should be seen in the context of their charge to preach to all nations (16:15–18), which it anticipates, and in the light of Christ's preaching, which it reflects.

St Mark includes here a reference to anointing the sick with oil. The Church sees in this a "hint" of the sacrament of the sick, instituted by our Lord and, later, "recommended and promulgated to the faithful by the Apostle James (cf. Jas 5:24ff)" (Council of Trent, *De sacr. extrem. unct.*, 1).

6:14–16 At the start of the Gospel, Mark proclaims Jesus to be the Christ, the Son of God. The Father also declares this at the Baptism of Jesus. However, except for the demons, whose testimony Jesus rejects, the people who encounter him are amazed by his doings but they fail to realize who he is (cf. 1:27; 2:7, 12; 4:41; etc.). These verses mark a further stage in this process which will reach its climax in Peter's profession of faith. But, even then, Jesus still has to keep on explaining to his disciples what his mission as Messiah really means.

6:17–29 Apostolic preaching was the source St Mark used for writing his Gospel. It looks as though Mark had no information about what Jesus did when his

s. Greek *his* **t.** Other ancient authorities read *he* said to Herod, "It is not lawful for you to have your brother's wife." [19]And Herodias had a grudge against him, and wanted to kill him. But she could not, [20]for Herod feared John, knowing that he was a righteous and holy man, and kept him safe. When he heard him, he was much perplexed; and yet he heard him gladly. [21]But an opportunity came when Herod on his birthday gave a banquet for his courtiers and officers and the leading men of Galilee. [22]For when Herodias' daughter came in and danced, she pleased Herod and his guests; and the king said to the girl, "Ask me for whatever you wish, and I will grant it." [23]And he vowed to her, "Whatever you ask me, I will give you, even half of my kingdom." [24]And she went out, and said to her mother, "What shall I ask?" And she said, "The head of John the baptizer." [25]And she came in immediately with haste to the king, and asked, saying, "I want you to give me at once the head of John the baptizer on a platter." [26]And the king was exceedingly sorry; but because of his oath and his guests he did not want to break his word to her. [27]And immediately the king sent a soldier of the guard and gave orders to bring his head. He went and beheaded him in the prison, [28]and brought his head on a platter, and gave it to the girl; and the girl gave it to her mother. [29]When his disciples heard of it, they came and took his body, and laid it in a tomb.

The apostles return Lk 9:10

[30]The apostles returned to Jesus, and told him all that they had done and taught. [31]And he said to them, "Come away by yourselves to a lonely place, and rest a while." For many were coming and going, and they had no leisure even to eat. [32]And they went away in the boat to a lonely place by themselves.

---

disciples were away from him; and so he fills this gap by covering the martyrdom of John the Baptist. This account, set in the context of the apostolic mission, shows the reader that a Christian's lot will often be like that of the Baptist or of Christ himself: preaching and bearing witness to the Gospel will have a good effect on many people, but that does not mean the Christian won't be at the mercy of the whims of the powerful: "By their eloquent and attractive example of a life completely transfigured by the splendour of moral truth, the martyrs and, in general, all the Chruch's saints, light up every period of history by reawakening its moral sense" (John Paul II, *Veritatis splendor,* 93).

6:30–44 We can see here how very busy Jesus' public ministry was. Such was his dedication to souls that St Mark twice (cf. 3:20) mentions that the disciples did not even have time to eat. The apostles also spent themselves in the service of others; after they return from their exhausting missionary work, Jesus wants to bring them away for a rest, but the crowds won't allow it.

In the miracle of the loaves Jesus' attitude sets an example for the Christian. When he sees the state of the people, he is filled with compassion and he gives

First miracle of the loaves and fish Mt 14:13–21; Lk 9:11–17; Jn 6:1–15

33 Now many saw them going, and knew them, and they ran there on foot from the towns, and got there ahead of them. 34 As he landed he saw a great throng, and he had compassion on them, because they were like sheep without a shepherd; and he began to teach them many things. 35 And when it grew late, his disciples came to him and said, "This is a lonely place, and the hour is now late; 36 send them away, to go into the country and villages round about and buy themselves something to eat." 37 But he answered them, "You give them something to eat." And they said to him, "Shall we go and buy two hundred denarii[u] worth of bread, and give it to them to eat?" 38 And he said to them, "How many loaves have you? Go and see." And when they had found out, they said, "Five, and two fish." 39 Then he commanded them all to sit down by companies upon the green grass. 40 So they sat down in groups, by hundreds and by fifties. 41 And taking the five loaves and the two fish he looked up to heaven, and blessed, and broke the loaves, and gave them to the disciples to set before the people; and he divided the two fish among them all. 42 And they all ate and were satisfied. 43 And they took up twelve baskets full of broken pieces and of the fish. 44 And those who ate the loaves were five thousand men.

Jesus walks on water Mt 14:22–33; Jn 6:16–21

45 Immediately he made his disciples get into the boat and go before him to the other side, to Bethsaida, while he dismissed the crowd. 46 And after he had taken leave of them, he went into the hills to pray. 47 And when evening came, the boat was out on the sea, and he was alone on the land. 48 And he saw that they were distressed in rowing, for the wind was against them. And about the fourth watch of the night he came to them, walking on the sea. He meant to pass by them, 49 but when they saw him walking on the sea they thought it was a ghost, and cried out; 50 for they all saw him, and were terrified. But immediately he spoke to them and said, "Take heart, it is I; have no fear." 51 And he got into the boat with them and the wind ceased. And they were

---

them nourishment for both soul and body—the spiritual nourishment of his teaching, and the bread as bodily food. These actions of Jesus are highly significant, for they mark the fulfilment of prophecies (cf. Ezek 31:1–31) according to which God himself was going to be the shepherd of his people, leading them to good pasture. The scene is also a figure of the new people of God, which gets its nourishment from the word of Christ and the bread of the Eucharist.

6:45–52 Jesus' actions reveal his divine power. That is what lies behind his miracles, as the apostles are gradually coming to realize. "Jesus, walking on the water, gives a new 'sign' of his presence, and promises to keep constant watch over his disciples and the Church" (John Paul II, Address, 25 November 1987).

u. The denarius was a day's wage for a labourer

utterly astounded, [52]for they did not understand about the loaves, but their
hearts were hardened.

Cures at Gennesaret Mt 14:34–36

[53]And when they had crossed over, they came to land at Gennesaret, and
moored to the shore. [54]And when they got out of the boat, immediately the
people recognized him, [55]and ran about the whole neighbourhood and began
to bring sick people on their pallets to any place where they heard he was.
[56]And wherever he came, in villages, cities, or country, they laid the sick in
the market places, and besought him that they might touch even the fringe of
his garment; and as many as touched it were made well.

The traditions of the elders. What defiles a man Mt 15:1–20

7 [1]Now when the Pharisees gathered together to him, with some of the
scribes, who had come from Jerusalem, [2]they saw that some of his
disciples ate with hands defiled, that is, unwashed. [3](For the Pharisees, and all
the Jews, do not eat unless they wash their hands,[v] observing the tradition of
the elders;* [4]and when they come from the market place, they do not eat
unless they purify[w] themselves; and there are many other traditions which they
observe, the washing of cups and pots and vessels of bronze.[x]) [5]And the
Pharisees and the scribes asked him, "Why do your disciples not live[y]
according to the tradition of the elders, but eat with hands defiled?" [6]And he
said to them, "Well did Isaiah prophesy of you hypocrites, as it is written,

> 'This people honours me with their lips,
> but their heart is far from me;
> [7]in vain do they worship me,
> teaching as doctrines the precepts of men.'

[8]You leave the commandment of God, and hold fast the tradition of men."

6:53–56 From 4:35 up to here, practically all the events reported have taken place during journeys round the Sea of Galilee. This paragraph summarizes two of the main features of this part of the Gospel—Christ's miracles, and the crowds' acknowledgment of Jesus, which astonishes his disciples.

7:1–23 This scene, covering Jesus' teaching on good moral conduct, draws from three distinct contexts—a controversy with Pharisees come down from Jerusalem (vv. 1–13), subsequent teaching to the crowd (vv. 14–15), and, as happened so often (cf. 4:10–20, 34; 9:28–29; etc.), an explanation given privately to his disciples (vv. 17–23).

The passage begins with these scribes criticizing Jesus for the actions of his disciples—failing to observe purification rites (v. 5). Conscious that some of his readers

v. One Greek word is of uncertain meaning and is not translated **w.** Other ancient authorities read *baptize* **x.** Other ancient authorities add *and beds* **y.** Greek *walk* **7:6–7** Is 29:13.

[9]And he said to them, "You have a fine way of rejecting the commandment of God, in order to keep your tradition! [10]For Moses said, 'Honour your father and your mother'; and 'He who speaks evil of father or mother, let him surely die'; [11]but you say, 'If a man tells his father or his mother, What you would have gained from me is Corban' (that is, given to God)[z]—[12]then you no longer permit him to do anything for his father or mother, [13]thus making void the word of God through your tradition which you hand on. And many such things you do."

[14]And he called the people to meet him, and said to them, "Hear me, all of you, and understand: [15]there is nothing outside a man which by going into him can defile him; but the things that come out of a man are what defile him."[a] [17]And when he had entered the house, and left the people, his disciples asked him about the parable. [18]And he said to them, "Then are you also without understanding? Do you not see that whatever goes into a man from outside cannot defile him, [19]since it enters, not his heart but his stomach, and so passes on?"[b] (Thus he declared all foods clean.) [20]And he said, "What comes out of a man is what defiles a man. [21]For from within, out of the heart of man, come evil thoughts, fornication, theft, murder, adultery, [22]coveting, wickedness, deceit, licentiousness, envy, slander, pride, foolishness. [23]All these evil things come from within, and they defile a man."

The Syrophoenician woman Mt 15:21–28

[24]And from there he arose and went away to the region of Tyre and Sidon.[c] And he entered a house, and would not have any one know it; yet he could not

---

are not of Jewish background, St Mark pauses to explain a few things about Pharisees. The Old Law (cf. Ex 30:17ff) specified rites to be performed by priests to ensure they had the moral cleanness to approach God; Jewish tradition had extended these rites to other areas (meals, for example) in order to give a religious meaning to all actions. This external cleanness was meant to be a sign of inner cleanness. However, by Christ's time the legalism attaching to all the various ceremonies established by human tradition had smothered the true meaning of divine worship. Jesus denounces this by using a text from Isaiah (Is 29:13) and by citing an instance where human tradition had become an excuse for not obeying a divine command (vv. 8–13).

At another point our Lord teaches the crowd about true cleanness. He does this by comparing free human choice and food. Later, his disciples ask him to explain the "parable" (v. 17). The core meaning of his teaching is then given (v. 19); as the authoritative interpreter, and Lord, of the Law, Christ declares all foods to be clean. However, the teaching goes deeper than this. The origin of sin and moral uncleanness should not be sought in things material, for when God created all things he saw that they were good (cf. Gen 1:31), but in the heart of man which, after original sin, was "changed for the worse" and became subject to the assaults of the passions. That does not mean that man cannot prove the victor (Gen 4:7) but that he does not find it easy (cf. *CCC*, 1707). See the RSV note **a** on v. 16.

z. Or *an offering* **a.** Other ancient authorities add verse 16, *If any man has ears to hear, let him hear* **b.** Or *is evacuated* **c.** Other ancient authorities omit *and Sidon.* **7:10** Ex 20:21; Deut 5:16; Ex 21:17; Lev 20:9.

be hid. 25But immediately a woman, whose little daughter was possessed by
an unclean spirit, heard of him, and came and fell down at his feet. 26Now the
woman was a Greek, a Syrophoenician by birth. And she begged him to cast
the demon out of her daughter. 27And he said to her, "Let the children first be
fed, for it is not right to take the children's bread and throw it to the dogs."
28But she answered him, "Yes, Lord; yet even the dogs under the table eat the
children's crumbs." 29And he said to her, "For this saying you may go your
way; the demon has left your daughter." 30And she went home, and found the
child lying in bed, and the demon gone.

Curing of a deaf man

31Then he returned from the region of Tyre, and went through Sidon to the Sea
of Galilee, through the region of the Decapolis. 32And they brought him a man
who was deaf and had an impediment in his speech; and they besought him to
lay his hand upon him. 33And taking him aside from the multitude privately, he put
his fingers into his ears, and he spat and touched his tongue; 34and looking up to
heaven, he sighed, and said to him, "Ephphatha," that is, "Be opened." 35And his
ears were opened, his tongue was released, and he spoke plainly. 36And he charged
them to tell no one; but the more he charged them, the more zealously they
proclaimed it. 37And they were astonished beyond measure, saying, "He has done
all things well; he even makes the deaf hear and the dumb speak."

7:24–30 Once more, Jesus goes off into pagan country. A Gentile woman (the evangelist specifies "a Greek, a Syrophoenician by birth": v. 26) asks him to cure her daughter. The detailed description of this encounter shows that faith in Jesus Christ should overcome all obstacles, even personal unworthiness. "Do not be discouraged. However unworthy a person is, however imperfect his prayer turns out to be, if it is offered with humility and perseverance, God always hears it" (Bl. J. Escrivá, *Furrow*, 468).

7:31–37 Here Jesus works a cure in a way that symbolizes the salvific power of his human nature. The liturgy of the Church used these gestures for a time in the rite of Baptism to symbolize Christ opening men's ears to the word of God.

This is the third miracle recorded by Mark where Jesus tells people to say nothing about it; this happened in connexion with the cure of a leper (1:44) and the raising of a person from the dead (5:43); here it involves the cure of a deaf man (v. 36) and in the next chapter a blind man (cf. 8:26)—the same sort of signs (cf. Mt 11:25; Lk 7:18–25; and notes) that the Baptist's disciples were told would be the marks of the Messiah. In all these instances St Mark records that the disciples were told to say nothing; Christ wanted people to remember that his mission as the Messiah had to take account of the cross.

Second miracle of the loaves Mt 15:32–39

8 [1]In those days, when again a great crowd had gathered, and they had
nothing to eat, he called his disciples to him, and said to them, [2]“I have
compassion on the crowd, because they have been with me now three days,
and have nothing to eat; [3]and if I send them away hungry to their homes, they
will faint on the way; and some of them have come a long way.” [4]And his
disciples answered him, “How can one feed these men with bread here in the
desert?” [5]And he asked them, “How many loaves have you?” They said, “Seven.”
[6]And he commanded the crowd to sit down on the ground; and he took the
seven loaves, and having given thanks he broke them and gave them to his
disciples to set before the people; and they set them before the crowd. [7]And
they had a few small fish; and having blessed them, he commanded that these
also should be set before them. [8]And they ate, and were satisfied; and they
took up the broken pieces left over, seven baskets full. [9]And there were about
four thousand people. [10]And he sent them away; and immediately he got into
the boat with his disciples, and went to the district of Dalmanutha.[d]

The leaven of the Pharisees and Herod Mt 16:1–12

[11]The Pharisees came and began to argue with him, seeking from him a sign
from heaven, to test him. [12]And he sighed deeply in his spirit, and said, “Why
does this generation seek a sign? Truly, I say to you, no sign shall be given to
this generation.” [13]And he left them, and getting into the boat again he
departed to the other side.

[14]Now they had forgotten to bring bread; and they had only one loaf with
them in the boat. [15]And he cautioned them, saying, “Take heed, beware of the

---

8:1–10 Both Matthew and Mark record a second multiplication of the loaves. Some details are very like those of the previous miracle (cf. 6:32–44). However, this one has features of its own: the people have come from far away (v. 3), there are seven loaves and seven baskets of scraps (vv. 5, 8) as compared with the twelve baskets of the previous one (cf. 6:43), etc. Jesus who was previously depicted as the Messiah of the new people of God now implies that the Gentiles, too, have a place in that people. This makes clearer the meaning of the two multiplications of the loaves: as Jesus told the Syrophoenician woman (about feeding bread to the dogs: cf. 7:27–30), salvation was designed first for Israel, then for all nations (cf. Acts 2:39; 3:26; 11:18; etc.). “All men are called to this catholic unity (of the People of God) […]. And in different ways to it belong, or are related, the Catholic faithful, others who believe in Christ, and finally all mankind, called by God’s grace to salvation” (Vatican II, *LG*, 13).

8:11–21 Elsewhere in the Gospels (cf. Mt 13:33 Lk 13:20–21;) Christ uses leaven as a simile to show how powerful his teaching is. Here leaven stands for the evil dispositions of Pharisees who do not believe in him and who ask for a sign to test

d. Other ancient authorities read *Magadan* or *Magdala*

leaven of the Pharisees and the leaven of Herod."[e] 16And they discussed it with
one another, saying, "We have no bread." 17And being aware of it, Jesus said
to them, "Why do you discuss the fact that you have no bread? Do you not yet
perceive or understand? Are your hearts hardened? 18Having eyes do you not
see, and having ears do you not hear? And do you not remember? 19When I
broke the five loaves for the five thousand, how many baskets full of broken
pieces did you take up?" They said to him, "Twelve." 20"And the seven for the
four thousand, how many baskets full of broken pieces did you take up?" And
they said to him, "Seven." 21And he said to them, "Do you not yet understand?"

Curing of a blind man at Bethsaida

22And they came to Bethsaida. And some people brought to him a blind man, and
begged him to touch him. 23And he took the blind man by the hand, and led him
out of the village; and when he had spit on his eyes and laid his hands upon him,
he asked him, "Do you see anything?" 24And he looked up and said, "I see men;
but they look like trees, walking." 25Then again he laid his hands upon his eyes;
and he looked intently and was restored, and saw everything clearly. 26And he
sent him away to his home, saying, "Do not even enter the village."

Peter's profession of faith Mt 16:13–20; Lk 9:18–21

27And Jesus went on with his disciples, to the villages of Caesarea Philippi;
and on the way he asked his disciples, "Who do men say that I am?" 28And

---

him (vv. 11–12); it also symbolizes the two-facedness of Herod, who equally fails to understand Jesus' miracles (6:14:16; cf. Lk 13:31–32). Our Lord warns his disciples against making the mistake of interpreting his actions in a human way, forgetting the true meaning of his salvific mission. The disciples simply fail to understand what Christ's actions mean.

8:22–26 As in the case of the deaf man (cf. 7:31–37), Jesus cures this man of blindness by means of gestures that the Church later used in sacramental liturgy. In the content of the Gospel, the cure of the blind man at Bethsaida marks the climax of the messianic signs worked by Christ (cf. the note on 7:31–37); so it is not surprising that what follows is Peter's profession of faith (8:29). Also the gradual nature of the blind man's cure may symbolize the path that Peter and the disciples (and indeed every man and woman) must follow: Our Lord cures our blindness until we "see everything clearly (v. 25) and dare to confess that Christ is the Son of God, and our Saviour." "Lord, give us light to see! We have more need of it than the blind man … who wanted to see the light but could not. Now, Lord, people do not want to see: what an incurable evil! In this, Lord, you must show your power and your mercy" (St Teresa of Avila, *Exclam.*, 8).

8:27–30 This passage records a key moment in Jesus' relationship with his disciples—when they acknowledge the fact that he is the Messiah. Jesus' conversation

e. Other ancient authorities read *the Herodians* **8:18** Jer 5:21.

they told him, "John the Baptist; and others say, Elijah; and others one of the
prophets." 29 And he asked them, "But who do you say I am?" Peter answered
him, "You are the Christ." 30 And he charged them to tell no one about him.

PART TWO: JESUS' MINISTRY ON THE WAY TO JERUSALEM

6. TEACHINGS ON THE CHRISTIAN LIFE

Jesus foretells his passion and resurrection.
Christian renunciation Mt 16:21–28; Lk 9:22–27

31 And he began to teach them that the Son of man must suffer many things,
and be rejected by the elders and the chief priests and the scribes, and be
killed, and after three days rise again. 32 And he said this plainly. And Peter

---

with his disciples shows how crucial Peter's reply is. From a human point of view, Jesus is the very best type of devout Jew—a prophet, or Elijah himself (cf 9:11). But Peter's reply is not just an opinion; it is a genuine profession of faith, the meaning of which is spelt out in Matthew 16: 16–17.

8:31–10:52 □□ After Peter's profession of faith the focus of the Gospel changes. From this point onwards Jesus increasingly gives attention to training his disciples, showing them that he needs to undergo the Passion in order to enter his glory (8:31–9:13). The three announcements of the Passion are a kind of repetitive theme of this part of the Gospel, interwoven with many teachings about the virtues and attitudes which should guide the disciples' lives—prayer (9:14–29), humility (9:33–50), poverty (10:17–31), etc.

8:31–9:50 □ Jesus now begins to reveal his role as the suffering Servant. This marks out the way of the cross which Christ accepted for himself (cf. 8:31) and which each Christian must follow (8:34). Jesus prepares his disciples for this event by his teaching (8:31–9:1; 9:30–32) and by his actions: the three disciples who will be witnesses to his agony in the garden of olives (14:33) are comforted by a vision of Jesus in glory (the Transfiguration: 9:2–13).

8:31–9:1 Jesus now begins to teach his disciples about what his mission involves: man's salvation will be brought about by Christ's passion and cross and therefore anyone who wants to follow him must be ready to renounce himself (vv. 34–38).

took him, and began to rebuke him. 33But turning and seeing his disciples, he
rebuked Peter, and said, "Get behind me, Satan! For you are not on the side of
God, but of men."

34And he called to him the multitude with his disciples, and said to them,
"If any man would come after me, let him deny himself and take up his cross
and follow me. 35For whoever would save his life will lose it: and whoever
loses his life for my sake and the gospel's will save it. 36For what does it profit
a man to gain the whole world and forfeit his life? 37For what can a man give
in return for his life?* 38For whoever is ashamed of me and of my words in
this adulterous and sinful generation, of him will the Son of man also be
ashamed, when he comes in the glory of his Father with the holy angels."

9 1And he said to them, "Truly, I say to you, there are some standing here
who will not taste death before they see the kingdom of God come with
power."

The Transfiguration Mt 17:1–13; Lk 9:28–36

2And after six days Jesus took with him Peter and James and John, and led
them up a high mountain apart by themselves; and he was transfigured before
them, 3and his garments became glistening, intensely white, as no fuller on
earth could bleach them. 4And there appeared to them Elijah with Moses; and
they were talking to Jesus. 5And Peter said to Jesus, "Master,[f] it is well that we

---

Christ's dialogue with Peter (vv. 31–33) sums up the whole paradox of what is involved in being a Christian: Peter finds it difficult to come to terms with the fact that Christ's victory in fact lies in the cross. Christ takes him to task because Peter's is a very narrow, human, point of view. We can be equally narrow-minded: "There is a kind of fear around, a fear of the Cross, of our Lord's Cross. What has happened is that people have begun to see as crosses all the unpleasant things that crop up in life, and they do not know how to take them as God's children should, with supernatural outlook. [...] In the Passion, the Cross is the emblem of the Redeemer: *in quo est salus, vita et resurrectio nostra*: there lies our salvation, our life and our resurrection" (Bl. J. Escrivá, *The Way of the Cross*, 2, 5).

9:2–13 In his transfiguration Jesus shows the reverse or, better, the outcome of his passion—resurrection and glorification. This event also explains what Christ's life involves: "I think that what we suffer in this life can never be compared to the glory, as yet unrevealed, which is waiting for us" (Rom 8:18).

Mark stresses that the disciples had difficulty in understanding the way of the Lord (vv. 9–10). And, apropos of Peter, who wants to anticipate the glory of heaven without undergoing the cross, the evangelist points out that "he did not know what to say" (v. 6). "Peter did not understand this when he wanted to remain with Christ on the mountain. It has been reserved for you, Peter, but for after death.

f. Or *Rabbi*

are here; let us make three booths, one for you and one for Moses and one for Elijah." [6]For he did not know what to say, for they were exceedingly afraid. [7]And a cloud overshadowed them, and a voice came out of the cloud, "This is my beloved Son;[g] listen to him." [8]And suddenly looking around they no longer saw any one with them but Jesus only.

[9]And as they were coming down the mountain, he charged them to tell no one what they had seen, until the Son of man should have risen from the dead. [10]So they kept the matter to themselves, questioning what the rising from the dead meant. [11]And they asked him, "Why do the scribes say that first Elijah must come?" [12]And he said to them, "Elijah does come first to restore all things; and how is it written of the Son of man, that he should suffer many things and be treated with contempt? [13]But I tell you that Elijah has come,* and they did to him whatever they pleased, as it is written of him."

Curing of an epileptic boy

Mt 17:14–20; Lk 9:37–43

[14]And when they came to the disciples, they saw a great crowd about them, and scribes arguing with them. [15]And immediately all the crowd, when they saw him, were greatly amazed, and ran up to him and greeted him. [16]And he asked them, "What are you discussing with them?" [17]And one of the crowd answered him, "Teacher, I brought my son to you, for he has a dumb spirit; [18]and wherever it seizes him, it dashes him down; and he foams and grinds his teeth and becomes rigid; and I asked your disiples to cast it out, and they were not able." [19]And he answered them, "O faithless generation, how long am I to be with you? How long am I to bear with you? Bring him to me." [20]And they brought the boy to him; and when the spirit saw him, immediately it convulsed the boy, and he fell on the ground and rolled about, foaming at the mouth. [21]And Jesus[h] asked his father, "How long has he had this?" And he said, "From childhood. [22]And it has often cast him into the fire and into the water, to destroy him; but if you can do anything, have pity on us and help us." [23]And Jesus said to him, "If you can! All things are possible to him who believes."

For now, Jesus says: 'Go down to toil on earth, to serve on earth, to be scorned and crucified on earth. Life goes down to be killed; Bread goes down to suffer hunger; the Way goes down to be exhausted on his journey; the Spring goes down to suffer thirst; and you refuse to suffer?" (St Augustine, *Serm.*, 78, 6; cf. *CCC*, 556).

9:14–29 Christ's miracle and his subsequent explanation (vv. 28–29) shows us the need for prayer to be backed by a solid faith. His dialogue with the boy's father shows the method Jesus uses to get that man to make a prayer full of faith. Our Lord responds to imperfect faith (v. 22) with a lament ("if you can …": v. 23). But that lament leads the boy's father to express his genuine faith :"I believe; help my unbelief" (v. 24).

g. Or *my Son, my* (or *the) Beloved* **h.** Greek *he*

[24]Immediately the father of the child cried out[i] and said, "I believe; help my
unbelief!" [25]And when Jesus saw that a crowd came running together, he
rebuked the unclean spirit, saying to it, "You dumb and deaf spirit, I command
you, come out of him, and never enter him again." [26]And after crying out and
convulsing him terribly, it came out, and the boy was like a corpse; so that
most of them said, "He is dead." [27]But Jesus took him by the hand and lifted
him up, and he arose. [28]And when he had entered the house, his disciples
asked him privately, "Why could we not cast it out?" [29]And he said to them,
"This kind cannot be driven out by anything but prayer and fasting."[j]

Second announcement of the Passion Mt 17:22–27; Lk 9:43–45

[30]They went on from there and passed through Galilee. And he would not have
any one know it; [31]for he was teaching his disciples, saying to them, "The Son
of man will be delivered into the hands of men, and they will kill him; and
when he is killed, after three days he will rise." [32]But they did not understand
the saying, and they were afraid to ask him.

Service to others. On leading others astray Mt 18:1–14; Lk 9:46–50; 17:1–2

[33]And they came to Capernaum; and when he was in the house he asked them,
"What were you discussing on the way?" [34]But they were silent; for on the
way they had discussed with one another who was the greatest. [35]And he sat
down and called the twelve; and he said to them, "If any one would be first, he
must be last of all and servant of all." [36]And he took a child, and put him in the
midst of them; and taking him in his arms, he said to them, [37]"Whoever
receives one such child in my name receives me; and whoever receives me,
receives not me but him who sent me."

9:30–32 From the time of Peter's profession of faith (8:31) up to when he reaches Jerusalem (11:1) Jesus seeks to keep away from the limelight (v. 30) in order to instruct his disciples about the significance of what is going to happen in Jerusalem. The evangelist shows that the disciples could not make out what Jesus meant (v. 32); we can see this from the fact that, when the moment of truth comes, they abandon him (14:50,71).

9:33–50 Jesus' teaching in these verses has to do mainly with the life of the Church. The first group of exhortations (vv 33–41) includes two episodes in which our Lord shows the sort of attitude a Christian should have—a readiness to serve others (vv. 33–35) and an open-mindedness to the growth of the Kingdom of God (vv. 38–40). Both episodes end with a novel doctrine which Jesus preached on many other occasions (cf. Mt 25: 40, 45): Christians should see Christ himself in the person of the needy. "It is necessary to emphasize that Christ, by revealing the loving-mercy of God, at the same time demands that man allow himself to be guided by love and mercy throughout his life" (John Paul II, *Div. in miser.*, 3).

i. Other ancient authorities add *with tears* **j.** Other ancient authorities omit *and fasting*

[38]John said to him, "Teacher, we saw a man casting out demons in your
name,[k] and we forbade him, because he was not following us." [39]But Jesus
said, "Do not forbid him; for no one who does a mighty work in my name will
be able soon after to speak evil of me. [40]For he that is not against us is for us.
[41]For truly, I say to you, whoever gives you a cup of water to drink because
you bear the name of Christ, will by no means lose his reward.
[42]"Whoever causes one of these little ones who believe in me to sin,[l] it
would be better for him if a great millstone were hung round his neck and he
were thrown into the sea. [43]And if your hand causes you to sin,[l] cut it off; it
is better for you to enter life maimed than with two hands to go to hell,[m] to the
unquenchable fire.[n] [45]And if your foot causes you to sin,[l] cut it off; it is better
for you to enter life lame than with two feet to be thrown into hell. [m,n] [47]And
if your eye causes you to sin, [l]pluck it out; it is better for you to enter the
kingdom of God with one eye than with two eyes to be thrown into hell,[m]
[48]where their worm does not die, and the fire is not quenched. [49]For every one
will be salted with fire.[o] [50]Salt is good; but if the salt has lost its saltness, how
will you season it? Have salt in yourselves, and be at peace with one another."

7. HEADING FOR JUDEA AND JERUSALEM

The indissolubility of marriage

Mt 19:1–12

10 [1]And he left there and went to the region of Judea and beyond the
Jordan, and crowds gathered to him again; and again, as his custom
was, he taught them.

The next part of the passage (vv. 42–50) consists of various exhorltations , quite severe ones, about the danger of scandal (cf. the note on Mt 18.1–14).

Some manuscripts add "where their worm does not die and the fire is not quenched" in vv. 44 and 46—words from Isaiah (66:24), forming a kind of chorus with v. 48. See the RSV note **n**.

10:1–52 □ The Gospel account now moves to Jesus' journey towards Judea and Jerusalem (10:1). This section begins with an argument with Pharisees (10:2–12) which will lead to an open confrontation in the Holy City (11:1–12:44). Jesus continues to prepare his disciples for his passion (10:32–45), though most of this section has to do with various aspects of Christian life—marriage, following Christ, detachment, etc.

10:1–12 This sort of scene is found often in the Gospel. The malevolent attitude of these Pharisees contrasts with the straightforwardness of the crowd, who are

k. Other ancient authorities add *who does not follow us* **l**. Greek *stumble* **m**. Greek *Gehenna*
n. Verses 44 and 46 (which are identical with verse 48) are omitted by the best ancient authorities
o. Other ancient authorities add *and every sacrifice will be salted with salt* **9:48** Is 66:24.

2And Pharisees came up and in order to test him asked, "Is it lawful for a
man to divorce his wife?" 3He answered them, "What did Moses command
you?" 4They said, "Moses allowed a man to write a certificate of divorce, and to
put her away." 5But Jesus said to them, "For your hardness of heart he wrote you
this commandment. 6But from the beginning of creation, 'God made them male
and female.' 7'For this reason a man shall leave his father and mother and be
joined to his wife,[p] 8and the two shall become one.'[q] So they are no longer two
but one.[q] 9What therefore God has joined together, let not man put asunder."
10And in the house the disciples asked him again about this matter. 11And
he said to them, "Whoever divorces his wife and marries another, commits
adultery against her; 12and if she divorces her husband and marries another,
she commits adultery."

Jesus and the children Mt 19:13–15; Lk 18:15–17

13And they were bringing children to him, that he might touch them; and the
disciples rebuked them. 14But when Jesus saw it he was indignant, and said to
them, "Let the children come to me, do not hinder them; for to such belongs
the kingdom of God. 15Truly, I say to you, whoever does not receive the
kingdom of God like a child shall not enter it." 16And he took them in his arms
and blessed them, laying his hands upon them.

---

attentive to Jesus' teaching. Christ knows how two-faced his opponents are; that is why he asks them what Moses "commanded" (v. 3). The Pharisees know that there is no such commandment, and therefore they reply that Moses "allowed" divorce (v. 4). Having established the rules of dialogue, Jesus explains that the true commandment is what God established at the moment of creation (Gen 2:24): "The love of the spouses requires, of its very nature, the unity and indissolubility of the spouses' community of persons, which embraces their entire life: 'so they are no longer two, but one flesh (Mt 19:6)'. They 'are called to grow continually in their communion through day-to-day fidelity to their marriage promise of total mutual self-giving' (John Paul II, *Fam. cons.*, 19) This human communion is confirmed, purified and completed by communion in Jesus Christ, given through the sacrament of Matrimony. It is deepened by lives of the common faith and by the Eucharist received together" (*CCC*, 1644)

10:13–16 This episode, full of spontaneity and vividly told, shows our Lord's attitude to children. It seems as if the evangelist cannot say enough (cf. v. 16) to describe Jesus' affection for them. But our Lord also uses the scene to make a point: the Kingdom of heaven belongs to those who receive it in a child-like way, that is, not as something one merits but as a gift from God our Father: "To be little you have to believe as children believe, to love as children love, to abandon yourself as children do …, to pray as children pray" (Bl. J. Escrivá, *Holy Rosary*, Preface).

p. Other ancient authorities omit *and be joined to his wife* **q.** Greek *one flesh* **10:4** Deut 24:1–4. **10:7–8** Gen 2:24.

The rich young man. Poverty and renunciation Mt 19:16–30; Lk 18:18–30
17And as he was setting out on his journey, a man ran up and knelt before him,
and asked him, "Good Teacher, what must I do to inherit eternal life?" 18And
Jesus said to him, "Why do you call me good? No one is good but God alone.
19You know the commandments: 'Do not kill, Do not commit adultery, Do not
steal, Do not bear false witness, Do not defraud, Honour your father and
mother.'" 20And he said to him, "Teacher, all these I have observed from my
youth." 21And Jesus looking upon him loved him, and said to him, "You lack
one thing; go, sell what you have, and give to the poor, and you will have
treasure in heaven; and come, follow me." 22At that saying his countenance
fell, and he went away sorrowful; for he had great possessions.
23And Jesus looked around and said to his disciples, "How hard it will be
for those who have riches to enter the kingdom of God!" 24And the disciples
were amazed at his words.* But Jesus said to them again, "Children, how hard
it is for those who trust in riches[r] to enter the kingdom of God! 25It is easier for
a camel to go through the eye of a needle than for a rich man to enter the
kingdom of God." 26And they were exceedingly astonished, and said to him,[s]
"Then who can be saved?" 27Jesus looked at them and said, "With men it is
impossible, but not with God; for all things are possible with God." 28Peter
began to say to him, "Lo, we have left everything and followed you." 29Jesus
said, "Truly, I say to you, there is no one who has left house or brothers or

---

10:17–31 This account has features similar to those seen in the calling of the disciples (1:16–20; 2:14)—the way our Lord looks at the young man and gives him an imperative command (v. 21). The evangelist also manages to convey Jesus' regard for the young man and his upright conduct (vv. 20–21), and the youth's sadness (v. 22) when he fails to respond generously to what God was asking of him.

The rich young man's failure to respond gives Jesus an opportunity to say something further about use of material things (vv. 23–31). Attachment to them may even be a form of idolatry (Mt 6:24; cf. Col 3:5) which can block a person's access to the Kingdom of God (Lk 6:20, 24). The Lord uses imagery (v. 25) which must have amused his listeners—the difficulty a camel would meet if it tried to squeeze through too narrow a space. Christian poverty, on the other hand, is something so valuable that St Francis of Assisi saw it as the "lady of his heart": "This is the virtue that allows the soul, still living in this world, to converse with the angels in heaven; it accompanied Christ on the cross, was buried with him in the tomb, rose with Christ, and with him ascended into heaven; souls in love with poverty receive, even in this life, the lightness to fly to heaven because it refines the powers of friendship, of humility and of love" (*Little Flowers*, 13).

In response to Peter's question, Jesus describes the positive side of self-surrender for his sake and that of the Gospel: the disciple will gain eternal life and

r. Other ancient authorities omit *for those who trust in riches* **s.** Other ancient authorities read *to one another* **10:19** Ex 20:12–16; Deut 5:16–20.

sisters or mother or father or children or lands, for my sake and for the gospel,
30who will not receive a hundredfold now in this time, houses and brothers and
sisters and mothers and children and lands, with persecutions, and in the age
to come eternal life.* 31But many that are first will be last, and the last first."

Third announcement of the Passion Mt 20:17–19; Lk 18:31–34

32And they were on the road, going up to Jerusalem, and Jesus was walking
ahead of them; and they were amazed, and those who followed were afraid.
And taking the twelve again, he began to tell them what was to happen to him,
33saying, "Behold, we are going up to Jerusalem; and the Son of man will be
delivered to the chief priests and the scribes, and they will condemn him to
death, and deliver him to the Gentiles; 34and they will mock him, and spit upon
him, and scourge him, and kill him; and after three days he will rise."

The sons of Zebedee make their request Mt 20:20–28

35And James and John, the sons of Zebedee, came forward to him, and said to
him, "Teacher, we want you to do for us whatever we ask of you." 36And he
said to them, "What do you want me to do for you?" 37And they said to him,
"Grant us to sit, one at your right hand and one at your left, in your glory."
38But Jesus said to them, "You do not know what you are asking. Are you able
to drink the cup that I drink, or to be baptized with the baptism with which I
am baptized?" 39And they said to him, "We are able." And Jesus said to them,
"The cup that I drink you will drink; and with the baptism with which I am
baptized, you will be baptized; 40but to sit at my right hand or at my left is not
mine to grant, but it is for those for whom it has been prepared." 41And when

---

in addition, because he is and knows he is a son of God and a brother to his brothers, he will be given everything back, a hundred times over. In this promise our Lord includes persecutions (v. 30), but as Peter and the apostles will discover (Acts 5:40–41) these will be a source of joy when they are borne for Christ.

10:32–45 As they make their way to Jerusalem, two events occur that are closely linked to one another. Jesus resolutely takes the road for Jerusalem (cf. v. 32). He is well aware of what is going to happen there (vv. 33–34) and of the redemptive meaning of his death (v. 45). He uses the image of the chalice and baptism (v. 38) to indicate the suffering he will undergo (cf. 14:36 and Rom 6:4–5). He associates his disciples with his own destiny but reminds them that, if he came to serve (v. 45), a spirit of service must distinguish them too (v. 43; cf. Jn 13:14–17): "The Church is not motivated by an earthly ambition but is interested in one thing only—to carry on the work of Christ under the guidance of the Holy Spirit, for he came into the world to bear witness to the truth, to save and not to judge, to serve and not to be served" (Vatican II, *GS*, 3).

the ten heard it, they began to be indignant at James and John. [42]And Jesus
called them to him and said to them, "You know that those who are supposed
to rule over the Gentiles lord it over them, and their great men exercise
authority over them. [43]But it shall not be so among you; but whoever would be
great among you must be your servant, [44]and whoever would be first among
you must be slave of all. [45]For the Son of man also came not to be served but
to serve, and to give his life as a ransom of many."

Bartimeus, the blind man of Jericho Mt 20:29–34; Lk 18:35–43

[46]And they came to Jericho; and as he was leaving Jericho with his disciples and
a great multitude, Bartimaeus, a blind beggar, the son of Timaeus, was sitting by
the roadside. [47]And when he heard that it was Jesus of Nazareth, he began to cry
out and say, "Jesus, Son of David, have mercy on me!" [48]And many rebuked him,
telling him to be silent; but he cried out all the more, "Son of David, have mercy
on me!" [49]And Jesus stopped and said, "Call him." And they called the blind man,
saying to him, "Take heart; rise, he is calling you." [50]And throwing off his mantle
he sprang up and came to Jesus. [51]And Jesus said to him, "What do you want me
to do for you?" And the blind man said to him, "Master,[t] let me receive my sight."
[52]And Jesus said to him, "Go your way; your faith has made you well." And
immediately he received his sight and followed him on the way.

PART THREE: JESUS' MINISTRY IN JERUSALEM

8. CLEANSING OF THE TEMPLE. CONTROVERSIES

The Messiah enters the Holy City Mt 21:1–11; Lk 19:28–40; Jn 12:12–19

11 [1]And when they drew near to Jerusalem, to Bethphage and Bethany, at
the Mount of Olives, he sent two of his disciples, [2]and said to them,

---

10:46–52 In his account of this miracle, Mark gives many little details about Bartimeus (v. 46) and his attitude to Jesus—his urgent and insistent request (vv. 47–48), the way he throws off his cloak to respond quickly to the call (v. 50), and his faith and simplicity in his conversation with our Lord (v. 51). As a result of his faith, his situation changes radically. He was blind and sitting by the roadside (v. 46) and now he gets his sight back and follows Jesus on his way (v. 52). "The faith he demands of us is this: we must keep in step with him, working generously and at the same time uprooting and getting rid of everything that gets in the way" (Bl. J. Escrivá, *Hom.*, 2, 198).

11:1–16:20 The last six chapters of St Mark's Gospel cover the final week of Jesus' life on earth, in Jerusalem. The importance that the evangelist gives to these

t. Or *Rabbi*

"Go into the village opposite you, and immediately as you enter it you will
find a colt tied, on which no one has ever sat; untie it and bring it. 3If any one
says to you, 'Why are you doing this?' say, 'The Lord has need of it and will
send it back here immediately.'" 4And they went away, and found a colt tied at
the door out in the open street; and they untied it. 5And those who stood there
said to them, "What are you doing, untying the colt?" 6And they told them

---

events can be seen from the many chronological and topographical details he supplies. On the first day (11:1–19) Jesus enters Jerusalem in triumph and proceeds to cleanse the temple. The Pharisees demand to know what authority he has to act in this way in the temple (11:28) and this marks the start of controversies with priests, scribes, elders, Herodians and Sadducees (11:27–12:40); this narrative breaks off to recount the eschatological discourse.

Alongside the controversies the evangelist reports that the religious leaders were looking for a way to arrest Jesus (11:18; 12:12; 14:1–2). Judas gives them the opportunity they need (14:10–11) and, from this point on, the evangelist describes the affronts Jesus suffers leading up to his death. However, Jesus dies not because his persecutors decide that he should; he dies because it is written that he should do so (14:21). So, it is not death that has the final word, but resurrection (14:28).

Whereas the first part of the Gospel concluded with Peter's profession of faith in Jesus as the Christ (cf. 8:29), this second part is rounded off by the words of the centurion acknowledging that Jesus is the "Son of God" (15:39)—the two titles of Jesus that Mark uses at the start of his Gospel (cf. 1:1).

11:1–12:44 □ The account begins with Jesus' entry into Jerusalem and then his purification of the temple and his controversies with various groups of Jews. The triumphal entry and the purification are actions expected of the promised Messiah (11:1–33). The parable of the wicked tenants (12:1–12) provides the key to interpret all the events the evangelist reports as happening on these days: Israel has rejected the gift of God, and therefore God is going to make a new people by means of a New Covenant based on his Son.

11:1–11 Jesus' entry into Jerusalem reveals him to be the promised Messiah (cf. Zech 9:9), and his gestures hint at how truly great he is. Like Bartimaeus previously (10:47–48) the crowds acknowledge him as the Messiah, the son of David. Jesus here anticipates a revision of that title which he will make more explicit later (12:35–37) by referring to himself as "the Lord" (v. 3), showing his lordship over all things. "From the beginning of Christian history, the assertion of Christ's lordship over the world and over history has implicitly recognized that man should not submit his personal freedom in an absolute manner to any earthly power, but only to God the Father and the Lord Jesus Christ" (*CCC*, 450).

what Jesus had said; and they let them go. [7]And they brought the colt to Jesus,
and threw their garments on it; and he sat upon it. [8]And many spread their
garments on the road, and others spread leafy branches which they had cut
from the fields. [9]And those who went before and those who followed cried out,
"Hosanna! Blessed is he who comes in the name of the Lord! [10]Blessed is the
kingdom of our father David that is coming! Hosanna in the highest!"
[11]And he entered Jerusalem, and went into the temple; and when he had
looked around at everything, as it was already late, he went out to Bethany
with the twelve.

The barren fig tree. The expulsion of the money-changers

Mt 21:12–22; Lk 19:45–48; Jn 2:13–25

[12]On the following day, when they came from Bethany, he was hungry. [13]And
seeing in the distance a fig tree in leaf, he went to see if he could find anything
on it. When he came to it, he found nothing but leaves, for it was not the
season for figs. [14]And he said to it, "May no one ever eat fruit from you again."
And his disciples heard it.
[15]And they came to Jerusalem. And he entered the temple and began to
drive out those who sold and those who bought in the temple, and he
overturned the tables of the money-changers and the seats of those who sold
pigeons; [16]and he would not allow any one to carry anything through the
temple. [17]And he taught, and said to them, "Is it not written, 'My house shall
be called a house of prayer for all the nations'? But you have made it a den of
robbers." [18]And the chief priests and the scribes heard it and sought a way to
destroy him; for they feared him, because all the multitude was astonished at
his teaching. [19]And when evening came they[u] went out of the city.
[20]As they passed by in the morning, they saw the fig tree withered away to
its roots. [21]And Peter remembered and said to him, "Master,[v] look! The fig tree
which you cursed has withered." [22]And Jesus answered them, "Have faith in
God. [23]Truly, I say to you, whoever says to this mountain, 'Be taken up and
cast into the sea,' and does not doubt in his heart, but believes that what he says

---

11:12–25 On the second day of the week Jesus acts in ways which further reveal him to be the Messiah: his apparently violent behaviour in the temple fulfils the prophecies about its need to be cleansed (Mal 3:1–5; Zech 14:21) in order to be a place of prayer for all the nations (Is 56:7).

This episode is set into another with which it is closely related—the cursing of the fig tree. By a symbolic gesture in the style of the prophets (Jer 19:1–13; Ezek 4:1–3; 5:1–6; etc.), Jesus indicates that Israel, like that fig tree, has failed to produce the fruit God expected (cf. 12:1–12); the destruction of the temple (cf. 13:2) is just a form of necessary purification. Christians need to guard against merely going through the motions of worshipping God; religion must come from

u. Other anceint authorities read *he* **v.** Or *Rabbi* **11:9** Ps 118:26. **11:17** Ps 56:7; Jer 7:11.

will come to pass, it will be done for him. 24Therefore I tell you, whatever you
ask in prayer, believe that you receive it, and you will. 25And whenever you
stand praying, forgive, if you have anything against any one; so that your
Father also who is in heaven may forgive you your trespasses."[w]

Jesus' authority Mt 21:23–27; Lk 20:1–8

27And they came again to Jerusalem. And as he was walking in the temple, the
chief priests and the scribes and the elders came to him, 28and they said to him,
"By what authority are you doing these things, or who gave you this authority
to do them?" 29Jesus said to them, "I will ask you a question; answer me, and I
will tell you by what authority I do these things. 30Was the baptism of John from
heaven or from men? Answer me." 31And they argued with one another, "If we
say, 'From heaven,' he will say, 'Why then did you not believe him?' 32But shall
we say, 'From men'?"—they were afraid of the people, for all held that John was
a real prophet. 33So they answered Jesus, "We do not know." And Jesus said to
them, "Neither will I tell you by what authority I do these things."

Parable of the wicked tenants Mt 21:33–46; Lk 20:9–19

12 1And he began to speak to them in parables. "A man planted a vineyard,
and set a hedge around it, and dug a pit for the wine press, and built a
tower, and let it out to tenants, and went into another country. 2When the time
came, he sent a servant to the tenants, to get from them some of the fruit of the

---

the heart, as the Fathers were well aware: "You also, if you do not wish to be condemned by Christ, … must be careful not to become a sterile tree, so that you can offer to Jesus, who made himself poor, the fruit of piety that he requires" (St Bede, *In Marci Evang. exp.*, in loc.). See the RSV note **w** (v. 26); this verse may come from Matthew 6:15.

11:27–33 The third day in Jerusalem begins at this point. The passage is made up of various teachings of Jesus, many of them given in the context of arguments with members of the Jewish establishment. These people were looking for a way to get rid of Jesus (cf. 11:18); hence their asking him to explain his behaviour in the temple. Jesus asks them to face the real question: Do they or do they not accept the ministry of John the Baptist as Precursor? For, accepting the Baptist also involves accepting Jesus' own ministry. As the evangelist points out, these men were not ready to recognize John, and their blindness will send Jesus to his death.

12:1–12 In this parable Jesus sums up the history of salvation, and his own life's work too. Using the allegory of the vineyard (cf. Is 5:1–7) he tells about all God's efforts to get the chosen people to produce fruit, and the resistance he met, especially from the leaders of Israel. Hence his decision to raise up a new people.

w. Other ancient authorities add verse 26, "*But if you do not forgive, neither will your Father who is in heaven forgive your trespasses*" **12:1** Is 5:1–7.

vineyard. 3And they took him and beat him, and sent him away empty-handed.
4Again he sent to them another servant, and they wounded him in the head,
and treated him shamefully. 5And he sent another, and him they killed; and so
with many others, some they beat and some they killed. 6He had still one other,
a beloved son; finally he sent him to them, saying, 'They will respect my son.'
7But those tenants said to one another, 'This is the heir; come, let us kill him,
and the inheritance will be ours.' 8And they took him and killed him, and cast
him out of the vineyard. 9What will the owner of the vineyard do? He will
come and destroy the tenants, and give the vineyard to others. 10Have you not
read this scripture:

'The very stone which the builders rejected
has become the head of the corner;
11this was the Lord's doing,
and it is marvellous in our eyes'?"

12And they tried to arrest him, but feared the multitude, for they perceived
that he had told the parable against them; so they left him and went away.

Tribute to Caesar Mt 22:15–22; Lk 20:20–26

13And they sent to him some of the Pharisees and some of the Herodians, to
entrap him in his talk. 14And they came and said to him, "Teacher, we know
that you are true, and care for no man; for you do not regard the position of
men, but truly teach the way of God. Is it lawful to pay taxes to Caesar, or not?

The reader of the Gospel knows that the "beloved Son" (v. 6) is Jesus himself (cf. 1:11; 9:7). Our Lord quotes Psalm 118 as a reference to his violent death on the cross and proclaims that that death will lead to the establishment of a new people with a New Covenant. Christ's death, then, means life for man: "We have not been killed or buried, nor raised from the dead after crucifixion […]. Christ was truly crucified and his body truly buried and raised from the dead; and to us it has been given, by grace, that by imitating what he suffered we may reach the truth of salvation" (Jerusalem Catechesis, *Catech.*, 20, 6).

12:13–17 Simple though it is, this scene shows the greatness of Jesus. Two hostile groups—Pharisees and Herodians—join forces in putting him to the test. The test is strengthened by the eulogy they make before posing a difficult question. The point they make is that if the Jews are a people meant to serve God, then if they paid Caesar's tax, would that not mean they were turning their back on God? Jesus' reply leaves them nonplussed (v. 17), and it shows what a Christian's attitude should be towards civil authority and just laws (cf. Rom 13:1–7). "Therefore," St Justin comments, "to God alone do we pray; and you, princes and kings, we serve most readily as regards other things […] and we pray for you" (*Apology, 1,* 17, 3).

12:10–11 Ps 118:22–23.

[15]Should we pay them, or should we not?" But knowing their hypocrisy, he
said to them, "Why put me to the test? Bring me a coin,[x] and let me look at it."
[16]And they brought one. And he said to them, "Whose likeness and inscription
is this?" They said to him, "Caesar's." [17]Jesus said to them, "Render to Caesar
the things that are Caesar's, and to God the things that are God's." And they
were amazed at him.

The resurrection of the dead Mt 22:23–33; Lk 20:27–40

[18]And Sadducees came to him, who say that there is no resurrection; and they
asked him a question, saying, [19]"Teacher, Moses wrote for us that if a man's
brother dies and leaves a wife, but leaves no child, the man[y] must take the
wife, and raise up children for his brother. [20]There were seven brothers; the
first took a wife, and when he died left no children; [21]and the second took her,
and died, leaving no children; and the third likewise; [22]and the seven left no
children. Last of all the woman also died. [23]In the resurrection whose wife will
she be? For the seven had her as wife."

[24]Jesus said to them, "Is not this why you are wrong, that you know neither
the scriptures nor the power of God? [25]For when they rise from the dead, they
neither marry nor are given in marriage, but are like angels in heaven. [26]And
as for the dead being raised, have you not read in the book of Moses, in the
passage about the bush, how God said to him, 'I am the God of Abraham, and
the God of Isaac, and the God of Jacob'? [27]He is not God of the dead, but of
the living; you are quite wrong."

The greatest commandment of all Mt 22:34–40; Lk 10:25–28

[28]And one of the scribes came up and heard them disputing with one another,
and seeing that he answered them well, asked him, "Which commandment is
the first of all?" [29]Jesus answered, "The first is, 'Hear, O Israel: The Lord our

---

12:18–27 Cf. the notes on Mt 22:23–33 and Lk 20:27–40.

12:28–34 Throughout these chapters Mark has reported the traps set by "the chief priests and the scribes and the elders" (11:27), the "Pharisees and Herodians" (12:13) and the Sadducees (12:18). Now, after Jesus' reply to the scribe, the evangelist notes that no one dared to ask our Lord any further questions (v. 34). However, the scribe's honest approach (cf. v. 28) is very different from the motivation behind the previous questions. This explains why the scribe is able to grasp the depth of Christ's answer and why he is open to the salvation which is only to be found in the Church. "The love of God is first in order of commandment, but the love of neighbour is first in order of action […]. Because you do not yet see God, by loving your neighbour you merit seeing him; by loving your neighbour you cleanse your eye for seeing God as John clearly says, 'If you do not

x. Greek *a denarius* **y.** Greek *his brother* **12:19** Deut 6:4. **12:26** Ex 3:6. **12:29** Deut 6:4.

God, the Lord is one; [30]and you shall love the Lord your God with all your
heart, and with all your soul, and with all your mind, and with all your
strength.' [31]The second is this, 'You shall love your neighbour as yourself.'
There is no other commandment greater than these." [32]And the scribe said to
him, "You are right, Teacher; you have truly said that he is one, and there is no
other than he; [33]and to love him with all the heart, and with all the under-
standing, and with all the strength, and to love one's neighbour as oneself, is
much more than all whole burnt offerings and sacrifices." [34]And when Jesus
saw that he answered wisely, he said to him, "You are not far from the kingdom
of God." And after that no one dared to ask him any question.

The divinity of the Messiah Mt 22:41–41; Lk 20:41–44

[35]And as Jesus taught in the temple, he said, "How can the scribes say that the
Christ is the son of David? [36]David himself, inspired by[z] the Holy Spirit,
declared,

'The Lord said to my Lord,
Sit at my right hand,
till I put thy enemies under thy feet.'

[37]David himself calls him Lord; so how is he his son?" And the great throng
heard him gladly.

Jesus censures the scribes Mt 23:1–12; Lk 20:45–47

[38]And in his teaching he said, "Beware of the scribes, who like to go about in
long robes, and to have salutations in the market places [39]and the best seats in
the synagogues and the places of honour at feasts, [40]who devour widows'
houses and for a pretence make long prayers. They will receive the greater
condemnation."

The widow's mite Lk 21:1–4

[41]And he sat down opposite the treasury, and watched the multitude putting
money into the treasury. Many rich people put in large sums. [42]And a poor

---

love your neighbour whom you see, how would you be able to love God whom you do not see?'" (St Augustine, *In Ioann. Ev.*, 17, 18).

12:35–37 Cf. the note on 11:11 and Mt 22:41–46.

12:38–40 Cf. the note on Mt 23:1–36.

12:41–44 As against the ostentation of the scribes (vv. 38–40) and the rich (v. 41), Jesus praises the honesty and generosity of a poor widow: "Didn't you see the light in Jesus' eyes when the poor widow left her alms in the temple? Give him

z. Or *himself, in* **12:31** Lev 19:18. **12:36** Ps 110:1.

widow came, and put in two copper coins, which make a penny. 43And he
called his disciples to him, and said to them, "Truly, I say to you, this poor
widow has put in more than all those who are contributing to the treasury.
44For they all contributed out of their abundance; but she out of her poverty has
put in everything she had, her whole living."

9. THE ESCHATOLOGICAL DISCOURSE

Announcement of the destruction of the temple Mt 24:1–2; Lk 21:5–6

13 1And as he came out of the temple, one of his disciples said to him,
"Look, Teacher, what wonderful stones and what wonderful buildings!"
2And Jesus said to him, "Do you see these great buildings? There will not be
left here one stone upon another, that will not be thrown down."

The beginning of tribulation.
Persecution on account of the Gospel Mt 10:16–22; 24:3–14; Lk 21:7–19

3And as he sat on the Mount of Olives opposite the temple, Peter and James
and John and Andrew asked him privately, 4"Tell us, when will this be, and

---

what you can: the merit is not in whether it is big or small, but in the intention with which you give it" (Bl. J. Escrivá, *The Way*, 829).

13:1–37 □ All the Synoptic Gospels report this discourse of our Lord (cf. Mt 24:1–25:46; Lk 21:5–37). It is called the "eschatological discourse" or the "discourse on the Parousia" because it covers events to do with the end of time. It is also described as an "apocalyptic discourse", given the kind of language it uses and its revelation of hidden things. It is not always easy to work out its meaning, but it certainly reinforces Jesus' recurring message to "take heed and be watchful" (cf. vv. 9, 23, 33, 35, 37).

13:1–2 The background to this discourse helps us understand what Jesus goes on to say. Thus, the Jews of Jesus' time—the apostles included—expected the day of God's Judgment (Is 13:6, 9; Zeph 1:15; etc.) to mean terror for the godless but glory for the chosen people. The splendour of the temple was simply a sign of that future glory. However, our Lord says that the temple is not going to last; it will be destroyed. At the same time the disciples must learn to interpret that event as a sign of the opposition they will meet in their mission of preaching the Gospel until the Son of man comes in glory. Throughout the discourse, these two events interweave—the destruction of the temple and the future history of the Church.

13:3–37 The opening verses (vv. 5–13) refer to "the beginning of the sufferings" (v. 8): the tribulation which will start prior to the destruction of Jerusalem (vv. 6–8)

what will be the sign when these are all to be accomplished?" [5]And Jesus
began to say to them, "Take heed that no one leads you astray. [6]Many will
come in my name, saying, 'I am he!' and they will lead many astray. [7]And
when you hear of wars and rumours of wars, do not be alarmed; this must take
place, but the end is not yet. [8]For nation will rise against nation, and kingdom
against kingdom; there will be earthquakes in various places, there will be
famines; this is but the beginning of the sufferings.

[9]"But take heed to yourselves; for they will deliver you up to councils, and
you will be beaten in synagogues; and you will stand before governors and
kings for my sake, to bear testimony before them. [10]And the gospel must first
be preached to all nations. [11]And when they bring you to trial and deliver you
up, do not be anxious beforehand what you are to say; but say whatever is
given you in that hour, for it is not you who speak, but the Holy Spirit. [12]And
brother will deliver up brother to death, and the father his child, and children
will rise against parents and have them put to death; [13]and you will be hated
by all for my name's sake. But he who endures to the end will be saved.

The great tribulation Mt 24:15–28; Lk 21:20–24

[14]"But when you see the desolating sacrilege set up where it ought not to be
(let the reader understand), then let those who are in Judea flee to the mountains;
[15]let him who is on the housetop not go down, nor enter his house, to take
anything away; [16]and let him who is in the field not turn back to take his mantle.
[17]And alas for those who are with child and for those who give suck in those

---

is like the tribulation that Christians will experience (vv. 9–13). In the both cases, our Lord's instruction is an invitation to hope.

The discourse then goes on (vv. 14–27) to describe the key moment—the Judgment. The "desolating sacrilege" (v. 14) is an expression taken from the prophet Daniel (Dan 9:27) referring to the profanation of the temple (cf. 1 Mal 1:54). Our Lord uses the expression to sum up the desperate situation the inhabitants of Jerusalem will find themselves in (vv. 14–20) at that time. Christians will experience similar anguish (vv. 21–25) prior to the coming of the Son of man in glory (vv. 26–27).

The final verses (vv. 28–37) indicate the attitude Christ's disciples should have (v. 37); they should be watchful, vigilant (vv. 33, 35, 37). One thing is certain: the Lord will come, just as surely as the fig tree goes through its seasons, just as the owner of the house will return as promised. The disciples must be vigilant. "He wished to hide this from us so that we might remain on our guard and be aware that this might happen to us during our life. He said very clearly that he would come again, but without stating at what moment. Thus, through all generations and at all times his coming is awaited ardently" (St Ephrem, *Super Diatess.*, 18, 15–17). In the liturgy of Advent, the Church encourages us to keep up this watchfulness.

13:14 Dan 9:27; 11:31; 12:11, **13:19** Dan 12:1; Joel 2:2.

days! [18]Pray that it may not happen in winter. [19]For in those days there will be such tribulation as has not been from the beginning of the creation which God created until now, and never will be. [20]And if the Lord had not shortened the days, no human being would be saved; but for the sake of the elect, whom he chose, he shortened the days. [21]"And then if any one says to you, 'Look, here is the Christ!' or 'Look, there he is!' do not believe it. [22]False Christs and false prophets will arise and show signs and wonders, to lead astray, if possible, the elect. [23]But take heed; I have told you all things beforehand.

The coming of the Son of man Mt 24:29–31; Lk 21:25–28

[24]"But in those days, after that tribulation, the sun will be darkened, and the moon will not give its light, [25]and the stars will be falling from heaven, and the powers in the heavens will be shaken. [26]And then they will see the Son of man coming in clouds with great power and glory. [27]And then he will send out the angels, and gather his elect from the four winds, from the ends of the earth to the ends of heaven.

The end will surely come—the lesson of the fig tree Mt 24:32–35; Lk 21:29–33

[28]"From the fig tree learn its lesson: as soon as its branch becomes tender and puts forth its leaves, you know that summer is near. [29]So also, when you see these things taking place, you know that he is near, at the very gates. [30]Truly, I say to you, this generation will not pass away before all these things take place. [31]Heaven and earth will pass away, but my words will not pass away.

The time of Christ's second coming Mt 24:36–41

[32]"But of that day or that hour no one knows, not even the angels in heaven, nor the Son, but only the Father. [33]Take heed, watch and pray;[a] for you do not know when the time will come. [34]It is like a man going on a journey, when he leaves home and puts his servants in charge, each with his work, and commands the doorkeeper to be on the watch. [35]Watch therefore—for you do not know when the master of the house will come, in the evening, or at midnight, or at cockcrow, or in the morning—[36]lest he come suddenly and find you asleep. [37]And what I say to you I say to all: Watch."

10. PASSION, DEATH AND RESURRECTION OF JESUS

The conspiracy against Jesus Mt 26:3–5; Lk 22:1–2; Jn 1:45–57

14 [1]It was now two days before the Passover and the feast of Unleavened Bread. And the chief priests and the scribes were seeking how to arrest

---

14:1–16:20 □ The last two chapters of the second Gospel focus very intensely on events. We notice, particularly, the roles played by the main actors in the drama—

a. Other ancient authorities omit *and pray* **13:24** Is 13:10. **13:25** Is 34:4; Joel 2:10. **13:26** Dan 7:13.

him by stealth, and kill him; 2for they said, "Not during the feast, lest there be a tumult of the people."

The anointing at Bethany and the treachery of Judas Mt 26:6–16; Lk 22:3–6; Jn 12:1–11

3And while he was at Bethany in the house of Simon the leper, as he sat at table, a woman came with an alabaster jar of ointment of pure nard, very costly, and she broke the jar and poured it over his head. 4But there were some who said to themselves indignantly, "Why was the ointment thus wasted? 5For this ointment might have been sold for more than three hundred denarii,[b] and given to the poor." And they reproached her. 6But Jesus said, "Let her alone; why do you trouble her? She has done a beautiful thing to me. 7For you always have the poor with you, and whenever you will, you can do good to them; but you will not always have me. 8She has done what she could; she has anointed my body beforehand for burying. 9And truly, I say to you, wherever the gospel is preached in the whole world, what she has done will be told in memory of her."

10Then Judas Iscariot, who was one of the twelve, went to the chief priests in order to betray him to them. 11And when they heard it they were glad, and promised to give him money. And he sought an opportunity to betray him."

---

the Jewish authorities who seem bent on bringing about Jesus' death, and the disciples, powerless witnesses of what is taking place, who not only fail to grasp the meaning of Christ's actions but even abandon him in his suffering at the critical moment. Yet in the midst of all this Jesus is at his most majestic. He knows what is going to happen to him and that it is good for him to suffer in this way. That is why it is he who takes the initiative in everything that happens. References to various passages from the Old Testament reveal to the apostles the meaning of these events: Jesus must die on the cross, but everything leads to the resurrection.

The saints have meditated much on the various stages of the Passion. "The remedy for all the evil brought about by our sins is to be found in the passion of Christ; but the passion can also be seen as an example or teaching. It shows the perfection of Christian life; he who wishes to be perfect must do no more than scorn what Christ scorned in being nailed to the cross, and desire what he desired on the cross: all the virtues are revealed there" (St Thomas Aquinas, *On the Creed*, 4, 919).

14:1–11 Almost from the start of our Lord's public ministry, some of the scribes and leading priests etc. "sought to destroy him" (3:6). They become much more determined about this towards the end (11:18; 12:12). Now they decide to arrest him "by stealth" (v. 1) and they find an ally in Judas, who from now on seeks an opportunity to betray him (v. 11). The intervening verses deal with the anointing of Jesus by a woman in Bethany (vv. 3–9). The evangelist stresses two things—the

b. The denarius was a day's wage for a labourer

Preparations for the Last Supper.
Judas' treachery foretold Mt 26:17–25; Lk 22:7–13; Jn 13:21–32
12And on the first day of Unleavened Bread, when they sacrificed the passover
lamb, his disciples said to him, "Where will you have us go and prepare for
you to eat the passover?" 13And he sent two of his disciples, and said to them,
"Go into the city, and a man carrying a jar of water will meet you; follow
him,* 14and wherever he enters, say to the householder, 'The Teacher says,
Where is my guest room, where I am to eat the passover with my disciples?'
15And he will show you a large upper room furnished and ready; there prepare
for us." 16And the disciples set out and went to the city, and found it as he had
told them; and they prepared the passover.
17And when it was evening he came with the twelve. 18And as they were at
table eating, Jesus said, "Truly, I say to you, one of you will betray me, one
who is eating with me." 19They began to be sorrowful, and to say to him one
after another, "Is it I?" 20He said to them, "It is one of the twelve, one who is
dipping bread in the same dish with me. 21For the Son of man goes as it is
written of him, but woe to that man by whom the Son of man is betrayed! It
would have been better for that man if he had not been born."

---

woman's generosity (v. 3) and the way people react. What the woman does is in line with customary Eastern hospitality, which honoured distinguished guests by offering then scented water. This refined and lavish gesture is interpreted by some as a waste (v. 4). Jesus, too, gives a different interpretation as to the meaning of her action (v. 8); but he goes on directly to say that she has made no mistake: the mistake lies with the men who judge her. In our relations with God, generosity is never a mistake; whereas calculation and meanness are always wrong: "Since he does not force our will, he takes only what he is given; but he does not give completely of himself until he sees that we have given all we have to him" (St Teresa of Avila, *Way of Perfection*, 48, 4).

14:12–21 Jesus' initiative in giving instructions for the preparation of the Passover (vv. 13–16) and, particularly, the mysterious warning in v. 21 show how intricately God's plans and human actions connect up: "Jesus' violent death was not the result of chance in an unfortunate coincidence of circumstances, but is part of the mystery of God's plan, as St Peter explains to the Jews of Jerusalem in his first sermon on Pentecost: 'This Jesus [was] delivered up according to the definite plan and foreknowledge of God' (Acts 2:23). This biblical language does not mean that those who handed him over were merely passive players in a scenario written in advance by God" (*CCC*, 599).

14:18 Ps 41:9.

The institution of the Eucharist Mt 26:26–29; Lk 22:14–20; 1 Cor 11:23–26

22 And as they were eating, he took bread, and blessed, and broke it, and gave
it to them, and said, "Take; this is my body." 23 And he took a cup, and when
he had given thanks he gave it to them, and they all drank of it. 24 And he said
to them, "This is my blood of the[c] covenant, which is poured out for many.
25 Truly, I say to you, I shall not drink again of the fruit of the vine until that
day when I drink it new in the kingdom of God."

The disciples will desert Jesus Mt 26:30–35; Lk 22:31–34; Jn 13:36–38

26 And when they had sung a hymn, they went out to the Mount of Olives.
27 And Jesus said to them, "You will all fall away; for it is written, 'I will strike
the shepherd, and the sheep will be scattered.' 28 But after I am raised up, I will
go before you to Galilee." 29 Peter said to him, "Even though they all fall away,
I will not." 30 And Jesus said to him, "Truly, I say to you, this very night, before
the cock crows twice, you will deny me three times." 31 But he said vehemently,
"If I must die with you, I will not deny you." And they all said the same.

Jesus' prayer and agony in the garden Mt 26:36–46; Lk 22:39–46

32 And they went to a place which was called Gethsemane; and he said to his
disciples, "Sit here, while I pray." 33 And he took with him Peter and James and

---

14:22–25 Of all the Synoptic Gospels, Mark's provides the briefest account of the institution of the Eucharist (cf. Mk 26:26–29; Lk 22:7–20 and notes). There is no doubt but that, in the light of Christ's death and resurrection, the sacrificial meaning of Christ's gestures and words at this point must have been very clear to the apostles: "Christ's death is both the *Paschal sacrifice* that accomplishes the definitive redemption of men, through 'the Lamb of God, who takes away the sin of the world' (Jn 1:29), and the *sacrifice of the New Convenant*, which restores man to communion with God by reconciling him to God through the 'blood of the convenant, which was poured out for many for the forgiveness of sins' (Mt 26:28)" (*CCC*, 613).

14:26–31 In the Jewish passover meal it is a custom to recite prayers called "Hallel", which include Psalms 113–118, the last part of these being recited at the end of the meal. At this point Jesus predicts that the disciples will leave him on his own and he comforts them by announcing his resurrection and telling them that his mission will start up again in Galilee. The evangelist records the protestations the apostles make (v. 31)—Peter's especially (vv. 29–31). Throughout his account St Mark makes note of how exactly these predictions are fulfilled—the flight of the disciples (14:40), Peter's denial (14:66–72) and the new mission to start in Galilee (16:7).

14:32–42 Alone in the garden of Gethsemane, Jesus becomes intensely aware of what lies ahead. The evangelist tells us that Jesus "began to be greatly depressed

c. Other ancient authorities insert *new* **14:27** Zech 13:7.

John, and began to be greatly distressed and troubled. [34]And he said to them,
“My soul is very sorrowful, even to death; remain here, and watch.”[d] [35]And
going a little farther, he fell on the ground and prayed that, if it were possible,
the hour might pass from him. [36]And he said, “Abba, Father, all things are
possible to thee; remove this cup from me; yet not what I will, but what thou
wilt.” [37]And he came and found them sleeping, and he said to Peter, “Simon,
are you asleep? Could you not watch[d] one hour? [38]Watch[d] and pray that you
may not enter into temptation; the spirit indeed is willing, but the flesh is
weak.” [39]And again he went away and prayed, saying the same words. [40]And
again he came and found them sleeping, for their eyes were very heavy; and
they did not know what to answer him. [41]And he came a third time, and said
to them, “Are you still sleeping and taking your rest? It is enough; the hour has
come; the Son of man is betrayed into the hands of sinners. [42]Rise, let us be
going; see, my betrayer is at hand.”

The arrest Mt 26:47–56; Lk 22:47–53; Jn 18:1–12

[43]And immediately, while he was still speaking, Judas came, one of the twelve,
and with him a crowd with swords and clubs, from the chief priests and the
scribes and the elders. [44]Now the betrayer had given them a sign, saying, “The
one I shall kiss is the man; seize him and lead him away safely.” [45]And when
he came, he went up to him at once, and said, “Master!”[e] And he kissed him.
[46]And they laid hands on him and seized him. [47]But one of those who stood by
drew his sword, and struck the slave of the high priest and cut off his ear.
[48]And Jesus said to them, “Have you come out as against a robber, with

---

and troubled” (v. 33) and the three disciples could not avoid falling asleep: “for their eyes were very heavy; and they did not know what to answer him” (v. 40). But Jesus pulls himself together and has recourse to prayer. Mark records this prayer of Son to Father (v. 36): “Abba, Father, all things are possible to thee.” Jesus addresses God using the same intimate name that a child give his father. So, his prayer is an act of self-abandonment and trust: “Filial trust is tested—it proves itself—in tribulation. The principal difficulty concerns the *prayer of petition*, for oneself or for others in intercession” (*CCC*, 2734).

14:43–52 This matter-of-fact account of Jesus’ arrest seems to imply that he was expecting it; he offers no resistance. Despite Judas’ act of betrayal and the cheap way these people came to arrest him (under cover of darkness), Jesus reads these events as the fulfilment of Scripture (cf. Is 52:13–53; Ps 41:10). Mark is the only evangelist to record the incident of the young man who escaped naked. Many commentators have taken it to be a reference to Mark himself. Whatever about that, it is an instance of a failed attempt to follow Christ—similar to Peter’s denial, which will occur shortly. At the hour of his surrender, Jesus is left quite alone.

d. Or *keep awake* **e.** Or *Rabbi*

swords and clubs to capture me? 49 Day after day I was with you in the temple
teaching, and you did not seize me. But let the scriptures be fulfilled." 50 And
they all forsook him, and fled.

51 And a young man followed him, with nothing but a linen cloth about his
body; and they seized him, 52 but he left the linen cloth and ran away naked.*

Jesus before the chief priests Mt 26:57–68; Lk 22:66–71; Jn 18:13–24

53 And they led Jesus to the high priests; and all the chief priests and the elders and
the scribes were assembled. 54 And Peter had followed him at a distance, right into
the courtyard of the high priest; and he was sitting with the guards, and warming
himself at the fire. 55 Now the chief priests and the whole council sought testimony
against Jesus to put him to death, but they found none. 56 For many bore false
witness against him, and their witness did not agree. 57 And some stood up and
bore false witness against him saying, 58 "We heard him say, 'I will destroy this
temple that is made with hands, and in three days I will build another, not made
with hands.' " 59 Yet not even so did their testimony agree. 60 And the high priest
stood up in the midst, and asked Jesus, "Have you no answer to make? What is it
that these men testify against you?" 61 But he was silent and made no answer.
Again the high priest asked him, "Are you the Christ, the Son of the Blessed?"
62 And Jesus said, "I am; and you will see the Son of man sitting at the right hand
of Power, and coming with the clouds of heaven." 63 And the high priest tore his
mantle, and said, "Why do we still need witnesses? 64 You have heard his
blasphemy. What is your decision?" And they all condemned him as deserving
death. 65 And some began to spit on him, and to cover his face, and to strike him,
saying to him, "Prophesy!" And the guards received him with blows.

14:53–72 This passage supports the tradition that Mark's Gospel incorporates Peter's memory of events. The opening verses (vv. 53–54) show the two protagonists—Jesus and Peter. Then a contrast is drawn between the two: Jesus is falsely accused but he admits the real truth and as a result is condemned to death by the high priest and abused by the servants (vv. 55–65); whereas they are right in what they say about Peter, Peter denies Jesus by telling a lie and avoids being implicated by the maid (vv. 66–72). This makes it clear that Peter's greatness comes not from his strength of character, but from his contrition (v. 72; cf. Jn 21:15–19). "He wept bitterly because he had love in his heart, and soon the sweetness of love displaced the bitterness of sorrow" (St Augustine, *Serm.*, 295, 3).

The climax of the passage comes in vv. 61–62. Jesus remained silent in the face of absurd accusations, but when the high priest asks the unambiguous question Jesus admits that he is the Messiah; not only that: he identifies himself with the transcendent Messiah foreseen by Daniel (Dan 7:13–14). Moreover, the words "I am" in Jesus' answer to Caiaphas can be interpreted as having a deeper meaning, for "I am" is a translation of the name of God himself (cf. Ex 3:14).

14:62 Dan 7:13; Ps 110:1.

Peter's denial Mt 26:69–75; Lk 22:54–62; Jn 18:15–18,25–27

66 And as Peter was below in the courtyard, one of the maids of the high priest
came; 67 and seeing Peter warming himself, she looked at him, and said, "You
also were with the Nazarene, Jesus." 68 But he denied it, saying, "I neither
know nor understand what you mean." And he went out into the gateway.[f]
69 And the maid saw him, and began again to say to the bystanders, "This man
is one of them." 70 But again he denied it. And after a little while the bystanders
said to Peter, "Certainly you are one of them; for you are a Galilean." 71 But he
began to invoke a curse on himself and to swear, "I do not know this man of
whom you speak." 72 And immediately the cock crowed a second time. And
Peter remembered how Jesus had said to him, "Before the cock crows twice,
you will deny me three times." And he broke down and wept.

Jesus before Pilate Mt 27:11–26; Lk 23:1–25; Jn 18:28–19:16

15 1 And as soon as it was morning the chief priests, with the elders and
scribes, and the whole council held a consultation; and they bound
Jesus and led him away and delivered him to Pilate.* 2 And Pilate asked him,
"Are you the King of the Jews?" And he answered him, "You have said so."
3 And the chief priests accused him of many things. 4 And Pilate again asked
him, "Have you no answer to make? See how many charges they bring against
you." 5 But Jesus made no further answer, so that Pilate wondered.
6 Now at the feast he used to release for them one prisoner whom they
asked. 7 And among the rebels in prison, who had committed murder in the
insurrection, there was a man called Barabbas. 8 And the crowd came up and

---

15:1–15 At the time, the trial and death of Jesus must have been disconcerting for all concerned—for the disciples, for the crowd, etc. The question arises: How was it possible for such a thing to happen? Mark gives a very plain account of events, reporting the part played by all those involved: the authorities of Israel hand Jesus over (v. 1) out of envy (v. 10), even at the expense of saving a murderer's life (v. 6); the crowd are just the mouthpiece of a blindness which condemns him to a violent death for no good reason at all (vv. 13–14); and then there is Pilate, an indolent man, who has regard for Jesus (v. 5) and seems to want to save him (v. 9), and yet he condemns him to death: why?—to please the crowd (v. 15).

In narrating the part played by the various characters and the attitude of Jesus himself, the evangelist lets us see the real explanation of events: man's sin is the cause of Jesus death, and Jesus accepts that death out of love for men, to make expiation for sin. That is how the Church reads the situation: "By embracing in his human heart the Father's love for men, Jesus 'loved them to the end' (Jn 13:1), for 'greater love has no man than this, that a man lay down his life for his friends' (Jn 15:13). In suffering and death his humanity became the free and perfect instrument of his divine love which desires the salvation of men. Indeed, out of love for his

f. Or *fore-court.* Other ancient authorities add *and the cock crowed.*

began to ask Pilate to do as he was wont to do for them. [9]And he answered them, "Do you want me to release for you the King of the Jews?" [10]For he perceived that it was out of envy that the chief priests had delivered him up. [11]But the chief priests stirred up the crowd to have him release for them Barabbas instead. [12]And Pilate again said to them, "Then what shall I do with the man whom you call the King of the Jews?" [13]And they cried out again, "Crucify him." [14]And Pilate said to them, "Why, what evil has he done?" But they shouted all the more, "Crucify him." [15]So Pilate, wishing to satisfy the crowd, released for them Barabbas; and having scourged Jesus, he delivered him to be crucified.

The crowning with thorns Mt 27:27–31; Jn 19:1–3

[16]And the soldiers led him away inside the palace (that is, the praetorium); and they called together the whole battalion. [17]And they clothed him in a purple cloak, and plaiting a crown of thorns they put it on him. [18]And they began to salute him, "Hail, King of the Jews!" [19]And they struck his head with a reed, and spat upon him, and they knelt down in homage to him.[20]And when they had mocked him, they stripped him of the purple cloak, and put his own clothes on him. And they led him out to crucify him.

The crucifixion and death of Jesus Mt 27:32–56; Lk 23:26–49; Jn 19:17–30

[21]And they compelled a passer-by, Simon of Cyrene, who was coming in from the country, the father of Alexander and Rufus, to carry his cross. [22]And they brought him to the place called Golgotha (which means the place of a skull). [23]And they offered him wine mingled with myrrh; but he did not take it. [24]And they crucified him, and divided his garments among them, casting lots for them, to decide what each should take. [25]And it was the third hour, when they crucified him. [26]And the inscription of the charge against him read, "The King

---

Father and for men, whom the Father wants to save, Jesus freely accepted his passion and death: 'No one takes [my life] from me, but I lay it down of my own accord' (Jn 10:18). Hence the sovereign freedom of God's Son as he went out to his death" (*CCC*, 609).

15:16–20 After reporting the way the Jews (leaders and people) reject Jesus, the evangelist now records rejection by the Gentile soldiers. They make fun of Jesus' kingship, but "the shame he endured has cleansed us of ours, the ropes which bound him have set us free, his crown of thorns has granted us the crown of the Kingdom, by his wounds we have been healed" (St Jerome, in *Cat. aurea*, in loc.).

15:21–41 Mark's account keeps up its matter-of-fact tone. He meticulously records the time of each event: Jesus was crucified at the third hour (v. 25), at the

15:24 Ps 22:18.

of the Jews." [27]And with him they crucified two robbers, one on his right and
one on his left.[g] [29]And those who passed by derided him, wagging their heads,
and saying, "Aha! You who would destroy the temple and build it in three
days, [30]save yourself, and come down from the cross!" [31]So also the chief
priests mocked him to one another with the scribes, saying, "He saved others;
he cannot save himself. [32]Let the Christ, the King of Israel, come down now
from the cross, that we may see and believe." Those who were crucified with
him also reviled him.

[33]And when the sixth hour had come, there was darkness over the whole
land[h] until the ninth hour. [34]And at the ninth hour Jesus cried out with a loud
voice, "Eloi, Eloi, lama sabachthani?" which means, "My God, my God, why
hast thou forsaken me?" [35]And some of the bystanders hearing it said,
"Behold, he is calling Elijah." [36]And one ran and, filling a sponge full of
vinegar, put it on a reed and gave it to him to drink, saying, "Wait, let us see
whether Elijah will come to take him down." [37]And Jesus uttered a loud cry,
and breathed his last. [38]And the curtain of the temple was torn in two, from top

---

sixth the earth was covered in darkness (v. 33), and at the ninth he died (v. 34). He also provides some anecdotal detail—for example, the reference to the son of Simon of Cyrene who would have been known to the readers of the Gospel (Rom 16:13). But it is the words of Jesus on the cross (v. 34) that give the evangelist the key to the meaning of what is going on—"Eloi, Eloi, lama sabachthani?", the first verse of Psalm 22. This psalm tells the story of a just man who is persecuted but who will win in the end: his sufferings will cause the Lord to be praised throughout the earth by a people yet unborn (Ps 22;9; vv. 31–32,36). The brutal treatment meted out to this just man and to Jesus includes: the insults of the people (Ps 22:8; v. 29), mockery on account of his reliance on God (Ps 22:9; vv. 31–32, 36), the dividing up of his clothes (Ps 22:19; v. 24), etc. Mark interprets two events as evidence of the success of Christ's mission—the tearing of the temple veil (v. 38), symbolizing the removal of barriers between the people of God and the Gentiles (cf. Ps 22:31), and a Gentile's act of faith in Jesus' divinity (v. 39), a signal of how all nations can believe in God (cf. Ps 22:28–30). This explains the paradox that Jesus tried to teach his disciples: he is the Messiah and the Son of God (cf. 1:1), but his victory is closely linked to the cross. "O what marvellous power of the cross! What ineffable glory of the Passion! In them we can see the trial of the Lord, the judgment of the world, and the power of the Crucified Christ. [...] For your cross is the fountain of all blessings and the origin of all graces: in it believers find strength in their weakness, glory in shame, life in death itself" (St Leo the Great, *Serm. 8 de Pass. Dom.*, 7).

See the RSV note **g** to v. 28.

g. Other ancient authorities insert verse 28, *And the scripure was fulfilled which says, "He was reckoned with the transgressors"* **h.** Or *earth* **15:29** Is 22:87–8. **15:34** Ps 22:2. **15:36** Ps 69:21.

to bottom. 39And when the centurion, who stood facing him, saw that he thus[i]
breathed his last, he said, "Truly this man was the Son[x] of God!"
40There were also women looking on from afar, among whom were Mary
Magdalene, and Mary the mother of James the younger* and of Joses, and
Salome, 41who, when he was in Galilee, followed him, and ministered to him;
and also many other women who came up with him to Jerusalem.

The burial of Jesus Mt 27:57–66; Lk 23:50–56; Jn 19:31–42

42And when evening had come, since it was the day of Preparation, that is, the
day before the sabbath, 43Joseph of Arimathea, a respected member of the
council, who was also himself looking for the kingdom of God, took courage
and went to Pilate, and asked for the body of Jesus. 44And Pilate wondered if
he were already dead; and summoning the centurion, he asked him whether he
was already dead.[j] 45And when he learned from the centurion that he was dead,
he granted the body to Joseph. 46And he bought a linen shroud, and taking him
down, wrapped him in the linen shroud, and laid him in a tomb which had
been hewn out of the rock; and he rolled a stone against the door of the tomb.
47Mary Magdalene and Mary the mother of Joses saw where he was laid.

The resurrection of Jesus. The empty tomb Mt 28:1–10; Lk 24:1–12; Jn 20:1–10

16 1And when the sabbath was past, Mary Magdalene, and Mary the
mother of James, and Salome, bought spices, so that they might go and
anoint him.* 2And very early on the first day of the week they went to the
tomb when the sun had risen. 3And they were saying to one another, "Who
will roll away the stone for us from the door of the tomb?" 4And looking up,
they saw that the stone was rolled back; for it was very large. 5And entering
the tomb, they saw a young man on the right side, dressed in a white robe; and
they were amazed. 6And he said to them, "Do not be amazed; you seek Jesus
of Nazareth, who was crucified. He has risen, he is not here; see the place
where they laid him. 7But go, tell his disciples and Peter that he is going before

---

15:42–47 Throughout this chapter, Mark has shown the attitudes of the various people involved. Now, from the crucifixion up to the end of his account (15:40–41, 47; 16:1–9), he recalls particularly the affection these women have for our Lord, and also the kindness of Joseph: "Joseph of Arimathea and Nicodemus visit Jesus secretly in ordinary times and in the time of triumph. But they are courageous in the face of authority, declaring their love for Christ *audacter*—'boldly'—in the time of cowardice. Learn" (Bl. J. Escrivá, *The Way*, 841).

16:1–8 In their earliest preaching (cf. Acts 2:22–32; 3:13–15; etc.) the apostles reminded people that "Christ died for our sins in accordance with the scriptures"

i. Other ancient authorities *cried out and* **x.** Or *a son* **j.** Other ancient authorities read *whether he had been some time dead*

you to Galilee; there you will see him, as he told you." [8]And they went out and
fled from the tomb; for trembling and astonishment had come upon them; and
they said nothing to any one, for they were afraid.

Jesus appears to Mary Magdalene Jn 20:11–18

[9]Now when he rose early on the first day of the week, he appeared first to
Mary Magdalene, from whom he had cast out seven demons. [10]She went and
told those who had been with him, as they mourned and wept. [11]But when they
heard that he was alive and had been seen by her, they would not believe it.

Jesus appears to two disciples Lk 24:13–35

[12]After this he appeared in another form to two of them, as they were walking
into the country. [13]And they went back and told the rest, but they did not
believe them.

(1 Cor 15:3–4). Mark has stressed (cf. 15:44–40) that our Lord truly died, and now he records that he truly rose (v. 6). The announcement made by the young man at the tomb contains instructions (v. 7) which sum up the life of the early Church: the disciples, Peter particularly, are to be witnesses of the resurrection and its meaning. The mission of the Church begins in Galilee. That region, which in Christ's time was a crossroads where Jews and Gentiles met, now becomes a symbol of the world-wide mission of the Church. And "the Church, spread throughout the whole world carefully guards the faith and preaching it has received, as though living in one and the same house; and its faith is the same in every place, as if the Church had one soul and one heart, and whatever it preaches, teaches and transmits, it does so in unison, as if from one mouth" (St Irenaeus, *Adv. haer.*, 1, 10, 2).

16:9–20 The second Gospel ends with a very summarized account of the appearances of the Risen Christ. These verses are stylistically different from the rest of the Gospel and are not to be found in some manuscripts (cf. RSV note **k** to v. 20). Even so, whether Mark closely copied from some document or whether these verses are a later addition, this passage is part of the canon and therefore is regarded as inspired.

The accent in this account is on the initial disbelief of the apostles. First (vv. 9–13) we are told of the appearances to Mary Magdalene and the disciples of Emmaus (cf. Lk 24:15–25); in both cases the narrator points out (vv. 11, 13) that their reaction was one of disbelief. The appearance to the Eleven (vv. 14–18) contains a summary of the mission of the apostles.

Finally, the last two verses (vv. 19–20) tell who Jesus is in the present age—the One who has been raised to the right hand of the Father and who is at work with his disciples confirming the message they bear.

Jesus appears to the Eleven.
The apostles' mission Mt 28:16–20; Lk 24:36–49; Jn 20:19–31
14Afterward he appeared to the eleven themselves as they sat at table; and he
upbraided them for their unbelief and hardness of heart, because they had not
believed those who saw him after he had risen. 15And he said to them, "Go
into all the world and preach the gospel to the whole creation. 16He who
believes and is baptized will be saved; but he who does not believe will be
condemned. 17And these signs will accompany those who believe: in my name
they will cast out demons; they will speak in new tongues; 18they will pick up
serpents, and if they drink any deadly thing, it will not hurt them; they will lay
their hands on the sick, and they will recover."

The ascension of our Lord Lk 24:50–53; Acts 1:6–11
19So then the Lord Jesus, after he had spoken to them, was taken up into
heaven, and sat down at the right hand of God.

The apostles go forth and preach
20And they went forth and preached everywhere, while the Lord worked with
them and confirmed the message by the signs that attended it. Amen.[k*]

---

k. Other ancient authorities omit verses 9–20. Some ancient authorities conclude Mark instead with the following: *But they reported briefly to Peter and those with him all that they had been told. And after this, Jesus himself sent out by means of them, from east to west, the sacred and imperishable proclamation of eternal salvation*

The Gospel according to St Luke

The third Gospel, along with the book of the Acts of the Apostles (cf. Acts 1:1), is attributed to "Luke, a physician from Antioch, a man familiar with the Greek language, as can be seen from his writings, a follower of the apostle Paul and his companion on his journeys" (St Jerome, *Of Famous Men*, 1); this is confirmed by an examination of his writing. The Gospel's prologue (1:1–4), written in excellent Greek style and similar to introductions in Greek history books, allows us to deduce that the author was not an eyewitness to the events he recounts, but that he was a conscientious writer who tried to be well-informed and to write an orderly account. Some passages in the Acts are written in the first person plural (Acts 16:10–17; 20:5–15; 21:1–18; 27:1–28:16), indicating that their author was with St Paul when the events occurred and he is usually identified as being the person the Apostle refers to in one of his letters as "Luke the beloved physician" (Col 4:14; cf. 2 Tim 4:11; Philem 24). Both books are addressed to Theophilus (Lk 1:3; Acts 1:1). We have no way of knowing whether this name refers to some person he knew or whether it is a general reference to Christians ("the beloved of God"), but in any case St Luke does seem to be writing especially for Christians of Gentile background.

Like the first evangelist, St Luke begins his book with episodes from Jesus' infancy. In the rest of his Gospel, which covers the public life of Jesus, Luke keeps to the general framework common to the Synoptic Gospels (Jesus' ministry in Galilee, his going up to Jerusalem, and his passion, death and resurrection there) but he gives more space than the others to Jesus' journey to the Holy City: it takes up ten chapters (9:51–19:27). The evangelist thereby graphically emphasizes the stages in the history of salvation which centre on Jesus Christ and on what he did in Jerusalem (his death, resurrection and ascension). Later, in fact, in the book of the Acts of the Apostles, he will describe how the preaching of the Gospel spread from Jerusalem to the neighbouring regions (Samaria and Judea), to Asia Minor and as far as Rome, the centre of the known world.

As in the other Gospels, the core of his message is Jesus Christ, but Luke has features which are his alone. His Gospel calls Jesus "the Prophet" (4:24; 7:16; 13:33; 24:19; etc.). He is the prophet *par excellence*, because no one can speak in God's name the way he does; and, like the prophets, he is anointed by the Spirit and guided by him (3:22; 4:14, 16–30; etc.). In the episodes to do with Jesus' infancy, Jesus is also called the "Saviour" (1:71, 77; 2:11, 30), because he is the one who is going to save the people from their sins; this salvation can already be seen in his actions towards people, especially his kindness towards the weak and towards sinners (7:50; 8:48, 50; 18:42;

19:9–10). The salvation which Jesus brings applies to *everyone*. Even in the infancy account we are told that Jesus is God's Saviour "in the presence of all peoples, a light for revelation to the Gentiles" (2:31–32), and both John the Baptist's mission (cf. 3:6) and Jesus' initial preaching in Nazareth (4:25–27) underline this universal scope of salvation. But it is, above all, in the episodes recounted in Jesus' journey to Jerusalem (9:51–19:27), many of which are to be found only in the third Gospel, that this aspect becomes most pronounced. In response to what God does in Christ, man needs to live a consistent *Christian life*, that is, he must respond to the Lord's call generously (5:11, 28; 18:22), every day (9:32), imitating the attitudes of Christ himself. Just as Jesus prays frequently, particularly at key moments in his life (3:21; 6:12; 9:29; 22:32; 23:34, the Christian should *pray* at all times (18:1; cf. 11:1–13; 23:40); following Christ's example, he should be *merciful* as the Father is merciful (6:36; cf. 15:1–32). Throughout the Gospel, other virtues are also stressed, such as *joy* (1:14, 28; 6:23; 15:7; 24:52; etc.), *poverty* (1:53; 4:18; 6:20; 12:13–21; 14:12–14; 16:9, 14–15, 19–31), etc. And the clearest example of this attitude of men and women towards God is that given by the *Blessed Virgin Mary*, the person who has received the greatest gifts from God (1:28–30) and who has best responded to them (1:45, 48).

Luke

Prologue

1 [1]Inasmuch as many have undertaken to compile a narrative of the things
which have been accomplished among us, [2]just as they were delivered to us
by those who from the beginning were eyewitnesses and ministers of the word,
[3]it seemed good to me also, having followed all things closely[a] for some time
past, to write an orderly account for you, most excellent Theophilus,* [4]that you
may know the truth concerning the things of which you have been informed.

1. THE INFANCY OF JOHN THE BAPTIST AND OF JESUS

The birth of John the Baptist foretold

[5]*In the days of Herod, king of Judea, there was a priest named Zechariah,[b] of
the division of Abijah; and he had a wife of the daughters of Aaron, and her

---

1:1–4 This prologue, which is very short and very elegantly written, explains why he wrote the book—to provides an orderly, documented (cf. v. 3) account of the life of Christ, starting at the beginning, and to show the salvific meaning of "the things which have been accomplished among us" (v. 1).

1:5–2:52 □ The infancy narrative in St Luke's Gospel consists of six episodes arranged in pairs, covering the birth and infancy of John the Baptist and Jesus—two annunciations (1:5–38), two births and circumcisions (1:39–2:21) and two scenes in the temple (2:22–52). The narratives also include canticles—the "Magnificat" (1:46–55), the "Benedictus" (1:68–79), the "Gloria" (2:14) and the "Nunc dimittis" (2:29–32)—which express the joy caused by God's actions in favour of men. Both narratives and canticles are full of Old Testament references which show that the salvation promised by God is now coming to pass (cf. 1:1).

The central scene of the whole group is the Annunciation to Mary and the Incarnation of the Word when the Blessed Virgin accepts her calling. These two dimensions—Christological and Mariological—are clear to see in each episode. The Child who is born in Bethlehem is the promised Saviour (1:71, 77; 2:11, 30), the Messiah, the Lord (1:76; 2:11, 26), whose mission is one of salvation (2:38); however, he will be a sign of contradiction, "for the fall and rising of many in Israel" (2:34); people can be saved only by believing in him. Alongside the Child we always find his Mother, who stands for that part of mankind faithful to God (1:46–56). She cooperates in God's saving plan (1:38) through her unwavering faith (1:45). On this account God not only associates her with her Son's mission

a. Or *accurately* **b.** Greek *Zacharias*

name was Elizabeth. [6]And they were both righteous before God, walking in all
the commandments and ordinances of the Lord blameless. [7]But they had no
child, because Elizabeth was barren, and both were advanced in years.
[8]Now while he was serving as priest before God when his division was on
duty, [9]according to the custom of the priesthood, it fell to him by lot to enter
the temple of the Lord and burn incense. [10]And the whole multitude of the
people were praying outside at the hour of incense. [11]And there appeared to
him an angel of the Lord standing on the right side of the altar of incense.
[12]And Zechariah was troubled when he saw him, and fear fell upon him. [13]But
the angel said to him, "Do not be afraid, Zechariah, for your prayer is heard,
and your wife Elizabeth will bear you a son, and you shall call his name John.

14 And you will have joy and gladness,
and many will rejoice at his birth;
15 for he will be great before the Lord,
and he shall drink no wine nor strong drink,
and he will be filled with the Holy Spirit,
even from his mother's womb.
16 And he will turn many of the sons of Israel to the Lord their God,
17 and he will go before him in the spirit and power of Elijah,
to turn the hearts of the fathers to the children,
and the disobedient to the wisdom of the just,
to make ready for the Lord a people prepared."

---

but also with the sufferings he will ultimately undergo in order to put God's plan of salvation into effect (2:35).

1:5–25 As on other occasions (cf. 2:1ff; 3:1ff), Luke, who is familiar with accepted ways of writing history, begins his account by setting the facts into the framework of secular history (v. 5). He will later link the annunciation to the Blessed Virgin to the annunciation to Zechariah (1:26), which occurred six months earlier.

Through the archangel, God enters the lives of Zechariah and his wife Elizabeth in a very unusual way. But what the angel proclaims impacts beyond the private sphere of the family (v. 14). Elizabeth, already advanced in years, is going to have a son who will be called John (v. 13)—a name which means "God is merciful"—and who will be exceptionally holy (v. 15), for his mission as precursor of the long awaited Messiah (v. 17) will make him an instrument of God's salvation (v. 16). "With John the Baptist, the Holy Spirit begins the restoration to man of 'the divine likeness', prefiguring what he would achieve with and in Christ. John's baptism was for repentance; baptism in water and the Spirit will be a new birth" (*CCC*, 720).

The whole scenario, in both form (divine intervention, disconcertion, proclamation, difficulty, sign) and content seems designed to parallel and prepare the

1:17 Mal 4:5.

[18]And Zechariah said to the angel, "How shall I know this? For I am an old man, and my wife is advanced in years." [19]And the angel answered him, "I am Gabriel, who stand in the presence of God; and I was sent to speak to you, and to bring you this good news. [20]And behold, you will be silent and unable to speak until the day that these things come to pass, because you did not believe my words, which will be fulfilled in their time." [21]And the people were waiting for Zechariah, and they wondered at his delay in the temple. [22]And when he came out, he could not speak to them, and they perceived that he had seen a vision in the temple; and he made signs to them and remained dumb. [23]And when his time of service was ended, he went to his home.

[24]After these days his wife Elizabeth conceived, and for five months she hid herself, saying, [25]"Thus the Lord has done to me in the days when he looked on me, to take away my reproach among men."

The annunciation and incarnation of the Son of God Mt 1:18–25

[26]In the sixth month the angel Gabriel was sent from God to a city of Galilee named Nazareth, [27]to a virgin betrothed to a man whose name was Joseph, of the house of David; and the virgin's name was Mary. [28]And he came to her and said, "Hail, full of grace,[b2] the Lord is with you!"[c] [29]But she was greatly troubled at the saying, and considered in her mind what sort of greeting this might be. [30]And the angel said to her,* "Do not be afraid, Mary, for you have found favour with God. [31]And behold you will conceive in your womb and bear a son, and you shall call his name Jesus.

---

way for the annunciation to Mary, thereby highlighting the latter event. Thus, Zechariah wanted to have children (v. 13) but was unable to have any; whereas the Blessed Virgin does not ask God for a child (cf. 1:34) but God gives her one; both Zechariah and Mary are disconcerted by the angel's greeting (1:12, 29), but Mary is not afraid (1:29) whereas Zechariah is (v. 12); finally, Zechariah has his doubts (v. 20) and asks for a sign (v. 18), whereas Mary believes (1:39) and is offered a sign even though she never asked for one (1:36).

1:26–38 This account is very tightly written. Almost every word carries remarkable depth of meaning. The Fathers and Church Tradition are not slow to notice this, and Christians re-live this mystery every day at the time of the Angelus.

The angel's message is about the unique, all-powerful action of God in being made flesh in order to save us. This divine action (cf. v. 35) is reminiscent of that of creation (cf. Gen 1:2), when the Spirit came down on the waters; and it reminds us of the time when the people of God believed and were able to recognize his presence by the cloud covering the ark of the Covenant (cf. Ex 40:34–36).

The attitude of our Lady (a "virgin" from Nazareth: v. 27) shows how a mere creature can co-operate in God's saving action. "Enriched from the first instant of

b². Or *O favoured one*. **c.** Other ancient authorities add "*Blessed are you among women!*"

32 He will be great, and will be called the Son of the Most High;
and the Lord God will give to him the throne of his father David,
33 and he will reign over the house of Jacob for ever;
and of his kingdom there will be no end."
34 And Mary said to the angel, "How can this be, since I have no husband?" 35
And the angel said to her,
"The Holy Spirit will come upon you,
and the power of the Most High will overshadow you;
therefore the child to be born[d] will be called holy,
the Son of God.
36 And behold, your kinswoman Elizabeth in her old age has also conceived a
son; and this is the sixth month with her who was called barren. 37 For with
God nothing will be impossible." 38 And Mary said, "Behold, I am the hand-
maid of the Lord; let it be to me according to your word." And the angel
departed from her.

The Visitation
39 In those days Mary arose and went with haste into the hill country, to a city
of Judah, 40 and she entered the house of Zechariah and greeted Elizabeth.

---

her conception with the splendor of an entirely unique holiness, the virgin of Nazareth is hailed by the heralding angel, by divine command, as 'full of grace' (cf. Lk 1:28). And to the heavenly messenger she replies, 'Behold the handmaid of the Lord, be it done unto me according to thy word' (Lk 1:38). Thus the daughter of Adam, Mary, consenting to the word of God, became the Mother of Jesus. Committing herself whole-heartedly and impeded by no sin to God's saving will, she devoted herself totally, as a handmaid of the Lord, to the person and work of her Son, under and with him, serving the mystery of redemption, by the grace of Almighty God. Rightly, therefore, the Fathers see Mary not merely as passively engaged by God, but as freely cooperating in the work of man's salvation through faith and obedience" (Vatican II, *LG*, 56).

1:39–56 Here we can see many other aspects of the greatness of Mary. Elizabeth, filled with the Holy Spirit, proclaims Mary as "the mother of my Lord" (v. 43). But this fact is also an object of faith and for this reason Elizabeth greets Mary in the way she does.

However, the Blessed Virgin's faith is not just a matter of personal virtue: it gives rise to the New Covenant: "Just as Abraham '*in hope believed against hope*, that he should become the father of many nations' (cf. Rom 4:18), so Mary, at the Annunciation, having professed her virginity ('How shall this be, since I have no husband?'), *believed* that through the power of the most High, by the power of the

d. Other ancient authorities add *of you* **1:37** Gen 18; Job 42:2.

41 And when Elizabeth heard the greeting of Mary, the babe leaped in her
womb; and Elizabeth was filled with the Holy Spirit 42 and she exclaimed with
a loud cry, "Blessed are you among women, and blessed is the fruit of your
womb! 43 And why is this granted me, that the mother of my Lord should come
to me? 44 For behold, when the voice of your greeting came to my ears, the
babe in my womb leaped for joy. 45 And blessed is she who believed that there
would be[e] a fulfilment of what was spoken to her from the Lord."

The Magnificat

46 And Mary said,
"My soul magnifies the Lord,
47 and my spirit rejoices in God my Saviour,
48 for he has regarded the low estate of his handmaiden.
For behold, henceforth all generations will call me blessed;
49 for he who is mighty has done great things for me,
and holy is his name.
50 And his mercy is on those who fear him
from generation to generation.
51 He has shown strength with his arm,
he has scattered the proud in the imagination of their hearts,
52 he has put down the mighty from their thrones,
and exalted those of low degree;
53 he has filled the hungry with good things,
and the rich he has sent empty away.
54 He has helped his servant Israel,
in remembrance of his mercy,
55 as he spoke to our fathers,
to Abraham and to his posterity for ever."*
56 And Mary remained with her about three months, and returned to her home.

Holy Spirit, she would become the mother of God's Son in accordance with the angel's revelation" (John Paul II, *Redempt. Mater*, 14).

The scene ends with Mary's *Magnificat* canticle. This poem, which evokes some passages of Old Testament (cf. 1 Sam 2:1–10) is a prayer in itself and a model of prayer: "In these sublime words, which are simultaneously very simple and wholly inspired by the sacred texts of the people of Israel, Mary's personal experience, the ecstasy of her heart, shines forth. In them shines a ray of the mystery of God, the glory of his ineffable holiness, the eternal *love which, as an irrevocable gift, enters into human history*" (ibid., 36).

e. Or *believed, for there will be* **1:46** 1 Sam 2:1–10.

The birth and circumcision of John the Baptist

57 Now the time came for Elizabeth to be delivered, and she gave birth to a son.
58 And her neighbours and kinsfolk heard that the Lord had shown great mercy
to her, and they rejoiced with her. 59 And on the eighth day they came to
circumcise the child; and they would have named him Zechariah after his
father, 60 but his mother said, "Not so; he shall be called John." 61 And they said
to her, "None of your kindred is called by this name." 62 And they made signs
to his father, inquiring what he would have him called. 63 And he asked for a
writing tablet, and wrote, "His name is John." And they all marvelled. 64 And
immediately his mouth was opened and his tongue loosed, and he spoke,
blessing God. 65 And fear came on all their neighbours. And all these things
were talked about through all the hill country of Judea; 66 and all who heard
them laid them up in their hearts, saying, "What then will this child be?" For
the hand of the Lord was with him.

The canticle of Zechariah

67 And his father Zechariah was filled with the Holy Spirit, and prophesied,
saying,

68 "Blessed be the Lord God of Israel,
for he has visited and redeemed his people,
69 and has raised up a horn of salvation* for us
in the house of his servant David,
70 as he spoke by the mouth of his holy prophets from of old,
71 that we should be saved from our enemies,
and from the hand of all who hate us;

1:57–80 The evangelist runs two accounts one after the other (1:57–2:21), to do with the birth and circumcision of the Baptist and then of Jesus. It is interesting to note the contrasts: John is born at home in a context of joy and wonder (vv. 58, 63–64, 66), whereas Jesus will be born away from home, a manger for a crib and acknowledged only by his parents and a few shepherds (2:1–20).

In the case of John the Baptist the Gospel centres more on his circumcision, because that is when God's special intervention is made manifest. When Zechariah (v. 63) does all that the angel commanded (1:13), his tongue is loosed: "Rightly was his tongue loosened because, being struck dumb through unbelief, his power of speech is returned through faith" (St Ambrose, *Com. on Lk*, in loc.).

God's involvement in events causes people to wonder what special mission God has planned for John. Zechariah, who knows that his son is the Precursor of the incarnate God (1:14–17), intones a canticle of praise to God (the *Benedictus*) in which he acknowledges God's saving actions towards Israel (vv. 68–75) culminating in the coming of the Lord himself, a coming for which Zechariah's son will prepare the way (vv. 76–79).

72 to perform the mercy promised to our fathers,
and to remember his holy covenant,
73 the oath which he swore to our father Abraham,
74 to grant us that we, being delivered from the hand of our enemies,
might serve him without fear,
75 in holiness and righteousness before him all the days of our life.
76 And you, child, will be called the prophet of the Most High;
for you will go before the Lord to prepare his ways,
77 to give knowledge of salvation to his people
in the forgiveness of their sins,
78 through the tender mercy of our God,
when the day shall dawn upon[f] us from on high
79 to give light to those who sit in darkness and in the shadow of death,
to guide our feet into the way of peace."
80 And the child grew and became strong in spirit, and he was in the wilderness
till the day of his manifestation to Israel.

The birth of Jesus Mt 1:18–25

2 1 In those days a decree went out from Caesar Augustus that all the world
should be enrolled. 2 This was the first enrolment, when Quirinius was
governor of Syria. 3 And all went to be enrolled, each to his own city. 4 And
Joseph also went up from Galilee, from the city of Nazareth, to Judea, to the

---

These two designations of God—Lord (v. 76) and Saviour (cf. vv. 69, 71, 77)—were also applied to Jesus by the angel in his message to the shepherds (v. 17).

2:1–21 The Gospel's account of Jesus' birth is a brief one. However, it does supply some details—the place of birth, Bethlehem, and how badly off the Holy Family were. These two things are also a lesson telling us that God uses the events of human history to steer things in accordance with his plans and to instruct us: "Is there any clearer way of declaring his mercy than by deigning to take on our miserable condition? Could there be anything more abounding in piety than that the Word of God should have made himself as one of such little worth as ourselves? Men ought to deduce from these facts what great concern God has for them; may they understand what God thinks and feels for them" (St Bernard, *Serm. 1 in Epiph. Dom.*, 2).

The angel's message to the shepherds indicates the significance of Jesus' birth. He is no ordinary child, but the Saviour, the Messiah, the Lord (v. 11), and his coming into the world brings the very best of gifts—praise of God's glory and peace among men (v. 14). Hence the great significance of the adoration of the shepherds (v. 17): "The shepherds are Israelites; the Magi, Gentiles. The first lived

f. Or *whereby the dayspring will visit.* Other ancient authorities read *since the dayspring has visited*
1:78 Mal 4:2. **1:79** Is 9:2.

city of David, which is called Bethlehem, because he was of the house and
lineage of David, 5to be enrolled with Mary, his betrothed, who was with child.
6And while they were there, the time came for her to be delivered. 7And she
gave birth to her first-born* son and wrapped him in swaddling cloths, and laid
him in a manger, because there was no place for them in the inn.

The adoration of the shepherds

8And in that region there were shepherds out in the field, keeping watch over their
flock by night. 9And an angel of the Lord appeared to them, and the glory of the
Lord shone around them, and they were filled with fear. 10And the angel said to
them, "Be not afraid; for behold, I bring you good news of a great joy which will
come to all the people; 11for to you is born this day in the city of David a Saviour,
who is Christ the Lord. 12And this will be a sign for you: you will find a babe
wrapped in swaddling cloths and lying in a manger." 13And suddenly there was
with the angel a multitude of the heavenly host praising God and saying,

14 "Glory to God in the highest,
and on earth peace among men with whom he is pleased!"[g]

15When the angels went away from them into heaven, the shepherds said to
one another, "Let us go over to Bethlehem and see this thing that has happened,
which the Lord has made known to us." 16And they went with haste, and found
Mary and Joseph, and the babe lying in a manger. 17And when they saw it they
made known the saying which had been told them concerning this child; 18and all
who heard it wondered at what the shepherds told them. 19But Mary kept all these
things, pondering them in her heart. 20And the shepherds returned, glorifying and
praising God for all they had heard and seen, as it had been told them.

The circumcision of Jesus Mt 1:25

21And at the end of eight days, when he was circumcised, he was called Jesus,
the name given by the angels before he was conceived in the womb.

The purification of Mary and the presentation of Jesus in the temple

22And when the time came for their purification according to the law of Moses,
they brought him up to Jerusalem to present him to the Lord 23(as it is written
in the law of the Lord, "Every male that opens the womb shall be called holy

---

nearby; the latter, far away. Yet both came to the cornerstore, Christ" (St Augustine, *Serm. de Nativ. Dom.*, 202, 1).

2:22–38 The Holy Family went up to Jerusalem to fulfil two prescriptions of the Law of Moses—the purification of the mother (cf. Lev 12:2–8) and the presentation and then redemption or buying back of the first-born (cf. Ex 13:2, 12–13). This is the occasion of Jesus' manifestation to Israel: "The *presentation of*

g. Other ancient authorities read *peace, good will among men* **2:23** Ex 13:2,12.

to the Lord") 24and to offer a sacrifice according to what is said in the law of
the Lord, "a pair of turtledoves, or two young pigeons."

Simeon's prophecy

25Now there was a man in Jerusalem, whose name was Simeon, and this man
was righteous and devout, looking for the consolation of Israel, and the Holy
Spirit was upon him. 26And it had been revealed to him by the Holy Spirit that
he should not see death before he had seen the Lord's Christ. 27And inspired
by the Spirit[h] he came into the temple; and when the parents brought in the
child Jesus, to do for him according to the custom of the law, 28he took him up
in his arms and blessed God and said,

29"Lord, now lettest thou thy servant depart in peace,
according to thy word;
30 for mine eyes have seen thy salvation
31 which thou hast prepared in the presence of all peoples,
32 a light for revelation to the Gentiles,
and for glory to thy people Israel."

33And his father and his mother marvelled at what was said about him;
34and Simeon blessed them and said to Mary his mother,

"Behold, this child is set for the fall *and rising of many in Israel,
and for a sign that is spoken against
35(and a sword will pierce through your own soul also),
that thoughts out of many hearts may be revealed."

Anna the prophetess

36And there was a prophetess Anna, the daughter of Phanuel, of the tribe of
Asher; she was of a great age, having lived with her husband seven years from
her virginity, 37and as a widow till she was eighty-four. She did not depart from
the temple, worshipping with fasting and prayer night and day. 38And coming
up at that very hour she gave thanks to God, and spoke of him to all who were
looking for the redemption of Jerusalem.

Jesus in the temple shows him to be the first-born Son who belongs to the Lord" (*CCC*, 534). Simeon and Anna, both of them well on in years, stand for the true Israel that awaits the coming of its Saviour and Redeemer (vv. 30, 38) and praises God for letting them see their hopes fulfilled (vv. 28, 38).

Simeon is depicted as a man led by the Holy Spirit (vv. 25, 26, 27); therefore, what he has to say carries special weight: he acknowledges Jesus as the expected Messiah, the "glory of Israel" but also "light of revelation" for all men. However, Christ's mission of salvation will be "a sign that is spoken against" set for the fall of many: "The sword of sorrow predicted for Mary announces Christ's perfect and unique oblation on the cross that will impart the salvation God had 'prepared in the presence of all peoples'" (*CCC*, 529).

h. *Or in the Spirit.*

The childhood of Jesus

39 And when they had performed everything according to the law of the Lord,
they returned to Galilee, to their own city, Nazareth. 40 And the child grew and
became strong, filled with wisdom; and the favour of God was upon him.

The finding in the temple

41 Now his parents went to Jerusalem every year at the feast of the Passover.
42 And when he was twelve years old, they went up according to custom; 43 and
when the feast was ended, as they were returning, the boy Jesus stayed behind
in Jerusalem. His parents did not know it, 44 but supposing him to be in the
company they went a day's journey, and they sought him among their kinsfolk
and acquaintances; 45 and when they did not find him, they returned to
Jerusalem, seeking him. 46 After three days they found him in the temple,
sitting among the teachers, listening to them and asking them questions; 47 and
all who heard him were amazed at his understanding and his answers. 48 And
when they saw him they were astonished; and his mother said to him, "Son,
why have you treated us so? Behold, your father and I have been looking for
you anxiously." 49 And he said to them, "How is it that you sought me? Did you
not know that I must be in my Father's house?"* 50 And they did not under-
stand the saying which he spoke to them.

The hidden life of Jesus at Nazareth Mt 2:23

51 And he went down with them and came to Nazareth, and was obedient to
them; and his mother kept all these things in her heart.
52 And Jesus increased in wisdom and in stature,[i] and in favour with God
and man.

2:41–50 Now that he has reached the age of twelve, Jesus, like all male children of Israel, has to make a pilgrimage to Jerusalem. The evangelist does not say much about this journey because he wants to focus on the conversation between Jesus and his Mother. His parents find him "listening to the teachers and asking them questions" (cf. v. 46), in such a way that all those present "were amazed at his understanding and his answers" (v. 47). This sets the scene for what follows: Jesus is no ordinary child, but the Son of God. In his dialogue with his Mother, Jesus seems surprisingly detached, but we must not forget that the Semitic mind was fond of contrasts and antitheses. The crux of the scene is really what Jesus says in v. 49, words that his parents did not understand (v. 50): "The *finding of Jesus in the temple* is the only event that breaks the silence of the Gospels about the hidden years of Jesus. Here Jesus lets us catch a glimpse of the mystery of his total consecration to a mission that flows from his divine sonship" (*CCC*, 529).

2:51–52 Luke ends his infancy narrative by summing up the life of the Holy Family during those years. He has already (cf. 2:19, 39–40) referred to these same

i. Or *years*

2. PRELUDE TO THE PUBLIC MINISTRY OF JESUS

The preaching of John the Baptist Mt 3:1–12; Mk 1:1–8; Jn 1:19–34

3 [1]In the fifteenth year of the reign of Tiberius Caesar, Pontius Pilate being
governor of Judea, and Herod being tetrarch of Galilee, and his brother
Philip tetrarch of the region of Ituraea and Trachonitis, and Lysanias tetrarch
of Abilene, [2]in the high-priesthood of Annas and Caiaphas, *the word of God
came to John the son of Zechariah in the wilderness; [3]and he went into all the
region about the Jordan, preaching a baptism of repentance for the forgiveness
of sins. [4]As it is written in the book of the words of Isaiah the prophet,

"The voice of one crying in the wilderness:
Prepare the way of the Lord,
make his paths straight.
[5]Every valley shall be filled,
and every mountain and hill shall be brought low,
and the crooked shall be made straight,
and the rough ways shall be made smooth;
[6]and all flesh shall see the salvation of God."

---

dispositions of the two leading figures in salvation history, Jesus and Mary. "His hidden years are not without significance, nor were they simply a preparation for the years which were to come after—those of his public life. [...] I have understood clearly that God wants our Lord's whole life to be an example for Christians. I saw this with special reference to his hidden life, the years he spent working side by side with ordinary men. Our Lord wants many people to ratify their vocation during years of quiet, unspectacular living" (Bl. J. Escrivá, *Hom.*, 1, 20).

3:1–4:13 □ Like the other evangelists, St Luke presents the "preparation for Jesus' ministry" by focusing on the Baptist (3:1–20) and on the temptations in the wilderness (3:21–22; 4:1–13). To this he adds the genealogy of Jesus (3:23–38). One feature of this Gospel is that it draws attention to the stages and places of salvation; to do so, it brings forward the imprisonment of the Baptist (that is, gives it an earlier position than the other Synoptics: 3:19–20; cf. Mt 14:3–4; Mk 6:17–18), in order to show more graphically that the stage of the Baptist precedes that of Jesus. Similarly, it places the last of the temptations of Jesus in Jerusalem (4:9), because Jerusalem is the place that lies at the centre of St Luke's account: there our Lord will be revealed as the light of the Gentiles (2:22–35), and there will make his departure (9:31), and there will start his mission to the whole world (24:47).

3:1–20 All four Gospels cover the activity of John the Baptist prior to the public life of Jesus. Luke's account is the most detailed and most orderly. Thus, he describes the Baptist's mission (vv. 3–6), the content of his message (vv. 7–14),

3:4–6 Is 40:3–5.

7He said therefore to the multitudes that came out to be baptized by him, "You brood of vipers!* Who warned you to flee from the wrath to come? 8Bear fruits that befit repentance, and do not begin to say to yourselves, 'We have Abraham as our father'; for I tell you, God is able from these stones to raise up children to Abraham. 9Even now the axe is laid to the root of the trees; every tree therefore that does not bear good fruit is cut down and thrown into the fire."

10And the multitudes asked him, "What then shall we do?" 11And he answered them, "He who has two coats, let him share with him who has none; and he who has food, let him do likewise." 12Tax collectors also came to be baptized, and said to him, "Teacher, what shall we do?" 13And he said to them, "Collect no more than is appointed you." 14Soldiers also asked him, "And we, what shall we do?" And he said to them, "Rob no one by violence or by false accusation, and be content with your wages."

15As the people were in expectation, and all men questioned in their hearts concerning John, whether perhaps he were the Christ, 16John answered them all, "I baptize you with water; but he who is mightier than I is coming, the thong of whose sandal I am not worthy to untie; he will baptize you with the Holy Spirit and with fire. 17His winnowing fork is in his hand, to clear his threshing floor, and to gather the wheat into his granary, but the chaff he will burn with unquenchable fire."

18So, with many other exhortations, he preached good news to the people.

---

his relationship with the coming Messiah (vv. 15–18) and his imprisonment (vv. 19–20). His account of the Baptist is given in the light of a passage from the book of Isaiah (Is 40:3–5). In that part of Isaiah the Jewish people are told that, after the exile in Babylon, there will be a new exodus and that they will have as guide not Moses but God himself; the people will make their way through the desert until they come to the new promised land.

The coming of the Lord is imminent; therefore people need to prepare their hearts, do penance for their sins, and change their lives in order to be able to receive the grace that the Messiah brings. For, salvation is not a matter of who you are, it is not something you get just because you are a son of Abraham (v. 8): it calls for a personal conversion which proves itself by deeds (vv. 11–14).

Finally, the Baptist stresses that he is not the Messiah, but that the Messiah is on the point of arriving and he will come endowed with the authority of supreme judge (that is, with authority such as only God has) and with a dignity such as no other man has: "Learn direct from John a lesson of humility. People take him for the Messiah, and he tells them he is not; it does not occur to him to use another's mistake to his own advantage. [...] He knows very well where their salvation lay; he knows that he was simply a lamp, and he wanted to ensure that the mind of pride did not put it out" (St Augustine, *Serm.,* 293, 3).

John the Baptist imprisoned

[19]But Herod the tetrarch, who had been reproved by him for Herodias, his brother's wife, and for all the evil things that Herod had done, [20]added this to them all, that he shut up John in prison.

Jesus is baptized Mt 3:13–17; Mk 1:9–11

[21]Now when all the people were baptized, and when Jesus also had been baptized and was praying, the heaven was opened, [22]and the Holy Spirit descended upon him in bodily form, as a dove, and a voice came from heaven, "Thou art my beloved Son;[j] with thee I am well pleased."[k]

The ancestry of Jesus Mt 1:1–17

[23]Jesus, when he began his ministry, was about thirty years of age, being the
son (as was supposed) of Joseph,* the son of Heli, [24]the son of Matthat, the son
of Levi, the son of Melchi, the son of Jannai, the son of Joseph, [25]the son of
Mattathias, the son of Amos, the son of Nahum, the son of Esli, the son of
Naggai, [26]the son of Maath, the son of Mattathias, the son of Semein, the son of
Josech, the son of Joda, [27]the son of Joanan, the son of Rhesa, the son of
Zerubbabel, the son of Shealtiel,[l] the son of Neri, [28]the son of Melchi, the son of
Addi, the son of Cosam, the son of Elmadam, the son of Er, [29]the son of Joshua,
the son of Eliezer, the son of Jorim, the son of Matthat, the son of Levi, [30]the son
of Simeon, the son of Judah, the son of Joseph, the son of Jonam, the son of
Eliakim, [31]the son of Melea, the son of Menna, the son of Mattatha, the son of
Nathan, the son of David, [32]the son of Jesse, the son of Obed, the son of Boaz, the
son of Sala, the son of Nahshon, [33]the son of Amminadab, the son of Admin, the

---

3:21–22 The Baptism of Jesus reveals the fact that he is the Son of God. This event, the Adoration by the Magi (Mt 2:11) and the first miracle which Jesus worked at the wedding in Cana (Jn 2:11) are the first three formal manifestations of Christ's divinity, as the liturgy reminds us on the feast of the Epiphany: "We venerate this holy day, lit up with three marvels: today, the star guides the Magi to the crib; today, the water is turned into wine at Cana; today, Christ was baptized by John in the Jordan in order to save us. Alleluia" (*Divine Office, Magnificat* antiphon, Second Vespers).

3:23–38 The genealogies given in Holy Scripture are not designed to be a detailed record of who a person's ancestors were; rather, what they show is that he belongs to a particular group (cf. the note on Mt 1:1–17). Whereas Matthew puts the accent on the messianic character of our Lord, Luke emphasizes his mission as Saviour of all mankind, and his priestly character. Following St Augustine, St Thomas sees Luke's genealogy as teaching us about Christ's priesthood: "St Luke narrates the genealogy of Christ in ascending order (after his baptism, not at the beginning [of

j. Or *my Son, my* (or *the*) *Beloved* **k.** Other ancient authorities read *today I have begotten thee*
l. Greek *Salathiel*

son of Arni, the son of Hezron, the son of Perez, the son of Judah, [34]the son of
Jacob, the son of Isaac, the son of Abraham, the son of Terah, the son of
Nahor, [35]the son of Serug, the son of Reu, the son of Peleg, the son of Eber, the
son of Shelah, [36]the son of Cainan, the son of Arphaxad, the son of Shem, the
son of Noah, the son of Lamech, [37]the son of Methuselah, the son of Enoch,
the son of Jared, the son of Mahalaleel, the son of Cainan, [38]the son of Enos,
the son of Seth, the son of Adam, the son of God.

Jesus fasts and is tempted in the wilderness Mt 4:1–11; Mk 1:12–13

4 [1]And Jesus, full of the Holy Spirit, returned from the Jordan, and was led by
the Spirit [2]for forty days in the wilderness, tempted by the devil. And he ate
nothing in those days; and when they were ended, he was hungry. [3]The devil said
to him, "If you are the Son of God, command this stone to become bread." [4]And
Jesus answered him, "It is written, 'Man shall not live by bread alone.'" [5]And the
devil took him up, and showed him all the kingdoms of the world in a moment of
time, [6]and said to him, "To you I will give all this authority and their glory; for
it has been delivered to me, and I give it to whom I will. [7]If you, then, will
worship me, it shall all be yours." [8]And Jesus answered him, "It is written,

'You shall worship the Lord your God,
and him only shall you serve.'"

[9]And he took him to Jerusalem, and set him on the pinnacle of the temple, and
said to him, "If you are the Son of God, throw yourself down from here; [10]for
it is written,

'He will give his angels charge of you, to guard you,'

[11]and

'On their hands they will bear you up,
lest you strike your foot against a stone.'"

[12]And Jesus answered him, "It is said, 'You shall not tempt the Lord your
God.'" [13]And when the devil had ended every temptation, he departed from
him until an opportune time.

---

his Gospel) in order to point out the Priest who takes away all sin at the same moment as John the Baptist bears witness to 'he who takes away the sins of the world'. The genealogy ascends from Abraham to God, with whom we are reconciled when we have become clean and purified" (*Summa theol.* 3, 31, 3 and 3).

4:1–13 At the start of his mission of salvation, our Lord is tempted by Satan (cf. the note on Mt 4:1–11). In the first temptation (vv. 3–4) the devil tests Jesus' divine filiation which God the Father has just proclaimed (cf. 3:22); in the second (vv. 5–8) Jesus is offered authority over the world provided he pays homage to Satan; in the third (vv. 9–12), the devil sets him on the pinnacle of the temple of Jerusalem and suggests that he throw himself off and use his power as Son of God to protect himself.

4:4 Deut 8:3. **4:8** Deut 6:13. **4:10–11** Ps 91:11–12. **4:12** Deut 6:16.

PART ONE: JESUS' MINISTRY IN GALILEE

3. THE START OF HIS MINISTRY IN GALILEE

14 And Jesus returned in the power of the Spirit into Galilee, and a report
concerning him went out through all the surrounding country.
15 And he taught
in their synagogues, being glorified by all.

Preaching in Nazareth

Mt 13:53–58; Mk 6:1–6

16 And he came to Nazareth, where he had been brought up; and he went to the
synagogue, as his custom was, on the sabbath day. *And he stood up to read;
17 and there was given to him the book of the prophet Isaiah. He opened the
book and found the place where it was written,

18 "The Spirit of the Lord is upon me,
because he has anointed me to preach good news to the poor.
He has sent me to proclaim release to the captives
and recovering of sight to the blind,
to set at liberty those who are oppressed,
19 to proclaim the acceptable year of the Lord."

Jesus defeats the devil here, as he will also do at "an opportune time" (v. 13), that is, in his passion and death (cf. the note on 22:1–6): his filial acceptance of the Father's plans will liberate men from the one who has the power of death, that is, the devil (cf. Heb 2:14). Jesus' victory over the tempter serves to encourage his disciples: if they trust in God, they will be able to defeat all temptation.

4:14–9:50 □□ In the first part of his Gospel Luke covers the beginnings of Jesus' public ministry in Galilee. The scene of Jesus in the synagogue of Nazareth (4:16–30) introduces his whole programme of action. The "today" of salvation (4:21), announced at this point, immediately takes effect with his miracle-working (4:38–41; 5:12–26; 7:1–23; 8:26–56, etc.), his forgiving of sins (5:17–26; 7:36–50), his acts of mercy (7:13; 9:11), etc.

The mission he has been given (4:18) is one of evangelizing. At the centre of his preaching we find the sermon on the mount (6:17–49) and the parables of the Kingdom (8:4–18). The evangelist likes to draw our attention to the power and uniqueness of Jesus' words (4:31–37; 5:17–26), which cause people to throng around him (4:37, 40, 42; 5:1, 15, 19, 29; etc.).

To put his plan of salvation into operation our Lord chooses disciples (5:1–11, 27–32; 6:12–16), and from them he selects the group of the twelve apostles. He gives special attention to training the apostles (8:10; 9:21; etc.); he reveals his glory to them (9:28–36) and sends them out to preach (9:1–6), on a mission which anticipates the world-wide mission of the Church (Acts 1:8).

4:18–19 Is 61:1–2.

[20]And he closed the book, and gave it back to the attendant, and sat down; and the
eyes of all in the synagogue were fixed on him. [21]And he began to say to them,
"Today this scripture has been fulfilled in your hearing." [22]And all spoke well of
him, and wondered at the gracious words which proceeded out of his mouth; and
they said, "Is not this Joseph's son?" [23]And he said to them, "Doubtless you will
quote to me this proverb, 'Physician, heal yourself; what we have heard you did
at Capernaum, do here also in your own country.'" [24]And he said, "Truly, I say to
you, no prophet is acceptable in his own country. [25]But in truth, I tell you, there
were many widows in Israel in the days of Elijah, when the heaven was shut up
three years and six months, when there came a great famine over all the land;
[26]and Elijah was sent to none of them but only to Zarephath, in the land of Sidon,
to a woman who was a widow. [27]And there were many lepers in Israel in the time
of the prophet Elisha; and none of them was cleansed, but only Naaman the
Syrian." [28]When they heard this, all in the synagogue were filled with wrath.
[29]And they rose up and put him out of the city, and led him to the brow of the hill
on which their city was built, that they might throw him down headlong. [30]But
passing through the midst of them he went away.

Finally, Jesus' discourse in the synagogue of Nazareth also includes reference to the universality of this mission of salvation (4:25–27), a universality which can also be seen in the episode of the centurion (7:1–10) but which will be the central theme of the next part of the Gospel (9:51–19:27).

4:14–6:11 □ The beginnings of Jesus' ministry include his preaching in the synagogues of Galilee (4:14–15) and Judea (4:44). Jesus' preaching will be remarkable for the authority with which he speaks (4:32), and his fame will keep spreading (5:15). It is no wonder that the representatives of official Judaism take issue with him (5:27–6:11).

4:14–30 The Holy Spirit was actively involved in Jesus' birth and infancy as reported in this Gospel, and now it is he who guides Jesus' ministry: after descending on him at his Baptism (3:22), he leads him into the wilderness (4:1) and empowers him for his mission in Galilee (v. 14).

In the synagogue of Nazareth Jesus reads Isaiah 61:1–2, where the prophet announces the coming of the Lord who will free his people from their afflictions: "These words of St Luke make up the *first messianic declaration*, from which flow the acts and words known in the Gospel. Through those words and works, Christ makes his Father present among men" (John Paul II, *Div. in mis.*, 3). Our Lord extends the meaning of the passage by asserting that the prophecy is fulfilled in him (v. 21). The message of salvation is nothing other than himself: "Since he is the 'Good News', there is a complete identity of message and messenger in Christ, an identity of saying, acting and being" (John Paul II, *Redempt. miss.*, 13). Also, his own countrymen reject him because he depicts himself as the Messiah—the first of many ways in which Jesus will suffer at the hands of his people.

In the synagogue in Capernaum Mk 1:21–28

31And he went down to Capernaum, a city of Galilee. And he was teaching
them on the sabbath; 32and they were astonished at his teaching, for his word
was with authority. 33And in the synagogue there was a man who had the spirit
of an unclean demon; and he cried out with a loud voice, 34"Ah![m] What have
you to do with us, Jesus of Nazareth? Have you come to destroy us? I know
who you are, the Holy One of God." 35But Jesus rebuked him, saying, "Be
silent, and come out of him!" And when the demon had thrown him down in
the midst, he came out of him, having done him no harm. 36And they were all
amazed and said to one another, "What is this word? For with authority and
power he commands the unclean spirits, and they come out." 37And reports of
him went out into every place in the surrounding region.

Curing of Peter's mother-in-law Mt 8:14–15; Mk 1:29–31

38And he arose and left the synagogue, and entered Simon's house. Now
Simon's mother-in-law was ill with a high fever, and they besought him for her.
39And he stood over her and rebuked the fever, and it left her; and immediately
she rose and served them.

Other cures Mt 8:16–17; Mk 1:32–34

40Now when the sun was setting, all those who had any that were sick with
various diseases brought them to him; and he laid his hands on every one of
them and healed them. 41And demons also came out of many, crying, "You are
the Son of God!" But he rebuked them, and would not allow them to speak,
because they knew that he was the Christ.

4:31–37 Even at this early stage in Jesus' preaching there are two things that impress his listeners: his words are accompanied by works which show his authority (v. 32) and they are able to work wonders (v. 35). These are the qualities that the Word of God has in the Old Testament, where we find God confirming his word by deeds (cf. Ex 19:3–6) and by his word calling things into existence (Gen 1:3ff).

4:38–41 All three Synoptic Gospels report the curing of Peter's mother-in-law immediately after other cures worked by Jesus on the same afternoon. Luke is the only one to refer to the disciples' petition (v. 38) and the compassion our Lord shows by "laying his hands on every one" (v. 40): "When the sick asked our Lord to cure them, he immediately did; he gives us to understand that he awaits the prayers of the faithful to heal the sufferings brought about by our sins" (St Jerome, in *Cat. aurea*, in loc.).

m. Or *Let us alone*

Jesus preaches in other cities in Judea Mk 1:35–39

42And when it was day he departed and went into a lonely place. And the
people sought him and came to him, and would have kept him from leaving
them; 43but he said to them, "I must preach the good news of the kingdom of
God to the other cities also; for I was sent for this purpose." 44And he was
preaching in the synagogues of Judea.[n]

The miraculous catch of fish and the calling of the first disciples Mt 4:18–25; Mk 1:16–20; Jn 1:35–51

5 1While the people pressed upon him to hear the word of God, he was
standing by the lake of Gennesaret. 2And he saw two boats by the lake; but
the fishermen had gone out of them and were washing their nets. 3Getting into
one of the boats, which was Simon's, he asked him to put out a little from the
land. And he sat down and taught the people from the boat. 4And when he had
ceased speaking, he said to Simon, "Put out into the deep and let down your
nets for a catch." 5And Simon answered, "Master, we toiled all night and took
nothing! But at your word I will let down the nets." 6And when they had done
this, they enclosed a great shoal of fish; and as their nets were breaking, 7they

---

4:42–44 As in many other places (cf. Lk 5:1, 15, 19, 29 etc.) the evangelist notes that huge crowds of people felt a desire to be with Jesus and hear his teaching. "Nobody can have all his desires satisfied in this life; no created thing can satisfy man's desire: God can satisfy in abundance, unto infinity" (St Thomas Aquinas, *On the Creed,* 12, 1012).

5:1–11 St Luke's account of the calling of Peter and the first disciples is slightly different from that of the other Gospels (cf. Mt 4:18–25; Mk 1:16–20; Jn 1:35–51). They are called early on in Christ's public life and all four Gospels show that it is a pressing call and that the disciples respond without delay. Luke shows very clearly the special relationship between Jesus and Peter (the dialogue which follows is between the two of them: cf. vv 3, 4, 5, 8, 10) for it will be Peter who will later be the captain of the boat of the Church. "Before becoming apostles, we are fishermen. After becoming apostles, we are fishermen still. The same profession, before and after. What has changed? There is a change inside our soul, now that Christ has come aboard, as he went aboard Peter's boat. Its horizon has opened wider. It feels a greater ambition to serve and an irrepressible desire to tell all creation about the *magnalia Dei* (Acts 2:11), the marvellous doings of our Lord, if only we let him work" (Bl. J. Escrivá, *Hom.*, 2, 264–5).

This scene gives us a glimpse of the future mission of the Church: when working on their own account the disciples will grow weary and fail to produce results (cf. v. 5); but when they work for Christ, the fruit will be out of all proportion to their efforts (cf. 6, 10).

n. Other ancient authorities read *Galilee*

beckoned to their partners in the other boat to come and help them. And they
came and filled both the boats, so that they began to sink. [8]But when Simon
Peter saw it, he fell down at Jesus' knees, saying, "Depart from me, for I am a
sinful man, O Lord." [9]For he was astonished, and all that were with him, at the
catch of fish which they had taken; [10]and so also were James and John, sons of
Zebedee, who were partners with Simon. And Jesus said to Simon, "Do not be
afraid; henceforth you will be catching men." [11]And when they had brought
their boats to land, they left everything and followed him.

Curing of a leper Mt 8:1–4; Mk 1:40–45

[12]While he was in one of the cities, there came a man full of leprosy; and when
he saw Jesus, he fell on his face and besought him, "Lord, if you will, you can
make me clean." [13]And he stretched out his hand, and touched him, saying, "I
will; be clean." And immediately the leprosy left him. [14]And he charged him
to tell no one; but "go and show yourself to the priest, and make an offering
for your cleansing, as Moses commanded, for a proof to the people."[o] [15]But so
much the more the report went abroad concerning him; and great multitudes
gathered to hear and to be healed of their infirmities. [16]But he withdrew to the
wilderness and prayed.

Curing of a paralyzed man Mt 9:1–8; Mk 2:1–12

[17]On one of those days, as he was teaching, there were Pharisees and teachers
of the law sitting by, who had come from every village of Galilee and Judea
and from Jerusalem; and the power of the Lord was with him to heal.[p] [18]And
behold, men were bringing on a bed a man who was paralyzed, and they
sought to bring him in and lay him before Jesus;[q] [19]but finding no way to bring
him in, because of the crowd, they went up on the roof and let him down with
his bed through the tiles into the midst before Jesus. [20]And when he saw their
faith he said, "Man, your sins are forgiven you." [21]And the scribes and the
Pharisees began to question, saying, "Who is this that speaks blasphemies? Who
can forgive sins but God only?" [22]When Jesus perceived their questionings, he

---

5:12–16 The ways that people in the Gospel address Jesus can often help us in our approach through prayer: "Jesus hears the prayer of faith, expressed in words [...] or in silence [...]. Healing infirmities or forgiving sins, Jesus always responds to a prayer offered in faith: 'Your faith has made you well; go in peace'" (*CCC*, 2616).

5:17–26 This miracle shows clearly that Jesus' authority on earth and the power of his word (v. 24) have a higher source (v. 17). The passage also teaches that the Lord rewards the faith of the paralytic's friends (v. 20): "How great is the Lord: through the merits of some he forgives others; and he praises the former, he forgives the latter" (St Ambrose, *Com. on Lk,* in loc.).

o. Greek *to them* **p.** Other ancient authorities read *was present to heal them* **q.** Greek *him* answered them, "Why do you question in your hearts? [23]Which is easier, to say, 'Your sins are forgiven you,' or to say, 'Rise and walk'? [24]But that you may know that the Son of man has authority on earth to forgive sins"—he said to the man who was paralyzed—"I say to you, rise, take up your bed and go home." [25]And immediately he rose before them, and took up that on which he lay, and went home, glorifying God. [26]And amazement seized them all, and they glorified God and were filled with awe, saying, "We have seen strange things today."

The calling of Matthew Mt 9:9–13; Mk 2:13–17

[27]After this he went out, and saw a tax collector, named Levi, sitting at the tax office; and he said to him, "Follow me." [28]And he left everything, and rose and followed him.

[29]And Levi made him a great feast in his house; and there was a large company of tax collectors and others sitting at table[r] with them. [30]And the Pharisees and their scribes murmured against his disciples, saying, "Why do you eat and drink with tax collectors and sinners?" [31]And Jesus answered them, "Those who are well have no need of a physician, but those who are sick; [32]I have not come to call the righteous, but sinners to repentance."

A discussion on fasting Mt 9:14–17; Mk 2:18–22

[33]And they said to him, "The disciples of John fast often and offer prayers, and so do the disciples of the Pharisees, but yours eat and drink." [34]And Jesus said to them, "Can you make wedding guests fast while the bridegroom is with them? [35]The days will come, when the bridegroom is taken away from them, and then they will fast in those days." [36]He told them a parable also: "No one tears a piece from a new garment and puts it upon an old garment; if he does, he will tear the new, and the piece from the new will not match the old. [37]And no one puts new wine into old wineskins; if he does, the new wine will burst the skins and it will be spilled, and the skins will be destroyed. [38]But new wine must be put into fresh wineskins. [39]And no one after drinking old wine desires new; for he says, 'The old is good.'"[s]

5:27–32 In this episode we can see something which is often reflected in Christ's life and that of the Church—the fact that Christ calls people irrespective of any merit they may have, and that the call should be responded to gratefully (v. 29), generously and promptly (v. 28; cf. 5:11).

5:33–39 The criticism made by the scribes and Pharisees gives Jesus an opportunity to say something about his own status and the scope of his teaching: his presence in the world is such a joyful thing that a penitential practice like fasting (vv. 34–35) can be left aside for later. His teaching calls for more profound interior penance, a renewal (v. 36–38); if someone gives it that reception, he will find it is like a mature wine

r. Greek *reclining* **s.** Other ancient authorities read *better*

The law of the sabbath

Mt 12:1–8; Mk 2:23–28

6 [1]On a sabbath,[t] while he was going through the grainfields, his disciples
plucked and ate some ears of grain, rubbing them in their hands. [2]But
some of the Pharisees said, "Why are you doing what is not lawful to do on the
sabbath?" [3]And Jesus answered, "Have you not read what David did when he
was hungry, he and those who were with him: [4]how he entered the house of
God, and took and ate the bread of the Presence, which it is not lawful for any
but the priests to eat, and also gave it to those with him?" [5]And he said to
them, "The Son of man is lord of the sabbath."

Curing of a man with a withered hand

Mt 12:9–14; Mk 3:1–6

[6]On another sabbath, when he entered the synagogue and taught, a man was there
whose right hand was withered. [7]And the scribes and the Pharisees watched him,
to see whether he would heal on the sabbath, so that they might find an accusation
against him. [8]But he knew their thoughts, and he said to the man who had the
withered hand, "Come and stand here." And he rose and stood there. [9]And Jesus
said to them, "I ask you, is it lawful on the sabbath to do good or to do harm, to
save life or to destroy it?" [10]And he looked around on them all, and said to him,
"Stretch out your hand." And he did so, and his hand was restored. [11]But they
were filled with fury and discussed with one another what they might do to Jesus.

(v. 39) and will have no desire to return to his previous lifestyle. But our Lord does not do away with fasting (cf. v. 35); he simply gives it more meaning: "The merit of our fasting does not derive solely from denying ourselves food; denying the body its nutrition is of no value if the soul does not give up iniquity and if the tongue does not cease to speak evil" (St Leo the Great, *Serm. 4 de Quadrag.*, 2).

6:1–11 In these two controversies about the sabbath, Jesus manifests his divine authority and power and teaches the true meaning of sabbath rest (cf. the notes on Mt 12:1–14; Mk 2:23–28; 3:1–6). But the scribes and Pharisees persist in their blindness (v. 11): "O Pharisee! You see the one who performs marvellous deeds and cures the sick by his superior power and you plot his death through envy!" (St Cyril, in *Cat. aurea.*, in loc.).

6:12–8:56 □ The establishment of the "college" of apostles marks the start of a new section of the Gospel. The apostles accompany Jesus on his mission in Galilee, a mission which involves preaching—especially to be seen in the sermon on the mount (6:17–49) and his parables discourse (8:4–18)—and Jesus' working of miracles. Luke reports practically the same miracles as the other two Synoptics, but only he narrates the miracle of the raising of the son of the widow of Nain, which our Lord works out of compassion (7:13), the virtue which sums up the teaching of the sermon on the mount (6:36).

t. Other ancient authorities read *On the second first sabbath* (on the second sabbath after the first)

4. JESUS' MIRACLES AND PREACHING IN GALILEE

Jesus chooses twelve apostles Mt 10:1–4; Mk 3:13–19

12In these days he went out into the hills to pray; and all night he continued in
prayer to God. 13And when it was day, he called his disciples, and chose from
them twelve, whom he named apostles: 14Simon, whom he named Peter, and
Andrew his brother, and James and John, and Philip and Bartholomew, 15and
Matthew, and Thomas, and James the son of Alphaeus, and Simon who was
called the Zealot, 16and Judas the son of James, and Judas Iscariot, who became
a traitor.

Preaching on the plain

17And he came down with them and stood on a level place, with a great crowd
of his disciples and a great multitude of people from all Judea and Jerusalem
and the sea coast of Tyre and Sidon, who came to hear him and to be healed of
their diseases; 18and those who were troubled with unclean spirits were cured.
19And all the crowd sought to touch him, for power came forth from him and
healed them all.

6:12–16 As on other occasions (9:28; 22:39; etc.), the evangelist records that Jesus prays in advance of an important event (v. 12). Our Lord will then proceed to establish the group of the twelve apostles. The choice of twelve, who are given the special title of apostles (v. 13), as also other snippets of information provided by the other Gospels (cf. the notes on Mt 10:1–4; Mk 3:13–19), points to Jesus' work being given continuity in the form of his Church. Jesus has been sent by the Father, and he gives the apostles a role in his mission: "That divine mission, which was committed by Christ to the apostles, is destined to last until the end of the world since the Gospel, which they were charged to hand on, is, for the Church, the principle of all its life for all time. For that very reason the apostles were careful to appoint successors in this hierarchically constituted society" (Vatican II, *LG*, 20).

6:17–19 At this point a discourse begins which is equivalent to, but much shorter than, the sermon on the mount in St Matthew (Mt 5:1–7:29). By recording that Jesus used to preach in level places easily accessible to the crowd, St Luke shows how close our Lord was to the people, and the fact that his message was addressed to everyone.

Apropos of the different "editions" of this sermon, one needs to remember that "The sacred authors, in writing the four Gospels, selected certain of the many elements which had been handed on, either orally or already in written form, others they synthesized or explained with an eye to the situation of the churches, the while sustaining the form of preaching, but always in such a fashion that they have told us the honest truth about Jesus" (Vatican II, *DV*, 19). In Luke's text we can distinguish

The Beatitudes and the woes Mt 5:1–12

20 And he lifted up his eyes on his disciples, and said:*
"Blessed are you poor, for yours is the kingdom of God.
21 "Blessed are you that hunger now, for you shall be satisfied.
"Blessed are you that weep now, for you shall laugh.
22 "Blessed are you when men hate you, and when they exclude you and
revile you, and cast out your name as evil, on account of the Son of man!
23 Rejoice in that day, and leap for joy, for behold, your reward is great in
heaven; for so their fathers did to the prophets.
24 "But woe to you that are rich, for you have received your consolation.
25 "Woe to you that are full now, for you shall hunger.
"Woe to you that laugh now, for you shall mourn and weep.
26 "Woe to you, when all men speak well of you, for so their fathers did to
the false prophets.

Love of enemies Mt 5:38–48

27 "But I say to you that hear, Love your enemies, do good to those who hate
you, 28 bless those who curse you, pray for those who abuse you. 29 To him who
strikes you on the cheek, offer the other also; and from him who takes away

---

three parts—the beatitudes and the woes (vv. 20–26), verses dealing with love for enemies (vv. 27–38), and teaching about integrity (vv. 39–49).

6:20–26 The eight beatitudes of the first Gospel (cf. Mt 5:3–12) are summed up in four by St Luke, but with four opposing woes. In both instances "The beatitude we are promised confronts us with decisive moral choices. It invites us to purify our hearts of bad instincts and to seek the love of God above all else. It teaches us that true happiness is not found in riches or well-being, in human fame or power, or in any human achievement—however beneficial it may be—such as science, technology and art, or indeed in any creature, but in God alone, the source of every good and of all love" (*CCC*, 1723).

6:27–38 These words, which here run on from the beatitudes, really contain the core of Jesus' teaching on the love and compassion that Christians should show others. Over the course of his life, and particularly through his death (cf. 23:34), Jesus himself set us an example to follow.

In the opening verses (27–30), our Lord lists various types of insult and how to deal with them. The Semitic style, which is very fond of contrasts, puts the focus on the teaching summarized in v. 31: "As you wish that men would do to you, do so to them". Verses 32–34 prepare the way for what our Lord says about the true motivation for that policy: that way of behaving befits a son of God who wants to copy his merciful Father (v. 36). Finally, Jesus' invitation to generosity (vv. 37–38) rounds off the idea of a reward in the next life, hinted at in v. 35.

your cloak do not withhold your coat as well. [30]Give to every one who begs
from you; and of him who takes away your goods do not ask them again.
[31]And as you wish that men would do to you, do so to them.

[32]"If you love those who love you, what credit is that to you? For even
sinners love those who love them. [33]And if you do good to those who do good
to you, what credit is that to you? For even sinners do the same. [34]And if you
lend to those from whom you hope to receive, what credit is that to you? Even
sinners lend to sinners, to receive as much again. [35]But love your enemies, and
do good, and lend, expecting nothing in return;[v] and your reward will be great,
and you will be sons of the Most High; for he is kind to the ungrateful and the
selfish. [36]Be merciful, even as your Father is merciful.

[37]"Judge not, and you will not be judged; condemn not, and you will not be
condemned; forgive, and you will be forgiven; [38]give, and it will be given to
you; good measure, pressed down, shaken together, running over, will be put
into your lap. For the measure you give will be the measure you get back."

Integrity Mt 7:1–5; 15–20; 24–27

[39]He also told them a parable: "Can a blind man lead a blind man? Will they
not both fall into a pit? [40]A disciple is not above his teacher, but every one
when he is fully taught will be like his teacher. [41]Why do you see the speck
that is in your brother's eye, but do not noticc the log that is in your own eye?
[42]Or how can you say to your brother, 'Brother, let me take out the speck that
is in your eye,' when you yourself do not see the log that is in your own eye?
You hypocrite, first take the log out of your own eye, and then you will see
clearly to take out the speck that is in your brother's eye.

[43]"For no good tree bears bad fruit, nor again does a bad tree bear good
fruit; [44]for each tree is known by its own fruit. For figs are not gathered from
thorns, nor are grapes picked from a bramble bush. [45]The good man out of the
good treasure of his heart produces good, and the evil man out of his evil
treasure produces evil; for out of the abundance of the heart his mouth speaks.

[46]"Why do you call me 'Lord, Lord,' and not do what I tell you? [47]Every
one who comes to me and hears my words and does them, I will show you
what he is like: [48]he is like a man building a house, who dug deep, and laid the
foundation upon rock; and when a flood arose, the stream broke against that
house, and could not shake it, because it had been well built.[w] [49]But he who

---

6:39–49 The discourse ends with a series of teachings which have a common denominator: external expressions of piety or virtue are not what matters, but rather one's inner disposition. "It is not a question of practising our religion or not, but rather of trying to practise the virtues and make our will conform to his so that the totality of our life is as His Majesty ordains; we want to do his will, not ours" (St Teresa of Avila, *Interior Castle*, 3, 2, 6).

v. Other ancient authorities read *despairing of no man* **w.** Other ancient authorities read *founded upon the rock* hears and does not do them is like a man who built a house on the ground without a foundation; against which the stream broke, and immediately it fell, and the ruin of that house was great."

The centurion's faith Mt 8:5–13; Jn 4:46–54

7 [1]After he had ended all his sayings in the hearing of the people he entered Capernaum. [2]Now a centurion had a slave who was dear[x] to him, who was sick and at the point of death. [3]When he heard of Jesus, he sent to him elders of the Jews, asking him to come and heal his slave. [4]And when they came to Jesus, they besought him earnestly, saying, "He is worthy to have you do this for him, [5]for he loves our nation, and he built us our synagogue." [6]And Jesus went with them. When he was not far from the house, the centurion sent friends to him, saying to him, "Lord, do not trouble yourself, for I am not worthy to have you come under my roof; [7]therefore I did not presume to come to you. But say the word, and let my servant be healed. [8]For I am a man set under authority, with soldiers under me: and I say to one, 'Go,' and he goes; and to another, 'Come,' and he comes; and to my slave, 'Do this,' and he does it." [9]When Jesus heard this he marvelled at him, and turned and said to the multitude that followed him, "I tell you, not even in Israel have I found such faith." [10]And when those who had been sent returned to the house, they found the slave well.

The son of the widow of Nain restored to life

[11]Soon afterward[y] he went to a city called Nain, and his disciples and a great crowd went with him. [12]As he drew near to the gate of the city, behold, a man who had died was being carried out, the only son of his mother, and she was a widow; and a large crowd from the city was with her. [13]And when the Lord saw her, he had compassion on her and said to her, "Do not weep." [14]And he came and touched the bier, and the bearers stood still. And he said, "Young man, I say to you, arise." [15]And the dead man sat up, and began to speak. And he gave him to his mother. [16]Fear seized them all; and they glorified God, saying, "A great prophet has arisen among us!" and "God has visited his

---

7:1–10 This episode is a very good example of the faith and humility needed in one's approach to Jesus. The account contrasts the praise given the centurion by the elders ("He is worthy to have you do this for him": v. 4) with the man's own sense of unworthiness (vv. 6–7); also, the faith of this Roman official, which he had already shown (v. 5), is now seen as nothing less than remarkable (vv. 8–9). The Church's liturgy uses the centurion's very words to express our own feelings just before receiving Communion, to help us have similar dispositions.

7:11–17 The third Gospel continually highlights God's mercy towards the needy, and the duty we all have to be compassionate towards one another (1;50, 54, 72,

x. Or *valuable* **y.** Other ancient authorities read *Next day* people!" [17]And this report concerning him spread through the whole of Judea and all the surrounding country.

Messengers from John the Baptist Mt 11:1–15

[18]The disciples of John told him of all these things. [19]And John, calling to him
two of his disciples, sent them to the Lord, saying, "Are you he who is to
come, or shall we look for another?" [20]And when the men had come to him,
they said, "John the Baptist has sent us to you, saying, 'Are you he who is to
come, or shall we look for another?'" [21]In that hour he cured many of diseases
and plagues and evil spirits, and on many that were blind he bestowed sight.
[22]And he answered them, "Go and tell John what you have seen and heard: the
blind receive their sight, the lame walk, lepers are cleansed, and the deaf hear,
the dead are raised up, the poor have good news preached to them. [23]And
blessed is he who takes no offence at me."

[24]When the messengers of John had gone, he began to speak to the crowds
concerning John: "What did you go out into the wilderness to behold? A reed
shaken by the wind? [25]What then did you go out to see? A man clothed in soft
raiment? Behold, those who are gorgeously apparelled and live in luxury are
in kings' courts. [26]What then did you go out to see? A prophet? Yes, I tell you,
and more than a prophet. [27]This is he of whom it is written,

> 'Behold, I send my messenger before thy face,
> who shall prepare thy way before thee.'

[28]I tell you, among those born of women none is greater than John; yet he who
is least in the kingdom of God is greater than he."* [29](When they heard this all
the people and the tax collectors justified God, having been baptized with the
baptism of John; [30]but the Pharisees and the lawyers rejected the purpose of
God for themselves, not having been baptized by him.)

78; 6:36; 10:33, 37; 15:20; etc.). Here, in a miracle which St Luke is the only one to report, Jesus' compassion towards those in pain is recorded. "[Christ] is the definitive incarnation of mercy, its living sign" (John Paul II, *Div. in mis.*, 8).

Having witnessed a miracle so similar to those worked by Elijah and Eliseus (cf. 1 Kings 17:17–24; 2 Kings 4:18–37), the people take Jesus to be a prophet. The text immediately goes on to show that St John the Baptist (cf. 7:18–19) senses (and St Peter later professes; cf. 9:20) that Jesus is much more than a prophet: he is the Messiah sent by God.

7:18–35 In his reply to John's disciples, Jesus shows that he is the promised Messiah, because he works the signs which the Old Testament associates with the messianic times (cf. the notes on Mt 11:1–15; Mk 7:31–37). He then goes on (vv. 24–30) to explain just how great a figure the Baptist is. He is great by reason of his lifestyle (vv. 24–25), but, above all, on account of his unique mission of coming

7:22 Is 29: 18–19; 35:5–6; 61:1. **7:27** Mal 3:1.

Jesus reproaches his contemporaries Mt 11:16–19

31"To what then shall I compare the men of this generation, and what are they
like? 32They are like children sitting in the market place and calling to one
another,

'We piped to you, and you did not dance;
we wailed, and you did not weep.'

33For John the Baptist has come eating no bread and drinking no wine; and
you say, 'He has a demon.' 34The Son of man has come eating and drinking;
and you say, 'Behold, a glutton and a drunkard, a friend of tax collectors and
sinners!' 35Yet wisdom is justified by all her children."

Forgiveness for a sinful woman

36One of the Pharisees asked him to eat with him, and he went into the
Pharisee's house, and sat at table. 37And behold, a woman of the city, who was
a sinner, when she learned that he was sitting at table in the Pharisee's house,
brought an alabaster flask of ointment, 38and standing behind him at his feet,
weeping, she began to wet his feet with her tears; and wiped them with the hair
of her head, and kissed his feet, and anointed them with the ointment. 39Now
when the Pharisee who had invited him saw it, he said to himself, "If this man
were a prophet, he would have known who and what sort of woman this is
who is touching him, for she is a sinner." 40And Jesus answering said to him,

---

directly before Christ (vv. 26–27). Still, he belongs to the time of the promise; now that that promise has found fulfilment in Jesus Christ, the gift of the Kingdom, that is, the divine filiation a person receives in Christ, is greater than the gift that John received (vv. 28–29).

Finally, Jesus compares the reception John's message got from the Pharisees and lawyers with the way his own message is received. The call to penance issued by the Baptist was accepted by the people and the tax collectors (cf. v. 29), but not by the Pharisees and teachers of the Law: this meant that they rejected God's plans for them (cf. v. 30). In vv. 31–35 Jesus implies that the same fate awaits his own message of salvation.

7:36–50 This scene gives a very good idea of Jesus' teaching method. It involves two subjects—Jesus' divinity, and the connexion between forgiveness and love. The account begins by introducing the characters and setting the scene. Simon sees Jesus as a teacher (v. 40) but doubts that he is a prophet (v. 39). However, Jesus shows him that he can divine things which are hidden—what Simon is thinking, and the woman's background. Therefore, the Pharisee should not be surprised (as some were: v. 49) that Jesus forgives sins, something only God can do. Our Lord uses the occasion to show the connexion between forgiveness and love. The key words come in v. 47 with its literary inversion: to someone who loves, much is forgiven; and, vice versa, a person to whom much is forgiven, loves much. "What

"Simon, I have something to say to you." And he answered, "What is it,
Teacher?" 41"A certain creditor had two debtors; one owed five hundred
denarii, and the other fifty. 42When they could not pay, he forgave them both.
Now which of them will love him more?" 43Simon answered, "The one, I
suppose, to whom he forgave more." And he said to him, "You have judged
rightly." 44Then turning toward the woman he said to Simon, "Do you see this
woman? I entered your house, you gave me no water for my feet, but she has
wet my feet with her tears and wiped them with her hair. 45You gave me no
kiss, but from the time I came in she has not ceased to kiss my feet. 46You did
not anoint my head with oil, but she has anointed my feet with ointment.
47Therefore I tell you, her sins, which are many, are forgiven, for she loved
much; but he who is forgiven little, loves little."* 48And he said to her, "Your
sins are forgiven." 49Then those who were at table with him began to say
among themselves, "Who is this, who even forgives sins?" 50And he said to the
woman, "Your faith has saved you; go in peace."

The holy women

8 1Soon afterward he went on through cities and villages, preaching and
bringing the good news of the kingdom of God. And the twelve were with
him, 2and also some women who had been healed of evil spirits and
infirmities: Mary, called Magdalene, from whom seven demons had gone out,
3and Joanna, the wife of Chuza, Herod's steward, and Susanna, and many
others, who provided for them[s] out of their means.

Parable of the sower. The meaning of parables Mt 13:1–23; Mk 4:1–20

4And when a great crowd came together and people from town after town
came to him, he said in a parable: 5"A sower went out to sow his seed; and as

---

the Lord appreciates is not the ointment but the affection; he is thankful for faith and praises humility. And you also, if you desire grace, must increase in love; pour out over the body of Christ your faith in the resurrection, the perfume of the holy Church and the balm of fraternal charity" (St Ambrose, *Com. on Lk*, in loc.).

8:1–3 By their dedication and the help they give our Lord, these women (cf. v. 3) cooperate in the apostolate of preaching the Kingdom of God (v. 1). Luke is the only evangelist to report on this and he gives the names of three of the women—Mary Magdalene, the first witness of the resurrection (Jn 20:11–18; Mk 16:9), Joanna, a well-to-do lady and also a witness of the resurrection (24;10), and Susanna, of whom this is the only mention.

8:4–18 The Synoptic Gospels record how Jesus preached in parables. The first two (cf. Mt 13:1–52; Mk 4:1–34) give the "parables of the Kingdom" all together in one long discourse. St Luke here summarizes the content of that whole

s. Other ancient authorities read *him*.

he sowed, some fell along the path, and was trodden under foot, and the birds
of the air devoured it. [6]And some fell on the rock; and as it grew up, it
withered away, because it had no moisture. [7]And some fell among thorns; and
the thorns grew with it and choked it. [8]And some fell into good soil and grew,
and yielded a hundredfold." As he said this, he called out, "He who has ears to
hear, let him hear."

[9]And when his disciples asked him what this parable meant, [10]he said, "To
you it has been given to know the secrets of the kingdom of God; but for
others they are in parables, so that seeing they may not see, and hearing they
may not understand. [11]Now the parable is this: The seed is the word of God.
[12]The ones along the path are those who have heard; then the devil comes and
takes away the word from their hearts, that they may not believe and be saved.
[13]And the ones on the rock are those who, when they hear the word, receive
it with joy; but these have no root, they believe for a while and in time of
temptation fall away. [14]And as for what fell among the thorns, they are those
who hear, but as they go on their way they are choked by the cares and riches
and pleasures of life, and their fruit does not mature. [15]And as for that in the
good soil, they are those who, hearing the word, hold it fast in an honest and
good heart, and bring forth fruit with patience.

Parable of the lamp Mk 4:21–25

[16]"No one after lighting a lamp covers it with a vessel, or puts it under a bed,
but puts it on a stand, that those who enter may see the light. [17]For nothing is
hid that shall not be made manifest, nor anything secret that shall not be
known and come to light. [18]Take heed then how you hear; for to him who has
will more be given, and from him who has not, even what he thinks that he has
will be taken away."

The true kinsmen of Jesus Mt 12:46–50; Mk 3:31–35; Lk 11:27–28

[19]Then his mother and his brethren* came to him, but they could not reach him
for the crowd. [20]And he was told, "Your mother and your brethren are standing

---

discourse; but he mentions that Jesus often used parables in his teaching (cf. 7:36–50; 10:25–37; 11:5–13; 12:13–21; etc.).

On the meaning of these parables, see the notes on Mt 13:1–52 and Mk 4:1–34.

8:19–21 What Jesus says here shows the role faith plays in the new order of things that Jesus has established by coming into the world. For Jesus and for the reader of Luke's Gospel (cf. 1:38) these words apply first and foremost to Mary, a model of faith. "Throughout her life and until her last ordeal when Jesus her son died on the cross, Mary's faith never wavered. She never ceased to believe in the fulfilment of God's word. And so the Church venerates in Mary the purest realization of faith" (*CCC*, 149).

8:10 Is 6:9–10.

outside, desiring to see you." [21]But he said to them, "My mother and my brethren are those who hear the word of God and do it."

The calming of the storm Mt 8:23–27; Mk 4:35–41

[22]One day he got into a boat with his disciples and he said to them, "Let us go across to the other side of the lake." So they set out, [23]and as they sailed he fell asleep. And a storm of wind came down on the lake, and they were filling with water, and were in danger. [24]And they went and woke him, saying, "Master, Master, we are perishing!" And he awoke and rebuked the wind and the raging waves; and they ceased, and there was a calm. [25]He said to them, "Where is your faith?" And they were afraid, and they marvelled, saying to one another, "Who then is this, that he commands even wind and water, and they obey him?"

The Gerasene demoniac Mt 8:28–34; Mk 5:1–20

[26]Then they arrived at the country of the Gerasenes,[a] which is opposite Galilee. [27]And as he stepped out on land, there met him a man from the city who had demons; for a long time he had worn no clothes, and he lived not in a house but among the tombs. [28]When he saw Jesus, he cried out and fell down before him, and said with a loud voice, "What have you to do with me, Jesus, Son of the Most High God? I beseech you, do not torment me." [29]For he had commanded the unclean spirit to come out of the man. (For many a time it had seized him; he was kept under guard, and bound with chains and fetters, but he broke the bonds and was driven by the demon into the desert.) [30]Jesus then asked him, "What is your name?" And he said, "Legion"; for many demons had entered him. [31]And they begged him not to command them to depart into the abyss. [32]Now a large herd of swine was feeding there on the hillside; and they begged him to let them enter these. So he gave them leave. [33]Then the demons came out of the man and entered the swine, and the herd rushed down the steep bank into the lake and were drowned.

[34]When the herdsmen saw what had happened, they fled, and told it in the city and in the country. [35]Then people went out to see what had happened, and they came to Jesus, and found the man from whom the demons had gone, sitting at the feet of Jesus, clothed and in his right mind; and they were afraid. [36]And those who had seen it told them how he who had been possessed with demons was healed. [37]Then all the people of the surrounding country of the Gerasenes[a] asked him to depart from them; for they were seized with great

---

8:22–25 This miracle clearly reveals Jesus' authority over the forces of nature. Cf. the notes on Mt 8:23–27 and Mk 4:35–41.

8:26–39 This episode shows Jesus' power over demons, and the fact that his mission extends to every sort of person. Cf. the notes on Mt 8:28–34 and Mk 5:1–20.

a. Other ancient authorities read *Gadarenes*, other *Gergesenes* fear; so he got into the boat and returned. [38]The man from whom the demons had gone begged that he might be with him; but he sent him away, saying, [39]"Return to your home, and declare how much God has done for you." And he went away, proclaiming throughout the whole city how much Jesus had done for him.*

Jairus' daughter is restored to life.
Curing of the woman with a hemorrhage Mt 9:18–26; Mk 5:21–43

[40]Now when Jesus returned, the crowd welcomed him, for they were all waiting for him. [41]And there came a man named Jairus, who was a ruler of the synagogue; and falling at Jesus' feet he besought him to come to his house, [42]for he had an only daughter, about twelve years of age, and she was dying.

As he went, the people pressed round him. [43]And a woman who had had a flow of blood for twelve years and had spent all her living upon physicians[b] and could not be healed by any one, [44]came up behind him, and touched the fringe of his garment; and immediately her flow of blood ceased. [45]And Jesus said, "Who was it that touched me?" When all denied it, Peter[c] said, "Master, the multitudes surround you and press upon you!" [46]But Jesus said, "Some one touched me; for I perceive that power has gone forth from me." [47]And when the woman saw that she was not hidden, she came trembling, and falling down before him declared in the presence of all the people why she had touched him, and how she had been immediately healed. [48]And he said to her, "Daughter, your faith has made you well; go in peace."

[49]While he was still speaking, a man from the ruler's house came and said, "Your daughter is dead; do not trouble the Teacher any more." [50]But Jesus on hearing this answered him, "Do not fear; only believe, and she shall be well." [51]And when he came to the house, he permitted no one to enter with him, except Peter and John and James, and the father and mother of the child. [52]And all were weeping and bewailing her; but he said, "Do not weep; for she is not dead but sleeping." [53]And they laughed at him, knowing that she was dead. [54]But taking her by the hand he called, saying, "Child, arise." [55]And her spirit returned, and she got up at once; and he directed that something should be

---

8:40–56 This miracle, which is to be found in the three Synoptic Gospels, shows the need for and power of faith in our approach to Jesus (cf. the notes on Mt 9:18–26 and Mk 5:21–43). But the Gospels like to show that faith can take many forms: "There are always sick people who, like Bartimeus, pray with great faith and have no qualms about confessing their faith at the top of their voices. But notice how, among those whom Christ encounters, no two souls are alike. This woman, too, has great faith, but she does not cry aloud; she draws near to Jesus without anyone even noticing. For her it is enough just to touch his garment, because she is quite certain she will be cured" (Bl. J. Escrivá, *Hom.*, 2, 199).

b. Other ancient authorities omit *and had spent all her living upon physicians* **c.** Other ancient authorities add *and those who were with him*

given her to eat. [56]And her parents were amazed; but he charged them to tell
no one what had happened.

5. JESUS TRAVELS WITH HIS APOSTLES

The mission of the apostles Mt 10:5–15; Mk 6:6–13

9 [1]And he called the twelve together and gave them power and authority
over all demons and to cure diseases, [2]and he sent them out to preach the
kingdom of God and to heal. [3]And he said to them, "Take nothing for your
journey, no staff, nor bag, nor bread, nor money; and do not have two tunics.
[4]And whatever house you enter, stay there, and from there depart. [5]And
wherever they do not receive you, when you leave that town shake off the dust
from your feet as a testimony against them." [6]And they departed and went
through the villages, preaching the gospel and healing everywhere.

Herod's opinion about Jesus Mt 14:1–2; Mk 6:14–16

[7]Now Herod the tetrarch heard of all that was done, and he was perplexed,
because it was said by some that John had been raised from the dead, [8]by some

---

In his account of the miracle, St Luke records that Peter was the spokesman of the disciples (v. 45), and he adds the little detail about Jesus' concern that the little girl be given something to eat (v. 55).

9:1–50 □ The mission of the apostles marks the start of a new section which focuses on Jesus' involvement with them. At the centre of this section comes Peter's profession of faith (vv. 18–21). Up to this point the apostles were in Jesus' company and helping him in his mission; from now on, Jesus devotes special attention to teaching them the meaning of what is going to happen in Jerusalem and the kind of life a disciple of his should lead.

9:1–6 This passage succinctly outlines how the apostles played a part in Jesus' mission and extended its range. Luke has already described the power and authority which marked Jesus' proclamation of the Gospel and his treatment of the sick; now we see that our Lord gives the Twelve these same powers (v. 1) and a share in his own mission (v. 2). The apostles fulfilled their assignment (v. 60) and they passed it on to the Church: "The whole Church is apostolic, in that she remains, through the successors of St Peter and the other apostles, in communion of faith and life with her origin; and in that she is 'sent out' into the whole world. All members of the Church share in this mission, though in various ways. 'The Christian vocation is, of its nature, a vocation to the apostolate as well' (Vatican, II, *AA*, 2)" (*CCC*, 863). Cf. the note on Lk 6:12–16.

9:7–9 Jesus' activity gives rise to a key question: "Who is this man?" The Gospel records that the people were unsure (vv. 7–8; cf. 9:18–19), that Herod was

that Elijah had appeared, and by others that one of the old prophets had risen.
9Herod said, "John I beheaded; but who is this about whom I hear such
things?" And he sought to see him.

The return of the apostles.
First miracle of the loaves and fish Mt 14:13–21; Mk 6:30–44; Jn 6:1–15
10On their return the apostles told him what they had done. And he took them
and withdrew apart to a city called Bethsaida. 11When the crowds learned it,
they followed him; and he welcomed them and spoke to them of the kingdom
of God, and cured those who had need of healing. 12Now the day began to
wear away; and the twelve came and said to him, "Send the crowd away, to go
into the villages and country round about, to lodge and get provisions; for we
are here in a lonely place." 13But he said to them, "You give them something to
eat." They said, "We have no more than five loaves and two fish—unless we are
to go and buy food for all these people." 14For there were about five thousand
men. And he said to his disciples, "Make them sit down in companies, about fifty
each." 15And they did so, and made them all sit down. 16And taking the five
loaves and the two fish he looked up to heaven, and blessed and broke them, and
gave them to the disciples to set before the crowd. 17And all ate and were
satisfied. And they took up what was left over, twelve baskets of broken pieces.

Peter's profession of faith Mt 16:13–20; Mk 8:27–30
18Now it happened that as he was praying alone the disciples were with him;
and he asked them, "Who do the people say that I am?" 19And they answered,

---

perplexed (v. 7), and that Peter acknowledged Jesus to be the Messiah (9:20). But it also points out that Herod asked the question out of mere curiosity (v. 9; cf. 23:8) whereas Peter made a genuine act of faith, putting his whole life behind it.

9:10–17 Christ's salvific actions are vividly symbolized in this miracle which lead to Peter's profession of faith. Prior to the miracle we see (v. 11) Jesus doing things typical of his messianic mission—proclaiming the Kingdom of God and working wonders (cf. 4:18). The miracle of the multiplication of the loaves adds a further feature: it shows the superabundance of gifts that betokens the messianic times (cf. Is 25:6; Ps 78:19–20; etc.). This feeding the people in a desert place (v. 12) is clearly evocative of the episodes during the Exodus when God nourished his people (cf. Ex 16), and it prefigures the Eucharist, the food given Christians as they makes their way towards God: "Communion with the Body and Blood of Christ increases the communicant's union with the Lord, forgives his venial sins and preserves him from grave sins. Since receiving this sacrament strengthens the bonds of charity between the communicant and Christ, it also reinforces the unity of the Church as the Mystical Body of Christ" (*CCC*, 1416).

9:18–21 The first three Gospels all report St Peter's profession of faith. Luke's account is more condensed than that of the other two evangelists (cf. the notes on

"John the Baptist; but others say, Elijah; and others, that one of the old
prophets has risen." [20]And he said to them, "But who do you say that I am?"
And Peter answered, "The Christ of God."

First announcement of the Passion Mt 16:21–24

[21]But he charged and commanded them to tell this to no one, [22]saying, "The
Son of man must suffer many things, and be rejected by the elders and chief
priests and scribes, and be killed, and on the third day be raised."

The need for self-denial Mt 16:24–28; Mk 8:31–9:1

[23]And he said to all, "If any man would come after me, let him deny himself
and take up his cross daily and follow me. [24]For whoever would save his life
will lose it; and whoever loses his life for my sake, he will save it. [25]For what
does it profit a man if he gains the whole world and loses or forfeits himself?
[26]For whoever is ashamed of me and of my words, of him will the Son of man
be ashamed when he comes in his glory and the glory of the Father and of the
holy angels. [27]But I tell you truly, there are some standing here who will not
taste death before they see the kingdom of God."

The Transfiguration Mt 17:1–9; Mk 9:2–13

[28]Now about eight days after these sayings he took with him Peter and John
and James, and went up on the mountain to pray. [29]And as he was praying, the
appearance of his countenance was altered, and his raiment became dazzling
white. [30]And behold, two men talked with him, Moses and Elijah, [31]who
appeared in glory and spoke of his departure, which he was to accomplish at
Jerusalem. [32]Now Peter and those who were with him were heavy with sleep
but kept awake, and they saw his glory and the two men who stood with him.

Mt 16:13–20; Mk 8:27–30). But Luke again points out this instance of Jesus praying (v. 18) at a key moment in his public ministry (cf. 3:21; 6;12; 9:28; etc.).

9:22–27 Jesus explains that his mission involves the cross. Therefore, anyone who wants to follow him can take no other road. It is something a Christian must do "every day" (v. 23): "You ask me, 'Why that wooden cross?' And I quote from a letter: 'As I raise my eyes from the microscope, my sight comes to rest on the cross—black and empty. That cross without a corpus is a symbol; it has a meaning others won't see. And I, tired out and on the point of abandoning my work, once again bring my eyes close to the lens and continue. For that lonely cross is calling for a pair of shoulders to bear it" (Bl. J. Escrivá, *The Way*, 277).

9:28–36 The Transfiguration is one of the few episodes in the Gospel that is chronologically linked to another: it happened "about eight days after" (v. 28; "seven days after" according to Mt 17:1 and Mk 9:2) Peter's profession of faith:

33And as the men were parting from him, Peter said to Jesus, “Master, it is well that we are here; let us make three booths, one for you and one for Moses and one for Elijah”—not knowing what he said. 34As he said this, a cloud came and overshadowed them; and they were afraid as they entered the cloud. 35And a voice came out of the cloud, saying, “This is my Son, my Chosen;[d] listen to him!” 36And when the voice had spoken, Jesus was found alone. And they kept silence and told no one in those days anything of what they had seen.

Curing of an epileptic boy Mt 17:14–20; Mk 9:14–29

37On the next day, when they had come down from the mountain, a great crowd met him. 38And behold, a man from the crowd cried, “Teacher, I beg you to look upon my son, for he is my only child; 39and behold, a spirit seizes him and he suddenly cries out; it convulses him till he foams, and shatters him, and will hardly leave him. 40And I begged your disciples to cast it out, but they could not.” 41Jesus answered, “O faithless and perverse generation, how long am I to be with you and bear with you? Bring your son here.” 42While he was coming, the demon tore him and convulsed him. But Jesus rebuked the unclean spirit, and healed the boy, and gave him back to his father. 43And all were astonished at the majesty of God.

Second announcement of the Passion Mt 17:22–27; Mk 9:30–32

But while they were all marvelling at everything he did, he said to his disciples, 44“Let these words sink into your ears; for the Son of man is to be delivered into the hands of men.” 45But they did not understand this saying,

---

“For a moment Jesus discloses his divine glory, confirming Peter’s confession. He also reveals that he will have to go by the way of the cross at Jerusalem in order to ‘enter into his glory’. Moses and Elijah had seen God’s glory on the Mountain; the Law and the Prophets had announced the Messiah’s suffering. Christ’s Passion is the will of the Father: the Son acts as God’s servant; the cloud indicates the presence of the Holy Spirit. ‘The whole Trinity appeared: the Father in the voice; the Son in the man; the Spirit in the shining cloud’ (St Thomas Aquinas, *Summa theol.,* 3, 45, 4 2)” (*CCC*, 555).

9:37–43 Apropos of this miracle, the other evangelists report Jesus’ teaching on the value of faith (cf. Mt 17: 14–20 and note) and prayer (cf. Mk 9:14–29 and note). St Luke, for his part, mentions the anxiety felt by the man over his only child (v. 38; cf. 7:12) and the people’s recognition of God (v. 43; cf. 4:32; 8:25; 11:14).

9:43–45 Once again, after moments of glory, Jesus reminds his disciples about his passion and death, and once again they fail to understand what he is saying: “No one should be scandalized to see how imperfect the apostles were. The mystery of

d. Other ancient authorities read *my Beloved*

and it was concealed from them, that they should not perceive it; and they were afraid to ask him about this saying.

Humility and tolerance Mt 18:1–14; Mk 9:33–50

46And an argument arose among them as to which of them was the greatest.
47But when Jesus perceived the thought of their hearts, he took a child and put
him by his side, 48and said to them, "Whoever receives this child in my name
receives me, and whoever receives me receives him who sent me; for he who
is least among you all is the one who is great."
49John answered, "Master, we saw a man casting out demons in your name,
and we forbade him, because he does not follow with us." 50But Jesus said to
him, "Do not forbid him; for he that is not against you is for you."

PART TWO: JESUS' MINISTRY ON THE WAY TO JERUSALEM

6. THE JOURNEY BEGINS

Samaritans refuse to receive Jesus

51When the days drew near for him to be received up, he set his face to go to
Jerusalem.* 52And he sent messengers ahead of him, who went and entered a
village of the Samaritans, to make ready for him; 53but the people would not

---

the cross lay in the future, and the grace of the Holy Spirit had not yet been given to them" (St John Chrysostom, *Hom. on Mt*, 65, 2).

9:46–50 Two episodes show the limited horizon of the apostles. Jesus contrasts it with the simplicity of the child and the need for open-heartedness—virtues much encouraged in early Christian writings: "You will be simple of heart and rich in spirit [...]. You will not praise yourself, but be humble in everything. You will not seek [your own] glory. You will not harbour evil intentions against your neighbour, nor fill your soul with recklessness" (*Epistle of Barnabas*, 19, 2–3).

9:51–9:27 □□ The three Synoptic Gospels mention Jesus' journey from Galilee to Jerusalem. However, Luke is the one who gives most space to it (almost ten chapters) and he includes many teachings of our Lord which are not to be found in the other Gospels—the parable of the Good Samaritan (10:25–37), the parables of God's mercy (15:1–32), that of the Pharisee and the tax collector (18:9–14), the conversion of Zacchaeus (19:1–10), etc. These passages show the special features

receive him, because his face was set toward Jerusalem.* [54]And when his
disciples James and John saw it, they said, "Lord, do you want us to bid fire
come down from heaven and consume them?"[e] [55]But he turned and rebuked
them.[f] [56]And they went on to another village.

Requirements for following Jesus Mt 8:18–22

[57]As they were going along the road, a man said to him, "I will follow you
wherever you go." [58]And Jesus said to him, "Foxes have holes, and birds of the
air have nests; but the Son of man has nowhere to lay his head." [59]To another
he said, "Follow me." But he said, "Lord, let me first go and bury my father."

---

of the third Gospel—its emphasis on God's mercy, the universal scope of the salvation preached by Jesus, the joy of conversion, etc.

By giving so much space to this journey up to Jerusalem, St Luke is showing very graphically the importance the Holy City has in salvation history. Thus, our Lord's public ministry begins in Galilee (4:14–9:50); from there he goes to Jerusalem via Samaria (9:51–9:27), and in Jerusalem our salvation is accomplished (19:28–24:53). In his second book, the Acts of the Apostles, he works in the other direction: we see the very early stages of the Church taking place in Jerusalem (Acts 1:1–7:60), from where it expands to Samaria (8:1–25) and out to the ends of the earth (8:26–28:31).

9:51–10:24 □ Jesus' journey towards Jerusalem recalls events of his earlier mission in Galilee. The rejection of him by the Samaritans (9:53) is reminiscent of the way he was treated in Nazareth (4:28–30); the mission of the seventy-two (10:1–12, 17–20) reminds us of that of the Twelve (9:1–6, 10); and Jesus' criticism of the cities (10:13–16) is like earlier reproaches he made about the unbelief of his own generation of Jews (7:31–35).

9:51–56 In setting his face towards Jerusalem, towards the cross, Jesus is voluntarily carrying out his Father's plan (cf. 9:31), which will bring him through his passion and death to glorious resurrection and ascension. At the start of his ministry Jesus was rejected by the people of Nazareth (cf. 4:16–30); as this new stage begins, it is the Samaritans who reject him—a further proof that his evangelizing and saving mission is no easy task.

9:57–62 As at the start of his ministry (cf. 5:1–11), there are also at this point people who feel called to follow Jesus. Peter and the other apostles left "all things" (cf. 5:11, 28) to follow him; but these people still have to detach themselves from something. One needs to be radical in order to follow Jesus: "Sometimes [the will] seems to be fixed on serving Christ, but at the same time seeks the applause and

e. Other ancient authorities add *as Elijah did* **f.** Other ancient authorities add *and he said, "You do not know what manner of spirit you are of; for the Son of man came not to destroy men's lives but to save them"* **9:54** 2 King 1: 10–12.

60But he said to him, "Leave the dead to bury their own dead; but as for you, go
and proclaim the kingdom of God." 61Another said, "I will follow you, Lord; but
let me first say farewell to those at my home." 62Jesus said to him, "No one who
puts his hand to the plough and looks back is fit for the kingdom of God."

The mission of the seventy disciples

10 1After this the Lord appointed seventy[g] others, and sent them on ahead
of him, two by two, into every town and place where he himself was
about to come. 2And he said to them, "The harvest is plentiful, but the
labourers are few; pray therefore the Lord of the harvest to send out labourers
into his harvest. 3Go your way; behold, I send you out as lambs in the midst of
wolves. 4Carry no purse, no bag, no sandals; and salute no one on the road.
5Whatever house you enter, first say, 'Peace be to this house!' 6And if a son of
peace is there, your peace shall rest upon him; but if not, it shall return to you.
7And remain in the same house, eating and drinking what they provide, for the
labourer deserves his wages; do not go from house to house. 8Whenever you
enter a town and they receive you, eat what is set before you; 9heal the sick in
it and say to them, 'The kingdom of God has come near to you.' 10But
whenever you enter a town and they do not receive you, go into its streets and
say, 11'Even the dust of your town that clings to our feet, we wipe off against
you; nevertheless know this, that the kingdom of God has come near.' 12I tell
you, it shall be more tolerable on that day for Sodom than for that town.

Jesus reproaches cities for their unbelief

Mt 11:20–24

13"Woe to you, Chorazin! woe to you, Bethsaida! for if the mighty works done
in you had been done in Tyre and Sidon, they would have repented long ago,

---

approval of men […]. It struggles to win future goods but without leaving behind those of the present life. A will like this will never enable us to achieve genuine holiness" (John Cassian, *Collationes*, 4, 12).

10:1–12 Jesus now sends another seventy disciples "into every town and place" (v. 1) with instructions very like those previously given the Twelve (cf. 9:1–5). The number 72 (cf. RSV note **g**) may be an allusion to the descendants of Noah (cf. Gen 10) who made up the nations prior to the scattering that followed the destruction of the tower of Babel. Anyway, this mission seems to point to the universal scope of Christ's mission. Jesus' words also show the urgency of evangelization. Urgency and universality are two features of the Church's missionary activity: "Today, all Christians, all the particular [local] churches and the universal Church, are asked to have the same courage that missionaries had in the past, and the same openness to listening to the voice of the Spirit" (John Paul II, *Redempt. miss.*, 30).

10:13–16 See the note on Mt 11:20–24.

sitting in sackcloth and ashes. [14]But it shall be more tolerable in the judgment for Tyre and Sidon than for you. [15]And you, Capernaum, will you be exalted to heaven? You shall be brought down to Hades.

[16]"He who hears you hears me, and he who rejects you rejects me, and he who rejects me rejects him who sent me."

The seventy return from their mission

[17]The seventy[g] returned with joy, saying, "Lord, even the demons are subject to us in your name!" [18]And he said to them, "I saw Satan fall like lightning from heaven.* [19]Behold, I have given you authority to tread upon serpents and scorpions, and over all the power of the enemy; and nothing shall hurt you. [20]Nevertheless do not rejoice in this, that the spirits are subject to you; but rejoice that your names are written in heaven."

Jesus gives thanks

Mt 11:25–30

[21]In that same hour he rejoiced in the Holy Spirit and said, "I thank thee, Father, Lord of heaven and earth, that thou hast hidden these things from the wise and understanding and revealed them to babes; yea, Father, for such was thy gracious will.[h] [22]All things have been delivered to me by my Father; and no one knows who the Son is except the Father, or who the Father is except the Son and any one to whom the Son chooses to reveal him."

[23]Then turning to the disciples he said privately, "Blessed are the eyes which see what you see! [24]For I tell you that many prophets and kings desired to see what you see, and did not see it, and to hear what you hear, and did not hear it."

10:17–20 The disciples have experienced the joy of sharing in Christ's mission and of seeing its effectiveness (v. 17). Our Lord, however, tells them that what they should really rejoice over is something much deeper—the fact that God has chosen them. "Don't doubt it: your vocation is the greatest grace our Lord could have given you. Thank him for it" (Bl. J. Escrivá, *The Way*, 913).

10:21–24 This passage, also found in St Matthew (cf. Mt 11:25–27), is traditionally called our Lord's "hymn of joy". It is one of those moments when Jesus rejoices to see humble people understanding and accepting the word of God: "Children do not worry about the wealth of their parents. However, the parents, if they hold the throne or have great riches, do not hesitate to satisfy all their little ones' desires [...]. Neither riches nor glory (not even the glory of heaven) fills the heart of a small child [...]. What he demands is love [...]. He can love only you, Jesus, and nothing more!" (St Thérèse of Lisieux, *Autobiography*, 9).

g. Other ancient authorities read *seventy-two* **h.** Or *so it was well-pleasing before thee*

7. FURTHER PREACHING

Parable of the good Samaritan Mt 22:34–40; Mk 12:28–34

25And behold, a lawyer stood up to put him to the test, saying, "Teacher, what
shall I do to inherit eternal life?" 26He said to him, "What is written in the law?
How do you read?" 27And he answered, "You shall love the Lord your God
with all your heart, and with all your soul, and with all your strength, and with
all your mind: and your neighbour as yourself." 28And he said to him, "You
have answered right; do this, and you will live."
29But he, desiring to justify himself, said to Jesus, "And who is my
neighbour?" 30Jesus replied, "A man was going down from Jerusalem to
Jericho, and he fell among robbers, who stripped him and beat him, and
departed, leaving him half dead. 31Now by chance a priest was going down
that road; and when he saw him he passed by on the other side. 32So likewise
a Levite, when he came to the place and saw him, passed by on the other side.
33But a Samaritan, as he journeyed, came to where he was; and when he saw
him, he had compassion, 34and went to him and bound up his wounds, pouring
on oil and wine; then he set him on his own beast and brought him to an inn,
and took care of him. 35And the next day he took out two denarii[i] and gave them
to the inn-keeper, saying, 'Take care of him; and whatever more you spend, I will
repay you when I come back.' 36Which of these three, do you think, proved
neighbour to the man who fell among the robbers?" 37He said, "The one who
showed mercy on him." And Jesus said to him, "Go and do likewise."

10:25–11:54 □ This is a section which contains very little narration of events; the evangelist concentrates on covering a range of Jesus' teachings, a rather mixed selection—on mercy, prayer, signs of Jesus, etc.

10:25–37 Jesus praises and concurs in the summary of the Law given by this Jewish scribe. However, by his parable of the Good Samaritan, he expands the horizons of that love of God which had become narrow as a result of legalism: our neighbour is not only someone whom we have an affinity with (through family, race, religion, etc.) but all those who are around us and require our help.

It may well be that our Lord brings a priest and a Levite into the parable in order to stress the limitations of legal rules. According to the Law of Moses (cf. Lev 21:1–4, 11–12; Num 19:11–22) contact with a dead body meant that a person contracted legal impurity. By his parable Jesus shows (and the scribe agrees with him) that compliance with legal prescriptions should never be allowed to smother compassion. But, in the background of the parable (we must remember that Jesus' answer is not at all what the teacher of the Law would have expected) we can see that our real neighbour is Jesus himself who has mercy on us (cf. vv. 36–37).

i. The denarius was a day's wage for a labourer **10:27** Deut 6:5; Lev 19:18.

Martha and Mary welcome our Lord

38 Now as they went on their way, he entered a village; and a woman named
Martha received him into her house. 39 And she had a sister called Mary, who
sat at the Lord's feet and listened to his teaching. 40 But Martha was distracted
with much serving; and she went to him and said, "Lord, do you not care that
my sister has left me to serve alone? Tell her then to help me." 41 But the Lord
answered her, "Martha, Martha, you are anxious and troubled about many
things; 42 one thing is needful.[j] Mary has chosen the good portion, which shall
not be taken away from her."

The Our Father Mt 6:9–13

11 1 He was praying in a certain place, and when he ceased, one of his
disciples said to him, "Lord, teach us to pray, as John taught his
disciples." 2 And he said to them, "When you pray, say:

"Father, hallowed be thy name. Thy kingdom come. 3 Give us each day our
daily bread;[k] 4 and forgive us our sins, for we ourselves forgive every one who
is indebted to us; and lead us not into temptation."

Effective prayer Mt 7:7–11

5 And he said to them, "Which of you who has a friend will go to him at
midnight and say to him, 'Friend, lend me three loaves; 6 for a friend of mine

---

10:38–42 The Gospel mentions this family on a number of occasions (cf. Jn 11:1–45; 12:1–9); Lazarus, Martha and Mary were friends of his. His answer to Martha is not meant as a rebuke but as warm praise for Mary's attention to his teaching: "The former busied herself, the latter got nourished; the former had many things to attend to, the latter concentrated on one. Both occupations were good" (St Augustine, *Serm.*, 103, 3). Christ's words, then, are an invitation to us to be contemplative souls in the midst of everyday affairs: "Understand this well: there is something holy, something divine hidden in the most ordinary situations, and it is up to each of you to discover it. [...] There is no other way. Either we learn to find our Lord in ordinary, everyday life, or else we shall never find him" (Bl. J. Escrivá, *Conversations*, 114).

11:1–4 St Matthew also records the Our Father, in the context of the sermon on the mount (cf. the note on Mt 6:1–18). By putting it into a different context (v. 1), Luke's Gospel shows the close connexion between Christians' prayer and that of Jesus, the Son of God: "The prayer that comes to us from Jesus is truly unique: it is 'of the Lord'. On the one hand, in the words of this prayer the only Son gives us the words the Father gave him (cf. Jn 17:7): he is the master of our prayer. On the other, as Word incarnate, he knows in his human heart the needs of his human brothers and sisters and reveals them to us: he is the model of our prayer" (*CCC*, 2765).

11:5–13 Our Lord adds some teachings about imprecatory prayer: he draws a comparison and spells out the effectiveness of this sort of prayer. Then, using the

j. Other ancient authorities read *few things are needful, or only one* **k.** Or *our bread for the morrow*

has arrived on a journey, and I have nothing to set before him'; 7and he will
answer from within, 'Do not bother me; the door is now shut, and my children
are with me in bed; I cannot get up and give you anything'? 8I tell you, though
he will not get up and give him anything because he is his friend, yet because
of his importunity he will rise and give him whatever he needs. 9And I tell you,
Ask, and it will be given you; seek, and you will find; knock, and it will be
opened to you. 10For every one who asks receives, and he who seeks finds, and
to him who knocks it will be opened. 11What father among you, if his son asks
for[1] a fish, will instead of a fish give him a serpent; 12or if he asks for an egg,
will give him a scorpion? 13If you then, who are evil, know how to give good
gifts to your children, how much more will the heavenly Father give the Holy
Spirit to those who ask him!"

The Kingdom of God and the kingdom of Satan Mt 12:22–37, 43–45; Mk 3:22–27

14Now he was casting out a demon that was dumb; when the demon had gone
out, the dumb man spoke, and the people marvelled. 15But some of them said,
"He casts out demons by Beelzebul, the prince of demons"; 16while others, to
test him, sought from him a sign from heaven. 17But he, knowing their
thoughts, said to them, "Every kingdom divided against itself is laid waste, and
house falls upon house. 18And if Satan also is divided against himself, how
will his kingdom stand? For you say that I cast out demons by Beelzebul.
19And if I cast out demons by Beelzebul, by whom do your sons cast them
out? Therefore they shall be your judges. 20But if it is by the finger of God that
I cast out demons, then the kingdom of God has come upon you. 21When a
strong man, fully armed, guards his own palace, his goods are in peace; 22but

---

image of the father, he assures Christians of the greatest gift of all, the Holy Spirit: "Through communion with him, the Holy Spirit makes us spiritual, he returns us to Paradise, brings us to the Kingdom of heaven and into adoption as sons, he gives us the confidence to call God Father and to participate in the grace of Christ, to be called a child of light and to partake in eternal glory" (St Basil, *De Spir. Sanct.*, 15, 36; cf. CCC, 736).

11:14–26 Jesus' enemies now come up with a very serious accusation: it is the devil who is working through him, Jesus. He refutes the accusation, at the same time warning them all of its gravity (cf. the notes on Mt 12:22–37; Mk 3:20–30). Then, he draws a comparison to point out the danger they are in (vv. 24–26): by God's action towards his people they have been set free from the power of evil but their obstinate rejection of God's action at work through Christ has turned them into a place where the evil one can operate unhindered. Elsewhere in the New Testament (cf. Heb 6:4–6; 2 Pet 2:20–22; etc) the sacred writers voice their concern lest Christians find themselves in a similar situation.

l. Other ancient authorities insert *bread, will give him a stone; or if he asks for* when one stronger than he assails him and overcomes him, he takes away his armour in which he trusted, and divides his spoil. [23]He who is not with me is against me, and he who does not gather with me scatters.

[24]"When the unclean spirit has gone out of a man, he passes through waterless places seeking rest; and finding none he says, 'I will return to my house from which I came.' [25]And when he comes he finds it swept and put in order. [26]Then he goes and brings seven other spirits more evil than himself, and they enter and dwell there; and the last state of that man becomes worse than the first."

Responding to the word of God Lk 8:19–21

[27]As he said this, a woman in the crowd raised her voice and said to him, "Blessed is the womb that bore you, and the breasts that you sucked!" [28]But he said, "Blessed rather are those who hear the word of God and keep it!"

The sign of Jonah Mt 12:38–42

[29]When the crowds were increasing, he began to say, "This generation is an evil generation; it seeks a sign, but no sign shall be given to it except the sign of Jonah. [30]For as Jonah became a sign to the men of Nineveh, so will the Son of man be to this generation. [31]The queen of the South will arise at the judgment with the men of this generation and condemn them; for she came from the ends of the earth to hear the wisdom of Solomon, and behold, something greater than Solomon is here. [32]The men of Nineveh will arise at the judgment with this generation and condemn it; for they repented at the preaching of Jonah, and behold, something greater than Jonah is here.

The lamp of the body, the light of the soul Mt 5:15; 6:22–23

[33]"No one after lighting a lamp puts it in a cellar or under a bushel, but on a stand, that those who enter may see the light. [34]Your eye is the lamp of your

---

11:27–28 The Tradition of the Church has interpreted these words as praising Mary's greatness. Over and above her physical motherhood, Jesus proclaims her spiritual fidelity: "It was a compliment to his Mother on her *fiat*, her 'be it done.' She lived it sincerely, unstintingly, fulfilling its every consequence, but never amid fanfare, rather in the hidden and silent sacrifice of each day" (Bl. J. Escrivá, *Hom.*, 1, 172).

11:29–32 These words of our Lord are a response to the impertinent request for a sign reported some verses earlier (11;16). The signs Jesus works, and his wisdom, are clear for all to see. Christ's life and preaching are an invitation to conversion, but his hearers, maybe, did not have the right dispositions; hence their failure to grasp what he is saying.

11:33–36 Further reproaches are made by Jesus, using the metaphor of light. If a person has healthy sight, he sees things clearly; similarly, in the moral life, a body; when your eye is sound, your whole body is full of light; but when it is not sound, your body is full of darkness. [35]Therefore be careful lest the light in you be darkness. [36]If then your whole body is full of light, having no part dark, it will be wholly bright, as when a lamp with its rays gives you light."

Jesus reproaches scribes and Pharisees Mt 23:1–36

[37]While he was speaking, a Pharisee asked him to dine with him; so he went in and sat at table. [38]The Pharisee was astonished to see that he did not first wash before dinner. [39]And the Lord said to him, "Now you Pharisees cleanse the outside of the cup and of the dish, but inside you are full of extortion and wickedness. [40]You fools! Did not he who made the outside make the inside also? [41]But give for alms those things which are within; and behold, everything is clean for you.

[42]"But woe to you Pharisees! for you tithe mint and rue and every herb, and neglect justice and the love of God; these you ought to have done, without neglecting the others. [43]Woe to you Pharisees! for you love the best seat in the synagogues and salutations in the market places. [44]Woe to you! for you are like graves which are not seen, and men walk over them without knowing it."

[45]One of the lawyers answered him, "Teacher, in saying this you reproach us also." [46]And he said, "Woe to you lawyers also! for you load men with burdens hard to bear, and you yourselves do not touch the burdens with one of your fingers. [47]Woe to you! for you build the tombs of the prophets whom your fathers killed. [48]So you are witnesses and consent to the deed of your fathers; for they killed them, and you build their tombs. [49]Therefore also the Wisdom of God said, 'I will send them prophets and apostles, some of whom they will kill and persecute,' [50]that the blood of all the prophets, shed from the foundation of the world, may be required of this generation, [51]from the blood

---

person whose approach is pure and straightforward is able to recognize God at work in the world. Because they lack simplicity, these people don't see that God is at work in the things Jesus is doing. Hence our Lord's invitation to them to take corrective action.

11:37–54 In this passage—one of the most hard-hitting in the Gospel—Jesus unmasks the vice which was largely responsible for official Judaism's rejection of his teaching. These are people who, under the guise of doing good, by keeping to the mere letter of the law, fail to be true to its spirit; they close themselves to the love of God and neighbour. Apparently very upright, they turn others away from fervent pursuit of God, by making virtue distasteful.

Our Lord points out three results of that sort of attitude: it can lead others to break the law without realizing it (v. 44), and can even cause the death of good men (vv. 48–51); and it can make salvation impossible (v. 52).

of Abel to the blood of Zechariah, who perished between the altar and the
sanctuary. Yes, I tell you, it shall be required of this generation. 52Woe to you
lawyers! for you have taken away the key of knowledge; you did not enter
yourselves, and you hindered those who were entering."
53As he went away from there, the scribes and the Pharisees began to press
him hard, and to provoke him to speak of many things, 54lying in wait for him,
to catch at something he might say.

8. ANNOUNCEMENT OF THE END

Various teachings Mt 10:16–42

12 1In the meantime, when so many thousands of the multitude had gathered
together that they trod upon one another, he began to say to his disciples
first, "Beware of the leaven of the Pharisees, which is hypocrisy. 2Nothing is
covered up that will not be revealed, or hidden that will not be known. 3Whatever
you have said in the dark shall be heard in the light, and what you have whispered
in private rooms shall be proclaimed upon the housetops.
4"I tell you, my friends, do not fear those who kill the body, and after that
have no more that they can do. 5But I will warn you whom to fear: fear him
who, after he has killed, has power to cast into hell;[m] yes, I tell you, fear him!
6Are not five sparrows sold for two pennies? And not one of them is forgotten
before God. 7Why, even the hairs of your head are all numbered. Fear not; you
are of more value than many sparrows.
8"And I tell you, every one who acknowledges me before men, the Son of
man also will acknowledge before the angels of God; 9but he who denies me
before men will be denied before the angels of God. 10And every one who
speaks a word against the Son of man will be forgiven; but he who blasphemes
against the Holy Spirit will not be forgiven. 11And when they bring you before
the synagogues and the rulers and the authorities, do not be anxious how or

---

12:1–14:35 □This new section also deals mainly with Jesus' teachings. But now the main subject is death, the end of the world, the after-life: Christ's words are a call to vigilance and hope (12:1–13:9; 13:22–30; 14:15–24). We also find here other themes close to Luke's heart—true poverty, humility, etc.

12:1–12 Here the evangelist brings together some directives of Jesus'. Although their content suggests that they were addressed to disciples, St Luke mentions that they were spoken to "many thousands" (v. 1). Obviously, then, what Jesus is saying applies to all Christians without exception.

The previous episode ended with Jesus' enemies deciding to "press him hard, and to provoke him" and to try to catch him unawares (cf. 11:53–54). Christ

m. Greek *Gehenna*

what you are to answer or what you are to say; [12]for the Holy Spirit will teach
you in that very hour what you ought to say."

Parable of the rich fool

[13]One of the multitude said to him, "Teacher, bid my brother divide the inheri-
tance with me." [14]But he said to him, "Man, who made me a judge or divider
over you?" [15]And he said to them, "Take heed, and beware of all covetousness;
for a man's life does not consist in the abundance of his possessions." [16]And
he told them a parable, saying, "The land of a rich man brought forth
plentifully; [17]and he thought to himself, 'What shall I do, for I have nowhere
to store my crops?' [18]And he said, 'I will do this: I will pull down my barns,
and build larger ones; and there I will store all my grain and my goods. [19]And
I will say to my soul, Soul, you have ample goods laid up for many years; take
your ease, eat, drink, be merry.' [20]But God said to him, 'Fool! This night your
soul is required of you; and the things you have prepared, whose will they be?'
[21]So is he who lays up treasure for himself, and is not rich toward God."

Trust in God's fatherly providence Mt 6:19–34

[22]And he said to his disciples, "Therefore I tell you, do not be anxious about
your life, what you shall eat, nor about your body, what you shall put on. [23]For
life is more than food, and the body more than clothing. [24]Consider the ravens:
they neither sow nor reap, they have neither storehouse nor barn, and yet God
feeds them. Of how much more value are you than the birds! [25]And which of
you by being anxious can add a cubit to his span of life?[n] [26]If then you are not
able to do as small a thing as that, why are you anxious about the rest?
[27]Consider the lilies, how they grow; they neither toil nor spin;[o] yet I tell you,

---

forewarns his disciples that they will be treated in the same sort of way. Therefore he exhorts them to have courage, and to seek to please God, not men.

12:13–21 In the same general context as that of the previous discourse (judging the things of the earth with one's eyes on heaven), Jesus now warns of the danger of setting one's heart on material wealth: "To have more is not the ultimate end of peoples, nor of each person. All growth [increase] is ambivalent. Although it is necessary to allow man to be more himself, it makes man a prisoner whenever it is turned into the supreme good that prevents him from seeing beyond it" (Paul VI, *Pop. prog.*, 19).

12:22–34 The key, radical, point in what Jesus says in these further teachings on the use of material things lies in the last verse: we centre our affections, our desires, our deepest feelings, our heart, on what we regards as our treasure, the thing we value most. Therefore, as against the empty-headed rich man who stored

n. Or *to his stature* **o.** Other ancient authorities read *Consider the lillies; they neither spin nor weave*

even Solomon in all his glory was not arrayed like one of these. 28But if God
so clothes the grass which is alive in the field today and tomorrow is thrown
into the oven, how much more will he clothe you, O men of little faith! 29And
do not seek what you are to eat and what you are to drink, nor be of anxious
mind. 30For all the nations of the world seek these things; and your Father
knows that you need them. 31Instead, seek his[p] kingdom, and these things shall
be yours as well.

32"Fear not, little flock, for it is your Father's good pleasure to give you the
kingdom. 33Sell your possessions, and give alms; provide yourselves with
purses that do not grow old, with a treasure in the heavens that does not fail,
where no thief approaches and no moth destroys. 34For where your treasure is,
there will your heart be also.

The need for vigilance; the parable of the steward Mt 24:42–51

35"Let your loins be girded and your lamps burning, 36and be like men who are
waiting for their master to come home from the marriage feast, so that they
may open to him at once when he comes and knocks. 37Blessed are those
servants whom the master finds awake when he comes; truly, I say to you, he
will gird himself and have them sit at table, and he will come and serve them.
38If he comes in the second watch, or in the third, and finds them so, blessed
are those servants! 39But know this, that if the householder had known at what
hour the thief was coming, he would have been awake and[q] would not have left
his house to be broken into. 40You also must be ready; for the Son of man is
coming at an hour you do not expect."

---

up treasure in vain (cf. 12:20–21), Jesus invites his disciples to build up treasure in heaven (v. 33) by being generous on earth.

At the same time he exhorts us not to be worried about the necessities of life, about food, clothes, health etc. (vv. 22–30): the Kingdom of God is what matters (v. 31). This sort of radical thinking is echoed by the Church in her call to holiness: "Therefore all the faithful are invited and obliged to holiness and the perfection of their own state of life. Accordingly let all of them see that they direct their affections rightly, lest they be hindered in their pursuit of perfect love by the use of worldly things and by an adherence to riches which is contrary to the spirit of evangelical poverty" (Vatican II, *LG*, 42). Cf. the note on Mt 5:17–48.

12:35–48 Here Jesus uses two images to encourage watchfulness—being dressed for business, and keeping the lamp lit (v. 35). To enable them to do certain kinds of work, or get ready for a journey, the Jews used a belt to hitch up the long-flowing robes they normally wore; so, "girding one's loins" means showing one is ready and is determined not to take things easy (cf. Jer 1:17; Eph 6:14; 1 Pet 1:13). And a person who has his "lamps burning" is keeping an eye out or waiting for

p. Other ancient authorities read *God's* **q.** Other ancient authorities omit *would have been awake and*

41 Peter said, "Lord are you telling this parable for us or for all?" 42 And the
Lord said, "Who then is the faithful and wise steward, whom his master will
set over his household, to give them their portion of food at the proper time?
43 Blessed is that servant whom his master when he comes will find so doing.
44 Truly I tell you, he will set him over all his possessions. 45 But if that servant
says to himself, 'My master is delayed in coming,' and begins to beat the
menservants and the maidservants, and to eat and drink and get drunk, 46 the
master of that servant will come on a day when he does not expect him and at
an hour he does not know, and will punish[r] him, and put him with the
unfaithful. 47 And that servant who knew his master's will, but did not make
ready or act according to his will, shall receive a severe beating. 48 But he who
did not know, and did what deserved a beating, shall receive a light beating.
Every one to whom much is given, of him will much be required; and of him
to whom men commit much they will demand the more.

Jesus brings division, not peace Mt 10:34–36

49 "I came to cast fire upon the earth; and would that it were already kindled!
50 I have a baptism to be baptized with; and how I am constrained until it is
accomplished! 51 Do you think that I have come to give peace on earth? No, I
tell you, but rather division; 52 for henceforth in one house there will be five
divided, three against two and two against three; 53 they will be divided, father
against son and son against father, mother against daughter and daughter
against her mother, mother-in-law against daughter-in-law and daughter-in-law
against her mother-in-law."

---

someone to arrive. Our Lord then uses two further comparisons (vv. 36–40) to show the way we should watch for him coming, as he surely will—like a servant expecting his master, or a householder watching out for a thief: both of them know that the "other" is going to come and that their life depends on the meeting.

In response to St Peter's question, Jesus says something about the responsibilities of office-holders (vv. 41–48), and people in general. He even makes certain distinctions, specifying that the faithful servant (vv. 43–44) will be treated differently from the cynic (vv. 45–46), as will a weak person (vv. 45–46) as compared with someone who is indifferent (v. 48).

12:49–53 Fire is often used in the Bible (cf., e.g., Deut 2:46) to express God's ardent love for men. Using this image and that of Baptism (cf. the note on Mt 10:16–42), Jesus reveals his uncontainable desire to give his life for love of mankind, and that Christians should follow his example: "O Jesus, strengthen our souls, open out the way for us, and, above all, intoxicate us with your Love. Make us into blazing fires to enkindle the earth with the heavenly fire you brought us" (Bl. J. Escrivá, *The Forge*, 31). However, Jesus is well aware that God has made him a "sign of contradiction" (cf. 2:34–35) and that this will be true also of his disciples.

r. Or *cut him in pieces* **12:53** Mic 7:6.

The signs of the times

Mt 5:25–26; 16:2–3

[54]He also said to the multitudes, "When you see a cloud rising in the west, you
say at once, 'A shower is coming'; and so it happens. [55]And when you see the
south wind blowing, you say, 'There will be scorching heat'; and it happens.
[56]You hypocrites! You know how to interpret the appearance of earth and sky;
but why do you not know how to interpret the present time?

[57]"And why do you not judge for yourselves what is right? [58]As you go
with your accuser before the magistrate, make an effort to settle with him on
the way, lest he drag you to the judge, and the judge hand you over to the
officer, and the officer put you in prison. [59]I tell you, you will never get out till
you have paid the very last copper."

The need for repentance

13 [1]There were some present at that very time who told him of the
Galileans whose blood Pilate had mingled with their sacrifices. [2]And he
answered them, "Do you think that these Galileans were worse sinners than all
the other Galileans, because they suffered thus? [3]I tell you, No; but unless you
repent you will all likewise perish. [4]Or those eighteen upon whom the tower
in Siloam fell and killed them, do you think that they were worse offenders
than all the others who dwelt in Jerusalem? [5]I tell you, No; but unless you
repent you will all likewise perish."

Parable of the barren fig tree

[6]And he told this parable: "A man had a fig tree planted in his vineyard; and he
came seeking fruit on it and found none. [7]And he said to the vinedresser, 'Lo,

---

12:54–59 In his complaint Jesus plays with two senses of the word "time"—time in the sense of season, and in the sense of a stage of salvation. Apparently the people he refers to were reasoning in two different ways: they were logical when judging earthly things, but illogical when it came to thinking about Him. The signs he had given—the miracles, his life and his teaching—should be enough to enable them to accept that he is the Messiah; yet they fail to do so.

13:1–5 Our Lord used current events to get his teaching across to the crowd. Here he tells them that these two tragedies (vv. 1, 4) should not be blamed on the sins of those who died; no, they are a call to conversion. The same holds good for us: lots of things that happen in our life are meant to get us to mend our ways: "Going over all the stages of history again, we will see that in each era the Lord has given a chance to repent to anyone who wanted to convert to him" (St Clement of Rome, *First Letter to Cor*, 7, 5).

13:6–9 In this parable Jesus teaches two things—the need to produce good fruit, and the patience and tender care God spends in helping us to be good.

these three years I have come seeking fruit on this fig tree, and I find none. Cut
it down; why should it use up the ground?' 8And he answered him, 'Let it
alone, sir, this year also, till I dig about it and put on manure. 9And if it bears
fruit next year, well and good; but if not, you can cut it down.'"

Jesus cures a woman on the sabbath

10Now he was teaching in one of the synagogues on the sabbath. 11And there
was a woman who had had a spirit of infirmity for eighteen years; she was bent
over and could not fully straighten herself. 12And when Jesus saw her, he
called her and said to her, "Woman, you are freed from your infirmity." 13And
he laid his hands upon her, and immediately she was made straight, and she
praised God. 14But the ruler of the synagogue, indignant because Jesus had
healed on the sabbath, said to the people, "There are six days on which work
ought to be done; come on those days and be healed, and not on the sabbath
day." 15Then the Lord answered him, "You hypocrites! Does not each of you
on the sabbath untie his ox or his ass from the manger, and lead it away to
water it? 16And ought not this woman, a daughter of Abraham whom Satan
bound for eighteen years, be loosed from this bond on the sabbath day?" 17As
he said this, all his adversaries were put to shame; and all the people rejoiced
at all the glorious things that were done by him.

Parables of the mustard seed and of the leaven Mt 13:31–35; Mk 4:30–32

18He said therefore, "What is the kingdom of God like? And to what shall I
compare it? 19It is like a grain of mustard seed which a man took and sowed in
his garden; and it grew and became a tree, and the birds of the air made nests
in its branches."

20And again he said, "To what shall I compare the kingdom of God? 21It is
like leaven which a woman took and hid in three measures of meal, till it was
all leavened."

13:10–17 Similar episodes are reported elsewhere in the Gospels (cf. Mt 12:9–14; Mk 3:1–6; Lk 6:6–11; 14:1–6): by performing cures on the sabbath Jesus shows his divine generosity and exposes the small-mindedness of those who take him to task for doing so. Here he also stresses that God made this day holy (cf. Ex 20:11; 23:12) and gave it to man as a day of rest; therefore it is a day for praising God, a day for joy—and a very good day to cure this afflicted woman (v. 16). The people's rejoicing (which the evangelist notes: v. 17)—affirms the goodness of what Jesus has done.

13:18–21 Cf. the note on Mk 4:1–34.

The narrow gate Mt 7:13–14:21–23

22 He went on his way through towns and villages, teaching, and journeying
toward Jerusalem. 23 And some one said to him, "Lord, will those who are saved
be few?" And he said to them, 24 "Strive to enter by the narrow door; for many,
I tell you, will seek to enter and will not be able. 25 When once the householder
has risen up and shut the door, you will begin to stand outside and to knock at
the door, saying, 'Lord, open to us.' He will answer you, 'I do not know where
you come from.' 26 Then you will begin to say, 'We ate and drank in your
presence, and you taught in our streets.' 27 But he will say, 'I tell you, I do not
know where you come from; depart from me, all you workers of iniquity!'
28 There you will weep and gnash your teeth, when you see Abraham and Isaac
and Jacob and all the prophets in the kingdom of God and you yourselves thrust
out. 29 And men will come from east and west, and from north and south, and
sit at table in the kingdom of God. 30 And behold, some are last who will be
first, and some are first who will be last."

Jesus' reply to Herod

31 At that very hour some Pharisees came, and said to him, "Get away from
here, for Herod wants to kill you." 32 And he said to them, "Go and tell that fox,
'Behold, I cast out demons and perform cures today and tomorrow, and the
third day I finish my course. 33 Nevertheless I must go on my way today and
tomorrow and the day following; for it cannot be that a prophet should perish
away from Jerusalem.'

Jerusalem admonished Mt 23:37–39

34 "O Jerusalem, Jerusalem, killing the prophets and stoning those who are sent
to you! How often would I have gathered your children together as a hen
gathers her brood under her wings, and you would not! 35 Behold, your house
is forsaken. And I tell you, you will not see me until you say, 'Blessed is he
who comes in the name of the Lord.' "

13:22–30 In response to a typical question from a rabbi, Jesus makes it very clear that salvation is not tied to a privilege of race: it is a reward for spiritual combat. "God desires all men to be saved" (1 Tim 2:4), but in order to attain salvation "the faithful should use the strength dealt out to them by Christ's gift, so that, following in his footsteps and conformed to his image, doing the will of God in everything, they may wholeheartedly devote themselves to the glory of God and to the service of their neighbour" (Vatican II, *LG*, 40).

13:31–35 As elsewhere (cf. 7:36; 12:37; etc.) Luke records here (v. 31) that Jesus had much contact with Pharisees and even when he criticized their doings his aim was simply to identify where they had gone wrong in order to help them to mend their ways.

13:35 Jer 22:5; Ps 118:26.

Jesus cures a dropsical man on the sabbath

14 [1]One sabbath when he went to dine at the house of a ruler who belonged to the Pharisees, they were watching him. [2]And behold, there was a man before him who had dropsy. [3]And Jesus spoke to the lawyers and Pharisees, saying, "Is it lawful to heal on the sabbath, or not?" [4]But they were silent. Then he took him and healed him, and let him go. [5]And he said to them, "Which of you, having an ass[s] or an ox that has fallen into a well, will not immediately pull him out on a sabbath day?" [6]And they could not reply to this.

A lesson about humility

[7]Now he told a parable to those who were invited, when he marked how they chose the places of honour, saying to them, [8]"When you are invited by any one to a marriage feast, do not sit down in a place of honour, lest a more eminent man than you be invited by him; [9]and he who invited you both will come and say to you, 'Give place to this man,' and then you will begin with shame to take the lowest place. [10]But when you are invited, go and sit in the lowest place, so that when your host comes he may say to you, 'Friend, go up higher'; then you will be honoured in the presence of all who sit at table with you. [11]For every one who exalts himself will be humbled, and he who humbles himself will be exalted."

This passage clearly shows how Jesus saw his life and his death: "Out of love for his Father and for men, whom the Father wants to save, Jesus freely accepted his passion and death: 'No one takes [my life] from me, but I lay it down of my own accord' (Jn 10:28). Hence the sovereign freedom of God's Son as he went out to his death" (*CCC*, 609). Jesus also knows that the failure of his mission to the Jews is only apparent: in due course they will acknowledge that he indeed is the Messiah that was to come (v. 35).

14:1–6 This account gives the distinct impression that the scenario was a set-up: the Pharisees invite Jesus, they put him in front of the man with dropsy, and wait to see what happens. In Jesus' time, if someone had dropsy, it was assumed that he had got it due to some sin, and therefore it was not lawful to work a cure on the sabbath. Jesus' line of argument also shows how he saw his mission to men: just as no one would fail to act to save his child or his donkey on the sabbath, Jesus cures this man because he sees our needs as his own.

14:7–11 Jesus takes occasion of this meal to get across various teachings. He uses the example of invited guests to say something about humility: "I was wondering once why our Lord so dearly loved this virtue of humility; and all of a sudden—without, I believe, my having previously thought of it—the following reason came into my mind: that it is because God is Sovereign Truth and to be humble is to walk in truth, for it is absolutely true to say that we have no good thing in

s. Other ancient authorities read *a son*

The right attitude to the poor

12He said also to the man who had invited him, "When you give a dinner or a
banquet, do not invite your friends or your brothers or your kinsmen or rich
neighbours, lest they also invite you in return, and you be repaid. 13But when
you give a feast, invite the poor, the maimed, the lame, the blind, 14and you
will be blessed, because they cannot repay you. You will be repaid at the
resurrection of the just."

Parable of the invited guests Mt 22:1–14

15When one of those who sat at table with him heard this, he said to him,
"Blessed is he who shall eat bread in the kingdom of God!" 16But he said to him,
"A man once gave a great banquet, and invited many; 17and at the time for the
banquet he sent his servant to say to those who had been invited, 'Come; for all
is now ready.' 18But they all alike began to make excuses. The first said to him, 'I
have bought a field, and I must go out and see it; I pray you, have me excused.'
19And another said, 'I have bought five yoke of oxen, and I go to examine them;
I pray you, have me excused.' 20And another said, 'I have married a wife, and
therefore I cannot come.' 21So the servant came and reported this to his master.
Then the householder in anger said to his servant, 'Go out quickly to the streets
and lanes of the city, and bring in the poor and maimed and blind and lame.'
22And the servant said, 'Sir, what you commanded has been done, and still there
is room.' 23And the master said to the servant, 'Go out to the highways and
hedges, and compel people to come in, that my house may be filled. 24For I tell
you, none of these men who were invited shall taste my banquet.'"

---

ourselves, but only misery and nothingness; and anyone who fails to understand this is walking in falsehood. He who best understands it is most pleasing to Sovereign Truth because he is walking in truth. May it please God, sisters, to grant us grace never to fail to have this knowledge of ourselves. Amen" (St Teresa of Avila, *Interior Castle*, 6, 10, 8).

14:12–14 Here Jesus continues to use the image of the banquet. Humility needs to be rounded off by the practice of charity. Even when giving a gift, one should primarily have God in mind (cf. 12:22–34 and note).

14:15–24 Jesus now uses the image of the banquet to describe the Kingdom of God. This parable describes the Church as a universal call to salvation. God chose Israel to mediate that salvation (cf. Is 45); but, when all was ready (v. 17) and God sent his Son, the first people to be issued with an invitation (Israel, the most deserving) said no. Therefore, God is going to found his Church with the despised of Israel (v. 21) and with pagans (v. 23).

Conditions for following Jesus Mt 10:37–38; 5:13

[25]Now great multitudes accompanied him; and he turned and said to them,
[26]“If any one comes to me and does not hate his own father and mother and
wife and children and brothers and sisters, yes, and even his own life, he
cannot be my disciple.* [27]Whoever does not bear his own cross and come after
me, cannot be my disciple. [28]For which of you, desiring to build a tower, does not
first sit down and count the cost, whether he has enough to complete it?
[29]Otherwise, when he has laid a foundation, and is not able to finish, all who see
it begin to mock him, [30]saying, ‘This man began to build, and was not able to
finish.’ [31]Or what king, going to encounter another king in war, will not sit down
first and take counsel whether he is able with ten thousand to meet him who
comes against him with twenty thousand? [32]And if not, while the other is yet a
great way off, he sends an embassy and asks terms of peace. [33]So therefore,
whoever of you does not renounce all that he has cannot be my disciple.

[34]“Salt is good; but if salt has lost its taste, how shall its saltness be
restored? [35]It is fit neither for the land nor for the dunghill; men throw it away.
He who has ears to hear, let him hear.”

9. PARABLES OF GOD’S MERCY

The lost sheep Mt 18:12–14

15 [1]Now the tax collectors and sinners were all drawing near to hear him.
[2]And the Pharisees and the scribes murmured, saying, “This man
receives sinners and eats with them.”

[3]So he told them this parable: [4]“What man of you, having a hundred sheep,
if he has lost one of them, does not leave the ninety-nine in the wilderness, and
go after the one which is lost, until he finds it? [5]And when he has found it, he

---

14:25–35 Now we are shown Jesus in another context. A great many people follow him (v. 25), but our Lord tells them that following him in the true sense is something much more radical than just being attracted by his teaching: “The doctrine that the Son of God came to teach [man] was contempt for all things, so that he might receive the price of the spirit of God in himself; for, in so far as his soul remains atttached to things [of this world], man is made incapable of receiving the spirit of God by pure transformation” (St John of the Cross, *Ascent of Mount Carmel*, 1, 5, 2).

15:1–32 □ All Jesus’ actions and words reveal the mercy of God towards men. However, “St Luke was the evangelist who dealt in most detail with these themes [of mercy] in the teachings of Christ, and for this reason his Gospel has earned the title, ‘the Gospel of mercy’” (John Paul II, *Div. in mis.*, 3). In this chapter St Luke includes three parables in which Jesus graphically describes the infinite and fatherly mercy of lays it on his shoulders, rejoicing. [6]And when he comes home, he calls together his friends and his neighbours, saying to them, 'Rejoice with me, for I have found my sheep which was lost.' [7]Just so, I tell you, there will be more joy in heaven over one sinner who repents than over ninety-nine righteous persons who need no repentance.

The lost coin

[8]"Or what woman, having ten silver coins,[t] if she loses one coin, does not light a lamp and sweep the house and seek diligently until she finds it? [9]And when she has found it, she calls together her friends and neighbours, saying, 'Rejoice with me, for I have found the coin which I had lost.' [10]Just so, I tell you, there is joy before the angels of God over one sinner who repents."

The prodigal son

[11]And he said, "There was a man who had two sons; [12]and the younger of them said to his father, 'Father, give me the share of property that falls to me.' And he divided his living between them. [13]Not many days later, the younger son gathered all he had and took his journey into a far country, and there he squandered his property in loose living. [14]And when he had spent everything, a great famine arose in that country, and he began to be in want. [15]So he went and joined himself to one of the citizens of that country, who sent him into his

---

God, the watchful care he takes of us as individual persons, and his joy over the conversion of the sinner. If we meditate on these teachings of our Lord, we will find they give us confidence: "What a sweet joy it is to think that God is just, that he takes our weakness into account, that he knows perfectly the limits of our fragile nature. What, then, have I to fear? God, infinitely just!, in his bounty deigned to forgive all the sins of the prodigal son; will he not also show such justice to me who am always by his side?" (St Thérèse of Lisieux, *Autobiography*, 8).

15:1–10 Jesus uses the criticism made by the Pharisees and scribes (v. 2) to show God's desire to save everyone, with no exceptions. Clearly, the culminating point of all God's doings in this regard is the Incarnation of Jesus Christ. Therefore, basing itself on this and other passages of the Gospel (cf. Jn 10:11), Christian Tradition sees Christ as this Good Shepherd: "He placed the sheep on his shoulders because, in taking on our human nature, he also took on our sins" (St Gregory the Great, *Hom. on Gospel*, 2, 14, 3).

15:11–32 This is one of Jesus' most beautiful parables. The mercy of God described in the foregoing parables is rounded out in this vivid description of the actions of the Father (vv. 20–24; 31–32). The parable focuses very much on what conversion involves: "*The process of conversion and repentance* was described by

t. The drachma, rendered here by *silver coin*, was about a day's wage for a labourer

fields to feed swine. 16And he would gladly have fed on[u] the pods that the
swine ate; and no one gave him anything. 17But when he came to himself he
said, 'How many of my father's hired servants have bread enough and to spare,
but I perish here with hunger! 18I will arise and go to my father, and I will say
to him, "Father, I have sinned against heaven and before you; 19I am no longer
worthy to be called your son; treat me as one of your hired servants.'" 20And
he arose and came to his father. But while he was yet at a distance, his father
saw him and had compassion, and ran and embraced him and kissed him.
21And the son said to him, 'Father, I have sinned against heaven and before
you; I am no longer worthy to be called your son.'[v] 22But the father said to his
servants, 'Bring quickly the best robe, and put it on him; and put a ring on his
hand, and shoes on his feet; 23and bring the fatted calf and kill it, and let us eat
and make merry; 24for this my son was dead, and is alive again; he was lost,
and is found.' And they began to make merry.
25"Now his elder son was in the field; and as he came and drew near to the
house, he heard music and dancing. 26And he called one of the servants and
asked what this meant. 27And he said to him, 'Your brother has come, and your
father has killed the fatted calf, because he has received him safe and sound.'
28But he was angry and refused to go in. His father came out and entreated
him, 29but he answered his father, 'Lo, these many years I have served you,
and I never disobeyed your command; yet you never gave me a kid, that I
might make merry with my friends. 30But when this son of yours came, who
has devoured your living with harlots, you killed for him the fatted calf!' 31And
he said to him, 'Son, you are always with me, and all that is mine is yours. 32It
was fitting to make merry and be glad, for this your brother was dead, and is
alive; he was lost, and is found.'"

Jesus in the parable of the prodigal son, the centre of which is the merciful father: the fascination of illusory freedom, the abandonment of the father's house; the extreme misery in which the son finds himself after squandering his fortune; his deep humiliation at finding himself obliged to feed swine, and still worse, at wanting to feed on the husks the pigs ate; his reflection on all he has lost; his repentance and decision to declare himself guilty before his father; the journey back; the father's generous welcome; the father's joy—all these are characteristic of the process of conversion. The beautiful robe, the ring and the festive banquet are symbols of that new life—pure, worthy and joyful—of anyone who returns to God and to the bosom of his family, which is the Church. Only the heart of Christ who knows the depths of his Father's love could reveal to us the abyss of his mercy in so simple and beautiful a way" (*CCC*, 1439).

v. Other ancient authorities add *treat me as one of your hired servants* **u.** Other ancient authorities read *filled his belly with*

10. VARIOUS TEACHINGS

The unjust steward

16 1 He also said to the disciples, "There was a rich man who had a
steward, and charges were brought to him that this man was wasting his
goods. 2 And he called him and said to him, 'What is this that I hear about you?
Turn in the account of your stewardship, for you can no longer be steward.'
3 And the steward said to himself, 'What shall I do, since my master is taking
the stewardship away from me? I am not strong enough to dig, and I am
ashamed to beg. 4 I have decided what to do, so that people may receive me
into their houses when I am put out of the stewardship.' 5 So, summoning his
master's debtors one by one, he said to the first, 'How much do you owe my
master?' 6 He said, 'A hundred measures of oil.' And he said to him, 'Take your
bill, and sit down quickly and write fifty.' 7 Then he said to another, 'And how
much do you owe?' He said, 'A hundred measures of wheat.' He said to him,

---

16:1–19:27 □ In this section we again find the sort of mixed themes found in the second part of Luke's Gospel. He recounts further parables (16:1–31), but in these Jesus' theme is the proper use of possessions, and the dangers of being well-to-do. Jesus will return to this theme later (18:18–30), in connexion with the failure of the rich young man to respond to his calling, and, in the positive sense, the conversion of Zacchaeus (19:1–10). Other parables (18:1–14) on prayer and humility have their counterpart in the words of warning in the middle of the section (17: 1–10). Finally, the eschatological announcement comes in both our Lord's explicit discourse on the subject (17:20–37) and in the parable of the pounds (19:11–27).

At the end of the section comes the third announcement of the passion (18:31–34) and the blind man of Jericho confessing Jesus as the Messiah (18:28)—both events preparing the reader for what we will soon see happening in Jerusalem.

16:1–15 We might find the parable of the unjust steward disconcerting because sometimes we read parables, which are designed to get across a message, as allegories in which every element or every character has significance. Our Lord, of course, presumes that we realize the steward is acting immorally; the point he wants to get across to his disciples is that they should be shrewd and resourceful in spreading the Kingdom of God: "What zeal men put into their earthly affairs! Dreaming of honours, striving for riches, bent on sensuality! Men and women, rich and poor, old and middle-aged and young and even children: all of them alike. When you and I put the same zeal into the affairs of our souls, then we'll have a living and working faith. And there will be no obstacle that we cannot overcome in our apostolic works" (Bl. J. Escriva, *The Way*, 317).

After this parable, the Gospel gives some maxims spoken by Jesus (vv. 9–15). They are prefaced by the very formal words, "I tell you" (v. 9), and although they

'Take your bill, and write eighty.' [8]The master commended the dishonest
steward for his prudence; for the sons of this world[w] are wiser in their own
generation than the sons of light.* [9]And I tell you, make friends for yourselves
by means of unrighteous mammon, so that when it fails they may receive you
into the eternal habitations.
[10]"He who is faithful in a very little is faithful also in much; and he who is
dishonest in a very little is dishonest also in much. [11]If then you have not been
faithful in the unrighteous mammon, who will entrust to you the true riches?
[12]And if you have not been faithful in that which is another's, who will give you
that which is your own? [13]No servant can serve two masters; for either he will
hate the one and love the other, or he will be devoted to the one and despise the
other. You cannot serve God and mammon."
[14]The Pharisees, who were lovers of money, heard all this, and they scoffed
at him. [15]But he said to them, "You are those who justify yourselves before
men, but God knows your hearts; for what is exalted among men is an
abomination in the sight of God.

The Law and the Gospel Mt 5:17,32; 11:12–13; 19:9; Mk 10:11

[16]"The law and the prophets were until John; since then the good news of the
kingdom of God is preached, and every one enters it violently. [17]But it is easier
for heaven and earth to pass away, than for one dot of the law to become void.
[18]"Every one who divorces his wife and marries another commits adultery,
and he who marries a woman divorced from her husband commits adultery.

---

cover a number of things, there is a common thread running through them: at all times, be we rich or poor, in important or trivial matters, our sights should be on God. Perhaps the core of what he says here comes in v. 13, which sees love of riches as a type of idolatry: "All bow down before wealth. Wealth is that to which the multitude of men pay an instinctive homage. They measure happiness by wealth; and by wealth they measure respectability. [...] It is a homage resulting from a profound faith. [...] that with wealth he may do all things. Wealth is one idol of the day and notoriety is a second. [...] Notoriety, or the making of a noise in the world—it may be called 'newspaper fame'—has come to be considered a great good in itself, and a ground of veneration" (John H. Newman, *Discourses to mixed congregations*, 5; cf. *CCC*, 1723).

16:16–18 Here the evangelist notes other sayings of our Lord, this time to do with salvation history (cf. v. 16). Jesus has not come to do away with the Law (v. 17) but to bring it to perfection: his teaching on the indissolubility of marriage (v. 18) is a further example of this.

w. Greek *age*

Lazarus and the rich man

19"There was a rich man, who was clothed in purple and fine linen and who
feasted sumptuously every day. 20And at his gate lay a poor man named
Lazarus, full of sores, 21who desired to be fed with what fell from the rich
man's table; moreover the dogs came and licked his sores. 22The poor man
died and was carried by the angels to Abraham's bosom. The rich man also
died and was buried; 23and in Hades, being in torment, he lifted up his eyes,
and saw Abraham far off and Lazarus in his bosom. 24And he called out,
'Father Abraham, have mercy upon me, and send Lazarus to dip the end of his
finger in water and cool my tongue; for I am in anguish in this flame.' 25But
Abraham said, 'Son, remember that you in your lifetime received your good
things, and Lazarus in like manner evil things, but now he is comforted here,
and you are in anguish. 26And besides all this, between us and you a great
chasm has been fixed, in order that those who would pass from here to you
may not be able, and none may cross from there to us.' 27And he said, 'Then
I beg you, father, to send him to my father's house, 28for I have five brothers,
so that he may warn them, lest they also come into this place of torment.' 29But
Abraham said, 'They have Moses and the prophets; let them hear them.' 30And
he said, 'No, father Abraham; but if some one goes to them from the dead,
they will repent.' 31He said to him, 'If they do not hear Moses and the prophets,
neither will they be convinced if some one should rise from the dead'."

On leading others astray

Mt 18:6–7; Mk 9:42

17 1And he said to his disciples, "Temptations to sin[x] are sure to come; but
woe to him by whom they come! 2It would be better for him if a

---

16:19–31 This parable disposes of two mistaken ideas—that of those who denied the survival of the soul after death (and, therefore, the Judgment and retribution in the next life), and the notion that material prosperity in this life is a reward for moral integrity, and that adversity is a punishment for wrongdoing.

Coming where it does in the Gospel, this parable is a very clear example of the doctrine on material wealth outlined a little earlier. We are not told that the rich man had done anything bad, but simply that he was very well dressed and kept a sumptuous table every day (v. 9); but because this was the only thing he lived for, he could not see Lazarus as his neighbour and could not hear the voice of God even when given some dramatic sign (vv. 29, 31). So, the parable is a call to temperance and to solidarity with others: "Wishing to come down to topics that are practical and of some urgency, the Council lays stress on respect for the human person: everyone should look upon his neighbour (without any exception) as another self, bearing in mind, above all, his life and the means necessary for living it in a dignified way, lest he follow the example of the rich man who ignored Lazarus, the poor man" (Vatican II, *GS*, 27).

17:1–10 This passage brings together a number of teachings Jesus gave his disciples (v. 1) and the apostles (v. 5), all of them to do with how Christians

x. Greek *stumbling blocks*

millstone were hung round his neck and he were cast into the sea, than that he should cause one of these little ones to sin.[y]

Forgiving offences Mt 18:15–17, 21–22

3Take heed to yourselves; if your brother sins, rebuke him, and if he repents,
forgive him; 4and if he sins against you seven times in the day, and turns to you
seven times, and says, 'I repent,' you must forgive him."

The power of faith Mt 21:21; Mk 11: 22–24

5The apostles said to the Lord, "Increase our faith!" 6And the Lord said, "If
you had faith as a grain of mustard seed, you could say to this sycamine tree,
'Be rooted up, and be planted in the sea,' and it would obey you.

Humble service

7"Will any one of you, who has a servant ploughing or keeping sheep, say to
him when he has come in from the field, 'Come at once and sit down at
table'? 8Will he not rather say to him, 'Prepare supper for me, and gird
yourself and serve me, till I eat and drink; and afterward you shall eat and
drink'? 9Does he thank the servant because he did what was commanded?
10So you also, when you have done all that is commanded you, say, 'We are
unworthy servants; we have only done what was our duty.'"

The ten lepers

11On the way to Jerusalem he was passing along between Samaria and Galilee.
12And as he entered a village, he was met by ten lepers, who stood at a
distance 13and lifted up their voices and said, "Jesus, Master, have mercy on

---

(particularly officeholders) should conduct themselves in the Church to come. He uses a very graphic image to show them the gravity of the sin of scandal (vv. 1–2), invites them to be magnanimous in pardoning offences (vv. 3–4), and urges them to avoid any kind of pride (vv. 7–10). The apostles realize that he is making heavy demands, but Christ teaches that nothing is impossible if we have faith in God (vv. 5–6).

17:11–19 To avoid the spread of disease, the Law of Moses laid down (Lev 13:45–46) that lepers should live away from other people and should let it be known that they suffered from this disease. That is why the ten lepers did not come right up to Jesus but instead begged his help by shouting from a distance (vv. 12–13).

These men faithfully obeyed what Jesus told them to do (v. 14) but only one of them—a Samaritan—showed gratitude as well as faith. Jesus describes this action as "giving praise to God" (v. 18) and says that it is the cause of this foreigner's

y. Greek *stumble*

us." [14]When he saw them he said to them, "Go and show yourselves to the priests." And as they went they were cleansed. [15]Then one of them, when he saw that he was healed, turned back, praising God with a loud voice; [16]and he fell on his face at Jesus' feet, giving him thanks. Now he was a Samaritan. [17]Then said Jesus, "Were not ten cleansed? Where are the nine? [18]Was no one found to return and give praise to God except this foreigner?" [19]And he said to him, "Rise and go your way; your faith has made you well."

The coming of the Kingdom of God

[20]Being asked by the Pharisees when the kingdom of God was coming, he answered them, "The kingdom of God is not coming with signs to be observed;* [21]nor will they say, 'Lo, here it is!' or 'There!' for behold, the kingdom of God is in the midst of you."[z]

The day of Christ's coming Mt 24:36–41

[22]And he said to the disciples, "The days are coming when you will desire to see one of the days of the Son of man, and you will not see it. [23]And they will say to you, 'Lo, there!' or 'Lo, here!' Do not go, do not follow them. [24]For as the lightning flashes and lights up the sky from one side to the other, so will the Son of man be in his day.[a] [25]But first he must suffer many things and be rejected by this generation. [26]As it was in the days of Noah, so will it be in the days of the Son of man. [27]They ate, they drank, they married, they were given in marriage, until the day when Noah entered the ark, and the flood came and destroyed them all. [28]Likewise as it was in the days of Lot—they ate, they drank, they bought, they sold, they planted, they built, [29]but on the day when Lot went out from Sodom fire and brimstone rained from heaven and destroyed them all—[30]so will it be on the day when the Son of man is revealed. [31]On that day, let him who is on the housetop, with his goods in the house, not come down to take them away; and likewise let him who is in the field not turn back. [32]Remember Lot's wife. [33]Whoever seeks to gain his life

---

salvation (healing: v. 19). So, this scene is another instance of something which Jesus proclaimed in his opening discourse in the synagogue of Nazareth (cf. 4:27). It also invites the reader to be grateful to God: "What better prayer can we think in our mind, or utter with our tongue, or express with our pen than 'Thanks be to God'? Nothing can be said more briefly than this, or heard more joyfully, or used more faithfully" (St Augustine, *Letters*, 41, 1).

17:20–37 Jesus' conversation with the Pharisees (vv. 20–21) and his subsequent discourse to his disciples (vv. 22–37) have much to reveal about the coming of the Kingdom of God. In both passages Jesus says that it is not something one can see with one's eyes (vv. 21, 23). The Pharisees were expecting some dramatic manifestation to

z. Or *within you* **a.** Other ancient authorities omit *in his day*

will lose it, but whoever loses his life will preserve it. 34I tell you, in that night
there will be two men in one bed; one will be taken and the other left. 35There
will be two women grinding together; one will be taken and the other left."[b]
37And they said to him, "Where, Lord?" He said to them, "Where the body is,
there the eagles[c] will be gathered together."

Persevering prayer. Parable of the unjust judge

18 1And he told them a parable, to the effect that they ought always to pray
and not lose heart. 2He said, "In a certain city there was a judge who
neither feared God nor regarded man; 3and there was a widow in that city who
kept coming to him and saying, 'Vindicate me against my adversary.' 4For a
while he refused; but afterward he said to himself, 'Though I neither fear God
nor regard man, 5yet because this widow bothers me, I will vindicate her, or
she will wear me out by her continual coming.'" 6And the Lord said, "Hear
what the unrighteous judge says. 7And will not God vindicate his elect, who
cry to him day and night? Will he delay long over them? 8I tell you, he will
vindicate them speedily. Nevertheless, when the Son of man comes, will he
find faith on earth?"

Parable of the Pharisee and the tax collector

9He also told this parable to some who trusted in themselves that they were
righteous and despised others: 10"Two men went up into the temple to pray, one

---

mark the establishment of God's kingdom, but Jesus tells them it is already come: "Jesus accompanies his words with many 'mighty works and wonders and signs' (Acts 2:22), which manifest that the kingdom is present in him" (*CCC*, 547).

However, as our Lord explained in many parables, the Kingdom is something that is designed to spread: "First announced to the children of Israel, this messianic kingdom is intended to accept men of all nations" (ibid., 543). Before it is definitively established Jesus must be rejected by his own generation (v. 25), but when he comes in glory as the Son of man it will all happen suddenly and take everyone by surprise: hence the need to be vigilant.

See the RSV note (and cf. Mt 24:40).

18:1–8 The parable of the unjust judge contains very vivid teaching about the need for and usefulness of perseverance in prayer. But our Lord also links effectiveness of prayer to faith (v. 8): "In order to pray, let us believe; and for our faith not to weaken, let us pray. Faith causes prayer to grow, and when prayer grows our faith is strengthened" (St Augustine, *Serm.*, 115, 1).

18:9–14 In addition to perseverance, prayer, which is contact with God, calls for humility. That is the message of this parable: "When we pray, do we speak from

b. Other ancient authorities add verse 36, "*Two men will be in the field; one will be taken and the other left*" **c.** Or *vultures*

a Pharisee and the other a tax collector. [11]The Pharisee stood and prayed thus
with himself, 'God, I thank thee that I am not like other men, extortioners,
unjust, adulterers, or even like this tax collector. [12]I fast twice a week, I give
tithes of all that I get.' [13]But the tax collector, standing far off, would not even
lift up his eyes to heaven, but beat his breast, saying, 'God, be merciful to me a
sinner!' [14]I tell you, this man went down to his house justified rather than the
other; for every one who exalts himself will be humbled, but he who humbles
himself will be exalted."

Jesus blesses the children Mt 19:13–15; Mk 10:13–16

[15]Now they were bringing even infants to him that he might touch them; and
when the disciples saw it, they rebuked them. [16]But Jesus called them to him,
saying, "Let the children come to me, and do not hinder them; for to such
belongs the kingdom of God. [17]Truly, I say to you, whoever does not receive
the kingdom of God like a child shall not enter it."

The rich young man. Christian poverty and renunciation Mt 19:16–30; Mk 10:17–31

[18]And a ruler asked him, "Good Teacher, what shall I do to inherit eternal
life?" [19]And Jesus said to him, "Why do you call me good? No one is good but
God alone. [20]You know the commandments: 'Do not commit adultery, Do not
kill, Do not steal, Do not bear false witness, Honour your father and mother.'"

---

the height of our pride and will, or 'out of the depths' of a humble and contrite heart? (Ps 30:14) He who humbles himself will be exalted; *humility* is the foundation of prayer. Only when we humbly acknowledge that 'we do not know how to pray as we ought' (Rom 8:26) are we ready to receive freely the gift of prayer. Man is a beggar before God" (*CCC*, 2559).

18:15–17 This episode tells us about two things—Jesus' regard for children (v. 16), and the need to be like children in order to enter the Kingdom of God (v. 17): "Why does he say that the children are suitable for the Kingdom of heaven? Perhaps because they are normally without malice, they do not know how to deceive, and they do not seek vengeance; they are not lustful, nor do they desire riches or harbour ambition. But the virtue in all this is not an ignorance of evil, but the rejection of evil; it does not consist in an inability to sin but in refusing to consent to sin. Moreover, Christ does not refer to childhood in itself, but to the innocence that children have in their simplicity" (St Ambrose, *Com. on Lk,* in loc.).

18:18–30 The three Synoptic Gospels include this scene which shows Jesus with the rich young man and then with his disciples. Luke's account is the most matter-of-fact but he manages to highlight the most important aspects of Christ's teaching, the kernel of which lies in what Jesus says to Peter at the end (v. 29):

18:20 Ex 20: 12–16; Deut 5:16–20.

[21]And he said, "All these I have observed from my youth." [22]And when Jesus
heard it, he said to him, "One thing you still lack. Sell all that you have and
distribute to the poor, and you will have treasure in heaven; and come, follow
me." [23]But when he heard this he became sad, for he was very rich. [24]Jesus
looking at him said, "How hard it is for those who have riches to enter the
kingdom of God! [25]For it is easier for a camel to go through the eye of a
needle than for a rich man to enter the kingdom of God." [26]Those who heard
it said, "Then who can be saved?" [27]But he said, "What is impossible with
men is possible with God." [28]And Peter said, "Lo, we have left our homes and
followed you." [29]And he said to them, "Truly, I say to you, there is no man who
has left house or wife or brothers or parents or children, for the sake of the
kingdom of God, [30]who will not receive manifold more in this time, and in the
age to come eternal life."

Third announcement of the Passion Mt 20:17–19; Mk 10:32–34

[31]And taking the twelve, he said to them, "Behold, we are going up to
Jerusalem, and everything that is written of the Son of man by the prophets
will be accomplished. [32]For he will be delivered to the Gentiles, and will be
mocked and shamefully treated and spit upon; [33]they will scourge him and kill
him, and on the third day he will rise." [34]But they understood none of these
things; this saying was hid from them, and they did not grasp what was said.

Curing of the blind man of Jericho Mt 20:29–34; Mk 10:46–52

[35]As he drew near to Jericho, a blind man was sitting by the roadside begging;
[36]and hearing a multitude going by, he inquired what this meant. [37]They told

---

someone who leaves all things for the sake of the Kingdom of God will receive much more than he has given up. Thus, "Jesus' call to the rich young man to follow him, in the obedience of a disciple and in the observance of the Commandments, is joined to the call to poverty and chastity" (*CCC*, 2053).

18:31–34 This is Jesus' third announcement about his passion and resurrection, and it is to be found in the three Synoptic Gospels. Luke records more such announcements than the others (cf. 9:22, 44; 12:50; 13:32; 17:25) and it is he too who reports the difficulty the disciples had in understanding what our Lord was saying (v. 34). This failure on their part should not surprise us. One can only make sense of suffering if one sees it in the light of Christ, who "by suffering for us not only gave us an example so that we might follow in his footsteps, but also opened up a way. If we follow this path, life and death are made holy and acquire a new meaning" (Vatican II, *GS*, 22).

18:35–43 Luke seems to be drawing on the blind man's own account of this episode: the man hears the crowd passing and he asks what is going on (v. 36).

him, "Jesus of Nazareth is passing by." [38]And he cried, "Jesus, Son of David, have mercy on me!" [39]And those who were in front rebuked him, telling him to be silent; but he cried out all the more, "Son of David, have mercy on me!" [40]And Jesus stopped, and commanded him to be brought to him; and when he came near, he asked him, [41]"What do you want me to do for you?" He said, "Lord, let me receive my sight." [42]And Jesus said to him, "Receive your sight; your faith has made you well." [43]And immediately he received his sight and followed him, glorifying God; and all the people, when they saw it, gave praise to God.

The conversion of Zacchaeus

19 [1]He entered Jericho and was passing through. [2]And there was a man named Zacchaeus; he was a chief tax collector, and rich. [3]And he sought to see who Jesus was, but could not, on account of the crowd, because he was small of stature. [4]So he ran on ahead and climbed up into a sycamore tree to see him, for he was to pass that way. [5]And when Jesus came to the place, he looked up and said to him, "Zacchaeus, make haste and come down; for I must stay at your house today." [6]So he made haste and came down, and received him joyfully. [7]And when they saw it they all murmured, "He has gone in to be the guest of a man who is a sinner." [8]And Zacchaeus stood and said to the Lord, "Behold, Lord, the half of my goods I give to the poor; and if I have defrauded any one of anything, I restore it fourfold." [9]And Jesus said to him, "Today salvation has come to this house, since he also is a son of Abraham. [10]For the Son of man came to seek and to save the lost."

When told that it is Jesus, he raises his voice in petition (vv. 37–39): "I fear that Jesus is departing and will not return" (cf. St Augustine, *Serm.*, 88, 13). But his faith is so strong that he manages to obtain his cure, causing all the people to praise God (v. 43).

19:1–10 This episode is more eloquent about the mercy of God than about the conversion of a sinner, a mercy so wonderfully described by our Lord in his parables (cf. 15:1–32). Zacchaeus is a son of Abraham (v. 9), but one who seemingly was not living up to what the Covenant entailed (cf. vv. 2, 7).

But Jesus has come to save even those who have gone astray (cf. 15:1–7 and Ezek 34:1): "I will seek the lost, and I will bring back the strayed, and I will bind up the crippled and I will strengthen the weak." Therefore, when Zacchaeus' curiosity leads him to climb up the tree, Jesus responds by calling him by name and inviting himself to Zacchaeus' house (v. 5). The outcome of this meeting with Jesus is joy (v. 6) and salvation (vv. 9–10).

Parable of the pounds Mt 25:14–30

11 As they heard these things, he proceeded to tell a parable, because he was near to Jerusalem, and because they supposed that the kingdom of God was to appear immediately. 12 He said therefore, "A nobleman went into a far country to receive kingly power[d] and then return. 13 Calling ten of his servants, he gave them ten pounds,[e] and said to them, 'Trade with these till I come.' 14 But his citizens hated him and sent an embassy after him, saying, 'We do not want this man to reign over us.' 15 When he returned, having received the kingly power,[d] he commanded these servants, to whom he had given the money, to be called to him, that he might know what they had gained by trading. 16 The first came before him, saying, 'Lord, your pound has made ten pounds more.' 17 And he said to him, 'Well done, good servant! Because you have been faithful in a very little, you shall have authority over ten cities.' 18 And the second came, saying, 'Lord, your pound has made five pounds.' 19 And he said to him, 'And you are to be over five cities.' 20 Then another came, saying, 'Lord, here is your pound, which I kept laid away in a napkin; 21 for I was afraid of you, because you are a severe man; you take up what you did not lay down, and reap what you did not sow.' 22 He said to him, 'I will condemn you out of your own mouth, you wicked servant! You knew that I was a severe man, taking up what I did not lay down and reaping what I did not sow? 23 Why then did you not put my money into the bank, and at my coming I should have collected it with interest?' 24 And he said to those who stood by, 'Take the pound from him, and give it to him who has the ten pounds.' 25 (And they said to him, 'Lord, he has ten pounds!') 26 'I tell you, that to every one who has will more be given; but from him who has not, even what he has will be taken away. 27 But as for these enemies of mine, who did not want me to reign over them, bring them here and slay them before me.' "

19:11–27 For those present, this parable would have reminded them of events of the time. Flavius Josephus recounts that, after the death of Herod (the year 4/3 BC), his son Archelaus went to Rome to get official confirmation of his royal title. However, some Jewish leaders also went to see Caesar to prevent the succession because they regarded Archelaus as a cruel man. And while Archelaus was in Rome, some of his retainers protected his interests at home (cf. *Ant.*, 17, 299–314; *Jewish War*, 2, 1–19).

Jesus uses this parable to correct the too human outlook of his disciples who were expecting him to dramatically reveal himself as the Messiah and establish the Kingdom of God (cf. v. 11). Jesus tells them that he will indeed come as King and Judge: his faithful followers should not worry about the enemies of the Kingdom (v. 14) but rather do everything they can to build up the inheritance left to them.

d. Greek *a kingdom* **e.** The mina, rendered here by *pound*, was about three months' wages for a labourer

PART THREE: THE JERUSALEM MINISTRY

11. CLEANSING OF THE TEMPLE. CONTROVERSIES

The Messiah enters the Holy City Mt 21:1–11; Mk 11:1–11; Jn 12:12–19

[28]And when he had said this, he went on ahead, going up to Jerusalem.
[29]When he drew near to Bethphage and Bethany, at the mount that is called
Olivet, he sent two of the disciples, [30]saying, "Go into the village opposite,
where on entering you will find a colt tied, on which no one has ever yet sat;
untie it and bring it here. [31]If any one asks you, 'Why are you untying it?' you
shall say this, 'The Lord has need of it.' " [32]So those who were sent went away
and found it as he had told them. [33]And as they were untying the colt, its owners
said to them, "Why are you untying the colt?" [34]And they said, "The Lord has
need of it." [35]And they brought it to Jesus, and throwing their garments on the colt
they set Jesus upon it. [36]And as he rode along, they spread their garments on the
road. [37]As he was now drawing near, at the descent of the Mount of Olives, the

---

19:28–24:53 □□ This account of the last week of Jesus' life is very like that in the two other Synoptics: it covers Jesus' entry into Jerusalem and the cleansing of the temple (19:28–48), his controversies with the Jewish authorities (20:1–44), the eschatological discourse (21:5–36) and the lengthy Passion narrative (22:1–23:56) and the resurrection (24:1–53). Within this, Luke emphasizes Jesus' piety (19:41–44) and mercy (22:51, 61; 23:28–29, 34, 43), his magnanimity (22:21–30, 47–53; 23:26–49; etc.) and his constant recourse to prayer (22:32, 39–46; 23:34, 46)—a model for the way a Christian should live.

The account ends with our Lord telling his apostles to stay in Jerusalem until the Holy Spirit comes, and the ascension (24:49–53), two events which also appear in the opening verses of the Acts of the Apostles (Acts 1:4–9), which recounts the public manifestation of the Church and its growth.

19:28–21:38 The cleansing of the temple and the controversies with the Jewish authorities prior to the passion are all reported in similar terms in the three Synoptics. St Luke makes a point of drawing our attention to the leaders' eagerness to dispose of Jesus (19:39, 47–48; 20:19, 20, 26). This fulfils the prophecy about Jesus being the cornerstone (20:18–19) "set for the fall and rising of many in Israel, and for a sign that is spoken against" (2:34). The eschatological discourse (21:5–36) is shorter than in the other two Synoptics, but much of what Luke does not put here is already covered in his narrative of Jesus' journey up to Jerusalem.

19:38 Ps 118:26.

whole multitude of the disciples began to rejoice and praise God with a loud
voice for all the mighty works that they had seen, [38]saying, "Blessed is the
King who comes in the name of the Lord! Peace in heaven and glory in the
highest!" [39]And some of the Pharisees in the multitude said to him, "Teacher,
rebuke your disciples." [40]He answered, "I tell you, if these were silent, the very
stones would cry out."

Jesus weeps over Jerusalem

[41]And when he drew near and saw the city he wept over it, [42]saying, "Would that
even today you knew the things that make for peace! But now they are hid from
your eyes. [43]For the days shall come upon you, when your enemies will cast up a
bank about you and surround you, and hem you in on every side, [44]and dash you
to the ground, you and your children within you, and they will not leave one stone
upon another in you; because you did not know the time of your visitation."*

Jesus in the temple Mt 21:12–17; Mk 11:15–19; Jn 2:13–25

[45]And he entered the temple and began to drive out those who sold, [46]saying
to them, "It is written, 'My house shall be a house of prayer'; but you have
made it a den of robbers."

19:28–40 This scene has elements and nuances that suggest the glorious manifestation of Jesus in Jerusalem. Jesus uses a donkey for his entry into Jerusalem, thereby fulfilling an ancient prophecy: "Rejoice greatly, O daughter of Zion! Shout aloud, O daughter of Jerusalem! Lo, your king comes to you; triumphant and victorious is he, humble and riding on an ass, on a colt, the foal of an ass" (Zech 9:9). The disciples' acclamation (v. 38) shows that they acknowledge him as King and Messiah, because the words they use are from a psalm about the enthronement of the Messiah (cf. Ps 118:26: "Blessed be he who enters in the name of the Lord"); and it also shows that they see him as Saviour (cf. Lk 2:11–14). The Pharisees, maybe because they fear a riot, criticize Jesus for allowing the demonstration. He replies in a phrase which sounds like a proverb: so obvious is his messiahship that if men refused to recognize it, nature would proclaim it.

19:41–44 Jesus' feelings about Jerusalem cause him to weep. Zechariah, the father of John the Baptist, was able to see (cf. 1:68, 78) a "visit" paid by God and his Messiah to his people in the events surrounding his son's birth; but now Jerusalem fails to make the connexion (vv. 42, 44). The destruction of the city by Titus, prophesied here by Jesus (vv. 43–44), is a sign of the temporary nature of the Old Covenant which will be replaced by the new one which will be born on Calvary.

19:45–48 What Jesus said would come to pass, now begins to happen: he cleanses the temple (cf. the notes on Mt 21:12–17; Mk 11:12–25) and the leaders of the people begin to plot his death.

47And he was teaching daily in the temple. The chief priests and the scribes
and the principal men of the people sought to destroy him; 48but they did not
find anything they could do, for all the people hung upon his words.

Jesus' authority Mt 21:23–27; Mk 11:27–33

20 1One day, as he was teaching the people in the temple and preaching
the gospel, the chief priests and the scribes with the elders came up
2and said to him, "Tell us by what authority you do these things, or who it is
that gave you this authority." 3He answered them, "I also will ask you a
question; now tell me, 4Was the baptism of John from heaven or from men?"
5And they discussed it with one another, saying, "If we say, 'From heaven,' he
will say, 'Why did you not believe him?' 6But if we say, 'From men,' all the
people will stone us; for they are convinced that John was a prophet." 7So they
answered that they did not know whence it was. 8And Jesus said to them,
"Neither will I tell you by what authority I do these things."

Parable of the wicked tenants Mt 21:33–46; Mk 12:1–12

9And he began to tell the people this parable: "A man planted a vineyard, and
let it out to tenants, and went into another country for a long while. 10When the
time came, he sent a servant to the tenants, that they should give him some of
the fruit of the vineyard; but the tenants beat him, and sent him away empty-
handed. 11And he sent another servant; him also they beat and treated
shamefully, and sent him away empty-handed. 12And he sent yet a third; this
one they wounded and cast out. 13Then the owner of the vineyard said, 'What
shall I do? I will send my beloved son; it may be they will respect him.' 14But
when the tenants saw him, they said to themselves, 'This is the heir; let us kill
him, that the inheritance may be ours.' 15And they cast him out of the vineyard
and killed him. What then will the owner of the vineyard do to them? 16He will
come and destroy those tenants, and give the vineyard to others." When they

---

20:1–8 This dialogue has the style of a rabbinical disputation, with our Lord winning the point. No one should be surprised that Jesus does not give these men an answer, "for Jesus has no time for calculations, for astuteness, for the cruelty of cold hearts, for attractive but empty beauty. What he likes is the cheerfulness of a young heart, a simple step, a natural voice, clean eyes, ears attentive to his affectionate word of advice" (Bl. J. Escrivá, *Hom.*, 1, 181).

20:9–19 Given the circumstances in which it was preached, this was a very outspoken parable (cf. the note on Mk 12:1–12). Jesus clearly identifies himself with the beloved son (v. 13; cf. 3:22) who is thrown out of the vineyard (v. 18), Jerusalem, to be put to death. And Jesus is also the cornerstone of the new house of God, causing those who reject him to stumble, and be condemned (vv. 17–18).

20:9 Is 5:7.

heard this, they said, "God forbid!" [17]But he looked at them and said, "What then is this that is written:

'The very stone which the builders rejected
has become the head of the corner'?

[18]Every one who falls on that stone will be broken to pieces; but when it falls on any one it will crush him."

[19]The scribes and chief priests tried to lay hands on him at that very hour, but they feared the people; for they perceived that he had told this parable against them.

Tribute to Caesar Mt 22: 15–22; Mk 12:13–17

[20]So they watched him, and sent spies, who pretended to be sincere, that they might take hold of what he said, so as to deliver him up to the authority and jurisdiction of the governor. [21]They asked him, "Teacher, we know that you speak and teach rightly, and show no partiality, but truly teach the way of God. [22]Is it lawful for us to give tribute to Caesar, or not?" [23]But he perceived their craftiness, and said to them, [24]"Show me a coin.[f] Whose likeness and inscription has it?" They said, "Caesar's." [25]He said to them, "Then render to Caesar the things that are Caesar's, and to God the things that are God's." [26]And they were not able in the presence of the people to catch him by what he said; but marvelling at his answer they were silent.

The resurrection of the dead Mt 22:23–33; Mk 12:18–27

[27]There came to him some Sadducees, those who say that there is no resurrection, [28]and they asked him a question, saying, "Teacher, Moses wrote for us that if a man's brother dies, having a wife but no children, the man[g] must take the wife and raise up children for his brother. [29]Now there were seven brothers; the first took a wife, and died without children; [30]and the second [31]and the third took her, and likewise all seven left no children and died. [32]Afterward the woman also died. [33]In the resurrection, therefore, whose wife will the woman be? For the seven had her as wife."

20:20–26 The Jewish authorities become increasingly clever in their attempts to do away with Jesus (v. 20) but Jesus wins in these confrontations (v. 26; cf. the note on Mk 12:13–17). The reply Jesus gives here, however, sets a permanent marker for how Christians should act: "We Christians try to pay our tributes and contributions to those to whom they are due, just as he [Jesus] taught us" (St Justin, *Apology*, 1,17, 1).

20:27–40 The Sadducees held to a literal interpretation of the "written Law" (the Pentateuch) and did not believe in the resurrection of the dead; whereas the Pharisees accepted what some other texts of Scripture (Dan 12:2–3) and oral tradition said about the resurrection.

f. Greek *denarius* **g.** Greek *his brother* **20:17** Ps 118: 22–23. **20:28** Deut 25:5.

34And Jesus said to them, "The sons of this age marry and are given in
marriage; 35but those who are accounted worthy to attain to that age and to the
resurrection from the dead neither marry nor are given in marriage, 36for they
cannot die any more, because they are equal to angels and are sons of God,
being sons of the resurrection. 37But that the dead are raised, even Moses
showed, in the passage about the bush, where he calls the Lord the God of
Abraham and the God of Isaac and the God of Jacob.* 38Now he is not God of
the dead, but of the living; for all live to him." 39And some of the scribes
answered, "Teacher, you have spoken well." 40For they no longer dared to ask
him any question.

The divinity of the Messiah Mt 22:41–46; Mk 12:35–37

41But he said to them, "How can they say that the Christ is David's son? 42For
David himself says in the Book of Psalms,

'The Lord said to my Lord,
Sit at my right hand,
43till I make thy enemies a stool for thy feet.'

44David thus calls him Lord; so how is he his son?"

Jesus condemns the scribes Mt 23:1–36; Mk 12:38–40

45And in the hearing of all the people he said to his disciples, 46"Beware of the
scribes, who like to go about in long robes, and love salutations in the market
places and the best seats in the synagogues and the places of honour at feasts,
47who devour widow's houses and for a pretence make long prayers. They will
receive the greater condemnation."

In response to the crafty question put by these Sadducees, Jesus explains some aspects of the resurrection of the dead (cf. the note on Mt 22:23–33): there will be no need for marriage because death will be no more (v. 36): the principle of the new life will be God himself (v. 38). "*For man*, this consummation will be the final realization of the unity of the human race, which God willed from creation […]. The beatific vision, in which God opens himself in an inexhaustible way to the elect, will be the ever-flowing well-spring of happiness, peace, and mutual communion" (*CCC*, 1045).

20:41–44 "Lord" was the word usually used among Greek-speaking Jews to refer to God: in this passage "Jesus ascribes this title to himself in a veiled way when he disputes with the Pharisees about the meaning of Psalm 110 […]. Throughout his public life, he demonstrated his divine sovereignty by works of power over nature, illnesses, demons, death and sin" (*CCC*, 447).

20:45–47 See the note on Mt 23:1–36.

20:37 Ex 3:6.

The widow's mite Mk 12:41–44

21 [1]He looked up and saw the rich putting their gifts into the treasury;
[2]and he saw a poor widow put in two copper coins. [3]And he said,
"Truly I tell you, this poor widow has put in more than all of them; [4]for they
all contributed out of their abundance, but she out of her poverty put in all the
living that she had."

Announcement of the destruction of the temple Mt 24:1–2; Mk 13:1–2

[5]And as some spoke of the temple, how it was adorned with noble stones and
offerings, he said, [6]"As for these things which you see, the days will come
when there shall not be left here one stone upon another that will not be
thrown down."

The beginning of tribulation.
Persecution on account of the Gospel Mt 24:3–4; Mk 13:3–13

[7]And they asked him, "Teacher, when will this be, and what will be the sign
when this is about to take place?" [8]And he said, "Take heed that you are not led
astray; for many will come in my name, saying, 'I am he!' and, 'The time is at
hand!' Do not go after them. [9]And when you hear of wars and tumults, do not be
terrified; for this must first take place, but the end will not be at once."

[10]Then he said to them, "Nation will rise against nation, and kingdom
against kingdom; [11]there will be great earthquakes, and in various places
famines and pestilences; and there will be terrors and great signs from heaven.
[12]But before all this they will lay their hands on you and persecute you,
delivering you up to the synagogues and prisons, and you will be brought
before kings and governors for my name's sake. [13]This will be a time for you
to bear testimony. [14]Settle it therefore in your minds, not to meditate before-
hand how to answer; [15]for I will give you a mouth and wisdom, which none of

---

21:1–4 The action of the widow (vv. 1–20) and what Jesus says in his explanation (vv. 3–4) are an enduring example of the sort of attitude we should have towards God: "The Lord does not take account of the amount offered him but of the affection with which it is offered. Almsgiving is not a matter of sparing a little from one's plenty, but of acting like that widow, who gave everything she had" (St John Chrysostom, *Hom. on Heb*, 1, 4).

21:5–36 All the Synoptic Gospels (cf. Mt 24:1–51; Mk 13:1–37 and notes) record this discourse of Jesus in front of the temple about the destruction of Jerusalem and the end of the world. Three interconnected subjects run through the discourse—the destruction of Jerusalem (which took place about forty years later), the signs of the end of the world, and the coming of Christ in glory and majesty. The language of the discourse is apocalyptic—full of images which are not easy to interpret.

your adversaries will be able to withstand or contradict. 16You will be
delivered up even by parents and brothers and kinsmen and friends, and some
of you they will put to death; 17you will be hated by all for my name's sake.
18But not a hair of your head will perish. 19By your endurance you will gain
your lives.

The great tribulation in Jerusalem Mt 24:15–28; Mk 13:14–23

20"But when you see Jerusalem surrounded by armies, then know that its
desolation has come near. 21Then let those who are in Judea flee to the
mountains, and let those who are inside the city depart, and let not those who
are out in the country enter it; 22for these are days of vengeance, to fulfil all
that is written. 23Alas for those who are with child and for those who give
suck in those days! For great distress shall be upon the earth and wrath upon
this people; 24they will fall by the edge of the sword, and be led captive
among all nations; and Jerusalem will be trodden down by the Gentiles, until
the times of the Gentiles* are fulfilled.

The coming of the Son of man Mt 24:29–31; Mk 13:24–27

25"And there will be signs in sun and moon and stars, and upon the earth distress
of nations in perplexity at the roaring of the sea and the waves, 26men fainting
with fear and foreboding of what is coming on the world; for the powers of the
heavens will be shaken. 27And then they will see the Son of man coming in a
cloud with power and great glory. 28Now when these things begin to take place,
look up and raise your heads, because your redemption is drawing near."

The end will surely come—the lesson of the fig tree Mt 24:32–35; Mk 13:28–31

29And he told them a parable: "Look at the fig tree, and all the trees; 30as soon
as they come out in leaf, you see for yourselves and know that the summer is

---

In the opening verses (vv. 5–7) Jesus announces the destruction of the temple. This will be accompanied by the appearance of false messiahs (v. 8) and by wars and revolutions (v. 9).

He then goes on (vv. 10–19) to tell his disciples about the difficulties they will encounter in spreading the Kingdom of God—persecution, misunderstanding, hatred etc. (vv. 12, 16, 17). But he promises to come to their aid (vv. 14–15); they will win victory on account of their perseverance (vv. 18–19).

The discourse goes on to deal with signs forewarning of the destruction of Jerusalem (vv. 20–24) which are signs of the end of the world leading up to the coming of Christ in glory (vv. 25–28).

Finally, using the image of the fig tree, our Lord assures them that all these things are going to happen. Hence his exhortation to vigilance through living a temperate life (v. 34) and a life of prayer (v. 36).

21:27 Dan 7:13–14.

already near. [31]So also, when you see these things taking place, you know that
the kingdom of God is near. [32]Truly, I say to you, this generation will not pass
away till all has taken place. [33]Heaven and earth will pass away, but my words
will not pass away.

The need for vigilance Mt 24:42–51

[34]"But take heed to yourselves lest your hearts be weighed down with
dissipation and drunkenness and cares of this life, and that day come upon you
suddenly like a snare; [35]for it will come upon all who dwell upon the face of the
whole earth. [36]But watch at all times, praying that you may have strength to
escape all these things that will take place, and to stand before the Son of man."

Jesus teaches in the temple

[37]And every day he was teaching in the temple, but at night he went out and
lodged on the mount called Olivet. [38]And early in the morning all the people
came to him in the temple to hear him.

12. THE PASSION, DEATH AND RESURRECTION OF JESUS

Judas' treachery Mt 26:3–5, 14–16; Mk 14:1–2, 10–11

22 [1] Now the feast of Unleavened Bread drew near, which is called the
Passover. [2]And the chief priests and the scribes were seeking how to
put him to death; for they feared the people.

[3]Then Satan entered into Judas called Iscariot, who was of the number of
the twelve; [4]he went away and conferred with the chief priests and captains
how he might betray him to them. [5]And they were glad, and engaged to give

---

22:1–24:53 □ The account of the passion, death and resurrection of Jesus is recounted in close focus by all the evangelists. In his account of the passion, Luke draws attention especially to Jesus' compassion: in the midst of his sufferings, he takes an interest in those around him; he cures the servant wounded by the sword (22:51), consoles the women (23:28ff) and promises Paradise to the repentant thief (23:43).

On the post-resurrection events, this is the Synoptic Gospel which has most to say about the appearances of Jesus. Unlike the others, he reports the appearances in Jerusalem, the city in which Christ suffered and died and from which salvation will spread throughout the world.

22:1–6 At the end of the third temptation in the wilderness the devil departed from Christ "until an opportune moment" (4:13). Now, availing himself of Judas (v. 3), he enters the scene again. It is his hour, the hour of the "power of darkness" (22:53). However, this apparent victory of the devil was in fact his defeat, because him money. 6So he agreed and sought an opportunity to betray him to them in the absence of the multitude.

Preparations for the Last Supper Mt 26:17–19; Mk 14:12–16

7Then came the day of Unleavened Bread, on which the passover lamb had to be sacrificed. 8So Jesus[h] sent Peter and John, saying, "Go and prepare the passover for us, that we may eat it." 9They said to him, "Where will you have us prepare it?" 10He said to them, "Behold, when you have entered the city, a man carrying a jar of water will meet you; follow him into the house which he enters, 11and tell the householder, 'The Teacher says to you, Where is the guest room, where I am to eat the passover with my disciples?' 12And he will show you a large upper room furnished; there make ready." 13And they went, and found it as he had told them; and they prepared the passover.

The institution of the Eucharist Mt 26:26–29; 14:22–25; 1 Cor 11:23–26

14And when the hour came, he sat at table, and the apostles with him. 15And he said to them, "I have earnestly desired to eat this passover with you before I suffer; 16for I tell you I shall not eat it[i] until it is fulfilled in the kingdom of God." 17And he took a cup, and when he had given thanks he said, "Take this, and divide it among yourselves; 18for I tell you that from now on I shall not drink of the fruit of the vine until the kingdom of God comes." 19And he took bread, and when he had given thanks he broke it and gave it to them, saying, "This is my body which is given for you. Do this in remembrance of me." 20And likewise the cup after supper, saying, "This cup which is poured out for you is the new covenant in my blood.[j]

Christ, through his death, crushed him who had power over death, thereby setting free all those whose fear of death was such that they spent their lives as slaves (cf. Heb 2:14–15).

22:7–20 Luke gives a more detailed account of the Passover meal than the other two Synoptics, whose narratives are more stylized. Preparations for the Passover involved a series of elaborate operations—sacrificing the lamb in the temple in the early afternoon, burning anything leavened that happened to be in the house, and assembling all the things needed for the meal (five types of bitter herbs, parsley, wine, oil, unleavened bread, honey, figs and olives). The instructions given by Jesus (vv. 10–12) may have been designed to ensure that the Sanhedrin did not know where exactly he was going to celebrate Passover.

The Passover meal was a kind of memorial ceremony: the meal (and the prayers said at it: Deut 26:5–10) was designed to evoke God's liberation of each member of his people. Our Lord's opening words (vv. 15–18) show that the old

h. Greek *he* **i.** Other ancient authorities read *never eat it again* **j.** Some ancient authorities omit *which is given for you. Do this in remembrance of me" 20And likewise the cup after supper, saying, "This cup which is poured out for you is the new covenant in my blood"*

The treachery of Judas foretold Mt 26:20–25; Mk 14:17–21; Jn 13:21–32
21“But behold the hand of him who betrays me is with me on the table. 22For
the Son of man goes as it has been determined; but woe to that man by whom
he is betrayed!” 23And they began to question one another, which of them it
was that would do this.

A dispute among the apostles
24A dispute also arose among them, which of them was to be regarded as the
greatest. 25And he said to them. “The kings of the Gentiles exercise lordship over
them; and those in authority over them are called benefactors. 26But not so with
you; rather let the greatest among you become as the youngest, and the leader as
one who serves. 27For which is the greater, one who sits at table, or one who
serves? Is it not the one who sits at table? But I am among you as one who serves.
28“You are those who have continued with me in my trials; 29as my Father
appointed a kingdom for me, so do I appoint for you 30that you may eat and drink
at my table in my kingdom, and sit on thrones judging the twelve tribes of Israel.

Peter's denial foretold Mt 26:30–35; Mk 14:26–31; Jn 13:36–38
31“Simon, Simon, behold, Satan demanded to have you,[k] that he might sift you[k]
like wheat, 32but I have prayed for you that your faith may not fail; and when you

---

rite has ceased to apply; by the words he pronounces over the bread and the wine (vv. 19–20) something new is established: his sacrificed body and his blood poured out establish the New Covenant between God and men, for their salvation. For this reason Jesus also establishes this rite as a memorial: “Do this in remembrance of me” (v. 19). “When the Church celebrates the Eucharist, she commemorates Christ's Passover, and it is made present: the sacrifice Christ offered once for all on the cross remains ever present. ‘As often as the sacrifice of the Cross by which “Christ our Pasch has been sacrificed” is celebrated on the altar, the work of our redemption is carried out’ (Vatican II, *LG*, 3)” (*CCC*, 1364).

22:21–30 Throughout his Gospel (and especially in his account of the passion), Luke likes to get across the idea that Jesus' way of dealing with difficulties sets an example for Christians. These two incidents, which contrast with the account of the meal, allow us to see how alone Jesus was and the feelings that inspire his life (very different to those of his disciples). Yet what he says to his disciples inspires hope. Even though they are still very small-minded (v. 24; cf. Mt 20:20–28; Mk 10:35–45 and notes), because they are associated with Christ's humiliation (v. 28) they will also be involved in his exaltation.

22:31–38 After the meal and before his arrest in Gethsemane, Jesus warns his disciples, particularly Peter, that their faith is going to be put to the test (vv. 31–32) because they do not yet grasp the redemptive meaning of his life and his death (vv.

k. The Greek word for *you* here is plural; in verse 32 it is singular

have turned again, strengthen your brethren." [33]And he said to him, "Lord, I am
ready to go with you to prison and to death." [34]He said, "I tell you, Peter, the
cock will not crow this day, until you three times deny that you know me."

Appeal to the apostles

[35]And he said to them, "When I sent you out with no purse or bag or sandals,
did you lack anything?" They said, "Nothing." [36]He said to them, "But now,
let him who has a purse take it, and likewise a bag. And let him who has no
sword sell his mantle and buy one. [37]For I tell you that this scripture must be
fulfilled in me, 'And he was reckoned with transgressors'; for what is written
about me has its fulfilment." [38]And they said, "Look, Lord, here are two
swords." And he said to them, "It is enough."

Jesus' prayer and agony in the garden Mt 26:36–46; Mk 14:32–42

[39]And he came out, and went, as was his custom, to the Mount of Olives; and the
disciples followed him. [40]And when he came to the place he said to them, "Pray
that you may not enter into temptation." [41]And he withdrew from them about a
stone's throw, and knelt down and prayed, [42]"Father, if thou art willing, remove
this cup from me; nevertheless not my will, but thine, be done." [43]And there
appeared to him an angel from heaven, strengthening him. [44]And being in an
agony he prayed more earnestly; and his sweat became like great drops of blood
falling down upon the ground.[l] [45]And when he rose from prayer, he came to the
disciples and found them sleeping for sorrow, [46]and he said to them, "Why do you
sleep? Rise and pray that you may not enter into temptation."

37–38). St Luke reports this episode in more detail than the other Synoptics and he includes Jesus' prayer for Peter. The Church has always held that the special help Jesus gave Peter "to keep this faith from every lapse and to strengthen his brothers in it" (*CCC*, 552) continues to be given to the bishop of Rome, Peter's successor.

22:39–46 Jesus' prayer in the garden of olives shows that he accepts his ignominious death in order to do what his Father has planned. This prayer must have lasted quite a long time, though St Luke reports only the key moments. Almost every verse of this passage mentions prayer; it begins and ends with Jesus' recommendation to pray in order not to enter into temptation; and Jesus himself sets us an example because "in an agony he prayed more earnestly" (v. 43). Our Lord's prayer is, then a perfect lesson in abandonment and union with God's will: "Are you suffering some great tribulation? Do you have reverses? Say very slowly, as if savouring the words, this powerful and manly prayer: 'May the most just and most lovable will of God be done, be fulfilled, be praised and eternally exalted above all things. Amen. Amen.' I assure you that you'll find peace" (Bl. J. Escrivá, *The Way*, 691).

l. Other ancient authorities omit verses 43 and 44 **22:37** Is 53:12.

The arrest Mt 26: 47–56; Mk 14:43–52; Jn 18:1–12

47While he was still speaking, there came a crowd, and the man called Judas,
one of the twelve, was leading them. He drew near to Jesus to kiss him; 48but
Jesus said to him, "Judas, would you betray the Son of man with a kiss?"
49And when those who were about him saw what would follow, they said,
"Lord, shall we strike with the sword?" 50And one of them struck the slave of
the high priest and cut off his right ear. 51But Jesus said, "No more of this!"
And he touched his ear and healed him. 52Then Jesus said to the chief priests
and captains of the temple and elders, who had come out against him,* "Have
you come out as against a robber, with swords and clubs? 53When I was with
you day after day in the temple, you did not lay hands on me. But this is your
hour, and the power of darkness."

Peter's denials Mt 26:69–75; Mk 14:66–72; Jn 18:15–18,25–27

54Then they seized him and led him away, bringing him into the high priest's
house. Peter followed at a distance; 55and when they had kindled a fire in the
middle of the courtyard and sat down together, Peter sat among them. 56Then
a maid, seeing him as he sat in the light and gazing at him, said, "This man
also was with him." 57But he denied it, saying, "Woman, I do not know him."
58And a little later some one else saw him and said, "You also are one of
them." But Peter said, "Man, I am not." 59And after an interval of about an
hour still another insisted, saying, "Certainly this man also was with him; for
he is a Galilean." 60But Peter said, "Man, I do not know what you are saying."
And immediately, while he was still speaking, the cock crowed. 61And the
Lord turned and looked at Peter. And Peter remembered the word of the Lord,

---

22:47–53 In their accounts of this episode, all four evangelists show the nobility and self-possession of Jesus and the drama of events that unfold—the crush of the crowds, the betrayal by Judas, the wounding of the high priest's servant, etc. In this context Luke focuses on two further aspects—the mercy of our Lord in healing the wounded servant (v. 51) and the apparent victory of the devil (v. 53).

22:54–71 Luke's account seeks to keep closest to the chronology of events: Jesus is taken at night to the house of Caiaphas; there, Peter denies him and the servants revile him; in the early morning there is a meeting of the Sanhedrin at which Jesus is condemned to death. As regards the events of the night, Luke is the only evangelist to mention the look that our Lord gives Peter (v. 61) which touches his heart and makes him contrite. This Gospel often mentions how Jesus looked at people (5:20, 27; 6:10, 20; etc.); this is something the saints have meditated on: "I often think, my Christ, how delectable and happy your eyes seem to those who love you, when you, my God, are pleased to look on them with love. I think that even one such gentle glance bestowed on souls whom you count as your own is

how he had said to him, "Before the cock crows today, you will deny me three
times." 62And he went out and wept bitterly.

Jesus abused by the guards Mt 26:67–68; Mk 14:65

63Now the men who were holding Jesus mocked him and beat him; 64they also
blindfolded him and asked him, "Prophesy! Who is it that struck you?" 65And
they spoke many other words against him, reviling him.

Jesus before the chief priests Mt 26:57–68; Mk 14:53–65; 18:13–24

66When day came, the assembly of the elders of the people gathered together,
both chief priests and scribes; and they led him away to their council, and they
said, 67"If you are the Christ, tell us." But he said to them, "If I tell you, you
will not believe; 68and if I ask you, you will not answer. 69But from now on
the Son of man shall be seated at the right hand of the power of God." 70And
they all said, "Are you the Son of God, then?" And he said to them, "You say
that I am." 71And they said, "What further testimony do we need? We have
heard it ourselves from his own lips."

Jesus before Pilate Mt 27:11–14; Mk 15:1–5; Jn 18:28–40

23 1Then the whole company of them arose, and brought him before
Pilate. 2And they began to accuse him, saying, "We found this man
perverting our nation, and forbidding us to give tribute to Caesar, and saying
that he himself is Christ a king."* 3And Pilate asked him, "Are you the King
of the Jews?" And he answered him, "You have said so." 4And Pilate said to
the chief priests and the multitudes, "I find no crime in this man." 5But they
were urgent, saying, "He stirs up the people, teaching throughout all Judea,
from Galilee even to this place."

---

sufficient reward for many years of service. [...] You know, my Lord, that I was often more terrified at thinking I might see your divine face turned from me in wrath on that fearful day of the last judgment than of all the pains and furies of hell that I could imagine" (St Teresa of Avila, *Exclam.*, 14).

The interrogation by the Sanhedrin clearly shows Jesus to have the dual title of the Christ and the Son of God. However, to accept Jesus as such one needs faith. The members of the Sanhedrin do not have faith (vv. 67–68) and they condemn Jesus to death.

23:1–25 St Luke's account of the trial of Jesus seems to grow out of the prayer of the Christians of Jerusalem: "In this city there were gathered together against thy holy servant Jesus, whom thou didst anoint, both Herod and Pontius Pilate, with the Gentiles and the peoples of Israel, to do whatever thy hand and thy plan had predestined to take place" (Acts 4:27–28). In line with this description St Luke presents the events in three scenes—Jesus before Pilate, before Herod, and again

Jesus before Herod

[6]When Pilate heard this, he asked whether the man was a Galilean. [7]And when he learned that he belonged to Herod's jurisdiction, he sent him over to Herod, who was himself in Jerusalem at that time. [8]When Herod saw Jesus, he was very glad, for he had long desired to see him, because he had heard about him, and he was hoping to see some sign done by him. [9]So he questioned him at some length; but he made no answer. [10]The chief priests and the scribes stood by, vehemently accusing him. [11]And Herod with his soldiers treated him with contempt and mocked him; then, arraying him in gorgeous apparel, he sent him back to Pilate. [12]And Herod and Pilate became friends with each other that very day, for before this they had been at enmity with each other.

Jesus is condemned to death Mt 27:15–26; Mk 5:6–15; Jn 19:4–16

[13]Pilate then called together the chief priests and the rulers and the people, [14]and said to them, "You brought me this man as one who was perverting the people; and after examining him before you, behold, I did not find this man guilty of any of your charges against him;* [15]neither did Herod, for he sent him back to us. Behold, nothing deserving death has been done by him; [16]I will therefore chastise him and release him."[m]

[18]But they all cried out together, "Away with this man, and release to us Barabbas"—[19]a man who had been thrown into prison for an insurrection started in the city, and for murder. [20]Pilate addressed them once more, desiring to release Jesus; [21]but they shouted out, "Crucify, crucify him!" [22]A third time he said to

---

before Pilate. Readers can judge from the facts as to who was responsible for what, but they know, as the evangelist does, that over and above the will of men is the plan of God.

In the first scene we can see immediately the shrewd way Jesus' accusers go about their business by changing the title given him in their accusation: the Sanhedrin condemned him for calling himself Christ and Son of God (22:66–71) but now they accuse him of calling himself King and subverting the people (v. 2). Pilate immediately sees how inconsistent they are, but he compromises. He takes the first chance he gets (vv. 6–7) to shed responsibility.

In the second scene, it is easy to see what the characters are like: Herod comes across as a frivolous, almost grotesque individual (vv. 8–9) and the chief priests and the scribes are bent on Jesus' being put to death (v. 10). In the face of such petty enemies our Lord remains aloof (v. 9).

Then, at Pilate's court once more, the governor, in his exchanges with Jesus' accusers, three times (vv. 14, 20, 22) makes it clear that Jesus is innocent. But on each occasion the crowd call for Jesus' death (vv. 18, 21, 23). Paradoxically Barabbas is set free (v. 25) even though he was guilty of sedition and murder (v. 19). The scene is an indictment of indolence.

See the RSV note.

m. Here, or after verse 19, other ancient authorities add verse 17, *Now he was obliged to release one man to them at the festival*

them, "Why, what evil has he done? I have found in him no crime deserving
death; I will therefore chastise him and release him." 23But they were urgent,
demanding with loud cries that he should be crucified. And their voices prevailed.
24So Pilate gave sentence that their demand should be granted. 25He released the
man who had been thrown into prison for insurrection and murder, whom they
asked for; but Jesus he delivered up to their will.

The crucifixion and death of Jesus Mt 27:32–56; Mk 15:21–41; Jn 19:17–30

26And as they led him away, they seized one Simon of Cyrene, who was coming
in from the country, and laid on him the cross, to carry it behind Jesus. 27And
there followed him a great multitude of the people, and of women who bewailed
and lamented him. 28But Jesus turning to them said, "Daughters of Jerusalem, do
not weep for me, but weep for yourselves and for your children. 29For behold,
the days are coming when they will say, 'Blessed are the barren, and the
wombs that never bore, and the breasts that never gave suck!' 30Then they will
begin to say to the mountains, 'Fall on us'; and to the hills, 'Cover us.' 31For if
they do this when the wood is green, what will happen when it is dry?"*

32Two others also, who were criminals, were led away to be put to death with
him. 33And when they came to the place which is called The Skull, there they
crucified him, and the criminals, one on the right and one on the left. 34And Jesus
said, "Father, forgive them; for they know not what they do." [n] And they cast lots
to divide his garments. 35And the people stood by, watching; but the rulers scoffed
at him, saying, "He saved others; let him save himself, if he is the Christ of God,
his Chosen One!" 36The soldiers also mocked him, coming up and offering him
vinegar, 37and saying, "If you are the King of the Jews, save yourself!" 38There
was also an inscription over him,[o] "This is the King of the Jews."

39One of the criminals who were hanged railed at him, saying, "Are you not
the Christ? Save yourself and us!" 40But the other rebuked him, saying, "Do
you not fear God, since you are under the same sentence of condemnation?

23:26–49 Like the other evangelists, Luke describes the crucifixion and death of Jesus as fulfilling God's plan: Jesus has become the suffering Servant (cf. the notes on Mt 27:32–56; Mk 15:21–41).

Jesus' behaviour throughout is depicted as an example every Christian should follow: it profoundly impresses the centurion, and it provokes the crowd to contrition (vv. 47–48). Jesus is a model of mercy and forgiveness: he consoles the women (vv. 28–29), pardons those who are going to put him to death (v. 35), and opens the gates of Paradise to the good thief (v. 43). In his other book, Luke shows us the first martyr, St Stephen, imitating our Lord's example (cf. Acts 7:60): "Forgiveness demonstrates the presence in the world of *the love which is more powerful than sin.* Forgiveness is also the fundamental condition for reconciliation,

n. Other ancient authorities omit the sentence *And Jesus . . . what they do* **o.** Other anceint authorities add *in letters of Greek and Latin and Hebrew* **23:30** Hos 10:8. **23:34** Ps 22:18. **23:36** Ps 69:21.

41And we indeed justly; for we are receiving the due reward of our deeds; but
this man has done nothing wrong." 42And he said, "Jesus, remember me when
you come in your kingly power."[p] 43And he said to him, "Truly, I say to you,
today you will be with me in Paradise."

44It was now about the sixth hour, and there was darkness over the whole
land[q] until the ninth hour, 45while the sun's light failed;[r] and the curtain of the
temple was torn in two. 46Then Jesus, crying with a loud voice, said, "Father,
into thy hands I commit my spirit!" And having said this he breathed his last.
47Now when the centurion saw what had taken place, he praised God, and said,
"Certainly this man was innocent!" 48And all the multitudes who assembled to
see the sight, when they saw what had taken place, returned home beating their
breasts. 49And all his acquaintances and the women who had followed him
from Galilee stood at a distance and saw these things.

The burial Mt 27:57–61; Mk 15:42–47; Jn 19:31–42

50Now there was a man named Joseph from the Jewish town of Arimathea. He
was a member of the council, a good and righteous man, 51who had not
consented to their purpose and deed, and he was looking for the kingdom of
God. 52This man went to Pilate and asked for the body of Jesus. 53Then he
took it down and wrapped it in a linen shroud, and laid him in a rock-hewn
tomb, where no one had ever yet been laid. 54It was the day of Preparation, and
the sabbath was beginning.[s] 55The women who had come with him from
Galilee followed, and saw the tomb, and how his body was laid; 56then they
returned, and prepared spices and ointments.

On the sabbath they rested according to the commandment.

---

not only in the relationship of God with man, but also in relationships between people" (John Paul II, *Div. in mis.*, 14).

Jesus gets all his strength from prayer. He twice turns to his Father God, and his last words are addressed to Him: "Father, into thy hands I commit my spirit" (v. 46). "All the troubles, for all time, of humanity enslaved by sin and death, all the petitions and intercessions of salvation history are summed up in this cry of the incarnate Word. Here the Father accepts them and, beyond all hope, answers them by raising his Son. Thus is fulfilled and brought to completion the drama of prayer in the economy of creation and salvation" (*CCC*, 2606).

23:50–56 The text supplies details which go to show that the one who is "buried" is the one who "rose": Jesus' body is placed in a tomb "where no one had ever been laid" (v. 53) and the women, too, were witnesses of "how his body was laid" (v. 55): "God did not prevent death from separating [Christ's] soul from the body in accordance with the necessary order of nature, but he reunited them once again, one to the other, by means of the resurrection so that he himself might become the

p. Greek *kingdom* **q.** Or *earth* **r.** Or *the sun was eclipsed.* Other ancient authorities read *the sun was darkened* **s.** Greek *was dawning* **23:46** Ps 31:5.

The resurrection of Jesus. The empty tomb
Mt 28:1–10; Mk 16:1–8; Jn 20:1–10

24 1But on the first day of the week, at early dawn, they went to the tomb,
taking the spices which they had prepared. 2And they found the stone
rolled away from the tomb, 3but when they went in they did not find the body.[t]
4While they were perplexed about this, behold, two men stood by them in
dazzling apparel; 5and as they were frightened and bowed their faces to the
ground, the men said to them, "Why do you seek the living among the dead?
He is not here, but has risen.[u] 6Remember how he told you, while he was still
in Galilee, 7that the Son of man must be delivered into the hands of sinful men,
and be crucified, and on the third day rise." 8And they remembered his words,
9and returning from the tomb they told all this to the eleven and to all the rest.
10Now it was Mary Magdalene and Joanna and Mary the mother of James and
the other women with them who told this to the apostles; 11but these words
seemed to them an idle tale, and they did not believe them. 12But Peter rose
and ran to the tomb; stooping and looking in, he saw the linen cloths by
themselves; and he went home wondering at what had happened.[v]

The road to Emmaus
Mk 16:12–13

13That very day two of them were going to a village named Emmaus, about
seven miles[w] from Jerusalem, 14and talking with each other about all these
things that had happened. 15While they were talking and discussing together,

---

point of contact between life and death, ending in himself the decomposition of the nature which produces death and inaugurating in himself the principle of reunion of the two separated parts" (St Gregory of Nyssa, *Oratio. catech.*, 16; cf. *CCC*, 625).

24:1–12 Of the Synoptics, Luke's Gospel is the one which goes into most detail about the announcement of the resurrection and about Jesus' appearances. Throughout, he records how difficult the disciples found it to accept that Jesus had risen.

The opening verses describe the women's reaction. They are disconcerted (v. 4) and frightened (v. 5) to find the tomb empty and meet the two brightly clad men. Only when reminded that everything had been predicted by Jesus are they moved to believe in the resurrection (vv. 7–8). The narrative then goes on to focus on the attitude of the disciples. They do not believe the women; but Peter (and possibly others: cf. 24:24) begins to think that maybe it is true; however, this does not lead to belief but just to wonder (v. 12).

24:13–35 The appearance to the disciples in Emmaus complements what has gone before: eventually, when they get back to Jerusalem, all the disciples already believe in the resurrection (vv. 34–35).

t. Other ancient authorities add *of the Lord Jesus* **u.** Other ancient authorities omit *He is not here, but has risen* **v.** Other ancient authorities omit verse 12 **w.** Greek *sixty stadia*; some ancient authorities read *a hundred and sixty stadia*

Jesus himself drew near and went with them. [16]But their eyes were kept from
recognizing him. [17]And he said to them, "What is this conversation which you
are holding with each other as you walk?" And they stood still, looking sad.
[18]Then one of them, named Cleopas, answered him, "Are you the only visitor
to Jerusalem who does not know the things that have happened there in these
days?" [19]And he said to them, "What things?" And they said to him,
"Concerning Jesus of Nazareth, who was a prophet mighty in deed and word
before God and all the people, [20]and how our chief priests and rulers delivered
him up to be condemned to death, and crucified him. [21]But we had hoped that
he was the one to redeem Israel. Yes, and besides all this, it is now the third day
since this happened. [22]Moreover, some women of our company amazed us.
They were at the tomb early in the morning [23]and did not find his body; and
they came back saying that they had even seen a vision of angels, who said that
he was alive. [24]Some of those who were with us went to the tomb, and found it
just as the women had said; but him they did not see." [25]And he said to them,
"O foolish men, and slow of heart to believe all that the prophets have spoken!
[26]Was it not necessary that the Christ should suffer these things and enter into
his glory?" [27]And beginning with Moses and all the prophets, he interpreted to
them in all the scriptures the things concerning himself.

[28]So they drew near to the village to which they were going. He appeared
to be going further, [29]but they constrained him, saying, "Stay with us, for it is
toward evening and the day is now far spent." So he went in to stay with them.
[30]When he was at table with them, he took the bread and blessed, and broke it,
and gave it to them. [31]And their eyes were opened and they recognized him;
and he vanished out of their sight. [32]They said to each other, "Did not our
hearts burn within us while he talked to us on the road, while he opened to us
the scriptures?" [33]And they rose that same hour and returned to Jerusalem; and
they found the eleven gathered together and those who were with them, [34]who
said, "The Lord has risen indeed, and has appeared to Simon!" [35]Then they

---

However, this appearance has a quality of its own. These two disciples were sad (v. 17), all hope gone (v. 21); in the last analysis, they had not grasped the mystery of Christ's life (vv. 19–24). When Jesus explains events to them in terms of fulfillment of the Scriptures, their hearts are set on fire (v. 32) and they want him to stay with them (vv. 28–29). Then, at the last moment they recognize him at the breaking of the bread.

This episode in a way helps to show the part Holy Scripture and the Eucharist play in the Church in nourishing our faith in Jesus: "The Church has always venerated the Holy Scriptures as she venerated the Body of the Lord, in so far as she never ceases, particularly in the sacred liturgy, to partake of the bread of life and to offer it to the faithful from the one table of the Word of God and the Body of Christ" (Vatican II, *DV*, 21).

told what had happened on the road, and how he was known to them in the
breaking of the bread.

Jesus appears to the disciples in the upper room Mt 28:16–20; Mk 16:14–18; Jn 20:19–31
36 As they were saying this, Jesus himself stood among them, and said to them,
"Peace to you!"[x] 37 But they were startled and frightened, and supposed that
they saw a spirit. 38 And he said to them, "Why are you troubled, and why do
questionings rise in your hearts?* 39 See my hands and my feet, that it is I
myself; handle me, and see; for a spirit has not flesh and bones as you see that
I have." 40 And when he had said this, he showed them his hands and his feet.[y]
41 And while they still disbelieved for joy, and wondered, he said to them,
"Have you anything here to eat?" 42 They gave him a piece of broiled fish,
43 and he took it and ate before them.

44 Then he said to them, "These are my words which I spoke to you, while
I was still with you, that everything written about me in the law of Moses and
the prophets and the psalms must be fulfilled." 45 Then he opened their minds
to understand the scriptures, 46 and said to them, "Thus it is written, that the
Christ should suffer and on the third day rise from the dead, 47 and that
repentance and forgiveness of sins should be preached in his name to all
nations,[z] beginning from Jerusalem. 48 You are witnesses of these things. 49 And
behold, I send the promise of my Father upon you; but stay in the city, until
you are clothed with power from on high."

24:36–53 Maybe we can see, in the account of Jesus' appearance, his "method" of teaching his disciples about aspects of the resurrection. Once the disciples have been convinced of the resurrection (cf. 24:34), our Lord shows them that he is not just a spirit (v. 37) but has flesh and blood (vv. 39, 41–43) and that he is the same person as he who died on the cross (vv. 39–40): "I for my part know very well and firmly believe that after his resurrection the Lord remained present in the flesh. And so when he appeared to Peter and his companions he said, 'Touch me and know that I am not an incorporeal spirit.' And all, when they touched him and believed, were convinced that he was present in body and soul [...]. Moreover, after his resurrection he ate and drank with them, as the man of flesh he was, even if, spiritually speaking, he was made one with the Father" (St Ignatius of Antioch, *Letter to the Smyrnaeans*, 3, 1–3).

After these proofs of his identity, and before his return to the Father, Jesus entrusts his disciples with their mission. These closing words of our Lord sum up

x. Other ancient authorities omit *and said to them, "Peace to you!"* **y.** Other ancient authorities omit verse 40 **z.** Or *nations. Beginning from Jerusalem you are witnesses*

The ascension of our Lord Mk 16:19; Acts 1:6–11

50Then he led them out as far as Bethany, and lifting up his hands he blessed
them. 51While he blessed them, he parted from them, and was carried up into
heaven.[a] 52And they worshipped him, and[b] returned to Jerusalem with great
joy, 53and were continually in the temple blessing God.

---

everything that St Luke will go on to describe in the book of the Acts of the Apostles: it is part of God's plan that the mystery of Christ, of which they are witnesses (v. 48) should be preached abroad (vv. 46–47), for the salvation of all mankind (v. 47). The apostolic mission will begin in Jerusalem (v. 47), where the "exodus" of Jesus reached its fulfillment (cf. 9:31) and where the mission of the Holy Spirit will begin (v. 49).

a. Other ancient authorities omit *and was carried up into heaven* **b.** Other ancient authorities omit *worshipped him, and*

The Gospel according to St John

From very early on, the Tradition of the Church attributed the authorship of the fourth Gospel to the apostle John, the son of Zebedee, the Lord's beloved disciple, who reclined on his breast during the last supper. It is very likely that a disciple of the apostle added something, given what is said at the end of the text: "this is the disciple who is bearing witness to these things, and who has written these things; and we know that his testimony is true" (Jn 21:24; cf. 13:23; 19:26; 20:2; 21:7). The apostle John must have written his Gospel around the end of the first century, after many years of meditating on and proclaiming the words and deeds of Jesus.

As compared with the first three Gospels, St John's has very characteristic features of its own. Christ's ministry is centred mainly in Judea, and the focus is particularly on what Jesus does in the temple of Jerusalem, to which he goes up at least three times in connexion with festivals (2:13; 7:10; 12:12). In contrast to the Synoptics, John has very little to say about Jesus' activity in Galilee, although he does focus on his passage through Samaria (4:1–42). In presenting his teaching this evangelist also shows a marked tendency to expound the deep meaning of Jesus' words and actions. He often sets Jesus' revelation in the framework of long discourses which are much more profound and require more work by the reader than is apparent at first sight. Also John concentrates on specific miracles, which he calls "signs"; because they provide him with a basis for particular teaching he wants to stress. He has written his Gospel as a testimony "that you may believe that Jesus is the Christ, the Son of God, and that believing you may have life in his name" (20:31).

Generally speaking, John follows the same order as the apostles used in their oral preaching. In doing so, he is in line with the Synoptic Gospels: Jesus begins his public ministry after being baptized in the Jordan by John the Baptist, he preaches and works miracles in Galilee and Jerusalem, and he ends his life on earth with his passion and glorious resurrection. Within this framework, John follows a plan of his own, expanding on certain ideas which recur throughout his book—the series of Jewish festivals which mark the stages of his account and show the Old Testament reaching fulfilment in the New; the themes of Life, the Bread of Life, the Light, Truth, Love etc., through which Christ's saving action is expressed. These ideas interweave throughout the Gospel and give it a solid structure and thematic consistency. Following the prologue with which his Gospel opens (1:1–18), and in which the main ideas of the book are summarized, we can distinguish two main parts. The first contains the gradual revelation of Jesus as the Messiah by means of his signs, meetings and discourses, in the face of a steadily increasing blindness on the part of those Jews who reject him (1:19–12:50); scholars usually call this part the "book of the signs". The second part shows Jesus' manifestation as the Messiah and Son of God, in his passion, death and resurrection, that is, in the "hour" of Jesus and the power of darkness (13:1–21:25); this is usually called the "book of Christ's glory".

The fourth Gospel has been described as the "spiritual Gospel" (Clement of Alexandria). Like the Synoptics, it is "Gospel", but it implies a deeper understanding of our Lord's life and teaching. In this sense it is a continuation or extension of those other Gospels. John teaches that Jesus is the Messiah, the *Son of God*, the eternal Word of the Father, who communicates his Spirit after his death and resurrection. This revelation of Christ demands *faith* of Christians if they are share in his Life, and it also requires them to have *communion in charity* with their fellow Christians in the Church under the guidance of Peter. This union with Christ and in the Church is guaranteed by the *sacraments*. The Blessed Virgin is a model of faith and, as Mother of the Church, she continues to give all Christians her motherly care.

John

Prologue

1 [1]In the beginning was the Word, and the Word was with God, and the Word was God.* [2]He was in the beginning with God; [3]all things were made through him, and without him was not anything made that was made. [4]In him was life,[a] and the life was the light of men. [5]The light shines in the darkness,* and the darkness has not overcome it.

[6]There was a man sent from God, whose name was John. [7]He came for testimony, to bear witness to the light, that all might believe through him. [8]He was not the light, but came to bear witness to the light.

[9]The true light that enlightens every man was coming into the world. [10]He was in the world, and the world was made through him, yet the world knew him not. [11]He came to his own home, and his own people received him not. [12]But to all who received him, who believed in his name, he gave power to become children of God; [13]who were born, not of blood nor of the will of the flesh nor of the will of man, but of God.

[14]And the Word became flesh and dwelt among us, full of grace and truth; we have beheld his glory, glory as of the only Son from the Father. [15](John bore witness to him, and cried, "This was he of whom I said, 'He who comes after me

---

1:1–18 These opening verses are both a prologue and a hymn in praise of Jesus Christ. As a prologue they mention the main themes that will be covered in the Gospel narrative. Jesus is the eternal Word of God and as such, in speaking to men, he communicates light, truth and life (vv. 1–10). Living among them he manifests to them his divine glory (vv. 15–18). Also mentioned are those who were witnesses of his earthly life—John the Baptist (vv. 6–7, 15) and the disciples, who believed in Jesus (v. 16), and also those who rejected him (v. 11). As a hymn to Jesus Christ, these verses proclaim the eternity and divinity of the Word (v. 1), his role in the work of creation (v. 3), his incarnation (v. 14), and his self-offering for the salvation of all men which makes those who believe in him children of God (vv. 9, 16). In other words, as St Paul does elsewhere (cf. Col 1:15–20; Phil 2:6–11), the evangelist tells us who Jesus Christ really is, where he comes from, how he came into the world and what he has done for mankind.

The content and some of the wording of the Prologue are very reminiscent of chapter 1 of the book of Genesis: 1) the opening words are the same ("In the beginning"), although the evangelist is referring to the absolute beginning, that is, eternity; 2) in both, the creative role of the Word of God is similar; in Genesis the creative work of God culminates in the creation of man in the image and likeness

a. Or *was not anything made. That which has been made was life in him* ranks before me, for he was before me.'") [16]And from his fulness have we all received, grace upon grace. [17]For the law was given through Moses; grace and truth came through Jesus Christ. [18]No one has ever seen God; the only Son,[b] who is in the bosom of the Father, he has made him known.

PART ONE: JESUS IS MANIFESTED AS THE MESSIAH BY HIS SIGNS AND WORDS

1. INTRODUCTION

The witness of John the Baptist

Mt 3:1–12; Mk 1:1–8; Lk 3:1–18

[19]And this is the testimony of John, when the Jews sent priests and Levites from Jerusalem to ask him, "Who are you?" [20]He confessed, he did not deny, but confessed, "I am not the Christ." [21]And they asked him, "What then? Are you Elijah?" He said, "I am not." "Are you the prophet?" And he answered, "No." [22]They said to him then, "Who are you? Let us have an answer for those who sent us. What do you say about yourself?" [23]He said, "I am the voice of one crying in the wilderness, 'Make straight the way of the Lord,' as the prophet Isaiah said."

---

of God; in the Gospel, the work of the Incarnate Word ends with man being raised up (re-created) to the status of a son or daughter of God.

1:19–12:50 □□ In this section of his Gospel St John shows Jesus gradually revealing himself through his miracles (which are signs of his divinity) and his words, in which he declares himself to be the Messiah, the Son of God, and equal to the Father. All this builds up in a dramatic crescendo to Jesus' "hour", which culminates in his death and resurrection, the subject of the second part of the Gospel. Given its content, the first part of John's Gospel has been well named "the book of the signs".

1:19–51 □ To introduce this first part of the Gospel we have the testimony of John (1:19–34; cf. 3:22–26) and the calling of the first disciples (1:35–51).

1:19–34 The Baptism of Jesus marks the start of his mission as the suffering Servant, and it anticipates the "Baptism" of his violent death by which he redeems the world from sin. The evangelist depicts the witness borne by the Baptist as a model for the testimony that Christians should give of what they have seen and

b. Other ancient authorities read *God* **1:23** Is 40:3.

[24]Now they had been sent from the Pharisees. [25]They asked him, "Then
why are you baptizing, if you are neither the Christ, nor Elijah, nor the
prophet?" [26]John answered them, "I baptize with water; but among you stands
one whom you do not know, [27]even he who comes after me, the thong of
whose sandal I am not worthy to untie." [28]This took place in Bethany beyond
the Jordan, where John was baptizing.

[29]The next day he saw Jesus coming toward him, and said, "Behold, the
Lamb of God, who takes away the sin of the world!* [30]This is he of whom I
said, 'After me comes a man who ranks before me, for he was before me.' [31]I
myself did not know him; but for this I came baptizing with water, that he
might be revealed to Israel." [32]And John bore witness, "I saw the Spirit
descend as a dove from heaven, and it remained on him. [33]I myself did not
know him; but he who sent me to baptize with water said to me, 'He on whom
you see the Spirit descend and remain, this is he who baptizes with the Holy
Spirit.' [34]And I have seen and borne witness that this is the Son of God."

The calling of the first disciples Mt 4:18–25; Mk 1:16–20; Lk 5:1–11

[35]The next day again John was standing with two of his disciples; [36]and he
looked at Jesus as he walked, and said, "Behold, the Lamb of God!" [37]The two
disciples heard him say this, and they followed Jesus. [38]Jesus turned, and saw
them following, and said to them, "What do you seek?" And they said to him,

---

experienced through their belief in Jesus. "All Christians by the example of their lives and the witness of the word, wherever they live, have an obligation to manifest the new man which they put on in Baptism, and to reveal the power of the Holy Spirit by whom they were strengthened at Confirmation, so that others, seeing their good works, might glorify the Father and more perfectly perceive the true meaning of human life and the universal solidarity of mankind" (Vatican II, *AG*, 11).

By calling Jesus the "Lamb of God" (v. 29), John is making reference to the redemptive sacrifice of Christ. Isaiah compared the sufferings of the Servant, the Messiah, to the sacrifice of a lamb (cf. Is 53:7); and the blood of the Passover lamb, smeared on the doors of houses, preserved from death the first-born of the Israelites in Egypt (cf. Ex 12:6–7). After Jesus' death and resurrection, his disciples, that is, Christians, bear witness to the fact that he is the true Paschal Lamb. We do this immediately before receiving Christ in Holy Communion, that is, at the point when we partake of "the marriage supper of the Lamb" (Rev 19:9).

The witness borne by John at Jesus' baptism also manifests the divinity of Jesus Christ and reveals the mystery of the Holy Trinity (cf. vv. 32–34).

1:35–51 This account of Jesus' meeting with his first disciples mentions some of our Lord's titles—Rabbi (Teacher), Messiah (Christ), Son of God, King of Israel, Son of man. Taken together they show that Jesus is the Messiah promised in the Old Testament and acknowledged in the Church.

"Rabbi" (which means Teacher), "where are you staying?"
39He said to them,
"Come and see." They came and saw where he was staying; and they stayed
with him that day, for it was about the tenth hour.
40One of the two who heard
John speak, and followed him, was Andrew, Simon Peter's brother.
41He first
found his brother Simon, and said to him, "We have found the Messiah"
(which means Christ).
42He brought him to Jesus. Jesus looked at him, and
said, "So you are Simon the son of John? You shall be called Cephas" (which
means Peter[c]).

43The next day Jesus decided to go to Galilee. And he found Philip and said
to him, "Follow me."
44Now Philip was from Bethsaida, the city of Andrew
and Peter.
45Philip found Nathanael, and said to him, "We have found him of
whom Moses in the law and also the prophets wrote, Jesus of Nazareth, the
son of Joseph."
46Nathanael said to him, "Can anything good come out of
Nazareth?" Philip said to him, "Come and see."
47Jesus saw Nathanael coming
to him, and said to him, "Behold, an Israelite indeed, in whom is no guile!"
48Nathanael said to him, "How do you know me?" Jesus answered him,
"Before Philip called you, when you were under the fig tree, I saw you."
49Nathanael answered him, "Rabbi, you are the Son of God! You are the King
of Israel!"
50Jesus answered him, "Because I said to you, I saw you under the
fig tree, do you believe? You shall see greater things than these."
51And he said
to him, "Truly, truly, I say to you, you will see heaven opened, and the angels
of God ascending and descending upon the Son of man."

The evangelist shows that some disciples came to know Jesus through the mediation of those who already followed him. That is how Christian apostolate works: "That's what it's all about—getting people to face Jesus and ask him: 'Lord, what do you want me to do?'" (Bl. J. Escrivá, *Hom.*, 1, 149).

"You shall be called Cephas" (v. 42): naming something is equivalent to taking possession of the thing named (cf. Gen 17:5; 32:29). "Cephas" is the Greek transcription of an Aramaic word meaning stone, rock, and from this point onwards Simon is called Peter. St John, writing in Greek, is explaining the meaning of the word used by Jesus. Cephas was not a proper name, but our Lord gave it to the apostle to indicate his role as his vicar, a role he will reveal later (cf. Mt 16:16–18).

The "greater things" (vv. 50–51) suggest Jesus' glorification. By evoking the dream of Jacob, in which the patriarch saw a ladder linking heaven and earth whereby the angels of God descended (Gen 28:62), and by his reference to the Son of man (cf. Dan 7:13), this passage reveals how Christ will attain his glory through his death on the cross. Thus we are shown that through his death Jesus will become the judge who will judge the world (the Son of man) and the way of salvation that will take men to heaven (the ladder).

c. From the word for *rock* in Aramaic and Greek respectively **1:51** Gen 28:12.

2. JESUS, THE AUTHOR OF THE NEW ECONOMY OF SALVATION: FIRST SIGNS OF FAITH

The wedding at Cana

2 [1]On the third day there was a marriage at Cana in Galilee, and the mother
of Jesus was there; [2]Jesus also was invited to the marriage, with his
disciples. [3]When the wine failed, the mother of Jesus said to him, "They have
no wine." [4]And Jesus said to her, "O woman, what have you to do with me?*
My hour has not yet come." [5]His mother said to the servants, "Do whatever he
tells you." [6]Now six stone jars were standing there, for the Jewish rites of
purification, each holding twenty or thirty gallons. [7]Jesus said to them, "Fill
the jars with water." And they filled them up to the brim. [8]He said to them,
"Now draw some out, and take it to the steward of the feast." So they took it.
[9]When the steward of the feast tasted the water now become wine, and did not
know where it came from (though the servants who had drawn the water

---

2:1–4:54 □ This section deals with Jesus' ministry in Galilee, Jerusalem and Samaria. The episodes are narrated in such a way that they cover one week, day by day. The unifying thread of the entire section is the fact that Jesus is revealing himself as the Messiah who is founding the new economy of grace, superior to the old system of the temple and the Law. We can see this in the water changed into wine at Cana in Galilee (2:9), in the evangelist's commentary on the episode of the cleansing of the temple ("he spoke of the temple of his body": 2:21), in the revelation to Nicodemus about being born again through Baptism (3:5), and in our Lord's conversation with the Samaritan woman, when he announces that true worship must be "in spirit and truth" (4:24). No one can remain indifferent to Jesus' revelation of himself; therefore, St John reports the initial faith of the disciples and the people, and the early reactions of some Jews against Jesus.

2:1–12 Through the miracle at the wedding feast of Cana, Jesus begins to manifest his glory and inaugurate the messianic times. The miracle or, as the text puts it, the "sign", of the water being changed into wine anticipates the Hour of Christ's glorification (v. 4). John shows the generous scale of our Lord's gift (more than 500 litres or, that is, over 100 gallons of wine); this largesse is a sign that the Messiah has come, and it is, in turn, a symbol of the supernatural gifts that he obtains for us. The presence of the Blessed Virgin at the miracle, as also her presence later at Calvary (19:25), shows our Mother's involvement in the work of Redemption. Mary cooperates in Jesus' work from beginning to end; she acts as a true mother, and in both episodes we can see her special solicitude towards everyone. At Cana she intercedes when "the hour" has not yet come; on Calvary she offers the Father the redemptive death of her Son, and accepts the mission Jesus confers on her to be the Mother of all believers, who are represented there knew), the steward of the feast called the bridegroom [10]and said to him, "Every man serves the good wine first; and when men have drunk freely, then the poor wine; but you have kept the good wine till now." [11]This, the first of his signs, Jesus did at Cana in Galilee, and manifested his glory; and his disciples believed in him.

[12]After this he went down to Capernaum, with his mother and his brethren* and his disciples; and there they stayed for a few days.

Cleansing of the temple Mt 21:12–17; Mk 11:15–19; Lk 19:45–48

[13]The Passover of the Jews was at hand, and Jesus went up to Jerusalem. [14]In the temple he found those who were selling oxen and sheep and pigeons, and the money-changers at their business. [15]And making a whip of cords, he drove them all, with the sheep and oxen, out of the temple; and he poured out the coins of the money-changers and overturned their tables. [16]And he told those who sold the pigeons, "Take these things away; you shall not make my Father's house a house of trade." [17]His disciples remembered that it was written, "Zeal for thy house will consume me." [18]The Jews then said to him, "What sign have you to show us for doing this?" [19]Jesus answered them, "Destroy this temple, and in three days I will raise it up." [20]The Jews then said, "It has taken forty-six years to build this temple, and will you raise it up in three days?" [21]But he spoke of the temple of his body. [22]When therefore he was raised from the dead, his disciples remembered that he had said this; and they believed the scripture and the word which Jesus had spoken.

[23]Now when he was in Jerusalem at the Passover feast, many believed in his name when they saw the signs which he did; [24]but Jesus did not trust

---

by the beloved disciple. "The heart of Mary, which suffers with all the unfortunate […], inspires her to take on the role of intercessor and to ask her Son for a miracle, even though no one asked her to do so […]. If the good Lady acted in that way without being asked, what would she not be willing to do when asked?" (St Alphonsus M. Ligouri, *Shortened Sermons*, 48, 2, 1).

The Church sees Jesus' presence at this wedding as being highly significant: it confirms the high value of marriage and proclaims that from this point onwards marriage will be an effective sign of the presence of Christ (cf. *CCC*, 1613).

On Jesus' "brethren" (v. 12) cf. Mt 12:46–50 and the note on same.

2:13–25 In his narrative St John links up Jesus' ministry with Jewish festivals. Here, the cleansing of the temple prior to the Passover is the centre of the first section of the Gospel and it has a deeper meaning than is apparent in the other Gospels: Jesus not only manifests himself as the Messiah (cf. Mt 21:12–13) but also shows that he is the new and definitive temple of God among men.

When Jesus compares the temple of Jerusalem to his own Body, he is revealing the deepest truth about himself—the Incarnation. The evangelist makes the point,

2:17 Ps 69:9.

himself to them, 25because he knew all men and needed no one to bear witness
of man; for he himself knew what was in man.

The visit of Nicodemus

3 1Now there was a man of the Pharisees, named Nicodemus, a ruler of the
Jews. 2This man came to Jesus[d] by night and said to him, “Rabbi, we know
that you are a teacher come from God; for no one can do these signs that you
do, unless God is with him.” 3Jesus answered him, “Truly, truly, I say to you,
unless one is born anew,[e] he cannot see the kingdom of God.” 4Nicodemus said
to him, “How can a man be born when he is old? Can he enter a second time
into his mother’s womb and be born?” 5Jesus answered, “Truly, truly, I say to
you, unless one is born of water and the Spirit, he cannot enter the kingdom of
God. 6That which is born of the flesh is flesh, and that which is born of the
Spirit is spirit.[f] 7Do not marvel that I said to you, ‘You must be born anew.’[e]
8The wind[f] blows where it wills, and you hear the sound of it, but you do not
know whence it comes or whether it goes; so it is with every one who is born
of the Spirit.” 9Nicodemus said to him, “How can this be?” 10Jesus answered
him, “Are you a teacher of Israel, and yet you do not understand this? 11Truly,
truly, I say to you, we speak of what we know, and bear witness to what we
have seen; but you do not receive our testimony. 12If I have told you earthly
things and you do not believe, how can you believe if I tell you heavenly
things? 13No one has ascended into heaven but he who descended from heaven,
the Son of man.[g] 14And as Moses lifted up the serpent in the wilderness, so

---

however, that we can grasp this truth only in the light of the events of the last Passover (v. 22).

3:1–21 Through Jesus’ conversation with Nicodemus (a member of the Sanhedrin of Jerusalem) John provides a clear revelation of who Jesus is, the nature of the salvation he brings us, and how we are to attain it—by the faith that comes in Baptism through the action of the Holy Spirit.

At the start of this dialogue (vv. 2–8), Jesus teaches the need to be born again of water and the Holy Spirit. The simile of being born again shows the new condition man finds himself in as a result of Baptism. A human being is changed into a being born of the Holy Spirit, becoming a child of God, with all the freedom that that involves: “Although there are two births, (Nicodemus) knew only one. One is from earth, the other from heaven; one is from the flesh, the other from the spirit; one is from mortality, the other from eternity; one is from male and female, the other from God and Church. But these two are each unique; neither the one nor the other can be repeated” (St Augustine, *In Ioann. Ev.*, 11, 6).

Jesus explains to Nicodemus that a person needs faith in order to be able to understand him (vv. 9–15).

d. Greek *him* **e.** Or *from above* **f.** The same Greek word means both *wind* and *spirit* **g.** Other ancient authorities add *who is in heaven* must the Son of man be lifted up, [15]that whoever believes in him may have eternal life."[h]

[16]For God so loved the world that he gave his only Son, that whoever believes in him should not perish but have eternal life. [17]For God sent the Son into the world, not to condemn the world, but that the world might be saved through him. [18]He who believes in him is not condemned; he who does not believe is condemned already, because he has not believed in the name of the only Son of God. [19]And this is the judgment, that the light has come into the world, and men loved darkness rather than light, because their deeds were evil. [20]For every one who does evil hates the light, and does not come to the light, lest his deeds should be exposed. [21]But he who does what is true comes to the light, that it may be clearly seen that his deeds have been wrought in God.

The Baptist again bears witness

[22]After this Jesus and his disciples went into the land of Judea; there he remained with them and baptized.* [23]John also was baptizing at Aenon near Salim, because there was much water there; and people came and were baptized. [24]For John had not yet been put in prison.*

He compares his future crucifixion to the bronze serpent which Moses set up on a staff, as a remedy devised by God to cure Israelites bitten by the poisonous snakes of the desert (Num 21:8–9). So, too, Jesus, raised up on the cross, is salvation for those who look on him with faith. "The words of Christ are at once words of judgment and grace, of life and death. For it is only by putting to death that which is old that we can come to newness of life. [...] No one is freed from sin by himself or by his own efforts, no one is raised above himself or completely delivered from his own weakness, solitude or slavery; all have need of Christ who is the model, master, liberator, saviour, and giver of life" (Vatican II, *AG*, 8).

The final words (vv. 16–21) summarize how the death of Jesus is the supreme sign of God's love for mankind. For those for whom the Gospel was initially written and for a person reading it now, these words are a pressing call to respond to God's love: "Let us remember with what love [the Lord] has shown us mercy and the greatness of God [...]: love draws forth love. [...] Let us strive to keep sight of this always, and awaken ourselves to love" (St Teresa of Avila, *Life*, 22, 14).

3:22–36 Again the Baptist states that Jesus is greater than he. The betrothal symbolism in which Jesus is the Bridegroom (cf. Mk 2:19) and the Church the Bride (cf. Eph 5:24–32; Rev 19:7–9) conveys the idea of Christ's union with the Church. The Baptist's joy shows that the Messiah has begun his work. His joy is full, now that Christ is calling men and they are following Him. He anticipates the joy that the Church feels when new members become part of the Body of Christ.

h. Some interpreters hold that the quotation continues through verse 21.

[25]Now a discussion arose between John's disciples and a Jew over purifying. [26]And they came to John, and said to him, "Rabbi, he who was with you beyond the Jordan, to whom you bore witness, here he is, baptizing, and all are going to him." [27]John answered, "No one can receive anything except what is given him from heaven. [28]You yourselves bear me witness, that I said, I am not the Christ, but I have been sent before him. [29]He who has the bride is the bridegroom; the friend of the bridegroom, who stands and hears him, rejoices greatly at the bridegroom's voice; therefore this joy of mine is now full. [30]He must increase, but I must decrease."[i]

[31]He who comes from above is above all; he who is of the earth belongs to the earth, and of the earth he speaks; he who comes from heaven is above all. [32]He bears witness to what he has seen and heard, yet no one receives his testimony; [33]he who receives his testimony sets his seal to this, that God is true. [34]For he whom God has sent utters the words of God, for it is not by measure that he gives the Spirit; [35]the Father loves the Son, and has given all things into his hand. [36]He who believes in the Son has eternal life; he who does not obey the Son shall not see life, but the wrath of God rests upon him.

Jesus and the Samaritan woman

4 [1]Now when the Lord knew that the Pharisees had heard that Jesus was making and baptizing more disciples than John [2](although Jesus himself did not baptize, but only his disciples), [3]he left Judea and departed again to Galilee. [4]He had to pass through Samaria. [5]So he came to a city of Samaria, called Sychar, near the field that Jacob gave to his son Joseph. [6]Jacob's well was there, and so Jesus, wearied as he was with his journey, sat down beside the well. It was about the sixth hour.

The concluding words of the chapter (vv. 31–36) reveal the divinity of Jesus and his role as the Christ. Jesus Christ is the only one who can reveal God the Father to mankind, because he is the Son of God. "Christ, the Son of God made man, is the Father's one, perfect and unsurpassable Word. In him he has said everything; there will be no other word than this one" (*CCC*, 65).

The actions and words of Jesus are truly human and they are at the same time the actions and words of God in human history, because the Incarnate Word is one with the Father and the Holy Spirit.

4:1–45 In Jerusalem the Pharisees' hostility towards Jesus begins to show itself. Our Lord moves off to the north, to Galilee, where the Pharisees had less influence, thereby avoiding their doing away with him before the time planned by God the Father.

In Jesus' unforgettable dialogue with the Samaritan woman, St John again presents the doctrine of grace, God's gift to men through the Holy Spirit after the

i. Some interpreters hold that the quotation continues through verse 36

[7]There came a woman of Samaria to draw water. Jesus said to her, "Give
me a drink." [8]For his disciples had gone away into the city to buy food. [9]The
Samaritan woman said to him, "How is it that you, a Jew, ask a drink of me,
a woman of Samaria?" For Jews have no dealings with Samaritans. [10]Jesus
answered her, "If you knew the gift of God, and who it is that is saying to you,
'Give me a drink,' you would have asked him, and he would have given you
living water." [11]The woman said to him, "Sir, you have nothing to draw with,
and the well is deep; where do you get that living water? [12]Are you greater than
our father Jacob, who gave us the well, and drank from it himself, and his
sons, and his cattle?" [13]Jesus said to her, "Every one who drinks of this water

---

Incarnation of his Son. As in his conversation with Nicodemus, Jesus uses ordinary language, with an immediate, material reference, to explain supernatural things. This deeper meaning contains the core of the Church's future teaching on the subject of sacraments. Just as water is essential for human life, the water which can truly assuage man's spiritual thirst is the grace of Christ. This episode also shows that the salvation which Christ brings is available to everyone. He loves all souls. Jesus asks the woman for water not just because he is thirsty but to show that he also thirsts for the salvation of man. Christ seeks man out and man makes himself available to Christ through prayer. "The wonder of prayer is revealed beside the well where we come seeking water: there, Christ comes to meet every human being. It is he who first seeks us and asks us for a drink. Jesus thirsts; his asking arises from the depths of God's desire for us. Whether we realize it or not, prayer is the encounter of God's thirst with ours. God thirsts that we may thirst for him (cf. St Augustine, *Quaest.*, 64,4)" (*CCC*, 2560).

The end of the passage refers to the plans of God (vv. 20–26). The Samaritans knew little about these plans because as they saw it revelation was to be found only in the Law of Moses; whereas the Jews knew much more about the Messiah because they accepted the entire Old Testament. But both Jews and Samaritans needed to be open to the new Revelation of Jesus Christ. Both peoples were waiting for the Messiah, and now that he had come a new and definitive Covenant was being established, one in which Gerizim, the mountain on which the Samaritans worshipped, and Jerusalem with its temple, would play no part: what the Father wants is for all of us to accept the Messiah, his Son, as the new Temple of God (cf. 2:21), where worship comes from man's heart and is stirred up by the Spirit of God himself (cf. Rom 8:15).

Apropos of the conversation of the Samaritan woman and the return of the disciples (vv. 30–42) we find another of the themes which recur in the fourth Gospel: Jesus has come to do the will of the Father. That will is that everyone who sees the Son and believes in him shall have eternal life and be raised up on the last day (cf. 6:39–40).

will thirst again, [14]but whoever drinks of the water that I shall give him will
never thirst; the water that I shall give him will become in him a spring of
water welling up to eternal life." [15]The woman said to him, "Sir, give me this
water, that I may not thirst, nor come here to draw."

[16]Jesus said to her, "Go, call your husband, and come here." [17]The woman
answered him, "I have no husband." Jesus said to her, "You are right in saying,
'I have no husband'; [18]for you have had five husbands, and he whom you now
have is not your husband; this you said truly." [19]The woman said to him, "Sir,
I perceive that you are a prophet. [20]Our fathers worshipped on this mountain;*
and you say that in Jerusalem is the place where men ought to worship."
[21]Jesus said to her, "Woman, believe me, the hour is coming when neither on
this mountain nor in Jerusalem will you worship the Father. [22]You worship
what you do not know; we worship what we know, for salvation is from the
Jews. [23]But the hour is coming, and now is, when the true worshippers will
worship the Father in spirit and truth, for such the Father seeks to worship him.
[24]God is spirit, and those who worship him must worship in spirit and truth."
[25]The woman said to him, "I know that Messiah is coming (he who is called
Christ); when he comes, he will show us all things." [26]Jesus said to her, "I who
speak to you am he."

[27]Just then the disciples came. They marvelled that he was talking with a
woman, but none said, "What do you wish?" or, "Why are you talking with
her?" [28]So the woman left her water jar, and went away into the city, and said
to the people, [29]"Come, see a man who told me all that I ever did. Can this be
the Christ?" [30]They went out of the city and were coming to him.

[31]Meanwhile the disciples besought him, saying, "Rabbi, eat." [32]But he
said to them, "I have food to eat of which you do not know." [33]So the disciples
said to one another, "Has any one brought him food?" [34]Jesus said to them,
"My food is to do the will of him who sent me, and to accomplish his work.
[35]Do you not say, 'There are yet four months, then comes the harvest'? I tell
you, lift up your eyes, and see how the fields are already white for harvest.
[36]He who reaps receives wages, and gathers fruit for eternal life, so that sower
and reaper may rejoice together. [37]For here the saying holds true, 'One sows
and another reaps.' [38]I sent you to reap that for which you did not labour;
others have laboured, and you have entered into their labour."

[39]Many Samaritans from that city believed in him because of the woman's
testimony, "He told me all that I ever did." [40]So when the Samaritans came to
him, they asked him to stay with them; and he stayed there two days. [41]And
many more believed because of his word. [42]They said to the woman, "It is no
longer because of your words that we believe, for we have heard for ourselves,
and we know that this is indeed the Saviour of the world."

[43]After the two days he departed to Galilee. [44]For Jesus himself testified
that a prophet has no honour in his own country. [45]So when he came to

Galilee, the Galileans welcomed him, having seen all that he had done in Jerusalem at the feast, for they too had gone to the feast.

Curing of a royal official's son Mt 8:5–13; Lk 7:1–10

46So he came again to Cana in Galilee, where he had made the water wine.
And at Capernaum there was an official whose son was ill. 47When he heard
that Jesus had come from Judea to Galilee, he went and begged him to come
down and heal his son, for he was at the point of death. 48Jesus therefore said
to him, "Unless you see signs and wonders you will not believe." 49The official
said to him, "Sir, come down before my child dies." 50Jesus said to him, "Go,
your son will live." The man believed the word that Jesus spoke to him and
went his way. 51As he was going down, his servants met him and told him that
his son was living. 52So he asked them the hour when he began to mend, and
they said to him, "Yesterday at the seventh hour the fever left him." 53The
father knew that was the hour when Jesus had said to him, "Your son will
live"; and he himself believed, and all his household. 54This was now the
second sign that Jesus did when he had come from Judea to Galilee.

3. JESUS REVEALS HIS DIVINITY

Curing of a paralyzed man

5 1After this there was a feast of the Jews, and Jesus went up to Jerusalem.
2Now there is in Jerusalem by the Sheep Gate a pool, in Hebrew called
Bethzatha,[j] which has five porticoes. 3In these lay a multitude of invalids,
blind, lame, paralyzed.[k] 5One man was there, who had been ill for thirty-eight

---

4:46–54 In this first section of his Gospel, John has chosen to report Jesus' miracles in Cana of Galilee. In the first of these, at the wedding, the miracle led people to believe in Him (cf. 2:1–11); but now a royal official (possibly a pagan from the court of Herod Antipas) puts faith in Jesus' word prior to seeing the miracle. Our Lord wants our faith in him to be based on the acceptance of what he says, and not on a desire for miracles. Miracles are a call to faith and a motive of credibility.

5:1–47 □ This section contains the cure of a paralyzed man at the pool of Bethzatha (also called the "Probatic" pool, because it was near the Probatic or Sheep Gate) and a discourse in which Jesus, as the Son, reveals that he acts in union with the Father. All this happens on "a feast of the Jews" (v. 1), maybe Passover or else Pentecost, fifty days after Passover. John is making it plain that Jesus is divine, as can be seen from both the miracle and the discourse. We also see here how some

j. Other ancient authorities read *Bethseda*, others *Bethsaida* **k.** Other ancient authorities insert, wholly or in part, *waiting for the moving of the water; 4for an angel of the Lord went down at certain seasons into the pool, and troubled the water: whoever stepped in first after the troubling of the water was healed of whatever disease he had* years. [6]When Jesus saw him and knew that he had been lying there a long time, he said to him, "Do you want to be healed?" [7]The sick man answered him, "Sir, I have no man to put me into the pool when the water is troubled, and while I am going another steps down before me." [8]Jesus said to him, "Rise, take up your pallet, and walk." [9]And at once the man was healed, and he took up his pallet and walked.

Now that day was the sabbath. [10]So the Jews said to the man who was cured, "It is the sabbath, it is not lawful for you to carry your pallet." [11]But he answered them, "The man who healed me said to me, 'Take up your pallet, and walk.'" [12]They asked him, "Who is the man who said to you, 'Take up your pallet, and walk'?" [13]Now the man who had been healed did not know who it was, for Jesus had withdrawn, as there was a crowd in the place. [14]Afterward, Jesus found him in the temple, and said to him, "See, you are well! Sin no more, that nothing worse befall you." [15]The man went away and told the Jews that it was Jesus who had healed him. [16]And this was why the Jews persecuted Jesus, because he did this on the sabbath. [17]But Jesus answered them, "My Father is working still, and I am working." [18]This was why the Jews sought all the more to kill him, because he not only broke the sabbath* but also called God his Father, making himself equal with God.

The authority of the Son of God

[19]Jesus said to them, "Truly, truly, I say to you, the Son can do nothing of his own accord, but only what he sees the Father doing; for whatever he does, that the Son does likewise. [20]For the Father loves the Son, and shows him all that

---

Jews begin openly to hate Jesus and plot his death because he has made himself out to be the Son of God (v. 18).

5:1–18 In curing the paralyzed man Jesus exercises a power that is exclusive to God. This enables him to be above the sabbath and to set men free from sin. Jesus' conversation with the man in the temple after the cure shows how important it is not to fall into sin again after receiving the grace of faith in Christ.

The Law of Moses made Saturday a weekly day of rest. The Jews regarded it as a form of imitating God's "rest" after creating the world. However, Jesus tells us that God does not cease to act after his work of creation. Therefore, by curing the paralytic on the sabbath and affirming that his Father is always working and he himself likewise (v. 17), Jesus is revealing in an implicit way that his own nature is divine. On this holy day he manifests the salvific action of God, his merciful love for man.

The New Vulgate omits vv. 3b–4 of the Vulgate, putting them in a footnote (as does the RSV). These verses are not to be found in important Greek codexes and papyri, nor do they appear in many early translations.

5:19–47 In this long discourse in which Jesus defends his actions we find some of St John's favourite themes: Christ reveals the Father and receives from him the power to give true Life.

he himself is doing; and greater works than these will he show him, that you
may marvel. 21For as the Father raises the dead and gives them life, so also the
Son gives life to whom he will. 22The Father judges no one, but has given all
judgment to the Son, 23that all may honour the Son, even as they honour the
Father. He who does not honour the Son does not honour the Father who sent
him. 24Truly, truly, I say to you, he who hears my word and believes him who
sent me, has eternal life; he does not come into judgment, but has passed from
death to life.

25"Truly, truly, I say to you, the hour is coming, and now is, when the dead
will hear the voice of the Son of God, and those who hear will live. 26For as the
Father has life in himself, so he has granted the Son also to have life in himself,
27and has given him authority to execute judgment, because he is the Son of man.
28Do not marvel at this; for the hour is coming when all who are in the tombs will
hear his voice 29and come forth, those who have done good, to the resurrection of
life, and those who have done evil, to the resurrection of judgment.

Jesus speaks of equality and at the same time distinction between the Father and the Son (vv. 19–30). They are equals: all the Son's authority is the authority of the Father, and the things the Son does are works of the Father. Yet Father and Son are distinct from one another. When Jesus Christ does things which are proper to God, he is thereby testifying that he is divine (cf. v. 36). The sign, the miracle, *par excellence* of Jesus is his own resurrection, which is the cause and first-fruit of our own resurrection (cf. 1 Cor 15:20ff). Through this he receives from the Father the power to judge: "Christ is Lord of eternal life. Full right to pass definitive judgment on the works and hearts of men belongs to him as redeemer of the world. He 'acquired' this right by his cross. The Father has given 'all judgment to the Son' (Jn 5:22). Yet the Son did not come to judge, but to save and to give the life he has in himself. By rejecting grace in this life, one already judges oneself, receives according to one's works, and can even condemn oneself for all eternity by rejecting the Spirit of love" (*CCC*, 679).

In the second part of the discourse (vv. 31–40) Jesus anticipates a possible objection from the Jews that evidence given in one's own cause is insufficient (cf. Deut 19:15); he says that his words are supported by four testimonies—that of John the Baptist (cf. 1:34), that of miracles, that of the Father (cf. 1:31–34; 12:28–30), and that of the Scriptures.

Finally (vv. 41–47), Jesus reproaches his listeners for three things which prevent them from acknowledging Him as the Messiah and Son of God—their lack of love of God, their desire for human glory and their misinterpretation of Scripture. To see who is truly Christ, one needs better dispositions that that: "That Christ you see is not Jesus. At best it is only the pitiful image that your blurred eyes are able to form … Purify yourself. Make your sight sharper with humility and penance. Then the pure light of love will not fail you. And you will have perfect vision. The image you see will really be his: Jesus himself" (Bl. J. Escrivá, *The Way*, 212).

30“I can do nothing on my own authority; as I hear, I judge; and my
judgment is just, because I seek not my own will but the will of him who sent
me. 31If I bear witness to myself, my testimony is not true; 32there is another
who bears witness to me, and I know that the testimony which he bears to me
is true. 33You sent to John, and he has borne witness to the truth. 34Not that the
testimony which I receive is from man; but I say this that you may be saved.
35He was a burning and shining lamp, and you were willing to rejoice for a
while in his light. 36But the testimony which I have is greater than that of John;
for the works which the Father has granted me to accomplish, these very works
which I am doing, bear me witness that the Father has sent me. 37And the
Father who sent me has himself borne witness to me. His voice you have never
heard, his form you have never seen; 38and you do not have his word abiding in
you, for you do not believe him whom he has sent. 39You search the scriptures,
because you think that in them you have eternal life; and it is they that bear
witness to me; 40yet you refuse to come to me that you may have life. 41I do not
receive glory from men. 42But I know that you have not the love of God within
you. 43I have come in my Father’s name, and you do not receive me; if another
comes in his own name, him you will receive. 44How can you believe, who
receive glory from one another and do not seek the glory that comes from the
only God? 45Do not think that I shall accuse you to the Father; it is Moses who
accuses you, on whom you set your hope. 46If you believed Moses, you would
believe me, for he wrote of me. 47But if you do not believe his writings, how
will you believe my words?”

4. JESUS IS THE BREAD OF LIFE

Miracle of the loaves and fish Mt 14:13–21; Mk 6:30–44; Lk 9:10–17

6 1After this Jesus went to the other side of the Sea of Galilee, which is the
Sea of Tiberias. 2And a multitude followed him, because they saw the
signs which he did on those who were diseased. 3Jesus went up into the hills,
and there sat down with his disciples. 4Now the Passover, the feast of the Jews,
was at hand. 5Lifting up his eyes, then, and seeing that a multitude was coming
to him, Jesus said to Philip, “How are we to buy bread, so that these people may

---

6:1–71 □ This chapter is the fourth section of the Gospel, structured very much like the previous one. First come two signs or miracles—the multiplication of the loaves and fish, and Jesus’ walking on the water, and then a discourse—that of the synagogue of Capernaum, in which Jesus reveals himself to be the Bread of Life. St John points out that this occurred when “the Passover, the feast of the Jews, was at hand” (v. 4), thereby implying that the Eucharistic banquet will be the New Passover. Many of Jesus’ followers were scandalized by his words: those who do not believe turn their backs on him (v. 66) and those who do believe become more staunch (v. 69).

eat?" 6This he said to test them, for he himself knew what he would do. 7Philip
answered him, "Two hundred denarii[l] would not buy enough bread for each of
them to get a little." 8One of his disciples, Andrew, Simon Peter's brother, said to
him, 9"There is a lad here who has five barley loaves and two fish; but what are
they among so many?" 10Jesus said, "Make the people sit down." Now there was
much grass in the place; so the men sat down, in number about five thousand.
11Jesus then took the loaves, and when he had given thanks, he distributed them
to those who were seated; so also the fish, as much as they wanted. 12And when
they had eaten their fill, he told his disciples, "Gather up the fragments left over,
that nothing may be lost." 13So they gathered them up and filled twelve baskets
with fragments from the five barley loaves, left by those who had eaten. 14When
the people saw the sign which he had done, they said, "This is indeed the prophet
who is to come into the world!"

15Perceiving then that they were about to come and take him by force to
make him king, Jesus withdrew again to the hills by himself.

Jesus walks on water Mt 14:22–33; Mk 6:45–52

16When evening came, his disciples went down to the sea, 17got into a boat,
and started across the sea to Capernaum. It was now dark, and Jesus had not
yet come to them. 18The sea rose because a strong wind was blowing. 19When
they had rowed about three or four miles,[m] they saw Jesus walking on the sea

---

6:1–15 The Gospel of St John reports only seven of Jesus' miracles. The sacred writer has chosen those most suited to his purpose of revealing particular facets of the mystery of Christ. The miracle of the multiplication of the loaves and fish, performed a few days before the Passover, prefigures the Christian Pasch and the mystery of the Eucharist and is placed directly before the discourse at Capernaum on the Bread of Life (6:26–58), in which Jesus promises to give himself as nourishment for our soul. The connexion between miracle and discourse is underlined by the words of v. 11, which are virtually the same as those used in the Synoptics and St Paul in their accounts of the institution of the Eucharist (cf. Mt 26:26; Mk 14:22; Lk 22:14 and 1 Cor 11:23–24).

The people's reaction to the miracle shows that those who benefit from it acknowledge Jesus to be the Prophet, the Messiah promised in the Old Testament (cf. Deut 18:15), but their concept of messianism is of an earthly and naturalistic kind: they want to make Jesus their king because they expect the Messiah to bring them earthly goods in abundance, and to set them free from Roman domination. Jesus will not allow the people to divert him from his mission; as he will later explain to Pilate, his Kingdom is "not of this world" (18:36).

6:16–21 This miracle, which is found also in Matthew and Mark, shows the disciples' faith to be still very weak. "The wind is an image of the temptations and

l. The denarius was a day's wage for a labourer **m.** Greek *twenty-five or thirty stadia* and drawing near to the boat. They were frightened, [20]but he said to them, "It is I; do not be afraid." [21]Then they were glad to take him into the boat, and immediately the boat was at the land to which they were going.

The people look for Jesus
[22]On the next day the people who remained on the other side of the sea saw that there had been only one boat there, and that Jesus had not entered the boat with his disciples, but that his disciples had gone away alone. [23]However, boats from Tiberias came near the place where they ate the bread after the Lord had given thanks. [24]So when the people saw that Jesus was not there, nor his disciples, they themselves got into the boats and went to Capernaum, seeking Jesus.

The discourse on the bread of life
[25]When they found him on the other side of the sea, they said to him, "Rabbi, when did you come here?" [26]Jesus answered them, "Truly, truly, I say to you, you seek me, not because you saw signs, but because you ate your fill of the loaves. [27]Do not labour for the food which perishes, but for the food which endures to eternal life, which the Son of man will give to you; for on him has God the Father set his seal." [28]Then they said to him, "What must we do, to be doing the works of God?" [29]Jesus answered them, "This is the work of God, that you believe in him whom he has sent." [30]So they said to him, "Then what

---

persecution that the Church will suffer through lack of love. Because, as St Augustine says, when the fire of love is cooled, the waves grow and the ship is capsized. However, wind, stormy weather, waves and darkness do not drive the ship off course or destroy it" (St Thomas Aquinas, *Com. on Jn*, in loc.). Jesus comes again to meet them and he shows them that he has the same power over the elements of nature as God has. The words "It is I" (*Ego sum* in the Latin, "I am") bring to mind the words God used to reveal his name to Moses (cf. 8:28). The miracle, and the discourse on the Bread of Life, will help to strengthen the disciples' faith.

6:22–25 Capernaum was the base Jesus used for his ministry in Galilee. The crowds look for Jesus and they find him there. Then, in the synagogue (v. 59) he will give his discourse on the Bread of Life (vv. 26–59), in which he reveals who he is, where he comes from and the good things he has for us—faith, the Eucharist and eternal life.

6:26–59 The discourse begins with an introduction in the form of a dialogue between Jesus and the Jews, in which our Lord reveals the messianic gifts he bears (vv. 26–34). The manna, the food the Israelites gathered every day on their journey through the desert (cf. Ex 16:13ff), was regarded by the Jews as symbolic of the

sign do you do, that we may see, and believe you? What work do you
perform? 31Our fathers ate the manna in the wilderness; as it is written, 'He
gave them bread from heaven to eat.'" 32Jesus then said to them, "Truly, truly,
I say to you, it was not Moses who gave you the bread from heaven; my Father
gives you the true bread from heaven. 33For the bread of God is that which
comes down from heaven, and gives life to the world." 34They said to him,
"Lord, give us this bread always."

35Jesus said to them, "I am the bread of life; he who comes to me shall not
hunger, and he who believes in me shall never thirst. 36But I said to you that you
have seen me and yet do not believe. 37All that the Father gives me will come to
me; and him who comes to me I will not cast out. 38For I have come down from
heaven, not to do my own will, but the will of him who sent me; 39and this is the

---

good things the Messiah would bring; that is why they ask him to work a similar wonder. But they could not have had the faintest suspicion that the manna was in fact a symbol of the great messianic gift which God intended to give to mankind—his own Son present in the Blessed Eucharist. In this dialogue Jesus tries to bring them to make an act of faith in him, intending then to openly reveal his eucharistic presence.

In the first part of the discourse (vv. 35–51), Jesus presents himself as the Bread of Life. Three mysteries are to be found here: 1) faith in Jesus Christ, which means "going towards Jesus" by accepting his signs (miracles) and his words; 2) the resurrection of believers, which begins in this life through faith and will reach its fulfillment at the end of time; 3) predestination—the plan our Father in heaven has for the salvation of all mankind. Jesus says that "they shall all be taught by God" (v. 45)—words evocative of Isaiah 54:13 and Jeremiah 31:41–34, where those prophets make reference to the future covenant which God will establish with his people when the Messiah comes, a covenant which the Messiah will seal with his blood and which will endure forever, a covenant which God will inscribe on their hearts.

In the second part of the discourse (vv. 52–59), Christ reveals the mystery of the Eucharist. There is such realism in what he says that it cannot be given a metaphorical or figurative interpretation. His listeners know exactly what Jesus is saying (v. 52) but they do not believe he can be speaking the truth. If they had thought he was speaking in symbols or metaphors, they would have taken it in their stride; no dispute would have arisen. Here we find the source of the Church's belief that Christ becomes present in this sacrament through changing his bread and wine into his Body and Blood. "The Council of Trent summarizes the Catholic faith by declaring: 'Because Christ our Redeemer said that it was truly his body that he was offering under the species of bread, it has always been the conviction of the Church of God, and this holy Council now declares again, that by the consecration of the bread and wine there takes place a change of the whole substance of the bread into the substance of the body of Christ our Lord and of the whole substance of the wine into the substance of his blood. This change the holy Catholic Church has fittingly and properly called transubstantiation' (DS 1642)" (*CCC*, 1376).

6:31 Ex 16:4.

will of him who sent me, that I should lose nothing of all that he has given me,
but raise it up on the last day. 40For this is the will of my Father, that every one
who sees the Son and believes in him should have eternal life; and I will raise
him up at the last day."
41The Jews then murmured at him, because he said, "I am the bread which
came down from heaven." 42They said, "Is not this Jesus, the son of Joseph,
whose father and mother we know? How does he now say, 'I have come down
from heaven'?" 43Jesus answered them, "Do not murmur among yourselves.
44No one can come to me unless the Father who sent me draws him; and I will
raise him up on the last day. 45It is written in the prophets, 'And they shall all
be taught by God.' Every one who has heard and learned from the Father
comes to me. 46Not that any one has seen the Father except him who is from
God; he has seen the Father. 47Truly, truly, I say to you, he who believes has
eternal life. 48I am the bread of life. 49Your fathers ate the manna in the
wilderness, and they died. 50This is the bread which comes down from heaven,
that a man may eat of it and not die. 51I am the living bread* which came down
from heaven; if any one eats of this bread, he will live for ever; and the bread
which I shall give for the life of the world is my flesh."
52The Jews then disputed among themselves, saying, "How can this man
give us his flesh to eat?"* 53So Jesus said to them, "Truly, truly, I say to you,
unless you eat the flesh of the Son of man and drink his blood, you have no life
in you; 54he who eats my flesh and drinks my blood has eternal life, and I will
raise him up on the last day. 55For my flesh is food indeed, and my blood is
drink indeed. 56He who eats my flesh and drinks my blood abides in me, and I
in him. 57As the living Father sent me, and I live because of the Father, so he
who eats me will live because of me. 58This is the bread which came from
heaven, not such as the fathers ate and died; he who eats this bread will live for
ever." 59This he said in the synagogue, as he taught in Capernaum.

The disciples' reaction

60Many of his disciples, when they heard of it, said, "This is a hard saying;
who can listen to it?" 61But Jesus, knowing in himself that his disciples
murmured at it, said to them, "Do you take offence at this? 62Then what if you
were to see the Son of man ascending where he was before?* 63It is the spirit

---

6:60–71 These verses show how the disciples received Jesus' words. In revealing the eucharistic mystery Jesus requires his disciples to believe what he says because it is he who has said it. His revelation should not be interpreted in a human way, that is, by focusing exclusively on what is visible to the senses or by having a natural as distinct from supernatural view of things: it should be interpreted as a revelation from God, who is "spirit" and "life" (v. 63). As on other occasions, the

6:45 Is 54:13.

that gives life, the flesh is of no avail; the words that I have spoken to you are
spirit and life. 64But there are some of you that do not believe." For Jesus knew
from the first who those were that did not believe, and who it was that should
betray him. 65And he said, "This is why I told you that no one can come to me
unless it is granted him by the Father."
66After this many of his disciples drew back and no longer went with him.
67Jesus said to the twelve, "Will you also go away?" 68Simon Peter answered
him, "Lord, to whom shall we go? You have the words of eternal life; 69and we
have believed, and have come to know, that you are the Holy One of God."
70Jesus answered them, "Did I not choose you, the twelve, and one of you is a
devil?" 71He spoke of Judas the son of Simon Iscariot, for he, one of the
twelve, was to betray him.

5. JESUS IS THE LIGHT OF THE WORLD

Jesus goes up to Jerusalem during the feast of Tabernacles

7 1After this Jesus went about in Galilee; he would not go about in Judea,
because the Jews[n] sought to kill him. 2Now the Jews' feast of Tabernacles
was at hand. 3So his brethren* said to him, "Leave here and go to Judea, that
your disciples may see the works you are doing. 4For no man works in secret
if he seeks to be known openly. If you do these things, show yourself to the
world." 5For even his brethren did not believe in him. 6Jesus said to them, "My

---

reference to future events, to the glory of his resurrection (v. 62), helps prepare the ground for the disciple's faith, and for our own: "Now I have told you before it takes place, so that when it does take place, you may believe" (14:29).

The promise of the Eucharist gave rise to disputes (6:52) and scandal (v. 61), and many people gave up following Jesus (v. 16). Peter, however, speaking for the Twelve, expresses his faith in Jesus as Messiah, just as he did at Caesarea Philippi (cf. Mt 16:13–20; Mk 8:27–30). Peter's profession of faith also symbolizes the communion in faith of those who believe in Christ, who find in the faith of Peter, and of his successors, the sure guarantee of the truth of what they believe.

7:1–10:21 □The fifth section of the Gospel contains almost four chapters. These cover Jesus' activity in Jerusalem during the celebration of the feast of Tabernacles, the occasion of another visit to the Holy City. In contrast to the meaning which this festival had for the Jews, Jesus is depicted as the Messiah who is installing a new salvific order centred on grace, an order superior to that which obtained among the Israelites, centred on the Law (cf. 1:17). Once more we are told that Jesus has been sent by the Father, and the sending of the Holy Spirit is spoken about (chap. 7). Jesus is the Judge who pardons the adulterous woman (chap. 8), and the Light of the world

n. Or *Judeans*

time has not yet come, but your time is always here. 7The world cannot hate
you, but it hates me because I testify of it that its works are evil. 8Go to the
feast yourselves; I am not [o] going up to this feast, for my time has not fully
come." 9So saying, he remained in Galilee.
10But after his brethren had gone up to the feast, then he also went up, not
publicly but in private. 11The Jews were looking for him at the feast, and
saying, "Where is he?" 12And there was much muttering about him among the
people. While some said, "He is a good man," others said, "No, he is leading
the people astray." 13Yet for fear of the Jews no one spoke openly of him.
14About the middle of the feast Jesus went up into the temple and taught.
15The Jews marvelled at it, saying, "How is it that this man has learning,[p] when
he has never studied?" 16So Jesus answered them, "My teaching is not mine,
but his who sent me; 17if any man's will is to do his will, he shall know
whether the teaching is from God or whether I am speaking on my own
authority. 18He who speaks on his own authority seeks his own glory; but he

---

who gives sight to the man born blind but who also condemns those who refuse to see (chap. 9). He is the Door by which people enter Eternal Life, and the Good Shepherd who lays down his life for all men (10:1–21).

7:1–30 In this passage St John plainly tells us that Jesus' relatives did not believe in him; we see, too, Jesus' refusal to look for human or earthly success (vv. 1–13). Jesus' relatives know that he is able to work wonders, but they do not believe in him. They do not see the true meaning of his miracles—which only shows that miracles, on their own, do not produce faith. (On Jesus' brethren, see the note on Mt 12:46–50; on the meaning of the word "world", see Jn 17:1–26 and note.)

Jesus has the status and authority of being the revealer of the Father (vv. 16–24). The Jews, who know that Jesus never attended the schools of the teachers of the Law, are amazed at his learning, and they ask a sly question: "How is it that this man has learning, when he has never studied?" (v. 15). They accuse him of being a false prophet. Jesus uses the occasion to state that his teaching comes from God. In order to discern this, one needs to have an upright intention. If people do not believe in him (despite his miracles), it is because they don't have the right dispositions. They are very prejudiced; they don't weigh up the evidence calmly: that is the only explanation for their attributing to demons the things that Jesus has done (cf. v. 20).

Jesus asks them to judge rightly and discover that he brings salvation—to try to grasp the profound meaning of his actions (vv. 25–30). That is the first step towards believing in his divinity. Accepting his teaching demands a mental and moral conversion: "He who desires, therefore, to fully understand and appreciate the words of Christ must strive to conform his entire life to him" (Thomas à Kempis, *Imitation of Christ*, 1, 1, 2).

o. Other ancient authorities add *yet* **p.** Or *this man knows his letters*

who seeks the glory of him who sent him is true, and in him there is no
falsehood. [19]Did not Moses give you the law? Yet none of you keeps the law.
Why do you seek to kill me?" [20]The people answered, "You have a demon!
Who is seeking to kill you?" [21]Jesus answered them, "I did one deed, and you
all marvel at it. [22]Moses gave you circumcision (not that it is from Moses, but
from the fathers), and you circumcise a man upon the sabbath. [23]If on the
sabbath a man receives circumcision, so that the law of Moses may not be
broken, are you angry with me because on the sabbath I made a man's whole
body well? [24]Do not judge by appearances, but judge with right judgment."
[25]Some of the people of Jerusalem therefore said, "Is not this the man
whom they seek to kill? [26]And here he is, speaking openly, and they say
nothing to him! Can it be that the authorities really know that this is the
Christ? [27]Yet we know where this man comes from; and when the Christ
appears, no one will know where he comes from." [28]So Jesus proclaimed, as
he taught in the temple, "You know me, and you know where I come from?
But I have not come of my own accord; he who sent me is true, and him you
do not know. [29]I know him, for I come from him, and he sent me." [30]So they
sought to arrest him; but no one laid hands on him, because his hour had not
yet come. [31]Yet many of the people believed in him; they said, "When the
Christ appears, will he do more signs than this man has done?"

Different opinions about Jesus

[32]The Pharisees heard the crowd thus muttering about him, and the chief
priests and Pharisees sent officers to arrest him. [33]Jesus then said, "I shall be
with you a little longer, and then I go to him who sent me; [34]you will seek me
and you will not find me; where I am you cannot come." [35]The Jews said to
one another, "Where does this man intend to go that we shall not find him?
Does he intend to go to the Dispersion among the Greeks and teach the

---

7:31–53 Here Jesus speaks about his glorification when he goes to the Father, and about the sending of the Holy Spirit. The feast of Tabernacles, in autumn, was a festival of joy and thanksgiving, commemorating God's protection of the Israelites during the forty years of the Exodus. Because it coincided with the end of the harvest, it was also called the feast of Ingathering. On each of the eight days of the festival, the high priest went to the pool of Siloam and used a golden cup to collect water which he took to the temple and sprinkled on the altar (in remembrance of the water which sprang up miraculously in the desert), asking God to send rain in plenty (cf. Ex 17:1–7). Meanwhile, a passage from the prophet Isaiah (Is 12:3) was chanted which told of the coming of the Saviour and of the outpouring of heavenly gifts that would accompany him. Ezekiel 47 was also read—a passage that spoke of the torrents of water that would pour out of the temple. Jesus now proclaims

Greeks? [36]What does he mean by saying, 'You will seek me and you will not find me,' and, 'Where I am you cannot come'?"

[37]On the last day of the feast, the great day, Jesus stood up and proclaimed, "If any one thirst, let him come to me and drink. [38]He who believes in me, as[q] the scripture has said, 'Out of his heart shall flow rivers of living water.'" [39]Now this he said about the Spirit, which those who believed in him were to receive; for as yet the Spirit had not been given, because Jesus was not yet glorified.

[40]When they heard these words, some of the people said, "This is really the prophet." [41]Others said, "This is the Christ." But some said, "Is the Christ to come from Galilee? [42]Has not the scripture said that the Christ is descended from David, and comes from Bethlehem, the village where David was?" [43]So there was a division among the people over him. [44]Some of them wanted to arrest him, but no one laid hands on him.

[45]The officers then went back to the chief priests and Pharisees, who said to them, "Why did you not bring him?" [46]The officers answered, "No man ever spoke like this man!" [47]The Pharisees answered them, "Are you led astray, you also? [48]Have any of the authorities or of the Pharisees believed in him? [49]But this crowd, who do not know the law, are accursed." [50]Nicodemus, who had gone to him before, and who was one of them, said to them, [51]"Does our law judge a man without first giving him a hearing and learning what he does?" [52]They replied, "Are you from Galilee too? Search and you will see that no prophet is to rise from Galilee." [53]They went each to his own house, [1]but Jesus went to the Mount of Olives.

---

that that time has come: "If any man thirst, let him come to me and drink" (v. 37). This invitation recalls words of divine Wisdom: "Come to me, you who desire me, and eat your fill" (Sir 24;19; cf. Prov 9:4–5) and is somewhat reminiscent of these words of St Augustine: "You made us for Yourself, and our hearts are restless until they rest in You" (*Confessions*, 1, 1, 1).

When Jesus speaks of "rivers of living water" flowing out of his heart, he is probably referring to the prophecy of Ezekiel 36:25ff where it is announced that in messianic times the people will be sprinkled with pure water and will be given a new Spirit and their heart of stone will be changed for a heart of flesh. That living water is a symbol of the Holy Spirit who is promised here and (in 19:34) bestowed under the symbol of the water that flows from Christ's side. The title of "the prophet" is a reference to Deuteronomy 18:18 which foretells the coming of a prophet during the last times, a prophet whom all must listen to (cf. 1:21; 6:14). "The Christ" ("the Messiah") was the title most used in the Old Testament to designate the Saviour whom God would send.

q. Or *let him come to me, and let him who believes in me drink. As* **7:42** Mic 5:2.

The adulterous woman

8 [2]Early in the morning he came again to the temple; all the people came to him, and he sat down and taught them. [3]The scribes and the Pharisees brought a woman who had been caught in adultery, and placing her in the midst [4]they said to him, "Teacher, this woman has been caught in the act of adultery. [5]Now in the law Moses commanded us to stone such. What do you say about her?" [6]This they said to test him, that they might have some charge to bring against him. Jesus bent down and wrote with his finger on the ground. [7]And as they continued to ask him, he stood up and said to them, "Let him who is without sin among you be the first to throw a stone at her." [8]And once more he bent down and wrote with his finger on the ground. [9]But when they heard it, they went away, one by one, beginning with the eldest, and Jesus was left alone with the woman standing before him. [10]Jesus looked up and said to her, "Woman, where are they? Has no one condemned you?" [11]She said, "No one, Lord." And Jesus said, "Neither do I condemn you; go, and do not sin again."[r*]

Jesus, the light of the world

[12]Again Jesus spoke to them, saying, "I am the light of the world; he who follows me will not walk in darkness, but will have the light of life." [13]The Pharisees then said to him, "You are bearing witness to yourself; your testimony is not true." [14]Jesus answered, "Even if I do bear witness to myself, my testimony is true, for I know whence I have come and whither I am going, but you do not know whence I have come or whither I am going. [15]You judge

---

8:1–11 Although this episode is absent from many ancient codexes, Church Tradition regards it as inspired and canonical. Its omission may have been due to the fact that some rigorists thought that, because it showed Jesus to be so merciful towards this woman, it might lead to a relaxation of moral rules.

At any event, the episode shows the way Jesus thinks (cf. 8:15): he, the Just One, does not condemn; whereas these people, who are sinners, judge that the woman should die. "It is important to recognize that we ought never be so carried away in our contemplation of divine mercy that we forget God's justice; neither do we consider divine justice without also taking God's mercy into account; because hope is not without [an element of] fear, nor fear without hope" (Fray Luis de Granada, *Life of Jesus Christ*, 13).

Jesus' reply (v. 7) refers to the way stoning was carried out: those who witnessed the crime had to throw the first stones, and then others joined in, to purge, in some way, the shame which the crime brought to the whole people (cf. Deut 17:7).

8:12–20 Jesus now reveals himself as the Light of the world. On the first night of the feast of Tabernacles the "court of the women" in the temple was filled with the

r. Some ancient authorities insert 7.53–8.11 either at the end of this gospel or after Lk 21.38, with variations of the text. Others omit it altogether

according to the flesh, I judge no one. [16]Yet even if I do judge, my judgment is
true, for it is not I alone that judge, but I and he[s] who sent me. [17]In your law it
is written that the testimony of two men is true; [18]I bear witness to myself, and
the Father who sent me bears witness to me." [19]They said to him therefore,
"Where is your Father?" Jesus answered, "You know neither me nor my
Father; if you knew me, you would know my Father also." [20]These words he
spoke in the treasury, as he taught in the temple; but no one arrested him,
because his hour had not yet come.

Jesus warns the unbelieving Jews

[21]Again he said to them, "I go away, and you will seek me and die in your
sin;* where I am going, you cannot come." [22]Then said the Jews, "Will he kill
himself, since he says, 'Where I am going, you cannot come'?" [23]He said to
them, "You are from below, I am from above; you are of this world, I am not
of this world. [24]I told you that you would die in your sins, for you will die in
your sins unless you believe that I am he." [25]They said to him, "Who are you?"
Jesus said to them, "Even what I have told you from the beginning.[t] [26]I have
much to say about you and much to judge; but he who sent me is true, and I
declare to the world what I have heard from him." [27]They did not understand
that he spoke to them of the Father. [28]So Jesus said, "When you have lifted up

---

bright light of high lamps which lit up the sky above the city. This light reminded the people of the bright cloud of God's presence which guided the Israelites through the wilderness during the Exodus. It was probably against the background of this custom that Jesus chose to depict himself as "the Light"—imagery also used elsewhere (Mk 4:16) to designate the Messiah (cf. Lk 1:78; 2:30–32).

Jesus applies this image to himself in two ways: he is the light that enlightens our minds, for he is the fullness of divine Revelation; and he is also the light that enlightens our hearts to enable us to accept that Revelation and live according to it. "In Christ and through Christ God has revealed himself fully to mankind and has definitively drawn close to it; at the same time, in Christ and through Christ man has acquired full awareness of his diginty, of the heights to which he is raised, of the surpassing worth of his own humanity, and of the meaning of his existence" (John Paul II, *Redempt. hom.*, 11).

8:21–59 Because the Jewish authorities persist in rejecting him, Jesus warns them that he is going to heaven, from where he has come, and they will keep on looking for the Messiah but they will not find him because they seek him outside of Jesus, nor can they follow him, for they do not believe in him (vv. 21–30). The words "I am he", which occur often in the Gospel, point to the fact that Jesus is divine. This was the name of God that was revealed to Moses: "I am who I am" (Ex 3:14). "The divine name, 'I Am' or 'He Is', expresses God's faithfulness: despite the

s. Other ancient authorities read *the Father* **t.** Or *Why do I talk to you at all?*

the Son of man, then you will know that I am he, and that I do nothing on my
own authority but speak thus as the Father taught me. 29And he who sent me
is with me; he has not left me alone, for I always do what is pleasing to him."
30As he spoke thus, many believed in him.

31Jesus then said to the Jews who had believed in him, "If you continue in
my word, you are truly my disciples, 32and you will know the truth, and the
truth will make you free." 33They answered him, "We are descendants of
Abraham, and have never been in bondage to any one. How is it that you say,
'You will be made free'?"

34Jesus answered them, "Truly, truly, I say to you, every one who commits
sin is a slave of sin. 35The slave does not continue in the house for ever; the son
continues for ever. 36So if the Son makes you free, you will be free indeed. 37I
know that you are descendants of Abraham; yet you seek to kill me, because
my word finds no place in you. 38I speak of what I have seen with my Father,
and you do what you have heard from your father."

39They answered him, "Abraham is our father." Jesus said to them, "If you
were Abraham's children, you would do what Abraham did, 40but now you
seek to kill me, a man who has told you the truth which I heard from God; this
is not what Abraham did. 41You do what your father did." They said to him,
"We were not born of fornication; we have one Father, even God."* 42Jesus

---

faithlessness of men's sin and the punishment it deserves, he keeps 'steadfast love for thousands' (Ex 34:7). By going so far as to give up his own Son for us, God reveals that he is 'rich in mercy' (Eph 2:4). By giving his life to free us from sin, Jesus reveals that he himself bears the divine name: 'When you have lifted up the Son of man, then you will realize that "I Am"' (Jn 8:28)" (*CCC*, 211).

Belief in Jesus must go further than superficial enthusiasm: it is a matter of being true disciples, in such a way that Jesus' words affect our lives in a permanent way. This deep faith will bring us to know the truth and live a truly free life (vv. 31–41): "You will know the truth and the truth will make you free" (v. 32). "According to Christian faith and the Church's teaching, 'only the freedom which submits to the Truth leads the human person to his true good. The good of the person is to be in the Truth and to do the Truth" (John Paul II, *Veritatis splendor*, 84).

The words "slave" and "sin" in v. 35 are reminiscent of the two sons of Abraham (cf. Gen 21:1–21), Ishmael, born of the slave woman Hagar; and Isaac, born of the free woman Sarah, who would be the heir to God's promises. Jesus shows that freedom is no longer based on descent from Abraham but on knowledge of the truth, which really means knowing Christ himself. Only knowledge of Christ can make us free, because it delivers us from the bondage of sin, the cause of every type of human slavery.

Those who knowingly oppose the truth revealed by Jesus in his deeds and words are acting as children of God's enemy, the devil (vv. 42–59). He is the father

said of them, "If God were your Father, you would love me, for I proceeded
and came forth from God; I came not of my own account, but he sent me.
[43]Why do you not understand what I say? It is because you cannot bear to hear
my word. [44]You are of your father the devil, and your will is to do your father's
desires. He was a murderer from the beginning, and has nothing to do with the
truth, because there is no truth in him. When he lies, he speaks according to his
own nature, for he is a liar and the father of lies. [45]But, because I tell the truth,
you do not believe me. [46]Which of you convicts me of sin? If I tell the truth,
why do you not believe me? [47]He who is of God hears the words of God; the
reason why you do not hear them is that you are not of God."

[48]The Jews answered him, "Are we not right in saying that you are a
Samaritan and have a demon?" [49]Jesus answered, "I have not a demon; but I
honour my Father, and you dishonour me. [50]Yet I do not seek my own glory;
there is One who seeks it and he will be the judge. [51]Truly, truly, I say to you,
if any one keeps my word, he will never see death." [52]The Jews said to him,
"Now we know that you have a demon. Abraham died, as did the prophets;
and you say, 'If any one keeps my word, he will never taste death.' [53]Are you
greater than our father Abraham, who died? And the prophets died! Who do
you claim to be?" [54]Jesus answered, "If I glorify myself, my glory is nothing;
it is my Father who glorifies me, of whom you say that he is your God. [55]But
you have not known him; I know him. If I said, I do not know him, I should be
a liar like you; but I do know him and I keep his word. [56]Your father Abraham
rejoiced that he was to see my day; he saw it* and was glad." [57]The Jews then
said to him, "You are not yet fifty years old, and have you seen Abraham?"[u]
[58]Jesus said to them, "Truly, truly, I say to you, before Abraham was, I am."*

---

of lies: he lied when he seduced our first parents, and he likewise deceives those people who yield to his temptations and stay lodged in their sins. The Son of God manifested himself "to destroy the works of the devil" (1 Jn 3:8). In opposition to the father of lies who promised Adam and Eve immortality, Jesus will keep his promise to give eternal life to those who accept his teachings and remain true to them (vv. 51).

Against the wild accusation that Jesus was possessed by the devil (cf. also Mt 12:24 and Mk 3:21–22) and that he was a Samaritan (v. 48), that is, a heretic, a breaker of the Law, St John shows us that Jesus is acting with great patience and leaving the dispute to the judgment of God. Jesus is not seeking human prestige but rather his Father's glory. Therefore he candidly states what he is—the fulfilment of the hopes of the Old Testament patriarchs. For Abraham, the first-fruits of messianic joy were the birth of his son Isaac, especially when, after he was put to the test, God restored to him that only son (Gen 22:11); this prefigured the resurrection of Christ after his redemptive sacrifice. Abraham rejoiced at the thought that he would see the day of salvation.

u. Other ancient authorities read *has Abraham seen you?*

[59]So they took up stones to throw at him; but Jesus hid himself, and went out of the temple.

Curing of the man born blind

9 [1]As he passed by, he saw a man blind from his birth. [2]And his disciples
asked him, "Rabbi, who sinned, this man or his parents, that he was born
blind?" [3]Jesus answered, "It was not that this man sinned, or his parents, but
that the works of God might be made manifest in him. [4]We must work the
works of him who sent me, while it is day; night comes, when no one can
work.* [5]As long as I am in the world, I am the light of the world." [6]As he said
this, he spat on the ground and made clay of the spittle and anointed the man's
eyes with the clay, [7]saying to him, "Go, wash in the pool of Siloam" (which
means Sent). So he went and washed and came back seeing. [8]The neighbours
and those who had seen him before as a beggar, said, "Is not this the man who
used to sit and beg?" [9]Some said, "It is he"; others said, "No, but he is like him."
He said, "I am the man." [10]They said to him, "Then how were your eyes opened?"
[11]He answered, "The man called Jesus made clay and anointed my eyes and said
to me, 'Go to Siloam and wash'; so I went and washed and received my sight."
[12]They said to him, "Where is he?" He said, "I do not know."

[13]They brought to the Pharisees the man who had formerly been blind.
[14]Now it was a sabbath day when Jesus made the clay and opened his eyes.
[15]The Pharisees again asked him how he had received his sight. And he said to
them, "He put clay on my eyes, and I washed, and I see." [16]Some of the
Pharisees said, "This man is not from God, for he does not keep the sabbath."
But others said, "How can a man who is a sinner do such signs?" There was
a division among them. [17]So they again said to the blind man, "What do you
say about him, since he has opened your eyes?" He said, "He is a prophet."

[18]The Jews did not believe that he had been blind and had received his
sight, until they called the parents of the man who had received his sight, [19]and

---

9:1–23 This miracle shows Jesus to be the light of the world—which supports what was said in the Prologue, "The true light that enlightens every man was coming into the world" (1:9). Jesus not only gives light to the eyes of the blind man: he also enlightens him interiorly, leading him to make an act of faith in Jesus' divinity (9:38). The episode also shows the mind-set of those who are spiritually blind.

Jesus corrects the opinion (prevalent at the time) that blindness and disease in general were traceable to one's own sins or those of one's parents. And by curing the blind man, he shows that he has come to take away the sin of the world, the ultimate cause of all mankind's misfortunes.

Using the broader etymology of the world "Siloam", John applies it to Jesus who is the One "sent" by the Father. Using words and gestures reminiscent of the

asked them, "Is this your son, who you say was born blind? How then does he
now see?" 20His parents answered, "We know that this is our son, and that he
was born blind; 21but how he now sees we do not know, nor do we know who
opened his eyes. Ask him; he is of age, he will speak for himself." 22His
parents said this because they feared the Jews, for the Jews had already agreed
that if any one should confess him to be Christ, he was to be put out of the
synagogue. 23Therefore his parents said, "He is of age, ask him."

The blindness of the Jews

24So for the second time they called the man who had been blind, and said to
him, "Give God the praise; we know that this man is a sinner." 25He answered,
"Whether he is a sinner, I do not know; one thing I know, that though I was
blind, now I see." 26They said to him, "What did he do to you? How did he
open your eyes?" 27He answered them, "I have told you already, and you
would not listen. Why do you want to hear it again? Do you too want to
become his disciples?" 28And they reviled him, saying, "You are his disciple,
but we are disciples of Moses. 29We know that God has spoken to Moses, but
as for this man, we do not know where he comes from." 30The man answered,
"Why, this is a marvel! You do not know where he comes from, and yet he
opened my eyes. 31We know that God does not listen to sinners, but if any one

---

miracle of Naaman, the Syrian general who was cured of leprosy by the prophet Eliseus (cf. 2 Kings 5:1ff), Jesus requires the man to show his faith "What an example of firm faith the blind man gives us! [...] What power could the water possibly contain that when the blind man's eyes were moistened with it they were cured? Surely some mysterious eye salve, or a precious medicine made up in the laboratory of some wise alchemist, would have done better? But the man believed; he acted upon the command of God, and he returned with eyes full of light" (Bl. J. Escrivá, *Hom.*, 2, 193).

In this episode we see examples of various attitudes people adopt towards Jesus and his miracles. The blind man, a straightforward person, believes in Jesus as God's envoy, prophet (v. 17; cf. 9:33) and Son of God (cf. 9:38); whereas self-centred people, who claim to have no need of salvation (people like these Pharisees) persist in not wanting to see or believe, despite the clear evidence before them.

Church Tradition has seen this miracle as symbolizing Baptism, in which water is used to cleanse the soul and give it the light of faith. "This blind man represents the human race [...]. If the blindness represents lack of faith, enlightenment represents faith. [...]. He washed his eyes in the pool whose name means 'Who has been sent': he was baptized in Christ" (St Augustine, *In Ioann. Ev.*, 44, 1–2).

9:24–41 From the exchange between the newly cured man and the Jewish authorities, we can see that a person who believes in Christ is doing God's will. "Give God the praise" (v. 24)—a solemn declaration, like an oath, exhorting

is a worshipper of God and does his will, God listens to him. [32]Never since the
world began has it been heard that any one opened the eyes of a man born blind.
[33]If this man were not from God, he could do nothing." [34]They answered him,
"You were born in utter sin, and would you teach us?" And they cast him out.
[35]Jesus heard that they had cast him out and having found him he said, "Do
you believe in the Son of man?"[v] [36]He answered, "And who is he, sir, that I
may believe in him?" [37]Jesus said to him, "You have seen him, and it is he who
speaks to you." [38]He said, "Lord, I believe"; and he worshipped him. [39]Jesus
said, "For judgment I came into this world, that those who do not see may see,
and that those who see may become blind." [40]Some of the Pharisees near him
heard this, and they said to him, "Are we also blind?" [41]Jesus said to them, "If
you were blind, you would have no guilt; but now that you say, 'We see,' your
guilt remains."

The Good Shepherd

10 [1]"Truly, truly, I say to you, he who does not enter the sheepfold by the
door but climbs in by another way, that man is a thief and a robber; [2]but
he who enters by the door is the shepherd of the sheep. [3]To him the gatekeeper
opens; the sheep hear his voice, and he calls his own sheep by name and leads
them out. [4]When he has brought out all his own, he goes before them, and the
sheep follow him, for they know his voice. [5]A stranger they will not follow, but
they will flee from him, for they do not know the voice of strangers." [6]This
figure Jesus used with them, but they did not understand what he was saying
to them.
[7]So Jesus again said to them, "Truly, truly, I say to you, I am the door of the
sheep. [8]All who came before me are thieves and robbers; but the sheep did not
heed them. [9]I am the door; if any one enters by me, he will be saved, and will

---

someone to tell the truth. The man's expulsion from the synagogue because of his faith in Christ acts as a reminder to Christians of their duty to stay faithful even at the risk of being rejected by others.

As in the case of the Samaritan woman, the blind man recognizes Jesus as being divine. The authorities for their part become increasingly obstinate; as they see it, belief in Jesus will mean perdition. He was not sent to condemn the world but to save it (cf. 3:17); but his presence among us already constitutes a kind of judgment, for each of us has to take a stand, either to accept or to reject him.

10:1–21 In this passage St John shows us that the way to salvation is through faith in Jesus and with the help of his grace. Jesus is the Gate whereby we enter eternal Life; he is the Good Shepherd who leads us and who has given up his life for us. All this imagery of shepherd, sheep and flock reminds us of the language of Old Testament prophets: the chosen people is the flock, and the Lord its shepherd (cf.

v. Other ancient authorities read *the Son of God*

go in and out and find pasture. 10The thief comes only to steal and kill and
destroy; I came that they may have life, and have it abundantly. 11I am the
good shepherd. The good shepherd lays down his life for the sheep. 12He who
is a hireling and not a shepherd, whose own the sheep are not, sees the wolf
coming and leaves the sheep and flees; and the wolf snatches them and scatters
them. 13He flees because he is a hireling and cares nothing for the sheep. 14I
am the good shepherd;* I know my own and my own know me, 15as the Father
knows me and I know the Father; and I lay down my life for the sheep. 16And
I have other sheep, that are not of this fold; I must bring them also, and they
will heed my voice. So there shall be one flock, one shepherd. 17For this reason
the Father loves me, because I lay down my life, that I may take it again. 18No
one takes it from me, but I lay it down of my own accord. I have power to lay
it down, and I have power to take it again; this charge I have received from my
Father."*

19There was again a division among the Jews because of these words.
20Many of them said, "He has a demon, and he is mad; why listen to him?"
21Others said, "These are not the sayings of one who has a demon. Can a
demon open the eyes of the blind?"

Ps 23). The prophets, particularly Jeremiah and Ezekiel, reacting to the infidelity of the kings and the priests (to whom the name of "shepherd" was also applied) promised that there would be new shepherds. In fact, Ezekiel says that God will raise up a unique Shepherd, a descendant of David, who will lead the sheep to pasture, where they will be quite safe (Ezek 24). Jesus describes himself as that Good Shepherd, who looks after his sheep. In other words, the ancient prophecies find their fulfilment in him. From very early on, Christians drew inspiration from this touching image of the Good Shepherd who has such love for each of us.

Christ describes himself as the door to the sheepfold, which is the Church (v. 7): "The Church is a sheepfold, the sole and necessary gateway to which is Christ. It is also a flock, of which God foretold that he would himself be the shepherd, and whose sheep, although watched over by human shepherds, are nevertheless at all times led and brought to pasture by Christ himself, the Good Shepherd and prince of shepherds, who gave his life for his sheep" (Vatican II, *LG*, 6).

Here we have yet another explicit reference to the redemptive value of Christ's sacrifice (cf. vv. 15–17). Jesus gives up his life even for those sheep who are not part of the flock of Israel. His mission extends to all mankind, for he calls all God's children to enter his Church (v. 16).

Finally (vv. 19–21), the evangelist tells us about the different reactions to what Jesus says (cf. 6:52; 7:12, 25–27, 31, 40, 43); reactions which are repeated throughout history. "Jesus: wherever you have passed not a heart has remained indifferent. You are either loved or hated. When an apostolic man follows you, carrying out his duty, is it surprising—if he is another Christ!—that he should provoke similar murmurs of aversion or of love?" (Bl. J. Escrivá, *The Way*, 687).

6. JESUS AND THE FATHER

Jesus and the Father are one

22It was the feast of the Dedication at Jerusalem; 23it was winter, and Jesus was walking in the temple, in the portico of Solomon. 24So the Jews gathered round him and said to him, "How long will you keep us in suspense? If you are the Christ, tell us plainly." 25Jesus answered them, "I told you, and you do not believe. The works that I do in my Father's name, they bear witness to me; 26but you do not believe, because you do not belong to my sheep. 27My sheep hear my voice, and I know them, and they follow me; 28and I give them eternal life, and they shall never perish, and no one shall snatch them out of my hand. 29My Father, who has given them to me,[w] is greater than all, and no one is able to snatch them out of the Father's hand. 30I and the Father are one."

An attempt to stone our Lord

31The Jews took up stones again to stone him. 32Jesus answered them, "I have shown you many good works from the Father; for which of these do you stone me?" 33The Jews answered him, "We stone you for no good work but for blasphemy; because you, being a man, make yourself God." 34Jesus answered them, "Is it not written in your law, 'I said, you are gods'? 35If he called them

---

10:22–42 □ This section is set during the feast of the Dedication of the Temple, which commemorated the cleansing of the temple by Judas Maccabeus after it was profaned by Antiochus IV Epiphanes (cf. 1 Mac 1:54; 4:36–59; 2 Mac 1:1–2:18). Jesus reveals himself as the Son of God, equal to the Father (10:22–42). Some of his listeners believe him, but others, particularly the Jewish authorities, reject what he says, to the point of wanting to arrest him (10:39). However, that will happen only when our Lord permits it.

10:22–30 As against people's doubts about Jesus being the Messiah, John highlights the fact that Jesus and the Father are one. This is central to belief in Jesus. People who will not accept that Jesus does his works at the Father's bidding cannot believe in him. Jesus gives his grace to all; but some people resist it. "I see thanks to sunlight; but if I close my eyes I can see nothing: [my blindness] is my fault, not the sun's, for in closing my eyes I shut out the sunlight" (St Thomas, *Com. on Jn*, in loc.).

10:31–42 It is only through divine revelation that we can know that Jesus and the Father are one in substance. The Jews realized that Jesus was saying he was God, but they interpreted his words as blasphemy and accused him of making himself out to be God when in fact he was a man. Jesus rejects their accusation on the basis of the testimony of Holy Scripture (the prophecies) and of his own works (miracles).

w. Other ancient authorities read *What my Father has given to me* **10:34** Ps 82:6.

gods to whom the word of God came (and scripture cannot be broken), [36]do
you say of him whom the Father consecrated and sent into the world, 'You are
blaspheming,' because I said, 'I am the Son of God'? [37]If I am not doing the
works of my Father, then do not believe me; [38]but if I do them, even though
you do not believe me, believe the works, that you may know and understand
that the Father is in me and I am in the Father." [39]Again they tried to arrest
him, but he escaped from their hands.
[40]He went away again across the Jordan to the place where John at first
baptized, and there he remained. [41]And many came to him; and they said,
"John did no sign, but everything that John said about this man was true."
[42]And many believed in him there.

7. JESUS IS THE LIFE OF THE WORLD

The raising of Lazarus

11 [1]Now a certain man was ill, Lazarus of Bethany, the village of Mary
and her sister Martha. [2]It was Mary who anointed the Lord with
ointment and wiped his feet with her hair, whose brother Lazarus was ill. [3]So
the sisters sent to him, saying, "Lord, he whom you love is ill." [4]But when
Jesus heard it he said, "This illness is not unto death; it is for the glory of God,
so that the Son of God may be glorified by means of it."
[5]Now Jesus loved Martha and her sister and Lazarus. [6]So when he heard
that he was ill, he stayed two days longer* in the place where he was. [7]Then
after this he said to the disciples, "Let us go into Judea again." [8]The disciples
said to him, "Rabbi, the Jews were but now seeking to stone you, and are you
going there again?" [9]Jesus answered, "Are there not twelve hours in the day?
If any one walks in the day, he does not stumble, because he sees the light of
this world. [10]But if any one walks in the night, he stumbles, because the light

---

11:1–57 □ In this chapter Jesus reveals himself as "Resurrection and Life" for those who believe in him. Martha's faith stands out, as does the reaction of the Jewish authorities: such is their hatred that they decide that Jesus must die. The evangelist's remark about the "Passover of the Jews" being at hand (11:55) suggests that these events announce the redemptive death of Christ and his glorious resurrection, that is, the Christian Passover.

11:1–44 The miracle of the raising of Lazarus, which is a sign of our future resurrection from the dead, proves Jesus' power over death. John begins his account by reporting the facts (vv. 1–16). In Christ's conversation with Martha (vv. 17–27) we find one of the most accurate definitions of who Jesus is; he is the Resurrection and the Life—the Resurrection because his own triumph over death is the cause of the resurrection of all men; the Life, because not only does he open

is not in him." [11]Thus he spoke, and then he said to them, "Our friend Lazarus
has fallen asleep, but I go to awake him out of sleep." [12]The disciples said to
him, "Lord, if he has fallen asleep, he will recover." [13]Now Jesus had spoken
of his death, but they thought that he meant taking rest in sleep. [14]Then Jesus
told them plainly, "Lazarus is dead; [15]and for your sake I am glad that I was
not there, so that you may believe. But let us go to him." [16]Thomas, called the
Twin, said to his fellow disciples, "Let us also go, that we may die with him."

[17]Now when Jesus came, he found that Lazarus[x] had already been in the
tomb four days. [18]Bethany was near Jerusalem, about two miles[y] off, [19]and
many of the Jews had come to Martha and Mary to console them concerning
their brother. [20]When Martha heard that Jesus was coming, she went to meet
him, while Mary sat in the house. [21]Martha said to Jesus, "Lord, if you had
been here, my brother would not have died. [22]And even now I know that
whatever you ask from God, God will give you." [23]Jesus said to her, "Your
brother will rise again." [24]Martha said to him, "I know that he will rise again
in the resurrection at the last day." [25]Jesus said to her, "I am the resurrection
and the life,[z] he who believes in me, though he die, yet shall he live, [26]and
whoever lives and believes in me shall never die. Do you believe this?" [27]She
said to him, "Yes, Lord; I believe that you are the Christ, the son of God, he
who is coming into the world."

---

the door to eternal life but he provides man with the nourishment of grace to help him on his way there. And so the Christian can say: "Lord, for your faithful people life is changed, not ended. When the body of our earthly dwelling lies in death we gain an everlasting dwelling place in heaven" (*Roman Missal*, first preface of the Dead). Martha sets us an example of faith: to be raised and to live with Christ, one must believe in him.

We can see how deeply Jesus feels from the way he weeps over Lazarus. This weeping shows him to be truly human and it also evidences God's love for man. "Jesus is your Friend—*the* friend—with a human heart, like yours, with most loving eyes that wept for Lazarus. And as much as he loved Lazarus, he loves you ..." (Bl. J. Escrivá, *The Way*, 422).

Jesus prays before working the miracle (vv. 38–44). Here we can see his role as Mediator. Jesus' attitude and feelings show us the way people who have been baptized should relate to God; Baptism has united us to Christ and made us children of God in him; we should always pray in a filial way and thank God our Father for all the good things he has given us. "Jesus' prayer, characterized by thanksgiving, reveals to us how to ask: *before* the gift is given, Jesus commits himself to the One who in giving gives himself. The Giver is more precious than the gift; he is the 'treasure'; in him abides his Son's heart; the gift is given 'as well' (cf. Mt 6:21, 33)" (*CCC*, 2604).

x. Greek *he* **y.** Greek *fifteen stadia* **z.** Other ancient authorities omit *and the life*

28When she had said this, she went and called her sister Mary, saying
quietly, "The Teacher is here and is calling for you." 29And when she heard it,
she rose quickly and went to him. 30Now Jesus had not yet come to the village,
but was still in the place where Martha had met him. 31When the Jews who
were with her in the house, consoling her, saw Mary rise quickly and go out,
they followed her, supposing that she was going to the tomb to weep there.
32Then Mary, when she came to where Jesus was and saw him, fell at his feet,
saying to him, "Lord, if you had been here, my brother would not have died."
33When Jesus saw her weeping, and the Jews who came with her also
weeping, he was deeply moved in spirit and troubled; 34and he said, "Where
have you laid him?" They said to him, "Lord, come and see." 35Jesus wept.
36So the Jews said, "See how he loved him!" 37But some of them said, "Could
not he who opened the eyes of a blind man have kept this man from dying?"

38Then Jesus, deeply moved again, came to the tomb; it was a cave, and a
stone lay upon it. 39Jesus said, "Take away the stone." Martha, the sister of the
dead man, said to him, "Lord, by this time there will be an odour, for he has
been dead four days." 40Jesus said to her, "Did I not tell you that if you would
believe you would see the glory of God?" 41So they took away the stone. And
Jesus lifted his eyes and said, "Father, I thank thee that thou hast heard me. 42I
knew that thou hearest me always, but I have said this on account of the people
standing by, that they may believe that thou didst send me." 43When he had
said this, he cried with a loud voice, "Lazarus, come out." 44The dead man
came out, his hands and feet bound with bandages, and his face wrapped with
a cloth. Jesus said to them, "Unbind him, and let him go."

The Sanhedrin decides on the death of Jesus Mt 26:3–5; Mk 14:1–2

45Many of the Jews therefore, who had come with Mary and had seen what he
did, believed in him; 46but some of them went to the Pharisees and told them
what Jesus had done. 47So the chief priests and the Pharisees gathered the
council, and said, "What are we to do? For this man performs many signs. 48If
we let him go on thus, every one will believe in him, and the Romans will
come and destroy our holy place[a] and our nation." 49But one of them,

---

11:45–57 Once again we see Jesus to be a sign of contradiction. Some people believe in him and some denounce him. Caiaphas' words, which have a dual meaning, as John points out, refer to the foundation of the new Israel, the Church, through the death of Christ on the cross. And so it happens that one of the last high priests of the Old Covenant prophesies the investiture of the High Priest of the New Covenant, which will be sealed in his own Blood.

When St John says that Christ was going to die "to gather into one the children of God who are scattered abroad" (v. 52), he is referring to what our Lord had said about the salvific effects of his death (cf. 10:16). The prophets had already

a. Greek *our place*

Caiaphas, who was high priest that year, said to them, "You know nothing at all; 50you do not understand that it is expedient for you that one man should die for the people, and that the whole nation should not perish."* 51He did not say this of his own accord, but being high priest that year he prophesied that Jesus should die for the nation, 52and not for the nation only, but to gather into one the children of God who are scattered abroad. 53So from that day on they took counsel how to put him to death.

54Jesus therefore no longer went about openly among the Jews, but went from there to the country near the wilderness, to a town called Ephraim; and there he stayed with the disciples.

55Now the Passover of the Jews was at hand, and many went up from the country to Jerusalem before the Passover, to purify themselves. 56They were looking for Jesus and saying to one another as they stood in the temple, "What do you think? That he will not come to the feast?" 57Now the chief priests and the Pharisees had given orders that if any one knew where he was, he should let them know, so that they might arrest him.

8. JESUS IS ACCLAIMED AS THE MESSIANIC KING

Mary anoints our Lord at Bethany Mt 26:6–16; Mk 14:3–11

12 *1Six days before the Passover, Jesus came to Bethany, where Lazarus was, whom Jesus had raised from the dead. 2There they made him a supper; Martha served, and Lazarus was one of those at table with him. 3Mary

---

announced the future assembling of Israelites faithful to God, to form the new people of Israel (cf. Is 43:5; Jer 23:3–5; Ezek 34:24; 37:21–24). These prophecies are fulfilled by the death of Jesus who, on being raised up on the cross, draws and gathers together the true people of God, made up of believers, whether Israelites or not (cf. 12:32). "All men are called to belong to the new People of God. This People therefore, whilst remaining one and only one, is to be spread throughout the whole world and to all ages in order that the design of God's will may be fulfilled: he made human nature one in the beginning and has decreed that all his children who were scattered should be finally gathered together as one. It was for this purpose that God sent his Son, whom he appointed heir of all things, that he might be teacher, king and priest of all, the head of the new and universal People of God's sons" (Vatican II, *LG*, 13).

The reference to the Passover (v. 55–57) sets the scene for the events that follow, and underlines the fact that Jesus is the new and definitive Passover.

12:1–50 □ This section brings to an end the first part of the Gospel which has focused on Jesus' revelation of himself by means of words and signs (miracles).

took a pound of costly ointment of pure nard and anointed the feet of Jesus and
wiped his feet with her hair; and the house was filled with the fragrance of the
ointment. 4But Judas Iscariot, one of his disciples (he who was to betray him),
said, 5"Why was this ointment not sold for three hundred denarii[b] and given to
the poor?" 6This he said, not that he cared for the poor, but because he was a
thief, and as he had the money box he used to take what was put into it. 7Jesus
said, "Let her alone, let her keep it for the day of my burial. 8The poor you
always have with you, but you do not always have me."
9When the great crowd of the Jews learned that he was there, they came,
not only on account of Jesus but also to see Lazarus, whom he had raised from
the dead. 10So the chief priests planned to put Lazarus also to death, 11because
on account of him many of the Jews were going away and believing in Jesus.

The Messiah's entry into Jerusalem

12The next day a great crowd who had come to the feast heard that Jesus was
coming to Jerusalem. 13So they took branches of palm trees and went out to
meet him, crying, "Hosanna! Blessed is he who comes in the name of the
Lord, even the King of Israel! 14And Jesus found a young ass and sat upon it;
as it is written,

The anointing at Bethany and his later triumphal entry into Jerusalem announce Christ's redemptive death and the glorification of the risen Jesus. Our Lord himself proclaims that the hour of his glorification through death on the cross and resurrection (vv. 23–33) has come. After Jesus' last invitation to people to believe in him, many do believe, but others prefer the praise of men (v. 42).

12:1–11 The anointing at Bethany, immediately prior to the Passover, anticipates the embalming that will be given to Christ's body before its burial. This scene is reported also by Matthew and Mark, but in John's account is given a more personal character. We are told the name of the woman who does the anointing (Mary: v. 3)—and the name of her critic (Judas: v. 4). The presence of Lazarus, recently raised from the dead, and the reference to Jesus' burial (v. 7) also suggest that Jesus is going to die in order to give life to all men.

The Tradition of the Church has seen in this gesture made by Lazarus' sister a sign of the generosity with which we should respond to Christ's love for mankind. "What a shining proof of magnanimity is this 'extravagance' on Mary's part! [...] Don't be mean and grudging with people who, without counting the cost, have given of their all, everything they have, for your sake" (Bl. J. Escrivá, *Hom.*, 2, 126).

12:12–19 Jesus' triumphal entry into Jerusalem anticipates his glorification when he rises from the dead. When the crowd use the words "Blessed is he who comes

b. The denarius was a day's wage for a labourer. **12:13** Ps 118:25.

[15]"Fear not, daughter of Zion;
behold, your king is coming,
sitting on an ass's colt!"

[16]His disciples did not understand this at first; but when Jesus was glorified,
then they remembered that this had been written of him and had been done to
him. [17]The crowd that had been with him when he called Lazarus out of the
tomb and raised him from the dead bore witness. [18]The reason why the crowd
went to meet him was that they heard he had done this sign. [19]The Pharisees
then said to one another, "You see that you can do nothing; look, the world has
gone after him."

Jesus announces his glorification

[20]Now among those who went up to worship at the feast were some Greeks.
[21]So these came to Philip, who was from Bethsaida in Galilee, and said to him,
"Sir, we wish to see Jesus." [23]Philip went and told Andrew; Andrew went with
Philip and they told Jesus. [23]And Jesus answered them, "The hour has come
for the Son of man to be glorified. [24]Truly, truly, I say to you, unless a grain of
wheat falls into the earth and dies, it remains alone; but if it dies, it bears much
fruit. [25]He who loves his life loses it, and he who hates his life in this world
will keep it for eternal life. [26]If any one serves me, he must follow me; and
where I am, there shall my servant be also; if any one serves me, the Father
will honour him.

[27]"Now is my soul troubled. And what shall I say? 'Father, save me from
this hour'? No, for this purpose I have come to this hour. [28]Father, glorify thy

---

in the name of the Lord" (Ps 118:26), they are acclaiming Jesus as the Messiah. The words "the King of Israel", not found in the Synoptics, underline Christ's royalty: the Messiah is the King *par excellence*, although his Kingdom is not of this world (cf. 11:36).

It is very significant that Jesus enters Jerusalem on an ass: he is the king of peace announced by the prophets (cf. Zech 9:9). It was only after his death and resurrection that his disciples grasped the true meaning of this sign—as the evangelist in fact points out (v. 16). Christ wins his kingdom by means of humility and the cross.

12:20–36 The "Greeks" who want to see Jesus stand for the Gentile world. This may be the reason behind the announcement of Jesus' imminent glorification, and the indication that his mission extends to the whole world: Jesus is, as it were, a seed that dies and, by dying, produces an abundant crop (v. 24). He attracts all men to himself (v. 32).

Now that our Lord's "hour" is imminent, John describes his prayer in a way reminiscent of that in the Garden of Olives as reported in the other Gospels. Jesus

12:15 Zech 9:9.

name." Then a voice came from heaven, "I have glorified it, and I will glorify
it again." [29]The crowd standing by heard it and said that it had thundered.
Others said, "An angel has spoken to him." [30]Jesus answered, "This voice has
come for your sake, not for mine. [31]Now is the judgment of this world, now
shall the ruler of this world be cast out; [32]and I, when I am lifted up* from the
earth, will draw all men to myself." [33]He said this to show by what death he
was to die. [34]The crowd answered him, "We have heard from the law that the
Christ remains for ever. How can you say that the Son of man must be lifted
up? Who is this Son of man?" [35]Jesus said to them, "The light is with you for
a little longer. Walk while you have the light, lest the darkness overtake you;
he who walks in the darkness does not know where he goes. [36]While you have
the light, believe in the light, that you may become sons of light."

The unbelief of the Jews

When Jesus had said this, he departed and hid himself from them. [37]Though
he had done so many signs before them, yet they did not believe in him; [38]it
was that the word spoken by the prophet Isaiah might be fulfilled:

---

is troubled and he turns as Son to the Father for the strength to be true to his mission. The "glory" refers to the holiness and power of God. The voice of the Father—something similar happened at the Baptism of Christ (cf. Mt 3:13–17 and par.) and at the Transfiguration (Mt 17:1–13 and par.)—formally ratifies the fact that the fullness of deity dwells in Jesus Christ (Col 2:9).

On the cross, the world and the ruler of this world will be judged (vv. 31–33). Nailed to the cross, Jesus is the supreme sign of contradiction for all men and women: those who acknowledge him as Son of God will be saved; those who reject him will be condemned (cf. 3:14–18).Therefore, every Christian should manifest the saving power of the cross "The Cross must also be inserted in the very heart of the world. Jesus wants to be raised on high, there: in the noise of the factories and workshops, in the silence of libraries, in the loud clamour of the streets, in the stillness of the fields, in the intimacy of the family, in crowded gatherings, in stadiums … Wherever there is a Christian striving to lead an honourable life, he should, with his love, set up the Cross of Christ, who attracts all things to himself" (Bl. J. Escrivá, *The Way of the Cross*, 11,3).

Jesus' revelation provokes his brethren to ask a question about the Messiah (v. 34). Although Jesus does not provide a direct explanation, he implies that his presence among them is light enough for them to glimpse the mystery of Christ and believe in him.

12:37–50 The evangelist explains why so many Jews failed to believe in Jesus despite seeking his miracles and despite hearing him preach. He quotes two passages from Isaiah. From the first (Is 53:1) we can see that faith is a gift from

12:38 Is 53:1.

"Lord, who has believed our report,
and to whom has the arm of the Lord been revealed?"
39 Therefore they could not believe. For Isaiah again said,
40 "He has blinded their eyes and hardened their heart,
lest they should see with their eyes and perceive with their heart,
and turn for me to heal them."
41 Isaiah said this because he saw his glory and spoke of him. 42 Nevertheless
many even of the authorities believed in him, but for fear of the Pharisees they
did not confess it, lest they should be put out of the synagogue: 43 for they
loved the praise of men more than the praise of God.
44 And Jesus cried out and said, "He who believes in me, believes not in me,
but in him who sent me. 45 And he who sees me sees him who sent me. 46 I have
come as light into the world, that whoever believes in me may not remain in
darkness. 47 If any one hears my sayings and does not keep them, I do not judge
him; for I did not come to judge the world but to save the world. 48 He who
rejects me and does not receive my sayings has a judge; the word that I have
spoken will be his judge on the last day. 49 For I have not spoken on my own
authority; the Father who sent me has himself given me commandment what
to say and what to speak. 50 And I know that his commandment is eternal life.
What I say, therefore, I say as the Father has bidden me."

God; it is an act whereby "man gives free obedience to God himself, consenting to and cooperating with his grace, which he might instead have resisted" (Vatican I, *Dei Filius*, 3). From the second (Is 6:9–10), referred to also in other New Testament books, John deduces that the unbelief of Jews, which could have been demoralizing for the first generation of Christians, was in fact something foreseen and predicted.

In contrast with the man blind from birth who, after Jesus cured him, refused to retract his profession of faith in Jesus even though the authorities threatened to expel him (cf. 9:35–41), we now meet people (vv. 42–43) who do not dare to openly believe in Jesus because it is just does not suit them to do so: John's comment about them is a permanent reproach to those who give too much weight to other people's opinion of them, putting their own reputation above the glory of God.

The Gospel concludes its coverage of Jesus' public ministry by summarizing the main themes of the preceding chapters—the need for faith in Christ (v. 55); the Father and Son are one yet distinct (v. 45); Jesus is Light and Life of the world (vv. 46, 50); men will be judged according to whether they accept or reject the Son of God (vv. 47–49).

12:40 Is 6:10.

PART TWO: JESUS IS MANIFESTED AS THE MESSIAH SON OF GOD IN HIS PASSION, DEATH AND RESURRECTION

9. THE LAST SUPPER

Jesus washes his disciples' feet

13 *[1] Now before the feast of the Passover, when Jesus knew that his hour had come to depart out of this world to the Father, having loved his own who were in the world, he loved them to the end. [2]And during supper, when the devil had already put it into the heart of Judas Iscariot, Simon's son, to betray him, [3]Jesus, knowing that the Father had given all things into his hands,

---

13:1–21:25 □□ Here we can see three sections, three themes—the Last Supper and farewell discourses; our Lord's passion and death; and his resurrection. In each Christ is again manifested and revealed and again people react differently—with faith or unbelief. This second part of John's Gospel is often called "the book of Christ's glory".

13:1–17:26 □ These chapters deal with Jesus' revelation to his disciples in the privacy of the Last Supper. In his account John mentions some things that are not in the other Gospels (the washing of the feet, for example) and he does not cover the institution of the Eucharist, reported by the Synoptics and St Paul, and about which John speaks in chapter 6. Up to this point, "life" and "light" were highlighted; now the key word is "love".

In 13:33–17:26 John gives the Last Supper discourse, also called the farewell discourse. It has three parts to it: 1) on Christ's departure and his return (13:33–38 and chap. 14); 2) on Christ and the Church (chaps. 15–16); 3) the priestly prayer of Christ (chap. 17). The basic themes are: love, which has its roots in Christ's love and becomes the Lord's commandment; the way Jesus consoles his disciples just before he leaves, by promising that he will return and that he will send the Holy Spirit; Christ's union with his own, like vine and branches, which is founded on love and on keeping his commandments.

13:1–20 This chapter begins by stressing the fact that the moment of truth has come. The Passover, which commemorated the liberation of the Israelites from bondage on Egypt, prefigured the liberation Jesus came to bring—the redemption of mankind from the slavery of sin, by means of his sacrifice on the cross.

What Jesus did for his own may be summed up in this sentence: "He loved them to the end" (v. 1). It shows the intensity of his love—which brings him even

and that he had come from God and was going to God, [4]rose from supper, laid aside his garments, and girded himself with a towel. [4]Then he poured water into a basin, and began to wash the disciples' feet, and to wipe them with the towel with which he was girded. [6]He came to Simon Peter, and Peter said to him, "Lord, do you wash my feet?" [7]Jesus answered him, "What I am doing you do not know now, but afterward you will understand." [8]Peter said to him, "You shall never wash my feet." Jesus answered him, "If I do not wash you, you have no part in me." [9]Simon Peter said to him, "Lord, not my feet only but also my hands and my head!" [10]Jesus said to him, "He who has bathed does not need to wash, except for his feet,[c] but he is clean all over; and you are clean, but not all of you." [11]For he knew who was to betray him; that was why he said, "You are not all clean."

[12]When he had washed their feet, and taken his garments, and resumed his place, he said to them, "Do you know what I have done to you? [13]You call me Teacher and Lord; and you are right, for so I am. [14]If I then, your Lord and Teacher, have washed your feet, you also ought to wash one another's feet. [15]For I have given you an example, that you also should do as I have done to you. [16]Truly, truly, I say to you, a servant[d] is not greater than his master; nor is he who is sent greater than he who sent him. [17]If you know these things, blessed are you if you do them. [18]I am not speaking of you all; I know whom I have chosen; it is that the scripture may be fulfilled, 'He who ate my bread has lifted his heel against me.' [19]I tell you this now, before it takes place, that when it does take place you may believe that I am he. [20]Truly, truly, I say to you, he who receives any one whom I send receives me; and he who receives me receives him who sent me."

---

to give up his life. At the washing of the feet, our Lord humbles himself to the point of performing a service befitting household servants. The passage is reminiscent of the hymn in St Paul's letter to the Philippians: "Christ Jesus, though he was in the form of God, … emptied himself taking the form of a servant …" (Phil 2:6–7). Cleaning his disciples' feet had a meaning which Peter could not appreciate at the time. By this simple, symbolical gesture, Jesus was indicating that he had come "not to be served but to serve", and his service consisted in "giving his life as a ransom for many" (Mk 10:45). This tells the apostles, and in them all who would later make up the Church, that humble service of others is what makes a disciple like the Master. "If, in the light of this attitude of Christ's, 'being a king' is truly possible only by 'being a servant', then 'being a servant' also demands so much spiritual maturity that it must really be described as 'being a king'" (John Paul II, *Redempt. hom.*, 21). On the "I am he" (v. 19), see the note on 8:21–59.

c. Other ancient authorities omit *except for his feet* **d.** Or *slave* **13:18** Ps 41:9.

The treachery of Judas foretold Mt 26:20–25; Mk 14:17–21; Lk 22:21–23

21 When Jesus had thus spoken, he was troubled in spirit, and testified, "Truly, truly, I say to you, one of you will betray me."
22 The disciples looked at one another, uncertain of whom he spoke.
23 One of his disciples, whom Jesus loved, was lying close to the breast of Jesus;
24 so Simon Peter beckoned to him and said, "Tell us who it is of whom he speaks."
25 So lying thus, close to the breast of Jesus, he said to him, "Lord, who is it?"
26 Jesus answered, "It is he whom I shall give this morsel when I have dipped it." So when he had dipped the morsel, he gave it to Judas, the son of Simon Iscariot.
27 Then after the morsel, Satan entered into him. Jesus said to him, "What you are going to do, do quickly,"
28 Now no one at the table knew why he said this to him.
29 Some thought that, because Judas had the money box, Jesus was telling him, "Buy what you need for the feast"; or, that he should give something to the poor.
30 So, after receiving the morsel, he immediately went out; and it was night.

The new commandment.
The disciples' desertion foretold Mt 26:30–35; Mk 14:26–31; Lk 22:31–34

31 When he had gone out, Jesus said, "Now is the Son of man glorified, and in him God is glorified;
32 if God is glorified in him, God will also glorify him in himself, and glorify him at once.
33 Little children, yet a little while I am with you. You will seek me; and as I said to the Jews so now I say to you, 'Where I

13:21–32 In this announcement of Judas' treachery we can see how it contrasts with Jesus' love for his beloved disciple (which shows his love for all those who are true disciples), and the love his disciples have for the Master.

"It was night" (v. 30)—a reference to darkness as an image of sin, of the power of darkness which now seems to have the upper hand (cf. Lk 22:53) and which opposes the true Light, Christ, whom the darkness has not overcome (cf. 1:5). The moment of Jesus' glorification has come—something that refers above all to the glory Christ will receive once he is raised up on the cross. The evangelist stresses that Christ's death marks the start of his victory, which at the same time is the glorification of the Father. Furthermore Christ's disciple will find that what makes him truly great is his imitation of Jesus' own obedience. St Paul spells this out when he says: "Far be it from me to glory except in the cross of the Lord Jesus Christ" (Gal 6:14).

13:33–38 The Lord's commandments can be summed up in just one—the New Commandment of love. This precept includes the entire law of the Church and it is the distinguishing mark of a Christian: "Anyone can bless himself with the sign of the cross of Christ: anyone can answer 'Amen'; anyone can sing Allelujah; anyone can be baptized, enter churches, build the walls of basilicas. But the only thing that distinguishes the children of God is charity. Those who practise charity are born of God; those who do not practise it are not born of God. It is indeed an

am going you cannot come.' 34A new commandment* I give to you, that you
love one another; even as I have loved you, that you also love one another.
35By this all men will know that you are my disciples, if you have love for one
another."
36Simon Peter said to him, "Lord, where are you going?" Jesus answered,
"Where I am going you cannot follow me now; but you shall follow afterward."
37Peter said to him, "Lord, why cannot I follow you now? I will lay down my life
for you." 38Jesus answered, "Will you lay down your life for me? Truly, truly, I
say to you, the cock will not crow, till you have denied me three times.

Jesus reveals the Father

14 1"Let not your hearts be troubled; believe[e] in God, believe also in me.
2In my Father's house are many rooms; if it were not so, would I have
told you that I go to prepare a place for you? 3And when I go and prepare a
place for you, I will come again and will take you to myself, that where I am
you may be also. 4And you know the way where I am going."[f] 5Thomas said
to him, "Lord, we do not know where you are going; how can we know the
way?" 6Jesus said to him, "I am the way, and the truth, and the life; no one
comes to the Father, but by me. 7If you had known me, you would have known
my Father also; henceforth you know him and have seen him."
8Philip said to him, "Lord, show us the Father, and we shall be satisfied."
9Jesus said to him, "Have I been with you so long, and yet you do not know

---

important sign, an essential difference. No matter what you have, if you do not have this one thing, everything else is of no avail; and if you lack everything, and have nothing else but charity, then you have kept the law" (St Augustine, *In Epist. Ioann. ad Parth.*, 5,7). However, the words "as I have loved you" (v. 34) give the precept new meaning. Christian love is measured not by just any man's heart but by the heart of Christ (cf. Mt 5:43–48).

The prediction of Peter's denial (the content of the conversation at this point) ties in with the conversation at the end of the Gospel where Jesus asks Peter if he loves him (21:15–19). Fidelity to Christ is a matter of love: "And what is the secret of perseverance? Love. Fall in Love, and you will not leave him" (Bl. J. Escrivá, *The Way*, 999).

14:1–14 Jesus' death means that he goes to the Father, with whom he is one because he is God. His revelation of the Father is preceded by the announcement that Jesus is going away to prepare a place in heaven for those who have believed in him and have been faithful to him. Jesus is, therefore, the way to the Father because he reveals the Father to us. The words in v. 6, St Augustine comments, are "as if he were saying, where do you want to go? I am the Way. Where do you want to reach? I am the Truth. Where do you hope to stay? I am the Life" (*Serm.*, 142, 1).

e. Or *you believe* **f.** Other ancient authorities read *where I am going you know, and the way you know*
g. Other ancient authorities add *me*

me, Philip? He who has seen me has seen the Father; how can you say, 'Show
us the Father'? 10Do you not believe that I am in the Father and the Father in
me? The words that I say to you I do not speak on my own authority; but the
Father who dwells in me does his works. 11Believe me that I am in the Father
and the Father in me; or else believe me for the sake of the works themselves.
12Truly, truly, I say to you, he who believes in me will also do the works
that I do; and greater works than these will he do; because I go to the Father.
13Whatever you ask in my name, I will do it, that the Father may be glorified
in the Son; 14if you ask[g] anything in my name, I will do it.

Promise of the Holy Spirit

15"If you love me, you will keep my commandments. 16And I will pray the
Father, and he will give you another Counsellor, to be with you for ever, 17even
the Spirit of truth, whom the world cannot receive, because it neither sees him
nor knows him; you know him, for he dwells with you, and will be in you.
18"I will not leave you desolate; I will come to you. 19Yet a little while, and
the world will see me no more, but you will see me; because I live, you will
live also. 20In that day you will know that I am in my Father, and you in me,
and I in you. 21He who has my commandments and keeps them, he it is who
loves me; and he who loves me will be loved by my Father, and I will love him
and manifest myself to him. 22Judas (not Iscariot) said to him, "Lord, how is it
that you will manifest yourself to us, and not to the world?" 23Jesus answered
him, "If a man loves me, he will keep my word, and my Father will love him,

---

And elsewhere he says: "Every man is capable of understanding the Truth and the Life but not all find the Way. The wise men of the world understand God as eternal life and as a truth which is knowable; [...] however, the word of God, which is Truth and Life in the presence of the Father, has become the Way on assuming a human nature. Look at his humility and you will attain God" (ibid., 141, 1 and 4).

Verse 9 is particularly revealing. To know Christ is to know God. Jesus is the face of God. "Christ's whole earthly life—his words and deeds, his silences and sufferings, indeed his manner of being and speaking—is *Revelation* of the Father. Jesus can say: 'Whoever has seen me has seen the Father' (Jn 14:9), and the Father can say: 'This is my Son, my Chosen; listen to him! Because our Lord became man in order to do his Father's will, even the least characteristics of his mysteries manifest 'God's love … among us' (1 Jn 4:9)" (*CCC*, 516).

14:15–31 Jesus announces that, after his resurrection, he will send the Holy Spirit to the apostles; and the Spirit will guide them, reminding them of Jesus' teachings and helping them to understand them. "Paraclete" (counsellor: vv 16, 26) means etymologically "called to be beside someone" to accompany, console, protect, defend. Hence the way it is often translated—Counsellor, Consoler, Advocate, etc.

g. Other ancient authorities add *me*

and we will come to him and make our home with him. [24]He who does not
love me does not keep my words; and the word which you hear is not mine but
the Father's who sent me.
[25]"These things I have spoken to you, while I am still with you. [26]But the
Counsellor, the Holy Spirit, whom the Father will send in my name, he will
teach you all things,* and bring to your remembrance all that I have said to
you. [27]Peace I leave with you; my peace I give to you; not as the world gives
do I give to you. Let not your hearts be troubled, neither let them be afraid.
[28]You heard me say to you, 'I go away, and I will come to you.' If you loved
me, you would have rejoiced, because I go to the Father; for the Father is
greater than I. [29]And now I have told you before it takes place, so that when it
does take place, you may believe. [30]I will no longer talk much with you, for
the ruler of this world is coming. He has no power over me; [31]but I do as the
Father has commanded me, so that the world may know that I love the Father.
Rise, let us go hence.

The vine and the branches

15 [1]"I am the true vine, and my Father is the vinedresser. [2]Every branch of
mine that bears no fruit, he takes away, and every branch that does bear
fruit he prunes that it may bear more fruit. [3]You are already made clean by the

---

Jesus describes the Holy Spirit as "another" Counsellor, because Christ is our Advocate and Mediator in heaven at his Father's side (cf. 1 Jn 2:1), and the Holy Spirit will be given to the disciples in his stead as an Advocate and a Protector. This passage reveals the mystery of the most Blessed Trinity.

The apostles are surprised (v. 22), because they think that Jesus is giving them something just for their own ears whereas it was commonly held by the Jews that the Messiah would manifest himself for all the world to see, as King and Saviour. Jesus, however, speaks about his being revealed to those who love him and who keep his commandments. But this manifestation does not involve just intellectual cognition; it means the indwelling of God in the Christian's soul (v. 23). God promised his presence in the midst of the people in the Old Testament. Here there is talk of a presence of the Father and the Son in each person, turning him or her into a temple of the Holy Spirit (cf. 2 Cor 6:16–17). Awareness of this indwelling of the Trinity in the human soul has been a source of great consolation to the saints: "It was a sweet dream that shed light throughout my life, converting it into a heaven on earth" (Bl. Elizabeth of the Trinity, *Letters*, 1906).

When the apostles receive the Holy Spirit, he will guide them to all truth and will help them understand Jesus' words. Along with the gift of the Holy Spirit we are given peace (v. 27), that is, reconciliation with God and with others.

15:1–8 This comparison of the chosen people to a vine was used in the Old Testament (Ps 80:9ff; Is 5:1–7; cf. Mt 21:33–43). Now, talking of the vine and its

word which I have spoken to you. [4]Abide in me, and I in you. As the branch
cannot bear fruit by itself, unless it abides in the vine, neither can you, unless
you abide in me. [5]I am the vine, you are the branches. He who abides in me,
and I in him, he it is that bears much fruit, for apart from me you can do
nothing. [6]If a man does not abide in me, he is cast forth as a branch and
withers; and the branches are gathered, thrown into the fire and burned. [7]If you
abide in me, and my words abide in you, ask whatever you will, and it shall be
done for you. [8]By this my Father is glorified, that you bear much fruit, and so
prove to be my disciples.

The law of love

[9]As the Father has loved me, so have I loved you; abide in my love. [10]If you
keep my commandments, you will abide in my love, just as I have kept my
Father's commandments and abide in his love. [11]These things I have spoken
to you, that my joy may be in you, and that your joy may be full.

[12]"This is my commandment, that you love one another as I have loved
you. [13]Greater love has no man than this, that a man lay down his life for his
friends. [14]You are my friends if you do what I command you. [15]No longer do
I call you servants,[h] for the servant[i] does not know what his master is doing;
but I have called you friends, for all that I have heard from my Father I have

---

branches, Jesus explains that he and those united to him form the new Israel of God, the Church, of which he is the head (cf. 1 Cor 3:9). One needs to be a part of the new Vine, the true Vine, Christ, if one is to bear fruit. It is not any longer just a matter of belonging to a community but of living the life of Christ, the life of grace. The image of the vine also helps us understand what the unity of the Church involves. It is the mystical Body of Christ in which all the members are closely united to the Head and thereby to one another (cf. 1 Cor 12:12–27; Rom 12:4–5; Eph 4:15–16).

15:9–17 Genuine love of Jesus involves making an effort to keep God's commandments. Particularly the commandment of brotherly love, following the example of Christ who went as far as to die for us. The persecutions and difficulties a follower of Christ inevitably meets up with should never shake his faith or discourage him. On the contrary, they should give him an opportunity to show his faith and to be consoled and comforted by the Holy Spirit.

Jesus speaks about the Paraclete three times during the Last Supper. On the first occasion (14:15ff), he says that he will be another Counsellor sent by the Father to stay with them for ever; then (14:26) he says that he himself, on behalf of the Father, will send the Spirit of truth to tell them all things; and on the third time (16:6–7) he reveals the whole plan of salvation and announces that his ascension into heaven will lead to the sending of the Holy Spirit.

h. Or *slaves* **i.** Or *slave*

made known to you. [16]You did not choose me, but I chose you and appointed
you that you should go and bear fruit and that your fruit should abide; so that
whatever you ask the Father in my name, he may give it to you. [17]This I
command you, to love one another.

A hostile world

[18]"If the world hates you, know that it has hated me before it hated you.* [19]If
you were of the world, the world would love its own; but because you are not
of the world, but I chose you out of the world, therefore the world hates you.
[20]Remember the word that I said to you, 'A servant[i] is not greater than his
master.' If they persecuted me, they will persecute you; if they kept my word,
they will keep yours also. [21]But all this they will do to you on my account,
because they do not know him who sent me. [22]If I had not come and spoken to
them, they would not have sin; but now they have no excuse for their sin. [23]He
who hates me hates my Father also. [24]If I had not done among them the works
which no one else did, they would not have sin; but now they have seen and
hated both me and my Father. [25]It is to fulfil the word that is written in their
law, 'They hated me without a cause.' [26]But when the Counsellor comes,
whom I shall send to you from the Father, even the Spirit of truth, who
proceeds from the Father, he will bear witness to me; [27]and you also are
witnesses, because you have been with me from the beginning.

The action of the Holy Spirit

16 [1]"I have said all this to you to keep you from falling away. [2]They will
put you out of the synagogues; indeed, the hour is coming when
whoever kills you will think he is offering service to God. [3]And they will do
this because they have not known the Father, nor me. [4]But I have said these

---

Verses 14 and 15, particularly, tell us things about the mystery of the Blessed Trinity; we learn that the three divine persons are equal: everything that the Father has belongs to the Son and the Spirit also has what is common to the Father and the Son, that is, the divine essence.

15:18–27 In the light of the apparent triumph of sin, Jesus teaches that there can be no agreement between himself and the sinful world: he who lives in sin hates the light (cf. 3:19–20). For this reason Christ has been, and the apostles will be, persecuted. Those who deny Jesus would not have sinned if he had not revealed himself through his works, if the Light had not overcome the darkness; but now they have no excuse; the rejection of Christ is the rejection of God's truth (cf. Ps 35:19).

16:1–15 Jesus teaches that those who neither know God nor acknowledge the Christ will persecute the disciples just as they persecuted Jesus himself and put

15:25 Ps 35:19; 69:4.

things to you, that when their hour comes you may remember that I told you of them.

"I did not say these things to you from the beginning, because I was with you. [5]But now I am going to him who sent me; yet none of you asks me, 'Where are you going?' [6]But because I have said these things to you, sorrow has filled your hearts. [7]Nevertheless I tell you the truth: it is to your advantage that I go away, for if I do not go away, the Counsellor will not come to you; but if I go, I will send him to you. [8]And when he comes, he will convince the world of sin and of righteousness and of judgment: [9]of sin, because they do not believe in me; [10]of righteousness, because I go to the Father, and you will see me no more;* [11]of judgment, because the ruler of this world is judged.

[12]"I have yet many things to say to you, but you cannot bear them now. [13]When the Spirit of truth comes, he will guide you into all the truth; for he will not speak of his own authority, but whatever he hears he will speak, and he will declare to you the things that are to come. [14]He will glorify me, for he will take what is mine and declare it to you. [15]All that the Father has is mine; therefore I said that he will take what is mine and declare it to you.

Fullness of joy

[16]"A little while, and you will see me no more; again a little while, and you will see me." [17]Some of his disciples said to one another, "What is this that he says to us, 'A little while, and you will not see me, and again a little while, and

---

him to death. The persecution and difficulties which those who follow Christ inevitably face should neither discourage nor scandalize them. On the contrary, his followers, consoled and comforted by the action of the Holy Spirit, will see these contradictions as opportunities to show their faith.

Jesus speaks of the Holy Spirit on three occasions during the Last Supper. In the first reference (14:15ff) he states that the Spirit will be another Consoler sent by the Father to be with them always; in the second (14:26) he says that he himself on behalf of his Father will send the Spirit of Truth who will teach them all things; and in the last (16:1–15) he reveals completely the plan of salvation and announces that the fruit of his ascension into heaven will be the sending of the Holy Spirit.

Verses 14–15 in particular disclose some aspects of the mystery of the Blessed Trinity. The equality of the three divine persons is revealed in saying that all that the Father possesses belongs to the Son, that all that the Son possesses belongs to the Father, and that the Holy Spirit too possesses what the Father and the Son share, that is, the divine essence.

16:16–33 The disciples could not grasp what Jesus meant. When he says that after suffering tribulation they will be filled with a joy they will never lose (cf. 17:13), this is primarily a reference to the joy of the resurrection (cf. Lk 24:41), but it also refers to their definitive encounter with Christ in heaven.

you will see me'; and, 'because I go to the Father'?" [18]They said, "What does
he mean by 'a little while'? We do not know what he means." [19]Jesus knew
that they wanted to ask him; so he said to them, "Is this what you are asking
yourselves, what I meant by saying, 'A little while, and you will not see me,
and again a little while, and you will see me'? [20]Truly, truly, I say to you, you
will weep and lament, but the world will rejoice; you will be sorrowful, but
your sorrow will turn into joy. [21]When a woman is in travail she has sorrow,
because her hour has come; but when she is delivered of the child, she no
longer remembers the anguish, for joy that a child[j] is born into the world. [22]So
you have sorrow now, but I will see you again and your hearts will rejoice, and
no one will take your joy from you. [23]In that day you will ask nothing of me.
Truly, truly, I say to you, if you ask anything of the Father, he will give it to
you in my name. [24]Hitherto you have asked nothing in my name; ask, and you
will receive, that your joy may be full.

[25]"I have said this to you in figures; the hour is coming when I shall no
longer speak to you in figures but tell you plainly of the Father. [26]In that day you
will ask in my name; and I do not say to you that I shall pray the Father for you;
[27]for the Father himself loves you, because you have loved me and have believed
that I came from the Father. [28]I came from the Father and have come into the
world; again, I am leaving the world and going to the Father."

[29]His disciples said, "Ah, now you are speaking plainly, not in any figure!
[30]Now we know that you know all things, and need none to question you; by this
we believe that you came from God." [31]Jesus answered them, "Do you now
believe? [32]The hour is coming, indeed it has come, when you will be scattered,
every man to his home, and will leave me alone; yet I am not alone, for the Father

---

The image of the woman giving birth (frequently used in the Old Testament to refer to intense pain) is also used, especially by the prophets, to mean the birth of the new messianic people (cf. Is 21:3; 26:17; Jer 30:6; Hos 13:13; Mic 4:9–10). The birth of the new people of God (the Church of Christ) involves intense pain, not only for Jesus, but also, to some degree, for the apostles. But this pain, like birth pains, will be made up for by the joy of the final coming of the Kingdom of Christ (cf. Rom 8:18).

After his resurrection our Lord will speak very clearly to the apostles, in such a way that they will have a better grasp of the mystery of his passion and of just how intense God's love is: so great is it that he sent his Son into the world. The strong faith of the disciples is based on the conviction that our Lord knows all things and can read all hearts, and on the victory won by Christ. Jesus also shows that even while he was with them he could read their hearts (cf. 2:25). Jesus' prediction that they will all abandon him, once it is read against the face of his resurrection, is a call to hope. In the face of tribulation and attacks from those who reject Christ, Jesus' words resound in their hearts: "I have overcome the world" (v. 33).

j. Greek *a human being*

is with me. 33I have said this to you, that in me you may have peace. In the world
you have tribulation; but be of good cheer, I have overcome the world."

The priestly prayer of Jesus

17 1When Jesus had spoken these words, he lifted his eyes to heaven and
said,* "Father, the hour has come, glorify thy Son that the Son may
glorify thee, 2since thou hast given him power over all flesh, to give eternal life
to all whom thou hast given him. 3And this is eternal life, that they know thee
the only true God, and Jesus Christ whom thou hast sent. 4I glorified thee on
earth, having accomplished the work which thou gavest me to do; 5and now,
Father, glorify thou me in thy own presence with the glory which I had with
thee before the world was made.*

6"I have manifested thy name to the men whom thou gavest me out of the
world; thine they were, and thou gavest them to me, and they have kept thy
word. 7Now they know that everything that thou hast given me is from thee;
8for I have given them the words which thou gavest me, and they have received
them and know in truth that I came from thee; and they have believed that thou
didst send me. 9I am praying for them; I am not praying for the world but for
those whom thou hast given me, for they are thine; 10all mine are thine, and
thine are mine, and I am glorified in them. 11And now I am no more in the
world, but they are in the world, and I am coming to thee. Holy Father, keep
them in thy name, which thou hast given me, that they may be one, even as we
are one. 12While I was with them, I kept them in my name, which thou hast
given me; I have guarded them, and none of them is lost but the son of
perdition, that the scripture might be fulfilled. 13But now I am coming to thee;

17:1–26 Jesus turns to the Father, addressing him in a moving dialogue in which, as Priest, he offers him the imminent sacrifice of his passion and death. This concluding part of the discourse is called Jesus' "Priestly Prayer".

In the opening verses of the Prayer (1–5) Jesus asks for the glorification of his holy human nature, and the acceptance by the Father, of his sacrifice on the cross. The word "glory" here means the splendour, power and honour which "belong to God". The glorification of Jesus has three dimensions to it: 1) it serves to reveal the glory of the Father because Christ, in obedience to God's redemptive decree, makes the Father known (v. 4); 2) it manifests Christ's divinity through his human nature (vv. 2 and 5); 3) it offers us the opportunity to attain eternal life—and this redounds to the glory of the Father and of Jesus Christ (vv. 2–3).

In the second part of the Prayer (vv. 6–19), Jesus prays for his disciples, whom he is going to send into the world to proclaim his work of redemption. He asks the Father to give them unity, perseverance, joy and holiness. By asking the Father to "keep them in thy name" (v. 11) he is asking for their perseverance in what he has taught them (v. 6) and in communion with him. One consequence of this communion and these things I speak in the world, that they may have my joy fulfilled in themselves. [14]I have given them thy word; and the world has hated them because they are not of the world, even as I am not of the world. [15]I do not pray that thou shouldst take them out of the world, but that thou shouldst keep them from the evil one.[k] [16]They are not of the world, even as I am not of the world. [17]Sanctify them in the truth; thy word is truth. [18]As thou didst send me into the world, so I have sent them into the world. [19]And for their sake I consecrate myself, that they also may be consecrated in truth.

[20]"I do not pray for these only, but also for those who believe in me through their word, [21]that they may all be one; even as thou, Father, art in me, and I in thee, that they also may be in us, so that the world may believe that thou hast sent me. [22]The glory which thou hast given me I have given to them, that they may be one even as we are one, [23]I in them and thou in me, that they may become perfectly one, so that the world may know that thou hast sent me and hast loved them even as thou has loved me. [24]Father, I desire that they also, whom thou hast given me, may be with me where I am, to behold my glory which thou has given me in thy love for me before the foundation of the world. [25]O righteous Father, the world has not known thee, but I have known thee;

---

is unity among his disciples, which is a reflection of the unity that exists among the three divine Persons.

Our Lord also prays for those who, though they live in the world, are not of the world, that they may be sanctified in God's truth (v. 17) and carry out the mission he has given them, just as he himself did what the Father sent him to do (v. 18). In St John's Gospel "world" has a number of meanings. First, it means the whole of creation and, within it, mankind, whom God loves most tenderly; but "world" also refers to the things of this world, which do not last and which can be at odds with the things of the spirit. So, Jesus' petition (v.15) is a call on us to take the steps necessary. "Be men and women of the world, but don't be worldly men and women" (Bl. J. Escrivá, *The Way*, 939).

In the third part of his Priestly Prayer (vv. 20–26), Christ prays for unity among all those who will believe in him over the course of the centuries. He wants the Church to be one as the Father and the Son are one. The first result of the unity of the Church will be the world believing in Christ and in his divine mission (vv. 21, 23). "Jesus Christ wishes his people to increase […] and he perfects its fellowship in unity: in the confession of one faith, in the common celebration of divine worship, and in the fraternal harmony of the family of God. […] The highest exemplar and source of this mystery is the unity, in the Trinity of Persons, of one God, the Father and the Son in the Holy Spirit" (Vatican II, *UR*, 2).

Following Christ's example, the same Council insisted on the need for prayer for the unity of Christians; it defines the prayer as "the soul of the whole ecumenical movement" (ibid., 8).

k. Or *from evil*

and these know that thou hast sent me. [26]I made known to them thy name, and I will make it known, that the love with which thou has loved me may be in them, and I in them."

10. THE PASSION AND DEATH OF JESUS

The arrest of Jesus Mt 26:47–56; Mk 14:43–52; Lk 22:47–53

18 [1]When Jesus had spoken these words, he went forth with his disciples
across the Kidron valley, where there was a garden, which he and his
disciples entered. [2]Now Judas, who betrayed him, also knew the place; for
Jesus often met there with his disciples. [3]So Judas, procuring a band of
soldiers and some officers from the chief priests and the Pharisees, went there
with lanterns and torches and weapons. [4]Then Jesus, knowing all that was to
befall him, came forward and said to them, "Whom do you seek?" [5]They
answered him, "Jesus of Nazareth." Jesus said to them, "I am he." Judas, who

---

18:1–19:42 □ The Gospel of John depicts the passion and death of Jesus as a glorification. He makes it very clear that it is in his passion that Christ is most clearly revealed as the Messiah King: when, on our Lord's saying "I am he," his opponents draw back and fall down (18:5–8); before Pilate, he declares himself to be a king (18:33–37; cf. 19:2–3, 19–22); and, throughout, his serene and majestic mien show that he is fully in control of events (18:4; 19:28): everything that is happening is in keeping with the Father's will (18:11; 19:30).

The Passion also marks the peak of the world's hatred of Jesus—the hour of the power of darkness, affecting even his disciples, for they leave him or deny him (18:25–27). But at the foot of the cross we also find the greatest of all professions of faith—that of the Blessed Virgin, whom our Lord gives as Mother to mankind, in the person of the beloved disciple (19:25–27). Christ is the new Passover Lamb who, by his redemptive death, takes away the sin of the world (19:31; cf. 1:29). From our Lord's side, along with blood, flows water, the symbol of Baptism and of the promised Holy Spirit (cf. 7:37–39).

18:1–12 Gethsemane is the first of the scenes where Christ's passion is depicted. John does not report our Lord's prayer in the Garden of Olives, but he is the only evangelist to tell us that the people who came to arrest Jesus drew back and fell down when he spoke (vv. 4–6). The text is evocative of Psalm 56:9: "My enemies will be turned back in the day when I call" and evidences the majesty of Christ; he surrenders himself voluntarily. "Had he not allowed himself to be taken by them, they would have been unable to effect their plan, but neither would he have done what he came to do. They in their rage sought to put him to death; he also sought us by dying for us" (St Augustine, *In Ioann. Ev.*, 112, 3).

betrayed him, was standing with them. [6]When he said to them, “I am he,” they
drew back and fell to the ground. [7]Again he asked them, “Whom do you seek?”
And they said, “Jesus of Nazareth,” [8]Jesus answered, “I told you that I am he; so,
if you seek me, let these men go.” [9]This was to fulfil the word which he had
spoken, “Of those whom you gavest me I lost not one.” [10]Then Simon Peter,
having a sword, drew it and struck the high priest’s slave and cut off his right ear.
The slave’s name was Malchus. [11]Jesus said to Peter, “Put your sword into its
sheath; shall I not drink the cup which the Father has given me?”

[12]So the band of soldiers and their captain and the officers of the Jews
seized Jesus and bound him.

Jesus before the chief priests. Peter’s denials Mt 26:57–75; Mk 14:53–72; Lk 22:54–71

[13]First they led him to Annas; for he was the father-in-law of Caiaphas, who
was high priest that year.* [14]It was Caiaphas who had given counsel to the
Jews that it was expedient that one man should die for the people.

[15]Simon Peter followed Jesus, and so did another disciple. As this disciple was
known to the high priest, he entered the court of the high priest along with Jesus,
[16]while Peter stood outside at the door. So the other disciple, who was known to
the high priest, went out and spoke to the maid who kept the door, and brought
Peter in. [17]The maid who kept the door said to Peter, “Are not you also one of this
man’s disciples?” He said, “I am not.” [18]Now the servants[l] and officers had made
a charcoal fire, because it was cold, and they were standing and warming
themselves; Peter also was with them, standing and warming himself.

[19]The high priest then questioned Jesus about his disciples and his
teaching. [20]Jesus answered him, “I have spoken openly to the world; I have
always taught in synagogues and in the temple, where all Jews come together;
I have said nothing secretly. [21]Why do you ask me? Ask those who have heard
me, what I said to them; they know what I said.” [22]When he had said this, one
of the officers standing by struck Jesus with his hand, saying, “Is that how you
answer the high priest?” [23]Jesus answered him, “If I have spoken wrongly,

---

18:13–27 The second scene of the Passion is the house of Annas. Jesus who had “released” Lazarus (11:44) is now himself bound. Isaac, too, was “bound” before his sacrifice (cf. Gen 22:9). During his interrogation, Jesus lays stress on the fact that he has always acted openly: everyone has had a chance to listen to him and to witness his miracles. The chief priests themselves have seen him in the temple and in the synagogues, but, not wishing to see or believe, they make out that his aims are hidden and sinister.

Peter’s denials are treated in less detail here than in the Synoptics, maybe because the early Christians were very familiar with the episode. After Jesus’ resurrection, the full scope of his forgiveness will become evident when he confirms Peter in his mission as leader of the apostles (cf. 21:15–17).

l. Or *slaves*

bear witness to the wrong; but if I have spoken rightly, why do you strike me?"
24Annas then sent him bound to Caiaphas the high priest.
25Now Simon Peter was standing and warming himself. They said to him,
"Are not you also one of his disciples?" He denied it and said, "I am not."
26One of the servants[1] of the high priest, a kinsman of the man whose ear Peter
had cut off, asked, "Did I not see you in the garden with him?" 27Peter again
denied it; and at once the cock crowed.

The trial before Pilate—Jesus is King Mt 27:11–14; Mk 15:1–15; Lk 23:1–5

28Then they led Jesus from the house of Caiaphas to the praetorium. It was
early. They themselves did not enter the praetorium, so that they might not be
defiled, but might eat the passover.* 29So Pilate went out to them and said,
"What accusation do you bring against this man?"* 30They answered him, "If
this man were not an evildoer, we would not have handed him over." 31Pilate
said to them, "Take him yourselves and judge him by your own law." The Jews
said to him, "It is not lawful for us to put any man to death."* 32This was to
fulfil the word which Jesus had spoken to show by what death he was to die.
33Pilate entered the praetorium again and called Jesus, and said to him,
"Are you the King of the Jews?" 34Jesus answered, "Do you say this of your
own accord, or did others say it to you about me?" 35Pilate answered, "Am I a
Jew? You own nation and the chief priests have handed you over to me; what
have you done?" 36Jesus answered, "My kingship is not of this world; if my
kingship were of this world, my servants would fight, that I might not be
handed over to the Jews; but my kingship is not from the world." 37Pilate said
to him, "So you are a king?" Jesus answered, "You say that I am a king. For
this I was born, and for this I have come into the world, to bear witness to the
truth. Every one who is of the truth hears my voice." 38Pilate said to him,
"What is truth?"

18:28–40 The trial before Pilate, which starts here and extends as far as 19:16, is given more prominence than in the other Gospels and is recounted in more detail. It is the central scene of the five in John's account. It highlights the majesty of Jesus Christ as the messianic King, contrasting with his rejection by the Jews.

There are seven stages in this trial; these are marked by Pilate's entrances and exits. First (vv. 29–32) the Jews indict Jesus in a general way as an "evildoer". There follows the dialogue between Pilate and Jesus (vv. 33–37), culminating with Christ's admission that he is King. Pilate then tries to save our Lord (vv. 38–40), asking the people whether they want him to release "the King of the Jews".

The central point of the account is the crowning with thorns, with the soldiers mockingly doing obeisance to Christ as "King of the Jews" (19:1–3). After this comes the shameful scene when our Lord is led out wearing the crown of thorns and draped in the purple robe—the *Ecce Homo*. The Jews' accusation now turns

1. Or *slaves*

After he had said this, he went out to the Jews again, and told them, "I find
no crime in him. 39But you have a custom that I should release one man for
you at the Passover; will you have me release for you the King of the Jews?"
40They cried out again, "Not this man, but Barabbas!" Now Barabbas was a
robber.

The scourging at the pillar and the crowning with thorns Mt 27:27–31; Mc 15:16–20

19 1Then Pilate took Jesus and scourged him. 2And the soldiers plaited a
crown of thorns, and put it on his head, and arrayed him in a purple
robe; 3they came up to him, saying, "Hail, King of the Jews!" and struck him
with their hands.

Pilate hands Jesus over Mt 27:15–26; Mk 15:6–15; Lk 23:13–25

4Pilate went out again, and said to them, "Behold, I am bringing him out to
you, that you may know that I find no crime in him." 5So Jesus came out,

---

on Jesus claiming to be the Son of God (19:4–7). Once again, Pilate, in the praetorium again, speaks with Jesus (vv. 19:8–12) and tries to probe further into his divine origin. The Jews then concentrate their hatred in a directly political accusation: "Everyone who makes him a king sets himself against Caesar" (9:12). Finally (19:13–16), in a very formal way, stating the exact time and place, Pilate points to Jesus and says, "Here is your King!" (19:14). The Jewish leaders openly reject him who was and is the genuine King spoken of by the prophets.

The trial begins with Jesus' first appearance before Pilate (vv. 28–40). When he was examined by the high priest, the charge was a religious one (of being the Son of God: cf. Mt 26:57–68). Now it is political; it is designed to involve the authority of the Roman empire: by declaring that he is the Messiah and the King of the Jews, Jesus (they claimed) was a revolutionary who conspired against Caesar. But, as Jesus explains to Pilate, his messianism transcends earthly power and glory.

19:1–3 This episode, set at the centre of the account, highlights Christ's kingship even though these soldiers are acclaiming him only out of mockery. Wearing the insignia of royalty, and despite this tragic parody, Christ still projects the majesty of the King of Kings. The image of Christ being ill-treated becomes in this way a source of prayer and atonement for the Christian. "Love involves suffering: how can anyone say that they love Christ if they remain unmoved by the sight of the suffering Christ?" (Fr Luis de Granada, *Libr. de la or.*, 1, 2, 4).

19:4–16 Pilate realizes that Jesus is innocent. He is not the subversive that his accusers wished to portray him as. Because the governor does not want to act as a judge of religious matters, the Jews move their charge into the political sphere, even though, by doing so, they go against their own inner convictions (they do not in fact accept Caesar as their king). Christ's majesty can be seen again in his reply to Pilate's question about where his authority comes from (vv. 8–11).

wearing the crown of thorns and the purple robe. Pilate said to them, "Here is the man!" 6When the chief priests and the officers saw him, they cried out, "Crucify him, crucify him!" Pilate said to them, "Take him yourselves and crucify him, for I find no crime in him." 7The Jews answered him, "We have a law, and by that law he ought to die, because he has made himself the Son of God."* 8When Pilate heard these words, he was the more afraid; 9he entered the praetorium again and said to Jesus, "Where are you from?"* But Jesus gave no answer. 10Pilate therefore said to him, "You will not speak to me? Do you not know that I have the power to release you, and the power to crucify you?" 11Jesus answered him, "You would have no power over me unless it had been given you from above; therefore he who delivered me to you has the greater sin."

12Upon this Pilate sought to release him, but the Jews cried out, "If you release this man, you are not Caesar's friend; every one who makes himself a king sets himself against Caesar." 13When Pilate heard these words, he brought Jesus out and sat down on the judgment seat at a place called The Pavement, and in Hebrew, Gabbatha. 14Now it was the day of Preparation for the Passover; it was abut the sixth hour. He said to the Jews, "Here is your King!" 15They cried out, "Away with him, away with him, crucify him!" Pilate said to them, "Shall I crucify your King?" The chief priests answered, "We have no king but Caesar." 16Then he handed him over to them to be crucified.

The crucifixion and death of Jesus Mt 27:32–56; Mk 15:21–41; Lk 23:26–49

17So they took Jesus, and he went out, bearing his own cross, to the place called the place of a skull, which is called in Hebrew Golgotha. 18There they crucified him, and with him two others, one on either side, and Jesus between

---

The evangelist notes that Jesus was condemned at the sixth hour, as if he wanted to stress that Jesus was the new Passover Lamb, because that was the time that leavened bread was replaced by unleavened bread in private houses, and the time when the lamb was officially sacrificed in the temple.

19:17–30 The scene of the crucifixion is a sort of summary of Jesus' life and teaching. The universal scope of Christ's kingship is symbolized by the "title" written in a number of languages (v. 19–20). The seamless garment which the soldiers avoid tearing (v. 24) symbolizes the unity of the Church and recalls Jesus' priestly prayer at the Last Supper. The presence of the Blessed Virgin and the beloved disciple (vv. 25–27), and the blood and water flowing from Christ's side (v. 24) remind us of the wedding at Cana and stand for the Christ and believers who become members of the Church through Baptism and the Eucharist. Christ's thirst (v. 28) reminds us of the incident at Jacob's well and the things Jesus said at the feast of Tabernacles, and it shows his desire to save all souls. The words he speaks as he gives up his spirit (v. 30) show that he really does die, and they imply

them. [19]Pilate also wrote a title and put it on the cross; it read, "Jesus of
Nazareth, the King of the Jews." [20]Many of the Jews read this title, for the place
where Jesus was crucified was near the city; and it was written in Hebrew, in
Latin, and in Greek. [21]The chief priests of the Jews then said to Pilate, "Do not
write, 'The King of the Jews,' but 'This man said, I am King of the Jews.'"
[22]Pilate answered, "What I have written I have written."

[23]When the soldiers had crucified Jesus they took his garments and made
four parts, one for each soldier; also his tunic. But the tunic was without seam,
woven from top to bottom; [24]so they said to one another, "Let us not tear it, but
cast lots for it to see whose it shall be." This was to fulfil the scripture,

> "They parted my garments among them,
> and for my clothing they cast lots."

[25]So the soldiers did this. But standing by the cross of Jesus were his mother,
and his mother's sister, Mary the wife of Clopas, and Mary Magdalene. [26]When
Jesus saw his mother, and the disciple whom he loved standing near, he said to
his mother, "Woman, behold, your son!" [27]Then he said to the disciple, "Behold,
your mother!" And from that hour the disciple took her to his own home.*

[28]After this Jesus, knowing that all was now finished, said (to fulfil the
scripture), "I thirst." [29]A bowl full of vinegar stood there; so they put a sponge full
of vinegar on hyssop and held it to his mouth. [30]When Jesus had received the
vinegar, he said, "It is finished"; and he bowed his head and gave up his spirit.

Jesus' side is pierced. His burial Mt 27:57–66; Mk 15:42–47; Lk 23:50–56

[31]Since it was the day of Preparation, in order to prevent the bodies from
remaining on the cross on the sabbath (for that sabbath was a high day), the

---

he is bestowing the Holy Spirit, as he often promised he would during his public life. And he also gives his Mother to be a Mother to his disciples, symbolized by the presence of the beloved disciple.

Jesus' words to his Mother and the disciple reveal his filial love for the Blessed Virgin. By declaring Mary to be the Mother of his beloved disciple, he is giving her a new role in the work of salvation, which reaches its climax at this point. In other words, he is establishing Mary's spiritual motherhood. "Entrusting himself to Mary in a filial manner, the Christian, like the Apostle John, 'welcomes' the Mother of Christ 'into his own home' and brings her into everything that makes up his inner life, that is to say, into his human and Christian 'I'" (John Paul II, *Redempt. Mater*, 45).

19:31–42 On the eve of Passover, the Passover lambs were sacrificed officially in the temple; in accordance with the Law (cf. Ex 12:46) no bone of them was to be broken. The reference to the preparation day (the Parasceve) and to the fact that the bones of the crucified men were not broken serve to emphasize that Christ is the true Passover Lamb who takes away the sins of the world.

19:24 Ps 22:18.

Jews asked Pilate that their legs might be broken, and that they might be taken away. [32]So the soldiers came and broke the legs of the first, and of the other who had been crucified with him; [33]but when they came to Jesus and saw that he was already dead, they did not break his legs. [34]But one of the soldiers pierced his side with a spear, and at once there came out blood and water. [35]He who saw it has borne witness—his testimony is true, and he knows that he tells the truth—that you also may believe. [36]For these things took place that the scripture might be fulfilled, "Not a bone of him shall be broken." [37]And again another scripture says, "They shall look on him whom they have pierced."

[38]After this Joseph of Arimathea, who was a disciple of Jesus, but secretly, for fear of the Jews, asked Pilate that he might take away the body of Jesus, and Pilate gave him leave. So he came and took away his body. [39]Nicodemus also, who had at first come to him by night, came bringing a mixture of myrrh and aloes, about a hundred pounds' weight. [40]They took the body of Jesus, and bound it in linen cloths with the spices, as is the burial custom of the Jews. [41]Now in the place where he was crucified there was a garden, and in the garden a new tomb where no one had ever been laid. [42]So because of the Jewish day of Preparation, as the tomb was close at hand, they laid Jesus there.

11. APPEARANCES OF THE RISEN CHRIST

The empty tomb Mt 28:1–10; Mk 16:1–8; Lk 24:1–12

20 [1]Now on the first day of the week Mary Magdalene came to the tomb early, while it was still dark, and saw that the stone had been taken

---

The blood and water overflowing from Christ's pierced side symbolize Baptism and the Eucharist, all the sacraments, and the Church herself. "Here was opened wide the door of life, from which the sacraments of the Church have flowed out, without which there is no entering in unto the life which is true life. [...] Here the second Adam with bowed head slept upon the cross, that thence a wife might be formed of him, flowing from his side while he slept. O, death, by which the dead come back to life! Is there anything purer than this blood, any wound more healing!" (St Augustine, *In Ioann. Ev.*, 120, 2).

The account of the Passover ends with a quotation from Zechariah (Zech 12:10). By including this prophetic text (v. 37), John is saying that the salvation wrought to Christ on the cross marks the fulfillment of God's promise of redemption. Everyone who looks on Jesus with faith receives the benefits of his passion; we can see this even in the fact that Joseph of Arimathea and Nicodemus, people who were previously afraid to confess Jesus, now do so boldly.

20:1–21:25 □ The last section of the Gospel completes the glorious manifestation of Jesus as Messiah and Son of God, which John has recounted in order to

19:36 Ex 12:46; Ps 34:20.

away from the tomb. [2]So she ran, and went to Simon Peter and the other
disciple, the one whom Jesus loved, and said to them, “They have taken the
Lord out of the tomb, and we do not know where they have laid him.” [3]Peter
then came out with the other disciple, and they went toward the tomb. [4]They
both ran, but the other disciple outran Peter and reached the tomb first; [5]and
stooping to look in, he saw the linen cloths lying there, but he did not go in.
[6]Then Simon Peter came, following him, and went into the tomb; he saw the
linen cloths lying, [7]and the napkin, which had been on his head, not lying with
the linen cloths but rolled up in a place by itself. [8]Then the other disciple, who
reached the tomb first, also went in, and he saw and believed; [9]for as yet they
did not know the scripture, that he must rise from the dead. [10]Then the
disciples went back to their homes.

The appearance to Mary Magdalene Mt 28:1–10; Mc 16:9–11

[11]But Mary stood weeping outside the tomb, and as she wept she stooped to
look into the tomb; [12]and she saw two angels in white, sitting where the body

---

strengthen the faith of believers. The section includes appearances of the risen Lord to the apostles, making them see the meaning of the Scriptures in the light of Jesus’ words and actions (20:8–9), and the gift of the Holy Spirit with thc power to forgive sins (20:22–23). The account of the miraculous draught of fish on the Sea of Tiberias (21:1–14) prefigures the multitude of peoples that the Church’s apostolate will win for Christ. The rest of chapter 21 fits into this ecclesiological setting; it tells how leadership of the Church was given to St Peter (21:15–19). The Gospel ends by confirming the truthfulness of the evangelist’s testimony: he saw and heard the things he has reported (21:24–25).

20:1–10 All four Gospels report the first testimonies of the holy women and the disciples regarding Christ’s glorious resurrection. These refer to two things—the empty tomb and the appearances of the risen Jesus. John makes it clear that, although Mary Magdalen was the first to go to the tomb, the apostles were the first to go in and the first to see the evidence that Christ had risen (the empty tomb, the linen cloths lying there, the napkin in a place apart). The beloved disciple checks that Jesus’ body is missing. The state of the tomb, especially the fact that the linen cloths are “lying there”, flattened, deflated, as it were, showed that this was not man’s work, and that Jesus’ body could not have been reanimated the way Lazarus’ had been. Hence the fact that “he saw” and “believed” (v. 8).

20:11–18 The Gospel teaches that Jesus reveals himself to those who truly seek him. Mary is a model for those who seek Jesus. In this scene Jesus appears as the “Good Shepherd” who “calls his own sheep by name” (10:3); he says “Mary” and they “know his voice” (10:4): “Rabboni”. Mary in turn, must bear witness to the resurrection and tell the others that she has seen the Lord. Moreover, the apostles are

of Jesus had lain, one at the head and one at the feet. [13]They said to her,
"Woman, why are you weeping?" She said to them, "Because they have taken
away my Lord, and I do not know where they have laid him." [14]Saying this, she
turned round and saw Jesus standing, but she did not know that it was Jesus.
[15]Jesus said to her, "Woman, why are you weeping? Whom do you seek?"
Supposing him to be the gardener, she said to him, "Sir, if you have carried him
away, tell me where you have laid him, and I will take him away." [16]Jesus said to
her, "Mary." She turned and said to him in Hebrew, "Rabboni!" (which means
Teacher). [17]Jesus said to her, "Do not hold me, for I have not yet ascended to the
Father; but go to my brethren and say to them, I am ascending to my Father and
your Father, to my God and your God."* [18]Mary Magdalene went and said to the
disciples, "I have seen the Lord"; and she told them that he had said these things
to her.

Jesus appears to the disciples Mt 28:16–20; Mk 16:14–18; Lk 24:36–49

[19]On the evening of that day, the first day of the week, the doors being shut
where the disciples were, for fear of the Jews, Jesus came and stood among
them and said to them, "Peace be with you." [20]When he had said this, he
showed them his hands and his side. Then the disciples were glad when they
saw the Lord. [21]Jesus said to them again, "Peace be with you. As the Father

---

no longer "servants" but "brethren" (v. 17): after the death and glorious resurrection of Jesus, those who believe in him receive the gift of divine sonship. (cf. 1:12), making them sons and daughters of God and brothers and sisters of Jesus.

20:19–31 The appearance of the glorified Jesus to the disciples and the outpouring of the Holy Spirit upon them is this Gospel's equivalent, as it were, of the Pentecost in the book of the Acts. The mission our Lord gives the apostles (vv. 22–23), very like that of the end of St Matthew's Gospel (Mt 28:18ff), shows the divine origin of the Church and her power to forgive sins. "Our Lord instituted the sacrament of Penance when, having risen from the dead, he breathed on his disciples saying, 'Receive the Holy Spirit … ' All the Fathers [of the Church] have said that the power to forgive or retain sins was passed on to the apostles and their rightful successors through our Lord's symbolic action and his clear words so that those who sinned after having received Baptism might be reconciled to the Church" (Council of Trent, *De sacr. paenitentia*, 1).

At the appearance Jesus makes eight days later (vv. 24–29), Thomas plays a key role. Just as Mary Magdalen is a model for all those who seek Jesus, Thomas has come to symbolize those who have their doubts about Christ's divinity and his humanity, but who later become fully convinced. The Risen One and the Crucified are the same. Our Lord again makes it clear that faith in him has to be based on the testimony of those who have seen him.

has sent me, even so I send you." [22]And when he had said this, he breathed on
them, and said to them, "Receive the Holy Spirit. [23]If you forgive the sins of
any, they are forgiven; if you retain the sins of any, they are retained."
[24]Now Thomas, one of the twelve, called the Twin, was not with them when
Jesus came. [25]So the other disciples told him, "We have seen the Lord." But he
said to them, "Unless I see in his hand the print of the nails, and place my finger
in the mark of the nails, and place my hand in his side, I will not believe."
[26]Eight days later, his disciples were again in the house, and Thomas was
with them. The doors were shut, but Jesus came and stood among them, and
said, "Peace be with you." [27]Then he said to Thomas, "Put your finger here,
and see my hands; and put out your hand, and place it in my side; do not be
faithless, but believing." [28]Thomas answered him, "My Lord and my God!"
[29]Jesus said to him, "Have you believed because you have seen me? Blessed
are those who have not seen and yet believe."
[30]Now Jesus did many other signs in the presence of the disciples, which are
not written in this book; [31]but these are written that you may believe that Jesus
is the Christ, the Son of God, and that believing you may have life in his name.

The miraculous catch of fish

21 *[1]After this Jesus revealed himself again to the disciples by the Sea of
Tiberias; and he revealed himself in this way. [2]Simon Peter, Thomas
called the Twin, Nathanael of Cana in Galilee, the sons of Zebedee, and two
others of his disciples were together. [3]Simon Peter said to them, "I am going
fishing." They said to him, "We will go with you." They went out and got into
the boat; but that night they caught nothing.

Verses 30–31 are the first epilogue or conclusion of this Gospel. They state John's purpose in writing this book—that people might believe that Jesus is the Messiah, the Christ announced by the prophets in the Old Testament, and the Son of God, and that that belief might lead us to share, even now, in eternal life.

21:1–14 This chapter (21:1–25) is an addition to the Gospel, written either by the evangelist himself or by some followers of his (cf. v. 21:24). The main theme of this passage is the Church. The communion that exists between the beloved disciple and Peter is highlighted. By recounting the mission that our Lord gives Peter to guide his Church, the beloved disciple implies that all his own testimony, written and oral, is supported by that authority.

The opening verses (vv. 1–14) bring to mind the first miraculous draught of fish (cf. Lk 5:1–11), when our Lord promised to make Peter a fisher of men. Now he is going to confirm him in his mission as the visible head of the Church. In this account we can see very clearly the love which enables the beloved disciple to recognize Jesus; Peter's faith; and an insistence on the fact that the Risen One is

[4]Just as day was breaking, Jesus stood on the beach; yet the disciples did not know that it was Jesus. [5]Jesus said to them, "Children, have you any fish?" They answered him, "No." [6]He said to them, "Cast the net on the right side of the boat, and you will find some." So they cast it and now they were not able to haul it in, for the quantity of fish. [7]That disciple whom Jesus loved* said to Peter, "It is the Lord!" When Simon Peter heard that it was the Lord, he put on his clothes, for he was stripped for work, and sprang into the sea. [8]But the other disciples came in the boat, dragging the net full of fish, for they were not far from the land, but about a hundred yards[m] off.

[9]When they got out on land, they saw a charcoal fire there, with fish lying on it, and bread. [10]Jesus said to them, "Bring some of the fish that you have just caught." [11]So Simon Peter went aboard and hauled the net ashore, full of large fish, a hundred and fifty-three of them; and although there were so many, the net was not torn. [12]Jesus said to them, "Come and have breakfast." Now none of the disciples dared ask him, "Who are you?" They knew it was the Lord. [13]Jesus came and took the bread and gave it to them, and so with the fish. [14]This was now the third time that Jesus was revealed to the disciples after he was raised from the dead.

Peter's primacy

[15]When they had finished breakfast, Jesus said to Simon Peter, "Simon, son of John, do you love me more than these?" He said to him, "Yes, Lord; you know that I love you." He said to them, "Feed my lambs." [16]A second time he said to him, "Simon, son of John, do you love me?" He said to him, "Yes, Lord; you know I love you." He said to him, "Tend my sheep."* [17]He said to him the third time, "Simon, son of John, do you love me?" Peter was grieved because he said to him the third time, "Do you love me?" And he said to him, "Lord, you know everything; you know that I love you." Jesus said to him, "Feed my

---

not a spirit but the same man as ate with them before and now eats with them again. Fathers and Doctors of the Church have often dwelt on the mystical meaning of this episode: the boat is the Church, whose unity is symbolized by the net which is not torn; Peter in the boat stands for supreme authority in the Church; and the number of fish signifies the number of the elect.

21:15–23 In contrast with Peter's denials during the passion, Jesus, the Good Shepherd who cures the wounded sheep, confers on Peter the primacy which he previously promised to give him. "Jesus entrusted a specific authority to Peter: 'I will give you the keys of the kingdom of heaven, and whatever you bind on earth shall be bound in heaven, and whatever you loose on earth shall be loosed in heaven (Mt 16:19). The 'power of the keys' designates authority to govern the house of God, which is the Church. Jesus, the Good Shepherd, confirmed this

m. Greek *two hundred cubits*

sheep. [18]Truly, truly, I say to you, when you were young, you girded yourself
and walked where you would; but when you are old, you will stretch out your
hands, and another will gird you and carry you where you do not wish to go."
[19](This he said to show by what death he was to glorify God.) And after this he
said to him, "Follow me."

[20]Peter turned and saw following them the disciple whom Jesus loved, who
had lain close to his breast at the supper and had said, "Lord, who is it that is
going to betray you?" [21]When Peter saw him, he said to Jesus, "Lord, what
about this man?" [22]Jesus said to him, "If it is my will that he remain until I
come, what is that to you? Follow me!" [23]The saying spread abroad among the
brethren that this disciple was not to die; yet Jesus did not say to him that he
was not to die, but, "If it is my will that he remain until I come, what is that to
you?"

Conclusion

[24]This is the disciple who is bearing witness to these things, and who has written
these thing; and we know that his testimony is true.

[25]But there are also many other things which Jesus did; were every one of
them to be written, I suppose that the world itself could not contain the books
that would be written.

---

mandate after his Resurrection: 'Feed my sheep' (Jn 21:15–17). The power to 'bind and loose' connotes the authority to absolve sins, to pronounce doctrinal judgments, and to make disciplinary decisions in the Church. Jesus entrusted this authority to the Church through the ministry of the apostles and in particular through the ministry of Peter, the only one to whom he specifically entrusted the keys of the kingdom" (*CCC*, 553).

In addition to Peter's authority we also see here the role of St John, who may well have written verses 20–23 to dispel the idea that the beloved disciple would not die.

21:24–25 The text appeals to the testimony of "the disciple whom Jesus loved" (v. 20), to guarantee the veracity of everything contained in this book (v. 24). Everything this Gospel says should be accepted by its readers as being absolutely true.

The Acts of the Apostles

From the middle of the second century onwards, St Luke's second book (cf. Acts 1:1) came to be called the Acts of the Apostles. There is no evidence that its author gave it this title; it isn't really an account of the apostles' activity but rather a kind of historical monograph describing the early stages of Christianity linked to the missionary work of the two most prominent apostles, Peter and Paul.

The book is very much of a piece with the third Gospel. If that Gospel covered the activity of Jesus as he made his way up to Jerusalem and accomplished his mission of redemption in the Holy City, the Acts of the Apostles begins at the point when Jesus, the Lord now raised to the right hand of God, sent his apostles out to be his witnesses to the ends of the earth (1:1–11). The book ends with St Paul's arrival in Rome, "preaching the kingdom of God and teaching about the Lord Jesus Christ quite openly and unhindered" (28:31). Luke recounts the main stages of this part of the history of salvation—the descent of the Holy Spirit on the Church, the early preaching in Jerusalem, the spread of Christianity to the neighbouring regions of Samaria and Judea, and the mission covering Asia Minor and reaching as far as Rome. But the book extends beyond this "external" description to cover the internal development of the early Church under the impulse of the Holy Spirit: it is he who gives life, strength and consolation to the faithful and he who, with the call to the Gentiles (10:1–11:8), leads the apostles to proclaim salvation to all mankind.

On account of this continuous presence of the Holy Spirit, this book has also been called the "Gospel of the Holy Spirit". It also contains a great deal of profound teaching about *Jesus Christ.* It emphasizes that all the aspects of the paschal mystery (passion, death, resurrection and ascension) in fact fulfil the plans God announced earlier in the Old Testament. It applies to Jesus many titles which show that he is divine and that his mission is a redemptive one: he is called Lord (2:36), Saviour (5:31), God's [suffering] Servant (3:13), the Righteous One (7:52), the Holy One (3:14) and, particularly, Christ (the Messiah), this last-mentioned becoming our Lord's proper name. The book is also an essential source for the history of the *Church* in the first thirty years of its life. We see the Church to be God's instrument for the fulfilment of the Old Testament promises: it is, therefore, the true Israel, a new and universal people, with an essentially missionary role. The *lifestyle of the early Christians* is outlined in a very moving way. It centres on prayer, the Eucharist and the teaching of the apostles, and it expresses itself in edifying attitudes and actions of detachment, harmony and love (2:42–47; 4:23–37; etc.). Luke proposes this lifestyle as a marker and model for future generations of disciples. It also acts as a discreet precedent for the apologias which came to be written in the two centuries which followed: the Christianity it portrays is a faith that is confident in God and in itself, a faith that has no time for the esoteric world of sects and no fear of public debate about its principles and convictions.

Acts

Prologue

1 [1]In the first book, *O Theophilus, I have dealt with all that Jesus began to
do and teach, [2]until the day when he was taken up, after he had given
commandment through the Holy Spirit to the apostles whom he had chosen.
[3]To them he presented himself alive after his passion by many proofs,
appearing to them during forty days, and speaking of the kingdom of God.
[4]And while staying[a] with them he charged them not to depart from Jerusalem,
but to wait for the promise of the Father, which, he said, "you heard from me,
[5]for John baptized with water, but before many days you shall be baptized with
the Holy Spirit."

The Ascension Mk 16:19; Lk 24:50–53

[6]So when they had come together, they asked him, "Lord, will you at this time
restore the kingdom of Israel?" [7]He said to them, "It is not for you to know
times or seasons which the Father has fixed by his own authority. [8]But you

---

1:1–5 Like his Gospel (cf. Lk 1:1–4) St Luke begins this book with a prologue, in the style of secular historians. This second volume of his work links up with the events recounted at the end of Luke's Gospel and sets about reporting the origins and early growth of Christianity, of which the protagonist of this book, the Holy Spirit, is the prime mover. The spiritual dimension of this book, which is one of a piece with the third Gospel, nourished the soul of the first generation of Christians, providing them with a chronicle of God's faithful and loving support of the new Israel, the Church. In writing his book, Luke works as a historian, but his account goes much deeper than mere history: "The Acts of the Apostles seems to give a purely historical account, confined to recording the early life and growth of the Church; if, however, we bear in mind that Acts was written by Luke, a doctor, who is himself praised in the Gospels (cf. 2 Cor 8:18), we will understand that his words act as medicine for the ailing soul" (St Jerome, *Letters*, 53, 9).

1:6–11 The apostles' question shows that they are still thinking in terms of earthly restoration of the Davidic dynasty. It would seem that for them—as for many Jews of their time—eschatological hope in the Kingdom went no further than expectation of a Jewish hegemony which would extend right across the Diaspora. In his reply to their question, our Lord tells them that that sort of mistaken expectation has been overtaken by events. God's plans go much much further and are on a higher plane; they have nothing to do with any sort of political empire; they aim to transform man through the action of the Holy Spirit.

a. Or *eating*

shall receive power when the Holy Spirit has come upon you; and you shall be
my witnesses in Jerusalem and in all Judea and Samaria and to the end of the
earth." 9And when he had said this, as they were looking on, he was lifted up,
and a cloud took him out of their sight. 10And while they were gazing into
heaven as he went, behold, two men stood by them in white robes, 11and said,
"Men of Galilee, why do you stand looking into heaven? This Jesus, who was
taken up from you into heaven, will come in the same way as you saw him go
into heaven."

PART ONE: THE CHURCH IN JERUSALEM

1. THE DISCIPLES IN JERUSALEM

The apostolic college

12Then they returned to Jerusalem from the mount called Olivet, which is near
Jerusalem, a sabbath day's journey away; 13and when they had entered, they
went up to the upper room, where they were staying, Peter and John and James
and Andrew, Philip and Thomas, Bartholomew and Matthew, James the son of

---

Our Lord's ascension into heaven helps explain the present condition of his risen body: "Christ's ascension into heaven signifies his participation, in his humanity, in God's power and authority. Jesus Christ is Lord: he possesses all power in heaven and on earth. [...] As Lord, Christ is also head of the Church, which is his Body. Taken up to heaven and glorified after he had thus fully accomplished his mission, Christ dwells on earth in his Church" (*CCC*, 668–669).

1:12–7:60 □ □ The first seven chapters of the book of Acts cover the life of the infant Church in Jerusalem. Once Matthias is elected to fill the vacancy in the group of the Twelve (1:15–26), there follows an account of the coming of the Holy Spirit at Pentecost (2:1–13) and the first apostolic preaching about Jesus Christ (2:14–41).

The account continues with the growth and clustering of the community around Peter and the other apostles. Miracles and extraordinary events (3:1–10; 5:1–16) mark the preaching of the Twelve. At various points St Luke inserts summaries which describe the spiritual vitality of the early Church (1:14; 2:42–47; 4:32–37; 5:12–16). The steady increase in the number of faithful (2:42, 47; 4:4; 5:14; 6:1) creates a need for deacons to be appointed (6:1–7). A persecution of the Church after the martyrdom of St Stephen brings this part to an end; the scene now moves to the regions adjoining Judea (8:1ff).

Alphaeus and Simon the Zealot and Judas the son of James. [14]All these with one accord devoted themselves to prayer, together with the women and Mary the mother of Jesus, and with his brethren.*

The election of Matthias

[15]In those days Peter stood up among the brethren (the company of persons was in all about a hundred and twenty), and said, [16]"Brethren, the scripture had to be fulfilled, which the Holy Spirit spoke beforehand by the mouth of David, concerning Judas who was guide to those who arrested Jesus. [17]For he was numbered among us, and was allotted his share in this ministry. [18](Now this man bought a field with the reward of his wickedness; and falling headlong[b] he burst open in the middle and all his bowels gushed out. [19]And it became known to all the inhabitants of Jerusalem, so that the field was called in their language Akeldama, that is, Field of Blood.) [20]For it is written in the Book of Psalms,

'Let his habitation become desolate,
and let there be no one to live in it';

and

'His office let another take.'

1:12–26 □ Luke introduces us to the group of the disciples, the core of the nascent Church, prior to the coming of the Holy Spirit. He specifically names the members of the "apostolic college" (1:13), which will be made up to its quota by the election of Matthias (1:26)—and Mary, the Mother of the Lord (1:14). Rather in the way that the Holy Spirit descended on Mary, full of grace (Lk 1:28), he will now descend on this group of people who come together to pray (1:14, 24).

1:12–14 In this description of the group of disciples prior to the coming of the Holy Spirit, we are told about two very specific things—their life of prayer, and the presence of Mary among them. "We are told this time and again in the passage narrating the lives of the first followers of Christ. 'All these with one accord devoted themselves to prayer'" (Bl. J. Escrivá, *Hom.*, 2, 242).

In its contemplation of and meditation on this "tableau", Tradition has seen evidence of the motherly care the Blessed Virgin exercises over the whole Church, both at its beginning and over the centuries.

1:15–26 The episode of the election of St Matthias tells important things about the constitution of the Church—such as the number of the Twelve and Peter's place in the community. It is Peter, to whom Jesus entrusted the task of confirming his brethren in the faith (Lk 22:32), who proposes the election of an apostle to take the place of Judas. This means that the college of apostles is filled prior to the coming of the Holy Spirit on the day when "the Church was openly displayed to the people" (Vatican II, *AG*, 4).

b. Or *swelling up* **1:20** Ps 69:25; 109:8.

[21]So one of the men who have accompanied us during all the time that the Lord
Jesus went in and out among us, [22]beginning from the baptism of John until the
day when he was taken up from us—one of these men must become with us a
witness to his resurrection."* [23]And they put forward two, Joseph called
Barsabbas, who was surnamed Justus, and Matthias. [24]And they prayed and said,
"Lord, who knowest the hearts of all men, show which one of these two thou
hast chosen [25]to take the place in this ministry and apostleship from which Judas
turned aside, to go to his own place." [26]And they cast lots for them, and the lot
fell on Matthias; and he was enrolled with the eleven apostles.

2. PENTECOST

The coming of the Holy Spirit

2 [1]When the day of Pentecost had come, they were all together in one place.
[2]And suddenly a sound came from heaven like the rush of a mighty wind,
and it filled all the house where they were sitting. [3]And there appeared to them
tongues as of fire, distributed and resting on each one of them. [4]And they were

---

Luke usually applies the term "apostles" only to the Twelve (cf., e.g., 6:6), or the Eleven plus Peter, whom he portrays as the head of the apostolic college (cf. 2:14). The main roles of the apostles throughout this book are: to be witnesses to Jesus' resurrection (cf. 1:22) and to do so through the ministry of the Word (6:4), supported by signs and miracles which render visible the salvation that they proclaim (2:14–21, 43; 3:11, 16; etc.). The Twelve are also responsible for the government of the Church—collecting resources for brethren in need, choosing people for the ministry of deacons (6:2–3), intervening to ensure the unity of the Church (15:2), etc.

Most of Luke's attention is concentrated on the figure of Peter, whom he mentions 56 times in this book. Peter is always at the centre of those scenes and episodes in which he appears with other apostles or disciples. In matters to do with the community at Jerusalem, Peter acts as the spokesman of the Twelve (2:14, 37; 5:29) and he plays a key role in the opening up of the Gospel to the pagans.

The college of the twelve apostles, whose head is Peter, endures in the episcopacy of the Church, whose head is the Pope, Peter's successor and the vicar of Jesus Christ: "Just as, in accordance with the Lord's decree, St Peter and the rest of the apostles constitute a unique apostolic college, so in like fashion the Roman pontiff, Peter's successor, and the bishops, the successors of the apostles, are related with and united to one another" (Vatican II, *LG*, 22).

2:1–47 □ In the book of the Acts, Pentecost marks the start of the spread of the Church: animated by the Holy Spirit, it constitutes the new people of God which begins to preach the Gospel to all nations and assemble together all those called

all filled with the Holy Spirit and began to speak in other tongues, as the Spirit gave them utterance.
5Now there were dwelling in Jerusalem Jews, devout men from every
nation under heaven. 6And at this sound the multitude came together, and they
were bewildered, because each one heard them speaking in his own language.
7And they were amazed and wondered, saying, "Are not all these who are
speaking Galileans? 8And how is it that we hear, each of us in his own native
language? 9Parthians and Medes and Elamites and residents of Mesopotamia,
Judea and Cappadocia, Pontus and Asia, 10Phrygia and Pamphylia, Egypt and
the parts of Libya belonging to Cyrene, and visitors from Rome, both Jews and
proselytes, 11Cretans and Arabians, we hear them telling in our own tongues
the mighty works of God." 12And all were amazed and perplexed, saying to
one another, "What does this mean?" 13But others mocking said, "They are
filled with new wine."

---

by God. The outpouring of the Holy Spirit also acts as a sign, a form of revelation; later on, St Peter will see the descent of the Holy Spirit on Cornelius and his family (10:44– 48; 11:15–17) as a clear indication that the Gentiles are called to Christ without any need of circumcision.

2:1–13 This account of the coming of the Holy Spirit is full of symbolism. Pentecost was one of the three great Jewish feasts: it was held fifty days after Passover and many Israelites went on pilgrimage to the Holy City for that day. It originated as a festival to celebrate the end of the grain harvest and to give thanks to God as well as make an offering of first–fruits. Later it was given the additional dimension of commemorating the promulgation of the Law given by God to Moses on Sinai. The noise, like that of a gale, and the fire (vv. 2–3), are in fact reminiscent of the way God manifested himself on Mount Sinai (cf. Ex 19:16, 18; Ps 29) when he gave the Israelites the Law and established them as his people. He manifests these same features now to his new people, the Church: the wind stands for the new spiritual way he will operate in human history (cf. *CCC*, 691); the "fire symbolizes the transforming energy of the Holy Spirit's actions" (*CCC*, 696).

The list given of the nationalities of those who heard the disciples (vv. 5, 9–11) and the fact that they all understood the language spoken by the apostles (vv. 4, 6, 8, 11) evoke, by way of contrast, the confusion of languages that occurred at Babel (cf. Gen 11:1–9): "Without doubt, the Holy Spirit was at work in the world before Christ was glorified. On the day of Pentecost, however, he came down on the disciples that he might remain with them forever; on that day the Church was openely displayed to the crowds and the spread of the Gospel among the nations, through preaching, was begun. Finally, on that day was foreshadowed the union of all peoples in the catholicity of the faith by means of the Church of the New Alliance, a Church which speaks every language, understands and embraces all tongues in charity, and thus overcomes the dispersion of Babel" (Vatican II, *AG*, 4).

Peter's address

14But Peter,* standing with the eleven, lifted up his voice and addressed them,
"Men of Judea and all who dwell in Jerusalem, let this be known to you, and give
ear to my words. 15For these men are not drunk, as you suppose, since it is only
the third hour of the day; 16but this is what was spoken by the prophet Joel:

17'And in the last days it shall be, God declares,
that I will pour out my Spirit upon all flesh,
and your sons and your daughters shall prophesy,
and your young men shall see visions,
and your old men shall dream dreams;
18 yea, and on my menservants and my maidservants in those days
I will pour out my Spirit; and they shall prophesy.
19 And I will show wonders in the heaven above
and signs on the earth beneath,
blood, and fire, and vapour of smoke;
20 the sun shall be turned into darkness
and the moon into blood,
before the day of the Lord comes,
the great and manifest day.
21 And it shall be that whoever calls on the name of the Lord
shall be saved.'

22"Men of Israel, hear these words: Jesus of Nazareth a man attested to you
by God with mighty works and wonders and signs which God did through him
in your midst, as you yourselves know—23this Jesus, delivered up according

---

2:14–41 Peter speaks on behalf of the Twelve, as he will do on so many occasions. His address is full of quotations from the Old Testament which he uses to explain what has just occurred: "The prophetic texts that directly concerns the sending of the Holy Spirit are oracles by which God speaks to the heart of his people in the language of the promise, with the accents of 'love and fidelity' (cf. Ezek 11:19; 36:25–28: 37:1–14; Jer 31:31–34; and Joel 3:1–5). St Peter will proclaim their fulfilment on the morning of Pentecost (cf. Acts 2:17–21). According to these promises, at the 'end time' the Lord's Spirit will renew the hearts of men, engraving a new law in them. He will gather and reconcile the scattered and divided peoples; he will transform the first creation, and God will dwell with men in peace" (*CCC*, 715).

In his address Peter outlines the content of the apostolic proclamation (the *kerygma*), which is what is proposed for people's belief. This proclamation gives testimony of the death and resurrection of Christ, and his subsequent glorification; it tells people the main points of Jesus' mission, a mission announced by John the Baptist, confirmed by miracles and rounded off by the appearances of the risen Lord and by the outpouring of the Holy Spirit; it signals the arrival of the messianic times foretold by the prophets, and it calls everyone to conversion, to prepare for the Parousia or the second coming of Christ in glory.

2:17–21 Joel 2:28–32.

to the definite plan and foreknowledge of God, you crucified and killed by the
hands of lawless men. [24]But God raised him up, having loosed the pangs of
death, because it was not possible for him to be held by it. [25]For David says
concerning him,

> "I saw the Lord always before me,
> for he is at my right hand that I may not be shaken;
> [26] therefore my heart was glad, and my tongue rejoiced;
> moreover my flesh will dwell in hope.
> [27] For thou wilt not abandon my soul to Hades,
> nor let thy Holy One see corruption.
> [28] Thou hast made known to me the ways of life;
> thou wilt make me full of gladness with thy presence."

[29]"Brethren, I may say to you confidently of the patriarch David that he
both died and was buried, and his tomb is with us to this day. [30]Being therefore
a prophet, and knowing that God had sworn with an oath to him that he would
set one of his descendants upon his throne, [31]he foresaw and spoke of the resur-
rection of the Christ, that he was not abandoned to Hades, nor did his flesh see
corruption. [32]This Jesus God raised up, and of that we all are witnesses. [33]Being
therefore exalted at the right hand of God, and having received from the Father
the promise of the Holy Spirit, he has poured out this which you see and hear.
[34]For David did not ascend into the heavens; but he himself says,

> 'The Lord said to my Lord, Sit at my right hand,
> [35]till I make thy enemies a stool for thy feet.'

[36]Let all the house of Israel therefore know assuredly that God has made him
both Lord and Christ, this Jesus whom you crucified."

Many baptisms

[37]Now when they heard this they were cut to the heart, and said to Peter and
the rest of the apostles, "Brethren, what shall we do?" [38]And Peter said to
them, "Repent, and be baptized every one of you in the name of Jesus Christ
for the forgiveness of your sins; and you shall receive the gift of the Holy
Spirit. [39]For the promise is to you and to your children and to all that are far
off, every one whom the Lord our God calls to him." [40]And he testified with
many other words and exhorted them, saying, "Save yourselves from this
crooked generation." [41]So those who received his word were baptized, and
there were added that day about three thousand souls.

The early Christians

[42]And they devoted themselves to the apostles' teaching and fellowship, to the
breaking of bread and the prayers.

2:42–47 This is the first of the three summaries contained in the early chapters of
Acts (cf. 4:32–37 and 5:12–16); it describes in simple words the key elements in

2:25–28 Ps 16:8–11. **2:30** Ps 132:11. **2:31** Ps 16:10. **2:34–35** Ps 110:1.

43 And fear came upon every soul; and many wonders and signs were done
through the apostles. 44 And all who believed were together and had all things in
common; 45 and they sold their possessions and goods and distributed them to
all, as any had need. 46 And day by day, attending the temple together and
breaking bread in their homes, they partook of food with glad and generous
hearts, 47 praising God and having favour with all the people. And the Lord
added to their number day by day those who were being saved.

3. THE APOSTLES' WORK IN JERUSALEM

Curing of a man lame from birth

3 1 Now Peter and John were going up to the temple at the hour of prayer, the
ninth hour.* 2 And a man lame from birth was being carried, whom they
laid daily at the gate of the temple which is called Beautiful to ask alms of
those who entered the temple. 3 Seeing Peter and John about to go into the
temple, he asked for alms. 4 And Peter directed his gaze at him, with John, and
said, "Look at us." 5 And he fixed his attention upon them, expecting to receive
something from them. 6 But Peter said, "I have no silver and gold, but I give
you what I have; in the name of Jesus Christ of Nazareth, walk." 7 And he took

---

the ascetical and liturgical-sacramental life of the early Christians. "This sequence is characteristic of the Church's prayer: founded on the apostolic faith; authenticated by charity; nourished in the Eucharist" (*CCC*, 2624).

3:1–5:42 □ Strengthened by the Holy Spirit they received at Pentecost, the apostles continue to preach the Gospel, confirming the truth of their message by wondrous works. Soon, however, opposition begins to come from the Jewish authorities (4:1–2; 5:17–18) and difficulties arise within the Church itself (5:1–11). Against this background, the text shows the optimistic attitude of the early believers, guided as they were by the Holy Spirit. The general public held them in high regard (5:51–16), important, upright men like Gamaliel understood them (5:34–39), the Spirit was helping them (4:31), and God was comforting them by increasing the number of believers and causing a growth in virtue in that early community (4:4, 32–37).

3:1–10 The New Testament miracles show that this was a time when divine grace was intensely concentrated. However, that does not mean that miracles do not continue to occur in the Christian economy of salvation. Depending on circumstances, and in different sorts of ways, miracles do continue to happen, performed because God is drawn by the interior dispositions of men and women of faith (cf. the note on 5:12–16).

him by the right hand and raised him up; and immediately his feet and ankles were made strong. [8]And leaping up he stood and walked and entered the temple with them, walking and leaping and praising God. [9]And all the people saw him walking and praising God, [10]and recognized him as the one who sat for alms at the Beautiful Gate of the temple; and they were filled with wonder and amazement at what had happened to him.

Peter's address in the temple

[11]While he clung to Peter and John, all the people ran together to them in the portico called Solomon's, astounded. [12]And when Peter saw it he addressed the people, "Men of Israel, why do you wonder at this, or why do you stare at us, as though by our own power or piety we had made him walk? [13]The God of Abraham and of Isaac and of Jacob, the God of our fathers, glorified his servant[c] Jesus, whom you delivered up and denied in the presence of Pilate, when he had decided to release him. [14]But you denied the Holy and Righteous One, and asked for a murderer to be granted to you, [15]and killed the Author of life, whom God raised from the dead. To this we are witnesses. [16]And his name, by faith in his name, has made this man strong whom you see and know; and the faith which is through Jesus[d] has given the man this perfect health in the presence of you all.

[17]"And now, brethren, I know that you acted in ignorance, as did also your rulers. [18]But what God foretold by the mouth of all the prophets, that his Christ should suffer, he thus fulfilled. [19]Repent therefore, and turn again, that your sins may be blotted out, that times of refreshing may come from the presence of the Lord, [20]and that he may send the Christ appointed for you, Jesus, [21]whom heaven must receive until the time for establishing all that God spoke by the mouth of his holy prophets from of old. [22]Moses said, 'The Lord God will raise up for you a prophet from your brethren as he raised me up. You shall listen to him in whatever he tells you. [23]And it shall be that every soul that does not listen to that prophet shall be destroyed from the people.' [24]And all the prophets who have spoken, from Samuel and those who came afterwards, also proclaimed these days. [25]You are the sons of the prophets and of the covenant which God gave to your fathers, saying to Abraham, 'And in your posterity shall all the families of the earth be blessed.' [26]God having raised up his servant,[c] sent him to you first, to bless you in turning every one of you from your wickedness."

3:11–26 This second address by St Peter contains two parts. In the first (vv. 12–16) the apostle explains that the miracle has been worked in the name of Jesus and through faith in his name; in the second (vv. 17–26), he moves his listeners to repentance. Then at the end (vv. 25–26) Peter mentions something ever-present in apostolic preaching (cf. 2:39): salvation is offered in the first instance to the chosen people, but it is available to all.

c. Or *child* **d.** Greek *him* **3:13** Ex 3:6. **3:22** Deut 18:15–18. **3:23** Lev 23:29; Deut 18:19. **3:25** Gen 22:18.

Peter and John are arrested

4 [1]And as they were speaking to the people, the priests and the captain of the
temple and the Sadducees came upon them, [2]annoyed because they were
teaching the people and proclaiming in Jesus the resurrection from the dead.*
[3]And they arrested them and put them in custody until the morrow, for it was
already evening. [4]But many of those who heard the word believed; and the
number of the men came to about five thousand.

Address to the Sanhedrin

[5]On the morrow their rulers and elders and scribes were gathered together in
Jerusalem, [6]with Annas the high priest and Caiaphas and John and Alexander,
and all who were of the high-priestly family. [7]And when they had set them in
the midst, they inquired, "By what power or by what name did you do this?"
[8]Then Peter, filled with the Holy Spirit, said to them, "Rulers of the people and
elders, [9]if we are being examined today concerning a good deed done to a
cripple, by what means this man has been healed, [10]be it known to you all, and
to all the people of Israel, that by the name of Jesus Christ of Nazareth, whom
you crucified, whom God raised from the dead, by him this man is standing
before you well. [11]This is the stone which was rejected by you builders, but
which has become the head of the corner. [12]And there is salvation in no one
else, for there is no other name under heaven given among men by which we
must be saved."

[13]Now when they saw the boldness of Peter and John, and perceived that
they were uneducated, common men, they wondered; and they recognized that
they had been with Jesus. [14]But seeing the man that had been healed standing
beside them, they had nothing to say in opposition. [15]But when they had
commanded them to go aside out of the council, they conferred with one
another, [16]saying, "What shall we do with these men? For that a notable sign
has been performed through them is manifest to all the inhabitants of
Jerusalem, and we cannot deny it. [17]But in order that it may spread no further
among the people, let us warn them to speak no more to any one in this name."

4:1–22 Jesus told his disciples (cf. Lk 21:12–15) that they would suffer persecution, and this is now borne out, as is the fact that he endows them with a wisdom which the powers that be cannot resist. The key words of the passage undoubtedly come at the end (vv. 19–20). Courage is something expected not only of people in prominent positions; we are all asked to have it: "Christians should approach those who are outside wisely, in 'the Holy Spirit, genuine love, truthful speech' (2 Cor 6:6–7), and should strive, even to the shedding of their blood, to spread the light of life with all confidence and apostolic courage. The disciple has a grave obligation to Christ, his Master, to grow daily in his knowledge of the truth he has received from him, to be faithful in announcing it and vigorous in defending it" (Vatican II, *DH*, 14).

4:11 Ps 118:22.

18So they called them and charged them not to speak or teach at all in the name
of Jesus. 19But Peter and John answered them, "Whether it is right in the sight
of God to listen to you rather than to God, you must judge; 20for we cannot but
speak of what we have seen and heard." 21And when they had further
threatened them, they let them go, finding no way to punish them, because of
the people; for all men praised God for what had happened. 22For the man on
whom this sign of healing was performed was more than forty years old.

The Church's thanksgiving prayer

23When they were released they went to their friends and reported what the
chief priests and the elders had said to them. 24And when they heard it, they
lifted their voices together to God and said, "Sovereign Lord, who didst make
the heaven and the earth and the sea and everything in them, 25who by the
mouth of our father David, thy servant,[c] didst say by the Holy Spirit,

'Why did the Gentiles rage,
and the peoples imagine vain things?
26The kings of the earth set themselves in array,
and the rulers were gathered together,
against the Lord and against his Anointed'—[e]

27for truly in this city there were gathered together against thy holy servant[c]
Jesus, whom thou didst anoint, both Herod and Pontius Pilate, with the
Gentiles, and the peoples of Israel, 28to do whatever thy hand and thy plan had
predestined to take place. 29And now, Lord, look upon their threats, and grant
to thy servants[f] to speak thy word with all boldness, 30while thou stretchest out
thy hand to heal, and signs and wonders are performed through the name of
thy holy servant[c] Jesus." 31And when they had prayed, the place in which they
were gathered together was shaken; and they were all filled with the Holy
Spirit and spoke the word of God with boldness.

4:23–31 This petition of the apostles and the whole community sets an example for Christians of all times—an example of prayer and reliance on supernatural resources. They ask God to give them the strength necessary to continue boldly to preach the Word and not to be cowed by persecution, and to give them the power to work miracles to back up their preaching. The Holy Spirit is mentioned twice, for "the Spirit who teaches the Church and recalls for her everything that Jesus said was also to form her in the life of prayer" (*CCC*, 2623). These first Christians have recourse to Holy Scripture in their prayer: "Like the inspired writers of the New Testament, the first Christian communities read the book of Psalms in a new way, singing in it the mystery of Christ. In the newness of the Spirit, they also composed hymns and canticles in the light of the unheard-of event that God accomplished in his Son: his incarnation, his death which conquered death, his

c. Or *child* **e.** Or *Christ* **f.** Or *slaves* **4:24** Ex 20:11; Ps 146:6. **4:25–26** Ps 2:1–2.

The way of life of the early Christians

32Now the company of those who believed were of one heart and soul, and no
one said that any of the things which he possessed was his own, but they had
everything in common.* 33And with great power the apostles gave their
testimony to the resurrection of the Lord Jesus, and great grace was upon them
all. 34There was not a needy person among them, for as many as were
possessors of lands or houses sold them, and brought the proceeds of what was
sold 35and laid it at the apostles' feet; and distribution was made to each as any
had need. 36Thus Joseph who was surnamed by the apostles Barnabas (which
means, Son of encouragement), a Levite, a native of Cyprus, 37sold a field
which belonged to him, and brought the money and laid it at the apostles' feet.

Deception by Ananias and Sapphira

5 1But a man named Ananias with his wife Sapphira sold a piece of property,
2and with his wife's knowledge he kept back some of the proceeds, and
brought only a part and laid it at the apostles' feet. 3But Peter said, "Ananias,
why has Satan filled your heart to lie to the Holy Spirit and to keep back part of
the proceeds of the land? 4While it remained unsold, did it not remain your
own? And after it was sold, was it not at your disposal? How is it that you have
contrived this deed in your heart? You have not lied to men but to God." 5When
Ananias heard these words, he fell down and died. And great fear came upon
all who heard of it. 6The young men rose and wrapped him up and carried him
out and buried him.

7After an interval of about three hours his wife came in, not knowing what
had happened. 8And Peter said to her, "Tell me whether you sold the land for
so much." And she said, "Yes, for so much." 9But Peter said to her, "How is it

---

resurrection and ascension to the right hand of the Father. Doxology, the praise of God, arises from this 'marvellous work' of the whole economy of salvation" (ibid., 2641).

4:32–37 In the first summary (cf. 2:42–47 and note), Luke mentioned mainly the prayer of the early Church; now he emphasizes the fact that they shared their possessions; and later (cf. 5:12–16) he focuses on signs and wonders worked by the apostles. He is well aware of the importance of being truly detached from possessions, as we can see from the example he gives (Barnabas: vv. 36–37) and the counter-example (Ananias and Sapphira: 5:1–11).

5:1–11 The reader cannot help being surprised by the baneful consequences that this sin has for the two culprits. But their sin is not just a sin of greed; the worst part about it is their attempt to deceive God, who is at work in the Church. St Ephrem comments that God punished Ananias and Sapphira in this way "not only because they stole and hid their crime, but also because they showed no

that you have agreed together to tempt the Spirit of the Lord? Hark, the feet of
those that have buried your husband are at the door, and they will carry you
out." [10]Immediately she fell down at his feet and died. When the young men
came in they found her dead, and they carried her out and buried her beside her
husband. [11]And great fear came upon the whole church,* and upon all who
heard of these things.

Growth of the Church

[12]Now many signs and wonders were done among the people by the hands of
the apostles. And they were all together in Solomon's Portico. [13]None of the
rest dared join them, but the people held them in high honour. [14]And more than
ever believers were added to the Lord, multitudes both of men and women,
[15]so that they even carried out the sick into the streets, and laid them on beds
and pallets, that as Peter came by at least his shadow might fall on some of
them. [16]The people also gathered from the towns around Jerusalem, bringing
the sick and those afflicted with unclean spirits, and they were all healed.

The apostles are arrested and miraculously freed

[17]But the high priest rose up and all who were with him, that is, the party of
the Sadducees, and filled with jealousy [18]they arrested the apostles and put
them in the common prison. [19]But at night an angel of the Lord opened the
prison doors and brought them out and said, [20]"Go and stand in the temple and
speak to the people all the words of this Life."* [21]And when they heard this,
they entered the temple at daybreak and taught.

Now the high priest came and those who were with him and called together
the council and all the senate of Israel, and sent to the prison to have them

---

shame, and sought to deceive those acting under the guidance of the Holy Spirit who knows all things" (*Cat. arm. sup. Act.*, in loc.). The severe punishment they receive befits the circumstances: the Church was in a foundational period, when people had a special duty to be faithful and when God was particularly supportive.

5:12–16 In this third summary Luke refers particularly to the apostles' power to work miracles. As in our Lord's case (cf. Mk 6:56; Lk 7:18–33; Acts 2:22), the miracles they work confirm to the people that the Kingdom of God has indeed come among them: "Without working miracles and marvellous signs, the disciples of Jesus could not have moved those who heard them to abandon their traditional religion and embrace new doctrines and truths, to risk their lives by accepting the new teachings preached to them" (Origen, *Against Celsus*, 1, 46).

5:17–33 This account contrasts two contrary orders given to the apostles—that of the angel (v. 20) and that of the Sanhedrin (v. 28); so the apostles' reply is very significant: if there is any clash, God must be obeyed rather than men.

brought. [22]But when the officers came, they did not find them in the prison, and they returned and reported, [23]"We found the prison securely locked and the sentries standing at the doors, but when we opened it we found no one inside." [24]Now when the captain of the temple and the chief priests heard these words, they were much perplexed about them, wondering what this would come to. [25]And some one came and told them, "The men whom you put in prison are standing in the temple and teaching the people."

The apostles before the Sanhedrin

[26]Then the captain with the officers went and brought them, but without violence, for they were afraid of being stoned by the people.

[27]And when they had brought them, they set them before the council. And the high priest questioned them, [28]saying, "We strictly charged you not to teach in this name, yet here you have filled Jerusalem with your teaching and you intend to bring this man's blood upon us." [29]But Peter and the apostles answered, "We must obey God rather than men. [30]The God of our fathers raised Jesus whom you killed by hanging him on a tree. [31]God exalted him at his right hand as Leader and Saviour, to give repentance to Israel and forgiveness of sins. [32]And we are witnesses to these things, and so is the Holy Spirit whom God has given to those who obey him."

[33]When they heard this they were enraged and wanted to kill them.

Gamaliel's intervention

[34]But a Pharisee in the council named Gamaliel, *a teacher of the law, held in honour by all the people, stood up and ordered the men to be put outside for a while. [35]And he said to them, "Men of Israel, take care what you do with these men. [36]For before these days Theudas arose, giving himself out to be somebody, and a number of men, about four hundred, joined him; but he was slain and all who followed him were dispersed and came to nothing. [37]After him Judas the Galilean arose in the days of the census and drew away some of the people after him; he also perished, and all who followed him were scattered. [38]So in the present case I tell you, keep away from these men and let

---

5:34–42 Gamaliel was St Paul's teacher at one point (cf. 22:3). He belonged to a moderate grouping among the Pharisees. He was a prudent man, impartial and religiously minded. The Fathers of the Church often propose him as an example of an upright man who is awaiting the Kingdom of God and one who dared to defend the apostles. The revolts of Theudas and Judas referred to in his speech are reported by Flavius Josephus (cf. *Ant.*, 18, 4–10; 20:169–172), but apparently they occurred around the time of Jesus' birth. Both Theudas and Judas had a considerable following; they revolted because they objected to God's chosen people, the Jews, being ruled and taxed by foreigners such as Herod and Imperial Rome.

them alone; for if this plan or this undertaking is of men, it will fail; [39]but if it is of God, you will not be able to overthrow them. You might even be found opposing God!"

The apostles are flogged

[40]So they took his advice, and when they had called in the apostles, they beat them and charged them not to speak in the name of Jesus, and let them go. [41]Then they left the presence of the council, rejoicing that they were counted worthy to suffer dishonour for the name. [42]And every day in the temple and at home they did not cease teaching and preaching Jesus as the Christ.

4. THE "DEACONS". ST STEPHEN

Appointment of the Seven

6 [1]Now in these days when the disciples were increasing in number, the Hellenists* murmured against the Hebrews because their widows were neglected in the daily distribution. [2]And the twelve summoned the body of the disciples and said, "It is not right that we should give up preaching the word of God to serve tables. [3]Therefore, brethren, pick out from among you seven men of good repute, full of the Spirit and of wisdom, whom we may appoint

---

Following Gamaliel's line of argument, the reader can see that the apostles were indeed engaged in God's work. However, the Sanhedrin were not impressed and, in punishing Jesus' disciples, they only bring about what our Lord had said would happen—that they would rejoice to suffer for his sake (cf. Mt 5:11–12; Mk 10:30; Lk 6:22–23). At the end of the passage, Luke tells us that the apostles were in no way deflected from their mission.

6:1–7:60 □St Luke now focuses on the Hellenists, writing along much the same lines as in the previous section (cf. the note on 3:1–5:42). The Christians of Hellenist background were experiencing difficulties of their own: within the Church, their widows were being neglected (6:1), and from the outside opposition was coming from the synagogue of the Freedmen (6:9). Luke sees the providence of God behind all these events. The difficulties of the Hellenists are solved by the appointment of "deacons", and just as persecution by Jews led to an increase in the number of disciples, including very many priests (6:7), this new persecution will lead to the martyrdom of Stephen, which will sow the seed of Saul's conversion: "If Stephen had not prayed to God, the Church would not have had Paul" (cf. St Augustine, *Serm.*, 315, 7).

6:1–7 At the start of this section we see two groups of disciples, identified by their background prior to conversion—the Hellenists and the Hebrews. Hellenists were to this duty. 4But we will devote ourselves to prayer and to the ministry of the word." 5And what they said pleased the whole multitude, and they chose Stephen, a man full of faith and of the Holy Spirit, and Philip, and Prochorus, and Nicanor, and Timon, and Parmenas, and Nicolaus, a proselyte of Antioch. 6These they set before the apostles, and they prayed and laid their hands upon them.

7And the word of God increased; and the number of the disciples multiplied greatly in Jerusalem, and a great many of the priests were obedient to the faith.

Stephen's arrest

8And Stephen, full of grace and power, did great wonders and signs among the people. 9Then some of those who belonged to the synagogue of the Freedmen (as it was called), and of the Cyrenians, and of the Alexandrians, and of those from Cilicia and Asia, arose and disputed with Stephen. 10But they could not withstand the wisdom and the Spirit with which he spoke. 11Then they secretly instigated men, who said, "We have heard him speak blasphemous words against Moses and God." 12And they stirred up the people and the elders and

---

Jews who had been born and lived for a time outside Palestine. They spoke Greek and had synagogues of their own where Greek translations of the Scriptures were used. They had a certain amount of Greek culture (the Hebrews would have had much less). The Hebrews were Jews born in Palestine; they spoke Aramaic and used the Hebrew Bible in synagogue. The difference of background naturally carried over into the Christian community for a while, but it would be wrong to see it as divisive, and even more wrong to imagine that there were two opposing groups in early Christianity.

This chapter deals with the apostles' establishment of the institution of "the Seven". This is the second defined group of disciples (the apostles themselves—"the Twelve"—made up the first) to be given a ministry in the Church. Luke uses the word *diakonia* to describe their duty or form of service, but he does not call these seven men appointed "to serve tables" (v. 2) "deacons". Nor do early Christian writers connect these seven to the deacons (in a later, technical sense) who, alongside priests and bishops, will soon go to make up the hierarchy of the Church. Therefore, we cannot say for sure whether the diaconal ministry, as we know it, derives directly from "the Seven". However, it is not impossible that the ministry described here helped to define the institution of the diaconate in its proper sense.

6:8–15 St Stephen is the first Christian martyr. That is why Luke gives him so much coverage: he tells us about his death (cf. also 7:54–60), concentrating particularly on how Stephen followed his Master in word and works. Stephen had the irresistible wisdom (v. 10) that Jesus promised his disciples (cf. Lk 21:15). Also, like Jesus (cf. Mt 26:57–68 and par.) he was accused by false witnesses (vv. 11–14). Later, before his death, Stephen (7:55–56) has a vision of the Son of man

the scribes, and they came upon him and seized him, and brought him before the council, [13]and set up false witnesses who said, "This man never ceases to speak words against this holy place and the law; [14]for we have heard him say that this Jesus of Nazareth will destroy this place, and will change the customs which Moses delivered to us." [15]And gazing at him, all who sat in the council saw that his face was like the face of an angel.

Stephen's address to the Sanhedrin

7 [1]And the high priest said, "Is this so?" [2]And Stephen said: "Brethren and fathers, hear me. The God of glory appeared to our father Abraham, when he was in Mesopotamia, before he lived in Haran, [3]and said to him, 'Depart from your land and from your kindred and go into the land which I will show you.' [4]Then he departed from the land of the Chaldeans, and lived in Haran. And after his father died, God removed him from there into this land in which you are now living; [5]yet he gave him no inheritance in it, not even a foot's length, but promised to give it to him in possession and to his posterity after him, though he had no child. [6]And God spoke to this effect, that his posterity would be aliens in a land belonging to others, who would enslave them and ill-treat them four hundred years. [7]'But I will judge the nation which they serve,'

---

in glory, in line with Jesus' prophecy (cf. Mt 26:64 and par.). And, finally, like Christ (cf. Lk 23:34, 46) he forgives those who have brought about his death and he abandons himself to God (7:59–60): "Therefore, it was fitting that he be the first martyr for Christ, and in giving example to future martyrs by his own glorious death, he not only bore testimony to the passion of Christ, but he imitated it, too, by his meekness and patient suffering" (St Cyprian, *De bono patientiae*, 16).

The "synagogue of the Freedmen (as it was called)" seems to be a reference to Jews from Hellenist parts of the Diaspora. These were probably the same Jews that a little further on disputed with Paul and wanted to kill him (9:29). Just as now they cannot resist Stephen's wisdom (v. 10), they will later be unable to stem the spread of the new faith.

7:1–53 Stephen's address is the longest one reported in Acts. It gives a summary of the history of Israel, divided into three periods—those of the patriarchs (vv. 1–16), of Moses (vv. 17–43), and of the building of the temple (vv. 44–50). It ends with a short section (vv. 51–53) where he brings his argument together.

Stephen does not defend himself directly. He answers his accusers with a Christian vision of salvation history, in which the temple and the Law have already fulfilled their purpose. He tells them that he continues to respect the Mosaic Law and the temple, but that, as a Christian, his idea of God's law is more universal and more profound, and his concept of the temple more spiritual, for God can be worshipped anywhere in the world. This approach, which respects and perfects the

7:3 Gen 12:1. **7:5** Deut 2:5; Gen 12:7; 17:8. **7:6–7** Gen 15:13–14. **7:7** Ex 3:12.

said God, 'and after that they shall come out and worship me in this place.'
8And he gave him the covenant of circumcision. And so Abraham became the
father of Isaac, and circumcised him on the eighth day; and Isaac became the
father of Jacob, and Jacob of the twelve patriarchs.

9"And the patriarchs, jealous of Joseph, sold him into Egypt; but God was
with him, 10and rescued him out of all his afflictions, and gave him favour and
wisdom before Pharaoh, king of Egypt, who made him governor over Egypt
and over all his household. 11Now there came a famine throughout all Egypt
and Canaan, and great affliction, and our fathers could find no food. 12But
when Jacob heard that there was grain in Egypt, he sent forth our fathers the
first time. 13And at the second visit Joseph made himself known to his
brothers, and Joseph's family became known to Pharaoh. 14And Joseph sent
and called to him Jacob his father and all his kindred, seventy-five souls; 15and
Jacob went down into Egypt. And he died, himself and our fathers, 16and they
were carried back to Shechem and laid in the tomb that Abraham had bought
for a sum of silver from the sons of Hamor in Shechem.

17"But as the time of the promise drew near, which God had granted to
Abraham, the people grew and multiplied in Egypt 18till there arose over Egypt
another king who had not known Joseph. 19He dealt craftily with our race and
forced our fathers to expose their infants, that they might not be kept alive.
20At this time Moses was born, and was beautiful before God. And he was
brought up for three months in his father's house; 21and when he was exposed,
Pharaoh's daughter adopted him and brought him up as her own son. 22And
Moses was instructed in all the wisdom of the Egyptians, and he was mighty
in his words and deeds.

23"When he was forty years old, it came into his heart to visit his brethren,
the sons of Israel. 24And seeing one of them being wronged, he defended the
oppressed man and avenged him by striking the Egyptian. 25He supposed that
his brethren understood that God was giving them deliverance by his hand, but
they did not understand. 26And on the following day he appeared to them as
they were quarrelling and would have reconciled them, saying, 'Men, you are
brethren, why do you wrong each other?' 27But the man who was wronging his

---

religious values of Judaism (because it realizes their true meaning and brings them to fulfilment), is reinforced by the way he presents the figure of Moses. He shows Moses as a "type" of Christ: Christ is the new Moses. Small elucidations of the Greek text of the Old Testament help in this direction: expressions like "they refused" or "deliverer" (v. 35) are not applied to Moses in the books of the Old Law, but they were used in that sense in the Judaism of Stephen's time, and he uses them here to suggest the figure of Christ. The Israelites' rebellious and hostile treatment of Moses, who had a mission from God, is being repeated—more gravely, and with more serious consequences—in their rejection of Jesus Christ.

7:10 Gen 41:10–46. **7:11** Gen 41:54. **7:18** Ex 1:7–8.

neighbour thrust him aside, saying, 'Who made you a ruler and a judge over
us? 28 Do you want to kill me as you killed the Egyptian yesterday?' 29 At this
retort Moses fled, and became an exile in the land of Midian, where he became
the father of two sons.

30 "Now when forty years had passed, an angel appeared to him in the
wilderness of Mount Sinai, in a flame of fire in a bush. 31 When Moses saw it
he wondered at the sight; and as he drew near to look, the voice of the Lord
came, 32 'I am the God of your fathers, the God of Abraham and of Isaac and
of Jacob.' And Moses trembled and did not dare to look. 33 And the Lord said
to him, 'Take off the shoes from your feet, for the place where you are
standing is holy ground. 34 I have surely seen the ill-treatment of my people
that are in Egypt and heard their groaning, and I have come down to deliver
them. And now come, I will send you to Egypt.'

35 "This Moses whom they refused, saying, 'Who made you a ruler and a
judge?' God sent as both ruler and deliverer by the hand of the angel that
appeared to him in the bush. 36 He led them out, having performed wonders and
signs in Egypt and at the Red Sea, and in the wilderness for forty years. 37 This
is the Moses who said to the Israelites, 'God will raise up for you a prophet
from your brethren as he raised me up.' 38 This is he who was in the con-
gregation in the wilderness with the angel who spoke to him at Mount Sinai,
and with our fathers; and he received living oracles to give to us. 39 Our fathers
refused to obey him, but thrust him aside, and in their hearts they turned to
Egypt, 40 saying to Aaron, 'Make for us gods to go before us; as for this Moses
who led us out from the land of Egypt, we do not know what has become of
him.' 41 And they made a calf in those days, and offered a sacrifice to the idol and
rejoiced in the works of their hands. 42 But God turned and gave them over to
worship the host of heaven, as it is written in the book of the prophets:

'Did you offer to me slain beasts and sacrifices,
forty years in the wilderness, O house of Israel?
43 And you took up the tent of Moloch,
and the star of the god Rephan,
the figures which you made to worship;
and I will remove you beyond Babylon.'

44 "Our fathers had the tent of witness in the wilderness, even as he who spoke
to Moses directed him to make it, according to the pattern that he had seen. 45 Our
fathers in turn brought it in with Joshua when they dispossessed the nations which
God thrust out before our fathers. So it was until the days of David, 46 who found
favour in the sight of God and asked leave to find a habitation for the God of
Jacob. 47 But it was Solomon who built a house for him. 48 Yet the Most High does
not dwell in houses made with hands; as the prophet says,

49 'Heaven is my throne,
and earth my footstool.

7:30 Ex 3:2–3. **7:32** Ex 3:6. **7:34** Ex 3:7–8. **7:35** Ex 2:14. **7:37** Deut 18:15. **7:40** Ex 32:1. **7:49–50** Is 66:1–2.

What house will you build for me, says the Lord,
or what is the place of my rest?
[50]Did not my hand make all these things?'
[51]"You stiff-necked people, uncircumcised in heart and ears, you always resist
the Holy Spirit. As your fathers did, so do you. [52]Which of the prophets did not
your fathers persecute? And they killed those who announced beforehand the
coming of the Righteous One, whom you have now betrayed and murdered,
[53]you who received the law as delivered by angels and did not keep it."

Martyrdom of St Stephen

[54]Now when they heard these things they were enraged, and they ground their
teeth against him. [55]But he, full of the Holy Spirit, gazed into heaven and saw
the glory of God, and Jesus standing at the right hand of God; [56]and he said,
"Behold, I see the heavens opened, and the Son of man standing at the right
hand of God." [57]But they cried out with a loud voice and stopped their ears and
rushed together upon him. [58]Then they cast him out of the city and stoned him;
and the witnesses laid down their garments at the feet of a young man named
Saul. [59]And as they were stoning Stephen, he prayed, "Lord Jesus, receive my
spirit." [60]And he knelt down and cried with a loud voice, "Lord, do not hold
this sin against them." And when he had said this, he fell asleep. [1a]And Saul
was consenting to his death.

PART TWO: THE CHURCH SPREADS BEYOND JERUSALEM

5. THE CHURCH IN SAMARIA

Persecution of the Church

8 [1b]And on that day a great persecution arose against the church in
Jerusalem; and they were all scattered throughout the region of Judea and
Samaria, except the apostles. [2]Devout men buried Stephen, and made great

---

7:54–60 St Luke's account, drawing as it does a parallel between the death of Jesus and that of Stephen (cf. the note on 6:8–15), also tells us something new: whereas Jesus addressed himself to God the Father (Lk 23:26), Stephen directs the same type of prayer to the Lord Jesus (v. 59), thereby confessing the divinity of Christ.

8:1–12:25 This part of the book tells about how persecution had the effect of sending Christians (but not the Twelve) away from Jerusalem into Judea, Samaria lamentation over him. 3But Saul laid waste the church, and entering house after house, he dragged off men and women and committed them to prison.

Philip's preaching in Samaria

4Now those who were scattered went about preaching the word. 5Philip went down to a city of Samaria, and proclaimed to them the Christ. 6And the multitudes with one accord gave heed to what was said by Philip, when they heard him and saw the signs which he did. 7For unclean spirits came out of many who were possessed, crying with a loud voice; and many who were paralyzed or lame were healed. 8So there was much joy in that city.

---

and Syria. There was not enough scope left in Jerusalem, and the Church now begins to open up to the Gentiles. We hear about the conversion of the Ethiopian (8:26–39) and of numerous Samaritans (8:14–17). There are fairly detailed accounts of the calling of Paul to be the Apostle of the Gentiles (9:15), and the conversion of Cornelius the centurion (chaps. 10–11)—events of exceptional significance as regards the Gospel's overcoming ethnic barriers. The section ends with the death of James the brother of John, and the arrest and miraculous release of St Peter.

8:1–40 □ The spread of the Church to Samaria marks a first step towards the fulfilment of what our Lord said at the Ascension (1:8). The spread of the faith is initially associated with the ministry of Philip, one of the seven deacons (8:5–8), but in the book of the Acts full reception of the Holy Spirit is always linked to the apostles and to union with the mother church of Jerusalem (8:14–17).

8:1–4 Stephen's execution marked the start of a violent persecution in Jerusalem. Conscious of the role that Paul would play in the early Church, Luke twice mentions his involvement in the persecution: "Christianity has been too often in what seemed deadly peril, that we should fear for it any new trial now [...] What is commonly a great surprise when it is witnessed is the particular mode by which, in the event, Providence rescues and saves His elect inheritance. Sometimes our enemy is turned into a friend; sometimes he is despoiled of that special virulence of evil which was so threatening; sometimes he falls to pieces of himself; sometimes he does just so much as is beneficial, and then is removed. Commonly the Church had nothing more to do than to go on in her own proper duties, in confidence and peace; to stand still and to see the salvation of God" (J.H. Newman, *Biglietto Speech*).

8:5–8 The first result of the persecution was that it led to a successful spread of the Gospel proclamation to Samaria: "The religion founded on the mystery of Christ's cross cannot be destroyed by any kind of cruelty. Persecutions do not tear down the Church; rather they build it up. The field of the Lord gives rich harvest:

Simon the magician
9But there was a man named Simon who had previously practised magic in the
city and amazed the nation of Samaria, saying that he himself was somebody
great. 10They all gave heed to him, from the least to the greatest, saying, "This
man is that power of God which is called Great." 11And they gave heed to him,
because for a long time he had amazed them with his magic. 12But when they
believed Philip as he preached good news about the kingdom of God and the
name of Jesus Christ, they were baptized, both men and women. 13Even Simon
himself believed, and after being baptized he continued with Philip. And
seeing signs and great miracles performed, he was amazed.

Peter and John in Samaria
14Now when the apostles at Jerusalem heard that Samaria had received the
word of God, they sent to them Peter and John, 15who came down and prayed
for them that they might receive the Holy Spirit; 16for it had not yet fallen on
any of them, but they had only been baptized in the name of the Lord Jesus.
17Then they laid their hands on them and they received the Holy Spirit.

---

when the ears of grain fall and die, they sprout up again in greater number" (St Leo the Great, *Serm. in natal. Apost. Petr. et Paul.*, 6).

8:9–13 Luke uses this episode of Simon Magus to show the difference between the genuine miracles worked by the apostles in the name of Jesus and with his power, and the real or apparent prodigies worked by a charlatan. "As in the times of Moses, a distinction is made here between kinds of prodigy. Magic was practised, but it was easy to identify genuine miracles [...]. Unclean spirits were cast out of many people whom they had taken over, and they cried out with a loud voice. This was the sign of their expulsion. Those who practised magic produced the very opposite effect, reinforcing the bonds that restrained possessed people" (St John Chrysostom, *Hom. on Acts*, 18, 3).

8:14–25 The apostles also oversaw the first spread of the Church outside Jerusalem. Tradition has seen in vv. 15–17 evidence of the origin of the sacrament of Confirmation: "The apostles, in fulfillment of the will of Christ, communicate the gift of the Holy Spirit to the neophytes by the laying on of hands, and so bring the grace of Baptism to completion in them (cf. Acts 8: 15–17; 19: 5–6). This explains why the doctrine of Baptism and the laying on of hands is recalled as one of the fundamental elements of Christian formation in the Letter to the Hebrews (cf. Heb 6:2). Catholic tradition has justifiably taken the act of the laying on of hands as the primitive origin of the sacrament of Confirmation, which, in a certain way, preserves the grace of Pentecost in the Church" (Paul VI, *Div. consort. nat*).

The sin of simony

[18]Now when Simon saw that the Spirit was given through the laying on of the
apostles' hands, he offered them money, [19]saying, "Give me also this power,
that any one on whom I lay my hands may receive the Holy Spirit." [20]But Peter
said to him, "Your silver perish with you, because you thought you could
obtain the gift of God with money!* [21]You have neither part nor lot in this
matter, for your heart is not right before God. [22]Repent therefore of this
wickedness of yours, and pray to the Lord that, if possible, the intent of your
heart may be forgiven you. [23]For I see that you are in the gall of bitterness and
in the bond of iniquity." [24]And Simon answered, "Pray for me to the Lord, that
nothing of what you have said may come upon me."

[25]Now when they had testified and spoken the word of the Lord, they returned
to Jerusalem, preaching the gospel to many villages of the Samaritans.

Philip baptizes an Ethiopian official

[26]But an angel of the Lord said to Philip, "Rise and go toward the south[g] to the
road that goes down from Jerusalem to Gaza." This is a desert road. [27]And he
rose and went. And behold, an Ethiopian, a eunuch, a minister of Candace the
queen of the Ethiopians, in charge of all her treasure, had come to Jerusalem
to worship [28]and was returning; seated in his chariot, he was reading the
prophet Isaiah. [29]And the Spirit said to Philip, "Go up and join this chariot."
[30]So Philip ran to him, and heard him reading Isaiah the prophet, and asked,
"Do you understand what you are reading?" [31]And he said, "How can I, unless
some one guides me?" And he invited Philip to come up and sit with him.
[32]Now the passage of the scripture which he was reading was this:

"As a sheep led to the slaughter
or a lamb before its shearer is dumb,
so he opens not his mouth.

8:26–40 The baptism of the Ethiopian official marks an important step in the spread of Christianity. This episode encapsulates the various stages in apostolate: Christ's disciple is moved by the Spirit (cf. vv. 29, 39) and readily obeys his instruction; he bases his preaching on Holy Scripture—as Jesus did in the case of the disciples of Emmaus—and then administers Baptism.

This account shows the importance Holy Scripture has for evangelization—and how necessary a guide is for its interpretation: "I can say from my own experience that I am neither more studious nor more saintly than the eunuch who left the royal palace and travelled up from Eygpt, from the ends of the earth, to the temple—a man whose love for divine knowledge was so great that he read the sacred texts as he journeyed in his carriage. And he, moreover, did not truly know him who is venerated by that book. Philip came to him and revealed Jesus who is hidden, imprisoned almost, in the words of the text [...] and in that moment the eunuch believed and was baptized, made one of the faithful and holy. I tell you this so that

g. Or *at noon* **8:32** Is 53: 7–8.

[33]In his humiliation justice was denied him.
Who can describe his generation?
For his life is taken up from the earth."
[34]And the eunuch said to Philip, "About whom, pray, does the prophet say this,
about himself or about some one else?" [35]Then Philip opened his mouth, and
beginning with this scripture he told him the good news of Jesus. [36]And as
they went along the road they came to some water, and the eunuch said, "See,
here is water! What is to prevent my being baptized?"[h] [38]And he commanded
the chariot to stop, and they both went down into the water, Philip and the
eunuch, and he baptized him. [39]And when they came up out of the water, the
Spirit of the Lord caught up Philip; and the eunuch saw him no more, and went
on his way rejoicing. [40]But Philip was found at Azotus, and passing on he
preached the gospel to all the towns till he came to Caesarea.

6. THE CONVERSION OF ST PAUL

Saul on his way to Damascus

9 [1]But Saul, still breathing threats and murder against the disciples of the
Lord, went to the high priest [2]and asked him for letters to the synagogues
at Damascus, so that if he found any belonging to the Way, men or women, he

---

you may see that no one can enter fully into the Holy Scriptures without having the help of someone to show him the way" (St Jerome, *Epist.*, 53, 5–6).

That guide is the reliable interpretation of the Church, to whom God entrusted the books which he inspired. That is why the Second Vatican Council teaches that "attention must be devoted to the content and unity of the whole of Scripture, taking into account the Tradition of the entire Church and the analogy of faith, if we are to derive their true meaning from the sacred texts. [...] All that has been said about the manner of interpreting Scripture is ultimately subject to the judgment of the Church which exercises the divinely conferred commission and ministry of watching over and interpreting the Word of God" (*DV*, 12).

See the RSV note **h**: v. 37 is missing from some Greek codexes and the better early translations. It may have derived from a profession of faith used in the ceremony of Baptism.

9:1–31 □ This is the first of three accounts of the calling of Saul to be found in this book (cf. 22:5–16; 26:10–18); it probably happened sometime between the years 34 and 36. When key events are involved St Luke does not mind repeating himself. In this first account he describes events from two different viewpoints—that of Paul (vv. 1–9) and that of Ananias (vv. 10–19). Then (vv. 19–30) he goes on to describe the apostles' spirited preaching.

h. Other ancient authorities add all or most of verse 37, *And Philip said, "If you believe with all your heart, you may." And he replied, "I believe that Jesus Christ is the Son of God."*

might bring them bound to Jerusalem. 3Now as he journeyed he approached
Damascus, and suddenly a light from heaven flashed about him. 4And he fell
to the ground and heard a voice saying to him, "Saul, Saul, why do you
persecute me?" 5And he said, "Who are you, Lord?" And he said, "I am Jesus,
whom you are persecuting;* 6but rise and enter the city, and you will be told
what you are to do." 7The men who were travelling with him stood speechless,
hearing the voice but seeing no one. 8Saul arose from the ground; and when
his eyes were opened, he could see nothing; so they led him by the hand and
brought him into Damascus. 9And for three days he was without sight, and
neither ate nor drank.

Ananias baptizes Saul

10Now there was a disciple at Damascus called Ananias. The Lord said to him
in a vision, "Ananias." And he said, "Here I am, Lord." 11And the Lord said to
him, "Rise and go to the street called Straight, and inquire in the house of Judas
for a man of Tarsus named Saul; for behold, he is praying, 12and he has seen a
man named Ananias come in and lay his hands on him so that he might regain
his sight." 13But Ananias answered, "Lord, I have heard from many about this
man, how much evil he has done to thy saints* at Jerusalem; 14and here he has
authority from the chief priests to bind all who call upon thy name." 15But the
Lord said to him, "Go, for he is a chosen instrument of mine to carry my name
before the Gentiles and kings and the sons of Israel; 16for I will show him how
much he must suffer for the sake of my name." 17So Ananias departed and
entered the house. And laying his hands on him he said, "Brother Saul, the Lord
Jesus who appeared to you on the road by which you came, has sent me that you
may regain your sight and be filled with the Holy Spirit." 18And immediately
something like scales fell from his eyes and he regained his sight. Then he rose
and was baptized, 19and took food and was strengthened.

9:1–19 From the very start of Paul's vocation, when Christ first appeared to him, Christ made him see very clearly the fact that He identified with Christians. This was something which the Apostle will later elaborate on when in his letters he speaks about the Mystical Body of Christ (1. Col 1: 18; Eph 1:22f). It is an idea which some Fathers highlight in their commentaries: Jesus "does not say, 'Why do you persecute my members?'; rather, he asks, 'Why do you persecute me?,' because he himself suffers the insults in his body, which is the Church" (St Bede, *Sup. Act. exp.*, in loc).

9:19–31 Luke records just how energetic Saul's preaching was: the same ardour which he previously showed in his persecution of Christians (9:12) he now puts into his controversies with Jews (v. 22) and Greeks (v. 29). But "the disciples were afraid that the Jews would cause Saul's martyrdom as they did Stephen's. [...] They sent him to preach the Gospel in his native city, where the risk would be less.

Paul begins his apostolate

For several days he was with the disciples at Damascus. [20]And in the synagogues immediately he proclaimed Jesus, saying, "He is the Son of God." [21]And all who heard him were amazed, and said, "Is not this the man who made havoc in Jerusalem of those who called on this name? And he has come here for this purpose, to bring them bound before the chief priests." [22]But Saul increased all the more in strength, and confounded the Jews who lived in Damascus by proving that Jesus was the Christ.

Paul flees from Damascus

[23]When many days had passed, the Jews plotted to kill him, [24]but their plot became known to Saul. They were watching the gates day and night, to kill him; [25]but his disciples took him by night and let him down over the wall, lowering him in a basket.

Barnabas and Paul in Jerusalem

[26]And when he had come to Jerusalem he attempted to join the disciples; and they were all afraid of him, for they did not believe that he was a disciple. [27]But Barnabas took him, and brought him to the apostles, and declared to them how on the road he had seen the Lord, who spoke to him, and how at Damascus he had preached boldly in the name of Jesus. [28]So he went in and out among them at Jerusalem, [29]preaching boldly in the name of the Lord. And he spoke and disputed against the Hellenists; but they were seeking to kill him. [30]And when the brethren knew it, they brought him down to Caesarea, and sent him off to Tarsus.

Growth of the Church

[31]So the church throughout all Judea and Galilee and Samaria had peace and was built up; and walking in the fear of the Lord and in the comfort of the Holy Spirit it was multiplied.

From this action of the apostles you can see that God does not do everything directly by his grace and that he often permits his disciples to apply the rule of prudence" (St John Chrysostom, *Hom. on Acts*, 21, 1).

After his account of this early activity of Paul, Luke breaks off (v. 31) to give an over-view of the steady progress of the Church as a whole and of the various communities that have grown up by a result of the Christians' flight from Jerusalem (cf. 2:41, 47; 4:4; 5:14; 6:1, 7; 11:21, 24; 16:5). Luke emphasizes the peace and consolation the Holy Spirit has brought them. This is a note of justified optimism and confidence in God's on-going help.

7. ST PETER'S ACTIVITY

Curing of a paralyzed man at Lydda
32Now as Peter went here and there among them all, he came down also to the
saints that lived at Lydda. 33There he found a man named Aeneas, who had been
bedridden for eight years and was paralyzed. 34And Peter said to him, "Aeneas,
Jesus Christ heals you; rise and make your bed." And immediately he rose. 35And
all the residents of Lydda and Sharon saw him, and they turned to the Lord.

Peter raises Tabitha to life
36Now there was at Joppa a disciple named Tabitha, which means Dorcas or
Gazelle. She was full of good works and acts of charity. 37In those days she fell
sick and died; and when they had washed her, they laid her in an upper room.
38Since Lydda was near Joppa, the disciples, hearing that Peter was there, sent
two men to him entreating him, "Please come to us without delay." 39So Peter
rose and went with them. And when he had come, they took him to the upper
room. All the widows stood beside him weeping, and showing coats and garments
which Dorcas made while she was with them. 40But Peter put them all outside
and knelt down and prayed; then turning to the body he said, "Tabitha, rise." And
she opened her eyes, and when she saw Peter she sat up. 41And he gave her his
hand and lifted her up. Then calling the saints and widows he presented her alive.
42And it became known throughout all Joppa, and many believed in the Lord.
43And he stayed in Joppa for many days with one Simon, a tanner.

9:32–12:25 □ Luke now moves on to St Peter's activity outside Jerusalem. The account given here seems to indicate that there were already quite a number of Christians in Lydda (9:32) and Joppa (9:36–38). But the main event of this journey by St Peter is the conversion of the centurion Cornelius (10:1–11:18)—the acceptance of people into the fold without requiring them to be circumcised. Throughout this account, St Luke (and, like him, St Peter himself in his speech in Jerusalem: 11:4–17), stresses that the initiative always came from the Holy Spirit. The importance of this event will be seen later at other points in the life of the early Church (15:3–11).

9:32–35 Jesus, too, cured a paralysed man (Mt 9:108 and par.), telling him to get up and carry his bed away with him. He did so in his own name, forgiving sins as only God can. St Peter, on the other hand, works the miracle in Jesus' name.

9:36–43 This passage is an abiding and beautiful example of how works of devotion are rewarded. "It is clear from the Acts of the Apostles that almsgiving delivers us from natural as well as spiritual death. Peter was called when Tabitha, 'who never tired of doing good or giving in charity,' became ill and died. As soon

The vision of the centurion Cornelius

10 1At Caesarea there was a man named Cornelius, a centurion of what
was known as the Italian Cohort, 2a devout man who feared God with
all his household, gave alms liberally to the people, and prayed constantly to
God. 3About the ninth hour of the day he saw clearly in a vision an angel of
God coming in and saying to him, "Cornelius." 4And he stared at him in terror,
and said, "What is it, Lord?" And he said to him, "Your prayers and your alms
have ascended as a memorial before God. 5And now send men to Joppa, and
bring one Simon who is called Peter; 6he is lodging with Simon, a tanner, whose
house is by the seaside." 7When the angel who spoke to him had departed, he
called two of his servants and a devout soldier from among those that waited
on him, 8and having related everything to them, he sent them to Joppa.

Peter's vision

9The next day, as they were on their journey and coming near the city, Peter
went up on the housetop to pray, about the sixth hour. 10And he became
hungry and desired something to eat; but while they were preparing it, he fell
into a trance 11and saw the heaven opened, and something descending, like a
great sheet, let down by four corners upon the earth. 12In it were all kinds of

---

as he arrived, in accordance with the love of apostolic charity, he was surrounded by the widows, crying and demanding his help […], pleading for the life of the dead woman more by gestures than by words. Peter believed that he could bring about what they asked for so insistently, and that the help of Christ would never be lacking to the poor he loved so much […]. Christ did not deprive Peter of his help; Peter, the man whom he promised in the Gospel to grant everything asked for in his name. Thus, death was overcome and the woman brought back to life; her resurrected body returned to the light of this world to the amazement of all. All good works and works of mercy have this same power" (St Cyprian, *De opere et eleem.*, 6).

10:1–48 The conversion of the pagan Cornelius to Christianity is one of the high points of the book of the Acts. It is an extremely important event, showing as it does that the Gospel is addressed to all mankind and that the power of the Holy Spirit knows no limits. That is why, as on other occasions, Luke tells the story twice—here, keeping to the order of events and giving a lot of detail, which stresses the main points and helps show their significance, and in the next chapter (11:1–18) when Peter justifies his action to the brethren in Jerusalem.

The account begins by presenting Cornelius as a devout man (vv. 2, 4) and a "God-fearer"—an expression with a very exact meaning, used to designate someone who worshipped the God of the Bible and who practised the main commandments of the Jewish Law without being formally converted to Judaism. Although God's gifts are unmerited, the angel tells the centurion that his deeds have won God's favour (cf. v. 4). "Do you notice how the work of the Gospel

animals and reptiles and birds of the air. [13]And there came a voice to him,
"Rise, Peter; kill and eat." [14]But Peter said, "No, Lord; for I have never eaten
anything that is common or unclean." [15]And the voice came to him again a
second time, "What God has cleansed, you must not call common." [16]This
happened three times, and the thing was taken up at once to heaven.*
[17]Now while Peter was inwardly perplexed as to what the vision which he
had seen might mean, behold, the men that were sent by Cornelius, having made
inquiry for Simon's house, stood before the gate [18]and called out to ask whether
Simon who was called Peter was lodging there. [19]And while Peter was pondering
the vision, the Spirit said to him, "Behold, three men are looking for you. [20]Rise
and go down, and accompany them without hesitation; for I have sent them."
[21]And Peter went down to the men and said, "I am the one you are looking for;
what is the reason for your coming?" [22]And they said, "Cornelius, a centurion, an
upright and God-fearing man, who is well spoken of by the whole Jewish nation,
was directed by a holy angel to send for you to come to his house, and to hear
what you have to say." [23]So he called them in to be his guests.

Peter in the house of Cornelius
The next day he rose and went off with them, and some of the brethren from
Joppa accompanied him. [24]And on the following day they entered Caesarea.
Cornelius was expecting them and had called together his kinsmen and close
friends. [25]When Peter entered, Cornelius met him and fell down at his feet and
worshipped him. [26]But Peter lifted him up, saying, "Stand up; I too am a man."
[27]And as he talked with him, he went in and found many persons gathered;
[28]and he said to them, "You yourselves know how unlawful it is for a Jew to
associate with or to visit any one of another nation; but God has shown me that

---

begins among the Gentiles? Through a devout man whose deeds made him worthy of such favour" (St John Chrysostom, *Hom. on Acts*, 22, 2).

Then the focus of the account shifts to Peter, who is given two instructions by the Holy Spirit—to eat the flesh of the animals shown to him (cf. vv. 13–18) and to go back with the messengers to meet Cornelius (cf. v. 20). Both instructions run contrary to Peter's normal Jewish practice, but he resists only one of them. His reaction (cf. v. 14) to the Lord's command is that of a good Jew who loves and keeps the divine law he has learned from infancy. He has always adhered to the rules about foods to be avoided etc. and has observed the Mosaic distinction between clean and unclean. However, Peter is docile to what the Holy Spirit tells him to do: therefore, although the vision puzzles him (cf. vv. 17, 19), he does not resist the order to travel with the people who have come looking for him. Once he reaches Cornelius' house, Peter realizes that God has been guiding his steps all the way (vv. 28–29). When he hears the centurion's explanation (cf. vv. 30–33), he grasps (v. 34) the full significance of what he heard Jesus say in his preaching, and

I should not call any man common or unclean. [29]So when I was sent for, I came without objection. I ask then why you sent for me."

[30]And Cornelius said, "Four days ago, about this hour, I was keeping the ninth hour of prayer in my house; and behold, a man stood before me in bright apparel, [31]saying, 'Cornelius, your prayer has been heard and your alms have been remembered before God. [32]Send therefore to Joppa and ask for Simon who is called Peter; he is lodging in the house of Simon, a tanner, by the seaside.' [33]So I sent for you at once, and you have been kind enough to come. Now therefore we are all here present in the sight of God, to hear all that you have been commanded by the Lord."

Peter preaches to Cornelius

[34]And Peter opened his mouth and said: "Truly I perceive that God shows no partiality, [35]but in every nation any one who fears him and does what is right is acceptable to him. [36]You know the word which he sent to Israel, preaching good news of peace by Jesus Christ (he is Lord of all), [37]the word which was proclaimed throughout all Judea, beginning from Galilee after the baptism which John preached: [38]how God anointed Jesus of Nazareth with the Holy Spirit and with power; how he went about doing good and healing all that were oppressed by the devil, for God was with him. [39]And we are witnesses to all that he did both in the country of the Jews and in Jerusalem. They put him to death by hanging him on a tree; [40]but God raised him on the third day and made him manifest; [41]not to all the people but to us who were chosen by God as witnesses, who ate and drank with him after he rose from the dead. [42]And he commanded us to preach to the people, and to testify that he is the one ordained by God to be judge of the living and the dead. [43]To him all the prophets bear witness that every one who believes in him receives forgiveness of sins through his name."

The baptism of Cornelius and his family

[44]While Peter was still saying this, the Holy Spirit fell on all who heard the word. [45]And the believers from among the circumcised who came with Peter

---

he realizes that, in the salvific plans of God, Jews and pagans are equal. This simple and important discovery required special divine intervention.

However, the action of the Holy Spirit goes much further than that of men. The angel had only told Cornelius to send for Peter and hear what he had to say (cf. vv. 5, 22, 33), and therefore Peter, in a concentrated speech, which gives a synthesis of the entire Gospel (vv. 37–43), preaches the truth of Christ Jesus. But at this point the Holy Spirit takes the initiative; manifesting himself in a way similar to that on the day of Pentecost (cf. v. 46), he steals a march on the apostle (cf. vv. 47–48); seeing this, Peter gives instructions for the first Gentiles to be baptized without the requirement of circumcision.

were amazed, because the gift of the Holy Spirit had been poured out even on
the Gentiles. 46For they heard them speaking in tongues and extolling God.
Then Peter declared, 47"Can any one forbid water for baptizing these people
who have received the Holy Spirit just as we have?" 48And he commanded
them to be baptized in the name of Jesus Christ. Then they asked him to
remain for some days.

In Jerusalem Peter justifies his conduct

11 1Now the apostles and the brethren who were in Judea heard that the
Gentiles also had received the word of God. 2So when Peter went up to
Jerusalem, the circumcision party criticized him, 3saying, "Why did you go to
uncircumcised men and eat with them?" 4But Peter began and explained to
them in order: 5"I was in the city of Joppa praying; and in a trance I saw a
vision, something descending, like a great sheet, let down from heaven by four
corners; and it came down to me. 6Looking at it closely I observed animals and
beasts of prey and reptiles and birds of the air. 7And I heard a voice saying to
me, 'Rise, Peter; kill and eat.' 8But I said, 'No, Lord; for nothing common or
unclean has ever entered my mouth.' 9But the voice answered a second time from
heaven, 'What God has cleansed you must not call common.' 10This happened
three times, and all was drawn up again into heaven. 11And that very moment
three men arrived at the house in which we were, sent to me from Caesarea.
12And the Spirit told me to go with them, making no distinction. These six
brethren also accompanied me, and we entered the man's house. 13And he told us
how he had seen the angel standing in this house and saying, 'Send to Joppa and
bring Simon called Peter; 14he will declare to you a message by which you will
be saved, you and all your household.' 15As I began to speak, the Holy Spirit fell
on them just as on us at the beginning. 16And I remembered the word of the Lord,
how he said, 'John baptized with water, but you shall be baptized with the Holy
Spirit.' 17If then God gave the same gift to them as he gave to us when we
believed in the Lord Jesus Christ, who was I that I could withstand God?" 18When
they heard this they were silenced. And they glorified God, saying, "Then to
the Gentiles also God has granted repentance unto life."

11:1–18 Peter's behaviour naturally perturbs the community of the circumcised. They criticise the apostle for sitting down to eat with uncircumcised people and for preaching the word of God to them (vv. 1, 3). In a long address, Peter explains that he has not acted on his own initiative; at every point all he did was to obey the Holy Spirit. The thing that is really new and important about the events narrated in the previous chapter is identified in vv. 15–16, where Peter establishes a link between what happened at the coming of the Holy Spirit at Pentecost (2:1ff) and his coming down on the Gentile converts (10:44–46) at Caesarea. This made it plain for all to see (cf. v. 18) that in order to become part of the Church one did not need first to become a member of the Jewish people by means of circumcision.

Beginning of the Church in Antioch

[19]Now those who were scattered because of the persecution that arose over
Stephen travelled as far as Phoenicia and Cyprus and Antioch, speaking the
word to none except Jews. [20]But there were some of them, men of Cyprus and
Cyrene, who on coming to Antioch spoke to the Greeks[i] also, preaching the Lord
Jesus. [21]And the hand of the Lord was with them, and a great number that
believed turned to the Lord. [22]News of this came to the ears of the church in
Jerusalem, and they sent Barnabas to Antioch. [23]When he came and saw the grace
of God, he was glad; and he exhorted them all to remain faithful to the Lord with
steadfast purpose; [24]for he was a good man, full of the Holy Spirit and of faith.
And a large company was added to the Lord. [25]So Barnabas went to Tarsus to
look for Saul; [26]and when he had found him, he brought him to Antioch. For a
whole year they met with[j] the church, and taught a large company of people; and
in Antioch the disciples were for the first time called Christians.

Antioch helps the Church in Judea

[27]Now in these days prophets came down from Jerusalem to Antioch. [28]And
one of them named Agabus stood up and foretold by the Spirit that there would
be a great famine over all the world; and this took place in the days of
Claudius. [29]And the disciples determined, every one according to his ability,
to send relief to the brethren who lived in Judea; [30]and they did so, sending it
to the elders by the hand of Barnabas and Saul.

11:19–30 This account links up with Acts 8:1–4, which describes how the Christians fled in different directions, an account of the persecution that followed the martyrdom of Stephen. We are now told about the spread of the Gospel to Antioch on the Orontes, the capital of the Roman province of Syria. Antioch was the first great city of the ancient world to hear the word of Jesus Christ. Along with Ephesus it was the most important city of the Empire, after Rome and Alexandria, with a population of around one hundred and fifty thousand, including a sizeable Jewish colony. In Antioch the Gospel was proclaimed not only to Jews and proselytes; preaching was addressed to all and sundry and was part of the normal everyday activity of the Hellenist Christians who had come to the city after the death of Stephen.

The Christian mission at Antioch played a key role in the spread of Christianity, because the centre of gravity of the Christian Church began to shift from Jerusalem to Antioch, which became the base for the evangelization of the pagan world. St Luke stresses the communion that existed between the two churches; the church of Jerusalem felt responsible for everything that happened in the mission-field, and the church of Antioch was the first to show consideration (cf. vv. 29–30) for the needs of the mother church.

Luke also records (v. 26) the origin of the name "Christians", a very appropriate description of the faithful: "Even though the holy apostles were our teachers and

i. Other ancient authorities read *Hellenists* **j.** Or *were guests of*

Persecution by Herod. Peter's arrest and miraculous deliverance

12 [1]About that time Herod the king laid violent hands upon some who
belonged to the church.* [2]He killed James the brother of John with the
sword; [3]and when he saw that it pleased the Jews, he proceeded to arrest Peter
also. This was during the days of Unleavened Bread. [4]And when he had seized
him, he put him in prison, and delivered him to four squads of soldiers to guard
him, intending after the Passover to bring him out to the people. [5]So Peter was
kept in prison; but earnest prayer for him was made to God by the church.
[6]The very night when Herod was about to bring him out, Peter was
sleeping between two soldiers, bound with two chains, and sentries before the
door were guarding the prison; [7]and behold, an angel of the Lord appeared,
and a light shone in the cell; and he struck Peter on the side and woke him,
saying, "Get up quickly." And the chains fell off his hands. [8]And the angel said
to him, "Dress yourself and put on your sandals." And he did so. And he said
to him, "Wrap your mantle around you and follow me." [9]And he went out and
followed him; he did not know that what was done by the angel was real, but

---

gave us the Gospel of the Saviour, we do not take our name from them; we are *Christians* because of Christ; on account of him we are given that name" (St Athanasius, *Or. 1 contra Arian.*, 2).

12:1–19 This Herod is the third prince of this name to appear in the New Testament. He was a grandson of Herod the Great (who built the new temple of Jerusalem and was responsible for the massacre of the Holy Innocents: cf. Mt 2:16) and a nephew of Herod Antipas, the tetrarch of Galilee at the time of our Lord's death. Known as Herod Agrippa I, he was a favourite of the emperor Caligula, who gradually increased his territory and allowed him to use the title of king. He was a sophisticated and diplomatic type of person, so bent on consolidating his power that he had become a master of intrigue and a clever opportunist. If the description given of Herod in vv. 1–4 is accurate, so too is the summary provided of the Church's attitude to the persecution and to Peter's imprisonment (cf. v. 5): "Notice the dispositions of the faithful towards their pastors. They don't cause a disturbance or rebel: they have recourse to prayer, which is the sure way to put things right. They don't say: we don't count, there is no point in our prayers for him (Peter). They prayed out of their love for him. And notice what their persecutors did without meaning to: they made some more resolute in trials, and others more zealous and more loving" (St John Chrysostom, *Hom. on Acts*, 26, 2).

The description of the miraculous release of Peter by an angel shows the loving care that God takes of his faithful (v. 11). This is the second instance of an angel liberating Peter from detention (cf. 5:19ff) and it bears out Church teaching about the mission of angels: "From infancy to death, human life is surrounded by their watchful care and intercession. 'Beside each believer stands an angel as protector

thought he was seeing a vision. [10]When they had passed the first and the
second guard, they came to the iron gate leading into the city. It opened to
them of its own accord, and they went out and passed on through one street;
and immediately the angel left him. [11]And Peter came to himself, and said,
"Now I am sure that the Lord has sent his angel and rescued me from the hand
of Herod and from all that the Jewish people were expecting."

[12]When he realized this, he went to the house of Mary, the mother of John
whose other name was Mark, where many were gathered together and were
praying. [13]And when he knocked at the door of the gateway, a maid named Rhoda
came to answer. [14]Recognizing Peter's voice, in her joy she did not open the gate
but ran in and told that Peter was standing at the gate. [15]They said to her, "You are
mad." But she insisted that it was so. They said, "It is his angel!" [16]But Peter
continued knocking; and when they opened, they saw him and were amazed.
[17]But motioning to them with his hand to be silent, he described to them how the
Lord had brought him out of the prison. And he said, "Tell this to James and to
the brethren." Then he departed and went to another place.

[18]Now when day came, there was no small stir among the soldiers over
what had become of Peter. [19]And when Herod had sought for him and could
not find him, he examined the sentries and ordered that they should be put to
death. Then he went down from Judea to Caesarea, and remained there.

Death of Herod

[20]Now Herod was angry with the people of Tyre and Sidon; and they came to
him in a body, and having persuaded Blastus, the king's chamberlain, they
asked for peace, because their country depended on the king's country for
food. [21]On an appointed day Herod put on his royal robes, took his seat upon

---

and shepherd leading him to life' (St Basil, *Adv. Eunomium*, 3,1)" (*CCC*, 336). But the account not only tells us about this protection: we also see that the early Christians were fully aware of the angels' role. "Drink at the clear fountain of the Acts of the Apostles. In the twelfth chapter, Peter is freed from prison by the ministry of angels and comes to the house of Mark's mother. Those inside don't want to believe the servant girl when she tells them Peter is at the door. '*Angelus eius est!*'—'It's his angel!' they say. See on what intimate terms the early Christians were with their guardian angels. And what about you?" (Bl. J. Escrivá, *The Way*, 570).

12:20–23 Herod Agrippa I must have died at Caesarea in the year 44 during the games in honour of the emperor Claudius. Luke's brief description agrees with that of Josephus. "When the king made his way to the theatre on the morning of the second day," the Jewish historian tells us, "the rays of sun struck his silver clothes and made them shine with such brilliance that the crowd acclaimed him and declared him to be a god saying, "Look with favour on us. Until now we have seen

the throne, and made an oration to them. 22And the people shouted, "The voice
of a god, and not of man!" 23Immediately an angel of the Lord smote him,
because he did not give God the glory; and he was eaten by worms and died.
24But the word of God grew and multiplied.

Barnabas and Paul return

25And Barnabas and Saul returned from[k] Jerusalem when they had fulfilled
their mission, bringing with them John whose other name was Mark.

PART THREE: THE SPREAD OF THE CHURCH AMONG THE GENTILES. MISSIONARY JOURNEYS OF ST PAUL

8. ST PAUL'S FIRST APOSTOLIC JOURNEY

Paul and Barnabas are sent on a mission

13 1Now in the church at Antioch there were prophets and teachers,
Barnabas, Symeon who was called Niger, Lucius of Cyrene, Manaen a
member of the court of Herod the tetrarch, and Saul. 2While they were

---

you only as a man, but from now on we will venerate you as a being greater than mortal nature'" (*Ant.*, 19, 344–345). The king accepted the blasphemous flattery of the crowd. But no sooner did he than he was smitten by terrible pains and died within five days. The painful and unexpected death of the king who had persecuted the Church is reminiscent of the death of Antiochus IV Ephiphanes, another declared enemy of God's elect and of the divine Law: "The all-seeing God, the God of Israel, struck him an incurable and unseen blow" (2 Mac 9:5).

13:1–20:38 □ □ We now get an account about how salvation reaches out from Jerusalem to the ends of the earth. St Paul is the man God chooses for this mission (cf. 9:15). This third part of the book describes his apostolic journeys, which extend the preaching of the Gospel and establish many new communities. From this point onwards, we should note, the missionary work of the church of Antioch becomes particularly important; however, the book of the Acts always makes a point of stressing that every new impulse to evangelization also involves Jerusalem (9:26; 15:2; 20:16; 21:15).

13:1–14:28 □ After a brief description of the community at Antioch (vv. 1–3), the account focuses on the first apostolic journey of St Paul and St Barnabas, in Asia Minor. They left Antioch in the spring of the year 45 and arrived back about four

k. Other ancient authorities read *to*

worshipping the Lord and fasting, the Holy Spirit said, "Set apart for me
Barnabas and Saul for the work to which I have called them." 3Then after
fasting and praying they laid their hands on them and sent them off.

Paul and Barnabas in Cyprus

4So, being sent out by the Holy Spirit, they went down to Seleucia; and from
there they sailed to Cyprus. 5When they arrived at Salamis, they proclaimed
the word of God in the synagogues of the Jews. And they had John to assist
them. 6When they had gone through the whole island as far as Paphos, they
came upon a certain magician, a Jewish false prophet, named Bar-Jesus. 7He
was with the proconsul, Sergius Paulus, a man of intelligence, who summoned
Barnabas and Saul and sought to hear the word of God. 8But Elymas the
magician (for that is the meaning of his name) withstood them, seeking to turn
away the proconsul from the faith. 9But Saul, who is also called Paul, filled
with the Holy Spirit, looked intently at him 10and said, "You son of the devil,
you enemy of all righteousness, full of all deceit and villainy, will you not stop
making crooked the straight paths of the Lord? 11And now, behold, the hand
of the Lord is upon you, and you shall be blind and unable to see the sun for a
time." Immediately mist and darkness fell upon him and he went about seeking
people to lead him by the hand. 12Then the proconsul believed, when he saw
what had occurred, for he was astonished at the teaching of the Lord.

---

years later. In the course of their journey they visited Cyprus and much of the region of Cilicia, Pamphylia, Lycaonia and Pisidia, preaching to Jews and Gentiles and founding communities in the places where they stopped. They will later return to these same places to confirm the Christians in the faith.

13:1–3 From this point onwards Luke's account centres on the church of Antioch and the spread of the apostolic message into the pagan world. The Antiochene church was a flourishing community with an organization structure similar to that of the Jerusalem church, yet different in some ways. It had ordained ministers who were responsible for its governance and who preached the Gospel and administered the sacraments (cf. v. 2). Alongside them were prophets and teachers, who also had a special role in the community. In the primitive Christian churches, "teachers" were disciples well versed in Holy Scripture who were given charge of catechesis. A second-century document describes the ideal Christian teacher: "I do not speak of passing things nor do I seek what is new, but as a disciple, one of the apostles, I have become a teacher of peoples. I do nothing more than pass on what was given to me to those who have been made disciples worthy of the truth" (Anon., *Letter to Diognetus*, 11, 1).

13:4–14 We are told in passing that Saul has changed his name and is now also known as Paul (v. 9). This is the name we will find from now on in the New

Paul and Barnabas cross into Asia Minor

[13]Now Paul and his company set sail from Paphos, and came to Perga in Pamphylia. And John left them and returned to Jerusalem; [14]but they passed on from Perga and came to Antioch of Pisidia.

Preaching in the synagogue of Antioch of Pisidia

And on the sabbath day they went into the synagogue and sat down. [15]After the reading of the law and the prophets, the rulers of the synagogue sent to them, saying, "Brethren, if you have any word of exhortation for the people, say it." [16]So Paul stood up, and motioning with his hand said:*

"Men of Israel, and you that fear God, listen. [17]The God of this people Israel chose our fathers and made the people great during their stay in the land of Egypt, and with uplifted arm he led them out of it. [18]And for about forty years he bore with[m] them in the wilderness. [19]And when he had destroyed seven nations in the land of Canaan, he gave them their land as an inheritance, for about four hundred and fifty years. [20]And after that he gave them judges until Samuel the prophet. [21]Then they asked for a king; and God gave them Saul the son of Kish, a man of the tribe of Benjamin, for forty years. [22]And when he had removed him, he raised up David to be their king; of whom he testified and said, 'I have found in David the son of Jesse a man after my heart, who will do all my will.' [23]Of this man's posterity God has brought to Israel

---

Testament. Paul's treatment of Bar-Jesus/Elymas is one of the very few punitive miracles in the New Testament; in fact, commentators point out that this punishment was designed as a corrective and it lasted only for a time: "Paul chooses to convert him by means of a miracle similar to that by which he himself was converted. The word 'for a time' is the word not of one who punishes but of one who converts" (St John Chrysostom, *Hom. on Acts,* 28, 1).

13:15–43 Paul's address in the synagogue of Antioch in Pisidia is an excellent example of his way of presenting the Gospel to a mixed congregation of Jews and proselytes. He gives a general outline of salvation history leading up to Jesus, the long-awaited Messiah in whom all the strands of this history and God's promises converge. The stages prior to Jesus Christ, including that of John the Baptist, are just points on a route. Earlier, provisional elements must now, in Christ, give way to a new and definitive situation.

The address contains the principal themes of apostolic preaching—God's saving initiative in the history of Israel (vv. 17–22); reference to the Precursor (vv. 24–25); proclamation of the Gospel or *kerygma* in the proper sense (vv. 26b-3la); mention of Jerusalem (v. 3lb); arguments from Holy Scripture (vv. 33–37) complementing apostolic teaching and tradition (vv. 38–39); and a final exhortation, eschatological in character, that is, announcing the future (vv. 40–41). In many

m. Other ancient authorities read *cared for* (Deut 1:31) **13:22** Ps 89:20; 1 Sam 13:14; Is 44:28.

a Saviour, Jesus, as he promised. [24]Before his coming John had preached a
baptism of repentance to all the people of Israel. [25]And as John was finishing
his course, he said, 'What do you suppose that I am? I am not he. No, but after
me one is coming, the sandals of whose feet I am not worthy to untie.'

[26]"Brethren, sons of the family of Abraham, and those among you that fear
God, to us has been sent the message of this salvation. [27]For those who live in
Jerusalem and their rulers, because they did not recognize him nor understand
the utterances of the prophets which are read every sabbath, fulfilled these by
condemning him. [28]Though they could charge him with nothing deserving
death, yet they asked Pilate to have him killed. [29]And when they had fulfilled
all that was written of him, they took him down from the tree, and laid him in
a tomb. [30]But God raised him from the dead; [31]and for many days he appeared
to those who came up with him from Galilee to Jerusalem, who are now his
witnesses to the people. [32]And we bring you the good news that what God
promised to the fathers, [33]this he has fulfilled to us their children by raising
Jesus; as also it is written in the second psalm,

> 'Thou art my Son,
> today I have begotten thee.'

[34]And as for the fact that he raised him from the dead, no more to return to
corruption, he spoke in this way,

> 'I will give you the holy and sure blessings of David.'

[35]Therefore he says also in another psalm,

> 'Thou wilt not let thy Holy One see corruption.'

[36]For David, after he had served the counsel of God in his own generation, fell
asleep, and was laid with his fathers, and saw corruption; [37]but he whom God
raised up saw no corruption. [38]Let it be known to you therefore, brethren, that
through this man forgiveness of sins is proclaimed to you, [39]and by him every
one that believes is freed from everything from which you could not be freed
by the law of Moses. [40]Beware, therefore, lest there come upon you what is
said in the prophets:

> [41]'Behold, you scoffers, and wonder, and perish;
> for I do a deed in your days,
> a deed you will never believe, if one declares it to you.'"

[42]As they went out, the people begged that these things might be told them
the next sabbath. [43]And when the meeting of the synagogue broke up, many
Jews and devout converts to Judaism followed Paul and Barnabas, who spoke
to them and urged them to continue in the grace of God.

---

respects this address is like those of St Peter (cf. 2; 14ff; 3:12ff), especially where it proclaims Jesus as Messiah and in its many quotations from Scripture, chosen to show that the decisive event of the resurrection confirms Christ's divinity.

13:33 Ps 2:7. **13:34** Is 55:3. **13:35** Ps 16:10. **13:41** Hab 1:5.

Paul and Barnabas preach to the pagans

44The next sabbath almost the whole city gathered together to hear the word of
God. 45But when the Jews saw the multitudes, they were filled with jealousy,
and contradicted what was spoken by Paul, and reviled him. 46And Paul and
Barnabas spoke out boldly, saying, "It was necessary that the word of God
should be spoken first to you. Since you thrust it from you, and judge
yourselves unworthy of eternal life, behold, we turn to the Gentiles. 47For so
the Lord has commanded us, saying,

'I have set you to be a light for the Gentiles,
that you may bring salvation to the uttermost parts of the earth.'"

48And when the Gentiles heard this, they were glad and glorified the word
of God; and as many as were ordained to eternal life believed. 49And the word
of the Lord spread throughout all the region. 50But the Jews incited the devout
women of high standing and the leading men of the city, and stirred up
persecution against Paul and Barnabas, and drove them out of their district.
51But they shook off the dust from their feet against them, and went to Icon-
ium. 52And the disciples were filled with joy and with the Holy Spirit.

Iconium evangelized. Persecution

14 1Now at Iconium they entered together into the Jewish synagogue, and
so spoke that a great company believed, both of Jews and of Greeks.
2But the unbelieving Jews stirred up the Gentiles and poisoned their minds
against the brethren. 3So they remained for a long time, speaking boldly for the
Lord, who bore witness to the word of his grace, granting signs and wonders

---

13:44–52 St Paul was hoping, maybe, that Christianity would flourish on the soil of Judaism, so that the entire synagogue would peacefully and religiously move into the Gospel—its natural home and fulfilment according to God's plans. His experience proved otherwise: he encountered the disconcerting mystery of the infidelity of a large part of the chosen people, his own people (cf. Rom 9:1–11:36). However, the evangelization of the pagan world was not a consequence of Jewish rejection of the Word; it stemmed from the universal nature of Christianity, which offers all men the only grace that brings salvation; it perfects the Mosaic Law and reaches out beyond the ethnic and geographical confines of Judaism.

14:1–18 Luke here describes Paul and Barnabas as "apostles" (v. 14). Even though Paul is not one of the group of the Twelve, for whom he normally reserves the name of "apostles", he is regarded, and regards himself, as an apostle by virtue of his unique vocation (cf. 1 Cor 15:9; 2 Cor 11:5) and his tireless preaching to the Gentiles. When the writings of the Fathers mention "the Apostle" without being any more specific than that, they mean St Paul, because he is the apostle most quoted and commented on, due to his many letters.

13:47 Is 49:6.

to be done by their hands. [4]But the people of the city were divided; some sided
with the Jews, and some with the apostles. [5]When an attempt was made by
both Gentiles and Jews, with their rulers, to molest them and to stone them,
[6]they learned of it and fled to Lystra and Derbe, cities of Lycaonia, and to the
surrounding country; [7]and there they preached the gospel.

Curing of a cripple at Lystra

[8]Now at Lystra there was a man sitting, who could not use his feet; he was a
cripple from birth, who had never walked. [9]He listened to Paul speaking; and
Paul, looking intently at him and seeing that he had faith to be made well, [10]said
in a loud voice, "Stand upright on your feet." And he sprang up and walked.
[11]And when the crowds saw what Paul had done, they lifted up their voices,
saying in Lycaonian, "The gods have come down to us in the likeness of men!"
[12]Barnabas they called Zeus, and Paul, because he was the chief speaker, they
called Hermes. [13]And the priest of Zeus, whose temple was in front of the city,
brought oxen and garlands to the gates and wanted to offer sacrifice with the
people. [14]But when the apostles Barnabas and Paul heard of it, they tore their
garments and rushed out among the multitude, crying, [15]"Men, why are you
doing this? We also are men, of like nature with you, and bring you good news,
that you should turn from these vain things to a living God who made the heaven
and the earth and the sea and all that is in them. [16]In past generations he allowed
all the nations to walk in their own ways; [17]yet he did not leave himself without
witness, for he did good and gave you from heaven rains and fruitful seasons,
satisfying your hearts with food and gladness." [18]With these words they scarcely
restrained the people from offering sacrifice to them.

Paul is stoned

[19]But Jews came there from Antioch and Iconium; and having persuaded the
people, they stoned Paul and dragged him out of the city, supposing that he

---

In this very summarized account of activity in Iconium (v. 17) we see that the apostolate's career absolutely bears out what was announced in the Gospel—signs accompanying preaching (v. 3; cf. Mk 16:15–18), Jesus as a sign of contradiction (v. 4; cf. Lk 2:34), etc.

The account of Paul's activity at Lystra (vv. 8–18) has features similar to Peter's activity. Peter, too, cured a lame man (3:1–10) and Peter, like Paul now (v. 15), had to correct Cornelius by telling him he was a mere man. The Fathers draw attention to this parallel: "Just as the lame man cured by Peter and John at the gate of the temple represents the Jewish people, the cripple cured at Lycaonia stands for all the Gentile peoples who, cut off from the Law and the temple, are gathered together by Paul's preaching" (St Bede, *Sup. Act. exp.*, in loc.).

14:19–28 Luke, following Pauline teaching (cf. v. 22), points out here that the Word of God is making progress, but he does not disguise the fact that a preacher's

14:15 Ex 20:11; Ps 146:6.

was dead. [20]But when the disciples gathered about him, he rose up and entered
the city; and on the next day he went on with Barnabas to Derbe.

Return journey to Antioch

[21]When they had preached the gospel to that city and had made many disciples,
they returned to Lystra and to Iconium and to Antioch, [22]strengthening the
souls of the disciples, exhorting them to continue in the faith, and saying that
through many tribulations we must enter the kingdom of God. [23]And when
they had appointed elders for them in every church, with prayer and fasting,
they committed them to the Lord in whom they believed.

[24]Then they passed through Pisidia, and came to Pamphylia. [25]And when
they had spoken the word in Perga, they went down to Attalia; [26]and from
there they sailed to Antioch, where they had been commended to the grace of
God for the work which they had fulfilled. [27]And when they arrived, they
gathered the church together and declared all that God had done with them,
and how he had opened a door of faith to the Gentiles. [28]And they remained no
little time with the disciples.

9. THE COUNCIL OF JERUSALEM

Dissension at Antioch; Judaizers

15 [1]But some men came down from Judea and were teaching the brethren,
"Unless you are circumcised according to the custom of Moses, you

---

way is a way of the cross: "Cross, toil, tribulation: such will be your lot as long as you live. That was the way Christ followed, and the disciple is not above his Master" (Bl. J. Escrivá, *The Way*, 699).

15:1–35 □These verses could be described as the centre of the book of the Acts, not only on account of their position but also because they report the episode that most explains the spread of the Gospel throughout the world. The passage has to do with the conversion of Cornelius, a pagan; all the implications of this event are spelt out with the help of the Holy Spirit. St Luke, in his typically tidy way, describes the cause of the disagreement (vv. 1–5), the way the meeting in Jerusalem develops (vv. 6–29) and its consequences for the Church (vv. 30–35).

15:1–5 Some Christians with a Pharisee background—"certain men [who] came from James" (Gal 2:12)—arriving in Antioch assert categorically that salvation is impossible unless a person is circumcised and practises the Law of Moses. They accept (cf. 11:18) that Gentile converts can be baptized and become part of the Church; they do not properly understand the new economy of the Gospel; they think that it is still necessary for people to become Jews first and keep to all the cannot be saved." [2]And when Paul and Barnabas had no small dissension and debate with them, Paul and Barnabas and some of the others were appointed to go up to Jerusalem to the apostles and the elders about this question.

Paul and Barnabas go to Jerusalem

[3]So, being sent on their way by the church, they passed through both Phoenicia and Samaria, reporting the conversion of the Gentiles, and they gave great joy to all the brethren. [4]When they came to Jerusalem, they were welcomed by the church and the apostles and the elders, and they declared all that God had done with them. [5]But some believers who belonged to the party of the Pharisees rose up, and said, "It is necessary to circumcise them, and to charge them to keep the law of Moses."

Peter's address to the council

[6]The apostles and the elders were gathered together to consider this matter. [7]And after there had been much debate, Peter rose and said to them, "Brethren, you know that in the early days God made choice among you, that by my mouth the Gentiles should hear the word of the gospel and believe.[8]And God who knows the heart bore witness to them, giving them the Holy Spirit just as he did to us; [9]and he made no distinction between us and them, but cleansed their hearts by faith. [10]Now therefore why do you make trial of God by putting a yoke upon the neck of the disciples which neither our fathers nor we have been able to bear? [11]But we believe that we shall be saved through the grace of the Lord Jesus, just as they will."

Mosaic precepts and rites. These claims not only unsettle the Christians of Antioch but they also compromise the spread of the Christian religion. The need arises, therefore, for an appeal to the apostles and elders in Jerusalem, who are in charge of the Church.

15:6–11 Luke records three important events connected with the question at issue—Peter's address (vv. 7–11), that of James (vv. 13–21), and the decree sent to the churches (vv. 23–29). Peter's contribution is brief but decisive. Drawing on what God had allowed him to see in connexion with the baptism of Cornelius (cf. chap. 10), he sums up a lengthy debate (v. 7) and offers a solution which coincides with Paul and Barnabas' view of the matter: it is grace and not the Law that saves, and therefore circumcision and the Law itself have been superseded by faith in Jesus Christ (v. 11): "No one can become holy after sin without Christ […]. As the fathers of old [the patriarchs of the Old Testament] were saved by their faith in the Christ who was to come, we too are saved by our faith in Christ who was born and suffered [for us]" (*Summa theol.*, 3, 61, 3 and 4).

James' speech

12And all the assembly kept silence; and they listened to Barnabas and Paul as
they related what signs and wonders God had done through them among the
Gentiles. 13After they finished speaking, James replied, "Brethren, listen to me.
14Symeon has related how God first visited the Gentiles, to take out of them
a people for his name. 15And with this the words of the prophets agree, as it is
written,

16'After this I will return,
And I will rebuild the dwelling of David, which has fallen;
I will rebuild its ruins,
and I will set it up,
17that the rest of men may seek the Lord,
and all the Gentiles who are called by my name,
18says the Lord, who has made these things known from of old.'

19Therefore my judgment is that we should not trouble those of the Gentiles
who turn to God, 20but should write to them to abstain from the pollutions of
idols and from unchastity and from what is strangled[n] and from blood. 21For
from early generations Moses has had in every city those who preach him, for
he is read every sabbath in the synagogues."

The council's decision

22Then it seemed good to the apostles and the elders, with the whole church,
to choose men from among them and send them to Antioch with Paul and
Barnabas. They sent Judas called Barsabbas, and Silas, leading men among the

---

15:12–21 Using proofs from Scripture, James goes along with the points made by Peter: God has desired to make himself a new people from among all the nations. However, he proposes that a small number of ritual precepts in the Old Testament (cf. Lev 17:7ff, 18:6ff) be adhered to in order not to scandalize Jews living in the Diaspora (v. 21). Later on, apropos of the question of meat sacrificed to idols (cf. 1 Col 8: 10) Paul will proclaim that Christians can do as they wish, but he asks them to take into account the susceptibilities of the weak.

15:22–29 The apostolic decree summarizes the whole question—the source of the problem and its solution. What is very interesting is the fact that the Holy Spirit is associated with the apostles' decision (v. 28). A Spanish theologian of the sixteenth century comments on this as follows: "We too should follow the path that the Apostle Paul saw as the best one for settling all questions about the doctrine of the faith [...]. The Gentiles could demand satisfaction from the council of Jerusalem because it seemed to deprive them of the freedom conferred on them by Jesus Christ. Their freedom was denied when the council imposed particular ceremonies

n. Other early authorities omit *and from what is strangled* **15:16** Jer 12:15. **15:16–17** Amos 9:11–12. **15:18** Is 45:21.

brethren, [23]with the following letter: "The brethren, both the apostles and the
elders, to the brethren who are of the Gentiles in Antioch and Syria and Cilicia,
greeting. [24]Since we have heard that some persons from us have troubled you
with words, unsettling your minds, although we gave them no instructions, [25]it
has seemed good to us in assembly to choose men and send them to you with
our beloved Barnabas and Paul, [26]men who have risked their lives for the sake
of our Lord Jesus Christ. [27]We have therefore sent Judas and Silas, who
themselves will tell you the same things by word of mouth. [28]For it has seemed
good to the Holy Spirit and to us to lay upon you no greater burden than these
necessary things: [29]that you abstain from what has been sacrificed to idols and
from blood and from what is strangled[n] and from unchastity. If you keep
yourselves from these, you will do well. Farewell."

Reception of the council's decree

[30]So when they were sent off, they went down to Antioch; and having gathered
the congregation together, they delivered the letter. [31]And when they read it,
they rejoiced at the exhortation. [32]And Judas and Silas, who were themselves
prophets, exhorted the brethren with many words and strengthened them.
[33]And after they had spent some time, they were sent off in peace by the
brethren to those who had sent them.[o] [35]But Paul and Barnabas remained in
Antioch, teaching and preaching the word of the Lord, with many others also.

---

on his disciples as necessary conditions, where no such necessity existed since faith alone was the basis of salvation. Christians of Jewish origin did not complain about the decision of the council because they could point to some passages of Holy Scripture that seemed to suggest that circumcision was necessary for salvation. A teaching valid for all time is given to us by the example of the respect shown to the council by all concerned: our unshakeable faith rests on the authority of the synods presided over by Peter and his legitimate successors. That is how it seems, they say, to the Holy Spirit and to ourselves. The decision of the council conforms itself exactly to the work of the Holy Spirit" (Melchor Cano, *De locis*, 5, 4).

15:30–35 Paul and Barnabas, accompanied by Judas and Silas (15:22, 27, 32), return to Antioch to reassure the community and give them the apostles' letter. Very soon after this they will set out to visit places evangelized during the first apostolic journey (15:39–41) to tell them what has happened. Some manuscripts add (v. 34): "But Silas decided to stay there, so that Judas went back to Jerusalem on his own."

n. Other early authorities omit *and from what is strangled* **o.** Other ancient authorities insert verse 34, *But it seemed good to Silas to remain there*

10. ST PAUL'S SECOND APOSTOLIC JOURNEY

Silas, Paul's new companion

36And after some days Paul said to Barnabas, "Come, let us return and visit the
brethren in every city where we proclaimed the word of the Lord, and see how
they are." 37And Barnabas wanted to take with them John called Mark. 38But
Paul thought best not to take with them one who had withdrawn from them in
Pamphylia, and had not gone with them to the work. 39And there arose a sharp
contention, so that they separated from each other; Barnabas took Mark with
him and sailed away to Cyprus, 40but Paul chose Silas and departed, being
commended by the brethren to the grace of the Lord. 41And he went through
Syria and Cilicia, strengthening the churches.

15:36–18:22 □ St Paul's second journey starts at this point. As in the previous one, Paul starts out from Antioch and returns there—three years later, towards the spring of 53. Luke's narrative takes up almost three chapters, bringing us up to 18:23, at which point the third apostolic journey starts.

Paul and Silas travel through Syria and Cilicia (where Paul grew up) to Derbe and Lystra, where Timothy joins them. They cross Asia Minor (a very extensive province) and reach Troas (16:8), where they take ship for Macedonia (16:10). After a crossing of 250 kms (150 miles), they reach Neapolis, and from there they sail to Philippi, a Roman colony in which the events reported in chapter 16 occur. From there they go on to Thessalonica (17:1), the seat of the governor of the Roman province of Macedonia. A riot causes them to move on to Beroea (17:10), but further attacks by Jews from Thessalonica force Paul to leave in a hurry for Athens (17:14). The book of the Acts records the famous speech in the Areopagus that Paul made during this visit. From here he moves on quickly to Corinth (18:11), where he spends quite an amount of time (perhaps eighteen months) and works very hard in his ministry (18:18). Corinth is his embarkation point for his return journey to Antioch, though he makes brief stops at Ephesus (18:19) and Caesarea (18:22).

15:36–41 The journey now begins, although Paul and Barnabas part company because of a disagreement over Mark. But in God's plans, it is all for the best: "Different people have different gifts, and that difference is itself a gift [...]. Bear in mind that there is nothing wrong in their going separate ways, if that helped to evangelize all the Gentiles. It was in fact a good thing. If they take different roads in order to teach and make converts, there is nothing wrong about that. We should focus not on their differences but on what unites them [...]. If only all our separations were motivated by eagerness to preach" (St John Chrysostom, *Hom. on Acts*, 34, 1–2).

Timothy joins Paul

16 [1]And he came also to Derbe and to Lystra. A disciple was there, named
Timothy, the son of a Jewish woman who was a believer; but his father
was a Greek. [2]He was well spoken of by the brethren at Lystra and Iconium.
[3]Paul wanted Timothy to accompany him; and he took him and circumcised
him because of the Jews that were in those places, for they all knew that his
father was a Greek.

A tour of the churches of Asia Minor

[4]As they went on their way through the cities, they delivered to them for
observance the decisions which had been reached by the apostles and elders
who were at Jerusalem. [5]So the churches were strengthened in the faith, and
they increased in numbers daily.

[6]And they went through the region of Phrygia and Galatia, having been
forbidden by the Holy Spirit to speak the word in Asia. [7]And when they had
come opposite Mysia, they attempted to go into Bithynia, but the Spirit of
Jesus did not allow them; [8]so, passing by Mysia, they went down to Troas.
[9]And a vision appeared to Paul in the night: a man of Macedonia was standing

---

16:1–10 To accompany him, St Paul now chooses Timothy, a young man who was later to give him much help in his apostolate (cf. 17:14ff, 18:5; 19:22; 20:4; etc.). Timothy's mother, Eunice, and his grandmother Lois (cf. 2 Tim 1:5) were Christians, and Timothy had received the faith from them. As St Luke explains (cf. v. 3), Paul circumcised Timothy, for reasons of pastoral prudence: "He took Timothy and circumcised him. Paul did not act without thinking; he took everything into account so as to act prudently. Timothy had undertaken to preach the Gospel to Jews everywhere; so, to ensure that his words did not lose their value because he was not circumcised, Paul decided that Timothy should undergo circumcision. He did not act in this way to uphold the rite of circumcision, which he had already argued should be abandoned, but rather to protect the preaching of the Gospel" (St Ephrem, *Cat. arm. sup. Act.*, in loc.).

No sooner do they start evangelizing than the Holy Spirit, here also called "the Spirit of Jesus", acts as their guide: "There is hardly a page in the Acts of the Apostles where we fail to read about him and the action by which he guides, directs and enlivens the life and work of the early Christian community. It is he who inspires the preaching of St Peter (cf. 4.8), who strengthens the faith of the disciples (cf. 4:31), who confirms with his presence the calling of the Gentiles (cf.10: 44–47), who sends Saul and Barnabas to the distant lands where they will open new paths for the teaching of Jesus (cf. 13:2–4). In a word, his presence and doctrine are everywhere" (Bl. J. Escrivá, *Hom.*, 1, 127).

In v. 10 Luke changes to the first person plural, to indicate that he was Paul's companion on this journey (cf. 16:10–17; 20:5–25; 21:1–18, 27:1–28:16).

beseeching him and saying, "Come over to Macedonia and help us."
10And
when he had seen the vision, immediately we sought to go on into Macedonia, concluding that God had called us to preach the gospel to them.*

Macedonia

11Setting sail therefore from Troas we made a direct voyage to Samothrace,
and the following day to Neapolis,
12and from there to Philippi, which is the
leading city of the district[x] of Macedonia, and a Roman colony.

The conversion of Lydia

We remained in this city some days;
13and on the sabbath day we went outside
the gate to the riverside, where we supposed there was a place of prayer;* and
we sat down and spoke to the women who had come together.
14One who
heard us was a woman named Lydia, from the city of Thyatira, a seller of
purple goods, who was a worshipper of God. The Lord opened her heart to
give heed to what was said by Paul.
15And when she was baptized, with her
household, she besought us, saying, "If you have judged me to be faithful to
the Lord, come to my house and stay." And she prevailed upon us.

Curing of a possessed girl. Imprisonment of Paul

16As we were going to the place of prayer, we were met by a slave girl who
had a spirit of divination and brought her owners much gain by soothsaying.
17She followed Paul and us, crying, "These men are servants of the Most High
God, who proclaim to you the way of salvation."
18And this she did for many
days. But Paul was annoyed, and turned and said to the spirit, "I charge you in
the name of Jesus Christ to come out of her." And it came out that very hour.

16:11–15 In this moving account of the conversion of Lydia we see the interaction of God's gift of vocation and human gratefulness. It is God who opens Lydia's heart (v. 14), for "nobody can give his assent to the preaching of the gospel in a truly salvific way, unless he acts under the light and inspiration of the Holy Spirit, who gives to all the strength to affirm and believe the truth" (Vatican I, *Dei Filius*, 3). But then Lydia shows her gratitude in deeds: "Look at Lydia's wisdom. See how humbly and gently she addresses the apostles: 'If you have judged me to be faithful to the Lord.' […] Notice how faith yields its fruit in her, and how she sees her calling as something priceless" (St John Chrysostom, *Hom. on Acts*, 35, 1).

16:16–24 In Greek mythology Python was a serpent which uttered the Delphic oracles; hence *spiritus pythonis*, "a spirit of divination" (v. 16), which the slave girl is said to have. St Paul judges that the devil is at work in her—and therefore casts him out: "The Apostles did not wish to receive the honour and praise of the evil spirit, just as our Lord rejected the demon who proclaimed him among the Jews"

x. The Greek text is uncertain

19 But when her owners saw that their hope of gain was gone, they seized
Paul and Silas and dragged them into the market place before the rulers; 20 and
when they had brought them to the magistrates they said, "These men are Jews
and they are disturbing our city. 21 They advocate customs which it is not lawful
for us Romans to accept or practise." 22 The crowd joined in attacking them; and
the magistrates tore the garments off them and gave orders to beat them with rods.
23 And when they had inflicted many blows upon them, they threw them into
prison, charging the jailer to keep them safely. 24 Having received this charge,
he put them into the inner prison and fastened their feet in the stocks.

The Baptism of the jailer

25 But about midnight Paul and Silas were praying and singing hymns to God,
and the prisoners were listening to them, 26 and suddenly there was a great earth-
quake, so that the foundations of the prison were shaken; and immediately all
the doors were opened and every one's fetters were unfastened. 27 When the
jailer woke and saw that the prison doors were open, he drew his sword and
was about to kill himself, supposing that the prisoners had escaped. 28 But Paul
cried with a loud voice, "Do not harm yourself, for we are all here." 29 And he
called for lights and rushed in, and trembling with fear he fell down before
Paul and Silas, 30 and brought them out and said, "Men, what must I do to be
saved?" 31 And they said, "Believe in the Lord Jesus, and you will be saved,

---

(St Ephrem, *Cat. arm. sup. Act.*, in loc.). This incident marks the first time Paul comes into conflict with non-Jews. But their reaction does not take the form of a riot, as happened elsewhere in Asia Minor (13:50; 14:5, 19): instead they bring a civil charge before local magistrates. The authorities seem to over-react (cf. vv. 22–24). Maybe that explains why St Paul later asks for a form of apology (cf. 16:35–40).

16:25–34 "The devotion and strength which fired the hearts of the apostles was expressed in prayer, and they even sang hymns in the prison itself. Their praise moved the earth, shook the foundations of the prison, opened the doors, and, in the end, set the captives free. In the same way, each member of the faithful who rejoices in all things, when he meets temptations, rejoices still in his own weakness, so that the power of Christ will live in him. And when he has done this, he praises God with hymns, just as Paul and Silas did in the darkness of the prison, and he sings with the Psalmist, 'You are my refuge and my joy in the troubles that surround me'!" (St Bede, *Sup. Act. exp.*, in loc.).

As elsewhere in the New Testament (16:5; 18:8; 1 Cor 1: 16), there is reference here to an entire household being baptized. The Church cites this fact in her pastoral practice: "The practice of infant Baptism is an immemorial tradition of the Church. There is explicit testimony to this practice from the second century on, you and your household." [32]And they spoke the word of the Lord to him and to all that were in his house. [33]And he took them the same hour of the night, and washed their wounds, and he was baptized at once with all his family. [34]Then he brought them up into his house, and set food before them; and he rejoiced with all his household that he had believed in God.

Release from jail and departure from Philippi

[35]But when it was day, the magistrates sent the police, saying, "Let those men go." [36]And the jailer reported the words to Paul, saying, "The magistrates have sent to let you go; now therefore come out and go in peace." [37]But Paul said to them, "They have beaten us publicly, uncondemned, men who are Roman citizens, and have thrown us into prison; and do they now cast us out secretly? No! let them come themselves and take us out." [38]The police reported these words to the magistrates, and they were afraid when they heard that they were Roman citizens; [39]so they came and apologized to them. And they took them out and asked them to leave the city. [40]So they went out of the prison, and visited Lydia; and when they had seen the brethren, they exhorted them and departed.

Difficulties with Jews in Thessalonica

17 [1]Now when they had passed through Amphipolis and Apollonia, they came to Thessalonica, where there was a synagogue of the Jews. [2]And Paul went in, as was his custom, and for three weeks[p] he argued with them from the scriptures, [3]explaining and proving that it was necessary for the Christ to suffer and to rise from the dead, and saying, "This Jesus, whom I proclaim to you, is the Christ." [4]And some of them were persuaded, and joined Paul and Silas; as did a great many of the devout Greeks and not a few of the leading

---

and it is quite possible that, from the beginning of the apostolic preaching, when whole 'households' received Baptism, infants may also have been baptized" (*CCC*, 1252).

16:35–40 Paul's decision to let it be known that he is a Roman citizen, and to claim his rights as such, shows that there is no justification for Christians' renouncing their secular status.

17:1–9 Thessalonica was the seat of the Roman governor of the province of Macedonia; it was almost 150 kilometres (90 miles) from Philippi. It was founded in the fourth century BC and was declared a "free city" by the emperor Augustus in 42 BC. It had a Jewish colony, as can be seen from the fact that there was a synagogue. Paul must have stayed many weeks there, in the course of which he received donations from the Christians of Philippi (cf. Phil 4; 16) and had to work to earn his keep (cf. 1 Thess 2:9). It was a period of difficulties (cf. vv. 5–8) and

p. Or *sabbaths*

women. [5]But the Jews were jealous, and taking some wicked fellows of the
rabble, they gathered a crowd, set the city in an uproar, and attacked the house
of Jason, seeking to bring them out to the people. [6]And when they could not
find them, they dragged Jason and some of the brethren before the city
authorities, crying, "These men who have turned the world upside down have
come here also, [7]and Jason has received them; and they are all acting against
the decrees of Caesar, saying that there is another king, Jesus." [8]And the people
and the city authorities were disturbed when they heard this. [9]And when they
had taken security from Jason and the rest, they let them go.

Reception in Beroea

[10]The brethren immediately sent Paul and Silas away by night to Beroea; and
when they arrived they went into the Jewish synagogue. [11]Now these Jews
were more noble than those in Thessalonica, for they received the word with
all eagerness, examining the scriptures daily to see if these things were so.
[12]Many of them therefore believed, with not a few Greek women of high
standing as well as men. [13]But when the Jews of Thessalonica learned that the
word of God was proclaimed by Paul at Beroea also, they came there too,
stirring up and inciting the crowds. [14]Then the brethren immediately sent Paul
off on his way to the sea, but Silas and Timothy remained there. [15]Those who
conducted Paul brought him as far as Athens; and receiving a command for
Silas and Timothy to come to him as soon as possible, they departed.

Paul in Athens

[16]Now while Paul was waiting for them at Athens, his spirit was provoked
within him as he saw that the city was full of idols. [17]So he argued in the

---

joys (cf. v. 4), as Paul would later recall in his letters to the Thessalonians (cf. 1 Thess 2:1–12; 2 Thess 3:7–8).

17:10–15 The Jews of Beroea receive Paul with more open minds than Jews elsewhere, and this leads them to believe in the Lord. Luke specifically notes their nobility, eagerness and diligence (cf. v. 11): "It is a fact that the teaching of the truth is received in different ways by different people, in accordance with the dispositions of each. The Word presents what is good and evil to all in the same way, so that one [person] who is well disposed to the message has his soul filled with light, while another, who decides not to turn his eyes towards the light of truth, remains living in the darkness of ignorance" (St Gregory of Nyssa, *On the Life of Moses*, 2, 65).

17:16–21 This account of Paul's stay at Athens is full of significant detail. Luke lets us see the Apostle's zeal and how it manifests itself in evangelizing Jews (v. 17) and pagans (v. 18). In the entire Tradition of the Church, especially in the early

synagogue with the Jews and the devout persons, and in the market place every
day with those who chanced to be there. 18Some also of the Epicurean and Stoic
philosophers met him. And some said, "What would this babbler say?" Others
said, "He seems to be a preacher of foreign divinities"—because he preached
Jesus and the resurrection. 19And they took hold of him and brought him to the
Areopagus, saying, "May we know what this new teaching is which you present?
20For you bring some strange things to our ears; we wish to know therefore what
these things mean." 21Now all the Athenians and the foreigners who lived there
spent their time in nothing except telling or hearing something new.

Paul's speech in the Areopagus

22So Paul, standing in the middle of the Areopagus, said: "Men of Athens, I
perceive that in every way you are very religious. 23For as I passed along, and
observed the objects of your worship, I found also an altar with this inscription,
'To an unknown god.' What therefore you worship as unknown, this I proclaim to
you. 24The God who made the world and everything in it, being Lord of heaven
and earth, does not live in shrines made by man, 25nor is he served by human
hands, as though he needed anything, since he himself gives to all men life and
breath and everything. 26And he made from one every nation of men to live on all
the face of the earth, having determined allotted periods and the boundaries of
their habitation, 27that they should seek God, in the hope that they might feel
after him and find him. Yet he is not far from each one of us, 28for

'In him we live and move and have our being';

as even some of your poets have said,

'For we are indeed his offspring.'

---

years, the Church has been very conscious that pagan peoples must have some knowledge of the Truth which prepares them to accept Christ, the only Truth: "I confess that by my prayers and [ascetic] efforts I seek to become a Christian, not because the doctrines of Plato are completely different to those of Christ, but because they are not entirely the same, as is the case with the thought of other philosophers (the Stoics, for example), poets or historians. Each one speaks well when he speaks according to the seed of the Divine Word that he possesses. But it is clear that those who do not agree on basic principles cannot provide sure knowledge or perfect wisdom. All the true and good things said by those thinkers belong to us as Christians [...]. Pagan writers can have only a cloudy view of reality, and that only because of the seed of the Word present in them" (St Justin, *Apology*, 2, 13, 2–5).

17:22–34 This is the longest of all Paul's reported addresses to a pagan audience (cf. 14:15ff) and it is probably the first model we have of Christian apologetic method; it tends to stress the reasonableness of Christianity, and it is well able to hold its own with the best in human thought. The speaker is clearly the same

29Being then God's offspring, we ought not to think that the Deity is like gold, or silver, or stone, a representation by the art and imagination of man. 30The times of ignorance God overlooked, but now he commands all men everywhere to repent, 31because he has fixed a day on which he will judge the world in righteousness by a man whom he has appointed, and of this he has given asssurance to all men by raising him from the dead."

32Now when they heard of the resurrection of the dead, some mocked; but others said, "We will hear you again about this." 33So Paul went out from among them. 34But some men joined him and believed, among them Dionysius the Areopagite and a woman named Damaris and others with them.

Paul in Corinth, with Aquila and Priscilla

18 1After this he left Athens and went to Corinth. 2And he found a Jew named Aquila, a native of Pontus, lately come from Italy with his wife Priscilla, because Claudius had commanded all the Jews to leave Rome. And he went to see them; 3and because he was of the same trade he stayed with them, and they worked, for by trade they were tentmakers. 4And he argued in the synagogue every sabbath, and persuaded Jews and Greeks.

Preaching to Jews and Gentiles

5When Silas and Timothy arrived from Macedonia, Paul was occupied with preaching, testifying to the Jews that the Christ was Jesus. 6And when they opposed and reviled him, he shook out his garments and said to them, "Your

---

person as wrote the Letter to the Romans, someone who has long experience of preaching the Gospel to pagans; his method consists of first teaching about the one, true, living God and then going on to proclaim Jesus Christ, the divine Saviour of all mankind (cf. 2 Tim 1:9–10).

After an introduction designed to catch the attention of listeners and highlight the central theme (vv. 22–23), the address can be divided into three parts: 1) God is the Lord of the world; he does not need to live in temples built by men (vv. 24–25); 2) man was created by God and is dependent on him for everything (vv. 26–27); 3) there is a special relationship between God and man which means that idolatry is an error (vv. 28–29). In conclusion, Paul exhorts his listeners to accept the truth about God, and to repent, bearing in mind the Last Judgment (vv. 30–31).

The quotation (in v. 28) is from the Stoic poet Aratus (third century BC), where it comes in the singular; the plural form used by the Apostle may refer to a similar verse in the hymn to Zeus written by Cleantes (also third century).

18:1–11 Paul must have arrived in Corinth very discouraged by what had happened in Athens, and with very few resources to live on. He will later write: "And I was with you in weakness and in much fear and trembling; and my speech blood be upon your heads! I am innocent. From now on I will go to the Gentiles." [7]And he left there and went to the house of a man named Titius[q] Justus, a worshipper of God; his house was next door to the synagogue. [8]Crispus, the ruler of the synagogue, believed in the Lord, together with all his household; and many of the Corinthians hearing Paul believed and were baptized. [9]And the Lord said to Paul one night in a vision, "Do not be afraid, but speak and do not be silent; [10]for I am with you, and no man shall attack you to harm you; for I have many people in this city." [11]And he stayed a year and six months, teaching the word of God among them.

Paul before Gallio

[12]But when Gallio was proconsul of Achaia, the Jews made a united attack upon Paul and brought him before the tribunal, [13]saying, "This man is persuading men to worship God contrary to the law." [14]But when Paul was about to open his mouth, Gallio said to the Jews, "If it were a matter of wrongdoing or vicious crime, I should have reason to bear with you, O Jews; [15]but since it is a matter of questions about words and names and your own law, see to it yourselves; I refuse to be a judge of these things." [16]And he drove them from the tribunal. [17]And they all seized Sosthenes, the ruler of the synagogue, and beat him in front of the tribunal. But Gallio paid no attention to this.

---

and my message were not in plausible words of wisdom, but in demonstration of the Spirit and power" (1 Cor 2:3–4). Corinth was a very cosmopolitan commercial city located on an isthmus between two gulfs (now joined by a canal). Ships came to Corinth from all parts. Low moral standards, concentration on money-making, and voluptuous worship of Aphrodite would suggest that it was not the best ground for sowing the Word of God, but the Lord can change people's hearts: St Justin writes, "The Jewish people, who held the prophecies as their possession and who waited continually for the coming of the Christ, did not recognize him when he came; and not only that: they abused and mistreated him. On the other hand, the Gentiles, who had never heard of him until the apostles moved out beyond Jerusalem and told them about his life and the prophecies of his coming, were filled with joy and faith; they renounced their idols and were consecrated through Christ to God unbegotten" (*Apology, 1*, 49, 5).

18:12–17 Gallio was a brother of the Stoic philosopher Seneca. We know that he began his proconsulship of Achaia, of which Corinth was the capital, in July 51. Paul must have appeared before Gallio around the end of 52. This is one of the best-established dates we have for the Apostle.

q. Other early authorities read *Titus*

Return to Antioch via Ephesus

18After this Paul stayed many days longer and then took leave of the brethren and sailed for Syria, and with him Priscilla and Aquila. At Cenchreae he cut his hair, for he had a vow. 19And they came to Ephesus, and he left them there; but he himself went into the synagogue and argued with the Jews. 20When they asked him to stay for a longer period, he declined; 21but on taking leave of them he said, "I will return to you if God wills," and he set sail from Ephesus.

22When he had landed at Caesarea, he went up and greeted the church, and then went down to Antioch.

11. ST PAUL'S THIRD APOSTOLIC JOURNEY

Galatia and Phrygia

23After spending some time there he departed and went from place to place through the region of Galatia and Phrygia, strengthening all the disciples.

18:18–22 This is Paul's first recorded visit to Ephesus, the capital of proconsular Asia and one of the most flourishing cities of the Empire. Its most famous building was the Artemision or temple of Diana (Artemis), one of the wonders of the ancient world. The city's huge theatre had a capacity of 23,000. On this journey, Paul does not stay long, but Ephesus will be the centre of his next missionary journey.

18:23–20:38 □ Paul's third missionary journey, like the others, starts at Antioch; it ends with the departure of the Apostle for Jerusalem. It was a long journey and Luke concentrates on what happened in Ephesus.

To start with, Paul visits the cities already evangelized in Galatia and Phrygia; this would have been in the final months of 53 and early 54. He then goes to Ephesus, where he stays almost three years and has no end of tribulations (cf. 2 Cor 1:9), so much as that he can write from Ephesus to the Corinthians in the spring of 57 to say that "we hunger and thirst, we are ill-clad and buffeted and homeless [...]; we have become, and are now, as the refuse of the world, the offscouring of all things" (1 Cor 4:11, 13). Despite or possibly because of these circumstances, his apostolate proves very fruitful and the Christian message spreads right across proconsular Asia—to important cities like Colossae, Laodicea, Hierapolis, etc. and to hundreds of towns; as Paul himself puts it, "a wide door for effective work has been opened to me" (1 Cor 16:9).

As a result of the silversmiths riot the Apostle leaves the city, heading for Macedonia and Achaia to visit the churches founded during his second journey—Philippi, Thessalonica, Corinth. He stays three months there, in the winter of 57/58. His return journey to Jerusalem, to bring the money collected, is through

Apollos in Ephesus and Corinth

24Now a Jew named Apollos, a native of Alexandria, came to Ephesus. He was an eloquent man, well versed in the scriptures. 25He had been instructed in the way of the Lord; and being fervent in spirit, he spoke and taught accurately the things concerning Jesus, though he knew only the baptism of John. 26He began to speak boldly in the synagogue; but when Priscilla and Aquila heard him, they took him and expounded to him the way of God more accurately. 27And when he wished to cross to Achaia, the brethren encouraged him, and wrote to the disciples to receive him. When he arrived, he greatly helped those who through grace had believed, 28for he powerfully confuted the Jews in public, showing by the scriptures that the Christ was Jesus.

Disciples of John the Baptist at Ephesus

19 1While Apollos was at Corinth, Paul passed through the upper country and came to Ephesus. There he found some disciples. 2And he said to them, "Did you receive the Holy Spirit when you believed?" And they said, "No, we have never even heard that there is a Holy Spirit." 3And he said, "Into

---

Macedonia, to escape a Jewish plot. He boards ship at Neapolis (the port nearest Philippi) and after stops at Troas, Miletus (where he meets up with the elders he had summoned from Ephesus), Tyre and Caesarea, he manages to reach Jerusalem in time for Pentecost.

18:24–28 This passage shows how effective (vv. 27–28) was the zeal of this married couple, Priscilla and Aquila (v. 26): "The Christian family's faith and evangelizing mission also possesses this Catholic missionary inspiration. The sacrament of marriage takes up and re-proposes the task of defending and spreading the faith, a task that has its roots in Baptism and Confirmation, and makes Christian married couples and parents witnesses of Christ 'to the ends of the earth' (Acts 1:8) […]. Just as at the dawn of Christianity Aquila and Priscilla were presented as a missionary couple, so today the Church shows forth her perennial newness and fruitfulness by the presence of Christian couples and families who dedicate at least part of their lives to working in missionary territories proclaiming the Gospel and doing 'service to their fellow man in the love of Jesus Christ'" (John Paul II, *Fam. consortio*, 54).

19:1–7 This presence in Ephesus of a group of disciples who had received only the baptism of John is open to various interpretations. They may have been people who followed the teachings of the Baptist (he had baptized them); Paul regarded them as incipient Christians. But in the New Testament being a Christian is always connected with receiving the Baptism of Jesus Christ and having the Holy Spirit (cf. 11:16; Jn 3:5; Rom 8:9; 1 Cor 12:3; Gal 3:2; etc.); Paul proceeds to bring them what then were you baptized?" They said, "Into John's baptism." [4]And Paul said, "John baptized with the baptism of repentance, telling the people to believe in the one who was to come after him, that is, Jesus." [5]On hearing this, they were baptized in the name of the Lord Jesus. [6]And when Paul had laid his hands upon them, the Holy Spirit came on them; and they spoke with tongues and prophesied. [7]There were about twelve of them in all.

Paul's preaching and miracles at Ephesus

[8]And he entered the synagogue and for three months spoke boldly, arguing and pleading about the kingdom of God; [9]but when some were stubborn and disbelieved, speaking evil of the Way before the congregation, he withdrew from them, taking the disciples with him, and argued daily in the hall of Tyrannus.[r] [10]This continued for two years, so that all the residents of Asia heard the word of the Lord, both Jews and Greeks.

[11]And God did extraordinary miracles by the hands of Paul, [12]so that handkerchiefs or aprons were carried away from his body to the sick, and diseases left them and the evil spirits came out of them. [13]Then some of the itinerant Jewish exorcists undertook to pronounce the name of the Lord Jesus over those who had evil spirits, saying, "I adjure you by the Jesus whom Paul preaches." [14]Seven sons of a Jewish high priest named Sceva were doing this. [15]But the evil spirit answered them, "Jesus I know, and Paul I know; but who are you?" [16]And the man in whom the evil spirit was leaped on them, mastered all of them, and overpowered them, so that they fled out of that house naked and wounded.

Books of magic burned

[17]And this became known to all residents of Ephesus, both Jews and Greeks; and fear fell upon them all; and the name of the Lord Jesus was extolled. [18]Many also of those who were now believers came, confessing and divulging

---

through these stages (vv. 5–6). As elsewhere in Acts (cf., e.g., 3: 1–10 and 14: 8–18; 12:1–12 and 16:25–34; etc.) we can see the parallel between Paul's and Peter's way of working (cf. 8:14–17).

19:8–20 Paul's activity in Ephesus as described here echoes that of Jesus in Galilee (vv. 11–12; cf. Mk 5:27–31), including the way that miracles confirm his preaching: "Did the disciples of Jesus learn to do miracles from their Master, and so convince the crowds who listened to them, or did they not perform any miracles at all? It would be completely absurd to say that they performed no miracles of any kind, and that in blind belief [...] they set about teaching the new doctrine everywhere. For, in that case, what could inspire and strengthen them to preach so completely new a doctrine? And if the disciples also carried out miracles, who can

r. Other ancient authorities add *from the fifth hour to the tenth* their practices. [19]And a number of those who practised magic arts brought their books together and burned them in the sight of all; and they counted the value of them and found it came to fifty thousand pieces of silver. [20]So the word of the Lord grew and prevailed mightily.

Paul's plans for further journeys

[21]Now after these events Paul resolved in the Spirit to pass through Macedonia and Achaia and go to Jerusalem, saying, "After I have been there, I must also see Rome." [22]And having sent into Macedonia two of his helpers, Timothy and Erastus, he himself stayed in Asia for a while.

The silversmiths' riot in Ephesus

[23]About that time there arose no little stir concerning the Way. [24]For a man named Demetrius, a silversmith, who made silver shrines of Artemis, brought no little business to the craftsmen. [25]These he gathered together, with the workmen of like occupation, and said, "Men, you know that from this business we have our wealth. [26]And you see and hear that not only at Ephesus but almost throughout all Asia this Paul has persuaded and turned away a considerable company of people, saying that gods made with hands are not gods. [27]And there is danger not only that this trade of ours may come into disrepute but also that the temple of the great goddess Artemis may count for nothing, and that she may even be deposed from her magnificence, she whom all Asia and the world worship."

---

say that they were magicians?; for what magician would be willing to meet with so much danger in order to spread a teaching that prohibited magic?" (Origen, *Against Celsus,* 1, 38).

19:21–40 The success of Paul's apostolate in Ephesus can be seen not only from the fact that the silversmiths saw him as a threat to their livelihood but also in the fact that he was on friendly terms with the magistrates, the Asiarchs (v. 31). We can notice that the self-interest of Demetrius and the silversmiths contrasts with the more circumspect attitude of the magistrate (vv. 35–40). The magistrate's words show that the Christian message can make a favourable impression on those who examine it calmly and closely.

Luke uses the term "way" (v. 23) to describe Christianity and the Church (cf. 9:2; 22:4; 24:14, 22). This term was probably fairly widely used, with this meaning, by Christians of the period. This word, "way", has biblical roots and refers to a religious and moral lifestyle and even a set of moral criteria: "What good reason there is for calling the preaching of the gospel 'the Way', for it is the route that does indeed lead to the Kingdom of heaven" (St John Chrysostom, *Hom. on Acts*, 41, 1).

[28]When they heard this they were enraged, and cried out, "Great is Artemis of the Ephesians!" [29]So the city was filled with the confusion; and they rushed together into the theatre, dragging with them Gaius and Aristarchus, Macedonians who were Paul's companions in travel. [30]Paul wished to go in among the crowd, but the disciples would not let him; [31]some of the Asiarchs also, who were friends of his, sent to him and begged him not to venture into the theatre. [32]Now some cried one thing, some another; for the assembly was in confusion, and most of them did not know why they had come together. [33]Some of the crowd prompted Alexander, whom the Jews had put forward. And Alexander motioned with his hand, wishing to make a defence to the people. [34]But when they recognized that he was a Jew, for about two hours they all with one voice cried out, "Great is Artemis of the Ephesians!" [35]And when the town clerk had quieted the crowd, he said, "Men of Ephesus, what man is there who does not know that the city of the Ephesians is temple keeper of the great Artemis, and of the sacred stone* that fell from the sky?[s] [36]Seeing then that these things cannot be contradicted, you ought to be quiet and do nothing rash. [37]For you have brought these men here who are neither sacrilegious nor blasphemers of our goddess. [38]If therefore Demetrius and the craftsmen with him have a complaint against any one, the courts are open, and there are proconsuls; let them bring charges against one another. [39]But if you seek anything further,[t] it shall be settled in the regular assembly. [40]For we are in danger of being charged with rioting today, there being no cause that we can give to justify this commotion." [41]And when he had said this, he dismissed the assembly.

Paul goes into Macedonia and begins his return journey

20 [1]After the uproar ceased, Paul sent for the disciples and having exhorted them took leave of them and departed for Macedonia. [2]When he had gone through these parts and had given them much encouragement, he came to Greece. [3]There he spent three months, and when a plot was made against him by the Jews as he was about to set sail for Syria, he determined to

---

20:1–12 The narrator now takes up the thread of the projected journey to Jerusalem and Rome (cf. 19:21). St Paul travels by land, through Macedonia (v. 2), to Greece. It was probably at this point, in Corinth, that he wrote the Letter to the Romans heralding his future visit to that city: names mentioned in that letter (Rom 16:21–23) occur also among the names of Paul's companions in v. 4.

In v. 7 we find the first explicit reference in Acts to the Christian custom of meeting on the first day of the week to celebrate the Eucharist (cf. 2:42; 1 Cor 10:16): "By a tradition handed down from the apostles, which took its origin from the very day of Christ's resurrection, the Church celebrates the pascal mystery every seventh day, which day is appropriately called the Lord's Day or Sunday" (Vatican II, *SC*, 106).

s. The meaning of the Greek is uncertain **t.** Other ancient authorities read *about other matters* return through Macedonia. [4]Sopater of Beroea, the son of Pyrrhus, accompanied him; and of the Thessalonians, Aristarchus and Secundus; and Gaius of Derbe, and Timothy; and the Asians, Tychicus and Trophimus. [5]These went on and were waiting for us at Troas, [6]but we sailed away from Philippi after the days of Unleavened Bread, and in five days we came to them at Troas, where we stayed for seven days.

Celebration of the Eucharist. Eutychus' fall and recovery

[7]On the first day of the week, when we were gathered together to break bread,* Paul talked with them, intending to depart on the morrow; and he prolonged his speech until midnight. [8]There were many lights in the upper chamber where we were gathered. [9]And a young man named Eutychus was sitting in the window. He sank into a deep sleep as Paul talked still longer; and being overcome by sleep, he fell down from the third storey and was taken up dead. [10]But Paul went down and bent over him, and embracing him said, "Do not be alarmed, for his life is in him." [11]And when Paul had gone up and had broken bread and eaten, he conversed with them a long time, until daybreak, and so departed. [12]And they took the lad away alive, and were not a little comforted.

From Troas to Miletus

[13]But going ahead to the ship, we set sail for Assos, intending to take Paul aboard there; for so he had arranged, intending himself to go by land. [14]And when he met us at Assos, we took him on board and came to Mitylene. [15]And sailing from there we came the following day opposite Chios; the next day we touched at Samos; and[u] the day after that we came to Miletus. [16]For Paul had decided to sail past Ephesus, so that he might not have to spend time in Asia; for he was hastening to be at Jerusalem, if possible, on the day of Pentecost.

Farewell address to the elders of Ephesus

[17]And from Miletus he sent to Ephesus and called to him the elders of the church. [18]And when they came to him he said to them:

20:13–38 Paul's address to the elders of Ephesus is his third great discourse reported in Acts, the others being to the Jews in Pisidian Antioch (13:16ff) and to pagans at Athens (17:22ff). It is, in effect, an emotional farewell to all the churches Paul had founded.

The address divides into two parts. The first (vv. 18–27) is a brief resume of Paul's life of dedication to the church at Ephesus, with hints at the difficulties he expects to meet in the immediate future; two parallel passages (vv. 18–21 and 26–27) frame a central passage (vv. 22–25). In the second part, the Apostle speaks movingly about the mission and role of elders; two series of recommendations (vv.

u. Other ancient authorities add *after remaining at Trogyllium*

"You yourselves know how I lived among you all the time from the first day that I set foot in Asia, [19]serving the Lord with all humility and with tears and with trials which befell me through the plots of the Jews; [20]how I did not shrink from declaring to you anything that was profitable, and teaching you in public and from house to house, [21]testifying both to Jews and to Greeks of repentance to God and of faith in our Lord Jesus Christ. [22]And now, behold, I am going to Jerusalem, bound in the Spirit, not knowing what shall befall me there; [23]except that the Holy Spirit testifies to me in every city that imprisonment and inflictions await me. [24]But I do not account my life of any value nor as precious to myself, if only I may accomplish my course and the ministry which I received from the Lord Jesus, to testify to the gospel of the grace of God. [25]And now, behold, I know that all you among whom I have gone about preaching the kingdom will see my face no more. [26]Therefore I testify to you this day that I am innocent of the blood of all of you, [27]for I did not shrink from declaring to you the whole counsel of God. [28]Take heed to yourselves and to all the flock, in which the Holy Spirit has made you guardians, to feed the church of the Lord[v] which he obtained with his own blood.[w] [29]I know that after my departure fierce wolves will come in among you, not sparing the flock; [30]and from among your own selves will arise men speaking perverse things, to draw away the disciples after them. [31]Therefore be alert, remembering that for three years I did not cease night or day to admonish every one with tears. [32]And now I commend you to God and to the word of his grace, which is able to build you up and to give you the inheritance among all those who are sanctified. [33]I coveted no one's silver or gold or apparel. [34]You yourselves know that these hands ministered to my necessities, and to those who were with me.* [35]In all things I have shown you that by so toiling one must help the weak, remembering the words of the Lord Jesus, how he said, 'It is more blessed to give than to receive.'"

[36]And when he had spoken thus, he knelt down and prayed with them all. [37]And they all wept and embraced Paul and kissed him, [38]sorrowing most of all because of the word he had spoken, that they should see his face no more. And they brought him to the ship.

28–31 and 33–35) hinge on the central verse (v. 32). The advice that Paul gives here is very like that found in his pastoral letters to Timothy and Titus.

At every point we can notice how tirelessly the Apostle worked; he sets a good example for us: "It is necessary that those who direct the community exercise their governing role in an appropriate way [...]. There is a danger that those dedicated to the care of others and to guiding them towards eternal life may, unbeknownst to themselves, lose their way. Therefore, those whose job it is to supervise must work harder than everyone else, must be more humble than those in their charge, must spend their lives in giving an example of service, and consider those whom they govern as entrusted to them by God" (St Gregory of Nyssa, *De instit. Christ.*).

v. Other ancient authorities read *of God* **w.** Or *with the blood of his Own*

PART FOUR: ST PAUL, IN IMPRISONMENT, BEARS WITNESS TO CHRIST

12. ST PAUL IN JERUSALEM

From Miletus to Caesarea

21 [1]And when we had parted from them and set sail, we came by a
straight course to Cos, and the next day to Rhodes, and from there to
Patara.[x] [2]And having found a ship crossing to Phoenicia, we went aboard, and
set sail. [3]When we had come in sight of Cyprus, leaving it on the left we sailed
to Syria, and landed at Tyre; for there the ship was to unload its cargo. [4]And
having sought out the disciples, we stayed there for seven days. Through the
Spirit they told Paul not to go* on to Jerusalem. [5]And when our days there
were ended, we departed and went on our journey; and they all, with wives and
children, brought us on our way till we were outside the city; and kneeling
down on the beach we prayed and bade one another farewell. [6]Then we went
on board the ship, and they returned home.

[7]When we had finished the voyage from Tyre, we arrived at Ptolemais; and
we greeted the brethren and stayed with them for one day. [8]On the morrow we
departed and came to Caesarea; and we entered the house of Philip the evangelist,

---

21:1–28:31 □ □ The third part of the book, starting with Paul's arrival in Jerusalem, deals with his imprisonment. As the Lord had announced (23:11), the Apostle is now going to bear witness to Christ and the Gospel from prison. St Luke gives a detailed account of his journey, as a prisoner, to Rome. With Rome as his base, the way is opened to spread the Gospel in all directions.

21:1–23:21 □ As regards Paul's last stay in Jerusalem, Luke recalls how he was received joyfully by the Christians (21:17)—but also how bitter some Jews still felt towards him (21:27:28). Paul avails himself of adverse circumstances to make an apologia for his ministry which is also an apologia for the Gospel (22:1–21). His accusers are so stubborn that it seems as if they will bring about his death; but everything that happens is part of God's providence; everything is designed to bring the Gospel to the Gentiles and to Rome (22:21; 23:11).

21:1–14 As Jesus had done in his time, St Paul sets his face for Jerusalem aware of what awaits him there. The Holy Spirit's words and warnings (vv. 4, 11; cf. 20:23) strengthen him in his resolve to accept the will of God and bear the trials that lie ahead (v. 13; cf. 20:23–24). The Apostle's serenity contrasts with the distress of those around him, which is understandable, given their affection for him. Many years of self-surrender lay behind Paul's supernatural composure. "The

x. Other ancient authorities add *and Myra*

who was one of the seven, and stayed with him. [9]And he had four unmarried
daughters, who prophesied.

The prophet Agabus

[10]While we were staying for some days, a prophet named Agabus came down
from Judea. [11]And coming to us he took Paul's girdle and bound his own feet
and hands, and said, "Thus says the Holy Spirit, 'So shall the Jews at Jerusalem
bind the man who owns this girdle and deliver him into the hands of the
Gentiles.'" [12]When we heard this, we and the people there begged him not to
go up to Jerusalem. [13]Then Paul answered, "What are you doing, weeping and
breaking my heart? For I am ready not only to be imprisoned but even to die
at Jerusalem for the name of the Lord Jesus." [14]And when he would not be
persuaded, we ceased and said, "The will of the Lord be done."

Paul arrives in Jerusalem and meets the Christians

[15]After these days we made ready and went up to Jerusalem. [16]And some of
the disciples from Caesarea went with us, bringing us to the house of Mnason
of Cyprus, an early disciple, with whom we should lodge.

[17]When we had come to Jerusalem, the brethren received us gladly. [18]On
the following day Paul went in with us to James; and all the elders were
present. [19]After greeting them, he related one by one the things that God had
done among the Gentiles through his ministry. [20]And when they heard it, they
glorified God. And they said to him, "You see, brother, how many thousands
there are among the Jews of those who have believed; they are all zealous for
the law, [21]and they have been told about you that you teach all the Jews who
are among the Gentiles to forsake Moses, telling them not to circumcise their
children or observe the customs. [22]What then is to be done? They will certainly
hear that you have come. [23]Do therefore what we tell you. We have four men
who are under a vow; [24]take these men and purify yourself along with them
and pay their expenses, so that they may shave their heads. Thus all will know
that there is nothing in what they have been told about you but that you
yourself live in observance of the law. [25]But as for the Gentiles who have
believed, we have sent a letter with our judgment that they should abstain from
what has been sacrificed to idols and from blood and from what is strangled[y]

---

wholehearted acceptance of the will of God is the sure way of finding joy and peace: happiness in the cross. It's then we realize that Christ's yoke is sweet and that his burden is not heavy" (Bl. J. Escrivá, *The Way*, 758). The example of Paul impressed the disciples and moved them to accept what God had allowed with an expression that recalls the words of Jesus in Gethsemane (v.14; cf. Lk 22:42)

21:15–26 Paul and his companions are received by James—probably James the Less—the head of the Church in Jerusalem at that time (cf. 12:17; 15:13; 1 Cor

y. Other early authorities omit *and from what is strangled* and from unchastity." [26]Then Paul took the men, and the next day he purified himself with them and went into the temple, to give notice when the days of purification would be fulfilled and the offering presented for every one of them.

Paul is arrested in the temple

[27]When the seven days were almost completed, the Jews from Asia, who had seen him in the temple, stirred up all the crowd, and laid hands on him, [28]crying out, "Men of Israel, help! This is the man who is teaching men everywhere against the people and the law and this place; moreover he also brought Greeks into the temple, and he has defiled this holy place." [29]For they had previously seen Trophimus the Ephesian with him in the city, and they supposed that Paul had brought him into the temple. [30]Then all the city was aroused, and the people ran together; they seized Paul and dragged him out of the temple, and at once the gates were shut. [31]And as they were trying to kill him, word came to the tribune of the cohort that all Jerusalem was in confusion. [32]He at once took soldiers and centurions, and ran down to them; and when they saw the tribune and the soldiers, they stopped beating Paul. [33]Then the tribune came up and arrested him, and ordered him to be bound with two chains. He inquired who he was and what he had done. [34]Some in the crowd shouted one thing, some another; and as he could not learn the facts because of the uproar, he ordered

---

15:7; Gal 1:19) and by the priests who assisted him in the government and pastoral care of the community. Luke usually distinguishes elders and apostles; here he mentions elders only, which suggests that the other apostles, including Peter, had already left the Holy City. The rulers of the Church in Jerusalem rejoice over the success of Paul's apostolate (v. 20), but they are also aware of rumours which are circulating (v. 21). There is a basis for these, because the Apostle did regard the Mosaic Law as being of secondary importance as regards salvation and he did not hold circumcision as absolutely necessary (cf. Gal 4:9; 5:11; Rom 2:25–29). However, the accusation was unjust: Paul never exhorted Christians of Jewish background not to circumcise their sons; and he himself ensured that Timothy was circumcised (cf. 16:3). In Corinth he came out in support of women following the Jewish custom of wearing the veil at liturgical ceremonies (cf. 1 Cor 11:2–16), and he himself had no difficulty about taking a Nazirite vow (cf. 18:18).

21:27–40 Some Jews who had come from Asia (v. 27) for the feast of Pentecost (cf. 20:16) stirred up the crowd against Paul. Their charges against him (v. 28) are very like those made against our Lord in his time (cf. Mt 26:61; 27:40) and against Stephen (cf. 6:11–14).

With the arrest of Paul by the tribune (v. 33), a new "chapter" of the book begins in which Luke gives a detailed account of the Apostle's imprisonment (21:33–22:29), his trial at Jerusalem and Caesarea (chaps. 23–26) and his journey to Rome (27:1–28:16) to appear before an imperial court.

him to be brought into the barracks. [35]And when he came to the steps, he was
actually carried by the soldiers because of the violence of the crowd; [36]for the
mob of the people followed, crying, "Away with him!"
[37]As Paul was about to be brought into the barracks, he said to the tribune,
"May I say something to you?" And he said, "Do you know Greek? [38]Are you
not the Egyptian, then, who recently stirred up a revolt and led the four
thousand men of the Assassins out into the wilderness?" [39]Paul replied, "I am
a Jew, from Tarsus in Cilicia, a citizen of no mean city; I beg you, let me speak
to the people." [40]And when he had given him leave, Paul, standing on the
steps, motioned with his hand to the people; and when there was a great hush,
he spoke to them in the Hebrew language, saying:

Paul defends himself before the crowd

22 [1]"Brethren and fathers, hear the defence which I now make before
you."
[2]And when they heard that he addressed them in the Hebrew language,
they were the more quiet. And he said:
[3]"I am a Jew, born at Tarsus in Cilicia, but brought up in this city at the feet
of Gamaliel, educated according to the strict manner of the law of our fathers,
being zealous for God as you all are this day. [4]I persecuted this Way to the
death, binding and delivering to prison both men and women, [5]as the high
priest and the whole council of elders bear me witness. From them I received
letters to the brethren, and I journeyed to Damascus to take those also who
were there and bring them in bonds to Jerusalem to be punished.

From this point onwards Paul will not be so much a tireless missionary and founder of churches as an imprisoned witness of the Gospel; but even in those circumstances he will manage to proclaim Christ.

22:1–21 Luke gives an account of Paul's address to the Jews of Jerusalem, the first of three speeches in his own defence (cf. 24:10–21; 26:1–23) in which the Apostle tries to show that there is no reason why Christianity should be opposed by Jews or by Romans. He presents himself as what he is—a Jew full of respect for his own people and their sacred traditions. He earnestly desires his brethren to realize that there are compelling reasons for his commitment to Jesus: "Many have come to believe in Christianity as if against their will; a certain spirit, appearing to them in dreams or by the light of day, changed their minds suddenly, and, having hated the Word, they have gone on to die for him" (*Against Celsus*, 1, 46).

However, this speech is not an apologia in the strict sense. His main purpose is not to answer charges of sacrilege but to use the occasion to bear witness to Jesus Christ, whose commandments validate Paul's actions. What he is really trying to do is to get his hearers to listen well and obey the voice of the Lord.

6“As I made my journey and drew near to Damascus, about noon a great light from heaven suddenly shone about me. 7And I fell to the ground and heard a voice saying to me, ‘Saul, Saul, why do you persecute me?’ 8And I answered, ‘Who are you, Lord?’ And he said to me, ‘I am Jesus of Nazareth whom you are persecuting.’ 9Now those who were with me saw the light but did not hear the voice of the one who was speaking to me. 10And I said, ‘What shall I do, Lord?’ And the Lord said to me, ‘Rise, and go into Damascus, and there you will be told all that is appointed for you to do.’ 11And when I could not see because of the brightness of that light, I was led by the hand by those who were with me, and came into Damascus.

12“And one Ananias, a devout man according to the law, well spoken of by all the Jews who lived there, 13came to me, and standing by me said to me, ‘Brother Saul, receive your sight.’ And in that very hour I received my sight and saw him. 14And he said, ‘The God of our fathers appointed you to know his will, to see the Just One and to hear a voice from his mouth; 15for you will be a witness for him to all men of what you have seen and heard. 16And now why do you wait? Rise and be baptized, and wash away your sins, calling on his name.’

17“When I had returned to Jerusalem and was praying in the temple, I fell into a trance 18and saw him saying to me, ‘Make haste and get quickly out of Jerusalem, because they will not accept your testimony about me.’ 19And I said, ‘Lord, they themselves know that in every synagogue I imprisoned and beat those who believed in thee. 20And when the blood of Stephen thy witness* was shed, I also was standing by and approving, and keeping the garments of those who killed him.’ 21And he said to me, ‘Depart; for I will send you far away to the Gentiles.’”

Paul, the Roman citizen

22Up to this word they listened to him; then they lifted up their voices and said, “Away with such a fellow from the earth! For he ought not to live.” 23And as they cried out and waved their garments and threw dust into the air, 24the tribune commanded him to be brought into the barracks, and ordered him to be examined by scourging, to find out why they shouted thus against him. 25But when they had tied him up with the thongs, Paul said to the centurion who was standing by, “Is it lawful for you to scourge a man who is a Roman citizen, and uncondemned?” 26When the centurion heard that, he went to the tribune and said to him, “What are you about to do? For this man is a Roman citizen.” 27So the tribune came and said to him, “Tell me, are you a Roman citizen?” And he said, “Yes.” 28The tribune answered, “I bought this citizenship for a large

---

22:22–29 Roman law allowed suspects and slaves to be put under the lash in order to extract confessions. Since Paul claims his rights as a Roman citizen, it may be that Lysias called the Sanhedrin together (v. 30) for the sole purpose of learning what the basis of the charges was.

sum." Paul said, "But I was born a citizen." 29So those who were about to examine him withdrew from him instantly; and the tribune also was afraid, for he realized that Paul was a Roman citizen and that he had bound him.

Speech before the Sanhedrin

30But on the morrow, desiring to know the real reason why the Jews accused him, he unbound him, and commanded the chief priests and all the council to meet, and he brought Paul down and set him before them.

23 1And Paul, looking intently at the council, said, "Brethren, I have lived before God in all good conscience up to this day." 2And the high priest Ananias commanded those who stood by him to strike him on the mouth. 3Then Paul said to him, "God shall strike you, you whitewashed wall! Are you sitting to judge me according to the law, and yet contrary to the law you order me to be struck?" 4Those who stood by said, "Would you revile God's high priest?" 5And Paul said, "I did not know, brethren, that he was the high priest; for it is written, 'You shall not speak evil of a ruler of your people.'"

6But when Paul perceived that one part were Sadducees and the other Pharisees, he cried out in the council, "Brethren, I am a Pharisee, a son of Pharisees; with respect to the hope and the resurrection of the dead I am on trial." 7And when he had said this, a dissension arose between the Pharisees and the Sadducees; and the assembly was divided. 8For the Sadducees say that there is no resurrection, nor angel, nor spirit; but the Pharisees acknowledge them all. 9Then a great clamour arose; and some of the scribes of the Pharisees' party stood up and contended, "We find nothing wrong in this man. What if a spirit or an angel spoke to him?" 10And when the dissension became violent, the tribune, afraid that Paul would be torn in pieces by them, commanded the soldiers to go down and take him by force from among them and bring him into the barracks.

11The following night the Lord stood by him and said, "Take courage, for as you have testified about me at Jerusalem, so you must bear witness also at Rome."

22:30–23:11 At various times throughout Acts, Luke likes to show that Paul's action, and what they lead to, in some way parallel what happened to Jesus. In connexion with the present charge and its hearing before the Sanhedrin, Luke recalls that Paul, like Jesus (Jn 18:22), was struck a blow on the instructions of the high priest to get him to tell the truth (v. 2).

However, from this point onwards the hearing takes a different course: Jesus did not answer the charges laid against him; whereas Paul brings up a subject which is calculated to set his judges against one another (v. 6) and he escapes judgment; God has a further mission for him (v. 11). From now on the prisoner will concentrate not on defending himself but on bearing witness to the Gospel.

23:5 Ex 22:28.

A Jewish plot against Paul

[12]When it was day, the Jews made a plot and bound themselves by an oath neither to eat nor drink till they had killed Paul. [13]There were more than forty who made this conspiracy. [14]And they went to the chief priests and elders, and said, "We have strictly bound ourselves by an oath to taste no food till we have killed Paul. [15]You therefore, along with the council, give notice now to the tribune to bring him down to you, as though you were going to determine his case more exactly. And we are ready to kill him before he comes near."

[16]Now the son of Paul's sister heard of their ambush; so he went and entered the barracks and told Paul. [17]And Paul called one of the centurions and said, "Bring this young man to the tribune; for he has something to tell him." [18]So he took him and brought him to the tribune and said, "Paul the prisoner called me and asked me to bring this young man to you, as he has something to say to you." [19]The tribune took him by the hand, and going aside asked him privately, "What is it that you have to tell me?" [20]And he said, "The Jews have agreed to ask you to bring Paul down to the council tomorrow, as though they were going to inquire somewhat more closely about him. [21]But do not yield to them; for more than forty of their men lie in ambush for him, having bound themselves by an oath neither to eat nor drink till they have killed him; and now they are ready, waiting for the promise from you."

13. FROM JERUSALEM TO ROME

Paul is moved to Caesarea

[22]So the tribune dismissed the young man, charging him, "Tell no one that you have informed me of this."

[23]Then he called two of the centurions and said, "At the third hour of the night get ready two hundred soldiers with seventy horsemen and two hundred

---

23:12–21 On other occasions the apostles were freed from prison by extraordinary means. Now God uses human means (help from his relatives) to make it possible for Paul to advance God's project. Both methods betoken the providence of God at work.

23:22–28:31 □ This is the last section of the book. Luke goes into quite a lot of detail about Paul's trial and his journey to Rome. Over the course of these pages we see that all who listen to what Paul has to say or who sit in judgement over him realize that he is innocent of the charges laid against him. Christianity is a religion which does not run counter to any of the principles underlying the Empire.

23:22–35 Luke gives a very succinct account of how it came about that Paul will be judged in accordance with the laws of Imperial Rome. What we read here about spearmen to go as far as Caesarea. [24]Also provide mounts for Paul to ride, and bring him safely to Felix the governor." [25]And he wrote a letter to this effect:

[26]"Claudius Lysias to his Excellency the governor Felix, greeting. [27]This man was seized by the Jews, and was about to be killed by them, when I came upon them with the soldiers and rescued him, having learned that he was a Roman citizen. [28]And desiring to know the charge on which they accused him, I brought him down to their council. [29]I found that he was accused about questions of their law, but charged with nothing deserving death or imprisonment. [30]And when it was disclosed to me that there would be a plot against the man, I sent him to you at once, ordering his accusers also to state before you what they have against him."

[31]So the soldiers, according to their instructions, took Paul and brought him by night to Antipatris. [32]And on the morrow they returned to the barracks, leaving the horsemen to go on with him. [33]When they came to Caesarea and delivered the letter to the governor, they presented Paul also before him. [34]On reading the letter, he asked to what province he belonged. When he learned that he was from Cilicia [35]he said, "I will hear you when your accusers arrive." And he commanded him to be guarded in Herod's praetorium.

The trial before Felix

24 [1]And after five days the high priest Ananias came down with some elders and a spokesman, one Tertullus. They laid before the governor their case against Paul; [2]and when he was called, Tertullus began to accuse him, saying:

"Since through you we enjoy much peace, and since by your provision, most excellent Felix, reforms are introduced on behalf of this nation, [3]in every way and everywhere we accept this with all gratitude. [4]But, to detain you no further, I beg you in your kindness to hear us briefly. [5]For we have found this man a pestilent fellow, an agitator among all the Jews throughout the world, and a ringleader of the sect of the Nazarenes. [6]He even tried to profane the temple, but we seized him.[z] [8]By examining him yourself you will be able to learn from him about everything of which we accuse him."

---

the judicial process as also the personalities involved (Felix, Festus etc.) fits in with what we know of the period from extrabiblical sources.

24:1–27 By being sent to Caesarea by the tribune Lysias, Paul has entered the jurisdiction of Roman law. The Jews fail to have him tried by the Sanhedrin. The Apostle's case will follow the Roman judicial process known as *cognitio extra ordinem* which also applied to criminal cases and eventually (in the second century) took over entirely from a system of trial before "permanent tribunals"

z. Other ancient authorities add *and we would have judged him according to our law. [7] But the chief captain Lysias came and with great violence took him out of our hands, [8] commanding his accusers to come before you*

9The Jews also joined in the charge, affirming that all this was so.
10And when the governor had motioned to him to speak, Paul replied:
"Realizing that for many years you have been judge over this nation, I
cheerfully make my defence. 11As you may ascertain, it is not more than twelve
days since I went up to worship at Jerusalem; 12and they did not find me disputing
with any one or stirring up a crowd, either in the temple or in the synagogues, or
in the city. 13Neither can they prove to you what they now bring up against me.
14But this I admit to you, that according to the Way, which they call a sect, I
worship the God of our fathers, believing everything laid down by the law or
written in the prophets, 15having a hope in God which these themselves accept,
that there will be a resurrection of both the just and the unjust. 16So I always
take pains to have a clear conscience toward God and toward men. 17Now after
some years I came to bring to my nation alms and offerings. 18As I was doing
this, they found me purified in the temple, without any crowd or tumult. But
some Jews from Asia—19they ought to be here before you to make an accu-
sation, if they have anything against me. 20Or else let these men themselves
say what wrongdoing they found when I stood before the council, 21except this
one thing which I cried out while standing among them, 'With respect to the
resurrection of the dead I am on trial before you this day.'"

(questiones perpetuae). The main difference between the two systems was that in the former the investigation was carried out by the emperor himself or by a magistrate acting on his behalf or by an imperial official, who was helped by a council. One other important difference was that this new system allowed the judge more initiative (the older system was accusatory in style): the judge had more investigative scope and greater freedom as regards sentencing.

Chapters 24 and 25 of the Acts of the Apostles is in fact an important source of information about the *cognitio extra ordinem* in criminal cases; it accurately reports the various roles and stages. We are told about the charge brought against Paul (cf. 23:35; 24:1); the correct terminology is used in connexion with the hearing before the judge on the tribunal (cf. 25:6, 17); there is mention of the magistrate's council (25:12); the allegations are described in some detail, and we can see the discretion that the magistrates Felix and Festus enjoyed in hearing the case and weighing up the facts. In his defence (v. 10–21) St Paul makes it clear (cf. vv. 14–16) that it is incorrect to see Christianity as just a sect of Judaism. Moreover, he asserts that he has always acted within the law and never in any way sought to undermine civil authority: Tertullian writes, "A Christian is an enemy of no man, least of all an enemy of the emperor. Christians know that the one God gave him [the emperor] his station [in life], and therefore they love, respect and honour him, seeking to save him along with the whole empire until the end of time" *(Lib. ad Scapulum*, 2).

See the RSV note **z** to v. 6.

22But Felix, having a rather accurate knowledge of the Way, put them off, saying, "When Lysias the tribune comes down, I will decide your case." 23Then he gave orders to the centurion that he should be kept in custody but should have some liberty, and that none of his friends should be prevented from attending to his needs.

A further appearance before Felix

24After some days Felix came with his wife Drusilla, who was a Jewess; and he sent for Paul and heard him speak upon faith in Christ Jesus. 25And as he argued about justice and self-control and future judgment, Felix was alarmed and said, "Go away for the present; when I have an opportunity I will summon you." 26At the same time he hoped that money would be given him by Paul. So he sent for him often and conversed with him. 27But when two years had elapsed, Felix was succeeded by Porcius Festus; and desiring to do the Jews a favour, Felix left Paul in prison.

Festus resumes the trial. Paul appeals to Caesar

25 1Now when Festus had come into his province, after three days he went up to Jerusalem from Caesarea. 2And the chief priests and the principal men of the Jews informed him against Paul; and they urged him, 3asking as a favour to have the man sent to Jerusalem, planning an ambush to kill him on the way. 4Festus replied that Paul was being kept at Caesarea, and that he himself intended to go there shortly. 5"So," said he, "let the men of authority among you go down with me, and if there is anything wrong about the man, let them accuse him."

25:1–12 A little earlier we saw the venality of Felix (cf. 24:26–27); the trial continues under his successor, Porcius Festus. Secular sources indicate that Festus was a good administrator. He held the position of governor of Judea for two or three years, until the year 62, when he died.

The text implies that Festus was indeed impartial. He has no intention of handing the prisoner over to the Jewish courts. But his political prudence leads him to take Paul's accusers' requests partly into account, and he gives the Sanhedrin a say in the trial. Festus was empowered to use the Sanhedrin as a *consilium*, a source of expert advice. It is in this sense that he invites Paul to agree to be tried in Jerusalem.

The governor's question to Paul (v. 10) is in fact a rhetorical one, because he is really informing Paul of a decision he has already made. Paul realizes this, so he appeals to Caesar in order to avoid being tried in unfavourable circumstances. An appeal (*provocatio*) to the supreme authority was a resource available to a Roman citizen who thought that a magistrate had used his coercive power improperly or arbitrarily; it went to the very heart of Roman thinking: it was seen as a real guarantee and proof of a citizen's political liberty. It should not be confused with an appeal against a sentence (*apellatio*); Paul had not been sentenced.

[6]When he had stayed among them not more than eight or ten days, he went down to Caesarea; and the next day he took his seat on the tribunal and ordered Paul to be brought. [7]And when he had come, the Jews who had gone down from Jerusalem stood about him, bringing against him many serious charges which they could not prove. [8]Paul said in his defence, "Neither against the law of the Jews, nor against the temple, nor against Caesar have I offended at all." [9]But Festus, wishing to do the Jews a favour, said to Paul, "Do you wish to go up to Jerusalem, and there be tried on these charges before me?" [10]But Paul said, "I am standing before Caesar's tribunal, where I ought to be tried; to the Jews I have done no wrong, as you know very well. [11]If then I am a wrongdoer, and have committed anything for which I deserve to die, I do not seek to escape death; but if there is nothing in their charges against me, no one can give me up to them. I appeal to Caesar." [12]Then Festus, when he had conferred with his council, answered, "You have appealed to Caesar; to Caesar you shall go."

Festus briefs Agrippa

[13]Now when some days had passed, Agrippa the king and Bernice arrived at Caesarea to welcome Festus. [14]And as they stayed there many days, Festus laid Paul's case before the king, saying, "There is a man left prisoner by Felix; [15]and when I was at Jerusalem, the chief priests and the elders of the Jews gave information about him, asking for sentence against him. [16]I answered them that it was not the custom of the Romans to give up any one before the accused met the accusers face to face, and had opportunity to make his defence concerning the charge laid against him. [17]When therefore they came together here, I made no delay, but on the next day took my seat on the tribunal and ordered the man to be brought in. [18]When the accusers stood up, they brought no charge in his case of such evils as I supposed; [19]but they had certain points of dispute with him about their own superstition and about one Jesus, who was dead, but whom Paul asserted to be alive. [20]Being at a loss how to investigate these questions, I asked whether he wished to go to Jerusalem and be tried there regarding them. [21]But when Paul had appealed to be kept in custody for the decision of the emperor, I commanded him to be held until I send him to

---

25:13–27 Herod Agrippa II was a son of Herod Agrippa I (cf. the note on 12:1–9) and therefore a great-grandson of Herod the Great. He was born in the year 27. Like his father, he had won favour with Rome and had been given territories in northern Palestine, which he was allowed to govern with the title of king. Bernice was his sister. Festus' words, on the two occasions when he addresses the king (vv. 14–21; 24–27), show that there is no basis to the charges laid against Paul. Agrippa's answer (v. 22) is reminiscent of a similar scene when the half-brother of his grandfather, Herod Antipas, expressed a desire to see Jesus (cf. Lk 9:9; 23:8). Commentators have not failed to see Providence at work throughout this trial:

Caesar." 22And Agrippa said to Festus, "I should like to hear the man myself." "Tomorrow," said he, "you shall hear him."

Paul before Agrippa

23So on the morrow Agrippa and Bernice came with great pomp, and they entered the audience hall with the military tribunes and the prominent men of the city. Then by command of Festus Paul was brought in. 24And Festus said, "King Agrippa and all who are present with us, you see this man about whom the whole Jewish people petitioned me, both at Jerusalem and here, shouting that he ought not to live any longer. 25But I found that he had done nothing deserving death; and as he himself appealed to the emperor, I decided to send him. 26But I have nothing definite to write to my lord about him. Therefore I have brought him before you, and, especially before you, King Agrippa, that, after we have examined him, I may have something to write. 27For it seems to me unreasonable, in sending a prisoner, not to indicate the charges against him."

Paul's speech in the presence of Agrippa

26 1Agrippa said to Paul, "You have permission to speak for yourself." Then Paul stretched out his hand and made his defence:

2"I think myself fortunate that it is before you, King Agrippa, I am to make my defence today against all the accusations of the Jews, 3because you are especially familiar with all customs and controversies of the Jews; therefore I beg you to listen to me patiently.

"Agrippa's conversation with the governor awakens a great desire in the king to hear Paul [...]. Such is the effect of all the machinations perpetrated against Paul. If they had not occurred, no judge would have deigned to listen to what he had to say, and none would have heard him out in such calm circumstances" (St John Chrysostom, *Hom. on Acts*, 51, 4).

26:1–23 In his address before Agrippa, Paul once more gives an account of the circumstances of his conversion. Paul's vocation and mission (vv. 16–18) are described in a style similar to the calling of the prophets of Israel (cf. Ezek 2:1; Is 42:6f). God makes his design known in an imperious command which radically changes the whole life of his chosen one. However, there is a special nuance here: Paul is a "witness", just as the Eleven were (cf. 1:8, 22; 3:15; etc.).

In the second part of the address (vv. 19–23) Paul describes how diligently he has tried to respond to the grace given him (cf. v. 22). In this he is an example for every Christian. "The grace of the Holy Spirit is given to each person with the hope that each will multiply and increase what he receives", writes St Gregory of Nyssa (*De instit. Christ.*). The same idea is expressed by St Teresa of Avila when she writes that "We must make a constant effort to serve, and we must try to be grateful, for God grants us new strength on that condition; if we do not

4“My manner of life from my youth, spent from the beginning among my
own nation and at Jerusalem, is known by all the Jews. 5They have known for a
long time, if they are willing to testify, that according to the strictest party of our
religion I have lived as a Pharisee. 6And now I stand here on trial for hope in the
promise made by God to our fathers, 7to which our twelve tribes hope to attain,
as they earnestly worship night and day. And for this hope I am accused by Jews,
O king! 8Why is it thought incredible by any of you that God raises the dead?

9“I myself was convinced that I ought to do many things in opposing the
name of Jesus of Nazareth. 10And I did so in Jerusalem; I not only shut up
many of the saints in prison, by authority from the chief priests, but when they
were put to death I cast my vote against them. 11And I punished them often in
all the synagogues and tried to make them blaspheme; and in raging fury
against them, I persecuted them even to foreign cities.

12“Thus I journeyed to Damascus with the authority and commission of the
chief priests. 13At midday, O king, I saw on the way a light from heaven,
brighter than the sun, shining round me and those who journeyed with me.
14And when we had all fallen to the ground, I heard a voice saying to me in the
Hebrew language, ‘Saul, Saul, why do you persecute me? It hurts you to kick
against the goads.’ 15And I said, ‘Who are you, Lord?’ And the Lord said, ‘I am
Jesus whom you are persecuting. 16But rise and stand upon your feet; for I
have appeared to you for this purpose, to appoint you to serve and bear witness
to the things in which you have seen me and to those in which I will appear to
you, 17delivering you from the people and from the Gentiles—to whom I send
you 18to open their eyes, that they may turn from darkness to light and from
the power of Satan to God, that they may receive forgiveness of sins and a
place among those who are sanctified by faith in me.’

19“Wherefore, O King Agrippa, I was not disobedient to the heavenly
vision, 20but declared first to those at Damascus, then at Jerusalem and
throughout all the country of Judea, and also to the Gentiles, that they should
repent and turn to God and perform deeds worthy of their repentance. 21For
this reason the Jews seized me in the temple and tried to kill me. 22To this day
I have had the help that comes from God, and so I stand here testifying both to
small and great, saying nothing but what the prophets and Moses said would
come to pass: 23that the Christ must suffer, and that, by being the first to rise
from the dead, he would proclaim light both to the people and to the Gentiles.”

---

use the treasure and great standing he gives us, he will take it away from us again and leave us very much the poorer, and His Majesty will give his treasures to those who truly struggle, and who make good use of them for themselves and others” (*Life*, 10, 6).

Reactions to Paul's speech

24And as he thus made his defence, Festus said with a loud voice, "Paul, you
are mad; your great learning is turning you mad." 25But Paul said, "I am not
mad, most excellent Festus, but I am speaking the sober truth. 26For the king
knows about these things, and to him I speak freely; for I am persuaded that none
of these things has escaped his notice, for this was not done in a corner. 27King
Agrippa, do you believe the prophets? I know that you believe." 28And Agrippa
said to Paul, "In a short time you think to make me a Christian!" 29And Paul said,
"Whether short or long, I would to God that not only you but also all who hear
me this day might become such as I am—except for these chains."

30Then the king rose, and the governor and Bernice and those who were
sitting with them; 31and when they had withdrawn, they said to one another, "This
man is doing nothing to deserve death or imprisonment." 32And Agrippa said to
Festus, "This man could have been set free if he had not appealed to Caesar."

Departure for Rome. Voyage to Crete

27 1And when it was decided that we should sail for Italy, they delivered
Paul and some other prisoners to a centurion of the Augustan Cohort,
named Julius. 2And embarking in a ship of Adramyttium, which was about to
sail to the ports along the coast of Asia, we put to sea, accompanied by
Aristarchus, a Macedonian from Thessalonica. 3The next day we put in at
Sidon; and Julius treated Paul kindly, and gave him leave to go to his friends
and be cared for. 4And putting to sea from there we sailed under the lee of
Cyprus, because the winds were against us. 5And when we had sailed across

---

26:24–32 Paul's apostolic zeal, as seen in this episode, has communicated itself to those who read it: "How admirably (St Paul) behaves! Imprisoned for spreading the teachings of Christ, he misses no opportunity to preach the Gospel. [...] Where did St Paul get all his strength from? *Omnia possum in eo qui me confortat!* (Phil 4:13): I can do all things, because God alone gives me this faith, this hope, this charity" (Bl. J. Escrivá, *Hom.*, 2, 270f).

27:1–44 This account of St Paul's sea journey (27:1–28:16) is so exact in its terminology and so detailed that it is regarded as an important source of information on seafaring in ancient times. The narrative (in the first person plural, from here to the end of the book) records the memories and maybe the notes taken at the time by someone who accompanied the Apostle on the voyage.

The account shows us the providential care God takes of Paul (vv. 24, 44) and the Apostle's own solicitude towards his travelling companions (vv. 34–36), not that they always reciprocated it (v. 42).

The Tradition of the Church has read this journey as having a spiritual application for the faithful: "Why did God not preserve the boat from shipwreck? So as to make them all see more clearly how serious their plight was—and know

the sea which is off Cilicia and Pamphylia, we came to Myra in Lycia. [6]There
the centurion found a ship of Alexandria sailing for Italy, and put us on board.
[7]We sailed slowly for a number of days, and arrived with difficulty off Cnidus,
and as the wind did not allow us to go on, we sailed under the lee of Crete off
Salmone. [8]Coasting along it with difficulty, we came to a place called Fair
Havens, near which was the city of Lasaea.

The voyage is resumed against Paul's advice

[9]As much time had been lost, and the voyage was already dangerous because the
fast had already gone by, Paul advised them, [10]saying, "Sirs, I perceive that the
voyage will be with injury and much loss, not only of the cargo and the ship, but
also of our lives." [11]But the centurion paid more attention to the captain and to
the owner of the ship than to what Paul said. [12]And because the harbour was not
suitable to winter in, the majority advised to put to sea from there, on the chance
that somehow they could reach Phoenix, a harbour of Crete, looking northeast
and southeast,[a] and winter there.

A storm

[13]And when the south wind blew gently, supposing that they had obtained their
purpose, they weighed anchor and sailed along Crete, close inshore. [14]But
soon a tempestuous wind, called the northeaster, struck down from the land;
[15]and when the ship was caught and could not face the wind, we gave way to
it and were driven. [16]And running under the lee of a small island called
Cauda,[b] we managed with difficulty to secure the boat; [17]after hoisting it up,
they took measures[c] to undergird the ship; then, fearing that they should run
on the Syrtis, they lowered the gear, and so were driven. [18]As we were
violently storm-tossed, they began next day to throw the cargo overboard;
[19]and the third day they cast out with their own hands the tackle of the ship.
[20]And when neither sun nor stars appeared for many a day, and no small
tempest lay on us, all hope of our being saved was at last abandoned.

Paul's vision. He rallies his companions

[21]As they had been long without food, Paul then came forward among them
and said, "Men, you should have listened to me, and should not have set sail

---

that their rescue was not due to human aid but to the strong arm of God, who protected their lives after the ship foundered. And so it is with the righteous: they fare well in the midst of storms and tempests, whether it be on the high seas or in a stormy bay. [...] On a ship in danger of being engulfed by the sea, the chained prisoners and the whole crew owe their lives to the presence of Paul. They learn the benefit of being with a devout and holy person. Interior, more baneful tempests often assail us. God can rescue us if we are as clever as these sailors and pay

a. Or *southwest and northwest* **b.** Other ancient authorities read *Clauda* **c.** Greek *helps*

from Crete and incurred this injury and loss. [22]I now bid you to take heart; for
there will be no loss of life among you, but only of the ship. [23]For this very
night there stood by me an angel of the God to whom I belong and whom I
worship, [24]and he said, ‘Do not be afraid, Paul; you must stand before Caesar;
and lo, God has granted you all those who sail with you.’ [25]So take heart, men,
for I have faith in God that it will be exactly as I have been told. [26]But we shall
have to run on some island.”

[27]When the fourteenth night had come, as we were drifting across the sea
of Adria, about midnight the sailors suspected that they were nearing land.
[28]So they sounded and found twenty fathoms; a little farther on they sounded
again and found fifteen fathoms. [29]And fearing that we might run on the rocks,
they let out four anchors from the stern, and prayed for day to come. [30]And as
the sailors were seeking to escape from the ship, and had lowered the boat into
the sea, under pretence of laying out anchors from the bow, [31]Paul said to the
centurion and the soldiers, “Unless these men stay in the ship, you cannot be
saved.” [32]Then the soldiers cut away the ropes of the boat, and let it go.

[33]As day was about to dawn, Paul urged them all to take some food, saying,
“Today is the fourteenth day that you have continued in suspense and without
food, having taken nothing. [34]Therefore I urge you to take some food; it will
give you strength, since not a hair is to perish from the head of any of you.”
[35]And when he had said this, he took bread, and giving thanks to God in the
presence of all he broke it and began to eat. [36]Then they all were encouraged
and ate some food themselves. [37](We were in all two hundred and seventy-six[d]
persons in the ship.) [38]And when they had eaten enough, they lightened the
ship, throwing out the wheat into the sea.

Shipwreck and rescue

[39]Now when it was day, they did not recognize the land, but they noticed a bay
with a beach, on which they planned if possible to bring the ship ashore. [40]So
they cast off the anchors and left them in the sea, at the same time loosening
the ropes that tied the rudders; then hoisting the foresail to the wind they made
for the beach. [41]But striking a shoal[e] they ran the vessel aground; the bow
struck and remained immovable, and the stern was broken up by the surf.
[42]The soldiers’ plan was to kill the prisoners, lest any should swim away and
escape; [43]but the centurion, wishing to save Paul, kept them from carrying out
their purpose. He ordered those who could swim to throw themselves
overboard first and make for the land, [44]and the rest on planks or on pieces of
the ship. And so it was that all escaped to land.

---

attention to advice from saints [...]. Even if we are caught in a storm, we will be rescued; even if we were fourteen days without God, we would survive; even if we were to fall into darkness and night, if we believe in him we will be saved” (St John Chrysostom, *Hom. on Acts*, 53:4–5).

d. Other ancient authorities read *seventy-six* or *about seventy-six* **e.** Greek *place of two seas*

Waiting in Malta

28 [1]After we had escaped, we then learned that the island was called Malta. [2]And the natives showed us unusual kindness, for they kindled a fire and welcomed us all, because it had begun to rain and was cold. [3]Paul had gathered a bundle of sticks and put them on the fire, when a viper came out because of the heat and fastened on his hand. [4]When the natives saw the creature hanging from his hand, they said to one another, "No doubt this man is a murderer. Though he has escaped from the sea, justice has not allowed him to live." [5]He, however, shook off the creature into the fire and suffered no harm. [6]They waited, expecting him to swell up or suddenly fall down dead; but when they had waited a long time and saw no misfortune come to him, they changed their minds and said that he was a god.

[7]Now in the neighbourhood of that place were lands belonging to the chief man of the island, named Publius, who received us and entertained us hospitably for three days. [8]It happened that the father of Publius lay sick with fever and dysentery; and Paul visited him and prayed, and putting his hands on him healed him. [9]And when this had taken place, the rest of the people on the island who had diseases also came and were cured. [10]They presented many gifts to us;[f] and when we sailed, they put on board whatever we needed.

Arrival in Rome

[11]After three months we set sail in a ship which had wintered in the island, a ship of Alexandria, with the Twin Brothers as figureheads. [12]Putting in at Syracuse, we stayed there for three days. [13]And from there we made a circuit and arrived at Rhegium; and after one day a south wind sprang up, and on the second day we came to Puteoli. [14]There we found brethren, and were invited

---

28:1–10 Humanitarian the natives of Malta indeed are (vv. 2, 10) but they also prove to be very superstitious (vv. 4, 6). Be that as it may, St Paul's experience here bears out our Lord's promises: "these signs will accompany those who believe: in my name they will cast out demons; they will speak in new tongues; they will pick up serpents, and if they drink any deadly thing, it will not hurt them; they will lay their hands on the sick, and they will recover" (Mk 16:17–18).

28:11–16 The text (cf. vv. 14–16) reveals the climate of human and supernatural brotherhood that obtained among the Christians of Rome. "How well the early Christians practised this ardent charity which went far beyond the limits of mere human solidarity or natural kindness. They loved one another, through the heart of Christ, with a love both tender and strong. [...] The principal apostolate we Christians must carry out in the world, and the best witness we can give of our faith, is to help bring about a climate of genuine charity within the Church. For who indeed could feel attracted to the Gospel if those who say they preach the

f. Or *honoured us with many honours*

to stay with them for seven days. And so we came to Rome. 15And the brethren there, when they heard of us, came as far as the Forum of Appius and Three Taverns to meet us. On seeing them Paul thanked God and took courage. 16And when we came into Rome, Paul was allowed to stay by himself, with the soldier that guarded him.

Paul and the Roman Jews

17After three days he called together the local leaders of the Jews; and when they had gathered, he said to them, "Brethren, though I had done nothing against the people or the customs of our fathers, yet I was delivered prisoner from Jerusalem into the hands of the Romans. 18When they had examined me, they wished to set me at liberty, because there was no reason for the death penalty in my case. 19But when the Jews objected, I was compelled to appeal to Caesar—though I had no charge to bring against my nation. 20For this reason therefore I have asked to see you and speak with you, since it is because of the hope of Israel that I am bound with this chain." 21And they said to him, "We have received no letters from Judea about you, and none of the brethren coming here has reported or spoken any evil about you. 22But we desire to hear from you what your views are; for with regard to this sect we know that everywhere it is spoken against."

23When they had appointed a day for him, they came to him at his lodging in great numbers. And he expounded the matter to them from morning till evening, testifying to the kingdom of God and trying to convince them about Jesus both from the law of Moses and from the prophets. 24And some were

---

Good News do not really love one another, but spend their time attacking one another, spreading slander and quarrelling?" (Bl. J. Escrivá, *Hom.,* 2, 225f).

28:17–28 Paul would have arrived in Rome around the year 61. He was allowed to stay in a private house—under what was called *custodia militaris*, which meant that the only restriction was that he was guarded by a soldier at all times. In keeping with his missionary custom, Paul immediately seeks out the Jews of the city, and his preaching has predictable results (v. 24). So, because many Jews will not listen to him, Paul announces that he is free of his self-imposed obligation to preach the Gospel first to the Jews (v. 28). What he says suggests that the Christians are those who have grasped the meaning of God's promises to the chosen people and that it is they who are the true Israel. Christ's disciples have not abandoned the Law; it is, rather, the Jews who have renounced their position as God's chosen nation. "We are the true, spiritual people of Israel, the tribe of Judah, the sons of Jacob, of Isaac and of Abraham, to whom God bore witness even when he was not circumcised, and who was blessed by God and called the father of many nations" (*Dialogue with Tryphon*, 11, 5).

See the RSV note **g** on v. 29.

convinced by what he said, while others disbelieved. [25]So, as they disagreed
among themselves, they departed, after Paul had made one statement: "The
Holy Spirit was right in saying to your fathers through Isaiah the prophet:

[26]'Go to this people, and say,
You shall indeed hear but never understand,
and you shall indeed see but never perceive.
[27]For this people's heart has grown dull,
and their ears are heavy of hearing,
and their eyes they have closed;
lest they should perceive with their eyes,
and hear with their ears,
and understand with their heart,
and turn for me to heal them.'

[28]Let it be known to you then that this salvation of God has been sent to the
Gentiles; they will listen."[g]

Paul's ministry in Rome

[30]And he lived there two whole years at his own expense,[h] and welcomed all
who came to him, [31]preaching the kingdom of God and teaching about the
Lord Jesus Christ quite openly and unhindered.

28:30–31 The apparently abrupt way the book ends shows in fact that the promise the Lord made to his apostles has been kept: they would be his witnesses "to the end of the earth" (1:8). To describe St Paul's attitude to his work of evangelization, Luke (cf. v. 31) uses the word "parrhēsia"—"straightforward simplicity, filial trust, joyous assurance, humble boldness, the certainty of being loved" (*CCC*, 2778).

g. Other ancient authorities add verse 29. *And when he had said these words, the Jews departed, holding much dispute among themselves* **h.** Or *in his own hired dwelling* **28:26–27** Is 6:9–10.

The Letters of St Paul

After the historical/narrative books (the Gospels and Acts) in the canon of the New Testament come sacred writings which expound the salvific power of Christ's divine work and which apply his teaching to the real-life circumstances of the Christians of the time; sometimes, also, these books tease out the theology of the original core of Christian revelation (cf. Vatican II, *DV*, 20). The most important of these books are the letters (fourteen in all) which carry the name of St Paul or, in the case of the Letter to the Hebrews, which evidence that apostle's influence and authority.

We know a great deal about St Paul from his letters and from the book of the Acts. A native of Tarsus, he received a solid education in Judaism and in Hellenic culture. A man of great energy, he devoted his entire life in pursuit of his convictions, first as a Pharisee and then as a Christian. After his conversion around the mid-30s AD, he spent some time in Damascus and on retreat in Arabia. He then went to Jerusalem, to meet the apostles, and in the year 45 or so he went back to Tarsus and from there to Antioch in Syria, proclaiming the Gospel and giving testimony of his Christian faith. Using Antioch as his base, he made three great apostolic journeys in the years 45–58 which brought him to Cyprus, Asia Minor (the Roman circumscription of that name) and Greece, and he was present at the council of Jerusalem (*c.* the year 49 or 50). In the year 58 he was arrested in Jerusalem and taken to Caesarea (on the coast of Palestine) and from there to Rome. He arrived in the Eternal City in the spring of 61 and after spending some two years in confinement he seems to have made further journeys to Asia Minor, Crete, Macedonia and very likely Spain. In the year 64 or 67 he died a martyr in Rome.

St Paul was chosen by God to preach Christ's salvation to the Gentiles. What his letters contain is not a system of ideas or a systemic theology but a lived experience of the mystery of Christ, a message which he wants to spread throughout the world and which he expounds to the communities or individuals to whom his letters are addressed. In pursuit of his purpose he makes use of all the literary recourses and debating skills at his command. He had only one purpose in mind—to preach the Gospel of Jesus Christ which is "the power of God for salvation to every one who has faith" (Rom 1:16). This is the teaching he expounds in each of his letters, presenting it from different angles to suit the circumstances and the mentality of the people he is addressing. The solid core of these letters is always the same: Jesus Christ is the Saviour of man and of the world—of every person (Jew or Gentile) and of all creation, even at the cosmic level.

His teaching has come down to us in the form of letters which, given their personal tone, with greetings, farewells, introductions for individuals etc., are very much like family letters. But at the same time these letters contain (more or less developed) expositions of teaching, so much so that they often seem more like treatises than letters. Be that as it may, in one way or another all of these letters seek to strengthen the faith of the people they are written for. The Church has received these letters as a divinely inspired source of Christian Revelation, as something that is of permanent value, as well as being a precious testimony of the Apostle's life and thought and that of his co-workers and of the early Christian communities.

St Paul's letters are usually grouped as follows—the earlier letters (1 and 2 Thessalonians); those which evidence a unity of style and teaching reflecting the Apostle's circumstances in the years 57–58 and which are called the "great letters" (Romans, Galatians, 1 and 2 Corinthians); those which were written by Paul during the years of his captivity (Ephesians, Philippians, Colossians and Philemon); and, finally those sent to governors or "pastors" of particular churches, hence their name of "pastoral letters" (1 and 2 Timothy, and Titus). However, these letters are traditionally arranged in our Bible by putting the letters addressed to communities first and following them with those sent to individual people. Within this arrangement, they appear in order of length and of the frequency of their use in Christian liturgy—with the exception of the Letter to the Hebrews, which is usually placed last.

The Letter to the Romans

During his third apostolic journey in the years 53–58 St Paul wrote letters to the Galatians and to the community at Corinth. The two letters to the Corinthians produced good results; the community enjoyed spiritual health and fervour. The news coming from the other local churches founded by the Apostle indicated that things were going well with the help of the grace of the Holy Spirit. In view of this, St Paul plans to extend his apostolic work to Spain (cf. Rom 15:28), spending a while at Rome en route, where there was by now a sizeable Christian community. To prepare the ground for his visit to Rome, he writes his Letter to the Romans from Corinth, in the winter of 57–58.

This text, the longest of all Paul's letters (it is not so much a letter as a doctrinal treatise), is also regarded as his most important text. In it he expounds key matters of doctrine regarding the redemptive work of Christ and the Christian life. He expands and develops what he already had to say in the Letter to the Galatians, and gives a more systematic account of the action of Jesus Christ the Saviour in the believer and of the implications that derive from it.

The Christian community at Rome was made up of converts from Judaism and paganism. St Paul felt it was important to spell out the effects of Christ's salvation for both these groups, showing them that now they have all become one. After a long greeting, in which he explains who Jesus is (1:1–17), he goes on to provide an overview of unredeemed mankind, estranged from God and his enemy ever since the fall of Adam. The moral degradation of the Gentiles and similar sins of the Jews all point to the absolute need for the redemption brought about by Christ to give them the forgiveness and grace of God (1:18–4:25).

Four ideas should be borne in mind in order to understand what he goes on to say—sin and death (5:12–21), man's sinful flesh and the Law (7:1–25). Unredeemed man is at the mercy of these four things and his only escape is through the redemption brought about by Christ Jesus. Salvation comes only from God through our Lord Jesus Christ, and a person has to grasp it through faith, an unmerited gift from God: he cannot obtain it though works alone, but once a person has obtained faith—through Baptism, which grafts the Christian onto Christ—he can and should do good with the help of the Holy Spirit who dwells in him and completes the work of Justification brought about by Christ and which makes him holy and an adoptive son of the Father (8:1–39). In this way he ceases to be an enemy of God and becomes his friend; he moves from a state of condemnation to a state of grace; he ceases to deserve the old condemnation because he has been re-created and is able to hope in the glory of the children of God.

In the second part of the letter (12:1–15:13) St Paul applies the teaching of the earlier part to the life and lifestyle of the Christian. This brings him on, as a conclusion, to the moral demands made by the Faith and by “life in the Spirit”, and their practical consequences for life in the midst of a world which is as yet unredeemed but which must be led to salvation.

The Letter to the Romans marks a culmination in the divine Revelation given us through the Apostle Paul.

The other letters in the New Testament help us to learn more about how to apply the teaching contained in this letter.

Romans

INTRODUCTION

Greeting

1 [1]Paul, a servant[a] of Jesus Christ, called to be an apostle, set apart for the
gospel of God [2]which he promised beforehand through his prophets in the
holy scriptures, [3]the gospel concerning his Son, who was descended from
David according to the flesh [4]and designated[a2] Son of God in power according
to the Spirit of holiness by his resurrection from the dead, Jesus Christ our
Lord, [5]through whom we have received grace and apostleship to bring about
the obedience of faith for the sake of his name among all the nations,
[6]including yourselves who are called to belong to Jesus Christ;

[7]To all God's beloved in Rome, who are called to be saints:

Grace to you and peace from God our Father and the Lord Jesus Christ.*

[8]First, I thank my God through Jesus Christ for all of you, because your faith
is proclaimed in all the world. [9]For God is my witness, whom I serve with my
spirit in the gospel of his Son, that without ceasing I mention you always in my
prayers, [10]asking that somehow by God's will I may now at last succeed in
coming to you.* [11]For I long to see you, that I may impart to you some spiritual
gift to strengthen you, [12]that is, that we may be mutually encouraged by each
other's faith, both yours and mine. [13]I want you to know, brethren, that I have
often intended to come to you (but thus far have been prevented), in order that I
may reap some harvest* among you as well as among the rest of the Gentiles. [14]I
am under obligation both to Greeks and to barbarians, both to the wise and to the
foolish: [15]so I am eager to preach the gospel to you also who are in Rome.

1:1–17 □ At the start of the letter Paul introduces himself and states his qualifications for preaching the Gospel. He goes on (vv. 16–17) to spell out the subject of this letter—justification (righteousness) through faith in Christ.

1:1–15 Three matters are being covered in the opening verses. 1) Paul introduces of himself as a servant of Jesus Christ (just as the ancient prophets were servants of God: cf. 1 Sam 3:9; Is 42:1) and are chosen by the Lord to preach the Gospel; this justifies his writing to the faithful at Rome, whom he has not yet met. 2) He expresses a desire to go there, reminds them that they have been called to be saints and praises them for their faith. 3) He points out that he and the Roman Christians have received the same calling; it is a call from Jesus Christ. Paul gives a brief

a. Or *slave* **a²** Or *constituted*

Theme of the letter
16 For I am not ashamed of the gospel: it is the power of God for salvation to
every one who has faith, to the Jew first and also to the Greek. 17 For in it the
righteousness of God is revealed through faith for faith; as it is written, "He
who through faith is righteous shall live."[b]

PART ONE: JUSTIFICATION BY JESUS CHRIST

1. JUSTIFICATION BY FAITH

The fault of the Gentiles, and their punishment
18 For the wrath of God is revealed from heaven against all ungodliness and
wickedness of men who by their wickedness suppress the truth. 19 For what can
be known about God is plain to them, because God has shown it to them.
20 Ever since the creation of the world his invisible nature, namely, his eternal
power and deity, has been clearly perceived in the things that have been made.

---

description of Christ and his work of redemption (vv. 2–4): that is what he has preached wherever he has been.

"Obedience of faith" (v. 5): that is, the acceptance of the Gospel, which transcends human intelligence; the Gospel can be accepted only through faith in God who has revealed it. St Paul sees himself as "under obligation", that is, a debtor (v. 14), because he realizes that all these peoples have a right to hear his preaching: that is what he has been sent to do—to preach.

1:16–17 Here the Apostle states the theme of the letter—justification (righteousness) which comes through faith. "The righteousness of God" means that action whereby the Lord saves sinful man by making him righteous or just in God's eyes. "Through faith for faith" means that the righteousness of God in man stems from and is nourished by faith.

1:18–11:36 □□ The doctrinal part of the letter focuses on the meaning, nature and consequences of the justification Christ has won for us. After stating that only through Christ and faith in him can man become righteous in God's sight (1:18–4:25), St Paul explains that, through Baptism, we come to partake of the reconciliation with God brought about by Christ's sacrifice, and what the consequences of that are—freedom, life in the Spirit, divine filiation (5:1–8:39). Finally, he shows what Israel's role is in the ultimate manifestation of God's work of justification (9:1–11:36).

b. Or *The righteous shall live by faith* **17:1** Hab 2.4.

So they are without excuse; [21]for although they knew God they did not honour
him as God or give thanks to him, but they became futile in their thinking and
their senseless minds were darkened. [22]Claiming to be wise, they became
fools, [23]and exchanged the glory of the immortal God for images resembling
mortal man or birds or animals or reptiles.

[24]Therefore God gave them up in the lusts of their hearts to impurity, to the
dishonouring of their bodies among themselves, [25]because they exchanged the
truth about God for a lie and worshipped and served the creature rather than
the Creator, who is blessed for ever! Amen.

[26]For this reason God gave them up to dishonourable passions. Their
women exchanged natural relations for unnatural, [27]and the men likewise gave
up natural relations with women and were consumed with passion for one
another, men committing shameless acts with men and receiving in their own
persons the due penalty for their error.

[28]And since they did not see fit to acknowledge God, God gave them up to
a base mind and to improper conduct. [29]They were filled with all manner of
wickedness, evil, covetousness, malice. Full of envy, murder, strife, deceit,
malignity, they are gossips, [30]slanderers, haters of God, insolent, haughty,
boastful, inventors of evil, disobedient to parents, [31]foolish, faithless, heartless,
ruthless. [32]Though they know God's decree that those who do such things
deserve to die, they not only do them but approve those who practise them.

1:18–4:25 □ In these chapters St Paul explains that justification through faith is the only way of salvation open to men: *all* are sinners—pagans on account of their idolatry and immorality (1:18–32) and Jews on account of their sins and transgressions of the Law (2:1–24). Despite circumcision and the promises, Jews are sinners in God's sight (cf. 2:25–3:38), and so too are the Gentiles: all need to be justified by God's grace, which he gives to those who believe in Christ (3:21–31). The promises God made to Abraham were also dependent not on works but on faith (4:1–25).

1:18–32 Paul is describing the idolatry of the time (vv. 18–23) and what it leads to (vv. 24–32). It is only by acknowledging God as the creator of all things that man is able to appreciate his own dignity and "become what he is". However, when man rejects God he incurs what the Apostle calls "the wrath of God" (v. 18). This "wrath" is a metaphorical expression often used in the Bible to indicate God's feelings when man distances himself and disobeys the divine law. It does not mean "anger" in the sense of a desire for revenge but rather, as we will go on to see, anger in the sense that God allows man to steep himself in sin and depravity because he respects man's freedom. In this sense "wrath" means punishment by God, particularly in the sense of never getting to see and enjoy God in his glory.

The "wickedness" (v. 18) spoken about here has to do with man's rejecting the truth even though he has a natural inclination to seek it and cherish it.

The Jews are guilty, too

2 1 Therefore you have no excuse, O man, whoever you are, when you judge
another; for in passing judgment upon him you condemn yourself, because
you, the judge, are doing the very same things. 2 We know that the judgment of
God rightly falls upon those who do such things. 3 Do you suppose, O man,
that when you judge those who do such things and yet do them yourself, you
will escape the judgment of God? 4 Or do you presume upon the riches of his
kindness and forbearance and patience? Do you not know that God's kindness
is meant to lead you to repentance? 5 But by your hard and impenitent heart
you are storing up wrath for yourself on the day of wrath when God's
righteous judgment will be revealed. 6 For he will render to every man
according to his works: 7 to those who by patience in well-doing seek for glory
and honour and immortality, he will give eternal life; 8 but for those who are
factious and do not obey the truth, but obey wickedness, there will be wrath

---

On the basis of vv. 19–20 and other passages of the Bible, the Church teaches that it is possible to attain "natural" knowledge of God from the material world. "The world and man bear witness to the fact that they contain within themselves neither their first beginning nor their last end; rather, they partake of that which is Being-in-itself, which has neither beginning nor end. Thus, by various 'ways' man can come to know of the existence of a reality which is the original cause and the final end of all things, 'which everybody calls God' " (St Thomas Aquinas, *Summa theol.*, 1, 2, 3)" (*CCC*, 34).

Behaviour similar to that mentioned in v. 32 can be seen in our own time when "broad sectors of public opinion justify certain crimes against life in the name of the rights of individual freedom" (John Paul II, *Evang. vitae*, 4).

2:1–24 St Paul now comments on Jews who judge Gentiles and condemn them out of hand as sinners. He reminds them that God is the only judge; only he knows whether a person has acted in accordance with his conscience or not; storing up "wrath for the day of wrath" (v. 5) means acting sinfully and thereby earning damnation. Jews, too, should acknowledge that they are sinners; they will prove that they do so if they do works of penance; they are able to do so thanks to the kindness of God, who grants them pardon.

The Jews were given the Law as a guide to moral conduct; but every human being is endowed with reason and therefore knows the principles of the natural moral law (cf. vv. 14–15) which "is written and recorded in the minds of all men, human reason itself, commanding that good be done and sin be avoided" (Leo XIII, *Libertas praest.*). "Deep within his conscience man discovers a law which he has not laid upon himself but which he must obey. Its voice, ever calling him to love and to do what is good and to avoid evil, tells him inwardly at the right moment: Do this, shun that" (Vatican II, *GS*, 16).

and fury. [9]There will be tribulation and distress for every human being who does evil, the Jew first and also the Greek, [10]but glory and honour and peace for every one who does good, the Jew first and also the Greek. [11]For God shows no partiality.

[12]All who have sinned without the law will also perish without the law, and all who have sinned under the law will be judged by the law. [13]For it is not the hearers of the law who are righteous before God, but the doers of the law who will be justified. [14]When Gentiles who have not the law do by nature what the law requires, they are a law to themselves, even though they do not have the law. [15]They show that what the law requires is written on their hearts, while their conscience also bears witness and their conflicting thoughts accuse or perhaps excuse them [16]on that day when, according to my gospel, God judges the secrets of men by Christ Jesus.

[17]But if you call yourself a Jew and rely upon the law and boast of your relation to God [18]and know his will and approve what is excellent, because you are instructed in the law, [19]and if you are sure that you are a guide to the blind, a light to those who are in darkness, [20]a corrector of the foolish, a teacher of children, having in the law the embodiment of knowledge and truth—[21]you then who teach others, will you not teach yourself? While you preach against stealing, do you steal? [22]You who say that one must not commit adultery, do you commit adultery? You who abhor idols, do you rob temples? [23]You who boast in the law, do you dishonour God by breaking the law? [24]For, as it is written, "The name of God is blasphemed among the Gentiles because of you."

Real circumcision, a matter of the heart

[25]Circumcision indeed is of value if you obey the law; but if you break the law, your circumcision becomes uncircumcision. [26]So, if a man who is uncircumcised keeps the precepts of the law, will not his uncircumcision be regarded as circumcision? [27]Then those who are physically uncircumcised but keep the law will condemn you who have the written code and circumcision

---

2:25–3:8 The argument about the need for Jews to be justified by faith now moves on to deal with circumcision (2:25–29) and with the promises made to them (3:1–8). As regards circumcision, Paul says that true circumcision is not that of the flesh, but "circumcision of the heart", that is, obedience to the law of God. And, since Gentiles too can keep that law without having to have it written down or having to be circumcised, that means that the rite of circumcision, as such, cannot make a person righteous.

As regards the promises of salvation, the Apostle defends the special status of the Jewish people: the divine promises were made only to them (3:2). Due to their unfaithfulness, some Jews have not seen these promises fulfilled, for they have not

2:24 Is 52:5; Ezek 36:20.

but break the law. [28]For he is not a real Jew who is one outwardly, nor is true circumcision something external and physical. [29]He is a Jew who is one inwardly, and real circumcision is a matter of the heart, spiritual and not literal. His praise is not from men but from God.

3 [1]Then what advantage has the Jew? Or what is the value of circumcision?
[2]Much in every way. To begin with, the Jews are entrusted with the oracles
of God. [3]What if some were unfaithful? Does their faithlessness nullify the
faithfulness of God? [4]By no means! Let God be true though every man be
false, as it is written,

"That thou mayest be justified in thy words,
and prevail when thou art judged."

[5]But if our wickedness serves to show the justice of God, what shall we say?
That God is unjust to inflict wrath on us? (I speak in a human way.) [6]By no
means! For then how could God judge the world? [7]But if through my
falsehood God's truthfulness abounds to his glory, why am I still being
condemned as a sinner? [8]And why not do evil that good may come?—as some
people slanderously charge us with saying. Their condemnation is just.

All are sinners—Jews and Gentiles alike

[9]What then? Are we Jews any better off?[c] No, not at all; for I[d] have already charged
that all men, both Jews and Greeks, are under the power of sin, [10]as it is written:

"None is righteous, no, not one;
[11]no one understands, no one seeks for God.
[12]All have turned aside, together they have gone wrong;
no one does good, not even one."

---

come to believe in Christ; that is not due to unfaithfulness on God's part. God allows it to happen in order to show that the only thing that justifies man is faith in Jesus Christ (vv. 3–6). Some Jews, it seems were arguing, somewhat ironically, that their own unfaithfulness or unbelief allowed God to show his justice or his saving will. St Paul rejects this: they deserve condemnation (vv. 7–8).

God is not being unjust when he condemns someone for not wanting to accept his salvation in Christ; his promise to justify the sinner is conditional: the sinner must freely accept grace.

3:9–20 Paul uses a series of quotations from the Old Testament to prove that all men are guilty of sin—and therefore that all need redemption (cf. 3:21–31): "What Revelation makes known to us is confirmed by our own experience. For when man looks into his own heart he finds that he is drawn towards what is wrong and sunk in many evils which cannot come from his good Creator. Often refusing to acknowledge God as his source, man has also upset the relationship which should

c. Or *at any disadvantage* **d.** Greek *we* **3:4** Ps 51:4. **3:10–12** Eccles 7:20; Ps 14:1–30.

[13]"Their throat is an open grave,
they use their tongues to deceive."
"The venom of asps is under their lips."
[14] "Their mouth is full of curses and bitterness."
[15] "Their feet are swift to shed blood,
[16] in their paths are ruin and misery,
[17] and the way of peace they do not know."
[18] "There is no fear of God before their eyes."

[19]Now we know that whatever the law says it speaks to those who are under
the law, so that every mouth may be stopped, and the whole world may be held
accountable to God. [20]For no human being will be justified in his sight by
works of the law, since through the law comes knowledge of sin.

Righteousness, a free gift through faith in Christ

[21]But now the righteousness of God has been manifested apart from law,
although the law and the prophets bear witness to it, [22]the righteousness of
God through faith in Jesus Christ for all who believe. For there is no
distinction; [23]since all have sinned and fall short of the glory of God, [24]they are
justified by his grace as a gift, through the redemption which is in Christ Jesus,
[25]whom God put forward as an expiation by his blood, to be received by faith.
This was to show God's righteousness, because in his divine forbearance he
had passed over former sins; [26]it was to prove at the present time that he
himself is righteous and that he justifies him who has faith in Jesus.

[27]Then what becomes of our boasting? It is excluded. On what principle?
On the principle of works? No, but on the principle of faith.* [28]For we hold
that a man is justified by faith apart from works of law. [29]Or is God the God of
Jews only? Is he not the God of Gentiles also? Yes, of Gentiles also, [30]since
God is one; and he will justify the circumcised on the ground of their faith and
the uncircumcised through their faith. [31]Do we then overthrow the law by this
faith? By no means! On the contrary, we uphold the law.

---

link him to his last end; and at the same time he has broken the right order that should reign within himself as well as between himself and other men and all creatures" (Vatican II, *GS*, 13).

3:21–31 The righteousness of God is the action by which God makes people righteous; it was originally announced in the books of the Old Testament and now it has been made manifest in Christ and in the Gospel. From now on, salvation will depend on faith in Jesus Christ, for it is he who has brought about our redemption. God patiently put up with men's sins; in the fullness of time he chose to manifest his grace and his goodness by making men—whether Jews or Gentiles—righteous by means of the sacrifice of the cross.

3:13 Ps 5:9; 140:3. **3:14** Ps 10:7. **3:15–17** Is 59:7–8; Prov 1:16. **3:18** Ps 36:1. **3:20** Ps 143:2.

Abraham's exemplary faith

4 [1]What then shall we say about[e] Abraham, our forefather according to the
flesh? [2]For if Abraham was justified by works, he has something to boast
about, but not before God. [3]For what does the scripture say? "Abraham believed
God, and it was reckoned to him as righteousness." [4]Now to one who works,
his wages are not reckoned as a gift but as his due. [5]And to one who does not
work but trusts him who justifies the ungodly, his faith is reckoned as right-
eousness. [6]So also David pronounces a blessing upon the man to whom God
reckons righteousness apart from works:

[7]"Blessed are those whose iniquities are forgiven, and whose sins
are covered;
[8] blessed is the man against whom the Lord will not reckon his sin."

[9]Is this blessing pronounced only upon the circumcised, or also upon the
uncircumcised? We say that faith was reckoned to Abraham as righteousness.
[10]How then was it reckoned to him? Was it before or after he had been
circumcised? It was not after, but before he was circumcised. [11]He received
circumcision as a sign or seal of the righteousness which he had by faith while
he was still uncircumcised. The purpose was to make him the father of all who
believe without being circumcised and who thus have righteousness reckoned

---

The "expiation" (v. 25) was the name given to the cover or mercy seat of the ark of the Covenant. It was regarded as God's throne, from where he spoke to Moses, and the place from which to implore God's pardon for sins by a rite of expiatory sacrifice on the feast of the Day of Atonement (or expiation) (cf. Lev 16:1–34; 23:26–32; Num 29:7–11). St Paul is saying that God has made Jesus, as it were, the true mercy seat; he is the only one to go to, to have sins forgiven.

Verse 28 formally spells out the basic thesis of the Letter to the Romans. No Human being can claim before God that he is justified or righteous because he has kept the precepts of the Law. It is God who makes a person just; such grace is unmerited. Man becomes just by accepting, through faith, the grace that God offers him through Jesus Christ.

4:1–25 The Apostle appeals to the authority of the Scriptures to ratify his teaching on justification. Abraham was not justified by works of the Law but rather by faith (vv. 1–8), as we can see from Genesis 15:16, confirmed by David in the psalms (vv. 6–8). When Paul says "it was reckoned to him" (v. 3), he is depicting God as a master who notes down in a ledger the merits and demerits of his servants. In the case of Abraham what he put down in the merits column was not his works but his faith; that is why he says his faith was reckoned as righteousness, that is, holiness (justice). This shows the gratuitiousness of justification and we can see, too, that the act of faith is the first step

e. Other ancient authorities read *was gained by* **4:3** Gen 15:6. **4:7–8** Ps 32:1–2. **4:9** Gen 15:6.

to them, [12]and likewise the father of the circumcised who are not merely circumcised but also follow the example of the faith which our father Abraham had before he was circumcised.

[13]The promise to Abraham and his descendants, that they should inherit the world, did not come through the law but through the righteousness of faith. [14]If it is the adherents of the law who are to be the heirs, faith is null and the promise is void. [15]For the law brings wrath, but where there is no law there is no transgression.

[16]That is why it depends on faith, in order that the promise may rest on grace and be guaranteed to all his descendants—not only to the adherents of the law but also to those who share the faith of Abraham, for he is the father of us all, [17]as it is written, "I have made you the father of many nations"—in the presence of the God in whom he believed, who gives life to the dead and calls into existence the things that do not exist. [18]In hope he believed against hope, that he should become the father of many nations; as he had been told, "So shall your descendants be." [19]He did not weaken in faith when he considered his own body, which was as good as dead because he was about a hundred years old, or when he considered the barrenness of Sarah's womb. [20]No distrust made him waver concerning the promise of God, but he grew strong in his faith as he gave glory to God, [21]fully convinced that God was able to do what he had promised. [22]That is why his faith was "reckoned to him as righteousness." [23]But the words, "it was reckoned to him," were written not for his sake alone, [24]but for ours also. It will be reckoned to us who believe in him that raised from the dead Jesus our Lord, [25]who was put to death for our trespasses and raised for our justification.

---

in justification. So it is not good works that produce justification; rather, it is justification that renders works good and meritorious for eternal life.

The Apostle also notes (vv. 9–12) that the righteousness given to Abraham was not the outcome of circumcision, for Abraham was justified (cf. Gen 15:6) even before he was circumcised (Gen 17). Paul points out (vv. 13–17a) that what Abraham believed in (the promise that God made about his having countless offspring, and in whom all the nations of the earth would be blessed: cf. Gen 12:1–3; 15:5–6) was independent of the Law, for it was made before God gave the Law to Moses, and it was addressed to all Abraham's descendants (not just the Jews), that is, all who have the same faith as he.

Abraham's belief in a promise which seemed impossible to keep is a model for Christian faith (cf. *CCC*, 144). The promise made to him is fulfilled in us when we believe in Christ, who died and rose for all men (vv. 22–25).

4:17 Gen 17:5. **4:22–23** Gen 15:6.

2. SALVATION AND THE CHRISTIAN LIFE

Reconciliation through Christ's sacrifice, the basis of our hope

5 Therefore, since we are justified by faith, we[f] have peace with God through
our Lord Jesus Christ. 2Through him we have obtained access[g] to this grace
in which we stand, and we[h] rejoice in our hope of sharing the glory of God.
3More than that, we[h] rejoice in our sufferings, knowing that suffering produces
endurance, 4and endurance produces character, and character produces hope,
5and hope does not disappoint us, because God's love has been poured into our
hearts through the Holy Spirit who has been given to us.
6While we were still weak, at the right time Christ died for the ungodly.
7Why, one will hardly die for a righteous man—though perhaps for a good
man one will dare even to die. 8But God shows his love for us in that while we
were yet sinners Christ died for us. 9Since, therefore, we are now justified by
his blood, much more shall we be saved by him from the wrath of God. 10For
if while we were enemies we were reconciled to God by the death of his Son,
much more, now that we are reconciled, shall we be saved by his life. 11Not
only so, but we also rejoice in God through our Lord Jesus Christ, through
whom we have now received our reconciliation.

5:1–8:39 □ In this part of the letter St Paul explains the effects of justification. Christ reconciles us with the Father by means of the sacrifice of his blood, and Christ's resurrection is the basis of our hope (5:1–11); we are set free from sin and death, and we are given back the life of grace and the eternal life which we lost through the sin of the first man (5:12–21); Christ gives us this life through Baptism (6:1–11). He also makes it possible for us to be set free of our personal sins (6:12–23) and from the slavery of the Law (the Law no longer applies to us: 7:1–6); nor will our sinful passions have power over us (7:14–25). The most important element in justification is the new life given us by the Holy Spirit (8:1–13). Through the action of the Spirit, Christians truly become children of God (8:14–30), and are filled with confidence and hope even in the midst of difficulties (8:31–39).

5:1–11 The new life which results from justification develops from faith and hope and produces peace. Peace does not consist in there being no difficulties but in standing one's ground, full of hope ("endurance produces character": v. 3), overcoming tribulation and through endurance staying true to God. We need to experience tribulation, because thereby we grow in virtue. "A person who hopes and strives for something is ready to put up with all the difficulties and disappointments involved in attaining it. For example, a sick person, if he ardently desires to regain his health, is quite happy to take the bitter medicine which will cure him" (St Thomas Aquinas, *Com. on Rom*, in loc.).

f. Other ancient authorities read *let us* **g.** Other ancient authorities add *by faith* **h.** Or *let us*

Adam's original sin
12Therefore as sin came into the world through one man and death through sin,
and so death spread to all men because all men sinned—*13sin indeed was in the
world before the law was given, but sin is not counted where there is no law. 14Yet
death reigned from Adam to Moses, even over those whose sins were not like the
transgression of Adam, who was a type of the one who was to come.
15But the free gift is not like the trespass. For if many died through one
man's trespass, much more have the grace of God and the free gift in the grace
of that one man Jesus Christ abounded for many.* 16And the free gift is not
like the effect of that one man's sin. For the judgment following one trespass
brought condemnation, but the free gift following many trespasses brings
justification. 17If, because of one man's trespass, death reigned through that
one man, much more will those who receive the abundance of grace and the
free gift of righteousness reign in life through the one man Jesus Christ.
18Then as one man's trespass led to condemnation for all men, so one man's
act of righteousness leads to acquittal and life for all men. 19For as by one
man's disobedience many were made sinners, so by one man's obedience
many will be made righteous. 20Law came in, to increase the trespass; but
where sin increased, grace abounded all the more, 21so that, as sin reigned in
death, grace also might reign through righteousness to eternal life through
Jesus Christ our Lord.

Baptism
6 1What shall we say then? Are we to continue in sin that grace may abound?
2By no means! How can we who died to sin still live in it? 3Do you not
know that all of us who have been baptized into Christ Jesus were baptized
into his death? 4We were buried therefore with him by baptism into death, so

---

5:12–21 All men are involved in Adam's sin which "is transmitted with human nature by propagation, not imitation, and is proper to each (person)" (*CCC*, 419). This is what is called "original sin". But just as sin entered the world through the action of one who bore all mankind within him, for all would be descended from him), so, too, righteousness reaches us through one man, the "new Adam", Jesus Christ, "the first-born of all creation" who is "the head of the body, the church" (Col 1:15–18). Through his obedience and submission to his Father's will, Jesus counters the disobedience and rebellion of Adam, restoring to us, superabundantly, the forgiveness and eternal life we lost through the sin of our first parents.

6:1–11 At Baptism the grace of Christ is given to man and frees him from sin. This sacrament joins a person to Christ; immersion in water symbolizes death and burial, taking away man's guilt; emerging from the water symbolizes the resurrection of Christ: the person renounces sin once and for all and is born to a

that as Christ was raised from the dead by the glory of the Father, we too might
walk in newness of life.

[5]For if we have been united with him in a death like his, we shall certainly
be united with him in a resurrection like his. [6]We know that our old self was
crucified with him so that the sinful body might be destroyed, and we might
no longer be enslaved to sin. [7]For he who has died is freed from sin. [8]But if we
have died with Christ, we believe that we shall also live with him. [9]For we
know that Christ being raised from the dead will never die again; death no
longer has dominion over him. [10]The death he died he died to sin, once for all,
but the life he lives he lives to God. [11]So you also must consider yourselves
dead to sin and alive to God in Christ Jesus.

Liberation from sin

[12]Let not sin therefore reign in your mortal bodies, to make you obey their
passions. [13]Do not yield your members to sin as instruments of wickedness,
but yield yourselves to God as men who have been brought from death to life,
and your members to God as instruments of righteousness. [14]For sin will have
no dominion over you, since you are not under law but under grace.

[15]What then? Are we to sin because we are not under law but under grace?
By no means!* [16]Do you not know that if you yield yourselves to any one as
obedient slaves, you are slaves of the one whom you obey, either of sin, which
leads to death, or of obedience, which leads to righteousness? [17]But thanks be
to God, that you who were once slaves of sin have become obedient from the
heart to the standard of teaching to which you were committed, [18]and, having
been set free from sin, have become slaves of righteousness. [19]I am speaking
in human terms, because of your natural limitations. For just as you once
yielded your members to impurity and to greater and greater iniquity, so now
yield your members to righteousness for sanctification.

[20]When you were slaves of sin, you were free in regard to righteousness. [21]But
then what return did you get from the things of which you are now ashamed? The
end of those things is death. [22]But now that you have been set free from sin and
have become slaves of God, the return you get is sanctification and its end,

---

new life. "Our previous sins have been rubbed out by the action of grace. Now, to stay dead to sin after Baptism, a personal effort is needed, even though God's grace continues to help us mightily" (St John Chrysostom, *Hom. on Rom,* 11, 1).

6:12–23 Using the image of slavery and freedom, the Apostle exhorts us to live in accordance with our new status as baptized, "sanctified" (cf. v. 22) persons. "He calls each and every one to holiness; he asks each and every one to love him: young and old, single and married, healthy and sick, learned and unlearned, no matter where they work, or where they are" (Bl. J. Escrivá, *Hom.,* 2, 294).

eternal life. 23For the wages of sin is death, but the free gift of God is eternal life in Christ Jesus our Lord.

The Christian is not bound by the Law

7 1Do you not know, brethren—for I am speaking to those who know the
law—that the law is binding on a person only during his life? 2Thus a
married woman is bound by law to her husband as long as he lives; but if her
husband dies she is discharged from the law concerning the husband.
3Accordingly, she will be called an adulteress if she lives with another man
while her husband is alive. But if her husband dies she is free from that law,
and if she marries another man she is not an adulteress.
4Likewise, my brethren, you have died to the law through the body of
Christ, so that you may belong to another, to him who has been raised from the
dead in order that we may bear fruit for God. 5While we were living in the
flesh, our sinful passions, aroused by the law, were at work in our members to
bear fruit for death. 6But now we are discharged from the law, dead to that
which held us captive, so that we serve not under the old written code but in
the new life of the Spirit.

The Law and concupiscence

7What then shall we say? That the law is sin? By no means! Yet, if it had not
been for the law, I should not have known sin. I should not have known what
it is to covet if the law had not said, "You shall not covet." 8But sin, finding
opportunity in the commandment, wrought in me all kinds of covetousness.
Apart from the law sin lies dead. 9I was once alive apart from the law, but

---

7:1–6 A person who lives in Christ is free of the Mosaic Law. Once a Christian, through Baptism, has partaken of the death of Christ, he is "dead" to the Law (symbolized in vv. 2–3 by the husband), that is, free of the Law—in the sense of freed to do good, to bear the fruit of a holy life, to "bear fruit for God" (v. 4) by virtue of his union with Christ.

The term "flesh" (v. 5) means both human weakness (and therefore the seat of disordered passions which encourage man to sin) and the condition of man after original sin. The grace of the cross sets us free from the tyranny of sin and enables us to see to serve God willingly, not for fear of punishment but out of filial love. That is the freedom of spirit which Christians practise—doing what God desires because we too deserve it.

7:7–13 The Apostle explains the ways that the Law, sin and man inter-relate, and what each of these is. The "Law" is the Law of Moses. The commandments of the Law make man conscious of sin, and sin (depicted here as personal power) uses the commandments to tempt man.

7:7 Ex 20:17; Deut 5:21.

when the commandment came, sin revived and I died; [10]the very commandment which promised life proved to be death to me. [11]For sin, finding opportunity in the commandment, deceived me and by it killed me. [12]So the law is holy, and the commandment is holy and just and good.

[13]Did that which is good, then, bring death to me? By no means! It was sin, working death in me through what is good, in order that sin might be shown to be sin, and through the commandment might become sinful beyond measure.

Interior struggle

[14]We know that the law is spiritual; but I am carnal, sold under sin. [15]I do not understand my own actions. For I do not do what I want, but I do the very thing I hate. [16]Now if I do what I do not want, I agree that the law is good. [17]So then it is no longer I that do it, but sin which dwells within me. [18]For I know that nothing good dwells within me, that is, in my flesh. I can will what is right, but I cannot do it. [19]For I do not do the good I want, but the evil I do not want is what I do. [20]Now if I do what I do not want, it is no longer I that do it, but sin which dwells within me.

[21]So I find it to be a law that when I want to do right, evil lies close at hand. [22]For I delight in the law of God, in my inmost self, [23]but I see in my members another law at war with the law of my mind and making me captive to the law of sin which dwells in my members. [24]Wretched man that I am! Who will deliver me from this body of death? [25]Thanks be to God through Jesus Christ our Lord! So then, I of myself serve the law of God with my mind, but with my flesh I serve the law of sin.

Paul also points out that the Law, although sin uses it to gain a hold on man, is not evil: it is something holy and just and good: "The Law is a pedagogy and prophecy of things to come" (St Irenaeus, *Adv. haer.*, 4, 15, 1: cf. *CCC,* 1964).

7:14–25 Here we have a vivid description of the interior struggle that everyone experiences, a "law", an inclination (distinct from the Law of Moses), which is at war with the law of the Spirit (v. 23), that is, the spiritual good which God's grace enables man to desire. The very expression "the law of sin which dwells in my members" (v. 23) emphasizes how strenuously evil desires refuse to follow the commands of our spirit. However, this "law of sin" is not irresistible. Our moral faculties are indeed impaired and they do incline us to commit sin, but that inclination is not itself a sin. "The new life received in Christian initiation has not abolished the frailty and weakness of human nature, nor the inclination to sin that tradition calls concupiscence, which remains in the baptized such that with the help of the grace of Christ they may prove themselves in the struggle of Christian life. This is the struggle of conversion directed towards holiness and eternal life to which the Lord never ceases to call us" (*CCC*, 1426).

Life in the Spirit

8 1There is therefore now no condemnation for those who are in Christ Jesus. 2For the law of the Spirit of life in Christ Jesus has set me free from the law of sin and death. 3For God has done what the law, weakened by the flesh, could not do: sending his own Son in the likeness of sinful flesh and for sin,[i] he condemned sin in the flesh, 4in order that the just requirement of the law might be fulfilled in us, who walk not according to the flesh but according to the Spirit. 5For those who live according to the flesh set their minds on the things of the flesh, but those who live according to the Spirit set their minds on the things of the Spirit. 6To set the mind on the flesh is death, but to set the mind on the Spirit is life and peace. 7For the mind that is set on the flesh is hostile to God; it does not submit to God's law, indeed it cannot; 8and those who are in the flesh cannot please God.

9But you are not in the flesh, you are in the Spirit, if in fact the Spirit of God dwells in you. Any one who does not have the Spirit of Christ does not belong to him. 10But if Christ is in you, although your bodies are dead because of sin, your spirits are alive because of righteousness. 11If the Spirit of him who raised Jesus from the dead dwells in you, he who raised Christ Jesus from the dead will give life to your mortal bodies also through his Spirit who dwells in you.

12So then, brethren, we are debtors, not to the flesh, to live according to the flesh—13for if you live according to the flesh you will die, but if by the Spirit you put to death the deeds of the body you will live.

Christians are children of God

14For all who are led by the Spirit of God are sons of God. 15For you did not receive the spirit of slavery to fall back into fear, but you have received the spirit of sonship. When we cry, "Abba! Father!" 16it is the Spirit himself

---

8:1–13 The Apostle specifies two ways whereby man may live in this world after original sin. The first is life according to the Spirit, whereby man seeks God above all things and, with the help of grace, fights the inclinations of his passions; the second is life according to the flesh, whereby man lets himself be defeated. "If he has the Spirit, a person belongs to Christ, he has Christ, he rivals the angels in dignity. With the Spirit, the flesh is crucified and a person enjoys the 'charms' of eternal life" (St John Chrysostom, *Hom. on Rom*, 13, 8).

8:14–30 The life of a Christian is a sharing in the life of Christ, God's only Son. By becoming, through adoption, a true child of God, a Christian has a right (so to speak) to share also in Christ's inheritance—eternal life in heaven (vv. 14–18). This divine life, begun in Baptism through rebirth in the Holy Spirit, develops under the guidance of the Spirit, who makes the Christian more and more like Christ (vv. 14, 26–27). So, our adoption as children of God is already a fact: we

i. Or *and as a sin offering*

bearing witness with our spirit that we are children of God, [17]and if children,
then heirs, heirs of God and fellow heirs with Christ, provided we suffer with
him in order that we may also be glorified with him.

[18]I consider that the sufferings of this present time are not worth comparing
with the glory that is to be revealed to us. [19]For the creation waits with eager
longing for the revealing of the sons of God;* [20]for the creation was subjected
to futility, not of its own will but by the will of him who subjected it in hope;
[21]because the creation itself will be set free from its bondage to decay and obtain
the glorious liberty of the children of God. [22]We know that the whole creation has
been groaning in travail together until now; [23]and not only the creation, but we
ourselves, who have the first fruits of the Spirit, groan inwardly as we wait for
adoption as sons, the redemption of our bodies. [24]For in this hope we were saved.
Now hope that is seen is not hope. For who hopes for what he sees? [25]But if we
hope for what we do not see, we wait for it with patience.

[26]Likewise the Spirit helps us in our weakness; for we do not know how to
pray as we ought, but the Spirit himself intercedes for us with sighs too deep for
words. [27]And he who searches the hearts of men knows what is the mind of the
Spirit, because[j] the Spirit intercedes for the saints according to the will of God.

[28]We know that in everything God works for good[k] with those who love
him,[l] who are called according to his purpose. [29]For those whom he foreknew
he also predestined to be conformed to the image of his Son, in order that he
might be the first-born among many brethren. [30]And those whom he predestined
he also called; and those whom he called he also justified; and those whom he
justified he also glorified.

---

already have the first-fruits of the Spirit (v. 23) but not until the end of time, when our bodies are resurrected in glory, will our redemption reach its full measure (vv. 23–25). "Divine filiation is a joyful truth, a consoling mystery. It fills all our spiritual life, it shows us how to speak to God, to know and to love our Father in heaven. And it makes our interior struggle overflow with hope and gives us the trusting simplicity of little children. More than that: precisely because we are children of God, we can contemplate in love and wonder everything as coming from the hands of our Father, God the Creator. And so we become contemplatives in the middle of the world, loving the world" (Bl. J. Escrivá, *Hom.*, 1, 65).

Meanwhile we are in a waiting situation—not free from suffering (v. 18), groans (v. 23) and weakness (v. 26)—a situation characterized by a certain tension between what we already have and are, and what we still yearn for. This yearning on mankind's part is something that all creation experiences, because it is subject to "futility" (v. 20), that is, to corruption and death, particularly to the disorder caused by sin. In God's plan, creation's destiny and man's are intimately linked; creation, too, awaits transfiguration at the end of the world (vv. 19–22).

j. Or *that* **k.** Other ancient authorities read *in everything he works for good, or everything works for good* **l.** Greek *God*

Trust in God

31 What then shall we say to this? If God is for us, who is against us? 32 He who
did not spare his own Son but gave him up for us all, will he not also give us
all things with him? 33 Who shall bring any charge against God's elect? It is
God who justifies; 34 who is to condemn? Is it Christ Jesus, who died, yes, who
was raised from the dead, who is at the right hand of God, who indeed
intercedes for us?[m] 35 Who shall separate us from the love of Christ? Shall
tribulation, or distress, or persecution, or famine, or nakedness, or peril, or
sword? 36 As it is written,

> "For thy sake we are being killed all the day long;
> we are regarded as sheep to be slaughtered."

37 No, in all these things we are more than conquerors through him who loved
us. 38 For I am sure that neither death, nor life, nor angels, nor principalities,
nor things present, nor things to come, nor powers, 39 nor height, nor depth, nor
anything else in all creation, will be able to separate us from the love of God
in Christ Jesus our Lord.

3. GOD'S PLAN FOR THE CHOSEN PEOPLE

The privileges of Israel and God's fidelity

9 1 I am speaking the truth in Christ, I am not lying; my conscience bears me
witness in the Holy Spirit, 2 that I have great sorrow and unceasing anguish in
my heart. 3 For I could wish that I myself were accursed and cut off from Christ
for the sake of my brethren, my kinsmen by race. 4 They are Israelites, and to them
belong the sonship, the glory, the covenants, the giving of the law, the worship,
and the promises; 5 to them belong the patriarchs, and of their race, according to
the flesh, is the Christ, who is God over all, blessed for ever.[n] Amen.

8:31–39 The omnipotence of Him who loves man to the point of giving his only Son up to death on man's account, will ensure that we emerge victorious from all attacks, dangers and trials. Provided Christians truly desire God's good things, they can be sure of attaining salvation because God will never fail to give us the graces we need. Nothing that happens to us can separate us from the Lord.

To make his point, St Paul lists a whole series of things more powerful than man (vv. 38–39): nothing, no one, no created thing is stronger than the love God has for mankind.

9:1–11:36 □ Going back to something touched on in 3:1–2, St Paul now examines more closely the Jewish people's privilege of having been given divine revelation. The gratuitous choice of Jacob to be heir of the promise, and the rejection of Esau

m. Or *It is Christ Jesus . . . for us* **n.** Or *Christ. God who is over all be blessed for ever* **8:36** Ps 44:22.

[6]But it is not as though the word of God had failed. For not all who are
descended from Israel belong to Israel, [7]and not all are children of Abraham
because they are his descendants; but "Through Isaac shall your descendants be
named." [8]This means that it is not the children of the flesh who are the children of
God, but the children of the promise are reckoned as descendants. [9]For this is
what the promise said, "About this time I will return and Sarah shall have a son."
[10]And not only so, but also when Rebecca had conceived children by one man,
our forefather Isaac, [11]though they were not yet born and had done nothing either
good or bad, in order that God's purpose of election might continue, not because
of works but because of his call, [12]she was told, "The elder will serve the
younger." [13]As it is written, "Jacob I loved, but Esau I hated."

Israel's vocation

[14]What shall we say then? Is there injustice on God's part? By no means! [15]For
he says to Moses, "I will have mercy on whom I have mercy, and I will have

---

(9:1–13), involves the revelation of the mystery of predestination, which is not at odds with man's freedom (9:14–33). The chosen people of Israel were unfaithful to their calling, and God's mercy has been extended to the Gentiles instead (10:1–21). However, not all Israel has been rejected; a remnant will be saved (11:1–12). The section closes by contrasting the new people of God and the old (11:13–24), to announce that divine Wisdom has already ordained the conversion of all Israel and the unity of all the faithful (11:25–36).

9:1–13 The Israelites were descendants of Jacob (Israel): all the privileges that God gave the Israelites over the course of time derived from that fact. However, what really shows the dignity of the chosen people is the fact that God himself chose to assume a human nature with all the features of the Jewish race. Jesus Christ, as true man, is an Israelite "according to the flesh, and he is true God because he is 'God over all, blessed for ever' (v. 5). This statement, which appears in the form of a "doxology" or paean of praise to God, was a solemn Old Testament form of exalting God (cf. Ps 41:14; 72:19; etc.). By calling Jesus Christ "God, blessed for ever", his divinity is being declared in a very explicit way.

The fact that God chose Israel to be the heir of the promise, and then chose Jacob over the head of the first-born Esau, is something Paul uses to explain why there is nothing surprising about the call of the Gentiles. God chooses according to the promises, not according to the flesh. The true Israel, therefore, is not the one that descends from Abraham "according to the flesh" but that created by the bonds with the Spirit.

9:14–33 St Paul produces proofs from Scripture to back up what he has been saying. Beginning with the selection of Israel to be the chosen people, he says that

9:7 Gen 21:12. **9.9** Gen 18:10. **9:12** Gen 25:23. **9:13** Mal 1:2–3. **9:15** Ex 33:9.

compassion on whom I have compassion." [16]So it depends not upon man's will
or exertion, but upon God's mercy. [17]For the scripture says to Pharaoh, "I have
raised you up for the very purpose of showing my power in you, so that my
name may be proclaimed in all the earth." [18]So then he has mercy upon
whomever he wills, and he hardens the heart of whomever he wills.

[19]You will say to me then, "Why does he still find fault? For who can resist
his will?" [20]But who are you, a man, to answer back to God? Will what is
moulded say to its moulder, "Why have you made me thus?" [21]Has the potter
no right over the clay, to make out of the same lump one vessel for beauty and
another for menial use? [22]What if God, desiring to show his wrath and to make
known his power, has endured with much patience the vessels of wrath made
for destruction, [23]in order to make known the riches of his glory for the vessels
of mercy, which he has prepared beforehand for glory, [24]even us whom he has
called, not from the Jews only but also from the Gentiles? [25]As indeed he says
in Hosea,

"Those who were not my people
I will call 'my people,'
and her who was not beloved
I will call 'my beloved.' "
[26]"And in the very place where it was said to them,
'You are not my people,'
they will be called 'sons of the living God.'"

[27]And Isaiah cries out concerning Israel: "Though the number of the sons
of Israel be as the sand of the sea, only a remnant of them will be saved; [28]for
the Lord will execute his sentence upon the earth with rigour and dispatch."

---

there is a profound mystery operating—the mystery of predestination. God chose Israel from a multitude of candidates; he hardened Pharaoh's heart and punished him (vv. 16–18); he saves one person and condemns another (cf. the simile of the pot: vv. 20–26): these are examples which point to the same mystery. God, who is almighty and all-knowing, not only knows what lies in the future: by his infallible will he can arrange events to bring about his purpose; divine wisdom, Scripture says, "reaches mightily from one end of the earth to the other, and she orders all things well" (Wis 8:1). The human mind cannot fathom this dovetailing of God's infallible plan and man's freedom. That is where the mystery lies—in the combination of three realities: the absolute freedom and generosity of God, in giving us his grace; God's desire that all should be saved through the death of Christ on the cross; and man's free response, on which God counts and to which he moves him and which he prepares him for with his grace. "To God, all moments of time are present in their immediacy. When therefore he establishes his eternal plan of 'predestination', he includes in it each person's free response to his grace" (*CCC*, 600).

9:17 Ex 9:16. **9:20** Is 29:16; 45:9. **9:21** Jer 18:6. **9:25** Hos 2:25. **9:26** Hos 1:10. **9:27–28** Is 10:22–23.

[29]And as Isaiah predicted,

> "If the Lord of hosts had not left us children,
> we would have fared like Sodom and been made like Gomorrah."

[30]What shall we say, then? That Gentiles who did not pursue righteousness have attained it, that is, righteousness through faith; [31]but that Israel who pursued the righteousness which is based on law did not succeed in fulfilling that law. [32]Why? Because they did not pursue it through faith, but as if it were based on works. They have stumbled over the stumbling stone, [33]as it is written,

> "Behold, I am laying in Zion a stone that will make men stumble,
> a rock that will make them fall;
> and he who believes in him will not be put to shame."

Israel's infidelity

10 [1]Brethren, my heart's desire and prayer to God for them is that they may be saved.* [2]I bear them witness that they have a zeal for God, but it is not enlightened. [3]For, being ignorant of the righteousness that comes from God, and seeking to establish their own, they did not submit to God's righteousness. [4]For Christ is the end of the law, that every one who has faith may be justified.

[5]Moses writes that the man who practises the righteousness which is based on the law shall live by it. [6]But the righteousness based on faith says, Do not say in your heart, "Who will ascend into heaven?" (that is, to bring Christ down) [7]or "Who will descend into the abyss?" (that is, to bring Christ up from the dead). [8]But what does it say? The word is near you, on your lips and in your heart (that is, the word of faith which we preach); [9]because, if you confess with your lips that Jesus is Lord and believe in your heart that God raised him from the dead, you will be saved. [10]For man believes with his heart and so is justified, and he confesses with his lips and so is saved. [11]The scripture says, "No one who believes in him will be put to shame." [12]For there

---

10:1–21 The Jews have no excuse for not invoking Christ as Lord; their unbelief is due to their rebelliousness, for the Good News has indeed reached them. From the very start, the apostles have done as the Lord told them: "Go into all the world and preach the gospel to the whole creation" (Mk 16:15–16). And Christ's disciples continue to do this. "The Church will evangelize the world above all through her conduct, by her life [...]. This law laid down by St Paul is as valid and relevent today. Preaching, the proclamation of the [Gospel] message, is indispensable. [...] The word is always present, especially when it is backed up by the power of God" (Paul VI, *Evang. nunt.*, 41–42)

Verses 9–10 show the need to give internal assent to the divinity of Jesus Christ and to profess it openly. The title of Lord, a word generally used in the Old Testament as a substitute for YHWH, is applied here to Jesus Christ, to indicate his divinity.

9:29 Is 1:9. **9:33** Is 8:14; 28:16. **10:5** Lev 18:5. **10:6–7** Deut 9:14; 30:12–13; Bar 3:29. **10:8** Deut 30:14. **10:11** Is 28:16.

is no distinction between Jew and Greek; the same Lord is Lord of all and
bestows his riches upon all who call upon him. 13For, "every one who calls
upon the name of the Lord will be saved."
14But how are men to call upon him in whom they have not believed? And
how are they to believe in him of whom they have never heard? And how are
they to hear without a preacher? 15And how can men preach unless they are
sent? As it is written, "How beautiful are the feet of those who preach good
news!" 16But they have not all obeyed the gospel; for Isaiah says, "Lord, who
has believed what he has heard from us?" 17So faith comes from what is heard,
and what is heard comes by the preaching of Christ.
18But I ask, have they not heard? Indeed they have; for
"Their voice has gone out to all the earth,
and their words to the ends of the world."
19Again I ask, did Israel not understand? First Moses says,
"I will make you jealous of those who are not a nation;
with a foolish nation I will make you angry."
20Then Isaiah is so bold as to say,
"I have been found by those who did not seek me;
I have shown myself to those who did not ask for me."
21But of Israel he says, "All day long I have held out my hands to a disobedient
and contrary people."

Part of Israel will be saved

11 1I ask, then, has God rejected his people? By no means! I myself am an
Israelite, a descendant of Abraham, a member of the tribe of Benjamin.
2God has not rejected his people whom he foreknew. Do you not know what
the scripture says of Elijah, how he pleads with God against Israel? 3"Lord,
they have killed thy prophets, they have demolished thy altars, and I alone am

---

11:1–12 The Apostle brings in the biblical theme of the "remnant of Israel"—a description used in prophetical preaching to mean those Israelites who stayed true to God at times of widespread unfaithfulness. He uses this idea to explain how it happened that only a minority of Jews have believed in Jesus. These are the "remnant of Israel" whom God has chosen so that the promises might find fulfilment in them.

It also happens in the history of the Church that there are times when many people turn their backs on God. In such moments of crisis, Christians need to trust in God's promises and remember that our Lord also wants to use a faithful "few" to help remedy the general situation: "I'll tell you a secret, an open secret: these world crises are crises of saints. God wants a handful of men 'of his own' in every human activity. Then … '*pax Christi in regno Christi*'—'the peace of Christ in the kingdom of Christ'" (Bl. J. Escrivá, *The Way*, 301).

10:15 Is 52:7. **10:16** Is 53:1. **10:18** Ps 19:4. **10:19** Deut 32:1. **10:21** Is 65:2. **11:2** Ps 94:14. **11:3** 1 Kings 19:10.

left, and they seek my life." [4]But what is God's reply to him? "I have kept for
myself seven thousand men who have not bowed the knee to Baal." [5]So too at
the present time there is a remnant, chosen by grace. [6]But if it is by grace, it is
no longer on the basis of works; otherwise grace would no longer be grace.
[7]What then? Israel failed to obtain what it sought. The elect obtained it, but
the rest were hardened, [8]as it is written,

"God gave them a spirit of stupor,
eyes that should not see and ears that should not hear,
down to this very day."

[9]And David says,

"Let their table become a snare and a trap,
a pitfall and a retribution for them;
[10]let their eyes be darkened so that they cannot see,
and bend their backs for ever."

[11]So I ask, have they stumbled so as to fall? By no means! But through their
trespass salvation has come to the Gentiles, so as to make Israel jealous. [12]Now
if their trespass means riches for the world, and if their failure means riches for
the Gentiles, how much more will their full inclusion mean!

The new chosen people

[13]Now I am speaking to you Gentiles. Inasmuch then as I am an apostle to the
Gentiles, I magnify my ministry [14]in order to make my fellow Jews jealous,
and thus save some of them. [15]For if their rejection means the reconciliation of
the world, what will their acceptance mean but life from the dead? [16]If the
dough offered as first fruits is holy, so is the whole lump; and if the root is
holy, so are the branches.
[17]But if some of the branches were broken off, and you, a wild olive shoot,
were grafted in their place to share the richness[o] of the olive tree, [18]do not
boast over the branches. If you do boast, remember it is not you that support
the root, but the root that supports you. [19]You will say, "Branches were broken

---

11:13–24 The conversion of the Gentiles should make the Jews jealous and lead them to change. The good olive tree stands for the faithful of the Old Testament and, now, the Israel of God that is the Church. The natural branches that have stayed on the tree are Jews who were converted to Christianity; broken off branches are the unbelieving Jews who rejected Christ; the wild branches grafted on to the tree are the Gentiles who sprang from a wild tree but have now come to take the place of the Jews who were unfaithful to grace; these Gentiles are now one in faith with the patriarchs and prophets and share in the blessings promised to them.

This comparison has a twofold purpose—on the one hand, to check boasting by Christians of Gentile background, for if the natural, selected branches have been cut off, this can much more easily happen with those who are mere grafts; on the

o. Other ancient authorities read *rich root* **11:4** 1 Kings 19:18. **11:8** Is 29:10; Deut 29:4. **11:10** Ps 69:22–23.

off so that I might be grafted in." [20]That is true. They were broken off because of
their unbelief, but you stand fast only through faith. So do not become proud, but
stand in awe. [21]For if God did not spare the natural branches, neither will he spare
you. [22]Note then the kindness and the severity of God: severity toward those who
have fallen, but God's kindness to you, provided you continue in his kindness;
otherwise you too will be cut off. [23]And even the others, if they do not persist in
their unbelief, will be grafted in, for God has the power to graft them in again.
[24]For if you have been cut from what is by nature a wild olive tree, and grafted,
contrary to nature, into a cultivated olive tree, how much more will these natural
branches be grafted back into their own olive tree.

The conversion of the Jews

[25]Lest you be wise in your own conceits, I want you to understand this mystery,
brethren: a hardening has come upon part of Israel, until the full number of the
Gentiles come in, [26]and so all Israel will be saved; as it is written,

"The Deliverer will come from Zion,
he will banish ungodliness from Jacob";
[27]"and this will be my covenant with them
when I take away their sins."

[28]As regards the gospel they are enemies of God, for your sake; but as regards
election they are beloved for the sake of their forefathers. [29]For the gifts and
the call of God are irrevocable. [30]Just as you were once disobedient to God but
now have received mercy because of their disobedience, [31]so they have now
been disobedient in order that by the mercy shown to you they also may[p]
receive mercy. [32]For God has consigned all men to disobedience, that he may
have mercy upon all.

[33]O the depth of the riches and wisdom and knowledge of God! How
unsearchable are his judgments and how inscrutable his ways!

[34]"For who has known the mind of the Lord,
or who has been his counsellor?"
[35]"Or who has given a gift to him
that he might be repaid?"

[36]For from him and through him and to him are all things. To him be glory for
ever. Amen.

---

other hand, Paul wants to raise the spirits of Christians of Jewish background: the branches of the wild olive have been successfully grafted on against nature, so it will be much easier, he tells them, for the natural branches to be reunited with the trunk from which they came.

11:25–36 St Paul announces that according to God's plans—and he does not go back on his promises (v. 29)—all nations will be converted in the end. "Together

p. Other ancient authorities add *now* **11:26–27** Is 59:20–21. **11:27** Jer 31:33; Is 27:9. **11:34** Is 40:13–14.

PART TWO: LIVING IN CHARITY

4. CHRISTIAN BEHAVIOUR

Solidarity in the mystical body of Christ

12 [1]I appeal to you therefore, brethren, by the mercies of God, to present
your bodies as a living sacrifice, holy and acceptable to God, which is
your spiritual worship. [2]Do not be conformed to this world[q] but be transformed
by the renewal of your mind, that you may prove what is the will of God, what
is good and acceptable and perfect.[r]
[3]For by the grace given to me I bid every one among you not to think of
himself more highly than he ought to think, but to think with sober judgment,
each according to the measure of faith which God has assigned him. [4]For as in
one body we have many members, and all the members do not have the same
function, [5]so we, though many, are one body in Christ, and individually
members one of another. [6]Having gifts that differ according to the grace given
to us, let us use them: if prophecy, in proportion to our faith; [7]if service, in our
serving; he who teaches, in his teaching; [8]he who exhorts, in his exhortation;
he who contributes, in liberality; he who gives aid, with zeal; he who does acts
of mercy, with cheerfulness.

---

with the prophets and that same apostle, the Church awaits the day, known to God alone, when all peoples will call on God with one voice and 'serve him shoulder to shoulder'" (Vatican II, *NA*, 4). The conversion of the Jews, which will follow that of the Gentiles, is a secret, a "mystery", according to the text (v. 25), which lies in the future; it will happen when God so decides; that is all we know. This does not mean that the conversion of the Jewish people has to be a sign of the end of the world. The Church begs the Lord to listen to her prayers "that the people you first made your own may arrive at the fullness of redemption" (*Roman Missal,* Liturgy of Good Friday, Prayer of the faithful).

The great goodness of God who allowed the disobedience of Jews and Gentiles in order to show mercy and compassion for them in their wretchedness calls forth ardent praise from the Apostle (vv. 33–36) for the mysterious plan of God

12:1–16:27 □ □ The revelation that all Christians form one body in Christ marks the start of the "moral" part of the letter, the central theme of which is life in keeping with charity (12:1–13:4) which has specific implications and must be lived in line with Christ's example (14:1–15:13). The Apostle's own life is in accord with this teaching (15:14–16:27).

12:1–13:14 □ St Paul spells out the general principle which should govern the Christian life: charity, love, is the bond which unites the members of Christ's

q. Greek *age* **r.** Or *what is the good and acceptable and perfect will of God*

Charity towards all

[9]Let love be genuine; hate what is evil, hold fast to what is good; [10]love one
another with brotherly affection; outdo one another in showing honour.
[11]Never flag in zeal, be aglow with the Spirit, serve the Lord. [12]Rejoice in your
hope, be patient in tribulation, be constant in prayer. [13]Contribute to the needs
of the saints, practise hospitality.

[14]Bless those who persecute you; bless and do not curse them. [15]Rejoice with
those who rejoice, weep with those who weep. [16]Live in harmony with one
another; do not be haughty, but associate with the lowly;[s] never be conceited.
[17]Repay no one evil for evil, but take thought for what is noble in the sight of all.
[18]If possible, so far as it depends upon you, live peaceably with all. [19]Beloved,
never avenge yourselves, but leave it[t] to the wrath of God; for it is written,
"Vengeance is mine, I will repay, says the Lord." [20]No, "if your enemy is hungry,
feed him; if he is thirsty, give him drink; for by so doing you will heap burning
coals upon his head." [21]Do not be overcome by evil, but overcome evil with good.

Body, the Church. We all form one body in Christ and we are members of one another (12:1–8); hence the need for brotherly love (12:9–21). In this context, obedience to authority, which comes from God and is at the service of God (13:1–7), should also be exercised in a spirit of love for God. For all these reasons love is the fullness of the Law (13:8–14).

12:1–8 In v.v. 1–2 the Apostle invites us to worship God in a spiritual way, as befitting the new status Baptism has given us. Christians are the new people of God and they are members of Christ in such a way that "through Baptism all of us have been made priests of our lives, 'to offer spiritual sacrifices acceptable to God through Jesus Christ' (1 Pet 2:15). Everything we do can be an expression of our obedience to God's will and so perpetuate the mission of the God-Man" (Bl. J. Escrivá, *Hom.,* 1, 96).

Paul explains the various "gifts" or charisms to be found in the Church, using the simile of a body to get across the variety of roles: each person has his or her own role and contributes to the welfare of all while also seeking personal spiritual good (cf. 1 Cor 12:12–31).

12:9–21 "Having spoken of the graces that are not shared by everyone, the Apostle teaches that charity is a gift common to all" (St Thomas Aquinas, *Com. on Rom,* in loc.). True charity takes different forms depending on the needs and capacity of each person; it always involves seeking good and avoiding evil (v. 9); it has to be exercised with those who are Christian (vv. 10–13) and those who are not of the same faith (vv. 17–21). "We have to understand everyone; we must live peaceably with everyone; we must forgive everyone. [...] That's how Christ will reign in our souls and in the souls of the people around us" (Bl. J. Escrivá, *Hom.,* 1, 182).

s. Or give yourselves to humble tasks **t.** Greek *give place* **12:17** Prov 3:4. **12:19** Deut 32:35. **12:20** Prov 25:21–22.

Submission to authority

13 [1]Let every person be subject to the governing authorities. For there is no
authority except from God, and those that exist have been instituted by
God. [2]Therefore he who resists the authorities resists what God has appointed,
and those who resist will incur judgment. [3]For rulers are not a terror to good
conduct, but to bad. Would you have no fear of him who is in authority? Then
do what is good, and you will receive his approval, [4]for he is God's servant for
your good. But if you do wrong, be afraid, for he does not bear the sword in vain;
he is the servant of God to execute his wrath on the wrongdoer. [5]Therefore one
must be subject, not only to avoid God's wrath but also for the sake of
conscience. [6]For the same reason you also pay taxes, for the authorities are
ministers of God, attending to this very thing. [7]Pay all of them their dues, taxes
to whom taxes are due, revenue to whom revenue is due, respect to whom
respect is due, honour to whom honour is due.

Love, the fullness of the Law

[8]Owe no one anything, except to love one another; for he who loves his
neighbour has fulfilled the law. [9]The commandments, "You shall not commit
adultery, You shall not kill, You shall not steal, You shall not covet," and any
other commandment, are summed up in this sentence, "You shall love your
neighbour as yourself." [10]Love does no wrong to a neighbour; therefore love
is the fulfilling of the law.

13:1–7 Charity also extends as far as one's duties to the State. Jesus himself declared in the presence of Pilate that all authority comes from God (Jn 19:11; cf. Prov 8:15–16; Wis 6:3). God, the author of the social order, created man as needing to live and develop within a community, thereby enabling him to achieve his final end perfectly and effectively. The early Christians set an example in this regard, even though they were victims of the State's persecution and hatred. "Christians live in their own countries, but are seen as outsiders; they play their part as citizens and endure all things [...]. They obey all the laws laid down, but go beyond the law in their lives. They love all men, and are persecuted by all. They are disowned and condemned [...]. They are dishonoured, and by dishonour they are glorified" (Anon., *Letter to Diognetus*, 5, 5–14).

13:8–14 After showing that love is the fullness of the Law, Paul concludes his exhortations to charity with an invitation to prepare for the coming of the Lord (vv. 11–14). Christ came into the world by his Incarnation; he also comes to souls through grace; and at the end of time he will come as Judge. Rising like the sun, he dispelled darkness when he came into the world, and he continues to dispel whatever darkness remains in souls to the degree that men give him mastery of their hearts. The Church uses this inspired text in the liturgy of Advent to help us prepare for the definitive coming of the Lord, at her annual celebration of his Birth.

13:9 Ex 20:13–14; Deut 5:17–18; Lev 19:18.

[11]Besides this you know what hour it is, how it is full time now for you to wake from sleep. For salvation is nearer to us now than when we first believed; [12]the night is far gone, the day is at hand. Let us then cast off the works of darkness and put on the armour of light; [13]let us conduct ourselves becomingly as in the day, not in revelling and drunkenness, not in debauchery and licentiousness, not in quarrelling and jealousy. [14]But put on the Lord Jesus Christ, and make no provision for the flesh, to gratify its desires.

5. SENSITIVITY TOWARDS OTHERS

Seeing things from the other person's point of view

14 [1]As for the man who is weak in faith, welcome him, but not for disputes over opinions.* [2]One believes he may eat anything, while the weak man eats only vegetables. [3]Let not him who eats despise him who abstains, and let not him who abstains pass judgment on him who eats; for God has welcomed him. [4]Who are you to pass judgment on the servant of another? It is before his own master that he stands or falls. And he will be upheld, for the Master is able to make him stand.

[5]One man esteems one day as better than another, while another man esteems all days alike. Let every one be fully convinced in his own mind. [6]He who observes the day, observes it in honour of the Lord. He also who eats, eats in honour of the Lord, since he gives thanks to God; while he who abstains, abstains in honour of the Lord and gives thanks to God. [7]None of us lives to himself, and none of us dies to himself. [8]If we live, we live to the Lord, and if we die, we die to the Lord; so then, whether we live or whether we die, we are the Lord's. [9]For to this end Christ died and lived again, that he might be Lord both of the dead and of the living.

14:1–15:13 □ In this section St Paul focuses on a particular case—the difference between those who are "strong" and those who are "weak" in faith (in connexion with the question of observance or not of Jewish practices). Love and mutual respect are the criteria that should apply here. One needs to see things from one's neighbour's point of view (14:1–12), avoid giving cause for scandal (14:13–23) and follow Christ's example in all things (15:1–13).

14:1–12 Paul asks the brethren to be open and responsive to one another (cf. 15:7). The Christian community at Rome included some people of Jewish background who abstained from food forbidden by the Old Law; whereas others, "strong" in the faith, knew that Christ had freed them from Mosaic observances (such as avoidance of certain kinds of food and keeping to the Jewish calendar with its sabbaths, full moons and other festivals). These regarded the former, who were

14:11 Is 45:23.

[10]Why do you pass judgment on your brother? Or you, why do you despise
your brother? For we shall all stand before the judgment seat of God; [11]for it
is written,

"As I live, says the Lord, every knee shall bow to me,
and every tongue shall give praise[u] to God."

[12]So each of us shall give account of himself to God.

Not leading others astray

[13]Then let us no more pass judgment on one another, but rather decide never to put
a stumbling block or hindrance in the way of a brother. [14]I know and am persuaded
in the Lord Jesus that nothing is unclean in itself; but it is unclean for any one who
thinks it unclean.* [15]If your brother is being injured by what you eat, you are no
longer walking in love. Do not let what you eat cause the ruin of one for whom
Christ died. [16]So do not let your good be spoken of as evil. [17]For the kingdom of
God is not food and drink but righteousness and peace and joy in the Holy Spirit;
[18]he who thus serves Christ is acceptable to God and approved by men. [19]Let us
then pursue what makes for peace and for mutual upbuilding. [20]Do not, for the
sake of food, destroy the work of God. Everything is indeed clean, but it is wrong
for any one to make others fall by what he eats; [21]it is right not to eat meat or drink
wine or do anything that makes your brother stumble.[v] [22]The faith that you have,
keep between yourself and God; happy is he who has no reason to judge himself
for what he approves. [23]But he who has doubts is condemned, if he eats, because
he does not act from faith; for whatever does not proceed from faith is sin.[w]

The example of Christ

15 [1]We who are strong ought to bear with the failings of the weak, and not
to please ourselves; [2]let each of us please his neighbour for his good, to

---

fewer in number, as "weak" because they saw them as being tied down by Mosaic precepts. The "weak", for their part, were scandalized by the freedom of spirit of the others, and regarded them as sinners. The "strong" in turn looked down on the "weak" and did not mind shocking them. Both sets of Christians were sinning against charity. St Paul addresses them both in fatherly tones, exhorting the weak not to falsely judge the strong, and appealing to the strong not to despise the weak (cf. v. 21 and 1 Cor 8:7–13).

14:13–23 Here we have further instruction on the need to avoid giving offence: it is not just a matter of not doing evil things: actions which are morally indifferent should also be avoided if they only disconcert others who are less well educated in the faith.

15:1–13 The Apostle again reminds us about our Lord's abnegation: he bore our sins in his body and by his wounds we have been healed (cf. 1 Pet 2:24; Is 53:5–6).

u. Or *confess* **v.** Other ancient authorities add *or be upset or be weakened* **w.** Other authorities, some ancient, insert here Ch 16:25–27

edify him. 3For Christ did not please himself; but, as it is written, "The reproaches
of those who reproached thee fell on me." 4For whatever was written in former
days was written for our instruction, that by steadfastness and by the encour-
agement of the scriptures we might have hope. 5May the God of steadfastness
and encouragement grant you to live in such harmony with one another, in
accord with Christ Jesus, 6that together you may with one voice glorify the
God and Father of our Lord Jesus Christ.

7Welcome one another, therefore, as Christ has welcomed you, for the glory
of God. 8For I tell you that Christ became a servant to the circumcised to show
God's truthfulness, in order to confirm the promises given to the patriarchs,
9and in order that the Gentiles might glorify God for his mercy. As it is written,

"Therefore I will praise thee among the Gentiles,
and sing to thy name";

10and again it is said,

"Rejoice, O Gentiles, with his people";

11and again,

"Praise the Lord, all Gentiles,
and let all the peoples praise him";

12and further Isaiah says,

"The root of Jesse shall come,
he who rises to rule the Gentiles;
in him shall the Gentiles hope."

13May the God of hope fill you with all joy and peace in believing, so that by
the power of the Holy Spirit you may abound in hope.

Our charity should be inspired by Christ's own sentiments (cf. Phil 2:5–8); no one should be excluded from it. Although Christ addressed the Jews in the first instance, he also received Gentiles. With the coming of God-made-man, the promises made to the Jews about the Gentiles also praising God have come true. In this way are shown the fidelity of God to his promises and his compassion for all men, because his blessings extend also to those who are not Israelites by race.

15:14–16:27 □ By way of an epilogue, St Paul first explains why he has written to the Christians at Rome (5:14–21), then he outlines his future plans (15:22–33), and he ends with a long, affectionate series of endorsements and greetings (16:1–24). The final words of the letter are in praise of God, through Jesus Christ (16:25–27). So, he ends his letter the way he began it—in the name of God and Jesus Christ.

15:3 Ps 69:9. **15:9** Ps 18:49. **15:10** Deut 32:43. **15:11** Ps 117:1. **15:12** Is 11:10.

6. CONCLUSION AND FAREWELL

Paul's ministry

14I myself am satisfied about you, my brethren, that you yourselves are full of goodness, filled with all knowledge, and able to instruct one another. 15But on some points I have written to you very boldly by way of reminder, because of the grace given me by God 16to be a minister of Christ Jesus to the Gentiles in the priestly service of the gospel of God, so that the offering of the Gentiles may be acceptable, sanctified by the Holy Spirit.* 17In Christ Jesus, then, I have reason to be proud of my work for God. 18For I will not venture to speak of anything except what Christ has wrought through me to win obedience from the Gentiles, by word and deed, 19by the power of signs and wonders, by the power of the Holy Spirit, so that from Jerusalem and as far round as Illyricum I have fully preached the gospel of Christ, 20thus making it my ambition to preach the gospel, not where Christ has already been named, lest I build on another man's foundation, 21but as it is written,

> "They shall see who have never been told of him,
> and they shall understand who have never heard of him."

Journeys planned

22This is the reason why I have so often been hindered from coming to you. 23But now, since I no longer have any room for work in these regions, and since I have longed for many years to come to you, 24I hope to see you in passing as I go to Spain, and to be sped on my journey there by you, once I have enjoyed your company for a little. 25At present, however, I am going to Jerusalem with aid for the saints. 26For Macedonia and Achaia have been pleased to make some contribution for the poor among the saints at Jerusalem; 27they were pleased to do it, and indeed they are in debt to them, for if the

---

15:14–21 The Apostle began the morality section of the letter by exhorting the Romans to offer God an acceptable sacrifice (12:1). Now he ends by explaining that his letter is part of the ministry of evangelization that Christ gave him. He was chosen to proclaim the Gospel of Christ to the nations (1:5) and to make them an offering acceptable to God. Previously only the Jewish people could be regarded as a priestly people (cf. Ex 19:5–6); now that Christ has come, the Gentiles, too, are an offering that is "acceptable", sanctified by the Holy Spirit (v. 16).

15:22–33 Paul regards his work in the eastern parts of the Roman empire as having attained a degree of maturity. The Gospel of Christ has been proclaimed from Jerusalem as far as Illyricum, that is, the eastern shore of the Adriatic Sea (v. 19). He now wants to plan a journey westward and he is counting on the Christians of Rome to help him (v. 24); and he wants to visit them to strengthen them in the faith (v. 32).

15:21 Is 52:15.

Gentiles have come to share in their spiritual blessings, they ought also to be
of service to them in material blessings. 28When therefore I have completed
this, and have delivered to them what has been raised,[x] I shall go on by way of
you to Spain; 29and I know that when I come to you I shall come in the
fullness of the blessing[y] of Christ.

30I appeal to you, brethren, by our Lord Jesus Christ and by the love of the
Spirit, to strive together with me in your prayers to God on my behalf, 31that I
may be delivered from the unbelievers in Judea, and that my service for
Jerusalem may be acceptable to the saints, 32so that by God's will I may come
to you with joy and be refreshed in your company. 33The God of peace be with
you all. Amen.

Greetings and recommendations

16 1I commend to you our sister Phoebe, a deaconess of the church at
Cenchreae, 2that you may receive her in the Lord as befits the saints, and
help her in whatever she may require from you, for she has been a helper of
many and of myself as well.

3Greet Prisca and Aquila, my fellow workers in Christ Jesus, 4who risked
their necks for my life, to whom not only I but also all the churches of the
Gentiles give thanks; 5greet also the church in their house. Greet my beloved
Epaenetus, who was the first convert in Asia for Christ. 6Greet Mary, who has
worked hard among you. 7Greet Andronicus and Junias, my kinsmen and my
fellow prisoners; they are men of note among the apostles, and they were in
Christ before me. 8Greet Ampliatus, my beloved in the Lord. 9Greet Urbanus,
our fellow worker in Christ, and my beloved Stachys. 10Greet Apelles, who is
approved in Christ. Greet those who belong to the family of Aristobulus.
11Greet my kinsman Herodion. Greet those in the Lord who belong to the
12Greet those workers in the Lord, Tryphaena and Tryphosa. Greet the beloved
Persis, who has worked hard in the Lord. 13Greet Rufus, eminent in the Lord,
also his mother and mine. 14Greet Asyncritus, Phlegon, Hermes, Patrobas,
Hermas, and the brethren who are with them. 15Greet Philologus, Julia, Nereus
and his sister, and Olympas, and all the saints who are with them. 16Greet one
another with a holy kiss. All the churches of Christ greet you.*

16:1–23 This long series of affectionate greetings shows that the early Christians formed one great family, in which each person saw the others as brothers and sisters. As we can see from the names given here, this family contained people from many different places and cultures—people from Asia Minor and Greece, Latins, Jews, etc.; people of humble condition, slaves and freedmen, and people with a certain social standing such as Prisca, Aristobulus and Narcissus; in other words, people of all backgrounds linked by a common faith and by charity, "families who lived in union with Christ and who made him known to others.

x. Greek *sealed to them this fruit* **y.** Other ancient authorities insert *of the Gospel*

17I appeal to you, brethren, to take note of those who create dissensions and
difficulties, in opposition to the doctrine which you have been taught; avoid
them. 18For such persons do not serve our Lord Christ, but their own appetites,[z]
and by fair and flattering words they deceive the hearts of the simple-minded.
19For while your obedience is known to all, so that I rejoice over you, I would
have you wise as to what is good and guileless as to what is evil; 20then the
God of peace will soon crush Satan under your feet. The grace of our Lord
Jesus Christ be with you.[a]

21Timothy, my fellow worker, greets you; so do Lucius and Jason and Sosi-
pater, my kinsmen.

22I Tertius, the writer of this letter, greet you in the Lord.

23Gaius, who is host to me and to the whole church, greets you. Erastus, the
city treasurer, and our brother Quartus, greet you.[b]

Doxology

25Now to him who is able to strengthen you according to my gospel and the
preaching of Jesus Christ, according to the revelation of the mystery which
was kept secret for long ages 26but is now disclosed and through the prophetic
writings is made known to all nations, according to the command of the eternal
God, to bring about the obedience of faith—27to the only wise God be glory
for evermore through Jesus Christ! Amen.

Small Christian communities which were centres for the spreading of the Gospel and its message. Families no different from other families of those times, but living with a new spirit, which spread to all those who were in contact with them. This is what the first Christians were, and this is what we have to be: sowers of peace and joy, the peace and joy that Jesus has brought to us" (Bl. J. Escrivá, *Hom.*, 1, 30).

Phoebe (vv. 1–2) was the bearer of the letter. She came from Cenchrae, the eastern port of Corinth, so it is very likely that Paul was writing from Corinth. Rufus (v. 13) may have been one of the sons of Simon of Cyrene (cf. Mk 15:21).

The reference in vv. 17–18 is probably to Judaizing preachers who wanted to maintain the distinction between clean and unclean food as well as other matters of Jewish observance; they used to infiltrate Christian communities by projecting themselves as very religious people and by preaching what they argued was a more perfect lifestyle.

See the RSV note on v. 24.

16:25–27 Unlike other letters, this one ends with an elaborate poem of praise, or doxology, addressed through Jesus Christ to God almighty and wise. A very early papyrus has these two verses at 15:33; other manuscripts put it at the end of chapter 14 and then repeat it as a conclusion to the letter. It is quite likely that these two changes arose from the fact that the liturgical reading of the letter normally omitted chapters 15 and 16, as being more familial in style.

z. Greek *their own belly* (Phil 3:19) **a.** Other ancient authorities omit this sentence **b.** Other ancient authorities insert verse 24, *The grace of our Lord Jesus Christ be with you all. Amen*

The Letters to the Corinthians

The city of Corinth, on the Greek isthmus of the same name, with its two ports (on the Aegean and the Adriatic seas), was the capital of the Roman province of Achaia and one of the main centres of Mediterranean trade. It had a very cosmopolitan population, with a wide variety of religions, and it was notorious for loose living.

The church of Corinth was founded by St Paul, with the help of Silas and Timothy, in the year 50 or 51, during his second apostolic journey (in the years 50–53; cf. Acts 18:1–18). The Apostle spent more than a year and a half evangelizing the city. On his third apostolic journey (in the years 53–58), it is very likely that, after sending (from Ephesus) his First Letter to the Corinthians, he made another brief visit to the city (cf. 2 Cor 1:15–24). Later still, after the Corinthians had received the Second Letter, he spent the winter of 57–58 with them (cf. Acts 20:1–3).

To judge from things Paul says in his letters, the Christian community of Corinth must have been one of the largest founded by him. Most of the Christians, it seems, there were of Gentile background, and most of them were ordinary people, though some were educated and well-to-do. There must also have been a considerable number of women. So, it was a community that included all sorts of people and one in which things were not easy, given the moral depravity that characterized the city.

This moral and cultural climate had its effect on the Christians. For one thing, they could not but compare the preachers of the Gospel with the many Greek philosophers and teachers to be found in the city; and they were not free from the temptation to link the Gospel with Greek philosophy. News from various quarters—Apollos (1 Cor 16:12), Chloe's people (1 Cor 1:11)—reached Paul at Ephesus and led him to write his First Letter to the Corinthians in the spring of the year 57. In this letter he uses the light of the Gospel to sort out difficulties that had arisen in that community; the Gospel granted to Paul by divine revelation (cf. 2:10) and given him by the Church was the good news that Christ died for our sins and rose again in accordance with the Scriptures (cf. 15:1–5). The source of divisions in the community at Corinth lay in the fact that they were interpreting the Gospel in a human way, assessing its effectiveness by its preacher's eloquence. Paul tells them that salvation does not come through that sort of human wisdom but through Jesus Christ, who died on the cross (cf. 1:22–23). In Christ alone will they find true wisdom and salvation (cf. 1:30).

Along with other matters Paul covers in this letter, such as Christians' recourse to civil courts (6:1–11), marriage and virginity (7:1–40), the lawfulness or not of eating meat from animals which may have been used in sacrifices to idols (8:1–10:33), and order in liturgical assemblies, the institution of the Eucharist, and charisms (11:1–14:40), the Apostle also deals with a subject in which Greek thought still influenced Christians—the resurrection of the dead (15:1–58). Apparently some of the Corinthian Christians thought that resurrection was something that had already happened in the spiritual sphere (which charismatic outpourings may have tended to bear out) so that there existed no need to hope in resurrection of the dead. St Paul does not mince his words in his reply: "If there is no resurrection of the dead, then Christ has not been raised; if Christ has not been raised, then our preaching is in vain and your faith is in vain. […] But in fact Christ has been raised from the dead, the first fruits of those who have fallen asleep" (15:16–20).

In the Second Letter to the Corinthians, written a little later, in the autumn of the year 57, there is a reference to some negative reactions to the first letter among the Corinthians. Paul concentrates mainly on the connexions between the evangelizer, the Gospel and the evangelized. The preacher's strength comes from the Holy Spirit; the Gospel is what must reconcile the evangelized with God and with the Apostle, because "all this is from God, who through Christ reconciled us to himself and gave us the ministry of reconciliation. […] We beseech you on behalf of Christ, be reconciled to God" (5:18–20). There may be something to the theory that this letter known to us as the Second Letter to the Corinthians includes, to some extent at least, two other letters written by Paul to this community—the so-called "tearful letter" (chaps. 10–13; cf. 2:4) in which the Apostle corrects those who have offended him, and another letter in which we see harmonious relations restored between Paul and the Corinthians (chaps. 1–9).

The Letters to the Corinthians are an inexhaustible source of information about St Paul himself and many aspects of Christian teaching: they contain a bold apologia for his ministry (1 Cor 1–4; 2 Cor 11–13), teaching about the Body of Christ and its members (1 Cor 12:12–27), the hymn to love (1 Cor 13:1–13), etc.

1 Corinthians

INTRODUCTION

Greeting

1 [1]Paul, called by the will of God to be an apostle of Christ Jesus, and our brother Sosthenes,

[2]To the church of God which is at Corinth, to those sanctified in Christ Jesus, called to be saints* together with all those who in every place call on the name of our Lord Jesus Christ, both their Lord and ours:

[3]Grace to you and peace from God our Father and the Lord Jesus Christ.

Thanksgiving

[4]I give thanks to God[a] always for you because of the grace of God which was
given you in Christ Jesus, [5]that in every way you were enriched in him with all
speech and all knowledge—[6]even as the testimony to Christ was confirmed
among you—[7]so that you are not lacking in any spiritual gift, as you wait for
the revealing of our Lord Jesus Christ; [8]who will sustain you to the end,
guiltless in the day of our Lord Jesus Christ. [9]God is faithful, by whom you
were called into the fellowship of his Son, Jesus Christ our Lord.

1:1–9 □ St Paul begins the letter with his usual greeting (vv. 1–3) and an act of thanksgiving to God (vv. 4–9).

1:1–9 In the Apostle's time letters usually opened with words like "N. sends greetings," but here Paul uses a more personal opening, which has a pronounced Christian ring to it: "Grace and peace" (v. 3). In his thanksgiving (vv. 4ff) he reminds the Corinthians that they have been given the grace of God in Christ, a grace that enriches them in every way—in wisdom and in special gifts (charisms) granted by God. Apparently the Christians at Corinth were richly endowed with both things, even if they sometimes failed to understand them properly. That is why these matters are the main themes of the letter. Paul also reminds the Corinthians that we still live in expectation of the day when Jesus Christ will be revealed (v. 7)—because some of them thought that they had already attained the fullness of resurrection.

a. Other ancient authorities read *my God*

PART ONE: CORRECTION OF ABUSES

1. DIVISIONS AMONG THE CORINTHIANS

An appeal for unity

[10]I appeal to you, brethren, by the name of our Lord Jesus Christ, that all of you agree and that there be no dissensions among you, but that you be united in the same mind and the same judgment. [11]For it has been reported to me by Chloe's people that there is quarrelling among you, my brethren. [12]What I mean is that each one of you says, "I belong to Paul," or "I belong to Apollos," or "I belong to Cephas,"* or "I belong to Christ." [13]Is Christ divided? Was Paul crucified for you? Or were you baptized in the name of Paul? [14]I am thankful[b] that I baptized none of you except Crispus and Gaius; [15] lest any one should say that you were baptized in my name. [16](I did baptize also the household of Stephanas. Beyond that, I do not know whether I baptized any one else.) [17]For Christ did not send me to baptize but to preach the gospel, and not with eloquent wisdom, lest the cross of Christ be emptied of its power.

The wisdom of the cross

[18]For the word of the cross is folly to those who are perishing, but to us who are being saved it is the power of God. [19]For it is written,

---

1:10–6:20 □ □In the first part of the letter St Paul takes the Christian community of Corinth to task over a number of abuses. First, he deals with divisions caused by their being swayed by human philosophy and then forgetting the Gospel preached to them, the Gospel of the cross (1:10–4:21). Then, in the light of that Gospel he judges the way the community is conducting itself: he deals with a case of incest (5:1–13), the right method to solve problems which arise among them (6:1–11), and the proper use of the body and sexuality (6:12–20).

1:10–4:21 □ After citing current divisions among the Christians at Corinth (1:10–17), the Apostle spells out their causes: they don't realize what true wisdom is (1:18–3:3), or what the true role of ministers is (3:4–4:13). Then come a series of admonitions (4:14–21).

1:10–17 From what the Apostle says, it seems that factions had developed among the Corinthians, each group built around some prominent Christian. This was causing divisions and was likely to undermine unity of faith. The Apostle points out that faith is not something that depends on preachers or on who performed one's baptism: it is based on Christ.

1:18–31 Human wisdom needs to be in line with the wisdom of God. If it goes astray and does not obey God, it becomes worldly wisdom which seeks only

b. Other ancient authorities read *I thank God* **1:19** Is 29:14; Ps 33:10.

"I will destroy the wisdom of the wise,
and the cleverness of the clever I will thwart."

20Where is the wise man? Where is the scribe? Where is the debater of this
age? Has not God made foolish the wisdom of the world? 21For since, in the
wisdom of God, the world did not know God through wisdom, it pleased God
through the folly of what we preach to save those who believe. 22For Jews
demand signs and Greeks seek wisdom, 23but we preach Christ crucified, a
stumbling block to Jews and folly to Gentiles, 24but to those who are called,
both Jews and Greeks, Christ the power of God and the wisdom of God. 25For
the foolishness of God is wiser than men, and the weakness of God is stronger
than men.

26For consider your call, brethren; not many of you were wise according to
worldly standards, not many were powerful, not many were of noble birth;
27but God chose what is foolish in the world to shame the wise, God chose
what is weak in the world to shame the strong, 28God chose what is low and
despised in the world, even things that are not, to bring to nothing things that
are, 29so that no human being might boast in the presence of God. 30He is the
source of your life in Christ Jesus, whom God made our wisdom, our right-
eousness and sanctification and redemption; 31therefore, as it is written, "Let
him who boasts, boast of the Lord."

Paul's preaching in Corinth

2 1When I came to you, brethren, I did not come proclaiming to you the
testimony[c] of God in lofty words or wisdom. 2For I decided to know

---

worldly things—the trappings of power, rational arguments. But true wisdom comes from God and it has manifested itself in the cross of Christ. The cross is the seat of wisdom and the judgment seat, the touchstone men must use to test authenticity. The cross bears out the words of Isaiah 29:14 (v. 19); simplicity and humility are necessary if a person is to understand the divine wisdom of the cross. "The preaching of the cross of Christ contains elements that seem impossible according to human reason—how God might die, or how the Almighty subjected himself to violent men. There are also elements contradictory to the prudence of this world—that one who could have avoided opposition decided not to flee" (St Thomas Aquinas, *Com. on 1 Cor,* in loc.).

It was God who chose these Corinthians to be Christians, and he did not make his choice by using human criteria. The power comes from God alone and thus leads to only one conclusion (v. 31): "Let him who boasts, boast of the Lord" (v. 31).

2:1–5 Even Paul's own preaching relies entirely on the wisdom of the cross of Christ: "Our spirit is set in one direction; the only direction for our intellect, will and heart is—towards Christ our Redeemer, towards Christ, the Redeemer of the

c. Other ancient authorities read *mystery* (or *secret*) **1:31** Jer 9:24.

nothing among you except Jesus Christ and him crucified.* 3And I was with you in weakness and in much fear and trembling; 4and my speech and my message were not in plausible words of wisdom, but in demonstration of the Spirit and of power, 5that your faith might not rest in the wisdom of men but in the power of God.

Divine wisdom

6Yet among the mature we do impart wisdom, although it is not a wisdom of this age or of the rulers of this age, who are doomed to pass away. 7But we impart a secret and hidden wisdom of God, which God decreed before the ages for our glorification. 8None of the rulers of this age understood this; for if they had, they would not have crucified the Lord of glory. 9But, as it is written,

"What no eye has seen, nor ear heard,
nor the heart of man conceived,
what God has prepared for those who love him,"

10God has revealed to us through the Spirit. For the Spirit searches everything, even the depths of God. 11For what person knows a man's thoughts except the spirit of the man which is in him? So also no one comprehends the thoughts of God except the Spirit of God. 12Now we have received not the spirit of the world, but the Spirit which is from God, that we might understand the gifts bestowed on us by God. 13And we impart this in words not taught by human wisdom but taught by the Spirit, interpreting spiritual truths to those who possess the Spirit.[d]

14The unspiritual[e] man does not receive the gifts of the Spirit of God, for they are folly to him, and he is not able to understand them because they are spiritually discerned. 15The spiritual man judges all things, but is himself to be judged by no one. 16"For who has known the mind of the Lord so as to instruct him?" But we have the mind of Christ.

---

world. We wish to look towards him—because there is salvation in no one else but him, the Son of God—repeating what Peter said: 'Lord, to whom shall we go? You have the words of eternal life' (Jn 6:68)" (John Paul II, *Redempt. hom.*, 7).

2:6–16 Divine wisdom, in which men are called to share, has devised the plan of salvation revealed by God himself through the Holy Spirit. The words of Isaiah 64:2–3 (v. 9) summarize the content of divine wisdom: it is all those gifts that surpass human understanding (cf. Eph 3:9) and which God has prepared from all eternity for those who love him. These gifts are in fact God's love for mankind. Because they are not fully obtained until the next life, Christian Tradition has read the words of Isaiah as a description of heaven.

d. Or *interpreting spiritual truths in spiritual language*; or *comparing spiritual things with spiritual*
e. Or *natural* **2:9** Is 64:4. **2:16** Is 40:13.

The Corinthians are still unspiritual

3 [1]But I, brethren, could not address you as spiritual men, but as men of the
flesh, as babes in Christ. [2]I fed you with milk, not solid food; for you were
not ready for it; and even yet you are not ready, [3]for you are still of the flesh.
For while there is jealousy and strife among you, are you not of the flesh, and
behaving like ordinary men?

Apostolic ministry

[4]For when one says, "I belong to Paul," and another, "I belong to Apollos," are
you not merely men?
[5]What then is Apollos? What is Paul? Servants through whom you believed,
as the Lord assigned to each. [6]I planted, Apollos watered, but God gave the
growth. [7]So neither he who plants nor he who waters is anything, but only God
who gives the growth. [8]He who plants and he who waters are equal, and each
shall receive his wages according to his labour. [9]For we are God's fellow
workers;[f] you are God's field, God's building.
[10]According to the grace of God given to me, like a skilled master builder I
laid a foundation, and another man is building upon it. Let each man take care
how he builds upon it. [11]For no other foundation can any one lay than that
which is laid, which is Jesus Christ. [12]Now if any one builds on the foundation
with gold, silver, precious stones, wood, hay, straw—[13]each man's work will
become manifest; for the Day* will disclose it, because it will be revealed with
fire, and the fire will test what sort of work each one has done. [14]If the work
which any man has built on the foundation survives, he will receive a reward.
[15]If any man's work is burned up, he will suffer loss, though he himself will be
saved, but only as through fire.
[16]Do you not know that you are God's temple and that God's Spirit dwells
in you? [17]If any one destroys God's temple,* God will destroy him. For God's
temple is holy, and that temple you are.
[18]Let no one deceive himself. If any one among you thinks that he is wise
in this age, let him become a fool that he may become wise. [19]For the wisdom

---

3:1–3 The Corinthians have not yet attained true wisdom and are still quite unspiritual—as can be seen from the divisions among them, which derive from the fact that they have confused the Gospel with the skills of preachers. As elsewhere (13;11; Gal 4;1,3; Eph 4;14; cf. also Heb 5:12–17) the Apostle uses the simile of the child and the adult to exhort them to have a more mature faith.

3:4–23 One instance of the overly human thinking of the Corinthians (v. 4) is their failure to understand the role of a minister: ministers are not working for themselves but to built up the whole Church; each Christian and the entire Church belong only to God and to Christ.

f. Or *fellow workers for God* **3:16** Ex 34:34. **3:19** Job 5:13.

of this world is folly with God. For it is written, "He catches the wise in their
craftiness," [20]and again, "The Lord knows that the thoughts of the wise are
futile." [21]So let no one boast of men. For all things are yours, [22]whether Paul
or Apollos or Cephas or the world or life or death or the present or the future,
all are yours; [23]and you are Christ's; and Christ is God's.

Servants of Christ

4 [1]This is how one should regard us, as servants of Christ and stewards of the
mysteries of God. [2]Moreover it is required of stewards that they be found
trustworthy. [3]But with me it is a very small thing that I should be judged by
you or by any human court. I do not even judge myself. [4]I am not aware of
anything against myself, but I am not thereby acquitted. It is the Lord who
judges me. [5]Therefore do not pronounce judgment before the time, before the
Lord comes, who will bring to light the things now hidden in darkness and will
disclose the purposes of the heart. Then every man will receive his commen-
dation from God.
[6]I have applied all this to myself and Apollos for your benefit, brethren, that
you may learn by us not to go beyond what is written, that none of you may be

---

The root of all apostolic work is God "who gives the growth" (v. 7). Man is God's instrument—servant, minister (v. 5), or fellow-worker (v. 9)—in that task, which can only be carried through if Jesus Christ is its foundation (v. 11). Paul develops these ideas with the help of two useful similes—God's field (vv. 6–9) and his building (vv. 9–17). If Christ is the foundation, then Christians must "not only be linked to Jesus Christ: they must, as it were, be glued to him [...]. He is the foundation and we are the building; he is the trunk of the vine and we are the branches; he is the husband and we the wife; he is the shepherd and we the flock" (St John Chrysostom, *Hom. on 1 Cor,* 8, 4). Extending the building metaphor, Paul appeals to ministers to act responsibly, reminding them that a Day of Judgment will come, the Day of the Lord (vv. 10–17).

Paul uses two biblical quotations (Job 5:13; Ps 94:11; cf. vv. 19–20) to show that an unspiritual approach is doomed to failure; whereas a person who has Christ has all things: "Mine are the heavens and mine is the earth. All the peoples are mine, the just and sinners. Mine are the angels, and the Mother of God: all things belong to me. And God himself is mine and for me, because Christ is mine and all for me. What do you seek and search for, my soul? All things are yours, and everything is for you. Do not put yourself down or pay attention only to the crumbs that fall from your Father's table" (St John of the Cross, *Prayer of the soul in love*).

4:1–7 It is not for believers to judge ministers; God is the Judge. The Church Magisterium has often applied v. 1 to the Christian priesthood. What ministers are asked to have, above all, is fidelity: "They are faithful who seek in all things the

3:20 Ps 94:11.

puffed up in favour of one against another. [7]For who sees anything different in
you? What have you that you did not receive? If then you received it, why do
you boast as if it were not a gift?

Trials experienced by apostles

[8]Already you are filled! Already you have become rich! Without us you have
become kings! And would that you did reign, so that we might share the rule
with you! [9]For I think that God has exhibited us apostles as last of all, like men
sentenced to death; because we have become a spectacle to the world, to
angels and to men. [10]We are fools for Christ's sake, but you are wise in Christ.
We are weak, but you are strong. You are held in honour , but we in disrepute.
[11]To the present hour we hunger and thirst, we are ill-clad and buffeted and
homeless, [12]and we labour, working with our own hands. When reviled, we bless;
when persecuted, we endure; [13]when slandered, we try to conciliate; we have
become, and are now, as the refuse of the world, the offscouring of all things.

Admonishment

[14]I do not write this to make you ashamed, but to admonish you as my beloved
children. [15]For though you have countless guides in Christ, you do not have
many fathers. For I became your father in Christ Jesus through the gospel. [16]I
urge you, then, be imitators of me. [17]Therefore I sent[g] to you Timothy, my
beloved and faithful child in the Lord, to remind you of my ways in Christ, as
I teach them everywhere in every church. [18]Some are arrogant, as though I
were not coming to you. [19]But I will come to you soon, if the Lord wills, and
I will find out not the talk of these arrogant people but their power. [20]For the
kingdom of God does not consist in talk but in power. [21]What do you wish?
Shall I come to you with a rod, or with love in a spirit of gentleness?

---

honour of God and the good of his members [followers]" (St Thomas Aquinas, *Com. on 1 Cor,* in loc.).

4:8–13 The Apostle writes in an ironical vein about the conceitedness of the Corinthian Christians. What really concerns him is that they should be loyal and abound in the grace of God even when its ministers are not held in the highest esteem. He goes on to give a dramatic outline of the hardships which Christ's followers are happy to bear.

4:14–21 Paul identifies the spiritual paternity of the Corinthians: it was he himself who begot them in the faith. That is why he is right to reproach them so severely; his aim is not to make them feel ashamed (that would serve no purpose) but to encourage them to acquire the virtues they need and to help build up the Church. That is what the saints have always done: "We ought to regard those under our

g. Or *am sending*

2. A CASE OF INCEST

Punishment of the sinner

5 1It is actually reported that there is immorality among you, and of a kind
that is not found even among pagans; for a man is living with his father's
wife.* 2And you are arrogant! Ought you not rather to mourn? Let him who
has done this be removed from among you.
3For though absent in body I am present in spirit, and as if present, I have
already pronounced judgment 4in the name of the Lord Jesus on the man who has
done such a thing. When you are assembled, and my spirit is present, with the
power of our Lord Jesus, 5you are to deliver this man to Satan* for the destruction
of the flesh, that his spirit may be saved in the day of the Lord Jesus.[h]
6Your boasting is not good. Do you not know that a little leaven leavens the
whole lump? 7Cleanse out the old leaven that you may be a new lump, as you
really are unleavened. For Christ, our paschal lamb, has been sacrificed. 8Let
us, therefore, celebrate the festival, not with the old leaven, the leaven of
malice and evil, but with the unleavened bread of sincerity and truth.

Obstinate sinners are to be shunned

9I wrote to you in my letter not to associate with immoral* men; 10not at all
meaning the immoral* of this world, or the greedy and robbers, or idolaters,

---

authority as our children. We place ourselves at their service as Jesus did" (St John Bosco, *Divine Office,* Reading, 31 Jan.).

5:1–13 □ St Paul now turns to a serious matter which is an obstacle to the Christian life of that community, the case of a Christian who has set up house with his stepmother.

5:1–8 The Corinthians are being very passive: they don't seem to realize how serious a sin incest is ("it corrupts family relationships and marks a regression towards animality": *CCC*, 2388); St Paul moves quickly and boldly to see that action is taken, by solemnly decreeing the excommunication of the sinner, for the community's own protection. He draws a comparison with the dough used to make unleavened bread for Passover: Christians likewise must rid themselves of any sinful behaviour they engaged in prior to their conversion. We are now in a permanent Passover, that of Christ.

5:9–13 He warns the Corinthians against associating with people who call themselves Christians but are taking no steps to give up sinning (he lists a number of sins). Christians should work for the salvation of all men; but if someone proves to be a danger to one's own soul, then he should be avoided.

h. Other ancient authorities omit *Jesus*

since then you would need to go out of the world. [11]But rather I wrote[i] to you
not to associate with any one who bears the name of brother if he is guilty of
immorality or greed, or is an idolater, reviler, drunkard, or robber—not even
to eat with such a one. [12]For what have I to do with judging outsiders? Is it not
those inside the church whom you are to judge? [13]God judges those outside.
"Drive out the wicked person from among you."

3. RECOURSE TO PAGAN COURTS

6 [1]When one of you has a grievance against a brother, does he dare go to law
before the unrighteous* instead of the saints? [2]Do you not know that the
saints will judge the world? And if the world is to be judged by you, are you
incompetent to try trivial cases? [3]Do you not know that we are to judge
angels? How much more, matters pertaining to this life! [4]If then you have such
cases, why do you lay them before those who are least esteemed by the
church? [5]I say this to your shame. Can it be that there is no man among you
wise enough to decide between members of the brotherhood, [6]but brother goes
to law against brother, and that before unbelievers?

[7]To have lawsuits at all with one another is defeat for you. Why not rather
suffer wrong? Why not rather be defrauded? [8]But you yourselves wrong and
defraud, and that even your own brethren.

[9]Do you not know that the unrighteous will not inherit the kingdom of God?
Do not be deceived; neither the immoral,* nor idolaters, nor adulterers, nor
sexual perverts,[j] [10]nor thieves, nor the greedy, nor drunkards, nor revilers, nor
robbers will inherit the kingdom of God. [11]And such were some of you. But

---

6:1–11 □ Another cause of scandal is that Christians are having recourse to pagan courts, instead of trying to settle disagreements within the Church.

6:1–11 The advice the Apostle gives here is in line with Jewish practice: lawsuits were brought before Jewish courts. But he also appeals for fraternity, and for good example to be given: there is no reason why disputes cannot be settled without going to pagan courts.

He rounds off a series of warnings by reminding them of their Christian dignity (v. 11)—their Baptism and its effects, and their need to reclaim their initial holiness. "The followers of Christ, called by God not in virtue of their works but by his design and grace, and justified in the Lord Jesus, have been made sons of God in the Baptism of faith and partakers of the divine nature, and so are truly sanctified. They must therefore hold on to and perfect in their lives that sanctification which they have received from God" (Vatican II, *LG*, 40).

i. Or *now I write* **j.** Two Greeks words are rendered by this expression **5:13** Deut 17:7; 19:19.

you were washed, you were sanctified, you were justified in the name of the Lord Jesus Christ and in the Spirit of our God.

4. FORNICATION, A GRAVE SIN

Respect for the body
12"All things are lawful for me," but not all things are helpful. "All things are lawful for me," *but I will not be enslaved by anything. 13"Food is meant for the stomach and the stomach for food"—and God will destroy both one and the other. The body is not meant for immorality,* but for the Lord, and the Lord for the body. 14And God raised the Lord and will also raise us up by his power.

Offence to Christ and the Holy Spirit
15Do you not know that your bodies are members of Christ? Shall I therefore take the members of Christ and make them members of a prostitute? Never! 16Do you not know that he who joins himself to a prostitute becomes one body with her? For, as it is written, "The two shall become one flesh."[k] 17But he who is united to the Lord becomes one spirit with him. 18Shun immorality.* Every other sin which a man commits is outside the body; but the immoral man sins against his own body. 19Do you not know that your body is a temple of the

---

6:12–20 □ The Apostle now deals with the gravity of sins of a sexual nature, showing that they have a profound effect upon the person and are incompatible with what it means to be a Christian.

6:12–14 The Apostle takes issue with a misinterpretation of freedom which seems to have been current among the Corinthians. Some of them seemed to think that because Christians were free of the Law, then they could do what they liked: but that was not true at all. The Apostle makes it clear that there are things that are quite inappropriate or that can only enslave man again. These Christians were dismissing everything to do with the body as unimportant; but the Apostle tells them that regulations about food and rules of sexual morality are not at all on the same level. The human body is an integral part of the person; it partakes of one's union with Christ and is destined for resurrection. Sexual morality is very important.

6:15–20 Sexual behaviour involves the whole person and a sexual relationship creates a deep union between the persons involved. A Christian is, body-and-soul, a member of Christ, and he profanes his body, which is a temple of the Holy Spirit, if he uses it for fornication. But St Paul concludes what he has to say on a positive note: "Glorify God in your body" (v. 20). That is the basis of chastity's greatness, whether in marriage or in virginity.

k. Greek *one flesh* **6:16** Gen 2:24.

Holy Spirit within you, which you have from God? You are not your own;
[20]you were bought with a price. So glorify God in your body.

PART TWO: ANSWERS TO VARIOUS QUESTIONS

5. MARRIAGE AND VIRGINITY

Relations between husband and wife

7 [1]Now concerning the matters about which you wrote. It is well for a man
not to touch a woman. [2]But because of the temptation to immorality, each
man should have his own wife and each woman her own husband.* [3]The
husband should give to his wife her conjugal rights, and likewise the wife to
her husband. [4]For the wife does not rule over her own body, but the husband
does; likewise the husband does not rule over his own body, but the wife does.
[5]Do not refuse one another except perhaps by agreement for a season, that you
may devote yourselves to prayer; but then come together again, lest Satan
tempt you through lack of self-control. [6]I say this by way of concession, not of
command. [7]I wish that all were as I myself am. But each has his own special
gift from God, one of one kind and one of another.

[8]To the unmarried and the widows I say that it is well for them to remain
single as I do. [9]But if they cannot exercise self-control, they should marry. For
it is better to marry than to be aflame with passion.

7:1–15:58 □ □ The second part of the letter deals with questions posed by the faithful of Corinth. These all in some way or other affect daily life—how married people should behave to one another, and whether or not to choose the way of marriage (7:1–40), purchases made in the city market (8:1–10:33), the celebration of the Eucharist (11:1–34), the channelling of spiritual gifts (12:1–14:40) and, finally, hope in the resurrection of the dead (1:1–58). The main criterion to be applied is mutual love, charity (13:1–13), and therefore to avoid any attitude or action which could cause scandal or seem to imply disregard for others. The doubts raised by some people about future resurrection lead St Paul to remind them about the content of the Gospel as preached ever since the beginning of the Church, and which is the basis of Christian faith (15:1–4).

7:1–40 □ It may be that the query some people raised about virginity and celibacy arose because they regarded marital relations as something evil and therefore thought that celibacy and virginity were obligatory for Christians. Paul will discuss all these matters, including the position of widows.

Indissolubility of marriage

[10]To the married I give charge, not I but the Lord, that the wife should not
separate from her husband [11](but if she does, let her remain single or else be
reconciled to her husband)—and that the husband should not divorce his wife.

The Pauline privilege

[12]To the rest I say, not the Lord, that if any brother has a wife who is an unbeliever,
and she consents to live with him, he should not divorce her. [13]If any woman has a
husband who is an unbeliever, and he consents to live with her, she should not
divorce him. [14]For the unbelieving husband is consecrated through his wife, and
the unbelieving wife is consecrated through her husband. Otherwise, your children
would be unclean, but as it is they are holy. [15]But if the unbelieving partner desires
to separate, let it be so; in such a case the brother or sister is not bound. For God
has called us[l] to peace. [16]Wife, how do you know whether you will save your
husband? Husband, how do you know whether you will save your wife?

Leading the life God has assigned

[17]Only, let every one lead the life which the Lord has assigned to him, and in
which God has called him. This is my rule in all the churches. [18]Was any one

---

7:1–9 The Apostle briefly describes the legitimacy of marriage. Absolutely speaking, celibacy is on a higher plane than marriage; but marriage is something good and holy for those who are called to it. To live a celibate life one needs a special grace from God. If people do not have that gift, it is better for them to live a married life: that also involves a gift (v. 7). "Marriage is a divine path on earth! […] Those who are called to the married state will, with the grace of God, find within their state everything they need to be holy, to identify themselves each day more with Jesus Christ, and to lead those with whom they live to God" (Bl. J. Escrivá, *Conversations*, 91).

7:10–11 As regards the indissolubility of marriage, the Apostle makes it clear that this is a matter of God's teaching and not just his own. "He (God) wills and he communicates the indisolubility of marriage as a fruit, a sign and a requirement of the absolutely faithful love that God has for man and that the Lord Jesus has for the Church. […] To bear witness to the inestimable value of the indissolubility and fidelity of marriage is one of the most precious and most urgent tasks of Christian couples in our time" (John Paul II, *Fam. consortio*, 20).

7:12–16 Church discipline follows the solution outlined by St Paul: when one of the spouses becomes a Christian, and the other ceases to cohabit or does not allow the Christian partner to practise his or her faith, the baptized partner is then free to contract a new marriage (cf. *Code of Canon Law*, 1143–1147).

7:17–24 Some Corinthians may have been misreading what it meant to be "reborn" through Baptism, claiming that it involved a total change, not only

l. Other ancient authorities read *you*

at the time of his call already circumcised? Let him not seek to remove the marks of circumcision. Was any one at the time of his call uncircumcised? Let him not seek circumcision.
19For neither circumcision counts for anything nor uncircumcision, but keeping the commandments of God.
20Every one should remain in the state in which he was called.
21Were you a slave when called? Never mind. But if you can gain your freedom, avail yourself of the opportunity.[x]
22For he who was called in the Lord as a slave is a freedman of the Lord. Likewise he who was free when called is a slave of Christ.
23You were bought with a price; do not become slaves of men.
24So, brethren, in whatever state each was called, there let him remain with God.

Excellence of virginity

25Now concerning the unmarried,[x2] I have no command of the Lord, but I give my opinion as one who by the Lord's mercy is trustworthy.
26I think that in view of the present[m] distress it is well for a person to remain as he is.
27Are you bound to a wife? Do not seek to be free. Are you free from a wife? Do not seek marriage.
28But if you marry, you do not sin, and if a girl[m2] marries she does not sin. Yet those who marry will have worldly troubles, and I would spare you that.
29I mean, brethren, the appointed time has grown very short; from now on, let those who have wives live as though they had none,
30and those who mourn as though they were not mourning, and those who rejoice as though they were not rejoicing, and those who buy as though they had no goods,
31and those who deal with the world as though they had no dealings with it. For the form of this world is passing away.

---

internal but external as well, in a person's life. The Apostle explains by giving two examples (circumcision and slavery) which show that external circumstances do not vitiate Christian life; in fact, God designs these circumstances as a positive help towards Christian living. The Christian calling does not take anyone out of his or her place, nor is there any reason why it should entail changing the external circumstances of one's life. "Our calling discloses to us the meaning of our existence. It means being convinced, through faith, of the reason for our life on earth. [...] All happenings and events now fall within their true perspective: we understand where God is leading us" (Bl. J. Escrivá, *Hom.*, 1, 45).

7:25–38 The excellence of virginity and celibacy has to do with the love of God: the unmarried person can dedicate himself or herself to God more fully than a married person can. "Both the sacrament of Matrimony and virginity for the Kingdom of God come from the Lord himself. It is he who gives them meaning and grants them the grace which is indispensable for living them out in conformity with his will" (*CCC*, 1620).

Verses 36–38 have to do with a society in which parents arranged their children's marriages.

x. Or *make use of your present condition instead* **x².** Greek *virgins* **m.** Or *present* **m².** Greek *virgin*

[32]I want you to be free from anxieties. The unmarried man is anxious about
the affairs of the Lord, how to please the Lord; [33]but the married man is
anxious about worldly affairs, how to please his wife, [34]and his interests are
divided. And the unmarried woman or girl[m2] is anxious about the affairs of the
Lord, how to be holy in body and spirit; but the married woman is anxious
about worldly affairs, how to please her husband. [35]I say this for your own
benefit, not to lay any restraint upon you, but to promote good order and to
secure your undivided devotion to the Lord.
[36]If any one thinks that he is not behaving properly toward his betrothed,[m2] if
his passions are strong, and it has to be, let him do as he wishes: let them marry—
it is no sin. [37]But whoever is firmly established in his heart, being under no
necessity but having his desire under control, and has determined this in his heart,
to keep her as his betrothed, he will do well. [38]So that he who marries his
betrothed[m2] does well; and he who refrains from marriage will do better.

Advice to widows
[39]A wife is bound to her husband as long as he lives. If the husband dies, she is
free to be married to whom she wishes, only in the Lord. [40]But in my judgment
she is happier if she remains as she is. And I think that I have the Spirit of God.

6. FOOD OFFERED TO IDOLS

Idols have no real existence
8 [1]Now concerning food offered to idols: we know that "all of us possess
knowledge." "Knowledge" puffs up, but love builds up. [2]If any one
imagines that he knows something, he does not yet know as he ought to know.
[3]But if one loves God, one is known by him.*

7:39–40 On the subject of widows, see also 1 Tim 5:3–16.

8:1–10:33 □ In pagan cults, part of the meat of animals sacrificed to idols could be sold later in the markets. Some Christians were afraid that if they bought this meat they were in some way partaking in idolatrous rites; they asked for a practical guideline. The Apostle deals with the general principles first: there is no objection to eating this sort of meat, because idols have no real existence (8:1–6), but charity will sometimes dictate that they abstain from it (8:7–13); he then illustrates the principles by telling them what he himself does (9:1–27) and quoting lessons from the history of Israel (10:1–13); finally, he solves some specific cases raised (10:14–33).

8:1–6 Apropos of the sense of scandal some Christians had, Paul reminds them that they must not rely solely on their own judgment; charity must always come

m2. Greek *virgin*

[4]Hence, as to the eating of food offered to idols, we know that "an idol has
no real existence," and that "there is no God but one." [5]For although there may
be so-called gods in heaven or on earth—as indeed there are many "gods" and
many "lords"—[6]yet for us there is one God, the Father, from whom are all
things and for whom we exist, and one Lord, Jesus Christ, through whom are
all things and through whom we exist.

Not scandalizing the weak

[7]However, not all possess this knowledge. But some, through being hitherto
accustomed to idols, eat food as really offered to an idol; and their conscience,
being weak, is defiled. [8]Food will not commend us to God. We are no worse
off if we do not eat, and no better off if we do. [9]Only take care lest this liberty
of yours somehow become a stumbling block to the weak. [10]For if any one
sees you, a man of knowledge, at table in an idol's temple, might he not be
encouraged, if his conscience is weak, to eat food offered to idols? [11]And so
by your knowledge this weak man is destroyed, the brother for whom Christ
died. [12]Thus, sinning against your brethren and wounding their conscience
when it is weak, you sin against Christ. [13]Therefore, if food is a cause of my
brother's falling, I will never eat meat, lest I cause my brother to fall.

The right of apostles to receive maintenance from the faithful

9 [1]Am I not free? Am I not an apostle? Have I not seen Jesus our Lord? Are
not you my workmanship in the Lord? [2]If to others I am not an apostle, at
least I am to you; for you are the seal of my apostleship in the Lord.
[3]This is my defence to those who would examine me.* [4]Do we not have the
right to our food and drink? [5]Do we not have the right to be accompanied by a
wife,[n]* as the other apostles and the brethren of the Lord and Cephas? [6]Or is it
only Barnabas and I who have no right to refrain from working for a living?
[7]Who serves as a soldier at his own expense? Who plants a vineyard without
eating any of its fruit? Who tends a flock without getting some of the milk?

---

into play. "The source of all the Corinthians' problems lay not in their lack of knowledge but in their lack of charity and of concern for their neighbour" (St John Chrysostom, *Hom. on 1 Cor,* 20, 2).

8:7–13 Charity requires that one abstain from food sacrificed to idols, if eating it can cause a scandal; causing someone to fall away is a price too great for freedom; Christ died for each and every one.

9:1–14 St Paul uses an example from his own life to show that in some situations charity requires that one should not exercise certain rights: in his apostolate, for example, he could have a woman to look after him but chose not to; also, he could have claimed financial support from the faithful (vv. 5–6).

n. Greek *a woman, a sister*

[8]Do I say this on human authority? Does not the law say the same? [9]For it
is written in the law of Moses, "You shall not muzzle an ox when it is treading
out the grain." Is it for oxen that God is concerned? [10]Does he not speak entirely
for our sake? It was written for our sake, because the ploughman should plough
in hope and the thresher thresh in hope of a share in the crop. [11]If we have sown
spiritual good among you, is it too much if we reap your material benefits? [12]If
others share this rightful claim upon you, do not we still more?

Nevertheless, we have not made use of this right, but we endure anything
rather than put an obstacle in the way of the gospel of Christ. [13]Do you not
know that those who are employed in the temple service get their food from
the temple, and those who serve at the altar share in the sacrificial offerings?
[14]In the same way, the Lord commanded that those who proclaim the gospel
should get their living by the gospel.

St Paul does not exercise that right

[15]But I have made no use of any of these rights, nor am I writing this to secure
any such provision. For I would rather die than have any one deprive me of my
ground for boasting. [16]For if I preach the gospel, that gives me no ground for
boasting. For necessity is laid upon me. Woe to me if I do not preach the
gospel! [17]For if I do this of my own will, I have a reward; but if not of my own
will, I am entrusted with a commission. [18]What then is my reward? Just this:
that in my preaching I may make the gospel free of charge, not making full use
of my right in the gospel.

[19]For though I am free from all men, I have made myself a slave to all, that
I might win the more. [20]To the Jews I became as a Jew, in order to win Jews;
to those under the law I became as one under the law—though not being
myself under the law—that I might win those under the law. [21]To those outside
the law I became as one outside the law—not being without law toward God
but under the law of Christ—that I might win those outside the law. [22]To the
weak I became weak, that I might win the weak. I have become all things to
all men, that I might by all means save some. [23]I do it all for the sake of the
gospel, that I may share in its blessings.

9:15–23 Paul's appreciation of his God-given calling, and his love for all souls, have led him to preach the Gospel without receiving anything in exchange. "Intrinsically linked to the sacramental nature of ecclesial ministry is its character as service. Entirely dependent on Christ who gives mission and authority, ministers are truly 'slaves of Christ' (Rom 1:1), in the image of him who freely took 'the form of a slave' (Phil 2:7) for us. Because the word and grace of which they are ministers are not their own, but are given to them by Christ for the sake of others, they must freely become the slaves of all" (*CCC*, 876).

9:9 Deut 25:4.

The need for asceticism

24Do you not know that in a race all the runners compete, but only one receives
the prize? So run that you may obtain it. 25Every athlete exercises self-control
in all things. They do it to receive a perishable wreath, but we an imperishable.
26Well, I do not run aimlessly, I do not box as one beating the air; 27but I
pommel my body and subdue it, lest after preaching to others I myself should
be disqualified.

The lesson of Israel's history

10 1I want you to know, brethren, that our fathers were all under the cloud,
and all passed through the sea, and all were baptized into Moses in the
cloud and in the sea, 2and all ate the same supernatural[o] food 3and all drank the
same supernatural[o] drink. 4For they drank from the supernatural[o] Rock which
followed them, and the Rock was Christ. 5Nevertheless with most of them God
was not pleased; for they were overthrown in the wilderness.
6Now these things are warnings for us, not to desire evil as they did. 7Do not
be idolaters as some of them were; as it is written, "The people sat down to eat
and drink and rose up to dance." 8We must not indulge in immorality as some of
them did, and twenty-three thousand fell in a single day. 9We must not put the
Lord[p] to the test, as some of them did and were destroyed by serpents; 10nor
grumble, as some of them did and were destroyed by the Destroyer. 11Now these
things happened to them as a warning, but they were written down for our
instruction, upon whom the end of the ages has come. 12Therefore let any one
who thinks that he stands take heed lest he fall. 13No temptation has overtaken
you that is not common to man. God is faithful, and he will not let you be tempted
beyond your strength, but with the temptation will also provide the way of escape,
that you may be able to endure it.

Idolatry and the Eucharist, incompatible

14Therefore, my beloved, shun the worship of idols. 15I speak as to sensible
men; judge for yourselves what I say. 16The cup of blessing which we bless, is

---

9:24–27 Every two years the Isthmus games were held in Corinth. That may have been why Paul used these terms and similes connected with sport to explain what the ascetical struggle involves.

10:1–13 The Corinthians and all Christians need to draw lessons from the history of Israel. Despite all the wonders God marked for his people during the Exodus, on account of their repeated infidelity most Israelites never reached the promised land. This is telling us something: if we rely on our own resources, we run the risk of being unfaithful to God and being rejected by him.

10:14–22 St Paul returns to the subject of food sacrificed to idols. Christians may not attend the banquets which take place at pagan shrines (even though idols

o. Greek *spiritual* **p.** Other ancient authorities read *Christ* **10:7** Ex 32:4,6.

it not a participation[q] in the blood of Christ? The bread which we break, is it not a participation in the body of Christ?
17Because there is one bread, we who are many are one body, for we all partake of the one bread.
18Consider the people of Israel; are not those who eat the sacrifices partners in the altar?
19What do I imply then? That food offered to idols is anything, or that an idol is anything?
20No, I imply that what pagans sacrifice they offer to demons and not to God. I do not want you to be partners with demons.*
21You cannot drink the cup of the Lord and the cup of demons. You cannot partake of the table of the Lord and the table of demons.
22Shall we provoke the Lord to jealousy? Are we stronger than he?

Practical solutions to certain questions

23"All things are lawful," but not all things are helpful. "All things are lawful," but not all things build up.
24Let no one seek his own good, but the good of his neighbour.
25Eat whatever is sold in the meat market without raising any question on the ground of conscience.
26For "the earth is the Lord's, and everything in it."
27If one of the unbelievers invites you to dinner and you are disposed to go, eat whatever is set before you without raising any question on the ground of conscience.
28(But if some one says to you, "This has been offered in sacrifice," then out of consideration for the man who informed you, and for conscience' sake—
29I mean his conscience, not yours—do not eat it.) For why should my liberty be determined by another man's scruples?
30If I partake with thankfulness, why am I denounced because of that for which I give thanks?

---

represent nothing), because that would amount to idolatry. The Apostle ratifies his teaching by drawing a comparison with the eucharistic sacrifice. What he says confirms two basic truths about the mystery of the Eucharist—its sacrificial character, adverted to here by drawing a parallel between it and pagan sacrifice (v. 21), and the real presence of Christ, as can be seen by the reference to the body and blood of Christ (v. 16). The *Catechism of the Catholic Church*, in a passage listing various names for the sacrament of the Eucharist, says that it is called the breaking of the bread to signify that "all who eat the one broken bread, Christ, enter into communion with him and form but one body in him" (*CCC*, 1329) and it is called Holy Communion "because by this sacrament we unite ourselves to Christ who makes us sharers in his Body and Blood to form a single body" (ibid., 1331).

10:23–33 Here Paul deals with some particular cases, applying the criteria previously mentioned—avoiding scandal and seeking the glory of God in all things. "Similarly, when the sun rises and when it sets, when you are asleep and when you are awake, give thanks to God, who made all these things and arranged them for your benefit, so that you could come to know and love and praise their creator" (St Basil, *Hom. on Julitta mart.*).

q. Or *communion* **10:26** Ps 24:1.

[31]So, whether you eat or drink, or whatever you do, do all to the glory of God. [32]Give no offence to Jews or to Greeks or to the church of God, [33]just as I try to please all men in everything I do, not seeking my own advantage, but that of many, that they may be saved.

7. THE CELEBRATION OF THE EUCHARIST

Women in church

11 [1]Be imitators of me, as I am of Christ. [2]I commend you because you remember me in everything and maintain the traditions even as I have delivered them to you. [3]But I want you to understand that the head of every man is Christ, the head of a woman is her husband, and the head of Christ is God. [4]Any man who prays or prophesies with his head covered dishonours his head, [5]but any woman who prays or prophesies with her head unveiled dishonours her head—it is the same as if her head were shaven. [6]For if a woman will not veil herself, then she should cut off her hair; but if it is disgraceful for a woman to be shorn or shaven, let her wear a veil. [7]For a man ought not to cover his head, since he is the image and glory of God; but woman is the glory of man. [8](For man was not made from woman, but woman from man. [9]Neither was man created for woman, but woman for man.) [10]That is why a woman ought to have a veil[r] on her head, because of the angels. [11](Nevertheless, in the Lord woman is not independent of man nor man of woman; [12]for as woman was made from man, so man is now born of woman. And all things are from God.) [13]Judge for yourselves; is it proper for a woman to pray to God with her head uncovered? [14]Does not nature itself teach you that for a man to wear long hair is degrading to him, [15]but if a woman has long hair, it is her pride? For her hair is given to her for a covering. [16]If any one is disposed to be contentious, we recognize no other practise, nor do the churches of God.

11:1–34 □ In this section of the letter Paul sorts out some matters raised by the Corinthians in connection with liturgical assemblies and also expounds teaching on the Eucharist.

11:1–16 Elsewhere St Paul stressed the essential equality of man and woman in Christ: "There is neither Jew nor Greek, there is neither slave nor free, there is neither male nor female; for you are all one in Christ Jesus" (Gal 3:28). Here he deals with the use of the veil by women at liturgical ceremonies; this was a matter of dispute among the Corinthians (v. 16). The Apostle replies in line with Jewish custom of his time, the "traditions" (v. 2) he passed on to them. It may well be that behind the matter of the veil lay other questions that went deeper than that of women's attire. Be that as it may, external behaviour does reflect a person's inner dispositions.

r. Greek *authority* (the veil being a symbol of this)

Abuses in the celebration of the Eucharist
17But in the following instructions I do not commend you, because when you
come together it is not for the better but for the worse. 18For, in the first place,
when you assemble as a church, I hear that there are divisions among you; and
I partly believe it, 19for there must be factions among you in order that those
who are genuine among you may be recognized. 20When you meet together, it
is not the Lord's supper that you eat.* 21For in eating, each one goes ahead
with his own meal, and one is hungry and another is drunk. 22What! Do you
not have houses to eat and drink in? Or do you despise the church of God and
humiliate those who have nothing? What shall I say to you? Shall I commend
you in this? No, I will not.

The institution of the Eucharist and its worthy reception
23For I received from the Lord what I also delivered to you, that the Lord Jesus
on the night when he was betrayed took bread, 24and when he had given
thanks, he broke it, and said, "This is my body which is for[s] you. Do this in
remembrance of me." 25In the same way also the cup, after supper, saying,
"This cup is the new covenant in my blood. Do this, as often as you drink it, in
remembrance of me." 26For as often as you eat this bread and drink the cup,
you proclaim the Lord's death until he comes.
27Whoever, therefore, eats the bread or drinks the cup of the Lord in an
unworthy manner will be guilty of profaning the body and blood of the Lord.
28Let a man examine himself, and so eat of the bread and drink of the cup.
29For any one who eats and drinks without discerning the body eats and drinks
judgment upon himself. 30That is why many of you are weak and ill, and some

---

11:17–22 St Paul now comes to a much more serious abuse. These Christians, who come from a variety of social and cultural backgrounds, used to combine the celebration of the Eucharist with a meal in common. This had led to abuses and discrimination. Very early on in the Church, the Eucharist was separated from these meals, which then became fraternal meals with no liturgical significance.

11:23–34 The teaching on the Eucharist which St Paul passes on here clearly shows the importance of apostolic Tradition (v. 23). Verses 23–25 and the accounts in Matthew, Mark and Luke constitute the New Testament's coverage of the institution of the Eucharist. The passage contains the basic elements of Christian faith in the mystery of the Eucharist—1) the institution of the sacrament by our Lord, and his real presence in it; 2) the institution of the Christian priesthood; 3) the Eucharist is the sacrifice of the New Testament.

"Do this in remembrance of me" (v. 24): this is not a matter of merely recalling the Lord's Supper, but of renewing his Passover sacrifice of Calvary which already, at the Last Supper, was made present in an anticipated way.

s. Other ancient authorities read *broken for*

have died.[t] [31]But if we judged ourselves truly, we should not be judged. [32]But
when we are judged by the Lord, we are chastened[u] so that we may not be
condemned along with the world.
[33]So then, my brethren, when you come together to eat, wait for one
another—[34]if any one is hungry, let him eat at home—lest you come together
to be condemned. About the other things I will give directions when I come.

8. GIFTS AND GRACES

Kinds of spiritual gifts

12 [1]Now concerning spiritual gifts, brethren, I do not want you to be
uninformed.* [2]You know that when you were heathen, you were led
astray to dumb idols, however you may have been moved. [3]Therefore I want
you to understand that no one speaking by the Spirit of God ever says "Jesus
be cursed!" and no one can say "Jesus is Lord" except by the Holy Spirit.
[4]Now there are varieties of gifts, but the same Spirit; [5]and there are varieties
of service, but the same Lord; [6]and there are varieties of working, but it is the
same God who inspires them all in every one. [7]To each is given the
manifestation of the Spirit for the common good. [8]To one is given through the
Spirit the utterance of wisdom, and to another the utterance of knowledge
according to the same Spirit, [9]to another faith by the same Spirit, to another
gifts of healing by the one Spirit, [10]to another the working of miracles, to

---

The words of vv. 27–32 are an unambiguous assertion that Jesus is present in the eucharistic species. This real presence explains why one needs to be prepared in body and soul to receive it, and why receiving it unworthily has such grave consequences (vv. 27–29).

The *Catechism of the Catholic Church* refers to this teaching when it says that "Anyone conscious of a grave sin must receive the sacrament of Reconciliation before coming to communion" (CCC, 1385; cf. CIC, 919, 1).

12:1–14:40 □ At this point St Paul broaches the subject of spiritual gifts or charisms, the exercise of which had lead to disorders in liturgical assemblies. He uses the opportunity to stress that charity is the greatest of all gifts.

12:1–11 Unusual phenomena were to be found in the church of Corinth—speaking in ecstasy or in strange tongues (cf. chap. 14). This sort of thing might be the result of genuine charisms, but it could also arise from pseudo-religious emotional states, as happened, among the pagans, at the temple of the goddess Python at Delphi, near Corinth. St Paul establishes here criteria for distinguishing whether or not the Spirit of God is at work in such phenomena: do the people involved or do they not acknowledge Jesus and speak his praise. The Apostle puts

t. Greek *have fallen asleep* (as in 15:6,20) **u.** Or *when we are judged we are being chastened by the Lord*

another prophecy, to another the ability to distinguish between spirits, to
another various kinds of tongues, to another the interpretation of tongues. 11All
these are inspired by one and the same Spirit, who apportions to each one
individually as he wills.

Unity and variety in the mystical body of Christ

12For just as the body is one and has many members, and all the members of
the body, though many, are one body, so it is with Christ. 13For by one Spirit
we were all baptized into one body—Jews or Greeks, slaves or free—and all
were made to drink of one Spirit.

14For the body does not consist of one member but of many. 15If the foot
should say, "Because I am not a hand, I do not belong to the body," that would
not make it any less a part of the body. 16And if the ear should say, "Because I
am not an eye, I do not belong to the body," that would not make it any less a
part of the body. 17If the whole body were an eye, where would be the hearing?
If the whole body were an ear, where would be the sense of smell? 18But as it
is, God arranged the organs in the body, each one of them, as he chose. 19If all
were a single organ, where would the body be? 20As it is, there are many parts,
yet one body. 21The eye cannot say to the hand, "I have no need of you," nor
again the head to the feet, "I have no need of you." 22On the contrary, the parts
of the body which seem to be weaker are indispensable, 23and those parts of
the body which we think less honourable we invest with the greater honour,
and our unpresentable parts are treated with greater modesty, 24which our more
presentable parts do not require. But God has so composed the body, giving
the greater honour to the inferior part, 25that there may be no discord in the

---

more value on other gifts and manifestations of the Spirit which he goes on to mention, because they are ministries and gifts which help to build up the community.

12:12–31 By applying to the Church the comparison of society with a body, Paul points out two important things—that Christ and the Church are one and the same (v. 12), and that the Holy Spirit is the Church (v. 13). The building-up of the Church derives from that life–giving power. This means that all members of the Church, whatever their position, have the same basic status and the same importance. The union that obtains between the different members of the Church and the way they act towards one another is something the Church has always believed in; technically it is called the "Communion of Saints": "this expression refers first to the 'holy things' ('*sancta*'), above all the Eucharist, by which 'the unity of believers, who form one body in Christ, is both represented and brought about' (Vatican II, *LG*, 3). The term 'communion of saints' refers also to the communion of 'holy persons' ('*sancti*') in Christ who 'died for all', so that what each one does or suffers in and for Christ bears fruit for all" (*CCC*, 960, 961).

body, but that the members may have the same care for one another. [26]If one member suffers, all suffer together; if one member is honoured, all rejoice together.

[27]Now you are the body of Christ and individually members of it. [28]And God has appointed in the church first apostles, second prophets, third teachers, then workers of miracles, then healers, helpers, administrators, speakers in various kinds of tongues. [29]Are all apostles? Are all prophets? Are all teachers? Do all work miracles? [30]Do all possess gifts of healing? Do all speak with tongues? Do all interpret? [31]But earnestly desire the higher gifts.

And I will show you a still more excellent way.*

Hymn to charity

13 [1]If I speak in the tongues of men and of angels, but have not love, I am a noisy gong or a clanging cymbal. [2]And if I have prophetic powers, and understand all mysteries and all knowledge, and if I have all faith, so as to remove mountains, but have not love, I am nothing. [3]If I give away all I have, and if I deliver my body to be burned,[v] but have not love, I gain nothing.

[4]Love is patient and kind; love is not jealous or boastful; [5]it is not arrogant or rude. Love does not insist on its own way; it is not irritable or resentful; [6]it does not rejoice at wrong, but rejoices in the right. [7]Love bears all things, believes all things, hopes all things, endures all things.

[8]Love never ends; as for prophecies, they will pass away; as for tongues, they will cease; as for knowledge, it will pass away. [9]For our knowledge is imperfect and our prophecy is imperfect; [10]but when the perfect comes, the imperfect will pass away. [11]When I was a child, I spoke like a child, I thought like a child, I reasoned like a child; when I became a man, I gave up childish ways. [12]For now we see in a mirror dimly, but then face to face. Now I know in part; then I shall understand fully, even as I have been fully understood. [13]So faith, hope, love abide, these three; but the greatest of these is love.

13:1–13 This wonderful hymn to charity is one of the most beautiful passages in Pauline writing. It sings the praises of love by focusing on three key aspects—the superiority of and absolute need for this gift (vv. 1–3), its features and practical expression (vv. 4–7), and the fact that it endures forever (vv. 8–13).

Love is the greatest of all God's gifts: all the rest are designed to bring us to perfection and everlasting happiness; but love (charity) is beatitude itself. "Charity, which is love of God, never diminishes; rather it always increases; the better one comes to know God, the more one loves him" (St Thomas Aquinas, *Com. on 1 Cor,* in loc.).

v. Other ancient authorities read *body that I may glory*

Prophecy, the gift of tongues, and interpretation of tongues

14 1Make love your aim, and earnestly desire the spiritual gifts, especially
that you may prophesy. 2For one who speaks in a tongue speaks not to
men but to God; for no one understands him, but he utters mysteries in the
Spirit. 3On the other hand, he who prophesies speaks to men for their
upbuilding and encouragement and consolation. 4He who speaks in a tongue
edifies himself, but he who prophesies edifies the church. 5Now I want you all
to speak in tongues, but even more to prophesy. He who prophesies is greater
than he who speaks in tongues, unless some one interprets, so that the church
may be edified.

6Now, brethren, if I come to you speaking in tongues, how shall I benefit
you unless I bring you some revelation or knowledge or prophecy or teaching?
7If even lifeless instruments, such as the flute or the harp, do not give distinct
notes, how will any one know what is played? 8And if the bugle gives an
indistinct sound, who will get ready for battle? 9So with yourselves; if you in
a tongue utter speech that is not intelligible, how will any one know what is
said? For you will be speaking into the air. 10There are doubtless many
different languages in the world, and none is without meaning; 11but if I do not
know the meaning of the language, I shall be a foreigner to the speaker and the
speaker a foreigner to me. 12So with yourselves; since you are eager for
manifestations of the Spirit, strive to excel in building up the church.

13Therefore, he who speaks in a tongue should pray for the power to
interpret. 14For if I pray in a tongue, my spirit prays but my mind is unfruitful.
15What am I to do? I will pray with the spirit and I will pray with the mind
also; I will sing with the spirit and I will sing with the mind. 16Otherwise, if
you bless[w] with the spirit, how can any one in the position of an outsider[x] say
the "Amen" to your thanksgiving when he does not know what you are saying?
17For you may give thanks well enough, but the other man is not edified. 18I
thank God that I speak in tongues more than you all; 19nevertheless, in church
I would rather speak five words with my mind, in order to instruct others, than
ten thousand words in a tongue.

14:1–25 St Paul is teaching the value of the gifts of the Holy Spirit. The gift of prophecy mentioned here is the ability to speak spontaneously and in God's name in order to console and edify one's listeners; it does not necessarily involve the prediction of future events or the disclosure of secret things. The Christian gift of tongues was a supernatural faculty to pray or chant the praise of God with great enthusiasm, using strange words: often an interpreter (who had the gift to understand what was being said) explained the meaning. Apparently pagans were very impressed by this gift, but St Paul downplays it.

w. That is, *give thanks to God* **x.** Or *him that is without gifts*

[20]Brethren, do not be children in your thinking; be babes in evil, but in thinking be mature. [21]In the law it is written, "By men of strange tongues and by the lips of foreigners will I speak to this people, and even then they will not listen to me, says the Lord." [22]Thus, tongues are a sign not for believers but for unbelievers, while prophecy is not for unbelievers but for believers. [23]If, therefore, the whole church assembles and all speak in tongues, and outsiders or unbelievers enter, will they not say that you are mad? [24]But if all prophesy, and an unbeliever or outsider enters, he is convicted by all, he is called to account by all, [25]the secrets of his heart are disclosed; and so, falling on his face, he will worship God and declare that God is really among you.

Regulation of liturgical assemblies

[26]What then, brethren? When you come together, each one has a hymn, a lesson, a revelation, a tongue, or an interpretation. Let all things be done for edification. [27]If any speak in a tongue, let there be only two or at most three, and each in turn; and let one interpret. [28]But if there is no one to interpret, let each of them keep silence in church and speak to himself and to God. [29]Let two or three prophets speak, and let the others weigh what is said. [30]If a revelation is made to another sitting by, let the first be silent. [31]For you can all prophesy one by one, so that all may learn and all be encouraged; [32]and the spirits of prophets are subject to prophets. [33]For God is not a God of confusion but of peace.

As in all the churches of the saints, [34]the women should keep silence in the churches. For they are not permitted to speak, but should be subordinate, as even the law says. [35]If there is anything they desire to know, let them ask their husbands at home. For it is shameful for a woman to speak in church. [36]What! Did the word of God originate with you, or are you the only ones it has reached?

[37]If any one thinks that he is a prophet, or spiritual, he should acknowledge that what I am writing to you is a command of the Lord. [38]If any one does not recognize this, he is not recognized. [39]So, my brethren, earnestly desire to prophesy, and do not forbid speaking in tongues; [40]but all things should be done decently and in order.

14:26–40 Apparently, during some of these assemblies the Corinthians got carried away by their own enthusiasm and were too easily impressed by religious exaltation. They need to take steps to avoid unruliness; so the Apostle gives some specific directives—applying to those who speak in tongues (vv. 27–28), those who prophesy (vv. 29–33), and to women (vv. 34–35). Finally he gives a short summary of what he has been saying (vv. 36–40).

As regards women (v. 34) he is not against their prophesying (cf. 11:15); he speaks as he does against the background of what was happening at their assemblies in Corinth "The prohibition is confined solely to the official function of preaching to the assembly. [...] It should not be forgotten that St Paul provides

14:21 Is 28:11–12.

9. THE RESURRECTION OF THE DEAD

Christ's resurrection and his appearances

15 [1]Now I would remind you, brethren, in what terms I preached to you the
gospel, which you received, in which you stand, [2]by which you are
saved, if you hold it fast—unless you believed in vain.
[3]For I delivered to you as of first importance what I also received, that
Christ died for our sins in accordance with the scriptures, [4]that he was buried,
that he was raised on the third day in accordance with the scriptures, [5]and that
he appeared to Cephas, then to the twelve. [6]Then he appeared to more than five
hundred brethren at one time, most of whom are still alive, though some have
fallen asleep. [7]Then he appeared to James, then to all the apostles. [8]Last of all,
as to one untimely born, he appeared also to me. [9]For I am the least of the
apostles, unfit to be called an apostle, because I persecuted the church of God.
[10]But by the grace of God I am what I am, and his grace toward me was not in
vain. On the contrary, I worked harder than any of them, though it was not I,
but the grace of God which is with me. [11]Whether then it was I or they, so we
preach and so you believed.

---

one of the strongest accounts of the fundamental equality of men and women as children [of God] in Christ to be found in the New Testament" (SCDF, *Inter insigniores*, 4, 2). Man and woman are essentially equal, but that does not mean there cannot be diversity of roles in the Church, in such a way that only males chosen by God have access to the priestly ministry; we must remember that "the greatest in the kingdom of heaven are not the [ordained] ministers but the saints" (ibid., 6, 30).

15:1–58 □ Some Christians at Corinth were disinclined to accept the resurrection of the dead, maybe because Greeks never had a belief of that sort (not even those Greeks who held that the soul was immortal) and they thought that salvation in Christ was complete once a person was baptized. St Paul explains the eschatological dimension.

15:1–11 Paul reminds them about the Good News preached by the apostles from the very start. This Gospel proclaims the historical fact of Christ's resurrection. This is the key argument in favour of Jesus' divinity and his redemptive mission from the Father. The resurrection of Christ is the central dogma of Christian belief—so important that the apostles' primary role is to bear witness to the resurrection. This text of St Paul is enhanced by the fact because it is the earliest written account (earlier than the Gospels) of our Lord's resurrection, which had taken place scarcely twenty years before. The Christian gets confirmation that Christ rose from the dead from the testimony of Holy Scripture and that of the apostles to whom Christ appeared alive and glorified.

The basis of our faith

[12]Now if Christ is preached as raised from the dead, how can some of you say
that there is no resurrection of the dead? [13]But if there is no resurrection of the
dead, then Christ has not been raised; [14]if Christ has not been raised, then our
preaching is in vain and your faith is in vain. [15]We are even found to be
misrepresenting God, because we testified of God that he raised Christ, whom
he did not raise if it is true that the dead are not raised. [16]For if the dead are not
raised, then Christ has not been raised. [17]If Christ has not been raised, your
faith is futile and you are still in your sins. [18]Then those also who have fallen
asleep in Christ have perished. [19]If for this life only we have hoped in Christ,
we are of all men most to be pitied.

The cause of our resurrection

[20]But in fact Christ has been raised from the dead, the first fruits of those who
have fallen asleep. [21]For as by a man came death, by a man has come also the
resurrection of the dead. [22]For as in Adam all die, so also in Christ shall all be
made alive. [23]But each in his own order: Christ the first fruits, then at his
coming those who belong to Christ. [24]Then comes the end, when he delivers
the kingdom to God the Father after destroying every rule and every authority
and power. [25]For he must reign until he has put all his enemies under his feet.
[26]The last enemy to be destroyed is death. [27]"For God[z] has put all things in
subjection under his feet." But when it says, "All things are put in subjection
under him," it is plain that he is excepted who put all things under him.

15:12–19 By rising from the dead, Christ completes the work of Redemption. His death on the cross brought victory over sin; but it was necessary also that he should rise from the dead, thereby conquering death, the product of sin (cf. Rom 5:12). "The Resurrection above all constitutes the confirmation of all Christ's works and teachings. All truths, even those most inaccessible to human reason, find their justication if Christ by his Resurrection has given the definitive proof of his divine authority, which he had promised" (*CCC*, 651).

15:20–34 The Apostle insists on the solidarity that exists between Christ and Christians: we are all members of one body, of which Christ is the head. Therefore, once the resurrection of Christ is affirmed, the resurrection of the just necessarily follows. Adam's disobedience brought death for all; Jesus, the new Adam, has merited that all should rise. The Christian's salvation will be perfected after death when his body rises at the end of time. St Paul is expounding the entire messianic and redemptive work of Christ: in keeping with the Father's plan, Christ has been made Lord of the universe, in fulfilment of the Scriptures (Ps 110:1 and 8:7). Christ's sovereignty over all creation comes about in history, but it will achieve its final, complete form after the Last Judgment. Every year, on the last

z. Greek *he* **15:25** Ps 110:1. **15:27** Ps 8:6. **15:32** Is 22:13.

28When all things are subjected to him, then the Son himself will also be
subjected to him who put all things under him, that God may be everything to
every one.
29Otherwise, what do people mean by being baptized on behalf of the dead?
If the dead are not raised at all, why are people baptized on their behalf? *
30Why am I in peril every hour? 31I protest, brethren, by my pride in you which
I have in Christ Jesus our Lord, I die every day! 32What do I gain if, humanly
speaking, I fought with beasts at Ephesus? If the dead are not raised, "Let us
eat and drink, for tomorrow we die." 33Do not be deceived: "Bad company
ruins good morals." 34Come to your right mind, and sin no more. For some
have no knowledge of God. I say this to your shame.

The manner of the resurrection of the dead
35But some one will ask, "How are the dead raised? With what kind of body
do they come?" 36You foolish man! What you sow does not come to life unless
it dies. 37And what you sow is not the body which is to be, but a bare kernel,
perhaps of wheat or of some other grain. 38But God gives it a body as he has
chosen, and to each kind of seed its own body. 39For not all flesh is alike, but
there is one kind for men, another for animals, another for birds, and another
for fish. 40There are celestial bodies and there are terrestrial bodies; but the
glory of the celestial is one, and the glory of the terrestrial is another. 41There
is one glory of the sun, and another glory of the moon, and another glory of the
stars; for star differs from star in glory.

Sunday in Ordinary Time, the Church celebrates the solemnity of Jesus Christ the King, to acknowledge his absolute sovereignty over all created things.

The meaning of v. 29 is not absolutely clear. It may have refer to a custom (one that did not last long) which involved associating with one's own Baptism friends and relatives who had already died.

15:35–58 Now that he has stated that the dead will rise, St Paul deals with how it will happen, using comparisons with plants, minerals and animals (vv. 36–41). Then he describes the properties of the risen body (vv. 42–44) referring in particular to one—its spirituality or subtlety: vv. 42–50. He then describes the circumstances in which the general resurrection will take place (vv. 51–53), and he ends with a hymn of joy and thanksgiving to God for all these wonderful things (vv. 54–58).

The risen body is called a "spiritual body" (v. 44) "not because it is converted into spirit, but because it is subject in a particular way to the spirit; so that it [the spiritual body] may be at home in heaven, all earthly weakness and imperfection is changed and converted into a heavenly stability" (St Augustine, *De fid. et symb.* 6).

[42]So is it with the resurrection of the dead. What is sown is perishable, what
is raised is imperishable. [43]It is sown in dishonour, it is raised in glory. It is
sown in weakness, it is raised in power. [44]It is sown a physical body, it is raised
a spiritual body. If there is a physical body, there is also a spiritual body.
[45]Thus it is written, "The first man Adam became a living being"; the last
Adam became a life-giving spirit. [46]But it is not the spiritual which is first but
the physical, and then the spiritual. [47]The first man was from the earth, a man
of dust; the second man is from heaven. [48]As was the man of dust, so are those
who are of the dust; and as is the man of heaven, so are those who are of
heaven. [49]Just as we have borne the image of the man of dust, we shall[a] also
bear the image of the man of heaven. [50]I tell you this, brethren: flesh and blood
cannot inherit the kingdom of God, nor does the perishable inherit the
imperishable.

[51]Lo! I tell you a mystery. We shall not all sleep, but we shall all be
changed, [52]in a moment, in the twinkling of an eye, at the last trumpet. For the
trumpet will sound, and the dead will be raised imperishable, and we shall be
changed. [53]For this perishable nature must put on the imperishable, and this
mortal nature must put on immortality. [54]When the perishable puts on the
imperishable, and the mortal puts on immortality, then shall come to pass the
saying that is written:

> "Death is swallowed up in victory."
> [55]"O death, where is thy victory?
> O death, where is thy sting?"

[56]The sting of death is sin, and the power of sin is the law. [57]But thanks be to
God, who gives us the victory through our Lord Jesus Christ.

[58]Therefore, my beloved brethren, be steadfast, immovable, always abounding
in the work of the Lord, knowing that in the Lord your labour is not in vain.

10. MESSAGES AND WORDS OF FAREWELL

Collection for the church of Jerusalem

16 [1]Now concerning the contribution for the saints:* as I directed the
churches of Galatia, so you also are to do. [2]On the first day of every
week, each of you is to put something aside and store it up, as he may prosper,

---

16: 1–24 □ The last chapter, an epilogue, summarizes some recommendations and greetings.

16:1–4 This is a reminder about the duty to give financial help to Christians in need, specifically those in Jerusalem. It is in line with advice Paul had received

a. Other ancient authorities read *let us* **15:45** Gen 2:7. **15:54** Is 25:8. **15:55** Hos 13:14.

so that contributions need not be made when I come. [3]And when I arrive, I will
send those whom you accredit by letter to carry your gift to Jerusalem. [4]If it
seems advisable that I should go also, they will accompany me.

Plans for the months ahead

[5]I will visit you after passing through Macedonia, for I intend to pass through
Macedonia, [6]and perhaps I will stay with you or even spend the winter, so that
you may speed me on my journey, wherever I go. [7]For I do not want to see you
now just in passing; I hope to spend some time with you, if the Lord permits.
[8]But I will stay in Ephesus until Pentecost, [9]for a wide door for effective work
has opened to me, and there are many adversaries.

[10]When Timothy comes, see that you put him at ease among you, for he is
doing the work of the Lord, as I am. [11]So let no one despise him. Speed him on
his way in peace, that he may return to me; for I am expecting him with the
brethren.

[12]As for our brother Apollos, I strongly urged him to visit you with the
other brethren, but it was not at all his will[b] to come now. He will come when
he has opportunity.

Exhortations and greetings

[13]Be watchful, stand firm in your faith, be courageous, be strong. [14]Let all that
you do be done in love.

[15]Now, brethren, you know that the household of Stephanas were the first
converts in Achaia, and they have devoted themselves to the service of the
saints; [16]I urge you to be subject to such men and to every fellow worker and
labourer. [17]I rejoice at the coming of Stephanas and Fortunatus and Achaicus,

---

from the apostles (cf. Gal 2:10): “Charitable action today can and should reach all men and all needs. […] This obligation binds first and foremost the more affluent individuals and nations” (Vatican II, *AA*, 8).

16:5–12 Paul mentions journeys he is planning, and his intention to stay in Corinth for an extended period. The strictures contained in this letter do not imply that the Corinthians were not devout Christians or that the Apostle did not have high regard for them.

Apollo was well known to the Christians of Corinth, because he had spent long periods among them (cf. Acts 19:1; 1 Cor 1:11–12).

16:13–24 St Paul summarizes the main points of his letter. Using military language, he reminds them that the Christian life is one of struggle against one’s passions and against the temptations of the devil, and that everything a Christian does should be inspired by charity.

b. Or *God’s will for him*

because they have made up for your absence; [18]for they refreshed my spirit as well as yours. Give recognition to such men.

[19]The churches of Asia send greetings. Aquila and Prisca, together with the church in their house, send you hearty greetings in the Lord. [20]All the brethren send greetings. Greet one another with a holy kiss.

[21]I, Paul, write this greeting with my own hand. [22]If any one has no love for the Lord, let him be accursed. Our Lord, come![c] [23]The grace of the Lord Jesus be with you. [24]My love be with you all in Christ Jesus. Amen.

"Let him be accursed" (v. 21): this is a form of words implying punishment and condemnation (cf. 12:3; Gal 1:8) in a very broad sense; it seems to have involved public exclusion from the Church; it is best read in conjunction with 12:3: "no one speaking by the Spirit of God ever says 'Jesus be cursed!'"

"Maranatha!: an Aramaic expression meaning "Come, our Lord!" According to the *Didache* (10, 6), this invocation was used in early Christian times at the end of the eucharistic prayer. It appears in Revelation 22:20 in a Greek translation.

c. Greek *Maranatha*

2 Corinthians

INTRODUCTION

Greeting

1 [1]Paul, an apostle of Christ Jesus by the will of God, and Timothy our brother.
To the church of God which is at Corinth, with all the saints who are in the
whole of Achaia:
[2]Grace to you and peace from God our Father and the Lord Jesus Christ.

Thanksgiving

[3]Blessed be the God and Father of our Lord Jesus Christ, the Father of mercies
and God of all comfort, [4]who comforts us in all our affliction, so that we may
be able to comfort those who are in any affliction, with the comfort with which
we ourselves are comforted by God. [5]For as we share abundantly in Christ's
sufferings, so through Christ we share abundantly in comfort too.[a] [6]If we are
afflicted, it is for your comfort and salvation; and if we are comforted, it is for
your comfort, which you experience when you patiently endure the same
sufferings that we suffer. [7]Our hope for you is unshaken; for we know that as
you share in our sufferings, you will also share in our comfort.
[8]For we do not want you to be ignorant, brethren, of the affliction* we experi-
enced in Asia; for we were so utterly, unbearably crushed that we despaired of life

---

1:1–11 □ This letter starts in the way typical of other letters of St Paul—a greeting in which the Apostle introduces himself, and an act of thanksgiving to God in the form of a hymn.

1:1–2 St Paul introduces himself in his usual way—"an apostle of Christ Jesus by the will of God"—but his description takes on special significance here because he will devote the letter to defending his apostolic calling.

1:3–11 The act of thanksgiving here is rather different from that in most of Paul's other letters, where he gives thanks to God for the favours granted the Christians to whom he is writing, to help them appreciate their calling; here he thanks God on his own behalf for consoling him in his distress. Yet he is thinking of his addressees. He shows them the deep solidarity that exists among all the members of Christ's mystical body, and between members and Head. This intimate communion and intercommunication allows the Apostle to say that his sufferings are "Christ's", and to speak of the close connexions between his sufferings and consolations, and those of the Christians of Corinth.

a. Or *For as the suffering of Christ abound for us, so also comfort abounds through Christ* itself. [9]Why, we felt that we had received the sentence of death; but that was to make us rely not on ourselves but on God who raises the dead; [10]he delivered us from so deadly a peril, and he will deliver us; on him we have set our hope that he will deliver us again. [11]You also must help us by prayer, so that many will give thanks on our behalf for the blessing granted us in answer to many prayers.

PART ONE: ST PAUL'S DEFENCE AGAINST HIS ENEMIES

1. HIS SIMPLICITY AND SINCERITY

The evidence of his actions and his letters
[12]For our boast is this, the testimony of our conscience that we have behaved in the world, and still more toward you, with holiness and godly sincerity, not by earthly wisdom but by the grace of God. [13]For we write you nothing but what you can read and understand; I hope you will understand fully, [14]as you have understood in part, that you can be proud of us as we can be of you, on the day of the Lord Jesus.

Why he has not visited Corinth
[15]Because I was sure of this, I wanted to come to you first, so that you might have a double pleasure;[b] [16]I wanted to visit you on my way to Macedonia, and

---

1:12–7:16 □□ In this part of the letter Paul explains to the Corinthians why he acted as he did, and he answers the criticisms some have levelled against him. Here we see, perhaps more clearly than anywhere else, how dedicated St Paul was to his ministry (1:12–2:17), how sincere he was in his actions (3:1–6:10), and his heartfelt feelings as regards the different ways Christians responded (6:11–7:16).

1:12–2:17 □ Apparently some Christians at Corinth have been accusing the Apostle of not daring to return to the city, even though he promised he would. They think this is a sign of weakness. St Paul justifies his behaviour.

1:12–14 The Apostle wants to regain the Corinthians' affection and trust, which was probably being eroded by the unrelenting defamation his opponents directed against him.

1:15–2:4 It is not clear what caused the postponement of the planned visit. More than likely, some unpleasant incidents during an earlier stay in Corinth had

b. Other ancient authorities read *favour*

to come back to you from Macedonia and have you send me on my way to
Judea. [17]Was I vacillating when I wanted to do this? Do I make my plans like
a worldly man, ready to say Yes and No at once? [18]As surely as God is faithful,
our word to you has not been Yes and No. [19]For the Son of God, Jesus Christ,
whom we preached among you, Silvanus and Timothy and I, was not Yes and
No; but in him it is always Yes. [20]For all the promises of God find their Yes in
him. That is why we utter the Amen through him, to the glory of God. [21]But it
is God who establishes us with you in Christ, and has commissioned us; [22]he
has put his seal upon us and given us his Spirit in our hearts as a guarantee.

[23]But I call God to witness against me—it was to spare you that I refrained
from coming to Corinth. [24]Not that we lord it over your faith; we work with
you for your joy, for you stand firm in your faith.

2 [1] I made up my mind not to make you another painful visit. [2]For if I cause
you pain, who is there to make me glad but the one whom I have pained?
[3]And I wrote as I did, so that when I came I might not suffer pain from those
who should have made me rejoice, for I felt sure of all of you, that my joy
would be the joy of you all. [4]For I wrote you out of much affliction and
anguish of heart and with many tears, not to cause you pain but to let you
know the abundant love that I have for you.

Forgiveness for those who offend us

[5]But if any one has caused pain, he has caused it not to me, but in some measure
—not to put it too severely—to you all. [6]For such a one this punishment by the
majority is enough; [7]so you should rather turn to forgive and comfort him, or
he may be overwhelmed by excessive sorrow. [8]So I beg you to reaffirm your

---

aggrieved both the Corinthians and the Apostle, and they may have led to some particularly serious offence against him personally (cf. 2:5–11). For this reason he considers it more prudent to write, in order to fix things up prior to a visit.

As elsewhere in this letter (cf. 3:3; 13:13), Paul refers explicitly to the promises of the Holy Trinity: it is God (the Father) who has given us our "commission" (anointed us with grace), thereby linking us to the Son, through the gift of the Holy Spirit in our hearts. A Christian is "sealed" in Baptism (cf. v. 22): he no longer belongs to himself but has become the property of Christ. "Because this seal indicates the indelible effect of the anointing with the Holy Spirit in the sacraments of Baptism, Confirmation and Holy Orders, the image of the seal (*sphragis*) has been used in some theological traditions to express the indelible 'character' imprinted by these three unrepeatable sacraments" (*CCC*, 698).

2:5–11 These words have often been seen as referring to the man guilty of incest whom the Apostle condemned in 1 Corinthians 5:1–5. But it is more likely that they concern someone who committed a serious personal offence against Paul or

love for him. 9For this is why I wrote, that I might test you and know whether
you are obedient in everything. 10Any one whom you forgive, I also forgive.
What I have forgiven, if I have forgiven anything, has been for your sake in the
presence of Christ, 11to keep Satan from gaining the advantage over us; for we
are not ignorant of his designs.

Paul's eagerness for news

12When I came to Troas to preach the gospel of Christ, a door was opened for
me in the Lord; 13but my mind could not rest because I did not find my brother
Titus there. So I took leave of them and went on to Macedonia.

14But thanks be to God, who in Christ always leads us in triumph, and
through us spreads the fragrance of the knowledge of him everywhere. 15For
we are the aroma of Christ to God among those who are being saved and
among those who are perishing, 16to one a fragrance from death to death, to
the other a fragrance from life to life. Who is sufficient for these things? 17For
we are not, like so many, pedlars of God's word; but as men of sincerity, as
commissioned by God, in the sight of God we speak in Christ.

2. THE IMPORTANCE OF APOSTOLIC OFFICE

Paul's letter of recommendation

3 1Are we beginning to commend ourselves again? Or do we need, as some
do, letters of recommendation to you, or from you? 2You yourselves are our
letter of recommendation, written on your[c] hearts, to be known and read by all
men; 3and you show that you are a letter from Christ delivered by us, written
not with ink but with the Spirit of the living God, not on tablets of stone but on
tablets of human hearts.

---

one of his co-workers during his visit to Corinth. The offender would have been a Judaizer who had the support of a minority in the Corinthian church. This offence may have been the main reason for this letter written "with many tears" (2:4) and for the dispatch of Titus to Corinth (cf. 2:13; 7:6–16).

2:12–17 Like the Apostle, a Christian should make Christ present among men: "He ought to act in such a way that those who know him sense 'the fragrance of Christ'. Men should be able to recognize the Master in his disciples" (Bl. J. Escrivá, *Hom.,* 1, 105).

3:1–6:10 □Another accusation made against Paul by some Corinthians was that he was proud and arrogant in the performance of his ministry. In the course of defending himself he uses the opportunity to explain the nature and purpose of that ministry and of Christian ministry in general.

c. Other ancient authorities read *our*

Christian ministry is greater than that of the Old Covenant
4Such is the confidence that we have through Christ toward God. 5Not that we
are competent of ourselves to claim anything as coming from us; our
competence is from God, 6who has made us competent to be ministers of a
new covenant, not in a written code but in the Spirit; for the written code kills,
but the Spirit gives life.
7Now if the dispensation of death, carved in letters on stone, came with
such splendour that the Israelites could not look at Moses' face because of its
brightness, fading as this was, 8will not the dispensation of the Spirit be attended
with greater splendour? 9For if there was splendour in the dispensation of
condemnation, the dispensation of righteousness must far exceed it in splendour.
10Indeed, in this case, what once had splendour has come to have no splendour
at all, because of the splendour that surpasses it. 11For if what faded away
came with splendour, what is permanent must have much more splendour.
12Since we have such a hope, we are very bold, 13not like Moses, who put a
veil over his face so that the Israelites might not see the end of the fading
splendour. 14But their minds were hardened; for to this day, when they read the
old covenant, that same veil remains unlifted, because only through Christ is
it taken away. 15Yes, to this day whenever Moses is read a veil lies over their

---

3:1–3 Presumably Paul's enemies arrived in Corinth bearing some sort of letter of recommendation. The Apostle can produce a much more eloquent and powerful letter—the Corinthians themselves: it was his preaching that led to their conversion: "no matter how uncivilized the people may be, even though they may not understand the language of the spoken word they do understand the language of good example and of virtue, which they see put into practice; and thus they come to greatly appreciate the values those disciples hold" (St John of Avila, *Audi, filia*, 34).

3:4–18 By his preaching and personal conduct, St Paul proclaimed a type of relationship with God in Christ that was superior to and exceeded anything man could achieve through the Law of Moses. Some Corinthians, following the Judaizers, thought that Paul had invented his message; he was just full of himself. So Paul appeals to God and shows that the New Covenant is superior to the Old; it follows that the apostolic ministry is superior to that of Moses. The New Law is "Spirit", because it is the Holy Spirit himself who, through grace, imbues the hearts of the faithful with charity, and charity is the fullness of the Law. The veil Moses used to cover his face when he came down from Mount Sinai after speaking to God (Ex 34:29–35) was a symbol of the temporary nature of the Law and its ministry. Only with the help of the light brought by Christ, the fullness of revelation, can one see the true meaning of the Old Covenant: "the books of the Old Testament, all of them caught up into the Gospel message, attain and show forth their full meaning in the New Testament and, in their turn, shed light on it and explain it" (Vatican II, *DV*, 16).

minds; [16]but when a man turns to the Lord the veil is removed. [17]Now the Lord is the Spirit, and where the Spirit of the Lord is, there is freedom. [18]And we all, with unveiled face, beholding[d] the glory of the Lord, are being changed into his likeness from one degree of glory to another; for this comes from the Lord who is the Spirit.*

Paul's sincere conduct

4 [1]Therefore, having this ministry by the mercy of God,[e] we do not lose heart. [2]We have renounced disgraceful, underhanded ways; we refuse to practise cunning or to tamper with God's word, but by the open statement of the truth we would commend ourselves to every man's conscience in the sight of God. [3]And even if our gospel is veiled, it is veiled only to those who are perishing. [4]In their case the god of this world has blinded the minds of the unbelievers, to keep them from seeing the light of the gospel of the glory of Christ, who is the likeness of God. [5]For what we preach is not ourselves, but Jesus Christ as Lord, with ourselves as your servants[f] for Jesus' sake. [6]For it is the God who said, "Let light shine out of darkness," who has shone in our hearts to give the light of the knowledge of the glory of God in the face of Christ.

The trials Paul has experienced

[7]But we have this treasure* in earthen vessels, to show that the transcendent power belongs to God and not to us. [8]We are afflicted in every way, but not crushed; perplexed, but not driven to despair; [9]persecuted, but not forsaken; struck down, but not destroyed; [10]always carrying in the body the death of Jesus, so that the life of Jesus may also be manifested in our bodies. [11]For while we live we are always being given up to death for Jesus' sake, so that the life of Jesus may be manifested in our mortal flesh. [12]So death is at work in us, but life in you.*

4:1–6 Unlike the false apostles, Paul's own aim is to teach the truth of Jesus Christ, without any dilution or compromise. If, in spite of everything, there are still those who cannot see the truth of the Gospel, the reason lies in their bad dispositions, which allow the devil to darken their minds.

St Paul often calls Jesus "Lord"—a clear assertion of Christ's divinity, for "Lord" was the word the Greeks normally used to translate the Hebrew name for God.

4:7–12 In some way these sufferings of the Apostle re-enact those of Jesus in his passion and death. But, in Christ, suffering and death are the path to the life of glory after resurrection. "Only those who travel by the rough and narrow path of tribulation are given entrance to the city of the saints, and allowed to stay and rest there, to reign with the King" (Pseudo-Macarius, *Hom.*, 12, 5).

d. Or *reflecting* **e.** Greek *as we have received mercy* **f.** Or *slaves* **3:16** Ex 34–34.

Paul is sustained by hope of heaven
[13]Since we have the same spirit of faith as he had who wrote, "I believed, and
so I spoke," we too believe, and so we speak, [14]knowing that he who raised the
Lord Jesus will raise us also with Jesus and bring us with you into his
presence. [15]For it is all for your sake, so that as grace extends to more and
more people it may increase thanksgiving, to the glory of God.
[16]So we do not lose heart. Though our outer nature is wasting away, our
inner nature is being renewed every day. [17]For this slight momentary affliction
is preparing for us an eternal weight of glory beyond all comparison, [18]because
we look not to the things that are seen but to the things that are unseen; for the
things that are seen are transient, but the things that are unseen are eternal.
5 [1]For we know that if the earthly tent we live in is destroyed, we have a
building from God, a house not made with hands, eternal in the heavens.
[2]Here indeed we groan, and long to put on our heavenly dwelling, [3]so that by
putting it on we may not be found naked. [4]For while we are still in this tent, we
sigh with anxiety; not that we would be unclothed, but that we would be further
clothed, so that what is mortal may be swallowed up by life. [5]He who has
prepared us for this very thing is God, who has given us the Spirit as a guarantee.
[6]So we are always of good courage; we know that while we are at home in
the body we are away from the Lord, [7]for we walk by faith, not by sight. [8]We
are of good courage, and we would rather be away from the body and at home
with the Lord. [9]So whether we are at home or away, we make it our aim to
please him. [10]For we must all appear before the judgment seat of Christ, so that
each one may receive good or evil, according to what he has done in the body.

4:13–5:10 Hope in the resurrection and in sharing the happiness of heaven encourages the Apostle to be resolute. Whereas the outer man (his perishable body) is wasting away due to tribulation and suffering, the inner man (the life of the soul) is growing and being renewed day by day, until the point comes when it reaches its full growth in heaven. This is something that can readily be seen in the lives of the saints: in the midst of sufferings of every kind, and despite the fact that their life on earth is wasting away, their soul is being rejuvenated, their joy ever on the increase.

In heaven the body will be glorified by God; it will be the soul's eternal mansion. St Paul compares man's mortal body to a garment; in eternal life it will be further clothed with glory and immortality. "This earth is not our homeland; we are passing through it, as pilgrims. [...] Our homeland is heaven, which we merit by the grace of God and our own good works" (St Alphonsus Liguori, *Shortened Sermons*, 16).

4:13 Ps 116:10.

The ministry of reconciliation

11Therefore, knowing the fear of the Lord, we persuade men; but what we are
is known to God, and I hope it is known also to your conscience. 12We are not
commending ourselves to you again but giving you cause to be proud of us, so
that you may be able to answer those who pride themselves on a man's
position and not on his heart. 13For if we are beside ourselves, it is for God;
if we are in our right mind, it is for you. 14For the love of Christ controls us,
because we are convinced that one has died for all; therefore all have died.
15And he died for all, that those who live might live no longer for themselves
but for him who for their sake died and was raised.

16From now on, therefore, we regard no one from a human point of view;
even though we once regarded Christ from a human point of view, we regard
him thus no longer. 17Therefore, if any one is in Christ, he is a new creation;[g]
the old has passed away, behold, the new has come. 18All this is from God,
who through Christ reconciled us to himself and gave us the ministry of
reconciliation; 19that is, in Christ God was reconciling[h] the world to himself,*
not counting their trespasses against them, and entrusting to us the message of
reconciliation. 20So we are ambassadors for Christ, God making his appeal
through us. We beseech you on behalf of Christ, be reconciled to God. 21For
our sake he made him to be sin* who knew no sin, so that in him we might
become the righteousness of God.

5:11–21 Paul explains what motivates his apostolic ministry—the love of Christ (v. 14), meaning both Christ's love for people and the people's love for Christ. In describing this love, Paul gives a concise account of Redemption: God has reconciled men to himself by means of Jesus Christ, who bore the sins of the world and died for all, so that no longer are men's sins imputed to them. Moreover, God has made the apostles ambassadors of Christ to bring men "the message of reconciliation" (v. 19), offering them God's friendship. This is the understanding that Paul now has of Jesus Christ, in contrast with what he knew before his conversion, when he saw Christ only "from a human point of view" (v. 16).

The death of Christ is the high price paid on man's behalf, as a ransom to set them free from bondage to sin, death and the devil. As a result, we now belong to Christ, we no longer belong to ourselves, and the new life (in grace and freedom) won by Christ needs to be lived through and for Him.

"He made him to be sin" (v. 21). Obviously St Paul does not mean that Christ was guilty of sin. "Christ had no sin in him; he bore the burden of sin, but he did not commit sin" (St Augustine, *Enarr. in Ps.*, 68, 1, 10). In line with the way the word "sin" is used in the Old Testament, this statement means "he made himself a victim for sin or an "offering/sacrifice for sin".

g. Or *creature* **h.** Or *in Christ God was reconciling*

Paul, a true servant of Christ

6 [1]Working together with him, then, we entreat you not to accept the grace of
God in vain. [2]For he says,

"At the acceptable time I have listened to you,
"and helped you on the day of salvation."

Behold, now is the acceptable time; behold, now is the day of salvation. [3]We
put no obstacle in any one's way, so that no fault may be found with our
ministry, [4]but as servants of God we commend ourselves in every way: through
great endurance, in afflictions, hardships, calamities, [5]beatings, imprisonments,
tumults, labours, watching, hunger; [6]by purity, knowledge, forbearance, kind-
ness, the Holy Spirit, genuine love, [7]truthful speech, and the power of God;
with the weapons of righteousness for the right hand and for the left; [8]in honour
and dishonour, in ill repute and good repute. We are treated as impostors, and yet
are true; [9]as unknown, and yet well known; as dying, and behold we live; as
punished, and yet not killed; [10]as sorrowful, yet always rejoicing; as poor, yet
making many rich; as having nothing, and yet possessing everything.

3. ST PAUL OPENS HIS HEART

His love for the Corinthians

[11]Our mouth is open to you, Corinthians; our heart is wide. [12]You are not
restricted by us, but you are restricted in your own affections. [13]In return—I
speak as to children—widen your hearts also.

6:1–10 Paul concludes his long defence of his apostolic ministry by saying that he has always tried to act as a worthy servant of God. He appeals to the Corinthians' sense of responsibility by quoting Isaiah 49:8; this is reminiscent of our Lord's preaching in the synagogue of Nazareth (cf. Lk 4:16–21). The "acceptable time" (v. 2) will last until Christ comes in glory at the end of the world; in the life of the individual, it will last until the hour of his death. Until then, every day is the "day of salvation", an opportunity to serve God; we should never let anything deflect us from our purpose: "Let nothing trouble you, / Let nothing frighten you, / Everything passes, / God never changes, / Patience / Obtains all; / He who has God / Wants for nothing: / God alone is enough" (St Teresa of Avila, *Poems*, 30).

6:11–7:16 □ St Paul pauses to express his affection for the faithful of Corinth. He is mindful and appreciative of the regard that most of them have for him (Titus had reported this). This section is a particularly valuable source of information about Paul's personality.

6:11–13 The love of God is what has motivated everything Paul has done. "Charity is a virtue that inflames and devours. It was what caused our Apostle to speak, what expanded his heart" (St John Chrysostom, *Hom. on 2 Cor,* 13, 1).

6:2 Is 49:8.

Contact with unbelievers

14Do not be mismated with unbelievers. For what partnership have righteousness
and iniquity? Or what fellowship has light with darkness? 15What accord has
Christ with Belial?[i] Or what has a believer in common with an unbeliever?
16What agreement has the temple of God with idols? For we are the temple of
the living God; as God said,

"I will live in them and move among them,
"and I will be their God,
"and they shall be my people.
17 Therefore come out from them,
and be separate from them, says the Lord,
and touch nothing unclean;
then I will welcome you,
18 and I will be a father to you,
and you shall be my sons and daughters,
says the Lord Almighty."

7 1Since we have these promises, beloved, let us cleanse ourselves from every
defilement of body and spirit, and make holiness perfect in the fear of God.

Paul's joy at the news brought by Titus

2Open your hearts to us; we have wronged no one, we have corrupted no one,
we have taken advantage of no one. 3I do not say this to condemn you, for I

6:14–7:1 The Old Testament forbade the yoking together of different kinds of animals (cf. Deut 22:10; Lev 19:19). Paul uses this as a simile to show the difference between a Christian and a pagan. "Belial": the etymology is unclear; it may mean "useless", "perverse" or "lawless" (cf. Deut 13:13: "base fellows", lit. "sons of Belial"); hence its frequent application to the devil.

7:2–16 St Paul wants to fully regain the trust and affection of the Corinthians. This passage links up with what he began to say to them in chapter 2 and then interrupted to make his long apologia. He explains his reason for writing—to move them to repentance, the genuineness of which they can prove to God by showing their affection for Paul. As we can see here, the purpose of correction should always be the good of the person corrected. "We should correct out of love," St Augustine teaches, "not out of a desire to hurt them, but with affectionate intention of getting them to change. If we correct others in that way, we shall be keeping very well the precept, 'If your brother sins against you, go and tell him his fault, between you and him alone' (Mt 18:15)" (*Serm.*, 82, 4).

i. Greek *Beliar* **6:16** Lev 26: 11–12; Ezek 37:27; Jer 31:1. **6:17** Is 52:11; Jer 51:45; Zeph 3:20. **6:18** 2 Sam 7:14; Jer 30:9; Is 43:6.

said before that you are in our hearts, to die together and to live together. [4]I
have great confidence in you; I have great pride in you; I am filled with
comfort. With all our affliction, I am overjoyed.

[5]For even when we came into Macedonia, our bodies had no rest but we
were afflicted at every turn—fighting without and fear within. [6]But God, who
comforts the downcast, comforted us by the coming of Titus, [7]and not only by
his coming but also by the comfort with which he was comforted in you, as he
told us of your longing, your mourning, your zeal for me, so that I rejoiced still
more. [8]For even if I made you sorry with my letter, I do not regret it (though
I did regret it), for I see that that letter grieved you, though only for a while.
[9]As it is, I rejoice, not because you were grieved, but because you were grieved
into repenting; for you felt a godly grief, so that you suffered no loss through
us. [10]For godly grief produces a repentance that leads to salvation and brings
no regret, but worldly grief produces death. [11]For see what earnestness this
godly grief has produced in you, what eagerness to clear yourselves, what
indignation, what alarm, what longing, what zeal, what punishment! At every
point you have proved yourselves guiltless in the matter. [12]So although I wrote
to you, it was not on account of the one who did the wrong, nor on account of
the one who suffered the wrong, but in order that your zeal for us might be
revealed to you in the sight of God. [13]Therefore we are comforted.

And besides our own comfort we rejoiced still more at the joy of Titus,
because his mind has been set at rest by you all. [14]For if I have expressed to
him some pride in you, I was not put to shame; but just as everything we said
to you was true, so our boasting before Titus has proved true. [15]And his heart
goes out all the more to you, as he remembers the obedience of you all, and the
fear and trembling with which you received him. [16]I rejoice, because I have
perfect confidence in you.

The previous letter he refers to (v. 8) and which was mentioned earlier (cf. 2:3) is not 1 Corinthians, but a letter subsequent to it. Some scholars are of the view that chaps. 10–13 of 2 Corinthians may belong to that intermediary letter.

PART TWO: THE COLLECTION FOR THE CHURCH OF JERUSALEM

The Macedonians' good example

8 [1]We want you to know, brethren, about the grace of God which has been
shown in the churches of Macedonia, [2]for in a severe test of affliction, their
abundance of joy and their extreme poverty have overflowed in a wealth of
liberality on their part. [3]For they gave according to their means, as I can testify,
and beyond their means, of their own free will, [4]begging us earnestly for the
favour of taking part in the relief of the saints—[5]and this, not as we expected,
but first they gave themselves to the Lord and to us by the will of God.
[6]Accordingly we have urged Titus that as he had already made a beginning, he
should also complete among you this gracious work.

Appeal for generosity

[7]Now as you excel in everything—in faith, in utterance, in knowledge, in all
earnestness, and in your love for us—see that you excel in this gracious work
also.

[8]I say this not as a command, but to prove by the earnestness of others that
your love also is genuine. [9]For you know the grace of our Lord Jesus Christ,
that though he was rich, yet for your sake he became poor, so that by his
poverty you might become rich. [10]And in this matter I give my advice: it is
best for you now to complete what a year ago you began not only to do but to

---

8:1–9:15 □□ The Apostle now concentrates on the collection in aid of the faithful of Jerusalem (Corinth was not the only Church founded by him which was contributing: cf. Rom 15:26; 1 Cor 16:1). In this part of the letter we can see particularly the way the Christian community pooled resources.

8:1–6 The Christians of Macedonia are generous people: they might have felt excused from helping their brothers on account of their own poverty; whereas in fact they are very open-handed in their almsgiving.

8:7–15 Jesus Christ is *the* example of detachment and generosity. He was God, and in need of nothing, yet by becoming man he voluntarily set aside the glory of his divinity (cf. Phil 2:6f), and lived on earth as a poor man—from his birth in poverty at Bethlehem to his death on the cross; sometimes he did not even have the bare necessities of life (cf. Lk 9:58). "From the very beginning Christians have brought, along with the bread and wine for the Eucharist, gifts to share with those in need. This custom of the *collection*, ever appropriate, is inspired by the example of Christ who became poor to make us rich" (*CCC*, 1351).

desire, [11]so that your readiness in desiring it may be matched by your completing it out of what you have. [12]For if the readiness is there, it is acceptable according to what a man has, not according to what he has not. [13]I do not mean that others should be eased and you burdened, [14]but that as a matter of equality your abundance at the present time should supply their want, so that their abundance may supply your want, that there may be equality. [15]As it is written, "He who gathered much had nothing over, and he who gathered little had no lack."

Paul praises Titus and Timothy

[16]But thanks be to God who puts the same earnest care for you into the heart of Titus. [17]For he not only accepted our appeal, but being himself very earnest he is going to you of his own accord. [18]With him we are sending the brother who is famous among all the churches for his preaching of the gospel; [19]and not only that, but he has been appointed by the churches to travel with us in this gracious work which we are carrying on, for the glory of the Lord and to show our good will. [20]We intend that no one should blame us about this liberal gift which we are administering, [21]for we aim at what is honourable not only in the Lord's sight but also in the sight of men. [22]And with them we are sending our brother whom we have often tested and found earnest in many matters, but who is now more earnest than ever because of his great confidence in you. [23]As for Titus, he is my partner and fellow worker in your service; and as for our brethren, they are messengers[j] of the churches, the glory of Christ. [24]So give proof, before the churches, of your love and of our boasting about you to these men.

Appeal for speediness

9 [1]Now it is superfluous* for me to write to you about the offering for the saints, [2]for I know your readiness, of which I boast about you to the people of Macedonia, saying that Achaia has been ready since last year; and your zeal

---

8:16–24 In addition to Titus, who very probably was also the bearer of this letter, two other brethren are referred to, but their names are not given. It is very difficult to say who they might have been. The suggestion has often been put forward that one of them was Luke, who could have been with St Paul at the time. Some people think that the third envoy could have been Apollos, who was well known to the Corinthians.

9:1–5 As before (cf. 8:1–5), Paul uses the rivalry between the two provinces of Greece to encourage the Corinthians' generosity. To the Macedonians Paul praised the zeal and promptness of the Corinthians, for being the first to organize the collection. Now he asks the latter not to embarrass him by failing to live up to his reports of them.

j. Greek *apostles* **8:15** Ex 16:18. **8:21** Prov 3:4.

has stirred up most of them. 3But I am sending the brethren so that our
boasting about you may not prove vain in this case, so that you may be ready,
as I said you would be; 4lest if some Macedonians come with me and find that
you are not ready, we be humiliated—to say nothing of you—for being so
confident. 5So I thought it necessary to urge the brethren to go on to you before
me, and arrange in advance for this gift you have promised, so that it may be
ready not as an exaction but as a willing gift.

Blessings to be expected

6The point is this: he who sows sparingly will also reap sparingly, and he who
sows bountifully will also reap bountifully. 7Each one must do as he has made
up his mind, not reluctantly or under compulsion, for God loves a cheerful
giver. 8And God is able to provide you with every blessing in abundance, so
that you may always have enough of everything and may provide in abundance
for every good work. 9As it is written,

"He scatters abroad, he gives to the poor;
his righteousness[k] endures for ever."

10He who supplies seed to the sower and bread for food will supply and
multiply your resources[l] and increase the harvest of your righteousness.[k] 11You
will be enriched in every way for great generosity, which through us will
produce thanksgiving to God; 12for the rendering of this service not only
supplies the wants of the saints but also overflows in many thanksgivings to
God. 13Under the test of this service, you[m] will glorify God by your obedience
in acknowledging the gospel of Christ, and by the generosity of your
contribution for them and for all others; 14while they long for you and pray for
you, because of the surpassing grace of God in you. 15Thanks be to God for his
inexpressible gift!

9:6–15 The Apostle's words remind us of what our Lord promises: "give, and it will be given to you; good measure, pressed down, shaken together, running over" (Lk 6:38). Alms given reluctantly or a service done reluctantly can never please anyone, particularly God our Lord: "If you give bread and it makes you sad to do so, you lose both the bread and the reward" (St Augustine, *Enarr. in Ps.*, 42, 8). Paul emphasizes the abundant divine blessings (both temporal and spiritual) that generous almsgiving brings.

k. Or *benevolence* **l.** Greek *sowing* **m.** Or *they* **9:7** Prov 22:8. **9:9** Ps 112:9.

PART THREE: PAUL JUSTIFIES HIS CONDUCT

4. A REPLY TO ACCUSATIONS

Paul's readiness to use his apostolic authority

10 [1]I, Paul, myself entreat you, by the meekness and gentleness of Christ—
I who am humble when face to face with you, but bold to you when I
am away!*—[2]I beg of you that when I am present I may not have to show
boldness with such confidence as I count on showing against some who
suspect us of acting in worldly fashion. [3]For though we live in the world we
are not carrying on a worldly war, [4]for the weapons of our warfare are not
worldly but have divine power to destroy strongholds. [5]We destroy arguments
and every proud obstacle to the knowledge of God, and take every thought
captive to obey Christ, [6]being ready to punish every disobedience, when your
obedience is complete.

[7]Look at what is before your eyes. If any one is confident that he is Christ's,
let him remind himself that as he is Christ's, so are we. [8]For even if I boast a
little too much of our authority, which the Lord gave for building you up and not
for destroying you, I shall not be put to shame. [9]I would not seem to be
frightening you with letters. [10]For they say, "His letters are weighty and strong,
but his bodily presence is weak, and his speech of no account." [11]Let such people
understand that what we say by letter when absent, we do when present.

10:1–13:10 □□ This is another passage in which St Paul explains and justifies himself. He uses a very direct and forthright style because any division between the Apostle and the community founded by him could seriously endanger the latter. Compared with the affectionate tone of the previous sections of the letter, one is surprised by Paul's tone here, where he appeals to his authority (10:1–11) and boasts of his work (11:2–12:18).

10:1–18 □ The Apostle takes issue with accusations levelled by people who have sought to discredit him in his absence. Apparently those detractors were of Jewish background and claimed that their knowledge of God was superior to the Apostle's.

10:1–11 Paul begins by defending himself against criticism that he has been fainthearted in his mission. He was perfectly aware of the apostolic authority Christ had given him and of the power at work within him. However, following his Master's example (cf. Mt 11:29), he preferred, if at all possible, to use this authority only to build up morale, not to criticize. He depicts his life as that of a soldier; he uses God's weapons—which are supernatural and irresistible—to defeat the lies, arrogance and disobedience of his enemies (cf. 6:7–8).

Paul's province includes Corinth

12 Not that we venture to class or compare ourselves with some of those who
commend themselves. But when they measure themselves by one another, and
compare themselves with one another, they are without understanding.
13 But we will not boast beyond limit, but will keep to the limits God has
apportioned us, to reach even to you. 14 For we are not overextending ourselves,
as though we did not reach you; we were the first to come all the way to you
with the gospel of Christ. 15 We do not boast beyond limit, in other men's
labours; but our hope is that as your faith increases, our field among you may
be greatly enlarged, 16 so that we may preach the gospel in lands beyond you,
without boasting of work already done in another's field. 17 "Let him who
boasts, boast of the Lord." 18 For it is not the man who commends himself that
is accepted, but the man whom the Lord commends.

5. THE APOSTLE'S GROUNDS FOR BOASTING

His zeal

11 1 I wish you would bear with me in a little foolishness. Do bear with me!
2 I feel a divine jealousy for you, for I betrothed you to Christ to present
you as a pure bride to her one husband. 3 But I am afraid that as the serpent
deceived Eve by his cunning, your thoughts will be led astray from a sincere
and pure devotion to Christ. 4 For if some one comes and preaches another
Jesus than the one we preached, or if you receive a different spirit from the one
you received, or if you accept a different gospel from the one you accepted,
you submit to it readily enough. 5 I think that I am not in the least inferior to
these superlative apostles. 6 Even if I am unskilled in speaking, I am not in
knowledge; in every way we have made this plain to you in all things.

10:12–18 Now—in a rather complicated style—Paul replies to criticism by pointing to his right to work as an apostle in Corinth. God has assigned him a territory—that is, the conversion of the Gentiles—and he has worked at it indefatigably. Quoting Jeremiah 9:22f (as he did also in 1 Corinthians 1:31) he points out how absurd it would be to try to boast about oneself or to push oneself forward, when the only valid endorsement comes from God.

11:1–12:18 □ Paul finds it distasteful to be singing his own praises, so he asks the disciples to forgive him. But he feels he must make this apologia in order to put a stop to the inroads being made by his enemies. He compares his credentials with theirs.

11:1–6 St Paul acts the part of the "bridegroom's friend" (cf. Jn 3:29), whose duty it is to guard the virginity of the bride and who sees the danger she is in from the

10:17 Jer 9:23–24.

Paul accepted no material support in payment for preaching

7 Did I commit a sin in abasing myself so that you might be exalted, because
I preached God's gospel without cost to you? 8 I robbed other churches by
accepting support from them in order to serve you. 9 And when I was with you
and was in want, I did not burden any one, for my needs were supplied by the
brethren who came from Macedonia. So I refrained and will refrain from
burdening you in any way. 10 As the truth of Christ is in me, this boast of mine
shall not be silenced in the regions of Achaia. 11 And why? Because I do not
love you? God knows I do!

12 And what I do I will continue to do, in order to undermine the claim of those
who would like to claim that in their boasted mission they work on the same
terms as we do. 13 For such men are false apostles, deceitful workmen, disguising
themselves as apostles of Christ. 14 And no wonder, for even Satan disguises
himself as an angel of light. 15 So it is not strange if his servants also disguise
themselves as servants of righteousness. Their end will correspond to their deeds.

Paul apologizes for boasting

16 I repeat, let no one think me foolish; but even if you do, accept me as a fool,
so that I too may boast a little. 17 (What I am saying I say not with the Lord's
authority but as a fool, in this boastful confidence; 18 since many boast of
worldly things, I too will boast.) 19 For you gladly bear with fools, being wise
yourselves! 20 For you bear it if a man makes slaves of you, or preys upon you,
or takes advantage of you, or puts on airs, or strikes you in the face. 21 To my
shame, I must say, we were too weak for that!

---

snares of her enemies. The "superlative apostles" or superapostles (v. 5) is a sarcastic reference to his opponents, who may have been claiming apostolic authority.

11:7–15 St Paul made a point of preaching the Gospel without payment, not exercising his right to be financially supported by the faithful: instead, he earned enough through work to support himself; this clearly showed how upright his intentions were (cf. 1 Cor 9:4–18).

11:16–21 The Apostle is being very ironical, caricaturing the foolishness of the Corinthians, who think themselves so sensible (cf. 1 Cor 1:18–4:21). Their foolishness led to their doing nothing about the harm caused by intruders.

11:21–33 St Paul begins his apologia proper, in which he points out his qualifications as against those of his opponents. On the score of race he is their equal (v. 22); as Christ's minister he is far better qualified, and to prove it he cites the physical suffering he has undergone in his apostolate. One cannot fail to be moved by this outline of his sufferings, an account which provides very valuable

What Paul has suffered for Christ

But whatever any one dares to boast of—I am speaking as a fool—I also dare
to boast of that. 22Are they Hebrews? So am I. Are they Israelites? So am I.
Are they descendants of Abraham? So am I. 23Are they servants of Christ? I
am a better one—I am talking like a madman—with far greater labours, far more
imprisonments, with countless beatings, and often near death. 24Five times I have
received at the hands of the Jews the forty lashes less one. 25Three times I have
been beaten with rods; once I was stoned. Three times I have been shipwrecked;
a night and a day I have been adrift at sea; 26on frequent journeys, in danger from
rivers, danger from robbers, danger from my own people, danger from Gentiles,
danger in the city, danger in the wilderness, danger at sea, danger from false
brethren; 27in toil and hardship, through many a sleepless night, in hunger and
thirst, often without food, in cold and exposure. 28And, apart from other things,
there is the daily pressure upon me of my anxiety for all the churches. 29Who is
weak, and I am not weak? Who is made to fall, and I am not indignant?

30If I must boast, I will boast of the things that show my weakness. 31The God
and Father of the Lord Jesus, he who is blessed for ever, knows that I do not
lie. 32At Damascus, the governor under King Aretas guarded the city of
Damascus in order to seize me, 33but I was let down in a basket through a
window in the wall, and escaped his hands.

Visions and revelations

12 1I must boast; there is nothing to be gained by it, but I will go on to
visions and revelations of the Lord. 2I know a man in Christ who
fourteen years ago was caught up to the third heaven—whether in the body or
out of the body I do not know, God knows. 3And I know that this man was

---

information not found in the Acts of the Apostles. It is very revealing that the evidence he provides to show his superiority as a minister of Christ is precisely his sufferings. (cf. Acts 9:15–16). Our Lord had already said, "If any man would come after me, let him deny himself and take up his cross daily and follow me" (Lk 9:23). Suffering, the cross, is something inseparable from the Christian life, and a sure sign that one is following in the Master's footsteps. This is another paradox of the Christian religion. Christ triumphed on the cross, and his apostles rejoice when they suffer for his sake.

12:1–10 From other letters and from the book of the Acts we know that Paul received many visions and revelations over the course of his life. The "thorn in the flesh" (v. 7) may be a reference to concupiscence rather than some particular illness or disability.

Christians can learn a lot about the ascetical struggle from vv. 8–10. This passage reminds us of the need to ask the Lord to help us when we experience difficulties, and to be fully trusting, and to abandon ourselves to God, who knows

caught up into Paradise—whether in the body or out of the body I do not know,
God knows—4and he heard things that cannot be told, which man may not utter.
5On behalf of this man I will boast, but on my own behalf I will not boast, except
of my weaknesses. 6Though if I wish to boast, I shall not be a fool, for I shall be
speaking the truth. But I refrain from it, so that no one may think more of me than
he sees in me or hears from me. 7And to keep me from being too elated by the
abundance of revelations, a thorn* was given me in the flesh, a messenger of
Satan, to harass me, to keep me from being too elated. 8Three times I besought
the Lord about this, that it should leave me; 9but he said to me, "My grace is
sufficient for you, for my power is made perfect in weakness." I will all the more
gladly boast of my weaknesses, that the power of Christ may rest upon me. 10For
the sake of Christ, then, I am content with weaknesses, insults, hardships,
persecutions, and calamities; for when I am weak, then I am strong.

Paul again apologizes for boasting

11I have been a fool! You forced me to it, for I ought to have been commended
by you. For I was not at all inferior to these superlative apostles, even though
I am nothing. 12The signs of a true apostle were performed among you in all
patience, with signs and wonders and mighty works. 13For in what were you
less favoured than the rest of the churches, except that I myself did not burden
you? Forgive me this wrong!*

14Here for the third time I am ready to come to you. And I will not be a
burden, for I seek not what is yours but you; for children ought not to lay up
for their parents, but parents for their children. 15I will most gladly spend and
be spent for your souls. If I love you the more, am I to be loved the less? 16But
granting that I myself did not burden you, I was crafty, you say, and got the
better of you by guile. 17Did I take advantage of you through any of those
whom I sent to you? 18I urged Titus to go, and sent the brother with him. Did
Titus take advantage of you? Did we not act in the same spirit? Did we not
take the same steps?

---

what is best for us. It also shows us what we should do when we feel our own weakness: we should trust in divine help. "God frees us from strife not by making our troubles disappear, […] but by helping us not to be overcome by suffering" (Origen, *De oratio,* 30, 1).

12:11–18 The only reason the Corinthians could possibly have for feeling less favoured than other churches (the Apostle tells them ironically) is because he was not a burden on them—but he does not plan to change that policy. He also takes issue with something his opponents must have been saying about him—that he himself may not exploit the Corinthians but that some of his co-workers do (v. 16). We are shown here that the virtue of patience and miracles (v. 12) are distinctive features of St Paul's writings.

6. THE APOSTLE'S NEXT VISIT

The reason for his apologia

19Have you been thinking all along that we have been defending ourselves before
you? It is in the sight of God that we have been speaking in Christ, and all for
your upbuilding, beloved. 20For I fear that perhaps I may come and find you not
what I wish, and that you may find me not what you wish; that perhaps there may
be quarrelling, jealousy, anger, selfishness, slander, gossip, conceit, and disorder.
21I fear that when I come again my God may humble me before you, and I may
have to mourn over many of those who sinned before and have not repented of
the impurity, immorality, and licentiousness which they have practised.

Preparation for his next visit

13 1This is the third time I am coming to you. Any charge must be
sustained by the evidence of two or three witnesses. 2I warned those
who sinned before and all the others, and I warn them now while absent, as I
did when present on my second visit, that if I come again I will not spare
them—3since you desire proof that Christ is speaking in me. He is not weak in
dealing with you, but is powerful in you. 4For he was crucified in weakness,
but lives by the power of God. For we are weak in him, but in dealing with you
we shall live with him by the power of God.

12:19–13:10 □ The letter ends by explaining why the Apostle is writing this apologia of himself. This section also includes suggestions on how they should prepare for his forthcoming visit.

12:19–21 The sins of others cause Paul great distress; this should encourage a Christian to atone to God our Lord for all the offences committed against him. "Don't ask Jesus to forgive only your own faults: don't love him with your heart alone. Console him for every offence that has been, is, and will be done to him. Love him with all the strength of all the hearts of all the men who have loved him most. Be daring: tell him you are carried away with more love than Mary Magdalene, more than Teresa and little Thérèse, more carried away than Augustine and Dominic and Francis, more than Ignatius and Xavier" (Bl. J. Escrivá, *The Way*, 402).

13:1–10 The Apostle shows that he is acting in line with Christ (vv. 1–4). During his life on earth our Lord chose to appear weak (especially by permitting his passion and death); but, by rising from the dead he revealed his divine power, which had previously been kept hidden. Similarly St Paul, who has appeared to be weak (by tolerating the rebellious types in Corinth), is now considering using his God-given apostolic authority. He appeals to them (vv. 5–10) to respond to grace. "Two things are needed if sin is to be avoided—a free will and the grace of God.

13:1 Deut 19:15.

[5]Examine yourselves, to see whether you are holding to your faith. Test
yourselves. Do you not realize that Jesus Christ is in you?—unless indeed you
fail to meet the test! [6]I hope you will find out that we have not failed. [7]But we
pray God that you may not do wrong—not that we may appear to have met the
test, but that you may do what is right, though we may seem to have failed.
[8]For we cannot do anything against the truth, but only for the truth. [9]For we are
glad when we are weak and you are strong. What we pray for is your improve-
ment. [10]I write this while I am away from you, in order that when I come I may
not have to be severe in my use of the authority which the Lord has given me
for building up and not for tearing down.

7. WORDS OF FAREWELL

[11]Finally, brethren, farewell. Mend your ways, heed my appeal, agree with
one another, live in peace, and the God of love and peace will be with you.
[12]Greet one another with a holy kiss. [13]All the saints greet you.
[14]The grace of the Lord Jesus Christ and the love of God and the fellowship
of[n] the Holy Spirit be with you all.

[...] Therefore, to show the necessity of these two things, the Apostle asks God for his grace and warns [the people] to use their free will to avoid evil and to do good" (St Thomas Aquinas, *Com. on 2 Cor,* in loc.).

13:11–13 Kissing was the normal form of greeting in the Middle East (cf. Lk 7:45). St Paul gives the kiss a religious meaning, making it a sign of supernatural love and unity of faith—a meaning it retains in the eucharistic liturgy.

The final greeting—which the liturgy has made into one of the opening prayers of the Mass—is an explicit statement of faith in the Blessed Trinity. St Thomas points out that this greeting includes reference to all necessary supernatural graces: "The grace of Christ, by which we are justified and saved; the love of God the Father, by which we are united to him; and the fellowship of the Holy Spirit, who distributes the divine gifts to us" (*Com. on 2 Cor,* in loc.).

n. Or *and participation in*

The Letter to the Galatians

Galatia was an inland region in Asia Minor corresponding to the central plains of modern Turkey. In St Paul's time the Roman province of Galatia also included, to the south, the territories of Lycaonia, in which were situated four cities we are very familiar with from the Acts of the Apostles—Derbe, Lystra, Iconium and Pisidian Antioch. In his first apostolic journey (in the years 45–49) Paul had made contact with the inhabitants of Galatia when he evangelized the southern part of the province. But it was mainly during his second journey (in the years 50–53) that he preached among them (Gal 4:13; Acts 16:1–8), perhaps because illness kept him there for a period. He was very warmly received (Gal 4:14), and he visited them again in the year 53 or 54 (Acts 18:23).

However, certain Judaeo-Christians, very set in their national and religious traditions, also found their way there; these were people who saw the basis of man's salvation as having to do with keeping the prescriptions of the Law of Moses. Very probably some of these "false brethren" (Gal 2:4) sought to amend St Paul's teaching among the communities founded by him during his second journey (Acts 16:6), as they had previously tried to do at the council of Jerusalem. We do not know exactly who these people were, but they were a constant threat and they even put pressure on the apostles (in Galatians 2:11–14 we learn that they got Simon Peter himself to back-track).

Once he became aware of the danger from the Judaizers, St Paul wrote this letter, a letter which has rightly been described as a cry of love and of pain. It was very probably written in Ephesus around the year 54/55 and it constitutes the best commentary we have on the decisions of the council of Jerusalem (Acts 15:23, 29), where it was laid down that Christians of Gentile background were under no obligation to keep Jewish prescriptions.

The main theme of the letter is Christians' freedom as regards the fulfilment of the complex rules and regulations of the Mosaic Law and the prescriptions added to it by the tradition of the scribes. Paul proclaims that Christ alone has the authority to justify and save men, and that therefore anyone who preaches another Gospel, anyone who changes the Gospel of Christ, is to be shunned (cf. 1:4–5:8). According to the Judaizers, for a man to be a Christian and belong to the true Israel, he had to be circumcised (cf. 5:2). St Paul reacts strongly (one could say, vehemently) against this idea: what he says is that a man is justified in God's eyes only through faith in Jesus Christ. A Christian's identity derives from being a son of God through faith in Christ Jesus (3:26–29). The work of our salvation lay in the fact that "when the time had fully come, God sent forth his Son, born of woman, born under the law, to redeem those who were under the law, so that we might receive adoption as sons. And because you are sons, God has sent the Spirit of his Son into our hearts, crying, 'Abba! Father!'" (4:4–6). This is the source of Christian freedom, the freedom of the sons of God, because "for freedom Christ has set us free" (5:1). The Christian life grows on the soil of freedom, on a basis of divine sonship and faith in Jesus Christ dead and risen (cf. 5:24). Christians live by the Spirit, and walk by the Spirit (5:25), and it is the Spirit who produces fruit in us (cf. 5:22–23).

Galatians

INTRODUCTION

Greeting

1 1Paul an apostle—not from men nor through man, but through Jesus Christ
and God the Father, who raised him from the dead—2and all the brethren
who are with me,
To the churches of Galatia:
3Grace to you and peace from God the Father and our Lord Jesus Christ, 4who
gave himself for our sins to deliver us from the present evil age, according to the
will of our God and Father; 5to whom be the glory for ever and ever. Amen.

A warning

6I am astonished that you are so quickly deserting him who called you in the
grace of Christ and turning to a different gospel—*7not that there is another
gospel, but there are some who trouble you and want to pervert the gospel of
Christ. 8But even if we, or an angel from heaven, should preach to you a
gospel contrary to that which we preached to you, let him be accursed. 9As we
have said before, so now I say again, If any one is preaching to you a gospel
contrary to that which you received, let him be accursed.
10Am I now seeking the favour of men, or of God? Or am I trying to please
men? If I were still pleasing men, I should not be a servant[a] of Christ.*

1:1–10 □ The introduction consists of greetings to the Galatians (vv. 1–5) and explains why he is writing—to warn them about a possible distortion of the Gospel (vv. 6–10).

1:1–5 In his greeting the Apostle states his credentials: like the other apostles, Jesus Christ chose him for his ministry (cf. Acts 9:1–18). This passage indicates the two main themes of the letter—the reaffirmation of his apostolic authority (v. 1) and the effectiveness of the Redemption of mankind achieved by Jesus Christ (v. 4). Chapters 1–2 deal with the first theme.

1:6–10 The "gospel of Christ" which Paul preached to the Galatians proclaimed Jesus Christ as the only source of salvation. The preachers who were leading the Galatians astray were claiming that salvation came through circumcision and obedience to the Law. On account of his teaching, Paul earned the hostility of those Jews. This showed that in his preaching his aim was not to please men but to serve God (cf. v. 10).

a. Or *slave*

PART ONE: THE GOSPEL PREACHED BY ST PAUL

1. ST PAUL ARGUES IN HIS OWN DEFENCE

Paul's vocation

[11]For I would have you know, brethren, that the gospel which was preached by
me is not man's[b] gospel. [12]For I did not receive it from man, nor was I taught
it, but it came through a revelation of Jesus Christ. [13]For you have heard of my
former life in Judaism, how I persecuted the church of God violently and tried
to destroy it; [14]and I advanced in Judaism beyond many of my own age among
my people, so extremely zealous was I for the traditions of my fathers. [15]But
when he who had set me apart before I was born, and had called me through
his grace, [16]was pleased to reveal his Son to[c] me, in order that I might preach
him among the Gentiles, I did not confer with flesh and blood, [17]nor did I go
up to Jerusalem to those who were apostles before me, but I went away into
Arabia; and again I returned to Damascus.

[18]Then after three years I went up to Jerusalem to visit Cephas, and remained
with him fifteen days. [19]But I saw none of the other apostles except James the
Lord's brother. [20](In what I am writing to you, before God, I do not lie!)
[21]Then I went into the regions of Syria and Cilicia. [22]And I was still not known

---

1:11–4:31 □ □ The Gospel that St Paul was preaching to the Gentiles did not require them to become Jews first and submit to all the rules and regulations of the Law. This policy was opposed by narrow-minded people who just could not accept the newness of the free gift of salvation brought by Jesus Christ. Against these people, Paul appeals to his authority as an apostle and to his communion with the other apostles (1:11–2:21) and he also shows, by using Scripture, that Christ alone and not the Law of Moses can save man (3:1–4:31).

1:11–2:21 □ To defend the supernatural nature of his mission and also the truth of the Gospel, St Paul recalls key points in his own life—his calling (1:11–24), his journey to Jerusalem along with Barnabas and Titus, probably in connexion with the council of the apostles (2:1–10), and the incident at Antioch (2:11–21).

1:11–24 This account of his calling confirms what Paul has taught. What he is saying is that his Gospel—though it follows on naturally as a variation on the teachings of the other apostles (cf. 1 Cor 15:3; Gal 2:2)—does not come from man but is something revealed by Jesus himself. Like that of other people given a mission by God (cf. Jer 1:5; Is 49:1–5; Lk 1:14; etc.), his vocation is a divine initiative; it is not something he merited.

"James, the Lord's brother" (v. 19): probably James the Less, the leader of the Christian community at Jerusalem.

b. Greek *according to man* **c.** Greek *in*

by sight to the churches of Christ in Judea; [23]they only heard it said, "He who once persecuted us is now preaching the faith he once tried to destroy." [24]And they glorified God because of me.

Visit to Jerusalem

2 [1]Then after fourteen years I went up again to Jerusalem with Barnabas, taking Titus along with me. [2]I went up by revelation; and I laid before them (but privately before those who were of repute) the gospel which I preach among the Gentiles, lest somehow I should be running or had run in vain. [3]But even Titus, who was with me, was not compelled to be circumcised, though he was a Greek. [4]But because of false brethren secretly brought in, who slipped in to spy out our freedom which we have in Christ Jesus, that they might bring us into bondage—[5]to them we did not yield submission even for a moment, that the truth of the gospel might be preserved for you. [6]And from those who were reputed to be something (what they were makes no difference to me; God shows no partiality)—those, I say, who were of repute added nothing to me; [7]but on the contrary, when they saw that I had been entrusted with the gospel to the uncircumcised, just as Peter had been entrusted with the gospel to the circumcised [8](for he who worked through Peter for the mission to the circumcised worked through me also for the Gentiles), [9]and when they perceived the grace that was given to me, James and Cephas and John, who were reputed to be pillars, gave to me and Barnabas the right hand of fellowship, that we should go to the Gentiles and they to the circumcised; [10]only they would have us remember the poor, which very thing I was eager to do.

The incident at Antioch

[11]But when Cephas came to Antioch I opposed him to his face, because he stood condemned. [12]For before certain men came from James, he ate with the

---

2:1–10 Some Christians of Jewish background thought that pagan converts to Christianity should observe the prescriptions of Mosaic Law, and were requiring of them that they be circumcised like all Jews. This became a subject of much controversy at Jerusalem. Having received a divine revelation, Paul sets out from Antioch with Titus and Barnabas and forthrightly tells the apostles at Jerusalem that salvation comes from Christ's redemption: if these Judaizers' ideas were accepted, it would empty Christ's life, death and resurrection of all value. Those in charge, the "pillars" of the Church, accept that Paul is right, and they see his mission to preach the Gospel to the Gentiles as a further proof of God's mercy.

St Paul was faithful to the charge (v. 10) about not forgetting to make collections for the poor (cf. 1 Cor 16:1–3; 2 Cor 8:1–15; 9:15; etc.). These collections were a sign of communion with the mother church of Jerusalem.

2:11–21 In matters of secondary importance (cf. Acts 16:3; 21:22–26; Rom 14:1–12; 1 Cor 10:23–30) St Paul would give way when necessary, but he never

Gentiles; but when they came he drew back and separated himself, fearing the
circumcision party. 13And with him the rest of the Jews acted insincerely, so
that even Barnabas was carried away by their insincerity. 14But when I saw that
they were not straightforward about the truth of the gospel, I said to Cephas
before them all, "If you, though a Jew, live like a Gentile and not like a Jew,
how can you compel the Gentiles to live like Jews?" 15We ourselves, who are
Jews by birth and not Gentile sinners, 16yet who know that a man is not
justified[d] by works of the law but through faith in Jesus Christ, even we have
believed in Christ Jesus, in order to be justified by faith in Christ, and not by
works of the law,* because by works of the law shall no one be justified. 17But
if, in our endeavour to be justified in Christ, we ourselves were found to be
sinners, is Christ then an agent of sin? Certainly not! 18But if I build up again
those things which I tore down, then I prove myself a transgressor. 19For I
through the law died to the law, that I might live to God. 20I have been
crucified with Christ; it is no longer I who live, but Christ who lives in me; and
the life I now live in the flesh I live by faith in the Son of God, who loved me
and gave himself for me. 21I do not nullify the grace of God; for if justification[e]
were through the law, then Christ died to no purpose.

---

budged as regards Christians' freedom from the works prescribed by the Mosaic Law. St Peter, by ceasing to eat with Gentiles, appeared to feel obliged to fulfil the prescriptions of the Law. That is why Paul reacts so vigorously. The men who "came from James" (v. 12) would have been Christians of Jewish background who had come from Jerusalem where James, "the brother of the Lord", had stayed on as head of that church. It is easy to understand why people in Jersualem continued with Mosaic observance. But St Paul proclaims the radical newness of the Christian faith *vis-á-vis* Judaism: only by adhering to Christ do we become pleasing to God; that is the only thing that justifies us in his eyes. If we were to go back now to observe the Mosaic Law (he is saying), we would be indicating that, having ceased to observe the Law when we embraced faith in Christ, we had sinned thereby and that Christ was the cause, the agent, of that sin (v. 17). If we cling to Christ through faith, he lives in us and in that way, with him and like him, we live for God. "In the believer Christ is formed gradually by faith in the depth of his heart. The believer is called to freedom under grace, to be gentle and humble of heart, not boasting about the merits of his deeds, because in themselves they don't have any value. [...] Christ is formed in him who assimilates the form of Christ, and he assimilates the form of Christ who unites himself to him in spiritual love" (St Augustine, *Com. on Gal,* 38).

d. Or *reckoned righteous*; and so elsewhere **e.** Or *righteousness* **2:16** Ps 143:2.

2. DOCTRINAL MATTERS

Justification by faith

3 [1]O foolish Galatians! Who has bewitched you, before whose eyes Jesus
Christ was publicly portrayed as crucified? [2]Let me ask you only this: Did
you receive the Spirit* by works of the law, or by hearing with faith? [3]Are you
so foolish? Having begun with the Spirit, are you now ending with the flesh?
[4]Did you experience so many things in vain?—if it really is in vain. [5]Does he
who supplies the Spirit to you and works miracles among you do so by works
of the law, or by hearing with faith?

[6]Thus Abraham "believed God, and it was reckoned to him as righteousness."
[7]So you see that it is men of faith who are the sons of Abraham. [8]And the
scripture, foreseeing that God would justify the Gentiles by faith, preached the
gospel beforehand to Abraham, saying, "In you shall all the nations be blessed."
[9]So then, those who are men of faith are blessed with Abraham who had faith.

[10]For all who rely on works of the law are under a curse; for it is written,
"Cursed be every one who does not abide by all things written in the book of
the law, and do them." [11]Now it is evident that no man is justified before God
by the law; for "He who through faith is righteous shall live";[f] [12]but the law
does not rest on faith, for "He who does them shall live by them." [13]Christ
redeemed us from the curse of the law, having become a curse for us—for it is
written, "Cursed be every one who hangs on a tree"—[14]that in Christ Jesus the

---

3:1–4:31 □The doctrinal part in the letter deals with the question of justification by faith in Jesus Christ and not by the works of the Mosaic Law, which was laid down to prepare the way for the law of Christ. In Christ the promises made by Abraham (3:1–29) are fulfilled. Consequently a Christian, a son of God, a freeman and not a slave, receives his inheritance through his faith (4:1–31).

3:1–14 It is Paul's love for the Galatians that causes him pain. They have forgotten that only Jesus, and not the Law, brings salvation. They well know that they received justification without having even heard mention of the Law, for the Holy Spirit came upon them prior to the arrival of the Judaizers (vv. 1–5). It would be enough for them to remember the many charisms shown among them.

Besides, there is the example of Abraham (vv. 6–9). The Lord promised that his descendants would be blessed; he established a Covenant with him and justified him not by the works of the Law (which had not yet been promulgated) but through his faith (cf. Rom 4). In the same way, all who have believed in God and will in the future believe in him as Abraham did, will be his true descendants and will also receive God's blessing.

f. Or *the righteous shall live by faith* **3:6** Gen 15:6. **3:8** Gen 12:3;18:18. **3:10** Deut 27:26. **3:11** Hab 2:4. **3:12** Lev 18.5. **3:13** Deut 21:23.

blessing of Abraham might come upon the Gentiles, that we might receive the promise of the Spirit through faith.

The Law and the promise

15To give a human example, brethren: no one annuls even a man's will,[g] or adds to it, once it has been ratified. 16Now the promises were made to Abraham and to his offspring. It does not say, "And to offsprings," referring to many; but, referring to one, "And to your offspring," which is Christ. 17This is what I mean: the law, which came four hundred and thirty years afterward, does not annul a covenant previously ratified by God, so as to make the promise void. 18For if the inheritance is by the law, it is no longer by promise; but God gave it to Abraham by a promise.

19Why then the law? It was added because of transgressions, till the offspring should come to whom the promise had been made; and it was ordained by angels through an intermediary. 20Now an intermediary implies more than one; but God is one.

21Is the law then against the promises of God? Certainly not; for if a law had been given which could make alive, then righteousness would indeed be by the law. 22But the scripture consigned all things to sin, that what was promised to faith in Jesus Christ might be given to those who believe.

23Now before faith came, we were confined under the law, kept under restraint until faith should be revealed. 24So that the law was our custodian

---

Finally, the Mosaic Law, far from bringing salvation, is rather a cause of spiritual death, insofar as every precept involves a penalty if it is not obeyed (vv. 10–14). Our Lord freed us from the curse of the Law by voluntarily taking on himself the punishment man's sin deserved (v. 13). Therefore, to submit to the Law once again would in effect be treating Christ's sacrifice as something superfluous.

3:15–29 Paul puts forward God's promise to the descendants of Abraham as an argument in favour of justification by faith. First he explains that the promise referred to Christ (vv. 15–16). Then he argues that it is an unalterable promise (vv. 17–18). God is "merciful and faithful" (cf. Ex 34:6) and he keeps his promises. This means that what God promised Abraham cannot be set aside by the Law of Moses, which was promulgated much later. It is the role of the Law to expose and punish transgressions committed prior to Christ's coming (vv. 19–22). This is not at odds with the promise of salvation made to Abraham; on the contrary, the Law identifies what is sin, and it also shows that sin can and should be expiated. Therefore the Law was given by God to be our custodian or teacher (*paedagogus*), to protect men and to guide them to Christ. In St Paul's time a *paedagogus* was a servant whose job it was to look after children and to bring them to school; once a child became of age, their custodian had no role to play (vv. 23–25). When Jesus

g. Or *covenant* (as in verse 17)

until Christ came, that we might be justified by faith. [25]But now that faith has come, we are no longer under a custodian; [26]for in Christ Jesus you are all sons of God, through faith. [27]For as many of you as were baptized into Christ have put on Christ. [28]There is neither Jew nor Greek, there is neither slave nor free, there is neither male nor female; for you are all one in Christ Jesus. [29]And if you are Christ's, then you are Abraham's offspring, heirs according to promise.

Divine sonship

4 [1]I mean that the heir, as long as he is a child, is no better than a slave, though he is the owner of all the estate; [2]but he is under guardians and trustees until the date set by the father. [3]So with us; when we were children, we were slaves to the elemental spirits of the universe. [4]But when the time had fully come, God sent forth his Son, born of woman, born under the law, [5]to redeem those who were under the law, so that we might receive adoption as sons. [6]And because you are sons, God has sent the Spirit of his Son into our hearts, crying, "Abba! Father!" [7]So through God you are no longer a slave but a son, and if a son then an heir.

[8]Formerly, when you did not know God, you were in bondage to beings that by nature are no gods; [9]but now that you have come to know God, or rather to be known by God, how can you turn back again to the weak and beggarly elemental spirits, whose slaves you want to be once more? [10]You observe days, and months, and seasons, and years! [11]I am afraid I have laboured over you in vain.

Christ brought about his Redemption (v. 26b), man became of age, and this meant he was no longer under the custodian. Through faith in Christ and by means of Baptism, man becomes a child of God and puts on Christ (v. 27). From this point on, all differences between men disappear (v. 28); all become descendants of Abraham and all partake of the promises made to him. "So there is only one race, the race of the children of God. There is only one colour, the colour of the children of God. And there is only one language, the language which speaks to the heart and to the mind, without the noise of words, making us know God and love one another" (Bl. J. Escrivá, *Hom.,* 1, 106).

4:1–11 St Paul here gives a summary of human history and personal history from the point of view of the salvation which God offers mankind. It includes Jews (who come under the Law) and pagans (who are slaves to the idols of this world). The coming of Christ changed the situation radically. History reached its peak; from this point on it is firmly orientated towards God. Christ, born a true man, and a Jew, by his work of redemption set Jews free from the yoke of the Law, and liberated Gentiles from the bondage of idolatry. In Christ, God offers everyone an equal opportunity to be his children, and to all he sends the Spirit of his Son (v. 6). "The birth of Christ is the beginning of the Christian people; the birth of the head

A fatherly appeal by Paul
[12]Brethren, I beseech you, become as I am, for I also have become as you are.
You did me no wrong; [13]you know it was because of a bodily ailment that I
preached the gospel to you at first; [14]and though my condition was a trial to
you, you did not scorn or despise me, but received me as an angel of God, as
Christ Jesus. [15]What has become of the satisfaction you felt? For I bear you
witness that, if possible, you would have plucked out your eyes and given them
to me. [16]Have I then become your enemy by telling you the truth?[h] [17]They
make much of you, but for no good purpose; they want to shut you out, that
you may make much of them. [18]For a good purpose it is always good to be
made much of, and not only when I am present with you. [19]My little children,
with whom I am again in travail until Christ be formed in you! [20]I could wish to
be present with you now and to change my tone, for I am perplexed about you.

The two covenants—Hagar and Sarah
[21]Tell me, you who desire to be under law, do you not hear the law? [22]For it is
written that Abraham had two sons, one by a slave and one by a free woman.
[23]But the son of the slave was born according to the flesh, the son of the free
woman through promise. [24]Now this is an allegory: these women are two
covenants. One is from Mount Sinai, bearing children for slavery; she is

---

is, at the same time, the birth of the body. […] Every man who believes […] no longer belongs to the ancestry of his father in the flesh, but to the seed of the Saviour, who made himself the Son of man so that we might become sons of God" (St Leo the Great, *Serm. 6 in Nat.*, 2).

As well as saying that Christ pre-existed as Son of God, Paul also asserts that he is truly human, "born of woman" (v. 4).

4:12–20 He reminds the Galatians of the time he spent among them preaching the Gospel; he wants to win them back to the Gospel, and to see them become one with Christ. To show them what he means, he asks them to imitate the sort of life they have seen him (Paul) leading. Christ's disciples should strive to become like Him. "For this reason we, who have been made like to him, who have died with him and risen with him, are taken up into the mysteries of his life, until we reign together with him; […] we are associated with his sufferings as the body with its head, suffering with him, that with him we may be glorified" (Vatican II, *LG*, 7).

4:21–31 Paul goes back again to the subject of Abraham to explain what the freedom won by Christ involves. Sarah, Abraham's wife, was barren and so, in line with the custom of the time, Abraham had a son (Ishmael) by a slave-woman,

h. Or *by dealing truly with you*

Hagar. [25]Now Hagar is Mount Sinai in Arabia;[i] she corresponds to the present
Jerusalem, for she is in slavery with her children. [26]But the Jerusalem above is
free, and she is our mother. [27]For it is written,

> "Rejoice, O barren one who does not bear;
> break forth and shout, thou who are not in travail;
> for the desolate one hath more children
> than she who hath a husband."

[28]Now we,[j] brethren, like Isaac, are children of promise. [29]But as at that time he
who was born according to the flesh persecuted him who was born according to
the Spirit, so it is now. [30]But what does the scripture say? "Cast out the slave and
her son; for the son of the slave shall not inherit with the son of the free woman."
[31]So, brethren, we are not children of the slave but of the free woman.

PART TWO: CHRISTIAN FREEDOM AND CHARITY

3. EXHORTATIONS

Christian freedom

5 [1]For freedom Christ has set us free; stand fast therefore, and do not submit
again to a yoke of slavery.
[2]Now I, Paul, say to you that if you receive circumcision, Christ will be of no
advantage to you. [3]I testify again to every man who receives circumcision that he
is bound to keep the whole law. [4]You are severed from Christ, you who would be

---

Hagar. But God promised Sarah that she would have a son, and he kept his promise: when Abraham was already an old man and past his strength, Sarah gave birth to Isaac (Gen 15:4; 17:19). Paul sees an allegorical meaning in the two wives of Abraham: the slave woman stands for the Jewish people subject to the Law; the free woman stands for the Church, the outcome of God's promise, because Christians are like Isaac: they exist by virtue of God's promise, not by virtue of the Law.

The words of v. 29 are a gloss on Genesis 21:9 in line with a rabbinical tradition about Ishmael ill-treating Isaac during play. St Paul points out that those who have been set free from the Law by the death of Christ are being oppressed by those who want to stay under the Law, the Jews. In this persecution, too, he sees a sign that the promises have been kept in Jesus Christ.

5:1–6:18 □□ St Paul shows the practical consequences for Christians of the salvation worked by Jesus. Without freedom we cannot act out of love, and love,

i. Other ancient authorities read *For Sinai is a mountain in Arabia* **j.** Other ancient authorities read *you*
4:27 Is 54:1. **4:30** Gen 21:10–12

justified by the law; you have fallen away from grace. [5]For through the Spirit, by
faith, we wait for the hope of righteousness. [6]For in Christ Jesus neither circum-
cision nor uncircumcision is of any avail, but faith working through love. [7]You
were running well; who hindered you from obeying the truth? [8]This persuasion is
not from him who calls you. [9]A little leaven leavens the whole lump. [10]I have con-
fidence in the Lord that you will take no other view than mine; and he who is
troubling you will bear his judgment, whoever he is. [11]But if I, brethren, still
preach circumcision, why am I still persecuted? In that case the stumbling block
of the cross* has been removed. [12]I wish those who unsettle you would mutilate
themselves!

The fruits of the Spirit and the works of the flesh

[13]For you were called to freedom, brethren; only do not use your freedom as
an opportunity for the flesh, but through love be servants of one another. [14]For
the whole law is fulfilled in one word, "You shall love your neighbour as
yourself." [15]But if you bite and devour one another take heed that you are not
consumed by one another.

[16]But I say, walk by the Spirit, and do not gratify the desires of the flesh. [17]For
the desires of the flesh are against the Spirit, and the desires of the Spirit are
against the flesh; for these are opposed to each other, to prevent you from doing

---

in turn, guides freedom and keeps it developing properly (5:1–6:10). The letter ends with an account of how he himself lives that freedom (6:11–18).

5:1–6:10 □ The moral part of the letter begins by reminding them that the law of Christ is a law of freedom, unlike the law of circumcision (5:1–12). Consequently the works required by the New Law, the works of the Spirit, are opposed to the works of the flesh, the works of sin (5:13–26). The basic precept of the law of Christ is charity (6:1–10).

5:1–12 The Christian's freedom is the outcome of Christ's salvific work, which reaches us through faith in Him. From now on, the Christian is moved by Christ's spirit to desire justice (holiness). It doesn't matter what he was before; that is, it doesn't matter whether he was Jew or Gentile. What matters is faith working through love (v. 6): "when we ask how good a man is, we do not ask what he believes or what he hopes for but what he loves. He who rightly loves, without doubt, rightly believes and hopes. He who does not love, vainly believes, even if the things he believes are true [...]. This is the faith of Christ which the Apostle commends, and which works through charity" (St Augustine, *Enchir.*, 177).

5:13–26 Christian freedom does not mean that everything is allowed, but that man is able to make his way towards God, his true and ultimate end. A person is free

what you would. 18But if you are led by the Spirit you are not under the law.
19Now the works of the flesh are plain: fornication, impurity, licentiousness,
20idolatry, sorcery, enmity, strife, jealousy, anger, selfishness, dissension, party
spirit, 21envy,[k] drunkenness, carousing, and the like. I warn you, as I warned you
before, that those who do such things shall not inherit the kingdom of God. 22But
the fruit of the Spirit is love, joy, peace, patience, kindness, goodness, faithfulness,
23gentleness, self-control; against such there is no law. 24And those who belong
to Christ Jesus have crucified the flesh with its passions and desires.

25If we live by the Spirit, let us also walk by the Spirit. 26Let us have no
self-conceit, no provoking of one another, no envy of one another.

Fraternal charity

6 1Brethren, if a man is overtaken in any trespass, you who are spiritual
should restore him in a spirit of gentleness. Look to yourself, lest you too
be tempted. 2Bear one another's burdens, and so fulfil the law of Christ. 3For
if any one thinks he is something, when he is nothing, he deceives himself.
4But let each one test his own work, and then his reason to boast will be in
himself alone and not in his neighbour. 5For each man will have to bear his
own load.

6Let him who is taught the word share all good things with him who teaches.

7Do not be deceived; God is not mocked, for whatever a man sows, that he
will also reap. 8For he who sows to his own flesh will from the flesh reap
corruption; but he who sows to the Spirit will from the Spirit reap eternal life.
9And let us not grow weary in well-doing, for in due season we shall reap, if
we do not lose heart. 10So then, as we have opportunity, let us do good to all
men, and especially to those who are of the household of faith.

---

when he is led by the Spirit of God, who strengthens him to curb the inclinations of the flesh denounced by the Law, and instead produces the fruit which is above the Law. "The fruits listed by the Apostle are produced in [the souls of] just people by the Holy Spirit, even in this life, and are full of sweetness and joy because they come from the Holy Spirit, who 'is the love of the Father and of the Son in the Trinity, and who fills all creatures with infinite gentleness' (St Augustine, *De Trinitate* 5, 9)" (Leo XIII, *Div. ill. mun.*).

6:1–10 Christians, too, have a Law to keep—the law of Christ, which is the law of sincere love, the law of the Spirit. "Jesus makes charity the *new commandment* (cf. Jn 13:34). By loving his own 'to the end' (Jn 13:1), he makes manifest the Father's love which he receives. By loving one another, the disciples imitate the love of Jesus which they themselves receive" (*CCC*, 1823).

Because they were keeping to what the Jewish Law laid down, some Galatians thought themselves better than others. Their pride stemmed from a lack of self-

k. Other ancient authorities add *murder* **5:14** Lev 19:18.

4. CONCLUSION

[11]See with what large letters I am writing to you with my own hand. [12]It is
those who want to make a good showing in the flesh that would compel you to
be circumcised, and only in order that they may not be persecuted for the cross
of Christ. [13]For even those who receive circumcision do not themselves keep
the law, but they desire to have you circumcised that they may glory in your
flesh. [14]But far be it from me to glory except in the cross of our Lord Jesus
Christ, by which[l] the world has been crucified to me, and I to the world. [15]For
neither circumcision counts for anything, nor uncircumcision, but a new
creation. [16]Peace and mercy be upon all who walk by this rule, upon the Israel
of God.

[17]Henceforth let no man trouble me; for I bear on my body the marks of
Jesus.

[18]The grace of our Lord Jesus Christ be with your spirit, brethren. Amen.

---

knowledge. That is why the Apostle calls for personal examination of conscience; a sincere examination, done in the presence of God, who sees all things. "Man himself is nothing more than vanity, and if he is somehow greater than himself, he is so by the grace of God our Lord alone" (St John of Avila, *Audi, filia*, 66).

6:11–18 □ The letter ends with some words in St Paul's own hand, which he has added at the bottom of the text written by a secretary at his dictation. In these verses the Apostle gives a brief summary of the teaching contained in the letter, and a vibrant farewell.

6:11–18 Paul unmasks the intentions of those who have been unsettling the Galatians. The circumcised were boasting about bearing on their bodies the sign of the Old Covenant, circumcision. Paul tells them that there is only one thing to rejoice about—the cross of our Lord Jesus Christ, by which the new Covenant was sealed and the Redemption accomplished.

That is why the cross has become the mark of the Christian. The soul was created, St Teresa Benedicta of the Cross (Edith Stein) comments, for union with God through the cross, was redeemed by the cross, "consumed and sanctified by the cross, so that it would be marked with the sign of the cross for all eternity" (*The Science of the Cross*, 337).

l. Or *through whom*

The Letter to the Ephesians

Ephesus was the most important city in Asia Minor in St Paul's time. The Apostle stayed there at the end of his second apostolic journey (in the years 50–53), and again at the start of his third journey (in the years 54–57). His second visit lasted more than two years (cf. Acts 19:20) and he did so much preaching that Jews and Greeks across the entire province were able to hear the Gospel.

The Letter to the Ephesians has a somewhat different form from St Paul's other letters. There are no references to people, no greetings, and even the word "Ephesus" is not to be found in some of the oldest and most important manuscripts—all of which leads one to think that this may have been a circular letter addressed to the churches in the Phrygian region (where Ephesus as well as Laodicea, Colossae etc. were located). The Letter to the Ephesians covers more or less the same subjects as the Letter to the Colossians, but they are dealt with more extensively, more deeply and more serenely; it may well be that both letters date from the same period. Information in the Bible and in extrabiblical sources indicate that Paul had come up against doctrines which say that the universe is ruled by powers intermediate between God and men—powers whose favour men should try to win by means of certain rites and ascetical practices. The Apostle takes issue with these exotic Gnostic-Greek doctrines by arguing that Christ is the head of all beings, be they heavenly or earthly; he is absolute Lord of all, and the Saviour of all; nothing that exists can withdraw itself from the overlordship of Jesus Christ, whose Body is the Church.

The letter begins with an elaborate hymn or canticle which praises the salvific plan of God, carried out by Christ, for the benefit of the elect, the Church and all mankind (1:3–14). Due to sin, all created beings are disorientated and divided among themselves and against God, but now, through the redemption worked by Christ, they have been led back to unity with one another and with God, for Christ, who has become man and is now in the glory of heaven, has been made the Head of all things (1:3–2:22). St Paul goes on to reflect on the reality and nature of the Church. She is the universal means of salvation: Christ has made her his body, his fullness, his immaculate bride; in order to apply to mankind the salvation he has brought about by his death and resurrection (3:1–20).

As is customary in the Apostle's writings, he draws moral and ascetical conclusions from his theology (4:1–6:24): all the faithful should live together in peace and love, for they form one body with Christ and are enlivened by one and the same Spirit. He goes on to draw practical conclusions—about the duties of married couples, parents and children, masters and slaves, etc. All should be equally demanding on themselves, because all derive strength from the Head who is Christ Jesus.

Ephesians

Greeting

1 [1]Paul, an apostle of Christ Jesus by the will of God, To the saints who are*
also faithful[a] in Christ Jesus:
[2]Grace to you and peace from God our Father and the Lord Jesus Christ.

PART ONE: THE MYSTERY OF GOD REVEALED

1. GOD'S PLAN OF SALVATION

Hymn of praise

[3]Blessed be the God and Father of our Lord Jesus Christ, who has blessed us
in Christ with every spiritual blessing in the heavenly places, [4]even as he chose

---

1:1–2 The letter begins very much like the previous ones—a greeting and a hymn of thanksgiving (cf. Rom 1:1ff; 1 Cor 1:1ff). See the RSV note: this letter might have been a circular letter to the churches of the Ephesus region. The text of the letter does not refer to the specific circumstances of any particular Christian community.

1:3–3:21 □ □ The central theme of the letter is the Church. The Church makes present the salvific mystery of God brought about in Jesus Christ, in favour of Jews and Gentiles (1:1–2:22). St Paul's ministry consists in helping to put the plan of salvation into effect, through preaching (3:1–13) and prayer (13:14–21). These chapters make up the first part or the doctrinal section of the letter.

1:3–2:22 □ Paul expounds the divine plan of salvation, viewing it in the context of the mystery of God's eternity and its historical expression through Christ and the Church. "Already present in figure at the beginning of the world, (the) Church was prepared in marvellous fashion in the history of the people of Israel and in the old Alliance. Established in this last age of the world, and made manifest in the outpouring of the Spirit, it will be brought to glorious completion at the end of time" (Vatican II, *LG,* 2).

1:3–14 A hymn of praise is included in this first part (vv. 3–10) which describes the benefits or blessings contained in God's plan of salvation, called by St Paul

a. Other ancient authorities read *who are at Ephesus and faithful*

us in him before the foundation of the world, that we should be holy and
blameless before him. 5He destined us in love[b] to be his sons through Jesus
Christ, according to the purpose of his will, 6to the praise of his glorious grace
which he freely bestowed on us in the Beloved. 7In him we have redemption
through his blood, the forgiveness of our trespasses, according to the riches of
his grace 8which he lavished upon us. 9For he has made known to us in all
wisdom and insight the mystery of his will, according to his purpose which he
set forth in Christ 10as a plan for the fullness of time, to unite* all things in
him, things in heaven and things on earth.

11In him, according to the purpose of him who accomplishes all things
according to the counsel of his will, 12we who first hoped in Christ have been
destined and appointed to live for the praise of his glory. 13In him you also, who
have heard the word of truth, the gospel of your salvation, and have believed in
him, were sealed with the promised Holy Spirit, 14who is the guarantee of our
inheritance until we acquire possession of it, to the praise of his glory.

Thanksgiving. The supremacy of Christ

15For this reason, because I have heard of your faith in the Lord Jesus and your
love[c] toward all the saints, 16I do not cease to give thanks for you, remem-
bering you in my prayers, 17that the God of our Lord Jesus Christ, the Father
of glory, may give you a spirit of wisdom and of revelation in the knowledge
of him, 18having the eyes of your hearts enlightened, that you may know what
is the hope to which he has called you, what are the riches of his glorious
inheritance in the saints, 19and what is the immeasurable greatness of his
power in us who believe, according to the working of his great might 20which
he accomplished in Christ when he raised him from the dead and made him sit
at his right hand in the heavenly places, 21far above all rule and authority and

---

"the mystery" (v. 9). This plan ranges from the eternal choice of each human being by God to the "recapitulation" of all things in Christ (v. 10). The letter then goes on to explain how this divine plan has affected Jews (vv. 11–12) and Gentiles (vv. 13–14).

1:15–23 The faith and charity of those to whom the letter is written are a proof of all the teachings he has given them. Therefore, he gives thanks to God and asks him to give them deep insight into the mystery of Christ. He depicts Jesus Christ as being above all earthly and heavenly powers and as being the Head of the Church. Through the Church, Christ becomes present in and fills the entire universe and extends to it the fruits of his work of redemption. "We need to come to see Christ himself in the Church. For it is Christ who lives in the Church, who teaches, governs and sanctifies through her" (Pius XII, *Mystici Corporis*, 43).

b. Or *before him in love, having destined us* **c.** Other ancient authorities omit *your love*

power and dominion, and above every name that is named, not only in this age
but also in that which is to come; [22]and he has put all things under his feet and
has made him the head over all things for the church, [23]which is his body, the
fullness of him who fills all in all.

Salvation, a free gift

2 [1]And you he made alive, when you were dead through the trespasses and
sins [2]in which you once walked, following the course of this world,
following the prince of the power of the air, the spirit that is now at work in the
sons of disobedience. [3]Among these we all once lived in the passions of our
flesh, following the desires of body and mind, and so we were by nature
children of wrath, like the rest of mankind. [4]But God, who is rich in mercy, out
of the great love with which he loved us, [5]even when we were dead through
our trespasses, made us alive together with Christ (by grace you have been
saved), [6]and raised us up with him, and made us sit with him in the heavenly
places in Christ Jesus, [7]that in the coming ages he might show the immeasurable
riches of his grace in kindness toward us in Christ Jesus. [8]For by grace you
have been saved through faith; and this is not your own doing, it is the gift of
God—[9]not because of works, lest any man should boast. [10]For we are his
workmanship, created in Christ Jesus for good works, which God prepared
beforehand, that we should walk in them.

Reconciliation of Jews and Gentiles in Christ

[11]Therefore remember that at one time you Gentiles in the flesh, called the
uncircumcision by what is called the circumcision, which is made in the flesh
by hands—[12]remember that you were at that time separated from Christ,
alienated from the commonwealth of Israel, and strangers to the covenants of
promise, having no hope and without God in the world. [13]But now in Christ
Jesus you who once were far off have been brought near in the blood of Christ.
[14]For he is our peace, who has made us both one, and has broken down the

---

2:1–10 In these verses we can see the merciful love of God. Despite the sinfulness in which they stood (vv. 1–3), the merciful power of God (vv. 4–5) has acted on both Jews and Gentiles to liken them to Christ in his glorious triumph (vv. 6–7). And all this has come about through the gratuitous gift of faith (vv. 8–10). The "prince of the power of the air" (v. 2) refers to the devil as the leader of superhuman powers which, according to a widely held notion at the time, dwelt in the earth's atmosphere.

2:11–22 The redemption brought about by Christ on the cross has had the effect of making peace between Jews and Gentiles and reconciling both of them with God (vv. 16–18). This redemption has brought something new into being—the Church, which St Paul depicts as a holy temple, founded on the prophets and apostles (vv. 19–22).

1:22 Ps 8:6.

dividing wall of hostility, [15]by abolishing in his flesh the law of command-
ments and ordinances, that he might create in himself one new man in place of
the two, so making peace, [16]and might reconcile us both to God in one body
through the cross, thereby bringing the hostility to an end. [17]And he came and
preached peace to you who were far off and peace to those who were near;
[18]for through him we both have access in one Spirit to the Father.
[19]So then you are no longer strangers and sojourners, but you are fellow
citizens with the saints and members of the household of God, [20]built upon the
foundation of the apostles and prophets, Christ Jesus himself being the
cornerstone, [21]in whom the whole structure is joined together and grows into
a holy temple in the Lord; [22]in whom you also are built into it for a dwelling
place of God in the Spirit.

2. PROCLAMATION OF THE MYSTERY OF CHRIST

Paul's mission

3 [1]For this reason I, Paul, a prisoner for Christ Jesus on behalf of you
Gentiles—[2]assuming that you have heard of the stewardship of God's grace
that was given to me for you, [3]how the mystery was made known to me by
revelation, as I have written briefly. [4]When you read this you can perceive my
insight into the mystery of Christ, [5]which was not made known to the sons of
men in other generations as it has now been revealed to his holy apostles and
prophets by the Spirit; [6]that is, how the Gentiles are fellow heirs, members of

---

In the plan of salvation the Christian is also made into a holy temple in whom the Trinity dwells. This indwelling gives a person a deeper knowledge of and a more intense love for the mystery of God: "The Trinity! Here we find our abode, the intimacy we desire so much, the home that we will never have to leave" (Bl. Elizabeth of the Trinity, *Heaven on Earth*, 1).

3:1–21 □ Paul feels urged to make known God's plan of salvation because once man comes to know that mystery, that is, once he has faith, he can partake of the fullness of divine life.

3:1–13 It is Paul's mission to proclaim to the Gentiles the revelation of the "mystery" (v. 3). "In the Symbol of the faith the Church confesses the mystery of the Holy Trinity and of the plan of God's 'good pleasure' for all creation: the Father accomplishes the 'mystery of his will' (Eph 1:9) by giving his beloved Son and his Holy Spirit for the salvation of the world and for the glory of his name. Such is the mystery of Christ, revealed and fulfilled in history according to the wisely ordered plan that St Paul calls the 'plan of the mystery' (Eph 3:9) and the

2:17 Is 57:19.

the same body, and partakers of the promise in Christ Jesus through the gospel.
[7]Of this gospel I was made a minister according to the gift of God's grace
which was given me by the working of his power. [8]To me, though I am the
very least of all the saints, this grace was given, to preach to the Gentiles the
unsearchable riches of Christ, [9]and to make all men see what is the plan of the
mystery hidden for ages in[d] God who created all things; [10]that through the
church the manifold wisdom of God might now be made known to the
principalities and powers in the heavenly places. [11]This was according to the
eternal purpose which he has realized in Christ Jesus our Lord, [12]in whom we
have boldness and confidence of access through our faith in him. [13]So I ask
you not to[e] lose heart over what I am suffering for you, which is your glory.

The Apostle's prayer

[14]For this reason I bow my knees before the Father, [15]from whom every family in
heaven and on earth is named, [16]that according to the riches of his glory he may
grant you to be strengthened with might through his Spirit in the inner man, [17]and
that Christ may dwell in your hearts through faith; that you, being rooted and
grounded in love, [18]may have power to comprehend with all the saints what is the
breadth and length and height and depth, [19]and to know the love of Christ which
surpasses knowledge, that you may be filled with all the fullness of God.

Doxology

[20]Now to him who by the power at work within us is able to do far more
abundantly than all that we ask or think, [21]to him be glory in the church and in
Christ Jesus to all generations, for ever and ever. Amen.

---

patristic tradition will call the 'economy of the Word incarnate' or the 'economy of salvation'" (*CCC*, 1066).

3:14–19 St Paul asks God to strengthen Christians and to have Christ dwell in their hearts through faith so that they appreciate how much Christ loves them and grow until they are filled with the fullness of God. He may indeed be trying to sum up all the richness of the mystery of Christ in a graphic way—as a cross whose extremities reach out in all four directions as if to embrace the whole world. "Everything comes under the influence of the work of redemption through the Word of God; the Son of God was crucified for all [mankind], and has drawn the sign of the cross on all things" (St Irenaeus, *Demos. predic. apost.*). Knowledge of salvation history and of the mystery of Christ is ultimately what gives us a notion of the scale of God's love. It is therefore the basis of the Christian life: "O Jesus, most meek, the greatest joy of our heart, our endless good, your love embraces us" (Lauds hymn, *Divine Office,* Solemn. Sac. Heart of Jesus).

3:20–21 Paul praises the power of God: his plan of salvation has far exceeded anything men might have sought or imagined.

d. Or *by* **e.** Or *I ask that I may not*

PART TWO: CHRISTIAN LIFE IN THE CHURCH

3. NEW LIFE IN CHIRST AND IN THE CHURCH

A call to unity

4 [1]I therefore, a prisoner for the Lord, beg you to lead a life worthy of the
calling to which you have been called, [2]with all lowliness and meekness,
with patience, forbearing one another in love, [3]eager to maintain the unity of
the Spirit in the bond of peace. [4]There is one body and one Spirit, just as you
were called to the one hope that belongs to your call, [5]one Lord, one faith, one
baptism, [6]one God and Father of us all, who is above all and through all and in
all. [7]But grace was given to each of us according to the measure of Christ's
gift. [8]Therefore it is said,

"When he ascended on high he led a host of captives,
and he gave gifts to men."

[9](In saying, "He ascended," what does it mean but that he had also descended
into the lower parts of the earth? [10]He who descended is he who also ascended
far above all the heavens, that he might fill all things.) [11]And his gifts were that
some should be apostles, some prophets, some evangelists, some pastors and
teachers, [12]to equip the saints for the work of ministry, for building up the body
of Christ, [13]until we all attain to the unity of the faith and of the knowledge of the
Son of God, to mature manhood, to the measure of the stature of the fullness of

---

4:1–6:24 □□ After explaining about God's saving plan (a mystery hidden, and now revealed through Jesus Christ, who has brought it into effect), St Paul moves on to discuss the moral implications involved in being a member of the Church. This is the moral section of the letter.

4:1–32 □ Christians can and should reflect in their behaviour what has come about through grace—that is, the fact that they are inserted into Christ and are part of his Body, the Church.

4:1–16 What was expounded in the earlier part of the letter shows the importance of unity in the Body of Christ, and that in turn means that Christians need to be humble and committed. The unity of the Church is based on the fact that there is only one God, one Lord, one faith, one Baptism (vv. 5–6), and it is sustained by the action of Christ, the Head of the Church, who provides the Church with ministers so that all its members can reach maturity in the one Body, to whose growth they contribute (vv. 11–16).

The quotation in v. 8 is from Psalm 68:19. Paul is saying that this psalm is fulfilled in Jesus Christ: through him, through his earthly life and his death,

4:8 Ps 68:18

Christ; [14]so that we may no longer be children, tossed to and fro and carried
about with every wind of doctrine, by the cunning of men, by their craftiness
in deceitful wiles. [15]Rather, speaking the truth in love, we are to grow up in
every way into him who is the head, into Christ, [16]from whom the whole body,
joined and knit together by every joint with which it is supplied, when each
part is working properly, makes bodily growth and upbuilds itself in love.

Spiritual renewal

[17]Now this I affirm and testify in the Lord, that you must no longer live as the
Gentiles do, in the futility of their minds; [18]they are darkened in their under-
standing, alienated from the life of God because of the ignorance that is in them,
due to their hardness of heart; [19]they have become callous and have given
themselves up to licentiousness, greedy to practise every kind of uncleanness.
[20]You did not so learn Christ!—[21]assuming that you have heard about him and
were taught in him, as the truth is in Jesus. [22]Put off your old nature which
belongs to your former manner of life and is corrupt through deceitful lusts, [23]and
be renewed in the spirit of your minds, [24]and put on the new nature, created after
the likeness of God in true righteousness and holiness.

Christian virtues

[25]Therefore, putting away falsehood, let every one speak the truth with his
neighbour, for we are members one of another. [26]Be angry but do not sin; do
not let the sun go down on your anger, [27]and give no opportunity to the devil.
[28]Let the thief no longer steal, but rather let him labour, doing honest work

---

through his humiliation and glorification, God's gifts reach us. Paul sees Jesus distributing the benefits of the Redemption from the glory of heaven which he has entered.

4:17–24 The new life in Christ is as it were the condition each Christian needs to have in order to contribute to the growth of Christ's Body. To live this new life, a person must get rid of his previous life of vanity and sin; he must be converted and put on Jesus Christ, the new man, and be faithful to him at all times. "The power of God is made manifest in our weakness and it spurs us on to fight, to battle against our defects, although we know that we will never achieve total victory during our pilgrimage on earth. The Christian life is a continuous beginning again each day. It renews itself over and over" (Bl. J. Escrivá, *Hom.,* 1, 114).

4:25–32 The first consequence of the new life is the practice of virtue: this makes for harmony among Christians as members of the Body of Christ. Christians do not have to turn their backs on the world in order to live in keeping with the Gospel. They should seek to find God in their own environment and try to change

4:25 Zech 8:16. **4:26** Ps 4:4.

with his hands, so that he may be able to give to those in need. 29Let no evil
talk come out of your mouths, but only such as is good for edifying, as fits the
occasion, that it may impart grace to those who hear. 30And do not grieve the
Holy Spirit of God, in whom you were sealed for the day of redemption. 31Let
all bitterness and wrath and anger and clamour and slander be put away from
you, with all malice, 32and be kind to one another, tenderhearted, forgiving one
another, as God in Christ forgave you.

4. CHRISTIAN HOLINESS

The purity of life of God's children

5 1Therefore be imitators of God, as beloved children. 2And walk in love, as
Christ loved us and gave himself up for us, a fragrant offering and sacrifice
to God.
3But fornication and all impurity or covetousness must not even be named
among you, as is fitting among saints. 4Let there be no filthiness, nor silly talk,
nor levity, which are not fitting; but instead let there be thanksgiving. 5Be sure of
this, that no fornicator or impure man, or one who is covetous (that is, an
idolater), has any inheritance in the kingdom of Christ and of God. 6Let no one
deceive you with empty words, for it is because of these things that the wrath of
God comes upon the sons of disobedience. 7Therefore do not associate with them,

Walking in the light

8for once you were darkness, but now you are light in the Lord; walk as
children of light 9(for the fruit of light is found in all that is good and right and
true), 10and try to learn what is pleasing to the Lord. 11Take no part in the

---

that environment by practising the Christian virtues, embodying Christ's life in their own, particularly by forgiving one another.

5:1–20 □ The consequences of new life in Christ are: vigilance and the constant effort a Christian should make to strive against sin in all its various forms (vv. 1–18), sincere devotion to the Lord, and charity (vv. 19–20).

5:1–7 Holiness means being like God, the Holy One. The way to holiness is to imitate Jesus Christ in his love and self-giving (vv. 1–2). Therefore, as on other occasions (cf. Rom 1:18–32; Gal 5:19–21; 1 Cor 6:9–10), St Paul strictly warns those who live a disorderly life, a life away from Christ, that they will not have a share in the kingdom of God.

5:8–20 Another practical consequence—one should live a clean life in which the works of light are to be found, as befits those who were given the light of Christ at

unfruitful works of darkness, but instead expose them. [12]For it is a shame even
to speak of the things that they do in secret; [13]but when anything is exposed by
the light it becomes visible, for anything that becomes visible is light.
[14]Therefore it is said,

"Awake, O sleeper, and arise from the dead,
and Christ shall give you light."*

[15]Look carefully then how you walk, not as unwise men but as wise,
[16]making the most of the time, because the days are evil. [17]Therefore do not be
foolish, but understand what the will of the Lord is. [18]And do not get drunk
with wine, for that is debauchery; but be filled with the Spirit, [19]addressing one
another in psalms and hymns and spiritual songs, singing and making melody
to the Lord with all your heart, [20]always and for everything giving thanks in
the name of our Lord Jesus Christ to God the Father.

5. CHRISTIAN FAMILY LIFE

Duties of husband and wife

[21]Be subject to one another out of reverence for Christ. [22]Wives, be subject to
your husbands, as to the Lord. [23]For the husband is the head of the wife as
Christ is the head of the church, his body, and is himself its Saviour. [24]As the
church is subject to Christ, so let wives also be subject in everything to their
husbands. [25]Husbands, love your wives, as Christ loved the church and gave
himself up for her, [26]that he might sanctify her, having cleansed her by the
washing of water with the word, [27]that he might present the church to himself
in splendour, without spot or wrinkle or any such thing, that she might be holy

---

Baptism and were filled with the Holy Spirit. "Whoever wants to remain faithful to his baptismal promises and resist temptations will want to adopt the means for doing so: self-knowledge, practice of an ascesis adapted to the situations that confront him, obedience to God's commandments, exercise of the moral virtues and fidelity to prayer" (*CCC*, 2340).

5:21–6:9 □ The Apostle looks at the new situation of people who have become part of Christ, be they husband or wife, parent or child, master or slave. The section also contains an exhortation to love, obedience, and respect for others: these virtues have a new dimension in that they now reflect Christ and the Church.

5:21–33 The basis of the supernatural majesty and dignity of Christian marriage is the fact that it reflects the union between Christ and his Church. In exhorting Christian married couples to live in keeping with their membership of the Church, the Apostle establishes an analogy whereby the husband represents Christ and the

and without blemish. [28]Even so husbands should love their wives as their own
bodies. He who loves his wife loves himself. [29]For no man ever hates his own
flesh, but nourishes and cherishes it, as Christ does the church, [30]because we
are members of his body. [31]"For this reason a man shall leave his father and
mother and be joined to his wife, and the two shall become one flesh." [32]This
mystery is a profound one, and I mean in reference to Christ and the church;
[33]however, let each one of you love his wife as himself, and let the wife see
that she respects her husband.

Advice to children and parents

6 [1]Children, obey your parents in the Lord, for this is right. [2]"Honour your
father and mother" (this is the first commandment with a promise), [3]"that
it may be well with you and that you may live long on the earth." [4]Fathers, do
not provoke your children to anger, but bring them up in the discipline and
instruction of the Lord.

Advice to servants and masters

[5]Slaves, be obedient to those who are your earthly masters, with fear and
trembling, in singleness of heart, as to Christ; [6]not in the way of eye-service,

---

wife, the Church: "For a Christian, marriage is not just a social institution, much less a mere remedy for human weakness. It is a real supernatural calling. A great sacrament, in Christ and in the Church, says St Paul. [...] It is a sacred sign that sanctifies, an action of Jesus; he fills the souls of husband and wife and invites them to follow him; he transforms their whole married life into an occasion for God's presence on earth" (Bl. J. Escrivá, *Hom.*, 1, 23).

When Paul exhorts wives to be "subject" to their husbands, he is taking account of the fact that a Christian wife, in the way she acts towards her husband, should be like the Church, who is obedient to Christ. The husband is equally required to be submissive to his wife, like Jesus, who gave himself up to death out of love for the Church. "Spouses are the permanent reminder to the Church of what happened on the Cross; they are for one another and for the children witnesses to the salvation in which the sacrament makes them sharers" (John Paul II, *Fam. consortio*, 13).

6:1–4 St Paul reminds them about the fourth commandment (cf. Ex 20:12; Deut 5:16). Keeping this commandment brings temporal advantages (peace and prosperity) as well as spiritual ones (cf. *CCC*, 2200). Then, in v. 4, the Apostle deals with the duties of parents. "Parents must regard their children as *children of God* and respect them as *human persons*. Showing themselves obedient to the will of the Father in heaven, they educate their children to fulfil God's law" (ibid., 2222).

6:5–9 In St Paul's time labour relations were based to a large extent on slavery. He spells out the proper basis for relations between masters and servants. By

5:31 Gen 2:24.

as men-pleasers, but as servants[f] of Christ, doing the will of God from the
heart, 7rendering service with a good will as to the Lord and not to men,
8knowing that whatever good any one does, he will receive the same again
from the Lord, whether he is a slave or free. 9Masters, do the same to them,
and forbear threatening, knowing that he who is both their Master and yours is
in heaven, and that there is no partiality with him.

6. CONCLUSION

Weapons for spiritual combat

10Finally, be strong in the Lord and in the strength of his might. 11Put on the
whole armour of God, that you may be able to stand against the wiles of the
devil. 12For we are not contending against flesh and blood, but against the
principalities, against the powers, against the world rulers of this present
darkness, against the spiritual hosts of wickedness in the heavenly places.
13Therefore take the whole armour of God, that you may be able to withstand
in the evil day, and having done all, to stand. 14Stand therefore, having girded
your loins with truth, and having put on the breastplate of righteousness, 15and
having shod your feet with the equipment of the gospel of peace; 16besides all
these, taking the shield of faith, with which you can quench all the flaming

---

emphasizing the dignity of the human person, he is clearly teaching that human relationships are made supernatural if they involve Christ. This teaching established conditions which, centuries later, would lead to the abolition of slavery.

6:10–24 □ The Apostle ends his letter urging the faithful on in their struggle against evil and reminding them of the weapons at their disposal.

6:10–20 Using imagery taken from the army, Paul invites everyone to put on the armour of God so as to be able to fend off the onslaught of evil; and he encourages them to persevere in prayer, and to pray for himself and his ministry. The "world rulers" (v. 12) are the angels who rebelled against God. Although Christ defeated them, we still have to contend against them. Among the many spiritual weapons available to us to fight against the snares of the enemy, prayer gets special mention (v. 18): "'We have not been commanded to work, to keep watch and to fast constantly, but it had been laid down that we are to pray without ceasing' (Evagrius Ponticus, *Pract.*, 49). This tireless fervour can come only from love. Against our dullness and laziness, the battle of prayer is that of humble, trusting and persevering love" (*CCC*, 2742).

f. Or *slaves* **6:2–3** Ex 20:12; Deut 5:16. **6:14** Is 11:59:17. **6:15** Is 52:7. **6:17** Is 49:2.

darts of the evil one. [17]And take the helmet of salvation, and the sword of the
Spirit, which is the word of God. [18]Pray at all times in the Spirit, with all
prayer and supplication. To that end keep alert with all perseverance, making
supplication for all the saints, [19]and also for me, that utterance may be given
me in opening my mouth boldly to proclaim the mystery of the gospel, [20]for
which I am an ambassador in chains; that I may declare it boldly, as I ought to
speak.

Conclusion and blessing

[21]Now that you also may know how I am and what I am doing, Tychicus the
beloved brother and faithful minister in the Lord will tell you everything. [22]I
have sent him to you for this very purpose, that you may know how we are,
and that he may encourage your hearts.

[23]Peace be to the brethren, and love with faith, from God the Father and the
Lord Jesus Christ. [24]Grace be with all who love our Lord Jesus Christ with
love undying.

6:21–24 The Apostle has not said anything in the letter about his own circumstances; he has asked the bearer of the letter to provide that news.

The Letter to the Philippians

Philippi was quite an important city in St Paul's time, in terms of both commerce and history. It was situated in Macedonia, on the border with Thrace, on the Via Engatia, a paved Roman road which crossed both these regions, and it was an obligatory stopover for people coming from Asia Minor to Europe via Greece. The church of Philippi was the first church founded by Paul once he set foot on European soil (cf. Acts 16:11–40). This foundation happened during his second journey, around the year 50 or 51. He would revisit Philippi, possibly twice, during his third journey (cf. Acts 20:1–3), although he does not seem to have spent long there.

Some twenty years earlier Philippi had received the title of Colonia Iulia Augusta Philippensis, and the *ius italicum* (Italian law) applied there. Many retired men of the Roman legions had established themselves there. Given the background of the city's inhabitants, most of the Christian faithful there must have been of Gentile origin. All greatly loved the Apostle and they were noted for their generosity (4:10–20).

St Paul mentions that he is writing from prison (1:3), perhaps from Rome or Ephesus. If it was in fact Rome, the letter must be dated between the years 60 and 63. If from Ephesus, it would have been written between 54 and 57. During the Apostle's imprisonment, the Philippians, ever ready to give him whatever help he needed, decided to send Epaphroditus with alms to alleviate his material needs (4:18) and to assist him while he was in prison (2:25). But Epaphroditus fell ill, so seriously ill that his life was in danger. Once he recovered, Paul decided to send him back home, to be a consolation to the Philippians (2:25–30). He used the opportunity to send them this letter, thanking them for their kindness, exhorting them to continue to live authentic Christian lives (3:7–4:23), and warning them to be on their guard against Judaizers, who were sowing discord everywhere and putting obstacles in the way of the Gospel (3:1–6).

The letter is very much a counterpoint to that written to the Galatians. St Paul extends himself in praise of Christ, of co-workers in the spread of the Gospel, and of the Philippians. These last mentioned have stayed faithful to the Gospel in spite of difficulties, and they are a source of joy to the Apostle. The general tone of the letter is one of exhortation rather than doctrine. He writes in a very moving way, sending them news of the spread of the Gospel. From his prison he encourages them to put his teachings into practice and to grow in the Christian virtues. Although it is a short letter, it does deal with important matters of doctrine—the eternal destiny of man; the attitude a Christian should have to things temporal; the deep mystery of Christ and the example he gave us during his life on earth. In this connexion the key doctrinal passage of the letter is the so-called "Christological hymn" (2:6–11); this may be a text the Philippians were already familiar with, and which the Apostle transcribes adding some little variant of his own. These verses praise Christ's *self-emptying* in his incarnation, life and death, and the glorious *exaltation* of his human nature after he rose from the dead.

Philippians

1. INTRODUCTION

Greeting

1 [1]Paul and Timothy, servants[a] of Christ Jesus,
To all the saints in Christ Jesus who are at Philippi, with the bishops[b] and deacons:
[2]Grace to you and peace from God our Father and the Lord Jesus Christ.

Thanksgiving. Paul's affection and love

[3]I thank my God in all my remembrance of you, [4]always in every prayer of
mine for you all making my prayer with joy, [5]thankful for your partnership in
the gospel from the first day until now. [6]And I am sure that he who began a
good work in you will bring it to completion at the day of Jesus Christ. [7]It is

---

1:1–4:23 □ □ In this letter St Paul is going to open his heart to the faithful at Philippi. He begins by saying how happy he feels, despite his imprisonment (1:1–26) when he thinks of them and of the Gospel. He asks them, despite his absence, to complete his joy by being united to one another in humility. Christ's own self-abasement stands as an example for them (1:27–2:18). Paul compensates for his absence from Philippi by sending some brethren (2:19–30) along with this letter in which, to strengthen their Christian life, he warns them about certain intruders, enlivens their hope in heaven and thanks them for the help they have given him (3:1–4:23).

1:1–26 □ One feature of this letter is that it shows, more vividly than any other, St Paul's affection and appreciation for the Christians of those communities he founded. In addition to the normal greeting (vv. 1–2) and act of thanksgiving for the fidelity of those he is writing to (vv. 3–11), the Apostle has also things to say about his personal circumstances (vv. 12–26).

1:1–2 In the apostles' time the terms "bishop" and "deacon" did not have the precise meaning they now have; however, their use here does show that, even at this early stage, local churches had some sort of hierarchical structure.

1:3–11 A sense of joy is one of the clearest features of this letter; the good spirit and conduct of the Philippians make the Apostle particularly happy. St Paul is so identified with our Lord that he can say he has the same sentiments as Christ has (v. 8).

a. Or *slaves* **b.** Or *overseers*

right for me to feel thus about you all, because I hold you in my heart, for you
are all partakers with me of grace, both in my imprisonment and in the defence
and confirmation of the gospel. [8]For God is my witness, how I yearn for you
all with the affection of Christ Jesus. [9]And it is my prayer that your love may
abound more and more, with knowledge and all discernment, [10]so that you
may approve what is excellent, and may be pure and blameless for the day of
Christ, [11]filled with the fruits of righteousness which come through Jesus
Christ, to the glory and praise of God.

Paul's own circumstances

[12]I want you to know, brethren, that what has happened to me has really served
to advance the gospel, [13]so that it has become known throughout the whole
praetorian guard[c] and to all the rest that my imprisonment is for Christ; [14]and
most of the brethren have been made confident in the Lord because of my imprisonment,* and are much more bold to speak the word of God without fear.

[15]Some indeed preach Christ from envy and rivalry, but others from good
will. [16]The latter do it out of love, knowing that I am put here for the defence
of the gospel; [17]the former proclaim Christ out of partisanship, not sincerely
but thinking to afflict me in my imprisonment. [18]What then? Only that in every
way, whether in pretence or in truth, Christ is proclaimed; and in that I rejoice.

[19]Yes, and I shall rejoice. For I know that through your prayers and the help
of the Spirit of Jesus Christ this will turn out for my deliverance, [20]as it is my
eager expectation and hope that I shall not be at all ashamed, but that with full
courage now as always Christ will be honoured in my body,* whether by life
or by death. [21]For to me to live is Christ, and to die is gain. [22]If it is to be life
in the flesh, that means fruitful labour for me. Yet which I shall choose I cannot
tell. [23]I am hard pressed between the two. My desire is to depart and be with
Christ, for that is far better. [24]But to remain in the flesh is more necessary on
your account. [25]Convinced of this, I know that I shall remain and continue with
you all, for your progress and joy in the faith, [26]so that in me you may have
ample cause to glory in Christ Jesus, because of my coming to you again.

1:12–26 Paul is content about his position in prison, because in fact it gives him good scope to spread the Gospel. We do not know whom he is referring to when he mentions people who are preaching Christ "from envy and rivalry" (v. 15); still, he is happy that the Gospel is being preached (cf. Mk 9:38–40).

Like Paul, the believer should try to identify himself with Christ (vv. 21–26). A Christian's life in this world, involving suffering and even death, is in some way Christ's own life: that is what the Christian should be aiming at. Death is "gain" (v. 21), because it means being able to see God face to face (cf. 1 Cor 13:12) and obtain everlasting union with Christ. This desire to see and enjoy God in heaven led to St Teresa of Avila to say: "I am living and yet I am not really living, for I place my hopes on such a higher life that I am dying because I do not die" (*Poems*, 2).

c. Greek *in the whole praetorium*

2. TEACHINGS

Appeal for steadfastness
27Only let your manner of life be worthy of the gospel of Christ, so that
whether I come and see you or am absent, I may hear of you that you stand
firm in one spirit, with one mind striving side by side for the faith of the
gospel, 28and not frightened in anything by your opponents. This is a clear
omen to them of their destruction, but of your salvation, and that from God.
29For it has been granted to you that for the sake of Christ you should not only
believe in him but also suffer for his sake, 30engaged in the same conflict
which you saw and now hear to be mine.

Unity and humility
2 1So if there is any encouragement in Christ, any incentive of love, any
participation in the Spirit, any affection and sympathy, 2complete my joy
by being of the same mind, having the same love, being in full accord and of
one mind. 3Do nothing from selfishness or conceit, but in humility count others
better than yourselves. 4Let each of you look not only to his own interests, but
also to the interests of others.

Hymn in praise of God's self-emptying
5Have this mind among yourselves, which was in Christ Jesus, 6who, though
he was in the form of God,* did not count equality with God a thing to be

---

1:27–2:18 □ Not everything was going well for the Philippians: there may have been a degree of persecution, and also rivalries had developed, caused (it seems) by some preachers. St Paul exhorts them to be steadfast (1: 27–30) and to have a unity based on Christ-like humility (2:1–18).

1:27–30 Sufferings and difficulties providentially give Christians a chance to become more fully identified with Christ and not be afraid to embrace his cross (v. 29). "Is it not true that as soon as you cease to be afraid of the Cross, of what people call the cross, when you set your will to accept the Will of God, then you find happiness, and all your worries, all your sufferings, physical or moral, pass away?" (Bl. J. Escrivá, *The Way of the Cross*, 2).

2:1–4 What makes the Apostle particularly happy is when Christians are at one with each other, in a union based on love and on the example set by Christ—the very best example of humility, as we can see from the verses that follow.

2:5–11 This is one of the earliest New Testament texts to reveal the divinity of Jesus Christ. It is possible that Paul is transcribing an early liturgical hymn with some extra touches of his own. The hymn extols the humiliation and exaltation of grasped, [7]but emptied himself,* taking the form of a servant,[d] being born in the likeness of men. [8]And being found in human form he humbled himself and became obedient unto death, even death on a cross. [9]Therefore God has highly exalted him and bestowed on him the name which is above every name, [10]that at the name of Jesus every knee should bow, in heaven and on earth and under the earth, [11]and every tongue confess that Jesus Christ is Lord, to the glory of God the Father.

The children of God, the light of the world

[12]Therefore, my beloved, as you have always obeyed, so now, not only as in my presence but much more in my absence, work out your own salvation with fear and trembling; [13]for God is at work in you, both to will and to work for his good pleasure.

[14]Do all things without grumbling or questioning, [15]that you may be blameless and innocent, children of God without blemish in the midst of a crooked and perverse generation, among whom you shine as lights in the

---

Christ. Conscious throughout of Christ's divinity, the Apostle focuses on his death on the cross, the supreme example of humility and obedience. Verses 6–8 bring to mind the contrast between Jesus and Adam; Adam, a mere man, sought to be like God (cf. Gen 3:5); Jesus, although he was God, "emptied himself" (v. 7). Christ's obedience even to death on the cross thereby makes up for the disobedience of the first man; therefore, God raised him above all creation. Verse 9 tells us that by raising Jesus and having him sit on his right hand, God the Father enabled his Humanity to manifest the glory of Divinity that is his—"the name which is above every name", that is, the name of God. "This expression 'he exalted him' does not mean that the nature of the Word was raised up […]. Terms such as 'humbled' and 'exalted' refer only to the sphere of humanity, since only what is humble can be exalted" (St Athanasius, *Oratio 1 contra arianos*, 1, 41). All created things are subject to his authority, and men should acknowledge the basic truth of Christian teaching: "Jesus Christ is Lord", that is, Jesus Christ is God.

2:12–18 Reflection on Christ's example should help his disciple to persevere generously in his service. A Christian's upright and straightforward life should be a beacon to those around him. Verse 13 shows that in all this we can count on the help of God's grace. "The truth that God is at work in all actions of his creatures is inseparable from faith in God the Creator. God is the first cause who operates in and through secondary causes. […] Far from diminishing the creature's dignity, this truth enhances it. Drawn from nothingness by God's power, wisdom and goodness, it can do nothing if it is cut off from its origin, for 'without a Creator the creature vanishes' (Vatican II, *GS*, 3, 6, 3). Still less can a creature attain its ultimate end without the help of God's grace" (*CCC*, 308).

d. Or *slave* **2:10–11** Is 45:23.

world, [16]holding fast the word of life, so that in the day of Christ I may be
proud that I did not run in vain or labour in vain. [17]Even if I am to be poured
as a libation upon the sacrificial offering of your faith, I am glad and rejoice
with you all. [18]Likewise you also should be glad and rejoice with me.

3. PLANS AND NEWS

Timothy's mission

[19]I hope in the Lord Jesus to send Timothy to you soon, so that I may be
cheered by news of you. [20]I have no one like him, who will be genuinely
anxious for your welfare. [21]They all look after their own interests, not those of
Jesus Christ. [22]But Timothy's worth you know, how as a son with a father he
has served with me in the gospel. [23]I hope therefore to send him just as soon
as I see how it will go with me; [24]and I trust in the Lord that shortly I myself
shall come also.

Epaphroditus' mission

[25]I have thought it necessary to send to you Epaphroditus my brother and
fellow worker and fellow soldier, and your messenger and minister to my
need, [26]for he has been longing for you all, and has been distressed because
you heard that he was ill. [27]Indeed he was ill, near to death. But God had
mercy on him, and not only on him but on me also, lest I should have sorrow
upon sorrow. [28]I am the more eager to send him, therefore, that you may
rejoice at seeing him again, and that I may be less anxious. [29]So receive him in
the Lord with all joy; and honour such men, [30]for he nearly died for the work
of Christ, risking his life to complete your service to me.

2:19–30 □ There is a rather sudden change of subject at this point, and the Apostle begins to mention various items of news.

2:19–24 Timothy had been the Apostle's co-worker in the evangelization of the Philippians—his companion on apostolic journeys (cf. Acts 16:1, 3, 10ff; 20:4) or his special envoy (cf. Acts 19:22).

2:25–30 Paul's imprisonment had a place in God's plans. It stirred the love and generosity of the Philippians to send Epaphroditus to minister to his needs. "Suffering exists in the world to bring forth love, to draw out acts of love for one's neighbour, to transform the whole of human civilization into the 'civilization of love'" (John Paul II, *Salvif. dolor.*, 30).

4. THE CHRISTIAN LIFE

A warning about Judaizers

3 [1]Finally, my brethren, rejoice in the Lord. To write the same things to you
is not irksome to me, and is safe for you.
[2]Look out for the dogs, look out for the evil-workers, look out for those
who mutilate the flesh. [3]For we are the true circumcision, who worship God in
spirit,[e] and glory in Christ Jesus, and put no confidence in the flesh. [4]Though
I myself have reason for confidence in the flesh also. If any other man thinks
he has reason for confidence in the flesh, I have more: [5]circumcised on the
eighth day, of the people of Israel, of the tribe of Benjamin, a Hebrew born of
Hebrews; as to the law a Pharisee, [6]as to zeal a persecutor of the church, as to
righteousness under the law blameless.

The righteousness of God exceeds that of the Law

[7]But whatever gain I had, I counted as loss for the sake of Christ. [8]Indeed I
count everything as loss because of the surpassing worth of knowing Christ
Jesus my Lord. For his sake I have suffered the loss of all things, and count
them as refuse, in order that I may gain Christ [9]and be found in him, not
having a righteousness of my own, based on law, but that which is through
faith in Christ, the righteousness from God that depends on faith; [10]that I may
know him and the power of his resurrection, and may share his sufferings,
becoming like him in his death, [11]that if possible I may attain the resurrection
from the dead.

3:1–4:23 □ After giving news about himself and his co-workers, St Paul charges the Philippians to be faithful and to make progress in the Christian life. And he sets himself as an example: first, to answer the Judaizers, he describes the change he experienced when he became a Christian (3:1–16); then he speaks about the goal they must strive to reach, that of heaven (3:17–21); finally he tells them of how happy and grateful he is when he thinks about them (4:1–20).

3:1–6 The Apostle spells out his Jewish pedigree to show the Philippians his moral authority and to put in their place the Judaizers who were claiming that circumcision was necessary for salvation (v. 2).

3:7–11 Everything in which he gloried prior to his conversion he now regards as worthless in comparison with the grace of knowing Christ. It is Christ who makes man righteous, not the Law of Moses (cf. Rom 3:21). Therefore, one needs to give up everything for Christ's sake, and to try to become increasingly like him in order to attain the glory of resurrection.

e. Other ancient authorities read *worship by the Spirit of God*

The spiritual athlete

[12]Not that I have already obtained this or am already perfect; but I press on to
make it my own, because Christ Jesus has made me his own.* [13]Brethren, I do
not consider that I have made it my own; but one thing I do, forgetting what
lies behind and straining forward to what lies ahead, [14]I press on toward the
goal for the prize of the upward call of God in Christ Jesus. [15]Let those of us
who are mature be thus minded; and if in anything you are otherwise minded,
God will reveal that also to you. [16]Only let us hold true to what we have
attained.

Citizens of heaven

[17]Brethren, join in imitating me, and mark those who so live as you have an
example in us. [18]For many, of whom I have often told you and now tell you
even with tears, live as enemies of the cross of Christ. [19]Their end is
destruction, their god is the belly, and they glory in their shame, with minds set
on earthly things.* [20]But our commonwealth is in heaven, and from it we await
a Saviour, the Lord Jesus Christ, [21]who will change our lowly body to be like
his glorious body, by the power which enables him even to subject all things
to himself.

Exhortation to perseverance and joy

4 [1]Therefore, my brethren, whom I love and long for, my joy and crown,
stand firm thus in the Lord, my beloved.
[2]I entreat Euodia and I entreat Syntyche to agree in the Lord. [3]And I ask
you also, true yokefellow, help these women, for they have laboured side by
side with me in the gospel together with Clement and the rest of my fellow
workers, whose names are in the book of life.

3:12–16 Growth in holiness always entails an effort. “You should always be unhappy with what you are, if you want to attain what you are not yet. For when you were content with yourself, you stayed where you were. If you say ‘enough,’ you are finished that very minute. Always grow, always work on, always advance” (St Augustine, *Serm.*, 169, 18).

3:17–21 Imitation of the saints (and not of those opposed to our Lord’s cross) is a sure and effective way to serve God and others. As fellow-citizens of heaven, Christians should always be joyful and confident; as children of God, their lives should be based on hope in the Lord’s coming and in the resurrection.

4:1–9 Being joyful is not incompatible with being in a difficult or painful situation. The Lord is always at the Christian’s side, taking providential care of him (v. 5). All the Christian need do is make his needs known in all simplicity (v. 6). All

[4]Rejoice in the Lord always; again I will say, Rejoice. [5]Let all men know your forbearance. The Lord is at hand. [6]Have no anxiety about anything, but in everything by prayer and supplication with thanksgiving let your requests be made known to God. [7]And the peace of God, which passes all understanding, will keep your hearts and your minds in Christ Jesus.

[8]Finally, brethren, whatever is true, whatever is honourable, whatever is just, whatever is pure, whatever is lovely, whatever is gracious, if there is any excellence, if there is anything worthy of praise, think about these things. [9]What you have learned and received and heard and seen in me, do; and the God of peace will be with you.

Thanks for help received

[10]I rejoice in the Lord greatly that now at length you have revived your concern for me; you were indeed concerned for me, but you had no opportunity. [11]Not that I complain of want; for I have learned, in whatever state I am, to be content. [12]I know how to be abased, and I know how to abound; in any and all circumstances I have learned the secret of facing plenty and hunger, abundance and want. [13]I can do all things in him who strengthens me.

[14]Yet it was kind of you to share my trouble. [15]And you Philippians yourselves know that in the beginning of the gospel, when I left Macedonia, no church entered into partnership with me in giving and receiving except you only; [16]for even in Thessalonica you sent me help[f] once and again. [17]Not that I seek the gift; but I seek the fruit which increases to your credit. [18]I have received full payment, and more; I am filled, having received from

---

earthly things, everything noble, have a divine value, and can bring one closer to God (v. 8). "Where your fellow man, your yearnings, your work and your affections are, there you have your daily encounter with Christ" (Bl. J. Escrivá, *Conversations*, 113).

4:10–20 The difficulties that may arise in a person's life are never an insuperable obstacle and should never take away one's peace. God will always give a Christian strength.

St Paul was touched by the Philippians' generosity (vv. 14–20). He is not asking them for donations: he can survive without them; he is interested in the good that will redound to them on account of their almsgiving. Since God is the one who rewards men for their actions, a person who gives alms will ultimately benefit more than he who receives them. As a reward for their almsgiving, they will receive the eternal glory won by Christ Jesus. "Whoever gives alms should do so with detachment and joy, for the less he keeps back for himself, the greater will his gain be" (St Leo the Great, *Serm. 10 de Quadrag.*, 5).

f. Other ancient authorities read *money for my needs*

Epaphroditus the gifts you sent, a fragrant offering, a sacrifice acceptable and
pleasing to God. 19And my God will supply every need of yours according to
his riches in glory in Christ Jesus. 20To our God and Father be glory for ever
and ever. Amen.

Words of farewell

21Greet every saint in Christ Jesus. The brethren who are with me greet you.
22All the saints greet you, especially those of Caesar's household.
23The grace of the Lord Jesus Christ be with your spirit.

4:21–23 "Those of Caesar's household" (v. 22): a reference to civil servants, employees of the imperial government, who had became converts to Christianity. So, the phrase can refer both to those living in Rome and to those based in any imperial city.

The Letter to the Colossians

Colossae, in St Paul's time, was a small city in Asia Minor, situated in southwest Phrygia. St Paul visited this region at least twice. The first time was during his second missionary journey when on his way from Lystra and Iconium to Galatia (cf. Acts 16:6); and then during his journey he spent a very short while there to encourage the disciples in the faith (cf. Acts 18:23). Yet nowhere in the book of the Acts is any reference to Paul's visiting Colossae. The Apostle himself seems to imply that he did not personally know the Colossians (2:1). It was Epaphras, a native of Colossae (4:12) and a disciple of Paul, who had received a commission to preach the Gospel there, as also in the nearby towns of Hierapolis and Laodicea (1:7; 4:13). The majority of Christians there were of Gentile background.

When the Apostle was in prison (at Rome, Ephesus or maybe Caesarea), Epaphras informed him about some matters at Colossae which were causing him concern: Jewish visitors were bringing in Gnostic ideas, which were finding some acceptance. Gnostic teachings began to spread in the Roman empire from around the middle or start of the first century AD, mainly through Jews with a poor grasp of their own tradition and who began to mix it with Hellenic philosophical or religious ideas which themselves had been influenced by notions from the East.

The main thing about Gnosticism was its dualistic idea of God, the world and man. Two opposite principles, good and evil, spirit and matter, lay at the basis of everything. Gnosticism projected itself at a higher Wisdom, superior to all other religions (including Judaism), which it regarded as adequate only for the general mass of people. The first traces of Gnosticism in Colossae seemingly sought to reconcile Christianity with this philosophy: for Gnostics, Christ, being man, was on a plane lower than that of (spiritually purer) angelic powers: so, Christ was an "eon", a being intermediate between God (Spirit) and matter.

This sort of doctrinal confusion spurred St Paul, moved by God, to spell out certain essential points of the faith, and to have the Colossians reject these other, heterodox, notions. He goes on to explore key aspects of the mystery of Christ's being (Christology); he also stresses Christ's infinite superiority over and his headship of all things, be they angels, powers or whatever (1:15–20). The Apostle uses very rich expressions, saying, for example, that in Christ "the whole fullness of deity dwells bodily" (2:9); although the language is very different, the content of this statement is very similar to St John's wording when he says that "the Word became flesh and dwelt among us" (Jn 1:14). Moreover, in the Letter to the Colossians we find new terms which seemingly were used by Hellenist Gnostics but which are here charged with special shades of meaning. Basically what St Paul says is that Jesus Christ is eternal God; he did not cease to be God when he took on a human nature; therefore he is lord of all mankind and lord of the angels.

In addition to these doctrinal matters, the letter also covers moral and disciplinary matters, such as the duties of married people to one another (3:18–21), masters and slaves (3:22–4:1) and advice on the practice of Christian virtues (3:12–17; 4:2–6).

Colossians

INTRODUCTION

Greeting

1 [1]Paul, an apostle of Christ Jesus by the will of God, and Timothy our brother,

[2]To the saints and faithful brethren in Christ at Colossae:

Grace to you and peace from God our Father.

Thanksgiving for the Colossians' response to the Gospel

[3]We always thank God, the Father of our Lord Jesus Christ, when we pray for
you, [4]because we have heard of your faith in Christ Jesus and of the love
which you have for all the saints, [5]because of the hope laid up for you in
heaven. Of this you have heard before in the word of the truth, the gospel
[6]which has come to you, as indeed in the whole world it is bearing fruit and
growing—so among yourselves, from the day you heard and understood the
grace of God in truth, [7]as you learned it from Epaphras our beloved fellow
servant. He is a faithful minister of Christ on our[a] behalf [8]and has made known
to us your love in the Spirit.

Prayer for advancement in holiness

[9]And so, from the day we heard of it, we have not ceased to pray for you,
asking that you may be filled with the knowledge of his will in all spiritual
wisdom and understanding, [10]to lead a life worthy of the Lord, fully pleasing
to him, bearing fruit in every good work and increasing in the knowledge of

---

1:1–14 □ Strange notions were beginning to circulate in the church of Colossae, thanks to certain preachers. On hearing of this, the Apostle writes this letter. As usual, the opening greeting is followed by an act of thanksgiving.

1:3–8 Colossae had not been evangelized by St Paul, but by Epaphras, a disciple and co-worker of the Apostle. Paul ratifies Epaphras' preaching and ministry, and rejoices at the Colossians' faith.

1:9–14 The Apostle's repeated prayer (vv. 9–11) emphasizes the need to distinguish sound teaching from the misleading teaching of the false apostles. Verses 12–14 encourage the Colossians to show their gratitude for the gifts God has given them in Christ. Freedom from sin (salvation) is to be found in Christ,

a. Other ancient authorities read *your*

God. [11]May you be strengthened with all power, according to his glorious might, for all endurance and patience with joy, [12]giving thanks to the Father, who has qualified us[b] to share in the inheritance of the saints in light. [13]He has delivered us from the dominion of darkness and transferred us to the kingdom of his beloved Son, [14]in whom we have redemption, the forgiveness of sins.

PART ONE: FAITH IN CHRIST, THE LORD OF ALL

1. CHRIST, THE FIRST-BORN

Hymn in praise of Christ, the head of all creation
[15]He is the image of the invisible God, the first-born* of all creation; [16]for in him all things were created, in heaven and on earth, visible and invisible, whether thrones or dominions or principalities or authorities—all things were created through him and for him. [17]He is before all things, and in him all things hold together. [18]He is the head of the body, the church; he is the beginning, the first-born from the dead, that in everything he* might be pre-

---

who is the manifestation of God's love for mankind. "He has revealed to us that God is love [...]. He has brought salvation to all by overcoming death and the power of sin on the cross, through his total obedience to love" (John Paul II, *Reconcil. et paen.*, 10).

1:15–2:23 □□ In line with the notions of the time, the Colossians thought that the world was ruled by powers superior to man which God had placed as mediators in the fulfillment of his plan. Some "philosophers" numbered Christ among these—powers which led the Apostle to declare the incomparable superiority of Christ and to warn the faithful about such philosophies.

1:15–29 □The body of the letter begins with an explanation of the superiority of Christ as regards the created world and the Church. It continues with a reflection on the conversion of the Colossians and on the ministry of Paul.

1:15–20 Paul extols the ministry of Christ and his mission of redemption. This passage is a sublime canticle celebrating Jesus Christ, the Lord of creation; no part of the universe fails to be affected by the redemption which flows from the cross. The first stanza (vv. 15–17) asserts that Christ's dominion embraces the entire cosmos, for he is its creator. The passage is reminiscent of the prologue to St

b. Other ancient authorities read *you*

eminent. [19]For in him all the fullness of God was pleased to dwell, [20]and
through him to reconcile to himself all things, whether on earth or in heaven,
making peace by the blood of his cross.

The effect of Christ's saving action

[21]And you, who once were estranged and hostile in mind, doing evil deeds,
[22]he has now reconciled in his body of flesh by his death, in order to present
you holy and blameless and irreproachable before him, [23]provided that you
continue in the faith, stable and steadfast, not shifting from the hope of the
gospel which you heard, which has been preached to every creature under
heaven, and of which I, Paul, became a minister.

Paul's response to his calling

[24]Now I rejoice in my sufferings for your sake, and in my flesh I complete
what is lacking* in Christ's afflictions for the sake of his body, that is, the
church, [25]of which I became a minister according to the divine office which
was given to me for you, to make the word of God fully known, [26]the mystery
hidden for ages and generations[c] but now made manifest to his saints. [27]To
them God chose to make known how great among the Gentiles are the riches

---

John's Gospel and the opening verses of Genesis. The second stanza (vv. 18–20) refers to a second creation worked by God through the grace Jesus won by dying on the cross. He is the Mediator and the Head of the Church. He has re-established peace and reconciled all things to God.

When it says that the Son is "the image of the invisible God" (v. 15), the text is asserting that there is identity of (divine) nature between Father and Son, and that the Son proceeds from the Father. The fact that he is called "the first–born" shows that he is above and is the head of all created beings, because he is not only prior to them: they were all created "in him", "through him" and "for him" (v. 16).

1:21–23 Christ's holy human nature is an instrument of salvation: through his passion and death, our Lord conquered sin and obtained the grace necessary to cleanse man from his faults and make it possible for him to appear in God's presence (v. 22). The incarnation of the Word means that the Christian faith is opposed to disembodied spiritualism. The human body and material things in general are not an obstacle to man's santification. "There is just one life, made of flesh and spirit. And it is this life which has to become, in both soul and body, holy and filled with God. We discover the invisible God in the most visible and material things" (Bl. J. Escrivá, *Conversations*, 114).

1:24–29 We can cooperate with God's plans not only by our actions and our prayers: our sufferings also play a part, and they give us a share in Christ's own

c. Or *from angels and men*

of the glory of this mystery, which is Christ in you, the hope of glory. 28Him
we proclaim, warning every man and teaching every man in all wisdom, that
we may present every man mature in Christ. 29For this I toil, striving with all
the energy which he mightily inspires within me.

2. DEFENCE OF THE FAITH

Paul's concern for the faithful

2 1For I want you to know how greatly I strive for you, and for those
at Laodicea, and for all who have not seen my face, 2that their hearts may
be encouraged as they are knit together in love, to have all the riches of assured
understanding and the knowledge of God's mystery, of Christ, 3in whom are
hid all the treasures of wisdom and knowledge.

A warning about empty philosophies

4I say this in order that no one may delude you with beguiling speech. 5For
though I am absent in body, yet I am with you in spirit, rejoicing to see your
good order and the firmness of your faith in Christ.

6As therefore you received Christ Jesus the Lord, so live in him, 7rooted and
built up in him and established in the faith, just as you were taught, abounding
in thanksgiving.

8See to it that no one makes a prey of you by philosophy and empty deceit,
according to human tradition, according to the elemental spirits of the
universe, and not according to Christ.

---

suffering. "The man who suffers [...] in the spiritual dimension of the work of redemption brings about, as Christ did, the salvation of all his brothers and sisters" (John Paul II, *Salvif. dolor.*, 27).

On the "mystery" of salvation (vv. 26–27), cf. Eph 1:3–14.

2:1–23 □ The Colossians were in danger of being led astray by preachers who claimed that they needed to be submissive to certain heavenly powers or angelic spirits (discovered through special revelation) and to conform to prescriptions like those of the Jewish Law. St Paul reacts against theories of this kind: Christ, he tells them, has set them free from this sort of thing (worship of the elements, empty philosophies) through his death on the cross.

2:1–8 Christ is the fullest manifestation of the "mystery" or divine plan for man's salvation. To counter the "beguiling speech" of false teachers, St Paul exhorts the Colossians to go deeper into the Gospel they have been given. An infinite treasure of wisdom and knowledge lies hidden in Christ (cf. v. 3); this means that reflection

Defence of sound teaching in the face of heresy
[9]For in him the whole fullness of deity dwells bodily, [10]and you have come to
fullness of life in him, who is the head of all rule and authority. [11]In him also
you were circumcised with a circumcision made without hands, by putting off
the body of flesh in the circumcision of Christ; [12]and you were buried with him
in baptism, in which you were also raised with him through faith in the
working of God, who raised him from the dead. [13]And you, who were dead in
trespasses and the uncircumcision of your flesh, God made alive together with
him, having forgiven us all our trespasses, [14]having cancelled the bond which
stood against us with its legal demands; this he set aside, nailing it to the cross.
[15]He disarmed the principalities and powers and made a public example of
them, triumphing over them in him.[d]

Rejection of false asceticism
[16]Therefore let no one pass judgment on you in questions of food and drink or
with regard to a festival or a new moon or a sabbath. [17]These are only a
shadow of what is to come; but the substance belongs to Christ. [18]Let no one
disqualify you, insisting on self-abasement and worship of angels, taking his
stand on visions, puffed up without reason by his sensuous mind, [19]and not
holding fast to the Head, from whom the whole body, nourished and knit
together through its joints and ligaments, grows with a growth that is from God.

---

on his life and teachings is an inexhaustible source of nourishment for the life of the soul. "One must go deep into Christ, for he is like a mine, rich in many seams of treasure; and the treasure is never ending, no matter how deep one goes, because from each seam, new veins of treasure branch out in every direction" (St John of the Cross, *Spiritual Canticle*, 37, 3).

2:9–15 Verse 9 enunciates the profound mystery of the Incarnation; cf. Jn 1:14. Christ is the only mediator because he is God and Man. The basic purpose of his mediation is to reconcile men to God, through forgiving their sins and giving them the life of grace, which is a participation in the life of God. Christ achieved his purpose by his death on the cross (v. 14). That death removed the burden posed by circumcision and "cancelled the charge-sheet" (which might be read against each Jew); through his cross and resurrection, Christ has also disarmed any force which (according to the thinking at the time) might threaten man.

2:16–23 On being baptized, every Christian dies with Christ to the spirits of the universe and is freed from the slavery of the Law and of sin. It makes no sense, then, to continue to be hidebound by precepts which no longer apply—much less to be afraid to use the good things of the world.

d. Or *in it* (that is, the cross)

[20]If with Christ you died to the elemental spirits of the universe, why do you
live as if you still belonged to the world? Why do you submit to regulations,
[21]"Do not handle, Do not taste, Do not touch" [22](referring to things which all
perish as they are used), according to human precepts and doctrines? [23]These
have indeed an appearance of wisdom in promoting rigor of devotion and self-
abasement and severity to the body, but they are of no value in checking the
indulgence of the flesh.[e]

PART TWO: CHRIST THE LORD

3. MORAL CONSEQUENCES

Seeking the things that are above

3 [1]If then you have been raised with Christ, seek the things that are above,
where Christ is, seated at the right hand of God. [2]Set your minds on things
that are above, not on things that are on earth. [3]For you have died, and your life
is hid with Christ in God. [4]When Christ who is our life appears, then you also
will appear with him in glory.

Avoiding sin

[5]Put to death therefore what is earthly in you: fornication, impurity, passion,
evil desire, and covetousness, which is idolatry. [6]On account of these the wrath

---

3:1–4:18 □□ Through Baptism a Christian is given a share in Christ's lordship: he is in a new situation whereby he increases in holiness, knowledge and love to the extent that he does everything "in the name of the Lord Jesus" (3:17).

3:1–4:6 □ This section deals with the spiritual and moral implications of the teaching expounded in the preceding chapters. The focus is mainly on self-denial (3:1–11), interpersonal relations (3:12–17), and family and social life (3:18–4:1).

3:1–4 Through Baptism the Christian shares in the glorious life of the risen Jesus, who therefore fills all dimensions of his life. "My love is crucified [...]. Neither the food that decays nor the pleasures of this world satisfy me. What I want is the bread of God, which is the flesh of Christ, born of the descendants of David, and I desire no other drink but his blood, which is the charity that is never corrupted" (St Ignatius of Antioch, *Letter to the Romans,* 6,1–9, 3).

3:5–11 The "old nature", the "old man": one who lets himself be led by disorderly passions. Christ's disciple, who has been made a new person and who lives for the

e. Or *are of no value, serving only to indulge the flesh*

of God is coming.[f] [7]In these you once walked, when you lived in them. [8]But
now put them all away: anger, wrath, malice, slander, and foul talk from your
mouth. [9]Do not lie to one another, seeing that you have put off the old nature
with its practises [10]and have put on the new nature, which is being renewed in
knowledge after the image of its creator. [11]Here there cannot be Greek and
Jew, circumcised and uncircumcised, barbarian, Scythian, slave, free man, but
Christ is all, and in all.

Progress in the spiritual life

[12]Put on then, as God's chosen ones, holy and beloved, compassion, kindness,
lowliness, meekness, and patience, [13]forbearing one another and, if one has a
complaint against another, forgiving each other; as the Lord has forgiven you, so
you also must forgive. [14]And above all these put on love, which binds everything
together in perfect harmony. [15]And let the peace of Christ rule in your hearts, to
which indeed you were called in the one body. And be thankful. [16]Let the word of
Christ dwell in you richly, teach and admonish one another in all wisdom, and
sing psalms and hymns and spiritual songs with thankfulness in your hearts to
God. [17]And whatever you do, in word or deed, do everything in the name of the
Lord Jesus, giving thanks to God the Father through him.

Morals in family life

[18]Wives, be subject to your husbands, as is fitting in the Lord.* [19]Husbands,
love your wives, and do not be harsh with them. [20]Children, obey your parents

---

Lord, has a new and more perfect knowledge of God and of the world; thanks to this he sees things from a better vantage point, has a "supernatural insight" which is nothing other than "allowing oneself to be moved and possessed by the powerful hand of the author of all good" (St Ignatius Loyola, *Letters*, 4561f).

3:12–17 The virtues that the Apostle lists here as characteristic of the new man are all expressions, in one way or another, of charity or love, which "binds everything together in perfect harmony" (v. 14). All genuinely human things can (and should) be sanctified if done well, out of love (v. 17). "I assure you, my sons, that when a Christian carries out with love the most insignificant everyday action, that action overflows with the transcendence of God. That is why I have told you repeatedly, and hammered away once and again on the idea, that the Christian vocation consists in making heroic verse out of the prose of each day. Heaven and earth seem to merge, my children, on the horizon. But where they really meet is in your hearts, when you sanctify your everyday lives" (Bl. J. Escrivá, *Conversations*, 116).

3:18–4:1 This application of the Apostle's teaching to family life is based on charity and the need to live in the presence of God. In this light, all human relationships acquire new meaning.

f. Other ancient authorities add *upon the sons of disobedience*

in everything, for this pleases the Lord. [21]Fathers, do not provoke your children,
lest they become discouraged. [22]Slaves, obey in everything those who are your
earthly masters, not with eyeservice, as men-pleasers, but in singleness of
heart, fearing the Lord. [23]Whatever your task, work heartily, as serving the
Lord and not men, [24]knowing that from the Lord you will receive the
inheritance as your reward; you are serving the Lord Christ. [25]For the wrong-
doer will be paid back for the wrong he has done, and there is no partiality.
4 [1]Masters, treat your slaves justly and fairly, knowing that you also have a
Master in heaven.

Apostolic responsibility

[2]Continue steadfastly in prayer, being watchful in it with thanksgiving; [3]and
pray for us also, that God may open to us a door for the word, to declare the
mystery of Christ, on account of which I am in prison, [4]that I may make it
clear, as I ought to speak.

[5]Conduct yourselves wisely toward outsiders, making the most of the time.
[6]Let your speech always be gracious, seasoned with salt, so that you may
know how you ought to answer every one.

4. CONCLUSION

Tychicus and Onesimus will give personal news of Paul

[7]Tychicus will tell you all about my affairs; he is a beloved brother and faithful
minister and fellow servant in the Lord. [8]I have sent him to you for this very
purpose, that you may know how we are and that he may encourage your
hearts, [9]and with him Onesimus, the faithful and beloved brother, who is one
of yourselves. They will tell you of everything that has taken place here.

4:2–6 Perseverance in prayer is something often mentioned in the New Testament as being a feature of the early Christians (cf. Lk 18;1; Rom 12:12; 1 Thess 5;17; etc.). Prayer gave them the strength to spread Christ's message far and wide by their word and example: "The true apostle is on the lookout for occasions of announcing Christ by word, either to unbelievers to draw them towards the faith, or to the faithful to instruct them, strengthen them, incite them to a more fervent life; 'for Christ's love urges us on' (2 Cor 5:14), and in the hearts of all should the Apostle's words find echo: 'Woe to me if I do not preach the Gospel' (1 Cor 9:16)" (Vatican II, *AA*, 6).

4:7–18 □ In carrying out his apostolic ministry St Paul is not working away on his own. The references to other people, those that occur here as well as those in other letters (cf. Rom 16:3–23; 1 Cor 16:19–20; Philem 23:24; 2 Tim 4:19–21) show the Apostle's regard for and loyalty to his co-workers.

Greetings from Paul's fellow workers
10 Aristarchus my fellow prisoner greets you, and Mark the cousin of
Barnabas* (concerning whom you have received instructions—if he comes to
you, receive him), 11 and Jesus who is called Justus. These are the only men of
the circumcision among my fellow workers for the kingdom of God, and they
have been a comfort to me. 12 Epaphras, who is one of yourselves, a servant[g] of
Christ Jesus, greets you, always remembering you earnestly in his prayers, that
you may stand mature and fully assured in all the will of God. 13 For I bear
him witness that he has worked hard for you and for those in Laodicea and in
Hierapolis. 14 Luke the beloved physician* and Demas greet you.

Greetings and final wishes
15 Give my greetings to the brethren at Laodicea, and to Nympha and the
church in her house. 16 And when this letter has been read among you, have it
read also in the church of the Laodiceans; and see that you read also the letter
from Laodicea. 17 And say to Archippus, "See that you fulfil the ministry which
you have received in the Lord."
18 I, Paul, write this greeting with my own hand. Remember my fetters.
Grace be with you.

4:7–9 Like the Letter to the Ephesians, this letter is being delivered by Tychicus. With him will go Onesimus, the runaway slave who was later converted to the faith and whom Paul sent to his master, Philemon (cf. Philem 10).

4:10–18 Of the names mentioned here, some are familiar to us (Mark, Barnabas, Luke, for example). Demas will later desert Paul because he is "in love with this present world" (2 Tim 2:10). Archippus may have been Philemon's son (cf. Philem 2). St Paul has been dictating his letter to a secretary; then, as was customary, he writes a few words of farewell in his own hand (cf. 1 Cor 16:21; 2 Thess 3:17).

g. Or *slave*

The Letters to the Thessalonians

The Letters to the Thessalonians, written some twenty years after the death of our Lord, are the earliest writings in the New Testament.

Accompanied by Silas and Timothy, St Paul came to Thessalonica, the capital of the Roman province of Macedonia, during the first stage of his second missionary journey (which covered the years 51–53), and there he preached the Gospel. He made many converts and founded a Christian community which was a source of holy pride to him. However, after only a few months he was forced to leave the city in a hurry due to trouble caused by some Jews (cf. Acts 17:1–9). This meant that new converts in the city were not catechized properly and their position was not helped by the persecution instigated by those Jews. Because of this, Paul sent Timothy from Athens (1 Tit 3:2) to confirm the Thessalonians in the faith and to learn how they were doing. Meanwhile, Paul made his way to Corinth, where he met up with Timothy again (cf. Acts 18:5) and he learned the happy news that the Thessalonians were persevering in the faith and in charity, despite difficulties and persecution. Timothy also told him about certain matters which were troubling them—the fate of the dead, and the time of the Lord's second coming or the Parousia. The Apostle then wrote, in the winter of 50–51, his First Letter, to round off his earlier preaching. He sent it via Timothy and in it he also sought to set their minds at rest on what happens to people who die in the faith. What he says is that these too will share in the resurrection of Christ; they will "rise first" (1 Thess 4:16).

However, some of the Thessalonians failed to understand the Apostle's teaching and they thought that the Parousia was something that was going to happen soon. When St Paul heard about this, he wrote the Second Letter a few months later to clear up these misunderstandings.

Basically the themes of these letters are: evangelization, the action of the Word of God, holiness of life and, particularly, the Parousia, and resurrection of the dead. What he tells them is that they should not worry about these things or waste time trying to find out more about them; they should strive to live holy lives and work away in the expectation of the definitive coming of Christ.

1 Thessalonians

Greeting

1 [1]Paul, Silvanus, and Timothy,* To the church of the Thessalonians in God
the Father and the Lord Jesus Christ:
Grace to you and peace.

1. THE APOSTLE REJOICES OVER THE CHURCH OF THESSALONICA

Thanksgiving for the Thessalonians' fidelity

[2]We give thanks to God always for you all, constantly mentioning you in our
prayers, [3]remembering before our God and Father your work of faith and
labour of love and steadfastness of hope in our Lord Jesus Christ. [4]For we
know, brethren beloved by God, that he has chosen you; [5]for our gospel came
to you not only in word, but also in power and in the Holy Spirit and with full
conviction. You know what kind of men we proved to be among you for your
sake. [6]And you became imitators of us and of the Lord, for you received the
word in much affliction, with joy inspired by the Holy Spirit; [7]so that you
became an example to all the believers in Macedonia and in Achaia. [8]For not
only has the word of the Lord sounded forth from you in Macedonia and
Achaia, but your faith in God has gone forth everywhere, so that we need not

---

1:1–5:28 □ □ This is the earliest of St Paul's letters that has come down to us. After greeting the community (which he himself founded), he makes an elaborate act of thanksgiving to God for the fruit of evangelization and the faithfulness of those Christians (1:2–3:13). Later, moved (it seems) by the Thessalonians' sorrow over the death of loved ones, he exhorts them to live a holy life in the hope of the second coming of Christ (4:1–5:28).

1:2–3:13 □ The Apostle's thanksgiving extends both to the spread of the Gospel in Thessalonica (1:2–2:16) and the reports he has received about how those Christians are persevering in the faith (2:17–3:10). The section ends with a prayer for the Thessalonians (3:11–13).

1:2–10 The Apostle's work of evangelization stands as an example of how the Christian message should be proclaimed. The initiative comes from God, and it is God who makes the preaching effective. It is God the Father who chooses the evangelizer, and he does so out of love (v. 4); his Son Jesus provides steadfastness in hope (v. 3); the Holy Spirit makes the preacher's word persuasive (v. 5) and fills say anything. [9]For they themselves report concerning us what a welcome we had among you, and how you turned to God from idols, to serve a living and true God, [10]and to wait for his Son from heaven, whom he raised from the dead, Jesus who delivers us from the wrath to come.

Gospel preaching in Thessalonica—the early days recalled

2 [1]For you yourselves know, brethren, that our visit to you was not in vain; [2]but though we had already suffered and been shamefully treated at Philippi, as you know, we had courage in our God to declare to you the gospel of God in the face of great opposition. [3]For our appeal does not spring from error or uncleanness, nor is it made with guile; [4]but just as we have been approved by God to be entrusted with the gospel, so we speak, not to please men, but to please God who tests our hearts. [5]For we never used either words of flattery, as you know, or a cloak for greed, as God is witness; [6]nor did we seek glory from men, whether from you or from others, though we might have made demands as apostles of Christ. [7]But we were gentle[a] among you, like a nurse taking care of her children. [8]So, being affectionately desirous of you, we were ready to share with you not only the gospel of God but also our own selves, because you had become very dear to us.

[9]For you remember our labour and toil, brethren; we worked night and day, that we might not burden any of you, while we preached to you the gospel of God. [10]You are witnesses, and God also, how holy and righteous and blameless was our behaviour to you believers; [11]for you know how, like a father with his children, we exhorted each one of you and encouraged you and charged you [12]to lead a life worthy of God, who calls you into his own kingdom and glory.

---

with joy those who listen to it, despite any obstacles that may arise (v. 6). The basic content of preaching is "the Gospel" (v. 5). "For the Church, to evangelize means to bring the Good News to all human environments, and, by its influence, to transform them from within, to renew humanity itself" (Paul VI, *Evang. nunt.*, 18).

2:1–12 St Paul and his companions arrived in Thessalonica from Philippi, where persecution had broken out (cf. Acts 16:19–40). Soon enough, jealousy led Jews in Thessalonica to provoke unrest, and they had to leave that city too. The Apostle recalls the difficulties he experienced, and he makes the point that he always acted in an upright way (he may in fact be answering criticism from Jews or pagans). He was like a mother to them, like a father, and irreproachable (vv. 7–12). In this, he sets an example for church ministers: "We are reliquaries of God, the house of God and, as it is said, creatures of God; great holiness comes with these names" (St John of Avila, *Talk*).

a. Other ancient authorities read *babes*

The Thessalonians' patience

13And we also thank God constantly for this, that when you received the word
of God which you heard from us, you accepted it not as the word of men but
as what it really is, the word of God, which is at work in you believers. 14For
you, brethren, became imitators of the churches of God in Christ Jesus which
are in Judea; for you suffered the same things from your own countrymen as
they did from the Jews, 15who killed both the Lord Jesus and the prophets, and
drove us out, and displease God and oppose all men 16by hindering us from
speaking to the Gentiles that they may be saved—so as always to fill up the
measure of their sins. But God's wrath has come upon them at last![b]

Paul's solicitude

17But since we were bereft of you, brethren, for a short time, in person not in
heart, we endeavored the more eagerly and with great desire to see you face to
face; 18because we wanted to come to you—I, Paul,* again and again—but
Satan hindered us. 19For what is our hope or joy or crown of boasting before
our Lord Jesus at his coming? Is it not you? 20For you are our glory and joy.

Timothy's mission to Thessalonica

3 1Therefore when we could bear it no longer, we were willing to be left
behind at Athens alone, 2and we sent Timothy, our brother and God's
servant in the gospel of Christ, to establish you in your faith and to exhort you,
3that no one be moved by these afflictions. You yourselves know that this is to

---

2:13–16 Preaching is truly the "word of God" (v. 13) not only because it faithfully passes divine Revelation on but also because God himself speaks through those who proclaim the Gospel (cf. 2 Cor 5:20). "The word of God is alive and active" (Heb 4:12). Therefore, "by the saving Word of God faith is aroused in the heart of unbelievers and is nourished in the heart of believers. By this faith then the congregation of the faithful begins and grows, according to the saying of the apostle: 'Faith comes from what is heard, and what is heard comes by the preaching of Christ' (Rom 10: 17)" (Vatican II, *PO*, 4). On God's wrath, see the note on Rom 1:18.

2:17–20 Paul delights in the fidelity of the Thessalonians. "Thanks to the work of the master, the disciple is obedient, in such a way that his good behaviour brings about improvement in the master; the fruit reveals the master's work. Moreover, the effort of the disciple to do good crowns the master in the judgment of Christ" (St Thomas Aquinas, *Com. on 1 Thess,* in loc.).

3:1–5 The disciple is no greater than his Master (cf. Mt 10:24). Ever since his first missionary journey, the Apostle has told people that "through many tribulations we must enter the kingdom of God" (Acts 14:22) and he makes the same point in his last letter: "all who desire to live a godly life in Christ Jesus will be persecuted" (2 Tim

b. Or *completely*, or *for ever*

be our lot. 4For when we were with you, we told you beforehand that we were to suffer affliction; just as it has come to pass, and as you know. 5For this reason, when I could bear it no longer, I sent that I might know your faith, for fear that somehow the tempter had tempted you and that our labour would be in vain.

Paul rejoices over the good reports brought by Timothy

6But now that Timothy has come to us from you, and has brought us the good news of your faith and love and reported that you always remember us kindly and long to see us, as we long to see you—7for this reason, brethren, in all our distress and affliction we have been comforted about you through your faith; 8for now we live, if you stand fast in the Lord. 9For what thanksgiving can we render to God for you, for all the joy which we feel for your sake before our God, 10praying earnestly night and day that we may see you face to face and supply what is lacking in your faith?

Paul's prayer for the Thessalonians

11Now may our God and Father himself, and our Lord Jesus, direct our way to you; 12and may the Lord make you increase and abound in love to one another and to all men, as we do to you, 13so that he may establish your hearts unblamable in holiness before our God and Father, at the coming of our Lord Jesus with all his saints.

2. A CALL TO HOLINESS, HOPE AND PRAYER

Holiness and purity

4 1Finally, brethren, we beseech and exhort you in the Lord Jesus, that as you learned from us how you ought to live and to please God, just as you are

---

3:12). "Being with Jesus means we shall most certainly come upon his Cross. [...] In this way Jesus fashions the souls of those he loves, while at the same time never failing to give them inner serenity and joy" (Bl. J. Escrivá, *Hom.,* 2, 301).

3:6–10 The fact that the Thessalonians are steadfast in the faith despite persecution is not due to their own merits alone; the main credit must go to the grace of God.

3:11–13 The exhortation to be vigilant for the second coming of the Lord (the Parousia) is an underlying theme of this letter. Since we do not know when that will happen (cf. 5:2), we should always be leading lives worthy of Christ, lives where love reigns supreme; this makes man irreproachable in God's sight.

4:1–5:28 □ The thought of the second coming of the Lord, it seems, leads the Apostle to the exhortations that make up the second section of the letter. They are

doing, you do so more and more. 2For you know what instructions we gave
you through the Lord Jesus. 3For this is the will of God, your sanctification:*
that you abstain from unchastity;* 4that each one of you know how to control
his own body in holiness and honour, 5not in the passion of lust like heathen
who do not know God; 6that no man transgress, and wrong his brother in this
matter,[c] because the Lord is an avenger in all these things, as we solemnly
forewarned you. 7For God has not called us for uncleanness, but in holiness.
8Therefore whoever disregards this, disregards not man but God, who gives his
Holy Spirit to you.

Charity and good use of time
9But concerning love of the brethren you have no need to have any one write
to you, for you yourselves have been taught by God to love one another; 10and
indeed you do love all the brethren throughout Macedonia. But we exhort you,
brethren, to do so more and more, 11to aspire to live quietly, to mind your own
affairs, and to work with your hands, as we charged you;* 12so that you may
command the respect of outsiders, and be dependent on nobody.

---

all designed to encourage the Thessalonians to progress steadily in holiness (4:1–12), and to enliven their hope in future resurrection (4:13–5:11). The section concludes with encouragement to live in peace and joy and to pray at all times (5:12–22).

4:1–8 The exhortations the Apostle now begins to make are based on God's call to holiness. Verse 3 echoes our Lord's sermon on the mount: "You, therefore, must be perfect, as your heavenly Father is perfect" (Mt 5:48). Holiness entails purity. Therefore, Christian chastity is not only a consequence of the dignity of the human person, who is created in the image of God; it is also a requirement of the new dignity which Baptism confers: the body of a baptized person is a temple of the Holy Spirit (cf. 1 Cor 6:19–20). "If one has the spirit of God, chastity is not a troublesome and humiliating burden, but a joyful affirmation" (Bl. J. Escrivá, *Hom.,* 2, 177).

4:9–12 Alongside love, as one of the key points of Christian living, Paul stresses the need to work. Similar advice is often found in early Christian documents: "If somebody wishes to settle among you, let him find a job and work and so feed himself. If he has no job, provide for him as your own prudent judgement allows, so that there may be no idle Christian among you" (*Didache*, 12, 3–5). Love of God gives meaning to work: "An inner effort on the part of the human spirit, guided by faith, hope and charity, is needed in order that through these points the *work* of the individual human being may *be given the meaning which it has in the eyes of God*" (John Paul II, *Labor. exerc.*, 24).

c. Or *defraud his brother in business*

The second coming of the Lord
[13]But we would not have you ignorant, brethren, concerning those who are
asleep, that you may not grieve as others do who have no hope.* [14]For since
we believe that Jesus died and rose again, even so, through Jesus, God will
bring with him those who have fallen asleep. [15]For this we declare to you by
the word of the Lord, that we who are alive, who are left until the coming of
the Lord, shall not precede those who have fallen asleep. [16]For the Lord
himself will descend from heaven with a cry of command, with the archangel's
call, and with the sound of the trumpet of God. And the dead in Christ will rise
first; [17]then we who are alive, who are left, shall be caught up together with
them in the clouds to meet the Lord in the air; and so we shall always be with
the Lord.* [18]Therefore comfort one another with these words.
5 [1]But as to the times and the seasons, brethren, you have no need to have
anything written to you. [2]For you yourselves know well that the day of the
Lord will come like a thief in the night. [3]When people say, "There is peace and
security," then sudden destruction will come upon them as travail comes upon
a woman with child, and there will be no escape. [4]But you are not in darkness,
brethren, for that day to surprise you like a thief. [5]For you are all sons of light
and sons of the day; we are not of the night or of darkness. [6]So then let us not
sleep, as others do, but let us keep awake and be sober. [7]For those who sleep
sleep at night, and those who get drunk are drunk at night. [8]But, since we

---

4:13–5:11 The religious instruction of the Thessalonians had been cut short because the Apostle had to leave the city in a hurry. One of the questions remaining in their minds can be put as follows: Will the dead be under any disadvantage *vis-à-vis* those who are still alive at the Lord's second coming? In his reply Paul tells us two things: we will have no advantage over the dead (vv. 15–18); and, besides, we do not know when the Parousia will happen (vv. 1–2). The fact that he uses the second person plural ("we who are alive, who are left": v. 15) does not mean that the Parousia will happen soon or that Paul thinks he will live to see the day. Some people will misinterpret what he says (cf. 2 Thess 2:1–2), claiming that the Second Coming is imminent even though Paul says elsewhere that he does not know when it will be (1 Thess 5:2ff; cf. 2 Thess 22–12; etc.).

"The day of the Lord" (v. 2), a wording which occurs a number of times in Holy Scripture, means that moment at which God will intervene decisively and irreversibly. According to St Paul and other New Testament texts it is the Day of Judgment, when Christ will come in glory as Judge of all (cf. 1 Cor 1:8; 2 Cor 1:14); each person, however, will meet our Lord face to face after his death (cf. 2 Cor 5:6; Phil 1:23).

A Christian should therefore be watchful at all times, because he never really knows which day will be his last.

5:8 Is 59:17; Wis 5:18–19.

belong to the day, let us be sober, and put on the breastplate of faith and love,
and for a helmet the hope of salvation. 9For God has not destined us for wrath,
but to obtain salvation through our Lord Jesus Christ, 10who died for us so that
whether we wake or sleep we might live with him. 11Therefore encourage one
another and build one another up, just as you are doing.

Various counsels

12But we beseech you, brethren, to respect those who labour among you and
are over you in the Lord and admonish you, 13and to esteem them very highly
in love because of their work. Be at peace among yourselves.[c2] 14And we
exhort you, brethren, admonish the idlers, encourage the fainthearted, help the
weak, be patient with them all. 15See that none of you repays evil for evil, but
always seek to do good to one another and to all. 16Rejoice always, 17pray
constantly, 18give thanks in all circumstances; for this is the will of God in
Christ Jesus for you. 19Do not quench the Spirit, 20do not despise prophesying,
21but test everything; hold fast what is good, 22abstain from every form of evil.

Closing prayer and farewell

23May the God of peace himself sanctify you wholly; and may your spirit and
soul and body be kept sound and blameless at the coming of our Lord Jesus
Christ. 24He who calls you is faithful, and he will do it.

25Brethren, pray for us.

26Greet all the brethren with a holy kiss.

27I adjure you by the Lord that this letter be read to all the brethren.

28The grace of our Lord Jesus Christ be with you.

5:12–22 These counsels include one to respect and venerate those who form the hierarchy of the Church. "Those who command serve those they seem to command. They do not command because they desire power but because they are charged to minister to the needs of others. They come before others through love, not pride, in order to look after them" (St Augustine, *The City of God*, 19, 14). Constant prayer (v. 17) will help a person to strive to put St Paul's advice into practice. "The Apostle commands us to pray at all times. For the saints, sleep itself is prayer. Nevertheless, we should set out particular times of prayer so that if we become absorbed in our work the timetable [of our day] will remind us to fulfil our duty" (St Jerome, *Letters*, 22, 37).

5:23–28 The sanctification which God works in man affects his entire being. In the last analysis, Christian holiness is the fullness of the order established by God at the Creation and re-established after man's sin. Therefore, the Apostle invokes God as "the God of peace" (and peace is, according to its theological definition, "tranquillity in order"). Holiness gives all man's faculties, physical as well as spiritual, their perfection and wholeness, thereby rounding off and perfecting the natural order, without changing it.

c2. Or *with them*

2 Thessalonians

Greeting

1 [1]Paul, Silvanus, and Timothy,
To the church of the Thessalonians in God our Father and the Lord Jesus Christ:

[2]Grace to you and peace from God the Father and the Lord Jesus Christ.

1. HOPE IN A DIVINE REWARD

Thanksgiving

[3]We are bound to give thanks to God always for you, brethren, as is fitting,
because your faith is growing abundantly, and the love of every one of you for
one another is increasing. [4]Therefore we ourselves boast of you in the
churches of God for your steadfastness and faith in all your persecutions and
in the afflictions which you are enduring.

[5]This is evidence of the righteous judgment of God, that you may be made
worthy of the kingdom of God, for which you are suffering—

1:1–3:18 □□ This second letter to the faithful at Thessalonica is in many respects like the previous one. Apparently, some Christians there did not properly understand parts of the Apostle's preaching, and their faith was weakening due to the persecution they were experiencing. St Paul gives them instruction about the retribution God will deal out to each person eventually, and about the timing of the Lord's second coming (1:3–2:17); then he exhorts them to pray and work (3:1–15).

1:3–2:17 □ After greeting the community, he encourages the Thessalonians, contrasting their faith and the prize their steadfastness will win (1:5, 7, 10) with the punishment their persecutors will meet in due course (1:6, 8; 2:12).

1:3–5 The Apostle is pleased to see that the Thessalonians are being steadfast in the face of difficulty and he reminds them that suffering has a place in God's plans. "By bringing about salvation through his suffering, Christ has elevated human suffering to the level of redemption. Thus, all men can participate, through their suffering, in the redemptive suffering of Christ" (John Paul II, *Salvif. dolor.*, 19).

Divine retribution

[6]since indeed God deems it just to repay with affliction those who afflict you,
[7]and to grant rest with us to you who are afflicted, when the Lord Jesus is
revealed from heaven with his mighty angels in flaming fire, [8]inflicting
vengeance upon those who do not know God and upon those who do not obey
the gospel of our Lord Jesus. [9]They shall suffer the punishment of eternal
destruction and exclusion from the presence of the Lord and from the glory of
his might, [10]when he comes on that day to be glorified in his saints, and to be
marvelled at in all who have believed, because our testimony to you was
believed.

Prayer for perseverance

[11]To this end we always pray for you, that our God may make you worthy of
his call, and may fulfil every good resolve and work of faith by his power, [12]so
that the name of our Lord Jesus may be glorified in you, and you in him,
according to the grace of our God and the Lord Jesus Christ.

The coming of the Lord

2 [1]Now concerning the coming of our Lord Jesus Christ and our assembling
to meet him, we beg you, brethren, [2]not to be quickly shaken in mind or
excited, either by spirit or by word, or by letter purporting to be from us, to the
effect that the day of the Lord has come.* [3]Let no one deceive you in any way;
for that day will not come, unless the rebellion comes first, and the man of

---

1:6–10 The Lord is just and he will give each his just reward. The threat of punishment should not be the primary reason for staying true to God; however, if one does offend him, one should not forget that one is in danger of damnation. That fate contrasts with the glory of heaven that awaits the just. "In Heaven, a great Love awaits you, with no betrayals and no deceptions. The fullness of love, the fullness of beauty and greatness and knowledge … And it will never cloy: it will satiate, yet still you will want more" (Bl. J. Escrivá, *The Forge*, 995).

1:11–12 The Greek translated here as "according to the grace of our God and the Lord Jesus Christ" (v. 12) could also be translated as "according to the grace of our God and Lord Jesus Christ"—which would mean that what we have here is a profession of faith in Christ as God and Lord.

2:1–12 Against those who were misleading the Thessalonians by telling them that the Second Coming was imminent, St Paul uses Old Testament images and symbols to assert that two things must happen first—"rebellion" or apostasy, and the appearance on the scene of the "man of lawlessness" (v. 3). Our Lord himself predicted this rebellion (cf. Mk 13:22); he said that when it had run its course, the

1:8 Ex 3:2; Is 66:15; Jer 10:25; Ps 79:6.

lawlessness[a]* is revealed, the son of perdition, [4]who opposes and exalts
himself against every so-called god or object of worship, so that he takes his
seat in the temple of God, proclaiming himself to be God. [5]Do you not
remember that when I was still with you I told you this? [6]And you know what
is restraining him now so that he may be revealed in his time. [7]For the mystery
of lawlessness is already at work; only he who now restrains it will do so until
he is out of the way.* [8]And then the lawless one will be revealed, and the Lord
Jesus will slay him with the breath of his mouth and destroy him by his
appearing and his coming. [9]The coming of the lawless one by the activity of
Satan will be with all power and with pretended signs and wonders, [10]and with
all wicked deception for those who are to perish, because they refused to love
the truth and so be saved. [11]Therefore God sends upon them a strong delusion,
to make them believe what is false, [12]so that all may be condemned who did
not believe the truth but had pleasure in unrighteousness.

The need for steadfastness

[13]But we are bound to give thanks to God always for you, brethren beloved by
the Lord, because God chose you from the beginning[b] to be saved, through
sanctification by the Spirit[c] and belief in the truth. [14]To this he called you
through our gospel, so that you may obtain the glory of our Lord Jesus Christ.
[15]So then, brethren, stand firm and hold to the traditions which you were
taught by us, either by word of mouth or by letter.

[16]Now may our Lord Jesus Christ himself, and God our Father, who loved
us and gave us eternal comfort and good hope through grace, [17]comfort your
hearts and establish them in every good work and word.

End would come, and the last Judgment. We do not know what the Apostle means by the "man of lawlessness"—maybe all the forces of evil taken together as a tool at the service of Satan, although the description of this adversary of God is very like that of the "Antichrist" of St John (cf. 1 Jn 2:18–22; cf. *CCC*, 675). Anyway, everyone has to choose between "love of the truth" (cf. v. 10) offered by Christ, and the pretended signs and teachings of the evil one. "All men are bound to seek the truth, especially in what concerns God and his Church, and to embrace it. And hold on to it as they come to know it" (Vatican II, *DH,* 1).

2:13–17 To avoid being led astray by unsound teaching, one must hold fast to the faith one received and to apostolic Tradition. By means of Tradition "the Church, in her doctrine, life and worship, perpetuates and transmits to every generation all that she herself is, all that she believes" (Vatican II, *DV*, 8).

a. Other ancient authorities read *sin* **b.** Other ancient authorities read *as the first converts* **c.** Or *of spirit* **2:8** Is 11:4.

2. PRAYER, WORK, FRATERNITY

Paul asks for prayers

3 [1]Finally, brethren, pray for us, that the word of the Lord may speed on and
triumph, as it did among you, [2]and that we may be delivered from wicked
and evil men; for not all have faith. [3]But the Lord is faithful; he will strengthen
you and guard you from evil.[d] [4]And we have confidence in the Lord about you,
that you are doing and will do the things which we command. [5]May the Lord
direct your hearts to the love of God and to the steadfastness of Christ.

Avoiding idleness. Earning one's living

[6]Now we command you, brethren, in the name of our Lord Jesus Christ, that
you keep away from any brother who is living in idleness and not in accord
with the tradition that you received from us. [7]For you yourselves know how
you ought to imitate us; we were not idle when we were with you, [8]we did not
eat any one's bread without paying, but with toil and labour we worked night
and day, that we might not burden any of you. [9]It was not because we have not
that right, but to give you in our conduct an example to imitate. [10]For even
when we were with you, we gave you this command: If any one will not work,
let him not eat. [11]For we hear that some of you are living in idleness, mere
busybodies, not doing any work. [12]Now such persons we command and exhort
in the Lord Jesus Christ to do their work in quietness and to earn their own
living. [13]Brethren, do not be weary in well-doing.

3:1–18 □ From this point onwards the letter focuses on certain things to do with the Thessalonians' lifestyle, particularly their attitude to work.

3:1–5 Some people have been led astray; the Apostle appeals to the Thessalonians to trust in God (v. 3). God is always faithful, but he wants us to reciprocate in kind: "God created us without our cooperation, but he has willed to save us only with our cooperation" (St Augustine, *Serm.*, 169, 13).

3:6–15 Some of the Thessalonians, wrongly thinking that the Parousia was about to happen, had given up working. So the Apostle reminds them that when he was among them he worked hard to keep himself and was a burden to none. Christians are bound "to perform their temporal duties faithfully in the spirit of the Gospel." (Vatican II, *GS,* 43). A Christian should work hard, in order to give glory to God, look after the needs of his family and serve the community. "Everyone, in his job, in whatever place he has in society, must feel obliged to make his work God's work, sowing everywhere the peace and joy of the Lord" (Bl. J. Escrivá, *Hom.,* 2, 70).

d. Or *the evil one*

14If any one refuses to obey what we say in this letter, note that man, and
have nothing to do with him, that he may be ashamed. 15Do not look on him
as an enemy, but warn him as a brother.

Words of farewell

16Now may the Lord of peace himself give you peace at all times in all ways.
The Lord be with you all.

17I, Paul, write this greeting with my own hand. This is the mark in every
letter of mine; it is the way I write. 18The grace of our Lord Jesus Christ be
with you all.

3:16–18 The words of farewell, in St Paul's own handwriting, have become a liturgical greeting in the Church.

The Letters to Timothy and Titus

The two Letters to Timothy and the Letter to Titus are given the common title of "Pastoral Letters", a name which was coined in the nineteenth century and has to do with the content and addressees of the letters.

Timothy and Titus were two fellow workers of the Apostle who were in charge of the local communities of Ephesus and Crete respectively. The letters are all about pastoral matters, giving rules and advice on the government of those communities, under threat at the time from false teachers. There are also guidelines about how the churches should be organized and about the role of ministers. The tone of all three letters is simple and familial, betokening the author's desire to train these men for their pastoral work.

Timothy accompanied St Paul like "a son with a father" (Phil 2:22). He was the son of a Gentile father and a Jewish mother who was a pious Christian (Acts 16:1). During his second missionary journey, on his way through Lystra, Paul received excellent reports about this young Christian man. After having him circumcised, he took him along as his co-worker in the foundation of the churches of Philippi and Thessalonica (Acts 16:12). We know that he was at Beroea with Paul (Acts 17:14) and that the Apostle sent him from Athens to Thessalonica (1 Thess 3:2). He appears again in Corinth alongside Paul (Acts 18:5) and was with him on his third journey at Ephesus (Acts 19:22), Macedonia (1 Cor 4:17; 2 Cor 1:1) and Asia Minor (Acts 20:4). During the Apostle's first imprisonment he was with him in prison (Phil 1:1; 2:19; Col 1:1); later, the Letter to the Hebrews speaks about Timothy's having been "released", though no information is given as to the circumstances of his imprisonment (Heb 13:23). Finally, on his last journey in the East, Paul charged him with the government of the church of Ephesus. Timothy's faithfulness to St Paul is something which really stands out; he must have been still very young when the Apostle was asking the Christians of Corinth to treat him with respect (1 Cor 16:11) and he could not have been much older when he was given charge of the church at Ephesus (1 Tim 4:12; 2 Tim 2:22).

From what the First Letter says, Timothy is in charge of a fairly well established Christian community, even though it is still experiencing natural growing-pains. The pagan environment, the doctrines of false teachers and easy-going moral standards threaten the stability of that infant church. Like Titus in Crete, Timothy is given the job of ensuring that the people hold on to the sound teaching they have received, and of helping the Christians to live good lives.

The tone of the Second Letter is more intimate and full of feeling, containing as it does very personal references. Paul exhorts Timothy time and again to persevere in preaching and in his work of ministry, careless of external difficulties or inner fatigue. He also gives him the job of consolidating the administration system of the local church.

The content of the Letter to Titus is very like that of the First Letter to Timothy, maybe because both were written around the same time. Titus was the son of pagan parents; he must have been a convert of St Paul, to judge from the affection the saint shows him (Tit 1:4). He accompanied Paul and Barnabas to the council of Jerusalem, even though he had not been circumcised (Gal 2:1–5). The Acts of the Apostles does not mention Titus, but we do know that, towards the end of the third missionary journey, he was sent to Corinth on two delicate missions—the first time, to bring some letter (2 Cor 2:13; 7:14), and then to organize a collection and deliver the Second Letter to the Corinthians (2 Cor 8:6, 16:23; 12:18). There is no evidence that he was with the Apostle during his first Roman captivity, but we do know that, some time after that, St Paul left Titus on Crete until Artemas and Tychicus relieved him (Tit 3:12). Like Timothy in the First Letter, Titus is charged with organizing the community on Crete, and defending it against false doctrines that some people were beginning to spread.

The central idea in the Pastoral Letters—and the one which crops up most often—is that of salvation. God is referred to as "the Saviour" (1 Tim 1:1; 2:3; 4:10; Tit 1:3; 2:10; 3:4), who with infinite love "desires all men to be saved and to come to the knowledge of the truth" (1 Tim 2:4). This divine plan has been revealed and put into effect by Jesus Christ, the only Mediator (1 Tim 2:5), who "came into the world to save sinners" (1 Tim 1:15; cf. 2:5–6). The Church extends and makes present the saving action of Christ, being the people redeemed from iniquity and purified by his sacrifice (cf. Tit 2:14). Christians attain their salvation by a life rich in good deeds (cf. Tit 3:4), which are an expression of their devotion to God. These, then, are the three basic ideas in the Pastoral Letters—Jesus Christ, the Church (depicted as a solid structure, having deacons, priests and bishops), and the practice of the Christian life.

These letters are somewhat different from the other Pauline letters: the vocabulary and style are different; the content is more moral or practical in emphasis, as against the predominantly theological pitch of other epistles; the hierarchical organization of the Church and the sort of false doctrines mentioned seem to apply to a later period in the Apostle's life; moreover, it is not easy to work out at what stage in Paul's life these letters were written. This has led some scholars to query whether the letters were in fact written by Paul. However, independently of whether they were written by a secretary or a more or less close disciple of St Paul, they do reflect the Apostle's mind and authority, and the Church holds them to be inspired and canonical.

1 Timothy

Greeting

1 [1]Paul, an apostle of Christ Jesus by command of God our Saviour and of Christ Jesus our hope,
[2]To Timothy, my true child in the faith:*
Grace, mercy, and peace from God the Father and Christ Jesus our Lord.

1. SOUND DOCTRINE

False teachers to be admonished

[3]As I urged you when I was going to Macedonia, remain at Ephesus that you
may charge certain persons not to teach any different doctrine, [4]nor to occupy
themselves with myths and endless genealogies* which promote speculations
rather than the divine training[a] that is in faith; [5]whereas the aim of our charge
is love that issues from a pure heart and a good conscience and sincere faith.
[6]Certain persons by swerving from these have wandered away into vain
discussion, [7]desiring to be teachers of the law, without understanding either
what they are saying or the things about which they make assertions.

1:1–6:21 □□ In this letter to his disciple Timothy, who he had left in charge of the church of Ephesus, St Paul seeks to help him to perform his ministry well. To this end, he urges him to defend sound doctrine (1:3–20) and instructs him as regards community prayer (2:1–15), the qualities ministers ought to have (3:1–16), how a minister should perform his teaching role, and how he and certain other Christians should conduct themselves (4:1–6:19).

1:3–20 □ After the greeting, instead of the act of thanksgiving to God found in almost all his letters (cf. 2 Tim 1:3), the Apostle moves on immediately to remind Timothy about the job he has been entrusted with (vv. 3–7) and he cites his own example as a guideline (vv. 8–17).

1:3–7 The false teachers mentioned here seem to have been converts from Judaism who were still very fixed in their old ideas and keen on legends about the patriarchs and other biblical heroes found in extrabiblical Jewish writings. The whole point about making sure that teaching is sound, is to help people grow in love (cf. v. 5). "Faith teaches the truth, and a pure faith gives rise to charity" (St John Chrysostom, *Hom. on 1 Tim,* 2, 1).

a. Or *stewardship*, or *order*

The purpose of the Law

8Now we know that the law is good, if any one uses it lawfully, 9understanding
this, that the law is not laid down for the just but for the lawless and
disobedient, for the ungodly and sinners, for the unholy and profane, for
murderers of fathers and murderers of mothers, for manslayers, 10immoral
persons, sodomites, kidnapers, liars, perjurers, and whatever else is contrary to
sound doctrine, 11in accordance with the glorious gospel of the blessed God
with which I have been entrusted.

Paul recalls his own conversion

12I thank him who has given me strength for this, Christ Jesus our Lord,
because he judged me faithful by appointing me to his service, 13though I
formerly blasphemed and persecuted and insulted him; but I received mercy
because I had acted ignorantly in unbelief, 14and the grace of our Lord
overflowed for me with the faith and love that are in Christ Jesus. 15The saying
is sure and worthy of full acceptance, that Christ Jesus came into the world to
save sinners. And I am the foremost of sinners; 16but I received mercy for this
reason, that in me, as the foremost, Jesus Christ might display his perfect
patience for an example to those who were to believe in him for eternal life.
17To the King of ages, immortal, invisible, the only God, be honour and glory
for ever and ever.[b] Amen.

Timothy's responsibilities

18This charge I commit to you, Timothy, my son, in accordance with the
prophetic utterances which pointed to you, that inspired by them you may

---

1:8–11 The Law of Moses is good as far as it goes; it tells one what is sinful but does not provide the wherewithal to conquer sin. The passage says that "the law is not laid down for the just" (v. 9), because the just man, like Abraham, for example, did not need the Law in order to please God. Abraham was motivated by a desire to be faithful to God.

1:12–17 The initiative lies with God when it comes to calling people to the priestly ministry; Paul knows this from his own experience, and he gives thanks to God. Verse 15 contains a succinct definition of Christ's work of redemption. It begins with a form of words (literally, "Word of honour which you can totally rely on") which serve to focus our intention on a statement of some importance. This truth, basic to our faith, is included in the Creed: "For us and for our salvation he came down from heaven."

1:18–20 In the New Testament "prophecy" does not normally have to do with the prediction of a future event. In this passage "prophetic utterances" (v. 18) may

b. Greek *to the ages of ages*

wage the good warfare, [19]holding faith and a good conscience. By rejecting conscience, certain persons have made shipwreck of their faith, [20]among them Hymenaeus and Alexander, whom I have delivered to Satan* that they may learn not to blaspheme.

2. REGULATIONS ABOUT PRAYER

God desires the salvation of all

2 [1]First of all, then, I urge that supplications, prayers, intercessions, and thanksgivings be made for all men, [2]for kings and all who are in high positions, that we may lead a quiet and peaceable life, godly and respectful in every way. [3]This is good, and it is acceptable in the sight of God our Saviour, [4]who desires all men to be saved and to come to the knowledge of the truth. [5]For there is one God, and there is one mediator between God and men, the man Christ Jesus, [6]who gave himself as a ransom for all,* the testimony to which was borne at the proper time. [7]For this I was appointed a preacher and apostle (I am telling the truth, I am not lying), a teacher of the Gentiles in faith and truth.

---

refer to the mission entrusted to Timothy when hands were laid on him (cf. 4:14; 2 Tim 1:6) and the words of exhortation the Apostle used when he instructed Timothy.

"Delivering to Satan" (cf. v. 20) means excommunicating them from the Church, a pastoral, medicinal recourse designed to protect the faithful and to reform the heretics themselves.

2:1–15 □ Here the Apostle discusses how worship should be organized, particularly as regards prayer and the various roles in liturgical assemblies.

2:1–7 St Paul orders that prayers be said for all, not just for friends and benefactors and not just for Christians. The Church helps people do as Paul suggests by providing the Prayers of the Faithful at Mass where "the people, exercising their priestly function, intercede for all humanity" (*Roman Missal*, General Introduction, 45). God's desire that all should be saved is a subject that appears so often in the Pastoral Letters that God is often given the title of "Saviour". "Knowledge of the truth" (v. 4) is knowledge of Christ, (cf. Jn 14:6; 1 Jn 5:20) and the Gospel message. But it is not just an intellectual grasp of truth; it is something that needs to have an impact on one's life.

Verses 5–6 are a confession of faith, a summary of the basic content of the Gospel message, the truths a person needs to know in order to be saved: Jesus Christ is the perfect and only mediator between God and mankind, because being true God and true man he has offered a sacrifice of infinite value (his life) to reconcile men to God.

Men at prayer, women at prayer

[8]I desire then that in every place the men should pray, lifting holy hands without anger or quarrelling; [9]also that women should adorn themselves modestly and sensibly in seemly apparel, not with braided hair or gold or pearls or costly attire [10]but by good deeds, as befits women who profess religion. [11]Let a woman learn in silence with all submissiveness. [12]I permit no woman to teach or to have authority over men; she is to keep silent. [13]For Adam was formed first, then Eve; [14]and Adam was not deceived, but the woman was deceived and became a transgressor. [15]Yet woman will be saved through bearing children,[c] if she continues[d] in faith and love and holiness, with modesty.

3. CHURCH OFFICE

Qualifications for bishops

3 [1]The saying is sure: If any one aspires to the office of bishop,* he desires a noble task. [2]Now a bishop must be above reproach, the husband of one wife, temperate, sensible, dignified, hospitable, an apt teacher, [3]no drunkard, not violent but gentle, not quarrelsome, and no lover of money. [4]He must manage his own household well, keeping his children submissive and respectful in every way; [5]for if a man does not know how to manage his own household, how can he care for God's church? [6]He must not be a recent convert, or he may be puffed up with conceit and fall into the condemnation of the devil;[f] [7]moreover he must be well thought of by outsiders, or he may fall into reproach and the snare of the devil.[f]

2:8–15 The essential equality of man and woman (which St Paul proclaims: cf. Gal 3:28) does not mean that they have the same roles within the Church. The Apostle refers to the divine plan of Creation and the biblical account of original sin using the forms of thinking prevalent in the Jewish world of the time.

3:1–16 □ The Apostle focuses on the qualities a church minister needs to have. This concerns not only the good of the faithful but also the image the Church projects to outsiders.

3:1–7 When the Pastoral Letters were being written, the titles and responsibilities attaching to the various church offices had not yet become fixed; whereas in the writings of St Ignatius of Antioch (second century) they are plain to see. The "bishops" referred to here were people who headed up particular communities. As ministers of the Church, their mission was to teach, preside and lead an exemplary life.

c. Or *by the birth of the child* **d.** Greek *they continue* **f.** Or *slander*

Qualifications for deacons

[8]Deacons likewise must be serious, not double-tongued, not addicted to much
wine, not greedy for gain; [9]they must hold the mystery of the faith with a clear
conscience. [10]And let them also be tested first; then if they prove themselves
blameless let them serve as deacons. [11]The women* likewise must be serious,
no slanderers, but temperate, faithful in all things. [12]Let deacons be the
husband of one wife, and let them manage their children and their households
well; [13]for those who serve well as deacons gain a good standing for
themselves and also great confidence in the faith which is in Christ Jesus.

The Church is God's household

[14]I hope to come to you soon, but I am writing these instructions to you so that,
[15]if I am delayed, you may know how one ought to behave in the household of
God, which is the church of the living God, the pillar and bulwark of the truth.

The mystery of our religion

[16] Great indeed, we confess, is the mystery of our religion:
He[h] was manifested in the flesh,
vindicated[i] in the Spirit,
seen by angels,
preached among the nations,
believed on in the world,
taken up in glory.

3:8–13 "Deacons" were ministers who performed their functions under those who presided. The origin of the diaconate probably goes back to the "seven men of good repute" who were elected to help the apostles (cf. Acts 6:1–6).

3:14–15 God acts in and through the Church the way a good father does within the family. The Church is not a purely human society where ministers can exercise their functions as they think fit; it is a household which belongs to God.

3:16 "The mystery of our religion" is spelt out in the form of a hymn, a sort of canticle in honour of Christ; it is the opposite of the "mystery of lawlessness" (2 Thess 2:7). This text may even have been a sort of counter to the idolatrous chants of pagan Ephesus: "Great is Artemis of the Ephesians" (Acts 19:28): St Paul begins: "Great is the mystery of our religion." This mystery brings about the reconciliation/union of men with God in Christ: he took our flesh without ceasing to be God; the nations of the earth will acknowledge him as the angels in heaven do; he dwells in the hearts of men through faith, but his abode is in heaven, at the Father's side.

h. Greek *Who*; other ancient authorities read *God*; others, *Which* **i.** Or *justified*

4. PASTORAL DIRECTIVES

What to do about false teachers

4 [1]Now the Spirit expressly says that in later times some will depart from the faith by giving heed to deceitful spirits and doctrines of demons, [2]through the pretensions of liars whose consciences are seared, [3]who forbid marriage* and enjoin abstinence from foods* which God created to be received with thanksgiving by those who believe and know the truth. [4]For everything created by God is good, and nothing is to be rejected if it is received with thanksgiving; [5]for then it is consecrated by the word of God and prayer.

[6]If you put these instructions before the brethren, you will be a good minister of Christ Jesus, nourished on the words of the faith and of the good doctrine which you have followed. [7]Have nothing to do with godless and silly myths. Train yourself in godliness; [8]or while bodily training is of some value, godliness is of value in every way, as it holds promise for the present life and also for the life to come. [9]The saying is sure and worthy of full acceptance. [10]For to this end we toil and strive,[j] because we have our hope set on the living God, who is the Saviour of all men, especially of those who believe.

[11]Command and teach these things.

Pastoral advice to Timothy

[12]Let no one despise your youth, but set the believers an example in speech and conduct, in love, in faith, in purity. [13]Till I come, attend to the public reading of scripture, to preaching, to teaching. [14]Do not neglect the gift you

---

4:1–6:21 □ The Apostle now turns to specific situations occurring in the life of the Ephesus community—false teachers, older people, widows, elders, slaves, the well-to-do . . . Pastoral care should extend to all aspects of church life.

4:1–11 Paul's advice to Timothy is that the practice of godliness is the way to hold on to sound teaching: "Interior life is strengthened by a daily struggle in your practices of piety, which you should fulfil—or rather which you should *live*—lovingly, for the path we travel as children of God is a path of Love" (Bl. J. Escrivá, *The Forge*, 83).

4:12–16 "Reading, preaching and teaching" (cf. v. 13): all three were features of the liturgical assembly in early Christian times. Priestly ordination was conferred by liturgical prayer (prophetic utterance) and the laying on of hands. The Apostle's pastoral advice also shows the importance of preaching through good example: "We speak through them [our good works], when we show them to others in our life. When our deeds speak, the language is alive" (St Anthony of Padua, *Serm.,* in *Divine Office*, 13 June).

j. Other ancient authorities read *suffer reproach*

have, which was given you by prophetic utterance when the council of elders laid their hands upon you. [15]Practise these duties, devote yourself to them, so that all may see your progress. [16]Take heed to yourself and to your teaching; hold to that, for by so doing you will save both yourself and your hearers.

The pastor and the faithful in general

5 [1]Do not rebuke an older man but exhort him as you would a father; treat younger men like brothers, [2]older women like mothers, younger women like sisters, in all purity.

Widows, their role and lifestyle

[3]Honour widows who are real widows.* [4]If a widow has children or grandchildren, let them first learn their religious duty to their own family and make some return to their parents; for this is acceptable in the sight of God. [5]She who is a real widow, and is left all alone, has set her hope on God and continues in supplications and prayers night and day; [6]whereas she who is self-indulgent is dead even while she lives. [7]Command this, so that they may be without reproach. [8]If any one does not provide for his relatives, and especially for his own family, he has disowned the faith and is worse than an unbeliever.

[9]Let a widow be enrolled if she is not less than sixty years of age, having been the wife of one husband; [10]and she must be well attested for her good deeds, as one who has brought up children, shown hospitality, washed the feet of the saints, relieved the afflicted, and devoted herself to doing good in every way. [11]But refuse to enrol younger widows; for when they grow wanton against Christ they desire to marry, [12]and so they incur condemnation for having violated their first pledge.* [13]Besides that, they learn to be idlers, gadding about from house to house, and not only idlers but gossips and busybodies, saying what they should not. [14]So I would have younger widows marry, bear children, rule their households, and give the enemy no occasion to revile us. [15]For some have already strayed after Satan. [16]If any believing

---

5:1–2 The Apostle now begins to list for Timothy some practical rules for the governance of the Christian community. Although they refer to particular circumstances, they have universal validity.

5:3–16 This passage contains specific rules for the organized groups of widows which were a type of institution in the early Church. Widows did charitable work and looked after the needy (cf. Acts 9:36–39). Some unhappy experiences (v. 15) may lie behind the Apostle's directive that young widows without children or special family commitments should marry again, to avoid the dangers of an idle life.

The reference in v. 11 to "growing wanton" may have to do with sexual desires but it could be a reference to short-lived youthful enthusiasm.

woman[1] has relatives who are widows, let her assist them; let the church not be burdened, so that it may assist those who are real widows.

Criteria for choosing elders

17Let the elders who rule well be considered worthy of double honour,
especially those who labour in preaching and teaching; 18for the scripture says,
"You shall not muzzle an ox when it is treading out the grain," and, "The
labourer deserves his wages." 19Never admit any charge against an elder except
on the evidence of two or three witnesses. 20As for those who persist in sin,
rebuke them in the presence of all, so that the rest may stand in fear. 21In the
presence of God and of Christ Jesus and of the elect angels I charge you to
keep these rules without favour, doing nothing from partiality. 22Do not be
hasty in the laying on of hands, nor participate in another man's sins; keep
yourself pure.

23No longer drink only water, but use a little wine for the sake of your stomach and your frequent ailments.

24The sins of some men are conspicuous, pointing to judgment, but the sins
of others appear later. 25So also good deeds are conspicuous; and even when
they are not, they cannot remain hidden.

Slaves and their moral obligations

6 1Let all who are under the yoke of slavery regard their masters as worthy of
all honour, so that the name of God and the teaching may not be defamed.
2Those who have believing masters must not be disrespectful on the ground
that they are brethren; rather they must serve all the better since those who
benefit by their service are believers and beloved.

Teach and urge these duties.

5:17–25 These words show that it would be a serious thing to lay hands on someone without proper screening. The Church has always tried to ensure that only suitable people and well-trained people receive ordination. "God never abandons his Church, leaving the faithful without a sufficient number of suitable ministers to meet their needs, if worthy [candidates] are encouraged and the unworthy rejected" (St Thomas Aquinas, *Summa theol., sup.*, 36, 4, 1).

In v. 18 St Paul quotes Deuteronomy 25:4 and then a saying of Jesus', recorded in Luke 10:7. It may well be that Paul is acknowledging the Gospel of St Luke as "Scripture". However, the quotation may come from some text earlier than the Gospel of Luke.

6:1–2 The Apostle is not tackling the social problem of slavery in a direct way (cf. Col 3:22–4:1). He provides two criteria on how slaves should conduct themselves—

l. Other ancient authorities read *man or woman*; others, simply *man* **5:18** Deut 25:4; Num 18:31; 2 Chron 15:7. **5:19** Deut 19:15.

False teachers described

3If any one teaches otherwise and does not agree with the sound words of our Lord Jesus Christ and the teaching which accords with godliness, 4he is puffed up with conceit, he knows nothing; he has a morbid craving for controversy and for disputes about words, which produce envy, dissension, slander, base suspicions, 5and wrangling among men who are depraved in mind and bereft of the truth, imagining that godliness is a means of gain. 6There is great gain in godliness with contentment; 7for we brought nothing into the world, and[m] we cannot take anything out of the world; 8but if we have food and clothing, with these we shall be content. 9But those who desire to be rich fall into temptation, into a snare, into many senseless and hurtful desires that plunge men into ruin and destruction. 10For the love of money is the root of all evils; it is through this craving that some have wandered away from the faith and pierced their hearts with many pangs.

An appeal to defend the faith

11But as for you, man of God, shun all this; aim at righteousness, godliness, faith, love, steadfastness, gentleness. 12Fight the good fight of the faith; take hold of the eternal life to which you were called when you made the good confession in the presence of many witnesses. 13In the presence of God who gives life to all things, and of Christ Jesus who in his testimony before Pontius Pilate made the good confession, 14I charge you to keep the commandment unstained and free from reproach until the appearing of our Lord Jesus Christ; 15and this will be made manifest at the proper time by the blessed and only Sovereign, the King of kings and Lord of lords, 16who alone has immortality

---

good example and fraternity. Gradually, a Christian spirit began to have such an influence on society that it helped to bring about the abolition of slavery because "the ferment of the Gospel has aroused and continues to arouse in the hearts of men an unquenchable thirst for human dignity" (Vatican II, *GS*, 26).

6:3–10 What he has to say about unmasking false teachers shows he is writing from long experience. These men are greedy (v. 10), whereas good teachers are content with basic provisions and shelter. Detachment has always been a requirement for apostolic success. "Our Lord, in loving the poor, loves those who love them. [...] So we too hope that, in trying to love the poor, we will come to be loved by God" (St Vincent de Paul, *Epist.*, in *Divine Office,* 27 September).

6:11–16 Paul stresses the duty to be loyal and to do one's duty as laid down; he calls God the Father and Jesus as witnesses—Jesus, who himself bore witness to his kingship before Pontius Pilate.

m. Other ancient authorities insert *it is certain that*

and dwells in unapproachable light, whom no man has ever seen or can see. To
him be honour and eternal dominion. Amen.

The right way to use wealth
17As for the rich in this world, charge them not to be haughty, nor to set their
hopes on uncertain riches but on God who richly furnishes us with everything
to enjoy. 18They are to do good, to be rich in good deeds, liberal and generous,
19thus laying up for themselves a good foundation for the future, so that they
may take hold of the life which is life indeed.

Words of farewell
20O Timothy, guard what has been entrusted to you. Avoid the godless chatter
and contradictions of what is falsely called knowledge, 21for by professing it
some have missed the mark as regards the faith.

Grace be with you.

The doxology or hymn of praise (vv. 15–16) may have come from the liturgy. Like the other hymn found in this letter (1:17 and 3:16) it shows how aware the early Christians were that man's true purpose in life is to give glory to God.

6:17–19 Material things are meant to be used with a sense of social responsibility, with detachment, because true wealth is that which never perishes (cf. Lk 12:33). "It is necessary to state once more the characteristic principle of Christian social doctrine: the goods of this world are *originally meant for all*. The right to private property is *valid and necessary*, but it does not nullify the value of this principle" (John Paul II, *Sollic. rei soc.*, 42).

6:20–21 These verses summarize the Letter. "What has been entrusted" is sometimes translated as "deposit" ("*depositum*" in Latin). A *depositum* was something (usually money) entrusted to someone to keep and protect it until the depositer claimed it back. St Paul applies the idea to Revelation and the faith, and it has passed on into theological tradition. "Preserve the gift of the Catholic faith inviolate and without stain. By your strength, what you have believed remains yours and is passed on to others" (St Vincent Lerins, *Common.*, 22).

2 Timothy

Greeting
1 [1]Paul, an apostle of Christ Jesus by the will of God according to the
promise of the life which is in Christ Jesus,
[2]To Timothy, my beloved child:
Grace, mercy, and peace from God the Father and Christ Jesus our Lord.

[3]I thank God whom I serve with a clear conscience, as did my fathers, when
I remember you constantly in my prayers. [4]As I remember your tears, I long
night and day to see you, that I may be filled with joy.

1. PREACHING THE GOSPEL MESSAGE

Response to grace
[5]I am reminded of your sincere faith, a faith that dwelt first in your grand-
mother Lois and your mother Eunice and now, I am sure, dwells in you.
[6]Hence I remind you to rekindle the gift of God that is within you through the
laying on of my hands; [7]for God did not give us a spirit of timidity but a spirit
of power and love and self-control.

1:1–4:22 □ □ This is very like the previous letter, focusing as it does on the Gospel which warrants putting up with any type of trial (1:6–2:13); it is a teaching that must be held on to, defended and spread (2:14–4:8). Throughout the letter the Apostle gives bits of news about himself and he finishes with some words of advice (4:9–22).

1:1–5 These lines show the Apostle's deep affection for his disciple. They are in a way reminiscent of the elders' farewell to Paul at Miletus (cf. Acts 20:27). The mention of Timothy's mother and grandmother also conveys the intimate tone of the letter and the appreciation that is due to those who passed the faith on to us. "For Christians a special gratitude is due to those from whom they have received the gift of faith, the grace of Baptism and life in the Church. These may include parents, grandparents, other members of the family, pastors, catechists, and other teachers or friends. 'I am reminded of your sincere faith, a faith that dwelt first in your grandmother Lois and your mother Eunice and now, I am sure, dwells in you'" (*CCC*, 2220).

1:6–2:13 □ The first section of the letter has to do with hardships suffered by St Paul, but these are seen from Jesus Christ's point of view and meant to be an encouragement to Timothy.

St Paul, herald of the Gospel

8Do not be ashamed then of testifying to our Lord, nor of me his prisoner, but share in suffering for the gospel in the power of God, 9who saved us and called us with a holy calling, not in virtue of our works but in virtue of his own purpose and the grace which he gave us in Christ Jesus ages ago, 10and now has manifested through the appearing of our Saviour Christ Jesus, who abolished death and brought life and immortality to light through the gospel. 11For this gospel I was appointed a preacher and apostle and teacher, 12and therefore I suffer as I do. But I am not ashamed, for I know whom I have believed, and I am sure that he is able to guard until that Day what has been entrusted to me.[a] 13Follow the pattern of the sound words which you have heard from me, in the faith and love which are in Christ Jesus; 14guard the truth that has been entrusted to you by the Holy Spirit who dwells within us.

Attitudes towards certain disciples

15You are aware that all who are in Asia* turned away from me, and among them Phygelus and Hermogenes. 16May the Lord grant mercy to the household of Onesiphorus, for he often refreshed me; he was not ashamed of my chains, 17but when he arrived in Rome he searched for me eagerly and found me—18may the Lord grant him to find mercy from the Lord on that Day—and you well know all the service he rendered at Ephesus.

Bearing one's share of suffering

2 1You then, my son, be strong in the grace that is in Christ Jesus, 2and what you have heard from me before many witnesses entrust to faithful men who

---

1:6–7 The rite of laying on hands, already mentioned by Paul (cf. 1 Tim 4:14), passed on the gift of apostolic ministry; it has become the sign used in the sacrament of Order.

1:8–14 The Holy Spirit has been present in the Church since the day of Pentecost, all the time acting in her to sanctify the faithful and to ensure that her pastors (particularly the successors of Peter) "will guard in a holy way the revelation, that is, the deposit of the faith, given them by the apostles, and pass it on faithfully to others" (Vatican I, *Pastor Aeternus*).

1:15–18 We do not know anything about these disciples who deserted St Paul but they were probably well known in Ephesus. Onesiphorus' faithfulness, on the other hand, must have been a consolation to the pastors of the Church.

2:1–7 Faithfulness has always been seen as a virtue essential for those who are assigned to be on guard, on watch. Hence its relevance for bishops (*episkopos*, in

a. Or *what I have entrusted to him*

will be able to teach others also. 3Share in suffering as a good soldier of Christ
Jesus. 4No soldier on service gets entangled in civilian pursuits, since his aim
is to satisfy the one who enlisted him. 5An athlete is not crowned unless he
competes according to the rules. 6It is the hard-working farmer who ought to
have the first share of the crops. 7Think over what I say, for the Lord will grant
you understanding in everything.

Jesus, the Apostle's model

8Remember Jesus Christ, risen from the dead, descended from David, as
preached in my gospel, 9the gospel for which I am suffering and wearing
fetters like a criminal. But the word of God is not fettered. 10Therefore I
endure everything for the sake of the elect, that they also may obtain salvation
in Christ Jesus with its eternal glory.

11 The saying is sure:
If we have died with him, we shall also live with him;
12 if we endure, we shall also reign with him;
if we deny him, he also will deny us;
13 if we are faithless, he remains faithful—
for he cannot deny himself.

2. DEFENDING THE GOSPEL

Avoiding useless arguments

14Remind them of this, and charge them before the Lord[b] to avoid disputing
about words, which does no good, but only ruins the hearers. 15Do your best
to present yourself to God as one approved, a workman who has no need to be
ashamed, rightly handling the word of truth. 16Avoid such godless chatter, for

---

Greek, means "watchman"). The soldier, the athlete and the farmer are three examples of people who work diligently and conscientiously.

2:8–13 The trials which St Paul was experiencing in prison on account of preaching the Gospel constitute an entitlement to heaven, for martyrdom makes a disciple like his master. Salvation is attained through the merits of Christ. The hymn in vv. 11–13 is a call to be faithful in adverse circumstances even if that means martyrdom. It shows the closeness there is between the baptized person and Christ who died and rose from the dead; it sings the praises of Christian perseverance grounded on enduring loyalty to the Lord.

2:14–4:8 □ Useless argument and disorderly conduct undermine sound teaching. The second section of the letter warns about these dangers.

b. Other ancient authorities read *God*

it will lead people into more and more ungodliness, [17]and their talk will eat its
way like gangrene. Among them are Hymenaeus and Philetus,* [18]who have
swerved from the truth by holding that the resurrection is past already.* They
are upsetting the faith of some. [19]But God's firm foundation stands, bearing
this seal: "The Lord knows those who are his," and, "Let every one who names
the name of the Lord depart from iniquity."

[20]In a great house there are not only vessels of gold and silver but also of
wood and earthenware, and some for noble use, some for ignoble. [21]If any one
purifies himself from what is ignoble, then he will be a vessel for noble use,
consecrated and useful to the master of the house, ready for any good work.

Patience towards those in error

[22]So shun youthful passions and aim at righteousness, faith, love, and peace,
along with those who call upon the Lord from a pure heart. [23]Have nothing to
do with stupid, senseless controversies; you know that they breed quarrels.
[24]And the Lord's servant must not be quarrelsome but kindly to every one, an
apt teacher, forbearing, [25]correcting his opponents with gentleness. God may
perhaps grant that they will repent and come to know the truth, [26]and they may
escape from the snare of the devil, after being captured by him to do his will.[c]

2:14–21 In contrast to errors and misconceptions, the emphasis here is on the solidarity of the Church. The metaphor of building is used. It was customary to attach a "foundation document" to the first stone; in the case of a temple or some religious building, the foundation document would indicate the building's origin and purpose. St Paul develops his building simile by envisaging two inscriptions on the foundation stone. The first, taken from Numbers 16:5, reminds Timothy that God does the choosing and he takes care of his own; the second, from Isaiah 26:13, affirms the need for holiness. "You are holy, O Church, my mother, because the Son of God, who is holy, founded you. You are holy because the Father, source of all holiness, so ordained it. You are holy, because the Holy Spirit, who dwells in the souls of the faithful, assists you" (Bl. J. Escrivá, homily, 4 June 1972, in *In Love with the Church*). On the other hand, just as different kinds of containers can be found in a house, no one should be scandalized to find sinners in the Church, or people whose behaviour leaves much to be desired; rather, one should pray for them.

2:22–26 This is an appeal for patience and serenity; when faced with error, one should try to get the other person to repent and mend his ways—try to avoid causing a break-up and the consequent danger of people being lost to the Church.

c. Or *by him, to do his* (that is, God's) *will* **2:19** Num 16:5; Is 26:13.

Preventing error from doing harm

3 1But understand this, that in the last days there will come times of stress.
2For men will be lovers of self, lovers of money, proud, arrogant, abusive,
disobedient to their parents, ungrateful, unholy, 3inhuman, implacable,
slanderers, profligates, fierce, haters of good, 4treacherous, reckless, swollen
with conceit, lovers of pleasure rather than lovers of God, 5holding the form of
religion but denying the power of it. Avoid such people. 6For among them are
those who make their way into households and capture weak women, bur-
dened with sins and swayed by various impulses, 7who will listen to anybody
and can never arrive at a knowledge of the truth. 8As Jannes and Jambres
opposed Moses, so these men also oppose the truth, men of corrupt mind and
counterfeit faith; 9but they will not get very far, for their folly will be plain to
all, as was that of those two men.

10Now you have observed my teaching, my conduct, my aim in life, my
faith, my patience, my love, my steadfastness, 11my persecutions, my suffer-
ings, what befell me at Antioch, at Iconium, and at Lystra, what persecutions
I endured; yet from them all the Lord rescued me. 12Indeed all who desire to
live a godly life in Christ Jesus will be persecuted, 13while evil men and
impostors will go on from bad to worse, deceivers and deceived.

Staying true to Holy Scripture

14But as for you, continue in what you have learned and have firmly believed,
knowing from whom you learned it 15and how from childhood you have been

---

3:1–13 The "last days" (v. 3) have begun already with the incarnation of Christ. Among the men burdened with sin (v. 2–5), those who do most harm are people who spread ideas which go against the faith and undermine good morals. Jannes and Jambres (v. 8) were, so Jewish tradition had it, the names of the Egyptian magicians summoned by Pharaoh to perform miracles in answer to the prodigies worked by Moses and Aaron in his presence (cf. Ex 7:11).

Paul's little autobiographical references (vv. 10–13), which Timothy would have been familiar with (Timothy came from Lystra), are designed to encourage the latter. "A true athlete wins despite the blows he suffers. Bear all things [adversity] for God, so that he, too, will bear us up" (St Ignatius of Antioch, *Letter to Polycarp*, 3, 1).

3:14–17 Paul is explicitly stating that all the books of the Bible are inspired by God. That is why they enjoy special authority in the Church: "the divinely revealed realities, which are contained and presented in the Holy Scriptures, have been written down under the inspiration of the Holy Spirit [...]. All that the inspired authors, or sacred writers, affirm should be regarded as affirmed by the Holy Spirit; we must acknowledge that the books of Scripture, firmly, faithfully and without error, teach that truth which God, for the sake of our salvation, wished to see confided to the Holy

acquainted with the sacred writings which are able to instruct you for salvation
through faith in Christ Jesus. 16All scripture is inspired by God and[d] profitable
for teaching, for reproof, for correction, and for training in righteousness,*
17that the man of God may be complete, equipped for every good work.

Dedication to preaching

4 1I charge you in the presence of God and of Christ Jesus who is to judge
the living and the dead, and by his appearing and his kingdom: 2preach the
word, be urgent in season and out of season, convince, rebuke, and exhort, be
unfailing in patience and in teaching. 3For the time is coming when people will
not endure sound teaching, but having itching ears they will accumulate for
themselves teachers to suit their own likings, 4and will turn away from
listening to the truth and wander into myths. 5As for you, always be steady,
endure suffering, do the work of an evangelist, fulfil your ministry.

The crown of righteousness

6For I am already on the point of being sacrificed;* the time of my departure
has come. 7I have fought the good fight, I have finished the race, I have kept
the faith. 8Henceforth there is laid up for me the crown of righteousness, which
the Lord, the righteous judge, will award to me on that Day, and not only to me
but also to all who have loved his appearing.

3. FINAL ADVICE

News and messages

9Do your best to come to me soon. 10For Demas, in love with this present
world, has deserted me and gone to Thessalonica; Crescens has gone to

---

Scriptures" (Vatican II, *DV*, 11). The Church and the saints encourage us to read the Scriptures: "Read the divine Scriptures very often, or, to say it better, never let the holy Scriptures fall from your hands" (St Jerome, *Letters*, 52, 7).

4:1–5 The solemnity of this exhortation is signalled by an opening form of words similar to that found in Greco-Roman wills, which laid on the heirs an obligation to carry out the testator's wishes: "I charge you most solemnly" or "I implore you."

4:6–8 Conscious that he will soon die, St Paul depicts death as an offering to God, like the libations of oil poured out on an altar of sacrifice. A Christian's life is a type of spiritual sport, a competition that God is watching, and one that He will judge.

4:9–22 □ The final section is very moving. It mainly consists of pieces of news. We can see here St Paul's state of mind when he is on the brink of martyrdom. The

d. Or *Every scripture inspired by God is also*

Galatia,[e] Titus to Dalmatia. [11]Luke alone is with me. Get Mark and bring him
with you; for he is very useful in serving me. [12]Tychicus I have sent to
Ephesus. [13]When you come, bring the cloak that I left with Carpus at Troas,
also the books, and above all the parchments. [14]Alexander the coppersmith did
me great harm; the Lord will requite him for his deeds. [15]Beware of him
yourself, for he strongly opposed our message. [16]At my first defence no one
took my part; all deserted me. May it not be charged against them! [17]But the
Lord stood by me and gave me strength to proclaim the message fully, that all
the Gentiles might hear it. So I was rescued from the lion's mouth. [18]The Lord
will rescue me from every evil and save me for his heavenly kingdom. To him
be the glory for ever and ever. Amen.

Greetings and final good wishes

[19]Greet Prisca and Aquila, and the household of Onesiphorus. [20]Erastus
remained at Corinth; Trophimus I left ill at Miletus. [21]Do your best to come
before winter. Eubulus sends greetings to you, as do Pudens and Linus* and
Claudia and all the brethren.

[22]The Lord be with your spirit. Grace be with you.

---

fact that he mentions so many disciples by name shows the Apostle's great-heartedness: he tried his best with each; some of them failed to persevere, but most did prove true. The book of the Acts and other letters tell us a bit more about some of these people; for others, this mention in 2 Timothy is all we know about them. Certainly they must all have been very much in the heart of St Paul, who became "all things to all men, that I might by all means save some" (1 Cor 9:22).

e. Other ancient authorities read *Gaul*

Titus

Greeting

1 [1]Paul, a servant[a] of God and an apostle of Jesus Christ, to further the faith
of God's elect and their knowledge of the truth which accords with
godliness, [2]in hope of eternal life which God, who never lies, promised ages
ago [3]and at the proper time manifested in his word through the preaching with
which I have been entrusted by command of God our Saviour;
[4]To Titus, my true child in a common faith:
Grace and peace from God the Father and Christ Jesus our Saviour.

1. TITUS' MISSION IN CRETE

Qualifications for elders

[5]This is why I left you in Crete, that you might amend what was defective, and
appoint elders* in every town as I directed you, [6]if any man is blameless, the
husband of one wife, and his children are believers and not open to the charge
of being profligate or insubordinate. [7]For a bishop, as God's steward, must be
blameless; he must not be arrogant or quick-tempered or a drunkard or violent
or greedy for gain, [8]but hospitable, a lover of goodness, master of himself,
upright, holy, and self-controlled; [9]he must hold firm to the sure word as

---

1:1–3:15 □□ In content and purpose this letter is very similar to the letters to Timothy. The Apostle wants to help his co-workers in administration of churches. This letter also contains instructions about how community should be structured (1:5–16) and about the duties of Christians, depending on their various circumstances (2:1–3:11).

1:1–4 The heading is particularly long and formal. It gives special emphasis to Paul's title (apostle) and the importance that preaching has.

1:5–16 □ Paul entrusts Titus with the task of organizing the Christian community of Crete in a hierarchical way and protecting it from false teachings that some people are beginning to spread.

1:5–9 As in 1 Timothy 3:2–7, Paul wants a minister to be a model of holiness for his flock, a man of irreproachable conduct, whose family life too is exemplary; a

a. Or *slave*

taught, so that he may be able to give instruction in sound doctrine and also to confute those who contradict it.

Attitudes towards false teachers

10For there are many insubordinate men, empty talkers and deceivers, especially
the circumcision party; 11they must be silenced, since they are upsetting whole
families by teaching for base gain what they have no right to teach. 12One of
themselves, a prophet of their own, said, "Cretans are always liars, evil beasts,
lazy gluttons." 13This testimony is true. Therefore rebuke them sharply, that
they may be sound in the faith, 14instead of giving heed to Jewish myths or to
commands of men who reject the truth. 15To the pure all things are pure, but to
the corrupt and unbelieving nothing is pure; their very minds and consciences
are corrupted. 16They profess to know God, but they deny him by their deeds;
they are detestable, disobedient, unfit for any good deed.

2. MORAL DEMANDS OF THE CHRISTIAN FAITH

Duties of Christians in different situations

2 1But as for you, teach what befits sound doctrine. 2Bid the older men be
temperate, serious, sensible, sound in faith, in love, and in steadfastness.
3Bid the older women likewise to be reverent in behaviour, not to be slanderers

---

man who is an upright and welcoming person, and someone who has a good understanding of the Gospel. The Church has always tried to have people of this calibre as ministers. Pastors "should abound in every spiritual good and bear a living witness of God to all" (Vatican II, *LG*, 41).

1:10–16 In Crete (as in Ephesus: cf. 1 Tim 1:6) some philosophers, a number of them of Jewish background, were having some success with their sophistry and fallacious arguments. Paul here has recourse to irony, quoting a verse from an early poet (perhaps Epimenides, sixth century BC); Cretans seemingly had a reputation for telling lies.

Purity of heart (cf. Mt 23:25–26) is the basis of Christian freedom, contrasting sharply with the hypocrisy of trying to combine Christian faith and reprehensible moral conduct.

2:1–3:11 □ Particular demands are made on each member of the community depending on his or her circumstances; but all should be devout and should help one another.

2:1–10 A key feature of Christian morality is that it can never be reduced to an abstract ethical code with no theological basis; rather, it flows directly from the or slaves to drink; they are to teach what is good, [4]and so train the young women to love their husbands and children, [5]to be sensible, chaste, domestic, kind, and submissive to their husbands, that the word of God may not be discredited. [6]Likewise urge the younger men to control themselves. [7]Show yourself in all respects a model of good deeds, and in your teaching show integrity, gravity, [8]and sound speech that cannot be censured, so that an opponent may be put to shame, having nothing evil to say of us. [9]Bid slaves to be submissive to their masters and to give satisfaction in every respect; they are not to be refractory, [10]nor to pilfer, but to show entire and true fidelity, so that in everything they may adorn the doctrine of God our Saviour.

The Incarnation, the basis of Christian ethics and piety

[11]For the grace of God has appeared for the salvation of all men, [12]training us to renounce irreligion and worldly passions, and to live sober, upright, and godly lives in this world, [13]awaiting our blessed hope, the appearing of the glory of our great God and Saviour[c] *Jesus Christ, [14]who gave himself for us to redeem us from all iniquity and to purify for himself a people of his own who are zealous for good deeds.

[15]Declare these things; exhort and reprove with all authority. Let no one disregard you.

Respect for lawful authority

3 [1]Remind them to be submissive to rulers and authorities, to be obedient, to be ready for any honest work, [2]to speak evil of no one, to avoid quarrelling, to be gentle, and to show perfect courtesy toward all men.

---

deep truth that one professes. "There is a connexion between purity of heart, of body and of faith: the faithful must believe the articles of the Creed 'so that by believing they may obey God, by obeying may live well, by living well may purify their hearts and with pure hearts may understand what they believe' (St Augustine, *De fide et symbolo*, 10,25)" (*CCC*, 2518).

2:11–15 The duties just outlined all point to a Christian lifestyle (v. 12) based on hope (v. 13). It is Christ who by his work of redemption won for us the grace to live and to hope in this way. We receive this grace from the Eucharist, which nourishes our soul and we celebrate "the Eucharist 'awaiting the blessed hope and the coming of our Saviour, Jesus Christ' (*Roman Missal*, embolism after the Our Father; cf. Tit 2:13), asking 'to share in your glory when every tear will be wiped away. On that day we shall see you, our God, as you are. We shall become like you and praise you for ever through Christ our Lord' (*Roman Missal*, EP3)" (*CCC*, 1404).

3:1–2 The freedom of the children of God which Christ has won for us does not mean that we may oppose lawful civil authority. And whenever a situation arises

c. Or *of the great God and our Saviour*

Renewal of the Christian life in the Holy Spirit
3For we ourselves were once foolish, disobedient, led astray, slaves to various
passions and pleasures, passing our days in malice and envy, hated by men and
hating one another; 4but when the goodness and loving kindness of God our
Saviour appeared, 5he saved us, not because of deeds done by us in right-
eousness, but in virtue of his own mercy, by the washing of regeneration and
renewal in the Holy Spirit, 6which he poured out upon us richly through Jesus
Christ our Saviour, 7so that we might be justified by his grace and become
heirs in hope of eternal life.* 8The saying is sure.

I desire you to insist on these things, so that those who have believed in God may be careful to apply themselves to good deeds;[d] these are excellent and profitable to men.

Further advice
9But avoid stupid controversies, genealogies, dissensions, and quarrels over the
law, for they are unprofitable and futile. 10As for a man who is factious, after
admonishing him once or twice, have nothing more to do with him, 11knowing
that such a person is perverted and sinful; he is self-condemned.

---

where Christians are obliged to oppose civil authority they must do so in a positive sense.

3:3–8 The theological basis of the social obligations just mentioned is the main point in this chapter. Each Christian should bear witness to salvation history, to the change-over from sin to grace, and the transition from an era of slavery and error to one of freedom and rebirth ushered in by Christ. In vv. 4–7 we have a poem in praise of Jesus Christ which sums up the Incarnation, the Redemption and the application of salvation to the individual Christian.

3:9–11 The "schismatic" (v. 10), literally a "heretic", refers to those false teachers who opposed the doctrine of Titus. In due course the meaning of certain terms would become better defined. "Heresy is the obstinate denial or doubt, after Baptism, of a truth which must be believed by divine and Catholic faith. Apostasy is the total repudiation of the Christian faith. Schism is the withdrawal of submission to the (Pope) or from communion with the members of the Church subject to him" (*Code of Canon Law*, 751).

d. Or *enter honourable occupations*

3. CONCLUSION

Final messages

[12]When I send Artemas or Tychicus to you, do your best to come to me at Nicopolis, for I have decided to spend the winter there. [13]Do your best to speed Zenas the lawyer and Apollos on their way; see that they lack nothing. [14]And let our people learn to apply themselves to good deeds,[d] so as to help cases of urgent need, and not to be unfruitful.

Words of farewell

[15]All who are with me send greetings to you. Greet those who love us in the faith.

Grace be with you all.

3:12–14 Tychicus accompanied St Paul on his third missionary journey (cf. Acts 20:4) and delivered the letters to the Ephesians and the Colossians. Apollos, too, is mentioned in Acts as a cultured and eloquent man (18:24–26); in addition to his evangelizing work in Ephesus, he contributed a lot to the church at Corinth (cf. 1 Cor 1:12; 3:4–6, 22; 4:6; 16:12).

3:12–15 □ The final instructions in the letter show the importance that the early Christians gave to hospitality.

The Letter to Philemon

Philemon was a well-to-do citizen of Colossae whom St Paul had converted to the Christian faith, and his house was the place where the local Christians used to assemble. Paul was very grateful for these facilities; he calls him his "fellow worker" (cf. v. 1) and shows him great affection and trust (cf. vv. 8, 17, 19, 21). Onesimus, one of Philemon's slaves, had escaped from his house, maybe after stealing some money or valuables (cf. v. 18). Fearing punishment, Onesimus does not want to go back to his master; he takes flight and makes contact with Paul, who at this time is in prison. Paul's kindness and zeal soon make Onesimus aware of the Gospel and he embraces the Christian faith.

Paul feels that the best thing for Onesimus to do is to go back to his master: both of them are now brothers in the Lord. Tychicus is about to go to Colossae with the Apostle's Letter to the Colossians and it is arranged that Onesimus will go with him (cf. Col 4:7–5). So, both these letters, Colossians and Philemon, would have been written at the same time during one of Paul's periods in captivity (at Rome, Ephesus or Caesarea, perhaps).

This very short letter is a masterpiece of its type; it exudes sensitivity and refined charity. The Apostle does not write in an authoritative tone (though he was entitled to do so); he makes a humble appeal to Philemon, on the grounds of his (Paul's) being an "old man" and "a prisoner for Christ Jesus" (v. 9).

Although this is first and foremost a family letter, it also contains important, albeit concise, teaching. The letter has been called the "magna charta" of Christian freedom (cf. the note on vv. 8–12). The Apostle does not directly confront the subject of slavery, which was a feature of the social structure of the time, but he provides the Christian principles which in due course will lead to the abolition of slavery, once Christian teaching manages to influence the civil laws of nations. These principles are based on the freedom which Christ won for us on the cross, making us truly children of God and brothers or sisters to one another.

Philemon

Greeting

1 1Paul, a prisoner for Christ Jesus, and Timothy our brother,
To Philemon our beloved fellow worker 2and Apphia our sister and Archippus
our fellow soldier, and the church in your house:
3Grace to you and peace from God our Father and the Lord Jesus Christ.

Thanksgiving

4I thank my God always when I remember you in my prayers, 5because I hear
of your love and of the faith which you have toward the Lord Jesus and all the
saints, 6and I pray that the sharing of your faith may promote the knowledge
of all the good that is ours in Christ. 7For I have derived much joy and comfort
from your love, my brother, because the hearts of the saints have been
refreshed through you.

A plea on behalf of Onesimus

8Accordingly, though I am bold enough in Christ to command you to do what
is required, 9yet for love's sake I prefer to appeal to you—I, Paul, an ambas-
sador[a] and now a prisoner also for Christ Jesus—10I appeal to you for my child,
Onesimus, whose father I have become in my imprisonment. 11(Formerly he was
useless to you, but now he is indeed useful[b] to you and to me.) 12I am sending

---

1–25 □ □ The brevity of this letter helps to show the format St Paul used for his letters—greetings; an act of thanksgiving to God, or a prayer; the message or content; and the words of farewell. This particular letter is useful for evaluating in a Christian way the social milieux in which Christians live.

1–3 Apphia and Archippus may have been members of Philemon's family, possibly his wife and son. Archippus had an important position in the church of Colossae (cf. Col 4:17).

4–7 Paul is saying that a Christian must not only love Christ and believe in him; he must also, through and in Christ, love and trust other Christians. By sharing the same faith, Christians attain communion with Christ and with other believers.

8–21 St Paul begot Onesimus in the faith, this fugitive slave of Philemon's. The Apostle is playing on the meaning of the word "onesimus" (= useful), to intercede on the man's behalf with his old master and to ask Philemon to take him back again. Events are now being viewed from a new standpoint, in the light of divine Providence: God knows how to draw good from evil (cf. Rom 8:28).

a. Or *an old man* **b.** The name Onesimus meant *useful* or (compare verse 20) *beneficial*

him back to you, sending my very heart.
13 I would have been glad to keep him with me, in order that he might serve me on your behalf during my imprisonment for the gospel;
14 but I preferred to do nothing without your consent in order that your goodness might not be by compulsion but of your own free will.
15 Perhaps this is why he was parted from you for a while, that you might have him back for ever,
16 no longer as a slave but more than a slave, as a beloved brother, especially to me but how much more to you, both in the flesh and in the Lord.
17 So if you consider me your partner, receive him as you would receive me.
18 If he has wronged you at all, or owes you anything, charge that to my account.
19 I, Paul, write this with my own hand, I will repay it—to say nothing of your owing me even your own self.
20 Yes, brother, I want some benefit from you in the Lord. Refresh my heart in Christ.
21 Confident of your obedience, I write to you, knowing that you will do even more than I say.

Words of farewell

22 At the same time, prepare a guest room for me, for I am hoping through your prayers to be granted to you.
23 Epaphras, my fellow prisoner in Christ Jesus, sends greetings to you,
24 and so do Mark, Aristarchus, Demas, and Luke, my fellow workers.
25 The grace of the Lord Jesus Christ be with your spirit.

The Apostle does not deal directly with the subject of slavery, which was something that was part of the social structure of the period; however, he does provide the Christian principles which would help to bring about its abolition in those places where Christian teaching came to imbue civil law. These principles are grounded on the freedom which Christ won for us on the cross making us truly children of God and brothers and sisters of those who share our faith. "The liberation brought about by Christ […] ought, of necessity, to have effects in the social sphere" (SCDF, *Libert. nunt.*, 4, 13). This is the "more" (v. 21) that Paul expects of Philemon: he should treat Onesimus as a true brother in the faith, on a level of equality, not discriminating against him on grounds of class or status. "Be convinced that justice alone is never enough to solve the great problems of mankind. When justice alone is done, don't be surprised if people get hurt. The dignity of man, who is a son of God, requires much more. Charity must penetrate and accompany justice because it sweetens and deifies everything: 'God is love' (1 Jn 4:16). Our motive in everything we do should be the love of God, which makes it easier for us to love our neighbour and which purifies and raises all earthly loves on to a higher level" (Bl. J. Escrivá, *Hom.,* 2, 172).

22–25 This passage carries greetings from those who were with St Paul at this time (they are mentioned in Colossians 4:10–14), and the usual final words of blessing.

The Letter to the Hebrews

From the point of view of its content, the Letter to the Hebrews is one of the most formal and important writings in the New Testament. Even though its present title dates probably from the second century, it very exactly describes what the book is about. It is very probable that the "Hebrews" to whom the letter is addressed were, firstly, Christians of Jewish background who were familiar with both the Greek language and Hebrew culture, and familiar, too, with the rites of Mosaic religion. The Letter to the Hebrews is of a kind intermediary between that of a letter and that of a written discourse or sermon (cf. 13:32: "word of exhortation"). And its structure and style of exposition is reminiscent of a short theological essay.

From an historical and doctrinal point of view, the letter links up content-wise with the corpus of Pauline writings. We find here a faithful echo of St Paul's preaching. However, the letter has literary features of its own which show it to be very original. From around the end of the fourth century onwards it came to be universally attributed to St Paul; but prior to then, although it was generally accepted as being Pauline by churches in the East, the same unanimity did not obtain in the West. This was due to the obvious difference in style, syntax and language as compared with the rest of St Paul's letters: Hebrews is written in excellent, polished Greek, unlike the spontaneous, vigorous Greek of St Paul. The author must have been an educated Christian of Jewish background, a person very familiar with Holy Scripture and with the theological issues being debated at the time the letter was written; and he must have been someone very close to St Paul in thinking and pastoral work. The content of the letter shows its author to be a man of Hellenist culture and great pastoral zeal and someone steeped in the religious life of the Jewish people and temple worship. The year 65 has been suggested as a possible date of composition, but it is not impossible that it was written later in the century. Given the reference in 13:24, "Those who come from Italy send you greetings", which can be read as "Those of Italy ...", Rome has been suggested as a possible place of composition. But it may well be that the greeting comes from a group of Christians who originated in Italy but were now based somewhere else (we do not know where) and that the letter was written in that place.

The main aim of the letter is to show the superiority of Christianity over the Old Covenant; however, neither the style nor the purpose of the writer is a polemical one. The text argues that the New Law perfects, fulfils and surpasses the Old Law. Central to it is the fact that it sees Christ's priesthood and sacrifice as being superior to that of the Levites. This is the doctrinal basis of the letter's exhortation to perseverance in the faith: that exhortation (which is inseparable from the letter's primary aim) is the other reason why it was written.

Hebrews

The greatness of the incarnate Son of God

1 [1]In many and various ways God spoke of old to our fathers by the prophets;
[2]but in these last days he has spoken to us by a Son, whom he appointed the
heir of all things, through whom also he created the world. [3]He reflects the
glory of God and bears the very stamp of his nature, upholding the universe by
his word of power. When he had made purification for sins, he sat down at the
right hand of the Majesty on high, [4]having become as much superior to angels
as the name he has obtained is more excellent than theirs.*

PART ONE: EXCELLENCE OF THE RELIGION REVEALED BY CHRIST

1. CHRIST IS GREATER THAN THE ANGELS

Proof from Holy Scripture

[5] For to what angel did God ever say,
"Thou art my Son,
today I have begotten thee"?
Or again,
"I will be to him a father,
and he shall be to me a son"?

1:1–4 The entire letter explores, from different angles, the subject announced in the prologue—the sublimity of Christ, the natural and eternal Son of God, universal Mediator, eternal Priest. He is the fullness of salvific revelation. "Christ, the Son of God made man, is the Father's one, perfect and unsurpassable Word. In him he has said everything; there will be no other word than this one" (*CCC*, 65). And St John of the Cross comments: "The Apostle gives us to understand that God has rendered himself dumb because he has nothing left to say: what he said before in part, through the prophets, he has now said completely through him [Christ]." (*Ascent of Mount Carmel*, 2, 22, 4). The epistle is an appeal to Christians to base their entire life on that faith.

1:5–10:18 □□ Although doctrinal and moral teachings are interwoven throughout this text, the first ten chapters are mainly doctrinal in character: the sacred writer

1:5 Ps 2:7; 2 Sam 7:14.

6And again, when he brings the first-born into the world, he says,
"Let all God's angels worship him."
7Of the angels he says,
"Who makes his angels winds,
and his servants flames of fire."
8But of the Son he says,
"Thy throne, O God,[a] is for ever and ever,
the righteous sceptre is the sceptre of thy[b] kingdom.
9Thou hast loved righteousness and hated lawlessness;
therefore God, thy God, has anointed thee
with the oil of gladness beyond thy comrades."
10And,
"Thou, Lord, didst found the earth in the beginning,
and the heavens are the work of thy hands;
11 they will perish, but thou remainest;
12 they will all grow old like a garment,
like a mantle thou wilt roll them up,
and they will be changed.[c]
But thou art the same,
and thy years will never end."
13 But to what angel has he ever said,

---

deals with Christ's superiority over the main figures in the Old Testament—angels (1:5–2:18), Moses (3:1–4:13), levitical priests (4:14–7:28)—and the form of worship that applied under the Old Law (8:1–10:18).

1:5–2:18 □ The case opens by explaining that Christ is greater than the angels. Because veneration of angels was widespread in the Jewish world, there was a danger that, on account of his human nature, Christ would be regarded as being on a level lower than that of these created beings.

1:5–14 The letter links a series of quotations from the Old Testament to show that Jesus Christ is the Messiah King and Son of God by nature, not by adoption (v. 5); the angels should worship him because their nature is lower than his (vv. 6–7): he has the prerogatives of the Messiah King, the Anointed One (vv. 8–9), and it was he who made the world (vv. 10–12). The role of the angels, on the other hand, is to serve God and worship him. "We say that they [the angels] rise up to bring the prayers of men to the purest places of the world, the heavens. [...] And from there they descend, carrying the benefits that God has given them for each man as he deserves. [...] And so we call them angels or messengers, because of their role" (Origen, *Against Celsus*, 5, 4).

a. Or *God is thy throne* **b.** Other ancient authorities read *his* **c.** Other ancient authorities add *like a garment* **1:6** Deut 32:43 Gk; Ps 97:7. **1:7** Ps 104:4. **1:8–9** Ps 45:6–7. **1:10–12** Ps 102:25–27. **1:13** Ps 110:1.

"Sit at my right hand,
till I make thy enemies
a stool for thy feet"?
14 Are they not all ministering spirits sent forth to serve, for the sake of those
who are to obtain salvation?

An appeal for faith

2 1 Therefore we must pay the closer attention to what we have heard, lest we
drift away from it. 2 For if the message declared by angels* was valid and
every transgression or disobedience received a just retribution, 3 how shall we
escape if we neglect such a great salvation? It was declared at first by the Lord,
and it was attested to us by those who heard him, 4 while God also bore witness
by signs and wonders and various miracles and by gifts of the Holy Spirit
distributed according to his own will.

Jesus, man's brother, was crowned with glory and honour above the angels

5 For it was not to angels that God subjected the world to come, of which we
are speaking. 6 It has been testified somewhere,
"What is man that thou art mindful of him,
or the son of man, that thou carest for him?
7 Thou didst make him for a little while lower than the angels,
thou hast crowned him with glory and honour,[d]
8 putting everything in subjection under his feet."
Now in putting everything in subjection to him, he left nothing outside his
control. As it is, we do not yet see everything in subjection to him. 9 But we see
Jesus, who for a little while was made lower than the angels, crowned with
glory and honour because of the suffering of death, so that by the grace of God
he might taste death for every one.

2:1–4 Here the writer inserts an appeal based on the teaching just given. If Jesus is above the angels, more obedience is due to his teaching than to "the message declared by angels" (v. 2), that is, the Law given to Moses on Sinai and which, according to a Jewish tradition, was given by angels (cf. Gal 3:19).

2:5–18 Christians ought to be faithful to Christ, because he, as well as being the cause and starting point of salvation, has been made the Master of all creation. To him as man all things have been subjected. In this sense the words of Psalm 8 apply to Christ, for he is the perfection of mankind, the perfect man, who through his obedience and humility, and his passion and death, merited to be crowned with glory and honour (cf. Phil 2:6–11; 1 Pet 2:21–25). Thus, through his sufferings, Christ is Lord, and everything, even death itself (cf. 1 Cor 15:22–28) has been made subject to him. His enemies have been made his footstool (cf. Ps 8:6; 110:1; Mt 22:24) and he will lead everything to the Father, and God will be all in everything.

d. Other ancient authorities insert *and didst set him over the works of thy hands* **2:6–9** Ps 8:4–6.

10 For it was fitting that he, for whom and by whom all things exist, in
bringing many sons to glory, should make the pioneer of their salvation perfect
through suffering.* 11 For he who sanctifies and those who are sanctified have
all one origin. That is why he is not ashamed to call them brethren, 12 saying,

> "I will proclaim thy name to my brethren,
> in the midst of the congregation I will praise thee."

13 And again,

> "I will put my trust in him."

And again,

> "Here am I, and the children God has given me."

14 Since therefore the children share in flesh and blood, he himself likewise
partook of the same nature, that through death he might destroy him who has
the power of death, that is, the devil, 15 and deliver all those who through fear
of death were subject to lifelong bondage. 16 For surely it is not with angels that
he is concerned but with the descendants of Abraham. 17 Therefore he had to
be made like his brethren in every respect, so that he might become a merciful
and faithful high priest in the service of God, to make expiation for the sins of
the people. 18 For because he himself has suffered and been tempted, he is able
to help those who are tempted.

2. CHRIST IS GREATER THAN MOSES

Moses' ministry and that of Christ compared

3 1 Therefore, holy brethren, who share in a heavenly call, consider Jesus, the
apostle and high priest of our confession. 2 He was faithful to him who
appointed him, just as Moses also was faithful in[e] God's house. 3 Yet Jesus has

---

In order to bring about men's salvation, Jesus needed to have a human nature, like them. God the Father "made his Son perfect" (cf. v. 10) in the sense that, by becoming man and therefore being able to suffer and die, he was fully equipped to be mankind's representative. Being God and Man, he is the only mediator between God and men; he exercises this mediation as high priest (cf. v. 17) and through love is able to bridge the unbridgeable abyss that separates the sinful stock of Adam from God.

Christ's priesthood consists in making atonement by a sacrifice of expiation and a peace-offering for the sins of men. In this way he makes satisfaction to God for us.

3:1–4:13 □ The Jews regarded Moses as the true founder, liberator and lawgiver of the chosen people. These two chapters teach that Jesus Christ, the "new Moses", is greater than Moses (cf. the notes on Mt 2:13–18; 4:1–11; 5:17–48; etc.).

3:1–6 The titles of "apostle" and "high priest" (v. 1) apply here to the Son's mission in the world: Jesus is God's messenger or envoy to man, and man's representative before God.

e. Other ancient authorities insert *all* **2:12** Ps 22:22. **2:13** Is 8:17–18; 2 Sam 23:3; Is 8:18. **2:16** Is 41:8–9.

been counted worthy of as much more glory than Moses as the builder of a house has more honour than the house. 4(For every house is built by some one, but the builder of all things is God.) 5Now Moses was faithful in all God's house as a servant, to testify to the things that were to be spoken later, 6but Christ was faithful over God's[f] house as a son. And we are his house if we hold fast our confidence and pride in our hope.[g]

The need for faith. The bad example given by the chosen people

7Therefore, as the Holy Spirit says,

"Today, when you hear his voice,
8do not harden your hearts as in the rebellion,
on the day of testing in the wilderness,
9where your fathers put me to the test
and saw my works for forty years.
10Therefore I was provoked with that generation,
and said, 'They always go astray in their hearts;
they have not known my ways.'
11As I swore in my wrath,
'They shall never enter my rest.'"*

12Take care, brethren, lest there be in any of you an evil, unbelieving heart,
leading you to fall away from the living God. 13But exhort one another every
day, as long as it is called "today," that none of you may be hardened by the
deceitfulness of sin. 14For we share in Christ, if only we hold our first
confidence firm to the end, 15while it is said,

"Today, when you hear his voice,
do not harden your hearts as in the rebellion."

The writer starts out from the faithfulness of Moses and, pre-eminently, of Jesus; he shows the superiority of the latter by using the simile of a house (sometimes in the sense of building, sometimes in that of family); the architect is greater than the house; the son is greater than the steward.

3:7–19 Because God rested when he finished his work of creation (cf. Gen 2:2), rest was prescribed in the Old Testament as a kind of imitation of what God did (cf. Ex 20:10–11). Similarly, the Exodus was seen as a kind of new creation, and it too was followed by a type of rest, that is, entry into the promised land. The author of the letter gives the Exodus a Christian interpretation: it is the Redemption whereby Christ, a new Moses, leads us to eternal rest.

The word of the Holy Spirit is enduring; it continues to apply "today" (v. 13). Therefore, the writer takes his cue from Psalm 95—which contains a reference to a rebellion by the Israelites, when they complained, in the wilderness, to God about the lack of water (cf. Ex. 17:1–7)—and appeals to his readers to imitate

f. Greek *his* **g.** Other ancient authorities insert *firm to the end* **3:5** Num 12:7. **3:15** Ps 95:7–11.

16Who were they that heard and yet were rebellious? Was it not all those who
left Egypt under the leadership of Moses? 17And with whom was he provoked
forty years? Was it not with those who sinned, whose bodies fell in the
wilderness? 18And to whom did he swear that they should never enter his rest,
but to those who were disobedient? 19So we see that they were unable to enter
because of unbelief.

Through faith we can attain God's 'rest'

4 1Therefore, while the promise of entering his rest remains, let us fear lest
any of you be judged to have failed to reach it. 2For good news came to us
just as to them; but the message which they heard did not benefit them,
because it did not meet with faith in the hearers.[h] 3For we who have believed
enter that rest, as he has said,

"As I swore in my wrath,
'They shall never enter my rest,' "

although his works were finished from the foundation of the world. 4For he has
somewhere spoken of the seventh day in this way, "And God rested on the
seventh day from all his works." 5And again in this place he said,

"They shall never enter my rest."

---

those who remained loyal and believed the promise that they would reach the Lord's "rest". God punished the Israelites for not believing in him and in Moses, and for all their complaints and disobedience: this fact should encourage the Christian to be steadfast at all times. "Conduct yourself well 'now' without looking back on 'yesterday' which is really gone, and without worrying about 'tomorrow', which for you may never come" (Bl. J. Escrivá, *The Way*, 253).

4:1–11 This chapter is a further appeal for fidelity and it develops the theme of that "rest" which the people of Israel failed to attain; not even when they gained entry to the promised land. The celebration promised in Psalm 95 (written after the Jews reached the promised land) still applies; the "day" is still here. The letter now extends the Moses/Jesus comparison to Israelites/Christians.

Moses appealed to the chosen people to stay faithful and thereby reach the place of rest (cf. Deut 12:9–10). He established the precept of sabbath rest (cf. Deut 5;12–15; Ex 20:8–11; 35:1–3; Num 15:32–36) to remind the Jews about God's rest after creating the world; it was to be a sign of the Covenant and a symbol of eternal rest. Christ promises in his Gospel a new and enduring rest—life in the Father's house (cf. Jn 14:1–3). Christians have been invited by God to enter eternal rest (v. 2): a new 'today' has begun, another opportunity to choose the path of fidelity and obtain entry into the true Promised Land.

h. Other manuscripts read *they were not united in faith with the hearers* **3:17** Num 14:29. **3:18** Num 14:22–23. **4:3** Ps 95–11. **4:4** Gen 2:2. **4:5** Ps 95:11.

6Since therefore it remains for some to enter it, and those who formerly
received the good news failed to enter because of disobedience, 7again he sets
a certain day, "Today," saying through David so long afterward, in the words
already quoted,

"Today, when you hear his voice,
do not harden your hearts."

8For if Joshua had given them rest, God[i] would not speak later of another day.
9So then, there remains a sabbath rest for the people of God; 10for whoever
enters God's rest also ceases from his labours as God did from his.

11Let us therefore strive to enter that rest, that no one fall by the same sort
of disobedience.

The power of God's word

12For the word of God is living and active, sharper than any two-edged sword,
piercing to the division of soul and spirit, of joints and marrow, and discerning the
thoughts and intentions of the heart. 13And before him no creature is hidden, but
all are open and laid bare to the eyes of him with whom we have to do.

3. CHRIST, OUR HIGH PRIEST, IS GREATER THAN THE PRIESTS OF THE MOSAIC LAW

Our confidence is based on Christ's priesthood

14Since then we have a great high priest who has passed through the heavens,
Jesus, the Son of God, let us hold fast our confession. 15For we have not a high
priest who is unable to sympathize with our weaknesses, but one who in every

---

4:12–13 To enter this rest, one needs to accept the Word of God. In these verses, the "word" may mean Revelation as a whole, which finds its fullest and most perfect form in Christ himself. "Such is the force and power of the Word of God that it can serve the Church as her support and vigour, and the children of the Church as strength for their faith, food for the soul, and a pure and lasting fount of spiritual life" (Vatican II, *DV*, 21).

4:14–7:28 □ The main theme of the letter—Christ, the High Priest—starts here; his priesthood is greater than that of priests of the Mosaic Law.

4:14–16 A Christian should put all his trust in the new high priest, Christ. He has entered heaven and he is well disposed to us, for he sympathizes with our weaknesses. "The enemies of our sanctification will be rendered powerless if the mercy of God goes before us. And if through our own fault and human weakness we should fall, the Lord comes to our aid and raises us up" (Bl. J. Escrivá, *Hom.,* 1,

i. Greek *he* **4:7** Ps 95:7.

respect has been tempted as we are, yet without sin. 16Let us then with confidence draw near to the throne of grace, that we may receive mercy and find grace to help in time of need.

Christ has been made high priest by God the Father

5 1For every high priest chosen from among men is appointed to act on
behalf of men in relation to God, to offer gifts and sacrifices for sins. 2He
can deal gently with the ignorant and wayward, since he himself is beset with
weakness. 3Because of this he is bound to offer sacrifice for his own sins as well
as for those of the people. 4And one does not take the honour upon himself, but
he is called by God, just as Aaron was. 5So also Christ did not exalt himself to be
made a high priest, but was appointed by him who said to him,

"Thou art my Son,
today I have begotten thee";*

6as he says also in another place,

"Thou art a priest for ever,
after the order of Melchizedek."

7In the days of his flesh, Jesus[j] offered up prayers and supplications, with
loud cries and tears, to him who was able to save him from death, and he was
heard for his godly fear. 8Although he was a Son, he learned obedience
through what he suffered; 9and being made perfect he became the source of
eternal salvation to all who obey him, 10being designated by God a high priest
after the order of Melchizedek.

---

7). The fact that Christ did not sin, which Holy Scripture attests to (cf. Jn 8:46; Rom 8:3; 2 Cor 5:21; 1 Pet 1:19; 2:21–24), is a logical consequence of his being God and of his human integrity and holiness. And the weakness of Christ, which he chose to experience out of love for us, is an invitation from God to ask him for strength not to sin.

5:1–10 Christ is the high priest, who really can free us from all sin. In fact, he is the only perfect Priest: other priests (in natural religions as well as the Jewish religion) are only prefigurements of Christ. Jesus Christ is the true priest, because he was chosen by God (v. 5), as Aaron was, but not according to the order of the levitical priesthood, to which Aaron belonged; Christ belongs to a higher order, the order of Melchizedek (cf. 5:11–14).

The words of v. 1 are a very good short definition of what a priest is; "the proper office of the priest is to be a mediator between God and man, in so far as, on the one hand, he gives the divine things to the people, from which the name 'sacerdos' [priest] comes, 'he who gives the sacred things …', and, on the other, he offers to God the prayers of the people, and makes reparation for the sins of the people against God" (St Thomas Aquinas, *Summa theol.*, 3, 22, 1).

j. Greek *he* **5:5** Ps 2:7. **5:6** Ps 110:4 **5:10** Ps 110:4.

The need for religious instruction

[11]About this we have much to say which is hard to explain, since you have become dull of hearing. [12]For though by this time you ought to be teachers, you need some one to teach you again the first principles of God's word. You need milk, not solid food; [13]for every one who lives on milk is unskilled in the word of righteousness, for he is a child. [14]But solid food is for the mature, for those who have their faculties trained by practise to distinguish good from evil.

6 [1]Therefore let us leave the elementary doctrine of Christ and go on to maturity, not laying again a foundation of repentance from dead works and of faith toward God, [2]with instruction[k] about ablutions, the laying on of hands, the resurrection of the dead, and eternal judgment. [3]And this we will do if God permits.[l]

The danger of apostasy and the need for perseverance

[4]For it is impossible to restore again to repentance those who have once been enlightened, who have tasted the heavenly gift, and have become partakers of the Holy Spirit, [5]and have tasted the goodness of the word of God and the powers of the age to come, [6]if they then commit apostasy, since they crucify the Son of God on their own account and hold him up to contempt. [7]For land which has drunk the rain that often falls upon it, and brings forth vegetation useful to those for whose sake it is cultivated, receives a blessing from God. [8]But if it bears thorns and thistles, it is worthless and near to being cursed; its end is to be burned.

5:11–6:3 The "word of righteousness" refers to the mystery of justification (cf. Rom 6:6; 9:30). Verses 1–3 of Chapter 6 provide a summary of the teachings which should be explained (and which need to be accepted) before a person is baptized; these are basic truths from which one can proceed to grow in knowledge of Jesus Christ.

6:4–12 A Christian runs the risk of parting company with basic doctrine if he fails to live in accordance with it. Therefore, the letter reminds us about what our Lord said about sinning against the Holy Spirit (cf. Mt 12:31–32 and par.); the same teaching is to be found in the Second Letter of St Peter (cf. 2 Pet 2:20–22).

Verse 6 refers to how apostates and all sinners are the cause of Christ's passion and death; as long as they persist in the sins, they are crucifying Christ again and are holding him up to contempt because they show they despise what he has done for them. "In her magisterial teaching of the faith and in the witness of her saints, the Church has never forgotten that 'sinners were the authors and the ministers of all the sufferings that the divine Redeemer endured' (*Roman Catechism*, 1, 5, 11). 'Nor did the demons crucify him; it is you with them who have crucified him and

k. Other ancient manuscripts read *of instruction* **l.** Other ancient manuscripts read *let us do this if God permits* **6:8** Gen 3:17:18.

[9]Though we speak thus, yet in your case, beloved, we feel sure of better
things that belong to salvation. [10]For God is not so unjust as to overlook your
work and the love which you showed for his sake in serving the saints, as you still
do. [11]And we desire each one of you to show the same earnestness in realizing the
full assurance of hope until the end, [12]so that you may not be sluggish, but
imitators of those who through faith and patience inherit the promises.

The promises made to Abraham were confirmed by oath and cannot be broken

[13]For when God made a promise to Abraham, since he had no one greater by
whom to swear, he swore by himself, [14]saying, "Surely I will bless you and
multiply you." [15]And thus Abraham,[m] having patiently endured, obtained the
promise. [16]Men indeed swear by a greater than themselves, and in all their
disputes an oath is final for confirmation. [17]So when God desired to show more
convincingly to the heirs of the promise the unchangeable character of his
purpose, he interposed with an oath, [18]so that through two unchangeable things,
in which it is impossible that God should prove false, we who have fled for refuge
might have strong encouragement to seize the hope set before us. [19]We have this
as a sure and steadfast anchor of the soul, a hope that enters into the inner shrine
behind the curtain, [20]where Jesus has gone as a forerunner on our behalf, having
become a high priest for ever after the order of Melchizedek.

Jesus Christ is a priest after the order of Melchizedek

7 [1]For this Melchizedek, king of Salem, priest of the Most High God, met
Abraham returning from the slaughter of the kings and blessed him; [2]and

---

crucify him still, when you delight in your vices and sins' (St Francis of Assisi, *Admon.* 5, 3)" (*CCC*, 598).

The parable of the good and barren land serves to reinforce the writer's appeal in vv. 7–8 and leads on to some words of encouragement (vv. 9–12).

6:13–20 "Through two unchangeable things" (v. 18): in promises made by God veracity is doubly involved: he is both the taker of the oath and its guarantor. The promise and God's oath, which acts as a kind of anchor, are a source of reassurance at all times. "Man must have hope, just as every boat has an anchor. But there is a difference between the anchor and [the virtue of] hope: the anchor weighs down, while hope draws us up towards God" (St Thomas Aquinas, *Com. on Heb,* in loc.).

In the Old Testament, the high priest entered the Holy of Holies of the temple once a year, on the Day of Atonement (cf. v. 19). By the sacrifice of the Cross, Christ entered the true sanctuary or shrine of heaven and gave all mankind access to it. Our hope is sure because it is based on the enduring value of Christ's sacrifice and priesthood.

7:1–3 To show the superiority of Christ's priesthood over the levitical priesthood, the writer uses two passages from the Old Testament referring to Melchizedek—

m. Greek *he* **6:13–14** Gen 22:16–17. **6:20** Ps 110:4. **7:1–10** Gen 14:17–20.

to him Abraham apportioned a tenth part of everything. He is first, by translation of his name, king of righteousness, and then he is also king of Salem, that is, king of peace. [3]He is without father or mother or genealogy, and has neither beginning of days nor end of life,* but resembling the Son of God he continues a priest for ever.

Melchizedek's priesthood is greater than that of Abraham's line

[4]See how great he is! Abraham the patriarch gave him a tithe of the spoils. [5]And those descendants of Levi who receive the priestly office have a commandment in the law to take tithes from the people, that is, from their brethren, though these also are descended from Abraham. [6]But this man who has not their genealogy received tithes from Abraham and blessed him who had the promises. [7]It is beyond dispute that the inferior is blessed by the superior. [8]Here tithes are received by mortal men; there, by one of whom it is testified that he lives. [9]One might even say that Levi himself, who receives tithes, paid tithes through Abraham, [10]for he was still in the loins of his ancestor when Melchizedek met him.

[11]Now if perfection had been attainable through the Levitical priesthood (for under it the people received the law), what further need would there have been for another priest to arise after the order of Melchizedek, rather than one named after the order of Aaron? [12]For when there is a change in the priesthood, there is necessarily a change in the law as well. [13]For the one of whom these things are spoken belonged to another tribe, from which no one has ever served at the altar. [14]For it is evident that our Lord was descended from Judah, and in connection with that tribe Moses said nothing about priests.

[15]This becomes even more evident when another priest arises in the likeness of Melchizedek, [16]who has become a priest, not according to a legal requirement concerning bodily descent but by the power of an indestructible life. [17]For it is witnessed of him,

"Thou art a priest for ever,
after the order of Melchizedek."

Genesis 14:17–20, where he appears for the first time, and Psalm 110, where he is depicted as being a "priest for ever", invested with a priesthood distinct from that of Levi (cf. v. 3).

7:4–19 The tithing and the blessing show that Melchisedek is greater than Abraham and, therefore, greater than Levi, his descendant (vv. 4–10). So, since Christ's priesthood is according to the order of Melchizedek, it is superior to the levitical priesthood. Moreover, the levitical priesthood could not ensure that the Mosaic Law, which it served, would manage to fulfil God's plan, and achieve man's salvation (vv. 11–14). The Law was designed, so to speak, to announce a future, better, law—that of Christ—one full of hope because it opens the gates of eternal life (vv. 15–19). "In place of the precepts of old we are given hope for the goods of the future, which make us part of the family of God" (Theodoret, *Interp. ad Heb,* in loc.).

7:11 Ps 110:4. **7:17** Ps 110:4.

18On the one hand, a former commandment is set aside because of its weak-
ness and uselessness 19(for the law made nothing perfect); on the other hand,
a better hope is introduced, through which we draw near to God.

Christ is perfect high priest and his priesthood endures forever

20And it was not without an oath. 21Those who formerly became priests took
their office without an oath, but this one was addressed with an oath,

"The Lord has sworn
and will not change his mind,
'Thou art a priest for ever.'"

22This makes Jesus the surety of a better covenant.

23The former priests were many in number, because they were prevented by
death from continuing in office; 24but he holds his priesthood permanently,
because he continues for ever. 25Consequently he is able for all time to save
those who draw near to God through him, since he always lives to make
intercession for them.

26For it was fitting that we should have such a high priest, holy, blameless,
unstained, separated from sinners, exalted above the heavens. 27He has no
need, like those high priests, to offer sacrifices daily, first for his own sins and
then for those of the people; he did this once for all when he offered up
himself. 28Indeed, the law appoints men in their weakness as high priests, but
the word of the oath, which came later than the law, appoints a Son who has
been made perfect for ever.

4. CHRIST'S SACRIFICE IS MORE EXCELLENT THAN ALL THE SACRIFICES OF THE OLD LAW

Christ is high priest of a New Covenant, which replaces the Old

8 1Now the point in what we are saying is this: we have such a high priest,
one who is seated at the right hand of the throne of the Majesty in heaven,

---

7:20–28 God's oath enhances the superiority of Christ's priesthood—by confirming that it endures forever and has no rival. Prior to Christ there were many priests but they all died (v. 23) and had their imperfections (v. 28). The unique, everlasting, priesthood of Christ is extended by the Christian ministerial priesthood. "The redemptive sacrifice of Christ is unique, accomplished once for all; yet it is made present in the Eucharistic sacrifice of the Church. The same is true of the one priesthood of Christ; it is made present through the ministerial priesthood without diminishing the uniqueness of Christ's priesthood" (*CCC*, 1545).

8:1–10:18 □ The text now demonstrates the superiority of Christ's priesthood from the point of view of sacrifice, which is the essential and specific function of

7:21 Ps 110:4.

2 a minister in the sanctuary and the true tent[n] which is set up not by man but
by the Lord. 3 For every high priest is appointed to offer gifts and sacrifices;
hence it is necessary for this priest also to have something to offer. 4 Now if he
were on earth, he would not be a priest at all, since there are priests who offer
gifts according to the law. 5 They serve a copy and shadow of the heavenly
sanctuary; for when Moses was about to erect the tent,[n] he was instructed by
God, saying, "See that you make everything according to the pattern which
was shown you on the mountain." 6 But as it is, Christ[o] has obtained a ministry
which is as much more excellent than the old as the covenant he mediates is
better, since it is enacted on better promises. 7 For if that first covenant had
been faultless, there would have been no occasion for a second.

8 For he finds fault with them when he says:

"The days will come, says the Lord,
when I will establish a new covenant with the house of Israel
and with the house of Judah;
9 not like the covenant that I made with their fathers
on the day when I took them by the hand
to lead them out of the land of Egypt;
for they did not continue in my covenant,
and so I paid no heed to them, says the Lord.
10 This is the covenant that I will make with the house of Israel
after those days, says the Lord:
I will put my laws into their minds,
and write them on their hearts,
and I will be their God,
and they shall be my people.
11 And they shall not teach every one his fellow
or every one his brother, saying, 'Know the Lord,'
for all shall know me,
from the least of them to the greatest.*
12 For I will be merciful toward their iniquities,
and I will remember their sins no more."

13 In speaking of a new covenant he treats the first as obsolete. And what is
becoming obsolete and growing old is ready to vanish away.

---

a priest. In Christ the Old Covenant finds its perfection and fulfilment: that covenant worshipped God by means of sacrifices and offerings; now that Christ has come, the New Covenant begins, with a new sacrifice and a new temple.

8:1–13 Christ exercises his priesthood in heaven, in a new sanctuary and a new tabernacle (tent) which are "true" (v. 2) unlike the sanctuary and tent of Moses (cf. Ex 25:40), which were only a prefigurement. In heaven, Christ the eternal priest is

n. Or *tabernacle* **o.** Greek *he* **8:5** Ex 25:40. **8:8–12** Jer 31:31–34.

The rites of the Old Covenant prefigure those of the New

9 [1]Now even the first covenant had regulations for worship and an earthly
sanctuary. [2]For a tent[p] was prepared, the outer one, in which were the lamp-
stand and the table and the bread of the Presence;[q] it is called the Holy Place.
[3]Behind the second curtain stood a tent[p] called the Holy of Holies, [4]having the
golden altar of incense and the ark of the covenant covered on all sides with gold,
which contained a golden urn holding the manna, and Aaron's rod that budded,
and the tables of the covenant; [5]above it were the cherubim of glory over-
shadowing the mercy seat. Of these things we cannot now speak in detail.
[6]These preparations having thus been made, the priests go continually into
the outer tent,[p] performing their ritual duties; [7]but into the second only the high
priest goes, and he but once a year, and not without taking blood which he
offers for himself and for the errors of the people. [8]By this the Holy Spirit
indicates that the way into the sanctuary is not yet opened as long as the outer
tent is still standing [9](which is symbolic for the present age). According to this
arrangement, gifts and sacrifices are offered which cannot perfect the con-
science of the worshipper, [10]but deal only with food and drink and various
ablutions, regulations for the body imposed until the time of reformation.

---

forever presenting to the Father the fruit of his sacrifice on the cross. "In the earthly liturgy we take part in a foretaste of that heavenly liturgy which is celebrated in the Holy City of Jerusalem toward which we journey as pilgrims, where Christ is sitting at the right hand of God, Minister of the holies and of the true tabernacle" (Vatican II, *SC*, 8; cf. *CCC*, 667).

The words of Jeremiah 31:31–34 have been borne out in the New Covenant established by Jesus: this is the covenant in which God truly forgives sins and remembers them no more.

9:1–10 To show the excellence of Christ's sacrifice, the letter now describes the sanctuary of the Old Covenant, the tent or tabernacle, in which the Lord dwelt during the period when the people of Israel were making their way through the wilderness, and in their early years in the promised land. It also refers to the sacrifice on the great Day of Atonement or Yom Kippur (cf. Lev 16:1–34; 23:26–32; Num 29:7–11), the day when all Israel was reconciled with its God by the purification and forgiveness of all the sins committed during the previous year and for which no atonement had been made.

Once the curtain or veil blocking the way to the inner tent ceases to exist, man is able to attain union with God, that is, holiness, symbolized by entry into the Holy of Holies. By his death Christ tore the curtain (cf. Mt 27:51). He is the Way (cf. Jn 14:6), the Gate (cf. Jn 10:7), by which man can enter the heavenly sanctuary.

p. Or *tabernacle* **q.** Greek *the presentation of the loaves*

Christ sealed the New Covenant with his blood once and for all
11But when Christ appeared as a high priest of the good things that have come,[r]
then through the greater and more perfect tent[p] (not made with hands, that is,
not of this creation) 12he[s] entered once for all into the Holy Place, taking not
the blood of goats and calves but his own blood, thus securing an eternal
redemption. 13For if the sprinkling of defiled persons with the blood of goats
and bulls and with the ashes of a heifer sanctifies for the purification of the
flesh, 14how much more shall the blood of Christ, who through the eternal
Spirit offered himself without blemish to God, purify your[t] conscience from
dead works to serve the living God.
15Therefore he is the mediator of a new covenant, so that those who are
called may receive the promised eternal inheritance, since a death has occurred
which redeems them from the transgressions under the first covenant.[u] 16For
where a will is involved, the death of the one who made it must be established.
17For a will[u] takes effect only at death, since it is not in force as long as the one
who made it is alive. 18Hence even the first covenant was not ratified without
blood. 19For when every commandment of the law had been declared by
Moses to all the people, he took the blood of calves and goats, with water and
scarlet wool and hyssop, and sprinkled both the book itself and all the people,
20saying, "This is the blood of the covenant which God commanded you."

9:11–28 As the RSV note **u** points out, the Greek word (*diatheke*) in vv. 15–17 can be translated as either "covenant" or "will". This word, which literally means "disposition", was the word used in Greek translations of the Old Testament for the Covenant made on Sinai. The author of the letter uses both these meanings—pact or last disposition (will, testament) to explain that Christ's death on the cross was a true covenant sacrifice, like that offered by Moses (vv. 18–22; cf. Ex 24:3–8). He also teaches that Christ's death is God's last disposition: he has willed to give man heaven as his inheritance (vv. 23–28). "Do you want to discover by yet another means the power of this blood [of Christ]? Notice where it flows from, and what its source is. It began to flow from the cross itself, and its source was the Lord's side. [...] The soldier pierced his side, the wall of the holy temple was breached, and I find the hidden treasure and rejoice over the richness I have found" (St John Chrysostom, *Baptismal Catechesis*, 3, 16).

Verses 27–28 deal with three basic Christian truths about the last things 1) the immutable decree of death; 2) the fact that there is a judgment immediately after death; and 3) the second coming of Christ. "Death is the end of man's earthly pilgrimage, of the time of grace and mercy which God offers him so as to work out his earthly life in keeping with the divine plan, and to decide his ultimate destiny" (*CCC*, 1013).

"Not to deal with sin": this means that the second coming of Christ will not be for the purpose of making expiation for sin or to be offered as a victim for sin.

r. Other manuscripts read *good things to come* **s.** Greek *through* **t.** Other manuscripts read *our* **u.** The Greek word here used means both *covenant* and *will* **9:19–20** Ex 24:6–8.

21And in the same way he sprinkled with the blood both the tent[p] and all the
vessels used in worship. 22Indeed, under the law almost everything is purified
with blood, and without the shedding of blood there is no forgiveness of sins.
23Thus it was necessary for the copies of the heavenly things to be purified
with these rites, but the heavenly things themselves with better sacrifices than
these. 24For Christ has entered, not into a sanctuary made with hands, a copy
of the true one, but into heaven itself, now to appear in the presence of God on
our behalf. 25Nor was it to offer himself repeatedly, as the high priest enters the
Holy Place yearly with blood not his own; 26for then he would have had to
suffer repeatedly since the foundation of the world. But as it is, he has
appeared once for all at the end of the age to put away sin by the sacrifice of
himself. 27And just as it is appointed for men to die once, and after that comes
judgment, 28so Christ, having been offered once to bear the sins of many, will
appear a second time, not to deal with sin but to save those who are eagerly
waiting for him.

The sacrifices of the Old Covenant could not take away sins

10 1For since the law has but a shadow of the good things to come instead
of the true form of these realities, it can never, by the same sacrifices
which are continually offered year after year, make perfect those who draw
near.* 2Otherwise, would they not have ceased to be offered? If the worship-
pers had once been cleansed, they would no longer have any consciousness of
sin. 3But in these sacrifices there is a reminder of sin year after year. 4For it is
impossible that the blood of bulls and goats should take away sins.

Christ's offering of himself has infinite value

5Consequently, when Christ[v] came into the world, he said,

> "Sacrifices and offerings thou hast not desired,
> but a body hast thou prepared for me;
> 6 in burnt offerings and sin offerings thou hast taken no pleasure.
> 7 Then I said, 'Lo, I have come to do thy will, O God,'
> as it is written of me in the roll of the book."

8When he said above, "Thou hast neither desired nor taken pleasure in
sacrifices and offerings and burnt offerings and sin offerings" (these are offered

---

10:1–18 Once again the Old Testament sacrifices are compared with the sacrifice of Christ (cf. 7:27; 9:9–10, 12–14), this time from the viewpoint of their efficacy. The writer uses Old Testament texts to show that Christ's sacrifice is greater than those of the Old Law: they had to be repeated, and they could not take away sin (v. 11), whereas Christ's sacrifice is unique and perfect (vv. 121–14).

The Mass is the renewal of this unique sacrifice of Christ's, but it is not a repetition in the manner in which the old sacrifices were repeated: "The sacrifice

p. Or *tabernacle* **v.** Greek *he* **10:5–9** Ps 40:6–8.

according to the law), [9]then he added, "Lo, I have come to do thy will." He abolishes the first in order to establish the second. [10]And by that will we have been sanctified through the offering of the body of Jesus Christ once for all.

[11]And every priest stands daily at his service, offering repeatedly the same sacrifices, which can never take away sins. [12]But when Christ[w] had offered for all time a single sacrifice for sins, he sat down at the right hand of God, [13]then to wait until his enemies should be made a stool for his feet. [14]For by a single offering he has perfected for all time those who are sanctified. [15]And the Holy Spirit also bears witness to us; for after saying,

> [16]"This is the covenant that I will make with them
> after those days, says the Lord:
> I will put my laws on their hearts,
> and write them on their minds,"

[17]then he adds,

> "I will remember their sins and their misdeeds no more."

[18]Where there is forgiveness of these, there is no longer any offering for sin.

PART TWO: FAITH AND PERSEVERANCE IN FAITH

5. A CALL FOR LOYALTY

Motives for staying loyal to Christ

[19]Therefore, brethren, since we have confidence to enter the sanctuary by the blood of Jesus, [20]by the new and living way which he opened for us through the curtain, that is, through his flesh, [21]and since we have a great priest over the house of God, [22]let us draw near with a true heart in full assurance of faith, with our hearts sprinkled clean from an evil conscience and our bodies washed

---

of Christ and the sacrifice of the Eucharist are *one single sacrifice*: 'The victim is one and the same: the same now offers through the ministry of priests, who then offered himself on the cross; only the manner of offering is different' (Council of Trent, DS 1743). 'In this divine sacrifice which is celebrated in the Mass, the same Christ who offered himself once in a bloody manner on the altar of the cross is contained and is offered in an unbloody manner' (ibid.)" (*CCC*, 1367).

10:19–13:25 □□ From here to the end of the letter the emphasis is more on morality; the keynote is an exhortation to a living, steadfast faith (10:19–11:40), which helps a person draw nearer to Christ in the midst of trials and tribulations; a person's conduct should always be guided by charity (12:1–13:19).

w. Greek *this one* **10:12–13** Ps 110:1. **10:16–17** Jer 31:33–34. **10:28** Deut 17:2–6.

with pure water. [23]Let us hold fast the confession of our hope without wavering,
for he who promised is faithful; [24]and let us consider how to stir up one
another to love and good works, [25]not neglecting to meet together, as is the
habit of some, but encouraging one another, and all the more as you see the
Day drawing near.

[26]For if we sin deliberately after receiving the knowledge of the truth, there
no longer remains a sacrifice for sins, [27]but a fearful prospect of judgment, and
a fury of fire which will consume the adversaries. [28]A man who has violated the
law of Moses dies without mercy at the testimony of two or three witnesses.
[29]How much worse punishment do you think will be deserved by the man who
has spurned the Son of God, and profaned the blood of the covenant by which he
was sanctified, and outraged the Spirit of grace? [30]For we know him who said,
"Vengeance is mine, I will repay." And again, "The Lord will judge his
people." [31]It is a fearful thing to fall into the hands of the living God.

[32]But recall the former days when, after you were enlightened, you endured
a hard struggle with sufferings, [33]sometimes being publicly exposed to abuse
and affliction, and sometimes being partners with those so treated. [34]For you
had compassion on the prisoners, and you joyfully accepted the plundering of
your property, since you knew that you yourselves had a better possession and
an abiding one. [35]Therefore do not throw away your confidence, which has a
great reward. [36]For you have need of endurance, so that you may do the will of
God and receive what is promised.

> [37] "For yet a little while,
> and the coming one shall come and shall not tarry;
> [38] but my righteous one shall live by faith,
> and if he shrinks back,
> my soul has no pleasure in him."

[39] But we are not of those who shrink back and are destroyed, but of those who
have faith and keep their souls.

10:19–11:40 □ Various reasons and outstanding examples are listed with a view to encouraging Christians to persevere in their faith in spite of difficulties.

10:19–39 Christians should put their trust in the efficacy of Christ's sacrifice and associate themselves with his priesthood through faith, hope and love (vv. 19–24). They should stay true to the faith they received and professed at Baptism and maintain the purity which it brings (vv. 25–31). The letter warns about the gravity and the danger of the sin of apostasy: it is an outrage against the Holy Spirit (cf. the note on 6:4–12 and Mt 12:22–27).

The author appeals to Christians to be steadfast (vv. 32–34) in the face of persecution. He asks his addressees to think back to and meditate on the beginning

10:30 Deut 32:35–36. **10:37** Is 26:20 Gk; Hab 2:3. **10:38** Hab 2:4.

The good example of the patriarchs

11 [1]Now faith is the assurance of things hoped for, the conviction of things
not seen. [2]For by it the men of old received divine approval. [3]By faith
we understand that the world was created by the word of God, so that what is
seen was made out of things which do not appear.
[4]By faith Abel offered to God a more acceptable sacrifice than Cain,
through which he received approval as righteous, God bearing witness by
accepting his gifts; he died, but through his faith he is still speaking. [5]By faith
Enoch was taken up so that he should not see death; and he was not found,
because God had taken him. Now before he was taken he was attested as
having pleased God. [6]And without faith it is impossible to please him. For
whoever would draw near to God must believe that he exists and that he
rewards those who seek him.* [7]By faith Noah, being warned by God con-
cerning events as yet unseen, took heed and constructed an ark for the saving
of his household; by this he condemned the world and became an heir of the
righteousness which comes by faith.
[8]By faith Abraham obeyed when he was called to go out to a place which he
was to receive as an inheritance; and he went out, not knowing where he was to
go. [9]By faith he sojourned in the land of promise, as in a foreign land, living in
tents with Isaac and Jacob, heirs with him of the same promise. [10]For he looked
forward to the city which has foundations, whose builder and maker is God. [11]By
faith Sarah herself received power to conceive, even when she was past the age,
since she considered him faithful who had promised. [12]Therefore from one man,
and him as good as dead, were born descendants as many as the stars of heaven
and as the innumerable grains of sand by the seashore.
[13]These all died in faith, not having received what was promised, but having
seen it and greeted it from afar, and having acknowledged that they were
strangers and exiles on the earth. [14]For people who speak thus make it clear

---

of their Christian calling. They should act like people who compete and struggle openly, not minding that they draw attention to themselves (cf. 1 Cor 4:9). The appeal to perseverance is supported by two quotations from Scripture. The first (at v. 37), according to the Greek text from Isaiah 26:21, reminds them that God will not be slow to judge the sinful. The second (at v. 32, from Habakkuk 2:4), which St Paul quotes in Romans 1:17 and Galatians 3:11, announces the future liberation of the people of Israel. The ancient prophecy has found fulfilment in Christ, "the coming one" (v. 37), that is, he who must come a second time. Therefore, the Christian should await the outcome of persecution loyally and cheerfully.

11:1–22 These verses contain heartfelt praise of our forefathers in the faith. First, the essence of faith is defined (v. 1): through Faith, the believer obtains a sure knowledge of God's promises and a hold on the good things of heaven. This type

11:5 Gen 5:21–24. **11:12** Gen 15:5–6; 22:17; Ex 32:13.

that they are seeking a homeland. [15]If they had been thinking of that land from
which they had gone out, they would have had opportunity to return. [16]But as
it is, they desire a better country, that is, a heavenly one. Therefore God is not
ashamed to be called their God, for he has prepared for them a city.
[17]By faith Abraham, when he was tested, offered up Isaac, and he who had
received the promises was ready to offer up his only son, [18]of whom it was said,
"Through Isaac shall your descendants be named." [19]He considered that God was
able to raise men even from the dead; hence, he did receive him back, and this was
a symbol. [20]By faith Isaac invoked future blessings on Jacob and Esau. [21]By faith
Jacob, when dying, blessed each of the sons of Joseph, bowing in worship over the
head of his staff. [22]By faith Joseph, at the end of his life, made mention of the
exodus of the Israelites and gave directions concerning his burial.[x]

The faith of Moses, the judges and the prophets
[23]By faith Moses, when he was born, was hid for three months by his parents,
because they saw that the child was beautiful; and they were not afraid of the
king's edict. [24]By faith Moses, when he was grown up, refused to be called the
son of Pharaoh's daughter, [25]choosing rather to share ill-treatment with the people
of God than to enjoy the fleeting pleasures of sin. [26]He considered abuse suffered
for the Christ greater wealth than the treasures of Egypt, for he looked to the
reward. [27]By faith he left Egypt, not being afraid of the anger of the king; for he
endured as seeing him who is invisible. [28]By faith he kept the Passover and
sprinkled the blood, so that the Destroyer of the first-born might not touch them.

---

of faith, which is necessary for salvation, includes in the first place acknowledging the existence of God and the creation of all things out of nothing (v. 3).

"He died, but through his faith he is still speaking": this is reminiscent of the passage in Genesis where God tells Cain that "The voice of your brother's blood is crying to me from the ground" (Gen 4:10). Abel is God's witness, his "martyr", because he confesses God's greatness by his faith, sacrifice and generosity.

On the basis of Genesis 5:21–24, a Jewish tradition built up to the effect that Enoch (v. 5) did not die, and that, like Elijah, he was in the presence of God preparing the way for the Messiah.

Abraham is the greatest Old Testament example of faith in God (vv. 8–19). "To obey (from the Latin *ob-audire*, to 'hear or listen to') in faith is to submit freely to the word that has been heard, because its truth is guaranteed by God, who is Truth itself. Abraham is the model of such obedience offered us by Holy Scripture. The Virgin Mary is its most perfect embodiment" (*CCC*, 144).

11:23–40 After the patriarchs, Moses was the figure most revered by the Jewish people; he was for them the founder and lawgiver of their nation (cf. 3:1–5). The central point of the teaching in this passage is the double choice that faith requires

x. Greek *bones* **11:18** Gen 21:12. **11:21** Gen 47:31 Gk.

[29]By faith the people crossed the Red Sea as if on dry land; but the Egyptians, when they attempted to do the same, were drowned. [30]By faith the walls of Jericho fell down after they had been encircled for seven days. [31]By faith Rahab the harlot did not perish with those who were disobedient, because she had given friendly welcome to the spies.

[32]And what more shall I say? For time would fail me to tell of Gideon, Barak, Samson, Jephthah, of David and Samuel and the prophets—[33]who through faith conquered kingdoms, enforced justice, received promises, stopped the mouths of lions, [34]quenched raging fire, escaped the edge of the sword, won strength out of weakness, became mighty in war, put foreign armies to flight. [35]Women received their dead by resurrection. Some were tortured, refusing to accept release, that they might rise again to a better life. [36]Others suffered mocking and scourging, and even chains and imprisonment. [37]They were stoned, they were sawn in two,[y] they were killed with the sword; they went about in skins of sheep and goats, destitute, afflicted, ill-treated—[38]of whom the world was not worthy—wandering over deserts and mountains, and in dens and caves of the earth.

[39]And all these, though well attested by their faith, did not receive what was promised, [40]since God had foreseen something better for us, that apart from us they should not be made perfect.

6. THE EXAMPLE OF CHRIST AND THE DUTIES OF CHRISTIANS

The example of Christ

12 [1]Therefore, since we are surrounded by so great a cloud of witnesses, let us also lay aside every weight, and sin which clings so closely, and let

---

us to make—on the one hand, giving up sinful pleasures and embracing the suffering of the people of God (vv. 24–25); on the other, despising "the treasures of Egypt" and opting for the "abuse suffered for the Christ" (v. 26). (The sufferings undergone by the chosen people in Egypt prefigure the sufferings of the Messiah.)

Then, evoking the exploits and suffering of those who came out victorious on account of their faith, the sacred writer mentions the testimony of faith given by heroes, judges, kings, prophets and martyrs in the period following the conquest of the promised land. Not in any strict chronological order he mentions the principal judges (Gideon, Barak, Samson and Jephthah), the greatest of the kings (David), and the most famous early prophet (Samuel). Finally he refers to exploits and other deeds inspired by faith and fidelity, without mentioning anyone by name.

12:1–13:25 □ Now that the reader has been reminded about the standards of faith and fidelity set by the righteous of the Old Testament, the moral lesson is drawn: Christians must be no less faithful.

y. Other manuscripts add *they were tempted*

us run with perseverance the race that is set before us,* [2]looking to Jesus the
pioneer and perfecter of our faith, who for the joy that was set before him
endured the cross, despising the shame, and is seated at the right hand of the
throne of God.
[3]Consider him who endured from sinners such hostility against himself, so
that you may not grow weary or fainthearted.

Perseverance in the midst of trials

[4]In your struggle against sin you have not yet resisted to the point of shedding
your blood. [5]And have you forgotten the exhortation which addresses you as
sons?—

> "My son, do not regard lightly the discipline of the Lord,
> nor lose courage when you are punished by him.
> [6] For the Lord disciplines him whom he loves,
> and chastises every son whom he receives."

[7]It is for discipline that you have to endure. God is treating you as sons; for
what son is there whom his father does not discipline? [8]If you are left without
discipline, in which all have participated, then you are illegitimate children and
not sons. [9]Besides this, we have had earthly fathers to discipline us and we
respected them. Shall we not much more be subject to the Father of spirits and
live? [10]For they disciplined us for a short time at their pleasure, but he
disciplines us for our good, that we may share his holiness. [11]For the moment

---

12:1–3 Our model is Christ. He is a perfect example of obedience, of faithfulness to his mission, of union with the Father, and of endurance in suffering. Christ is depicted as a strong, unselfish athlete who runs a good race (cf. 1 Cor 9:24; Phil 2:16; 1 Tim 6:12; 2 Tim 2:5); he starts and finishes at the right time; he does not flag and he attains victory. Christians should try to live as he does. What the writer says here is very similar to Philippians 2:5–9: "Have the mind among yourselves, which was in Christ Jesus …". His example helps Christians put up with criticism from others and reminds them that they should not be surprised if, instead of success and joy, they encounter humiliation and hostility (cf. Mt 10:24–25; Jn 15:20).

12:4–13 Following Jesus' example, Christians should strive to avoid sin and put up with tribulation and persecution, because if such adversity arises, it means that the Lord permits it for our good. "God is my Father, even though he may send me suffering. He loves me tenderly, even while wounding me. […] And I, who also wish to fulfil the most holy Will of God, following in the footsteps of the Master, can I complain if I too meet suffering as my travelling companion? It will be a sure sign of my sonship, because God is treating me as he treated his own divine Son" (Bl. J. Escrivá, *The Way of the Cross*, 1, 1).

12:5–6 Prov 3:11–12.

all discipline seems painful rather than pleasant; later it yields the peaceful fruit of righteousness to those who have been trained by it.

12 Therefore lift your drooping hands and strengthen your weak knees, 13 and
make straight paths for your feet, so that what is lame may not be put out of joint but rather be healed.

Striving for peace. Purity. Reverent worship

14 Strive for peace with all men, and for the holiness without which no one will
see the Lord. 15 See to it that no one fail to obtain the grace of God; that no
"root of bitterness" spring up and cause trouble, and by it the many become
defiled; 16 that no one be immoral or irreligious like Esau, who sold his
birthright for a single meal. 17 For you know that afterward, when he desired to
inherit the blessing, he was rejected, for he found no chance to repent, though he sought it with tears.

18 For you have not come to what may be touched, a blazing fire, and
darkness, and gloom, and a tempest, 19 and the sound of a trumpet, and a voice
whose words made the hearers entreat that no further messages be spoken to
them. 20 For they could not endure the order that was given, "If even a beast
touches the mountain, it shall be stoned." 21 Indeed, so terrifying was the sight
that Moses said, "I tremble with fear." 22 But you have come to Mount Zion and
to the city of the living God, the heavenly Jerusalem, and to innumerable
angels in festal gathering, 23 and to the assembly[z] of the first-born who are
enrolled in heaven, and to a judge who is God of all, and to the spirits of just
men made perfect, 24 and to Jesus, the mediator of a new covenant, and to the
sprinkled blood that speaks more graciously than the blood of Abel.

12:14–29 Christians are exhorted to live a life which is acceptable worship of God (cf. v. 28). The sacred text dramatically contrasts two scenes—that of the establishment of the Covenant on Sinai (cf. Ex 19:12–16; 20:18), and the vision of the heavenly city on Mount Zion, the dwelling place of the angels and saints.

The central point in the writer's argument is based on the key moment of the Covenant—the shedding of our Lord's blood, which ratifies the Covenant and cleanses mankind from sin (cf. Ex 24:8; Heb 9:12–14, 20; 1 Pet 1:2). This blood "speaks more graciously than the blood of Abel" (cf. v. 24; cf. 11:4), for "the shedding of Abel's blood called for vengeance whereas the blood of Christ claims forgiveness" (St Thomas Aquinas, *Com. on Heb,* in loc.). Then, quoting the prophet Haggai (v. 26), the sacred writer shows that just as the earth trembled at Sinai when God sealed the Covenant with Moses, so did the earth, and heavens too, when the New Covenant was made (cf. Mt 27:51–52). If the Old Covenant required obedience and reverential fear (vv. 20–21), the much greater importance and dignity of the New demands greater union with the Lord (v. 25) and a life in the grace of God which enables us to offer him acceptable worship (v. 28).

z. *Or angels, and to the festal gathering and assembly* **12:20** Ex 19:12–13. **12:21** Deut 9:19. **12:12** Is 35:3; Job 4:3–4. **12:13** Prov 4:26 Gk.

25 See that you do not refuse him who is speaking. For if they did not escape when they refused him who warned them on earth, much less shall we escape if we reject him who warns from heaven. 26 His voice then shook the earth; but now he has promised, "Yet once more I will shake not only the earth but also the heaven." 27 This phrase, "Yet once more," indicates the removal of what is shaken, as of what has been made, in order that what cannot be shaken may remain. 28 Therefore let us be grateful for receiving a kingdom that cannot be shaken, and thus let us offer to God acceptable worship, with reverence and awe; 29 for our God is a consuming fire.

Duties towards others—charity, hospitality, fidelity in marriage

13 1* Let brotherly love continue. 2 Do not neglect to show hospitality to strangers, for thereby some have entertained angels unawares. 3 Remember those who are in prison, as though in prison with them; and those who are ill-treated, since you also are in the body. 4 Let marriage be held in honour among all, and let the marriage bed be undefiled; for God will judge the immoral and adulterous. 5 Keep your life free from love of money, and be content with what you have; for he has said, "I will never fail you nor forsake you." 6 Hence we can confidently say,

"The Lord is my helper,
I will not be afraid;
what can man do to me?"

Religious duties—obeying lawful pastors; religious worship

7 Remember your leaders, those who spoke to you the word of God; consider the outcome of their life, and imitate their faith. 8 Jesus Christ is the same yesterday and today and for ever. 9 Do not be led away by diverse and strange

---

13:1–6 Faithfulness to Christ means being faithful to him as a person and to his teaching.

Verse 2 alludes to episodes in the lives of Abraham and Sarah (cf. Gen 17), Lot (cf. Gen 19), Manoah (cf. Judg 13:3–22) or Tobit (cf. Tob 12:1–20), who gave hospitality to wayfarers who turned out to be angels.

The sacred writer uses some words spoken by Moses (cf. Deut 31:6), ratified by a further quotation from Psalm 118:6, to call to mind that it is God himself who has told man he will never abandon him. "Put your faith in God and offer him your veneration and love. He will answer for you and do all things for the best" (Thomas à Kempis, *Imitation of Christ*, 21, 2–3).

13:7–19 These verses are an appeal to readers to hold on to the faith they have received (vv. 7–9) and to ensure that their works of charity (v. 16) are evidence of

12:26 Hag 2:6. **12:29** Deut 4:24; Is 33:14. **13:5** Deut 31:6; Josh 1:5. **13:6** Ps 118:6.

teachings; for it is well that the heart be strengthened by grace, not by foods,
which have not benefited their adherents.* 10We have an altar from which
those who serve the tent[a] have no right to eat. 11For the bodies of those animals
whose blood is brought into the sanctuary by the high priest as a sacrifice for
sin are burned outside the camp. 12So Jesus also suffered outside the gate in
order to sanctify the people through his own blood. 13Therefore let us go forth
to him outside the camp and bear the abuse he endured.* 14For here we have
no lasting city, but we seek the city which is to come. 15Through him then let
us continually offer up a sacrifice of praise to God, that is, the fruit of lips that
acknowledge his name. 16Do not neglect to do good and to share what you
have, for such sacrifices are pleasing to God.

17Obey your leaders and submit to them; for they are keeping watch over
your souls, as men who will have to give account. Let them do this joyfully,
and not sadly, for that would be of no advantage to you.

18Pray for us, for we are sure that we have a clear conscience, desiring to act
honourably in all things. 19I urge you the more earnestly to do this in order that
I may be restored to you the sooner.

---

the faith they profess (v. 15) and the supernatural meaning of their lives (v. 14). Finally, the writer asks for prayer for himself (vv. 17–19). Verse 8 is a wonderful expression of faith summing up the basis of all Christian living. Christ's teaching is as immutable as he himself is, and it will eventually transform the world. All aspects of human life—work, family and social life, affections, suffering—acquire in Christ a new and enduring meaning. "The Church believes that Christ, who died and was raised for the sake of all, can show man the way and strengthen him through the Spirit in order to be worthy of his destiny: nor is there any other name under heaven given among men by which they can be saved. The Church likewise believes that the key, the centre and the purpose of the whole of man's history is to be found in its Lord and Master. She also maintains that beneath all that changes there is much that is unchanging, much that has its ultimate foundation in Christ, who is the same yesterday, and today, and forever" (Vatican II, *GS*, 10).

Verses 11–13 should be read against the background of the Old Testament rites of the Day of Atonement (cf. 9:1–10 and note). Jesus Christ, crucified outside the walls of Jerusalem, has fulfilled what was prefigured by the sacrificed victims that were burned outside the camp. By sacrificing the heifer and the male goat to atone for the sins of the people, the high priest was enabled to enter the sanctuary; so too the shedding of Christ's blood has opened the way to the sanctuary of heaven. But Christ's going out of the city also means leaving Jewish worship behind and declaring it to be no longer valid.

a. Or *tabernacle*

Words of farewell
[20]Now may the God of peace who brought again from the dead our Lord Jesus,
the great shepherd of the sheep, by the blood of the eternal covenant, [21]equip
you with everything good that you may do his will, working in you[b] that which
is pleasing in his sight, through Jesus Christ; to whom be glory for ever and
ever. Amen.
[22]I appeal to you, brethren, bear with my word of exhortation, for I have
written to you briefly. [23]You should understand that our brother Timothy has
been released, with whom I shall see you if he comes soon. [24]Greet all your
leaders and all the saints. Those who come from Italy send you greetings.
[25]Grace be with all of you. Amen.

13:20–25 The letter ends in the same sort of way as the Pauline letters do—with a doxology and some words of farewell. Jesus Christ is described as the "great Shepherd" (v. 20; cf. 1 Pet 2:25); once again we can glimpse a parallel between the Exodus/Old Covenant and entry into heaven.

"Those who come from Italy": as many Fathers and early commentators thought, this letter was probably written from Rome.

b. Other ancient authorities read *us*

The Catholic Letters

The canon of the books of the New Testament includes, along with the Pauline corpus (the thirteen letters of St Paul and the Letter to the Hebrews), a group of seven others which Tradition usually calls the "Catholic Letters"—that written by St James, two by St Peter, three by St John and one by St Jude. Apparently the reason for grouping them together is not because they are similar in doctrine or style, but simply to distinguish them from the body of Pauline letters. This grouping already existed from around the end of the fourth century AD (cf. Eusebius of Caesarea, *Eccl. Hist.*, 3, 25, 2–3). The books have not always been given this position in the New Testament: the great Vatican and Sinaitic codexes place them after the book of the Acts of the Apostles; from the time of St Jerome onwards, all bibles place them immediately after the writings of St Paul, just before the book of Revelation. Nor were they all in the same sequence as now: we often find St Peter's two letters coming first; however, from St Jerome onwards most manuscripts place them where they normally appear in printed bibles.

The name "catholic" was applied by Origen to the First Letter of Peter, the first of John and that of Jude. Later, Eusebius and St Jerome extended the title to cover all seven letters. It seems that they were given this name because they were addressed to the whole Church and not to particular communities or persons, as St Paul's letters were. By extension, the title was applied as to 1 and 2 John, even though those letters were sent to specific individuals.

Each letter has its own content and purpose and there is very little common to them all. St Augustine says that they were written to refute errors which were beginning to raise their head (cf. *De fide et operibus*, 14, 21). Certainly, they all evidence the teaching and catechesis which was being given to the first communities of Christians. For the most part, using a pastoral tone, they deal with doctrinal instruction and moral teaching, all aimed at encouraging people to live deeply Christian lives.

The Letter of St James

The Letter of James normally comes first in the group of "catholic" letters. It has received relatively little commentary over the centuries, probably because it has to do more with moral than doctrinal matters. From the sixteenth century onwards it has come in for more attention from exegetes and theologians in connexion with the whole question of faith and works (cf. 2:14–26). This sparsity of early commentaries and the complexity of the letter's language (a very educated Greek, with a clearly Semitic background) explain why scholars nowadays continue to query its authorship, date of composition, etc. In recent decades, it should be said, this letter has been attracting a lot of attention, on account of the fact that it faithfully reflects the spontaneity that marked the transmission of the Christian message among the early communities of the Church, and because it very clearly shows the continuity between the Old and New Testaments.

The letter begins with a short passage in which the author introduces himself: "James, a servant of God and of the Lord Jesus Christ" (1:1). Tradition identifies him with St James, the Lord's "brother" and bishop of Jerusalem. Some scholars also identify him with one of the Twelve, James, the son of Alphaeus. This James was a relative of Jesus, the son of one of the women named Mary who were with the Blessed Virgin at the foot of the cross. When St Peter went off to Rome, James stayed as head of the community at Jerusalem and in that capacity he received a visit from St Paul after his conversion. He was martyred around the year 62 at the instigation of the high priest Annas II (cf. Flavius Josephus, *Ant.*, 20, 9; Eusebius of Caesarea, *Eccl. Hist.*, 2, 23, 19–23).

The letter is addressed to "the twelve tribes in the Dispersion" (1:1), that is, the Christians of the Diaspora, who lived outside Palestine among the Gentiles. Anything we know about the circumstances in which it was written comes from the letter itself: that is, certain defects were beginning to appear which threatened the spiritual health of those communities. There is debate about the date of composition, but it was probably written in the 60s AD, although some scholars propose a later date.

What gives unity to the letter is its teaching on consistency between a believer's faith and life: one's behaviour should always reflect the faith one professes. However, the letter does not have the structure of a formal treatise. Like Jewish wisdom writing, the order it follows could best be described as a "psychological" and "pedagogical" one. Thus, one word suggests some other theme which uses the same sort of language; so, the same idea is repeated a number of times (in concentric circles, so to speak) in the form of short maxims etc. This style helps the listener or reader to remember the teaching better. The letter is full of exhortations and admonitions—on how to behave in the face of contradictions and temptations; on being fair-minded in one's views on people, and not talking behind their backs; on detachment from wealth, and concern for the needy; on the practice of prayer; on correction of those who have gone astray. Many of these exhortations are very reminiscent of Jesus' words in the Gospels, particularly the sermon on the mount in St Matthew's Gospel—1:12 (cf. Mt 5:11–12); 2:5 (cf. Mt 5:3); 2:13 (cf. Mt 5:7; 5:12 (cf. Mt 5:37; etc.).

A key element in the letter is its teaching on faith and works, which complements what St Paul has to say about this, particularly in Romans and Galatians. However, it looks at the subject from a different angle: St Paul says that faith acts through love (Gal 5:6), but, arguing as he is against Judaizers, he does not accept that the works of the Old Law are necessary: what really matters is faith. But James' main point is that faith needs to be reflected in one's behaviour; hence his famous statement, "a man is justified by works and not by faith alone" (2:24).

Another feature of the letter is its teaching on the sacrament of the anointing of the sick instituted by the Lord.

James

Greeting

1 [1]James, a servant of God and of the Lord Jesus Christ,
To the twelve tribes* in the Dispersion:
Greeting.

1. OPENING INSTRUCTIONS

The value of suffering

2Count it all joy, my brethren, when you meet various trials, 3for you know that
the testing of your faith produces steadfastness. 4And let steadfastness have its
full effect, that you may be perfect and complete, lacking in nothing.
5If any of you lacks wisdom, let him ask God, who gives to all men generously
and without reproaching, and it will be given him. 6But let him ask in faith, with
no doubting, for he who doubts is like a wave of the sea that is driven and tossed
by the wind. 7,8For that person must not suppose that a double-minded man,
unstable in all his ways, will receive anything from the Lord.
9Let the lowly brother boast in his exaltation, 10and the rich in his humili-
ation, because like the flower of the grass he will pass away. 11For the sun rises

---

1:1–5:20 □□ This text seems to be not so much a letter addressed to particular people, as a short treatise or homily in the style of wisdom writing. The advice given in the text follows no particular order. First there are instructions about being patient in the midst of trials and about the dignity of the poor (1:2–2:13). The author then shows that faith needs to be accompanied by works (2:14–26); and then he goes on to give some specific pieces of advice (3:1–5:20)—notably warnings addressed to the well-to-do (5:1–6), and words about the value of prayer and anointing of the sick.

1:1 "In the Dispersion", or diaspora: the term orginally meant Jews domiciled outside Palestine. Here it very probably means Jewish converts to Christianity.

1:2–2:13 □ These instructions all point to the need for there to be no discontinuity between one's faith and one's actions.

1:2–12 The problem of the suffering experienced by the just as compared with the prosperity in this life of the ungodly is one often dealt with in the Old Testament,

with its scorching heat and withers the grass; its flower falls, and its beauty perishes. So will the rich man fade away in the midst of his pursuits.
12Blessed is the man who endures trial, for when he has stood the test he will receive the crown of life which God has promised to those who love him.

The source of temptation

13Let no one say when he is tempted, "I am tempted by God"; for God cannot be
tempted with evil and he himself tempts no one; 14but each person is tempted
when he is lured and enticed by his own desire. 15Then desire when it has
conceived gives birth to sin; and sin when it is full-grown brings forth death.
16Do not be deceived, my beloved brethren. 17Every good endowment and
every perfect gift is from above, coming down from the Father of lights with
whom there is no variation or shadow due to change.[a] 18Of his own will he
brought us forth by the word of truth that we should be a kind of first fruits of
his creatures.

Doers of the word, not hearers only

19Know this, my beloved brethren. Let every man be quick to hear, slow to
speak, slow to anger, 20for the anger of man does not work the righteousness
of God. 21Therefore put away all filthiness and rank growth of wickedness and
receive with meekness the implanted word, which is able to save your souls.
22But be doers of the word, and not hearers only, deceiving yourselves.*
23For if any one is a hearer of the word and not a doer, he is like a man who
observes his natural face in a mirror; 24for he observes himself and goes away
and at once forgets what he was like. 25But he who looks into the perfect law,

---

particularly in the Psalms and the book of Job. But it was not fully and finally solved until the coming of Jesus Christ. "It is therefore through Christ, and in Christ, that light is thrown on the riddle of suffering and death which, apart from his Gospel, overwhelms us" (Vatican II, *GS*, 22). The wisdom St James refers to in v. 5 is, then, the wisdom of the cross (cf. 1 Cor 1:18ff).

Verse 12 seems to echo our Lord's words in the sermon on the mount: "Blessed are you when men revile you …".

1:13–18 From God only good can come. We must not attribute to God our inclination to sin. Nor is it correct to say that because God gave us freedom, he is the cause of our sin. Sin happens when we give in to temptation, to the pull of our passions. And so when we pray in the Our Father "Lead us not into temptation", we are asking God "not to allow us to take the way that leads to sin" (*CCC*, 2846).

1:19–27 The writer uses strong imagery to remind the reader of the need to apply the teaching he has received to his daily life (cf. Mt 7:24; Lk 11:28).

a. Other ancient authorities read *variation due to a shadow of turning*

the law of liberty, and perseveres, being no hearer that forgets but a doer that
acts, he shall be blessed in his doing.
26 If any one thinks he is religious, and does not bridle his tongue but
deceives his heart, this man's religion is vain. 27 Religion that is pure and
undefiled before God and the Father is this: to visit orphans and widows in
their affliction, and to keep oneself unstained from the world.

Impartiality

2 1 My brethren, show no partiality as you hold the faith of our Lord Jesus
Christ, the Lord of glory. 2 For if a man with gold rings and in fine clothing
comes into your assembly, and a poor man in shabby clothing also comes in,
3 and you pay attention to the one who wears the fine clothing and say, "Have a
seat here, please," while you say to the poor man, "Stand there," or, "Sit at my
feet," 4 have you not made distinctions among yourselves, and become judges with
evil thoughts? 5 Listen, my beloved brethren. Has not God chosen those who are
poor in the world to be rich in faith and heirs of the kingdom which he has
promised to those who love him? 6 But you have dishonoured the poor man. Is it
not the rich who oppress you, is it not they who drag you into court? 7 Is it not they
who blaspheme that honourable name which was invoked over you?*
8 If you really fulfil the royal law, according to the scripture, "You shall love
your neighbour as yourself," you do well. 9 But if you show partiality, you
commit sin, and are convicted by the law as transgressors. 10 For whoever
keeps the whole law but fails in one point has become guilty of all of it. 11 For
he who said, "Do not commit adultery," said also, "Do not kill." If you do not
commit adultery but do kill, you have become a transgressor of the law. 12 So
speak and so act as those who are to be judged under the law of liberty. 13 For
judgment is without mercy to one who has shown no mercy; yet mercy
triumphs over judgment.

"The perfect law, the law of liberty" (v. 25) is the good news brought by Jesus Christ, who has made us children of God and set us free from every kind of servitude—both that of the Old Law and subjection to devil, sin and death.

2:1–13 Apparently a good many of those to whom this letter was originally addressed were people of modest means. The Law of Moses condemned discrimination among people; our Lord corrected certain restrictive interpretations of that Law and formulated a "new commandment" (cf. Jn 13:34).

Both in the Old Law and in the New "to transgress one commandment is to infringe all the others. One cannot honour another person without blessing God his Creator. One cannot adore God without loving all men, his creatures" (*CCC*, 2069).

2:8 Lev 19:18. **2:11** Ex 20:13–14.

2. FAITH AND GOOD WORKS

Faith without good works is dead

14What does it profit, my brethren, if a man says he has faith but has not
works? Can his faith save him?* 15If a brother or sister is ill-clad and in lack
of daily food, 16and one of you says to them, "Go in peace, be warmed and
filled," without giving them the things needed for the body, what does it profit?
17So faith by itself, if it has no works, is dead.
18But some one will say, "You have faith and I have works." Show me your
faith apart from your works, and I by my works will show you my faith. 19You
believe that God is one; you do well. Even the demons believe—and shudder.

Examples from the Bible

20Do you want to be shown, you shallow man, that faith apart from works is
barren? 21Was not Abraham our father justified by works, when he offered his
son Isaac upon the altar? 22You see that faith was active along with his works,
and faith was completed by works, 23and the scripture was fulfilled which says,
"Abraham believed God, and it was reckoned to him as righteousness"; and he

---

2:14–26 □ The central idea is summed up here: faith is dead unless it produces works. The example of various Old Testament figures is cited.

2:14–19 Faith without good works cannot bring about salvation (cf. Mt 7:21). The example in vv. 15–16 is similar to that in 1 John: "if any one has the world's goods and sees his brother in need, yet closes his heart to him, how does the love of God abide in him?" (3:17). The conclusion drawn is similar, too: "Little children, let us not love in word or speech but in deed and in truth" (3:18). St Paul for his part says: "the kingdom of God does not consist in talk but in power", that is, in deeds (1 Cor 4:20). Works are the yardstick for measuring whether a Christian's life is genuine or not; they show whether he or she has true faith and love; "just as we know the life of the body through its movements, we come to see the life of faith through good works. The body is given life by the soul through which it moves and feels; likewise, charity is the life-force of faith […]. Just as the body dies when the soul leaves it, faith dies when the ardour of charity is cooled" (St Bernard, *Serm 2, Pasc.*, 1).

When a person is in mortal sin, Christian teaching describes him as having "dead faith" (cf. 17). "The gift of faith remains in one who has not sinned against it; […] when it is deprived of hope and love, faith does not fully unite the believer to Christ and does not make him a living member of his Body" (*CCC,* 1815).

2:20–26 St James supports his argument with Genesis 15:6 (a passage also used by Paul to show Abraham's faith) and the episode of Rahab (Josh 2:1–21; 6:17–25). The justification being spoken about here is the moral perfection which

2:23 Gen 15:6; Is 41:8.

was called the friend of God. 24You see that a man is justified by works and not
by faith alone. 25And in the same way was not also Rahab the harlot justified by
works when she received the messengers and sent them out another way? 26For
as the body apart from the spirit is dead, so faith apart from works is dead.

3. PRACTICAL APPLICATIONS

Controlling one's tongue

3 1Let not many of you become teachers, my brethren, for you know that we
who teach shall be judged with greater strictness. 2For we all make many
mistakes, and if any one makes no mistakes in what he says he is a perfect
man, able to bridle the whole body also. 3If we put bits into the mouths of
horses that they may obey us, we guide their whole bodies. 4Look at the ships
also; though they are so great and are driven by strong winds, they are guided
by a very small rudder wherever the will of the pilot directs. 5So the tongue is
a little member and boasts of great things. How great a forest is set ablaze by
a small fire!

6And the tongue is a fire. The tongue is an unrighteous world among our
members, staining the whole body, setting on fire the cycle of nature,[b] and set
on fire by hell.[c] 7For every kind of beast and bird, of reptile and sea creature,
can be tamed and has been tamed by humankind, 8but no human being can
tame the tongue—a restless evil, full of deadly poison. 9With it we bless the
Lord and Father, and with it we curse men, who are made in the likeness of
God. 10From the same mouth come blessing and cursing. My brethren, this
ought not to be so. 11Does a spring pour forth from the same opening fresh

---

presupposes faith and which is attained, once a person has grace, by the practice of virtue. In Paul (Rom 4:1–25; Gal 3:6–9) justification means the union with God through grace, but also the practice of charity (cf. Gal 5:6).

3:1–5:6 □ Here a number of specific applications are given of the principle that one's behaviour should be consistent with one's faith.

3:1–12 Sins of the tongue are easy to commit but they can do a great deal of harm. St James provides examples to show how a tiny cause can lead to disproportionately large effects. Therefore, a person should always have God's presence and his neighbour's good in mind when speaking: "Every good Christian must act more promptly to save the position of his neighbour, and not condemn it; if he cannot save it, he should enquire how his neighbour understands it, and if he misunderstands his position he should be corrected through love; if that is not enough, all the appropriate means should be put into action to ensure that his

b. Or *wheel of birth* **c.** Greek *Gehenna*

water and brackish? [12]Can a fig tree, my brethren, yield olives, or a grapevine figs? No more can salt water yield fresh.

True and false wisdom

[13]Who is wise and understanding among you? By his good life let him show his works in the meekness of wisdom. [14]But if you have bitter jealousy and selfish ambition in your hearts, do not boast and be false to the truth. [15]This wisdom is not such as comes down from above, but is earthly, unspiritual, devilish. [16]For where jealousy and selfish ambition exist, there will be disorder and every vile practise. [17]But the wisdom from above is first pure, then peaceable, gentle, open to reason, full of mercy and good fruits, without uncertainty or insincerity. [18]And the harvest of righteousness is sown in peace by those who make peace.

The source of discord

4 [1]What causes wars, and what causes fightings among you? Is it not your passions that are at war in your members? [2]You desire and do not have; so you kill. And you covet[d] and cannot obtain; so you fight and wage war. You do not have, because you do not ask. [3]You ask and do not receive, because you ask wrongly, to spend it on your passions. [4]Unfaithful creatures! Do you not know that friendship with the world is enmity with God? Therefore whoever wishes to be a friend of the world makes himself an enemy of God. [5]Or do you suppose it is in vain that the scripture says, "He yearns jealously over the spirit which he has made to dwell in us"? [6]But he gives more grace; therefore it says, "God opposes the proud, but gives grace to the humble." [7]Submit yourselves therefore to God. Resist the devil and he will flee from you. [8]Draw near to God

---

neighbour, through a perfect understanding of his situation, is saved" (St Ignatius Loyola, *Spir. exer.*, 22).

3:13–18 Unlike worldly wisdom, true wisdom produces meekness, mercy and peace (cf. Mt 5:5, 7, 9).

4:1–12 St James lists the main causes of disunity among Christians—greed and envy (vv. 1–3); disordered love for things of the world, and pride (vv. 4–10); and, stemming from that, gossip and defamation (vv. 11–12).

The quotation as given in v. 5 is not to be found in the Bible. St James may be referring not so much to a specific passage as to an idea that often occurs in the Bible when it depicts God as a jealous lover (e.g. Ex 20:5; 34:14; Zech 1:14; 8:2; etc.). The quotation in v. 6 comes from Proverbs 3:34. The defining idea is that "to recognize one's own sin, and, moreover, [...] to recognize oneself as a sinner, capable and inclined towards sinfulness, is an indispensable condition for returning to God" (John Paul II, *Reconc. et paen.*, 13).

d. Or *you kill and you covet* **4:6** Prov 3:34.

and he will draw near to you. Cleanse your hands, you sinners, and purify your
hearts, you men of double mind. [9]Be wretched and mourn and weep. Let your
laughter be turned to mourning and your joy to dejection. [10]Humble yourselves
before the Lord and he will exalt you.
[11]Do not speak evil against one another, brethren. He that speaks evil
against a brother or judges his brother, speaks evil against the law and judges
the law. But if you judge the law, you are not a doer of the law but a judge.
[12]There is one lawgiver and judge, he who is able to save and to destroy. But
who are you that you judge your neighbour?

Trust in divine providence

[13]Come now, you who say, "Today or tomorrow we will go into such and such
a town and spend a year there and trade and get gain"; [14]whereas you do not
know about tomorrow. What is your life? For you are a mist that appears for a
little time and then vanishes. [15]Instead you ought to say, "If the Lord wills, we
shall live and we shall do this or that." [16]As it is, you boast in your arrogance.
All such boasting is evil. [17]Whoever knows what is right to do and fails to do
it, for him it is sin.

A warning to the rich

5 [1]Come now, you rich, weep and howl for the miseries that are coming upon
you. [2]Your riches have rotted and your garments are moth-eaten. [3]Your gold
and silver have rusted, and their rust will be evidence against you and will eat
your flesh like fire. You have laid up treasure[e]* for the last days. [4]Behold, the
wages of the labourers who mowed your fields, which you kept back by fraud,
cry out; and the cries of the harvesters have reached the ears of the Lord of
hosts. [5]You have lived on the earth in luxury and in pleasure; you have fattened
your hearts in a day of slaughter. [6]You have condemned, you have killed the
righteous man; he does not resist you.

4:13–17 The expressions "If the Lord wills", "God willing" (also used by St Paul: cf. 1 Cor 4:19) has passed into popular Christian speech; it shows a readiness to leave one's future in God's hands, trusting in divine providence.

5:1–6 In tones reminiscent of the prophets, St James reproves the well-to-do for their pride, greed and pleasure-seeking, warning them that the judgment of God is near at hand. The description of the lifestyle of these rich people brings to mind the parable of Lazarus and the rich man (cf. Lk 16:19ff). The Church has constantly reminded people of the need to get rid of unjust inequalities (frequently denounced in Scripture). Those who have plenty of material resources should use them to benefit others. In this regard, the Church teaches that "[men ...] are morally obliged not to keep capital in reserve and unproductive. Looking at it another way, they must have regard for the common good before all other things

e. Or *will eat your flesh, since you have stored up fire*

4. FINAL COUNSELS

A call for constancy

[7]Be patient, therefore, brethren, until the coming of the Lord. Behold, the
farmer waits for the precious fruit of the earth, being patient over it until it
receives the early and the late rain. [8]You also be patient. Establish your hearts,
for the coming of the Lord is at hand. [9]Do not grumble, brethren, against one
another, that you may not be judged; behold, the Judge is standing at the doors.
[10]As an example of suffering and patience, brethren, take the prophets who
spoke in the name of the Lord. [11]Behold, we call those happy who were
steadfast. You have heard of the steadfastness of Job, and you have seen the
purpose of the Lord, how the Lord is compassionate and merciful.

On oath-taking

[12]But above all, my brethren, do not swear, either by heaven or by earth or
with any other oath, but let your yes be yes and your no be no, that you may
not fall under condemnation.

The value of prayer. The sacrament of the Anointing of the Sick

[13]Is any one among you suffering? Let him pray. Is any cheerful? Let him sing
praise. [14]Is any among you sick? Let him call for the elders of the church, and
let them pray over him, anointing him with oil in the name of the Lord; [15]and

---

[…]. The right to private property must not be conceived of without reference to the common good. It is subordinate to the universal end of all material goods" (SCDF, *Libert. consc.*, 87).

5:7–20 □ This section contains concluding words of advice about patience, swearing oaths, prayer for and anointing of the sick.

5:7–11 As at the start of his letter, St James appeals for patience—a serene and hope-filled attitude to events: "It may be said that it is through patience that man possesses his soul [cf. Lk 21: 29], because patience destroys at the root all the tribulations that deprive the soul of peace" (St Thomas Aquinas, *Summa theol.*, 2–2, 136, 2, 2).

5:12 This exhortation is almost an exact copy of the words of our Lord, "Let what you say be simply 'yes' or 'no', anything more than that comes from the evil one" (Mt 5:37). "Discretion in calling upon God is allied with a respectful awareness of his presence, which all our assertions either witness to or mock" (*CCC*, 2153).

5:13–18 Prayer is a necessary and effective counter to sadness ("suffering": v. 13). "Sadness is the end product of selfishness. If we truly want to live for God, we will

5:7 Deut 11:14; Jer 5:24. **5:11** Ps 103:8; 111:4.

the prayer of faith will save the sick man, and the Lord will raise him up; and
if he has committed sins, he will be forgiven.* 16Therefore confess your sins
to one another, and pray for one another, that you may be healed. The prayer
of a righteous man has great power in its effects. 17Elijah was a man of like
nature with ourselves and he prayed fervently that it might not rain, and for
three years and six months it did not rain on the earth. 18Then he prayed again
and the heaven gave rain, and the earth brought forth its fruit.

Concern for one another

19My brethren, if any one among you wanders from the truth and some one
brings him back, 20let him know that whoever brings back a sinner from the
error of his way will save his soul from death and will cover a multitude of
sins.

---

never lack cheerfulness, even when we discover our errors and wretchedness. Cheerfulness finds its way into our life of prayer, so much so that we cannot help singing for joy. For we are in love, and singing is a thing that lovers do" (Bl. J. Escrivá, *Hom.*, 2, 92).

The Magisterium of the Church teaches that this text (vv. 14–15) promulgates the sacrament of the Anointing of the Sick (see the note on Mk 6:6–13). "The sacrament of Anointing of the Sick has as its purpose the conferral of a special grace on the Christian experiencing the difficulties inherent in the condition of grave illness or old age" (*CCC*, 1527).

5:19–20 This is a call for apostolic zeal. "(God) prizes one soul that by his mercy, and our diligence and prayer, we may have gained for him, than all the other services we can render him" (St Teresa of Avila, *Foundations,* 1, 7).

The First Letter of St Peter

The First Letter of St Peter shows us the mission and cohesiveness of the early Church in the midst of a society estranged from God. It provides markers about the way Christians should behave *vis-à-vis* the world, that is, how they should operate in a hostile environment. Baptism and the cross are the two points of reference which we keep meeting in this letter.

From very early times this letter was unanimously accepted having been written by the apostle Peter. However, it may have been redacted by Silvanus (also called Silas in the Acts of the Apostles) or some other disciple commissioned to record St Peter's teaching. Therefore the date of composition is usually put around the year 64 or 67, the possible years of Peter's martyrdom (though a later date is possible). It is addressed to Christian communities living in various parts of Asia Minor. The environment there was hostile, which meant that Christians' perseverance was at risk. Many of them were converts from paganism, probably recent ones. Hence the constant reminders about Baptism (1:3, 23; 2:2; 3:21). As we can see from the final greetings, the letter was written in "Babylon" (5:13), that is, Rome, the capital of the empire, as it used to be called symbolically (cf. Rev 14:8; 16:19; 17:5; 18:2; 10, 21).

The main aim of the apostle seems to be to console Christians and exhort them to stay true to the faith in the midst of difficulties and persecution. The obstacles they come up against, they are told, should be put to good use—to purify them, being aware that it is God, not men, who is our judge. The letter teases out this profound and consoling idea—that a Christian is part of Christ and shares in his paschal mystery. Just as Jesus, in order to redeem men, suffered his passion and death and then was raised to imperishable life, so too Christians will attain their salvation and that of many others through coping with various kinds of contradictions. Jesus Christ is their model, and it is also he who makes fully meaningful the persecutions a Christian suffers (4:12–19).

Although he explicitly mentions Baptism only once, the writer does refer to it repeatedly. These references allow us to see elements of the baptismal liturgy and the catechesis given to those who request Baptism. The main points the letter makes in its teaching on Baptism are: Baptism involves a rebirth; it liberates a person from sin (this liberation was prefigured in the release of the Israelites from bondage in Egypt); it brings about salvation (prefigured in Noah). Thus, Baptism is the basis of the sacred writer's exhortations to his readers/listeners to stay firm in the faith (5:9). He also reminds them about other teachings concerning Jesus, the Church and the Christian life. We might mention particularly the teaching about the "royal priesthood" of the faithful (2:9), the universal scope of the redemption wrought by Christ (3:18–22), and giving testimony of one's faith to one's fellow citizens through one's example (3:15–16).

1 Peter

Greeting

1 [1]Peter, an apostle of Jesus Christ, To the exiles of the Dispersion in Pontus,
Galatia, Cappadocia, Asia, and Bithynia,* [2]chosen and destined by God the
Father and sanctified by the Spirit for obedience to Jesus Christ and for
sprinkling with his blood:

May grace and peace be multiplied to you.

Praise and thanksgiving to God

[3]Blessed be the God and Father of our Lord Jesus Christ! By his great mercy
we have been born anew to a living hope through the resurrection of Jesus
Christ from the dead, [4]and to an inheritance which is imperishable, undefiled,
and unfading, kept in heaven for you, [5]who by God's power are guarded
through faith for a salvation ready to be revealed in the last time. [6]In this you
rejoice,[a] though now for a little while you may have to suffer various trials, [7]so
that the genuineness of your faith, more precious than gold which though
perishable is tested by fire, may redound to praise and glory and honour at the

---

1:1–5:14 □ □ St Peter writes this letter mainly for Christians of Gentile background. In it, after thanking God for having saved us through Jesus Christ (1:3–12), he looks at some aspects of Christian life that follow on from Baptism—the call to holiness (1:13–2:10), the exemplary way a Christian should behave in everyday life (2:11–3:12), patience in times of trouble, be it great or small (3:13–4:19), and, finally, the way priests should behave towards their flock and vice versa (5:1–11). The letter ends by giving some information on Peter's situation at the time of writing (5:12–14).

1:1–2 The regions mentioned in v. 1 were in Asia Minor (present-day Turkey). Verse 2 amounts to a profession of faith in the Blessed Trinity: to the Father it attributes election from all eternity; to the Son, redemption; to the Holy Spirit, sanctification.

1:3–12 This letter was written to people who lived in a world hostile to Christian believers. Here St Peter expands on what he said in (v. 2), pointing out why they should feel consoled and should persevere in the faith: by his choice of them, God the Father has ear-marked for them a wonderful inheritance in heaven (vv. 3–5); to attain this, they need to love and believe in Christ in spite of trials (vv. 6–9); the Holy Spirit, who announced in the Old Testament that salvation would flow from the sufferings of Christ, now proclaims (through the preachers of the Gospel) that

a. Or *Rejoice in this*

revelation of Jesus Christ. 8Without having seen[b] him you[c] love him; though you do not now see him you[c] believe in him and rejoice with unutterable and exalted joy. 9As the outcome of your faith you obtain the salvation of your souls.

10The prophets who prophesied of the grace that was to be yours searched and inquired about this salvation; 11they inquired what person or time was indicated by the Spirit of Christ* within them when predicting the sufferings of Christ and the subsequent glory. 12It was revealed to them that they were serving not themselves but you, in the things which have now been announced to you by those who preached the good news to you through the Holy Spirit sent from heaven, things into which angels long to look.

1. A CALL TO HOLINESS

Christians are called to be saints

13Therefore gird up your minds, be sober, set your hope fully upon the grace that is coming to you at the revelation of Jesus Christ. 14As obedient children, do not be conformed to the passions of your former ignorance, 15but as he who called you is holy, be holy yourselves in all your conduct; 16since it is written, "You shall be holy, for I am holy."

The blood of Christ has ransomed us

17And if you invoke as Father him who judges each one impartially according to his deeds, conduct yourselves with fear throughout the time of your exile.
18You know that you were ransomed from the futile ways inherited from your

---

salvation has arrived. "If I experience pain, relief will come in due course. If I am offered tribulation, it will serve for my purification. Does gold shine in the craftman's furnance? It will shine later when it forms part of the collar, when it is jewellery. But, for the time being, it puts up with being in the fire because when it sheds its impurities it will acquire its brilliant shine" (St Augustine, *Enarr. in Ps*, 61, 11).

1:13–2:10 □ The body of the letter really begins here. As a consequence of the new life that Baptism confers, Christians are called to seek holiness.

1:13–16 With the Exodus-theme as a background, St Peter reminds us that Christians are the new chosen people, set free from the bondage of sin and called to attain holiness, with God himself as our model. On the call of all mankind to holiness, see the notes on Mt 5:17–48 and Lk 12:22–34.

1:17–21 Freedom from sin, and holiness derive from the sacrifice of Christ. St Peter uses the imagery and terminology of slave redemption to explain what

b. Other ancient authorities read *known* **c.** Or omit *you* fathers, not with perishable things such as silver or gold, [19]but with the precious blood of Christ, like that of a lamb without blemish or spot. [20]He was destined before the foundation of the world but was made manifest at the end of the times for your sake. [21]Through him you have confidence in God, who raised him from the dead and gave him glory, so that your faith and hope are in God.[d]

Brotherly love

[22]Having purified your souls by your obedience to the truth for a sincere love of the brethren, love one another earnestly from the heart. [23]You have been born anew, not of perishable seed but of imperishable, through the living and abiding word of God; [24]for

> "All flesh is like grass
> and all its glory like the flower of grass.
> The grass withers, and the flower falls,
> [25] but the word of the Lord abides for ever."

That word is the good news which was preached to you.

Like newborn babies

2 [1]So put away all malice and all guile and insincerity and envy and all slander. [2]Like newborn babes, long for the pure spiritual milk, that by it you may grow up to salvation; [3]for you have tasted the kindness of the Lord.

The priesthood that all believers share

[4]Come to him, to that living stone, rejected by men but in God's sight chosen and precious; [5]and like living stones be yourselves built into a spiritual house,

---

Christ's sacrifice means, but the price of redeeming the slave in this instance "was calculated in terms not of money but of blood, for Christ died for us" (St Ambrose, *Com. on Lk,* 12, 6–7).

1:22–25 Fraternal love is one of the main proofs of holiness. The validity of the precept of brotherly love is confirmed by the image of the flower of grass taken from Isaiah 40:6–8 (cf. Jas 1:9–11) which contrasts the fleetingness of earthly things with the enduring nature of the word of God.

2:1–3 The liturgy applies this text to the newly baptized; they are like babies recently born to the new life of grace; it prays "God of mercy, you wash away our sins in water, you give us new birth in the Spirit, and redeem us in the blood of Christ. As we celebrate Christ's resurrection, increase our awareness of these blessings, and renew your gift of life within us" (*Roman Missal*, 2nd Sunday of Easter).

2:4–10 Baptism makes a member a member of a spiritual building, the Church, whose cornerstone is Christ. Unlike those who reject faith, believers form the new

d. Or *so that your faith is hope in God* **1:24–25** Is 40:6–8 **2:3** Ps 34:8.

to be a holy priesthood, to offer spiritual sacrifices acceptable to God through
Jesus Christ. 6For it stands in scripture:
"Behold, I am laying in Zion a stone, a cornerstone chosen and
precious,
and he who believes in him will not be put to shame."
7To you therefore who believe, he is precious, but for those who do not believe,
"The very stone which the builders rejected
has become the head of the corner,"
8and
"A stone that will make men stumble,
a rock that will make them fall";
for they stumble because they disobey the word, as they were destined to do.
9But you are a chosen race, a royal priesthood, a holy nation, God's own
people,[e] that you may declare the wonderful deeds of him who called you out of
darkness into his marvellous light. 10Once you were no people but now you are
God's people; once you had not received mercy but now you have received mercy.

2. THE OBLIGATIONS OF CHRISTIANS

Setting an example for pagans

11Beloved, I beseech you as aliens and exiles to abstain from the passions of
the flesh that wage war against your soul. 12Maintain good conduct among the

---

Israel, the true people of God. In this holy people, there is only one priest, Jesus Christ, and only one sacrifice—that offered by him on the cross and which is renewed in the Mass. But all Christians, through the sacraments of Baptism and Confirmation, share in Christ's priesthood and are thereby equipped to mediate in a priestly way between God and man, and to take an active part in divine worship. "All their works, prayers and apostolic undertakings, family and married life, daily work, relaxation of mind and body, if they are accomplished in the Spirit—indeed even the hardships of life if patiently borne—all these become spiritual sacrifices acceptable to God through Jesus Christ. In the celebration of the Eucharist these may most fittingly be offered to the Father along with the body of the Lord. And so, worshipping everywhere by their holy actions, the laity consecrate the world itself to God" (Vatican I, *LG*, 34).

2:11–3:12 □This section consists of some instructions about the exemplary way Christians should behave in a hostile world.

2:11–12 The exemplary lives of Christians will bring their friends and colleagues to praise God: "In the same way your light must shine in the sight of men, so that,

e. Greek *a people for his possession* **2:6** Is 28:16. **2:7** Ps 118:22. **2:8** Is 8:14–15. **2:9** Ex 19:5–6; Is 43:20–21. **2:10** Hos 2:23.

Gentiles, so that in case they speak against you as wrongdoers, they may see
your good deeds and glorify God on the day of visitation.

Obedience to civil authority
13Be subject for the Lord's sake to every human institution,[f] whether it be to
the emperor as supreme, 14or to governors as sent by him to punish those who
do wrong and to praise those who do right. 15For it is God's will that by doing
right you should put to silence the ignorance of foolish men. 16Live as free
men, yet without using your freedom as a pretext for evil; but live as servants of
God. 17Honor all men. Love the brotherhood. Fear God. Honour the emperor.

Duties towards masters. Christ's example
18Servants, be submissive to your masters with all respect, not only to the kind
and gentle but also to the overbearing. 19For one is approved if, mindful of
God, he endures pain while suffering unjustly. 20For what credit is it, if when
you do wrong and are beaten for it you take it patiently? But if when you do
right and suffer for it you take it patiently, you have God's approval. 21For to
this you have been called, because Christ also suffered for you, leaving you an
example, that you should follow in his steps. 22He committed no sin; no guile
was found on his lips. 23When he was reviled, he did not revile in return; when
he suffered, he did not threaten; but he trusted to him who judges justly. 24He
himself bore our sins in his body on the tree,[g] that we might die to sin and live
to righteousness. By his wounds you have been healed. 25For you were

---

seeing your good works, they may give the praise to your Father in heaven" (Mt 5:16).

2:13–17 "The duty of obedience requires all to give due honour to authority, and to treat those who are charged to exercise it with respect, and, insofar as it is deserved, with gratitude and good-will" (*CCC*, 1900).

2:18–25 Patient endurance of unjust suffering rests on the example set by our Lord. Verses 21–25 are a beautiful hymn to Christ on the cross; Christ's sufferings fulfil the prophecies about the Servant of Yahweh in the book of Isaiah (52:13–53:12). However great the trials Christians may suffer, they will never be as severe or as undeserved as those of our Lord.

"Shepherd and Guardian of your souls" (v. 25). The messianic prophecies about the suffering servant include the image of the scattered flock (cf. Is 53:6), to which Jesus alludes in his allegory of the Good Shepherd (cf. Jn 10:11–16). St Peter, to whom our Lord gave charge of his flock (cf. Jn 21:15–19), seems to have been particularly fond of this pastoral simile.

f. Or *every institution ordained for men* **g.** Or *carried up . . . to the tree* **2:22** Is 53:9. **2:24** Is 53:12 Gk. **2:25** Is 53:6; Ezek 34:5.

straying like sheep, but have now returned to the Shepherd and Guardian of your souls.

Exemplary family life

3 [1]Likewise you wives,* be submissive to your husbands, so that some, though
they do not obey the word, may be won without a word by the behaviour of
their wives, [2]when they see your reverent and chaste behaviour. [3]Let not yours be
the outward adorning with braiding of hair, decoration of gold, and wearing of
fine clothing, [4]but let it be the hidden person of the heart with the imperishable
jewel of a gentle and quiet spirit, which in God's sight is very precious. [5]So once
the holy women who hoped in God used to adorn themselves and were
submissive to their husbands, [6]as Sarah obeyed Abraham, calling him lord. And
you are now her children if you do right and let nothing terrify you.
[7]Likewise you husbands, live considerately with your wives, bestowing
honour on the woman as the weaker sex, since you are joint heirs of the grace
of life, in order that your prayers may not be hindered.

Love of the brethren

[8]Finally, all of you, have unity of spirit, sympathy, love of the brethren, a
tender heart and a humble mind. [9]Do not return evil for evil or reviling for
reviling; but on the contrary bless, for to this you have been called, that you
may obtain a blessing. [10]For

"He that would love life
and see good days,
let him keep his tongue from evil
and his lips from speaking guile;
[11] let him turn away from evil and do right;
let him seek peace and pursue it.
[12] For the eyes of the Lord are upon the righteous,
and his ears are open to their prayer.
But the face of the Lord is against those that do evil."

3:1–7 The counsels and appeals contained in this passage are designed to steer spouses' mutual love towards a search for each other's greater good—that is, conversion. To counter the mores of the time, the apostle appeals to married couples to act in a Christian way; he gives some practical advice based on the equal dignity of husband and wife (v. 7).

3:8–12 Love is the virtue that must govern the Christian life; this theological virtue influences all the moral virtues. St Peter ends his appeal with a quotation from Psalm 34:13–17, a psalm which he already quoted earlier (cf. 2:3).

3:10–12 Ps 34:12–16.

3. THE CHRISTIAN'S ATTITUDE TO SUFFERING

Undeserved suffering is a blessing
[13]Now who is there to harm you if you are zealous for what is right? [14]But
even if you do suffer for righteousness' sake, you will be blessed. Have no fear
of them, nor be troubled, [15]but in your hearts reverence Christ as Lord. Always
be prepared to make a defence to any one who calls you to account for the
hope that is in you, yet do it with gentleness and reverence; [16]and keep your
conscience clear, so that, when you are abused, those who revile your good
behaviour in Christ may be put to shame. [17]For it is better to suffer for doing
right, if that should be God's will, than for doing wrong.

Christ's suffering and glorification
[18]For Christ also died[h] for sins once for all, the righteous for the unrighteous,
that he might bring us to God, being put to death in the flesh but made alive in
the spirit; [19]in which he went and preached to the spirits in prison, [20]who
formerly did not obey, when God's patience waited in the days of Noah, during
the building of the ark, in which a few, that is, eight persons, were saved through
water. [21]Baptism, which corresponds to this, now saves you, not as a removal of
dirt from the body but as an appeal to God for a clear conscience, through the
resurrection of Jesus Christ, [22]who has gone into heaven and is at the right
hand of God, with angels, authorities, and powers subject to him.

3:13–4:19 □ This part of the letter deals with how a Christian, through his suffering, shares in the redemptive mystery of Christ.

3:13–17 These verses introduce a new theme which takes us up to the end of the letter. They seem to be directed to people who are surprised to encounter persecution even though they are doing good (v. 13). If we act in a way consistent with our faith, those who criticize us unjustly may come to see their mistake and mend their ways (v. 16).

3:18–22 This passage may include parts of a Creed used in early Christian baptismal instruction. It very clearly states the essentials about belief in Jesus Christ, as preached by the apostles from the beginning, and it later found its way into the Apostles' Creed. Verse 19 brings in the Church's belief in the descent of Christ into hell, a manifestation of the fact that salvation reaches all, irrespective of the age in which they live: "In his human soul united to his divine person, the dead Christ went down to the realm of the dead. He opened heaven's gates for the just who had gone before him" (*CCC*, 637).

h. Other ancient authorities read *suffered* **3:14–15** Is 8:12–13.

The Christian has broken with sin

4 [1]Since therefore Christ suffered in the flesh, arm yourselves with the same thought, for whoever has suffered in the flesh[i] has ceased from sin,* [2]so as to live for the rest of the time in the flesh no longer by human passions but by the will of God. [3]Let the time that is past suffice for doing what the Gentiles like to do, living in licentiousness, passions, drunkenness, revels, carousing, and lawless idolatry. [4]They are surprised that you do not now join them in the same wild profligacy, and they abuse you; [5]but they will give account to him who is ready to judge the living and the dead. [6]For this is why the gospel was preached even to the dead, that though judged in the flesh like men, they might live in the spirit like God.

A call for charity

[7]The end of all things is at hand; therefore keep sane and sober for your prayers. [8]Above all hold unfailing your love for one another, since love covers a multitude of sins. [9]Practise hospitality ungrudgingly to one another. [10]As each has received a gift, employ it for one another, as good stewards of God's varied grace: [11]whoever speaks, as one who utters oracles of God; whoever renders service, as one who renders it by the strength which God supplies; in order that in everything God may be glorified through Jesus Christ. To him belong glory and dominion for ever and ever. Amen.

The Christian meaning of suffering

[12]Beloved, do not be surprised at the fiery ordeal which comes upon you to prove you, as though something strange were happening to you. [13]But rejoice

---

4:1–6 A Christian's lifestyle should be different from that of an unbaptized person, even if that leads to misunderstanding and unjust criticism. In due course, the Judgment will come and it will show everyone in his or her true light.

Verse 6 is difficult to interpret. Peter may be referring to our Lord's descent into the bosom of Abraham, or to Christians who have died without seeing, in this life, the final victory of Christ. In either case, he would be speaking about those who stayed faithful to God and whose lives seemed folly to people without a spiritual outlook. The text is reminiscent of Wisdom 3:1–4.

4:7–11 The incarnation of Jesus Christ marked the beginning of the last days, a period which extends to the end of the world and the Last Judgment. That is why St Peter urges the practice of prayer and charity, and also hospitality.

4:12–19 St Peter now returns to the main theme of this part of the letter. Christians who share in Christ's sufferings also share in his exaltation. "God wants to open our eyes to all the mercy he shows us through what the world calls

i. Other ancient authorities add *for us*; some *for you*

in so far as you share Christ's sufferings, that you may also rejoice and be glad
when his glory is revealed. [14]If you are reproached for the name of Christ, you
are blessed, because the spirit of glory[j] and of God rests upon you. [15]But let
none of you suffer as a murderer, or a thief, or a wrongdoer, or a mischief-
maker; [16]yet if one suffers as a Christian, let him not be ashamed, but under
that name let him glorify God. [17]For the time has come for judgment to begin
with the household of God; and if it begins with us, what will be the end of
those who do not obey the gospel of God? [18]And

"If the righteous man is scarcely saved,
where will the impious and sinner appear?"

[19]Therefore let those who suffer according to God's will do right and entrust
their souls to a faithful Creator.

4. FINAL EXHORTATIONS

To priests

5 [1]So I exhort the elders among you, as a fellow elder and a witness of the
sufferings of Christ as well as a partaker in the glory that is to be revealed.
[2]Tend the flock of God that is your charge,[k] not by constraint but willingly,[l] not
for shameful gain but eagerly, [3]not as domineering over those in your charge
but being examples to the flock. [4]And when the chief Shepherd is manifested
you will obtain the unfading crown of glory.

To all the faithful

[5]Likewise you that are younger be subject to the elders. Clothe yourselves, all
of you, with humility toward one another, for "God opposes the proud, but
gives grace to the humble."

---

dishonour, and how greatly honoured we are in being dishonoured when we seek to give honour to God" (St John of Avila, *Letters,* 58).

5:1–14 □ The final part of the letter consists of exhortations to priests and faithful in which the theme of Christ's sufferings is still present.

5:1–4 These exhortations are reminiscent of our Lord's when he spoke about the Good Shepherd (Jn 10:11) and when he told St Peter after the resurrection, "Feed my lambs ... Feed my sheep" (Jn 21:15–17).

5:5–11 In the face of trials which God permits, the apostle appeals for a solidarity among the faithful based on humility and docility (vv. 5–6). The ascetical effort to

j. Other ancient authorities insert *and of power* **k.** Other ancient authorities add *exercising the oversight* **l.** Other ancient authorities add *as God would have you* **4:18** Prov 11:31 Gk. **5:5** Prov 3:34.

[6]Humble yourselves therefore under the mighty hand of God, that in due
time he may exalt you. [7]Cast all your anxieties on him, for he cares about you.
[8]Be sober, be watchful. Your adversary the devil prowls around like a roaring
lion, seeking some one to devour. [9]Resist him, firm in your faith, knowing that
the same experience of suffering is required of your brotherhood throughout
the world. [10]And after you have suffered a little while, the God of all grace,
who has called you to his eternal glory in Christ, will himself restore, establish,
and strengthen[m] you. [11]To him be the dominion for ever and ever. Amen.

Words of farewell

[12]By Silvanus, a faithful brother as I regard him, I have written briefly to you,
exhorting and declaring that this is the true grace of God; stand fast in it. [13]She
who is at Babylon,* who is likewise chosen, sends you greetings; and so does
my son Mark. [14]Greet one another with the kiss of love.
Peace to all of you that are in Christ.

---

resist temptation is backed up by trust in the Lord (vv. 7–11). Christians, "firm in the faith" (cf. v. 9), will resist the attacks of the enemy. The trials they suffer serve to purify them and are a pledge of the glory God will give them: "This momentary affliction is preparing for us an eternal weight of glory beyond all comparison" (2 Cor 4:17).

5:12–14 Like other letters in the New Testament, this one ends with good wishes from the church where the writer is based, and some words of blessing.

Silvanus, called Silas in Acts 15:22, had accompanied St Paul during his second apostolic journey through Asia Minor and Greece (Acts 15:36–18:22). He could have been the bearer of the letter, or the secretary who took down Peter's dictation or even the editor of ideas the apostle gave him.

"Babylon" (v. 13): a figurative way of referring to Rome, the archetypal idolatrous and worldly city of the time (cf. Rev 16:19; 17:5; etc.).

The Mark referred to is the author of the second Gospel. Tradition says that he acted as St Peter's interpreter in Rome. The apostle calls him "son", using it in a spiritual sense.

m. Other ancient authorities read *restore, establish, strengthen and settle*

The Second Letter of St Peter

The Second Letter of Peter helps us to see the effort the first Christians made to practise the faith handed on to them by the apostles in an environment that constantly threatened their fidelity. Hope in the second, definitive, coming of Christ inspires the entire letter.

In the initial greeting the author identifies himself as Simon Peter, an apostle of Jesus Christ. Further on there are additional references which indicate that that apostle is the author. However, internal analysis makes it more difficult to attribute the letter to Peter: its vocabulary and style are markedly different from that of the First Letter of Peter, using as it does expressions which would be more appropriate to a later period. This explains why up to the fourth century the letter found difficulty in being accepted into the Church's canon of inspired books. It also has many similarities of style and content with the Letter of St Jude, to which it probably owes something. None of the theories advanced to solve these difficulties succeeds in explaining questions raised about its authorship, date and addressees. However, irrespective of whether it was written by St Peter, using a secretary or editor, or by an anonymous disciple of his who wished to convey teachings in line with those of the apostle, the Tradition of the Church has associated the Second Letter of Peter with the person of that apostle.

The letter is addressed to Christians in general, even though some expressions imply that it was originally addressed to Christian communities in Greece or Asia Minor. The dates of composition that have been suggested run from the year 60 to the end of the first century.

The letter refutes certain erroneous theories put forward by false teachers about Christ's second coming and makes relevant moral exhortations; other prominent features of the letter are its teaching on the inspiration of Scripture (1:19–21) and its appreciation of the writings of St Paul (3:15–16). But its main teaching has to do with the Parousia. This will indeed happen, it says, because our Lord revealed that it would and the Scriptures support this. Arguing against those who say that the Parousia is being delayed, it teaches that time is something very relative when compared with the eternity of God, for whom "one day is as a thousand years, and a thousand years as one day" (3:8), and that if God is delaying the end of time it is on account of his mercy, for he "does not wish that any should perish" (3:9).

2 Peter

Greeting

1 [1]Simon Peter, a servant and apostle of Jesus Christ,
To those who have obtained a faith of equal standing with ours in the righteousness of our God and Saviour Jesus Christ:[a]
[2]May grace and peace be multiplied to you in the knowledge of God and of Jesus our Lord.

1. A CALL TO FIDELITY

Divine largesse

[3]His divine power has granted to us all things that pertain to life and godliness, through the knowledge of him who called us to[b] his own glory and excellence, [4]by which he has granted to us his precious and very great promises, that through these you may escape from the corruption that is in the world because of passion, and become partakers of the divine nature.*

1:1–3:18 □ □ This letter, which is somewhat like the Letter of Jude, seeks to strengthen people's hope in the second coming of our Lord. A Christian needs to develop the faith he has received and he should trust apostolic teaching (1:3–21), guarding against false teachers who because they do not expect any second coming, give themselves over to licentious living and encourage others to do the same; this will earn them divine condemnation (2:1–22). In fact, even though our Lord's second coming may seem to have been delayed, it will indeed come about (3:1–16), so one needs to be watchful (3:17–18).

1:1–2 "Knowledge" of God and of Jesus Christ is obtained through a sound faith and conduct consistent with it (cf. 1:5–11). The author emphasizes this point from the very start, because he wants to warn people about false teachings which undermine the faith.

1:3–21 □ Against those who say that there will be no second coming, the sacred writer exhorts the faithful to hold on to the teaching they have received from the apostles.

1:3–4 Almighty God chose his apostles and endowed them with abundant graces so that all could become "partakers of the divine nature" (v. 4). This participation, which happens at Baptism, is a key feature of the Christian calling. It was for this

a. Or *of our God and the Saviour Jesus Christ* **b.** Or *by*

Christian virtues

[5]For this very reason make every effort to supplement your faith with virtue,
and virtue with knowledge, [6]and knowledge with self-control, and self-control
with steadfastness, and steadfastness with godliness, [7]and godliness with
brotherly affection, and brotherly affection with love. [8]For if these things are
yours and abound, they keep you from being ineffective or unfruitful in the
knowledge of our Lord Jesus Christ. [9]For whoever lacks these things is blind
and shortsighted and has forgotten that he was cleansed from his old sins.
[10]Therefore, brethren, be the more zealous to confirm your call and election,
for if you do this you will never fall; [11]so there will be richly provided for you
an entrance into the eternal kingdom of our Lord and Saviour Jesus Christ.

Spiritual testimony

[12]Therefore I intend always to remind you of these things, though you know
them and are established in the truth that you have. [13]I think it right, as long as
I am in this body,[c] to arouse you by way of reminder, [14]since I know that the
putting off of my body[c] will be soon, as our Lord Jesus Christ showed me.
[15]And I will see to it that after my departure you may be able at any time to
recall these things.

The Transfiguration, an earnest of the Second Coming

[16]For we did not follow cleverly devised myths when we made known to you
the power and coming of our Lord Jesus Christ, but we were eyewitnesses of
his majesty.* [17]For when he received honour and glory from God the Father

---

that the Word became flesh: "The Son of God became man so that we might become God" (St Athanasius, *De incarn. Verbi*, 54, 3; cf. *CCC*, 460).

1:5–11 We must respond to God's initiative with faith and the practice of virtue if we are to reach the goal and the fullness to which we are called. Faith and love are "the origin and end of our lives. Faith is the beginning; love, the end. Both, bonded together, bring us to God, and everything else related to perfection and holiness flows from them" (St Ignatius of Antioch, *Letter to the Ephesians,* 14, 1–2).

1:12–15 This passage sums up the purpose of the letter (which is a kind of spiritual testimony)—to remind people of the Christian truths and to encourage them to practise virtue. The ephemeral nature of man's life is evoked by the use of the simile of a tent (not apparent in the RSV's v. 13 where the word used is "body"; in the Neovulgate, "tabernaculum" = tent); cf. also 2 Cor 5:1.

1:16–18 The transfiguration of Jesus Christ was a proof of the doctrine of Christ's second coming. At the transfiguration our Lord gave the disciples a fleeting

c. Greek *tent*

and the voice was borne to him by the Majestic Glory, "This is my beloved
Son,[d] with whom I am well pleased," [18]we heard this voice borne from heaven,
for we were with him on the holy mountain.

Prophecy and the Second Coming
[19]And we have the prophetic word made more sure. You will do well to pay
attention to this as to a lamp shining in a dark place, until the day dawns and
the morning star rises in your hearts. [20]First of all you must understand this,
that no prophecy of scripture is a matter of one's own interpretation, [21]because
no prophecy ever came by the impulse of man, but men moved by the Holy
Spirit spoke from God.[e]

2. FALSE TEACHERS DENOUNCED

The harm they do
2 [1]But false prophets also arose among the people, just as there will be false
teachers among you, who will secretly bring in destructive heresies, even
denying the Master who bought them, bringing upon themselves swift
destruction. [2]And many will follow their licentiousness, and because of them
the way of truth will be reviled. [3]And in their greed they will exploit you with

---

glimpse of his divinity; at the end of time it will be manifested in all its fullness and forever.

1:19–21 The prophets' testimony is another guarantee of the truth of the Parousia, being as it is the word of God. Verse 21 makes it clear that there is such a thing as biblical interpretation. Scripture has been written under the inspiration of the Holy Spirit; God and the human author are involved in the writing of the sacred books in such a way that the end product is, at one and the same time, entirely of God's making and entirely of man's. However, as the sacred writer adds (v. 20), Holy Scripture must not be interpreted in an arbitrary way. "The task of giving an authentic interpetation of the Word of God, whether in its written form or in the form of Tradition, has been entrusted to the living teaching office of the Church alone. Its authority in this matter is exercised in the name of Jesus Christ" (Vatican II, *DV*, 10).

2:1–22 □ Before refuting the basic error of the false teachers (their denial of the Parousia), the sacred writer denounces their moral misconduct—their greed and sexual immorality.

2:1–3 The Old Testament contains many warnings about false teachers who sowed confusion among the people. Christians should not be surprised to encounter them, but the writer bemoans the damage they do.

d. Or *my son, my* (or *the*) *Beloved* **e.** Other authorities read *moved by the Holy Spirit holy men of God spoke* false words; from of old their condemnation has not been idle, and their destruction has not been asleep.*

The punishment that awaits them

4For if God did not spare the angels when they sinned, but cast them into hell[f]
and committed them to pits of nether gloom to be kept until the judgment; 5if
he did not spare the ancient world, but preserved Noah, a herald of righteous-
ness, with seven other persons, when he brought a flood upon the world of the
ungodly; 6if by turning the cities of Sodom and Gomorrah to ashes he condemned
them to extinction and made them an example to those who were to be ungodly;
7and if he rescued righteous Lot, greatly distressed by the licentiousness of the
wicked 8(for by what that righteous man saw and heard as he lived among them,
he was vexed in his righteous soul day after day with their lawless deeds), 9then
the Lord knows how to rescue the godly from trial, and to keep the unrighteous
under punishment until the day of judgment, 10and especially those who
indulge in the lust of defiling passion and despise authority.

Their arrogance and immorality

Bold and wilful, they are not afraid to revile the glorious ones, 11whereas
angels, though greater in might and power, do not pronounce a reviling
judgment upon them before the Lord. 12But these, like irrational animals,
creatures of instinct, born to be caught and killed, reviling in matters of which
they are ignorant, will be destroyed in the same destruction with them,
13suffering wrong for their wrongdoing. They count it pleasure to revel in the

---

2:4–10 Eternal punishment awaits false teachers and the ungodly, whereas God gives salvation to those who stay faithful, as he did in the case of Noah and Lot. Lot's experience should encourage us to persevere in doing good, even in a hostile environment.

Apparently, the main sin of the false teachers and the one which most perverted the faithful was that of lust (v. 10), as happened in Sodom and Gomorrah. This vice so clouds the mind that a person who becomes steeped in it ends up despising the authority of God (v. 10: literally "lordship": *dominatio*; cf. Jude 8–10). On the other hand, chastity "is a virtue that honours the human person and enables him to express and appreciate a love that is true and not self-seeking, generous, and respectful of others" (SCDF, *Pers. hum*, 12).

2:10–19 The parallel passage in St Jude (vv. 8–16) clarifies the meaning of some of the terms used in this passage, which describes the perverse behaviour of the false teachers.

"The glorious ones" (v. 10) can mean all of the angelic world or else only the fallen angels who rule the world, whose dignity is seen as lower than that of the angels who minister in the presence of the Lord (cf. Jude 8–10).

f. Greek *Tartarus*

daytime. They are blots and blemishes, revelling in their dissipation,[g] carous-
ing with you. 14They have eyes full of adultery, insatiable for sin. They entice
unsteady souls. They have hearts trained in greed. Accursed children! 15Forsaking
the right way they have gone astray; they have followed the way of Balaam,
the son of Beor, who loved gain from wrongdoing, 16but was rebuked for his
own transgression; a dumb ass spoke with human voice and restrained the
prophet's madness.

17These are waterless springs and mists driven by a storm; for them the nether
gloom of darkness has been reserved. 18For, uttering loud boasts of folly, they
entice with licentious passions of the flesh men who have barely escaped from
those who live in error. 19They promise them freedom, but they themselves are
slaves of corruption; for whatever overcomes a man, to that he is enslaved.

Apostasy, a grave sin

20For if, after they have escaped the defilements of the world through the
knowledge of our Lord and Saviour Jesus Christ, they are again entangled in them
and overpowered, the last state has become worse for them than the first. 21For
it would have been better for them never to have known the way of righteousness
than after knowing it to turn back from the holy commandment delivered to them.
22It has happened to them according to the true proverb, The dog turns back to his
own vomit, and the sow is washed only to wallow in the mire.

3. THE SECOND COMING OF CHRIST

The teaching of Tradition

3 1This is now the second letter that I have written to you, beloved, and in
both of them I have aroused your sincere mind by way of reminder; 2that

---

Balaam was seen as the epitome of the evil and avaricious person because he led the Israelites into idolatry and fornication (cf. Num 31:16; Rev 2:14), whereas he had previously blessed them (Num 22:1–24:25).

2:20–22 The sacred writer uses two popular proverbs (v. 22)—one taken from Proverbs 26:11—to show the serious situation of those who return to a life of sin after knowing the saving teaching of Christ. To the ungodly and to those who lead others astray the writer applies what our Lord had said about a person who, after a devil had been cast out of him, fell under his sway once more: "the last state of that man becomes worse than the first" (Mt 12:45).

3:1–18 □ The truth of faith most directly denied by the false teachers was the second coming of the Lord; by rejecting it, they were writing off the moral demands of Christianity.

g. Other ancient authorities read *love feasts* **2:22** Prov 26:11.

you should remember the predictions of the holy prophets and the commandment of the Lord and Saviour through your apostles.

Mistaken notions

[3]First of all you must understand this, that scoffers will come in the last days
with scoffing, following their own passions [4]and saying, "Where is the
promise of his coming? For ever since the fathers fell asleep, all things have
continued as they were from the beginning of creation."

True teaching about the End

[5]They deliberately ignore this fact, that by the word of God heavens existed
long ago, and an earth formed out of water and by means of water, [6]through
which the world that then existed was deluged with water and perished. [7]But
by the same word the heavens and earth that now exist have been stored up for
fire, being kept until the day of judgment and destruction of ungodly men.
[8]But do not ignore this one fact, beloved, that with the Lord one day is as a
thousand years, and a thousand years as one day. [9]The Lord is not slow about
his promise as some count slowness, but is forbearing toward you,[h] not
wishing that any should perish, but that all should reach repentance. [10]But the

---

3:1–2 The author appeals to people to live a Christian life based on the sound criteria given them by the Lord through the apostles: "What was handed on by the apostles comprises everything that serves to make the People of God live their lives in holiness and increase their faith" (Vatican II, *DV*, 8).

3:3–4 The false prophets referred to in the letter deny the second coming of Christ on the grounds that things are still the same, none of the catastrophes they expected has occurred (they had thought they were imminent).

"The fathers" (v. 4) may mean the first generation of Christians or possibly also Old Testament forebears. According to the false teachers, if between long ago and now no great change has occurred, then that is a good indication that no such change will occur in the future, either.

3:5–10 The sacred writer makes it very clear that time is something very relative compared with the eternity of God (v. 8) and that if God postpones the end of time he does so out of mercy (v. 9). One thing is certain: one needs to be watchful, because the day of the Lord will come without warning (v. 10). The author reproaches the false teachers for their lack of faith: by his word God created the world, and at his word the great flood came—a punishment which altered the face of the earth (vv. 5–6). Therefore, we must believe that a word from him will cause creation to undergo so great a change that "new heavens and a new earth" will come into being (cf. vv. 7, 10, 12–13).

h. Other ancient authorities read *on your account*

day of the Lord will come like a thief, and then the heavens will pass away with a loud noise, and the elements will be dissolved with fire, and the earth and the works that are upon it will be burned up.

Moral lessons to be drawn

11Since all these things are thus to be dissolved, what sort of persons ought you to be in lives of holiness and godliness, 12waiting for and hastening[i] the coming of the day of God, because of which the heavens will be kindled and dissolved, and the elements will melt with fire! 13But according to his promise we wait for new heavens and a new earth in which righteousness dwells.

14Therefore, beloved, since you wait for these, be zealous to be found by him without spot or blemish, and at peace. 15And count the forbearance of our Lord as salvation. So also our beloved brother Paul wrote to you according to the wisdom given him, 16speaking of this* as he does in all his letters. There are some things in them hard to understand, which the ignorant and unstable twist to their own destruction, as they do the other scriptures.

Final exhortation and doxology

17You therefore, beloved, knowing this beforehand, beware lest you be carried away with the error of lawless men and lose your own stability. 18But grow in the grace and knowledge of our Lord and Saviour Jesus Christ. To him be the glory both now and to the day of eternity. Amen.

3:11–16 Hope in the second coming of the Lord and in a radical transformation of this world, should not cause Christians to lose interest in things around them. "Far from diminishing our concern to develop this earth, the expectancy of a new earth should spur us on, for it is here that the body of a new human family grows, foreshadowing in some way the age which is to come" (Vatican II, *GS*, 39).

The reference to the writings of St Paul (vv. 15–15) is clear evidence of the fact that, from the beginning of Christianity, unity in matters of faith was considered essential.

3:17–18 The letter ends with a very succinct summary of some of its main points —pastoral concern, the means to defend oneself against false teachers, and belief in the divinity of Christ.

i. Or *earnestly desiring* **3:13** Is 65:17; 66:22.

The Letters of St John

According to a tradition which goes back to the second century, the apostle St John wrote these three letters at Ephesus on his return from exile on the island of Patmos, towards the end of the first century.

The First Letter of John carries no heading, unlike the other letters in the New Testament (with the exception of the Letter to the Hebrews) and unlike the general style of letters in the Classical world. There is no mention of the author or of the addressees, and none of the usual opening greetings. Nor are there words of farewell at the end. However, the style, structure, language and ideas in this letter all show that it fits in very well with the style of the fourth Gospel. The fact that addressees are not mentioned suggests that it was a kind of circular letter sent to a number of Christian communities. It is likely that it was written, after the fourth Gospel, to the Christian communities of Asia Minor mentioned in the book of Revelation (Rev 2:1–3:22).

From what it says one gathers that certain false teachers (antichrists, deceivers, children of the devil, as they are called: cf. 2:18, 26; 3:7, 10; 4:1) have sprung up in those young churches. Even though they have been cut off, their false ideas continue to threaten the purity of Christian faith and morals. The apostle writes to denounce this doctrinal and moral waywardness and thereby strengthen the believers' faith. Against those who were sowing discord and error, he tells them to stay in communion with God in the faith they have received; and, to counteract errors about Christ, he asserts the truth of the divinity and humanity of Jesus. Communion with God in Christ makes the Christian a child of God who should love his brethren. Charity, love, is the central theme of the letter. St John uses the noun "love" very often (eighteen times). And he uses the verb "to love" twenty-eight times. Twice we find the sublime statement that "God is love" (4:8, 16). As St Augustine says, in this letter the apostle John "said many things, practically all of them to do with charity" (*In Epist. Ioann. ad Parth.*, prologue). Basically what this letter is saying is that true belief in Jesus Christ, the Son of God, underpins Christian love, which leads a person to love his or her neighbour and to forgive offences.

The Second and Third Letters of St John are very much in line with the format of the letter-style of the Classical world: they start with a standard layout giving the sender's name, that of the addressee(s), and a greeting, and they end with a formal farewell. In both letters the writer introduces himself as "the elder" (2 Jn 1; 3 Jn 1). The Second Letter is addressed to "the elect lady and her children" (v. 1), a figurative way of referring to a local church, very probably one in Asia Minor. The Third Letter is addressed to a Christian called Gaius (v. 1), and perhaps through him to a group of Christian faithful.

Although not without some difficulty, Tradition has attributed these letters to St John, who would have written them towards the end of the first century.

The Second Letter was written as a word of warning at a time when the danger from heretics was not as great as that revealed in 1 John. The counsel the writer gives is along the same lines as that contained in the First Letter. The Third Letter, although it does not contain new teachings, is a valuable testimony to the fidelity of the early Christian communities and a model of the type of letters of commendation mentioned elsewhere in the New Testament (cf. Acts 18:27; 2 Cor 3:3).

1 John

Prologue

1 1*That which was from the beginning, which we have heard, which we have
seen with our eyes, which we have looked upon and touched with our
hands, concerning the word of life—2the life was made manifest, and we saw
it, and testify to it, and proclaim to you the eternal life which was with the
Father and was made manifest to us—3that which we have seen and heard we
proclaim also to you, so that you may have fellowship* with us; and our
fellowship is with the Father and with his Son Jesus Christ. 4And we are
writing this that our joy[a] may be complete.

1:1–5:21 □□ Although this letter carries no greeting or words of farewell, the writer and his addressees were obviously very close. The main subject is communion with God, with Christ and with one's brethren (1:1–4). To encourage this communion, St John lets his thoughts run on a number of themes which seem to be linked in concentric circles and are examined with greater depth as the letter develops. They look rather like the key points of a baptismal catechesis whereby the Christian can discern what is true communion and what is not. Communion with God is attained by walking in the light, in sincerity, by keeping the commandments and abiding in the truth of Christ and in Christ himself (1:5–2:29). This communion with God is a form of sonship and requires a person to break with sin and to practise the commandment of brotherly love with deeds (3:1–24). It is a communion which means one has to profess the truth concerning Christ, love as God loves, and believe in God's goodness in giving us his Son (4:1–5:12). The letter ends by reaffirming the power of prayer and the sense of confidence that faith confers (5:14–21).

1:1–4 The prologue, which states the basic theme of the document, has many similarities to that of the Fourth Gospel (Jn 1:1–18): Jesus is the Word of life made manifest to men. Commenting on this passage, the *Catechism of the Catholic Church* says: "The transmission of the Christian faith consists primarily in proclaiming Jesus Christ in order to lead others to faith in him. From the beginning, the first disciples burned with the desire to proclaim Christ: 'We cannot but speak of what we have seen and heard' (Acts 4:20)" (no. 425).

a. Other ancient authorities read *your*

1. UNION WITH GOD

God is light

5This is the message we have heard from him and proclaim to you, that God is
light and in him is no darkness* at all.

Walking in the light. Rejecting sin

6If we say we have fellowship with him while we walk in darkness, we lie and
do not live according to the truth; 7but if we walk in the light, as he is in the
light, we have fellowship with one another, and the blood of Jesus his Son
cleanses us from all sin. 8If we say we have no sin, we deceive ourselves, and
the truth is not in us. 9If we confess our sins, he is faithful and just, and will
forgive our sins and cleanse us from all unrighteousness. 10If we say we have
not sinned, we make him a liar, and his word is not in us.

2 1My little children, I am writing this to you so that you may not sin; but if
any one does sin, we have an advocate with the Father, Jesus Christ the
righteous; 2and he is the expiation for our sins, and not for ours only but also
for the sins of the whole world.

Keeping the commandments

3And by this we may be sure that we know him, if we keep his command-
ments.* 4He who says "I know him" but disobeys his commandments is a liar,
and the truth is not in him; 5but whoever keeps his word, in him truly love for

---

1:5–2:29 □ This section explains the nature of union with God and the demands it involves.

1:5 The simile of light helps to show what revelation involves: God is light, Jesus Christ has made him known to us, and Christian revelation is the splendour, the shining, of that light.

1:6–2:2 To lead a life of union with God, a Christian needs to acknowledge that he is a sinner and to strive to avoid sin. If he does so, Christ, who is our advocate with the Father (2:1), will cleanse him from all sin through his blood (1:7). Divine mercy operates when a person confesses his faults. The penance imposed in the sacrament of Reconciliation helps us to become more like Christ, who is the One who alone made expiation for our sins; he did so once for all (cf. *CCC*, 1460).

2:3–11 The entire letter is saying that "knowing God" is no mere intellectual exercise: it means being united to God by faith and love, living the life of grace.

The novelty of the "new commandment" lies not in the precept (which is to be found in the Old Testament: cf. Lev 19:18) but in the standard that Jesus sets—

God is perfected. By this we may be sure that we are in him: [6]he who says he
abides in him ought to walk in the same way in which he walked.
[7]Beloved, I am writing you no new commandment, but an old commandment which you had from the beginning; the old commandment is the word
which you have heard. [8]Yet I am writing you a new commandment, which is
true in him and in you, because[b] the darkness is passing away and the true light
is already shining. [9]He who says he is in the light and hates his brother is in the
darkness still. [10]He who loves his brother abides in the light, and in it[c] there is
no cause for stumbling. [11]But he who hates his brother is in the darkness and
walks in the darkness, and does not know where he is going, because the
darkness has blinded his eyes.

The Apostle's confidence in the faithful

[12]I am writing to you, little children, because your sins are forgiven for his
sake. [13]I am writing to you, fathers, because you know him who is from the
beginning. I am writing to you, young men, because you have overcome the
evil one. I write to you, children, because you know the Father. [14]I write to
you, fathers, because you know him who is from the beginning. I write to you,
young men, because you are strong, and the word of God abides in you, and
you have overcome the evil one.

Detachment from the world

[15]Do not love the world or the things in the world. If any one loves the world,
love for the Father is not in him. [16]For all that is in the world, the lust of the
flesh and the lust of the eyes and the pride of life, is not of the Father but is of

---

"even as I have loved you" (Jn 13:34) and in the fact that it covers everyone: we must love everyone, friends and enemies, without distinction of race or culture or social status. "What is the perfection of love? It consists of loving your enemies, and loving them so that they become your brothers" (St Augustine, *In Epist. Ioann. ad Parth.*, 1, 9).

2:12–14 These verses can be taken as an appeal to all Christians, whatever their position. "Little children" and "children" could refer to people recently baptized, whereas "fathers" and "young men" could mean people who have already passed through different stages of the faith and are now mature enough to bring others to the Church or have experience of overcoming the temptations of the world with the help of grace.

2:15–17 Here "world" has a pejorative meaning, in the sense of enemy of God and man and including everything that is hostile to God—the kingdom of sin. "The pride of life" (v. 16): this more or less parallels the Latin; the original Greek says

b. Or *that* **c.** Or *him*

the world. 17And the world passes away, and the lust of it; but he who does the will of God abides for ever.

Not listening to heretics

18Children, it is the last hour;* and as you have heard that antichrist is coming,
so now many antichrists have come; therefore we know that it is the last hour.
19They went out from us, but they were not of us; for if they had been of us,
they would have continued with us; but they went out, that it might be plain
that they all are not of us. 20But you have been anointed by the Holy One, and
you all know.[d] 21I write to you, not because you do not know the truth, but
because you know it, and know that no lie is of the truth. 22Who is the liar but
he who denies that Jesus is the Christ? This is the antichrist, he who denies the
Father and the Son. 23No one who denies the Son has the Father. He who
confesses the Son has the Father also. 24Let what you heard from the
beginning abide in you. If what you heard from the beginning abides in you,
then you will abide in the Son and in the Father. 25And this is what he has
promised us,[e] eternal life.

26I write this to you about those who would deceive you; 27but the anointing
which you received from him abides in you, and you have no need that any
one should teach you; as his anointing teaches you about everything, and is
true, and is no lie, just as it has taught you, abide in him.

---

something like "the arrogance of earthly things". "St John distinguishes three kinds of covetousness or concupiscence […]. In the Catholic catechetical tradition, the ninth commandment forbids carnal concupiscence; the tenth forbids coveting another's goods" (*CCC*, 2514).

2:18–29 The fact that there are heretics around suggests that our Lord's prediction about the coming of the anti-Christ (cf. Mt 24:15–28 and par.; 2 Thess 2:1–12) is being fulfilled and that the "last hour" has begun (v. 18). The early Christians had a lively desire to see the second coming of Christ; in this age everything that happens is a preparation for the second coming.

"Anointed by the Holy One" (vv. 20 and 27): the action of the Father and the Son through the Holy Spirit on the soul of the Christian as a consequence of Baptism. Christians have no need to hear teachings other than through the Church: guided by the Holy Spirit they have the certainty that faith gives "when 'from the bishops to the last of the faithful' (St Augustine, *De praed. sanct.*, 14, 27) they manifest a universal consent in matters of faith and morals" (Vatican II, *LG*,12). This is the supernatural appreciation of the faith, sometimes called *sensus fidelium*.

Verse 22 contains a basic tenet of the faith: to be a Christian a person must believe that Jesus who dwelt among us, is the Messiah and the Son of God.

d. Other ancient authorities read *you know everything* **e.** Other ancient authorities read *you*

28 And now, little children, abide in him, so that when he appears we may have
confidence and not shrink from him in shame at his coming. 29 If you know that
he is righteous, you may be sure that every one who does right is born of him.

2. LIVING AS GOD'S CHILDREN

We are children of God

3 1 See what love the Father has given us, that we should be called children of
God; and so we are. The reason why the world does not know us is that it
did not know him. 2 Beloved, we are God's children now; it does not yet appear
what we shall be, but we know that when he appears we shall be like him, for
we shall see him as he is.

A child of God does not sin

3 And every one who thus hopes in him purifies himself as he is pure.

4 Every one who commits sin is guilty of lawlessness; sin is lawlessness.
5 You know that he appeared to take away sins, and in him there is no sin. 6 No
one who abides in him sins;* no one who sins has either seen him or known
him. 7 Little children, let no one deceive you. He who does right is righteous,
as he is righteous. 8 He who commits sin is of the devil; for the devil has sinned
from the beginning. The reason the Son of God appeared was to destroy the
works of the devil. 9 No one born of God commits sin; for God's[f] nature abides

---

3:1–24 □ In this second section St John's exhortations are based on the fact that the Christian is a child of God.

3:1–2 Divine filiation is a marvellous fact whereby God gratuitously gives men a strictly supernatural status, an intimacy with God which makes them *domestici Dei*, "members of the household of God" (Eph 2:19). "This is the great boldness of the Christian faith—to proclaim the value and dignity of human nature and to affirm that we have been created to achieve the dignity of children of God, through the grace that raises us up to a supernatural level" (Bl. J. Escrivá, *Hom.,* 1, 133).

3:3–10 The prospect of seeing God (cf. v. 2) is the hope which sustains Christians and encourages them to keep on the road to holiness and fight against sin. The false teachers that St John had to contend with claimed to have special knowledge of God (*gnosis*) which put them beyond good and evil so that they paid no attention to sin; to identify these heretics, the apostle has recourse to our Lord's words, "the tree is known by its fruit" (Mt 12:33). The criteria for distinguishing children of God are: the practice of righteousness (that is, striving for holiness and fighting against sin) and brotherly love (v. 10).

f. Greek *his*

in him, and he cannot sin because he is[g] born of God. [10]By this it may be seen who are the children of God, and who are the children of the devil: whoever does not do right is not of God, nor he who does not love his brother.

Loving one another

[11]For this is the message which you have heard from the beginning, that we should love one another, [12]and not be like Cain who was of the evil one and murdered his brother. And why did he murder him? Because his own deeds were evil and his brother's righteous. [13]Do not wonder, brethren, that the world hates you. [14]We know that we have passed out of death into life, because we love the brethren. He who does not love abides in death. [15]Any one who hates his brother is a murderer, and you know that no murderer has eternal life abiding in him. [16]By this we know love, that he laid down his life for us; and we ought to lay down our lives for the brethren. [17]But if any one has the world's goods and sees his brother in need, yet closes his heart against him, how does God's love abide in him? [18]Little children, let us not love in word or speech but in deed and in truth.

[19]By this we shall know that we are of the truth, and reassure our hearts before him [20]whenever our hearts condemn us; for God is greater than our hearts, and he knows everything. [21]Beloved, if our hearts do not condemn us, we have confidence before God; [22]and we receive from him whatever we ask, because we keep his commandments and do what pleases him. [23]And this is his commandment, that we should believe in the name of his Son Jesus Christ and love one another, just as he has commanded us. [24]All who keep his

---

3:11–24 Those who do not practise brotherly love are as murderous as Cain (v. 12). The model of this love is Christ, who gave his life for us (vv. 13–16). Brotherly love should express itself in deed and in truth (vv. 17–18) and it leads a person to have serene confidence in God, who knows all things (vv. 19–22). "I consider that this is the pearl sought by the merchant described in the Gospel, who, when he found it, sold all that he had and bought it (cf. Mt 13:46). This is the precious pearl—charity. Without, it, anything else you have does you no good; and if you do possess it, you have all that you need [...]. You may tell me, 'I have not seen God'; but can you say, 'I have not seen man'? Love your brother. If you love your brother whom you see, you will also see God, because you will see charity and God dwells within charity' (St Augustine, *In Epist. Ioann. ad Parth.*, 5, 7).

Using an example very similar to that in James 2:15–16, St John, in vv. 17–18, points out that genuine love is expressed in deeds.

God's commandments are summed up in two things (vv. 22–24) – faith in Jesus Christ and love for the brethren. "We cannot truly love one another without faith in Christ, nor can we truly believe in the name of Jesus Christ without fraternal charity" (St Bede, *In 1 Epist. Ioann.*, in loc.).

g. Or *for the offspring of God abide in him, and they cannot sin because they are* commandments abide in him, and he in them. And by this we know that he abides in us, by the Spirit which he has given us.

3. FAITH IN CHRIST. BROTHERLY LOVE

Faith in Christ, not in false prophets

4 [1]Beloved, do not believe every spirit, but test the spirits* to see whether
they are of God; for many false prophets have gone out into the world. [2]By
this you know the Spirit of God: every spirit which confesses that Jesus Christ
has come in the flesh is of God, [3]and every spirit which does not confess Jesus
is not of God. This is the spirit of antichrist, of which you heard that it was
coming, and now it is in the world already. [4]Little children, you are of God,
and have overcome them; for he who is in you is greater than he who is in the
world. [5]They are of the world, therefore what they say is of the world, and the
world listens to them. [6]We are of God. Whoever knows God listens to us, and
he who is not of God does not listen to us. By this we know the spirit of truth
and the spirit of error.

God is love. Brotherly love, the mark of Christians

[7]Beloved, let us love one another; for love is of God, and he who loves is born
of God and knows God. [8]He who does not love does not know God; for God
is love. [9]In this the love of God was made manifest among us, that God sent

---

4:1–5:12 □ In this section the central themes of the letter are developed further in a kind of triptych in which belief in Jesus Christ is the framework into which the commandment of love is set.

4:1–6 Belief that the Son of God truly became man is the distinguishing mark of the Christian. "The first heresies denied not so much Christ's divinity as his true humanity (Gnostic Docetism). From apostolic times the Christian faith has insisted on the true incarnation of God's Son 'come in the flesh'" (*CCC*, 465).

4:7–21 The thread of the argument here is as follows: God is love and he loved us before we loved him (vv. 7–10); brotherly love is the response that God's love calls for (vv. 11–16). When our love is perfect, we feel no fear (vv. 17–18); brotherly love is an expression, a sign, of love of God (vv. 19–21).

The central theme of the letter is summed up in the words "God is love" (vv. 8, 16). "Even if nothing else were said in praise of love in all the pages of this epistle, even if nothing else were said in all the pages of Holy Scripture, and the only thing we heard from the mouth of the Holy Spirit were 'God is love,' we would need to search no more" (St Augustine, *In Epist. Ioann ad Parth.*, 7, 4). "By sending his only Son and the Spirit of Love in the fullness of time, God has revealed his innermost secret. God himself is an eternal exchange of love, Father, Son and Holy

his only Son into the world, so that we might live through him. 10In this is
love, not that we loved God but that he loved us and sent his Son to be the
expiation for our sins. 11Beloved, if God so loved us, we also ought to love one
another. 12No man has ever seen God; if we love one another, God abides in us
and his love is perfected in us.
13By this we know that we abide in him and he in us, because he has given
us of his own Spirit. 14And we have seen and testify that the Father has sent his
Son as the Saviour of the world. 15Whoever confesses that Jesus is the Son of
God, God abides in him, and he in God. 16So we know and believe the love
God has for us. God is love, and he who abides in love abides in God, and God
abides in him. 17In this is love perfected with us, that we may have confidence
for the day of judgment, because as he is so are we in this world. 18There is no
fear in love, but perfect love casts out fear. For fear has to do with punishment,
and he who fears is not perfected in love. 19We love, because he first loved us.
20If any one says, "I love God," and hates his brother, he is a liar; for he who
does not love his brother whom he has seen, cannot[h] love God whom he has
not seen. 21And this commandment we have from him, that he who loves God
should love his brother also.

Everyone who believes in Jesus overcomes the world

5 1Every one who believes that Jesus is the Christ is a child of God, and
every one who loves the parent loves the child. 2By this we know that we
love the children of God, when we love God and obey his commandments.
3For this is the love of God, that we keep his commandments. And his
commandments are not burdensome. 4For whatever is born of God overcomes
the world; and this is the victory that overcomes the world, our faith. 5Who is
it that overcomes the world but he who believes that Jesus is the Son of God?

Testimony borne to Christ

6This is he who came by water and blood, Jesus Christ, not with the water only
but with the water and the blood. 7And the Spirit is the witness, because the

---

Spirit, and he has destined us to share in that exchange" (*CCC*, 221). Christ's incarnation and redemptive death are the supreme proof of this love.

5:1–5 Through faith in Jesus Christ, a person is made a child of God at Baptism. This leads him to love his fellow men, his brothers and sisters (it is axiomatic that a person who loves his father also loves his brothers and sisters), to keep the commandments, and to share in Christ's victory over the world.

5:6–12 Seemingly some Gnostics were saying that Jesus of Nazareth became the Son of God through Baptism, and stopped being the Son of God prior to his

h. Other ancient authorities read *how can he*

Spirit is the truth. [8]There are three witnesses,* the Spirit, the water, and the blood; and these three agree. [9]If we receive the testimony of men, the testimony of God is greater; for this is the testimony of God that he has borne witness to his Son. [10]He who believes in the Son of God has the testimony in himself. He who does not believe God has made him a liar, because he has not believed in the testimony that God has borne to his Son. [11]And this is the testimony, that God gave us eternal life, and this life is in his Son. [12]He who has the Son has life; he who has not the Son of God has not life.

4. CONCLUSION

[13]I write this to you who believe in the name of the Son of God, that you may know that you have eternal life.

Prayer for sinners

[14]And this is the confidence which we have in him, that if we ask anything according to his will he hears us. [15]And if we know that he hears us in whatever we ask, we know that we have obtained the requests made of him. [16]If any one sees his brother committing what is not a mortal sin, he will ask, and God[i] will give him life for those whose sin is not mortal. There is sin which is mortal; I do not say that one is to pray for that. [17]All wrongdoing is sin, but there is sin which is not mortal.

---

passion. St John meets these errors head on and, by his reference ("water and blood") to Christ's Baptism and to his death on the cross, he asserts that these events are inseparable from the testimony borne by the Spirit and that if one denied them one would be calling God a liar (cf. v. 10).

5:13–21 □ After a short conclusion (v. 13), which takes up the central theme of the letter, St John adds, by way of an appendix, a few final words of counsel.

5:14–17 The sacred writer comes back to the theme of confidence in prayer and urges the need to pray for sinners.

"Sin which is mortal" (v. 16), sin which leads to death, is an expression reminiscent of the sin against the Holy Spirit (cf. Mt 12:31–32) and the sin of apostasy (cf. Heb 6:4–8). "John seems to wish to emphasize the incalculable seriousness of what constitutes the very essence of sin, namely the rejection of God. This is manifested above all in *apostasy* and *idolatry*—repudiating faith in revealed truth and making certain created realities equal to God, raising them to the status of idols or false gods" (John Paul II, *Reconcil. et paen.*, 17). If St John does not expressly command prayers to be offered for such sinners, that does not

i. Greek *he*

The Christian's confidence as a child of God

18We know that any one born of God does not sin, but He who was born of
God keeps him, and the evil one does not touch him.
19We know that we are of God, and the whole world is in the power of the
evil one.
20And we know that the Son of God has come and has given us under-
standing, to know him who is true; and we are in him who is true, in his Son
Jesus Christ. This is the true God and eternal life. 21Little children, keep
yourselves from idols.

---

mean that they are beyond recovery, if we take the omnipotence and mercy of God into account.

5:18–21 Jesus Christ, true God and true man, is also eternal life, because only in him can we attain that life. In his closing words, St John appeals to Christians to realize what a great thing it is to be a child of God: "Recognize your dignity, Christian, and since you have been brought to partake in the divine nature, do not think of returning to the old ways of vice through your bad behaviour. Think about the head and body of which you now form part. Never forget that you were freed from the power of darkness, and led into the light and the Kingdom of God" (St Leo the Great, *Serm. 1 in Nativ.*, 3).

2 John

Greeting
1The elder* to the elect lady* and her children, whom I love in the truth, and
not only I but also all who know the truth, 2because of the truth which abides
in us and will be with us for ever:
3Grace, mercy, and peace will be with us, from God the Father and from
Jesus Christ the Father's Son, in truth and love.

The law of love
4I rejoiced greatly to find some of your children following the truth, just as we
have been commanded by the Father. 5And now I beg you, lady, not as though
I were writing you a new commandment, but the one we have had from the
beginning, that we love one another. 6And this is love, that we follow his
commandments; this is the commandment, as you have heard from the
beginning, that you follow love.

Precautions against heretics
7For many deceivers have gone out into the world, men who will not
acknowledge the coming of Jesus Christ in the flesh; such a one is the deceiver

---

1–13 □□ This letter is very much in keeping with the letter-style of the time (greeting, body of letter, farewell). It contains advice to a Christian community on subjects dealt with more extensively in 1 John—brotherly love, keeping the commandments (vv. 4–6), and precautions against deceivers (vv. 7–11).

1–3 The "elect lady": probably a metaphor meaning a particular church of Asia Minor.

The word "truth", occurring four times in this short passage, means the revelation of God which reaches its climax in Jesus Christ and which includes all the truths in which we must believe. But the "truth" is also, and above all, an interior principle of supernatural life: "loving the truth" means "loving in Christ".

4–6 All the commandments reduce to love of God and love of neighbour. "Listen now to a simple precept: love and do what you like. If you keep quiet, do so out of love; if you speak out, do so out of love; if you correct someone, do so out of love; if you forgive, do so out of love" (St Augustine, *In Epist. Ioann. in Parth.*, 7, 8). Tradition is so definite on this point that anyone who teaches otherwise is a liar and a deceiver.

7–11 These verses are in fact a summary of things said in 1 John. They show how to identify these heretics—by the fact that they do not acknowledge the divinity of Jesus Christ incarnate.

and the antichrist. [8]Look to yourselves, that you may not lose what you[a] have worked for, but may win a full reward. [9]Any one who goes ahead and does not abide in the doctrine of Christ does not have God; he who abides in the doctrine has both the Father and the Son. [10]If any one comes to you and does not bring this doctrine, do not receive him into the house or give him any greeting; [11]for he who greets him shares his wicked work.

Conclusion and greetings

[12]Though I have much to write to you, I would rather not use paper and ink, but I hope to come to see you and talk with you face to face, so that our joy may be complete.

[13]The children* of your elect sister greet you.

In the Middle East hospitality and greetings were not mere marks of courtesy or good manners: they involved a real sense of solidarity and close affinity. Hence the warning that reception (vv. 10–11) of these people could imply complicity in their evil deeds and the risk of giving scandal to other members of the Church.

On the "antichrist" (v. 7), see 1 Jn 2:18–29.

12–13 The greeting sent in v. 13 comes from members of the church from which John is writing, probably that of Ephesus.

a. Other ancient authorities read *we*

3 John

Greeting

[1]The elder to the beloved Gaius, whom I love in the truth.
[2]Beloved, I pray that all may go well with you and that you may be in
health; I know that it is well with your soul.

Praise of Gaius

[3]For I greatly rejoiced when some of the brethren arrived and testified to the
truth of your life, as indeed you do follow the truth. [4]No greater joy can I have
than this, to hear that my children follow the truth.
[5]Beloved, it is a loyal thing you do when you render any service to the
brethren, especially to strangers, [6]who have testified to your love before the
church. You will do well to send them on their journey as befits God's service.
[7]For they have set out for his sake and have accepted nothing from the heathen.
[8]So we ought to support such men, that we may be fellow workers in the truth.

1–15 □□ This letter is very similar in form to the previous one. It was written in connexion with disagreements which had arisen in a Christian community. St John praises Gaius, to whom the letter is addressed, for his hospitable reception of the apostle's envoys (vv. 3–8), and he condemns the behaviour of Diotrephes (vv. 9–10), while recommending someone called Demetrius (vv. 11–12).

1–2 An ancient Christian text (*Apostolic Constitutions*, 7, 46) mentions a Gaius as bishop of Pergamum and a Demetrius (v. 12) as bishop of Philadelphia, but there is doubt as to the historical reliability of those data. From what the letter says, Gaius does not seem (at least, not so far) to have held any hierarchical office; he seems to have been simply a prominent Christian, faithful to his responsibilities in the Church.

3–8 "For his sake": literally "for the name", meaning "for Christ" (cf. Acts 5:41; Phil 2:9–10; Jas 2:7).

"Fellow workers in the truth" (v. 8): the Second Vatican Council applies these words to lay people when explaining how their apostolate and the ministry of pastors complement one another: "The apostolate of the Church and of each of its members aims primarily at announcing to the world by word and action the message of Christ and communicating to it the grace of Christ. The principal means of bringing this about is the ministry of the word and of the sacraments. Committed in a special way to the clergy, it leaves room however for a highly important part for the laity, the part namely of 'helping on the cause of truth'" (*AA*, 6).

Diotrephes' misconduct

9I have written something to the church; but Diotrephes, who likes to put himself first, does not acknowledge my authority. 10So if I come, I will bring up what he is doing, prating against me with evil words. And not content with that, he refuses himself to welcome the brethren, and also stops those who want to welcome them and puts them out of the church.

Commendation of Demetrius

11Beloved, do not imitate evil but imitate good. He who does good is of God; he who does evil has not seen God. 12Demetrius* has testimony from every one, and from the truth itself; I testify to him too, and you know my testimony is true.

Conclusion and farewell

13I had much to write to you, but I would rather not write with pen and ink; 14I hope to see you soon, and we will talk together face to face.

15Peace be to you. The friends greet you. Greet the friends, every one of them.

9–12 These verses contrast the behaviour of Diotrephes with that of Demetrius. Here we have a further example of the Church's concern that pastors should behave properly: "In exercising his office of father and pastor the bishop should be with his people as one who serves, a good shepherd who knows his sheep and whose sheep know him, a true father who excels in his love and solicitude for all" (Vatican II, *CD*, 16).

Verse 11 is a resume of the teaching contained in various passages of 1 John: he who does right is showing that he is of God.

13–15 "Peace be to you": the normal Jewish greeting, which the apostles continued to use in their letters, giving it a Christian meaning.

The Letter of St Jude

Taking issue with false teachers who say that a Christian's freedom *vis-à-vis* the Law means that he is free from moral obligations, this short letter is an exhortation to fidelity in the faith, and an exposition of the moral implications of the Gospel.

The author introduces himself to his readers as "Jude, a servant of Jesus Christ and brother of James" (v. 1). His description of himself as "brother of James" gives him a certain status, because James, a relative of our Lord, had been in charge of the church of Jerusalem (cf. the introduction to the Letter of St James, above). The name Jude (not Judas Iscariot) appears alongside that of James and other "brothers" of Jesus, that is, as one of our Lord's relatives, in Matthew 13:55 and Mark 6:3; it is possible that he was one of the Twelve, the "Judas the son of James" (Lk 6:16; Acts 1:13), or "Thaddeus" (Mt 10:3; Mk 3:18). The letter does not specify whom it is addressed to, but it was probably written originally for Christian converts from Judaism. We do not know when it was written; maybe around the year 70.

The author seeks to exhort the faithful to put up a fight for the faith delivered to them (v. 3), reminding them that the apostles warned them in advance that ungodly people would appear on the scene, people given to licentiousness (vv. 17–18). Maybe the author wrote the letter because he had learned that people like this had already wormed their way into those Christian communities (v. 4).

From the letter we can see that the errors being spread had mainly to do with morality: these people were "perverting the grace of our God into licentiousness" (v. 4), and proposing a false interpretation of Christian freedom—something that St Paul also took issue with (cf., e.g., Rom 6:1–15; 1 Cor 6:12ff; Gal 5:13ff). Sins of intemperance (vv. 4, 8, 11, 13, 23) and greed (vv. 11, 16) are the ones which come in for most mention.

The problem of false teachers and their evil influence is also dealt with in the Second Letter of St Peter; the two letters display a great similarity in ideas and even terminology, especially in Jude 4–8 and 2 Peter 2:1–3:3. A comparison of the two texts leads one to think that the Letter of Jude influenced 2 Peter, a letter which elaborates on and nuances some of the things it says. The author of the Letter of St Jude uses arguments taken from biblical and extrabiblical tradition and quotes some passages from apocryphal writings such as the *Assumption of Moses* (v. 9) and the *Book of Enoch* (vv. 7, 14–15).

Jude

Greeting and blessing
[1]Jude, a servant of Jesus Christ and brother of James,
To those who are called, beloved in God the Father and kept for Jesus Christ:
[2]May mercy, peace, and love be multiplied to you.

His reason for writing
[3]Beloved, being very eager to write to you of our common salvation, I found it
necessary to write appealing to you to contend for the faith which was once for all
delivered to the saints. [4]For admission has been secretly gained by some who long
ago were designated for this condemnation, ungodly persons who pervert the grace
of our God into licentiousness and deny our only Master and Lord, Jesus Christ.[a]

1. FALSE TEACHERS DENOUNCED

The punishment that awaits them
[5]Now I desire to remind you, though you were once for all fully informed, that
he[b] who saved a people out of the land of Egypt, afterward destroyed those
who did not believe. [6]And the angels that did not keep their own position but

---

1–25 □□ In this letter we find themes similar to those of 2 Peter, but dealt with more briefly. After explaining why he feels obliged to write (vv. 3–4), St Jude reminds his readers that God punished those whose blasphemous and licentious conduct some of them are now imitating (vv. 5–16), and, as against that, he encourages the faithful to stay steadfast in faith and love (vv. 17–23). He concludes with solemn words praising God through Jesus Christ (vv. 24–25).

1–2 In the way he describes his addressees, the writer provides a description of what a Christian is: his life starts with a call from God, it develops thanks to the grace of God, and reaches its culmination in Jesus Christ.

3–4 The author warns the faithful about false teachers who, using the pretext of the freedom won by Christ, claim that there is no great need to struggle against sin. To understand the true nature of freedom, we need to contemplate Jesus Christ. "Freedom finds its true meaning when it is put to the service of the truth which redeems, when it is spent in seeking God's infinite Love which liberates us from all forms of slavery" (Bl. J. Escrivá, *Hom.*, 2, 27).

5–16 □ This part of the letter unmasks the "ungodly persons" and announces the end that awaits them.

a. Or *the only Master and our Lord Jesus Christ* **b.** Ancient authorities read *Jesus* or *the Lord* or *God*

left their proper dwelling have been kept by him in eternal chains in the nether
gloom until the judgment of the great day;* 7just as Sodom and Gomorrah and
the surrounding cities, which likewise acted immorally and indulged in
unnatural lust, serve as an example by undergoing a punishment of eternal fire.

Their immorality

8Yet in like manner these men in their dreamings defile the flesh, reject authority,
and revile the glorious ones.[c] 9But when the archangel Michael, contending with
the devil, disputed about the body of Moses, he did not presume to pronounce a
reviling judgment upon him, but said, "The Lord rebuke you."* 10But these men
revile whatever they do not understand, and by those things that they know by
instinct as irrational animals do, they are destroyed. 11Woe to them! For they walk
in the way of Cain, and abandon themselves for the sake of gain to Balaam's
error, and perish in Korah's rebellion. 12These are blemishes[d] on your love feasts,
as they boldly carouse together, looking after themselves; waterless clouds,
carried along by winds; fruitless trees in late autumn, twice dead, uprooted; 13wild
waves of the sea, casting up the foam of their own shame; wandering stars for
whom the nether gloom of darkness has been reserved for ever.

The judgment of God

14It was of these also that Enoch in the seventh generation from Adam pro-
phesied, saying, "Behold, the Lord came with his holy myriads, 15 to execute

---

5–7 The three biblical examples given (Num 14:35; Gen 6:1–2 and 19:4–25) seem to refer to three vices—unbelief, pride and lust. See also 2 Pet 2:4–10. The existence of hell (cf. v. 7) and the other "last things" is standard Christian teaching, revealed to man not in order to strike terror into him but to encourage a change of heart and perseverance in doing good: "Only within this eschatological vision can the full extent of sin be seen, and can one feel impelled in a decisive way towards penance and reconciliation" (John Paul II, *Reconcil. et paen.*, 26).

8–13 To illustrate the sinfulness of these offences against the angels, the sacred writer uses a popular legend recorded in the apocryphal *Assumption of Moses*, according to which, when St Michael was preparing to bury Moses' body, the devil tried to wrest it from him. St Michael prevented him from doing so, but he did the devil no hurt; he simply appealed to the judgment of God.

The writer provides three further biblical examples to show the evildoing of the false teachers—Cain (Gen 4:3), Balaam (Num 31:16; Rev 2:14; cf. 2 Pet 2:15), and Korah and his followers who rebelled against Moses (Num 16).

The false teachers are quite happy to attend Christian assemblies, but they lead an immoral life and cause scandal.

14–16 Here the letter actually quotes the Book of Enoch, an apocryphal text written many years before Jesus Christ and which contains legends to do with

c. Greek *glories* **d.** Or *reefs* **9:** Zech 3:2.

judgment on all, and to convict all the ungodly of all their deeds of ungodliness which they have committed in such an ungodly way, and of all the harsh things which ungodly sinners have spoken against him." [16]These are grumblers, malcontents, following their own passions, loud-mouthed boasters, flattering people to gain advantage.

2. EXHORTATION

False teachers were predicted

[17]But you must remember, beloved, the predictions of the apostles of our Lord Jesus Christ; [18]they said to you, "In the last time there will be scoffers, following their own ungodly passions." [19]It is these who set up divisions, worldly people, devoid of the Spirit.

Faith, hope and charity

[20]But you, beloved, build yourselves up on your most holy faith; pray in the Holy Spirit; [21]keep yourselves in the love of God; wait for the mercy of our Lord Jesus Christ unto eternal life.

---

obscure Old Testament passages (the book is mentioned at other places in the letter). In the apocalyptic language of this sort of literature, future events are spoken of as if they had already happened. St Jude uses the book to illustrate his teaching about the punishment of the ungodly.

17–25 □ To counter the errors of the false teachers, this part of the letter is an exhortation to guard the faith, to practise virtue and to set good example.

17–19 These warnings can be traced back to what Christ himself said: "False Christs and false prophets will arise and show great signs and wonders, so as to lead astray, if possible, even the elect" (Mt 24:24).

"In the last time": an expression referring to the messianic age, which began with the coming of Christ (cf. Gal 4:4).

20–21 As elsewhere in the New Testament, an invocation of the Blessed Trinity is combined with an exhortation to the three theological virtues (faith, hope and love): "The theological virtues relate directly to God. They dispose Christians to live in a relationship with the Holy Trinity. They have the One and Triune God for their origin, motive and object" (*CCC*, 1812).

Attitude towards waverers

[22]And convince some, who doubt; [23]save some, by snatching them out of the fire; on some have mercy with fear, hating even the garment spotted by the flesh.[e]

Final doxology

[24]Now to him who is able to keep you from falling and to present you without blemish before the presence of his glory with rejoicing, [25]to the only God, our Saviour through Jesus Christ our Lord, be glory, majesty, dominion, and authority, before all time and now and for ever. Amen.

22–23 Christians should always show kindness to those who break with sound teaching, while avoiding putting their own souls at risk. "It is a feature of those who are perfect that they hate in sinners only their sins; and that they love these same persons" (St Augustine, *Contra Adimant.*, 17, 5).

24–25 The doxology or hymn of praise addressed to God the Father through Jesus Christ shows that Jesus is the mediator of both our salvation and our praise of the Father. From the beginning, the Church has had the custom of addressing liturgical prayer to the Father through Jesus Christ.

e. The Greek text in this sentence is uncertain at several points

The Revelation to John (The Apocalypse)

The book of Revelation comes last in the collection of books in Holy Scripture and it is the only prophetical book in the New Testament. The Church has recourse to it often, particularly in the Liturgy, to sing the praises of the victory of the risen Christ and the splendour of the heavenly Jerusalem, a symbol of the Church in glory. A certain parallel is noticeable between the book of Revelation and the first book in the Bible, that of Genesis. In the latter we are shown how things began through the creative action of God. In the Apocalypse, which uses a symbolism very similar to that in Genesis, we are told at length about the new creation (cf. Rev 21:1–5), inaugurated by the redemption wrought by Christ, a re-creation which will reach its climax when Christ comes again at the end of time. The last chapters of Revelation refer specifically to the river that irrigated Paradise (cf. Gen 2:6; Rev 22:1) and to the tree of life (cf. Gen 2:9; Rev 22:14).

In the first century BC and the first century AD, particularly in times of tribulation, many texts were written, first Jewish and then Christian, which carried the title of "Apocalypse" (Revelation) and which fit in a genre of what is now called "apocalyptic writing". These books have two features in common: (a) they deal with the last times, when good will triumph and evil will be defeated; and (b) they use symbolism taken from the animal kingdom, the stars, special numbers, etc., to describe past and present times and to project from them into the future. The Apocalypse of John shares these features, but it really owes more to the prophetical oracles of the Old Testament. Like the other apocalyptic writings, it is a book of consolation, written at a time of exceptional stress and difficulty. It is also a text, valid for all times, encouraging the reader to holiness of life and faithfulness to Jesus Christ.

The name of the author of the book of Revelation is John (1:1). Many attempts have been made to work out who exactly this man was. From the second century onwards Tradition has identified him with St John, the apostle and evangelist. The book is similar in many ways to the fourth Gospel, and it is very likely that the authority of the apostle John must be attributed to both books. The book of Revelation is addressed to "the seven churches that are in Asia (1:4)—Ephesus, Smyrna, Pergamum, Thyatira, Sardis, Philadelphia and Laodicea (cf. 1:11), the number seven symbolizing the Church universal. The writer's purpose is to put Christians on their guard against the great dangers which threatened the faith and, at the same time, to console and encourage those who were feeling the strain of tribulation, due mainly to the terrible persecution unleashed by the emperor Domitian (in the years 81–96) and by some Jews. In these circumstances the author tries to console Christians and to buoy up their hope in the ultimate victory of Christ.

Over the course of the centuries many interpretations have been offered to explain this book. Most of them have seen it as being simply a prophecy about the last times. However, the Apocalypse provides a theological overview of all history, putting the stress on its transcendental and religious meaning. St John shows us the position of the Church at the time when he was writing, and he also gives a panoramic view of the last age; but he stresses that these last times have already begun with the coming of Jesus Christ, the Son of God made man. This is a viewpoint very much in line with the fourth Gospel, which also depicts the last epoch, and eternal life as well, as having already started and as being on its way to plenitude. We are shown the cosmic battle between good and evil, but the ultimate victory of Christ is also shown to be already in place.

The doctrinal centre of the book, then, has to do with both comings of the Lord—the first coming, with Christ's triumph over death, and the second coming, the Parousia, with the definitive establishment of his Kingdom at the end of time. It also contains moral exhortations (these come mainly in the first part of the book) and teachings about the redemption brought about by Christ, the majesty of God, the Church, angels and the Blessed Virgin Mary.

Revelation

Prologue

1 [1]The revelation of Jesus Christ, which God gave him to show to his servants
what must soon take place; and he made it known by sending his angel to
his servant John, [2]who bore witness to the word of God and to the testimony
of Jesus Christ, even to all that he saw. [3]Blessed is he who reads aloud the
words of the prophecy, and blessed are those who hear, and who keep what is
written therein; for the time is near.

PART ONE: LETTERS TO THE SEVEN CHURCHES

Address and greeting

[4]John to the seven churches that are in Asia:*
Grace to you and peace from him who is and who was and who is to come,
and from the seven spirits who are before his throne, [5]and from Jesus Christ
the faithful witness, the first-born of the dead, and the ruler of kings on earth.

1:1–3 "The revelation of Jesus Christ" (v. 1). This book contains a revelation which the Lord Jesus, risen and in glory, is making to his Church through the apostle St John. After an introduction which gives the book's title, names the addressees and identifies God as the source of its message (1:1–20), there come the letters to the seven churches (2:1–3:22) and details of God's plans for the future of the world and the Church (4:1–22:21).

After his resurrection Jesus continues to speak to his Church through the apostles, in this instance St John (vv. 1–2). When the author says these events will take place "soon", he does not mean at an approximate date; what he wants to do is strengthen Christians' faith and their conviction that Christ will definitively overcome evil; his victory has in fact already begun. Happy are those who believe this and stay loyal.

1:4–3:22 □ □ The book is written for the whole Church, as symbolized by these seven churches of Asia Minor. The sacred writer first explains how he was given the divine revelation and told to make it known (1:4–20); then he reports what the Lord is saying to each church in its particular circumstance—what needs to be corrected and what is promised to those who overcome evil.

1:4–8 The revelation comes from God who is almighty and all-knowing (as seen from the mention of the divine name—"he who is and who was and who is to

To him who loves us and has freed us from our sins by his blood [6]and made us a kingdom, priests to his God and Father, to him be glory and dominion for ever and ever. Amen. [7]Behold, he is coming with the clouds, and every eye will see him, every one who pierced him; and all tribes of the earth will wail on account of him. Even so. Amen.

[8]"I am the Alpha and the Omega," says the Lord God, who is and who was and who is to come, the Almighty.

Reason for writing

[9]I John, your brother, who share with you in Jesus the tribulation and the kingdom and the patient endurance, was on the island called Patmos on account of the word of God and the testimony of Jesus. [10]I was in the Spirit on the Lord's day, and I heard behind me a loud voice like a trumpet [11]saying, "Write what you see in a book and send it to the seven churches, to Ephesus and to Smyrna and to Pergamum and to Thyatira and to Sardis and to Philadelphia and to Laodicea."

---

come"—and of the spirits who serve him [v. 4]) and from Jesus Christ, who died and rose again, the ruler of history, the Redeemer of man and the Lord of his Church.

Not content with setting us free from our sins, our Lord gave us a share in his kingship and priesthood; therefore he deserves to be praised for ever and ever. "The baptized, by regeneration and the anointing of the Holy Spirit, are consecrated to be a spiritual house and a holy priesthood, that through all the works of Christian men they may offer spiritual sacrifices and proclaim the perfection of him who has called them out of darkness into his marvellous light" (Vatican II, *LG*, 10).

Although the text speaks in the present tense—"he is coming in the clouds" (v. 7) —it should be read as referring to the future: the prophet was seeing future events as if they were actually happening (cf. Dan 7:13). This will be the day of final victory, when those who crucified Jesus, "every one who pierced him" (cf. Zech 12:10; Jn 19:37), and those who rejected him over the course of history, will be astonished by the majesty and glory of the crucified One.

1:9–20 The island of Patmos was a penitentiary. The Lord's day (v. 10), Sunday, is the day which the Church, ever since the apostolic age keeps as its holy day in place of the Jewish sabbath (Saturday), because it was the day Jesus rose from the dead. The scene painted in the vision has a liturgical quality: we are given to understand that the writer received the vision during the celebration of a Sunday liturgy—the liturgy on earth linking up with that of heaven.

In the vision the lampstands (v. 12) symbolize the churches at prayer; they remind us of the seven-branched candlestick (the *menorah*) which used to burn in the temple of Jerusalem. Jesus Christ, as Son of man (cf. Dan 7:13), is the eschatological Judge and the features mentioned symbolize his priesthood ("long robe": cf. Ex 28:4; Zech 3:4); his kingship ("golden girdle": cf. 1 Mac 10:89); his eternity

1:7 Dan 7:13; Zech 12:10.

[12]Then I turned to see the voice that was speaking to me, and on turning I saw seven golden lampstands, [13]and in the midst of the lampstands one like a son of man,* clothed with a long robe and with a golden girdle round his breast; [14]his head and his hair were white as white wool, white as snow; his eyes were like a flame of fire, [15]his feet were like burnished bronze, refined as in a furnace, and his voice was like the sound of many waters; [16]in his right hand he held seven stars, from his mouth issued a sharp two-edged sword, and his face was like the sun shining in full strength.

[17]When I saw him, I fell at his feet as though dead. But he laid his right hand upon me, saying, "Fear not, I am the first and the last, [18]and the living one; I died, and behold I am alive for evermore, and I have the keys of Death and Hades. [19]Now write what you see, what is and what is to take place hereafter. [20]As for the mystery of the seven stars which you saw in my right hand, and the seven golden lampstands, the seven stars are the angels of the seven churches and the seven lampstands are the seven churches.

Letter to the church of Ephesus

2 [1]To the angel of the church in Ephesus write: 'The words of him who holds the seven stars in his right hand, who walks among the seven golden lampstands.

[2]"'I know your works, your toil and your patient endurance, and how you cannot bear evil men but have tested those who call themselves apostles but are not, and found them to be false; [3]I know you are enduring patiently and bearing up for my name's sake, and you have not grown weary. [4]But I have this against you, that you have abandoned the love you had at first. [5]Remember then from what you have fallen, repent and do the works you did at first. If not,

---

("white hair": cf. Dan 7:9); his divine wisdom ("eyes like a flame of fire": cf. 2:18); and his power ("feel like burnished bronze": cf. Dan 10:6; "sound of many waters": cf. Ezek 43:2). The Lord holds the churches in his hand to show that he protects them.

2:1–7 Ephesus was the foremost city of Asia Minor. Because its church was the foremost in the region, Christ is depicted as the Lord of all the churches. He praises the church's patience and endurance in staying loyal to the true faith, and he criticizes it for its lack of fervour: if it does not pay heed, it will lose its pre-eminent position. The Nicolaitans (v. 6), seemingly, held that it was possible to be a Christian and yet worship idols. St Francis de Sales comments: "He did not accuse them of lacking in love, rather that they were no longer as fervent, open or fruitful as they had been in the beginning; in the same way as we would describe a man who was strong, cheerful and brave, as being sad and timid if he became defeated" (*Treatise on the love of God*, 4, 22).

1:13 Dan 7:13; 10:5. **1:14** Dan 7:9; 10:6. **1:15** Dan 10:6; Ezek 1:24.

I will come to you and remove your lampstand from its place, unless you repent.
[6]Yet this you have, you hate the works of the Nicolaitans, which I also hate. [7]He
who has an ear, let him hear what the Spirit says to the churches. To him who
conquers I will grant to eat of the tree of life, which is in the paradise of God.'

Letter to the church of Smyrna

[8]"And to the angel of the church in Smyrna write: 'The words of the first and
the last, who died and came to life.

[9]"'I know your tribulation and your poverty (but you are rich) and the
slander of those who say that they are Jews and are not, but are a synagogue of
Satan. [10]Do not fear what you are about to suffer. Behold, the devil is about to
throw some of you into prison, that you may be tested, and for ten days* you
will have tribulation. Be faithful unto death, and I will give you the crown of
life. [11]He who has an ear, let him hear what the Spirit says to the churches. He
who conquers shall not be hurt by the second death.'

Letter to the church of Pergamum

[12]"And to the angel of the church in Pergamum write: 'The words of him who
has the sharp two-edged sword.

[13]"'I know where you dwell, where Satan's throne is; you hold fast my
name and you did not deny my faith even in the days of Antipas my witness,
my faithful one, who was killed among you, where Satan dwells. [14]But I have
a few things against you: you have some there who hold the teaching of
Balaam, who taught Balak to put a stumbling block before the sons of Israel,
that they might eat food sacrificed to idols and practise immorality. [15]So you
also have some who hold the teaching of the Nicolaitans. [16]Repent then. If not,
I will come to you soon and war against them with the sword of my mouth.
[17]He who has an ear, let him hear what the Spirit says to the churches. To him
who conquers I will give some of the hidden manna, and I will give him a
white stone, with a new name written on the stone which no one knows except
him who receives it.'

2:8–11 Smyrna was a city renowned for its ritual worship of the Roman emperor: appropriately, the vision presents Christ as the only true God, "the first and the last" (v. 8). It encourages the Christians of Smyrna to be steadfast in the midst of persecution from Jews.

2:12–17 Pergamum, which was famous for its many temples, had a monumental altar dedicated to Zeus. The Christians of the city were tempted to take part in pagan religious celebrations. Some even encouraged such involvement, as Balaam in his time tried to lead the Jews astray (cf. Num 31:16). They are reminded that Christ is the Judge and carries a sword of punishment.

Letter to the church of Thyatira

18“And to the angel of the church in Thyatira write: ‘The words of the Son of
God, who has eyes like a flame of fire, and whose feet are like burnished bronze.
19“‘I know your works, your love and faith and service and patient endurance,
and that your latter works exceed the first. 20But I have this against you, that
you tolerate the woman Jezebel, who calls herself a prophetess and is teaching
and beguiling my servants to practise immorality* and to eat food sacrificed to
idols. 21I gave her time to repent, but she refuses to repent of her immorality.*
22Behold, I will throw her on a sickbed, and those who commit adultery with
her I will throw into great tribulation, unless they repent of her doings; 23and I
will strike her children dead. And all the churches shall know that I am he who
searches mind and heart, and I will give to each of you as your works deserve.
24But to the rest of you in Thyatira, who do not hold this teaching, who have
not learned what some call the deep things of Satan,* to you I say, I do not lay
upon you any other burden; 25only hold fast what you have, until I come. 26He
who conquers and who keeps my works until the end, I will give him power
over the nations, 27and he shall rule them with a rod of iron, as when earthen
pots are broken in pieces, even as I myself have received power from my
Father; 28and I will give him the morning star.* 29He who has an ear, let him
hear what the Spirit says to the churches.’

Letter to the church of Sardis

3 1“And to the angel of the church in Sardis write: ‘The words of him who
has the seven spirits of God and the seven stars.
“‘I know your works; you have the name of being alive, and you are dead.
2Awake, and strengthen what remains and is on the point of death, for I have
not found your works perfect in the sight of my God. 3Remember then what
you received and heard; keep that, and repent. If you will not awake, I will
come like a thief, and you will not know at what hour I will come upon you.
4Yet you have still a few names in Sardis, people who have not soiled their
garments; and they shall walk with me in white, for they are worthy. 5He who
conquers shall be clad thus in white garments, and I will not blot his name out
of the book of life; I will confess his name before my Father and before his
angels. 6He who has an ear, let him hear what the Spirit says to the churches.’

2:18–29 Thyatira was a small city noted for smelting, weaving and dyeing. Lydia came from there (cf. Acts 16:13–15). Christ is depicted to these Christians as the powerful Son of God, and they are exhorted not to engage in idolatrous practices.

3:1–6 Sardis was an important hub in the highway system and was noted for its licentious lifestyle. To this Christian community Christ is portrayed as the one who sends the Spirit who can change them from within. The church is accused of giving the appearance of being Christian whereas many of its members are living in sin and have no spiritual life.

2:26–27 Ps 2:8–9.

Letter to the church of Philadelphia

7"And to the angel of the church in Philadelphia write: 'The words of the holy
one, the true one, who has the key of David, who opens and no one shall shut,
who shuts and no one opens.

8"'I know your works. Behold, I have set before you an open door, which
no one is able to shut; I know that you have but little power, and yet you have
kept my word and have not denied my name. 9Behold, I will make those of the
synagogue of Satan who say that they are Jews and are not, but lie—behold,
I will make them come and bow down before your feet, and learn that I have
loved you. 10Because you have kept my word of patient endurance, I will keep
you from the hour of trial which is coming on the whole world, to try those
who dwell upon the earth. 11I am coming soon; hold fast what you have, so
that no one may seize your crown. 12He who conquers, I will make him a pillar
in the temple of my God; never shall he go out of it, and I will write on him the
name of my God, and the name of the city of my God, the new Jerusalem
which comes down from my God out of heaven, and my own new name.*
13He who has an ear, let him hear what the Spirit says to the churches.'

Letter to the church of Laodicea

14"And to the angel of the church in Laodicea write: 'The words of the Amen,
the faithful and true witness, the beginning of God's creation.

15"'I know your works: you are neither cold nor hot. Would that you were
cold or hot! 16So, because you are lukewarm, and neither cold nor hot, I will
spew you out of my mouth. 17For you say, I am rich, I have prospered, and I
need nothing; not knowing that you are wretched, pitiable, poor, blind, and
naked. 18Therefore I counsel you to buy from me gold refined by fire, that you
may be rich, and white garments to clothe you and to keep the shame of your
nakedness from being seen, and salve to anoint your eyes, that you may see.
19Those whom I love, I reprove and chasten; so be zealous and repent.
20Behold, I stand at the door and knock; if any one hears my voice and opens

---

3:7–13 Philadelphia was the gateway to the region of Phrygia. It had suffered an earthquake around the year 17 AD, and when it was rebuilt it was renamed Neocaesarea, but the name did not catch on. Now it is promised a new name (v. 12) which will endure. The faithful in this city are reminded that Christ has the keys to the Kingdom of God, and they are assured that many Jews there will be converted.

3:14–22 Laodicea was a prosperous city, located near hot springs. Christ is depicted as God who is true to his promises and who expects ardent love. "Fight against the softness that makes you lazy and careless in your spiritual life. Remember that it might well be the beginning of lukewarmness … and, in the words of the Scripture, God will vomit out the lukewarm" (Bl. J. Escrivá, *The Way*, 325).

3:7 Is 22:22.

the door, I will come in to him and eat with him, and he with me. [21]He who
conquers, I will grant him to sit with me on my throne, as I myself conquered
and sat down with my Father on his throne. [22]He who has an ear, let him hear
what the Spirit says to the churches.'"

PART TWO: ESCHATOLOGICAL VISIONS

1. INTRODUCTORY VISION

God in majesty

4 [1]After this I looked, and lo, in heaven an open door! And the first voice,
which I had heard speaking to me like a trumpet, said, "Come up hither,
and I will show you what must take place after this." [2]At once I was in the
Spirit, and lo, a throne stood in heaven, with one seated on the throne! [3]And he
who sat there appeared like jasper and carnelian, and round the throne was a
rainbow that looked like an emerald.* [4]Round the throne were twenty-four
thrones, and seated on the thrones were twenty-four elders,* clad in white
garments, with golden crowns upon their heads. [5]From the throne issue flashes
of lightning, and voices and peals of thunder, and before the throne burn seven
torches of fire, which are the seven spirits of God; [6]and before the throne there
is as it were a sea of glass, like crystal.

4:1–22:21 □ □ After Christ's message to each of the churches, God's plan for mankind and the Church is revealed as having been made manifest to the author of the book in a series of visions. First there is an elaborate vision of heaven, which acts as an introduction to what follows (4:1–5:14). Then come other visions which cover events in time prior to the last battle (6:1–11:14), culminating in visions of the battle in which evil is defeated forevermore and the Kingdom of God and the heavenly Jerusalem are manifested in all their splendour (11:15–22:15). The book concludes with an epilogue which swears to the truth of its contents (22:16–21).

4:1–5:14 □ This great vision of heaven includes God in majesty (4:1–11) and the risen Christ, who reveals to man the mysterious plans of God (5:1–18).

4:1–11 Here we find imagery taken from the Old Testament: the throne reminds us of the visions of Isaiah 6:1 and Ezekiel 1:26–28; the rainbow is the sign of God's Covenant in Genesis 9:7–17; the thunder and lightning appear in the theophany on Sinai (Ex 19:16); the sea of glass and the four living creatures are part of the description of the temple of Jerusalem in 1 Kings 7:23–26 and Ezekiel

And round the throne, on each side of the throne, are four living creatures,*
full of eyes in front and behind: [7]the first living creature like a lion, the second
living creature like an ox, the third living creature with the face of a man, and
the fourth living creature like a flying eagle. [8]And the four living creatures,
each of them with six wings, are full of eyes all round and within, and day and
night they never cease to sing,

"Holy, holy, holy,* is the Lord God Almighty,
who was and is and is to come!"

[9]And whenever the living creatures give glory and honour and thanks to him
who is seated on the throne, who lives for ever and ever, [10]the twenty-four
elders fall down before him who is seated on the throne and worship him who
lives for ever and ever; they cast their crowns before the throne, singing,

[11] "Worthy art thou, our Lord and God,
to receive glory and honour and power,
for thou didst create all things,
and by thy will they existed and were created."

The sealed scroll and the Lamb

5 [1]And I saw in the right hand of him who was seated on the throne a
scroll* written within and on the back, sealed with seven seals; [2]and I saw
a strong angel proclaiming with a loud voice, "Who is worthy to open the
scroll and break its seals?" [3]And no one in heaven or on earth or under the
earth was able to open the scroll or to look into it, [4]and I wept much that no
one was found worthy to open the scroll or to into it. [5]Then one of the elders

---

10:14. These images and other symbolism such as that of colours are used to describe the majesty of God and the praise that he receives in heaven from the patriarchs and apostles. The Church links her liturgy to this heavenly praise: "It is especially in the sacred liturgy that our union with the heavenly Church is best realized; in the liturgy, through the sacramental signs, the power of the Holy Spirit acts on us, and with community rejoicing we celebrate together the praise of the divine majesty, when all those of every tribe and tongue and people and nation who have been redeemed by the blood of Christ and gathered together into one Church glorify, in one common song of praise, the one and triune God" (Vatican II, *LG*, 50).

5:1–14 The sealed scroll symbolizes God's mysterious plan for each individual and for human history as a whole. If a person does not know about this plan, he is steeped in ignorance and anguish. But Christ, because he redeemed man by his death on the cross and won victory over death, has revealed God's plans to man. "Christ the Lord, Christ the new Adam, in the very revelation of the mystery of the Father and of his love, fully reveals man to himself and brings to light his most high calling" (Vatican II, *GS*, 22). Christ in glory deserves the same worship as the Father.

4:7 Ezeh 1:10. **4:8** Is 6: 2–3; Ezek 1:18; Ex 3:14.

said to me, "Weep not; lo, the Lion of the tribe of Judah, the Root of David,
has conquered, so that he can open the scroll and its seven seals."
6And between the throne and the four living creatures and among the elders,
I saw a Lamb standing, as though it had been slain, with seven horns and with
seven eyes,* which are the seven spirits of God sent out into all the earth; 7and
he went and took the scroll from the right hand of him who was seated on the
throne. 8And when he had taken the scroll, the four living creatures and the
twenty-four elders fell down before the Lamb, each holding a harp, and with
golden bowls full of incense, which are the prayers of the saints; 9and they
sang a new song, saying,

> "Worthy art thou to take the scroll and to open its seals,
> for thou wast slain and by thy blood didst ransom men for God
> from every tribe and tongue and people and nation,
> 10 and hast made them a kingdom and priests to our God,
> and they shall reign on earth."

11Then I looked, and I heard around the throne and the living creatures and the
elders the voice of many angels, numbering myriads of myriads and thousands of
thousands, 12saying with a loud voice, "Worthy is the Lamb who was slain, to
receive power and wealth and wisdom and might and honour and glory and
blessing!" 13And I heard every creature in heaven and on earth and under the earth
and in the sea, and all therein, saying, "To him who sits upon the throne and to the
Lamb be blessing and honour and glory and might for ever and ever!" 14And the
four living creatures said, "Amen!" and the elders fell down and worshipped.

2. EVENTS PRIOR TO THE FINAL OUTCOME

Christ opens the first six seals. Vision of the four horsemen

6 *1Now I saw when the Lamb opened one of the seven seals, and I heard one
of the four living creatures say, as with a voice of thunder, "Come!" 2And
I saw, and behold, a white horse, and its rider had a bow; and a crown was
given to him, and he went out conquering and to conquer.

6:1–11:14 □Through the image of the Lamb opening the seven seals one by one (6:1–7:17), the author is showing the deep meaning of history under the lordship of Christ and why so many misfortunes afflict mankind. Our sense of expectation increases the nearer we get to the opening of the seventh seal (cf. 8:1). When that moment comes, seven trumpets begin to sound, also one by one, symbolizing the voice of God (8:2–11:14). Only at the seventh trumpet blast will the mystery of the End be revealed (cf. 10:7); meanwhile, the reader is kept in suspense as he sees the hand and power of God at work throughout the course of history.

3When he opened the second seal, I heard the second living creature say,
"Come!" 4And out came another horse, bright red; its rider was permitted to
take peace from the earth, so that men should slay one another; and he was
given a great sword.
5When he opened the third seal, I heard the third living creature say,
"Come!" And I saw, and behold, a black horse, and its rider had a balance* in
his hand; 6and I heard what seemed to be a voice in the midst of the four living
creatures saying, "A quart of wheat for a denarius,[a] and three quarts of barley
for a denarius;[a] but do not harm oil and wine!"
7When he opened the fourth seal, I heard the voice of the fourth living
creature say, "Come!" 8And I saw, and behold, a pale horse, and its rider's
name was Death, and Hades followed him; and they were given power over a
fourth of the earth, to kill with sword and with famine and with pestilence and
by wild beasts of the earth.
9When he opened the fifth seal, I saw under the altar the souls of those who
had been slain for the word of God and for the witness they had borne; 10they
cried out with a loud voice, "O Sovereign Lord, holy and true, how long before
thou wilt judge and avenge our blood on those who dwell upon the earth?"
11Then they were each given a white robe and told to rest a little longer, until
the number of their fellow servants and their brethren should be complete, who
were to be killed as they themselves had been.
12When he opened the sixth seal, I looked, and behold, there was a great
earthquake; and the sun became black as sackcloth, the full moon became like
blood, 13and the stars of the sky fell to the earth as the fig tree sheds its winter
fruit when shaken by a gale; 14the sky vanished like a scroll that is rolled up,
and every mountain and island was removed from its place. 15Then the kings
of the earth and the great men and the generals and the rich and the strong, and
every one, slave and free, hid in the caves and among the rocks of the
mountains, 16calling to the mountains and rocks, "Fall on us and hide us from
the face of him who is seated on the throne, and from the wrath of the Lamb;
17for the great day of their wrath has come, and who can stand before it?"

6:1–17 Once the first four seals are opened, four horsemen appear. The first stands for Jesus Christ and the others symbolize war, famine and pestilence. When the fifth seal is broken (v. 9), the glory of the martyrs is revealed and, at the opening of the sixth, the tribulations which Jesus said would mark the end of the world. "The inspired evangelist not only saw the devastation brought about by sin, war, starvation and death; he saw, before all other things, the victory of Christ. There can be no doubt but that the journey of the Church through the centuries is a *via crucis*, but it has also been, at the same time, a triumphant procession. The Church of Christ, the people of Christian faith and love, are always those who bring light, salvation and peace to a humanity without hope. Jesus Christ, yesterday and today, one and the same forever" (Pius XII, Address, 15 November 1946).

a. The denarius was a day's wage for a labourer **6:16** Hos 10:8.

The great multitude of the saved

7 1After this I saw four angels standing at the four corners of the earth,
holding back the four winds of the earth, that no wind might blow on earth
or sea or against any tree. 2Then I saw another angel ascend from the rising of
the sun, with the seal of the living God, and he called with a loud voice to the
four angels who had been given power to harm earth and sea, 3saying, “Do not
harm the earth or the sea or the trees, till we have sealed the servants of our
God upon their foreheads.” 4And I heard the number of the sealed, a hundred
and forty-four thousand* sealed, out of every tribe of the sons of Israel,
5twelve thousand sealed out of the tribe of Judah, twelve thousand of the tribe
of Reuben, twelve thousand of the tribe of Gad, 6twelve thousand of the tribe
of Asher, twelve thousand of the tribe of Naphtali, twelve thousand of the tribe
of Manasseh, 7twelve thousand of the tribe of Simeon, twelve thousand of the
tribe of Levi, twelve thousand of the tribe of Issachar, 8twelve thousand of the
tribe of Zebulun, twelve thousand of the tribe of Joseph, twelve thousand
sealed out of the tribe of Benjamin.

9After this I looked, and behold, a great multitude which no man could
number, from every nation, from all tribes and peoples and tongues, standing
before the throne and before the Lamb, clothed in white robes, with palm
branches in their hands, 10and crying out with a loud voice, “Salvation belongs
to our God who sits upon the throne, and to the Lamb!” 11And all the angels
stood round the throne and round the elders and the four living creatures, and
they fell on their faces before the throne and worshipped God, 12saying,
“Amen! Blessing and glory and wisdom and thanksgiving and honour and
power and might be to our God for ever and ever! Amen.”

13Then one of the elders addressed me, saying, “Who are these, clothed in
white robes, and whence have they come?” 14I said to him, “Sir, you know.” And
he said to me, “These are they who have come out of the great tribulation;* they
have washed their robes and made them white in the blood of the Lamb.

15 Therefore are they before the throne of God,
and serve him day and night within his temple;
and he who sits upon the throne will shelter them with his presence.
16 They shall hunger no more, neither thirst any more;
the sun shall not strike them, nor any scorching heat.
17 For the Lamb in the midst of the throne will be their shepherd,
and he will guide them to springs of living water;
and God will wipe away every tear from their eyes.”

7:1–17 The suspense is heightened by the insertion of two visions prior to the opening of the seventh seal. The first vision shows God’s protection of Christians —a great number, one hundred and forty-four thousand, making up the new people of God. The second vision (vv. 9–17) shows the glory enjoyed after death

7:16 Is 49:10. **7:17** Ezek 34:23; Ps 23:2; Is 25:89.

The opening of the seventh seal

8 [1]When the Lamb opened the seventh seal, there was silence in heaven for
about half an hour. [2]Then I saw the seven angels who stand before God, and
seven trumpets were given to them. [3]And another angel came and stood at the
altar with a golden censer; and he was given much incense to mingle with the
prayers of all the saints upon the golden altar before the throne; [4]and the
smoke of the incense rose with the prayers of the saints from the hand of the
angel before God. [5]Then the angel took the censer and filled it with fire from
the altar and threw it on the earth;* and there were peals of thunder, voices,
flashes of lightning, and an earthquake.
[6]Now the seven angels who had the seven trumpets made ready to blow them.

The first six trumpet calls. The three woes

[7]The first angel blew his trumpet, and there followed hail and fire, mixed with
blood, which fell on the earth; and a third of the earth was burnt up, and a third
of the trees were burnt up, and all green grass was burnt up.
[8]The second angel blew his trumpet, and something like a great mountain,
burning with fire, was thrown into the sea; [9]and a third of the sea became
blood, a third of the living creatures in the sea died, and a third of the ships
were destroyed.
[10]The third angel blew his trumpet, and a great star fell from heaven,
blazing like a torch, and it fell on a third of the rivers and on the fountains of
water. [11]The name of the star is Wormwood. A third of the waters became
wormwood, and many men died of the water, because it was made bitter.

---

by those whom Christ has redeemed. "The blood of the Lamb, offered in sacrifice for all, has worked its saving power in every corner of the world, bringing grace and salvation to this 'great crowd'. Having undergone trials and been purified by the blood of Christ, the redeemed are safe in the Kingdom of God, where they praise and worship him for all time" (John Paul II, Homily, 1 November 1981).

8:1–6 The silence after the opening of the seventh seal is a sign of anxious expectation of revelation, and it allows the prayer of the saints (symbolized by the incense) to reach God: "Contemplative prayer *is silence*, the 'symbol of the world to come' (St Isaac of Nineveh, *Tract. Myst.*, 66) or 'silent love' (John of the Cross). Words in this kind of prayer are not speeches; they are like kindling that feeds the fire of love. In this silence, unbearable to the 'outer' man, the Father speaks to us his incarnate Word, who suffered, died and rose; in this silence the Spirit of adoption enables us to share in the prayer of Jesus" (*CCC*, 2717).

8:7–9:21 The trumpet blasts stand for the will of God heralding and inflicting punishment for the sins of mankind. The first four trumpet blasts (8:7–12) announce calamities similar to those caused by the plagues of Egypt, though much

12The fourth angel blew his trumpet, and a third of the sun was struck, and a
third of the moon, and a third of the stars, so that a third of their light was dark-
ened; a third of the day was kept from shining, and likewise a third of the night.
13Then I looked, and I heard an eagle crying with a loud voice, as it flew in
midheaven, "Woe, woe, woe to those who dwell on the earth, at the blasts of
the other trumpets which the three angels are about to blow!"
9 1And the fifth angel blew his trumpet, and I saw a star* fallen from heaven
to earth, and he was given the key of the shaft of the bottomless pit; 2he
opened the shaft of the bottomless pit, and from the shaft rose smoke like the
smoke of a great furnace, and the sun and the air were darkened with the
smoke from the shaft. 3Then from the smoke came locusts on the earth, and
they were given power like the power of scorpions of the earth; 4they were told
not to harm the grass of the earth or any green growth or any tree, but only
those of mankind who have not the seal of God upon their foreheads; 5they
were allowed to torture them for five months, but not to kill them, and their
torture was like the torture of a scorpion, when it stings a man. 6And in those
days men will seek death and will not find it; they will long to die, and death
will fly from them.
7In appearance the locusts were like horses arrayed for battle; on their heads
were what looked like crowns of gold; their faces were like human faces, 8their
hair like women's hair, and their teeth like lions' teeth; 9they had scales like

---

worse. Now these misfortunes affect the various elements created by God—land, sea, waters of the earth, and the firmament.

The motif of the eagle (8:13), symbolizing perhaps an angel, creates a climate of expectation and anxiety as to what the three remaining trumpet calls will bring.

The fifth and sixth trumpet blasts directly impact on mankind, producing effects more horrific than the previous ones (9:1–21). The fallen star symbolizes Satan (cf. Lk 10:18), whom God allows to release for a period the demons incarcerated in the bowels of the earth (according to the thinking of the time), in order to wreak havoc on those who refuse to acknowledge God. These demons have a truly frightening appearance, and on top of that their leader is called Destruction (Abaddon: 9:11). At the end of the Apocalypse, after Christ's victory, the author sees Satan and his followers being once again entombed in the abyss.

Now the angels of death appear (9:15). Only God has power over them. In the last analysis, as in the case of the calls to penance addressed to the churches of Asia Minor (cf. 2:5, 16, 21; 3:3; etc.), all the punishments described in the Apocalypse are designed to move people to repentance. But people persist in evil-doing: they turn away from God to worship idols, which are really only scarecrows compared with the infinite majesty of the living God (cf., e.g., Ps 115; Jer 10:3–5). Sadly, punishment sometimes only has the effect of hardening people's hearts, as happened to the pharaoh when he refused to let the Israelites leave Egypt.

iron breastplates, and the noise of their wings was like the noise of many
chariots with horses rushing into battle. [10]They have tails like scorpions, and
stings, and their power of hurting men for five months lies in their tails. [11]They
have as king over them the angel of the bottomless pit; his name in Hebrew is
Abaddon, and in Greek he is called Apollyon.[b]

[12]The first woe has passed; behold, two woes are still to come.

[13]Then the sixth angel blew his trumpet, and I heard a voice from the four
horns of the golden altar before God, [14]saying to the sixth angel who had the
trumpet, "Release the four angels who are bound at the great river Euphrates."*
[15]So the four angels were released, who had been held ready for the hour, the
day, the month, and the year, to kill a third of mankind. [16]The number of the
troops of cavalry was twice ten thousand times ten thousand; I heard their
number. [17]And this was how I saw the horses in my vision: the riders wore
breastplates the color of fire and of sapphire[c] and of sulphur, and the heads of
the horses were like lions' heads, and fire and smoke and sulphur issued from
their mouths. [18]By these three plagues a third of mankind was killed, by the
fire and smoke and sulphur issuing from their mouths. [19]For the power of the
horses is in their mouths and in their tails; their tails are like serpents, with
heads, and by means of them they wound.

[20]The rest of mankind, who were not killed by these plagues, did not repent
of the works of their hands nor give up worshipping demons and idols of gold
and silver and bronze and stone and wood, which cannot either see or hear or
walk; [21]nor did they repent of their murders or their sorceries or their immorality*
or their thefts.

The seer is given a little scroll to eat

10 [1]Then I saw another mighty angel coming down from heaven, wrapped
in a cloud, with a rainbow over his head, and his face was like the sun,
and his legs like pillars of fire. [2]He had a little scroll open in his hand. And he
set his right foot on the sea, and his left foot on the land, [3]and called out with

---

10:1–11 Before the seventh trumpet blast, the sacred writer inserts a further vision (the seer is once again back on earth). This insertion helps heighten the suspense and prepares the reader to face up to what will happen when the third woe comes and the seventh trumpet call announces the events of the End (cf. 11;14–15). Man can never know God's plans in their totality, the plans proclaimed by the seven trumpet calls, but God does make them known to John the seer. That revelation is symbolized by the little open scroll, which is different from the scroll we saw in 5:2. This open scroll symbolizes the divine revelation made to the prophets. The symbolism of eating a document is not new (cf. Ezek 2:8–3:3). It means that God is speaking through Holy Scripture promising blessing and chastisement. The reader must accept as true everything he reads in the book.

b. Or *Destroyer* **c.** Greek *hyacinth* **9:20** Deut 5:4, 23; Ps 115: 4–7; Ps 135:15–17.

a loud voice, like a lion roaring; when he called out, the seven thunders sounded. 4And when the seven thunders had sounded, I was about to write, but I heard a voice from heaven saying, "Seal up what the seven thunders have said, and do not write it down." 5And the angel whom I saw standing on sea and land lifted up his right hand to heaven 6and swore by him who lives for ever and ever, who created heaven and what is in it, the earth and what is in it, and the sea and what is in it, that there should be no more delay, 7but that in the days of the trumpet call to be sounded by the seventh angel, the mystery of God,* as he announced to his servants the prophets, should be fulfilled.

8Then the voice which I had heard from heaven spoke to me again, saying, "Go, take the scroll which is open in the hand of the angel who is standing on the sea and on the land." 9So I went to the angel and told him to give me the little scroll; and he said to me, "Take it and eat; it will be bitter to your stomach, but sweet* as honey in your mouth." 10And I took the little scroll from the hand of the angel and ate it; it was sweet as honey in my mouth, but when I had eaten it my stomach was made bitter. 11And I was told, "You must again prophesy about many peoples and nations and tongues and kings."

Death and resurrection of the two witnesses

11 *1Then I was given a measuring rod like a staff, and I was told: "Rise and measure the temple of God and the altar and those who worship there, 2but do not measure the court outside the temple; leave that out, for it is given over to the nations, and they will trample over the holy city for forty-two months.* 3And I will grant my two witnesses* power to prophesy for one thousand two hundred and sixty days, clothed in sackcloth."

11:1–14 These verses contain the prophecy of the seer who has eaten the scroll, a prophecy about the tribulation the Church will undergo as a prelude to the events of the End that follow the seventh and final trumpet blast (11:15ff). The Church is symbolized by the temple and the altar of Jerusalem, which God protects. The rest of the city is that part of mankind which does not belong to the Church and before whom the Church bears witness to the point of martyrdom. The two witnesses stand for the testimony given by the Church. In the last analysis all the tribulation is caused by the forces of evil, that is, the beast (the antichrist), which makes its appearance in the Holy City (v. 7).

Over a limited period (that is, the period of history symbolized by the forty-two months, the one thousand two hundred and seventy days or the three days and a half) there are points when the forces of evil prevail, causing many people to waver. Simultaneously the witnesses of the true God come on the scene, preaching penance (vv. 3–6), and for this they suffer martyrdom to the great delight of their foes (vv. 7–10). But God steps in on the martyrs' side and sweeps them up to heaven; he decimates their foes, and in their terror the survivors praise God (vv. 11–13).

10:5–6 Dan 12:7; Gen 14:22; 19; Neh 9:6. **11:4** Zech 4:3,11–14.

4These are the two olive trees and the two lampstands which stand before the Lord of the earth. 5And if any one would harm them, fire pours out from their mouth and consumes their foes; if any one would harm them, thus he is doomed to be killed. 6They have power to shut the sky, that no rain may fall during the days of their prophesying, and they have power over the waters to turn them into blood, and to smite the earth with every plague, as often as they desire. 7And when they have finished their testimony, the beast that ascends from the bottomless pit will make war upon them and conquer them and kill them, 8and their dead bodies will lie in the street of the great city* which is allegorically[d] called Sodom and Egypt, where their Lord was crucified. 9For three days and a half men from the peoples and tribes and tongues and nations gaze at their dead bodies and refuse to let them be placed in a tomb, 10and those who dwell on the earth will rejoice over them and make merry and exchange presents, because these two prophets had been a torment to those who dwell on the earth. 11But after the three and a half days a breath of life from God entered them, and they stood up on their feet, and great fear fell on those who saw them. 12Then they heard a loud voice from heaven saying to them, "Come up hither!" And in the sight of their foes they went up to heaven in a cloud. 13And at that hour there was a great earthquake, and a tenth of the city fell; seven thousand people were killed in the earthquake, and the rest were terrified and gave glory to the God of heaven.

14The second woe has passed; behold, the third woe is soon to come.

3. CHRIST'S VICTORY OVER THE POWERS OF EVIL. THE CHURCH IN GLORY

The seventh trumpet call

15Then the seventh angel blew his trumpet, and there were loud voices in heaven, saying, "The kingdom of the world has become the kingdom of our

---

11:15–22:15 □ The sounding of the seventh trumpet opens a new section in which we are shown, firstly, the climax of the confrontation between Satan and the powers of evil, on the one side, and Christ and the Church on the other (12:1–16:16); then come the battles of the End-time and, following the victory of Christ, the full and permanent establishment of his kingship (16:17–22:5).

11:15–19 These verses, which proclaim the definitive coming of the Kingdom of Christ, are a sort of introduction to the whole section. The voices in heaven, symbolizing divine revelation, announce that God's plan has come to fruition, his plan that Christ should reign over the entire universe for ever and ever. The words of Psalm 2 are thereby fulfilled. In fact "she is, on earth, the seed and the

d. Greek *spiritually*

Lord and of his Christ, and he shall reign for ever and ever." 16And the twenty-
four elders who sit on their thrones before God fell on their faces and
worshipped God, 17saying,

"We give thanks to thee, Lord God Almighty, who art and who wast,
that thou hast taken thy great power and begun to reign.
18 The nations raged, but thy wrath came,
and the time for the dead to be judged,
for rewarding thy servants, the prophets and saints,
and those who fear thy name, both small and great,
and for destroying the destroyers of the earth."

19Then God's temple in heaven was opened, and the ark of his covenant was
seen within his temple; and there were flashes of lightning, voices, peals of
thunder, an earthquake, and heavy hail.

The woman pursued by the dragon

12 *1And a great portent appeared in heaven, a woman clothed with the
sun, with the moon under her feet, and on her head a crown of twelve
stars; 2she was with child and she cried out in her pangs of birth, in anguish for
delivery. 3And another portent appeared in heaven; behold, a great red dragon,
with seven heads and ten horns, and seven diadems upon his heads. 4His tail
swept down a third of the stars of heaven, and cast them to the earth. And the
dragon stood before the woman who was about to bear a child, that he might
devour her child when she brought it forth; 5she brought forth a male child,

---

beginning of that kingdom. While she slowly grows to maturity, the Church longs for the completed kingdom and, with all her strength, hopes and desires to be united in glory with her king" (Vatican II, *LG*, 5). The final victory of Christ is revealed as an already present reality—and this causes the entire people of God (as represented by the twenty-four elders; cf. 4:4) to worship him and give him thanks. The vision reveals God's dwelling-place as heaven and shows that he has stayed true to his Covenant.

12:1–17 God's faithfulness to his Covenant is manifested in the victory of Christ and his Church over the forces of evil. The final confrontation is described, the struggle between the dragon or serpent and the beasts on the one side, and the Messiah, the Woman and her children on the other (cf. 12:1–13:18). Then the Lamb appears, Christ in glory, and the Last Judgment will be proclaimed (cf. 14:1–20).

This theme will follow the thread of the seven bowls or plagues (cf. 15:1–16:16). Then follows a new description of the contenders, and the last battles (cf. 16:17–20:15).

Three confrontations with the dragon are described—that of the Messiah born of the Woman (1–6); that of St Michael and his angels (1:7–12); and that of the

12:5 Is 66:7; Ps 2:9.

one who is to rule all the nations with a rod of iron, but her child was caught
up to God and to his throne, [6]and the woman fled into the wilderness, where
she has a place prepared by God, in which to be nourished for one thousand
two hundred and sixty days.

[7]Now war arose in heaven, Michael and his angels fighting against the
dragon; and the dragon and his angels fought, [8]but they were defeated and
there was no longer any place for them in heaven. [9]And the great dragon was
thrown down, that ancient serpent, who is called the Devil and Satan, the
deceiver of the whole world—he was thrown down to the earth, and his angels
were thrown down with him. [10]And I heard a loud voice in heaven, saying,
"Now the salvation and the power and the kingdom of our God and the authority
of his Christ have come, for the accuser of our brethren has been thrown down,
who accuses them day and night before our God. [11]And they have conquered him
by the blood of the Lamb and by the word of their testimony, for they loved not
their lives even unto death. [12]Rejoice then, O heaven and you that dwell therein!
But woe to you, O earth and sea, for the devil has come down to you in great
wrath, because he knows that his time is short!"

[13]And when the dragon saw that he had been thrown down to the earth, he
pursued the woman who had borne the male child. [14]But the woman was given
the two wings of the great eagle that she might fly from the serpent into the
wilderness, to the place where she is to be nourished for a time, and times, and
half a time.* [15]The serpent poured water like a river out of his mouth after the
woman, to sweep her away with the flood. [16]But the earth came to the help of
the woman, and the earth opened its mouth and swallowed the river which the
dragon had poured from his mouth. [17]Then the dragon was angry with the
woman,* and went off to make war on the rest of her offspring, on those who
keep the commandments of God and bear testimony to Jesus. And he stood[e]
on the sand of the sea.

Woman and the rest of her offspring (13–17). These confrontations are not presented as being in chronological order, but as separate pictures set alongside each other because they are closely connected: in each the same enemy, the devil, battles against God's plans and against those whom God uses to implement them.

The mysterious figure of the Woman is depicted with features which are applicable to Israel, to the Church and to the Blessed Virgin. It is easier to understand the passage if one views it in the context of Revelation as a whole, where we learn that the Blessed Virgin personifies both Israel and the Church (cf. Lk 1:26–31; 2:35; Gal 4:24). As long as the Church is making her pilgrim way on earth "The Mother of Jesus in the glory which she possesses in body and soul in heaven is the image and beginning of the Church as it is to be perfected in the world to come. Likewise she shines forth on earth, until the day of the Lord shall come, a sign of certain hope and comfort to the pilgrim People of God" (Vatican II, *LG*, 68).

e. Other ancient authorities read *And I stood*, connecting the sentence with 13.1

The beasts given authority by the dragon

13 [1]And I saw a beast* rising out of the sea, with ten horns and seven heads, with ten diadems upon its horns and a blasphemous name upon its heads. [2]And the beast that I saw was like a leopard, its feet were like a bear's, and its mouth was like a lion's mouth. And to it the dragon gave his power and his throne and great authority. [3]One of its heads seemed to have a mortal wound, but its mortal wound was healed, and the whole earth followed the beast with wonder. [4]Men worshipped the dragon, for he had given his authority to the beast, and they worshipped the beast, saying, "Who is like the beast, and who can fight against it?"

[5]And the beast was given a mouth uttering haughty and blasphemous words, and it was allowed to exercise authority for forty-two months; [6]it opened its mouth to utter blasphemies against God, blaspheming his name and his dwelling, that is, those who dwell in heaven. [7]Also it was allowed to make war on the saints and to conquer them.[f] And authority was given it over every tribe and people and tongue and nation, [8]and all who dwell on earth will worship it, every one whose name has not been written before the foundation of the world in the book of life of the Lamb that was slain. [9]If any one has an ear, let him hear:

> [10]If any one is to be taken captive,
> to captivity he goes;
> if any one slays with the sword,
> with the sword must he be slain.

Here is a call for the endurance and faith of the saints.

The beast rising from out of the earth

[11]Then I saw another beast* which rose out of the earth; it had two horns like a lamb and it spoke like a dragon. [12]It exercises all the authority of the first

---

13:1–10 Satan, the serpent of old, launches his attack through the beasts he endows with his power (v.1; cf. v.11). The beasts stand for those who over the course of history have embodied the powers of evil in one way or another. The first beast (vv. 1–10) symbolizes political power taken to such an extreme that it supplants God; the second (vv. 11–12) stands for those forces of evil who defend, justify and propagate that deification of power by giving it an acceptable face. The beasts are depicted as having features found in the prophets' descriptions of the enemies of Israel, and they can be read as referring to the Roman empire; but that empire is also seen as the symbolic tool of a diabolical power that ceaselessly hovers over mankind and will become more virulent as the End approaches. "Idolatry is an extreme form of the disorder produced by sin. The substitution of the worship of creatures for the adoration of the living God deforms relationships between people and leads to various forms of oppression" (SCDF, *Libert. consc.*, 39).

13:11–18 Further on (cf. 16:13; 19:20) this second beast is identified with the false prophet because his role consists in leading men astray and getting them to

f. Other ancient authorities omit this sentence **13:10** Jer 15:2; 43:11.

beast in its presence, and makes the earth and its inhabitants worship the first
beast, whose mortal wound was healed. 13It works great signs, even making
fire come down from heaven to earth in the sight of men; 14and by the signs
which it is allowed to work in the presence of the beast, it deceives those who
dwell on earth, bidding them make an image for the beast which was wounded
by the sword and yet lived; 15and it was allowed to give breath to the image of
the beast so that the image of the beast should even speak, and to cause those
who would not worship the image of the beast to be slain. 16Also it causes all,
both small and great, both rich and poor, both free and slave, to be marked on
the right hand or the forehead, 17so that no one can buy or sell unless he has
the mark, that is, the name of the beast or the number of its name. 18This calls
for wisdom: let him who has understanding reckon the number of the beast,
for it is a human number, its number is six hundred and sixty-six.[g*]

The Lamb and his entourage

14 1Then I looked, and lo, on Mount Zion stood the Lamb, and with him a
hundred and forty-four thousand who had his name and his Father's
name written on their foreheads. 2And I heard a voice from heaven like the
sound of many waters and like the sound of loud thunder; the voice I heard
was like the sound of harpers playing on their harps, 3and they sing a new song
before the throne and before the four living creatures and before the elders. No
one could learn that song except the hundred and forty-four thousand who had
been redeemed from the earth. 4It is these who have not defiled themselves
with women, for they are chaste;[h*] it is these who follow the Lamb wherever

---

worship the first beast. Because he has real (but evil) power he is able to work prodigies similar to those performed by the prophets (for example, Elijah, who brought fire down from heaven: cf. 1 Kings 18:38) and can even seem to vie with the power of the life-giving Spirit by breathing life into the images of the beast. He symbolizes those regimes and ideologies which reject God and put man on a pedestal. Materialism works in the same deceptive way as the beast does, for "though it sometimes also speaks of the 'spirit' and of 'questions of the spirit', as for example in the fields of culture or morality, it does so only insofar as it considers certain facts as derived from matter (*epiphenomena*), since according to this system matter is the one and only form of being. It follows, according to this interpretation, that religion can only be understood as a kind of 'idealistic illusion', to be fought with the most suitable means and methods according to circumstances of time and place, in order to eliminate it from society and from man's very heart" (John Paul II, *Dom. et Viv.*, 56).

14:1–5 The book now turns to the Lamb (Christ) and will then go on to speak about the Judgment in anticipation of the Lamb's victory. In opposition to the powers of evil and the active hostility offered God and the Church at the instigation of Satan stands the risen Christ with his followers who sing in praise of his glory and triumph. Mount

g. Other ancient authorities read *six hundred and sixteen* **h.** Greek *virgins* he goes; these have been redeemed from mankind as first fruits for God and the Lamb, 5and in their mouth no lie was found, for they are spotless.

Proclamation and symbols of the Judgment

6Then I saw another angel flying in midheaven, with an eternal gospel to proclaim to those who dwell on earth, to every nation and tribe and tongue and people; 7and he said with a loud voice, "Fear God and give him glory, for the hour of his judgment has come; and worship him who made heaven and earth, the sea and the fountains of water."

8Another angel, a second, followed, saying, "Fallen, fallen is Babylon the great, she who made all nations drink the wine of her impure passion."

9And another angel, a third, followed them, saying with a loud voice, "If any one worships the beast and its image, and receives a mark on his forehead or on his hand, 10he also shall drink the wine of God's wrath, poured unmixed into the cup of his anger, and he shall be tormented with fire and sulphur in the presence of the holy angels and in the presence of the Lamb. 11And the smoke of their torment goes up for ever and ever; and they have no rest, day or night, these worshippers of the beast and its image, and whoever receives the mark of its name."

12Here is a call for the endurance of the saints, those who keep the commandments of God and the faith of Jesus.

13And I heard a voice from heaven saying, "Write this: Blessed are the dead who die in the Lord henceforth." "Blessed indeed," says the Spirit, "that they may rest from their labours, for their deeds follow them!"

The harvest and the vintage

14Then I looked, and lo, a white cloud, and seated on the cloud one like a son of man, with a golden crown on his head, and a sharp sickle in his hand. 15And

---

Zion stands for the Church, protected by Christ and gathered about him. The assembly includes all those who belong to Christ and to the Father and who therefore bear the mark which shows them to be children of God. They are so numerous that it is impossible to count them, but their number is defined and God has it in his mind—the people of God represented by a number which is the result of multiplying 12 (tribes) by 12 (apostles) by 1000 (standing for a number on a huge scale): cf. 7:3–8. They are not yet in heaven; they are on earth, where they praise God, uniting their voices to the praise of the heavenly liturgy.

14:6–13 Three angels announce the Judgment; Christ, the Son of man will pronounce it (14:14); and three other angels will carry it out (14:15–20). All men are capable of acknowledging and loving their Creator: those who do so will be rewarded on the day of Judgment. This is the "eternal gospel" (v. 6).

14:14–20 This preview of the Last Judgment is presented in two scenes—the harvest (cf. vv. 14–16) and the vintage (vv. 17–20)—in line with the prophecy of Joel about

another angel came out of the temple, calling with a loud voice to him who sat
upon the cloud, "Put in your sickle, and reap, for the hour to reap has come,
for the harvest of the earth is fully ripe." 16So he who sat upon the cloud swung
his sickle on the earth, and the earth was reaped.

17And another angel came out of the temple in heaven, and he too had a sharp
sickle. 18Then another angel came out from the altar, the angel who has power
over fire, and he called with a loud voice to him who had the sharp sickle, "Put in
your sickle, and gather the clusters of the vine of the earth, for its grapes are ripe."
19So the angel swung his sickle on the earth and gathered the vintage of the earth,
and threw it into the great wine press of the wrath of God; 20and the wine press
was trodden outside the city, and blood flowed from the wine press, as high as
a horse's bridle, for one thousand six hundred stadia.[i]

The hymn of the saved

15 1Then I saw another portent in heaven, great and wonderful, seven
angels with seven plagues, which are the last, for with them the wrath of
God is ended.

2And I saw what appeared to be a sea of glass mingled with fire, and those
who had conquered the beast and its image and the number of its name,
standing beside the sea of glass with harps of God in their hands. 3And they
sing the song of Moses,* the servant of God, and the song of the Lamb, saying,

"Great and wonderful are thy deeds,
O Lord God the Almighty!
Just and true are thy ways,
O King of the ages![j]
4Who shall not fear and glorify thy name, O Lord?

---

how God will judge nations hostile to Israel: "Let the nations bestir themselves, and come up to the valley of Jehoshapat; for there I will sit to judge all the nations round about. Put in the sickle, for the harvest is ripe. Go in, tread, for the winepress is full. The vats overflow, for their wickedness is great" (Joel 4:12–13).

15:1–4 The third portent (cf. the two others in 12:1, 3) heralds the final outcome of the contention between the powers of evil and the Church of Jesus Christ. This is symbolized by the number seven being repeated three times, after the seven seals (cf. 5:1) and the seven trumpet calls (cf. 8:2). The sea of glass is somewhat reminiscent of the passage of the Red Sea during the Exodus, and the molten or bronze sea used in the temple of Jerusalem in purification rites (cf. 4:6–7). At any event, once again we have the Church's prayer of praise preceding God's intervention "Praise is the form of prayer which recognizes most immediately that God is God. It lauds God for his own sake and gives him glory, quite beyond what he does, but simply because He Is. It shares in the blessed happiness of the pure of heart who love God in faith before seeing him in glory" (*CCC*, 2639).

i. About two hundred miles **j.** Other ancient authorities read *the nations*

For thou alone art holy.
All nations shall come and worship thee,
for thy judgments have been revealed."

The seven bowls of plagues

[5]After this I looked, and the temple of the tent of witness in heaven was
opened, [6]and out of the temple came the seven angels with the seven plagues,
robed in pure bright linen, and their breasts girded with golden girdles. [7]And
one of the four living creatures gave the seven angels seven golden bowls full
of the wrath of God who lives for ever and ever; [8]and the temple was filled
with smoke from the glory of God and from his power, and no one could enter
the temple until the seven plagues of the seven angels were ended.
16 [1]Then I heard a loud voice from the temple telling the seven angels, "Go
and pour out on the earth the seven bowls of the wrath of God."
[2]So the first angel went and poured his bowl on the earth, and foul and evil
sores came upon the men who bore the mark of the beast and worshipped its
image.
[3]The second angel poured his bowl into the sea, and it became like the
blood of a dead man, and every living thing died that was in the sea.
[4]The third angel poured his bowl into the rivers and the fountains of water,
and they became blood. [5]And I heard the angel of water say,

"Just art thou in these thy judgments,
thou who art and wast, O Holy One.
[6]For men have shed the blood of saints and prophets,
and thou hast given them blood to drink.
It is their due!"

15:5–16:21 The tent, like the ark in 11:19, symbolizes the presence of God, who takes decisive action (15:5) through his angels. The seven golden bowls are the devices used to pour the plagues over the world; that is why they are said to be full of the wrath of God, that is, full of the divine justice which will now be made fully manifest. Thus, the golden bowls are also a symbol of the prayers of the saints (which have caused God to intervene: cf. 5:8) and their results—the victory of good, and punishment of the powers of evil. Strictly speaking the *bowls* symbolize the prayers of the saints; their *content* is not the plagues as such but the outcome of prayer—action on God's part which serves to console the righteous (the perfume of incense) and punish the beast's followers, those who work iniquity (the wrath of God).

The imagery used to describe the punishment inflicted by God derives from the plagues of Egypt. The first four have to do with the elements of nature (cf. 16:2–9 and 8:7–13), the fifth and sixth with historical forces (cf. 16:10–16 and 9:1–21) and the seventh with the final climax. But this time the punishment affects not just one third of everything but absolutely everything. Sin is on the increase. Evils are the fruit of sin, and God's wrath expresses itself by allowing men to follow the

[7]And I heard the altar cry,
"Yea, Lord God the Almighty,
true and just are thy judgments!"
[8]The fourth angel poured his bowl on the sun, and it was allowed to scorch
men with fire; [9]men were scorched by the fierce heat, and they cursed the
name of God who had power over these plagues, and they did not repent and
give him glory.
[10]The fifth angel poured his bowl on the throne of the beast, and its kingdom
was in darkness; men gnawed their tongues in anguish [11]and cursed the God
of heaven for their pain and sores, and did not repent of their deeds.
[12]The sixth angel poured his bowl on the great river Euphrates, and its water
was dried up, to prepare the way for the kings from the east. [13]And I saw,
issuing from the mouth of the dragon and from the mouth of the beast and
from the mouth of the false prophet, three foul spirits like frogs; [14]for they are
demonic spirits, performing signs, who go abroad to the kings of the whole
world, to assemble them for battle on the great day* of God the Almighty.
[15]("Lo, I am coming like a thief! Blessed is he who is awake, keeping his
garments that he may not go naked and be seen exposed!") [16]And they
assembled them at the place which is called in Hebrew Armageddon.*
[17]The seventh angel poured his bowl into the air, and a loud voice came out
of the temple, from the throne, saying, "It is done!" [18]And there were flashes
of lightning, voices, peals of thunder, and a great earthquake such as had never
been since men were on the earth, so great was that earthquake. [19]The great
city was split into three parts, and the cities of the nations fell, and God
remembered great Babylon, to make her drain the cup of the fury of his wrath.
[20]And every island fled away, and no mountains were to be found; [21]and great
hailstones, heavy as a hundred-weight, dropped on men from heaven, till men
cursed God for the plague of the hail, so fearful was that plague.

---

desires of their idolatrous hearts (cf. Rom 1:18–32). As history advances, the signs are that sin is on the increase; sin is the ultimate cause of the new plagues which threaten the world. "It must be added that on the horizon of contemporary civilization—especially in the form that is most developed in the technical and scientific sense—*the signs and symptoms of death* have become particularly present and frequent. One has only to think of the arms race and of the inherent danger of nuclear self-destruction. Moreover, everyone has become more and more aware of the grave situation of vast areas of our planet, marked by death-dealing poverty and famine. It is a question of problems that are not only economic but also and above all ethical. But on the horizon of our era there are gathering ever darker 'signs of death': a custom has become widely established—in some places it threatens to become almost an institution—of taking the lives of human beings even before they are born or before they reach the natural point of death" (John Paul II, *Dom. et Viv.*, 57).

The great harlot and the beast

17 [1]Then one of the seven angels who had the seven bowls came and said to me, “Come, I will show you the judgment of the great harlot* who is seated upon many waters, [2]with whom the kings of the earth have committed fornication, and with the wine of whose fornication* the dwellers on earth have become drunk.” [3]And he carried me away in the Spirit into a wilderness, and I saw a woman sitting on a scarlet beast which was full of blasphemous names, and it had seven heads and ten horns. [4]The woman was arrayed in purple and scarlet, and bedecked with gold and jewels and pearls, holding in her hand a golden cup full of abominations and the impurities of her fornication; [5]and on her forehead was written a name of mystery: “Babylon the great, mother of harlots and of earth’s abominations.” [6]And I saw the woman, drunk with the blood of the saints and the blood of the martyrs of Jesus.

When I saw her I marveled greatly. [7]But the angel said to me, “Why marvel? I will tell you the mystery of the woman, and of the beast with seven heads and ten horns that carries her. [8]The beast that you saw was, and is not, and is to ascend from the bottomless pit and go to perdition; and the dwellers on earth whose names have not been written in the book of life from the foundation of the world, will marvel to behold the beast, because it was and is not and is to come. [9]This calls for a mind with wisdom: the seven heads are seven hills on which the woman is seated; [10]they are also seven kings, five of whom have fallen, one is, the other has not yet come, and when he comes he must remain only a little while. [11]As for the beast that was and is not, it is an eighth but it belongs to the seven, and it goes to perdition. [12]And the ten horns that you saw are ten kings who have not yet received royal power, but they are to receive authority as kings for one hour, together with the beast. [13]These are of one mind and give over their power and authority to the beast; [14]they will make war on the Lamb, and the Lamb will conquer them, for he is Lord of lords and King of kings, and those with him are called and chosen and faithful.”

[15]And he said to me, “The waters that you saw, where the harlot is seated, are peoples and multitudes and nations and tongues. [16]And the ten horns that you saw, they and the beast will hate the harlot; they will make her desolate

---

17:1–18 The blowing of the seventh trumpet (11:15) revealed the protagonists of the struggle (12:1–18), how it affects the Church (13:1–18), and how the Church is saved by Jesus Christ (14:1–20) who has power to judge and punish (15:1–18). Now we are given a close-up of God’s enemies—the harlot and the beast—and their punishment (18:1–24). The great harlot is the city of Rome, described in a sort of riddle (v. 9) using images which in the book of Isaiah were applied to Tyre and Nineveh (cf. Is 23:16–17; Nahum 3:4). The “many waters”, as explained in 17:15, stand for the peoples over whom the great harlot holds sway. The city is also called Babylon because that city is the symbol of the cities hostile to God (cf. 17:5; Is 21:9; Jer 51:1–19) and a byword for licentious living. The beast, with its and naked, and devour her flesh and burn her up with fire, [17]for God has put it into their hearts to carry out his purpose by being of one mind and giving over their royal power to the beast, until the words of God shall be fulfilled. [18]And the woman that you saw is the great city which has dominion over the kings of the earth."

The fall of Babylon announced

18 [1]After this I saw another angel coming down from heaven, having great authority; and the earth was made bright with his splendour. [2]And he called out with a mighty voice,

"Fallen, fallen is Babylon the great!
It has become a dwelling place of demons,
a haunt of every foul spirit,
a haunt of every foul and hateful bird;
[3]for all nations have drunk[k] the wine of her impure passion,
and the kings of the earth have committed fornication with her,
and the merchants of the earth have grown rich with the wealth of her wantonness."

[4]Then I heard another voice from heaven saying,

"Come out of her, my people,
lest you take part in her sins,
lest you share in her plagues;
[5]for her sins are heaped high as heaven,
and God has remembered her iniquities.
[6]Render to her as she herself has rendered,
and repay her double for her deeds;
mix a double draught for her in the cup she mixed.
[7]As she glorified herself and played the wanton,
so give her a like measure of torment and mourning.

---

seven heads and horns, stands for the antichrist as embodied in the emperors who persecute the Church. Of these, the sixth, in power when St John was writing, would be Domitian (ruled 81–96), and the previous five: Caligula (37–41), Claudius (41–54), Nero (54–68), Vespasian (69–79) and Titus (79–81); the seventh would be Nerva (96–98). The beast is number eight although the writer identifies it with one of the seven (v. 11)—probably with Nero who, according to a contemporary legend, was going to reappear. The ten kings (v. 12) symbolize those whom Rome established as kings in the nations it conquered, and who were subject to the emperor.

18:1–24 These verses describing the downfall of Rome follow the prophetical style of foretelling a future event by reporting it as something that has already happened. First the fall of the city is proclaimed (vv. 1–3), the people of God are

k. Other ancient authorities read *fallen by*

Since in her heart she says, 'A queen I sit,
I am no widow, mourning I shall never see,'
[8] so shall her plagues come in a single day,
pestilence and mourning and famine,
and she shall be burned with fire;
for mighty is the Lord God who judges her."

[9]And the kings of the earth, who committed fornication and were wanton
with her, will weep and wail over her when they see the smoke of her burning;
[10]they will stand far off, in fear of her torment, and say,

"Alas! alas! thou great city,
thou mighty city, Babylon!
In one hour has thy judgment come."

[11]*And the merchants of the earth weep and mourn for her, since no one
buys their cargo any more, [12]cargo of gold, silver, jewels and pearls, fine linen,
purple, silk and scarlet, all kinds of scented wood, all articles of ivory, all
articles of costly wood, bronze, iron and marble, [13]cinnamon, spice, incense,
myrrh, frankincense, wine, oil, fine flour and wheat, cattle and sheep, horses
and chariots, and slaves, that is, human souls.

[14] "The fruit for which thy soul longed has gone from thee,
and all thy dainties and thy splendour are lost to thee,
never to be found again!"

[15]The merchants of these wares, who gained wealth from her, will stand far
off, in fear of her torment, weeping and mourning aloud,

[16] "Alas, alas, for the great city
that was clothed in fine linen, in purple and scarlet,
bedecked with gold, with jewels, and with pearls!
[17] In one hour all this wealth has been laid waste."

And all shipmasters and seafaring men, sailors and all whose trade is on the
sea, stood far off [18]and cried out as they saw the smoke of her burning,

---

exhorted to leave the city and its degradation, the reason for its punishement is given (vv. 4–8), and the lamentations of those in league with the city are described (vv. 9–17). Then we see the joy felt by those who suffered under its yoke and now witness God giving it its just deserts (v. 20). Among the sins imputed to the city and which have caused its ruin is unbridled sexual indulgence (cf. vv. 7, 12–14). This sort of lifestyle degrades a society and makes it self-destruct, as can be seen from history and in our own time. It was something denounced by Pius XI when he said that "the greatest disease of the modern age, the source of all the evils we condemn, is the lack of reflection, the effusive attachment to and the feverish demand for external things, the immoderate desire for riches and pleasures, which bit by bit deprives the soul of its most noble ideals, submerges it in the most base and transitory things, and renders it incapable of contemplating the eternal realities" (*Mens nostra*, 5).

"What city was like the great city?"
19 And they threw dust on their heads, as they wept and mourned, crying out,
"Alas, alas, for the great city
where all who had ships at sea grew rich by her wealth!
In one hour she has been laid waste.
20 Rejoice over her, O heaven,
O saints and apostles and prophets,
for God has given judgment for you against her!"
21 Then a mighty angel took up a stone like a great millstone and threw it into
the sea, saying,
"So shall Babylon the great city be thrown down with violence,
and shall be found no more;
22 and the sound of harpers and minstrels, of flute players and
trumpeters,
shall be heard in thee no more;
and a craftsman of any craft
shall be found in thee no more;
and the sound of the millstone
shall be heard in thee no more;
23 and the light of a lamp
shall shine in thee no more;
and the voice of bridegroom and bride
shall be heard in thee no more;
for thy merchants were the great men of the earth,
and all nations were deceived by thy sorcery.
24 And in her was found the blood of prophets and of saints,
and of all who have been slain on earth."

Songs of victory in heaven

19 1 After this I heard what seemed to be the mighty voice of a great multi-
tude in heaven, crying,
"Hallelujah! Salvation and glory and power belong to our God,
2 for his judgments are true and just;

19:1–10 The righteous rejoice to see their enemy overwhelmed; the praises they sing end in three loud "Hallelujahs" (= praise the Lord), and their song, which blends with that of the Church in heaven celebrates not only the destruction and defeat of evil but also the definitive installation of the Kingdom of God, a kingdom of love which is depicted as a wedding feast celebrating the imminent nuptials of the Lamb. This marriage, viewed from the end of history, reveals the Church in all ages as well as the purpose and daily mission of Christians—to prepare their wedding garment (by good works, praise of God, and a holy life) so as to gain access to the wedding feast.

he has judged the great harlot who corrupted the earth
with her fornication,
and he has avenged on her the blood of his servants."
3Once more they cried,
"Hallelujah! The smoke from her goes up for ever and ever."
4And the twenty-four elders and the four living creatures fell down and
worshipped God who is seated on the throne, saying, "Amen. Hallelujah!"
5And from the throne came a voice crying,
"Praise our God, all you his servants,
you who fear him, small and great."
6Then I heard what seemed to be the voice of a great multitude, like the sound
of many waters and like the sound of mighty thunderpeals, crying,
"Hallelujah! For the Lord our God the Almighty reigns.
7Let us rejoice and exult and give him the glory,
for the marriage of the Lamb* has come,
and his Bride has made herself ready;
8it was granted her to be clothed with fine linen, bright and
pure"—
for the fine linen is the righteous deeds of the saints.
9And the angel said[l] to me, "Write this: Blessed are those who are invited
to the marriage supper of the Lamb." And he said to me, "These are true words
of God." 10Then I fell down at his feet to worship him, but he said to me, "You
must not do that! I am a fellow servant with you and your brethren who hold
the testimony of Jesus. Worship God." For the testimony of Jesus is the spirit
of prophecy.

The first battle—the beast is destroyed

11Then I saw heaven opened, and behold, a white horse! He who sat upon it is
called Faithful and True, and in righteousness he judges and makes war. 12His
eyes are like a flame of fire, and on his head are many diadems; and he has a
name inscribed which no one knows but himself. 13He is clad in a robe dipped
in[m] blood, and the name by which he is called is The Word of God. 14And the
armies of heaven, arrayed in fine linen, white and pure, followed him on white
horses. 15From his mouth issues a sharp sword with which to smite the nations,
and he will rule them with a rod of iron; he will tread the wine press of the fury
of the wrath of God the Almighty. 16On his robe and on his thigh he has a
name inscribed, King of kings and Lord of lords.
17Then I saw an angel standing in the sun, and with a loud voice he called
to all the birds that fly in midheaven, "Come, gather for the great supper of

---

19:11–21 The prophetical account of the fall of Rome, given in the form of a proclamation, is followed by a description of Christ endowed with power (vv. 11–16) to

l. Greek *he said* **m.** Other ancient authorities read *sprinkle with* **19:15** Ps 2:9.

God, [18]to eat the flesh of kings, the flesh of captains, the flesh of mighty men, the flesh of horses and their riders, and the flesh of all men, both free and slave, both small and great.” [19]And I saw the beast and the kings of the earth with their armies gathered to make war against him who sits upon the horse and against his army. [20]And the beast was captured, and with it the false prophet who in its presence had worked the signs by which he deceived those who had received the mark of the beast and those who worshipped its image. These two were thrown alive into the lake of fire that burns with sulphur. [21]And the rest were slain by the sword of him who sits upon the horse, the sword that issues from his mouth; and all the birds were gorged with their flesh.

The thousand-year reign of Christ and his people

20 [1]Then I saw an angel coming down from heaven, holding in his hand the key of the bottomless pit and a great chain. [2]And he seized the dragon, that ancient serpent, who is the Devil and Satan, and bound him for a thousand years, [3]and threw him into the pit, and shut it and sealed it over him, that he should deceive the nations no more, till the thousand years were ended. *After that he must be loosed for a little while.

[4]Then I saw thrones, and seated on them were those to whom judgment was committed. Also I saw the souls of those who had been beheaded for their testimony to Jesus and for the word of God, and who had not worshipped the beast or its image and had not received its mark on their foreheads or their hands. They came to life, and reigned with Christ a thousand years. [5]The rest of the dead did not come to life until the thousand years were ended. This is

---

conquer permanently and decisively the forces of evil which have sustained the great city. Their defeat is narrated in reverse order to that in which they appear later in the book: the first to be conquered are the kings of the earth (vv. 17–18), then the beast and the false prophet (vv. 20–21; cf. 17:16–17); finally, in a second eschatological battle Christ defeats the ancient enemy, Satan (cf. 20:1–10; 13:2). Not until this happens will the General Judgment take place (20:11–15). The depiction of Christ as the glorious victor (vv. 15–16) is similar to that at the start of the book: attention is focussed on different parts of the body (though not in any systematic way: cf. 1:5, 12–16); he seems to be the same person as the rider on the white horse mentioned when the first of the seven seals was about to be opened (cf. 6:2). “The whole of man’s history has been the story of dour combat with the powers of evil, stretching, so our Lord tells us, from the very dawn of history until the last day. Finding himself in the midst of the battlefield, man has to struggle to do what is right, and it is at great cost to himself, and aided by God’s grace, that he succeeds in achieving his own inner integrity” (Vatican II, *GS*, 37).

20:1–6 The harlot (Rome) has been defeated (chap. 18) and the beast and his false prophet, too, the forces of persecution (chap. 19); there remains the dragon whom

the first resurrection. [6]Blessed and holy is he who shares in the first resurrection! Over such the second death has no power, but they shall be priests of God and of Christ, and they shall reign with him a thousand years.

The second battle—Satan is overthrown

[7]And when the thousand years are ended, Satan will be loosed from his prison
[8]and will come out to deceive the nations which are at the four corners of the earth, that is, Gog and Magog, to gather them for battle; their number is like
the sand of the sea. [9]And they marched up over the broad earth and surrounded the camp of the saints and the beloved city; but fire came down from heaven[n]
and consumed them, [10]and the devil who had deceived them was thrown into the lake of fire and sulphur where the beast and the false prophet were, and they will be tormented day and night for ever and ever.

The Last Judgment of the living and the dead

[11]Then I saw a great white throne and him who sat upon it; from his presence
earth and sky fled away, and no place was found for them. [12]And I saw the

---

we saw in chapter 12 and whose defeat marks the final outcome of the war that started there. The battle between Satan and God is described in two scenes; the first tells of how Satan is brought under control for a time only (vv. 1–3); the second describes his last assault on the Church, and what happens to him in the end (20:7–10). Between these two scenes comes the reign of Christ and his followers, which lasts a thousand years (vv. 4–6). One interpretation (St Augustine's) of the thousand-year reign is that it is the period between the Incarnation of the Son of God and his second coming at the end of time, a period during which the devil's scope is limited and the devil is in some way enchained; although "he desires to do us harm, he cannot do so because his power is subject to another's power [...]. He who gives him the ability to tempt, also gives his mercy to the one who is tempted. He has restricted the devil's ability to tempt people" (*De Serm. Dom. in monte*, 2, 9, 34). The "first resurrection" (v. 6) is Baptism.

20:7–10 God will allow the devil to act in a very intense way, especially during the last days. Our Lord also said that these times would be marked by tribulation the like of which had never been seen before (cf. Mt 24:21–22). And St Paul refers to the "man of lawlessness" who will take his seat in the temple and proclaim himself God (cf. 2 Thess 2:3–8). Gog and Magog symbolize powers which wreak vast destruction (cf. Ezek 38–39). The throwing of the devil into the fiery lake means his defeat; never again will evil affect the world. In that fire, along with the beast and the false prophet, the ungodly will suffer for ever more—a further instance of Scripture's teaching the everlasting duration of this punishment (cf., e.g., Mt 18:8; 25:41, 46; Mk 9:43, 48).

20:11–15 Now that the devil, the root of all evil, is removed from the scene we are shown the resurrection of the dead and the General Judgment. The Judgment

n. Other ancient authorities read *from God*, *out of heaven*, or *out of heaven from God*

dead, great and small, standing before the throne, and books were opened. Also another book was opened, which is the book of life. And the dead were judged by what was written in the books, by what they had done.
13And the sea gave up the dead in it, Death and Hades gave up the dead in them, and all were judged by what they had done.
14Then Death and Hades were thrown into the lake of fire. This is the second death, the lake of fire;
15and if any one's name was not found written in the book of life, he was thrown into the lake of fire.

A new world comes into being. The new Jerusalem

21 1Then I saw a new heaven and a new earth; for the first heaven and the first earth had passed away, and the sea was no more.*
2And I saw the holy city, new Jerusalem, coming down out of heaven from God, prepared as a bride adorned for her husband;
3and I heard a loud voice from the throne saying, "Behold, the dwelling of God is with men. He will dwell with them, and they shall be his people,[o] and God himself will be with them;[p]
4he will wipe away every tear from their eyes, and death shall be no more, neither shall there be mourning nor crying nor pain any more, for the former things have passed away."

---

is described by using the metaphor of two books—one for recording the actions of men (cf. Dan 7:10); the other, a special book, for the names of those predestined to eternal life (cf. Dan 12:1): the Apocalypse is in this way teaching us about two truths which are always closely connected—that we are free, and that there is a grace of predestination. The "second death" (v. 14) is eternal damnation. The Last Judgment is a truth of faith on which Paul VI had this to say: "Christ ascended into heaven, and will come again, in glory, to judge the living and the dead, each according to his merits: those who responded to the Love and Piety of God will enter eternal life; those who rejected him to the very end, into unquenchable fire [...]. We believe in eternal life. We believe that souls who die in the grace of Christ, those who must be purified in Purgatory, as well as those carried directly by Jesus to heaven like the Good Thief, make up the people of God beyond death, who will triumph fully on the day of the Resurrection when their souls will be united once more with their bodies" (*Creed of the People of God*, 12 and 28).

21:1–22:5 Now that all the forces of evil, including death, have been vanquished, the writer turns to contemplate the establishment of the Kingdom of God in all its fullness. Thus, the climax of the book shows a new world inhabited by a new race, a renewed mankind—the new Jerusalem (vv. 1–4; cf. Is 65:12–25)—and whose establishment is guaranteed by the eternal and almighty word of God (vv. 5–8). That mankind—the people of God—is portrayed as the Bride of the Lamb; a detailed description shows a wonderful city in which God the Father and Christ

o. Other ancient authorities read *peoples* **p.** Other ancient authorities add *and be their God* **21:3** Lev 26:11–12; Ezek 37:27; Zech 3:4. **21:4** Is 25:8.

5And he who sat upon the throne said, "Behold, I make all things new."
Also he said, "Write this, for these words are trustworthy and true." 6And he
said to me, "It is done! I am the Alpha and the Omega, the beginning and the
end. To the thirsty I will give from the fountain of the water of life without
payment. 7He who conquers shall have this heritage, and I will be his God and
he shall be my son. 8But as for the cowardly, the faithless, the polluted, as for
murderers, fornicators, sorcerers, idolaters, and all liars, their lot shall be in the
lake that burns with fire and sulphur, which is the second death."*

9Then came one of the seven angels who had the seven bowls full of the seven
last plagues, and spoke to me, saying, "Come, I will show you the Bride, the wife
of the Lamb." 10And in the Spirit he carried me away to a great, high mountain,
and showed me the holy city Jerusalem coming down out of heaven from God,
11having the glory of God, its radiance like a most rare jewel, like a jasper, clear
as crystal. 12It had a great, high wall, with twelve gates, and at the gates twelve
angels, and on the gates the names of the twelve tribes of the sons of Israel were
inscribed; 13on the east three gates, on the north three gates, on the south three
gates, and on the west three gates. 14And the wall of the city had twelve foun-
dations, and on them the twelve names of the twelve apostles of the Lamb.

15And he who talked to me had a measuring rod of gold to measure the city and
its gates and walls. 16The city lies foursquare, its length the same as its breadth; and
he measured the city with his rod, twelve thousand stadia;[q] its length and breadth

---

reign (21:9–22:5). The vision is similar to that of the prophet Ezekiel when he saw the new Jerusalem and the future temple (cf. Ez 40:1–42:26). But here the emphasis is on the City coming down from heaven—meaning that the long-desired complete establishment of the messianic kingdom is going to be brought about by the power of God and in line with his will. The names of the tribes of Israel and of the twelve apostles are given, to convey the continuity between the ancient chosen people and the Church of Christ, and at the same time to show that the Church is something new and is founded on the twelve apostles of the Lord (cf. Eph 2:20). The positioning of the gates shows the universality of the Church; they give ease of access to people from all points of the compass; this is what St Augustine means when he says that "outside the catholic Church one can find everything except salvation" (*Sermo ad Caesar.*, 6). Surprisingly there is no temple in the City (whereas there was one in Ezekiel's vision), because there is no longer any need for God to have a dwelling place, since the blessed contemplate God the Father and the Lamb directly. If the water of life is the symbol of the Holy Spirit (cf. 21:6), some Fathers and modern commentators have reason to see a Trinitarian meaning in this passage: the Holy Spirit, who proceeds from the Father and the Son, is represented by the power which flows out from the throne of God and the Lamb.

This passage in the book of Revelation nourishes the Church in faith and hope, not only in St John's own time but also in every generation as she makes her pilgrim

q. About fifteen hundred miles **21:7** 2 Sam 7:14. **21:12** Ezek 48:31; Ex 28:21.

and height are equal. [17]He also measured its wall, a hundred and forty-four cubits
by a man's measure, that is, an angel's. [18]The wall was built of jasper, while the
city was pure gold, clear as glass. [19]The foundations of the wall of the city were
adorned with every jewel; the first was jasper, the second sapphire, the third agate,
the fourth emerald, [20]the fifth onyx, the sixth carnelian, the seventh chrysolite, the
eighth beryl, the ninth topaz, the tenth chrysoprase, the eleventh jacinth, the twelfth
amethyst. [21]And the twelve gates were twelve pearls, each of the gates made of a
single pearl, and the street of the city was pure gold, transparent as glass.

[22]And I saw no temple in the city, for its temple is the Lord God the
Almighty and the Lamb. [23]And the city has no need of sun or moon to shine
upon it, for the glory of God is its light, and its lamp is the Lamb. [24]By its light
shall the nations walk; and the kings of the earth shall bring their glory into it,
[25]and its gates shall never be shut by day—and there shall be no night there;
[26]they shall bring into it the glory and the honour of the nations. [27]But nothing
unclean shall enter it, nor any one who practises abomination or falsehood, but
only those who are written in the Lamb's book of life.

22 [1]Then he showed me the river of the water of life, bright as crystal,
flowing from the throne of God and of the Lamb [2]through the middle of
the street of the city; also, on either side of the river, the tree of life[r] with its
twelve kinds of fruit, yielding its fruit each month; and the leaves of the tree
were for the healing of the nations. [3]There shall no more be anything accursed,
but the throne of God and of the Lamb shall be in it, and his servants shall
worship him; [4]they shall see his face, and his name shall be on their foreheads.
[5]And night shall be no more; they need no light of lamp or sun, for the Lord
God will be their light, and they shall reign for ever and ever.

The visions come to an end

[6]And he said to me, "These words are trustworthy and true. And the Lord, the
God of the spirits of the prophets, has sent his angel to show his servants what
must soon take place. [7]And behold, I am coming soon."

---

way. As the Second Vatican Council put it, "we know neither the moment of the consummation of the earth and of man nor the way the universe will be transformed. The form of this world, distorted by sin, is passing away and we are taught that God is preparing a new dwelling and a new earth in which righteousness dwells, whose happiness will fill and surpass all the desires of peace arising in the hearts of men. Then with death conquered the sons of God will be raised in Christ, and what was sown in weakness and dishonour will put on the imperishable: charity and its works will remain and all of creation, which God made for man, will be set free from its bondage to decay" (*GS*, 39).

22:6–15 The wonderful description of the Church just given contrasts sharply with her present position on earth—so much so that one can glimpse that future glory

r. Or *the Lamb. In the midst of the street of the city, and on either side of the river, was the tree of life,* etc.

Blessed is he who keeps the words of the prophecy of this book.
8I John am he who heard and saw these things. And when I heard and saw
them, I fell down to worship at the feet of the angel who showed them to me;
9but he said to me, "You must not do that! I am a fellow servant with you and
your brethren the prophets, and with those who keep the words of this book.
Worship God."
10And he said to me, "Do not seal up the words of the prophecy of this
book, for the time is near. 11Let the evildoer still do evil, and the filthy still be
filthy, and the righteous still do right, and the holy still be holy."
12"Behold, I am coming soon, bringing my recompense, to repay every one
for what he has done. 13I am the Alpha and the Omega, the first and the last,
the beginning and the end."
14Blessed are those who wash their robes,[s] that they may have the right to
the tree of life and that they may enter the city by the gates. 15Outside are the
dogs and sorcerers and fornicators and murderers and idolaters, and every one
who loves and practises falsehood.

4. EPILOGUE

16"I Jesus have sent my angel to you with this testimony for the churches. I am
the root and the offspring of David, the bright morning star."

Prayer of the Spirit and the Bride. Words of warning and farewell

17The Spirit and the Bride say, "Come." And let him who hears say, "Come."
And let him who is thirsty come, let him who desires take the water of life
without price.

---

only if one trusts those who speaks on God's behalf (vv. 6–9). St John is conscious of having put down his text in the way that the prophets spoke their message; they were inspired by "the God of the spirits of the prophets" (v. 6). This is why he presents his book as a "prophecy". It is a prophecy pronounced not as an esoteric secret but as something for all to hear (the book must be kept open) so it can lead them to a change of heart, because the redemption won by Christ has opened up the final stage in the process of salvation. This is what is meant by the words "what must soon take place" (v. 6). The passage, then, is an appeal for continuous progress towards holiness (cf. v. 11). "No one deserves to be called good who does not strive to be better; and when you begin not to want to be better, you cease to be good" (St Bernard, *Letters*, 91).

22:16–21 □ Jesus Christ solemnly confirms the authenticity of the prophetical content of the book. Then it is confirmed by the praying Church (v. 17) and by the

s. Other ancient authorities read *do his commandments*

[18]I warn every one who hears the words of the prophecy of this book: if any
one adds to them, God will add to him the plagues described in this book,
[19]and if any one takes away from the words of the book of this prophecy, God
will take away his share in the tree of life and in the holy city, which are
described in this book.
[20]He who testifies to these things says, "Surely I am coming soon." Amen.
Come, Lord Jesus!
[21]The grace of the Lord Jesus be with all the saints.[t] Amen.

---

author of the written text (vv. 18–19); and, once more, before the words of farewell, it is confirmed by Christ.

22:17–21 The Bride is the Church who, in reply to Christ's promise (cf. 22:12), ardently desires and prays for his coming. She is inspired by the Holy Spirit, the voices of both Church and Spirit fusing in a single cry. Every Christian is invited to join in this prayer and to discover in the Church the gift of the Spirit, symbolized by the water of life (21:6); this gift allows Christians a foretaste of the good things of the Kingdom.

This hope is not in vain, for it is founded on Christ's victory and prefigured in that of the Woman: "Victory over the 'prince of this world' (Jn 14:30) was won once for all at the Hour when Jesus freely gave himself up to death to give us his life. This is the Judgment of this world, and the prince of this world is 'cast out' (Jn 12:31; Rev 12:11). 'He pursued the woman'(cf. Rev 12:13–16) but had no hold on her: the new Eve, 'full of grace' of the Holy Spirit, is preserved from sin and the corruption of death (the Immaculate Conception and the Assumption of the Most Holy Mother of God, Mary, ever virgin). 'Then the dragon was angry with the woman, and went off to make war on the rest of her offspring' (Rev 12:17). Therefore the Spirit and the Church pray: 'Come, Lord Jesus' (Rev 22:17, 20), since his coming will deliver us from the Evil One" (*CCC*, 2835).

t. Other ancient authorities omit *all*; others omit *the saints*

Explanatory Notes

Asterisks in the text of the New Testament refer to these 'Explanatory Notes' in the RSVCE.

THE GOSPEL ACCORDING TO MATTHEW

1:1: The genealogy is given to show that Jesus had the descent required for messiahship, i.e. from Abraham and, in particular, from David the king.

1:16: Joseph's, not Mary's, descent is given here, as the Jews did not usually reckon descent through the mother. Joseph was the legal and presumed father, and it was this fact that conferred rights of inheritance, in this case, the fulfilment of the messianic promises.

1:25: This means only that Joseph had nothing to do with the conception of Jesus. It implies nothing as to what happened afterwards.

3:2, *Repent* implies an internal change of heart.

3:6: Not Christian baptism but a preparation for it.

3:15: Though without sin, Jesus wished to be baptized by John, as this was the final preparation for his messianic mission.

5:17: Jesus came to bring the old Law to its natural fulfilment in the new while discarding what had become obsolete; cf. Jn 4:21.

5:29: An exaggeration to emphasize the need to avoid occasions of sin.

5:32, *unchastity*: The Greek word used here appears to refer to marriages which were not legally marriages, because they were either within the forbidden degrees of consanguinity (Lev 18:6–16) or contracted with a Gentile. The phrase *except on the ground of unchastity* does not occur in the parallel passage in Lk 16:18. See also Mt 19:9 (Mk 10:11–12), and especially 1 Cor 7:10–11, which shows that the prohibition is unconditional.

6:6: This does not, of course, exclude public worship but ostentatious prayer.

6:24, *mammon*: i.e., riches.

8:3: The miracles of Jesus were never performed to amaze people and shock them into belief. They were worked with a view to a real strengthening of faith in the recipient or beholder, from whom the proper dispositions were required.

8:29, *before the time:* Before the day of judgment the demons are permitted by God to tempt men and even to possess them.

10:5: The Gospel, the messianic salvation, had first to be preached and offered to the chosen people, Israel. Later it would be offered to the Gentiles.

11:3: The Baptist expected more obvious signs of the Messiah. By quoting the prophet Isaiah, Jesus showed that he was indeed inaugurating the messianic kingdom—but by doing good rather than by glorious manifestations or sudden punishments.

11:27: This shows a profound relationship between the Son and the Father, far superior to adoptive sonship.

12:14: The Pharisees regarded healing as work and so forbade it on the sabbath.

12:24, *Beelzebul:* Name of a Canaanite god meaning "the Prince-god." The Jews interpreted this name as "Prince of demons," because for them all false gods were demons.

12:31: To attribute to the devil the works of the Holy Spirit seems to imply a hardness of heart which precludes repentance.

12:46, *brethren*: The Greek word or its Semitic equivalent was used for varying degrees of blood relationship; cf. Gen 14:14; 29:12; Lev 10:4.

12:48: Jesus puts the work of salvation before family relationships. It is not said, however, that he refused to see them.

13:12: To those well-disposed Jews who have made good use of the old Covenant will now be given the perfection of the New. On the other hand, from those who have rejected God's advances will now be taken away even that which they have, because the old Covenant is passing away.

13:52: This is Matthew's ideal: that the learned Jew should become the disciple of Jesus and so add the riches of the new Covenant to those of the Old, which he already possesses; cf. verse 12.

13:55: See note on Mt 12:46.

14:33: Their realization of his Godhead was the prelude to Peter's confession of faith at Caesarea Philippi (Mt 16:16).

15:5: By dedicating his property to God, i.e. to the temple, a man could avoid having to help his parents, without actually giving up what he had. The scribes held such a vow to be valid without necessarily approving it.

15:24: See note on 10:5.

16:14: The title of prophet had a messianic significance because the gift of prophecy, which had been extinct since Malachi, was expected to return at the beginning of the messianic era, especially by an outpouring of the Spirit as foretold by the prophet Joel and as realized in Acts 2:16.

16:16: The context shows that Peter recognizes the sonship of Jesus as divine and not adoptive like ours. Mark and Luke in the parallel passages mention only the confession of the messiahship.

16:18: The name "Peter" comes from the Greek word for "rock." Jesus makes him the foundation on which the Church is to be built. The word "church" means "assembly' or "society" of believers. The Hebrew equivalent is used in the Old Testament to indicate the chosen people. In applying it to the church Jesus shows it to be the messianic community foretold by the prophets. See note on Mt 18:18.

16:25, *life* (both times): A play on the word "life"—natural and supernatural; cf. Mk 8:35–36.

17:4: Peter thought the glorious messianic kingdom had come. In fact, Jesus allowed this glimpse of his glory to strengthen them for the coming passion.

18:9, *Gehenna* (see footnote b) was the name of a valley south of Jerusalem where human sacrifice had once been practised; cf. 2 Chron 33:6. Later it became a cursed place and refuse dump, and the name came to symbolize the Christian place of punishment.

18:18: To the other apostles is given a share in the authority given to Peter.

19:9: This appears to refer to the case in Mt 5:32, though the Greek word for "except" is different.

19:11–12: Jesus means that a life of continence is to be chosen only by those who are called to it for the sake of the kingdom of God.

21:9: The crowd openly recognize Jesus as the Messiah and he allows it for the first time.

21:23: They object to the assumption of authority implicit in the manner of his entry into the city and in his expulsion of the sellers from the temple.

21:33–44: This parable is really an allegory in which almost every detail represents something in God's dealings with Israel.

22:11: The wedding garment represents the dispositions necessary for admission to the kingdom.

23:5, *phylacteries*: Little leather boxes containing, on a very small scroll, the principal words of the law; cf. Deut 6:4–9. Taking the command literally, they fastened these to their arms and their foreheads.

23:9: i.e., "Do not use the title without reference to God's universal fatherhood." He cannot mean that the title is never to be used by a son to his father.

24:1–25:46: The "eschatological discourse," as it is called, deals with the fall of Jerusalem and the end of the world. The two themes seem to be inextricably intermingled in the Gospels as we now have it, but it is possible that originally they were in separate discourses. However, the fusion of the two does bring out their connexion. The one prefigures the other. Moreover, in the reverse direction, so to speak, the language used to describe the day of the Lord in Joel and elsewhere is here applied to the fall of Jerusalem, the details of which must therefore not be taken too literally (24:29).

25:29: See note on 13:12.

26:17: The Passover was celebrated this year on the Friday evening (Jn 18:28). Jesus must have anticipated the passover meal because he would be dead the following day and because the meal prefigured his death.

26:26: The details of the Eucharist are superimposed on the ritual of the Passover.

26:51: It was Peter, as John in his later Gospel tells us (Jn 18:10), though Matthew is reluctant to say so.

26:59: They sought evidence against him and this was necessarily false.

26:64–65: For the first time Jesus speaks clearly of his own identity. Caiaphas evidently understands him to claim divinity.

27:46: Jesus applies Psalm 22 (Vulgate 21) to himself.

27:66: The sealing and guarding only helped to make the subsequent resurrection more obvious.

28:1–20: The resurrection appearances. There are divergent traditions in the Gospels, Galilean and Judean. Paul adds his own record (1 Cor 15). The accounts do not easily fit together, but this is surely evidence of their genuineness. There is no attempt to produce an artificial conformity.

THE GOSPEL ACCORDING TO MARK

1:34: Throughout his ministry Jesus forbade the demons and those he healed of their infirmities to reveal his identity as Messiah, because the people, with their ideas of a national leader to come, were only too prone to mistake his true mission.
2:14, *Levi*: Mark does not identify him with Matthew the apostle; cf. Mt 9:9.
3:31, *brethren*: See note on Mt 12:46.
4:12, *so that . . .* : One might rephrase this: "So that the scripture might be fulfilled"; cf. Jn 18:32; 19:24, 28. It was not God's intention to prevent their understanding. Matthew avoids this difficulty by writing, "I speak to them in parables, *because* seeing they do not see" (Mt 13:13).
5:43: Knowing their nationalistic views about the Messiah to come, Jesus wished to avoid a tumult.
7:3: Mark, writing for Gentiles, explains these Jewish customs.
8:36, *life*: See note on Mt 16:25.
9:13, Elijah has come: i.e., in the person of the Baptist (Mt 11:14).
10:24, *amazed at his words*: The Old Testament often records God's offers of material rewards for observance of his laws. This was because the future life was not yet revealed. It was therefore taken for granted, in spite of contrary evidence, that riches were a sign of God's favour.
10:30: Some of the reward will be given in this life.
14:13: It was unusual for a man to carry water; it was a woman's task.
14:51–52: This young man is usually supposed to have been the evangelist himself.
15:1: The Jews could not execute Jesus without the Roman governor's permission.
15:40, *the younger*, or "the Less."
16:1: There had been no time on the Friday to anoint him before the sabbath rest.
16:9–20: This passage is regarded as inspired and canonical scripture even if not written by Mark. As it is missing from some important manuscripts, it is possible that Mark did not write it. On the other hand, he would hardly have left his Gospel unfinished at verse 8. Many think that the original ending was lost at a very early date and that this ending was composed at the end of the apostolic period to take its place.

THE GOSPEL ACCORDING TO LUKE

1:3, *Theophilus* is again referred to in Acts 1:1, but nothing is known of him.
1:5–2:52: The "Infancy Gospel;" as it is called, is written in a markedly Semitic style which differs from that of the rest of the Gospel. It appears to be based on the reminiscences of Mary.
1:30: The words of the angel are drawn from messianic passages in the Old Testament.
1:46–55; The *Magnificat* is based on the song of Hannah (1 Sam 2:1–10), and other Old Testament passages which describes God's favour towards Israel and especially towards the poor and lowly.
1:69, *a horn of salvation*: i.e., a mighty saviour.
2:7, *first-born*: The term connotes possession of certain rights, privileges and obligations; cf. Ex 13:1–2, 11–16. The word is used even in modern times without necessarily implying subsequent births.
2:34, *for the fall*: i.e., in the sense that by rejecting his claims many would sin grievously.
2:49: Jesus stresses the priority of his duty to his Father, which involves a high degree of independence of earthly ties.
3:2: See note on Jn 18:13.
3:7, *brood of vipers*: This epithet seems to have been directed mainly at the Pharisees; cf. Mt 3:7.
3:23: This genealogy, more universalist than that of Matthew, goes back to Adam, the ancestor of all men, and then to God, his Maker. Like Matthew, however, it gives the genealogy of Joseph, though Mary may well have been of the family of David.
4:16–30: This account of the visit to the synagogue seems to be composed of the details of more than one visit. Luke is trying here to underline the contrast between Christ's offer of salvation and the people's refusal of it.
6:20–49: Luke's discourse is shorter than that of Matthew because it does not contain Matthew's additional material collected from other occasions, or his details which would interest only Jews.
7:28: John, by virtue of his office, belonged to the old dispensation, the time of preparation for the kingdom. In terms of spiritual status, even the humbler members of the kingdom were superior to him.

7:47: The preceding parable suggests that she loved much because she had been forgiven much. Jesus now implies that her love is a sign rather than a cause of forgiveness, thus confirming the point of the parable.
8:19, *brethren*: See note on Mt 12:46.
8:39: There was no reason for secrecy (to avoid popular disturbance) in a non-Jewish area.
9:51: Here begins the "travel narrative" of Luke, which continues up to the Passion.
received up: i.e., into heaven; cf. 2 Kings 2:9–11; Acts 1:2, 11. The term here includes his passion, death, resurrection and ascension.
9:53: The Samaritans worshiped on Mount Gerizim, when orthodox Jews, of course, went to Jerusalem, and to Jerusalem only for sacrifice.
10:18: Jesus refers to the fall of the angels (cf. Rev 12:9), while he speaks of his conquest of the forces of evil.
14:26: Christ's disciples must be prepared to part from anyone who prevents them from serving him.
16:8: The master commended his foresight without approving what he actually did.
17:20: At that time, many people were expecting to see the kingdom inaugurated with striking manifestations; cf. 19:11.
19:41–44: These moving words spoken over the city are full of scriptural allusions. Moreover, the details given could apply as well to the siege of 587 BC as to that of AD 70. It is not safe, therefore, to argue from this passage that the fall of the city had already taken place when Luke wrote his Gospel.
20:37: As elsewhere (1 Cor 15:13–19), survival after death is linked with the resurrection of the body.
21:24, *the times of the Gentiles*: i.e., those during which the Gentiles will take the place of the unbelieving people of Israel. Evidently, therefore, the end of the world does not coincide with the fall of Jerusalem. St Paul says that the Jews will be converted before the end (Rom 11:26).
22:52: Matthew and Mark describe the arrest first, before Christ's words. Luke and John both put his address to the soldiers and officials before the arrest, doubtless to stress his command over events.
23:2: They purposely produce political charges, as these alone would interest Pilate.
23:14: Luke, writing for Gentiles, makes it clear that Pilate wanted to release Jesus.
23:31: One does not burn green wood. The meaning is that, if an innocent man is thus punished, what must the guilty (dry wood) expect.
24:38: Luke stresses this episode for the benefit of his Greek readers, for whom the resurrection of the body was both impossible and absurd; cf. Acts 17:32.

THE GOSPEL ACCORDING TO JOHN

1:1: John begins by giving his Gospel a theological background. By speaking at once of "the Word" he implies that his readers are familiar with the term. To Gentiles it indicated some form of divine revelation or self-expression. Jews would equate it with the divine Wisdom described in Proverbs, which already appears as something more than a divine quality and has some relation with the visible world. In Sirach and Wisdom the idea is further developed. In the last-named book, Wisdom appears as a pre-existing person, taking part in the creation of the world and having a mission to reveal God to his creatures; cf. Wisdom 7:22–8:1.
1:5, *light . . . darkness*: One of the familiar themes of the Gospel.
1:29: John applies to Jesus the messianic prophecy of Is 53:6–7, perhaps worded more explicitly by the evangelist in later years.
2:4, *what have you to do with me?* While this expression always implies a divergence of view, the precise meaning is to be determined by the context, which here shows that it is not an unqualified refusal, still less a rebuke.
2:12, *brethren*: See note on Mt 12:46.
3:22, *baptized*: A baptism like that of John. The time for baptism "in the Spirit" had not yet come.
3:24: From the other Gospels we learn that, after John was arrested, Jesus withdrew from Judea.
4:20, *this mountain*: Gerizim, on which the Samaritans worshiped.
5:18, *broke the sabbath*: i.e., broke the sabbath as interpreted by them; see note on Mt 12:14.
6:51: Jesus is the "living bread," both as Word of God (verses 32ff) and as sacrificial victim for the salvation of man.
6:52: A natural question to ask. Jesus answers, not by explaining it away, but by re-emphasizing the reality, though not, of course, in the crude sense implied in their question.

6:62: When Jesus ascends into heaven they will know that he spoke the truth.
7:3, *brethren*: See note on Mt 12:46.
7:53–8:11: This passage, though absent from some of the most ancient manuscripts, is regarded as inspired and canonical by the Church. The style suggests that it is not by St John, and that it belongs to the Synoptic Tradition.
8:21, *die in your sin*: Theirs is that sin against the truth which is the sin against the Holy Spirit; cf. Mt 12:31.
8:41: They mean, "We are not idolaters," and protest their fidelity to God their Father: see notes on Rev 14:4 and 17:2.
8:56, *he saw* it either in prophetic vision while on earth or by some special privilege after death.
8:58: The present tense indicates Christ's eternal existence as God.
9:4: Jesus explains in advance the purpose of the miracle.
10:14, *the good shepherd*: The name has messianic significance; cf. Ezek 34.
10:18. Throughout the Gospel, Jesus insists that he is master of his own life and no one takes it from him; cf. 18:6 (at his arrest); 19:11 (before Pilate); 19:30 (on the cross).
11:6, *stayed two days longer*: This is explained in verse 15.
11:50: Caiaphas agreed that, as Jesus was not (in their opinion) the Messiah, any popular insurrection now could only end in disaster; so it was better, he argued, to do away with him. He was unconscious of the deeper meaning of his words, namely that Jesus must die for the salvation of man.
12:1: Here begins the last week of Jesus' public life. This is described in great detail, as was the first week in chapter 1.
12:32, *lifted up*: i.e., on the cross; but the words also contain a reference to his going up into heaven. The two mysteries are inseparable.
13:1: John begins here to unfold the mystery of the love of Jesus for "his own." Note the solemn introduction to the "hour" of his passion and death.
13:34, *new commandment*: Jesus gives a new depth to the familiar commandment of the Old Testament. The standard now is, "as I have loved you."
14:26, *all things*: After Jesus has gone to his Father, the Holy Spirit will complete his revelation to the world.
15:18: Jesus contrasts the love his disciples have with the hatred the world bears them.
16:10: Jesus is taken from them because they did not receive him.
17:1–16: The priestly prayer of Jesus, before his sacrifice.
17:5: Declares his pre-existence.
18:13: According to Jewish law the high-priesthood was for life. The Romans had deposed Annas, the legal holder, in AD 15, and appointed another in his place, but many Jews continued to recognize Annas.
18:28: They would have contracted a legal impurity by entering the house of a pagan.
18:29: See note on Lk 23:2.
18:31: Crucifixion was a Roman not a Jewish punishment.
19:7: At last, because of Pilate's reluctance, they produce the real charge.
19:8–9: Pilate is afraid and asks Jesus where he comes from—not his country but his mysterious origins, as implied in the charge.
19:27, *took her to his own home*: Joseph must now have been dead.
20:17: The death and resurrection of Jesus had put an end to the ordinary familiar relationships of human life, and the time of lasting companionship had not yet come.
21:1–25: This chapter was added later, either by the evangelist or by a disciple; cf. 20:30–31 and 21:24.
21:7: John remembered a similar miracle before; cf. Lk 5:6.
21:15–17: The threefold question addressed to Peter alone corresponds to the threefold denial. Jesus gives Peter charge over his flock.

THE ACTS OF THE APOSTLES

1:1, *the first book*: i.e., St Luke's Gospel.
1:14, *brethren*: See note on Mt 12:46.
1:22: An apostle must be a witness to Christ's resurrection.
2:14: Peter assumes the leadership in public. In this discourse we have the earliest form of the apostolic preaching.

3:1: In the early days, the first Christians observed the prescriptions of the Jewish Law.
4:2: The Sadducees did not believe in the resurrection of the dead.
4:32, *everything in common*: They freely shared what was theirs individually; cf. Acts 5:4.
5:11 church: i.e., the Christian and messianic community, a term borrowed from the Old Testament.
5:20, *Life*: cf. Acts 9:2, "the Way." These terms recall the words of Jesus, 'I am the way, and the truth, and the life" (Jn 14:6).
5:34, *Gamaliel*: teacher of St Paul; cf. Acts 22:3.
6:1, *Hellenists*: Greek-speaking Jews of the Dispersion, who had their own synagogues in Jerusalem and read the scriptures in Greek.
8:20: Hence the word "simony," meaning "buying and selling spiritual powers and privileges."
9:5: Jesus identifies himself with his followers.
9:13, *saints*: i.e., Christians, made holy by Baptism.
10:16: The vision was to prepare Peter for his reception of Cornelius the Gentile and his household into the Church; cf. also Acts 15.
12:1: The second wave of persecution; cf. Acts 8:1.
13:16–41 This first recorded sermon of Paul is similar to that of Peter in Acts 2:14–36.
16:10: This is the first of the passages in Acts in which the story is told in the first person plural, indicating that Luke, the author, was there. The manuscript Codex Bezae, however, has a "we" passage in 11:28.
16:13: Being a Roman colony, Philippi had no synagogue within its walls.
19:35, *the sacred stone* or statue of the goddess which according to legend came down from heaven. Possibly a meteorite.
20:7: Celebration of the Eucharist on the Lord's day, i.e. Saturday evening, according to the Jewish way of reckoning a day from sunset to sunset.
20:34: Paul insisted on working for his living, though recognizing the apostle's right to support by the faithful; cf. 1 Cor 9:4–7.
21:4, *told Paul not to go*: This was not a command. The Holy Spirit enlightened them about what lay before Paul and they naturally wished to spare him; cf. verse 11.
22:20, *thy witness*: Greek, "martyr." Witnessing by one's death (i.e. martyrdom) is the supreme example.

THE LETTER OF PAUL TO THE ROMANS

1:1–7: The opening address and salutation are very much in the style of contemporary letter-writing, giving the name of the sender and recipient, and following this with greetings.
1:10: Paul did not found the church at Rome.
1:13, *harvest*: Perhaps those who founded the church at Rome had confined themselves largely to Jews and had not made much headway with Gentiles.
3:27: Above all it is faith, not works alone, that will justify both Jew and Gentile, and (as is made clear later) faith in Jesus.
5:12: Physical death is a sign of spiritual death; though physical death remains after justification.
5:15: The *felix culpa* praised in the *Exsultet* at the Easter Vigil.
6:4, *buried*: Immersed in the water of Baptism.
6:15: As before in the case of the Law (Rom 2:17–29), so now in the case of grace. Paul says it is not a licence to sin.
7:13–25: Man under the law of Moses and perhaps man under the natural law too.
8:19: Material creation too shares man's destiny, made as it was for him. Many ancient philosophers thought matter to be evil, and that the spirit should be freed from it.
9:19–24: Paul's words here, taken by themselves, seem to leave no room for moral responsibility; but they must be taken in conjunction with other passages; see chapters 1–2.
10:1: Paul is afraid he has spoken too strongly of their sins, so he declares his love for Israel.
14:1–15:13: Paul is tolerant of the Jewish Christians' reluctance to abandon the ritual prescriptions of the law of Moses, while being equally insistent that they shall not be forced on Gentile Christians.
14:14: Conscience is the ultimate guide.
15:15–16: Paul again justifies his writing to a church he did not found.
16:16, *all the churches of Christ greet you*: A remarkable salutation, not used elsewhere.

THE FIRST LETTER OF PAUL TO THE CORINTHIANS

1:2, *saints*: A word commonly used for Christians in Paul's letters and in Acts.
1:12, *Cephas*: i.e., Peter. It does not follow from this that he had ever been to Corinth, but it does indicate his authority there.
2:1–2: Paul's failure at Athens convinced him that lofty words and worldly wisdom were less effective than Jesus crucified.
3:13, *the Day*: i.e., the day of the Lord, God's searching judgments.
3:16, *God's temple*: The dignity of the Christian.
5:1, *father's wife*: Evidently his stepmother.
5:5, *to Satan*: not only excommunicated, but in some sense given over to suffering, for his own good.
5:9–10, *immoral*: Literally, "fornicators."
5:11, *guilty of immorality*: Literally, "a fornicator."
6:1, *the unrighteous*: i.e., civil courts in which the judges were, of course, pagans.
6:9, *the immoral*: Literally, "fornicators."
homosexuals: Greek has, "effeminate or sodomites." The apostle condemns not the inherent tendencies of such, but the indulgence of them.
6:12: This saying is possibly an exaggeration of the freedom from the Mosaic law which Christians enjoyed. The saying had been applied to sinful practices, as is clear from the following verses.
6:13, 18, *immorality*: i.e., sexual immorality.
7:2: Note Paul's insistence on equality of man and woman in certain aspects of christian marriage, and his recognition that the unmarried state is also a gift from God.
8:1–13: Animals sacrificed to pagan gods were often sold as meat in the market. Could Christians buy such meat? Paul allows it so long as scandal is avoided.
9:3: Paul sets great store by the fact that he has earned his living and waived his right to support by the faithful. He uses this as an authentication of his apostolate.
9:5, *a wife*: Greek, "a woman, or a sister." This could mean either a woman who is a Christian, or a wife who is a Christian. There were pious women who ministered to the apostles (Lk 8:3). As many of the apostles must have been married, they may have been ministered to by their wives; though it is possible they had left their wives in answer to the Lord's command to leave all (Lk 18:28–29).
brethren: See note on Mt 12:46.
10:20: Paul appears to forbid partaking in sacrificial meals. In verse 27 he says they may eat meat offered to idols if it is at an ordinary meal, unless it would cause scandal to any one present.
11:20: There was apparently a common meal before the Eucharist at which food and drink were to be shared. Paul condemns the abuses that had crept in.
12:1: The spiritual gifts here referred to were common in the first age of the Church and helped to establish it on a firm basis.
12:31: Love, however, is far superior to these gifts.
15:13: Again, the resurrection of the dead is linked with Christ's resurrection; cf. Rom 8:11.
15:29: Apparently a custom of vicarious baptism for those who had died without it. Paul mentions it without approving it.
16:1: The collection to be made everywhere for the poor Christians in Jerusalem.

THE SECOND LETTER OF PAUL TO THE CORINTHIANS

1:8, *affliction*: Possibly the disturbance at Ephesus (Acts 19:23–41), or perhaps a serious illness.
3:18: Cleansed in baptism through the power of the Holy Spirit, our soul shines with the reflected glory of God.
4:7, *this treasure*: i.e., the apostolate.
4:12: i.e., we suffer, if necessary, even unto death, that you may have (spiritual) life.
5:19: Or, "God was reconciling the world to himself through Christ."
5:21, *made him to be sin*: i.e., "Sending his own Son in the likeness of sinful flesh and for sin, he condemned sin in the flesh" (Rom 8:3).
9:1, *superfluous*: Yet Paul goes on to do so at some length, exhorting them to be generous.
10:1: Paul is referring ironically to what some people are saying about him; see verse 10.
12:7, *a thorn*: Perhaps some form of sickness or disability, or the opposition of Israel to his teaching.
12:13: Paul ironically asks forgiveness for not being a charge on them as the other apostles were.

THE LETTER OF PAUL TO THE GALATIANS

1:6: After the greeting there is no commendation, as was usual, but rather strong rebuke.
1:10: No doubt Paul was accused of exempting Gentile converts from the law of Moses in order to curry favour.
2:16, *works of the Law*: Paul is contrasting not faith with good works but faith in Jesus Christ with observance of the law of Moses.
3:2, *Spirit*: He probably refers to the outward manifestations of the Spirit, such as the gift of the tongues.
5:11, *stumbling block of the cross*: So far as the Jews were concerned, this would consist largely in the exemption of converts from the obligations of the law of Moses

THE LETTER OF PAUL TO THE EPHESIANS

1:1, *To the saints who are*: The addition "at Ephesus" is doubtful. The letter may have been a form of encyclical.
1:10, *to unite*: Or, "to sum up." This is one of the chief themes of the letter. Men are to be under Christ as head of the Mystical Body, and even irrational creatures must be in some way under him as the cornerstone of creation.
2:14, *dividing wall*: A metaphor taken from the wall that divided the court of the Gentiles from the court of the Israelites in the temple.
3:3, *the mystery*: i.e., that the Gentiles were to be admitted to the Church on a basis of equality.
5:14: Apparently a fragment of an early Christian hymn; cf. 1 Tim 3:16.

THE LETTER OF PAUL TO THE PHILIPPIANS

1:14, *because of my imprisonment*: i.e., because I continue to preach in their midst, though in prison.
1:20, *honoured in my body*: i.e., through my sufferings.
2:6, *in the form of God*: The Greek shows that divine attributes and therefore nature are implied here. It is not the divine nature he set no store by, but equality of treatment and recognition of his divinity.
2:7, *emptied himself* of this external recognition which was his right.
3:12, *made me his own*: On the road to Damascus.
3:19: These Judaizers made holiness a question of distinction of foods and set great store by circumcision.

THE LETTER OF PAUL TO THE COLOSSIANS

1:15, *first-born*: Born of the Father before all ages. The reference here is to the divine person of the Word; see verse 16.
1:18: His human nature.
1:24, *what is lacking*: Christ's sufferings were, of course, sufficient for our redemption, but we may all add ours to his, in order that the fruits of his redemption may be applied to the souls of men.
3:18–4:5: The whole passage corresponds closely to Eph 5:22–6:9.
4:10: Mark, the evangelist, and, probably, the John Mark of Acts 12:25.
4:14: Luke, the evangelist.

THE FIRST LETTER OF PAUL TO THE THESSALONIANS

1:1: Paul joins with himself two who had evangelized Thessalonica with him.
2:18, *I, Paul*: He distinguishes himself from Silvanus and Timothy.
4:3, *sanctification*: with special reference to the practice of purity which was specially difficult to those newly converted from paganism.
immorality: i.e., sexual immorality.
4:11: The Thessalonians thought that the second coming of Christ was at hand and tended to neglect their daily duties. He corrects this misconception.

4:13: Paul tells them that those who died before Christ's Second Coming are no worse off than those who will still be alive at his coming.
4:17: i.e., we who are alive shall go out to meet him and accompany him back on his return to this earth.

THE SECOND LETTER OF PAUL TO THE THESSALONIANS

2:2: Paul warns against over eagerness to expect the Second Coming, and specifies various signs to be looked for first.
2:3, *the man of lawlessness*: i.e., Antichrist.
2:7: Evil will operate secretly till the final unmasking.

THE FIRST LETTER OF PAUL TO TIMOTHY

1:2: Timothy, son of a Greek father and a Jewish mother, was already a Christian when Paul met him (Acts 16:1). A close association ensued.
1:4, *myths and endless genealogies*: A reference to the Jewish legends and spurious pedigrees added by false Judaizers to the Biblical narratives; cf. the Book of Jubilees.
1:20, *delivered to Satan*: A form of excommunication; see note on 1 Cor 5:5
2:6, *ransom for all*: This is why Paul wants prayers for all (verse 1).
3:1, *bishop*: At this time an office probably not distinct from that of priest.
3:11, *women*: i.e., deaconesses.
4:3, *forbid marriage*: As some Gnostics did.
abstinence from foods: As practised by Judaizers.
5:3, *real widows*: i.e., with no one to help and support them.
5:12: Paul had no objection to widows marrying again; cf. 1 Cor 7:8–9. But the widows here had clearly made some sort of vow or promise to serve the Church in singleness. Paul recommended that younger widows should marry again (verse 14).

THE SECOND LETTER OF PAUL TO TIMOTHY

1:15, *Asia*: The Roman province of that name, now in western Turkey.
2:18: They explained the resurrection by saying it was the rising to newness of life in Baptism, thus ignoring a bodily resurrection, a doctrine the Greeks found very hard to accept; cf. Acts 17:32.
3:16: Paul refers to the Old Testament scriptures.
4:6, *on the point of being sacrificed*: Literally, "poured out in sacrifice" as a drink offering or libation.
4:21, *Linus*: According to tradition, the successor of Peter in the see of Rome.

THE LETTER OF PAUL TO TITUS

1:5, *elders*: Each Christian community was ruled by a body of elders.
2:13, *God and Saviour*: Both terms appear to refer to Jesus Christ.
3:5–7: A brief and clear statement of the doctrine of justification.

THE LETTER TO THE HEBREWS

1:1–4: A contrast between the progressive and piecemeal revelation of the old dispensation and the complete revelation of the new given by a single representative—no mere prophet but the Son of God himself.
2:2, *angels*: The Covenant of Sinai was thought to have been given through the angels.
2:10, *suffering*: The divinely appointed means of progress towards God; cf. verse 18.
3:11: Those who murmured against God in the desert were excluded from the promised land (the "rest"). Christians should be aware lest, by offending God, they be excluded from heaven, the true rest, of which the promised land was a type.

5:1–5: If Jesus was to be mediator, he had to have a human nature like ours and, moreover, he could not appoint himself, but had to be appointed by God.
6:4, *impossible*: The apostasy referred to in verse 6 is clearly thought of as so deliberate as to preclude any real possibility of repentance; or there may be a reference here to the impossibility of being baptized a second time.
7:3, *without father*: i.e., the father is not mentioned in scripture.
neither beginning of days nor end of life: So too here, they are not mentioned in scripture either. Thus his priesthood can be taken to foreshadow or symbolize the Christian priesthood. "You are a priest for ever after the order of Melchizedek" (Ps 110:4; cf. Heb 7:17).
8:11: This verse merely means that knowledge of God will be commonly shared, and is not literally intended to exclude the ministry of teaching in the messianic times.
10:1ff.: The sacrifices of the old law, being imperfect, were repeated, and did at least keep alive a sense of sin. Contrast with Christ's sacrifice (verse 14).
11:6: Here is stated the minimum necessary for salvation.
12:1ff: After explaining to the preceding chapters how we are redeemed through faith in Jesus Christ, the author now exhorts his readers to run the race with perseverance.
13:1ff: Moral exhortation.
13:9: Again the warning against false doctrine, especially the Judaizers' teachings; cf. Phil 3:19; 1 Tim 1:4; 4:3.
13:13: i.e., "Let us leave the observances of Judaism behind us."

THE LETTER OF JAMES

1:1, *twelve tribes*: i.e., Jewish Christians outside Palestine.
1:22: This is the main theme of the letter.
2:1–7: These are hard words, but no harder than those of Jesus.
2:10: In keeping the Law. We must keep the whole Law. We cannot pick and choose.
2:14: Good works are necessary beside faith.
5:3: The "treasure" they have laid up is described in the following verses.
5:13–15: This passage is the scriptural basis for the sacrament of Anointing of the Sick.

THE FIRST LETTER OF PETER

1:1: See note on Jas 1:1. Baptism is the main theme of this letter, which may in fact, have been a baptismal address.
1:11, *Spirit of Christ*: Christ, as the eternally existing Word, is envisaged as inspiring the prophets of old.
3:1–6: Peter's teaching on the behaviour and status of women corresponds to that of Paul, though without Paul's forthrightness.
4:1, *ceased from sin*: Peter means that a continual acceptance of suffering is incompatible with a proneness to sin.
5:13, *Babylon*: Rome was as full of iniquity as ancient Babylon; cf. Rev 17:9.

THE SECOND LETTER OF PETER

1:4, *partakers of the divine nature*: A strong expression to describe the transformation of human nature by divine grace.
1:16–18: A reference to the transfiguration.
2:3: Much of the material of this chapter appears to be from the letter of Jude.
3:16: *this* seems to refer to the theme of the end of the world and the second coming of Christ, about which Paul had written in his letters to the Thessalonians.

THE FIRST LETTER OF JOHN

1:1–7: Note the likeness with John's Gospel 1:1–18.
1:3, *fellowship*: A Johannine theme.
1:5, *light . . . darkness*: Another familiar theme in John's Gospel.
2:3: cf. the words of Jesus, "If you love me, you will keep my commandments" (Jn 14:15).
2:18, *the last hour*: John exhorts his readers to hold fast, as though the end were at hand.
3:6, *sins*: i.e., remains in sin, or has a habit of sin.
4:1, *test the spirits*: i.e., examine those who claim to have special gifts from the Holy Spirit; cf.1 Cor 14:32.
5:8, *There are three witnesses*: After these words, the Vulgate adds the following: "in heaven, the Father, the Word, and the Holy Ghost. And these three are one. And these are three that give testimony on earth." This passage, known as the Comma Johanneum or "The Three Heavenly Witnesses," is first found in the Latin (fourth century), and does not appear in any Greek New Testament manuscript before the sixteenth century. It is probably a marginal gloss which found its way into the text.

THE SECOND LETTER OF JOHN

1, *The elder*: Perhaps the head of the group or "college" of elders that presided over each Christian community. John was head not only of the Ephesus community but of all the communities in the province of Asia.
the elect lady: Probably not an individual lady but a particular church or community in Asia.
13, *children*: i.e., the Christians of Ephesus.

THE THIRD LETTER OF JOHN

12, *Demetrius*: Evidently a leading Christian, recommended to Gaius.

THE LETTER OF JUDE

6: It is not clear to what Jude refers. Perhaps Gen 6:2 or the apocryphal Enoch, chapters 6–15.
9: Apparently a reference to another apocryphal work, the Assumption of Moses.

THE REVELATION TO JOHN

1:4–8: Describes the glorious coming and reign of the Messiah.
1:13, *son of man* refers to Dan 7:13. The Messiah is described in symbolic terms.
2:10, *ten days*: Not literally. It means the persecution will be short.
2:20–21, *immorality* here seems to mean idolatry rather than sexual excess.
2:24, *deep things of Satan*: The doctrine of the Nicolaitans. *They* called them the "deep things of God."
2:28, *morning star*: Probably Christ himself.
3:12, *new name*: cf. Is 62:2. Perhaps it was "the Word," or perhaps it is not to be revealed till the last day.
4:3: John describes God in symbolic terms.
4:4, *elders*: They perform a priestly and royal task, since they praise God and share in the government of the world.
4:6, *four living creatures*: cf. Ezek 1:4–25: the four angles who preside over the government of the world. But in Christian tradition these symbols are used for the four evangelists.
4:8, *Holy, holy, holy*: Quoted in the Sanctus at Mass.
5:1, *a scroll*: This contained God's designs, kept secret till now; being written on both sides, nothing could be added.
5:6: The seven horns and seven eyes symbolize Christ's full power and knowledge.

6:1: Begins the account of the destruction of the Roman Empire, chapters 6–9.
6:5, *balance*: Symbol of famine. The balance was to measure rations.
7:4, *a hundred and forty-four thousand*: A symbolic number, i.e., 12 (the sacred number) squared and multiplied by 1,000 to denote a multitude. It is the Church, the spiritual Israel, that is meant.
7:14, *the great tribulation*: The Neronian persecution?
8:5: Coals from the altar of burnt offering were brought to the altar of incense.
9:1, *star*: A fallen angel.
9:14, *Euphrates*: The region of the Parthians.
9:21, *immorality*: See note on 2:20–21.
10:7, *mystery of God*: i.e., the establishment of the kingdom of God following on the destruction of Israel's enemies.
10:9, *bitter . . . sweet*: The scroll related both the sufferings and the victories of Christ's Church.
11:1–19: The Jerusalem here described stands for the Church, which is to be persecuted by the Romans.
11:2: The three and a half years' persecution of the Jews by Antiochus Epiphanes 168–165 BC had become the standard time of a persecution.
Three and a half years = 42 months = 1,260 days (verse 3).
11:3, *two witnesses*: As they have yet to die, possibly they are Elijah and Enoch.
11:8, *the great city*: i.e., Rome.
12:1–6: The *child* brought forth is the Messiah; the *dragon* is the devil; the *woman* who gave birth to the Messiah is Israel, and then becomes the Christian Church, which continually gives birth to the faithful.
12:14, *a time, and times, and half a time*: This is the three and a half years of 11.2.
12:17: Mary; the mother of the Messiah, must also be included in the meaning.
13:1, *a beast*: This symbolizes the material forces of evil, arrayed against the Church.
13:11, *another beast*: i.e., the false prophets.
13:18, *six hundred and sixty-six*: The letters of Nero's name plus the title of Caesar, given their numerical meaning in Hebrew and added together, make 666.
14:4: Although tradition tends to take this literally, the context and Old Testament metaphor suggest that it means they have kept free from idolatry.
14:8, *Babylon*: i.e., Rome.
15:3–4: The song of Moses in Ex 15:1–18 celebrated victory over Pharaoh. This is seen as foreshadowing the triumph of the Lamb.
16:14, *the great day* on which all the Gentile armies shall be gathered to give battle.
16:16, *Armageddon*: i.e., Megiddo, where Josiah was defeated by the king of Egypt; cf. 2 Kings 23:29.
17:1, *great harlot*: i.e., Rome.
17:2, *fornication*: i.e., idolatry.
18:11–20: The description abruptly assumes the language of Ezekiel's prophecy of the destruction of Tyre, another city notorious for its sins (Ezek 27:1–28).
19:7, *marriage of the Lamb*: i.e., final establishment of the kingdom of God. The spouse is the Church.
20:3: The destruction of the dragon must coincide in time with that of the beast (19:20), so that the first resurrection with the reign of the martyrs refers to the revival and expansion of the Church after the years of persecution.
21:1: Creation will be renewed one day, free from corruption and illumined by God's glory.
21:8, *second death*: i.e., eternal damnation.

List of changes in the Revised Standard Version for the Catholic Edition

For "brother" read "brethren" in Mt 12:46, 47 (note), 48, 49; 13:55; Mk 3:31, 32, 33, 34; Lk 8:19, 20, 21; Jn 2:12; 7.3, 5, 10; Acts 1:14; 1 Cor 9:5.

	TEXT		FOOTNOTES	
	RSV	RSVCE	RSV	RSVCE
Mt 1:19	divorce her	send her away		
Mt 18:24			[f]Delete existing note and substitute:	[f]A talent was more than fifteen years' wages of a labourer
Mt 18:28			[g]Delete existing note and substitute:	[g]The denarius was a day's wage for a labourer
Mt 19:9		. . . commits adultery; and he who marries a divorced woman commits adultery."[k]		[k]Other ancient authorities omit *and he . . . adultery*
Mt 20:2			[m]Delete existing note and substitute:	[m]The denarius was a day's wage for a labourer
Mt 21:44		[q]+[44] And he who falls on this stone will be broken to pieces; but when it falls on any one, it will crush him		[q]Other ancient authorities omit verse 44
Mt 25:15			[d]Delete existing note and substitute:	[d]A talent was more than fifteen years' wages of a labourer
Mt 27:24		[l]this righteous man's blood		[l]Other ancient authorities omit *righteous* or *man's*
Mk 6:37			[u]Delete existing note and substitute:	[u]The denarius was a day's wage for a labourer
Mk 9:29		[j]+ and fasting		[j]Other ancient authorities omit *and fasting*

	TEXT		FOOTNOTES	
	RSV	RSVCE	RSV	RSVCE
Mk 10:24		[r]+ for those who trust in riches		[r]Other ancient authorities omit *for those . . . in riches*
Mk 13:33		[a]+ and pray		[a]Other ancient authorities omit *and pray*
Mk 14:5			[b]Delete existing note and substitute:	[b]The denarius was a day's wage for a labourer
Mk 16:9–20		[k](Insert into the text after verse 8) [9]Now when he rose early on the first day of the week, he appeared first to Mary Magdalene, from whom he had cast out seven demons. [10]She went and told those who had been with him, as they mourned and wept. [11]But when they heard that he was alive and had been seen by her, they would not believe it. [12]After this he appeared in another form to two them, as they were walking into the country. [13]And they went back and told the rest, but they did not believe them. [14]Afterwards he appeared to the eleven themselves as they sat at a table; and he upbraided them for their unbelief and hardness of heart, because they had not believed those who saw him after he had risen. [15]And he said to them, "Go into all the world and preach the gospel to the whole creation. [16]He who believes and is baptized will be saved; but he who does not believe will be condemned. [17] And these signs will accompany those who believe: in my name they will cast out demons; they will speak in new tongues; [18] they will pick up serpents, and if they drink any deadly thing, it will not hurt them;		[k]Other ancient authorities omit verses 9–20. Some ancient authorities conclude Mark instead with the following: *But they reported briefly to Peter and those with him all that they had been told. And after this, Jesus himself sent out by means of them, from east to west, the sacred and imperishable proclamation of eternal salvation.*

	TEXT		FOOTNOTES	
	RSV	RSVCE	RSV	RSVCE
		they will lay their hands on the sick, and they will recover." [19]So then the Lord Jesus, after he had spoken to them, was taken up into heaven, and sat down at the right hand of God. [20]And they went forth and preached everywhere, while the Lord worked with them and confirmed the message by the signs that attended it. Amen.		
Mk 16:9–20	O favoured one	full of grace[b2]		[b2]Or *O favoured one*
Lk 1:28				[b]Other ancient authorities omit *and had spent . . . physicians*
Lk 8:43		[b]+ and had spent all her living upon physicians		
Lk 10:35			[i]Delete existing note and substitute:	[i]The denarius was a day's wage for a labourer
Lk 15:8			[t]Delete existing note and substitute:	[t]The dracma, rendered here by *silver coin*, was about a day's wage for a labourer
Lk 19:13			[e]Delete existing note and substitute:	[e]The mina, rendered here by *pound*, was about three months' wages for a labourer
Lk 22:19–20		[j]+ which is given for you. Do this in remembrance of me." [20]And likewise the cup after supper, saying, "This cup which is poured out for you is the new covenant in my blood.		[j]Some ancient authorities omit *which is given . . . blood*
Lk 24:5		[u]+ He is not here, but has risen.		[u]Other ancient authorities omit *He is . . . has risen*

	TEXT		FOOTNOTES	
	RSV	RSVCE	RSV	RSVCE
Lk 24:12		[v]+[12] But Peter rose and ran to the tomb; stooping and looking in, he saw the linen cloths by themselves; and he went home wondering at what had happened.		[v]Other ancient authorities omit verse 12
Lk 24:36		[x] + and said to them, "Peace to you!"		[x]Other ancient authorities omit *and said . . . to you*
Lk 24:40		[y]+[40]And when he had said this, he showed them his hands and feet.		[y]Other ancient authorities omit verse 40
Lk 24:51		[a]+ and was carried up into heaven.		[a]Other ancient authorities omit *and was . . . heaven*
Lk 24:52		[b] + worshipped him, and		[b]Other ancient authorities omit *worshipped him, and*
Jn 6:7			[l]Delete existing note and substitute:	[l]The denarius was a day's wage for a labourer
Jn 7:52		[r](Insert into the text here) [53] They went each to his 8 own house, [1] but Jesus went to the Mount of Olives. [2]Early in the morning he came again to the temple; and he sat down and taught them. [3]The scribes and the Pharisees brought a woman who had been caught in adultery, and placing her in the midst [4]they said to him, "Teacher, this woman has been caught in the act of adultery. [5]Now in the law Moses commanded us to stone such. What do you say about her?" [6] This they said to test him, that they might have some charge to bring against him. Jesus bent down and wrote with his finger on the ground. [7]And as they continued to ask him, he stood up and		[r]Some ancient authorities insert 7:53–8:11 either at the end of this gospel or after Lk 21:38, with variations of the text. Others omit it altogether

	TEXT		FOOTNOTES	
	RSV	RSVCE	RSV	RSVCE
Jn 7:52		said to them, "Let him who is without sin among you be the first to throw a stone at her." [8]And once more he bent down and wrote with his finger on the ground. [9]But when they heard it, they went away, one by one, beginning with the eldest, and Jesus was left alone with the woman standing before him. [10]Jesus looked up and said to her, "Woman, where are they? Has no one condemned you?" [11]She said, "No one, Lord." And Jesus said, "Neither do I condemn you: go, and do not sin again."		
Jn 12:5			[b]Delete existing note and substitute:	[b]The denarius was a day's wage for a labourer
Rom 1:4		designated[a2]		[a2]Or *constituted*
Rom 5:5	which	who		
Rom 8:11	which	who		
Rom 9:5	. . . Christ, God who is over all be blessed for ever.[n]	. . . Christ, who is God over all, blessed for ever.[n]	[n]Or *Christ, who is God over all, blessed for ever*	[n]Or *Christ, God who is over all be blessed for ever*
1 Cor 3:9	fellow workers for God [f]	God's fellow workers[f]	[f]Or *God's fellow workers*	[f]*Or fellow workers for God*
1 Cor 4:6	to live according to Scripture	not to go beyond what is written		
1 Cor 7:25		the unmarried[x2]		
1 Cor 7:28		a girl[m2]		[x2]Greek *virgins*
1 Cor 7:34		girl[m2]		[m2]Greek *virgin*
1 Cor 7:36		betrothed[m2]		
1 Cor 7:37		betrothed[m2]		
1 Cor 7:38		betrothed[m2]		

	TEXT		FOOTNOTES	
	RSV	RSVCE	RSV	RSVCE
1 Cor 9:5			[n]Delete existing note and substitute:	[n]Greek a *woman*, a *sister*
Eph 1:14	which	who		
Eph 5:32	I take it to mean	I mean in reference to		
Phil 2:5	you have	was		
1 Thess 4:4	how to take a wife for himself	how to control his own body		
1 Thess 5:13		among yourselves[c2]		[c2]Or *with them*
Heb 11:19	hence, figuratively speaking, he did receive him back	hence he did receive him back, and this was a symbol		
Rev		(Title) THE REVELATION TO JOHN (THE APOCALYPSE)		
Rev 6:6			[a]Delete existing note and substitute:	[a]The denarius was a day's wage for a labourer

Sources quoted in the Commentary

1. DOCUMENTS OF THE CHURCH

Trent, Council of

Doctrine on the sacrament of Extreme Unction, ss. XIV, 25 November 1551

Doctrine on the sacrament of Penance, ss. XIV, 25 November 1551

Vatican, First Council of

Dei Filius: Dogmatic Constitution, 24 April 1870

Pastor Aeternus: Dogmatic Constitution, 18 July 1870

Vatican, Second Council of

AA: *Apostolicam actuositatem*: Decree on the apostolate of lay people, 18 November 1965

AG: *Ad gentes*: Decree on the Church's missionary activity, 7 December 1965

CD: *Christus Dominus*: Decree on the pastoral office of bishops, 28 October 1965

DG: *Dignitatis humanae*: Decree on religious freedom, 7 December 1965

DV: *Dei Verbum*: Dogmatic constitution on divine revelation, 18 November 1965

GS: *Gaudium et spes*: Pastoral constitution on the Church in the modern world, 7 December 1965

LG: *Lumen gentium*: Dogmatic constitution on the Church, 21 November 1964

PO: *Presbyterorum ordinis*: Decree on the training of priests, 7 December 1965

SC: *Sacrosanctum Concilium*: Constitution on the sacred Liturgy, 4 December 1963

UR: *Unitatis redintegratio,* Decree on ecumenism, 21 November 1964

NA: *Nostra aetate*: Decree on the relation of the Church to non-Christian religions, 28 October 1965

Leo XIII

Libertas praestantissimum: Encyclical, 20 June 1888

Divinum illud munus, Encyclical, 9 May 1897

Pius XI

Mens nostra, Encyclical, 20 December 1929

Pius XII

Mystici Corporis, Encyclical, 29 June 1943

Address, 15 November 1946

Paul VI

Populorum Progressio: Encyclical on the development of peoples, 26 March 1967

Creed of the People of God: Solemn profession of faith, 30 June 1968

Divinae consortium naturae: Apostolic constitution, 15 August 1971

Evangelii nuntiandi: Apostolic exhortation, 8 December 1975

John Paul II

Address, 25 November 1987

Dives in misericordia: Encyclical on the mercy of God, 30 November 1980

Dominum et Vivificantem: Encyclical on the Holy Spirit in the life of the Church and of the world, 18 May 1986

Evangelium vitae: Apostolic letter on the value and inviolability of human life, 25 March 1995

Familiaris consortio: Apostolic exhortation on the duties of the Christian family, 22 November 1981

Homily, 1 November 1981

Laborem exercens: Encyclical on human work, 14 September 1981

Reconciliatio et poenitentia: Apostolic exhortation on reconciliation and penance, 2 December 1984

Redemptor hominis: Encyclical, 4 March 1979

Redemptoris Mater: Encyclical, 25 March 1987

Redemptoris missio: Encyclical, 7 December 1990

Salvifici doloris: Apostolic letter, 11 February 1984

Sollicitudo rei socialis: Encyclical on the twentieth anniversary of *Populorum Progressio,* 30 November 1987

Veritatis splendor: Apostolic letter on certain fundamental questions of the Church's moral teaching, 6 August 1993

Congregation for the Doctrine of the Faith (SCDF)

Inter insigniores: Declaration, 15 October 1976

Libertatis conscientia: Instruction on Christian freedom and liberation, 22 March 1986

Libertatis nuntius: Instruction, 6 August 1984

Persona humana: Declaration on sexual ethics, 29 December 1975

Other

CCC: *Catechism of the Catholic Church,* Dublin, 1994

Code of Canon Law: *Codex Iuris Canonici auctoritate Ioannis Pauli PP II promulgatus,* Vatican City, 1983; English edition, London, 1983

2. LITURGICAL TEXTS

Roman Missal: Missale Romanum, editio typica altera, Vatican City, 1975

The Divine Office, London, Sydney, Dublin, 1974

3. THE FATHERS, ECCLESIASTICAL WRITERS AND OTHER AUTHORS

Alphonsus Mary Liguori, St

Shortened sermons

Ambrose, St

Letters: *Epistulae,* PL16, 913–1342

Com. on Lk: *Expositio Evangelii secundum Lucam*: PL 15,1607–1944

Anon.

Epistle of Barnabas

Apostolic Constitutions

Didache, or Teaching of the Twelve Apostles

Letter to Diognetus

Jerusalem Catechesis: *Catecheses (Mystagogiae)*: PG 33, 331–1180

Catena aurea: A. Guarienti (ed.), *St Thomae Aquinatis Catena Aurea in Quattuor Evangelia,* Turin, 1953.

Athanasius, St

De incarnatione Verbi: PG 25, 3–96

Orationes tres contra arianos: PG 26,12–468

Augustine, St

Confessiones: PL 32, 659–868

Contra Adimantum Manichaei discipulum liber I: PL 42,129–172

De civitate Dei libri XXII: PL 41,13–804

De fide et symbolo liber I: PL 40,181–196

De sermone Domini in monte libri II: PL 34,1229–1308

Enarrationes in Psalmos: PL 38–39

Enchiridion ad Laurentium: PL 40, 231–290

Letters: *Epistolae*: PL 33

Com. in Gal: *Expositio epistolae ad Galatas*: PL 35, 2105–2148

Tractatus in Epistolam Ioannis ad Parthos: PL 35, 1977–2062

Tractatus in Evangelium Ioannis: PL 35, 1379–1970

Sermo ad Caesariensis ecclesiae plebem: PL 43, 689–698

Sermones: PL 36–37

Basil, St

Adversus Eunomium: PG 29, 497–669

Homilia in martyrem Julittam: PG 31, 237–261

Liber de Spiritu Sancto: PG 32, 67–217

Bede, St

In Marci Evangelium expositio: PL 92,131–302

In primam Epistolam Sancti Ioannis: PL 93, 85–120

Super Acta Apostolorum expositio: PL 92, 937–996

Benedict, St

Regula: PL 66, 215–932

Bernard, St

Letters: *Epistolae*: PL 182, 62–722

Liber de diligendo Deo: PL 182, 973–1000

Sermo 1 in Epiphania Domini: PL 183, 141–147

Sermo 2 Paschae: PL 183, 283–288

Cano, Melchor

De locis theologicis

Cassian, John

Collationes XXIV: PL 49, 477–1328.

Catherine of Siena, St

Letters

Clement of Rome, St

First Letter to Cor: *Epistula Clementis ad Corinthios I*

Cyprian, St

De bono patientiae: PL 4, 621–637

De opere et eleemosynis: PL 4, 601–622

Elizabeth of the Trinity
Heaven on Earth and *Letters* in *Obras completas,* ed. A. Aparicio, Burgos, 1984
Ephrem, St
Cat. arm. sup. Acts: *Commentarii in Acta Apostolorum,* ed. F. C. Conybeare in Foakes-Jackson and Lake, *The Acts of the Apostles. The beginnings of Christianity*, London, 1926
Super Diatess.: *Commentarii in Diatessaron*
Eusebius of Caesarea
Ecclesiastical History
Francis of Assisi, St
Little Flowers
Francis de Sales, St
Treatise on the Love of God
Gregory of Nyssa, St
De instituto Christiano: PG 46, 287–306
On the Life of Moses: De vita Mosis: PG 44, 297–430
Oratio catechetica magna: PG 45, 9–106.
Gregory the Great, St
Hom. on Gospel: XL Homiliarum in Evangelia libri duo: PL 76,1075–1312
Ignatius Loyola, St
Spiritual Exercises
Letters: *Epistolas*: *I.* Iparranguirre and C. de Dalmases (eds), *San Ignacio de Loyola. Obras,* Madrid, 1991
Ignatius of Antioch, St
Letter to the Corinthians
Letter to the Ephesians
Letter to Polycarp
Letter to the Romans
Letter to the Smyrnaeans
Irenaeus, St
Adversus haereses
Demonstratio praedicationis apostolicae
Jerome, St
Com. in Mt: *Commentariorum in Evangelium S. Matthaei libri quatuor*: PL 26,15–218
Letters: *Epistulae*: PL 22, 325–1244
Of Famous Men: De vivis illustribus
John of Avila, St
Audi, filia
Letters: *Epistolas,* ed. L. Sala Balust, F. Martin Hernández: *Obras completas del Santo Maestro Juan de Ávila,* vol. 5, Madrid, 1970
Talk: *Plática,* in ibid., vol. 6, Madrid, 1970
John Chrystostom, St
Baptismal Catechesis: *Catecheses ad illuminandos*: A. Wenger (ed.), *Huit catéchèses baptismales* (SC 50), Paris, 1970
Homiliae in Mattheum: PG 57,13–472
Homiliae in Acta Apostolorum: PG 60,13–384
Homiliae in Epistulam ad Romanos: PG 60, 391–682
Homiliae in Epistulam primam ad Corinthios: PG 61, 9–381
Homiliae in Epistulam secundam ad Corinthios: PG 61, 382–610
Homiliae in Epistulam primam ad Timotheum: PG 62, 501–600
Homiliae in Epistulam ad Hebraeos: PG 63, 9–236
John of the Cross, St
Ascent of Mount Carmel
Prayer of the Soul in Love
Spiritual Canticle
Josemaría Escrivá, Blessed
Conversations
The Forge
Furrow
Holy Rosary
In Love with the Church
The Way
The Way of the Cross
Hom., 1: *Christ Is Passing By*
Hom., 2: *Friends of God*
John B. M. Vianney, St
Sermon on prayer
Josephus, Flavius
Ant.: *Antiquitates Iudaicae*
The Jewish War
Justin Martyr, St
Apology, First and Second
Dialogus cum Tryphone Iudaeo
Leo the Great, St
Homiliae in natalitium Apostolorum Petri et Pauli: PL 54, 422–428
Sermo in Nativitate Domini I: PL 54, 190–193
Sermo in Nativitate Domini VI: PL 54, 212–216
Sermo in Epiphaniae Solemnitate III: PL 54, 240–244
Sermo de Quadragesima IV: PL 54, 274–281
Sermo de Quadragesima X: PL 54, 297–301
Sermo de Passione Domini VIII: PL 54, 337–342
Luis de Granada
Libro de la oración y meditación: A. Huerga (ed.), *Fray Luis de Granada. Obras completas,* Madrid, 1994.
Life of Jesus Christ
Newman, Cardinal John Henry
Biglietto Speech
Discourses to mixed congregations
Origen
Against Celsus: *Contra Celso*: GCS 2–3 (1899)
De oratione: GCS 3 (1899) 297–403
Peter, Chrysologus, St
Sermones: PL 52, 183–680

Pseudo–Macarius
Homilia: PL 34, 449–822
SCDF
See Congregation for the Doctrine of the Faith in Section 1 above
Teresa of Avila
Exclamations of the Soul to God
The Foundations
Interior Castle
Life
Poems
Way of Perfection
Teresa Benedicta, St (Edith Stein)
The Science of the Cross
Tertullian
De oratione: CSEL 20 (1890) 180–200
Liber ad Scapulum: CSEL 76 (1957)
Theodoret of Cyrus
Interpretatio ad Hebraeos: PG 82, 673–785
Thérèse of Lisieux, St
Autobiography
Thomas à Kempis
The Imitation of Christ
Thomas Aquinas, St
On the Creed: *Expositio in Credum*
Com. on 1 Cor: *Super Epistolam primam ad Corinthios*
Com. on 2 Cor: *Super Epistolam secundam ad Corinthios*
Com. on Heb: *Super Epistolam ad Hebraeos*
Com. on Mt: *Super Evangelium Matthaei lectura*
Com. on Jn: *Super Evangelium Ioannis lectura*
Com. on Rom: *Super Epistolam ad Romanos*
Com. on Thess: *Super Epistolam primam ad Thessalonicenses*
Summa theologiae
Vincent Lerins, St
Commonitorium: PL 50, 637–686

Headings added to the Biblical Text

for this edition

MATTHEW

Part Three: Jesus' ministry in Jerusalem

10. CLEANSING OF THE TEMPLE. CONTROVERSIES
The Messiah enters the Holy City 21:1
Jesus in the temple 21:12
The cursing of the fig tree 21:18
The authority of Jesus is questioned 21:23
Parable of the two sons 21:28
Parable of the wicked tenants 21:33
Parable of the marriage feast 22:1
Tribute to Caesar 22:15
The resurrection of the dead 22:23
The greatest commandment of all 22:34
The divinity of the Messiah 22:41
Jesus indicts scribes and Pharisees 23:1
Jerusalem admonished 23:37

11. THE ESCHATOLOGICAL DISCOURSE
Announcement of the destruction of the temple 24:1
The beginning of tribulations. Persecution on account of the Gospel 24:3
The great tribulation 24:15
The coming of the Son of man 24:29
The end will surely come—the lesson of the fig tree 24:32
The time of the second coming of Christ 24:36
Vigilance. Parable of the faithful servant 24:42
Parable of the wise and foolish maidens 25:1
Parable of the talents 25:14
The Last Judgment 25:31

12. THE PASSION, DEATH AND RESURRECTION OF JESUS
The last announcement of the Passion. The conspiracy against Jesus 26:1
The anointing at Bethany. Judas betrays Jesus 26:6
Preparations for the Last Supper and announcement of Judas' treachery 26:17
The institution of the Eucharist 26:26
The disciples' desertion foretold 26:30
Gethsemane—the agony in the garden 26:36
The arrest of Jesus 26:47
Jesus before the chief priests 26:57
Peter's denials 26:69
Jesus is brought before Pilate 27:1
Judas' despair and death 27:3
Jesus' trial before Pilate 27:11
The crowning with thorns 27:27
The crucifixion and death of Jesus 27:32
The burial of Jesus 27:57
Jesus rises from the dead and appears to the women 28:1
The soldiers are bribed 28:1
Appearance in Galilee. The mission to the world 28:16

MARK

1. PRELUDE TO THE PUBLIC MINISTRY OF JESUS
The ministry of John the Baptist 1:1
Jesus is baptized 1:9
The tempting of Jesus 1:12

Part One: Jesus' ministry in Galilee

2. JESUS BEGINS HIS MINISTRY
Jesus begins to preach and calls his first disciples 1:14
Jesus in the synagogue of Capernaum 1:21
Curing of Peter's mother-in-law 1:29
Jesus cures many sick people 1:32
Jesus goes to a lonely place to pray 1:35
Curing of a leper 1:40
Curing of a paralyzed man 2:1
The calling of Matthew 2:13
A discussion on fasting 2:18
The law of the sabbath 2:23
Curing of the man with a withered hand 3:1
Cures beside the Sea of Galilee 3:7
Jesus chooses twelve apostles 3:13
Jesus' relatives are concerned about him 3:19
Allegations of the scribes. Sin against the Holy Spirit 3:22
The true kinsmen of Jesus 3:31

3. PARABLES OF THE KINGDOM OF GOD
Parable of the sower. The meaning of parables 4:1
Parables of the lamp and the measure 4:21
Parables of the seed and of the mustard seed 4:26
The end of the parables discourse 4:33

4. MIRACLES AND ACTIVITY IN GALILEE
The calming of the storm 4:35
The Gerasene demoniac 5:1
Jairus' daughter is restored to life. Curing of the woman with a hemorrhage 5:21
No prophet is honoured in his own country 6:1

5. JESUS JOURNEYS WITH HIS APOSTLES
The mission of the Twelve 6:7
Opinions about Jesus 6:14
The martyrdom of John the Baptist 6:17
The apostles return 6:30
First miracle of the loaves and fish 6:33
Jesus walks on water 6:45
Cures at Gennesaret 6:53
The traditions of the elders. What defiles a man 7:1
The Syrophoenician woman 7:24
Curing of a deaf man 7:31
Second miracle of the loaves 8:1
The leaven of the Pharisees and Herod 8:11
Curing of a blind man at Bethsaida 8:22
Peter's profession of faith 8:27

Part Two: Jesus' ministry on the way to Jerusalem

6. TEACHINGS ON THE CHRISTIAN LIFE
Jesus foretells his passion and resurrection. Christian renunciation 8:31
The Transfiguration 9:2
Curing of an epileptic boy 9:14
Second announcement of the Passion 9:30
Service to others. On leading others astray 9:33

7. HEADING FOR JUDEA AND JERUSALEM
The indissolubility of marriage 10:1
Jesus and the children 10:13
The rich young man. Poverty and renunciation 10:17
Third announcement of the Passion 10:32
The sons of Zebedee make their request 10:35
Bartimeus, the blind man of Jericho 10:46

Part Three: Jesus' ministry in Jerusalem

LUKE

Part One: Jesus' ministry in Galilee

Part Two: Jesus' ministry on the way to Jerusalem

Part Three: The Jerusalem ministry

JOHN

Prologue

Part One: Jesus is manifested as the Messiah by his signs and words

1. INTRODUCTION
The witness of John the Baptist 1.19
The calling of the first disciples 1.35

2. JESUS THE AUTHOR OF THE NEW ECONOMY OF SALVATION: FIRST SIGNS OF FAITH
The wedding at Cana 2:1
Cleansing of the temple 2:13
The visit of Nicodemus 3:1
The Baptist again bears witness 3:22
Jesus and the Samaritan woman 4:1
Curing of a royal official's son 4:46

3. JESUS REVEALS HIS DIVINITY
Curing of a paralyzed man 5:1
The authority of the Son of God 5:19

4. JESUS IS THE BREAD OF LIFE
The miracle of the loaves and fish 6:1
Jesus walks on water 6:16
The people look for Jesus 6:22
The discourse on the bread of life 6:25
The disciples' reaction 6:60

5. JESUS IS THE LIGHT OF THE WORLD
Jesus goes up to Jerusalem during the feast of the Tabernacles 7:1
Different opinions about Jesus 7:32
The adulterous woman 8:2
Jesus, the light of the world 8:12
Jesus warns the unbelieving Jews 8:21
Curing of the man born blind 9:1
The blindness of the Jews 9:24
The Good Shepherd 10:1

6. JESUS AND THE FATHER
Jesus and the Father are one 10:22
An attempt to stone our Lord 10:31

7. JESUS IS THE LIFE OF THE WORLD
The raising of Lazarus 11.1
The Sanhedrin decides on the death of Jesus 11.45

8. JESUS IS ACCLAIMED AS THE MESSIANIC KING
Mary anoints our Lord at Bethany 12:1
The Messiah's entry into Jerusalem 12:12
Jesus announces his glorification 12:20
The unbelief of the Jews 12:36

Part Two: Jesus is manifested as the Messiah Son of God in his passion, death and resurrection

9. THE LAST SUPPER
Jesus washes his disciples' feet 13:1
The treachery of Judas foretold 13:21
The new commandment. The disciples' desertion foretold 13:31
Jesus reveals the Father 14:1
Promise of the Holy Spirit 14:15
The vine and the branches 15:1
The law of love 15:9
A hostile world 15:18
The action of the Holy Spirit 16:1
Fullness of joy 16:16
The priestly prayer of Jesus 17:1

10. THE PASSION AND DEATH OF JESUS
The arrest of Jesus 18:1
Jesus before the chief priests. Peter's denials 18:13
The trial before Pilate. Jesus is King 18:28
The scourging at the pillar and the crowning with thorns 19:1
Pilate hands Jesus over 19:12
The crucifixion and death of Jesus 19:17
Jesus' side is pierced. His burial 19:31

11. APPEARANCES OF THE RISEN CHRIST
The empty tomb 20:1
The appearance to Mary Magdalene 20:11
Jesus appears to the disciples 20:19
The miraculous catch of fish 21:1
Peter's primacy 21:15
Conclusion 21:24

ACTS

Prologue 1:10
The Ascension 1:6

Part One: The Church in Jerusalem

1. THE DISCIPLES IN JERUSALEM
The apostolic college 1:12
The election of Matthias 1:15

2. PENTECOST
The coming of the Holy Spirit 2:1
Peter's address 2:14
Many baptisms 2:37
The early Christians 2:42

3. THE APOSTLES' WORK IN JERUSALEM
Curing of a man lame from birth 3:1
Peter's address in the temple 3:11
Peter and John are arrested 4:1
Address to the Sanhedrin 4:5
The Church's thanksgiving prayer 4:23
The way of life of the early Christians 4:32
Deception by Ananias and Sapphira 5:1
Growth of the Church 5:12

ROMANS

INTRODUCTION
Greeting 1.1
Theme of the letter 1:16

Part One: Justification by Jesus Christ

1. JUSTIFICATION BY FAITH
The fault of the Gentiles, and their punishment 1:18
The Jews are guilty, too 2:1
Real circumcision, a matter of the heart 2:25
All are sinners—Jews and Gentiles alike 2:9
Righteousness, a free gift through faith in Christ 3:21
Abraham's exemplary faith 4:1

2. SALVATION AND THE CHRISTIAN LIFE
Reconciliation through Christ's sacrifice, the basis of our hope 5:1
Adam's original sin 5:12
Baptism 6:1
Liberation from sin 6:12
The Christian is not bound by the Law 7:1
The Law and concupiscence 7:7
Interior struggle 7:14
Life in the Spirit 8:1
Christians are children of God 8:14
Trust in God 8:31

3. GOD'S PLAN FOR THE CHOSEN PEOPLE
The privileges of Israel and God's fidelity 9:1
Israel's vocation 9:14
Israel's infidelity 10:1
Part of Israel will be saved 11:1
The new chosen people 11:13
The conversion of the Jews 11:25

Part Two: Living in charity

4. CHRISTIAN BEHAVIOUR
Solidarity in the mystical body of Christ 12:1
Charity towards all 12:9
Submission to authority 13:1
Love, the fullness of the Law 13:8

5. SENSITIVITY TOWARDS OTHERS
Seeing things from the other person's point of view 14.1
Not leading others astray 14.13
The example of Christ 15.1

6. CONCLUSION AND FAREWELL
Paul's ministry 15:14
Journeys planned 15:22
Greetings and recommendations 16:1
Doxology 16:25

1 CORINTHIANS

INTRODUCTION
Greeting 1:1
Thanksgiving 1:4

Part One: Correction of abuses

1. DIVISIONS AMONG THE CORINTHIANS
An appeal for unity 1:10
The wisdom of the cross 1:18
Paul's preaching in Corinth 2:1
Divine wisdom 2:6
The Corinthians are still unspiritual 3:1
Apostolic ministry 3:4
Servants of Christ 4:1
Trials experienced by apostles 4:8
Admonishment 4:14

2. A CASE OF INCEST
Punishment of the sinner 5:1
Obstinate sinners are to be shunned 5:9

3. RECOURSE TO PAGAN COURTS

4. FORNICATION, A GRAVE SIN
Respect for the body 6:12
Offence to Christ and the Holy Spirit 6:15

Part Two: Answers to various questions

5. MARRIAGE AND VIRGINITY
Relations between husband and wife 7:1
Indissolubility of marriage 7:10
The Pauline privilege 7:12
Leading the life God has assigned 7:17
Excellence of virginity 7:25
Advice to widows 7:39

6. FOOD OFFERED TO IDOLS
Idols have no real existence 8:1
Not scandalizing the weak 8:7
The right of apostles to receive maintenance from the faithful 9:1
St Paul does not exercise that right 9:15
The need for asceticism 9:24
The lesson of Israel's history 10:1
Idolatry and the Eucharist, incompatible 10:14
Practical solutions to certain questions 10:23

7. THE CELEBRATION OF THE EUCHARIST
Women in church 11:1
Abuses in the celebration of the Eucharist 11:17
The institution of the Eucharist and its worthy reception 11:23

8. GIFTS AND GRACES
Kinds of spiritual gifts 12:1
Unity and variety in the mystical body of Christ 12:12
Hymn to charity 13:1
Prophecy, the gift of tongues, and interpretation of tongues 14:1
Regulation of liturgical assemblies 14:26

9. THE RESURRECTION OF THE DEAD
Christ's resurrection and his appearances 15:1
The basis of our faith 15:12
The cause of our resurrection 15:20
The manner of the resurrection of the dead 15:35

10. MESSAGES AND WORDS OF FAREWELL
Collection for the church of Jerusalem 16:1
Plans for the months ahead 16:5
Exhortations and greetings 16:13

2 CORINTHIANS

INTRODUCTION
Greeting 1:1
Thanksgiving 1:3

Part One: St Paul's defence against his enemies

1. HIS SIMPLICITY AND SINCERITY
The evidence of his actions and his letters 1:12
Why he has not visited Corinth 1:15
Forgiveness for those who offend us 2:5
Paul's eagerness for news 2:12
Paul's sincere conduct 4:1
The trials Paul has experienced 4:7
Paul is sustained by hope of heaven 4:13
The ministry of reconciliation 5:11
Paul, a true servant of Christ 6:1

2. THE IMPORTANCE OF APOSTOLIC OFFICE
Paul's letter of recommendation 3:12
Christian ministry is greater than that of the Old Covenant 3:4

3. ST PAUL OPENS HIS HEART
His love for the Corinthians 6:11
Contact with unbelievers 6:14
Paul's joy at the news brought by Titus 7:2

Part Two: The collection for the church of Jerusalem

The Macedonians' good example 8:1
Appeal for generosity 8:7
Paul praises Titus and Timothy 8:16
Appeal for speediness 9:1
Blessings to be expected 9:6

Part Three: Paul justifies his conduct

4. A REPLY TO ACCUSATIONS
Paul's readiness to use his apostolic authority 10:1
Paul's province includes Corinth 10:12

5. THE APOSTLE'S GROUNDS FOR BOASTING
His zeal 11:1
Paul accepted no material support in payment for preaching 11:7
Paul apologizes for boasting 11:16
What Paul has suffered for Christ 11:21
Visions and revelations 12:1
Paul again apologizes for boasting 12:11

6. THE APOSTLE'S NEXT VISIT
The reason for his apologia 12:19
Preparation for his next visit 13:1

7. WORDS OF FAREWELL

GALATIANS

INTRODUCTION
Greeting 1:1
A warning 1:6

Part One: The Gospel preached by St Paul

1. ST PAUL ARGUES IN HIS OWN DEFENCE
Paul's vocation 1:11
Visit to Jerusalem 2:1
The incident at Antioch 2:11

2. DOCTRINAL MATTERS
Justification by faith 3:1
The Law and the promise 3:15
Divine sonship 4:1
A fatherly appeal by Paul 4:12
The two covenants—Hagar and Sarah 4:21

Part Two: Christian freedom and charity

3. EXHORTATIONS
Christian freedom 5:1
The fruits of the Spirit and the works of the flesh 5:13
Fraternal charity 6:1

4. CONCLUSION

EPHESIANS

Greeting 1:1

Part One: The mystery of God revealed

1. GOD'S PLAN OF SALVATION
Hymn of praise 1:3
Thanksgiving. The supremacy of Christ 1:15
Salvation, a free gift 2:1
Reconciliation of Jews and Gentiles in Christ 2:11

2. PROCLAMATION OF THE MYSTERY OF CHRIST
Paul's mission 3:1
The Apostle's prayer 3:14
Doxology 3:20

Part Two: Christian life in the Church

3. NEW LIFE IN CHIRST AND IN THE CHURCH
A call to unity 4:1
Spiritual renewal 4:17
Christian virtues 4:25

4. CHRISTIAN HOLINESS
The purity of life of God's children 5:1
Walking in the light 5:8

5. CHRISTIAN FAMILY LIFE
Duties of husband and wife 5:21
Advice to children and parents 6:1
Advice to servants and masters 6:5

6. CONCLUSION
Weapons for spiritual combat 6:10
Conclusion and blessing 6:21

PHILIPPIANS

1. INTRODUCTION
Greeting 1:1
Thanksgiving. Paul's affection and love 1:3
Paul's own circumstances 1:12

2. TEACHINGS
Appeal for steadfastness 1:27
Unity and humility 2:1
Hymn in praise of God's self-emptying 2:5
The children of God, the light of the world 2:12

3. PLANS AND NEWS
Timothy's mission 2:19
Epaphroditus' mission 2:25

4. THE CHRISTIAN LIFE
A warning about Judaizers 3:1
The righteousness of God exceeds that of the Law 3:7
The spiritual athlete 3:12
Citizens of heaven 3:17
Exhortation to perseverance and joy 4:1
Thanks for help received 4:10
Words of farewell 4:21

COLOSSIANS

INTRODUCTION
Greeting 1:1
Thanksgiving for the Colossians' response to the Gospel 1:3
Prayer for advancement in holiness 1:9

Part One: Faith in Christ, the Lord of all

1. CHRIST, THE FIRST-BORN
Hymn in praise of Christ, the head of all creation 1:15
The effect of Christ's saving action 1:21
Paul's response to his calling 1:24

2. DEFENCE OF THE FAITH
Paul's concern for the faithful 2:1
A warning about empty philosophies 2:4
Defence of sound teaching in the face of heresy 2:9
Rejection of false asceticism 2:16

Part Two: Christ the Lord

3. MORAL CONSEQUENCES
Seeking the things that are above 3:1
Avoiding sin 3:5
Progress in the spiritual life 3:12
Morals in family life 3:18
Apostolic responsibility 4:2

4. CONCLUSION
Tychicus and Onesimus will give personal news of Paul 4:7
Greetings from Paul's fellow workers 4:10
Greetings and final wishes 4:15

1 THESSALONIANS

Greeting 1.1

1. THE APOSTLE REJOICES OVER THE CHURCH OF THESSALONICA
Thanksgiving for the Thessalonians' fidelity 1:2
Gospel preaching in Thessalonica—the early days recalled 2:1
The Thessalonians' patience 2:13
Paul's solicitude 2:17
Timothy's mission to Thessalonica 3:1
Paul rejoices over the good reports brought by Timothy 3:6
Paul's prayer for the Thessalonians 3:11

2. A CALL TO HOLINESS, HOPE AND PRAYER
Holiness and purity 4:1
Charity and good use of time 4:9
The second coming of the Lord 4:13
Various counsels 5:12
Closing prayer and farewell 5:23

2 THESSALONIANS

Greeting 1:1

1. HOPE IN A DIVINE REWARD
Thanksgiving 1:3
Divine retribution 1:6
Prayer for perseverance 1:11
The coming of the Lord 2:1
The need for steadfastness 2:13

2. PRAYER, WORK, FRATERNITY
Paul asks for payers 3:1
Avoiding idleness. Earning one's living 3:6
Words of farewell 3:16

1 TIMOTHY

Greeting 1:1

1. SOUND DOCTRINE
False teachers to be admonished 1:3
The purpose of the Law 1:8
Paul recalls his own conversion 1:12
Timothy's responsibilities 1:18

2. REGULATIONS ABOUT PRAYER
God desires the salvation of all 2:1
Men at prayer, women at prayer 2:8

3. CHURCH OFFICE
Qualifications for bishops 3:1
Qualifications for deacons 3:8
The Church is God's household 3:14
The mystery of our religion 3:16

4. PASTORAL DIRECTIVES
What to do about false teachers 4:1
Pastoral advice to Timothy 4:12
The pastor and the faithful in general 5:1
Widows, their role and lifestyle 5:3
Criteria for choosing elders 5:17
Slaves and their moral obligations 6:1
False teachers described 6:3
An appeal to defend the faith 6:11
The right way to use wealth 6:17
Words of farewell 6:20

2 TIMOTHY

Greeting 1:1

1. PREACHING THE GOSPEL MESSAGE
Response to grace 1:5
St Paul, herald of the Gospel 1:8
Attitudes towards certain disciples 1:15
Bearing one's share of suffering 2:1
Jesus, the Apostle's model 2:8

2. DEFENDING THE GOSPEL
Avoiding useless arguments 2:14
Patience towards those in error 2:22
Preventing error from doing harm 3:1
Staying true to Holy Scripture 3:14
Dedication to preaching 4:1
The crown of righteousness 4:6

3. FINAL ADVICE
News and messages 4:9
Greetings and final good wishes 4:19

TITUS

PHILEMON

HEBREWS

JAMES

1 PETER

Greeting 1:1
Praise and thanksgiving to God 1:3

1. A CALL TO HOLINESS
Christians are called to be saints 1:13
The blood of Christ has ransomed us 1:17
Brotherly love 1:22
Like newborn babies 2:1
The priesthood that all believers share 2:4

2. THE OBLIGATIONS OF CHRISTIANS
Setting an example for pagans 2:11
Obedience to civil authority 2:13
Duties towards masters. Christ's example 2:18
Exemplary family life 3:1
Love of the brethren 3:8

3. THE CHRISTIAN'S ATTITUDE TO SUFFERING
Undeserved suffering is a blessing 3:13
Christ's suffering and glorification 3:18
The Christian has broken with sin 4:1
A call for charity 4:7
The Christian meaning of suffering 4:12

4. FINAL EXHORTATIONS
To priests 5:1
To all the faithful 5:5
Words of farewell 5:12

2 PETER

Greeting 1:1

1. A CALL TO FIDELITY
Divine largesse 1:3
Christian virtues 1:5
Spiritual testimony 1:12
The Transfiguration, an earnest of the Second Coming 1:16
Prophecy and the Second Coming 1:19

2. FALSE TEACHERS DENOUNCED
The harm they do 2:1
The punishment that awaits them 2:4
Their arrogance and immorality 2:10
Apostasy, a grave sin 2:20

3. THE SECOND COMING OF CHRIST
The teaching of Tradition 3:1
Mistaken notions 3:3
True teaching about the End 3:5
Moral lessons to be drawn 3:11
Final exhortation and doxology 3:17

1 JOHN

Prologue 1:1

1. UNION WITH GOD
God is light 1:5
Walking in the light. Rejecting sin 1:6
Keeping the commandments 2:3
The Apostle's confidence in the faithful 2:12
Detachment from the world 2:15
Not listening to heretics 2:18

2. LIVING AS GOD'S CHILDREN
We are children of God 3:1
A child of God does not sin 3:3
Loving one another 3:11

3. FAITH IN CHRIST. BROTHERLY LOVE
Faith in Christ, not in false prophets 4:1
God is love. Brotherly love, the mark of Christians 4:7
Everyone who believes in Jesus overcomes the world 5:1
Testimony borne to Christ 5:6

4. CONCLUSION
Prayer for sinners 5:14
The Christian's confidence as a child of God 5:18

2 JOHN

Greeting 1
The law of love 4
Precautions against heretics 7
Conclusion and greetings 12

3 JOHN

Greeting 1
Praise of Gaius 3
Diotrephes' misconduct 9
Commendation of Demetrius 11
Conclusion and farewell 13

JUDE

Greeting and blessing 1
His reason for writing 3

1. FALSE TEACHERS DENOUNCED
The punishment that awaits them 5
Their immorality 6
The judgment of God 14

2. EXHORTATION
False teachers were predicted 17
Faith, hope and charity 20
Attitude towards waverers 22
Final doxology 24

REVELATION

Prologue 1:1

Part One: Letters to the seven churches

Address and greeting 1:4
Reason for writing 1:9
Letter to the church of Ephesus 2:1
Letter to the church of Smyrna 2:8
Letter to the church of Pergamum 2:12
Letter to the church of Thyatira 2:18
Letter to the church of Sardis 3:1
Letter to the church of Philadelphia 3:7
Letter to the church of Laodicea 3:14

Part Two: Eschatological visions

1. INTRODUCTORY VISION

God in majesty 4:1
The sealed scroll and the Lamb 5:1

2. EVENTS PRIOR TO THE FINAL OUTCOME

Christ opens the first six seals. Vision of the four horsemen 6:1
The great multitude of the saved 7:1
The opening of the seventh seal 8:1
The first six trumpet calls. The three woes 8:7
The seer is given a little scroll to eat 10:1
Death and resurrection of the two witnesses 11:1

3. CHRIST'S VICTORY OVER THE POWERS OF EVIL. THE CHURCH IN GLORY

The seventh trumpet call 11:15
The woman pursued by the dragon 12:1
The beasts given authority by the dragon 13:1
The beast rising from out of the earth 13:11
The Lamb and his entourage 14:1
Proclamation and symbols of the Judgment 14:6
The harvest and the vintage 14:14
The hymn of the saved 15:1
The seven bowls of plagues 15:5
The great harlot and the beast 17:1
The fall of Babylon announced 18:1
Songs of victory in heaven 19:1
The first battle—the beast is destroyed 19:11
The thousand-year reign of Christ and his people 20:1
The second battle—Satan is overthrown 20:7
The Last Judgment of the living and the dead 20:11
A new world comes into being. The new Jerusalem 21:1
The visions come to an end 22:6

4. EPILOGUE

Prayer of the Spirit and the Bride. Words of warning and farewell of 22:17

Subject Index